A BIRNBAUM TRAVEL GUIDE

Alexandra Mayes Birnbaum
EDITORIAL CONSULTANT

Lois Spritzer
Executive Editor

Laura L. Brengelman
Managing Editor

Mary Callahan
Senior Editor

Patricia Canole
Gene Gold
Jill Kadetsky
Susan McClung
Beth Schlau
Associate Editors

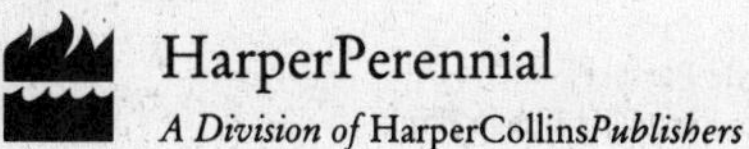

For Perry Wachtel, who helped more than he knows.

FIRST EDITION

ISSN 0749-2561 (Birnbaum Travel Guides)
ISSN 0883-248X (Caribbean)
ISBN 0-06-278103-0 (pbk.)

93 94 95 96 97 98 CC/CW 10 9 8 7 6 5 4 3 2 1

Cover design © Drenttel Doyle Partners
Cover photograph © Magnus Pietz/The Image Bank

BIRNBAUM TRAVEL GUIDES

Bahamas, and Turks & Caicos
Berlin
Bermuda
Boston
Canada
Cancun, Cozumel & Isla Mujeres
Caribbean
Chicago
Disneyland
Eastern Europe
Europe
Europe for Business Travelers
France
Germany
Great Britain
Hawaii
Ireland
Italy
London
Los Angeles
Mexico
Miami & Ft. Lauderdale
Montreal & Quebec City
New Orleans
New York
Paris
Portugal
Rome
San Francisco
Santa Fe & Taos
South America
Spain
United States
USA for Business Travelers
Walt Disney World
Walt Disney World for Kids, By Kids
Washington, DC

Contributing Editors

Cathy Beason
Janet Bennett
Ron Butler
Kevin Causey
Barbara Currie
Mary Dempsey
Charlanne Fields
Michael Finn
Lou Garcia
Alice Garrard
Martha Watkins Gilkes
Ian Glass
Joel Glass
Charles Gnaegy
Jack Gold
Sylvano Guerrero
Steven Gutkin
Sandra Hart
Ben Harte
Edward Holland
David Jacobs
Mark Kalish
Anne Kalosh
Delinda Karle
Laura Kelly
Peter Kramer
Jane Kronholtz
Catherine J. Langevin
Suzanne Lavanes
Richard Lee
Mary Dell Lucas
Wendy Luft
J. P. MacBean
Rob MacGregor
Thérèse Margolis
Karen Matusic
Erica Meltzer
Anne Millman
Lee Moncaster
Mike Morgan
Robin Nelson
Tamara Newell
Larry O'Connor
Joseph Petrocik
Kybran L. Phillips
Susan Pierres
Ann Pleshette
Maria Polvay
Linda Post
Virginia Puzo
Stacy Ritz
Allen Rokach
Alexandra Roll
Ruth Sanchez
Taryn Schneider
David P. Schulz
Laurie S. Senz
Marcia Y. Skyers-James
Molly Arost Staub
Kendric W. Taylor
Tony Tedeschi
Steve Wasserstein
Karen Weiner
Laurie Werner
Leslie Westbrook

Maps

B. Andrew Mudryk, Mark Stein Studios

Contents

Getting Ready to Go

Practical information for planning your trip.

Island-by-Island Hopping

Thorough, qualitative guides to all the islands and the most popular Caribbean coastal destinations. Each section offers a comprehensive report on the island or area's most compelling attractions and amenities — highlighting our top choices in every category.

Diversions

A selective guide to a variety of unexpected pleasures, pinpointing the best places in which to pursue them.

Foreword

My husband, Steve Birnbaum, was one of those people who occasionally went around the Caribbean clucking under his breath, pointing at new hotels and resort developments, sorrowfully describing them with paragraphs that began, "You should have seen how it used to be . . ." The truth of the matter is that although even I do, in fact, treasure memories of beaches without high-rises on their periphery and remember inland trails before they became four lanes of macadam, the good old Caribbean days weren't always that wonderful for visitors.

But the extensive development of the Caribbean area during the past several decades — and its increasing appeal to US travelers — has made it one of the most important travel magnets on this planet. Although often referred to as a single destination, the Caribbean encompasses countless cultures, and the marvelous blending of all these influences has spawned an environment that is both unique and compelling. It has been our aim to produce a guide that accurately reflects the diversity and allure of this vast canvas, complete with all the appropriate bouquets and blemishes. (Because the US government's ban on travel to Cuba for most US citizens was still in effect at press time, we do not cover this Caribbean country.)

What's more, the broadening sophistication of island travelers and the (often wrenching) maturation of the islands themselves have made it essential that Caribbean guidebooks also evolve in very fundamental ways in order to keep pace with readers and their needs. That's why we've tried to create a guide that's specifically organized, written, and edited for the more demanding modern traveler, one for whom qualitative information is infinitely more desirable than mere quantities of unappraised data.

For years, dating back as far as Herr Baedeker, travel guides have tended to be encyclopedic, much more concerned with demonstrating expertise in geography and history than with a real analysis of the sorts of things that actually concern a typical modern tourist. I think you'll notice a different, more contemporary tone to our text, as well as an organization and focus that are distinctive and more functional. Early on, we realized that giving up the encyclopedic approach precluded our listing every single route and restaurant, a realization that helped define our overall editorial focus. Similarly, when we discussed the possibility of presenting certain information in other than strict geographic order, we found that the new format enabled us to arrange data in a way that best answers the questions travelers typically ask.

Travel guides are, understandably, reflections of personal taste, and putting one's name on a title page obviously puts one's preferences on the line. But I think I ought to amplify just what "personal" means. I don't believe in the sort of personal guidebook that's a palpable misrepresentation on its face. It is, for example, hardly possible for any single travel writer to visit thousands of restaurants (and nearly as many hotels) in any given year and provide accurate appraisals of each. And even if it were physically possible for one human being to survive such an itinerary, it would of necessity have to be done at a dead sprint, and the perceptions derived therefrom would probably be less valid than those of any other intelligent individual visiting the same establishments. It is, therefore, impossible (especially in a large, annually revised and updated guidebook *series* such as we offer) to have only one person provide all the data on the entire world.

I also happen to think that such individual orientation is of substantially less value to readers. Visiting a single hotel for just one night, or eating one hasty meal in a random restaurant hardly equips anyone to provide appraisals that are of more than passing interest. We have, therefore, chosen what I like to describe as the "thee and me" approach to restaurant and hotel evaluation and, to a somewhat more limited degree, to the sites and sights we have included in our text. What this really reflects is personal sampling tempered by intelligent counsel from informed local sources, and these additional friends-of-the-editor are almost always residents of the island and/or area about which they are consulted.

In addition, very precise editing and tailoring keep our text fiercely subjective. So what follows is the gospel according to Birnbaum, and represents as much of our own taste and instincts as we can manage. It is probable, therefore, that if you like your beaches largely unpopulated and your mountainsides mostly uncrowded, prefer small hotels with personality to high-rise anonymities, and can't tolerate fresh fish that's been relentlessly overcooked, we're likely to have a long and meaningful relationship.

I should also point out something about the person to whom this guidebook is directed. Above all, he or she is a "visitor." This means that such elements as restaurants have been specifically picked to provide the visitor with a representative, enlightening, stimulating, and, above all pleasant experience. Since so many extraneous considerations can affect the reception and service accorded a regular restaurant patron, our choices can in no way be construed as an exhaustive guide to island dining. We think we've listed all the best places, in various price ranges, but they were chosen with a visitor's enjoyment in mind.

Other evidence of how we've tried to tailor our text to reflect modern travel habits is most apparent in the section we call DIVERSIONS. Where once it was common for travelers to spend an island visit nailed to a single spot, seeing only the obvious sights, the emphasis today is more likely to be directed toward pursuing some special interest often found off the beaten track. Therefore, we have collected these exceptional experiences so that it is no longer necessary to wade through a pound or two of superfluous prose just to find unexpected pleasures and treasures.

Finally, I also should point out that every good travel guide is a living enterprise; that is, no part of this text is carved in stone. In our annual revisions, we refine, expand, and further hone all our material to serve your travel needs better. To this end, no contribution is of greater value to us than your personal reaction to what we have written, as well as information reflecting your own experiences while using the book. Please write to us at 10 E. 53rd St., New York, NY 10022.

We sincerely hope to hear from you.

Alexandra Mayes Birnbaum

ALEXANDRA MAYES BIRNBAUM, editorial consultant to the *Birnbaum Travel Guides*, worked with her late husband Stephen Birnbaum as co-editor of the series. She has been a world traveler since childhood and is known for her lively travel reports on radio on what's hot and what's not.

pursuing some special interest off the beaten track. Therefore, we have collected their experiences [illegible] and it is no longer necessary to wade through a [illegible] of [illegible] just to find [illegible] [illegible] and [illegible].

Finally, I also should point out that every good travel guide is a living enterprise. [illegible] part of [illegible] [illegible] [illegible], expand, and further [illegible] all our [illegible] [illegible]. [illegible] [illegible] [illegible] [illegible] [illegible] [illegible] information [illegible] [illegible] experiences while using the book. Please write to us at 10 E. 53rd St., New York, NY 10022.

We sincerely hope to hear from you.

Caribbean

UNITED STATES
FLORIDA
Miami
Gulf of Mexico
ATLANTIC OCEAN
BAHAMAS
Tropic of Cancer
Havana
CUBA
Isle of Pines
To Mexico and Belize (see inset below)
GREATER A
Cayman Islands
HAITI
Kingston
JAMAICA
Isla Mujeres
Cancún
Cozumel
MEXICO
BELIZE
0 miles 99
0 kilometers 165
CARIBBE
Providencia
San Andrés
NICARAGUA
COSTA RICA
PANAMA
0 miles 200
0 kilometers 300
Santa Marta
Cartagena
COLOMBIA
N
84°
80°
76°
24°
20°
16°
12°
88°

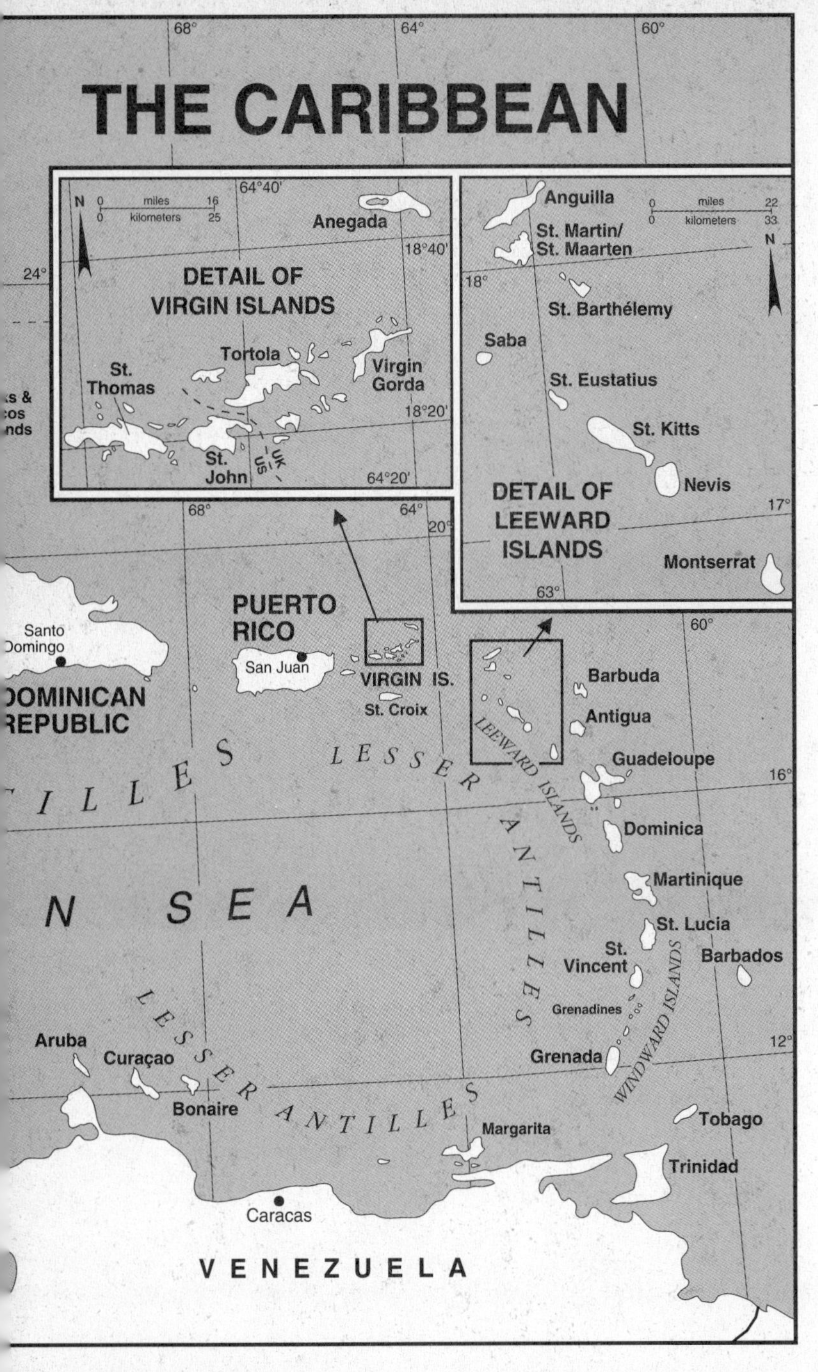

THE CARIBBEAN
DETAIL OF VIRGIN ISLANDS
miles
kilometers
Anegada
Tortola
Virgin Gorda
St. Thomas
St. John
UK
US
DETAIL OF LEEWARD ISLANDS
Anguilla
St. Martin/ St. Maarten
St. Barthélemy
Saba
St. Eustatius
St. Kitts
Nevis
Montserrat
PUERTO RICO
San Juan
VIRGIN IS.
St. Croix
Santo Domingo
DOMINICAN REPUBLIC
LESSER ANTILLES
LEEWARD ISLANDS
Barbuda
Antigua
Guadeloupe
Dominica
Martinique
St. Lucia
St. Vincent
Barbados
Grenadines
Grenada
WINDWARD ISLANDS
SEA
Aruba
Curaçao
Bonaire
Margarita
Tobago
Trinidad
Caracas
VENEZUELA

How to Use This Guide

A great deal of care has gone into the organization of this guidebook, and we believe it represents a real breakthrough in the presentation of travel material.

Our text is divided into three basic sections, in order to present information in the best way on every possible aspect of a Caribbean vacation. We feel that our main job is to highlight what's where and to provide basic information — how, when, where, how much, and what's best — to assist you in making the most intelligent choices possible.

Here is a brief summary of what you can expect to find in each section. We believe that you will find both your travel planning and on-island enjoyment enhanced by having this book at your side.

GETTING READY TO GO

A mini-encyclopedia of practical travel facts with all the precise data necessary to create a successful trip to the Caribbean. Here you will find how to get where you're going, plus selected resources — including useful publications, and companies and organizations specializing in discount and special-interest travel — providing a wealth of information and assistance useful both before and during your trip.

ISLAND-BY-ISLAND HOPPING

Individual reports on every island and Caribbean country offer short-stay guides with a consistent format: An essay introduces each subject island or nation as a historic entity and a functioning contemporary place to live and visit; *At-a-Glance* presents a site-by-site survey of the most important, interesting, and sometimes most offbeat sights to see and things to do. *Sources and Resources* is a concise listing of pertinent tourist information, such as the address of the local tourist office, which sightseeing tours to take, and where the best nightlife, scuba diving, golf, tennis, fishing, and swimming are to be found. The *Best on the Island* section is just that: our choice of each island's very best places to eat and sleep on a variety of budgets.

DIVERSIONS

This section is designed to help travelers find the best places in which to engage in a variety of exceptional experiences for the mind and body, without having to wade through endless pages of unrelated text. In every case, our particular suggestions are intended to guide you to that special place where the quality of experience is likely to be highest.

To use this book to full advantage, take a few minutes to read the table of contents and random entries in each section to get a firsthand feel for how it all fits together. You will find that the sections of this book are building blocks, designed to help you put together the best possible trip. Use them selectively as a tool; a source of ideas; a reference work for accurate facts; and a guidebook to the best buys, the most exciting sights, the most pleasant accommodations, the tastiest foods — *the best travel experience* that you can possibly have.

Getting Ready to Go

When to Go

For most of the Caribbean, the best weather — and the peak travel season — is from mid-December through mid-April. In the southern Caribbean of the Netherlands Antilles and the coastal waters of Venezuela and Colombia, the high season starts earlier, in November.

Although summers on some Caribbean islands can be hot, travel during the off-seasons and shoulder seasons (the months immediately before and after the peak months) offers relatively fair weather and smaller crowds. During these periods, travel also is less expensive.

The *Weather Channel* (2600 Cumberland Pkwy., Atlanta, GA 30339; phone: 404-434-6800) provides current weather forecasts. Call 900-WEATHER from any touch-tone phone in the US; the 95¢ per minute charge will appear on your phone bill.

Traveling by Plane

SCHEDULED FLIGHTS

Leading airlines offering flights between the US and the Caribbean include *Aeroméxico, Air France, Air Jamaica, ALM, American, Avianca, BWIA, Cayman Airways, Continental, Delta, Dominicana, Haiti Trans Air, Lacsa, Mexicana, Northwest, TACA, TWA, United,* and *Viasa.*

FARES The great variety of airfares can be reduced to the following basic categories: first class, business class, coach (also called economy or tourist class), excursion or discount, and standby, as well as various promotional fares. For information on applicable fares and restrictions, contact the airlines listed above or ask your travel agent. Most airfares are offered for a limited time period. Once you've found the lowest fare for which you can qualify, purchase your ticket as soon as possible.

RESERVATIONS Reconfirmation is strongly recommended for all international flights (although it is not usually necessary on domestic flights). It is essential that you confirm your round-trip reservations — *especially the return leg* — as well as any flights within the Caribbean.

SEATING Airline seats usually are assigned on a first-come, first-served basis at check-in, although you may be able to reserve a seat when purchasing your ticket. Seating charts often are available from airlines and are included in the *Airline Seating Guide* (Carlson Publishing Co., PO Box 888, Los Alamitos, CA 90720; phone: 310-493-4877).

SMOKING US law prohibits smoking on flights scheduled for 6 hours or less within the US and its territories (including Puerto Rico and the US Virgin Islands) on both domestic and international carriers. These rules do not apply to nonstop flights between the US and international destinations. A free wallet-size guide that describes the rights of nonsmokers is available from *ASH* (*Action on Smoking and Health;* DOT Card, 2013 H St. NW, Washington, DC 20006; phone: 202-659-4310).

SPECIAL MEALS When making your reservation, you can request one of the airline's alternate menu choices for no additional charge. Call to reconfirm your request 24 hours before departure.

BAGGAGE On a major international airline, passengers usually are allowed to carry on board one bag that will fit under a seat or in an overhead bin. Passengers also can check two bags in the cargo hold, measuring 62 inches and 55 inches in combined dimensions (length, width, and depth) with a per-bag weight limit of 70 pounds. There may be charges for additional, oversize, or overweight luggage, and for special equipment or sporting gear. Note that baggage allowances may vary for children (depending on the percentage of full adult fare paid) and on flights within the Caribbean. Check that the tags the airline attaches are correctly coded for your destination.

CHARTER FLIGHTS

By booking a block of seats on a specially arranged flight, charter operators frequently offer travelers bargain airfares. If you do fly on a charter, however, read the contract's fine print carefully. Charter operators can cancel a flight or assess surcharges of 10% of the airfare up to 10 days before departure. You usually must book in advance (no changes are permitted, so invest in trip cancellation insurance); also make your check out to the company's escrow account. For further information, consult the publication *Jax Fax* (397 Post Rd., Darien, CT 06820; phone: 203-655-8746).

DISCOUNTS ON SCHEDULED FLIGHTS

COURIER TRAVEL In return for arranging to accompany some kind of freight, a traveler may pay only a portion of the total airfare and a small registration fee. One agency that matches up would-be couriers with courier companies is *Now Voyager* (74 Varick St., Suite 307, New York, NY 10013; phone: 212-431-1616).

Courier Companies

Courier Travel Service (530 Central Ave., Cedarhurst, NY 11516; phone: 516-763-6898).

Discount Travel International (169 W. 81st St., New York, NY 10024; phone: 212-362-3636; and 940 10th St., Suite 2, Miami Beach, FL 33139; phone: 305-538-1616).

Excaliber International Courier (c/o *Way to Go Travel,* 6679 Sunset Blvd., Hollywood, CA 90028; phone: 213-466-1126).

F.B. On Board Courier Services (10225 Ryan Ave., Suite 103, Dorval, Quebec H9P 1A2, Canada; phone: 514-633-0740).

Halbart Express (147-05 176th St., Jamaica, NY 11434; phone: 718-656-8279).

International Adventures (60 E. 42nd St., New York, NY 10165; phone: 212-599-0577).

Midnight Express (925 W. High Park Blvd., Inglewood, CA 90302; phone: 310-672-1100).

Publications

Insider's Guide to Air Courier Bargains, by Kelly Monaghan (The Intrepid Traveler, PO Box 438, New York, NY 10034; phone: 212-304-2207).

Travel Secrets (PO Box 2325, New York, NY 10108; phone: 212-245-8703).

Travel Unlimited (PO Box 1058, Allston, MA 02134-1058; no phone).

World Courier News (PO Box 77471, San Francisco, CA 94107; no phone).

CONSOLIDATORS AND BUCKET SHOPS These companies buy blocks of tickets from airlines and sell them at a discount to travel agents or to consumers. Since many bucket shops operate on a thin margin, before parting with any money check the company's record with the Better Business Bureau.

Bargain Air (655 Deep Valley Dr., Suite 355, Rolling Hills, CA 90274; phone: 800-347-2345).

Council Charter (205 E. 42nd St., New York, NY 10017; phone: 800-800-8222 or 212-661-0311).

International Adventures (60 E. 42nd St., New York, NY 10165; phone: 212-599-0577).

Travac Tours and Charters (989 Ave. of the Americas, New York, NY 10018; phone: 800-872-8800 or 212-563-3303).

Unitravel (1177 N. Warson Rd., St. Louis, MO 63132; phone: 800-325-2222 or 314-569-0900).

LAST-MINUTE TRAVEL CLUBS For an annual fee, members receive information on imminent trips and other bargain travel opportunities. Despite the names of these clubs, you don't have to wait until literally the last minute to make travel plans.

Discount Travel International (114 Forest Ave., Suite 203, Narberth, PA 19072; phone: 215-668-7184).

Last Minute Travel (1249 Boylston St., Boston, MA 02215; phone: 800-LAST-MIN or 617-267-9800).

Moment's Notice (425 Madison Ave., New York, NY 10017; phone: 212-486-0500, -0501, -0502, or -0503).

Spur-of-the-Moment Cruises (411 N. Harbor Blvd., Suite 302, San Pedro, CA 90731; phone: 800-4-CRUISES in California; 800-343-1991 elsewhere in the US; or 310-521-1070).

Traveler's Advantage (3033 S. Parker Rd., Suite 900, Aurora, CO 80014; phone: 800-548-1116 or 800-835-8747).

Vacations to Go (1502 Augusta, Suite 415, Houston, TX 77057; phone: 713-974-2121 in Texas; 800-338-4962 elsewhere in the US).

Worldwide Discount Travel Club (1674 Meridian Ave., Miami Beach, FL 33139; phone: 305-534-2082).

GENERIC AIR TRAVEL These organizations operate much like an ordinary airline standby service, except that they offer seats on not one but several scheduled and charter airlines. One pioneer of generic flights is *Airhitch* (2790 Broadway, Suite 100, New York, NY 10025; phone: 212-864-2000).

BARTERED TRAVEL SOURCES Barter is a common means of exchange between travel suppliers. Bartered travel clubs such as *Travel World Leisure Club* (225 W. 34th St., Suite 909, New York, NY 10122; phone: 800-444-TWLC or 212-239-4855) offer discounts to members for an annual fee.

CONSUMER PROTECTION

Passengers with complaints who are not satisfied with the airline's response can contact the US Department of Transportation (DOT; Consumer Affairs Division, 400 7th St. SW, Room 10405, Washington, DC 20590; phone: 202-366-2220). If you have a complaint against a travel service in the Caribbean, contact the local tourist authorities. Also see *Fly Rights* (Publication #050-000-00513-5; US Government Printing Office, PO Box 371954, Pittsburgh, PA 15250-7954; phone: 202-783-3238).

Traveling by Ship

Your cruise fare usually includes all meals, recreational activities, and entertainment. Shore excursions are available at extra cost, and can be booked in advance or once you're on board. An important factor in the price of a cruise is the location and size of your cabin; for information on ships' layouts and facilities, consult the charts issued by the *Cruise Lines International Association* (*CLIA;* 500 Fifth Ave., Suite 1407, New York, NY 10110; phone: 212-921-0066).

Most cruise ships have a doctor on board, plus medical facilities. The US Public Health Service (PHS) also inspects all passenger vessels calling at US ports; for the most recent summary or a particular inspection report, write to Chief, Vessel Sanitation Program, National Center for Environmental Health (1015 N. America Way, Room 107, Miami, FL 33132; phone: 305-536-4307). For further information, consult *Ocean and Cruise News* (PO Box 92, Stamford, CT 06904; phone: 203-329-2787). And for a free listing of travel agencies specializing in cruises, contact the *National Association of Cruise Only Agencies* (*NACOA;* PO Box 7209, Freeport, NY 11520; phone: 516-378-8006).

In addition to the cruise lines listed below, US and local Caribbean companies specializing in chartered yachts are discussed in the individual island reports in ISLAND-BY-ISLAND HOPPING.

Cruise Lines

Carnival Cruise Lines (3655 NW 87th Ave., Miami, FL 33178-2428; phone: 800-327-9501).

Chandris Celebrity *and* ***Chandris Fantasy Cruises*** (5200 Blue Lagoon Dr., Miami, FL 33126; phone: 800-437-3111).

Clipper Cruises (7711 Bonhomme Ave., St. Louis, MO 63105; phone: 800-325-0010).

Club Med (3 E. 54th St., New York, NY 10022; phone: 800-CLUB-MED or 212-750-1687).

Commodore Cruise Line (800 Douglas Rd., Suite 600, Coral Gables, FL 33134; phone: 800-237-5361, 800-327-5617, or 305-529-3000).

Costa Cruises (80 SW 8th St., Miami, FL 33130; phone: 800-322-8263 for information; 800-462-6782 for reservations).

Crown Cruise Line (800 Douglas Rd., Suite 600, Coral Gables, FL 33134; phone: 800-237-5361 or 800-327-5617).

Crystal Cruises (2121 Ave. of the Stars, Los Angeles, CA 90067; phone: 800-446-6645).

Cunard (555 Fifth Ave., New York, NY 10017; phone: 800-5-CUNARD or 800-221-4770).

Dolphin Cruise Line (901 S. America Way, Miami, FL 33132; phone: 800-222-1003).

Epirotiki Lines (551 Fifth Ave., New York, NY 10176; phone: 212-599-1750 in New York State; 800-221-2470 elsewhere in the US).

Holland America Line (300 Elliot Ave. W., Seattle, WA 98119; phone: 800-426-0327).

Norwegian Cruise Line (95 Merrick Way, Coral Gables, FL 33134; phone: 800-327-7030).

Princess Cruises (10100 Santa Monica Blvd., Los Angeles, CA 90067; phone: 800-421-0522).

Regency Cruises (260 Madison Ave., New York, NY 10016; phone: 212-972-4774 in New York State; 800-388-5500 elsewhere in the US).

Renaissance Cruises (1800 Eller Dr., Suite 300, Ft. Lauderdale, FL 33335-0307; phone: 800-525-2450).

Royal Caribbean Cruise Lines (1050 Caribbean Way, Miami, FL 33132; phone: 800-432-6559 in Florida; 800-327-6700 elsewhere in the US).

Royal Cruise Line (1 Maritime Plaza, Suite 1400, San Francisco, CA 94111; phone: 800-792-2992 in California; 800-227-4534 elsewhere in the US).

Seabourn Cruise Line (55 Francisco St., Suite 710, San Francisco, CA 94133; phone: 800-929-9595).

Sun Line (1 Rockefeller Plaza, Suite 315, New York, NY 10020; phone: 800-468-6400 or 212-397-6400).

Windstar Cruises (300 Elliott Ave. W., Seattle, WA 98119; phone: 800-258-7245).

Touring by Car

Although it may seem that a car is unnecessary for an island stay, even where a car is not essential, driving still is a highly desirable way to explore.

Requirements and driving regulations vary throughout the Caribbean. On some islands, a US driver's license is the only requirement; on others, an International Driver's Permit (IDP) is required or strongly advised — particularly where a foreign language is spoken. You can obtain an IDP from US branches of the *American Automobile Association (AAA)*. Some islands also require the purchase of a local license or driving permit (from island authorities or car rental companies); insurance requirements also vary. On some islands, driving is on the left side of the road — steering wheels in rental cars may be on either side. In some parts of the Caribbean, it is inadvisable to drive far afield after dark due to increasing road incidents involving assaults and robberies of tourists.

MAPS

Road maps are available from Caribbean tourist offices, bookstores, and specialists such as *Map Link* (25 E. Mason St., Suite 201, Santa Barbara, CA 93101; phone: 805-965-4402). *Map Link* also offers broader geographical overview maps, such as the Greater and Lesser Antilles *Nelles Verlag* maps.

AUTOMOBILE CLUBS AND BREAKDOWNS

To protect yourself in case of breakdowns while driving in the Caribbean, and for travel information and other benefits, consider joining a reputable automobile club. The largest of these is the *American Automobile Association* (*AAA;* 1000 AAA Dr., Heathrow, FL 32746-5063; phone: 407-444-7000). Before joining this or any other automobile club, check whether it has reciprocity with clubs in the countries or on the islands you plan to visit.

GASOLINE

Many of the islands follow the British system of measurement, and gasoline is sold by the British or "imperial" gallon (equal to 1.2 US gallons). On other islands, gasoline is sold by the liter (which is slightly more than 1 quart; approximately 3.7 liters to 1 US gallon).

RENTING A CAR

You can rent a car through a travel agent or international rental firm before leaving home, or from a local company once in the islands. Reserve in advance.

Most car rental companies require a credit card, although some will accept a substantial cash deposit. The minimum age to rent a car is set by the company; some impose special conditions on drivers above a certain age. Electing to pay for collision damage waiver (CDW) protection will add to the cost of renting a car, but releases you from financial liability for the vehicle. Additional costs include drop-off charges or one-way service fees.

International Car Rental Companies

Avis (phone: 800-331-1084).
Budget (phone: 800-472-3325).
Hertz (phone: 800-654-3001).
National (phone: 800-227-3876).
Thrifty (phone: 800-367-2277).

Package Tours

A package is a collection of travel services that can be purchased in a single transaction. Its principal advantages are convenience and economy — the cost is usually lower than that of the same services bought separately. Tour programs generally can be divided into two categories: escorted or locally hosted (with a set itinerary) and independent (usually more flexible).

When considering a package tour, read the brochure *carefully* to determine what is included and other conditions. Check the company's record with the Better Business Bureau. The *United States Tour Operators Association* (*USTOA;* 211 E. 51st St., Suite 12B, New York, NY 10022; phone: 212-944-5727) also can be helpful in determining a package tour operator's reliability. As with charter flights, always make your check out to the company's escrow account.

Many tour operators offer packages focused on special interests such as archaeology, nature study, and various outdoor activities such as hiking and camping. *All Adventure Travel* (PO Box 4307, Boulder, CO 80306; phone: 800-537-4025 or 303-499-1981) represents such specialized packagers; some also are listed in the *Specialty Travel Index* (305 San Anselmo Ave., Suite 313, San Anselmo, CA 94960; phone: 415-459-4900 in California; 800-442-4922 elsewhere in the US). Also note that *TourScan* (PO Box 2367, Darien, CT 06820; phone: 800-962-2080 or 203-655-8091) includes a list of available package tours to the Caribbean in their *Island Vacation Catalog.*

Package Tour Operators

Adventure Tours (9819 Liberty Rd., Randallstown, MD 21133; phone: 410-922-7000 in Baltimore; 800-638-9040 elsewhere in the US).

AIB Tours (3798 W. Flagler St., Coral Gables, FL 33134; phone: 800-232-0242 in Florida; 800-242-8687 elsewhere in the US).

American Express Vacations (offices throughout the US; phone: 800-241-1700 or 404-368-5100).

American Wilderness Experience (PO Box 1486, Boulder, CO 80306; phone: 800-444-0099 or 303-444-2622).

Backroads Bicycle Touring (1516 5th St., Berkeley, CA 94710-1713; phone: 800-245-3874, 800-462-2848, or 510-527-1555).

Barron Adventures (PO Box 3180, Long Beach, CA 90803; phone: 310-592-2050).

Caiman Expeditions (3449 E. River Rd., Tucson, AZ 85718; phone: 800-365-ADVE or 602-299-1047).

Caribbean Concepts (575 Underhill Blvd., Syosset, NY 11791; phone: 516-496-9800 in Nassau County; 800-423-4433 elsewhere in the US).

Ecosummer Expeditions (936 Peace Portal Dr., PO Box 8014-240, Blaine, WA 98230; phone: 800-688-8605 or 206-332-1000; and 1516 Duranleau St., Vancouver, BC V6H 3S4, Canada; phone: 604-669-7741).

Fling Vacations (999 Postal Rd., Allentown, PA 18103; phone: 800-523-9624).

Forum Travel International (91 Gregory La., Suite 21, Pleasant Hill, CA 94523; phone: 510-671-2900).

GoGo Tours (69 Spring St., Ramsey, NJ 07446-0507; phone: 201-934-3500).

GWV International (300 1st Ave., Needham, MA 02194; phone: 800-225-5498 or 617-449-5460).

International Expeditions (1 Environs Park, Helena, AL 35080; phone: 800-633-4734 or 205-428-1700).

Lost World Adventures (1189 Autumn Ridge Dr., Marietta, GA 30066; phone: 800-999-0558 or 404-971-8586).

Mountain Travel-Sobek (6420 Fairmount Ave., El Cerrito, CA 94530; phone: 510-527-8100 in California; 800-227-2384 elsewhere in the US).

Nature Expeditions International (PO Box 11496, Eugene, OR 97440; phone: 800-869-0639 or 503-484-6529).

Questers Tours & Travel (257 Park Ave. S., New York, NY 10010; phone: 800-468-8668 or 212-673-3120).

Slickrock Adventures (PO Box 1400, Moab, UT 84532; phone: 801-259-6996).

Trans National Travel (2 Charlesgate W., Boston, MA 02215; phone: 800-262-0123).

Travel Impressions (465 Smith St., Farmingdale, NY 11735; phone: 800-284-0044).

Trek America (PO Box 470, Blairstown, NJ 07825; phone: 800-221-0596 or 908-362-9198).

Venezuela Connection (975 Osos St., San Luis Obispo, CA 93401; phone: 800-345-7422 or 805-543-8823).

Victor Emanuel Nature Tours (PO Box 33008, Austin, TX 78764; phone: 800-328-VENT or 512-328-5221).

Wildland Adventures (3516 NE 155th St., Seattle, WA 98155; phone: 800-345-4453 or 206-365-0686).

Insurance

The first person with whom you should discuss travel insurance is your own insurance broker. You may discover that the insurance you already carry protects you adequately while traveling and that you need little additional coverage. If you charge travel services, the credit card company also may provide some insurance coverage (and other safeguards).

Types of Travel Insurance

Baggage and personal effects insurance: Protects your bags and their contents in case of damage or theft anytime during your travels.

Personal accident and sickness insurance: Covers cases of illness, injury, or death in an accident while traveling.

Trip cancellation and interruption insurance: Guarantees a refund if you must cancel a trip; may reimburse you for the extra travel costs incurred for catching up with a tour or traveling home early.

Default and/or bankruptcy insurance: Provides coverage in the event of default and/or bankruptcy on the part of the tour operator, airline, or other travel supplier.

Flight insurance: Covers accidental injury or death while flying.

Automobile insurance: Provides collision, theft, property damage, and personal liability protection while driving your own or a rented car.

Combination policies: Include any or all of the above.

Disabled Travelers

Make travel arrangements well in advance. Specify to all services involved the nature of your disability to determine if there are accommodations and facilities that meet your needs.

Organizations

ACCENT on Living (PO Box 700, Bloomington, IL 61702; phone: 309-378-2961).

Access: The Foundation for Accessibility by the Disabled (PO Box 356, Malverne, NY 11565; phone: 516-887-5798).

American Foundation for the Blind (15 W. 16th St., New York, NY 10011; phone: 800-232-5463 or 212-620-2147).

Information Center for Individuals with Disabilities (Ft. Point Pl., 1st Floor, 27-43 Wormwood St., Boston, MA 02210; phone: 800-462-5015 in Massachusetts; 617-727-5540 or 617-727-5541 elsewhere in the US; TDD: 617-345-9743).

Mobility International USA (*MIUSA;* PO Box 3551, Eugene, OR 97403; phone: 503-343-1284, both voice and TDD; main office: 228

Borough High St., London SE1 1JX, England; phone: 44-71-403-5688).

National Rehabilitation Information Center (8455 Colesville Rd., Suite 935, Silver Spring, MD 20910; phone: 301-588-9284).

Paralyzed Veterans of America (*PVA;* PVA/ATTS Program, 801 18th St. NW, Washington, DC 20006; phone: 202-872-1300 in Washington, DC; 800-424-8200 elsewhere in the US).

Partners of the Americas (1424 K St. NW, Suite 700, Washington, DC 20005; phone: 800-322-7844 or 202-628-3300).

Royal Association for Disability and Rehabilitation (*RADAR;* 25 Mortimer St., London W1N 8AB, England; phone: 44-71-637-5400).

Society for the Advancement of Travel for the Handicapped (*SATH;* 347 Fifth Ave., Suite 610, New York, NY 10016; phone: 212-447-7284).

Travel Information Service (MossRehab Hospital, 1200 W. Tabor Rd., Philadelphia, PA 19141-3099; phone: 215-456-9600; TDD: 215-456-9602).

Publications

Access Travel: A Guide to the Accessibility of Airport Terminals (Consumer Information Center, Dept. 578Z, Pueblo, CO 81009; phone: 719-948-3334).

Air Transportation of Handicapped Persons (Publication #AC-120-32; US Department of Transportation, Distribution Unit, Publications Section, M-443-2, 400 7th St. SW, Washington, DC 20590).

The Diabetic Traveler (PO Box 8223 RW, Stamford, CT 06905; phone: 203-327-5832).

Directory of Travel Agencies for the Disabled and ***Travel for the Disabled,*** both by Helen Hecker (Twin Peaks Press, PO Box 129, Vancouver, WA 98666; phone: 800-637-CALM or 206-694-2462).

Guide to Traveling with Arthritis (Upjohn Company, PO Box 989, Dearborn, MI 48121).

The Handicapped Driver's Mobility Guide (*American Automobile Association,* 1000 AAA Dr., Heathrow, FL 32746; phone: 407-444-7000).

Handicapped Travel Newsletter (PO Box 269, Athens, TX 75751; phone: 903-677-1260).

Handi-Travel: A Resource Book for Disabled and Elderly Travellers, by Cinnie Noble (*Canadian Rehabilitation Council for the Disabled,* 45 Sheppard Ave. E., Suite 801, Toronto, Ontario M2N 5W9, Canada; phone: 416-250-7490, both voice and TDD).

Incapacitated Passengers Air Travel Guide (*International Air Transport Association,* Publications Sales Department, 2000 Peel St., Montreal, Quebec H3A 2R4, Canada; phone: 514-844-6311).

Ticket to Safe Travel (*American Diabetes Association,* 1660 Duke St., Alexandria, VA 22314; phone: 800-232-3472 or 703-549-1500).

Travel for the Patient with Chronic Obstructive Pulmonary Disease (Dr. Harold Silver, 1601 18th St. NW, Washington, DC 20009; phone: 202-667-0134).

Travel Tips for Hearing-Impaired People (*American Academy of Otolaryngology,* 1 Prince St., Alexandria, VA 22314; phone: 703-836-4444).

Travel Tips for People with Arthritis (*Arthritis Foundation,* 1314 Spring St. NW, Atlanta, GA 30309; phone: 800-283-7800 or 404-872-7100).

Traveling Like Everybody Else: A Practical Guide for Disabled Travelers, by Jacqueline Freedman and Susan Gersten (Modan Publishing, PO Box 1202, Bellmore, NY 11710; phone: 516-679-1380).

Package Tour Operators

Accessible Journeys (35 W. Sellers Ave., Ridley Park, PA 19078; phone: 215-521-0339).

Accessible Tours/Directions Unlimited (Lois Bonnani, 720 N. Bedford Rd., Bedford Hills, NY 10507; phone: 800-533-5343 or 914-241-1700).

Beehive Business and Leisure Travel (1130 W. Center St., N. Salt Lake, UT 84054; phone: 800-777-5727 or 801-292-4445).

Classic Travel Service (8 W. 40th St., New York, NY 10018; phone: 212-869-2560 in New York State; 800-247-0909 elsewhere in the US).

Dialysis at Sea Cruises (611 Barry Pl., Indian Rocks Beach, FL 34635; phone: 800-775-1333 or 813-596-4614).

Evergreen Travel Service (4114 198th St. SW, Suite 13, Lynnwood, WA 98036-6742; phone: 800-435-2288 or 206-776-1184).

Flying Wheels Travel (143 W. Bridge St., PO Box 382, Owatonna, MN 55060; phone: 800-535-6790 or 507-451-5005).

Good Neighbor Travel Service (124 S. Main St., Viroqua, WI 54665; phone: 608-637-2128).

The Guided Tour (7900 Old York Rd., Suite 114B, Elkins Park, PA 19117-2339; phone: 800-783-5841 or 215-782-1370).

Hinsdale Travel (201 E. Ogden Ave., Hinsdale, IL 60521; phone: 708-325-1335 or 708-469-7349).

MedEscort International (ABE International Airport, PO Box 8766, Allentown, PA 18105; phone: 800-255-7182 or 215-791-3111).

Prestige World Travel (5710-X High Point Rd., Greensboro, NC 27407; phone: 800-476-7737 or 919-292-6690).

Sprout (893 Amsterdam Ave., New York, NY 10025; phone: 212-222-9575).

Weston Travel Agency (134 N. Cass Ave., PO Box 1050, Westmont, IL 60559; phone: 708-968-2513 in Illinois; 800-633-3725 elsewhere in the US).

Single Travelers

The travel industry is not very fair to people who vacation by themselves — they often end up paying more than those traveling in pairs. Services catering to singles match travel companions, offer travel arrangements with shared accommodations, and provide useful information and discounts. Also consult publications such as *Going Solo* (Doerfer Communications, PO Box 123, Apalachicola, FL 32329; phone: 904-653-8848) and *Traveling on Your Own,* by Eleanor Berman (Random House, Order Dept., 400 Hahn Rd., Westminster, MD 21157; phone: 800-733-3000).

Organizations and Companies

Contiki Holidays (300 Plaza Alicante, Suite 900, Garden Grove, CA 92640; phone: 800-466-0610 or 714-740-0808).

Gallivanting (515 E. 79th St., Suite 20F, New York, NY 10021; phone: 800-933-9699 or 212-988-0617).

Globus *and* ***Cosmos*** (5301 S. Federal Circle, Littleton, CO 80123; phone: 800-221-0090 or 800-556-5454).

Jane's International *and* ***Sophisticated Women Travelers*** (2603 Bath Ave., Brooklyn, NY 11214; phone: 718-266-2045).

Marion Smith Singles (611 Prescott Pl., N. Woodmere, NY 11581; phone: 516-791-4852, 516-791-4865, or 212-944-2112).

Partners-in-Travel (11660 Chenault St., Suite 119, Los Angeles, CA 90049; phone: 310-476-4869).

Singles in Motion (545 W. 236th St., Riverdale, NY 10463; phone: 718-884-4464).

Singleworld (401 Theodore Fremd Ave., Rye, NY 10580; phone: 800-223-6490 or 914-967-3334).

Solo Flights (63 High Noon Rd., Weston, CT 06883; phone: 203-226-9993).

Suddenly Singles Tours (161 Dreiser Loop, Bronx, NY 10475; phone: 718-379-8800 in New York City; 800-859-8396 elsewhere in the US).

Travel Companion Exchange (PO Box 833, Amityville, NY 11701; phone: 516-454-0880).

Travel Companions (Atrium Financial Center, 1515 N. Federal Hwy., Suite 300, Boca Raton, FL 33432; phone: 800-383-7211 or 407-393-6448).

Travel in Two's (239 N. Broadway, Suite 3, N. Tarrytown, NY 10591; phone: 914-631-8301 in New York State; 800-692-5252 elsewhere in the US).

Older Travelers

Special discounts and more free time are just two factors that have given older travelers a chance to see the world at affordable prices. Many travel suppliers offer senior discounts — sometimes only to members of certain senior citizen organizations, which offer other benefits. Prepare your itinerary with one eye on your own physical condition and the other on a topographical map, and remember that it's easy to overdo when traveling.

Publications

Going Abroad: 101 Tips for Mature Travelers (*Grand Circle Travel,* 347 Congress St., Boston, MA 02210; phone: 800-221-2610 or 617-350-7500).

The Mature Traveler (GEM Publishing Group, PO Box 50820, Reno, NV 89513-0820; phone: 702-786-7419).

Take a Camel to Lunch and Other Adventures for Mature Travelers, by Nancy O'Connell (Bristol Publishing Enterprises, PO Box 1737, San Leandro, CA 94577; phone: 510-895-4461 in California; 800-346-4889 elsewhere in the US).

Travel Tips for Older Americans (Publication #044-000-02270-2; Superintendent of Documents, US Government Printing Office, PO Box 371954, Pittsburgh, PA 15250-7954; phone: 202-783-3238).

Unbelievably Good Deals & Great Adventures That You Absolutely Can't Get Unless You're Over 50, by Joan Rattner Heilman (Contemporary Books, 180 N. Michigan Ave., Chicago, IL 60601; phone: 312-782-9181).

Organizations

American Association of Retired Persons (*AARP;* 601 E St. NW, Washington, DC 20049; phone: 202-434-2277).

Golden Companions (PO Box 754, Pullman, WA 99163-0754; phone: 208-858-2183).

Mature Outlook (Customer Service Center, 6001 N. Clark St., Chicago, IL 60660; phone: 800-336-6330).

National Council of Senior Citizens (1331 F St. NW, Washington, DC 20004; phone: 202-347-8800).

Package Tour Operators

Elderhostel (PO Box 1959, Wakefield, MA 01880-5959; phone: 617-426-7788).

Evergreen Travel Service (4114 198th St. SW, Suite 13, Lynnwood, WA 98036-6742; phone: 800-435-2288 or 206-776-1184).

Gadabout Tours (700 E. Tahquitz Canyon Way, Palm Springs, CA 92262; phone: 800-952-5068 or 619-325-5556).

Grand Circle Travel (347 Congress St., Boston, MA 02210; phone: 800-221-2610 or 617-350-7500).

Grandtravel (6900 Wisconsin Ave., Suite 706, Chevy Chase, MD 20815; phone: 800-247-7651 or 301-986-0790).

Interhostel (UNH Division of Continuing Education, 6 Garrison Ave., Durham, NH 03824; phone: 800-733-9753 or 603-862-1147).

OmniTours (104 Wilmont Rd., Deerfield, IL 60015; phone: 800-962-0060 or 708-374-0088).

Saga International Holidays (222 Berkeley St., Boston, MA 02116; phone: 800-343-0273 or 617-262-2262).

Money Matters

Although several islands use US currency as their official means of exchange, local currencies are used throughout most of the Caribbean; these fluctuate in value in relation to the US dollar. (A listing of each island's currency, and the rate of exchange at press time, is provided in ISLAND-BY-ISLAND HOPPING.) On some islands that have their own currencies, US dollars may be welcome and even preferred to local currency, although this is not the case in Colombia, Mexico, and Venezuela, where using US currency means negotiating the exchange rate for every small purchase.

Exchange rates are posted in international newspapers such as the *International Herald Tribune.* Foreign currency information and related services are provided by banks and companies such as *Thomas Cook Foreign Exchange* (for the nearest location, call 800-621-0666 or 312-236-0042); *Harold Reuter and Company* (200 Park Ave., Suite 332E, New York, NY 10166; phone: 212-661-0826); and *Ruesch International* (for the nearest location, call 800-424-2923 or 202-408-1200). In the Caribbean, you will find the official rate of exchange posted in banks, airports, money exchange houses, hotels, and some shops. Since you will get more local currency for your US dollar at banks and money exchanges, don't change more than $10 at other commercial establishments. Ask how much commission you're being charged and the exchange rate, and don't buy money on the black market (it may be counterfeit). Estimate your needs carefully; if you overbuy, you lose twice — buying and selling back.

TRAVELER'S CHECKS AND CREDIT CARDS

It's wise to carry traveler's checks while on the road, since they are replaceable if stolen or lost. You can buy traveler's checks at banks and some are available by mail or phone. Although most major credit cards enjoy wide domestic and international acceptance, not every hotel, restaurant, or shop in the Caribbean accepts all (or in some cases any) credit cards. When making purchases with a credit card, note that the rate of exchange depends on when the charge is processed; most credit card companies charge a 1% fee for converting foreign currency charges. Keep a separate list of all traveler's checks (noting those that you have cashed) and the names and numbers of your credit cards. Both traveler's check and credit card companies have international numbers to call for information or in the event of loss or theft.

CASH MACHINES

Automated teller machines (ATMs) are increasingly common worldwide. Most banks participate in one of the international ATM networks; cardholders can withdraw cash from any machine in the same network using either a "bank" card or, in some cases, a credit card. At the time of this writing, most ATMs belong to the *CIRRUS* or *PLUS* network. For further information, ask at your bank branch.

SENDING MONEY ABROAD

Should the need arise, it is possible to have money sent to you via the services provided by *American Express* (*MoneyGram;* phone: 800-926-9400 or 800-666-3997 for information; 800-866-8800 for money transfers) or *Western Union Financial Services* (phone: 800-325-4176).

If you are down to your last cent and have no other way to obtain cash, the nearest US Consulate will let you call home to set these matters in motion.

Accommodations

For specific information on hotels, resorts, and other selected accommodations see the individual chapters in ISLAND-BY-ISLAND HOPPING. A particularly appealing option is to stay at one of the all-inclusive resorts located throughout the Caribbean. These properties offer packages that include airfare, accommodations, meals, local transportation, recreational activities, entertainment, and other extras.

RENTAL OPTIONS

An attractive accommodations alternative for the visitor content to stay in one spot is to rent one of the numerous properties available throughout the Caribbean. For a family or group, the per-person cost can be reasonable. To have your pick of the properties available, make inquiries at least 6 months in advance. The *Worldwide Home Rental Guide* (369 Montezuma, Suite 297, Santa Fe, NM 87501; phone: 505-984-7080) lists rental properties and managing agencies.

Rental Property Agents

At Home Abroad (405 E. 56th St., Suite 6H, New York, NY 10022-2466; phone: 212-421-9165).

Condo World (4230 Orchard Lake Rd., Suite 3, Orchard Lake, MI 48323; phone: 800-521-2980 or 313-683-0202).

Creative Leisure (951 Transport Way, Petaluma, CA 94954; phone: 800-4-CONDOS or 707-778-1880).

Hideaways International (PO Box 4433, Portsmith, NH 03802-4433; phone: 800-843-4433 or 603-430-4433).

La Cure Villas (11661 San Vicente Blvd., Suite 1010, Los Angeles, CA 90049; phone: 800-387-2726 or 416-968-2374).

Rent a Home International (7200 34th Ave. NW, Seattle, WA 98117; phone: 206-789-9377).

VHR Worldwide (235 Kensington Ave., Norwood, NJ 07648; phone: 201-767-9393 in New Jersey; 800-633-3284 elsewhere in the US).

Villa Leisure (PO Box 209, Westport, CT 06881; phone: 800-526-4244 or 203-222-7397).

Villas and Apartments Abroad (420 Madison Ave., Suite 1105, New York, NY 10017; phone: 212-759-1025 in New York State; 800-433-3020 elsewhere in the US).

Villas International (605 Market St., Suite 510, San Francisco, CA 94105; phone: 800-221-2260 or 415-281-0910).

HOME EXCHANGES

For comfortable, reasonable living quarters with amenities that no hotel could possibly offer, consider trading homes with someone abroad. The following companies provide information on exchanges:

Home Base Holidays (7 Park Ave., London N13 5PG, England; phone: 44-81-886-8752).

Intervac US/International Home Exchange (PO Box 590504, San Francisco, CA 94159; phone: 800-756-HOME or 415-435-3497).

Loan-A-Home (2 Park La., Apt. 6E, Mt. Vernon, NY 10552; phone: 914-664-7640).

Vacation Exchange Club (PO Box 650, Key West, FL 33041; phone: 800-638-3841 or 305-294-3720).

Worldwide Home Exchange Club (138 Brompton Rd., London SW3 1HY, England; phone: 44-71-589-6055; or 806 Brantford Ave., Silver Spring, MD 20904; phone: 301-680-8950).

HOME STAYS

The *United States Servas Committee* (11 John St., Room 407, New York, NY 10038; phone: 212-267-0252) maintains a list of hosts throughout the world willing to accommodate visitors free of charge. The aim of this nonprofit cultural program is to promote international understanding and peace, and *Servas* emphasizes that member travelers should be interested mainly in their hosts, not in sightseeing, during their stays.

ACCOMMODATION DISCOUNTS

The following organizations offer discounts of up to 50% on accommodations throughout the Caribbean:

Entertainment Publishing (2125 Butterfield Rd., Troy, MI 48084; phone: 800-477-3234 or 313-637-8400).

International Travel Card (6001 N. Clark St., Chicago, IL 60660; phone: 800-342-0558 or 312-465-8891).

Privilege Card (5395 Roswell Rd., Suite 200, Atlanta, GA 30342; phone: 404-262-0222).

Quest International (402 E. Yakima Ave., Suite 1200, Yakima, WA 98901; phone: 800-325-2400 or 509-248-7512).

World Hotel Express (14900 Landmark Blvd., Suite 116, Dallas, TX 75240; phone: 800-866-2015 or 214-991-5482 for information; 800-580-2083 for reservations).

Mail

Always use airmail and allow at least 10 days for delivery between the Caribbean and the United States. Stamps are available at post offices, most hotel desks, and from public vending machines. If your correspondence is especially important, you may want to send it via one of the international courier services, such as *Federal Express* or *DHL Worldwide Express.*

You can have mail sent to you care of your hotel (marked "Guest Mail, Hold for Arrival") or to a post office ("c/o General Delivery" — indicated as *a/c Poste Restante* on French-speaking islands or *a/c Lista de Correos* in Spanish-speaking destinations). *American Express* offices also will hold mail for customers ("c/o Client Letter Service"); information is provided in their pamphlet *Travelers' Companion.* US Embassies and Consulates abroad will hold mail for US citizens *only* in emergency situations.

Telephone

Most of the developed islands have direct and relatively efficient phone service, although service may be spotty on more remote islands and in backcountry areas of coastal countries. Public telephones are widely available — in restaurants, hotel lobbies, post offices, booths on the streets, and at most tourist centers. There also may be telephone offices from which long-distance calls can be made. The number of digits in phone numbers varies throughout the Caribbean.

For information on making telephone calls within individual islands or countries, or from the US to the Caribbean, see ISLAND-BY-ISLAND HOPPING. The procedures for calling between islands and from the Caribbean to the US are as follows:

Between Islands

- When calling from a location in the 809 area code to another island in the 809 coverage area, dial 1 + the local number.
- When calling from a location within the 809 area code to one outside of the 809 coverage area, dial 011 (international access code) + the country code + the city code (if applicable) + the local number.
- When calling from an international calling area outside of the 809 area code to another location in the Caribbean (whether in the 809 coverage area or not), dial the international access code + the country code + the city code + the local number.

To the US

- From a location within the 809 area code, you can dial directly 1 + the area code + the local number.
- If calling from a location outside of the 809 area code, dial an international access code + a US country code (both vary from one island or country to another) + the area code + the local number.

The procedure for reaching a local or international operator also varies throughout the Caribbean. For operator-assisted calls between islands or countries in the Caribbean, usually you will dial a direct number or the international access code followed by the number for the international operator. For the applicable procedures, contact the island tourist authorities.

In a number of Caribbean nations, you can charge international calls to a telephone company credit card number, and in Puerto Rico and the US Virgin Islands pay phones that take major credit cards (*American Express, MasterCard, Visa,* and so on) are increasingly common.

Long-distance telephone services that help you avoid the surcharges that hotels routinely add to phone bills are provided by *American Telephone and Telegraph* (*AT&T Communications,* International Information Service, 635 Grant St., Pittsburgh, PA 15219; phone: 800-874-4000), *MCI* (323 3rd St. SE, Cedar Rapids, IA 52401; phone: 800-444-3333), *Metromedia Communications Corp.* (1 International Center, 100 NE Loop 410, San Antonio, TX 78216; phone: 800-275-0200), and *Sprint* (offices throughout the US; phone: 800-877-4000). Some hotels still may charge a fee for line usage.

AT&T's Language Line Service (phone: 800-752-6096) provides interpretive services for telephone communications in French, Spanish, and many other foreign languages. Also useful are the *AT&T 800 Travel Directory* (available at *AT&T Phone Centers* or by calling 800-426-8686), the *Toll-Free Travel & Vacation Information Directory* (Pilot Books, 103 Cooper St., Babylon, NY 11702; phone: 516-422-2225), and *The Phone Booklet* (Scott American Corporation, PO Box 88, W. Redding, CT 06896; phone: 203-938-2955). A company called *Boatphone* (PO Box 1516, St. John's, Antigua, West Indies; phone: 800-BOAT-FON or 809-462-5051) offers cellular phone service on many Caribbean islands.

EMERGENCY NUMBERS

Below are the numbers to call in the Caribbean in the event of an accident or medical emergency.

Anguilla: Dial 911 for emergency assistance.
Antigua: Dial 999 or 911 for emergency assistance.
Aruba: Dial 100 for emergency assistance.
Barbados: Dial 115 for an ambulance; 112 for the police.
Belize: Dial 90 for emergency assistance.
Bonaire: Dial 11 for emergency assistance.
British Virgin Islands: Dial 999 for emergency assistance.

Cayman Islands: Dial 911 for emergency assistance.

Colombia: For emergency assistance in Cartagena, dial 118. In Santa Marta, dial 116 for an ambulance; 112 for the police. In San Andrés or Providencia, there are no emergency numbers; the individual hospitals or police departments must be called.

Curaçao: Dial 89337 for an ambulance; 44444 for the police.

Dominica: Dial 999 for emergency assistance; 448-2889 for an ambulance; 448-2222 for the police.

Dominican Republic: Dial 682-3743 for an ambulance; 682-2151 for the police.

Grenada: Dial 440-2113 for an ambulance; 440-2244 for the police.

Guadeloupe: Dial 590-820005 for Pointe-à-Pitre and 590-811155 for Basse-Terre.

Haiti: Dial 114 for emergency assistance.

Jamaica: Dial 119 for emergency assistance.

Martinique: Dial 552000 for an ambulance; 635151 for the police.

Mexico: Dial 06 for emergency assistance.

Montserrat: Dial 911 for an ambulance; 999 for the police.

Puerto Rico: Dial 343-2250 for an ambulance; 343-2020 for the police.

Saba: Dial 63237 for emergency assistance.

St. Barthélemy: Dial 276035 for an ambulance; 875040 for the police.

St. Eustatius: Dial 82333 for emergency assistance.

St. Kitts/Nevis: Dial 911 for emergency assistance.

St. Lucia: Dial 999 for emergency assistance.

St. Maarten: Dial 22111 for an ambulance; 22222 for the police.

St. Martin: Dial 875007 for an ambulance; 875040 for the police.

St. Vincent and the Grenadines: Dial 456-1185 for an ambulance; 999 for the police.

Trinidad and Tobago: Dial 999 for emergency assistance.

US Virgin Islands: Dial 922 for an ambulance; 915 for the police.

Venezuela: In Caracas only, dial 165 for the police; elsewhere, dial 103 for a local operator.

Electricity

Like the US, some islands use 110-volt, 60-cycle, alternating current (AC). Where 220-volt, 50-cycle, direct current (DC) is standard, you will need electrical converters to operate appliances designed for use in the US. To be fully prepared, pack a wall socket adapter for any outlets that have nonstandard plug configurations. (Information on local electricity standards can be found in ISLAND-BY-ISLAND HOPPING.)

Staying Healthy

For information on current health conditions, call the Centers for Disease Control and Prevention's *International Health Requirements and Recom-*

mendations Information Hotline: 404-332-4559. The US Public Health Service recommends diphtheria and tetanus shots for people traveling in the Caribbean. In addition, children should be inoculated against measles, mumps, rubella, and polio.

In some areas of the Caribbean (such as Mexico) it is not safe to drink the tap water — do not even brush your teeth with it. Stick to bottled and canned drinks or use water purification tablets. Milk sold in stores is pasteurized and safe to drink, but beware of spoilage due to improper refrigeration. Avoid unpasteurized or uncooked dairy products, unpeeled fruit, or any uncooked vegetables. And do *not* buy food from street vendors.

When swimming, the undertow (a current running back down the beach after a wave has washed ashore) can knock you down, and riptides (currents running against the tide) can pull you out to sea. If you see a shark, swim away quictly and smoothly. Also bcwarc of cels, Portuguese man-of-war (and other jellyfish), sea urchins, and razor sharp coral reefs.

In some areas of the Caribbean, Chagas' disease, malaria, and yellow fever can be transmitted through insect bites. (At the time of this writing, outbreaks of malaria had occurred in Haiti and rural areas of the Dominican Republic; yellow fever had been reported on Trinidad and Tobago.) Use a strong insect repellent; antimalarial tablets and a yellow fever inoculation are advisable. Bites from snakes, spiders, and scorpions, or any wild animal can be serious and must be treated immediately.

The best hospitals are affiliated with universities in major cities (such facilities generally have properly screened blood donors for infectious diseases). The next best alternative is to seek treatment at a private, rather than government-owned, hospital. Ask at your hotel for the house physician or for help in reaching a doctor or contact the US Consulate. Pharmacies usually are not open around the clock; if you need a prescription filled during off-hours, go directly to a local hospital.

Be extremely cautious about injections in the Caribbean because reusable syringes and needles are still common, and sterilization procedures may be inadequate. If you have a condition that requires occasional injections, bring a supply of syringes with you or buy disposable syringes.

In an emergency: Go to the emergency room of the nearest hospital or dial one of the numbers for emergency assistance listed above.

Additional Resources

International Association of Medical Assistance to Travelers (*IAMAT;* 417 Center St., Lewiston, NY 14092; phone: 716-754-4883).

International Health Care Service (440 E. 69th St., New York, NY 10021; phone: 212-746-1601).

International SOS Assistance (PO Box 11568, Philadelphia, PA 19116; phone: 800-523-8930 or 215-244-1500).

Medic Alert Foundation (2323 Colorado Ave., Turlock, CA 95380; phone: 800-ID-ALERT or 209-668-3333).

TravMed (PO Box 10623, Baltimore, MD 21285-0623; phone: 800-732-5309 or 410-296-5225).

Consular Services

The American Services section of the US Consulate is a vital source of assistance and advice for US citizens abroad. If you are injured or become seriously ill, the consulate can direct you to sources of medical attention and notify your relatives. If you become involved in a dispute that could lead to legal action, the consulate is the place to turn. In cases of natural disasters or civil unrest, consulates handle the evacuation of US citizens if necessary.

US Embassies and Consulates in the Caribbean

Anguilla, Antigua, Barbuda, British Virgin Islands, Montserrat, St. Kitts and Nevis: US Embassy, Queen Elizabeth Hwy., St. John's, Antigua, WI (phone: 809-462-3505, -3506, -3511, and -3512).

Barbados, Dominica, St. Lucia, St. Vincent and the Grenadines: US Consulate, Alico Bldg., Cheapside, Bridgetown, Barbados (phone: 809-431-0225).

Cayman Islands: US Consulate, PO Box 1749, George Town, Grand Cayman (phone: 809-949-8440).

Dominican Republic: US Embassy, Calle César Nicolás Penson and Calle Leopoldo Navarro, Santo Domingo, Dominican Republic (phone: 809-541-2171).

Grenada: US Embassy, Point Salines, St. George's, Grenada (phone: 809-444-1173).

Haiti: US Embassy, Harry Truman Blvd., Port-au-Prince, Haiti (phone: 509-220354).

Jamaica: US Embassy, Jamaica Mutual Life Centre, 2 Oxford Rd., 3rd Floor, Kingston 5, Jamaica (phone: 809-929-4850).

Martinique, Guadeloupe, St. Martin, St. Barthélemy: US Consulate, 14 Rue Blenac, B.P. 561, Fort-de-France, Martinique 97206 (phone: 596-631303).

Netherlands Antilles (Bonaire, Curaçao, Saba, St. Eustatius, and St. Maarten): US Consulate General, Curaçao, JB #1 Gorsiraweg, Roosevelt House, Willemstad, Curaçao (phone: 599-961-3066).

Trinidad and Tobago: US Embassy, 15 Queen's Park West, Port-of-Spain, Trinidad (phone: 809-622-6371).

The US State Department operates a 24-hour *Citizens' Emergency Center* travel advisory information hotline (phone: 202-647-5225). **In an emergency, call 202-647-4000 and ask for the duty officer.**

Entry Requirements and Customs Regulations

ENTERING THE ISLANDS

All of the islands and countries described in this guide require visitors to produce some legal documentation. The only universal requirement is proof of citizenship, such as a birth certificate, an affidavit of birth, voter's registration card, or valid passport. Those forms of identification without a photograph also must be accompanied by some form of official photo ID; however, a driver's license alone *will not* suffice as proof of citizenship. Officials at some destinations also may require a return or ongoing ticket, proof of pre-arranged accommodations, and/or sufficient funds.

Several Caribbean governments also require tourist cards, and many impose limits on the length of stay. For longer stays or entry for work or study, visas (issued by consulates) generally are required. Tourist cards should be obtained before departure from a consulate, government tourist office, airline, or travel agent, although in some cases, this can be done on arrival. For information on specific entry requirements, see ISLAND-BY-ISLAND HOPPING.

Most Caribbean nations impose limitations on the quantities of specific items (such as tobacco products and liquor) that may be imported duty-free. For information on customs regulations, contact island tourist authorities in the US.

RETURNING TO THE US

You must declare to the US Customs official at the point of entry everything you have acquired in the islands. The standard duty-free allowance for US citizens is $400 (if your trip is shorter than 48 continuous hours, or you have been out of the US within 30 days, it is cut to $25). However, the allowance is more generous for travelers returning from certain Caribbean destinations. For information on duty-free goods and allowances, see DIVERSIONS. Families traveling together may make a joint declaration.

The Generalized System of Preferences (which applies to some Caribbean countries) allows US citizens to bring certain goods into the US duty-free. Antiques (at least 100 years old) and paintings or drawings done entirely by hand also are duty-free.

A flat 10% duty is assessed on the next $1,000 worth of merchandise; additional items are taxed at a variety of rates (see *Tariff Schedules of the United States* in a library or any US Customs Service office). With the exception of gifts valued at $50 or less sent directly to the recipient, items shipped home are dutiable. Some articles are duty-free only up to certain limits. The $400 allowance includes 1 carton of (200) cigarettes, 100 cigars (not Cuban), and 1 liter of liquor or wine (for those over 21); the $25 allowance includes 10 cigars, 50 cigarettes, and 4 ounces of perfume. To avoid paying duty unnecessarily, before your trip, register the serial numbers of any expensive equipment you are bringing along with US Customs.

Forbidden imports include articles made of the furs or hides of animals on the endangered species list. In addition, you must obtain a permit from the appropriate government agency in order to take original artifacts out of any Caribbean island or country.

For further information, consult *Know Before You Go; International Mail Imports; Travelers' Tips on Bringing Food, Plant, and Animal Products into the United States; Importing a Car; GSP and the Traveler; Pocket Hints; Currency Reporting;* and *Pets, Wildlife, US Customs;* all available from the US Customs Service (PO Box 7407, Washington, DC 20044). For tape-recorded information on travel-related topics, call 202-927-2095 from any touch-tone phone.

DUTY-FREE SHOPS **Located in international airports, these provide bargains on the purchase of foreign goods. But beware: Not all foreign goods are automatically less expensive. You *can* get a good deal on some items, but know what they cost elsewhere.**

For Further Information

The Caribbean tourist authorities in the US are the best sources of travel information. Offices generally are open on weekdays, during normal business hours.

The only Caribbean island that does not have its own tourism information office is Dominica; it relies on the Caribbean Tourism Organization (20 E. 46th St., New York, NY 10017; phone: 212-682-0435), a central tourist information bureau for the region. The best places for tourist information in the Caribbean are listed in the *Sources and Resources* sections of the individual chapters in ISLAND-BY-ISLAND HOPPING.

Island Tourist Offices in the US

Anguilla

Anguilla Tourist Information and Reservation Office, c/o *Medhurst & Associates,* 271 Main St., Northport, NY 11768 (phone: 800-553-4939 or 516-261-1234).

Antigua

Antigua Department of Tourism

121 SE 1st St., Suite 1001, Miami, FL 33131 (phone: 305-381-6762).

610 Fifth Ave., Suite 311, New York, NY 10020 (phone: 212-541-4117).

Aruba

Aruba Tourism Authority

24 Salzebo St., Miami, FL 33134-5033 (phone: 305-567-2720).

1000 Harbor Blvd., Weehawken, NJ 07087 (phone: 800-TO-ARUBA or 201-330-0800).

Barbados

Barbados Board of Tourism

3440 Wilshire Blvd., Suite 1215, Los Angeles, CA 90010 (phone: 213-380-2198).

800 2nd Ave., New York, NY 10017 (phone: 212-986-6516).

Belize

Belize Tourist Board, 415 7th Ave., 18th Floor, New York, NY 10001 (phone: 212-268-8798).

Bonaire

Bonaire Government Tourist Office, 444 Madison Ave., Suite 2403, New York, NY 10022 (phone: 800-U-BONAIR or 212-832-0779).

British Virgin Islands

British Virgin Islands Tourist Board

1686 Union St., Suite 305, San Francisco, CA 94123 (phone: 800-232-7770 or 415-775-0344).

370 Lexington Ave., Room 416, New York, NY 10017 (phone: 212-696-0400).

Cayman Islands

Cayman Islands Department of Tourism

3440 Wilshire Blvd., Suite 1202, Los Angeles, CA 90010 (phone: 213-738-1968).

6100 Blue Lagoon Dr., Suite 150, Miami, FL 33126 (phone: 305-266-2300).

9252 W. Bryn Mawr Ave., Rosemont, IL 60018 (phone: 708-678-6446).

420 Lexington Ave., Suite 2733, New York, NY 10170 (phone: 212-682-5582).

2 Memorial City Plaza, 820 Gessner, Suite 170, Houston, TX 77024 (phone: 713-461-1317).

Colombia

At press time, the Colombian Government Tourist Office in the US had been closed, and Colombian Consulates in the US had assumed its responsibilities. Limited tourist information also was available from the Colombian Embassy, Press and Information Department, 2118 Leroy Pl. NW, Washington, DC 20008 (phone: 202-387-8338).

Curaçao

Curaçao Tourist Board

330 Biscayne Blvd., Suite 808, Miami, FL 33132 (phone: 800-445-8266 or 305-374-5811).

400 Madison Ave., Suite 311, New York, NY 10017 (phone: 212-751-8266).

Dominican Republic

Dominican Republic Tourist Information Center, 1 Times Sq. Plaza, 11th Floor, New York, NY 10036 (phone: 212-768-2482).

French West Indies (Guadeloupe, Martinique, St. Barthélemy, St. Martin)

French Government Tourist Office

9454 Wilshire Blvd., Suite 303, Beverly Hills, CA 90212-2967 (phone: 310-271-2358).

645 N. Michigan Ave., Suite 630, Chicago, IL 60611-2836 (phone: 312-337-6301).

628 Fifth Ave., New York, NY 10020 (phone: 212-757-1125).

2305 Cedar Spring Rd., Suite 205, Dallas, TX 75201 (phone: 214-720-4011).

Grenada

Grenada Tourist Office

820 2nd Ave., Suite 900D, New York, NY 10017 (phone: 212-687-9554).

Guadeloupe

See French West Indies, above.

Haiti

At press time, the Haitian National Office of Tourism in the US remained closed; information was available from the Haitian Consulate.

Consulate General of Haiti, 271 Madison Ave., 17th Floor, New York, NY 10016 (phone: 212-697-9767).

Embassy of Haiti, 2311 Massachusetts Ave. NW, Washington, DC 20008 (phone: 202-332-4091).

Jamaica

Jamaica Tourist Board

3440 Wilshire Blvd., Suite 1207, Los Angeles, CA 90010 (phone: 213-384-1123).

1320 S. Dixie Hwy., Suite 1100, Coral Gables, FL 33146 (phone: 305-665-0557).

300 W. Wieuca Rd. NE, Bldg. 1, Suite 100A, Atlanta, GA 30342 (phone: 800-327-9857 or 404-250-9971).

36 S. Wabash Ave., Suite 1210, Chicago, IL 60603 (phone: 312-346-1546).

801 2nd Ave., 20th Floor, New York, NY 10017 (phone: 212-688-7650).

8214 Westchester Dr., Suite 500, Dallas, TX 75225 (phone: 214-361-8778).

Martinique

See French West Indies, above.

Mexico (Cancún, Cozumel)

Mexican Government Tourism Office

10100 Santa Monica Blvd., Suite 224, Los Angeles, CA 90067 (phone: 213-203-8191).

128 Aragon Ave., Coral Gables, FL 33134 (phone: 305-443-9160).

70 E. Lake St., Suite 1413, Chicago, IL 60601 (phone: 312-565-2778).

405 Park Ave., Suite 1402, New York, NY 10022 (phone: 212-755-7261).

2707 N. Loop W, Suite 450, Houston, TX 77008 (phone: 713-880-5153).

1911 Pennsylvania Ave. NW, Washington, DC 20006 (phone: 202-728-1750).

Montserrat

Montserrat Tourist Board, c/o *Pace Advertising and Marketing,* 485 Fifth Ave., New York, NY 10017 (phone: 212-818-0100).

Puerto Rico

Government of Puerto Rico Tourism Company

3575 W. Cahuenga Blvd., Suite 560, Los Angeles, CA 90068 (phone: 213-874-5991).

200 SE 1st St., Suite 700, Miami, FL 33131 (phone: 305-381-8915).

575 Fifth Ave., 23rd Floor, New York, NY 10017 (phone: 800-223-6530 or 212-599-6262).

Saba/St. Eustatius

Saba and St. Eustatius Tourist Information Office, 271 Main St., Northport, NY 11768 (phone: 516-261-7474).

St. Barthélemy

See French West Indies, above.

St. Kitts/Nevis

St. Kitts/Nevis Tourism Office, 414 E. 75th St., 5th Floor, New York, NY 10021 (phone: 212-535-1234).

St. Lucia

St. Lucia Tourist Board, 820 2nd Ave., Suite 900E, New York, NY 10017 (phone: 212-867-2950).

St. Maarten

St. Maarten Tourist Office, 275 7th Ave., 19th Floor, New York, NY 10001-6788 (phone: 212-989-0000).

St. Martin

See French West Indies, above.

St. Vincent and the Grenadines

St. Vincent and the Grenadines Tourist Board

801 2nd Ave., 21st Floor, New York, NY 10017 (phone: 212-687-4981).

6505 Covercreek Pl., Dallas, TX 75240 (phone: 214-239-6451).

Trinidad and Tobago

Trinidad and Tobago Tourist Board, 25 W. 43rd St., Suite 1508, New York, NY 10036 (phone: 800-232-0082 or 212-719-0540).

US Virgin Islands

US Virgin Islands Division of Tourism

3460 Wilshire Blvd., Suite 412, Los Angeles, CA 90010 (phone: 213-739-0138).

2655 Le Jeune Rd., Suite 907, Coral Gables, FL 33134 (phone: 305-442-7200).

225 Peachtree St. NE, Suite 760, Atlanta, GA 30303 (phone: 404-688-0906).

122 S. Michigan Ave., Suite 1270, Chicago, IL 60603 (phone: 312-461-0180).

1270 Ave. of the Americas, Suite 1208, New York, NY 10020 (phone: 212-332-2222).

900 17th St. NW, Suite 500, Washington, DC 20006 (phone: 202-293-3707).

Venezuela

Consulate of Venezuela, 7 E. 51st St., New York, NY 10022 (phone: 212-826-1660).

Embassy of Venezuela, 1099 30th St. NW, Washington, DC 20007 (phone: 202-342-6809).

Island-by-Island Hopping

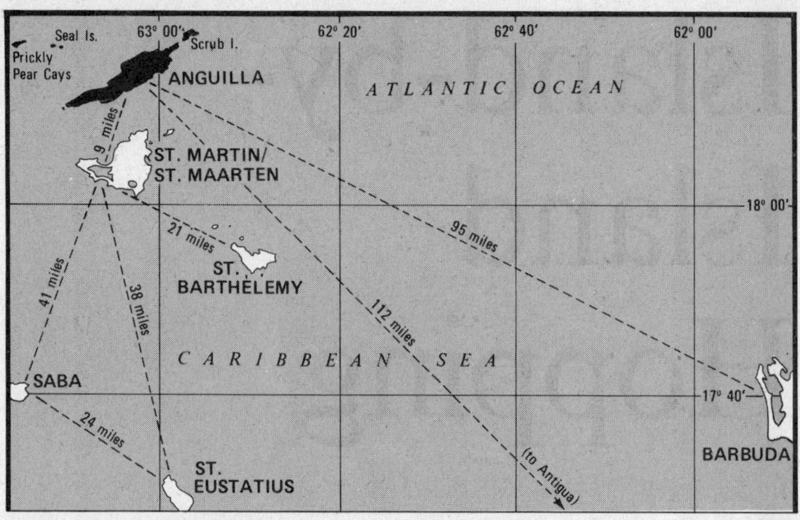

63° 00′
62° 20′
62° 40′
62° 00′
Seal Is.
Prickly Pear Cays
Scrub I.
ANGUILLA
ATLANTIC OCEAN
9 miles
ST. MARTIN/ ST. MAARTEN
18° 00′
95 miles
21 miles
ST. BARTHELEMY
41 miles
38 miles
112 miles
CARIBBEAN SEA
SABA
17° 40′
24 miles
(to Antigua)
BARBUDA
ST. EUSTATIUS

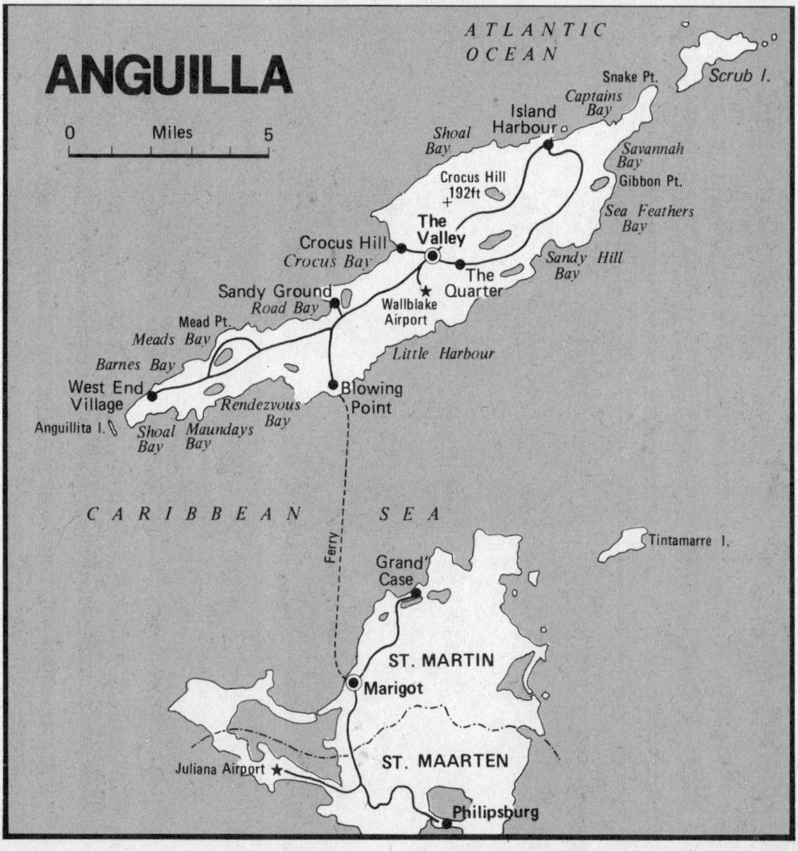

ANGUILLA

ATLANTIC OCEAN
0 Miles 5
Scrub I.
Snake Pt.
Captains Bay
Island Harbour
Shoal Bay
Savannah Bay
Crocus Hill 192ft
Gibbon Pt.
Sea Feathers Bay
The Valley
Crocus Hill
Crocus Bay
Sandy Hill Bay
The Quarter
Sandy Ground
Road Bay
Wallblake Airport
Mead Pt.
Meads Bay
Little Harbour
Barnes Bay
West End Village
Blowing Point
Rendezvous Bay
Anguillita I.
Shoal Bay
Maundays Bay
CARIBBEAN SEA
Tintamarre I.
Ferry
Grand' Case
ST. MARTIN
Marigot
ST. MAARTEN
Juliana Airport
Philipsburg

Anguilla

For its first four and a half centuries, Anguilla (pronounced An-*gwil*-la) lazed away its days in what seemed — to the outside world, at least — a content, nearly comatose, state. In fact, none of the islanders probably noticed when Columbus, sailing by in 1493, gave the island its name (the Spanish word for "eel," because of its long, narrow shape and serpentine shoreline).

The island's Arawak Indian residents continued their quiet existence until 1650, when the first British settlers arrived. In the 18th century, Anguillans were stung twice by French attacks. Both times, the invaders were forced to retreat, and the island continued to avoid interaction with the outside world.

For the next century and a half, no one — except Anguillans — thought much about the island. Even the islanders failed to react at first when, in 1825, the British government made a single Crown Colony of St. Kitts, Nevis, and Anguilla.

But during the 1950s, the Anguillans began to mutter; and in 1966, when Britain made an associated state of the three-island colony without giving Anguilla a say in its own government, the islanders objected loudly. Prodded by what they perceived as subjugation to a "foreign" power — the legislature in distant St. Kitts — Anguillans seceded from the alliance.

The cry of the "eel" brought international media attention, especially after neighboring islands talked of sending expeditionary forces. To forestall any precipitous local action, the Crown dispatched a "peacekeeping force" in 1969. To their surprise, they were greeted warmly by the Anguillans, who were waving Union Jacks instead of submachine guns. When the dust had settled, no lives had been lost (the one barrage reported turned out to be photographers' flashbulbs rather than gunfire). In response to its subjects' wishes, in 1971 Britain once more took Anguilla under its colonial wing. In February 1976, a new and separate constitution providing a ministerial system of government, with elected representatives handling most island affairs, went into effect. Soon after that Anguilla, now wide awake, took its first look at tourism as a potential source of income, even prosperity.

There were two major drawbacks at the start: near total obscurity and a dearth of accommodations for comfort-craving (let alone luxury-seeking) guests. In the late 1970s, the island had fewer than 150 rooms for visitors. On the other hand, though, Anguilla's bone-dry climate and isolation blessed the island with spectacular natural attractions: truly glorious beaches, incredibly clear water, and undisturbed reefs alive with fantastic fish.

Aware of others' mistakes, the government declared itself "committed to development of a *controlled* tourist industry" and began exploring possibilities. Today, low-rise first class and luxury hotels, villas, and condominiums dot the island, and others are quietly popping up on a regular basis. While the government is sincerely determined "to preserve peace and tranquillity," the island is no longer "the Caribbean's best-kept secret." In fact, Anguilla's small, serene, and select hotels are among the most talked-about in the Caribbean. In every sense, tourism is becoming big business.

The rise in development on the island has been a mixed blessing. The good news is that there are now enough rooms to house almost all the visitors eager to enjoy Anguilla's unique blend of sophistication and unspoiled beaches. The bad news is that petty crime has made an appearance. But locals still feel secure enough to leave their homes and cars unlocked at night, and rooms at the elegant *Cap Juluca* have no keys.

Even the most fertile imagination could not describe Anguilla as bustling or exciting, but the quiet atmosphere is a large part of its appeal. Besides sunning, lazy snorkeling, sailing, or picnicking, there really isn't much to do. More comforts and diversions may be on the way, but for now, if the sun, the sand, the sea, and a stack of paperbacks are *really* all you need for a perfect vacation, have we got an island for you . . .

Anguilla At-a-Glance

FROM THE AIR

Anguilla, northernmost of the British Leeward Islands, stretches for 16 miles from southwest to northeast, with small Scrub Island off its northeastern end and minuscule Anguillita Island off its southwestern tip. The French/Dutch island of St. Martin/St. Maarten is 4 miles south; St. Kitts is 70 miles south and slightly east; Puerto Rico is 150 miles due west. Anguilla is only 3 miles across at its widest point, and the shining white coral beaches that notch its coasts make for an undulating shoreline. The island rises only 213 feet above sea level, and has no cities, no rivers, no streams or rushing waterfalls; the land is dry, with several salt ponds and a few palm trees, but mostly short, sparse vegetation. The island's 8,000 inhabitants make their living lobstering, fishing, building hotels or the famed Anguillan boats, and working for the government or in the tourism industry.

Anguilla's main road leads from West End, a village in the southwest, to The Quarter, a small settlement at the island's midpoint; the road then loops northeast up to Island Harbour and back again. At a number of places, auxiliary roads branch off north and south toward beaches and fishing villages. The island's central area is called The Valley. It's the administrative center for Anguilla's elected ministerial government and the new home of the Department of Tourism office. Sandy Ground at Road Bay, the island's principal port of entry, is on the north coast. Ferries to

Marigot on St. Martin leave from Blowing Point on the south coast. Wallblake Airport is in the middle of the island near The Quarter and The Valley.

SPECIAL PLACES

On Anguilla, beaches definitely get top billing: With more than 33 from which to choose, you probably won't even have time to see them all.

DREAM BEACH

Shoal Bay Our vote for the island's most superb strand goes to this stunning, sweeping, silvery beach — literally one of the enormous beauties of this island. And much of the time it's enchantingly empty. The only crowds are offshore and underwater — clouds of iridescent fish that dart about the astonishing coral gardens. The drop-off and reef beyond lure experienced divers. There are shady trees to laze under when you've had enough sun and sea, but bring *everything* with you — masks, flippers, beach towels, cover-ups. Nearby beach bars provide drinks and food.

But don't just stop here. Many vacationers visit several beaches before settling on one or two favorites — you'll need a car or a mini-moke (an open-air jeep) to do this, although hitchhiking is perfectly acceptable. On the south shore, sweeping Rendezvous Bay is among the most beautiful. During the summer of 1986, some 3,000 pieces of ancient pottery, as well as some human remains from a large Amerindian settlement (possibly dating back to 100 BC), were found during excavations for a hotel on the beach here. Along the south coast to the west of Rendezvous Bay, facing the rolling hills of St. Martin, are the white shores of secluded Cove Bay (where you may share the clear water only with fishing boats) and Maunday's Bay. The latter is very good for shelling, and is the site of *Cap Juluca,* a sparkling, super-luxury resort sprawling over 179 acres of land and water. At the northeastern edge of Anguilla is Captain's Bay, one of the most secluded beaches on the island, with coral outcrops bracketing a romantic stretch of white sand. You're unlikely to find another soul here. There is also good snorkeling at Shoal Bay West, Mimi Bay, Little Harbour, Limestone Bay, Sea Feather, and at Little Bay, on the northern end of Crocus Bay, which is accessible by boat or via steep cliffs from the road's edge. Framed by the island's largest hill, vast Crocus Bay is the departure point of many Anguillan boat races — the island's favorite sport — but otherwise is very peaceful. Sandy Ground, on Road Bay, between the Salt Pond and the sea, is a small harborside village that is one of the island's prettiest. While Sandy Ground and Shoal Bay are the most commercial of Anguilla's many beaches, they are, by any standards, clean, uncrowded, and picturesque.

Still under way above Shoal Bay is the excavation of a cave known as The Fountain, which contains a large stalagmite and a number of interesting petroglyphs. Few people are aware of Anguilla's many archaeological digs (23 aboriginal sites have been discovered so far), some dating from as early as the 2nd millennium BC. Anguilla has established a 3½-acre national park around The Fountain; the *Anguilla Museum,* which was scheduled to open at press time, is housed in the Old Customs House next to the post office in The Valley. It features exhibits on Anguilla's archaeological finds and on the island's history. For additional information, contact the Anguilla Tourist Information Office (phone: 2759 or 2451; 800-553-4939 from the US).

EXTRA SPECIAL **The most fun place on this most peaceful of islands just might be Scilly Cay (pronounced *Silly Key*), an acre or so of coral, sand, exotic plants, and complete privacy that's just a 2-minute boat ride from Island Harbor Jetty. It's a perfect place to spend a day swimming, snorkeling, soaking up the sun, and feasting on the delicious barbecued lobster, crayfish, and chicken creations (the recipe for the sauce is a closely guarded secret) served at the *Gorgeous Scilly Cay* restaurant (open for lunch only; see *Eating Out*). Just stand on the dock and wave — they'll send a boat for you.**

Sources and Resources

TOURIST INFORMATION

Information about Anguilla can be obtained at the Department of Tourism office in The Valley (phone: 2759 or 2451; 800-553-4939 from the US). You also can write to the Director of Tourism (The Valley, Anguilla, BWI). The office will reply immediately, but allow at least 2 weeks for mailed correspondence. Publications available from the Anguilla Department of Tourism include *Anguilla, The Basic Facts,* a booklet filled with historical information; hotel and villa rate brochures that are updated annually; and a sketchy map of the island. Additional tourist maps may be purchased at hotels and at shops in town; a very detailed map is available at the Department of Lands and Survey. For information on Anguilla tourist offices in the US, see GETTING READY TO GO.

LOCAL COVERAGE *The Chronicle,* published on St. Maarten, arrives daily except Sundays, and currently is the best local source of summarized world and local news. Two publications produced on Anguilla, *What We Do in Anguilla* and *Anguilla Life,* are useful sources of local news and events.

RADIO AND TELEVISION

There is one FM radio station on Anguilla (ZGF) and two AM stations (the government station, Radio Anguilla, and the privately owned Caribbean Beacon). Caribbean Television International is available island-wide; cable TV, beamed in 24 hours a day via US satellite, reaches most of Anguilla.

TELEPHONE

When calling from the US, dial 809 (area code) + 497 (country code) + (local number). To call from another Caribbean island, the code may vary, so call the local operator. When dialing on Anguilla, use only the local number unless otherwise indicated.

ENTRY REQUIREMENTS

All visitors are required to show some sort of identification with a photo. If you're staying overnight, you'll be asked for proof of citizenship (a valid passport is preferred, although a birth certificate or voter's registration card, along with a government-approved photo ID such as a driver's license, is accepted) and a return or ongoing ticket. There is a $6 departure tax at the airport. If you are taking a day trip to St. Martin, there is a $1.15 departure tax at Blowing Point and a $2 departure tax at Marigot.

CLIMATE AND CLOTHES

Anguilla is in the path of the easterly trade winds, which means cooling breezes and low humidity throughout the year. The average temperature, year-round, is 80F (27C). Rainfall is light but erratic, and may fall at any time of year. The wettest months are usually September through December and sometimes April and May. You'll need only light, casual sports clothes (lots of beachwear), unless you feel like dressing up for dinner at the *Mallìouhana* hotel or at *Cap Juluca's Pimms* restaurant.

MONEY

Anguilla's official currency is the Eastern Caribbean Dollar (EC), valued at about $2.68 EC to $1 US. Prices in shops usually are quoted in $EC, but hotels and restaurants more often use $US, and most have $US currency for change. Be sure to ask which "dollars" are meant. Traveler's checks, and often personal checks, are readily accepted, and credit cards are being accepted more frequently in most hotels. Barclays Bank International has a branch in The Valley, and there are three other commercial banks: Anguilla National, Caribbean Commercial, and Scotia Bank. Several off-shore banks are registered for business. Banking hours are 8 AM to 3 PM on weekdays and 8 AM to 5 PM on Fridays; closed Saturdays, Sundays, and holidays. There is also an American Express office in The Valley. All prices in this chapter are quoted in US dollars.

LANGUAGE

English.

TIME

Atlantic standard time is maintained all year. It's 1 hour ahead of eastern standard time in winter (when it's noon on the US East Coast, it's 1 PM on Anguilla), and the same as eastern daylight saving time in summer.

CURRENT

In most places, outlets are 110 AC, the same current used in the US. Check with your hotel ahead of time to be sure; if a converter is required for your American appliances, bring one along.

TIPPING

The 10% or 15% service charge added to hotel bills takes care of everyone, although waiters/waitresses and bartenders do not object to a little something more; if you are pleased with the service, show it. Taxi drivers need not be tipped, either, but if they have given you special service or a good tour, a 10% to 15% tip is a nice way of showing your appreciation. Young boys help arriving visitors with baggage (in their wheelbarrows) at Blowing Point, and $1 will usually make them very happy. There are no official porters at Wallblake Airport, but you probably won't need one; your cab driver can always double as a porter. If someone else should help with your bag, a smile and a heartfelt thank you is all he or she probably expects.

GETTING AROUND

CAR RENTAL Varying vintages are available; newer models with air conditioning go for about $90 per day or $240 a week, with unlimited mileage. You pay for gas, plus an additional $7.50 per day for collision damage waiver at some places. Rates are lower in summer. With the island's many unpaved roads and grazing goats, you may want to opt for a jeep. *Maurice Connors Car Rental* has the largest selection (phone: 6433 or 6541). Other car rental firms include *Bennie's,* which represents *Avis* (phone: 2221; 800-331-1084 from the US), a short taxi ride from Blowing Point; *Budget* (phone: 2217; 800-472-3325 from the US); *Apex* (phone: 2642); *National* (phone: 2433); *Jedell's* (phone: 2747); *Triple "K"* (phone: 2934); and *Island Car Rentals* on the Airport Road (phone: 2723 or 2312; 4330 after 5 PM). The two full-service gas stations are in The Valley and on the way to Blowing Point. Driving is on the left, and there are no street signs (and only six traffic lights). Visitors must obtain an Anguillan driver's license by presenting a home license and paying about $7.50 at the car rental agency. Mopeds, scooters, and motorbikes may be rented but are fairly expensive. Call *Boo's* (phone: 2323). *Note:* The police now use radar to check how fast you're driving, so be sure to keep within the posted speed limit (usually 30 mph) to avoid paying a $35 fine.

FERRY SERVICES Regular ferry service links Blowing Point, Anguilla, and Marigot, French St. Martin, from about 7 AM to 10:30 PM or so daily.

Powerboats, most built by Anguilla's famed craftsmen, the ferries make the trip in about 20 minutes. During the day, a ferryboat departs every 30 minutes or so and one-way fare is $9. At night the fare is $10 one way and service is decreased.

SEA EXCURSIONS Pretty, palm-tufted Sandy Island and the even more remote Prickly Pear Cays used to be ideal escape sites, but have become crowded with day-trippers from St. Martin. Both still offer good snorkeling and beach bars that grill lobster, chicken, and ribs for lunch. A boat will take you there from Sandy Ground at 10 AM and bring you back later in the day. Ask at the small jetty by *Johnno's* or contact Neville Connors at *Sandy Island Enterprises* (phone: 6395).

TAXI A sociable way to get acquainted with the island and to learn something of its lore. Drivers will show you every nook and cranny in a couple of hours. The going rate for an around-the-island tour is $40. This includes about 2½ hours of sightseeing, after which the driver will drop you at a lunch spot or beach of your choice and pick you up at an appointed time. From Blowing Point (where the ferry from Marigot on St. Martin comes in) the established one-way cab fare to Shoal Bay is $15; to Sandy Ground, $12; to Meads Bay, $12; and to Island Harbour, $17. From the airport, the set one-way fares are $18 to *Cap Juluca,* $14 to *Malliouhana,* and $10 to the *Shoal Bay* resort and *Shoal Bay Villas.* These rates are for two passengers; there is an extra charge of $3 for each extra person.

TOURS Local tour operators include *Bennie's Tours* (phone: 2788), *Paradise Ventures* (phone: 2107), and *Bertram's* (phone: 2256). *Bennie's* offers a "transfer" service for visitors traveling to and from St. Martin, including taxis and boats, for $50 round-trip per person by day, $65 at night.

INTER-ISLAND FLIGHTS

American Eagle runs two flights daily from its San Juan, Puerto Rico, hub direct to Anguilla. *Windward Island Airways* (*WINAIR*), *Air Anguilla, Tyden Air,* and *LIAT* schedule daily flights from St. Maarten's Juliana Airport to Anguilla. The 6-minute flight costs about $35. *LIAT* also offers regular service to Anguilla from Antigua, Nevis, St. Thomas, and St. Kitts. *Air Anguilla* flies daily to St. Thomas, St. Croix, San Juan, and St. Kitts. *Tyden Air* and *Air Anguilla* also offer flightseeing excursions (about $100) and charter service to most Caribbean islands. It's a good idea to check for last-minute schedule changes and to be flexible enough to accommodate the elasticity of island time. For airline reservations and travel arrangements, contact *J. N. Gumbs Travel Agency* (phone: day, 2238; night, 2838), *Malliouhana Travel & Tours* (phone: 2431), or *Bennie's* (phone: 2788).

SPECIAL EVENTS

Carnival is a week-long holiday climaxing on the first Monday in August and featuring boat races, sports events, costume parades, music competitions, and nonstop partying. The island's three national holidays are *Anguilla Day* (May 30), marking the commencement of its secession from its partnership with St. Kitts and Nevis; *Constitution Day* (August 7); and *Separation Day* (December 19). Other holidays include *New Year's Day, Good Friday, Easter Monday, Whitmonday, Labour Day* (May 1), the *Queen's Official Birthday* (early June), *August Monday* (the first Monday in August), *August Thursday* (the first Thursday in August), *Christmas,* and *Boxing Day* (December 26).

SHOPPING

Serious shoppers head for St. Martin, but a few spots on Anguilla offer clothing and handicrafts. For high fashion, the island's top shop is the *Malliouhana* hotel boutique. The Valley post office's stamps appeal to collectors. If you're in the market for a traditional hand-built Anguillan racing boat, contact Ron Webster (phone: 4465); for a super-strong wooden craft made with the WEST System, contact David Carty (phone: 2616). Small models and other souvenirs and local crafts are sold at *Bertram's Shop* (phone: 2256) and *Bencraft* (no phone), both at Sandy Ground. Splendid shells are Anguilla's best souvenirs — yours for the finding on all island beaches, especially the north side of Rendezvous Bay and Maunday's Bay. Here are some other places to explore (many shops are closed Saturdays and Sundays):

BEACH STUFF All the togs you'll need for sunning and swimming can be found in a new hot pink and turquoise shop perched above the harbor at Sandy Ground. Road Bay (phone: 6814).

CARIBBEAN STYLE A lively, extensive collection of Caribbean arts and crafts. Above *Koal Keel* restaurant in The Valley (no phone).

CHEDDIE'S CARVING STUDIO Cheddie exhibits and sells his carvings in a white house trimmed in blue and green. Sculptures made from local mahogany and driftwood range in price from $50 to $2,000. The Cove (phone: 6027).

DEVONISH–COTTON GIN ART GALLERY Features some fine oils and watercolors by owner Courtney Devonish and other local artists, plus ceramics. Historic cotton gin machinery is exhibited, too. Wallblake (phone: 2949).

HALLMARK Small stocks of brand-name English bone china, porcelain, perfume, and linen, as well as Caribbean souvenirs. British goods sell at below-US prices. Closed off-season. On the Airport Rd. near the National Bank of Anguilla (no phone).

JAVA WRAPS A small link in the growing chain of Caribbean stores selling stunning Indonesian batik clothing. In the orange and purple-trimmed building on George Hill Rd. (phone: 5497).

SPORTS

BOATING Sailboat racing ranks as the island's "national" sport. The ad hoc races that set sail from Sandy Ground, Shoal Bay, or Crocus Bay are often accompanied by beachside barbecues, jump-up partying, and betting. Scheduled races take place on *Anguilla Day, New Year's Day,* and *Easter*. For a closer look at the Anguillan boats made by the island's famed master builders, visit the fishing village of Island Harbour. Those who prefer sailing to spectating can make arrangements with *Enchanted Island Cruises* (phone: 3111; fax: 3079) for a day cruise to Prickly Pear Cays or to any of the other lovely secluded coves aboard the 50-foot catamaran *Wildcat* ($80 for adults, $50 for children under 12, including snorkeling equipment, lunch, and drinks). A 2-hour sunset cruise, including wine and hors d'oeuvres, is $60 per adult, $30 for children under 12. Charters also are available for up to 30 people. *Suntastic Cruises* (phone: 3400, or 6847 evenings) sails its 37-foot sloop *Skybird* and the power cruiser *Sunbird* to Prickly Pear; a day trip, including lunch, drinks, and snorkeling gear, costs $70; a sunset cruise, complete with drinks and snacks, $50. Similar trips aboard *Ragtime*, a 28-foot sailboat, cost $55 and $35, respectively (phone: 6395; fax: 6234). *Classic Yacht Charters* (phone: 2367), under Captain Tom's helm, offers half-day sails for $35 per person for two or more. *Sandy Island Enterprises* (phone: 6395, 6433, or 6845) offers assorted trips aboard the *Shauna I* and *Shauna II;* a 2-hour glass-bottom boat tour, including open bar and snorkeling equipment, costs $20. Other day, sunset, and overnight cruises are offered by *Princess Soya Catamaran Cruises* (phone: 2671), *Mike's Glass-Bottom Boat Cruises* (phone: 2051 or 4155), and *Smitty's* (phone: 4300).

SNORKELING AND SCUBA With at least five new dive sites (artificial reefs created when ships were hauled from the Sandy Ground Harbor and sunk offshore, encouraging coral growth and attracting a variety of fish), Anguilla offers plenty of underwater adventure. Check with your hotel for information on scuba diving packages. *Tamariain Water Sports* (PO Box 247, The Valley, Anguilla, WI; phone: 2020, 2798, or 2900; fax: 5125) offers a variety of *PADI*-certified courses and a Medic First Aid course. Also available are resort scuba courses plus dive and/or snorkel trips around Anguilla and to nearby cays. Classes and dives offer personal attention, with a maximum of 12 divers to a boat. A one-tank dive costs $35; a two-tank dive, $60; and resort courses, $80. The *Tamariain* retail shop carries snorkeling and diving equipment for sale and rent. There are branches at both the *Malliouhana* resort and at Sandy Ground next to *Johnno's.* Sailboats, snorkeling gear, and other water sports equipment are available for rent from *Sandy Island Enterprises* (phone: 6395). *Shoal Bay Watersports* (phone: 2596), next to the *Reefside* restaurant, also has snorkeling equipment and Sunfish. Guides from these establishments and various island fishermen will take you to nearby cays and along the secret coves of Anguilla's splendid coast. Although there are no wall dives here, there are deep dives (130 feet on coral) and at least a dozen excellent dive sites. There is also good diving off Prickly Pear Cays and 2½ miles northwest at Dog Island, where the southeast shore drops off from 20 to about 80 feet. The reefs surrounding West and Mid cays, off Anguillita Island, and between Scrub Island and Anguilla's eastern end are also worthwhile. Prickly Pear Cays, Scrub Island, Sandy Island, and Little Bay are best for snorkeling, but you won't even need a boat to get to the offshore reefs at Shoal Bay.

SPORT FISHING Trips with local skippers and fishermen can be arranged through hotels at about $30 per person a day. Or try *Mike's Glass-Bottom Boat Cruises* (phone: 2051 or 4155). Ask about bringing your own tackle.

SWIMMING AND SUNNING The beaches are absolutely superb (see *Special Places*). There is no organized lifeguard system, so you should observe common-sense safety rules: Don't swim out too far alone and beware of currents, especially near reefs (coral scratches take an annoyingly long time to heal in tropical climates). Generally, the waters here are calm, clear, and safe even for children. Note that topless and nude bathing are not allowed on Anguilla.

TENNIS There are 4 courts at the *Malliouhana,* 3 at *Cap Juluca,* and 2 each at *Cinnamon Reef*, *Casablanca*, and *Coccoloba Plantation* (which has a *Peter Burwash International Tennis* program). *Mariners, Carimar, CoveCastles, Rendezvous Bay, Pelicans,* and *Sea Grape* have 1 court each. To book courts at the *Scouts Headquarters*, south of St. Mary's Anglican Church, contact *Anguilla Drug Store* in The Valley (phone: 2738).

WINDSURFING AND WATER SKIING Offered by *Sandy Island Enterprises* (phone: 6395, 2804, or 8645), *Tamariain* (phone: 2020, 2798, or 2900), and the major hotels.

NIGHTLIFE

Although this is a quiet island, there is usually live music somewhere every night of the week. The best sources of local entertainment information are the "Day & Night" listings in *Anguilla Life* magazine and the "Weekly Music Menu" in *What We Do in Anguilla.* There is live music most nights at *Cap Juluca's Pimms* restaurant, on Thursday nights at *Lucy's Harbour View,* on Tuesday and Friday nights at *Pom Pom,* and twice a week at *Coccoloba Plantation* and *Mariners. Cinnamon Reef* frequently has music, particularly on Fridays at the manager's poolside cocktail party and West Indian barbecue. On Saturday and Wednesday nights, as well as Sundays from noon on, *Johnno's Beach Bar* at Sandy Ground is *the* place to be; the music is good and loud, and the flavor decidedly local. Wednesday and

Sunday afternoons, *Gorgeous Scilly Cay* and *Uncle Ernie's Shoal Bay Beach Bar* feature live music and a great party atmosphere. (See *Eating Out* for details on the above restaurants.) Local bands include *North Sound, the Mussington Brothers, Spraka, Dumpa and the Angvibes, Sleepy and the All Stars,* and *Keith and the Mellow Tones.* One of the best local singers is Banky Banx, a guitarist who performs at the *Mallihouana* and other spots; his records and tapes, which are a big hit throughout the Caribbean, are sold in shops all over the island. In addition, several of the beach bars and small restaurants set up local string and scratch bands some afternoons and evenings, especially if there is an occasion, such as a small cruise ship anchored offshore; most hotels offer nightly entertainment in season. There is one dance club in town, *Red Dragon Disco* in South Hill (phone: 2687); it starts jumping after midnight Saturdays and Sundays. Makeshift clubs and dance halls often pop up overnight, and then fade away just as quickly. To find the latest spot, ask at your hotel or, better yet, consult your cab driver. For a real "night on the town," a group can charter *Mystic Boat* (phone: 6289) for a night run from Blowing Point to St. Martin; price depends on the number of people in the group. Or take a late afternoon ferry to Marigot for drinks and dinner, then return to Anguilla on the 10:45 PM boat. There have been some reports of crime in Marigot at night, so be sure to take appropriate precautions.

Best on the Island

CHECKING IN

Little Anguilla's building boom has made headlines in a variety of sources, among them TV's "Lifestyles of the Rich and Famous." In deference to both government wishes and owner preference, new properties are low-rise and high-quality; traditional cottage and villa architecture — shaped to fit the land as well as the island's beach-oriented, outdoor-indoor vacation style — remains dominant. A different architectural style (replicating an Arawak Indian village) characterizes the luxurious villas at the *Arawak Beach Resort* at Big Spring, set to open at press time.

Rates can run as high as $3,000 per day for a 5-bedroom villa at *Cap Juluca,* $1,140 for a 2-bedroom suite at the *Malliouhana,* or $790 for 3 bedrooms at *CoveCastles* (see *A Regal Resort and Some Special Havens,* below). We classify $400 or more per day for a double room without meals in winter as very expensive, $250 to $400 as expensive, $150 to $250 as moderate, and below $150 as inexpensive. Clearly, Anguilla is no bargain if you crave top-of-the-line digs. Nonetheless, there are some bed and breakfast accommodations that cost less than $100 a night, a list of which may be obtained from the tourist offices in New York and Anguilla. An 8% government tax is added to all hotel rates, plus a 10% service charge. Rates are reduced by 30% to 60% in summer, making this a great off-season bargain spot.

Many vacationers who stay at a hotel one season arrange to rent an apartment or cottage the following year. A reliable on-island rental agency is *Sunshine Villas,* run by Judy and Jim Henderson (phone: 6149; fax: 6021). A rate list for apartments, villas, and cottages is also available from the Department of Tourism. Because they are so popular here, we have included choice villa properties in our list of available accommodations.

Reservations for all hotels, guesthouses, and villas can be made by writing to *Anguilla Vacations* (6201 Leesburg Pike, Falls Church, VA 22044; phone: 703-534-8512), *Inns of Anguilla* (phone: 3180; 800-223-9815 from the US; fax: 5381), or by calling the Anguilla Tourist Information Office in Northport, NY (phone: 516-261-1234 in New York; 800-553-4939 from elsewhere in the US). When on Anguilla, use only the local numbers listed below. For information about dialing from elsewhere, see "Telephone" earlier in this chapter.

For an unforgettable island experience, we begin with our favorites, followed by our recommendations of cost and quality choices of hotels large and small, listed by price category.

A REGAL RESORT AND SOME SPECIAL HAVENS

Cap Juluca One of the Caribbean's super-luxury resorts, spread over 179 acres of stunning southwestern coast and overlooking the smoky mountains of St. Martin. Named for the Arawak rainbow god, *Juluca* is exquisitely Moroccan, with Moorish arches, domes, and flowered courtyards. There are 78 luxury doubles; 14 one- and two-bedroom suites featuring terraces and baths with decor that's straight out of the *Arabian Nights,* complete with huge tubs for two people; and 6 spacious and splendidly appointed private villas with 3 to 5 bedrooms and private pools. The restaurant, *Pimms,* offers *the* most romantic dining on Anguilla (see *Eating Out*). There's also tennis, a pool, and a full range of water sports. A new, complimentary program, offered during school holidays in spring and summer, features lunch, games, and supervised activities for children ages 3 to 9 years. Maunday's Bay (phone: 6779 or 6666; 800-323-0139 from the US).

CoveCastles Designed by renowned New York architect Myron Goldfinger, this ultramodern complex features 4 three-bedroom and 8 two-bedroom villas. The elegant appointments are the epitome of understated luxury: large rattan furniture upholstered with raw silk, hand-embroidered cotton sheets, flower arrangements, and ceiling fans. Each villa has 2 large baths and cable TV. Sports facilities include complimentary snorkeling equipment, a lighted tennis court, a lovely beach, windsurfing and Sunfish sailing, and a yacht that may be chartered for day trips. The dining room serves first-rate presentations of French, creole, and Italian dishes; meals also may be ordered and delivered to the villas. Closed from the end of

August through mid-October. West Shoal Bay (phone: 6801; 800-348-4716 from the US).

Malliouhana In a soaring white Moorish structure perched on a cliff overlooking Meads Bay at the northwestern reaches of the island, this resort is one of the Caribbean's most elegant and distinguished. Here is an authentic tropical hideaway, with food and wine of high quality, and a luxurious landscape that more than makes up for an island that's otherwise rather flat and undistinguished. Owned and managed by the British magnate Leon Roydon and his wife, Annette, this Mediterranean-feeling oasis has 50 units and a fully outfitted exercise center. The doubles, suites, and 2- and 3-bedroom villas are all stunningly furnished and decorated. There are 3 swimming pools (no chlorine), 4 Laykold tennis courts, a water sports center, and a renowned restaurant created by the late Jo Rostang, chef-owner of the first-rate *Bonne Auberge* in Antibes (see *Eating Out*). It's perfect for the kind of traveler for whom escapism is an art; the price may be high, but then so is the quality of the experience. Meads Bay (phone: 6111 or 6741; 800-372-1323 from the US).

EXPENSIVE

Carimar Beach Club These 23 well-appointed 1-, 2-, and 3-bedroom units, with full kitchens, ceiling fans, and patios or balconies, share Meads Bay with the posh *Malliouhana* hotel. Daily maid service is provided and there's cable TV in the clubhouse. There are 2 tennis courts, plus complimentary snorkeling equipment; other water sports can be arranged. Meads Bay (phone: 6881; 800-235-8667 from the US; fax: 6882).

Casablanca This resort on the site of the former *Merrywig* hotel faces 3 miles of white sand beach. The 76 rooms and suites have separate seating areas, air conditioning, ceiling fans, in-room safes, and private patios with views of sand, sea, and St. Martin. All water sports are offered; other leisure facilities include a health club with sea views, a freshwater pool, and 2 lighted tennis courts; a 9-hole golf course (the island's first) is slated to open this year. Continental fare is served in the elegant *Casablanca* restaurant (see *Eating Out*), and there's also the casual *Café Americain* (where complimentary afternoon tea is served), a poolside grill, a beachside bar, and 24-hour room service. Rendezvous Bay West (phone: 6999; 800-231-1945 from the US; fax: 6899).

Cinnamon Reef New Yorker Richard Hauser and his son, Scott, make each guest feel at home. The Moorish-arched main building is surrounded by 14 private, luxury villas and 4 beachfront suites that open onto 4 garden suites that expand to 2-bedroom, 2-bath accommodations. Each cottage has a sea view, oversize bedroom, sunken living room with ceiling fans, dressing room with hair dryer, spacious bathroom, and breezy patio. Sports facilities include a 60-by-40-foot freshwater swimming pool, 2 Deco Turf tennis courts, most water sports, and an 8-foot Jacuzzi. Continental breakfast is complimentary, and one of the best restaurants around, the *Palm Court* (see *Eating Out*), is here as well. Closed September. Little Harbour (phone: 2727; 800-223-1108 from the US; fax: 3727).

Coccoloba Plantation Straddling the beautiful white sand beaches of Meads and Barnes bays, this luxury resort has a handsome pool with swim-up bar and a good restaurant (it badly needs an overall renovation, however). Accommodations are in 50 air conditioned, 1-bedroom beachfront cottages with seaview patios. There are also 2 additional pools, water sports facilities, *Peter Burwash International* tennis on 2 lighted courts, and an exercise room. Barnes Bay (phone: 6871 or 6872; 800-833-3559 from the US; fax: 6332).

Frangipani This beachfront condominium complex on the northwest coast of the island has 8 luxury studios and 1-, 2-, and 3-bedroom suites, with another 28 in the works. The guestrooms are set in a pink Spanish/Mediterranean-style villa on a 2-mile beach that looks out to the Prickly Pear Cays. Each has a large terrace, full kitchen, washer/dryer, air conditioning, and ceiling fans. Continental breakfast is served each morning on the terraces; private cooks are also available to prepare West Indian dinners. Also on the premises are facilities for snorkeling, water skiing, fishing, and sailing; future plans call for tennis courts, a pool, and a restaurant. Only American Express accepted. Meads Bay (phone: 6442; 800-892-4564 from the US; fax: 6440).

Pineapple Beach Club Nestled on lovely Rendezvous Bay facing St. Martin and distant Saba, this 27-room property (formerly the *Anguilla Great House*) has recently become the island's first all-inclusive resort. A dramatic pool area leads to the spectacular beach. The rooms, which have cove ceilings (the walls slant upward to a flat-topped apex) and ceiling fans, are set in 5-unit gingerbread-style buildings; the 2 studios (with kitchenettes) may be combined with adjacent double rooms or rented on their own. There's live entertainment 3 times a week in season and a bar by the pool. The meal plan has a "Dine-Around" option, where guests may eat at the resort's *Old Caribe,* a fine open-air dining spot with bar (see *Eating Out*) or at any of 4 nearby restaurants. All meals, snacks, land and water sports (plus instruction), entertainment, taxes, airport transfers, and tips are included in the rate. Rendezvous Bay (phone: 6061; 800-345-0271 from the US; fax: 6019).

MODERATE

Mariners On one of Anguilla's most picturesque beaches, this charming West Indian–style resort draws yachtspeople, local dignitaries, and expatriates to its friendly bar, breezy gazebo, and restaurant, the *Beach Terrace* (see *Eating Out*). The 67 units are distributed among 25 gingerbread cottages with cove ceilings and wide verandahs bearing handsome deck furniture; each cottage has 2 double rooms connected by a studio with kitchen facilities and a foldaway bed (all have private baths). There is also live entertainment several times weekly, fishing charters, yacht cruises, lighted tennis courts, a swimming pool, a Jacuzzi, and water sports. All-inclusive packages and diving programs are available. Sandy Ground (phone: 2671 or 2815; 800-848-7938 from the US; fax: 2901).

Rainbow Reef Villas These 4 perfectly private, isolated, and quiet 2-bedroom villas overlook the sea. All have kitchens and verandahs, and are furnished with good-looking Haitian rattan. The beach, which is better for snorkeling than lazy swimming because of a coral reef, is outfitted with barbecue facilities and a gazebo. Six days' housekeeping service is included in the weekly rate. Sea Feather Bay (phone: 2817; fax: 3091).

Rendezvous Bay Guests will enjoy the casual atmosphere and warm hospitality of the Gumbs family, who makes everyone feel right at home. The 30 rooms are simple and clean, each with a private bath. The dining room, where meals are served family-style, has a reputation for good Anguillan cooking. Flanked by lovely dunes, its vast crescent of white sand beach is one of the best on the island. Snorkeling and fishing equipment and tennis are available. Rendezvous Bay (phone: 6549; fax: 6026).

Shoal Bay Resort This property, adorned with wood trellises dripping with bougainvillea, has 26 well-appointed 1-bedroom units, each with a full kitchen, living area, patio or terrace, and a foldaway bed. It's next to *Shoal Bay Villas* on a spectacular beach. Shoal Bay (phone: 2011; 800-223-9815 from the US; fax: 3355).

Shoal Bay Villas On glorious Shoal Bay, this is a small condominium resort with 2 miles of beach that is the stuff that island dreams are made of. The 13 attractive units range from studios to duplex suites (for up to four people), each with patio or terrace. There's also the *Reefside,* a good, reasonably priced restaurant; a pool; and a small water sports concession. Shoal Bay (phone: 2051; 800-722-7045 from the US; fax: 3631).

La Sirena Offers attractively furnished 2-, 3-, and 4-bedroom villas (totaling 20 rooms) with ocean views and 2 and 3 baths. Each also has a verandah or patio, kitchen facilities, and lounge or living/dining room. The 2 swimming pools, a bar in the open-air lobby, and a good restaurant serving local and continental food are other pluses. Only 300 feet from Meads Bay Beach (phone: 6827; 800-331-9358 from the US; fax: 6829).

INEXPENSIVE

Inter Island Here are 14 simple but clean rooms with bath, a family-style restaurant, and gracious West Indian hospitality. No frills and a bit far from the beach (you may need a car), it's nonetheless an excellent spot for the price. Lower South Hill (phone: 6259).

EATING OUT

Island mutton stewed with island vegetables, and fresh fish and spiny lobster caught by the fishing boats that sail out of Island Harbour, Crocus Bay, and Sandy Ground, are staples here. Yet some of the finest French cooking methods, paired with Caribbean ingredients, are also in evidence. Expect to pay $80 or more for a meal for two, not including wine, tip, or drinks, in those restaurants listed below as expensive, $50 to $80 in those listed as moderate, and under $50 at spots described as inexpensive. A 10% service charge is usually added to all food and beverage tabs. Some restaurants charge a fee for using credit cards, and many close in September and October, so call ahead. When calling on Anguilla use only the local numbers listed below. For information about dialing from elsewhere, see "Telephone" earlier in this chapter.

VERY EXPENSIVE

Malliouhana The ambience of this hotel dining room is elegant and romantic — soft lights, sea breezes, and fresh flowers. The imaginative menu was created by the late Jo Rostang, former chef-owner of the very popular *La Bonne Auberge* in Antibes; currently, the kitchen is overseen by his son Michel Rostang, whose eponymous Paris restaurant has earned two Michelin stars. Among the excellent offerings are fresh salmon in croissant pastry with a compote of onions, terrine of foie gras, *farcis de crayfish aux cèpes et aux épinards* (crayfish stuffed with mushrooms and spinach), and the prized *volaille de Bresse* (duck or chicken roasted on a spit). There is also a vast wine cellar, reported to hold some 35,000 bottles. The price for all this is rather dear (dinner for two will run from $175 to $200), but it's well worth it. Open daily for breakfast, lunch, and dinner. Reservations necessary (and hard for non-guests to get in high season). Major credit cards accepted. Meads Bay (phone: 6111 or 6741).

EXPENSIVE

Barrel Stay This thatch-roofed beachside bar and restaurant with barrel stays for tables features French-creole food, including a good fish soup, fresh red snapper in "Portuguese" sauce (tomatoes, onions, green peppers), barbecued lobster, Hawaiian ham steaks, and a creamy chocolate mousse. Open daily for breakfast, lunch, and dinner. Reservations advised. Major credit cards accepted. Sandy Ground (phone: 2831).

Beach Terrace Lunch or dinner on this breezy West Indian porch overlooking the very white sand beach at Sandy Ground is a memorable island experience. Lunches feature salads, soups, and hamburgers as well as fresh grilled fish of the day and lobster. Poached snapper or grouper in lemon butter sauce, seafood salads, and chicken baked with coconut and ginger are regular dinner offerings, but don't miss the lobster grilled with fresh basil butter. Thursday is barbecue night, and on Saturday there is a traditional West Indian dinner, both with live music. Open daily for lunch and dinner. Reservations unnecessary. Major credit cards accepted. At the *Mariners* resort, Sandy Ground (phone: 2671).

Casablanca Exquisite French fare with nouvelle touches is served indoors or alfresco, with a view of the sea and St. Martin. Recommended starters are goat cheese terrine and crayfish salad with ravioli; entrées include quails with sea grapes, and monkfish cooked in rice paper; and for dessert, try the *tarte tatin* made with papaya. Open daily for lunch and dinner. Reservations advised. Major credit cards accepted. At the *Casablanca* resort (phone: 6999).

Le Fish Trap Certainly among the island's top two or three dining spots, it overlooks the beach at Island Harbour. The menu combines continental fare with creole favorites to produce truly original dishes, many — including steak *au poivre* — flambéed tableside. Also noteworthy: crab cakes, seafood pasta, crayfish grilled with garlic butter or steamed on a bed of leeks, duck in raspberry vinegar sauce, and a remarkable tomato pie. If you can manage dessert, try the fresh raspberry *bavarois.* Open daily for lunch and dinner. Reservations necessary. Major credit cards accepted. Island Harbour (phone: 4488).

La Fontana This popular seaside trattoria combines Italian cooking with local ingredients; some tables are on the terrace, others on the sand. Try the tricolored roasted peppers and the "Padre Carmine" (grilled chicken served with primavera vegetables), named after the owner's father. Open daily for lunch and dinner. Reservations advised. Major credit cards accepted. Shoal Bay (phone: 3492).

Gorgeous Scilly Cay Don't miss this experience, especially on a Sunday when locals, day-trippers from St. Martin, and half the island's restaurateurs gather at this eatery on a private island reached via a 2-minute boat ride from the Island Harbour dock. The menu is limited — grilled chicken, lobster, prawns, or a combination marinated in a dynamite secret sauce. There's live music Wednesdays and Sundays. Wear your bathing suit and expect a fun time. Reservations unnecessary. No credit cards accepted. Open for lunch and early dinner; closed Mondays. Island Harbour (phone: 5123).

Hibernia A popular French retreat with consistently good food served in a setting that makes guests feel as if they're in a private, typically Anguillan home overlooking the water. Oriental influences have been added to the menu. Profiteroles filled with lobster and crab make a fine starter; entrées such as grilled crayfish served with ginger/vanilla sauce, and Thai broth aswim with seafood showcase the chef's skills. Homemade soursop sorbet provides a fine finish. Open for lunch and dinner; closed Mondays. Reservations advised. Major credit cards accepted. Island Harbour (phone: 4290).

Mango's One of the hottest spots on the island, this small eatery is great for people watching. The setting — an open-air structure on Barnes Bay — is spare, yet charming; the fare is simple, yet superb. Menu highlights include grilled meat, chicken, and the freshest of fish, as well as such creative appetizers as pumpkin-shrimp bisque. Open daily for dinner only. Reservations essential (book days ahead). Major credit cards accepted. Barnes Bay (phone: 6479).

Palm Court In a pretty and spacious gallery of the *Cinnamon Reef* hotel, this dining spot offers outstanding food, among the best in the Caribbean. Chefs Didier Rochat (trained by French culinary star Roger Vergé) and Vernon Hughes bring prize-winning techniques to the menu, which features West Indian and contemporary Caribbean fare. Lunches feature an interesting selection of salads, such as warm shrimp salad with sesame vinaigrette; slightly sautéed red snapper with a soy *beurre blanc* sauce is just one of the outstanding dinner entrées. The many-layered tiramisù is splendid, too. Monday night is "jump-up," with a manager's cocktail party and a steel band. There's live music most nights. Open daily for lunch and dinner. Reservations advised. Major credit cards accepted. Little Harbour (phone: 2727 or 2781).

Pimms Diners at *Cap Juluca*'s breezy Moorish-style oasis overlooking Maunday's Bay can watch the sun set behind a faux Moroccan village. The restaurant features light lunches of fresh fish and lobster, a special fish pie, pasta of the day (which might be seafood ravioli in Noilly Prat), superb salads, cold soups, and grilled meat. Dinners give full rein to chef Erwin Pascher's many talents; the menu includes lobster cake, gazpacho with avocado mousse, steaks and chops with innovative sauces, and grilled salmon with a lovely banana curry sauce. The *crème brûlée* and ovals of white and dark chocolate mousse in mint-raspberry *coulis* are sinfully good conclusions. There is also a pleasant bar area. Open daily for lunch and dinner. Reservations necessary. American Express only accepted. Maunday's Bay (phone: 6914).

MODERATE

Arlo's The island's best Italian restaurant, it offers lobster served with fettuccine in a tomato-cream sauce, scallops with roasted red pepper and a vodka sauce over angel hair pasta — and great pizza. Open for dinner only; closed Sundays. Reservations advised. MasterCard and Visa accepted. South Hill (phone: 6810).

Koal Keel One of the island's newest — and best — dining rooms is in a restored historic house that dates from 1780. The owners set an elegant table (the unusual decor, which includes a sleigh bed in the center of the room, adds to the charm) and offer service as impressive as the menu. Among the many choices are smoked grouper on a bed of leeks, rock-oven–baked chicken, and such sinful desserts as coconut tart and crêpes Mikado (filled with ice cream and crowned with chocolate sauce). Open daily for lunch and dinner. Reservations advised. Major credit cards accepted. The Valley (phone: 2930).

Lucy's Harbour View Perched on a hill overlooking Road Bay and the lagoon, this place is best at dusk, when you can watch the glorious Anguilla sunset. Vivacious Anguillan chef Lucy Connor creates dishes of kid and stewed mutton, conch soup, curried goat or chicken, and whole red snapper, all creole style, and all famous on the island. Service is not speedy, so come before your normal mealtime and enjoy a rum punch and the spectacular view. Live entertainment on Thursday nights. Open daily for lunch and dinner. Reservations advised. Major credit cards accepted. South Hill (phone: 6253).

Old Caribe West Indian fare is served at this informal eatery on a fine beach. The lunch menu features salads, burgers, and fish and chips; the prix fixe dinner includes such novelties as coconut meatballs and island grouper cooked and served in a cabbage leaf. Open daily for lunch and dinner. Reservations unnecessary. Major credit cards accepted. At the *Pineapple Beach Club,* Rendezvous Bay (phone: 6061).

Old House Set in a charming West Indian–style house on George Hill, this popular place dispenses fine local fare. The catch of the day here might include "old wife" or "hind" (yellowtail or grouper, respectively) prepared Anguillan-style (with tomatoes, onions, lemon, butter, fresh thyme, and chibble). Barbecued chicken, pork, and beef are also featured, along with salads and sandwiches. There's an excellent kids' menu as well. Open daily for lunch and dinner. Reservations advised. Major credit cards accepted. George Hill (phone: 2228).

Paradise Café Formerly the *Oasis* snack bar, this place serves Asian and French fare, including breast of duck with mandarin pancakes, Chinese stuffed ravioli, and Thai curry dishes. Open daily for lunch and dinner. Reservations advised for dinner. Major credit cards accepted. Katouche Bay, near *CoveCastles* (phone: 3210).

Pom Pom Under the same ownership as *Lucy's Harbour View* (see above), this beachside spot offers the same creole fare for dinner, including red snapper and curried goat, but its lunches are lighter, with salads, burgers, and barbecued ribs. Live entertainment sparks up the atmosphere on Tuesday and Friday nights. Open daily for lunch and dinner. Reservations unnecessary. Major credit cards accepted. Road Bay (phone: 2253).

Riviera Another pretty beachside bistro, featuring seafood with a Japanese touch: sushi, sashimi, and oysters (when available) sautéed in soy sauce and sake, and the island's best fish soup, thick and chunky with a properly piquant *rouille*. The friendly bar attracts visiting yachtspeople and coin collectors. Happy hour is 6 to 7 PM. Open daily for lunch and dinner. Reservations advised. Major credit cards accepted. Sandy Ground (phone: 2833).

Roy's For a taste of English heaven and everything you ever wanted to know about Anguilla's goings-on, visit this eatery on quiet Crocus Bay, the only pub on the island. The fish and chips are fresh and cooked to perfection, the Sunday roast beef is rare and delectable, and the Yorkshire pudding is coveted by British expatriates. There's a lovely terrace, and you'll never be lonely at the bar. Closed Mondays; dinner only on Saturdays. Reservations advised. MasterCard and Visa accepted. Crocus Bay (phone: 2470).

Smugglers This open-air spot with a nautical theme is perched over the water, with lights shining on the sea so diners can watch bobbing fishing boats and snapping fish. Besides steaks, chops, fresh fish, and the complimentary salad bar, there are 10 lobster dishes. The lobster *exotique*, from southeast Asia, is particularly notable — the tender meat is served in a sweet-and-sour sauce flavored with pineapple, ginger, and bamboo shoots. Save room for the apple pie made with custard and calvados. The prime attractions, though, may be charming French owner Marysa West and her 13-year-old daughter Maribelle, who works harder than most servers yet never stops smiling. Open for dinner only; closed Sundays. Reservations advised. Major credit cards accepted. The Forest (phone: 3728).

Trader Vic's What was originally a thatch-roofed beach bar and grill has now expanded into a vast restaurant across the road, which dispenses proper meals and occasionally a good buffet with a live band. The à la carte menu features fish or conch soup, grilled lobster, crayfish, grouper, snapper, and barbecued chicken or ribs. Lunches are still served at the very pleasant beach bar. Open daily for lunch and dinner. Reservations unnecessary. No credit cards accepted (no phone).

INEXPENSIVE

Johnno's Beach Bar Everyone on the island, locals and visitors alike, seems to turn up at this large tin-roofed shack to dance or just to hang out with friends. The menu features barbecued chicken, fish, and ribs. Things get really busy around 8 PM Wednesday, Thursday, Saturday, and Sunday nights, when a local band attracts a large crowd. Open for breakfast, lunch, and dinner; closed Mondays. Reservations unnecessary. No credit cards accepted. Sandy Ground (phone: 2728).

Uncle Ernie's Shoal Bay Beach Bar With three tables on the terrace and another seven on the sand, this shack on the beach between *Shoal Bay Villas* and *Trader Vic's* is one of the most popular places on booming Shoal Bay. You can get a beer and barbecued chicken, ribs, or catch of the day, all served with a smile. Live music adds to the flavor on Sundays between 2 and 7

PM and sometimes on Wednesdays. Open daily for lunch and dinner. Reservations unnecessary. No credit cards accepted. The Valley (no phone).

Other restaurants/snack bars serving "local" food include *Cora's Pepper Pot* in Short Cove (for *rôti,* a full West Indian meal wrapped into a hamburger-size pastry), *Millie's Cross Roads* near the government buildings in The Valley (try her stewed conch), the *Round Rock Café* on Shoal Bay (for Eunice's famous "goat water"), *The Palm* (for stewed lobster), and *Amy's Bakery* (for chicken and chips as well as cakes, pies, and pizza). If you crave Chinese, the tiny *Oriental* restaurant in The Quarter is open later than most. For picnics on the beach or fancy take-out fare (especially if you're staying in a villa), *Fat Cat Gourmet* offers escargot, quiche, chili, pasta salads, chicken or conch stew, and pastries for takeout or catering (phone: 2752).

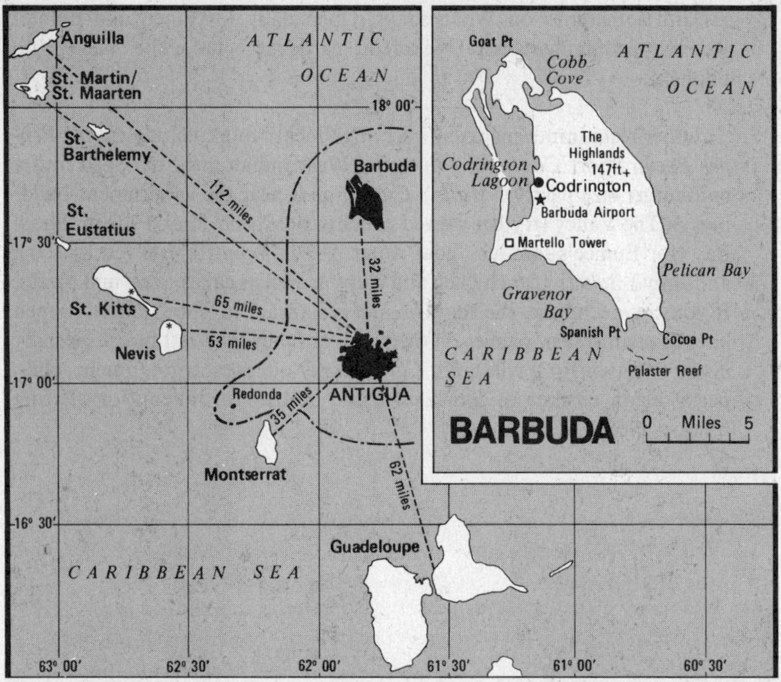

Anguilla
ATLANTIC OCEAN
St. Martin/ St. Maarten
18° 00′
St. Barthelemy
Barbuda
112 miles
St. Eustatius
17° 30′
32 miles
St. Kitts
65 miles
Nevis
53 miles
17° 00′
Redonda
ANTIGUA
35 miles
Montserrat
62 miles
16° 30′
Guadeloupe
CARIBBEAN SEA
63° 00′
62° 30′
62° 00′
61° 30′
61° 00′
60° 30′

Goat Pt
Cobb Cove
ATLANTIC OCEAN
The Highlands 147ft
Codrington Lagoon
Codrington
Barbuda Airport
Martello Tower
Pelican Bay
Gravenor Bay
Spanish Pt
Cocoa Pt
CARIBBEAN SEA
Palaster Reef
BARBUDA
0 Miles 5

ANTIGUA
Prickly Pear I.
Boon Pt
Humphry's Bay
Hodges Bay
Dickenson Bay
Cedar Grove
Long I.
ATLANTIC OCEAN
422ft
V.C. Bird Airport
Parham
Ft. James
Gt. Bird I.
St. John's Hbr
Harbour
Guana I.
ST. JOHN'S
526ft
Green Bay
Guana Bay
Parham
Crump I.
Long Bay
Indian Town Pt.
Five Islands Harbour
Devils Bridge
Sea View Farm
Willkie's Village
Nonsuch Bay
Green I.
Bolans
All Saints
271ft
Boggy Peak 1319ft
Fig Tree Drive
Freetown
York I.
Mill Reef
Liberta
Half Moon Bay
Johnson's Point
Willoughby Bay
Falmouth
English Harbour Town
Cades Bay
Old Road
Curtain Bluff
Shirley Hts 487ft
Marmora Bay
Falmouth Hbr
Nelson's Dockyard
English Hbr
0 Miles 5
CARIBBEAN SEA

Antigua

Antiguans claim their island has a beach for every day of the year, and travelers flying into Antigua get a good glimpse of the necklace of beautiful white sand beaches that nearly surround the island. The magnificent beaches are complemented by crystal clear, azure blue water, and from the air the sparkling sea would excite even the most lackadaisical vacationer.

Antigua (pronounced An-*tee*-gah) is a perfect island for vacationers who want to be in the sunshine beside the sea almost every day, because of all the eastern Caribbean islands, Antigua receives the least rainfall. Formerly a British colony, some of the Old World traditions linger, such as afternoon tea in some of the hotels, and cricket, one of the island's most popular sports. In fact, cricket might be the best metaphor for island life — not just because so much about the island is so determinedly British, but because, like that game, it is devoted to doing things in the fullness of time, with great enthusiasm but little rush.

Before the British settled on the island, it was inhabited by Indians: first the Siboney, or "stone people"; then the Arawak, a pastoral South American tribe; and finally the warlike Carib, who harassed European settlers here as late as the 1700s. Antigua was discovered by Columbus in 1493, during his second voyage into the Caribbean. Although he never came ashore, he did stop long enough to name it after Santa María la Antigua of Seville.

About 130 years later, a group of Englishmen sailed over from nearby St. Kitts and settled the island on behalf of England. Antigua has been British ever since, except for one brief year (1666) when the French took possession.

During the next 200 years, the British built forts on the shoreline and a major naval installation at English Harbour while waiting for the French to come back. They never did. But in 1784 a dashing young naval captain named Horatio Nelson arrived and took command of the yard. Under his command was the captain of the HMS *Pegasus,* Prince William Henry, Duke of Clarence (he later became King William IV). Clarence House, which sits on a hill opposite the yard, was built for the young prince while he was serving there. As naval vessels grew larger and as skirmishes between Britain and France diminished, Antigua's importance as a naval base receded and the yard was officially abandoned in the early 19th century. Nelson's Dockyard, after 150 years of neglect, has been faithfully restored and is now a museum and active yacht marina. Work also has begun on the restorations of the fortifications atop Shirley Heights, which overlooks English Harbour.

But while Antigua's history and way of life are both relatively tranquil, there is still lots to do besides watch the gulls soar on the trade breezes.

Virtually all the first class hotels have tennis courts, and several sponsor annual tournaments. The island has one 18-hole and two 9-hole (one private) golf courses. And the local waters are unexcelled for sports and activities: miles of reefs for snorkeling and diving, and numerous coves for sailing Sunfish. For serious deep-water sailors there is *Race Week,* held each spring in late April or early May. At day's end, a peripatetic night bird may while away the evenings at Antigua's clubs and casinos.

Antigua At-a-Glance

FROM THE AIR

During the dry season (February through April), Antigua gradually turns dusty and brown. But when the rains come, it becomes as green and lush as the Vermont countryside in June. From its shores you can see Guadeloupe, Montserrat, Nevis, and St. Kitts. Antigua is small — a scant 108 square miles — as are the other two islands that make up the state — Barbuda, 32 miles due north and measuring 68 square miles, and Redonda, a half-mile square of rock pinnacle that juts from the sea 20 miles to the southwest. There are about 63,000 people on Antigua, 1,500 on Barbuda, and only seagulls on Redonda.

SPECIAL PLACES

Though the focal point of sightseeing on the island is Nelson's Dockyard, the completely restored 18th-century naval yard on the southern side of Antigua, most visitors will begin their tour in St. John's, the island's capital and major city.

ST. JOHN'S There are three major attractions here: the farmers' market at the southern edge of town, the *Museum of Antigua and Barbuda,* and St. John's Cathedral. The bustling outdoor market is best seen on a Saturday morning, when the colorful fruit and vegetable stands are set up early in the morning and everyone turns out to shop. From the market, it is just a short taxi ride to Newgate Street for the museum and the cathedral. The *Museum of Antigua and Barbuda* (Long St.; phone: 463-1060) is a collection of early Indian items from some 120 prehistoric and historic sites on the island. While not elaborate or extensive, it does exhibit some interesting archaeological artifacts, and has displays about significant island historical facts and relationships. Originally built in 1683, St. John's Cathedral (on Church St.) has been rebuilt twice, in 1745 and again in 1845. The exterior is stone, but the interior is cased in pitch pine (which helped it survive subsequent earthquakes). The gates were constructed in 1789.

ELSEWHERE ON THE ISLAND

At the village of Falmouth, just north of Nelson's Dockyard, is an area that used to be devoted to producing sugar. Several antique stone sugar mill towers have been converted into private homes; you can see most of them from the road. From Falmouth, the route to the dockyard is well marked.

NELSON'S DOCKYARD The British navy used the dockyard continuously from 1707 until 1899, when ships became too large to negotiate the relatively tortuous entrance to the harbor. The impressive installation saw its finest moments during the command of Captain Horatio Nelson, from 1784 to 1787. During his stay, Nelson established a fast friendship with Prince William Henry, Duke of Clarence (later King William IV). Clarence House, visible across the harbor from the dockyard, was built for the duke. It is sometimes open to the public.

The main buildings are the *Admiral's House,* now a museum; the Officers' Quarters, which have undergone minor restoration; the *Admiral's Inn,* a hotel and restaurant constructed of bricks that came to Antigua as ships' ballast; and the *Copper and Lumber Store,* now a charming and unusual inn (see *Checking In* for details on the latter two). The dockyard complex, including the museum, is open daily from 6 AM to 6 PM. Admission charge (phone: 460-1053, 460-1379, or 460-1380). A good guide to the dockyard's history is *The Story of English Harbour,* by Desmond Nicholson. Published by the *Museum of Antigua and Barbuda,* it can be purchased at the museum or at local bookstores for $6.

SHIRLEY HEIGHTS Just north of Nelson's Dockyard is the town of English Harbour; the ridge of hills above the town was fortified in 1787 by General William Henry Shirley and came to be known as Shirley Heights. After leaving the yard, return to the crossroads at English Harbour and bear right for the road to the summit of Shirley Heights. Along the way, extensive fortifications, barracks, and powder magazines are visible; they were used to guard the dockyard from invaders. (They did their job well, for Antigua never was attacked.) The *Antigua Historical Society* has now identified all the ruins and has published a complete map of the facilities along the route; it is available at the *Museum of Antigua and Barbuda.* A small museum contains artifacts from the British era as well as some Arawak relics. The restaurant on the bluff provides light refreshment and a stunning view of the English Harbour.

FIG TREE DRIVE The best drive in Antigua is along the beautiful but hard-to-find Fig Tree Drive. It has no fig trees, first of all; fig is the Antiguan name for banana. To complicate matters, it's unmarked — there are a limited number of road signs on the whole island. Typical directions (which are perfectly clear once you're following them): "Fig Tree Drive is the major road opposite the pink coral Catholic church just outside the town of Liberta, north of Falmouth. You can't miss it." Bearing southwest at the church, the road winds through Antigua's rain forest and the hilliest section of the island, rising and falling steeply around Fig Tree Hill — farmland verdant with banana, mango, and coconut groves — before descending to Old Road and the Curtain Bluff area. No major sights, but a pleasant drive.

PARHAM HARBOUR One of the island's older waterfront villages, it is in the midst of a major restoration. Plans for this town near the airport include building a boardwalk that will feature restaurants, shops, and several historic sites; there is no projected completion date as yet. For more information, contact the *Museum of Antigua and Barbuda* (phone: 463-1060).

Sources and Resources

TOURIST INFORMATION

The tourist office on Antigua is on Long Street in St. John's. There also are information centers at V. C. Bird International Airport, Heritage Quay, and at the passenger ship terminal in St. John's (central phone for all: 462-0029, 462-0480, or 462-1005). For information about Antigua tourist offices in the US, see GETTING READY TO GO.

LOCAL COVERAGE The tourist office and hotel desks carry information on entertainment, restaurants, sightseeing, and special events. The *Antigua and Barbuda Activities Guide* and other locally produced brochures are available at a small price; the glossy, magazine-style *Antigua and Barbuda Adventure* is free.

The *Worker's Voice,* the *Nation,* and the *Outlet* are the island's newspapers. The Sunday *New York Times* (and, occasionally, the weekday edition) arrives several days late.

RADIO AND TELEVISION

The ABS (Antigua Broadcasting Service) handles TV and radio for both Antigua and Barbuda. Other radio stations are ZDK and Radio Lighthouse; for TV, Channel CTV.

TELEPHONE

When calling from the US, dial 809 (area code) + (local number). To call from another Caribbean island, the code may vary, so call the local operator. When calling on Antigua, dial the local number (note that all telephone numbers on the island begin with 46).

ENTRY REQUIREMENTS

US and Canadian citizens need a passport or other proof of citizenship (a birth certificate or voter's registration card plus a photo ID) and an onward or return ticket. A smallpox vaccination is not required unless you are coming from a contaminated area.

CLIMATE AND CLOTHES

Temperatures range from an average low of 73F (23C) in the winter to a high of 85F (30C) in the summer and fall. Except in September, there's a constant trade wind of 19 to 30 miles per hour, making for cool, pleasant evenings. There are few days without sun, and the annual rainfall averages only 45 inches. September, October, and November are the wettest months, when there are daily showers that usually last 10 minutes or less.

While many islands are completely casual, Antigua is not. Swimwear is for the beach only. Sightseeing or shopping requires casual street clothes (not shorts). The British tradition of men dressing for dinner (jackets and ties or just jackets) still survives during the winter season in a few deluxe hotels like *Curtain Bluff, Jumby Bay,* and *Half Moon Bay*. Restaurants are a different story; they all are casual and the "shirtjack" (a loose-fitting men's cotton shirt) usually suffices.

MONEY

The official currency of the island, the Eastern Caribbean dollar (called Bee Wee or EC), is valued at about $2.68 to the US dollar. Banks exchange at exactly the day's exchange rate; hotels and shops will change at a bit less. US and Canadian dollars are accepted everywhere. Credit cards (principally American Express and Visa) and traveler's checks are now accepted at all major hotels and at many shops and restaurants. All prices in this chapter are quoted in US dollars.

Banking hours are 8 AM to 1 PM Mondays through Thursdays and 3 to 5:30 PM on Fridays. Banks are closed Saturdays, Sundays, and holidays.

LANGUAGE

English has been spoken here since the 1630s. However, when Antiguans exchange pleasantries — liberally sprinkled with local colloquialisms — in their lilting accents, it may seem as if they're speaking another language.

TIME

Antigua is on atlantic standard time, 1 hour ahead of New York in winter; in summer, when daylight saving time is in effect in the US, noon in New York also is noon in Antigua.

CURRENT

Most hotels operate on 110 volts, 60 cycles — the same as in the US and Canada. However, some have 220-volt outlets (and to confuse matters a bit more, many of these have 110-volt shaver outlets). However, most hotels that have 220-volt outlets maintain an inventory of transformers and adapters for guests.

TIPPING

The 10% service charge added to the bill at virtually all Antiguan hotels and restaurants covers all but very special service. When a service charge is not included (if in doubt, ask), tip waiters 10% to 15%, hotel maids $1 per room per day, bellboys and airport porters 50¢ per bag. Taxi drivers get about 10% of the fare.

GETTING AROUND

BUS Public transport exists, but on a strictly informal basis; buses run "sometime in the morning" and "sometime in the afternoon." Tourists seldom use them, but for those with unlimited time, buses are an inexpensive way to travel.

CAR RENTAL The best way to get around for visitors who plan on staying for any length of time and want to travel around the island. Driving is on the left, and an Antiguan driver's license is required; it can be obtained at the airport or the police station in St. John's for about $12 with a valid US license. Rates for rental cars are about $50 to $55 a day, and about $250 a week. Insurance is extra. There are no mileage fees with rental cars.

All rental firms on the island are locally owned but represent international chains as well as independent operations. Among the best: *Avis* (phone: 462-2840), *Budget* (phone: 462-3009), *Capital Rentals* (phone: 462-0863), *Carib Car Rentals* (phone: 462-2062), *Dollar* (phone: 462-0362), *National* (phone: 462-2113), and *Village Car Rentals* (phone: 462-3751). During certain holiday peak times — *Christmas, Easter, Antigua Sailing Week* — reserve ahead.

SEA EXCURSIONS Lunch, all-day, and evening cocktail cruises are becoming very popular in Antigua. A number of yachts and the pirate-ship-shaped *Jolly Roger* (phone: 462-2064) offer such trips. The *Curtain Bluff* hotel has its own yacht. Buffet or barbecue cruises, with lunch, rum punches, swimming, and lots of music, cost about $50 per person; dinner cruises with dancing run about the same. Reservations can be made through most hotels. Day trips to Barbuda can be arranged through *Falcon* (phone: 462-4792).

TAXI Always available at the airport, in St. John's, at the deep-water harbor, and at the hotels. The rates are fixed by law (no meters). From the airport to St. John's, expect to pay about $12; to the most distant hotel, about $25. The trip from St. John's to Nelson's Dockyard will run about $25. Printed information on official taxi fares to all destinations is available at tourist offices on the island. Fares also may be confirmed with the official taxi dispatchers at the airport and harbor; be sure to check whether the quoted figure is in US or EC currency.

Touring by taxi is one of the best ways to see the island. Antiguan taxi drivers on the whole are friendly and informative, particularly since the government has provided them with an information booklet detailing much of the island's history, natural resources, and general facts, figures, tidbits, and trivia. A full tour of Nelson's Dockyard, Shirley Heights, Fig Tree Drive, and shopping in St. John's will cost about $70. Taxis are usually easy to arrange; for assistance, contact the *United Taxi Association* (phone: 461-1876).

INTER-ISLAND FLIGHTS

BWIA flies between San Juan and Antigua, and *LIAT* provides air links to most other Caribbean islands.

SPECIAL EVENTS

Antigua has three special celebrations: *Tennis Week, Race Week,* and *Summer Carnival. Tennis Week,* held at several topflight hotels in early January, features a week-long series of amateur men's and women's tournaments, pro-ams, and professional men's singles and doubles tourneys. There's also a *Women's Tennis Week* in early April.

In late April, Antigua's festive spirit turns to the sea for *Race Week,* 7 days of ocean racing and shoreside parties. It's a delightful mixture of breathtaking scenes and breathtaking rum, and the evening parties shift from hotel to hotel. The last day, called *Dockyard Day,* is a landlubber's delight. It features tugs-of-war between sailing crews, a greased pole race, and spinnaker flying. When the sun sets, Lord Nelson's Ball begins. Amid drinking and dancing, the week's awards are presented.

At the end of July and in early August is *Summer Carnival,* a week to 10 days of fetes, steel bands, Carnival Queen and calypso competitions, parades, and more fetes.

More sedate and official holidays observed by bank and state include *New Year's Day, Good Friday, Easter, Whitmonday, Independence Day* (November 1), *Christmas,* and *Boxing Day* (December 26).

SHOPPING

Liquor prices are among the lowest in the Caribbean, except for French wines and certain French cognacs. Cavalier, the local rum, is about $3 for 26 ounces, an outstanding bargain in anyone's book. (Local liquor stores generally carry cards showing cost, including extra duty, for those people wishing to bring back more than a single liter.) Prices on European imports, gold jewelry, and lead crystal are no better than those found elsewhere in the Caribbean (and usually no less than in mainland discount outlets), but Sea Island cotton products (all made in Japan) are excellent buys.

Island-made bead necklaces are sold on beaches, at the dockyard, or wherever else a "bead lady" can set up shop. A favorite souvenir is a warri board (an Antiguan game that you are guaranteed to learn during your stay).

Shopping hours are from 8 AM to noon and 1 to 4 PM Mondays through Fridays; on Thursdays and Saturdays some shops close for the afternoon. The local tourist guides give details on numerous other shops; below are our favorites in St. John's.

BASE ANTIGUA Offers an exclusive line of brilliantly colored women's fashions, all designed and made by local artisans. In the heart of Red Cliff Quay (phone: 462-0920).

COCO SHOP A great place for fabrics; also pottery. St. Mary's St. (phone: 462-1128).

GOLDSMITTY Look for fine handmade jewelry. *Red Cliff Quay Shopping Centre* (phone: 462-4601).

HARMONY HALL Sister to *Harmony Hall Gallery* on Jamaica, this complex of stores includes an arts center and a clothing boutique featuring crafts and fashions by Caribbean artists. Located in Freetown near Half Moon Bay (phone: 460-4120).

JACARANDA Featuring silk-screened and batik items, and island herbs and spices. Redcliff St. (phone: 462-1888).

SCENT SHOP What else? A scentsational array of more than 100 perfumes graces this nose-pleasing place. High St. (phone: 462-0303).

WINDJAMMER CLOTHING CO. Casual tropical wear is the specialty. *Red Cliff Quay Shopping Centre* (phone: 462-2607).

SPORTS

Since beaches are Antigua's main draw, it's only natural that most of the island's visitors can be found on or near one of the 365 stretches of sand that dot the island's perimeter. There is, however, a continued commitment to cricket and soccer and a rapidly growing interest in tennis, squash, and basketball.

BOATING Most hotels have Sunfish or Sailfish available (often without cost to guests). Individual day charters are offered by several companies, including *Black Swan* (phone: 460-5000), *Holiday Adventure* (phone: 461-0361), *Wadadli Watersports* (phone: 462-2890), *Jolly Roger Pirate Cruises* (phone: 462-2064), and *Bucanero* (phone: 464-8587). A quick check with *Nicholson Yacht Charters* (phone: 463-1530; 800-662-6066 from the US) will determine what is available at Nelson's Dockyard. *Nicholson* handles over 80 charter yachts, and more often than not, at least one or two are in for provisioning. Prices vary according to the boat's size and the length of the trip. Also check with the *Catamaran* hotel (phone: 463-1036); many privately owned charter yachts are docked there, and the staff will know what is available.

CRICKET Antigua's main sporting passion is played on pitches (fields) ranging from exquisitely manicured greens to vacant lots. Cricket is a spectator sport that also is a social event, much like *Carnival.* Matches are played Thursday afternoons, Saturdays, and Sundays.

CYCLING Rentals are available from *Sun Cycles* in Hodges Bay (phone: 461-0324).

GOLF There are no true championship courses on Antigua, but two layouts here offer diversion for the average player. *Cedar Valley* (phone: 462-0161), just outside St. John's, is a 6,077-yard, 18-hole, par 70 course. The *Half Moon Bay* resort has a 9-hole, par 34 course that stretches 2,140 yards. Rentals: clubs $6; carts $15; greens fees $16; caddies $10. Hourly lessons are available at $25. Weekly greens fees are available at both courses.

HIKING Because of limited public transportation, it is best to plan *round-trip* walking tours. For the stout of heart, a trek up the face of Monk's Hill (opposite the *Catamaran* hotel) offers a look at the forts atop the hill and a spectacular view of the island. *Warning:* Start early, take your time, and bring water and a snack. The *Historical and Archaeological Society* also occasionally arranges hikes and interesting excursions. For details, contact the society at the *Museum of Antigua and Barbuda* (Long St.; phone: 462-4930).

HORSEBACK RIDING The *St. James's Club* (phone: 463-1430 or 463-1113) leads guided excursions through the southeast countryside. *Charlie's* at Half Moon Bay (no phone) also has horses available.

HORSE RACING None of the "thoroughbreds" that parade to the post at the flat-racing course (look for a field with a rail around it by the west end of the runway at Bird Airport) would qualify for US races, but that doesn't keep the betting action from being fast and furious, or the local improvers of the breed from putting on the ritz. Races are held on all public holidays (approximately every 6 weeks). For information, contact Kenny Sumwell (phone: 462-6000 or 462-4337).

SNORKELING AND SCUBA The special lure of the waters off Antiguan beaches is that they are rather calm, suffer no heavy breakers or dangerous undertow, but still boast an abundance of reefs. Most hotels offer fins and masks free or for a nominal fee. For serious diving, the reefs and wrecks off Antigua's northeast, south, and west coasts provide good diving and make excellent day-trip destinations. Several hotels maintain their own equipment, including *Curtain Bluff, Club Antigua, Long Bay, Royal Antiguan,* and the *St. James's Club.* Dive operators include *Dive Antigua* (phone: 462-3483), *Dive Runaway* (phone: 462-2626), *Long Bay* (phone: 460-2005), *Jolly Dive* (phone: 462-0061), *Dockyard Divers* (phone: 460-1058), *Pirate Divers* (phone: 462-3094), and *Aquanaut* (phone: 460-5000). Single-tank dives cost around $55.

The waters off Barbuda — 32 miles north of Antigua — also provide excellent diving grounds, strewn with wrecks, although diving facilities on this isle are very limited.

SPORT FISHING Among the hotels operating sport fishing boats are *Runaway, Blue Waters Beach,* and *Long Bay;* half-day deep-sea trips cost about $150, inshore trips about $50 per person. The *Catamaran Club* (phone: 460-1036) also offers trips, and *Overdraft,* a fishing boat, is available for charter; contact Frankie Nunes (phone: 462-0649) to make the arrangements.

SWIMMING AND SUNNING Still the supreme interest and pastime of vacationers, and with good reason. The beaches are many and excellent. Because three-quarters of the island rests comfortably inside the Caribbean Sea, and that which does not is well protected by reefs, there are rarely heavy breakers or dangerous undertows. The Caribbean side of the island, however, is better protected than the Atlantic side. For calm waters in the Atlantic, seek out places like Half Moon Bay where one end is like a clear swimming pool; the other end is rougher and good only for experienced swimmers and body-surfers. All beaches on Antigua are public. Antigua's neighbor island, Barbuda, is all beach (the best place for shelling, by the way). Unfortunately, Barbuda has limited accommodations (see *Checking In*), but, time permitting, visitors to Antigua should consider a day trip.

TENNIS Antigua has a wide choice of places to play, many with lessons, pro shops, and equipment.

CHOICE COURTS

Curtain Bluff The small, select site of a well-attended annual spring tournament, it has the atmosphere of a private club. Facilities include 4 hard-surface plus 1 artificial grass court — all championship caliber — a teaching alley, a resident pro, a pro shop, and teaching equipment (phone: 462-8400/1/2).

The island's other tennis sites include *St. James's Club* (5 lighted courts), *Half Moon Bay* (5 courts), and the *Ramada Renaissance* (8 courts, 4 lighted). All have resident pros and complete shops. Other hotels — *Blue Waters Beach, Hawksbill Beach, Galleon Beach, Galley Bay, Halcyon Cove,* and *Club Antigua* — also offer tennis, though with fewer facilities. The *Temo Sports Centre* at English Harbour (phone: 460-1781) is a sports complex with 2 lighted tennis courts, squash courts, and a friendly bar. *Half Moon Bay,* the *Anchorage,* and *Halcyon Cove* host the annual *Tennis Week*'s professional tournaments each January. Most hotels don't charge guests for court time.

WATER SKIING Offered by some of the hotels and listed on the tourist office's activities chart. Cost is about $25 per person for a half hour.

WINDSURFING With constant winds blowing in from the ocean, it's the ideal water sport in Antigua. There are several established international windsurfing schools and an annual *Windsurfing Antigua* event. *Patrick's Wind-*

surfing School (phone: 462-3094), *Windsurfing Lord Nelson* (phone: 462-3094), *Paradise Watersports* (phone: 462-4158), and *Wadadli Watersports* (phone: 462-2980) offer lessons and rental equipment.

NIGHTLIFE

In season, most hotels offer some entertainment every night: a steel band, limbo dancers, dance band, or a display of fire eating. There are several casinos: one with adjacent lounge entertainment at the *Ramada Renaissance* hotel; a small, European-style casino next to the disco at the glitzy *St. James's Club;* one with a lounge and nightclub at the *Halcyon Cove;* and *King's Casino* in Heritage Quay. They operate every night and feature blackjack, craps, roulette, and one-armed bandits. Independent clubs and discos, like local restaurants, seem to sprout during the height of the winter season and then disappear, sometimes permanently.

Best on the Island

CHECKING IN

Antigua offers a staggering diversity of resort facilities and accommodations. The choices range from simple inns that charge about $75 a night, to the *K Club* on Barbuda, where a night's lodging will run in the neighborhood of $1,700. The island also has a number of self-contained housekeeping units. A listing — not always including rates, however — is available from the Department of Tourism. Summer rates (in effect from April 16 to December 15) are 30% to 45% lower; a room for two at *Jumby Bay,* which costs $895 (including all meals) in mid-January, will cost $650 or so in July. Expect to pay at least $500 for a room for two (MAP, including breakfast and dinner) in high season at hotels listed as very expensive; from $350 to $500 at establishments we call expensive; $170 to $350 in places in the moderate category; and $75 to $160 at places labeled inexpensive. There's a 6% tax on all hotel bills. When calling on Antigua use only the local numbers listed below. For information about dialing from elsewhere, see "Telephone" earlier in this chapter.

For an unforgettable island experience, we begin with our favorite, followed by our recommendations of cost and quality choices of accommodations, listed by area and price category.

A SPECIAL HAVEN

Curtain Bluff Celebrating 32 years of sole ownership, this property is dedicated to (at most) 120 guests, who enjoy the best of island sport and don't mind being very comfortable and personally catered to while they do. Along the beach-lined edges of a breeze-catching peninsula that pokes into the Caribbean on the island's south side, this peaceful oasis offers not only pleasing rooms (the prettiest are the pastel suites), all with porches or balconies looking out on sea, surf, and sky, but impeccably maintained Sunfish sailboats, water skiing, snorkel and scuba gear (with their own compressor on the premises and rock pools and reefs just offshore), plus 4 Har-Tru tennis courts with a wintertime resident pro (see *Tennis* in this chapter). Nothing flashy — just quality down to its tennis socks. Also available are squash courts and a workout room. Of more than passing interest, the annual spring *Antigua Sailing Week,* an international regatta, is cosponsored by the hotel. The beach bar, shaded by plume-fronded palms, is where most daytime action is centered. Later, it all moves to the covey of buildings set among lush foliage that house the patio bar, lounge, and breeze-conditioned dining room (jackets and ties requested for dinner). Chef Ruedi Portman is well known for his imaginative island cuisine. The wine cellar is one of the best-stocked in the Caribbean. In season, a different island band (flute, steel, calypso) plays almost every night. Closed from June 1 to October 1. Old Rd. (phone: 462-8400, 462-8401, or 462-8402; 212-289-8888 from the US; fax: 462-8409).

VERY EXPENSIVE

Half Moon Bay This country-club-style, 100-room resort on the island's most beautiful white sand beach was bought by the owners of *Curtain Bluff* early last year; extensive upgrading and renovation was planned at press time, and it is scheduled to reopen for the winter season. The complex includes a golf course, tennis courts, all water sports (except scuba diving), a pool, and a restaurant. Half Moon Bay (phone: 460-4300, 460-4305, or 460-4306; 800-223-6510 from the US; fax: 460-4306).

Jumby Bay A maximum of 76 guests have the entire 300 acres of this private island 1 mile north of Antigua to themselves. There are 12 cottages, 14 rooms in a Spanish-style villa, and 12 rondavels (cottages with an extra sitting room that can be used as a bedroom); amenities include 2 beaches, water sports, tennis, and fine food and drink (see *Eating Out*). Open November through August (phone: 462-6000; 800-421-9016 from the US; fax: 462-6000, ext. 144).

St. James's Club This glitter-dome-by-the-sea features an activity-rich environment and is certainly comfortable, but part of the premium price is returned only in the intangibles of seeing and being seen. Dress accordingly. There are 90 suites and studios, plus a private yacht club on a 100-acre point at Mamora Bay. Rates cover use of 2 big pools, sun decks, beaches, snorkel gear, windsurfers, sailboats, gym, and 5 tennis courts; scuba, jet skiing, water skiing, sport fishing, and riding (from the club's own stable of quarter horses) cost extra. Other amenities include a hair salon, 24-hour room service, 4 restaurants, a nightclub/disco, and a small European-style casino. Mamora Bay (phone: 460-5000; 800-274-0008 from the US; fax: 460-3015).

EXPENSIVE

Blue Waters Beach One of the few places with air conditioned rooms, it's pleasant in an Old English sort of way. The hotel has 67 rooms, 2 restaurants, and dancing or entertainment nightly during the winter season. The food is consistently good. Facilities include all water sports, a tennis court, and a pool. Soldiers Bay (phone: 462-0290; fax: 462-0293).

Carlisle Bay Club This 112-room complex features 1-bedroom beachfront condos with kitchens. Facilities include a restaurant, a freshwater pool, and 10 tennis courts. Old Rd. (phone: 462-1377).

Galley Bay Here are 31 double rooms in what seems to be a very remote setting. Actually, it is only 5 miles from St. John's and is a favorite celebrity hangout. Excellent beach and water sports, also a tennis court and horseback riding. At Galley Bay (phone: 462-0302; 800-223-6510 from the US; fax: 462-0302).

Halcyon Cove Beach This 154-room establishment offers lots of activities, a pool, tennis, all water sports, the *Warri Pier* for lunch and drinks (be prepared for slow service), nightly entertainment and/or dancing, and a casino. On Dickenson Bay (phone: 462-0256; 800-255-5859 from the US; fax: 462-0271).

Hawksbill Beach An impressive 37-acre beachfront site and among the island's top resorts — there are 84 deluxe, superior, and standard guestrooms, plus a separate greathouse with accommodations for up to eight guests (reserve 6 months to a year in advance). The resort has its own beach and coral reef for offshore snorkeling, most other water sports, a pool, and tennis. On the south coast, a half-hour's drive from the airport (phone: 462-0301; 800-327-6511 from the US; fax: 462-1515).

Hodges Bay Club Gleaming Mediterranean villas shelter 26 smartly comfortable 1- and 2-bedroom apartments (with cathedral ceilings, Italian tile floors, balconies or terraces, deluxe kitchens) overlooking a pretty if narrow white sand beach; double bedroom rentals are also available. Nearby Prickly Pear Island offers first-rate snorkeling and picnicking. Secluded, yet handy to golf course, airport, and St. John's. Hodges Bay (phone: 462-2300; 800-432-4229 from the US; fax: 462-1962).

Long Bay Small, pleasant, and somewhat isolated on the northeastern coast of the island, this family-owned-and-operated property is right at the water's edge; 20 balconied rooms and 6 cottages face a lagoon. All water sports, including scuba diving. Long Bay (phone: 463-2005; 800-225-4255 from the US; fax: 463-2439).

Ramada Renaissance This 8-story property offers 282 rooms in the main buildings, plus 12 one-bedroom and 18 two-bedroom suites in adjacent cottages. It offers little in the way of island ambience, but plenty of big-hotel amenities. All the rooms are air conditioned, and have radio/TV sets and VCRs, mini-bars, and refrigerators. There are 3 restaurants on the premises, 3 lounges, and a European-style casino. Other amenities include all water sports, 8 tennis courts (4 lighted), a swimming pool, and a yacht marina. On Deep Bay (phone: 462-3733; 800-228-2828 from the US; fax: 462-3732).

Sandals One of the all-inclusive couples-only Sandals resorts, this 149-room property has an island ambience; the lobby features an indoor waterfall, lush foliage, and tropical birds in cages. Facilities include 3 restaurants, a swimming pool, tennis courts, scuba diving, 1,500 feet of white sand beach, and all water sports. Dickenson Bay (phone: 462-0267; 800-SANDALS from the US; fax: 462-4135).

MODERATE

Blue Heron Beach A friendly enclave on a sandy, reef-protected beach fine for swimming and snorkeling, it has 40 rooms, all with balcony or verandah, plus a beach bar, breezy cocktail lounge, and a restaurant particularly strong on authentic West Indian dishes. Johnson's Point Beach (phone: 462-8564; fax: 462-8005).

Brown's Bay Villas Here are 7 beachfront villas overlooking Nonesuch Bay; each accommodates up to 6 people and has a full kitchen. The atmosphere is casual and comfortable, and there is a pool and a tennis court. On the east coast next to *Harmony Hall* (phone/fax: 462-3803).

Club Antigua If you love company and have been searching for a reasonably priced Caribbean vacation, this 487-room resort (formerly the *Jolly Beach*) has your number. A highly organized activities schedule takes hold of the tour-package client from arrival to departure. Guests can swim, frolic, or play tennis and other sports, and there's a mini-gym for children. Room rate includes all meals, drinks, and activities. Larger rooms are comfortable, if rather institutional in decor; smaller size units are downright tight. Off-season tour packages, including airfare, are among the best bargains of all time. Jolly Beach (phone: 462-0061; 800-777-1250 from the US; fax: 462-1827).

Copper and Lumber Store Unique setting and authentic 18th-century decor (Oriental rugs, antique four-poster beds, nautical memorabilia, period furniture) for 14 opulent suites in meticulously reconstructed Nelson's Dockyard warehouse. All have admirably modern kitchens. No sports facilities, but transport to the beach across the harbor is provided. The restaurant offers English specialties and some island dishes. Nelson's Dockyard (phone: 460-1058; fax: 460-1529).

Heritage Located in the heart of St. John's, it's convenient to lots of duty-free shopping and restaurants. The 3 studio and 16 one-bedroom suites are air conditioned and have kitchens. Special rates are available for businesspeople, and amenities include TV sets in all the rooms, conference and meeting facilities, a nearby beach, and golf and tennis by arrangement. Heritage Quay (phone: 462-1247; fax: 809-462-2262).

Pineapple Beach Club This beachfront property has 128 rooms, 2 restaurants, and 2 bars, in addition to an array of water sports facilities, a swimming pool, and 6 tennis courts. Transfers to the airport are included in the all-inclusive rate. Long Bay, St. John's (phone: 463-2006; 800-345-0356 from the US; fax: 463-2452).

Siboney Beach Club Almost hidden by palms and bougainvillea, this property features 12 suites in a greenery-laden 3-story building with a pool and small restaurant-lounge. An informal, congenial setting where the service can be as relaxed as the atmosphere, and the food is surprisingly good. If it's intimacy you crave, this is it. Try for top-floor balcony suites. On Dickenson Bay (phone: 462-3356; 800-533-0234 from the US; fax: 462-3356).

INEXPENSIVE

Admiral's Inn This delightful 200-year-old hostelry is the heart of Nelson's Dockyard. When the ships are in, you'll find millionaires and boat bums drinking and eating side by side at the bar or in the courtyard. The 14 rooms — not all air conditioned — are small but well appointed. The restaurant's great for almost any type of food (see *Eating Out*). No beach, but the management runs visitors to one across the harbor. English Harbour (phone: 460-1027; 800-621-1270 from the US; fax: 460-1534).

Falmouth Harbour Beach Apartments Run by the *Admiral's Inn* folks, these 28 suites — each with a kitchen and maid service — are a bargain. The beach is just minutes away. English Harbour (phone: 460-1027; 800-223-5695 from the US; fax: 463-1534).

BARBUDA

VERY EXPENSIVE

Coco Point Lodge An elegant, expensive (some say even eccentric) enclave on a 146-acre peninsula with a wonderful 2-mile-long white beach. There are 30 nicely decorated rooms, all of which open onto the beach. A perfect place to escape from civilization, there are no phones here and the only form of nighttime entertainment is a band that plays on Saturday nights. Most activities revolve around the sand and sea — swimming, snorkeling, sunning, and just plain relaxing. Dinners are served on an open-air terrace with a view of the sea. Many of the guests have been coming here for years, and the place has the air of a private club. Guests are flown from the Antigua airport to the resort's private airstrip. Note that no credit cards are accepted. Reservations are made through the owner, Patrick Kelly, in New York: *Coco Point Lodge,* 200 Madison Ave., New York, NY 10016 (phone: 212-696-4750).

K Club On one of the biggest, whitest, and most beautiful beaches in the Caribbean, this property has 35 rooms in 23 bungalows. Created by the well-known fashion designer Krizia, the decor is in white and aqua, and the rooms are spacious and private, with large bathrooms. This is the place for peace and solitude. The rate includes fine dining at the hotel's restaurant (alcoholic beverages are extra). No TV sets, no children under 12. Arrive by plane from Antigua and the hotel will drive you the 8 miles to the resort (phone: 460-0300; 800-83K-CLUB from the US; fax: 460-0305).

MODERATE

Palmetto A comfortable, lower-priced lodging alternative on Barbuda, this recently opened beachfront hotel offers 9 air conditioned cottages with kitchens, 24 guestrooms, and 3 villas. A restaurant, tennis court, pool, and bar are other featured amenities, and a variety of water sports is available. On Palmetto Point, 15 minutes from the main town (phone/fax: 460-0440).

EATING OUT

Like most Caribbean food, native Antiguan fare tends to be spicy, with sauces that are highly influenced by East Indian and creole recipes. A wide variety of curries is found on most island menus. Antiguan restaurants change names, locations, and phone numbers at the drop of a hat, so confirm that your choice is still around before heading off to dine. Expect to pay around $90 for two at the restaurants we list as expensive, about $40 at moderate spots, and not more than $20 at places in the inexpensive category. Most restaurants include a service charge on the bill, so check before deciding on any additional gratuity. When calling on Antigua, use only the local numbers listed below. For information about dialing from elsewhere, see "Telephone" earlier in this chapter.

ST. JOHN'S

EXPENSIVE

Chez Pascal Owned by Lyon-born Pascal Hilliat, it serves the best French fare on the island. Open for dinner only; closed Sundays and September 15 through November 15. Reservations advised. Major credit cards accepted. Tanner and Cross Sts. (phone: 462-3232).

MODERATE

Calypso Café A pleasant, open-air spot for sandwiches, salads, fish, or chicken. Open for lunch and dinner; closed Sundays. Reservations unnecessary. Major credit cards accepted. Redcliff St. (phone: 462-1965).

Lemon Tree Located in the heart of St. John's, this air conditioned place offers a wide range of prices, and menu choices to suit most tastes. Lively entertainment most evenings. Open for lunch and dinner; closed Sundays. Reservations necessary. Major credit cards accepted. Long St. (phone: 462-1969).

Redcliff Tavern Family-owned and -operated, this casual dining spot in the center of St. John's puts a strong emphasis on good, simple seafood dishes. There's also a bar that serves snacks along with drinks. Open for lunch and dinner. Closed Sundays. Reservations advised for dinner. Major credit cards accepted. In the *Red Cliff Quay Shopping Centre* (phone: 461-4557).

Spanish Main In a large 160-year-old home, this businessmen's luncheon haunt serves continental dishes in comfortable surroundings. Sunday brunch is roast beef and Yorkshire pudding. Live entertainment on some evenings. Open daily for breakfast, lunch, and dinner. Reservations advised. No credit cards accepted. At East and St. Mary's Sts. (phone: 462-0660).

INEXPENSIVE

Brother B's *The* place for a local lunch, it features outdoor tables and a West Indian menu with a special dish each day (try the pepper pot). It will be crowded, so expect to linger a while. A very casual, local lunch for one will run only slightly more than $3. Open for breakfast, lunch, and dinner; closed Sundays. Reservations unnecessary. No credit cards accepted. Long St. and Soul Alley (phone: 462-0616).

Speedy Joe's They serve a hearty meal quickly here; perfect when you don't have a lot of time. Open for breakfast, lunch, and dinner; dinner only on Sundays. Reservations advised. No credit cards accepted. At Nevis St. and Corn Alley (phone: 462-1142).

ELSEWHERE ON THE ISLAND

EXPENSIVE

Admiral's Inn In the 200-year-old inn, this dining place is delightfully decorated, with an open courtyard. The continental-island menu usually features fish and seafood dishes (try the lobster). The rum punch is excellent. Open daily for breakfast, lunch, and dinner; closed September 1 through October 15. Reservations advised for dinner in season. Major credit cards accepted. Nelson's Dockyard (phone: 463-1027).

Beach Pavilion, Jumby Bay This lovely spot on Long Island offers fine French, Italian, American, and native Caribbean food served in the luxury setting of the *Jumby Bay* hotel, accessible only by boat (a 15-minute ride from Jumby Bay Pier). There's also a good selection of fine Italian wines. Open daily for lunch and dinner. Reservations necessary. No credit cards accepted. Long Island (phone: 462-6000).

Le Bistro One of Antigua's most elegant dining spots, with a distinctly French-toned menu, which changes every 4 months. Some specialties include lobster bisque or onion soup to start; rack of lamb, Dover sole in cream and spinach sauce, red snapper with fennel, and veal and beef entrées; crème caramel, peach melba, and chocolate mousse pie to finish. Open for dinner only; closed Mondays and May 15 through August 1. Reservations necessary. Major credit cards accepted. Hodges Bay near the *Hodges Bay Club* (phone: 462-3881).

Clouds Specializing in French and European food, it has a panoramic view. Open for dinner only; closed Sundays. Reservations necessary. Major credit cards accepted. On the grounds of the *Halcyon Cove* hotel (phone: 462-0256).

Coconut Grove Sitting underneath coconut trees on a beautiful beach, this tropical, open-air eatery specializes in seafood dishes, particularly lobster. There is live entertainment some evenings. Open daily. Reservations necessary. Major credit cards accepted (no phone).

Colombo's Every sort of pasta imaginable — all homemade (the Italian Flag appetizer starts you off with three; *tagliatelle al pesto* is ambrosial). Entrées of veal, tournedos Rossini, suckling pig (different choices each evening), are followed by fruit ices or ice creams, if you've a cranny left. Open daily for lunch and dinner. Reservations advised. Major credit cards accepted. At the *Galleon Beach Club* (phone: 460-1024).

La Perruche Featuring an open-air dining room and a fine view of Falmouth Harbour; the fare includes seafood and other fresh island ingredients. Open for dinner only. Reservations advised. Major credit cards accepted. English Harbour (phone: 460-3013).

MODERATE

Alberto's A choice dining spot, run by Alberto himself, with an open-air tropical setting and fresh seafood always on the menu. Specialties include conch salad, snapper, linguine with clams, and stuffed clams. Open for dinner only; closed Mondays. Reservations necessary. American Express and MasterCard accepted. Near Nelson's Dockyard (phone: 460-3007).

French Quarter Featuring Cajun and American choices, it's air conditioned, but the abundant greenery gives an outdoor effect. Open for dinner only; closed Sundays and September. Entertainment most evenings. Reservations unnecessary. Major credit cards accepted. On Runaway Bay (phone: 462-2565).

Jaws Patrons enjoy a breathtaking view as they dine on steaks, fresh seafood, pasta, and local specialties. There is a dance floor and a DJ. Open daily for dinner. Reservations advised. Major credit cards accepted. Five Islands, Deep Bay (phone: 462-2428).

Pari's Pizza This garden under cover has a relaxed and informal atmosphere. Delicious pizza is the specialty, with daily specials such as pasta or ribs. Open daily for lunch and dinner. Reservations unnecessary. Major credit cards accepted. Dickenson Bay at Tradewinds Hill (phone: 462-1501).

Shirley Heights Lookout Housed in a restored 18th-century fortification with a spectacular view of Nelson's Dockyard and English Harbour, its specialties include lobster and fresh fish dishes, as well as familiar standbys such as burgers and fries. Open daily for lunch and dinner; steel band and barbecue every Sunday afternoon. Reservations advised. Major credit cards accepted. Shirley Heights (phone: 460-1274).

70° 00'
69° 30'
69° 00'
68° 30'
68° 00'
CARIBBEAN SEA
ARUBA
12° 30'
NETHERLAND'S ANTILLES
42 miles
BONAIRE
CURAÇAO
30 miles
12° 00'
Paraguana
Peninsula
Punto
Fijo
Ferry
170 miles
11° 30'
Coro
La Vela
de Coro
290 miles
(to Caracas)
(to Caracas)
VENEZUELA

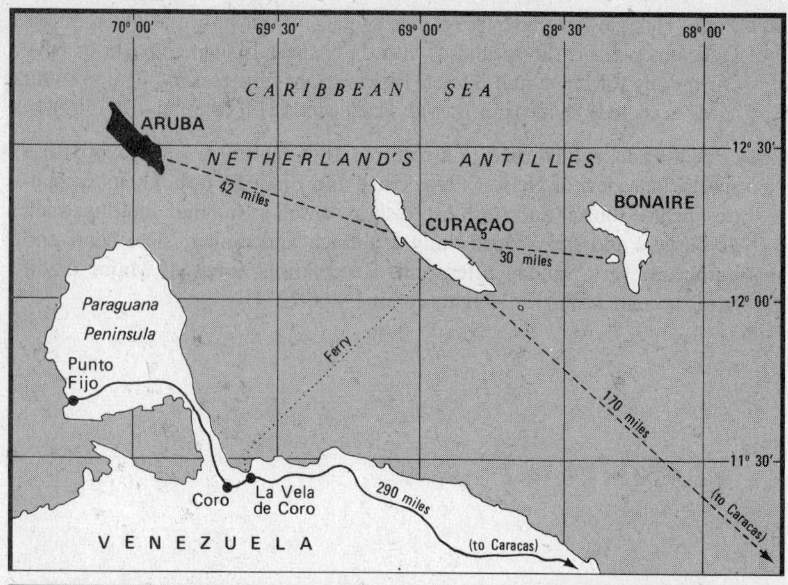

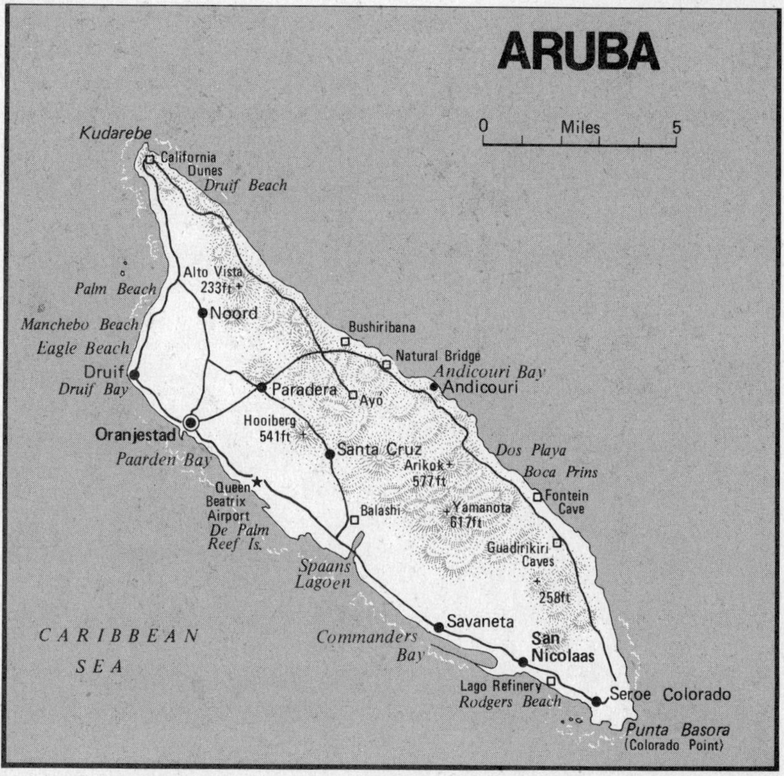

ARUBA
0
Miles
5
Kudarebe
California
Dunes
Druif Beach
Alto Vista
233ft
Palm Beach
Noord
Manchebo Beach
Eagle Beach
Bushiribana
Natural Bridge
Andicouri Bay
Andicouri
Druif
Druif Bay
Paradera
Ayó
Hooiberg
541ft
Oranjestad
Paarden Bay
Santa Cruz
Dos Playa
Arikok
577ft
Boca Prins
Queen
Beatrix
Airport
Fontein
Cave
Balashi
Yamanota
617ft
De Palm
Reef Is.
Guadirikiri
Caves
Spaans
Lagoen
258ft
CARIBBEAN
SEA
Savaneta
Commanders
Bay
San
Nicolaas
Lago Refinery
Rodgers Beach
Seroe Colorado
Punta Basora
(Colorado Point)

Aruba

Potential visitors once saw Aruba as a less developed and smaller version of Curaçao. There are similarities: Both islands are dry (cacti far outnumber palms), Dutch, and autonomous (citizens of Willemstad and Oranjestad enjoy the same rights and privileges as their fellow Netherlanders in Amsterdam); both offer duty-free shopping and casinos; and both have economies that were substantially bolstered by the oil industry.

But Aruba no longer lives in Curaçao's shadow. Tremendous investments in Aruba's tourism sector during the past several years have turned this 70-square-mile bit of land into one of the Caribbean's fastest-growing destinations. Aruba boasts more than 7,100 hotel rooms, both in the thoroughly modern properties on Palm Beach, a 5-mile stretch of pure white sand that outstrips any strand Curaçao has to offer, and in the first class hotels on smaller Eagle Beach and Druif Bay (both south of Palm, near Oranjestad). Aruba has 10 casinos, with 2 more under construction and, in season, there are shows most nights in its many hotel nightclubs. In sum, Aruba now caters to vacationers (over 500,000 annually) in a big way, which is good news to some travelers and less so to those who crave privacy and quiet.

Aruba was discovered in 1499 by Alonso de Ojeda, who claimed the island for Spain. There is still some question about whether he christened it Oro Uba — Spanish for "gold was there" — or whether the name came from *ora,* the Carib word for shell, or from *oubao,* meaning well-planned island. The Spanish did not consider the island worth colonizing, and, therefore, allowed its Arawak Indian population to remain alive. Although some 2,000 Indians were rounded up and shipped off to labor as slaves in the mines of Hispaniola — where the indigenous tribes had been exterminated — Arawak features survive on the faces of many Aruba natives.

In 1636, nearing victory in their 80-year war with Spain, the Dutch turned their attention to the Caribbean. They assessed the area and took over this neglected territory with little opposition from the Spanish. With the exception of a brief period during the early 19th century when the British flag flew over these islands, the Dutch have been in peaceful residence ever since. Of the 70,000 people who live on Aruba today, 75% were born on the island; the rest are Dutch, British, North American, or Venezuelan.

For a time it looked as though Aruba's fortune lay in gold, discovered in 1825 and mined successfully near Balashi. By 1916, though, the yield shrank to the point of unprofitability. But with the opening in 1924 of Exxon's Lago Oil Refinery — then the world's largest — the island began to prosper as never before.

Exxon closed its Aruba refinery in 1985, however, and Arubans embraced tourism as a way to replace lost jobs and bolster the island's economy. Even with the reopening of the oil refinery in 1990 by the Coastal Corporation, Arubans remain interested in seeing tourism flourish.

It seems to be doing just that — not strictly because of the sleek hotels and casinos, the extraordinary beaches, and bright, warm sea, but because Arubans make their island an especially pleasant place to visit. They personally bridge the gap between their red-roofed cottages and the tall hotels; they are a friendly people, and they want visitors not only to see their island but to understand it. For this reason, taxi touring here is worth the extra investment. In the course of a half-day tour, you will very likely learn a little Papiamento (*bon dia* for good morning; *masha danki* means thank you), hear about Aruban courtship (before a man may call on a woman seriously, he must build a house), and make at least one Aruban friend — your driver.

You also will learn that Aruban smiles are genuine; they mean *bon bini* — welcome.

Aruba At-a-Glance

FROM THE AIR

Aruba, shaped like a dolphin swimming northwest to southeast toward South America, is the smallest and westernmost of the Dutch "ABC" islands that lie just off the Venezuelan coast (Bonaire and Curaçao are the others). Fifteen miles north of Venezuela and 42 miles west of Curaçao, Aruba is 19.6 miles long and 6 miles at its widest point.

The mouth of the dolphin is Rodgers Bay, near the Seroe Colorado residential area at the island's southern point; its right fin is the capital city of Oranjestad, on the west coast; and the end of its tail is a lighthouse on the island's northern tip. Queen Beatrix Airport lies a mile southeast of the capital. Jets make the flight from New York in 4 hours; from Miami, in 2½ hours.

The best way to see Aruba from the air is by helicopter (*Happy Island Helicopters;* phone: 37664) or aboard one of the small *Air Aruba* or *ALM* commuter planes that make several flights a day between Aruba, Bonaire, and Curaçao. These low-flying craft reveal the dolphin in all its diversity, with windswept divi-divi trees along the southern shore, the surf crashing along the east coast, desolate dunes on the northern tip, and all manner of sailing craft at anchor at the southern corner.

SPECIAL PLACES

ORANJESTAD Millions of guilders have been spent on a recently completed face-lift of the capital, whose quaint Dutch architecture and tempting shopping opportunities make it one of the busiest towns in the Caribbean. Caya G.F. Betico Croes, its main avenue and most fashionable shopping street, is lined on either side with banks, offices, and shops that offer good duty-free buys from all over the world. Allow at least half a day to explore the city — and travel on foot. Head for the harbor and walk along the wharf where the local fishing boats and island schooners are moored. Every morning, fresh fish and produce are sold directly from these boats. Stroll along L.G. Smith Boulevard (named for an early Lago oil refinery general manager) to Wilhelmina Park, a showcase of tropical gardening on the waterfront. Afterward, eat lunch at one of any number of interesting restaurants in the area. Or buy some Dutch cheese and fresh fruit and head north to the picnic grove at Manchebo, or a half mile farther to Eagle Beach, which has palm-thatch picnic shelters. Should you choose to tour Oranjestad in the afternoon, remember: Many shops are closed between noon and 2 PM. After shopping, relax with cocktails on the *Bali* floating restaurant, then dine at one of the city's fine restaurants (see *Eating Out*).

ELSEWHERE ON THE ISLAND

The recommended route for touring Aruba heads north out of Oranjestad along Eagle Beach and Palm Beach to the northernmost tip of the island and continues clockwise. Along the way you will see:

DE OLDE MOLEN This old windmill was brought from Holland, piece by piece, and reconstructed; it's now a restaurant (see *Eating Out*).

CALIFORNIA DUNES At the northernmost tip of the island, the California Lighthouse stands on this desolate site (it's not open to the public).

CUNUCU The interior countryside — the flat landscape here — is marked by cactus, huge boulders, aloe and divi-divi trees (the latter, permanently bent by the wind, look as though their branches are blowing away), and pastel houses enclosed by cactus fences.

HOOIBERG (MT. HAYSTACK) This, Aruba's most prominent mountain, is at the center of the island. Several hundred carved steps climb up to its peak, a 541-foot height from which Venezuela is visible on clear days. Mt. Yamanota (617 feet) and Mt. Arikok (577 feet) are less accessible.

CASA BARI AND AYO Here, to the northeast of Hooiberg, are building-size stacks of diorite boulders that look as though they've been dumped on the landscape just to puzzle geologists and impress travelers.

BUSHIRIBANA On the northeast coast are abandoned gold mines and the ruins of a pirate's castle that legend dates to 1499.

NATURAL BRIDGE Along the east coast, the pounding surf has carved a bridge out of the coral rock.

ARIKOK NATIONAL PARK Site of the island's best-preserved Indian drawings, it's near the mountain of the same name.

BOCA PRINS Another coastal attraction; it's traditional to slide down the dunes here (wear tough jeans and sneakers).

FONTEIN AND GUADIRIKI CAVES These inland caves are decorated with still-undeciphered ancient Indian drawings.

SAN NICOLAAS In the southeast, Aruba's "second city," near Seroe Colorado, is a modern community designed and built for North Americans who came to work for Exxon's Lago Oil Refinery, now the Coastal Aruba Oil Refinery. Visitors are welcome at the *Aruba Golf Club* (phone: 42006), just north of San Nicolaas.

SAVANETA Aruba's oldest town, slightly more than midway between San Nicolaas and Balashi. This is where the Dutch reestablished control of the island in 1816. There is still a Dutch marine camp at Commander's Bay.

BALASHI Here are the 19th-century ruins of a gold smelting work and its accompanying settlement. Built during Aruba's "gold rush," it is northwest of Spaans Lagoen, a bit southeast of the island's center.

Sources and Resources

TOURIST INFORMATION

The Aruba Tourism Authority's Oranjestad office (172 L.G. Smith Blvd., PO Box 1019; phone: 23777; fax: 34702) has a very helpful staff and an excellent collection of maps, guides, and brochures. For information on Aruba tourist offices in the US, see GETTING READY TO GO.

LOCAL COVERAGE *Aruba Holiday,* a green, tabloid-size monthly guide to vacation activities, shopping, restaurants, and nightlife, is distributed free at the tourist bureau, airport, and hotels. *Aruba Today* and *The News* are both free English-language newspapers distributed at the front desk of most hotels. The *Miami Herald* and *The New York Times* normally reach Aruban newsstands on the day of publication.

RADIO AND TELEVISION

Aruba has some locally produced television and radio shows in Dutch, English, Papiamento, and Spanish. US TV programs, including CNN, also are available at most hotels. Trans-World Radio broadcasts newscasts in English four times daily.

TELEPHONE

When calling from the US, dial 011 (international access code) + 297 (country code) + 8 (city code) + (local number). To call from another Caribbean island, the access code may vary, so call the local operator.

When calling from a phone on Aruba, use only the local number unless otherwise indicated.

ENTRY REQUIREMENTS

For US and Canadian citizens, the only documents required are some proof of citizenship (a passport, or a birth certificate or a voter's registration card plus a photo ID; a driver's license alone is *not* acceptable) and an ongoing or return ticket. There is a $10 departure tax at the airport.

CLIMATE AND CLOTHES

Aruba is one of the few places in the world where newspapers don't publish weather reports. Since only about 24 inches of rain fall annually, the island guarantees one of the most stable all-year climates in all of the Caribbean. Temperatures rarely fall below 75F (24C) or rise above 85F (30C), and the trade winds rarely stop blowing. The winds keep the humidity down and blow mosquitoes and other insects away from the island (though bites are not unknown). Casual, lightweight resortwear is right for daytime in all seasons. Leave your raincoat at home and use the space for extra swimsuits and scarves. Islanders do not wear shorts or slacks in town, but it's okay for visitors. Bathing suits, however, are strictly for beach or poolside. In the evenings, especially in the casinos in season, women tend to dress up a bit and men occasionally wear jackets.

MONEY

Although US dollars are accepted everywhere, the official currency is the Netherlands Antilles florin or guilder (NAf); $1 US equals approximately 1.77 NAf. There's really no advantage to changing your dollars, but banks are open from 8 AM to 4 PM on weekdays. Shops give no discount for payment in US dollars and, like most restaurants and hotels, honor major credit cards. All prices in this chapter are quoted in US dollars.

LANGUAGE

There probably isn't a more linguistically versatile island in the Caribbean. Arubans speak Dutch (the official language), Spanish, English, Portuguese, and — as if that weren't enough — Papiamento, the local language that's a mixture of all the above and a few words left over from the days of the Arawak. But you'll have no trouble getting along in English.

TIME

Aruba is on atlantic standard time all year round. When it's noon in New York it's 1 PM in Aruba; when the eastern US is on daylight saving time, the hour is the same in both places.

CURRENT

At 110 volts, 60 cycles, converters and adapters are not necessary.

TIPPING

Hotels add an 11% service charge on rooms and a 10% to 15% service charge on food and beverages. Some restaurants add 10% to 15% to cover service; if not, that's the right amount to tip. Airport porters get at least 50¢ for each bag carried. There is no need to tip taxi drivers except for special services, such as carrying an unusually heavy load.

GETTING AROUND

BUS The yellow public buses run every 20 to 30 minutes daily (except on Sundays and holidays) between town and the hotels on Eagle Beach and Palm Beach. One-way fare is 90¢, round trip is $1.50. The bus leaves from the parking lot on Zoutmanstraat (just behind the mustard-colored government building across from the *Harbourtown Mall*). There's also a free shopping tour bus (you'll know it by its wild colors). It departs every hour starting from the *Holiday Inn* at 9:15 AM and stops at all the major hotels on its way toward town. The last bus is at 3:15 PM. The bus runs only one way; you'll have to get back on your own.

CAR RENTAL Plenty of cars are available, and renting one is the most pleasant and flexible way to see the island, shop, and dine out. Roads are good and clearly marked, and US or Canadian driver's licenses are valid. Rates range from about $30 to $65 a day, depending on the type of car. Hotels can make the arrangements for guests who haven't reserved a car ahead of time. Rental companies in Oranjestad include *Avis* (phone: 28787), *Budget* (phone: 28600), *Hertz* (phone: 24545), *National* (phone: 21967 or 24641), *Dollar* (phone: 22783 or 25651), and a number of local agencies, including *Hedwina's* (phone: 26442 or 37393) and *Marco's* (phone: 25295).

MOTORCYCLES AND MOPEDS Rates vary according to the vehicle. Scooters run from $15 to $30 per day, less for rentals of several days or longer. Motorcycles cost from $35 to $55 per day. Contact *Nelson Motorcycle Rental* (phone: 26801), *George's Cycle & Jeeps* (phone: 25975 or 31235), *Ron's Motorcycle Rental* (phone: 62090), *Semver Cycle Rental* (phone: 66851), or *Pardo Cycle Rental* (phone: 24573).

SEA EXCURSIONS The *Atlantis Submarine* (phone: 36090) takes up to 46 passengers 50 to 90 feet below the sea to Barcadera Reef. The 50-minute plunge in the modern, air conditioned sub costs $68 for adults, $34 for children. Some hotels have discount coupons. *DePalm* (phone: 24400 or 24545) offers a glass-bottom boat cruise with views of coral reefs, tropical fish, and shipwrecks for $15 per person, and a 3-hour sailing and snorkeling cruise on the trimaran *Seaventure* for $23 per person, which includes an open bar, snacks, and snorkeling equipment. The operator also offers sunset and moonlight cruises. *Pelican* (phone: 31228) is the other major tour operator offering day and evening cruises. *Red Sail Sports* (phone: 31603) offers snorkeling and buffet lunch cruises ($50 per person) aboard a 53-foot state-of-the-art catamaran, as well as cocktail, sunset, and moonlight sails (each $27.50 per person).

SIGHTSEEING TOURS Aruba cab drivers are genial and informative and can serve as superb guides. Hotels can recommend a good driver and make arrangements. A 1-hour taxi tour is about $30 for up to four passengers. *DePalm* (phone: 24400 or 24545), Aruba's largest operator, offers both island excursions and sailing tours. *Pelican* (phone: 23888) has excellent tours. Julio Maduro of *Corvalou Tours* runs fascinating 5-hour archaeological, historical, bird watching, and botanical treks into Aruba's back country for $40 per person, $70 per couple (phone: 21149). Eppie Boerstra of *Marlin Booster Tracking* (phone: 41513) offers wildlife and archaeology tours in five different languages. *Friendly Tours* (phone: 23230) offers daily morning and afternoon island bus tours that include a trip to the Tunnel of Love caves for $20 per person. *Watapana Tours* (phone: 35191) runs a 4-hour daytime tour that includes a swim and snorkel at Baby Beach for $29 per person, and an evening tour of Aruba's hottest clubs for $30 per person (including drinks).

TAXI Taxis aren't metered, so agree on the rate with the driver before getting in. The fare from the airport to most resort hotels is $12 to $14 for up to four people. Unless your hotel includes ground transfers in your room rate, you will need to take a taxi to your hotel, or rent a car.

INTER-ISLAND FLIGHTS

Air Aruba, the island's official airline, and *ALM* provide connecting service between Aruba, Bonaire, and Curaçao. *General Travel Bureau* (phone: 26609 or 34717), *Pelican* (phone: 31228), and *DePalm* (phone: 24400 or 24545) offer air excursions to both Curaçao and Caracas, Venezuela.

SPECIAL EVENTS

Carnival celebrations are the year's biggest events. Festivities usually begin in the middle of January with the *Tumba Contest* for musicians. For the next few weeks there are children's parades and other festivities; the climax is the *Grand Parade* (held on February 13 this year) and *Jump-up,* an outdoor party with lots of music and dancing (check the exact date of the latter with the tourist office). Banks and stores are closed on the following holidays (although when cruise ships are in port, some stores open for a few hours): *New Year's, Carnival Monday* (the day after the *Grand Parade*), *National Flag and Anthem Day* (March 18), *Good Friday, Easter, Easter Monday,* the *Queen's Birthday* (April 30), *Labor Day* (May 1), *Ascension Day, St. John's Day* (June 24), *San Nicolaas Day* (December 5), *Christmas,* and *Boxing Day* (December 26). The annual *Aruba Jazz and Latin Music Festival* is held in June at *Mansur Stadium.* Special annual sporting events include the *Aruba Hi-Winds Pro-Am Windsurfing Tournament* (first week of June), *Aruba Annual Mini-Marathon* (third week of

June), and the *Pan American Race of Champs, International Drag Racing* (second week of November).

SHOPPING

Technically, Aruba is not a free port, but the duty on most items is so low (3.3%) that Caya G.F. Betico Croes, Oranjestad's shopping hub, is a center for bargains from all over the world. But not all the prices are rock-bottom, so be sure to check stateside prices before you leave home. With that in mind, shop for: Royal Copenhagen porcelain; Delft Blue pottery; Dutch, Swedish, and Danish silver and pewter; Swiss watches; liquor and liqueurs; Madeira embroidery; Italian woodcarvings; French perfume; British woolens; Indonesian spices; Hummel figurines; and much, much more. *Seaport Village* in Oranjestad is a complex with over 85 stores, boutiques, and eateries. For last-minute, no-hassle shopping, most hotels house branches of one or two downtown stores with smaller selections, same prices. Most downtown stores are open Mondays through Saturdays, 8 AM to 6 PM, although some close for lunch between noon and 2 PM.

Here are some well-known emporia worthy of a shopper's attention. Stores are in Oranjestad unless otherwise noted.

ARTISTIC BOUTIQUE An interesting assortment of Indonesian imports, including ivory pieces and unusual earrings. 25 Caya G.F. Betico Croes (phone: 23142).

ARUBA TRADING COMPANY The best place in town for perfume. It also sells cosmetics, jewelry, and both men's and women's clothes. 12 Caya G.F. Betico Croes (phone: 22600 or 32125).

DEWIT'S Gift items, toys, and books. 94 Caya G.F. Betico Croes (phone: 21273).

D'ORSY'S There are several branches of this well-stocked perfume and cosmetics purveyor on the island. *Seaport Village Mall* (phone: 33709), 4 Havenstraat (phone: 31233), and 1 Emmastraat (phone: 37818). One branch is called *Perfume Palace,* 47 L.G. Smith Blvd. (phone: 34769).

LITTLE SWITZERLAND An islands-wide favorite, it offers an array of jewelry, crystal, watches, and gift items. 14 Caya G.F. Betico Croes (phone: 21192).

PALAIS ORIENTAL A wide selection of crystal. 72 Caya G.F. Betico Croes (phone: 21422).

SPRITZER & FUHRMANN A superb selection of fine jewelry and gifts. Two locations: 34A Caya G.F. Betico Croes (phone: 24360); and *Holiday Inn,* 230 L.G. Smith Blvd., Palm Beach (phone: 24461).

SPORTS

BOATING Most hotels have Sunfish for loan or rent (about $21 an hour); larger craft can be chartered from boat owners (ask at your hotel or the tourist board). *Aruba Nautical Club* marina in Balashi, at the mouth of Spanish Lagoon between Oranjestad and San Nicolaas, offers reef-protected, all-weather mooring for yachts. Members of other yacht clubs are welcome for a modest fee, charged according to size of craft; for information write to the club (Box 161, Oranjestad; phone: 23022). Farther down the shore, docking facilities also are available for $20 per day at *Bucuti Yacht Club* (31 Bucutiweg, Oranjestad; phone: 23793).

Pedalboats and sea jeeps also are popular at Aruba resorts. The *pedalos* rent for $7 per half hour, $10 per hour. Jet skis and Waverunners are fun to buzz around in; they cost about $45 per half hour for the two-seater, $35 for the single-seater. Check at your hotel's water sports facility.

CYCLING Mountain bikes can be rented at *Pablitos Bike Rental* (*La Quinta Beach;* phone: 35010) for $3 an hour, $8 a half day, and $12 a day.

DUNE SLIDING A sport unique to Aruba at Boca Prins on the north coast; wear sneakers and your strongest pair of jeans.

FITNESS *Body Friction* (136A L.G. Smith Blvd.; phone: 24642) is a complete fitness center; guests may use the facility for $7 a day. It's open Mondays through Fridays from 9 AM to 9 PM and Saturdays from 8 AM to 2 PM. The *Hyatt Regency, La Cabaña, Sonesta,* and the *Holiday Inn Aruba* allow non-guests to buy day passes to their health spas.

GOLF The *Aruba Golf Club* near San Nicolaas, on the eastern end of the island (phone: 42006), bills itself as an 18-hole course but, in fact, there are 11 Astroturf holes played different ways. The par 72 course is not plush, but it has 25 sand traps, goats, and lots of cacti. Greens fees are $7.50 for 9 holes, $10 for 18 holes. There are no caddies, but golf carts are available for $6 for 9 holes, $12 for 18 holes; club rentals are available. Golfers should also check the status of the Robert Trent Jones, Jr. 18-hole golf course in Arashi (phone: 24693), which began construction last year.

HORSEBACK RIDING Horses are available for $15 an hour at *Rancho El Paso* (phone: 23310) and *Rancho Campo* (phone: 20290).

LANDSAILING Combine a go-cart with a windsurfboard and the result is a fast-moving sailcart that just about flies over *Aruba Sailcart*'s (phone: 35133) huge dirt field. Helmets, gloves, and instruction — all you need to enjoy this fun and thrilling new sport — are provided. Wear clothes that are easy to wash — or that you don't care about very much. Single-seat carts cost $15 per half hour; two-seaters cost $20.

SNORKELING AND SCUBA The clear, warm, Aruban waters offer visibility up to 100 feet, and there is a good variety of coral, lacy sea fans, sponges, and multicolored tropical fish for divers to see and photograph. A favorite dive is the 400-foot sunken German freighter *Antilla,* which was scuttled off the northwestern tip of the island during World War II; another popular dive site is the wreck of the *Pedenales,* an oil tanker lying in only 25 feet of water. Arrangements for equipment rental, diving trips, and instruction can be made through your hotel. *Red Sail Sports* (phone: 31603), *DePalm* (phone: 24400 or 24545), and *Pelican* (phone: 31228) operate hotel concessions. Prices run about $60 for a beginner's course; guided trips for the experienced diver with a "C card" are about $30 for a one-tank dive, $48 for a two-tank dive. Snorkel trips run about $20 (includes equipment). For snorkeling on your own, equipment can be rented for $10 a day. Some tour operators add a 10% service charge. For those desiring an underwater experience that doesn't include getting wet, there's the *Atlantis Submarine* (see *Sea Excursions*).

SPORT FISHING Aruba's waters are best for sailfish, wahoo, blue and white marlin, tuna, and bonito. Fishing charters can be arranged through your hotel, at the pier next to the *Bali* restaurant, or through *DePalm* (phone: 24400 or 24545), *Pelican* (phone: 31228), *Red Sail Sports* (phone: 31603), or *Pinxter Real Estate* (phone: 33350). The cost of a half-day's fishing on a boat that takes up to six passengers (four can fish at the same time) runs from $220 to $300, including bait, tackle, soft drinks, and beer. The annual international *White Marlin Tournament,* held at the end of October, lures anglers from the US and South America.

SWIMMING AND SUNNING Gleaming white beaches stretch along the island's western and southwestern shores, which are known as the Turquoise Coast. The best are two strands above Oranjestad: Palm Beach, with a gentle slope that makes it especially good for kids and less adventurous swimmers; and Eagle Beach, closer to town, with thatch-roofed shelters for picnicking.

TENNIS A different game here because of the relentless trade winds, but it's popular, and there are courts at most of the principal hotels on the beach strip: the *Radisson Aruba Caribbean, Americana Aruba, Aruba Beach Club, Aruba Concorde, Aruba Palm Beach, Divi Aruba Beach, Tamarijn Aruba Beach, Holiday Inn,* and *Hyatt Regency;* the *Hyatt Regency* and *Holiday Inn* seem to have the best wind shields. Several hotels have tennis pros, and a number of the courts are lighted for night play. Tennis is free to hotel guests during the day; some hotels charge about $2 per hour for night lighting. Games can be arranged by non-guests when courts are not in use.

WATER SKIING Available at most oceanfront hotels. The charge is about $30 for two or three laps; lessons are available.

WINDSURFING *Red Sail Sports* (phone: 31603) offers equipment and instruction for both beginners and advanced windsurfers. Two-hour beginner lessons cost $44, advanced lessons run $33 an hour. "Fanatic" boards (with a special, high-tech design) are available for rent at $33 for 2 hours, $55 per day. *Pelican* (phone: 31228) rents boards for $30 a day; lessons cost $40.

NIGHTLIFE

Aruba's lively nightlife is centered around its 10 casinos. The plushest and most popular are the *Royal Cabaña Casino* at *La Cabaña All-Suite Beach Resort* (with the largest gaming facility in the Caribbean); the *Hyatt Regency Aruba Casino*, with live entertainment nightly; and the *Crystal Casino* at the *Sonesta.* Those who feel lucky may also try their hands at blackjack, craps, roulette, or the slot machines at the casinos of the *Radisson Aruba Caribbean, Americana Aruba, Aruba Palm Beach, Aruba Concorde, Harbourtown,* and *Holiday Inn; Aruba Palm Beach* also has a special room set aside for baccarat. The *Alhambra Casino* is part of an entertainment complex that also includes the *Aladdin Theater,* 14 shops, several restaurants, and a nightclub. It's near the *Divi Aruba Beach* and *Manchebo Beach* hotels. Low betting limits and the absence of high rollers and junket players give Aruba's casinos a pleasantly relaxed atmosphere. Casinos open for action after lunch and keep going until the small hours. *Note:* No one under 18 is admitted.

Non-gamblers can dance, drink, and watch a show in any of the hotel cocktail lounges or supper clubs. The *Americana*'s *Jardin Brésilien* lounge features live bands, while its *Las Palmas* nightclub stages cabaret shows. The *Aruba Palm Beach*'s *Player's Lounge* is a lively venue for drinks, dancing, and occasional entertainment. Cabaret shows and comedy are featured at the *Tropicana* nightclub at the *Royal Cabaña Casino.* The *Holiday Inn* has its *Palm Beach Room* and *L'Esprit* nightclub for dining, dancing, and a show (best on folkloric Sundays). Hotel supper clubs require reservations, as they sometimes close for guests-only parties. *Tamarijn Aruba Beach*'s outdoor bar spotlights local music. Most hotels have theme nights, featuring lavish buffets and entertainment, as regular weekly events; they range from "Pirate Night" on Mondays at the *Divi Aruba Beach* to "Fajitas & Ritas Night" on Fridays at the *Hyatt Regency Aruba.* There are also a number of popular dance clubs, although they don't get hopping until after 11 PM. The best ones are *Papas & Beer* (84 Palm Beach Rd.; phone: 60300), where bands perform; *La Visage* (152A L.G. Smith Blvd.; phone: 33418), which caters to a younger crowd; and *Desires* in the *Sonesta* hotel, where the beat is a combination of Latin and top 40. Every Tuesday evening from 6:30 to 8:30 PM, the *Bon Bini* festival is held in the outdoor courtyard of the *Fort Zoutman Museum,* located 1 block north of the *Harbourtown Mall. Bon bini* is Papiamento for "welcome," and this event was designed to introduce visitors to all things Aruban, from folk dancing to crafts to music to food, for only $1. For more information, call the tourist office (phone: 23777).

Best on the Island

CHECKING IN

In winter, expect to pay $250 or more per day without meals for a double room in a hotel listed below as very expensive, $160 and up in those places listed as expensive, from $120 to $160 in moderate places, and from $90 to $120 in inexpensive hotels. There's a 5% hotel tax, and most hotels add an 11% service charge. When calling from a phone on Aruba, use only the local numbers listed below; for information about calling from elsewhere, see "Telephone" earlier in this chapter.

PALM BEACH

VERY EXPENSIVE

Hyatt Regency Aruba This $57-million property, Aruba's top deluxe resort, has 360 rooms located on 12 beachfront acres on Palm Beach. It boasts a multilevel water display with cascading waterfalls, a slide, gardens, and a lagoon filled with tropical fish. The resort offers all water sports, with instruction available. There are also 4 restaurants, a modern health and fitness facility, and a casino with live entertainment. Rooms are decked out in Southwestern decor and boast all the creature comforts. 85 L.G. Smith Blvd. (phone: 31234; 800-233-1234 from the US; fax: 21682).

EXPENSIVE

Americana Aruba Here is a lively, rejuvenated place with handsome public areas, 419 moderate-size guestrooms, 2 tennis courts, a swimming pool, a spacious beach, water sports, a beauty salon, and a shopping arcade. There are also 3 restaurants and a theater-style nightclub and casino. 83 L.G. Smith Blvd. (phone: 24500; 800-223-2848 from the US; fax: 23191).

Aruba Concorde At press time, Hilton had assumed management of this hotel (the island's tallest), and $16.5 million was being poured into renovations. Plans include refurbishing the 475 rooms in a tropical motif; the pool, casino, and lobby were also slated for major upgrading. 77 L.G. Smith Blvd. (phone: 24466; 800-428-9933 from the US; fax: 33403).

Aruba Holiday Inn A long-overdue renovation is in the works for this 7-story property, which is popular with budget travelers and groups. There are 600 rooms (ask for a refurbished room or one in the newer north wing) and 4 restaurants. The casino and nightclub provide popular evening entertainment, while the beach — with its gamut of water sports — is the main daytime attraction. The hotel also has a shopping arcade and complete spa/health club. 230 L.G. Smith Blvd. (phone: 23600; 800-HOLIDAY from the US; fax: 25165).

Aruba Palm Beach This striking high-rise with 200 king-size rooms, all with private balconies, features Moorish lines, a lovely pink color scheme, and beautiful gardens. It boasts a 1,200-foot beach, tennis, a freshwater pool, water sports, 2 restaurants, and the stylish *Dutch Master Room* supper club and casino. 79 L.G. Smith Blvd. (phone: 23900; 800-345-2782 from the US; fax: 21941).

Mill Resort Located adjacent to *De Olde Molen* (The Old Mill) restaurant, a well-known Palm Beach landmark, is a complex of 99 apartment-style suites. Junior 1- and 2-bedroom luxury suites are available. There is a restaurant offering international fare for lunch and dinner, and breakfast is served poolside. The resort has tennis and racquetball courts, a health club, a playground, a gym, aerobics and jazz center, and a mini-market. 330 L.G. Smith Blvd. (phone: 37700; fax: 37271).

Playa Linda A stylish timeshare resort with a club-like atmosphere and full hotel services, it has 191 studio, 1-, and 2-bedroom apartments. Low-rise with a peaceful atmosphere (no charter groups, no casino), it's within strolling distance of brighter lights. There's a small market, a restaurant, a drugstore, a beach, and water sports; tennis can be arranged. 87 L.G. Smith Blvd. (phone: 31000; 201-617-8877 from New Jersey; 800-346-7084 from elsewhere in the US; fax: 25210).

Radisson Aruba Caribbean At press time, Radisson had just taken over the management of this 400-room, 23-suite property, and much-needed renovations were being planned. Aruba's first high-rise resort, it is set in exotic tropical gardens and features 4 restaurants, a lounge where afternoon tea is served, the *Fandango* nightclub, a casino, a health and fitness center, 4 lighted tennis courts, and a complete water sports center. 81 L.G. Smith Blvd. (phone: 33555; 800-777-1700 from the US; fax: 23260).

EAGLE BEACH

EXPENSIVE

La Cabaña All-Suite Beach A recent addition to the Aruba hotel scene, this 440-suite beachside resort is built in a horseshoe around a huge free-form pool facing the beach. All guestrooms have full kitchens, Jacuzzis, and soothing tropical decor. There's an elaborate gambling complex with a 14,000-square-foot casino (the largest in the Caribbean); also a complete fitness center, 5 restaurants, and water sports facilities. This is a good family place, with a supervised children's program and a video arcade to occupy teens. Palm Beach (phone: 39000; 212-251-1710 from New York; 800-835-7193 from elsewhere in the US; fax: 35474).

Costa Linda This new 5-story oceanfront resort has 155 two- and three-bedroom suites. Features include 4 whirlpools, 2 pools (1 for kids), tennis courts, a fitness center, a restaurant, a nightclub, a shopping arcade, and water sports. Eagle Beach (phone: 24693; 201-617-8877 from New Jersey; 800-346-7084 from elsewhere in the US; fax: 36040).

MANCHEBO AND DRUIF BAY BEACHES

VERY EXPENSIVE

Divi Aruba Beach Formerly known as the *Divi-Divi Beach* resort, this pleasantly rambling low-rise with Spanish architectural accents has lanais and casitas with patios right on the wide, white beach. The 6 superlative suites and 202 air conditioned rooms all have balconies or patios. Features include 2 freshwater pools, tennis courts, an outdoor bar, and informal, relaxed dining. Try *The Red Parrot* for excellent French fare. The *Alhambra Casino,* Aruba's most unusual (and only freestanding) casino with a number of boutiques, is just up the street. 93 L.G. Smith Blvd. (phone: 23300; 800-22-DORAL from the US; fax: 34002).

Dutch Village This sleek townhouse offers all the comforts, inside and out, including satellite TV and Jacuzzis in every one of its 97 studio and 1- and 2-bedroom apartments, plus a swimming pool, tennis, shops, a restaurant, and a bar. Guests have exchange privileges with the *Divi Aruba Beach* and *Tamarijn Aruba Beach* hotels. 64 L.G. Smith Blvd. (phone: 24150; 800-367-3484 from the US; fax: 34002).

EXPENSIVE

Best Western Manchebo Beach Considered by many to be the best and least crowded on the coast, this friendly, informal resort has a wide beach and 71 modern, air conditioned rooms. Guests have exchange privileges at the *Talk of the Town.* The *French Steak House* is its first-rate restaurant (see *Eating Out*); there's outdoor dancing at night. 55 L.G. Smith Blvd. (phone: 23444; 800-223-1108 or 800-528-1234 from the US; fax: 32446).

Tamarijn Aruba Beach Formerly the *Divi Tamarijn Beach,* all of this property's 236 rooms, including those in the 70-room addition, are within only a few barefoot steps of its 2,000-foot beach; there's an appealing Andalusian decor (red tile roofs, white walls) inside and out. Other pluses: a pool, 2 Jacuzzis, the intimate *Bunker Bar* directly on the ocean, and nightly music by local groups. There is an exchange arrangement with the *Divi Aruba Beach* hotel just up the shore. L.G. Smith Blvd. (phone: 24150; 800-22-DORAL from the US; fax: 34002).

MODERATE

Bushiri Bounty This beachfront property has 150 rooms and a staff that's eager to please (it's part of the Aruba Hospitality Trades Training Center). A refurbishing of the guestrooms was completed recently. Rates include use of the pool, complete water sports facilities, tennis, all meals at either of the hotel's 2 restaurants, and nightly entertainment. 35 L.G. Smith Blvd.

(phone: 25216; 800-GO-BOUNTY from the US; 800-438-2686 from Canada or Puerto Rico; fax: 26789).

La Quinta Beach This quiet, relaxed low-rise has 45 one- or two-bedroom suites, each with a TV set and VCR, a living and dining room, and a kitchenette with a microwave oven. A pool, restaurant, mini-market, and water sports facilities also are on the grounds. Eagle Beach (phone: 35010; 800-223-9815 from the US; fax: 26263).

ELSEWHERE ON THE ISLAND

EXPENSIVE

Sonesta Beach Club and Casino Located in the heart of Oranjestad, this place has 300 air conditioned rooms and a canal flowing through its lobby. Boats whisk guests to the resort's 40-acre private island out in the bay, where they have full use of the beach club. There are also 3 restaurants — the *Sea Breeze,* on the island; the *Desires* lounge; and the *Crystal Casino,* which is attached to the *Seaport Village* shopping complex — and a spa and fitness center. The choice for those who want to be in town, yet enjoy the beach. There's also a wonderful and free supervised children's program. 82 L.G. Smith Blvd. (phone: 36000; 800-SONESTA from the US; fax: 21627).

INEXPENSIVE

Best Western Talk of the Town Best known for its excellent restaurant (see *Eating Out*), this property is popular with budget travelers. There are 62 nicely done rooms overlooking the Caribbean and surrounding an attractive pool patio. The atmosphere is homey, not luxurious. Some of the rooms have kitchenettes; the 1- and 2-bedroom suites feature kitchenettes and TV sets. Not on the beach, but with a pool and an outdoor whirlpool; there's also a bar, a snack bar, and Caribbean entertainment most nights. Guests have full exchange privileges at *Manchebo Beach.* A 6-minute drive from town, it's a bit out of the way. 2 L.G. Smith Blvd., Oranjestad (phone: 23380; 800-223-1108 or 800-528-1234 from the US; fax: 32446).

EATING OUT

Perhaps because it grows so little of its own food, Aruba is notably short on native dishes. Its tastiest native recipes are *stob* (a lamb or goat stew) and *sopito de pisca* (a fish chowder with onions, tomatoes, garlic, peppers, and a bouquet of spices). If you like fish, try it — preferably with *funchi,* a sort of cornmeal pudding. Favorite Aruban snacks include *cala* (bean fritters), *pastechi* (a meat-stuffed turnover), and *ayacas* (a leaf-wrapped meat roll served mostly at *Christmas*). The most exotic eating around is Indonesian (from other onetime Dutch islands), and its most spectacular form is the *rijsttafel* (rice table), which may be loaded with 25 or more different herbed and spiced shrimp, meat, vegetables, pickles, and fruit dishes — some very hot — to be piled around and eaten with a mountain of rice. A number of Aruban restaurants do a scaled-down version; they also offer other Indonesian specialties like *nasi goreng* (a one-plate *rijsttafel* of meat, shrimp, chicken, and vegetables crowned with a fried egg), *bami goreng* (the same, with a base of Chinese noodles instead of rice), and *Java honde portie* (literally "a hound's portion" of rice, beef, vegetables, and fried eggs, all seasoned with curry). Also of Dutch island origin: *keshi yena* (Edam cheese stuffed with a savory mixture of shrimp or meat or chicken with tomatoes, onions, olives, pickles, and raisins) and *capucijners* (mixed beans, meat, marrow, bacon, onions, and pickles). Portions tend to be enormous — or larger.

Most of the big hotels have a terrace restaurant that's casual at lunch and fancier (both dress and menu) at night, plus a more expensive specialty restaurant and/or supper club. In town there are a number of good Aruban and Oriental places. You'll also find Argentinean, Mexican, German, Italian, French — even New York deli–style fare if you look. Major credit cards are generally accepted. In the listings that follow, dinner — without wine, drinks, or 10% to 15% service charge — at a restaurant described as expensive runs $60 or more for two; $30 to $60 at places described as moderate; and less than $30 at spots in the inexpensive category. When calling from a phone on Aruba, use only the local numbers listed below. For information about dialing from elsewhere, see "Telephone" earlier in this chapter.

PALM BEACH

EXPENSIVE

La Vie en Rose First-rate French food served in an elegant setting. Open daily for dinner only. Reservations advised. Major credit cards accepted. Located in the *Paradise Beach Village* complex on L.G. Smith Blvd., Eagle Beach (phone: 35955).

MODERATE

Bon Appetit This lovely place has wood beams, white tablecloths, and a gracious owner/host, Max Croes, who enjoys personally serving his flaming Max dessert (vanilla ice cream mixed with caramel, topped with milk chocolate, nuts, and whipped cream and then flambéed with Grand Marnier). House specialties are enormous prime ribs, roast rack of lamb for two, West Indian prawn curry, and shrimp scampi à la Chivas. Open for dinner only; closed Sundays. Reservations advised. Major credit cards accepted. 29 Palm Beach (phone: 65241).

Buccaneer Very popular, it specializes in fish and seafood served in an attractive atmosphere accented by dramatic aquariums. Open for dinner only; closed Sundays. There may be a line, but they won't take reservations. Major credit cards accepted. Gasparito St. (phone: 26172).

Chalet Suisse International fare served in a pleasant Swiss chalet–style building (what else?), overlooking the beach. Open for dinner only; closed Sundays. Reservations advised. Major credit cards accepted. 246 L.G. Smith Blvd. (phone: 35054).

Old Cunucu House International and local dishes are served in a restored country house with live entertainment Friday and Saturday nights. Open daily for dinner. Reservations advised. Major credit cards accepted. 150 Palm Beach, just inland from the resorts (phone: 61666).

De Olde Molen This really is an old windmill, built in Holland in 1804, knocked down, shipped, and reassembled in Aruba in 1960. It's tourist-oriented but nonetheless loaded with cozy atmosphere. The continental menu (steaks, lobster, veal cordon bleu) is not surprising, but it's good. Open for dinner only; closed Sundays. Reservations advised. Major credit cards accepted. Off Palm Beach Dr. (phone: 22060).

Papiamento Delicately lit ficus and palm trees grace the garden patio of this family-run restaurant, located in a 130-year-old home. The menu features creative continental and Caribbean favorites flavored with garden-fresh herbs. Lovers should request the "Honeymoon" room, a cozy alcove for dinner tête-à-tête. Try the Dover sole meunière; the Caribbean lobster, shrimp, and snapper cooked on a hot marble stone and served tableside; or the chateaubriand for two. Open daily for dinner. Reservations advised. Major credit cards accepted. 61 Washington Noord (phone: 64544).

INEXPENSIVE

La Paloma Northern Italian specialties are served here; try the veal cacciatore or the chicken topped with eggplant and mozzarella cheese. There's pasta and fresh seafood too. Open for dinner only; closed Tuesdays. Reservations advised. Major credit cards accepted. 39 Noord, a 5-minute drive from Palm Beach (phone: 62770).

ORANJESTAD

EXPENSIVE

Chez Mathilde Enjoy fine French fare in a 19th-century Aruban house. Small, romantic, and tastefully decorated dining rooms complement the fine food. Jackets suggested for men. Open daily; no lunch on Sundays. Reservations advised. Major credit cards accepted. 23 Havenstraat (phone: 34968).

MODERATE

Dynasty This eatery serves Japanese and Thai food at both cooking tables and conventional seating areas. Open daily for lunch and dinner. Reservations advised. Major credit cards accepted. At the *Harbourtown Hotel,* L.G. Smith Blvd. (phone: 36288).

Le Petit Café A local favorite, it specializes in steaks cooked on hot stones right at your table. Open daily for lunch and dinner. Reservations unnecessary. Major credit cards accepted. 7 Schelpstraat (phone: 26577).

Talk of the Town At dinner, this hotel dining room presents a bill of fare that includes escargots *la bourguignonne,* crabmeat crêpes, veal cordon bleu, broiled lobster, and excellent Caribbean frogs' legs, all served by candlelight. Open for lunch and dinner; closed Mondays. Reservations advised. Major credit cards accepted. At the *Talk of the Town Hotel,* 2 L.G. Smith Blvd. (phone: 23380).

Waterfront Fresh seafood is the specialty here; try the crab or the Maine lobster, and don't miss some of the best fresh-baked cornmeal bread on Aruba. Open daily for lunch and dinner. Reservations advised. Major credit cards accepted. *Harbourtown Mall,* L.G. Smith Blvd. (phone: 35858).

INEXPENSIVE

Bali Sea Palace Floating Restaurant This Oriental houseboat features an exotic atmosphere and tasty fare, including a 20-dish *rijsttafel.* Lunches, drinks, and snacks also are served at tables on the pier. The food's good; the atmosphere's touristy but fun. Open daily for lunch and dinner. Reservations advised. Major credit cards accepted. Off L.G. Smith Blvd. (phone: 22131).

Boonoonoonoos This spot specializes in Caribbean fare, with such indigenous dishes as sea terrine, curried goat, Jamaican jerk pork, and roast chicken Barbados (topped with plaintains and coconut). Traditional continental items are offered as well. Open daily; no lunch on weekends; no dinner on Sundays. Reservations advised for dinner. Major credit cards accepted. 18-A Wilhelminastraat (phone: 31888).

Coco Plum Hearty Aruban dishes such as *keshi yena,* fish soup, or red snapper *crioyo* (prepared in a creole-style sauce) are served at this pleasant, casual alfresco eatery. Open for breakfast, lunch, and dinner; closed Sundays. No reservations. Major credit cards accepted. 100 Caya G.F. Betico Croes (phone: 31176).

Mama's & Papa's Aruban specialties — *bakijow stoba seroe patrishi* (stewed cod), *kreeft di cay reef* (broiled lobster), and *keshi yena* (stuffed cheese) — are served indoors or alfresco at this truly native-style eatery. Open for dinner only; closed Sundays. Reservations unnecessary. Major credit cards accepted. *Dakota Shopping Center* (phone: 26537).

ELSEWHERE ON THE ISLAND

MODERATE

French Steak House Straightforwardly French, with an emphasis on quality rather than show-off cuisine, this place serves excellent escargots, filet mignon, and chateaubriand. The dining room is candlelit, but no jackets or ties are required. Open for dinner; closed Wednesdays. Reservations advised. Major credit cards accepted. *Manchebo Beach* hotel (phone: 23444).

Nueva Marina Pirata Surveying the water from a private pier where fresh fish is landed daily, this open-air café specializes in seafood Aruba-style — in a creole tomato sauce spiked with peppers, onions, herbs, and spices. Good down-home *funchi* (cornmeal pudding) accompanies each meal. Affable service; good prices. Open for dinner only; closed Tuesdays. Reservations advised. Major credit cards accepted. Spanish Lagoon (phone: 27372).

INEXPENSIVE

Brisas del Mar Arubans recommend this very casual, friendly place for its fresh fish, seafood, and island dishes; fried plantains and *pan bati* (corn-millet pancake) go well with whatever is ordered. Open for lunch and dinner; no lunch on Mondays. Reservations necessary. Major credit cards accepted. In Savaneta, by the sea just west of San Nicolaas (phone: 47718).

Mi Cushina This place offers local food served in a homey atmosphere and prepared by Arubans. Open for lunch and dinner; closed Thursdays. Reservations advised in season. Major credit cards accepted. 24 Noord Cura Cabai, near San Nicolaas (phone: 48335).

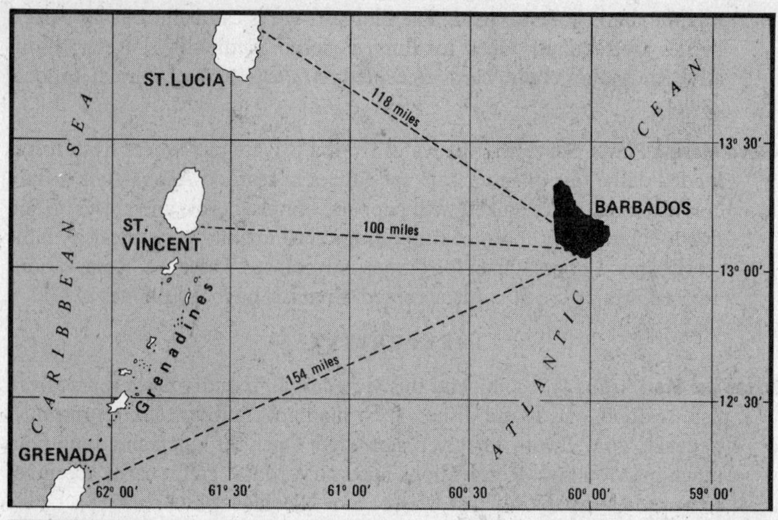

ST.LUCIA
CARIBBEAN SEA
ST. VINCENT
Grenadines
GRENADA
118 miles
100 miles
154 miles
BARBADOS
ATLANTIC OCEAN
13° 30′
13° 00′
12° 30′
62° 00′
61° 30′
61° 00′
60° 30
60° 00′
59° 00′

BARBADOS
Miles
0
5
ATLANTIC
OCEAN
Archer's Bay
ST. LUCY
Spring Hall
Fairfield
Gay's Cove
Maycock's Bay
St. Nicholas Abbey
Cherry Tree Hill
Colleton
Morgan Lewis Mill
ST. PETER
Farley Hill
ST. ANDREW
Greenland
Speightstown
Chalky Mt. 549ft
Turner's Hall
Bruce
Platinum Coast
Mt. Hillaby 1115ft
ST. JAMES
ST. JOSEPH
Bathsheba
Tent Bay
ST. THOMAS
Bath
Conset Bay
Holetown
Welchman Hall Gully
Blackmans
Harrison's Cave
Villa Nova
St. John's Church
Codrington College
Paynes Bay
ST. JOHN
Three Houses
Gun Hill
Drax Hall
Kendal
ST. MICHAEL
ST. GEORGE
ST. PHILIP
Marchfield
Windsor
Sam Lord's Castle
The Crane
Crane Beach
Deep Water Hbr
Bridgetown
Foul Bay
Carlisle Bay
Museum
CHRIST CHURCH
Needham's Point
Hastings
St. Lawrence
Christ Church
Paradise Beach
Grantley Adams International Airport
Worthing
Rockley Beach
Oistins
Oistins Bay
Scarboro
Long Bay
Silver Sands

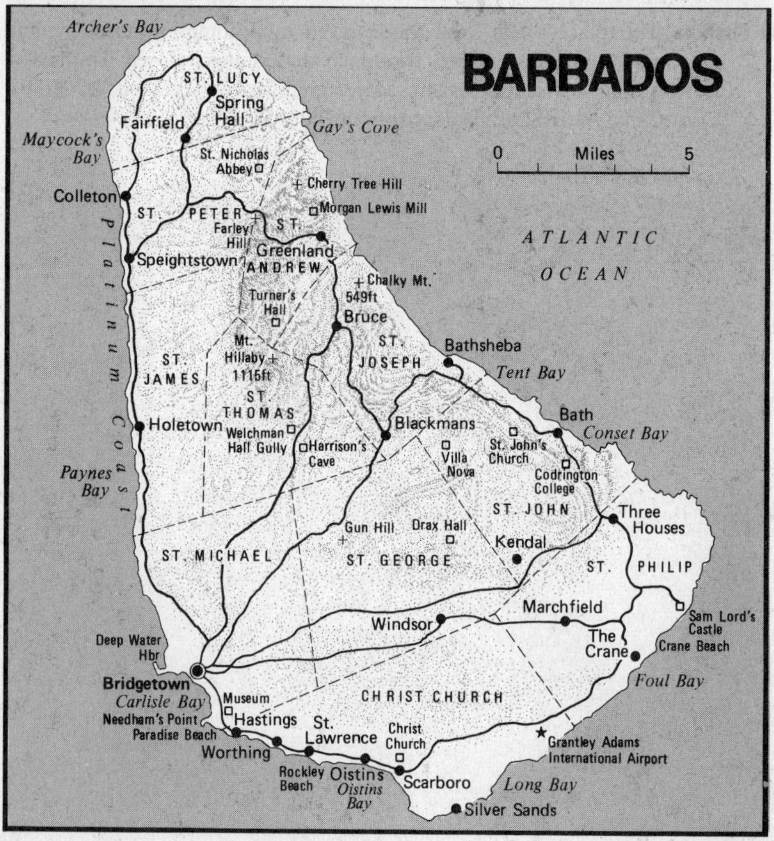

Barbados

If you were going to design a pleasure island, chances are it would look a good deal like Barbados: a west coast lined with white beaches and a sea so clear and gentle it looks like polished tourmaline; an east coast pounded by the Atlantic Ocean; southern cane fields that ripple as breezes comb across them; and craggy northern highlands where cool morning mists burn off to reveal sweeps of valley and sea framed by majestic mahogany trees.

Barbados has seaside villages and English country churches that date from the 17th century. Its prettiest hotels, built of pink coral stone, have rambling gardens and lush landscaping, and since the trade winds are steady and the climate kind, their leeward sides are often terraced and open to fresh air and the view. The beach life is superlative; the nightlife first-rate; golf is good; and there are several superior setups for learning and playing squash and tennis. You also can hike, bike, or ride horseback through the hills of St. Michael or rolling St. Philip Parish. There are plenty of land sites (historic, botanic, and scenic) to explore when you're tired of seeing the sea, and spectator sports (cricket, soccer, horse racing, polo) to watch when you've done enough playing yourself. And it's all pleasantly accessible thanks to the island's compact size.

Although Barbados has been independent since 1966, reminders of the British Empire are everywhere — Nelson's statue on Bridgetown's Trafalgar Square, the middies and wide-brimmed boaters worn by the Harbour Police, and afternoon tea laid out as a matter of course in the lounge of a number of St. James coast hotels. There's also the *Police Band,* resplendent in their white caps and tunics, offering a concert from the gingerbread-frilled Victorian bandstand on the Esplanade; white-wigged magistrates hurrying by on their way to court; and kids in uniforms trooping home from school — all reflective of a system of government, justice, and education built on the British model.

The pervasiveness of British customs on the island is not surprising, considering that Barbados was ruled continuously by Great Britain for over 350 years. Pedro a Campos, the Portuguese sailor said to have discovered the island in 1536, named it Los Barbados — "the bearded ones" — for the banyan trees, with their shaggy, exposed roots, that he sighted on the shore. But presumably because it lay on the Spanish (rather than the Portuguese) side of the line of demarcation established by a papal bull in 1493, he failed to claim the island for Portugal. As a result, the island was not settled by Europeans until English expeditionaries arrived in the early 1600s.

Compared to that of its neighbor islands, Barbados's history has been fairly free of strife. Its extreme easterly position, upwind of all the other

Lesser Antilles, made it relatively difficult to approach from the west and undoubtedly served as protection from attack by buccaneers. The island's planters, many of whom were either criminals shipped out as indentured servants or dissenters forced to emigrate from England for religious or political reasons, treated the African slaves imported to help cultivate their cane fields in a relatively humane manner, although there were brief slave uprisings in 1672, 1696, and 1702. The island's history, however, is not without some spicy tales. One story concerns a man named Sam Lord, who earned the wherewithal to build the magnificent house known as *Sam Lord's Castle* — now the centerpiece of Marriott's Barbados resort — via the unscrupulous practice of "wrecking," i.e., luring ships onto shoals by hanging lanterns in palms along the shore to simulate port lights, and relieving them of their cargoes.

Today's Bajans are much more hospitable. Their openness and friendliness toward tourists make the island's atmosphere especially appealing. But then Barbados has known tourism for several hundred years. As early as the 17th century, visitors came to the island for their health. In 1751, George Washington accompanied Lawrence, his tubercular half brother, on a visit to Bridgetown. The island was not kind to the future first US president — there he contracted the smallpox that marked him for life. Still, he declared the place "a delight" and himself "enraptured with the beautiful prospects."

Today's visitors are delighted, too, which pleases their hosts, whose love of and pride in their island is deep. Bajans are sure — in the nicest possible way — that "Bim" (as they call their homeland) is the best place in the Caribbean, even in the world. As one Bajan put it: "Barbados is where life feels right to me." Bajans want visitors to feel that way too. There has been some trouble in paradise, however. While crime once was virtually nonexistent here, at press time the US State Department warns of a prevalence of crimes — purse-snatching, pickpocketing, sexual assault, and armed robbery — against tourists in Barbados. And while the island's standard of living remains high, Barbados also faces a budget deficit and other economic problems.

So Barbados is not quite the perfect island. Neither is it the perfect destination for everyone. Downtown Bridgetown is worthwhile for shopping, but it's certainly not sugar-coated pretty. Glitter addicts won't find Vegas shows or gambling; but history buffs will find greathouses and antique churches and lots more to explore. Winter prices will seem astronomical to some; for others the peace and the place will be worth every penny; and still others will wait for summer, when prices drop by at least a third, for the best of both worlds. For some people, jackets for dinner (de rigueur here) are stuffy; for others, they're just a stylish touch.

Preferences differ, but for many people, Barbados combines all that's necessary for the perfect Caribbean vacation. This island could be where "life feels right" to you, too.

Barbados At-a-Glance

FROM THE AIR

Barbados's bright green cane and cotton fields, neatly framed by hedgerows, look like a tropical translation of rural England, reflecting the country's longtime British ties. The easternmost island of the West Indies, it lies outside the main arc of the Caribbean's Windward Islands chain, about 100 miles due east of St. Vincent and about 340 miles north of Guyana on the north coast of South America. It is small — 166 square miles, 21 miles long by 14 miles at its widest point — and relatively densely populated, with about 254,000 inhabitants.

The island is shaped like a pear, stem end pointing north, with its capital, Bridgetown (pop. 90,000), on the curve of the southwestern coast. Just inland from the southern coast, 11 miles east and slightly south of the city's center, near Seawell, is Grantley Adams International Airport. The 2,100-mile jet flight from New York takes just over 4 hours; the flight from Miami (about 1,610 miles) takes about 3¼ hours.

The island is rimmed by beaches. Its eastern edge, above a coast surf-combed by a dark blue Atlantic Ocean, is hilly and rugged; Bathsheba, a small fishing village, sits at the midpoint of its shoreline. The land along the western coast — on which Bridgetown and the centuries-old settlements of Holetown and Speightstown, as well as most resort hotels are located — is gentle and rolling, washed by a calmer leeward sea.

SPECIAL PLACES

Except for traffic-tangled Bridgetown, Barbados is the ideal place to explore by car, provided you don't attempt a shortcut from one main route to another without *very explicit* directions or a good map. In Barbados all numbered routes — laid out in a fan-like pattern — lead to or from Bridgetown. Though sometimes narrow, they are reasonably well marked with crossroad signs, and people are pleasant when visitors stop to ask directions. With this in mind, we suggest a two-part itinerary consisting of a sightseeing/shopping morning in Bridgetown, using hotel bus and/or taxi transport, and a day's drive around the island — preferably self-driven, but otherwise in a taxi with a congenial driver — including lunch and sunbathing on the east coast. (The waters can be rough here, so unless you're a strong swimmer, don't go in alone.) The east coast is great for body-surfing, too.

BRIDGETOWN Barbados's capital is an architectural hodgepodge with a network of one-way streets that — in rush hours — seems to epitomize the triumph of car over man. Luckily, the city's few points of interest are within strolling distance of each other and of Broad Street's in-bond (duty-free) shopping. Aim to arrive at Trafalgar Square, the heart of town, at about 10 AM, when the worst of the morning rush hour is over. Like its London namesake, the square (really the area between the edge of the inner harbor and the public buildings across Trafalgar Street) honors Nelson's 1805 naval victory and is endowed with a statue of the great admiral. This Horatio was sculpted and installed in 1813, some 30 years before its British counterpart. (Considerably more popular with Bajans is the huge statue of the Freed Slave Bussa, which stands at a crossroads on St. Barnabas Highway just outside Bridgetown.) Other landmarks in and around the square: Fountain Garden, with its magnificent three-dolphin fountain, commemorating the advent of piped water in 1865; a memorial cenotaph to the dead of World Wars I and II; and an arch erected in 1987 at the Bay Street entrance to Bridgetown to commemorate the 21st anniversary of independence.

Facing the north side of the square, the great, gray, Victorian-Gothic public buildings (1874) house the Assembly (on the right) and the Senate (in the left-hand towered building). These buildings are open to the public when the Senate and Assembly are not in session. The jarringly modern Financial Building dominates the square's east end.

The square's southern boundary is the edge of the old harbor, better known as the Careenage, because from the earliest days, ships were brought in here and careened (tipped on their sides) to have their bottoms scraped, caulked, and painted. Nowadays, island fishing boats berth beside elegant sailing yachts. Keep an eye out for the Bajan Harbour policemen, who wear sailor suits with blue-collared middies and wide-brimmed straw hats.

St. Michael's Cathedral (Anglican) is around the corner and to the right behind the Financial Building. Completed in 1665 and rebuilt after hurricanes in 1780 and 1831, it is said to be the place where George Washington worshiped when he visited Barbados with his brother in 1751. Today it offers cool moments on a hot day and a chance to inspect a collection of antique memorial tablets.

That's about it for urban sightseeing (elapsed time: about three-quarters of an hour). Proceed to Broad Street for an hour of intense shopping. If time permits, continue the spree by taking a taxi to nearby *Pelican Village* and the *Handicraft Emporium* (see *Shopping*). Then head for the Garrison Savannah (via cab), where the *Barbados Museum,* once the Old Military Prison, built by the Royal Engineers in 1820, features a copy of George Washington's *Barbados Journal,* relics of slavery, geological and archaeological specimens, plantation furniture, china and silver, and West Indian prints dating from the 17th century. A Children's Gallery contains lovely dollhouses and historical models. The museum is open Mondays through Saturdays from 10 AM to 6 PM. There's an admission charge (phone: 435-6900). Nearby lunch choices are the *Brown Sugar* and the *Ocean View* (see *Eating Out*).

Also of interest at the Garrison Savannah is the *National Cannon Collection,* an outdoor display of 30 cannons, dating from 1680 to 1870, that were rescued from around the island. The collection is located on a scenic spot that's especially popular with photographers.

On the way out Bay Street, Carlisle Bay and the Esplanade Pavilion (where the *Barbados Police Band* holds its concerts) are on the right. A little farther along, across from the entrance to the *Barbados Yacht Club,* Chelsea Road turns off to the left; on its near corner stands the structure apocryphally called "the George Washington House," where — historians agree — it is highly unlikely that either George or his brother ever slept.

ELSEWHERE ON THE ISLAND

Most organized tours travel counterclockwise through Oistins Town, then out to *Sam Lord's,* up the east coast, west across the island, and head back through Speightstown and Holetown. Those touring on their own should do just the opposite: Get an early start, drive north along the island's western edge, and continue clockwise, visiting:

HOLETOWN This little St. James coast community is the island's oldest British settlement. An obelisk marks the spot where the British ship *Orange Blossom* landed in 1627. St. James Church, one of the Caribbean's oldest (dating to 1660), is located here. It looks as though it has been transported — bell tower and all — from England, except for its tropical poinsettia hedge, which blooms bright red at *Christmas.*

GOLD COAST The shore of St. James and St. Peter parishes, it's lined with the island's plushest hotels and winter homes.

SPEIGHTSTOWN Once a major sugar port and still a fishing town, this place features old houses, a picturesque restored church (St. Peter's), and a bustling waterfront. The vendors who sell their piles of produce and crafts on Church Street, the main thoroughfare, remain undaunted by the town's modern shopping mall.

From here turn east on Highway 1 to cross the island and visit:

ST. NICHOLAS ABBEY In St. Peter, this Jacobean greathouse, built between 1650 and 1660, is notable for its architecture and antiques, including a stunning 1810 Coalport dinner service and an extensive collection of Wedgwood medallions. The home movie taken by the owner's father of the voyage from Britain and 1920s plantation life is worth the price of admission; open 10 AM to 3:30 PM Mondays through Fridays (phone: 422-8725).

FARLEY HILL A national park on Highway 1, St. Peter Parish, with gardens, rich green lawns, and enormous trees surrounding the shell of a once splendid greathouse, partially rebuilt during the filming of *Island in the Sun* in the late 1950s, and later destroyed again by fire. A monument commemorates the dedication of the park by Queen Elizabeth II; there are picnic tables, lookout points, stunning views. Open daily from 8:30 AM to 6 PM; admission charge (phone: 422-3555).

BARBADOS WILDLIFE RESERVE Across from the entrance to Farley Hill, this mahogany forest reserve is operated under the auspices of the Barbados Primate Research Center, and is home to rare green monkeys (said to have been brought from West Africa 3 centuries ago), deer, hares, tortoises, and various birds. Its most recent addition is Grenade Hall, a botanic reserve. Open daily from 10 AM to 5 PM. Admission charge (phone: 422-8826).

MORGAN LEWIS MILL Turn left (north) below Farley Hill and follow the signs to the only remaining windmill on Barbados with its working parts intact. It's open to the public daily from 8 AM to 4 PM. Admission charge.

EAST COAST HIGHWAY This wide, scenic road follows the ocean shore south; about halfway down there's a snack bar and picnic place at Barclay's Park.

ANDROMEDA GARDENS A terraced collection of exotic tropical plants and a great view of the Bathsheba coast are the highlights here. Open daily from 9 AM to 5 PM; admission charge. Hwy. 3, Bathsheba, St. Joseph (phone: 433-9261).

BATHSHEBA This small fishing village, a favorite Sunday beach area for Bajans, gives the coast its name. Nearby Tent Bay is home port for a fleet of fishing boats.

ST. JOHN'S CHURCH Built during the mid-1600s in the parish of the same name, this church on Highway 3B is known for its English look and the tomb of Ferdinand Paleologus, the Emperor Constantine's last descendant.

CODRINGTON COLLEGE This stately, gray stone Georgian seminary of the Anglican Community of the Resurrection opened in 1745. Located on Consett Bay in St. John, its campus features an avenue of palms and stunning ocean views. Open daily from 9 AM to 5 PM; admission charge.

SAM LORD'S CASTLE Once the elegant home of the celebrated 19th-century rogue, this structure in St. Philip is now the centerpiece of Marriott's Barbados resort hotel complex. Open daily from 8:30 AM to 5 PM; admission charge.

Other notable sites on the island include the following:

FRANCIA PLANTATION A stately plantation home in St. George's, now open to the public. Still in operation as a vegetable plantation, it boasts exquisite tropical gardens and orchards. Located between Gun Hill and St. George's Church in St. George, it's open weekdays from 10 AM to 4 PM. There's an admission charge (phone: 429-0474).

TURNER'S HALL WOODS Part of the Barbados National Trust, this comprises the last remaining 45 acres of the natural forest that once covered the island. It's inhabited by birds and monkeys, and features a boiling spring. Open daily. St. Andrew.

WELCHMAN HALL GULLY This is the Thomas Parish site of the National Trust's developing Botanical Garden with many marked, tropical specimens. Occasionally you'll sight wild monkeys. Worthwhile — if you're a flower lover. Open daily from 9 AM to 5 PM; admission charge. Hwy. 2 (phone: 438-6671).

HARRISON'S CAVE The spectacular caverns are endowed with great cream and crystal rooms, subterranean streams, pools, and waterfalls. The cave is wonderfully easy to explore thanks to an electric tram that carries visitors down and out again. Open daily from 9 AM to 4 PM; admission charge. Next to Welchman Hall (phone: 438-6640).

FLOWER FOREST Designed as a living legacy for future generations, this serene 50-acre garden spot features exotic flowers, specimen fruit and spice trees, and a glorious view. Light snacks and fruit are sold. Open daily from 9 AM to 5 PM; admission charge. Richmond Rd., St. Joseph (phone: 433-8152).

GUN HILL A lookout point as famous for its 17th-century carved lion as for one of the best views of the island. Open daily from 9 AM to 5 PM; admission charge.

BARBADOS ZOOLOGICAL PARK Located in St. Philip at Oughterson Plantation, it contains a collection of Caribbean wildlife, including several endangered species of parrots. The greathouse at the center of the park is full of antiques and interesting curios. Open daily from 10 AM to 5 PM. Admission charge (phone: 423-6203).

SOUTH POINT LIGHTHOUSE Located on the windswept landscape of the south coast and painted in red and white rings, this iron structure is believed to be the only remaining lighthouse of its kind. Though its components were manufactured in England, it was first constructed in Barbados, where it was lit in April 1852. The interior is not open to the public.

SUNBURY PLANTATION HOUSE A 300-year-old estate house with an impressive collection of mahogany furniture, antiques, and carriages. There's a casual restaurant and, on certain nights, elegant dinners are served in the house's dining room (call for the schedule and to make reservations). Open daily from 10 AM to 4:30 PM; admission charge. (phone: 423-6270).

VILLA NOVA In St. John Parish, this historic greathouse was once owned by Anthony Eden, Earl of Avon and a former British prime minister. Open from 9 AM to 4 PM Mondays through Fridays; admission charge (phone: 433-1524).

EXTRA SPECIAL **On Wednesday afternoons from mid-January through the first week of April, a different greathouse is open each week for public touring, affording a close look at island antiques as well as the elegant lifestyle of the historic homes' current**

residents. Tickets (about $4) benefit the National Trust. Watch the Sunday papers, call the National Trust (phone: 436-9033), or ask at the tourist office or your hotel activities desk for specifics.

Sources and Resources

TOURIST INFORMATION

On Barbados, the tourism office (phone: 427-2623/4) is in the Harbour Industrial Park near the Deep Water Harbour in Bridgetown. There also are tourist information centers at Grantley Adams International Airport and on the cruise ship pier at the Deep Water Harbour.

The Barbados Board of Tourism supplies information on attractions and accommodations. It also publishes a season-by-season list of rates and facilities at island hotels and guesthouses along with details on summer and winter package plans. The tourism board has two offices in the US (see GETTING READY TO GO).

LOCAL COVERAGE The *Barbados Advocate* is the island's daily paper. *The Nation* is published six times a week and appears as the *Sun* on Sundays. Given a 2- or 3-day time lag, Miami and other US papers (*USA Today* and the *Wall Street Journal*) and the *International Herald Tribune* also are generally available. *The Bajan,* a monthly magazine, focuses on local happenings, history, and people. *Caribbean Week* covers regional news.

The solid *Official Guide to Barbados* (sightseeing tips, sports, and entertainment information) is distributed free at the tourist office. The board's compact *Things You Should Know* brochure covers a good deal of useful information (transport companies and costs, shopping, restaurants, nightspots, and so on). The *Visitor,* a tourist-oriented tabloid published by *The Nation,* highlights current nightlife, restaurants, and sightseeing, as does the weekly *Sun Seeker,* published by the *Advocate;* both are distributed free at hotels, the board of tourism, and other tourist areas.

RADIO AND TELEVISION

Barbados Rediffusion radio BBS-FM, YESS 104.1 FM, the Voice of Barbados, Radio Liberty on 98.1 FM, and the Caribbean Broadcasting Corporation (daily radio, morning CNN news from the US, and evening TV) are the island's broadcast media.

TELEPHONE

The area code for Barbados is 809.

ENTRY REQUIREMENTS

US and Canadian citizens need only proof of citizenship (a birth certificate or voter's registration card along with a driver's license or other government-approved photo ID), although passports ensure easy re-entry home.

A ticket for onward or return transportation is also required. There is a $12.50 departure tax.

CLIMATE AND CLOTHES

Constant sea breezes temper the heat of the sun, which, according to official Barbadian records, shines more than 3,000 hours per (8,760-hour) year. Winter temperatures range from 68F (20C) to 85F (29C); summer temperatures 75F (25C) to 87F (31C). Showers are frequent but brief, and thanks to the trade winds, the air seldom stays muggy for long. Wettest months are September, October, and November; February and March are driest. Rooms at most hotels and guesthouses are at least partially air conditioned.

In terms of attire, only Bermuda is trimmer — a circumstance that, on both islands, can probably be traced to the lingering British influence. The effect is well groomed rather than stuffy: Bajans aren't all that keen on knee socks and walking shorts, but they do appreciate guests neatly turned out. Bare (but not topless) is beautiful on beaches only. Customarily, sun worshipers slip into a shirt or cover-up for lunch on a hotel terrace; a shirt and pants or a skirt or sport dress for daytime sightseeing; something roughly equivalent to what you'd wear on a warm evening at a country club at night. Only a few of the posher hotels (*Sandy Lane* and *Coral Reef Club,* for example) suggest men wear dinner jackets and black tie on some evenings during the winter season; otherwise, most hotels and restaurants request jackets, but not necessarily ties, after dark. In summer, dress is less formal.

MONEY

The Barbados dollar is pegged to the US dollar; at press time, the official exchange rate was $2 Barbados to $1 US. Shops accept both US and Canadian dollars, as well as traveler's checks, but don't offer discounts on purchases paid with them. Some of the larger stores and a number of hotels and restaurants also honor American Express, Diners Club, Visa, and MasterCard, although they may add a 5% surcharge. There usually is little difference between the exchange rate offered by banks and that given in hotels, shops, and restaurants. All prices in this chapter are quoted in US dollars.

Banking hours at Barclays are 8 AM to 3 PM Mondays through Thursdays; on Fridays, 8 AM to 5 PM. Most other banks are open 9 AM to 3 PM Mondays through Thursdays, and from 9 AM to 1 PM and 3 to 5 PM on Fridays. All banks are closed on weekends and holidays. The Barbados National Bank operates an exchange bureau at the airport daily from 8 AM to noon.

LANGUAGE

Bajans speak English with their own special island lilt.

TIME

Barbados time is 1 hour ahead of eastern standard time (when it's noon in New York, it's 1 PM in Bridgetown), or the same as eastern daylight saving time.

CURRENT

110 volts, 50 cycles; compatible with American and Canadian appliances. Some hotels also have 220 volts.

TIPPING

The extra 10% added to your bill in most hotels and restaurants covers all but special services. When a service charge is not included, tip waiters 10% to 15%, hotel maids $1 to $2 per room per day, bellboys 50¢ per bag (but not less than $1 per trip for one or two people), and about $1 for a special errand. Airport porters also should be tipped 50¢ per bag; and taxi drivers, 10% of the fare.

GETTING AROUND

BICYCLES *M. A. Williams Bicycle Rentals* (phone: 427-3955) in Hastings rents bikes for about $9 per day. Also try *Fun Seekers* (phone: 435-8206).

BUS Bajans use buses a lot, and more tourists should, too, since they reach many major interest points and are comfortable and reliable (if not wildly colorful as buses are on other islands). Bus route No. 1 travels the west coast road from Bridgetown to Speightstown and beyond; Nos. 6 and 7 run between Bridgetown and Bathsheba and Bridgetown and Codrington College, respectively. Fare is 75¢ no matter how long the ride, and exact change is required. Ask at the Barbados Transport Board (Roebuck St.; phone: 436-6820) for current schedule information.

Jitney buses, owned and operated by a number of hotels, shuttle guests to and from Bridgetown for sightseeing and shopping several times a day. In some cases, the service is free; in others, there's a small charge.

CAR RENTAL A great way to get around once you get the hang of keeping left (a bit of practice in a parking lot generally does the trick). During summer, rates range from about $50 per day for a mini-moke to about $65 per day for an automatic-shift four-passenger car, with unlimited mileage, and basic insurance. Gas, at about $2.50 per gallon, is extra. If you don't have a credit card, you'll be asked for a substantial deposit. Rental cars are often in short supply, so early booking is advised.

Some local firms are *National of Barbados* (phone: 426-0603), *L. E. Williams* (phone: 427-1043, 427-6006, or 427-6007), *Courtesy* (phone: 431-4161), *Dear's Garage* (phone: 429-9277), and *Sunny Isle* (phone: 435-7979). *Barbados Rent a Car* (phone: 425-1388) has a booth at the airport. Check the tourist office for a complete listing. Car rental companies issue visitor's driving permits for about $5.

ISLAND-HOPPING TRIPS One-day flying and longer sailing expeditions to nearby Martinique, St. Lucia, St. Vincent, the Grenadines, Grenada, and Tobago cost about $240 to $300 per person, including transfers, airfare, lunch, and sightseeing, and are operated by *Caribbean Safari Tours* (phone: 427-5100) in Bridgetown.

SEA EXCURSIONS Lunch and cocktail cruises are offered by a number of sailing ships. The *Jolly Roger* (phone: 436-6424), for about $52 per person, provides a snorkeling stop and barbecue, open bar, entertainment by the crew, and transportation from your hotel. For about the same price, the *Bajan Queen* (phone: 436-2149) makes similar trips; the catamaran *Irish Mist* (phone: 436-9201) offers slightly more serene day and evening trips.

SIGHTSEEING BUS TOURS *L. E. Williams,* one of the main (and oldest) tour companies, offers a day tour that covers the island (80 miles) and includes lunch for about $50 (phone: 427-1043, 427-6006, or 427-6007). Other island firms, such as *Dear's Garage* (phone: 429-9277) and *Johnson's* (phone: 426-4205), also organize tours. A unique expedition is the *Cosmic Tour* (phone: 429-6195), which views the universe with telescope and binoculars from various vantage points (subject to weather conditions). Numerous other tours are available. Be sure to confirm what is included, as some require additional fees for certain sites or for lunch.

SIGHTSEEING HELICOPTER EXCURSIONS For a breathtaking (if pricey) view of the island and great photo opportunities, contact *Bajan Helicopters* (phone: 431-0069). Cost is $60 for 20 minutes, $90 for 30 minutes.

SIGHTSEEING TAXI TOURS A good way to get a close-up of the island for those who prefer not to drive. Bajan drivers are friendly, dignified, and proud of their country. A day's trip with one of them provides visitors with a more personalized feel for the country than a routine bus tour. A 6- to 7-hour tour costs about $80 to $90 for a party of two, three, or four. Optional side trips: a stop for a soda or a rum and Coke at Barclay's Park scenic overlook; or lunch and a swim at *Marriott's Sam Lord's Castle* or the *Crane Beach* hotel.

TAXI Readily available at the airport, at stands in downtown Bridgetown, at the Deep Water Harbour, and outside hotels. They are not metered; but rates are fixed, and drivers carry lists of standard fares to which passengers can refer. From the airport, a taxi ride to a south coast hotel in Oistins will cost between $6 and $8; to *Sam Lord's Castle,* about $12; to the *Barbados Hilton* or *Grand Barbados,* about $15; to the center of Bridgetown, about $15; and to a hotel on the St. James coast, between $20 and $22.

INTER-ISLAND FLIGHTS

American Airlines and *BWIA* fly between Barbados and San Juan. *Air Martinique, BWIA,* and *LIAT* provide air links to other Caribbean islands.

SPECIAL EVENTS

Barbados's big annual bash is *Crop Over,* a 2-week (mid-July to early August) succession of parties, parades, craft displays, plantation fairs, and open-air concerts enjoyed by both Bajans and island visitors. Its climax is the historically rooted *Kadooment* — a day of "jump-up" partying, singing, and dancing with a parade starting from the *National Stadium* and winding up in a central plantation yard.

The official national holidays observed by banks and most businesses include *New Year's Day, Errol Barrow Day* (January 21), *Good Friday, Easter Sunday, Whitmonday, May Day* (May 1), *Kadooment* (first Monday in August), *UN Day* (first Monday in October), *Independence Day* (November 30), *Christmas,* and *Boxing Day* (December 26).

SHOPPING

For best buys (20% to 50% below stateside prices) on classic imports — English bone china, crystal, Japanese cameras and binoculars, perfumes, liquor, watches, jewelry, and clothes (especially British sweaters, tweeds, and sportswear), in-bond (duty-free) sections of major department stores and specialty shops on and around Bridgetown's Broad Street are where it's at. In these designated areas, merchandise is tagged with two prices: in-bond and take-away. The in-bond one is always lowest, but the take-away tag may still represent a saving over what you'd pay back home. For in-bond savings on liquor and tobacco products, visitors must shop at least 24 hours before scheduled departure time and select from display merchandise; purchases are then delivered directly to their plane or ship. All other duty-free items can be taken as they are paid for, provided the purchaser shows proof of being a visitor (airline ticket and passport or ID). *Mall 34, Norman Centre, Da Costas,* and the *Galleria* are air conditioned malls on Broad Street. Several smaller malls have sprung up along the south coast, *Hastings Plaza, Sandy Bank,* and *Quayside Centre* among them. These newer shopping havens also have restaurants and bars, and parking is much easier. The selection, however, may not be as extensive as in the central shopping area.

Visitors staying at a west coast hotel can save time and their feet by shopping in-bond departments of *Louis L.Bayley, Cave Shepherd, India House,* and others at the *Sunset Crest Shopping Centre; Cave Shepherd* also has a Speightstown branch. The stocks aren't quite as large as those downtown, but neither are the crowds, and the prices are the same. The smaller, double-decked *Skyway Shopping Plaza* at Hastings, handy to South Shore hotels, is stronger on crafts and souvenirs than in-bond buys. There also are coveys of shops (branches and independent boutiques) at the *Hilton* and *Sam Lord's.* A wander through the *Chattel Village* in St. Lawrence Gap is a must for the visiting shopper. These attractive shops, replicas of quaint "Bajan houses," are painted in an array of pastel colors and are filled with local arts and crafts.

A dozen boutiques — many in hotel gardens or lobby niches — offer sleek sportswear and resort clothes at prices that range from expensive to outrageous. No need to go into town; just start in the Speightstown neighborhood, or at the south edge of the city, and browse your way down the coast road. Shopping hours are from 8 AM to 4 PM, weekdays; 8 AM to 1 PM on Saturdays.

ANTIQUARIA Large and small antiques, maps, prints, glassware, china, and decorative items. Spring Garden Hwy., St. Michael (phone: 426-0635).

ARTICRAFTS Featuring the work of local artists. *Norman Centre* (phone: 427-5767).

BARBADOS HANDICRAFT CENTER All sorts of local crafts. Bridge St. (phone: 436-6128 or 427-5056).

BEST OF BARBADOS For top-quality island crafts. There are four branches located at *Da Costas Mall* (phone: 431-0013), *Sam Lord's* (phone: 423-7350), *Mall 34* (phone: 436-1416), and *Flower Forest* (phone: 433-8322).

CAVE SHEPHERD Featuring imported fashions. Broad St. (phone: 431-2121).

COTTON DAYS DESIGN Carol Cadogan sells her tropical sportswear at Bridge House, Cavans La. (phone: 431-0414) and at her design studio at Rose Cottage, Lower Bay St. (phone: 427-7191).

FLY FISH INC. This company sells an unusual souvenir — the island's national dish flash-frozen or vacuum-packed, with a reusable freezer gelpack (approved by major airlines for carry-on). It's also one of the few places that has fresh tropical floral bouquets that have been approved for airline carry-on. (For bouquets including roses, azaleas, camellias, gardenias, or syringa, a certificate from the US Department of Agriculture is needed for importation. All other flora can be imported without a certificate, but will be inspected at port of entry into the US.) At the airport departure lounge (phone: 428-1645).

LA GALERIE ANTIQUE China, linens, tapestries, Barbadian furniture. Paynes Bay (phone: 432-6094).

HANDICRAFT EMPORIUM Stacked to its warehouse rafters with fairly priced woven work, khuskhus, and pandanus mats, hats, rugs, and baskets. Princess Alice Hwy. (phone: 426-4391).

HARRISON'S Imported fashions and china. 1 Broad St. (phone: 431-5500).

LOUIS L. BAYLEY Jewelry specialists. *Da Costas Mall,* Broad St. (phone: 431-0029).

ORIGINS Fashionable island clothing from local designers. Next to the *Waterfront Café* on the Careenage (phone: 436-8522).

PELICAN ART GALLERY Featuring the works of Bajan artists. *Pelican Village.*

SIMON More "Caribbean" resortwear. St. James (phone: 432-6242).

THE WENTS & FRIENDS Interesting assortment of pottery, hand-painted clothing, woodcarvings, and paintings from local artists. Christ Church (phone: 426-8879).

Y. DE LIMA An eclectic selection of watches, jewelry, furniture, and appliances. 20 Broad St. (phone: 426-4644).

SPORTS

Sun, sand, and sea constitute 90% of what lures visitors to the island, but when the untoward urge to activity strikes, Barbados offers a number of worthwhile alternatives.

BOATING Most hotels have Sunfish, Sailfish, and/or Hobie Cats for loan or rent right on the beach, and most can book sailing yachts for day and party cruising. Individual charters, skippered or bareboat, aren't easy to arrange on the spur of the moment; but ask your hotel travel desk, or call the commodore at the *Barbados Cruising Club* (phone: 426-4434). From January through May, the *Barbados Cruising Club* and the *Barbados Yacht Club* (phone: 427-1125) sponsor frequent regattas.

For a truly breathtaking underwater view of the coral reefs, make reservations on the submarine *Atlantis* (phone: 436-8929). A 1-hour dive costs about $70.

CRICKET Inscrutable to most US spectators, it ranks as the number one sport and national passion, with Barbados fielding championship teams at both West Indian and World Test Match levels. The *Advocate* carries match schedules in season (June to January). Though the sport is played on several fields throughout the island, the main one is *Kensington Oval* in Fontabelle, St. Michael (phone: 436-1397).

GOLF A round on the championship 18 at *Sandy Lane* (phone: 432-1405 or 432-1145) will cost $40 for greens fees, about $18 for club rental, about $35 for a cart, and $20 and up for a caddie. There also are two 9-hole courses, one at *Rockley* resort and another at *Heywoods.*

HIKING The Barbados National Trust (phone: 436-9033) and the Duke of Edinburgh Award Scheme sponsor free hikes across Barbados every Sunday. If you're keen on walking on your own, you might take the public bus to Codrington College and follow the abandoned railway right-of-way along the east coast to the *Atlantis* hotel at Tent Bay (a nice place for an island lunch); bus back from nearby Bathsheba.

HORSEBACK RIDING On hill trails and along beaches in St. Michael Parish and in the countryside around *Sam Lord's* in St. Philip, it's as scenic as it is athletic. English saddles predominate, but some western saddles are available. Contact *Brighton Riding Stable* for beach rides (St. Michael; phone: 425-9381). *Caribbean International Riding Centre* (St. Joseph; phone: 433-

1453) offers 1-hour countryside rides or a selection of other rides, including lunch at Sunbury Plantation house. Rates, with guide, run about $27 per hour, including transportation to and from hotels.

SNORKELING AND SCUBA The *Eastern Caribbean Diving Association* is having a big impact on the development of diving on the island. In addition to assisting with the operation of a decompression chamber, the association is involved in marine conservation, and was instrumental in establishing minimum standards for safe operating by scuba diving shops. Borrow or rent masks and flippers for a small fee at most west coast hotels. For diving, reefs off the west and south coasts make intriguing day-trip destinations. Visit the coral reef of the three-zoned (for scientific research; for snorkeling, scuba, and glass-bottom boat trips; for swimming, skiing, sailing, and water sports) *Folkestone National Marine Reserve, Park, and Marine Museum* at Holetown (phone: 422-2871). For experienced divers, the deliberately sunk freighter *Stavronikita* beyond the reef is an added attraction, offering an opportunity for some fabulous underwater photography. Some hotels have their own diving facilities. Check *Dive Boat Safari* at the *Hilton* (phone: 427-4350 or 429-8216, nights), *Blue Reef Watersports* at *Glitter Bay* (phone: 422-3133), *The Dive Shop* at the *Grand Barbados* (phone: 426-9947; 426-2031 at night), *Shades of Blue* at the *Coral Reef Club* (phone: 422-3215), and *Jolly Roger Watersports* at the *Sunset Crest Club* (phone: 432-7090). The *Underwater Barbados Scuba Diving Shop* is near the *Coconut Court* hotel in Christ Church (phone: 426-0655) and *Exploresub Barbados* on St. Lawrence Gap offers dive packages with the *Divi Southwinds Beach* hotel (phone: 435-6542). Other operations include *Sandy Beach Water Sports* (*Sandy Beach;* phone: 435-8000) and *Willie's Water Sports* at *Heywoods* (phone: 422-1834). Introductory lessons are about $30; dives about $40 each.

SPECTATOR SPORTS There's soccer from January to June throughout the island; polo July to February at Holder's and St. James; and horse racing on occasional Saturdays from January to May and from July to November at the Garrison Savannah. The latter features snack booths (fried flying fish is the big seller), steel bands, and all the trappings of a small carnival.

SPORT FISHING Not one of Barbados's best sporting attractions, but blue marlin, barracuda, dolphin, wahoo, tuna, and occasional cobia are caught in waters north and south of Barbados. Contact *Ocean Hunter* (phone: 428-3050) or *Blue Jay Charters* (phone: 422-2098). The rate is about $300 for a half day, $600 for a full day for up to six people.

SQUASH *Heywoods* and *Rockley* resorts have 2 air conditioned squash courts each. The *Pineapple Beach Club* and the *Seaview* hotel also have squash facilities. Use is free to guests; others pay about $6 per hour. The *Barbados Squash Club* (phone: 427-7913) in Christ Church charges about $10 per 45 minutes.

SURFING Bajans do their surfing at Rockley Beach on the southwest coast between Worthing and St. Lawrence, at Enterprise Beach near Oistins, and at Bathsheba.

SWIMMING AND SUNNING While not very wide (exceptions: the *Hilton*'s broad expanse, shored up by stone jetties; and Crane Beach, considered by some to be one of the world's best), beaches are pink-tinged coral sand. The majority of hotels command their own stretches of sand (though, technically, all island beaches are public); guests of those that don't are usually just across the road from a beach they can think of as theirs. Most are endowed with chaises, snack and drink bars — all the life-sustaining essentials — so there's not much beach hopping. Barbados has two coasts: the surf-pounded east and the serene west, where most hotels are. Western waters are so clear and buoyant that even real swimming seems to cause unnecessary splashing; so you tend to float a lot and/or paddle about on float boards provided by hotels. But if you're west-based, you ought to try to make it to the east coast at least once — if only to view the drama of the Atlantic surf. There's swimming on the broad-beached eastern shoreline northwest from Bathsheba, but no regular lifeguard service; don't try it alone. *Marriott's Sam Lord's Castle* and the *Crane Beach* hotel offer wave-bathing that's safer, with lifeguards on duty.

TENNIS The *Casuarina Beach Club, Marriott's Sam Lord's Castle, Hilton, Rockley, Heywoods, Crane Beach, Ginger Bay,* and *Divi Southwinds Beach* hotels all have courts. *Sandy Lane* not only has courts and pros in attendance, but a setup suitable for exhibition matches. The 4 courts at the *Sunset Crest Club* near Holetown are lighted, as are those at *Sam Lord's, Heywoods, Rockley,* and *Divi Southwinds Beach.* Most hotels charge about $5 per hour of court time. The charge is $3 per hour to play on the government's grass court at the Garrison Savannah and $8 per hour at the *Paragon Tennis Club.*

WATER SKIING Best on calm western waters. If your hotel doesn't have its own setup, they'll make arrangements with the nearest facility — possibly *Blue Reef Watersports* at *Glitter Bay* (phone: 422-3133) or *Jolly Roger Watersports* (phone: 432-7090) at the *Sunset Crest Club,* both in St. James; or *Willie's Water Sports* at *Heywoods* (phone: 422-1834). Cost is about $15 per person per quarter hour.

WINDSURFING Growing ever more popular at south shore beach hotels. *Jolly Roger Watersports* (phone: 432-7090), *Surf and Sail* (phone: 436-3549), and other St. James coast shops offer board rentals and instruction.

NIGHTLIFE

When the sun goes down, even the most laid-back visitor may give in to the temptation to "jump-up" (dance) into the beckoning Barbadian night. During the winter season, the larger hotels (particularly *Marriott's Sam*

Lord's and the *Hilton*) feature elaborate entertainment. Steel bands and calypso singers are showcased at various nightspots and hotels around the island. Among the most popular island bands, the *Merrymen, Spice, Jade, Ivory, Second Avenue, Split Ends, KGB, Splashband, Square One,* and *Private Eye* rank highest; watch the local papers for when and where they'll be performing.

Those with stout hearts and cast-iron stomachs can dance at sea aboard the *Jolly Roger*'s *Sundowner Calypso Cruise* or the slightly more sedate *Bajan Queen.* On land, clubs for the energetic include the *Club Miliki* at *Heywoods,* and, in Bridgetown, the *Warehouse* (above the *Waterfront Café;* phone: 436-2897), *Septembers* (on Lower Bay St.; phone: 429-5574), and *Harbour Lights* (Upper Bay St.; phone: 436-7225). *Club Needham's* (on Needham's Point near the *Hilton;* phone: 428-3333), a multilevel, open-air nightclub set amid the ruins of a 350-year-old English fort, is open Thursday, Friday, and Saturday nights; the evening views are spectacular. In St. Lawrence Gap, try *After Dark* (phone: 435-6547) or *The Horizon* (next to *Pisces* restaurant; no phone). Clubs in Barbados generally charge an admission fee of about $5.

Throughout the year, there are must-see historical performances such as *1627 and All That,* staged by the talented *Barbados Dance Theatre* (phone: 435-6900) every Thursday and Sunday night at the *Barbados Museum* (phone: 427-0201 or 800-435-1627 from the US). The performance is accompanied by a delicious Bajan buffet. The *Barracks* at the *Island Inn* (phone: 426-4188) has a piano bar, and the *Plantation Garden Theatre* restaurant (phone: 428-5048), outside Bridgetown, offers Caribbean dining and entertainment, including *Plantation Tropical Spectacular II,* a performance tracing the island's history and roots given on Monday and Saturday nights, and *Barbados by Night,* a variety show with everything from fire-eaters to dancers presented on Wednesday and Friday nights.

The assortment of British-style pubs on the island includes *Limers* (St. Lawrence Gap; phone: 435-6554); the *Ship Inn* (St. Lawrence Gap; phone: 435-6961); the *Coach House* (Paynes Bay, St. James; phone: 432-1163); the *Boatyard* (Lower Bay St., Carlisle Bay; 436-2622), a nautical hangout; and the *Bamboo Beach Bar* (St. James; phone: 432-0910). Baxter's Road (Bridgetown) never seems to close — traditional Saturday night strolls up and down its food stall–lined length provide everyone with a real taste of Bajan nightlife, which usually starts to heat up after 10 PM.

Best on the Island

CHECKING IN

Barbados hotels are among the pleasantest, prettiest, and best run in the Caribbean. With their sea views, gardens, beaches, and relaxed atmosphere, staying in one is like being the house guest of rather well-off friends. In summer, when rates drop 30% to 50% from winter season highs, a number offer top-of-the-line elegance and comfort at bargain basement prices. More moderately priced south coast apartment hotels that ask $80 to $110 EP (without meals) daily for two between December 15 and *Easter* tend to be either older places that have seen better days or newer hotels with small rooms designed to handle a continuous stream of charter groups. Suites and apartments with kitchenettes — especially those on the southern shores of Christ Church — often make up in the reasonableness of their cost what they lack in comfort and/or style, but the tasteful-though-barefoot alternative really doesn't exist. Villa suites, apartments (quite a few in hotels), and rental cottages with their own cooking facilities (from $275 a week in summer, about $400 and *way* up in winter) do offer some savings potential. The tourist board issues seasonal lists of apartment and cottage rentals. In addition, the Barbados Hotel Association has set up a central reservations number in the US (phone: 800-462-2526). Given all this, the places below are recommended. Those listed as inexpensive ask $70 to $80 for a double room without meals in winter; places in the moderate category charge $110 to $200; expensive hotels cost $200 to $300; and very expensive places cost $300 or more (sometimes *much* more, but meals are generally included). The Modified American Plan (includes breakfast and dinner) can be added for about $40 per person per day. A number of hotels offer only MAP rates during the winter season, but several offer dine-around plans that allow some variety. All hotel and rental rates are subject to a 5% government tax and a 10% service charge. All telephone numbers are in the 809 area code unless otherwise indicated.

ST. JAMES

All hotels in St. James sit on Highway 1 alongside the beach.

VERY EXPENSIVE

Coral Reef Club This classic resort, on 12 beautifully landscaped acres, offers 75 cottages and suites. The reception lobby and lounge are open-air and very tropical, and there's a lovely restaurant overlooking sea and gardens; also good tennis and water sports. Family-owned and run with a special touch (phone: 422-2372; fax: 422-1776).

Glitter Bay Ensconced on what was once the Cunard estate, this quietly splendid condominium complex, part of the Pemberton chain, exudes luxury and chic in its Moorish modern design, flowered landscaping, palms, and sweep of blue sea. With free water sports, boating, and tennis; golf and riding arranged. There's a patio-surrounded freshwater pool and an excellent restaurant, *Piperade* (see *Eating Out*). Each of the 87 suites has a full kitchen, air conditioned bedroom(s), fan-cooled living room, and terrace or balcony (phone: 422-5555; fax: 422-3940).

Royal Pavilion A luxury resort on a beautiful 1,200-foot beach. Sister of *Glitter Bay,* it has 75 oceanfront suites and offers complimentary water sports, tennis on 2 lighted, Astroturf courts, a pool, a beachfront snack bar, and a fine restaurant (phone: 422-4444; fax: 422-3940).

Sandy Lane This, the island's most luxurious hotel, boasts a carefully preserved original façade and 110 sumptuous rooms with every modern comfort. There are also 18 oversize ocean-view luxury units, a restaurant serving continental fare, tennis courts, and the island's only 18-hole course, which recently received extensive manicuring. The establishment, managed by the Forte Hotels group, offers all the special amenities, from Rolls-Royce airport pickup to fluffy monogrammed bathrobes. In-season prices are high; but less costly packages are offered (phone: 432-1311; fax: 432-2954).

EXPENSIVE

Barbados Beach Village A comfortable and popular informal beachfront resort with 89 rooms (61 double, 28 suites with kitchenettes), a restaurant, 2 bars, and entertainment most nights. Management warns that the layout of units is inconvenient for disabled guests (phone: 425-1440; fax: 424-0996).

Colony Club A rambling, coral stone house with 76 villa rooms in the garden and near the beach, its attractive public rooms have seascape views. Super waterside terrace for breakfast, lunch, stay-all-day beach life; pleasant service. Good summer packages (phone: 422-2335; fax: 422-1726).

Pineapple Beach Club This all-inclusive resort, formerly the *Divi St. James,* is now owned by the island's largest conglomerate, which also owns the *Rockley Beach* resort. Here are 147 guestrooms, beach, fitness center, and squash and tennis courts, as well as a continental restaurant and a bar. All meals and beverages, water sports, live entertainment nightly, tours, and airport departure transfers are included in the rate (phone: 432-7840; 407-994-5640 from Florida; 800-345-0356 from the US; fax: 407-994-6344).

Settlers Beach Coolly luxurious villa apartments circle a swimming pool set in neat, green lawns and gardens by the sea. Each of the 22 villas has 2 bedrooms, a living room/dining area, and a full kitchen (cooks are available). All sports, shopping nearby. The beach restaurant serves excellent lunches and dinners. Exchange dining, too (phone: 422-3052; fax: 422-1937).

MODERATE

Inn on the Beach A garden-edged pool, a patio, and the beach are the focus of this compact set of 20 smallish but bright efficiency studios — each with kitchenette and ocean view. The outdoor dining room and bar attract a lively afternoon clientele (phone: 432-0385; fax: 432-2440).

ST. PETER

VERY EXPENSIVE

Cobblers Cove A gracious, small (39 lovely suites), air conditioned hostelry made special and charming by little touches and attention to detail. This luxurious member of the Relais & Châteaux group includes villa rooms with balconies or patios surrounding a pretty, pink main house, once a private home. The beach — one of the best coves on Barbados — pool, and bar are within steps of each other. All rooms have kitchenettes, but most guests prefer to dine on the terrace, where they can enjoy excellent continental cooking as well as Bajan specialties, while basking in tropical breezes. Good summer packages (phone: 422-2291; fax: 422-1460).

EXPENSIVE

Heywoods The first full-scale luxury resort on the island's scenic northern end, it has 7 handsome buildings (a total of 288 air conditioned rooms and suites) set among palms and gardens on an old sugar plantation site. There are 3 freshwater pools, a mile-long white beach with all water sports, 5 lighted tennis courts, 2 air conditioned squash courts, and a 9-hole golf course. In addition, there's a crafts market, several boutiques, a choice of bars, restaurants from informal to elegant, and an appealing disco. Caring staff under Wyndham management (phone: 422-4900; fax: 422-1581).

INEXPENSIVE

Sandridge A small set of balconied, air conditioned hotel rooms, studios, suites (some duplexes) with kitchenettes, made attractive by the surrounding gardens, pool, appealing beach bar, restaurant, and helpful staff (phone: 422-2361; fax: 422-1965).

ST. PHILIP

EXPENSIVE

Crane Beach What once was an impossibly run-down, turn-of-the-century hotel is now one of the island's most appealing. Its site, though remote, is spectacular, overlooking the Atlantic, with pool and surf beach. The 18 air conditioned rooms and antiques-decorated apartments (all with four-poster beds, kitchenettes, tiled baths, vistas) may be the island's handsomest. There's also a 6-bedroom villa. The *Panoramic* dining room (see *Eating Out*) features fresh seafood, fine wines (phone: 423-6220; fax: 423-5343).

Ginger Bay This small, intimate place has 16 rooms on the Atlantic Ocean, a pool, a lighted tennis court, and *Ginger's,* an good outdoor restaurant. Guests get to the beach through a cave on the grounds (phone: 423-5810; fax: 423-6629).

Marriott's Sam Lord's Castle The old rascal's elegant mansion — beautifully kept and thoughtfully screened from the 234-room complex — is the centerpiece of this pleasant resort. The hotel buildings, open-air dining room, sports, and beach are just through the trees beyond. Surf swimming, lighted tennis, nearby riding, and evening entertainment are big features. To our mind, choicest of the resort's rooms are in the "Castle" (furnished with antiques and four-poster beds) and the sleek buildings closest to the sea (phone: 423-7350; fax: 423-5918).

ST. MICHAEL

EXPENSIVE

Grand Barbados A stunning, deluxe 133-room beachfront resort, it offers wonderful service and attention to detail. All rooms have satellite TV, phone, hair dryer, and mini-bar. There are 2 executive floors with additional amenities. Complimentary water sports for guests. A range of menus is offered at 2 restaurants (phone: 426-0890; fax: 436-9823).

Island Inn Originally part of a garrison where British troops were based, this small, elegant 25-room inn (now all-inclusive) has been restored with original stone ballast work and furnished with antiques and reproductions. Elegant surroundings, nice bar, restaurant, swimming pool, and conference facilities for 220 (phone: 436-6393; fax: 437-8035).

Sandals Barbados Formerly the *Cunard Paradise Beach,* this beachside property recently was acquired by the Sandals chain, which specializes in all-inclusive resorts for couples. It was still being renovated as we went to press, but it is set to open early this year (phone: 305-284-1300 from Florida; 800-SANDALS from the US; fax: 305-284-1336).

CHRIST CHURCH

EXPENSIVE

Divi Southwinds Beach Here's a smart, 20-acre hotel-condominium complex with tennis courts, a good-looking central pool with an elevated, open-air restaurant, 2 additional pools, and its own beach club (with bar) on St. Lawrence Beach just across the road. The guestrooms include pleasantly stylish air conditioned studios, double rooms, and 1- and 2-bedroom duplex suites, with living rooms, kitchens, and balconies. *Exploresub Barbados* is one of its best attractions (see *Sports*); good dive packages also are offered year-round (phone: 428-7181; 800-367-3484 from the US; fax: 428-4674).

MODERATE

Asta Set in a 2½-acre garden on Palm Beach, this property has 60 apartments, each with a fully equipped kitchen. There are also 2 big blue pools, a small market, a boutique, a gameroom, and a restaurant (phone: 427-2541; fax: 426-9566).

Casuarina Beach Club This immensely popular casual resort has 131 air conditioned rooms, a good-size pool, and a choice of water sports, as well as tennis. Dover (phone: 428-3600; fax: 428-1970).

Rockley Clusters of smart studios and townhouse apartments are scattered around a 9-hole golf course in the hills. There's a country club atmosphere here with pools, tennis courts (lighted, with a pro), squash courts, and water sports at a beach club with its own restaurant, bar, and shuttle service. There's also a supermarket, boutique, bar, restaurant, and disco (phone: 435-7880; fax: 435-8015).

Seaview A small, romantic beachfront hotel that feels like a plantation house. The 18 guestrooms have four-poster beds and mahogany furniture; 8 have ocean views. There's also a lighted tennis court, a pool, an air conditioned squash court, and 2 restaurants, including the *Virginian* (see *Eating Out*). Main road, Hastings (phone: 426-1450; fax: 436-1333).

INEXPENSIVE

Ocean View A venerable but very appealing hotel on the sea in Hastings. Big pluses: Old World charm, agreeable service, pin-neat housekeeping, popular Bajan dining room overlooking the sea. There's also a reef-rimmed beach; the rooms (some air conditioned) are in all sorts of shapes (phone: 427-7821; fax: 427-7826).

Sea Foam Haciendas These 12 modest but pleasant 2-bedroom apartments are especially good for large families, since they can be interconnected. They feature full kitchens, including microwaves and coolers to bring to the beach; a quiet stretch of Worthing Beach is right outside (phone: 435-7380; 800-462-2526 from the US; fax: 435-7384).

EATING OUT

Native Bajan cookery is interesting rather than exotic. The tourist board's emblem, a flying fish, is also the national dish, broiled, baked, deep-fried, stuffed, and served in stew. Delicate and moist, it sounds rather exotic and tastes delicious. Other favorite seafoods: sea eggs (sea urchins, often minced and deviled with bread crumbs and spices), crab backs, langouste (lobster), dolphin, and kingfish. Most meat (except goat and some poultry) is imported and is generally only so-so. Bajans also fancy pudding (sausage stuffed with mashed sweet potato and spices, with or without blood added), *souse* (a mélange of pig parts pickled with onion, cucumber, and pepper), and more generally appealing side dishes like *coo coo* (cornmeal and okra), *jug jug* (green peas and guinea corn flour), and cassava pone, a *Christmas* specialty. Among island-grown fruits: paw paw (papaya), soursop (luscious in ice cream), avocado, banana, and coconut (super in milk sherbet). Guava is another — stewed, made into preserves, or cooked down and cooled into "cheese."

Mauby, a non-alcoholic liquor brewed from bark, sugar, and spices, is sold down by the Careenage, in neighborhood bars, and is often made and served in Bajan homes; it is spicy and pleasant (if you like liqueurs, you'll probably like it). *Falernum,* brewed from sugar, is a specialty liqueur. But Barbados rum — the world's smoothest, richest, and best — has no rivals. It turns up in punches, mixed with soda or tonic, and in daiquiris. The "rum snap" and rum cocktail are traditional drinks. Mount Gay brand has fueled generations of yachtsmen, and is sold in a variety of grades from everyday Eclipse to superior, oldest, and darkest Sugar Cane Brandy. Cockspur is another excellent brand. Generally, prices on bottles to take home are half what they cost in the US.

Most of the island's best restaurants fall under one of two headings: continental and expensive, or Bajan and not so. Some combine the two. It's easy to run up a check for $75 or more for two at *Reid's,* while a feast on a pair of flying fish at the *Ocean View* will cost only about $15 per couple. Lunches are even less. Dinner for two (not including wine, drinks, or tip) at those places listed as expensive will cost $65 or more; dinner for two at a moderate restaurant will run $30 to $50; at an inexpensive place, from $15 to $25. All telephone numbers are in the 809 area code unless otherwise indicated.

ST. MICHAEL

EXPENSIVE

Brown Sugar Behind the *Island Inn,* its smart setting is an ideal place to sample Bajan specialties like pumpkin soup, pepper pot, and soursop ice cream. There's a very popular noon buffet. Open for lunch and dinner; no lunch on weekends. Reservations necessary. Major credit cards accepted. Off Hilton Rd. (phone: 426-7684).

MODERATE

Waterfront Café Overlooking the yachts moored in the Careenage, this hot spot attracts an eclectic crowd of sailors, tourists, and well-heeled residents. The menu includes sandwiches and local dishes (flying fish, pepper pot). Live entertainment (usually jazz, but also guitar, piano, and Dixieland). Open for lunch and dinner; closed Sundays. Reservations necessary Thursday nights, when the popular *VSOP Dixieland Jazz Band* plays. Major credit cards accepted. Overlooking the waterfront, in Bridgetown (phone: 427-0093).

CHRIST CHURCH

EXPENSIVE

Ile de France Excellent French fare served in an elegant setting. Open for dinner only; closed Mondays. Reservations advised. Major credit cards accepted. In the *Windsor House Hotel,* Hastings (phone: 435-6869).

Josef's Its continental menu rates high marks for unusually good meat dishes (veal cordon bleu and Viennoise, filet béarnaise), as well as kingfish Caribe, dolphin meunière, flying fish creole, and barracuda in hollandaise sauce (a must). Open for lunch and dinner; no lunch on Saturdays; closed Sundays. Reservations necessary. MasterCard and Visa accepted. St. Lawrence Gap (phone: 435-6541).

da Luciano Italian food in a handsomely restored antique mansion. Try the *misto mare* (mixed marinated seafood). Open daily for dinner only. Reservations advised. Major credit cards accepted. "Staten," Hastings (phone: 427-5518).

Pisces Delicious fish and seafood in a small, pretty house on the shore at St. Lawrence Gap. Recommended: flying fish in wine sauce, snapper Caribe, nutmeg ice cream. Open daily for dinner. Reservations advised. Major credit cards accepted. Hwy. 7 (phone: 435-6564).

MODERATE

Captain's Carvery at the Ship Inn Nestled next to a cozy pub, it features a Bajan buffet at lunch, international buffets at dinner. Open daily. Reservations necessary. Major credit cards accepted. St. Lawrence Gap (phone: 435-6961).

Flamboyant An appealing little house on the South Coast road run by a husband and wife, with a unique menu of European and island dishes. Friendly; good rum punches, too. Open for dinner daily. Reservations advised. Major credit cards accepted (phone: 427-5588).

Ocean View A pretty green and white seaside dining room, it has a limited — but very good — Bajan and continental menu (savory soup, crisp flying fish). Open daily for lunch and dinner. Reservations necessary. Major credit cards accepted. Hastings (phone: 427-7821).

Plantation Garden Theatre Located at St. Lawrence Gap, Bajan food is served in a tropical atmosphere. Folkloric and calypso cabaret dinner shows are presented. Price includes hotel transfers, dinner, and show. Open 8:30 AM to 4 PM; until 11 PM on show nights. Reservations necessary. Major credit cards accepted (phone: 428-5048 or 428-2986).

Virginian The menu is a mix of fresh seafood, continental, and Bajan dishes — each prepared to order. Lobster and flying fish (several ways), shrimp, and prime ribs, are specialties; don't miss the yam croquettes or the Virginian crêpe finale. Open daily for dinner. Reservations unnecessary. Major credit cards accepted. In the *Seaview* hotel (phone: 427-7963).

Witch Doctor Tasty island cookery in a quaint setting. Favorites are split pea and pumpkin soup, fish fritters, chicken *piri-piri* (marinated in lime, garlic, and chili peppers, then baked), and ice cream with homemade rum-raisin topping. Open daily for dinner only. Reservations unnecessary. MasterCard and Visa accepted. St. Lawrence Gap (phone: 435-6581).

ST. JAMES

EXPENSIVE

Bagatelle Great House A lovely old estate house that has been transformed into a fine dining place. The setting is romantic, the food traditional Caribbean. Open daily for dinner. Reservations necessary. Major credit cards accepted. Bagatelle, St. Thomas (phone 421-6767).

La Cage aux Folles In palatial surroundings at Parish Bay, the menu features French, Chinese, and Caribbean fare. Open for dinner only; closed Tuesdays. Reservations necessary; reserve *way* ahead. Visa and MasterCard accepted. Parish Bay (phone: 424-2424).

Carambola Dine by candlelight on a seaside cliff at this open-air dining spot, which has a tropical atmosphere (except during the rainy season). There's a prize-winning chef and an extensive wine list, mostly with French vintages. Open for dinner only; closed Sundays. Reservations advised. Major credit cards accepted. Derricks (phone: 432-0832).

Château Créole Set in what was once a private home off the West Coast Road. The menu is international, with some creole and Bajan additions. The emphasis is on seafood; homemade ice cream and pies are featured desserts. Open daily for dinner. Reservations advised. Major credit cards accepted. Next to the *Glitter Bay* hotel (phone: 422-4116).

The Fathoms Dine outside on the beachfront deck, or in the airy, wood-and-tile rooms at this surfside eatery. The menu focuses on seafood prepared with interesting sauces, and the servings are ample. (But try to save room for the first-rate desserts.) Exotic tropical drinks are also featured. Open for lunch and dinner. Reservations advised for dinner. Major credit cards accepted. Paynes Bay (phone: 432-2568).

Koko's This real find offers adventurous "nu-Bajan" cuisine. Try the *koq-ka-doo* (chicken stuffed with banana and rum sauce) or the shrimp kristo (sailing in little *christophine* — squash — boats). Open daily for dinner only. Reservations advised. Major credit cards accepted. Overlooking the sea at Prospect (phone: 424-4557).

Piperade Elegant European and island cooking in a romantic island setting. Chef's pâté, shrimp *Barbade, callaloo,* and filets of beef are all commendable. Music accompanies your meal. Open daily for breakfast, lunch, and dinner. Reservations advised. Major credit cards accepted. In the garden of the *Glitter Bay* hotel (phone: 422-4111).

Raffles Easily the west coast's coziest, most exotic restaurant, it doesn't stop at creating the best in island atmosphere, but also delivers some of Barbados's best food, including specialties such as Bajan blackened fish and coconut pie. Given such attributes, it's a highly popular place. Open for dinner only; closed Sundays. Reservations necessary. Major credit cards accepted. Holetown (phone: 432-6557).

Reid's In a covered garden setting, with a highly polished mahogany bar, this place caters to a social, chic crowd. The menu includes lobster, shrimp creole, roast duckling, and a variety of veal and beef dishes. Open for dinner only; closed Mondays. Reservations advised. MasterCard and Visa accepted. In Derricks, across from the *Coconut Creek* hotel (phone: 432-7623).

Treasure Beach A popular spot offering island specialties in a charming, intimate setting. Open daily for breakfast, lunch, and dinner. Reservations advised for dinner. Major credit cards accepted. Paynes Bay (phone: 432-1346).

MODERATE

Coach House An attractive gathering place, popular for its informal atmosphere and simple, excellent food at reasonable prices. Live entertainment heats things up at night, and those so inclined can dance. Check the local listings. Open for lunch and dinner; dinner only on Saturdays. Reservations necessary for dinner. Major credit cards accepted. Paynes Bay near Sandy Lane (phone: 432-1163).

ELSEWHERE ON THE ISLAND

EXPENSIVE

Panoramic Formerly known as the *Pavilion,* it's a really fine dining room in the *Crane* hotel. Specialties: fresh fish, seafood (including langouste done with just the right touch), and a well-thought-out wine list. Large Sunday brunch. Open daily for breakfast, lunch, and dinner. Reservations advised. Major credit cards accepted. St. Philip (phone: 423-6220).

INEXPENSIVE

Atlantis Enid Maxwell sets out one of the island's best Sunday brunches, a buffet laden with Bajan treats such as dolphin, flying fish, turtle steaks, pumpkin fritters, pickled breadfruit, and incredible pies — all made from scratch in her family-staffed kitchen. Open daily for lunch and dinner. Reservations necessary for Sunday brunch. American Express only accepted. Overlooking Tent Bay near Bathsheba, St. Joseph (phone: 433-9445).

Kingsley Club Once a plantation owners' private club, now a charming little inn offering splendid prix fixe lunches. Specialties include split pea and pumpkin soup, baked yam casserole, and sinfully good coconut meringue pie. Open daily for breakfast, lunch, and dinner. Reservations advised. Major credit cards accepted. Near Bathsheba, in Cattlewash-on-Sea (phone: 433-9422).

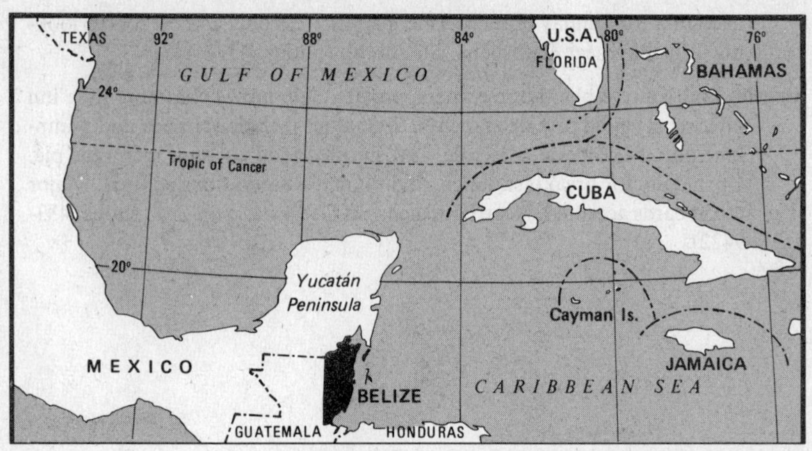
TEXAS
92°
88°
84°
U.S.A.
80°
76°
FLORIDA
BAHAMAS
GULF OF MEXICO
24°
Tropic of Cancer
CUBA
20°
Yucatán
Peninsula
Cayman Is.
MEXICO
JAMAICA
BELIZE
CARIBBEAN SEA
GUATEMALA
HONDURAS

Yucatán
Peninsula
MEXICO
Chetumal
Corozal
Corozal
Bay
Lamanai
Orange Walk
Rio Hondo
New R.
Ambergris
Cay
San Pedro
Crooked
Tree
Altun
Ha
Great
Barrier
Reef
CARIBBEAN SEA
Belize R.
Hattieville
Belize
City
Turneffe Is.
Lighthouse
Reef
Belmopan
San Ignacio
Xunantunich
Mullins
River
Dangriga
(Stann Creek)
Augustine
Victoria
Peak
3,680ft
Glover Reef
Caracol
Maya Mts
BELIZE
Seine Bight
Placencia
Big Creek
0
Miles
50
Lubaantun
San
Antonio
GULF OF HONDURAS
Punta Gorda
Barranco
Sarstoon
R.
GUATEMALA
HONDURAS

Belize

South of Mexico's Yucatán Peninsula and northeast of Guatemala is the small, wedge-shaped, developing country of Belize, formerly known as British Honduras. It's one of the few places in the Caribbean with literally hundreds of pristine, untouched islands. Even Ambergris Caye, the largest and most developed of these, has mile-long stretches of empty beach, perfect for sunning and swimming. Some of the world's best fishing can be enjoyed in the mangrove swamps and clear flat areas around the cays (pronounced *keys*), and the barrier reef — longest in the Western Hemisphere and second longest in the world — provides great diving.

But Belize is far more than the typical fun-in-the-sun, tropical Caribbean getaway. Primarily English-speaking, it offers US tourists the opportunity to explore a Central American country with relative ease. Not far from the beach are dense jungle, majestic karstic mountains, and rain forest. And its history is just as fascinating as its geography. This tiny country has been a melting pot for immigrants from Africa, the Caribbean, Mexico, Central America, Europe, and Asia for 300 years; British pirates, former slaves from East India, and Yucatán refugees from the War of the Castes all have left their mark here. However, Belize can trace its native culture and ancestry to well before that — to the mysterious ancient Maya, whose immense cities still stand throughout the region. Even while European settlements were being established on Belize's coast, Maya towns existed undetected just a few miles inland, protected by the thick jungle that only the Indians knew how to penetrate with ease. And while many of the early European settlements have been long since washed away, the mammoth religious structures of the Maya — their great temples and pyramids — endure.

Although Spain had claimed this part of the New World for itself, the area's lack of gold, the fierce resistance of the Maya, and the navigational hazards of the barrier reef kept its involvement here at a minimum. In fact, the first white men to colonize Belize were from Great Britain in the early 17th century — and even then only because they were shipwrecked off its coast.

These first British settlers discovered that Belize's swamps and jungles were rich in timber, and almost every type of fish in the Caribbean could be found feeding off the reef. The jungles also were full of game. Trade in logwood, which produces a dye, and then the lumber trade proved almost as profitable as pirating and, with slaves to supply the labor, were easier and safer.

English soldiers and sailors established logging camps here in the 1690s, and soon afterward Britain challenged Spain's claim to the area. The English government encouraged immigration, providing some limited financial and military support. By 1745, slaves accounted for 71% of the population, and by 1800 the number had risen to 86%. With the shift in economic activity from logwood to mahogany, more slaves, land, and capital were needed, and in 1787 the settlers began to pass a series of laws that soon resulted in a dozen settlers owning four-fifths of all the land.

The country abolished slavery in 1838, but because most of the land was controlled by "mahogany lords," the freed men were forced to seek employment with their former masters, who passed a system of labor laws designed to keep workers under firm control. In addition, the practice of "advancing" wages bound workers to their employers by keeping them in debt. This system of land and labor control lasted into the middle of the 20th century.

Belize became British Honduras in 1862 because local British residents feared attacks by mestizos (people of mixed Spanish and Maya ancestry) and Spaniards from Mexico escaping the War of the Castes (1848–58), a conflict between Mexico's original Indian residents and Spanish colonists. Three years earlier, Great Britain and Guatemala had signed a treaty fixing the borders of Guatemala and Belize. However, boundary problems exist to this day, as both Mexico and Guatemala continue to claim that, as inheritors of the Spanish lands in the area, they are entitled to Belizean territory. (In late 1991, Guatemala established diplomatic relations with Belize, and at press time the two countries were negotiating a treaty to give Guatemala partial access to Belizean territorial waters in the Caribbean. Guatemala has said that if this agreement is reached, it will abandon its claim to the rest of the country, but Belizeans remain wary.)

Along with British immigration came the beginnings of a Caribbean influence. The earliest Caribbean immigration was involuntary — slave labor brought from Jamaica in the early 1700s to work in the lumber industry. Since then, Belize has become a mosaic of ethnic groups, cultures, and customs. While the country's population was just 6,000 in 1840, it had jumped to over 25,000 by 1861; to 60,000 by 1942; and today stands at about 190,000. The main groups are mestizos (now the majority), Creoles (people of mixed black and white heritage), and Garifuna (the progeny of escaped African slaves and Carib Indians). There also are a number of people of Spanish and East Indian descent, some Chinese and Arabs, and a small Mennonite community of European origin. The most recent immigrants are some 4,700 Salvadoran and Guatemalan refugees who resettled in Belize in the late 1980s, fleeing wars in their countries.

After a slow process of evolution toward more representative government, a constitution written in 1964 provided total self-government for the first time. As early as 1961, the British government had made it plain that British Honduras (the name "Belize" was officially adopted in 1971) could become independent whenever it wished. However, because of a well-founded fear that without Britain's protection their country would soon be overrun by neighboring Guatemala, Belizeans chose to retain their British ties. After Britain agreed to retain a small protective military presence in the country, Belize declared itself an independent nation on September 21, 1981, and it has managed its own affairs with pride and enthusiasm ever since.

Belize guards its environment as fiercely as it does its freedom. More than 25 wildlife and archaeological reserves have been established in the past 10 years, including the 100,000-acre Cockscomb Basin, the world's first and only jaguar sanctuary. One major strategy to reconcile the growing influx of visitors with the country's environmental needs is ecotourism, which encourages people to explore regions without harming the resident wildlife.

Unless ecotourism is successful, Belize probably will not remain an unspoiled destination much longer. More and more North Americans are discovering its lush, almost virgin coastline and its secluded Maya ruins. While not offering much in the way of creature comforts, Belize does promise adventure and the chance to experience one of the last vestiges of nature in the wild.

Belize At-a-Glance

FROM THE AIR

Belize is a patchwork of subtropical lowlands, marshes, and swamps, with mountains and forests to the west, and beaches, the massive barrier reef, and some 200 offshore cays and islands to the east. It is on the Caribbean coast of the Yucatán Peninsula, separated from Mexico in the north by the Río Hondo and from Guatemala to the southwest by the Sarstoon River. The tiny nation is only 184 miles north to south and 75 miles east to west at its widest point, a total of 9,000 square miles of landmass, one-third of which is used for farming and ranching. The rest is rugged jungle terrain, mountains, and swamps; 266 square miles of offshore cays; and about 300 miles of rivers.

The first view of Belize from the air is of the 185-mile-long barrier reef — second in the world in size only to Australia's Great Barrier Reef. Interspersed are cays and islands of all sizes stretched like a chain set in the blue-green Caribbean Sea. The desolate swamps and deep jungles in the north, dotted with small towns and villages, gradually give rise to the vast Maya Mountains in the southwest. These are topped by Victoria Peak, which, at 3,680 feet, is the highest peak in the entire Cockscomb Mountain range. The country is traversed by a number of rivers: The New River runs parallel to the Río Hondo in the north, and there are several small rivers in the south. The Belize River originates in Guatemala and crosses the country's central region from west to east.

The country sits on a vast continental block of limestone that extends 800 miles north to south, and about 400 miles across. This ledge slopes at a downward angle, so that Belize City on the Caribbean coast is only 18 inches above sea level, and high water easily flows inland, causing bad flooding.

Most visitors will arrive at Phillip S.W. Goldson International Airport, 10 miles north of Belize City. Belize has some 190,000 inhabitants, of whom 60,000 live in Belize City. In addition to Belize City, there are seven towns (including Belmopan, the capital), and 160 villages and settlements of varying size. There is more jungle and mountain than rural or urban life, even including the resorts on the coast and the cays.

SPECIAL PLACES

BELIZE CITY Hot, humid, and an interesting mixture of British colonial architecture and small-town ambience, this community is the only real city in the country. It is filled with old, mostly wooden buildings and houses that give the entire place a tumbledown feel, the effect broken only occasionally by Victorian government buildings.

The most colorful things about the city are its street names: The Queen's Square uses animal names such as Antelope, Armadillo, and Seagull Streets; the Mesopotamia area has Middle Eastern names like Euphrates, Cairo, and Tigris; and the Caribbean Shores area relies on church figures for names.

The city's small business and shopping area is located on the few blocks on either side of the Belize Swing Bridge. On the southern side of the bridge are Albert and Queen Streets, which make up the commercial district, and Regent Street, which houses most of the government buildings. On Regent Street is St. John's Cathedral. Built between 1812 and 1826, it was the first Anglican church in Central America. A block away, on Southern Foreshore near the Swing Bridge, is the Baron Bliss Institute, dedicated to the multimillionaire who left $2 million to Belize in the 1920s; it contains carved stone monuments from the ancient Maya ceremonial center of Caracol, in the Maya Mountains. The institute's library is open to the public daily from 9 AM to noon and from 3 to 5 PM (phone: 2-77267).

Located on the northern side of the Swing Bridge is the Fort George neighborhood, the city's classiest area, with fine old plantation-style homes lining the waterfront. Standing center stage is the *Radisson Fort George* hotel (2 Marine Parade), which opened in 1953. At the northeast end of the bridge is the Paslow Building, an interesting bit of colonial architecture. It contains the post office, which in turn houses the Belize Philatelic Bureau. With drawings of wildlife, shells, historical events, the British royal family, and Belizean patriots, Belizean stamps are unusual and inexpensive mementos. The nearby *Book Centre* (144 N. Front St.; phone: 2-77457) is a good source for American newspapers and magazines as well as books on Belizean history.

For an interesting excursion, drop in on George Gabb, reputedly Belize's best carver. His studio, on the Northern Highway going out of town (it's just after the Texaco station), is open every day from 8 AM to 6:30 PM. The genial Gabb will demonstrate how he carves the native ziricote hardwood, which, when cut across the grain, reveals a brown and black "rose" on a white background.

BELMOPAN The capital of Belize was carved out of the jungle in the late 1960s after Hurricane Hattie seriously damaged Belize City in 1961. It was occupied by the government in July 1970. At first, many of the Belizeans who worked in Belmopan commuted from Belize City, but over the years the town's population has grown to about 7,000, and now the capital has developed a personality of its own. Its Assembly Building, which dominates the government complex, was designed to represent a Maya temple. On Mondays, Wednesdays, and Fridays from 1:30 to 4 PM, the Archaeology Commission conducts guided tours through its vault, which houses a collection of artifacts from the country's archaeological sites. (There is no museum within the country.) Call ahead to make arrangements (phone: 8-22106).

GUANACASTE NATIONAL PARK About 2 miles outside Belmopan, at the juncture of the Western and Hummingbird Highways, this park offers 50 acres of forest. The name comes from the colossal guanacaste tree growing on the southwestern edge of the park; it rises to a height of about 400 feet, masked in huge orchids and bromeliads that cling to its branches like giant *Christmas* ornaments. Hundreds of other tree species thrive here, too, including the unusual mammee apple, bookut, and quamwood. Be sure to bring a swimsuit — a dip in the clean, bubbling Belize River is a must (no phone).

BELIZE ZOO In 1982, American biologist Sharon Matola started this zoo with a few primitive pens nestled among the trees. Today, it's an outstanding example of the habitat-style zoo, with more than 100 species of native animals residing in spacious patches of forest veiled in wire mesh. Pebbled paths pass the homes of howler monkeys, crocodiles, jaguars, marguays, king vultures, great black hawks, toucans, pacas, anteaters, and many other beautiful, exotic creatures. Matola, who still runs the zoo, implores visitors to respect the animals with clever, hand-painted wooden signs with messages such as "I'm a great black hawk, but guys who take shots at me are Great Big Turkeys!" The zoo is open daily from 10 AM to 4:30 PM; there's an admission charge. Take the Western Highway 28 miles west of Belize City, then look for the little wooden sign (no phone).

CAYO DISTRICT This area — Belize's wealthiest — stretches from just west of Belmopan to the Guatemalan border. Savvy adventurers are discovering the region's jungle lodges, guest ranches, Maya ruins, and picturesque byways. A popular day trip is to Mountain Pine Ridge, a national forest reserve encompassing hundreds of miles of natural pine, bald hills, orchids, wildlife, and rivulets. Its most famous attraction is the 1,000-foot

Hidden Valley Falls, which actually tumble 1,300 feet into the valley below. There are 15 miles of roads to cover here, and a picnic should be the order of the day. All necessary facilities are available for travelers, campers, and day-trippers.

Some of Belize's most compelling scenery lies in Cayo at Spanish Lookout, where Mennonite farmlands cover the landscape. It's reached by a 6-mile trek over a very rocky, rutted road that angles north from the Western Highway west of Belmopan. You can see straw-hatted Mennonite farmers driving horse-drawn buggies laden with watermelon and corn.

San Ignacio, the capital of the district, sits on the bank of the Macal River (a branch of the Belize River) in the misty foothills of the Maya Mountains 72 miles west of Belize City. The town can be the jumping-off point for a variety of activities, including exploring Maya ruins, mountain climbing, canoeing and swimming in the Macal River, and horseback riding. High-quality accommodations abound in the area (see *Checking In*). Local hotels and *Mountain Equestrian Trails (MET;* Mountain Pine Ridge Rd.; phone: 92-3310; fax: 82-3235) offer tours into the Maya Mountains and to Tikal in Guatemala. *MET* also can arrange horseback riding trips.

XUNATUNICH About 80 miles southwest of Belize City, near the Guatemalan border, this archaeological site (whose name is pronounced *Shoo*-na-*too*-nich) is dominated by its impressive, 130-foot El Castillo pyramid. The climb to the top is challenging, but the panoramic view of Belize's mountains and Guatemala provides ample reward. One of the best excavated and most popular of the country's ruins, the site is filled with stone buildings that are more than 1,400 years old and boasts an extensive sampling of artifacts from the ancient Maya civilization. Admission charge. To reach the site, drive southwest on the Western Highway from San Ignacio about 2 miles to the small village of Succotz, then cross the Macal River via the hand-cranked ferry (give the ferry operator a small tip), which operates daily from 9 AM to noon and 1 to 5 PM.

A WORD ABOUT ARTIFACTS

Remember that Maya artifacts are not to be removed from any ruin, and the authorities are very strict about enforcing this rule. This includes items that locals may attempt to sell to you, illegally. Government permits are required for any artifact that is taken from the country.

DANGRIGA (STANN CREEK) On a lovely stretch of sand, Dangriga rests along the sea 105 miles south of Belize City. Though accessible by the Southern Highway, the road's rough dirt surface wreaks havoc on cars and passengers alike, and bus service is inconvenient, so the town is best reached by air (*Maya Airways* has daily service). Most of its 8,000 residents are

Garifuna, who first settled here in 1823 — the event is celebrated here annually (see *Special Events*). The barrier reef is a short boat ride from Dangriga, and fishing, swimming, snorkeling, or diving excursions can be arranged through the *Pelican Beach* resort (phone: 5-22044), the *Bone Fish* hotel (phone: 5-22165), the *Rio Mar* (phone: 5-22201), and the *Sophie* hotel (phone: 5-22789). Hotel staff can help visitors find Benjamin, the famous Belizean painter who lives and works here.

A few miles south of Dangriga, on the beach, is the Garifuna village of Hopkins, and the world's first and only jaguar preserve is in Cockscomb Basin, 30 miles south. Ask at the *Pelican Beach* for information about the park.

PLACENCIA South of Dangriga, this tiny fishing village is strung along the beach of a narrow, 16-mile peninsula. It's reached by boat from either Mango Creek or Big Creek, where there's also an airstrip (stand under the palm tree to wait for your flight). It's also possible to drive here in a four-wheel-drive vehicle, but the access road is not in good condition, especially when it's raining. The beaches here are the loveliest in Belize; lately, Americans and Europeans have made this a trendy place for swimming, sunbathing, diving, fishing, and nightlife. There are several good hotels here, particularly the *Rum Point Inn* (see *Checking In*), and nearby Seine Bight, north of Placencia, is an interesting Garifuna village.

PUNTA GORDA Flanked by hills on the west and northwest, Punta Gorda lies at the southern end of Belize. The capital of the Toledo district, its population is primarily a mixture of Garifuna, Creole, Maya, East Indian, and Chinese. The town overlooks the Bay of Honduras, with Guatemala and Honduras only a few miles across the sea. Though Punta Gorda (nicknamed P.G. by Belizeans) is not designed for the tourist trade, it's worth a look, with its funky clapboard homes, roosters wandering the streets, and corner groceries advertising fresh pig snouts and gibnut (a large rodent considered a delicacy). There are no good hotels here, but hard-core adventurers will find plenty to do, as some of Central America's most remote Maya ruins and villages rest in the hills just above town. Also, boats can be hired to Livingston, Guatemala, for river trips to little-explored areas.

A few miles away from the huge promontory at the southern end of Punta Gorda is the site of the former Toledo settlement, home of US Civil War refugees, and nearby are several picturesque Maya villages. There is a primitive hotel, *Bol's Hilltop* (phone: 7-22144), in the village of San Antonio. A mile north of San Pedro Colombia is the path to the ancient Maya ceremonial center of Lubaantun. The mile-long trail to the site is very muddy, except in the dry season. The site itself, however, which is made up of temples built from stone blocks, is well worth the effort. Several miles north of the Punta Gorda–San Antonio turnoff and a few miles south of Big Falls is the trail into Nim Li Punit, a Maya ceremonial center noted for its carved stone monuments, or stelae, which show ancient rulers "letting blood" into braziers to appease the gods.

ALTUN HA Only 30 miles north of Belize City is the ancient Maya ceremonial center of Altun Ha. It was here that a carved jade head — 6 inches long and weighing 10 pounds — of the sun god Kinich Ahau was unearthed during the 1960s by a *Royal Ontario Museum* team. While an important find, it was only one of many artifacts (including bowls and jade objects) discovered in these 3 square miles of ruins. Drive toward Orange Walk on the Northern Highway. Turn right at Maskall Road (also the old highway to Orange Walk) and continue on for about 15 minutes. There is a sign on the left marking the site.

CROOKED TREE WILDLIFE SANCTUARY Located 33 miles northwest of Belize City and 2 miles off the Northern Highway, this wildlife refuge consists of a network of lagoons, swamps, and waterways that provide a variety of habitats for Belize's flora and fauna. There are herons, snowy and great egrets, and all five species of kingfishers, crocodiles, black howler monkeys, coatimundi (a tropical mammal related to the raccoon), and many other animals. Further information can be obtained from the Belize Audubon Society (PO Box 1001, Belize City; phone: 2-77369). Visitors can now stay at the *Crooked Tree* resort (phone: 2-77745).

LAMANAI Hidden in the jungle of northern Belize, about 50 miles northwest of Belize City, is the fascinating ancient trading and ceremonial center of Lamanai, with spectacular temples and masks still intact. The city was probably first inhabited some 3,500 years ago. During the 1970s, a team of archaeologists uncovered more than 700 buildings here. Of those, a 112-foot temple is perhaps the most impressive. Because Lamanai is spread out along miles of the New River lagoon and can be reached only by a 2- to 3-hour boat ride, a guide is necessary. Nearby *Maruba* resort (phone: 3-22199; see *Checking In*) offers excellent tours, complete with gourmet picnic lunch.

About 30 miles upriver from Lamanai, and 66 miles north of Belize City, is Orange Walk Town. Though it doesn't offer much of interest to travelers, 3 miles west of here is Cuello, the oldest Maya site yet discovered, dating from 2500 BC. It is on Yo Creek Road, behind the Cuello Brothers Rum Distillery, Central America's largest.

COROZAL A Maya stronghold known as Chetumal until the middle of the 19th century, Corozal is the northernmost town in Belize. In addition to its location on Corozal Bay, which is ideal for swimming and fishing, it has Santa Rita Corozal, a Maya ruin, and, nearby, Cerros Maya, another archaeological site accessible only by boat; make arrangements at *Tony's Inn* (phone: 4-22055), *Adventure Inn* (phone: 4-22187), or *Menzies Travel and Tours* (phone: 4-22725).

EXTRA SPECIAL More than 75% of the visitors to Belize spend their vacations on one of the offshore islands such as Cay Caulker, Turneffe Island, Glover's Reef, or St. George's Cay. But Ambergris Caye is the most popular with visitors from the US. The 30-mile-long island sits 36 miles northeast of Belize City, just 15 minutes away by small plane. (Both ***Island Air*** and ***Tropic Air*** have daily regularly scheduled flights from Belize City.) Arrivals land on the 2,500-foot paved strip that is just a few steps from the heart of the island's only village, San Pedro, population 4,000. The streets of San Pedro are pure white sand, and almost everything is just a short, easy stroll away. Most of the places to stay are within a quarter mile of the landing strip. Many resorts are spread out both north and south of the village and can be reached only by boat.

What's most exciting about Ambergris Caye is the magnificent barrier reef just 300 yards offshore. Nearly 185 miles long, it is the longest reef in the Western Hemisphere and a diver's paradise. Underwater visibility is more than 100 feet at Ambergris Caye, and what a spectacle there is: crimson parrot fish and yellowtail damselfish; zebra-striped sergeant majors; green moray eels (peaceful, unless provoked); and many more sea creatures, gliding and darting amid a staggering variety of coral and sea plants. Off the southern tip of the island, an underwater national park was created to protect the natural beauty of the area. Snorkeling equipment rental, glass-bottom boats, and diving trips can be arranged through most of the hotels in San Pedro.

At night stroll over to the ***Navigator Bar,*** at the ***Barrier Reef*** hotel (Main St.; phone: 26-2075). Here you will find a mix of locals, Americans, and visiting British troops who have come for rest and recuperation from their mainland bases. With its white sand floor, bamboo decor, formica tables, and hi-fi tapes, this is ***the*** nighttime gathering place of Ambergris Caye. Other favorite watering holes are the ***Tackle Box*** (on the end of a pier at the ***Coral Beach*** hotel; phone: 26-2013) and the bar at ***Ramón's Village.***

Sources and Resources

TOURIST INFORMATION

The Belize Tourist Board (83 North Front St., Belize City; phone: 2-77213; fax: 2-77490) can provide literature, maps, advice, and help. Newspapers are in English, and there is a tourist guide of sorts, but it's not very helpful. For information about Belize tourist offices in the US, see GETTING READY TO GO.

Note: Due to an increase in robberies and related assaults in Belize, the

US State Department cautions visitors to Belize not to walk alone on city streets at night, wear jewelry or carry valuables, or travel alone to remote tourist sites. For up-to-date travel advisory information, check with the US State Department's Citizens' Emergency Center (phone: 202-647-5225).

LOCAL COVERAGE The *Amandala,* the *Reporter,* the *Belize Times, Liberty,* and the *San Pedro Sun* are the major weekly newspapers. The *People's Pulse,* another weekly paper, the *Belize Review,* a monthly, and *Belize Currents,* a bimonthly, also carry information on local events and activities.

RADIO AND TELEVISION

The Broadcasting Corporation of Belize and KREM Radio broadcast in English and Spanish.

TELEPHONE

When calling from the US dial 011 (international access code) + 501 (country code) + (city code) + (local number). To call from anywhere else, the access code may vary, so contact the local operator. When calling from one city in Belize to another, dial 0 + (city code) + (local number). When dialing within a city, use only the four- or five-digit local number. The city code for Belize City is 2. The telephone numbers listed in this chapter include city codes.

ENTRY REQUIREMENTS

To enter Belize, US and Canadian citizens must have a current passport; the immigration office at the point of entry will stamp a visa in your passport. Crossing the border from Mexico or Guatemala to Belize is a fairly simple process, although it can take an hour or more if there are crowds. When you leave Mexico, you must relinquish your Mexican tourist card. If you plan to return to Mexico from Belize, you will be issued a new tourist card upon re-entry. Another option is to stop at the Mexican Embassy in Belize City (20 Park St.; phone: 2-30193) to pick up a replacement card.

Note, however, that travel between Mexico and Belize can be difficult unless you're driving your own car. There are no car rental companies in the area on either side of the border, and taxi fares are quite expensive ($15 to $25 just to cross the border). Buses run regularly and are much cheaper, but the trip can be uncomfortable and slow.

CLIMATE AND CLOTHES

Belize is a subtropical area with temperatures ranging from the mid-70s in January to the upper 90s in August. At midday, shade temperatures of 95F to 100F are not uncommon. Rainfall in the northern part of the country averages 50 inches per year, but in the south 200 inches per year is normal. The rainy season generally runs from June through December, and the driest period is from February through May. During the rains, Belize is susceptible to hurricanes, and the humidity hovers around 80%.

Extremely light, informal clothing is the norm, and with good reason. Although some businessmen do wear jackets and ties, it is unnecessary. Women tend to wear summery dresses to dinner, although tropical safari gear might be more appropriate the rest of the time. Shorts are fine on the offshore islands, but not in town.

MONEY

The official currency is the Belize dollar (BZ), which has been stabilized at $1 US to $2 BZ. Banks generally are open from 8 AM to 1 PM weekdays; on Fridays they're also open from 3 to 6 PM. Hotels usually will exchange currency with little or no commission. If arriving from Mexico, do not exchange Mexican pesos if possible, as the exchange rate is very poor in Belize. All prices in this chapter are quoted in US dollars.

LANGUAGE

English is the official language, but it comes with a variety of accents, British, Caribbean, and Spanish among them. Many Belizeans speak Spanish, Chinese, Maya, or creole, and there are several German-speaking Mennonite settlements.

TIME

The country is on central standard time, which means that for most of the year it has the same time as Chicago; when the US switches to daylight saving time, however, Belize does not.

CURRENT

Most of Belize uses 110-volt, 60-cycle current, just like the US.

TIPPING

Very few restaurants add a service charge, so plan to add 15% if you're satisfied. Many hotels add a 10% service charge, but the staff rarely receives this; leave hotel maids about $1 per day. Taxi drivers should be tipped (about 10% of the fare), and hotel bellhops and airport porters get about 50¢ per bag.

GETTING AROUND

Within the cities (once again, a relative term), transportation is easy, but once in the countryside, roads are extremely variable. The main highway in northern Belize is very good, and the Western Highway, now that it is paved, also makes for good driving. The Hummingbird Highway south from Belmopan may be the worst road in the country, but it passes through some of the most magnificent scenery. The Southern Highway is also treacherous, as it is composed of a hard dirt that can damage a car's suspension and chassis even in good weather; during the rainy season, the road often floods.

BUS Long-haul buses between towns and villages aren't very comfortable, but they do try to maintain some type of schedule. Fares range from $1 to $4, according to the destination. Local Belize City buses are about 50¢. Bus service to Belize is available from Guatemala City (the fare is about $12), and from Chetumal, Mexico (fare $3.50), but note that crossing the border by bus can be difficult and time-consuming.

CAR RENTAL Many of the country's roads have been improved recently, and all major roads in the north are paved. If you decide to drive, expect to pay $70 to $125 a day (less if you rent for several days) with unlimited mileage. Gas will cost about $2.50 a gallon. Beware of rental companies offering seemingly bargain rates on big, old, American gas-guzzlers. By the time you've paid for gas, you've spent more than if you'd rented a new four-wheel-drive vehicle. Besides, you'll need the four-wheel-drive if you decide to venture off the beaten path — and you should. All the major car rental companies are in Belize City; however, some hotel owners will rent their car (or a friend's) if you decide you need a vehicle in an outlying area. The best rental company in Belize City is *Budget Rent-A-Car* (771 Bella Vista; phone: 2-32435; fax: 2-30237). Other good firms are *World Auto Rentals* (Phillip S.W. Goldson International Airport; phone: 25-2586; fax: 2-32940), *National* (126 Freetown Rd.; phone: 25-2294; fax: 2-31586), or *Hertz* (Northern Hwy., 2½ miles from Belize City; phone: 2-32981; fax: 2-32053). A valid US driver's license is all that is needed to drive in Belize.

FERRY The *Andrea I* and *II* run afternoons from Belize City to Ambergris Caye. The trip is $10 one way. The boats can be boarded at the waterfront at the *Bellevue* hotel on Southern Foreshore.

TAXI There are no meters, but the rates are set by the government. However, if you are leaving from a hotel, check what the fare should be beforehand, as taxi drivers here have been known to overcharge. From Phillip S.W. Goldson International Airport to Belize City the fare is $20, and there are always cabs. Watch out for drivers who will compute the fare in Belize dollars and try to collect in US dollars.

INTER- AND INTRA-ISLAND FLIGHTS

Tropic Air (San Pedro, Ambergris Caye; phone: 26-2012; 800-422-3435 from the US; fax: 26-2338) has several regularly scheduled flights each day from Belize City to San Pedro on Ambergris Caye and can arrange charters to anywhere in the country. It also flies on an irregular schedule to Tikal, Guatemala. *Maya Airways* (Belize City; phone: 2-72312; 800-522-3419 from the US; fax: 2-30585) has daily scheduled flights to towns in southern and northern Belize, and infrequent service to other destinations within the country. *Island Air* (phone: 26-2435 in San Pedro or 2-31140 in Belize City; fax: 26-2192) also has daily scheduled flights to San Pedro.

SPECIAL EVENTS

National Day is the big holiday in Belize. It kicks off on September 10 with parades, floats, sports activities, patriotic rallies, and beauty contests. The celebrations culminate on September 21, Belize's *Independence Day.* The second week in November is devoted to tourism, with booths, displays, and food. The arrival of the Garifuna from Honduras is celebrated on November 19 in Dangriga and nearby villages with costumed dancers, booths, and displays. On March 9, a regatta is held on the Belize River to honor Baron Bliss, the country's major benefactor. The *Fiesta de San José* (held in March or April) at San José Succotz climaxes with a reenactment of a battle between the Moors and the Spaniards. In July, the *Fiesta del Virgen del Carmen,* at Benque Viejo del Carmen, features costumes and much dancing in the streets.

SHOPPING

Belize is not exactly a shopper's paradise. The in-bond stores do carry watches, perfume, and other imports at duty-free prices, but it is hardly comparable to other free ports in the Caribbean. There are nice rosewood carvings, and woodwork carved from ziricote, the two-tone wood native to the area. The government operates *Cottage Craft Industries* (26 Albert St., Belize City; phone: 2-72359). Good buys include straw goods made from jipijapa straw in the Punta Gorda area, jewelry made from Belizean black coral, and slate sculptures by Maya villagers. And though you may be tempted, remember, it's illegal to bring tortoiseshell items into the US.

SPORTS

Fishing in the nation's rivers and off the coast is the main attraction, closely followed by scuba diving and snorkeling in and around the barrier reef.

CLIMBING The Maya Mountains, in the southwest, present a challenge to even experienced climbers. Victoria's Peak, at 3,680 feet, crowns the Cockscomb Range. The Chief Forest Officer at the Ministry of Natural Resources (Belmopan, Belize; phone: 8-22333) will put you in touch with a qualified guide.

HORSEBACK RIDING For guided tours and trail rides ($60 per person for a half-day's riding; $100 for a full day), contact the *Mountains Equestrian Trails* (Mile 8, Mountain Pine Ridge RA, Cayo District; mailing address: PO Box 1158, Belize City, Belize, Central America).

HUNTING A license is required, and you must be accompanied by a guide holding a government concession. Jaguars and ocelots are protected by law, but the Belize jungles abound with other game animals, such as wild pig, deer, game birds, and waterfowl. Ask the Chief Forest Officer, Ministry of Natural Resources (see above), for details and recommendations. Also contact the Commissioner of Police in Belmopan (phone: 8-22224) if you plan to bring firearms into the country.

SNORKELING AND SCUBA Boasting the second-longest barrier reef in the world and with three of the four authentic coral atolls in the Caribbean, Belize offers every conceivable underwater terrain to divers — from the novice to the most experienced. Experienced divers shouldn't miss Jacques Cousteau's famous Belize Blue Hole cave surrounded by coral reef, considered by some to be one of the Seven Underwater Wonders of the World. Most hotels, especially on Ambergris Caye, Turneffe, Glover's Reef, and Lighthouse Reef, offer year-round open water certification with internationally certified instructors using state-of-the-art equipment. The *Aggressor Fleet* operates the *Belize Aggressor I* and *II,* offering the serious diver Belize's best.

The dive shops in San Pedro are very well equipped with state-of-the-art diving equipment. The minimum cost for a boat, with guide, is about $50 a day with two dives. *Reef Divers, Ltd.* (phone: 26-2173; 800-426-0226 from the US), *Ramon's* (phone: 26-2071; 601-649-1990 in the US), *Sun Breeze* (phone: 26-2191 or 26-2347), *Journey's End* (phone: 26-2173; 800-447-0474 from the US), *Victoria House* (phone: 26-2067; 800-247-5159 from the US), and *Paradise* resort (phone: 26-2021) in San Pedro on Ambergris Caye have full-time internationally certified dive masters/guides. Several one- and two-boat operators are also certified. Check before you make reservations. Try snorkeling; it is readily available, and like scuba here, truly spectacular.

SPORT FISHING Any fish in the Caribbean can be caught off the coast of Belize: deep sea for bills and wahoo; reef fishing for barracuda, grouper, and snapper; flat fishing, light tackle and fly fishing for bone and tarpon; and river fishing for tarpon and snook. The barrier reef paralleling the coast harbors a huge variety of game fish, with simple offshore fishing lodges. For more information, contact *Turneffe Island Lodge* (phone: 800-338-8149 from the US), *Journey's End* (phone: 800-447-0474 from the US), *Paradise* hotel (phone: 2-62083), or *El Pescador* (phone: 26-2398). *Angler Adventures* (PO Box 872, Old Lyme, CT 06371; phone: 203-434-9624) offers fishing safari trips. The *Belize River Lodge* (phone: 2-52002), on the Belize River, runs both deep-sea and light tackle trips.

Average cost for a boat, guide, and equipment is about $125 per day for up to four persons. Most of the hotels and resorts have facilities available, and private guides can be hired. For information, contact the *Belize Tourism Industry Association* (phone: 2-75717 or 2-78709; fax: 2-78710).

SWIMMING AND SUNNING Swimming is good off the sandy beaches of the cays and on the southeast coast. Sunbathing on your very own cay is tops.

TENNIS The two nicest courts are at the *Pickwick Club* in Belize City, but it is open only to members and their guests. The only hotel with tennis courts is *Journey's End* on Ambergris Caye.

NIGHTLIFE

Belize City is not a night town. There's dancing late in the evenings at the *Château Caribbean* and *Bellevue* hotels, and quiet music and conversation at the bar of the *Fort George* hotel or *Villa* hotel, overlooking the harbor. *Legends* (30 Queen St.; phone: 2-30436) is currently a favorite after-dark gathering place, as is the *Hard Rock Café* (35 Queen St.; phone: 2-32041), although it's not a member of the world-famous chain. But perhaps the best nightclub in Belize is the *Cahal Pech* disco in San Ignacio (phone: 92-2736). Named for nearby ruins and perched on a hill overlooking the Maya Mountains about a quarter mile from the *San Ignacio* hotel, it's a scenic spot that rocks well into the wee hours.

Best in the Country

CHECKING IN

Belize has no luxury hotels, and US travelers may find that none of its accommodations suit sophisticated tastes. But visitors seeking local character, charm, and hospitality will find them in abundance. Jungle lodges and beach villas, many owned and run by American expatriates, offer the chance to get to know this fascinating country on a personal level. Meals are festive events; the owners and guests dine together at one big table, discussing the latest issues in local politics and conservation. In Belize City, several larger chain hotels provide more modern facilities. Offshore, Ambergris Caye offers many comfortable motels and guesthouses, as well as resorts. Lighthouse Reef and the Turneffe Isles have only one lodge each, and visitors may well feel as if they're living on their own private island.

Many accommodations in Belize have no air conditioning; ask in advance. Generally, air conditioning is unnecessary in the winter, but summer can be suffocatingly hot.

In winter, with the exception of some resorts on Ambergris Caye and some fishing resorts, which can be very pricey ($300 or more a night), expect to pay $90 to $150 for a double room, including meals, in hotels we describe as expensive. Places in the moderate range cost between $55 and $90; inexpensive accommodations will cost less than $55 a night. Prices are reduced somewhat in the summer, but the strict Caribbean winter/summer seasonal rate changes don't affect Belize as much as the island nations. All Belize hotels add a 5% room tax, and some will add a 10% service charge. The telephone numbers listed below include city codes. Remember to dial zero before the city code when calling from one city in Belize to another; when calling within a single city use only the local number (the last four or five digits). For information about dialing from elsewhere, see "Telephone" earlier in this chapter.

BELIZE CITY

EXPENSIVE

Belize River Lodge A unique, 12-room lodge for the angler. This hotel sits on the fish-packed Belize River, and guests are taken on fishing excursions, overnight if desired. There's a pleasant restaurant featuring native cooking. Package rates include guides, boats, and all meals. Located in Ladyville, near Phillip S.W. Goldson International Airport, but accessible only by boat (the lodge provides transportation). Advance reservations are necessary (phone: 25-2002; fax: 25-2298).

Biltmore Plaza One of the newer large hotels in Belize. This 90-room property has a cozy atmosphere, with a gazebo, and a fish pond and garden inside a central plaza. There's also a pool, a restaurant, and a bar. On Northern Rd., only 6½ miles from Phillip S.W. Goldson International Airport (phone: 2-32302; 800-327-3573 from the US; fax: 2-32301).

Holiday Inn Villa Belize Recently renovated, this modern hostelry has 41 tastefully decorated rooms, many with splendid ocean views. All have private baths, air conditioning, and plush carpets. *Top of the Town,* the fifth-floor restaurant, is one of the best in the city (see *Eating Out*). 13 Cork St. (phone: 2-32800; 800-HOLIDAY from the US; fax: 2-30276).

Radisson Fort George One of Belize's more comfortable properties, with 70 air conditioned rooms (30 in a newer, 7-story glass wing), all with private bath. The hotel is run in a proper British manner. Most popular among businesspeople and older tourists, it makes a good home base for touring the country. There is a gift shop, a spacious starched-white-tablecloth restaurant with a picture-window view of the harbor, a lounge with music on weekends, and a pool. Marine Parade (phone: 2-77400; 800-333-3333 from the US; fax: 2-73820).

Ramada Royal Reef This 4-story establishment has 120 air conditioned guestrooms, including a presidential suite. On-premises amenities include a pool, a restaurant, a gift shop, a travel agency, and a marina. There are also conference rooms that can accommodate up to 400. Located on the edge of the waterfront on what was originally the Barrach Green, where Charles Lindbergh landed his *Spirit of St. Louis* (phone: 2-32670; 800-228-9898 from the US; fax: 2-32660).

MODERATE

Bellevue Once a colonial private home, this place now has 38 air conditioned guestrooms. Its elegant restaurant is very popular among locals and visitors (see *Eating Out*). Amenities include a pool and the *Laughing Parrot,* an outdoor bar. 5 Southern Foreshore Rd. (phone: 2-77051; fax: 2-73253).

Château Caribbean It's a converted mansion overlooking the sea, with 25 clean rooms, air conditioning, and private baths. Off-street parking is also provided, a nice extra. There's also a very good restaurant and bar. 6 Marine Parade (phone: 2-30800; fax: 2-30900).

Royal Orchid Nestled in the heart of the city, this place has 22 comfortable, air conditioned rooms. There's a beautiful restaurant on the top floor that offers a full view of the city. Corner of New Rd. and Douglas Jones Rd. (phone: 2-32783; fax: 2-32789).

INEXPENSIVE

Belize Guest House An old colonial-style dwelling that sits on the edge of the sea. There are 6 rooms: 2 with private bath; 3 air conditioned. Suzuki jeep rental available. A cabaña on the shore also can be rented. 2 Hudson St. (phone: 2-77569).

Colton House Perhaps the best bargain in Belize City, this gem is located a block from the sea in the city's best neighborhood. The 1930s house is inviting, featuring colonial decor and a spacious front porch with swings. The 4 extra-large rooms have high ceilings and individual entrances, and 2 have private baths. 9 Cork St. (phone: 2-44666).

Fort Street Guest House Belize City's first bed and breakfast establishment is in a charming colonial building. There are 6 rooms, all with private bath, and an elegant restaurant (see *Eating Out*). 4 Fort St. (phone: 2-30116; fax: 2-78808).

Mom's Triangle Inn Simple, clean accommodations in a converted colonial building. The 6 rooms all have a private bath, and there is a good casual restaurant (see *Eating Out*). 11 Handyside St. (phone: 2-45523).

AMBERGRIS CAYE

VERY EXPENSIVE

Captain Morgan's Retreat This resort features cabañas located directly on the beach, and a lush, tropical ambience. There's a restaurant and bar, but the main attractions here are the beach (there are oversized hammocks for lolling about), the sea, and the great coral reef. Reef, deep-sea, and fly fishing; scuba diving; snorkeling; and day sailing trips can be arranged. The resort is accessible only by boat (the hotel picks up guests in San Pedro several times a day). On the north side of Ambergris Caye (phone: 26-2527; 800-447-2931 from the US).

Journey's End Caribbean Club Featured on "Lifestyles of the Rich & Famous," and featuring a private coconut-palm-fringed beach, lighted tennis court, oversize swimming pool, Hobie Cats for sailing, a dining room, and a couple of bars. Its two buildings hold 30 individual units and 40 hotel rooms with lagoon frontage. Accessible by boat (pickup is in San Pedro), and thanks to a nearby airstrip, by plane. North of San Pedro (phone: 26-2173; 800-447-0474 from the US; fax: 26-2028).

EXPENSIVE

Belize Yacht Club Beautiful Mediterranean-style condos, with 52 one-bedroom units and 26 two-bedroom units. Great marina and a large pier with electricity, water, telephone, and refueling facilities. Half-mile south of San Pedro Town, Ambergris Caye (phone: 26-2493; fax: 26-2423).

El Pescador With 12 double rooms and 2 large suites, this remote hostelry is accessible only by boat (the hotel picks up guests in San Pedro). Life here is devoted to fisherfolk. All the rooms have twin beds and private facilities, plus verandahs offering striking views of the sea. Three miles north of San Pedro (phone/fax: 26-2398).

Ramón's Village A favorite of young, single Americans and Europeans, this place has an upbeat, often uproarious, atmosphere. Forty cozy, thatch-roofed bungalows rest on a palmy beach, plus there's a swimming pool and a bar. San Pedro (phone: 26-2071; 800-624-4215; fax: 26-2214).

Victoria House This upscale resort in a beach setting has 26 units — 7 standard hotel rooms, 10 thatch-roofed cabañas, 8 deluxe rooms, and 1 honeymoon suite (in a cabaña). There also is a restaurant and a bar. Two miles south of San Pedro (phone: 26-2067; 800-247-5159 from the US).

MODERATE

Paradise Here is a Tahitian-style resort on Ambergris Caye, offering 18 units in thatch-roofed and bamboo huts, all with private facilities. There is a pleasant, family-style dining room, and a bar in a separate building. Fishing and diving facilities are also available. Write to PO Box 888, Belize City (phone: 26-2083).

San Pedro Holiday Caters primarily to deep-sea fishermen, though divers come, too; more than 90% of its business is repeat, a very good sign. Cooking is done by the owner, and meals are served in a homey, unpretentious dining room. On the beach at San Pedro (phone: 26-2014; fax: 26-2295).

Sun Breeze This 34-room property features a beachfront setting, air conditioned rooms, a restaurant, a "barefoot" bar and grill, and a dive shop. San Pedro (phone: 26-2191; fax: 26-2346).

INEXPENSIVE

Coral Beach Family-run and catering to divers, it has comfortable accommodations in 11 rooms. San Pedro (phone: 26-2001; fax: 26-2864).

OTHER CAYS

EXPENSIVE

Lighthouse Reef An island lover's paradise, this resort on the secluded Northern Cay is surrounded by postcard-perfect white sand, coconut palms, and iridescent turquoise sea. It's favored by divers, who can join up to 5 daily dives to the surrounding atolls. Accommodations are in 5 spacious, modern cabañas, 4 suites, and 1 villa with clay tile floors and air conditioning. A good restaurant and friendly staff complete the inviting picture. Weekly packages only. Northern Cay (phone: 800-423-3114 from the US).

Turneffe Island Lodge Fishing is the focus of this remote (accessible only by boat) resort 30 miles off the coast. All 8 rooms have private baths. There is a restaurant, bar, and beach. Week-long packages only, including guides, boats, accommodations, and meals. Cay Bokel (phone: 800-338-8149 from the US; fax: 3-0276).

MODERATE

Manta Nine small, simple cottages strung along the beach of an unnamed island within Glover's Reef, one of the 4 newly forming atolls in the Western Hemisphere. Popular with scuba divers, it features weekly packages, including meals and boat transport to the island (phone: 2-31895; 800-342-0053 from the US; fax: 2-32764).

ELSEWHERE IN THE COUNTRY

EXPENSIVE

Blancaneaux Lodge Film director Francis Ford Coppola's stunning mountain retreat opened last spring. It features 8 thatch-roof cottages decorated in an African motif and perched in the Mountain Pine Ridge forest, and there is a main building with 6 additional rooms and a huge circular restaurant that serves pizza. The wilds of the jungle are right outside, including lovely waterfalls and dense greenery. This is the perfect place to get away from it all in style. Located 2 hours from the Maya ruins of Caracol, the property is on a dirt road off the Western Highway (phone: 2-34495; fax: 2-31657).

Blue Marlin Lodge Located 35 miles south/southeast of Phillip S.W. Goldson International Airport, with 13 rooms. The barrier reef is 120 feet off the beach. This spot boasts some of the finest, most accessible diving in Belize. South Water Cay, Dangriga (phone: 5-22243; fax: 5-22296).

Chaa Creek Cottages Belize's most elegant jungle lodge, in a stunning setting in the jungle-clad hills of the Cayo District. Owned by an Englishman and his American wife, it is unsurpassed for service and surroundings. Nineteen stucco cabañas, with red stone floors, soaring thatch roofs and gleaming oak dressers, are sprinkled along a hill overlooking the Macal River. Swimming, bird watching, horseback riding, and trips to area ruins and Mountain Pine Ridge are available. Located near the village of Benque Viejo, about 20 minutes southwest of San Ignacio off the Western Highway (phone: 92-2037; fax: 92-2501).

Chan Chich Lodge Built in the center of a Maya ruin in northwestern Belize and surrounded by virgin jungle, this place offers 12 individual thatch-roofed cabañas, beautiful landscaping, a bar, and a dining room. Río Bravo (phone: 2-77031; 800-343-8009 from the US; fax: 2-77062).

duPlooy's Riverside Cottages Located in western Belize, there are 9 cottages set on 20 acres of rolling hills, surrounded by lush tropical growth and framed on the eastern and northern sides by the Macal River. Tours can be arranged. Big Eddy, San Ignacio (phone: 92-2188; 800-359-0747 from the US; fax: 92-2057).

Maruba This remote jungle resort and spa bills itself as being "for the experienced traveler." Located in the heart of the Maya jungle, it features modern facilities, a pool, a restaurant that serves local fare, a bar, a Japanese hot tub, tropical gardens, and an informal atmosphere. Jungle trips on the Northern River and day trips to Lamanai, Altun Ha, and other points of interest in the interior are offered. There's also superb fishing and health spa packages. Located 40 miles north of Belize City near the Crooked Tree Wildlife Sanctuary. At the 40½-mile mark of the Old Northern Hwy., Maskall Village (phone: 3-22199; 713-799-2013 from the US; fax: 713-795-8573).

Rum Point Inn A very special place along some of the prettiest coastline in Belize. The 8 futuristic-looking cabañas have gardens and Guatemalan sling chairs. A short stroll away is the picturesque dining room, where innkeepers George and Corol Bevier provide insights on Belize. To get here, guests take a 20-minute boat ride through mangrove islands teeming with wildlife. On the beach, just north of the village of Placencia (phone: 6-22017; 800-747-1381 from the US; fax: 6-22017; 504-464-0325 from the US).

MODERATE

Maya Mountain Lodge Another guest ranch with guestrooms and garden cottages (14 units in all) and delicious food. A number of guided archaeological and natural history tours are offered, as well as hiking, canoeing, and horseback riding. PO Box 46, San Ignacio (phone: 92-2164).

Pelican Beach A very pleasant, family-run place right on the beach with 20 rooms. The owners are hospitable and helpful. Just north of Dangriga (phone: 5-22044; fax: 5-22570).

Turtle Inn Small, but very nice, with 6 thatch-roofed bungalows and a 2-bedroom house on the beach. Meals are included in the price. Placencia (phone: 62-2069).

Warrie Head Lodge This beautiful, 137-acre working farm on the Belize River is a little over an hour's drive from Belize City. It has 500 acres of unspoiled riverside, an adjoining forest, and 10 simple guestrooms. Tours to archaeological sites, reserves, and a zoo can be arranged. Teakettle Village, Cayo (phone: 2-77185, 2-77363, or 2-77364).

Windy Hill This complex with 14 cottages is only a few minutes from the Maya ruins at Xunantunich and Tikal, Guatemala. The staff will provide tours to the Mt. Pine Ridge Forest, the Rio Frio Caves, and the swirling waters of the Mopan and Macal rivers. Graceland Ranch, San Ignacio (phone: 92-2017; fax: 92-3080).

INEXPENSIVE

Adventure Inn This place features 15 pleasant, thatch-roofed bungalows overlooking beautiful Corozal Bay, in Consejo Shores, 7 miles north of Corozal. Box 35, Corozal Town (phone: 4-22187; 800-552-3419 from the US; fax: 4-22243).

Nabitunich Here are 8 charming cottages built on a hillside overlooking the Belize River, outside of San Ignacio (phone: 9-22061).

Traveller's Inn Despite its location next to the bus stop, this establishment is the only first-rate lodging in Punta Gorda, the southernmost town in Belize. Its 8 second-floor rooms feature plush carpets, contemporary dressers and armoires, air conditioning, and cable TV. It also boasts the only fancy restaurant in town. 53 Main St., Punta Gorda (phone: 7-22568).

Tony's Inn A cheery, comfortable motel on a lovely slice of beach in the northern town of Corozal. There are 40 rooms, all with modern decor and some with air conditioning and cable TV. It also has a congenial staff and the best restaurant in town. Located at the south end of Corozal (phone: 4-22055; fax: 4-22829).

EATING OUT

Fine dining has not yet arrived in Belize, yet this developing country has much to offer in the way of charming eateries. On the cays, it's mainly seafood, with shrimp, lobster, conch, and fish (usually snapper or grouper) — ceviche, too — headlining the menus. Order lobster and conch only in season — July through October for lobster; October through June for conch. (If seafood is offered out of season, it's a good bet that the restaurant obtained it illegally from poachers.)

Most hotels prepare meals for their guests, and many will accommodate non-guests if notified in advance. In the jungle lodges, cooks depend on fresh-from-the-garden vegetables and herbs, and tropical fruits culled from the bush country. The official Belizean dish is beans and rice cooked with coconut milk, which can be delicious. Curries, johnnycakes, Tex-Mex fare, and Chinese food are also ubiquitous. For dessert, try a custard apple — it's sweet and creamy, something like pudding. Belikin beer, the only Belizean beer, consumed in great quantities by locals and visitors, is delicious. It costs only $1 a bottle in most places, except on Ambergris Caye, where the price can be double or even triple that. Imported US beer costs $3 and up.

Meal prices are high by Central American standards, but low compared to most Caribbean islands. The cost of a three-course dinner for two, not including drinks or wine, at an expensive place costs $25 or more; expect to pay from $15 to $25 at moderate places; under $15 at inexpensive places. Reservations are rarely necessary in any restaurant, unless you're dining at the restaurant of the hotel you're not staying at. When calling from one place to another in Belize, remember to dial zero before the area code. For information about calling from elsewhere, see "Telephone" earlier in this chapter.

BELIZE CITY

EXPENSIVE

Bellevue Featuring one of the most extensive, and most highly acclaimed, menus in Belize, this lovely dining room with a fine view of the harborfront features such imaginative dishes as rockfish olé (stuffed with capers, olives, onions and garlic), grouper doria (with cucumbers and cream), and ménage à trois (sautéed snapper, lobster, and shrimp). Breakfast and lunch are also tops. Open daily. Major credit cards accepted. *Bellevue Hotel,* 5 Southern Foreshore Rd. (phone: 2-77051; fax: 2-73253).

Fort Street In an delightful colonial-style house decorated with flickering oil lamps, eyelet tablecloths, and fresh flowers, this elegant eatery presents fresh seafood, steaks, and chicken. The variable menu, which is printed on a chalkboard, might include such delicacies as Cajun shrimp, kingfish with sour cream and pineapple, or snapper *tic tick* (baked in foil with onions and peppers). Open for lunch and dinner; closed Sundays. MasterCard and Visa accepted. 4 Fort St. (phone: 2-30116; fax: 2-78808).

Top of the Town The classy dining room on the fifth floor of the *Holiday Inn Villa* is Belize's highest restaurant; the resulting view of Belize City and the surrounding area is delightful. The menu features delicious seafood dishes. Open daily for lunch and dinner. Major credit cards accepted. 13 Cork St. (phone: 2-32800).

INEXPENSIVE

Macy's In 1988, the queen of England ate gibnut (a large rodent whose white meat is considered a delicacy) here and made this funky hole-in-the-wall nationally famous. In addition to the regal gibnut, there's oxtail stew, fried chicken, beans and rice, steamed snapper, and fresh-squeezed papaya and watermelon juices. Open daily for lunch and dinner. No credit cards accepted. 18 Bishop St. (phone: 2-73419).

Mom's This longtime gathering spot for American expatriates will cure homesickness. BLTs, fried chicken, mashed potatoes, and an irresistible bread pudding are among the offerings. Open daily for lunch and dinner. MasterCard and Visa accepted. In *Mom's Triangle Inn,* 11 Handyside St. (phone: 2-45523).

AMBERGRIS CAYE

EXPENSIVE

Jade Garden San Pedro's much-talked-about Chinese restaurant is in a beautiful old house right on the beach. The fare, which ranges from good to great, includes curries, sweet-and-sour dishes, chow meins, and egg foo yung, as well as fresh seafood. Open daily for lunch and dinner. Closed during the month of October. Major credit cards accepted. Located on the sea, about 1½ miles north of the San Pedro airstrip (phone: 26-2506).

MODERATE

Elvi's Kitchen Extremely popular with locals and tourists alike, this colorful place has a sand floor and a tree growing through the roof. Diners feast on burgers, steaks, rice and beans, and whatever the catch of the day might be. Open for lunch and dinner; closed Sundays. Major credit cards accepted. Pescador Dr., San Pedro (phone: 26-2176 or 26-2404).

Mary Ellen's Little Italy The island's best Italian eatery is in a romantic seaside venue. Owned by an attorney from Tennessee, it features lasagna and spaghetti, plus more unusual offerings like shrimp manicotti with white cream sauce. Open for lunch and dinner; closed Wednesdays in summer. Major credit cards accepted. Barrier Reef Dr., San Pedro (phone: 26-2866).

INEXPENSIVE

Fido's Island Grill Eventually, everyone who comes to San Pedro ends up here (or so the story goes). The restaurant is parked right in the middle of town, and its rambling wood floors and palm thatching make for a comfortable, inviting atmosphere. The quick, filling fare includes Buffalo wings, tuna sandwiches, burritos, fish 'n' chips, and chili dogs. Open for lunch and dinner; closed Wednesdays. No credit cards accepted. Barrier Reef Dr., San Pedro (phone: 26-2056).

ELSEWHERE IN THE COUNTRY

INEXPENSIVE

Brenda's Soulful Belizean home cooking by a Placencia woman in her backyard. Offerings depend on what's available — and what Brenda's in the mood for — but they're sure to be scrumptious, filling, and a good buy. Her cream pies are legendary. Open daily for lunch and dinner (except when

Brenda doesn't feel like cooking). No credit cards accepted. Located near the Placencia post office, but if you get lost, anyone can show you the way (phone: 6-23137).

Caladium Restaurant A choice lunch spot for government employees, this quaint eatery sits in downtown Belmopan. The chalkboard menu outside announces daily specials such as pork chops, fried chicken, gibnut, meatballs, BLTs, cheeseburgers, and heavenly milkshakes. Open daily for lunch and dinner. No credit cards accepted. Market Sq., Belmopan (phone: 8-22754).

Eva's If ever there was a restaurant that embodied Belize, this is it. The downtown San Ignacio eatery sits at the center of jungle comings-and-goings, catering to every person — farmer, drifter, tourist, or archaeologist — who passes through. The food — typical Belizean fare such as stew chicken, and beans and rice — comes in second to the atmosphere, but it's still good. Open daily for lunch and dinner. No credit cards accepted. 22 Burns Ave., San Ignacio (phone: 92-2267).

Kingfisher This big, weathered, clapboard building on the sea in Placencia is the place for drinking Belikin, swapping fish tales, and eating fresh seafood. Open for lunch and dinner; closed Thursdays and during the month of October. Visa and American Express accepted (phone: 6-23175).

Serendib Small but very clean, with wood paneled walls and ceiling, this is the place for both local fare and Oriental dishes. Deep-fried lobster, rice and curry, chow mein, deviled shrimp, and pepper steak are just a few of the specialties. Open for lunch and dinner; closed Sundays. No credit cards accepted. 27 Burns Ave., San Ignacio (phone: 92-2302).

Bonaire

Sleepy little Bonaire has been quietly blooming as a tourist destination for decades. In 1960, a mere 1,555 visitors found their way to its sun-warmed shores. By 1991, that figure had multiplied by more than thirtyfold: Some 49,000 people vacationed here, many of them return visitors. And the number of tourists continues to grow. Today, Bonaire rates a place on the savviest list of about-to-be-discovered Caribbean destinations — for good, if not immediately obvious, reasons.

Bonaire is hardly a stereotypical tropical resort. At last count, it boasted a little over 1,000 hotel and condo rooms, and a smattering of duty-free shops. But the sudden surge of serious investment interest in Bonaire already is being felt, with the development of several new small properties and a few larger projects.

Salty, sandy, and dry, Bonaire's hilly north end is desert, covered with countless species of cactus, century plants, and intriguingly contorted prickly-pear trees. Though a few sections of the island's flat southern end are dotted with mangrove marshes, it is an overall desert-like area. Ashore, Bonaire is as intriguing to photographers and naturalists as it is offshore to the hundreds of divers who come to explore its watery depths.

Over the ages, live coral has grafted itself to the island's volcanic limestone base, which slopes steeply into the sea. As a result, Bonaire is surrounded by coral formations and sea gardens, and most of the island's 86 dive sites lie immediately offshore. Moreover, Bonaire offers waters with visibility of 60 to more than 100 feet, nine first-rate diving operations, and a government dedicated to protecting its environment, on land and under the sea. (In 1991, the government appointed a marine park manager, who oversees offshore conservation efforts.)

The discovery of these submarine attractions and tourism's subsequent arrival represent the end of a nearly 5-century search by the island's various owners for a viable economic base. Ever since 1499, when the island was discovered by Europeans — led not by Columbus, but by Amerigo Vespucci, who also sailed for the Spanish — governments and private entrepreneurs have tried a variety of ventures on Bonaire. The Spanish, after an unrewarding search for their favorite substance, gold, relied on the island as a source of wood, salt, and meat. They stripped it of its hardwoods and dyewoods, "panned" and dried salt from the sea around it, and hunted its wild goats and sheep.

The Dutch, who arrived in 1623, were no more successful in finding a lucrative use for the island. Nor were the British, who took over Bonaire in the early 19th century. In 1810, they leased the island to a US merchant, Joseph Foulke, who also failed to make good. When the Dutch returned in 1816, they tried harvesting salt, building ships, making brick and tile,

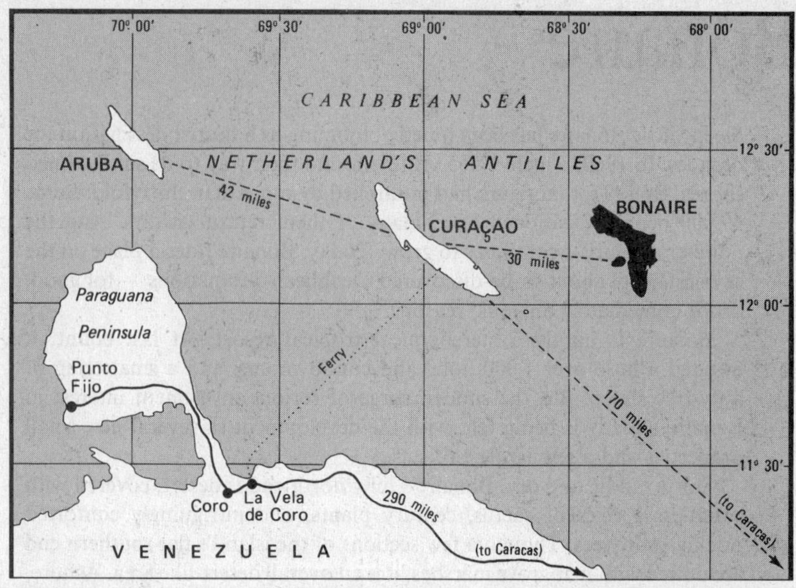
70° 00′
69° 30′
69° 00′
68° 30′
68° 00′
CARIBBEAN SEA
12° 30′
12° 00′
11° 30′
ARUBA
NETHERLAND'S ANTILLES
42 miles
BONAIRE
CURAÇAO
30 miles
Paraguana
Peninsula
Punto
Fijo
Ferry
170 miles
Coro
La Vela
de Coro
290 miles
(to Caracas)
VENEZUELA
(to Caracas)

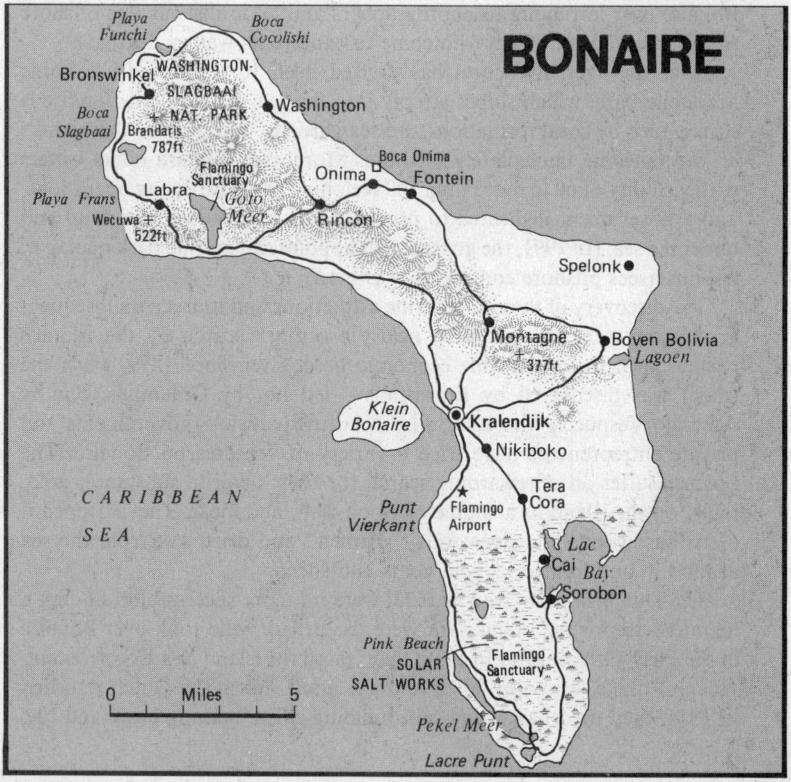

BONAIRE
Playa
Funchi
Boca
Cocolishi
WASHINGTON-
SLAGBAAI
NAT. PARK
Bronswinkel
Washington
Boca
Slagbaai
Brandaris
787ft
Flamingo
Sanctuary
Boca Onima
Onima
Fontein
Playa Frans
Labra
Wecuwa
522ft
Goto
Meer
Rincón
Spelonk
Montagne
377ft
Boven Bolivia
Lagoen
Klein
Bonaire
Kralendijk
Nikiboko
CARIBBEAN
SEA
Tera
Cora
Punt
Vierkant
Flamingo
Airport
Lac
Cai
Bay
Sorobon
Pink Beach
SOLAR
SALT WORKS
Flamingo
Sanctuary
0
Miles
5
Pekel Meer
Lacre Punt

raising stock (sheep, horses, and cattle), and weaving hats. Nothing worked. In recent years, Bonaire's men, unable to sustain themselves on the proceeds of the salt lake and the wild goat population, were forced to find work elsewhere, mostly in the oil refineries of Curaçao, Aruba, and Venezuela.

Neighbors on the sister islands and South America, who probably learned about Bonaire from the migrants, began to go there to get away from it all. They fished and lazed and took home tales of the stunning flocks of migratory flamingos at Goto Meer and Pekel Meer. Bird watchers followed; they eventually catalogued 189 species that live on the island in addition to the flamingos — warblers, doves, hummingbirds, sea swallows, gulls, green parrots, white and blue heron, native Bonairean "lorikeets" or parakeets, and dozens more.

The island's first hotel, the *Zeebad* — originally an internment camp for German prisoners during World War II, now the *Divi Flamingo Beach* resort and casino — opened in 1952. The second, the *Bonaire Beach* hotel (now the *Sunset Beach*), opened in 1962, about the time that the full tourist potential of the island began to be realized. Then the first scuba divers arrived, and with them the awareness that Bonaire's future lay less on its dry land than in the fabulous world below the surface of the sea around it.

Bonaire is a diver's paradise, but it has other attractions, too: its white sand beaches; its natural park; its eerie, sea-carved grottoes; and the petroglyphs left behind by the Caiquetio Indians, its original inhabitants. The sun shines all year, and the capital, Kralendijk (pronounced *Krawl*-in-dike), with its colorful, toy-like houses, is appealing. Residents are courteous and friendly; they seem genuinely happy to see visitors. Their *bon bini* — Papiamento for "welcome" — is genuine. This hospitality and the unspoiled nature attract not only bird watchers and divers, but those who just want to enjoy the serenity — and perhaps snorkel a bit, too.

Bonaire At-a-Glance

FROM THE AIR

The top of a 24-mile-long volcanic ridge off the South American coast, Bonaire is shaped like a rough crescent, with its back to the trade winds blowing from the northeast. Its windward coast is surf-pounded and wild, but on the leeward side the crescent encloses a natural, protected harbor, with the uninhabited island of Klein Bonaire in the center. In its calm, clear waters a startling variety of marine life flourishes in depths easily managed by snorkelers and novice scuba divers. Beaches stretch to the south and north, but inland, the two halves of the island are quite different. The south is flat and desert-like, and the southern tip is marked by ponds of contrasting colors, where salt is manufactured by solar evaporation.

The northern half of the island is hilly with much more greenery, especially within 13,500-acre Washington-Slagbaai National Park on the north coast.

The island is 38 miles east of Curaçao, 80 miles east of Aruba, and 50 miles north of the coast of Venezuela. With an area of 112 square miles and only 11,000 inhabitants, Bonaire is one of the most sparsely populated Caribbean islands and consequently one of the most unspoiled. Its capital city, Kralendijk, its major hotels, and its Flamingo Airport are on the leeward side near the center of the crescent.

The trip from New York — including flight connecting time — takes about 7 hours, or 5 hours nonstop; from Miami, nonstop flights now make the trip in about 2½ hours.

SPECIAL PLACES

KRALENDIJK A clean, well-kept town, its name means "coral dike" or "reef." Many of the bright buildings are noteworthy examples of Dutch colonial architecture. A half-hour walk can take it all in: the fish market that looks like a Greek temple; the duty-free shops of Kaya Grandi; the waterfront with its promenade and a lighthouse; the pier lined with fishing boats and island sloops; the old fort with three ancient cannon.

BONAIRE MARINE PARK This underwater preserve incorporates the entire coastline surrounding both Bonaire and the offshore island of Klein Bonaire, down to 200 feet. The area is protected by law, and visitors may not take *anything,* alive or dead, from its reefs. Established in 1979, it is one of the few successful efforts in marine conservation in the Caribbean.

ELSEWHERE ON THE ISLAND

An island tour falls naturally into two circuits, northern and southern.

NORTHERN ROUTE Driving northward from Kralendijk, you take a paved road that follows the shoreline along low coral cliffs. Every half mile or so there's a place to park and look; it's also possible to leave the car behind to walk along cactus-lined cliffside paths with views of curving beaches. One of these paths, carved from the coral rock, is known as the Thousand Steps (though there aren't really that many). It leads down to one of Bonaire's finest sites for scuba or snorkeling.

The main road continues north along an extraordinary section where a grotto in the hillside forms a natural arch along the roadway. Long ago, the ocean surface, now 30 or 40 feet lower, had been at the level of the roadbed. Over the centuries, waves and tides ate into soft coral rock and created this series of caves that extend deeply inland in some places.

The road turns inland, winds uphill, then dips again to one of Bonaire's most beautiful sites — Goto Meer, a lake that might have been lifted intact from the Scottish moors, except that it's saltwater, with an island in its center. Flocks of flamingos stand along the lake's irregular shoreline.

Follow the road along the lake to Rincón, the oldest town on the island, with its distinctive pastel buildings. Stop at *Verona's* bar and restaurant near the center of town (Kaya Para Mira; no phone) for a beer or soft drink, or sample some of the unique, homemade flavors at *Prisca's Ice Cream* shop (phone: 6334) on Kaya Komkomber. The locals will probably stare at you appraisingly; simply say hello and tell them where you're from, and the curtain of aloofness disappears. Bonaireans are friendly and courteous, but they probably won't start a conversation without an invitation.

Those who want to make a day of this excursion should turn left at the sign to Washington-Slagbaai National Park, at the northern tip of the island. This 13,500-acre tract is a preserve interlaced by miles of well-marked, rugged dirt roads. The park is untouched; there's no point in going unless you take the time to explore. There are two mapped-out routes: a 15-mile trail marked by green arrows, and a 22-mile one marked by yellow arrows. Pick up an *Excursion Guide,* available at the entrance for about $6; it describes the park's geography, history, geology, and plant and animal life. Watch for goats, donkeys, and iguanas. Though no hunting, fishing, or overnight camping is permitted, Boca Slagbaai (Slaughter Bay) is a favorite with picnickers. Bird watchers will see the most species in the morning. Top birding spots include Salina Mathijs, a salt flat popular with flamingos; the watering hole at Poos di Mangel; and Bronswinkel Well at the foot of Mt. Brandaris.

Along the park's shores are hidden bathing beaches and rocky caves. Swimming, snorkeling, and scuba diving are permitted. Incidentally, the name Washington originated when this area was all one plantation to which the owners had given the name "America." The most important place in "America" was where the workers got their pay, and they called that "Washington." The park is open to the public from 8 AM to 5 PM daily, except holidays, but no one is admitted after 3:30 PM; admission charge. Near the entrance is a small museum whose featured exhibit, in addition to cooking utensils and pottery, is an antique hearse.

If you want to skip the park, turn right from Rincón and head to Onima, on the eastern coast, the site of interesting grottoes. Continue on the paved road for 2 or 3 miles east from Rincón, and then, at the roadside sign, turn left along a dirt road toward Boca Onima. At the end of the road is a parking area along a cliff face, perhaps 50 feet high, honeycombed with odd formations. It's well worth walking a quarter mile or so along the cliff base to look at the patterns carved in the volcanic rock by centuries of wind and water. Once back at the parking area, follow the sign saying "Indian Inscriptions" to the nearby shallow, open caves. The caves' ceilings are inscribed with pink-red petroglyph designs painted by Caiquetio Indians at least 500 years ago. These patterns, which have never been deciphered by archaeologists, are repeated in various caves on Bonaire.

When returning to Kralendijk, take a short detour via Seroe Largu (pronounced "Largo") for a special view of the city, the western shoreline, and, just offshore, the island of Klein Bonaire. This observation point is memorable. Some night when there's bright moonlight, drive out again. It takes only a few minutes, and the reward is splendid: the lights of Kralendijk and the boats in the bay; the lovely coastline; the moon reflected on the water; and a glow on the horizon from the lights of Curaçao, 40 miles away.

SOUTHERN ROUTE The tour south from Kralendijk is totally different. Head down the highway past the airport and the shore homes; about 5 miles away are radio towers belonging to one of the world's most powerful transmitters: the 810,000-watt Trans-World Radio.

After a shoreline drive that features hundreds of sea birds, the road reaches the AKZO Antilles International Salt Company's salt mountains, great pyramids of dazzling white sea salt. They are produced by a distillation process that starts with sea water flowing into a rectangular pond, where the sunshine and trade winds evaporate some of the water; the residue is then pumped to a second pond, where more water is evaporated. This continues in pond after pond, each pond assuming a different hue because of the amount of salt, until the water is completely evaporated. Flocks of pink flamingos feed in these multicolored ponds; they love the briny water and the algae. At two points along the way, the government has restored the tiny, tar-roofed huts where the slaves who worked in the salt ponds slept during the week. On weekends they hiked to their homes in Rincón, 7 miles away. (Slavery was abolished here in 1863.)

The drive now leads past Pink Beach, an incredibly soft stretch of white sand with a pink hue at the water line, followed by Willemstoren, the oldest lighthouse on Bonaire (unfortunately not open to the public). Continue to the Maracultura Foundation (phone: 2595), an aquaculture research center on the south shore that is experimenting with ways to farm fish, shrimp, and conch. Tours are offered Mondays through Saturdays at 10 AM and 12:30 PM; small admission charge. The road eventually leads to Sorobon, site of the island's only naturalist (clothing optional) resort, and Lac Bay. The road along this part of the island is bordered by mangrove swamps, unique to this part of Bonaire.

If you've brought a bathing suit or picnic lunch, take a 4-mile drive off the main road to Cai, a little settlement on Lac Bay. The swimming and snorkeling here are delightful, and there are shelters to provide shade for a picnic. The drive back to Kralendijk passes through two villages with the exotic names of Tera Cora and Nikiboko.

Sources and Resources

TOURIST INFORMATION

The Tourism Corporation of Bonaire has an office in Kralendijk (12 Kaya Simón Bolívar; phone: 8322 or 8649; fax: 8408). For information about Bonaire tourist offices in the US, see GETTING READY TO GO.

LOCAL COVERAGE *Bonaire Holiday* has up-to-date information on events, shopping, and sightseeing. It's available free at the airport, tourist office, and hotels. *Dutch Caribbean,* a free newspaper published Mondays through Saturdays, has information on Bonaire, as well as Aruba and Curaçao; it is distributed free in hotels.

For background reading, Dr. J. Hartog's *History of Bonaire* is available in paperback; so is the *Antillean Fish Guide* and the colorful, informative *Guide to the Bonaire Marine Park* by Tom van't Hof. All are available in island bookstores.

RADIO AND TELEVISION

Trans-World Radio has English newscasts three times a day.

TELEPHONE

When calling from the US, dial 011 (international access code) + 5997 (country code) + (local number). To call from another Caribbean island, the access code may vary, so contact the local operator.

ENTRY REQUIREMENTS

Proof of citizenship (a passport, or an original or notarized birth certificate or voter's registration card with photo ID) and an ongoing ticket are all that US and Canadian citizens need.

CLIMATE AND CLOTHES

Constant cloudless days (yearly rainfall totals only about 22 inches) keep the temperature about 82F (28C), although the thermometer sometimes may reach as high as 90F (33C) in September or as low as 74F (23C) in January. The island's heat and humidity are well tempered by trade winds blowing from the northeast at an average 16 mph. Casual resortwear is the general rule for both men and women. You'll need some type of long-sleeve cover-up to slip on when you've had enough sun. Shorts or slacks are okay for women in town, but bikinis should be confined to the beach or pool. Short-sleeve sport shirts are always permissible. *Note:* Salt water and the constant Antillean breeze make simple hairdos nearly essential for women; ditto head scarves for the beach and sightseeing drives.

MONEY

The Netherlands Antilles florin, or guilder (NAf), is the official monetary unit, with a rate of exchange of approximately 1.77 NAf to $1 US. US dollars and traveler's checks are acceptable everywhere; Canadian dollars are somewhat less negotiable, so they should be exchanged for florins. Banking hours are 8:30 AM to 4 PM, Mondays through Fridays. Stores offer no discounts for payment in US dollars. Major credit cards are honored in most shops, hotels, and restaurants. All prices in this chapter are quoted in US dollars.

LANGUAGE

Bon bini might be the first words you hear; that's "welcome" in Papiamento, the language unique to the Netherlands Antilles. But don't worry, almost everyone connected with tourism understands and speaks English. Dutch is the official language, but — since South America is so close — Spanish is also widely spoken.

TIME

Bonaire is on atlantic standard time, which puts its clocks an hour ahead of eastern standard time (when it's noon in New York, it's 1 PM in Bonaire). During daylight saving time, the hour is the same in both places.

CURRENT

Outlets are 127 volts, 50 cycles. American appliances work, though a bit slowly; adapters are recommended.

TIPPING

A 10% to 15% service charge is added to most hotel bills to take care of chambermaids and other staff, and to restaurant checks. An additional tip is not needed unless some special service has been provided. Taxi drivers appreciate tips (10% of the fare) but it's not mandatory. Give airport porters and other bellhops about 50¢ per bag.

GETTING AROUND

BUS There are no public buses.

CAR RENTAL The roads are narrow but in good to excellent condition, and with bird watching to do, numerous beaches to visit, and many diving sites just offshore (look for yellow markers beside the road), it's nice to have your own wheels. It's not expensive; daily rates, with unlimited mileage, range from about $28 to $60, depending on the size of the car, plus a government tax of $2 per day. US and Canadian driver's licenses are valid for driving on the island; the driver must be at least 21. For reservations from the US, call *Avis* (phone: 800-331-1212) or *Budget* (phone: 800-472-3325); on the island, *Avis* (phone: 5795), *Budget* (phone: 8300 or 8315), *Dollar* (phone: 5600 or 8888), *A. B. Car Rentals* (phone: 8980), or *Island Car Rentals* (phone: 5111) can meet your needs. *Bonaire Bicycle and Motorbike* (phone: 8226) and *S. F. Wave Touch* (phone: 4246) rent scooters for about $26 a day, including free pickup and delivery.

SEA EXCURSIONS There are 4-hour evening sails aboard the 60-foot Siamese junk *Samur* (phone: 5433) for $30 per person. The *Samur* also offers snorkel cruises ($35 per person), sunset cruises ($25 per person), and barbecue trips to the uninhabited island of Klein Bonaire, off Kralendijk ($45 per person). Half-day snorkel cruises and sunset cruises also are offered aboard the 42-foot cutter *Oscarina* (phone: 8290) and the 37-foot trimaran *Woodwind* (phone: 8285). Glass-bottom boat tours are available aboard the *Bonaire Dream* at the Harbour Village marina (phone: 7500); the 1½-hour trip costs $15 for adults; $7.50 for children.

Dive-Inn at the *Sunset Beach* hotel (phone: 8448, ext. 200) runs seagoing tours (diving, snorkeling, fishing, and sailing). Rates often include transport, beverages, and lunch, and vary according to sport and destination. *Captain Don's Habitat* (phone: 8290), *Dive-Inn,* and *Dive Bonaire* (phone: 8285) offer water taxi rides to Klein Bonaire; for about $6 per person, they'll take passengers over in the morning, leave them for a few hours of snorkeling, beaching, and picnicking, and pick them up in the afternoon.

SIGHTSEEING BUS TOURS *Bonaire Sightseeing* (phone: 8311 or 8778); and *Ayubi's Tours* (phone: 5338) offer a choice of 2-hour guided trips: a northern tour (not including Washington-Slagbaai National Park) and a southern tour, at $12 per person. *Bonaire Sightseeing* also offers a 3-hour guided town and country tour for $17 per person, a 3-hour tour of Washington-Slagbaai National Park for $25 per person, and a full-day tour of the park for $45 per person (minimum four people).

TAXI The cabs are unmetered; government-established rates are posted in hotels and the airport, and each driver has a list. Fare from the airport to your hotel will run $6 to $10 per cab (four-person maximum). Rates increase 25% from 7 PM to midnight, and 50% from midnight to 6 AM. Hotels can get a cab in a matter of minutes, or you can call the central dispatcher at 8100. Drivers are good guides to island attractions and will take a party of up to four on a half-day tour for about $60 for the northern route, $40 for the southern route.

INTER-ISLAND FLIGHTS

ALM and *Air Aruba* offer flights from Bonaire to Aruba, Curaçao, and Caracas (Venezuela). Direct charters are available as well.

SPECIAL EVENTS

Bonaire's biggest wingding is the *October International Sailing Regatta,* 5 days of racing, steel band music, dancing, and feasting not only for the crews of participating working fishing boats, yachts, sloops, Sunfish, and Sailfish, but for the entire island and visitors. There's also lots of folk dancing and singing on *Dia de San Juan* (St. John's Day, June 23) and *Dia de San Pedro* (St. Peter's Day, June 29). *Carnival* time from late February to early March is observed with costumed parades and more dancing. The *Nikonos Shootout* (held June 20–27) is an annual event for underwater camera buffs. More photography occurs, this time on land, during the *Birdwatching Olympics* (Sept. 20–26). Official holidays, when banks and shops are closed (although some shops stay open when there's a cruise ship in port), include *New Year's Day, Carnival Monday* (March 2), *Ash*

Wednesday, the *Queen's Birthday* and *Rincón Day* (April 30), *Good Friday, Easter, Labor Day* (May 1), *Ascension Day* (May 28), *Whitmonday, Kingdom Day* (December 15), *Christmas,* and *Boxing Day* (December 26).

SHOPPING

Bonaire shopping — like that in Curaçao and Aruba — though technically not entirely duty-free, offers substantial savings on a long list of imported luxuries: Swiss watches, English china, French perfume, Danish silver, Scandinavian crystal, jewelry, and more. On the whole, Bonaire's inventory doesn't begin to compare with that of its sister islands, though some Curaçao/Aruba stores have Bonaire branches. Store hours are 8 AM to noon and 2 to 6 PM daily except Sundays. The following stores are in Kralendijk unless otherwise noted.

ARIES BOUTIQUE Good buys in 14K and 18K gold jewelry, watches, Delft china, and semi-precious gems. Dutch specialty foods are also on sale here. 33 Kaya Grandi (phone: 8091).

CARIBBEAN ARTS & CRAFTS A good place for locally crafted black coral, Mexican onyx, painted wooden fish, sterling silver jewelry, Peruvian tapestries, and decorative stone carvings. 38A Kaya Grandi (phone: 5051).

D'ORSY'S You'll find a good selection of duty-free perfume and famous-name cosmetics. *Harborside Mall* (phone: 5488).

FUNDASHON ARTE INDUSTRIA BONARIANO Local crafts and souvenirs at a not-for-profit workshop. J.A. Abraham Blvd. (no phone).

KI BO KE PAKUS The "do-what-you-want" shop is the island's best boutique, offering a good selection of bikinis, dashikis, caftans, and pareos at nice prices. At the *Divi Flamingo Beach* hotel (phone: 8239).

LITTMAN JEWELERS This is the place to shop for fine jewelry and watches. 33 Kaya Grandi (phone: 8160).

SPRITZER & FUHRMANN A local branch of the well-known island chain of very fine jewelry shops. 31 Kaya Grandi (phone: 5488).

THINGS BONAIRE A little bit of everything can be found here, from Indonesian clothing and jewelry to Delftware to hats and visors. At the *Sunset Beach* hotel (phone: 8190); and 38C Kaya Grandi (phone: 8423).

SPORTS

BIRD WATCHING Bird watchers flock to Bonaire and for good reason: close to 190 species live here. The roseate flamingos are the most famous, and there are pelicans, parrots, herons, doves, cuckoos, and such exotic birds as the groove-billed ani, the black-whiskered vireo, and the bananaquit. Birding is best on the northern part of the island in valleys, ponds, and Washington-Slagbaai National Park. Flamingo sanctuaries are at Goto Meer on the northern coast and at Pekel Meer on the southwest coast. The largest colony lives at the salt flats at the southern end. For flamingo watching, take binoculars and a telephoto lens for your camera. A listing of most of the species of Bonaire birds is available at the tourist offices in New York and Bonaire.

BOATING If you're on Bonaire at *International Regatta* time in October, you're likely to be recruited by one of the skippers as crew or just ballast. A Sunfish can be rented at your hotel for about $15 an hour; use of a windsurfer with instruction is about $20 per hour. The *Harbour Village Marina* has 72 slips for various types of vessels.

SNORKELING AND SCUBA Bonaire is ideal for snorkeling, and scuba is the island's varsity sport. Divers come from everywhere to take part or to take advanced certification courses. Novices come to learn the sport and be certified by one of the island's teaching and training facilities. The island is special for diving because it is a coral reef itself. You don't have to travel offshore to find the dive spots; most are right off the beach or a very short boat ride away. The fringing reef starts just offshore and slopes gently downward at a 45-degree angle. Visibility in these calm waters is generally 60 to 100 feet, sometimes more. Of special interest is the *Hilma Hooker,* a 238-foot freighter wrecked off the southwest coast that swarms with fish and other sea creatures. It is only 50 feet from the surface and can be viewed by snorkelers as well as divers. A decompression chamber is available next to the St. Franciscus Hospital in Kralendijk (phone: 8187 or 8900). Anyone planning to dive in the Bonaire Marine Park must purchase a $10 dive tag, which entitles you to 1 calendar year of unlimited diving. Tags can be purchased at any dive shop or at the park headquarters in the Old Fort in Kralendijk (phone: 8444).

Captain Don Stewart, leader of Bonaire's determined movement to preserve its reefs and marine life, runs *Captain Don's Habitat* (phone: 8290; 800-327-6709 from the US), a five-star scuba training facility with multilingual instructors; it is rated one of the Caribbean's best. Another *PADI* five-star training facility is *Sand Dollar Dive and Photo* at the *Sand Dollar Beach Club.* It offers scuba instruction in four languages (English, Spanish, French, and Dutch/Papiamento) through the instructor level and several beginner and advanced courses, including one in underwater photography.

Similar scuba programs are offered by *Dive Bonaire* (with 11 dive boats and complete underwater-photography facilities) at the *Divi Flamingo Beach* resort and casino; the *Dive-Inn* at the *Sunset Beach* hotel (phone: 8448, ext. 200), Bruce Bowker of the *Carib Inn; Great Adventures Bonaire* at the *Harbour Village Beach* resort; and *Neal Watson Undersea Adventures* at the *Coral Regency* resort. All local dive centers offer many boat dive and shore dive packages; prices vary. A unique diving opportunity is offered by Dee Scarr (phone: 8529), whose "Touch the Sea" underwater tours emphasize close yet nonintrusive interaction with sea creatures large and small. Cost is $75 per dive per person (minimum two people). Or put on a mask and fins and swim out on your own (but never alone). Just don't spearfish or collect any coral or other marine souvenirs while underwater — it's strictly against the law. (It's okay to pick up shells on the beach.)

Dive packages are available through *Bonaire Tours* (phone: 908-566-8866 from New Jersey; 800-526-2370 from elsewhere in the US).

SPORT FISHING Local skippers are prepared to take visitors in search of dorado, yellowfin tuna, sea bass, grouper, marlin, sailfish, bonito, and pompano. A half day on a skippered boat costs about $275 for four to six people; a full day runs about $375. Make arrangements through your hotel or contact *Captain Rich* (phone: 5111) or *Piscatur Charters* (phone: 8774).

SWIMMING AND SUNNING Few hotels have beautiful beaches. The best are found at *Sunset Beach* and *Harbour Village*. In general, Bonaire's shore is lined by low coral cliffs, with paths and stairways leading down to small coves of sandy beaches. A few of these spots have changing facilities, but most are too secluded to require them. No beach is ever crowded, even those in front of the hotels. In addition to the beaches just above and below Kralendijk, others worth a special visit include Pink Beach on the southwest coast, Sorobon and Cai on Lac Bay on the southeast coast, where you can watch the conch fishermen and help yourself to conch shells for souvenirs; and on the northern end of the island, the coastline of Washington-Slagbaai National Park, including Playa Funchi, black coral Boca Bartol, and Playa Chiquito (Little Beach), walled on three sides by low coral cliffs.

TENNIS Not a major drawing card on Bonaire, but there are 2 courts at the *Sunset Beach* hotel, 2 courts at the *Sand Dollar Beach Club,* and 1 court at the *Divi Flamingo Beach.* Non-guests can play for free during the day and for $10 per hour in the evenings at *Divi Flamingo Beach;* free tennis clinics are here Tuesday and Wednesday mornings from 8:30 to 10 AM.

WINDSURFING *Lac Bay,* a shallow protected cove on the east coast, is ideal for windsurfing, especially for novices (there's no way to be blown out to sea). *Windsurfing Bonaire* (phone/fax: 5363) offers courses and board rentals and arranges free hotel pickup and drop-off. Lessons cost $20; board rentals $20 an hour, $40 for a half day.

NIGHTLIFE

Most is at the hotels, with performances by local folk dancers, a steel band, or a local combo. The *Divi Flamingo Beach*'s informal gaming room — billed as "The World's First Barefoot Casino" — opens at 8 PM daily except Sundays and occasionally has entertainment. The island has one downtown nightclub/disco (not to worry, Régine), called *E Wowo* ("The Eye" in Papiamento). The *Divi Flamingo Beach* resort and casino and the

Sunset Beach hotel plan something a little different each evening during the winter season, with music and dancing several nights a week. Happy hours and special theme nights featuring international buffets are also specialties, all pleasantly casual. For downtown mingling, stop in any evening, except Mondays, at *Karels* bar, located on the waterfront across from the *Zeezicht* restaurant.

Best on the Island

CHECKING IN

The majority of Bonaire's hotel rooms are concentrated on the shore in or near Kralendijk. To keep hotel architecture and commercial growth in harmony with the island's simple beauties and relaxed atmosphere, expansion is being firmly controlled. Hotel prices range from expensive ($160 and up a night for a double room, without meals, in winter) to moderate (between $100 and $160 a night), to inexpensive (less than $100 a night). There is an additional government room tax of about $4 per person per night, and most hotels add a 10% to 15% service charge. A list of inexpensive guesthouses and rental apartments is available from the tourist office. When calling from a phone on Bonaire, use only the local numbers listed below. For information about dialing from elsewhere, see "Telephone" earlier in this chapter.

EXPENSIVE

Captain Don's Habitat This property offers a wide variety of accommodations, including 11 two-bedroom cottages, 30 deluxe oceanfront hotel rooms, and 15 oceanfront luxury villas. Rooms and villas are air conditioned and feature terraces and cable TV. The *Kunuku Terrace Bar,* the casual *Faucets* restaurant, and *Captain Don's Habitat Dive Center* (see "Snorkeling and Scuba") round out the amenities. Northern coast (phone: 8290; 305-373-3341 from Miami; 800-327-6709 from elsewhere in the US; fax: 8240).

Coral Regency An all-suite property, it has 32 one- and two-bedroom suites, each with a full kitchen, air conditioning, private patio or balcony, and direct-dial telephones. Dive facilities, a casual restaurant, seaside bar, gift shop, and pool complete the picture. Next to *Captain Don's Habitat* (phone: 5580; 800-327-8150 from the US; fax: 5680).

Divi Flamingo Beach With-it, yet slightly off the beaten track, this is a pleasantly informal place with a genuinely personal feeling. There are 145 air conditioned rooms, some with balconies over the water; there are also 40 deluxe studios with kitchenettes in the on-premises *Club Flamingo* complex, which includes a separate dive shop/pier next to the main resort. The 2 open-air dining rooms, *Chibi Chibi* (see *Eating Out*) and *Calabas Terrace,* overlook the beach and sea. There's also a bar with local entertainment, a casino, 2 freshwater pools, and a Jacuzzi; scuba diving is offered by *Dive Bonaire.* The all-inclusive package is a good value. Between the airport and town at the edge of the sea (phone: 8285; 800-367-3484 from the US; fax: 8238).

Harbour Village Beach All 72 rooms and 30 apartments at this upscale property have air conditioning, direct-dial telephones, cable TV, and balconies or patios overlooking the marina or the beach. There is a pool, water sports, and 2 restaurants and bars. On the northwest coast at the marina (phone: 7500; 800-424-0004 from the US; fax: 7507).

Sand Dollar Beach Club Overlooking the ocean, the 85 luxury studio, 1-, 2-, and 3-bedroom condominium units have air conditioning and complete kitchens. Two tennis courts, a pool, the *Green Parrot* restaurant (see *Eating Out*), and the *PADI* five-star *Sand Dollar Dive and Photo Shop* are also on the premises. On the northwest coast (phone: 8738; 617-821-1012 from Massachusetts; 800-766-6016 from elsewhere in the US; fax: 8760).

MODERATE

Sorobon Beach An unusual "naturalist's" resort, it has 20 one-bedroom cottages with kitchenettes, but no air conditioning. Facilities include a beach and a restaurant. The big draw: Clothing is optional. On Lac Bay (phone: 8080; 800-828-9356 from the US; fax: 5363).

Sunset Beach A popular group destination, this 2-story property with 120 old-looking but amenity-laden rooms and suites is a link in the Golden Tulip hotel chain. There is a nice beach, 2 bars, dining room, coffee shop, beach pavilion for lunch; also shops, mini-golf, pool, tennis courts, and playground. *Dive-Inn* operates a full water sports program on the premises. On the northwest coast (phone: 8448; 800-344-4439 from the US; fax: 8118).

INEXPENSIVE

Buddy Dive Resort These 10 tiny apartments are along the ocean; each has a kitchenette, a shower, and twin beds. Only 5 are air conditioned; none have phones or TV sets. A new building with 15 one-, two-, and three-bedroom apartments opened last year, and a second complex with another 15 units is set to open this year. *Buddy Watersports Center* offers scuba diving and other water sports. On the northwest coast (phone: 8065; 800-359-0747 from the US; fax: 8647).

Carib Inn Once a private home, it now is the base for Bruce Bowker's scuba operation, with a pool, patio, and 7 nicely renovated, unpretentious rooms (5 with full kitchens), 1 sizable seaview suite with kitchen, and 1 efficiency apartment for rent to divers. This friendly roost is one of the island's best buys. In 1973, Bruce was Bonaire's first "imported" scuba instructor, and his hospitality is much of the inn's appeal. About 1½ miles outside of Kralendijk (phone: 8819; fax: 8819).

Sunset Inn Across the street from a small beach, this small complex offers 7 air conditioned rooms or 1-bedroom suites. All rooms have a TV set, a telephone, and a refrigerator. There's good snorkeling offshore, and car rentals are available at excellent rates. Just outside of town (phone: 8448; 800-344-4439 from the US; fax: 8118).

EATING OUT

Food on Bonaire is generally acceptable, simply cooked, but there's not much variety. The *Sunset Beach* and *Divi Flamingo Beach* hotels try for international standards, and feature good, fresh fish, plus an occasional *rijsttafel* — the traditional Indonesian "rice table" made up of many deliciously spiced dishes. *Harbour Village Beach,* one of the newer hotels, offers a good combination of continental, American, and native Caribbean fare. Hotels also serve native island dishes, but they don't always put them on the menu, so it's a good idea to ask about unlisted specials. Worth sampling: *keshi yena,* a tasty, if hefty, mixture of chicken and beef, cooked with onions and tomatoes, then baked in a round of Edam cheese; *stobi,* a casserole of lamb served with rice and banana fritters; goat stew (nicely seasoned, it tastes a lot like veal); and fish chowder. Dinner for two (including tip but not drinks) will cost $45 or more at a restaurant in the expensive category; $25 to $45 at places listed as moderate; and less than $25 at inexpensive eateries. Our recommendations are all in or near Kralendijk. When calling from a phone on Bonaire, use only the local numbers listed below. For information about dialing from elsewhere, see "Telephone" earlier in this chapter.

EXPENSIVE

Bistro des Amis Cozily French, this place specializes in escargots, coquilles St-Jacques, and other such Gallic specialties. Open for dinner only; closed Sundays. Reservations advised. American Express and Visa accepted. 4 Kaya L.D. Gerharts (phone: 8003 or 8700).

Kasa Coral Start off the day with a breakfast buffet of familiar American dishes. Lunch entrées are mostly native dishes, while dinner is a prix fixe menu offering varied selections such as fresh seafood and rack of lamb. Open daily. Reservations advised. Major credit cards accepted. In the *Harbour Village Beach* resort (phone: 7500).

Raffles Formerly *Le Chic,* this Kralendijk restaurant in an old Bonairean home now features Indonesian and continental cooking. The chef is especially well known for his sweet-and-sour shrimp and mango parfait. Open for dinner only; closed Mondays. Reservations advised. Major credit cards accepted. 5 Kaya C.E.B. Hellmund (phone: 8617).

MODERATE

Chibi Chibi Alfresco dining in a 2-story wood building overlooking the beach. Highlights include an extensive wine list, seafood specialties, and international coffees to complement fabulous desserts. Open daily for dinner only. Reservations advised. Major credit cards accepted. At the *Divi Flamingo Beach* resort (phone: 8285).

Den Laman This seafood spot has an inviting bar, aquarium decor, and a salad bar; there's dancing and live entertainment several times a week. Open for dinner only; closed Tuesdays. Reservations advised. Major credit cards accepted. Shoreside between the *Sunset Beach* hotel and the *Sand Dollar Beach Club* (phone: 8955).

Green Parrot Located on the beach, this is the perfect spot for sunset viewing. Burgers, seafood, steaks, and local specialties are served in a casual atmosphere. There's entertainment Saturday nights. Open daily for breakfast, lunch, and dinner. Dinner reservations advised. Major credit cards accepted. At the *Sand Dollar Beach Club* (phone: 5454).

Playa Lechi Tropical dining in an attractive "beach hut." Offerings include surf and turf and a Bonairean Night once a week featuring a buffet of island specialties and a floor show with local music. Open daily for dinner only. Reservations unnecessary. Major credit cards accepted. At the *Sunset Beach* hotel (phone: 8448).

Richard's Fast becoming a favorite of locals and visitors alike, chef Bonito specializes in seafood; his most popular dish is shrimp *primavera.* This casual alfresco eatery boasts lots of greenery and a gleaming wood bar. Boaters can dock at the pier out front. Open for happy hour and dinner nightly except Mondays. Reservations advised. Major credit cards accepted. 60 Abraham Blvd. (phone: 5263).

Zeezicht That's Dutch for "sea view"; it's a popular bistro right on the waterfront — good for sampling local specialties, including conch stew, goat curry, or fresh fish platters. Open daily for breakfast, lunch, and dinner. Happy hour features live entertainment from 4:15 to 5:15 PM nightly. Reservations advised. Major credit cards accepted. 10 Curaçaostraat (phone: 8434).

INEXPENSIVE

Great China The menu here features a wide variety of Chinese specialties, seafood, and Indonesian dishes. Open for lunch and dinner; closed Tuesdays. Reservations unnecessary. Major credit cards accepted. Kaya Grandi (phone: 8886).

Mona Lisa A convivial atmosphere plus an authentic Dutch menu that features fresh fish and seafood are the drawing cards at this eatery. Open daily for lunch and dinner. Reservations unnecessary. American Express accepted. 15 Kaya Grandi (phone: 8718).

Rendezvous This place offers a café atmosphere and seafood dishes, salads, steaks, and good desserts. Espresso and cappuccino are served in the bar. Open for dinner only; closed Tuesdays. Reservations advised. Major credit cards accepted. Kerkweg (phone: 8454 or 8539).

British Virgin Islands

The British Virgin Islands appear on most maps as a spray of dots not far from Puerto Rico; the general impression is that the cartographer spattered ink over a quarter inch of parchment, which makes for frustrating map reading. Sailors, however, have had no trouble finding the 50 landmasses — rocks, cays, fragments, spits, volcanic atolls, as well as full-fledged islands — that make up the group. For years — indeed, centuries — boats have sailed around and through them, putting in at completely empty cays for a night's rest or to await richly laden galleons on their way to Europe, as 17th- and 18th-century pirates were fond of doing. Over 200 ships have run aground here over the centuries and tales of sunken treasure abound, especially off the Anegada Reefs. (Robert Louis Stevenson's *Treasure Island* is popularly believed to be BVI's Norman Island, but some think it's actually a tiny cay called Dead Chest off Peter Island, because of the book's famed ditty "Fifteen men on the Dead Man's Chest — Yo-ho-ho, and a bottle of rum!")

Christopher Columbus discovered the entire Virgin Islands chain in 1493, although it was forgotten almost immediately. In 1595 Sir Francis Drake sailed into the channel south of Tortola that now bears his name. Within 30 years, the English had established a legal claim to at least some of the islands, although the claim was disputed — by the Spanish and the Dutch primarily — until 1672, when Tortola was annexed by the English government.

In the meantime, Tortola became a pirates' haven, and there was much coming and going from many of the smaller cays. By the end of the 17th century, Tortola had begun to attract English planters as well; they firmly established the British right to the island. By 1850 or so, a Quaker colony had been established, the planters far outnumbered the pirates, and the Quakers and the planters tried to form their own constitutional government.

Occasional talk of independence through the years notwithstanding, the British Virgin Islands remain linked to the British Commonwealth. The governor is appointed by the queen, but laws are made and administered by a locally elected chief minister and Legislative Council. You'll find a portrait of the queen in most hotels and shops and British courtesy everywhere. But, oddly enough, you'll find only US currency in the British Virgin Islands.

Even more than their sisters, the US Virgin Islands, the British Virgins are for tourists who want sun, sea, and nature. Fewer than ten of the islands have accommodations for tourists, although yachtspeople and day sailors in the know often drop anchor off several of the others. The uninhabited coves of Fallen Jerusalem, Great Dog, Ginger, Norman, and little Prickly Pear are especially beckoning to the carefree bareboat visitor, while the seven relatively "built-up" British Virgin Islands (those with five or more guestrooms) are ready for vacationers who yearn for tranquil cottage resorts at the edge of the sea.

Development for tourism proceeds with great caution because much of the pleasure these cays and islands give tourists is in their isolation and tiny size. The BVI have been much less commercial than other islands because of transportation difficulties; no major airlines have direct flights from North America, so ferries or small planes must be used. However, a new cruise ship dock in Road Town is expected to berth up to two ships daily, and the airport will be enlarged by the end of this year to accommodate jets flying direct from the US.

Despite these developments, it is likely that these islands still will remain the province of those lucky people who sail around them. The British Virgin Islands offer a quiet retreat, without hotel chains, fancy restaurants, or casinos, but with magnificent scenery, perfect sailing conditions, personalized hotels, secluded beaches, and welcoming, friendly islanders.

British Virgin Islands At-a-Glance

FROM THE AIR

The British Virgin Islands are made up of more than 50 islands, rocks, and cays, many of which are clustered around the Sir Francis Drake Channel, a historic waterway 20 miles long and 5 miles wide. The chain lies 60 miles east of Puerto Rico and directly northeast of St. John, one of the US Virgin Islands. Only 16 of the islands are inhabited; the entire country has a population of approximately 12,000 people and a total area of only 59 square miles. The major inhabited islands in the chain are Tortola, with the islands' capital, Road Town; Virgin Gorda; Beef Island (connected to Tortola by a bridge); Anegada; and Jost Van Dyke.

SPECIAL PLACES

TORTOLA Road Town, the capital of the BVI and home of about half of its residents, is where most activity begins and ends on Tortola. There are about a dozen shops to browse through all along Main Street, a colorful market at the edge of town, and any number of sailing craft to take you away for the day. Several of the old, colorful wooden buildings have been preserved, even though a shopping plaza and several modern government buildings have gone up in the city center. The Virgin Island Historical Society's small *Folk Museum* (Main St.) has a pictorial display of island history, artifacts from the Taíno Indian and plantation eras, and items from the famous shipwreck of the *Rhone* (see *Snorkeling and Scuba* below). The Botanic Garden, on the outskirts of town, has a fine collection of tropical flora and fauna on 2.8 acres. It makes a very pleasant outing.

To explore the island, head west from Road Town toward Sage Moun-

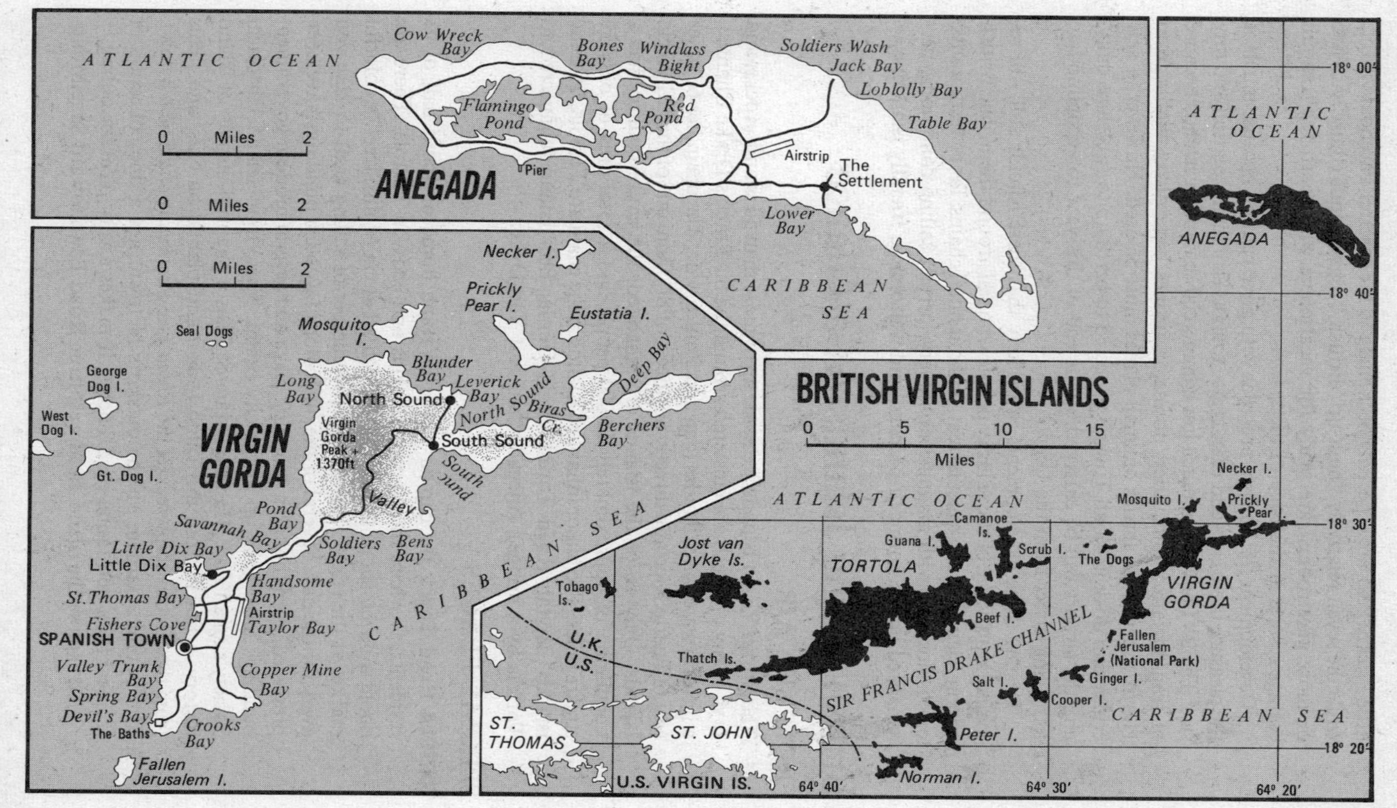

ANEGADA
ATLANTIC OCEAN
0 Miles 2
0 Miles 2
Cow Wreck Bay
Bones Bay
Windlass Bight
Soldiers Wash
Jack Bay
Loblolly Bay
Table Bay
Flamingo Pond
Red Pond
Pier
Airstrip
The Settlement
Lower Bay
CARIBBEAN SEA
VIRGIN GORDA
0 Miles 2
Necker I.
Prickly Pear I.
Eustatia I.
Mosquito I.
Seal Dogs
George Dog I.
West Dog I.
Gt. Dog I.
Blunder Bay
Leverick Bay
Long Bay
North Sound
North Sound
Biras Cr.
Deep Bay
Bercher Bay
Virgin Gorda Peak + 1370ft
South Sound
South Sound
Valley
Pond Bay
Savannah Bay
Little Dix Bay
Little Dix Bay
Soldiers Bay
Bens Bay
Handsome Bay
Airstrip
Taylor Bay
St. Thomas Bay
Fishers Cove
SPANISH TOWN
Valley Trunk Bay
Spring Bay
Devil's Bay
The Baths
Crooks Bay
Copper Mine Bay
Fallen Jerusalem I.
CARIBBEAN SEA
ATLANTIC OCEAN
ANEGADA
18° 00′
18° 40′
BRITISH VIRGIN ISLANDS
0 5 10 15
Miles
ATLANTIC OCEAN
Necker I.
Mosquito I.
Prickly Pear
Camanoe Is.
Guana I.
Scrub I.
The Dogs
Jost van Dyke Is.
TORTOLA
VIRGIN GORDA
Tobago Is.
Beef I.
Fallen Jerusalem (National Park)
U.K.
U.S.
Thatch Is.
SIR FRANCIS DRAKE CHANNEL
Salt I.
Ginger I.
Cooper I.
CARIBBEAN SEA
ST. THOMAS
ST. JOHN
Peter I.
Norman I.
U.S. VIRGIN IS.
64° 40′
64° 30′
64° 20′
18° 30′
18° 20′

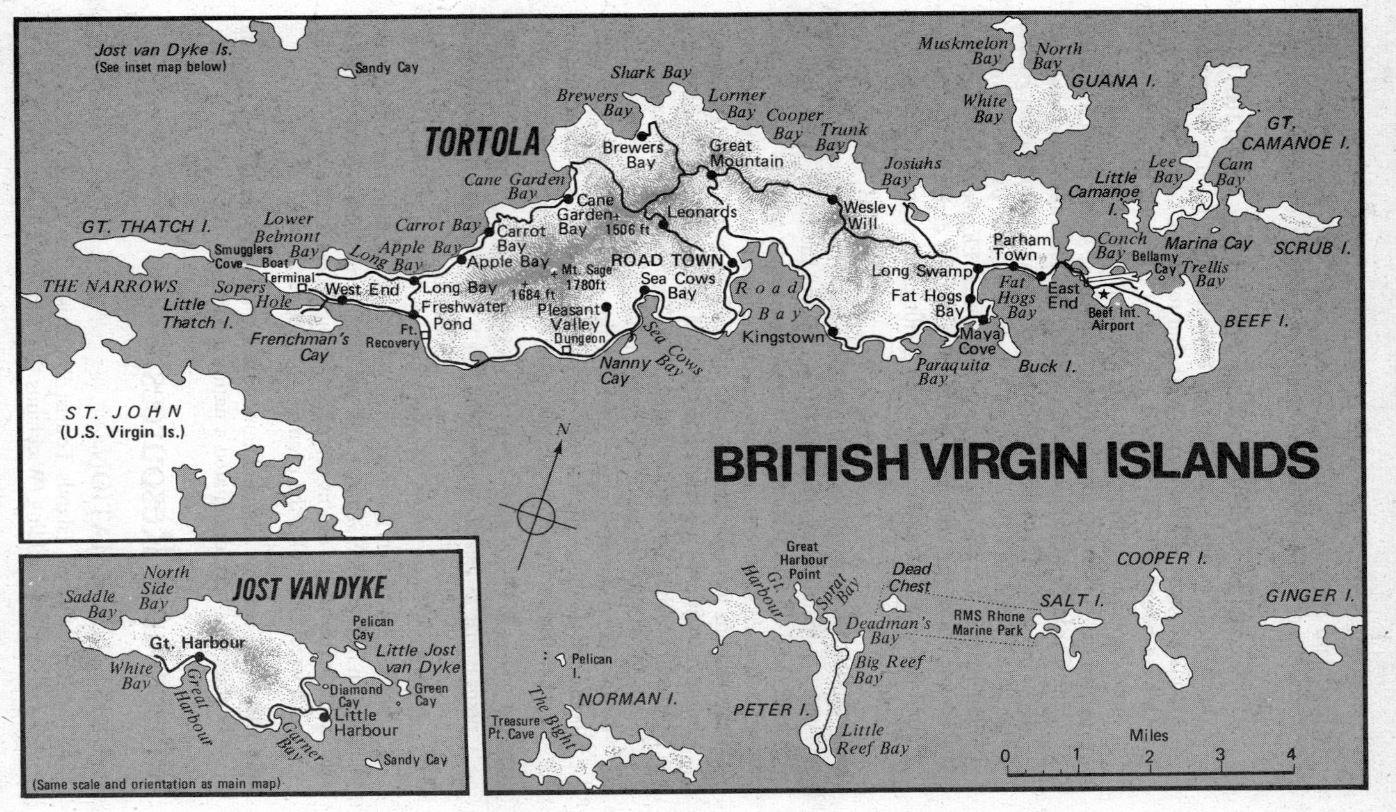
BRITISH VIRGIN ISLANDS
TORTOLA
Jost van Dyke Is.
(See inset map below)
Sandy Cay
Shark Bay
Brewers Bay
Lormer Bay
Cooper Bay
Trunk Bay
Josiahs Bay
Muskmelon Bay
North Bay
White Bay
GUANA I.
GT. CAMANOE I.
Lee Bay
Cam Bay
Little Camanoe I.
Conch Bay
Marina Cay
SCRUB I.
Bellamy Cay
Trellis Bay
Beef Int. Airport
BEEF I.
East End
Parham Town
Long Swamp
Fat Hogs Bay
Maya Cove
Buck I.
Paraquita Bay
Wesley Will
Kingstown
Road Bay
Great Mountain
Leonards
ROAD TOWN
Sea Cows Bay
Nanny Cay
Pleasant Valley
Dungeon
Mt. Sage 1780ft
1506 ft
1684 ft
Cane Garden Bay
Carrot Bay
Apple Bay
Long Bay
Freshwater Pond
Ft. Recovery
West End
Boat Terminal
Smugglers Cove
Lower Belmont Bay
Sopers Hole
Frenchman's Cay
GT. THATCH I.
Little Thatch I.
THE NARROWS
ST. JOHN
(U.S. Virgin Is.)
N
Great Harbour Point
Gt. Harbour
Sprat Bay
Dead Chest
Deadman's Bay
Big Reef Bay
Little Reef Bay
PETER I.
RMS Rhone Marine Park
SALT I.
COOPER I.
GINGER I.
Pelican I.
NORMAN I.
The Bight
Treasure Pt. Cave
Miles
0
1
2
3
4
JOST VAN DYKE
Saddle Bay
North Side Bay
Gt. Harbour
White Bay
Great Harbour
Pelican Cay
Little Jost van Dyke
Diamond Cay
Green Cay
Little Harbour
Garner Bay
Sandy Cay
(Same scale and orientation as main map)

tain, the island's highest point (1,780 feet) and the focal point of Sage Mountain National Park. On its slopes, what was once a primeval rain forest makes the ideal spot for a picnic overlooking the neighboring islands and cays.

The coast road continues west past Fort Recovery, built in 1660 by the Dutch. Just beyond the anchorage at Sopers Hole (if you're thirsty, have a drink at *Pusser's Landing*) is West End town, the takeoff point for St. Thomas–bound ferries. Around the island's western tip lie the north shore's splendidly unspoiled white beaches: Smuggler's Cove, with its garden of snorkeling reefs; sweeping Long Bay; Apple Bay; Carrot Bay; Cane Garden Bay (where *Stanley's Beach Bar* sets up frosty drinks and snacks); beautifully protected Brewer's Bay (which features campgrounds and the remnants of a rum distillery); and Josiah's Bay near Tortola's eastern end. Turn south and cross the Queen Elizabeth Bridge to Beef Island, site of Beef International Airport, launch departures for Marina and Bellamy cays, and untrammeled shelling and sunning beaches. Then head back to Road Town.

VIRGIN GORDA The highlight of a visit to this island (third-largest in the chain, with a population of about 1,000) is a trip to the Baths, where gigantic rocks and boulders, shaped by volcanic pressures millions of years ago, have formed strange entrances to water grottoes and shaded pools. Crawl through one formation to find yourself ankle-deep in cool water; through another to find a long stretch of sand and sunlight. Virgin Gorda boasts some 20 beaches; favorites include Spring, Trunk, and Devil's bays. There is also a 1,370-foot mountain peak in the north. An abandoned 17th-century copper mine on the southeast tip, with its chimney and boiler house still standing, offers fine photo opportunities from your car; the area is scheduled for reinforcement but currently it's unsafe to walk around.

ANEGADA The only coral island of the group (the rest are volcanic), its highest point is just 28 feet above sea level. It's home to a human population of only 250, as well as to a rare species of rock iguana. Dozens of shipwrecks off the reefs tempt divers. One of the sunken ships, the *Paramatta,* has rested 30 feet down for more than 100 years; another, the 18th-century British frigate HMS *Astrea,* sank in 1808. There is also a Greek freighter, sunk in the middle of this century. Although there is little left of the sites, each wreck still holds the promise of hidden treasure.

JOST VAN DYKE On this island, Diamond Cay, home to terns, pelicans, and boobies, has been designated a national park.

Sources and Resources

TOURIST INFORMATION

The British Virgin Islands Tourist Board is in the Joseph Josiah Smith Social Security Building (Wickhams Cay I in Road Town; phone: 43134;

fax: 43866). For information about BVI tourist offices in the US, see GETTING READY TO GO.

LOCAL COVERAGE The *Welcome* is a most informative free bimonthly guide. The *Island Sun* and *BVI Beacon* are the weekly BVI newspapers. Florence Lewisohn's *Tales of Tortola and the British Virgin Islands* and Vernon Pickering's *History of the British Virgin Islands* (available at island shops) are readable histories. *The Cruising Guide to the Virgin Islands* is almost as valuable to landlubbers as to sailors.

RADIO AND TELEVISION

ZBVI-AM (780) is the main island station; the FM station ZROD is another option. Channel 10 picks up programming from the CBS affiliate in St. Thomas, while cable TV beams 18 channels throughout the area.

TELEPHONE

When calling from the US, dial 809 (area code) + 49 (country code) + (local number). To call the British Virgin Islands from another Caribbean island, the code may vary, so contact the local operator. When calling within the British Virgin Islands, use only the local number unless otherwise indicated.

ENTRY REQUIREMENTS

A current passport is the preferred entry document, but proof of citizenship (birth certificate or voter's registration card, along with a photo ID) is acceptable. An ongoing or return ticket is also required. There is a departure tax of $5 per person leaving by air; $4 per person leaving by sea.

WARNING **Currently, there is a law prohibiting members of the Jamaican Rastafarian movement from entering the BVI (purportedly because of concerns about drug smuggling). Rastafarians who must visit for a specific reason, such as business (vacations don't qualify), must have an island official file an application in advance with the immigration authorities. Also, there have been reports of immigration officials turning away tourists wearing clothes or hair styles (such as dreadlocks) that are commonly worn by Rastafarians, even if the tourists are not from Jamaica and not members of the sect. For more information, contact the tourist office in New York before you leave (phone: 212-696-0400 or 800-853-8530).**

CLIMATE AND CLOTHES

The British Virgin Islands enjoy temperatures that range from 77 to 90F (25 to 32C) all year. The air is cooled by trade winds, especially at night, when temperatures drop as much as 10 degrees. Comfortable and casual are the fashion bywords here. Men (except those staying at *Little Dix Bay* or *Peter Island*) can leave their jackets and ties at home.

MONEY

The US dollar is used throughout the islands.

LANGUAGE

The queen's English is spoken, often with a West Indian lilt.

TIME

Atlantic standard time is in effect all year. In winter, when it's noon in the BVI, it's 11 AM in the US eastern standard time zone; when daylight saving time is in effect, the hour is the same in both places.

CURRENT

Outlets are 110 volts, 60 cycles; American appliances need no converter.

TIPPING

All hotels add a 10% to 15% service charge to bills; anything additional is up to you. The standard 10% to 15% is expected in restaurants and by cabbies.

GETTING AROUND

CAR RENTAL Only the coolest and surest drivers should take on the roller coaster hills and hairpin turns of the roads in the British Virgin Islands. Vehicles range from Land Rovers, jeeps, and mini-mokes to six- and eight-passenger Suzukis and air conditioned automatic sedans. On Tortola, contact *Avis* (opposite police headquarters; phone: 43322, 42193, or 800-228-0668); *National* at Duffs Bottom (phone: 43197) or at Nanny Cay (phone: 45345); *Caribbean Car Rental* (at *Maria's Inn;* phone: 42595); *Anytime Car Rental* (at the *Wayside Inn;* phone: 42875 or 43107); *Alphonso's* (in Fish Bay; phone: 43137 or 44886); *Budget* (Wickhams Cay; phone: 42639, after hours 42531); *Island Suzuki* (near Nanny Cay; phone: 43666); or *International Car Rentals* (at *International Motors* in Road Town; phone: 42516 or 42517). On Virgin Gorda, try *Hertz* (phone: 55803 or 800-654-3001), *Andy's Taxi* (phone: 55252 or 55353), *Speedy's Car Rental* (phone: 55235 or 55240), or *Mahogany* (phone: 55542 or 55469). Rates begin at about $40 a day, including unlimited mileage; weekly and monthly rates are available. A valid US driver's license and a temporary BVI driver's license (good for 30 days; available at police headquarters or the rental agency for $10) are required. Renters must be over 25 years of age, and, remember, driving is on the left.

FERRY SERVICES Travel between Tortola and Virgin Gorda is mainly by local ferry service. *Smith's Ferry* (phone: 44430, 42355, or 54495) and *Speedy's Fantasy* (phone: 55240 or 55235) both operate from Road Town in Tortola to the Virgin Gorda Yacht Harbour, about a half-hour trip. *Smith's, Speedy's,* and *Native Son* (phone: 54617) travel between Road Town or

West End in Tortola and St. Thomas. The *North Sound Express* (phone: 42746) goes from Beef Island to the *Bitter End Yacht Club* on Virgin Gorda. *Peter Island Boat* (phone: 42561) links that island and Tortola. Individual arrangements can be made for separate trips.

SEA EXCURSIONS The 80-foot traditional schooner *White Squall II,* out of the *Village Cay* marina (phone: 42564) and the catamaran *Patouche II,* at Wickhams Cay I (phone: 60222 or 42845) offer half- and full-day snorkeling trips to Norman Island caves; half-days are $40 and $48, full-days $68 per person; rates include lunch, drinks, and snorkel gear. Day sails to Cooper Island aboard 30- to 50-foot yachts for $75 per person, including drinks, are available through *Misty Isle Charters* (phone: 55643); 1-week flotilla sailings, where several boats sail together under the lead of owner Cliff Couture's 50-foot vessel *Shenanigan,* also are offered. The catamaran *Ppalu* (phone: 42771, ext. PPALU) offers excursions to Anegada, the Baths, Cooper Island, and Norman Island.

SIGHTSEEING TOURS Tours are offered by *Travel Plan Tours* (phone: 42872), *Mahogany* (phone: 55542, 55469, or 55322 nights), *Style's Taxi* (phone: 42260 or 43341 at night), or *Andy's Taxi* (phone: 55252 or 55353). A 2½-hour tour of Tortola for one to three people runs about $50; $12 for each additional passenger. *Scato's Bus Service* (phone: 42365) conducts economical minibus tours (on 26-seaters) for the budget-minded.

TAXI Cabs are readily available only on Tortola, Virgin Gorda, and Anegada; rates are fixed, so ask in advance. "Safaris," attractive open buses painted bright colors, are available on Virgin Gorda (*Mahogany Taxi Service*; phone: 55542 or 55469) and Tortola (*BVI Taxi*; phone: 42875 or 42322). A minibus seating 26 (*Scato's;* phone: 42365) is available in Tortola for budget-minded groups. You have to call for safaris and minibuses; they cannot be hailed in the street.

INTER-ISLAND FLIGHTS

American Eagle, Sunaire, and *LIAT* offer frequent daily flights from San Juan to Tortola and Virgin Gorda. *Sunaire* also flies from the BVI to St. Croix and St. Thomas. *LIAT* flies to Tortola from Antigua and St. Martin. *Virgin Islands Seaplane Shuttle* flies from St. Thomas and St. Croix to Tortola.

SPECIAL EVENTS

The *Spring Regatta* in April on Tortola draws yachts and hordes of spectators from all the Caribbean islands as well as the US. The *Inter-Airline Regatta,* on Tortola in late September or early October, is an airline-sponsored event attracting airline employees from far and wide. Virgin Gorda holds a 3-day festival at *Easter,* while the *BVI Summer Festival* in August is a 2-week bonanza of beauty contests, singing, dancing, and parades. Banks and offices close for *New Year's Day, Commonwealth Day* (Mar. 14), *Easter Monday, Whitmonday,* the *Queen's Official Birthday* (early June), *Territory Day* (July 1), *St. Ursula's Day* (October 21), the *Prince of Wales's Birthday* (November 14), *Christmas,* and *Boxing Day* (December 26).

SHOPPING

Selections pale beside those in the neighboring USVI, but while Road Town is not a duty-free port, there's no duty on British imports, and some items are bargains. Per-bottle prices on liquor are sometimes lower than those on St. Thomas or St. Croix, but because of the 1-liter limit (as opposed to the 1-gallon USVI duty-free allowance), most US citizens buy their booze in Charlotte Amalie or Christiansted. Island goods include handmade shell jewelry, cotton resortwear, coral creations, local ceramics, and interesting artwork. Most shops are on Road Town's Main Street, with a few more in shopping arcades built into marina developments. Best for buying, browsing on Tortola:

A.H. RIISE Smaller version of the St. Thomas company with bargain-basement liquor prices. O'Neal Complex, Port Purcell (phone: 44483 or 46615).

AMPLE HAMPER All sorts of edible and potable temptations from Great Britain and the islands. Columbus Centre, Wickhams Cay I (phone: 54684).

CARINA CORALS These works of art made from crushed coral are often presented as official gifts to visiting dignitaries. At the *Courtyard Gallery,* Main St. (no phone).

CAROUSEL GIFT SHOP Locally made crafts, including attractive pottery and costume jewelry with island themes. Main St. (phone: 44542).

COLLECTOR'S CORNER An enormous selection of cut and uncut larimar, a bluish stone mined in the Dominican Republic; also handmade shell jewelry. Columbus Centre, Wickhams Cay I (phone: 43550).

KIDS IN DE SUN Ideal for indulgent grandmas, with fashions including tiny Java Wraps batiks. Main St. (phone: 46268).

SAMARKAND Handmade jewelry plus a small selection of BVI collector silver coins, which can be purchased as is or set into mountings. Main St. (phone: 46415).

SUNNY CARIBBEE HERB & SPICE COMPANY Exotic spices, jams and jellies, mustard, vinegar, herbs, tea, coffee, and hot sauces from all over the Caribbean. Main St. (phone: 42178).

On Virgin Gorda, at Yacht Harbour, *Island Woman* (phone: 55237) has Java Wraps clothing and Indonesian crafts; *Kaunda's* (phone: 46737) and the *Virgin Gorda Craft Shop* (phone: 55137) feature Caribbean crafts.

SPORTS

BOATING The British Virgins are among the world's best sailing areas, with more than 300 bareboats, almost 100 charter yachts, and the most developed marinas and shore facilities in the Caribbean. More than 70% of the visitors to the BVI are on sailing vacations. Among the dozen yacht charter firms in Road Town, tops in quality of boats and expertise of personnel, is Ginny and Charlie Cary's the *Moorings,* the largest yacht operation in the Caribbean (phone: 42331; or write 19345 US 19N, Suite 402, Clearwater, FL 34624; phone: 800-535-7289 from the US or 800-535-1446 outside the US). Also recommended are the *Trimarine Boat Company* (phone: 42490; fax: 45774), and *Tropic Island Yacht Management* (phone: 42450; 800-356-8938 from the US). The sailboat *Take Two* may be chartered by guests of the *Prospect Reef* resort. Steve Colgate's *Offshore Sailing School* (phone: 45119; 800-221-4326 from the US) at the *Treasure Isle* hotel offers courses year-round. The *Sopers Hole Marina* (phone: 54553; fax: 54560) offers charters and related services at the multicolored complex at West End. Long-term rentals of bareboats and all-inclusive charters also are available from the *Bitter End Yacht Club* (phone: 42746) in Virgin Gorda. *The Cruising Guide to the Virgin Islands,* published by *Cruising Guide Publications* (2274 S.R. 580, Suite B, Clearwater, FL 34623; phone: 813-796-2469 in Florida) provides invaluable background for sailing, scuba diving, and snorkeling; it can be ordered direct from the publisher for $16.50 (plus $3.50 shipping and handling).

CAMPING *Brewer's Bay Campground,* Tortola (phone: 43463), is on a beautiful beach. Rates are $20 a night for two, including a tent and basic equipment; $7 for a bare site. There's a bar, restaurant, and commissary; snorkeling gear, tours, and baby-sitters are available. *Anegada Beach Campground* (phone: 58038) charges $20 to $30 a night, less in summer. On Jost Van Dyke, *Tula's N&N Campground* (phone: 59301 or 59302; fax: 775-9296) charges $25 and up per couple per night for a tent site and $15 for a bare site, less in summer; there's also a restaurant, snack bar, and live entertainment.

HIKING Sage Mountain National Park, which peaks at 1,780 feet, is an interesting place to hike on Tortola. Check with the tourist board or with *Shadows Ranch* (phone: 42262), which offers exploration on foot or on horseback. A bonus for bird watchers: A list of some 143 BVI birds is available from the National Park Trust (phone: 43904).

HORSE RACING There's betting, music, food, and fun at Tortola's makeshift *Little A Race Track* (phone: 44442) one Sunday a month, as well as on holidays and during the *BVI Summer Festival* in August. Check local publications for racing schedules.

HORSEBACK RIDING Ellis Thomas at Sea Cows Bay (phone: 44442) and the *Shadows Ranch* (phone: 42262) both offer a 2-hour ride for $30 per person, and a jaunt through Sage Mountain National Park for $40 per person.

SNORKELING AND SCUBA There's excellent snorkeling at Virgin Gorda around the Baths and at a dive site called the Indians near Peter and Norman islands. Marina Cay and Cooper Island have good snorkeling from their beaches. Anegada Island, just off the Anegada Reef, has excellent scuba diving and snorkeling sites, although there's not much left of some of the 300-odd ships wrecked here. The most popular dive site in the British Virgin Islands is the wreckage of the RMS *Rhone,* now a British National Monument, close to the western point of Salt Island, a little over 5 miles from Road Town, Tortola. Destroyed by an 1867 hurricane that sank 75 ships and killed at least 500 people, the *Rhone* is one of the Caribbean's most intriguing wrecks. It is broken in half, both parts adorned with colorful fans, corals, sponges, and gorgonians. A huge variety of tame fish cruise through the ship's interior and upright wreckage. It can be reached by commercial dive boat or private charter. Other popular dive sites (there are well over 60) include Blonde Rock, between Dead Chest and Salt Island; Painted Walls (shallow); the wreck of the *Chikuzen* north of Beef Island; and Brenners Bay near Norman. Among the larger dive outfits are *Baskin in the Sun* (with outlets at the *Prospect Reef, Long Beach Bay,* and *Sebastian's* hotels, Road Town; phone: 800-233-7938 from the US); the *Sopers Hole Marina* (Tortola; phone: 42858 or 42859; fax: 45853); *Underwater Safaris,* at the *Moorings* (Road Town; phone: 43235 or 43965; 800-537-7032 from the US); *Blue Water Divers* (Nanny Cay; phone: 43878); and *Island Diver Ltd.* (at the *Village Cay* marina; phone: 43878 or 52367). In Virgin Gorda, try *Kilbride's Underwater Tours* (North Sound, Virgin Gorda; phone: 59638), and *Dive BVI* (Virgin Gorda Yacht Harbour, Leverick Bay, and Peter Island; phone: 55513; 800-848-7078 from the US). Most of these outfits also offer snorkeling excursions, as do *King Charters* (phone: 45820), and *Caribbean Images* (phone: 52563), which also runs a glass-bottom boat tour from the *Prospect Reef* hotel. Figure about $25 per person for a half-day of snorkeling.

SURFING Apple Bay is the place. Surfboards are available at *Sebastian's on the Beach* (phone: 54212); *Bomba's Shack* is the hangout for the surfing crowd.

SWIMMING AND SUNNING Although almost all of the British Virgin Islands' beaches are lovely, in our opinion, this one is the fairest of them all.

A DREAM BEACH

Cane Garden Bay Acknowledged to be one of the handsomest stretches (1½ miles) of fine, white beach in all the British Virgins, this is the place we choose to spend lazy, sun-filled days. You have to bring your own snorkel gear, but you can buy a nice island lunch at *Quito's* or *Rhymer's*

Beach Bar. For a slightly more formal lunch, walk along the bay to the *Sugar Mill* hotel, well known for its fine restaurant. Except for a tire-and-rope swing, there are no sports facilities. Activities are limited to sunning, splashing, and feeling pleased you came.

Other splendid strands include Smuggler's Cove, with its snorkeling reefs and the mile-long white sands of Long Bay. But the lazing is lovely and the swimming fine on a dozen lesser-known strands as well. Virgin Gorda is ringed with glorious beaches such as Devil's Bay, Spring Bay, and Trunk Bay. And dozens more on the BVI's small cays and uninhabited isles await discovery.

TENNIS On Virgin Gorda, *Little Dix Bay* has 7 courts overseen by *Peter Burwash International* (for guests only), *Biras Creek* has 2 courts, and guests at the *Bitter End Yacht Club* have visiting privileges at *Biras Creek*'s courts. On Tortola, *Prospect Reef* has 6 courts, *Mariner Inn* has 2, *Long Bay Beach* and *Frenchman's Cay* each have 1. *Treasure Isle* guests may use the *Mariner Inn* courts across the street. There are also courts at the *Guana Island Club, Necker Island,* and *Peter Island* resorts.

NIGHTLIFE

For those who have energy left after a day of sun and sea and dinner, there's lots of action after dark. In Road Town on Tortola, the *Paradise Pub* at the *Fort Burt Marina* (phone: 42608) has live entertainment (reggae, jazz, or rock) Saturday nights; *Fort Burt* (at the marina; phone: 42587) jumps on Wednesdays; and the *Santa Maria* restaurant (Wickhams Cay; phone: 42771) has something going on Tuesdays through Sundays. Look for night action at *Treasure Isle* on Mondays and Fridays.

Elsewhere on Tortola, *Pusser's Landing* (West End; phone: 57369) offers dancing (often to a BVI fungi band) till early morning. The *Long Bay Beach* resort offers entertainment on Tuesdays and Thursdays. *Bomba's Shack* (phone: 54148) on the beach has local bands Wednesday nights and Sunday afternoons, but partyers really get going monthly on full-moon night. *Sebastian's* (Apple Bay; phone: 54212) offers a West Indian fungi band Sunday nights. At Cane Garden Bay, there is reggae at *Rhymer's Beach Bar* (phone: 54639 or 54215) Sunday nights and a steel band at *Stanley's* at Cave Garden Bay (phone: 54520) nightly except Sundays. Quito Rhymer sings folk music at his *Gazebo* (phone: 54837) four times a week after dinner.

On other islands, Virgin Gorda's *Bath & Turtle* (phone: 55239), *Bitter End's Clubhouse* (phone: 42746), and *Pusser's Leverick Bay* (phone: 57369) feature dance music (live and taped) into the wee hours. There's night action at the *Virgin Queen* (Virgin Gorda; phone: 42310) on Fridays. *Foxy's,* at Great Harbour on Jost Van Dyke (phone: 59275), is another popular nightspot, and *Neptune's Treasure* on Anegada has a local band on Tuesday nights (no phone). For a special treat, arrange to take a dinghy over to tiny Bellamy Cay at Beef Island to *The Last Resort* (phone: 52520 or Channel 16), where Tony Snell has entertained the boating crowd with risqué one-man shows for more than 2 decades; dinner is 7:30 PM, cabaret at 9:30 PM.

Best on the Islands

CHECKING IN

Throughout the British Virgin Islands are some 90 hotels and guesthouses. Although a few of the larger hotels offer special packages that can cut costs considerably, most do not. Expect to pay from about $450 to $690 for a double room (with all meals included) in winter at the hotels we've listed as very expensive. Rooms in the expensive category will run from about $200 to $425 a night EP (without meals). Our moderate selections will cost $100 to $190 a night, and expect to pay anywhere from $60 to $100 for a double room without meals in an inexpensive hotel. Rates drop by as much as 50% in summer. Modified American Plan (including breakfast and dinner) and American Plan (all meals included) rates at places that aren't all-inclusive are higher, of course. A 7% accommodation tax is added to hotel bills; service charges vary from 10% to 15%. Private homes also are available for rent; check with the tourist board for listings. Many luxurious hotels do not have air conditioning, since the trade winds and ceiling fans are sufficient for most people. When calling from a phone within the British Virgin Islands, use only the local numbers listed below. For information on dialing from elsewhere, see "Telephone" earlier in this chapter. The central telephone number for making British Virgin Islands hotel reservations from the US is 800-223-4483 (fax: 212-655-5671 in New York City).

For an unforgettable island experience, we begin with our favorites, followed by our recommendations of cost and quality choices of hotels large and small, listed by area and price category.

A REGAL RESORT, A SPECIAL HAVEN, AND ENCHANTED PRIVATE ISLANDS

Little Dix Bay There's sort of a fresh-air exhilaration about life at this 500-acre Rockresort complex on Virgin Gorda. The guests that gather on its sunny crescent of beach are younger and more active than their counterparts at *Caneel Bay* on St. John; they generally love sailing, sunning, swimming, and snorkeling in their own home bay and picnic trips to the island's other blissful beaches; there's also *Peter Burwash* tennis, horseback riding, and biking. The resort's central building is composed of terraces topped with peaked roofs that look like giant beach hats. But during the day you won't find many people under them; everybody's up and about. At night, everyone gathers in the *Sugar Mill* bar for drinks. Sometimes there's music, dancing, or local entertainment during and after dinner. The moonrises are spectacular. Our favorite rooms are those in the shingle-topped, hexagonal stilt-houses west of the main buildings, with patios and hammocks underneath; inside, you'll find all the traditional Rockresort comforts. Its carefree, open-air life makes this a particularly good place for a family holiday. Little Dix Bay (phone: 55555; 800-928-3000 from the US).

Biras Creek This Virgin Gorda retreat feels far away because it is — a 15-minute taxi ride plus a boat ride (both complimentary) from the Virgin Gorda airstrip. But what a place to soak up sun and unwind. The resort's 150 acres reach from a blue bay on one side, up and over a hill, and then down again to the sea on the other. The 33 beachside suites in 16 cottages and 3 private suites with sunken tubs are luxury in depth right down to their shaggy rugs. Nothing showy, but lots of the kind of fine contemporary decor for which the Scandinavians are famous (plus a little island flavor thrown in for good measure). The suites feature airy bedrooms, sitting rooms (with small fridges stocked with rum and ginger ale), patios facing the sea, and discreetly walled outdoor showers that give you the feeling you're bathing in a waterfall. At the glittering beach, there's sunbathing, swimming, snorkeling, sailing, and a bar made out of a weathered boat hull. A permanent dock can accommodate 10 yachts of up to 60 feet long. There's also a small nature sanctuary and 2 tennis courts just a short stroll away. It's a 5-mile hike (or bike trip) to town (bikes are free), but day sailing trips to other beaches are more fun and often include memorable picnics. At cocktail time, everyone sleeks up and gathers in the castle-shaped clubhouse on the heights for drinks, sunset viewing, and dinner (see *Eating Out*). The wine list here — 161 different vintages of US, German, Austrian, French, and Italian origin — is said to rival any in the Caribbean. North Sound (phone: 43555 or 43556; 800-223-1108 from the US; fax: 43557).

Guana Island Club Green-clad and hilly, this 850-acre island prides itself on "comfortably casual atmosphere, lots of space and privacy." A maximum of 30 guests are lodged in whitewashed cottages that cling to the central ridge. For complete privacy, guests can rent the entire island for about $7,400 a day. Seven shining beaches, a salt pond populated by a flock of flamingos, a nature preserve, unusual flora and fauna, and intriguing mountain trails provide daytime diversion; the more energetic can indulge in snorkeling, sailing, fishing, windsurfing, water skiing, tennis, and croquet; scuba diving can be arranged. All on-premises activities and three meals a day are included. The island is a 10-minute launch ride from Beef Island International Airport on Tortola (phone: 42354; 914-967-6050 from New York; 800-54-GUANA from elsewhere in the US).

Necker Island Advertised simply as "The Island," this 74-acre hideaway, surrounded by its own unspoiled coral reef and flanked by 3 white sand beaches, may indeed be the ultimate in luxurious retreats. Its owner, Richard Branson, the multimillionaire whiz kid of Virgin Records and

Virgin Atlantic Airways, originally bought this island for his family and friends but then decided to lease it out — the entire island with 10-bedroom villa — when he's not there. The villa, a remarkable Balinese-style structure, was built from rock that was blasted from the top of Devil's Hill, where it perches, entirely surrounded by terraces with breathtaking views. The sun filters through a lush tropical garden in the center of the spectacular open space that comprises a living, dining, and bar area; above it, a gallery library bulges with books and games for all tastes. The young Canadian managers, Barbara and Dan Reid, are longtime island residents and former managers of the *Bitter End Yacht Club* on Virgin Gorda. First class meals can be enjoyed on the breezy deck, under the retractable roof in the dining room, or at poolside. Other amenities include an exercise room, Jacuzzis, tennis, windsurfing, sailing dinghies, water skiing, aquascooters, fishing equipment, full-size snooker table, facilities for small meetings and conferences, and an open bar and wine cellar. The daily rate of $10,900, includes all of the above, plus all meals for 16 to 20 people. Guests are met at Beef Island International Airport on Tortola or on Virgin Gorda and are ferried over (less than 30 minutes; phone: 42757 or 44492 on Tortola; 800-542-0004 or 800-241-6759 from the US).

Peter Island Simple, sleek, and supremely first class, this place acquired its Scandinavian ambience from the source: The 8 neat 2-unit A-frames that house the resort's 32 original guestrooms were all prefabbed in Norway, shipped out — with all their luxurious garnishes — on the former owner's boats, then reassembled on Sprat Bay with the main clubhouse and marina. The marina and its facilities for sailing, scuba, and fishing are top-notch. There is a meeting room that accommodates 50, a fitness center, an up-to-the-minute water sports center, and a freshwater swimming pool. The Scandinavian-style clubhouse — with its deck, bar, and rotisserie dining room — combines eye-pleasing looks and body-cradling comfort. But the adjacent sea and the palm trees that border it are appealingly West Indian, as are the 20 additional rooms in a beach house just over the hill on Dead Man's Bay, one of the island's most beautiful bays. Sports include swimming, snorkeling (at a special beach), cruising, windsurfing, Sunfish and Squib sailing, and 4 Laykold tennis courts with *Peter Burwash International* instructors. The crowd that gathers for dinner each evening at *Tradewinds* is tanned and glowing; jackets are requested. Less formal is the resort's *Deadman's Bay Beach Bar* restaurant. Several nights a week a band comes over from Road Town to play for dancing (phone: 42561; 800-346-4451 from the US).

TORTOLA

EXPENSIVE

Long Bay Beach This low-rise complex sprawls up a hillside overlooking a truly beautiful mile-long beach, the sea, and nearby islands. The family-friendly resort has 62 rooms and 8 two-bedroom units, either beachfront cabañas or hillside villas. There's also a tennis court, a saltwater swimming pool, 2 bars, and 2 excellent restaurants — the *Garden* restaurant (see *Eating Out*) for more formal dining, and the *Beach* restaurant. Be prepared to climb up and down steep hills. Long Bay (phone: 54252; 800-729-9599 from the US).

Sunset House On a hillside above Long Bay with a spectacular view, this place feels like a private, modern home. There are only 5 rooms in the main house (each with a private balcony) and another 2 on the beach. The chef cooks in the common kitchen or at the pool. Other features include ceiling fans, a pool with bar, and a Jacuzzi. Long Bay (phone: 42550; 800-835-8530 or 800-232-7770 from the US; fax: 45866).

MODERATE

Fort Recovery Built around an unexcavated round fort tower dating from the Dutch occupation in about 1630, this complex offers 10 air conditioned suites with 1, 2, or 4 bedrooms. All units feature full kitchens and daily maid service. Several accommodations are right on the beach; one unit, *The Big House,* boasts a private art collection including (the owner claims) some genuine works by Georgia O'Keeffe. Construction of a health center is scheduled to be completed this year. Fort Recovery Estate (phone: 54467; 800-367-8455 from the US; fax: 54036).

Mariner Inn Originally designed for bareboaters, this 40-room property has attracted other vacationers as well. Highlights include 2 tennis courts, a pool, a dive shop, yacht charters, a full-service marina with slips for 140 yachts (many available for charter), a specialty food shop, a good restaurant (see *Eating Out*), and a lively bar overlooking the marina, all within walking distance of Road Town. There's free transportation to *Treasure Isle,* which shares facilities. Wickhams Cay II, Road Town (phone: 42331; 800-535-7289 from the US; fax: 42226).

Prospect Reef The largest resort (44 acres) in the British Virgin Islands boasts a freshwater junior Olympic-size pool and dive tank, stone-terraced sea pools, 2 children's pools, 2 restaurants, and 2 bars. The 131 comfortable, attractive units include studios (with kitchenettes), suites, and 2-bedroom villas; some have air conditioning. Other amenities: a large shopping arcade, 6 tennis courts and a pro shop (lessons are available), and a fitness center. Sporting equipment is complimentary, and scuba, snorkeling, sailing, and deep-sea fishing trips can be arranged. Road Town (phone: 43311; 800-356-8937 from the US; fax: 45595).

Sebastian's on the Beach Located on a lovely north shore beach, this is one of Tortola's older properties, with lots of island flavor and no pretensions. The 26 rooms all have private baths, ceiling fans, and refrigerators; beachfront and rooms facing the back have king- or queen-size beds; the less deluxe courtyard rooms are a bargain. The restaurant serves simple fare and creole specialties (see *Eating Out*); there's also a friendly beach bar. Apple Bay (phone: 54212; 305-266-5256 from Florida; 800-336-4870 from elsewhere in the US; fax: 54466).

Sugar Mill Built on the ruins of a 300-year-old sugar mill on 5 acres at Apple Bay, this complex has 4 two-bedroom suites, 4 one-bedroom apartments, and 12 studios (most with kitchenettes), plus an air conditioned villa. The estate has a circular freshwater pool, a commendable restaurant (see *Eating Out*), and its own small beach with a shaded bar. Apple Bay (phone: 54355; 800-462-8834 from the US; fax: 54696).

Treasure Isle One of Tortola's first hotels, this 15-acre complex is a 5-minute drive from the center of Road Town. The property, on a hillside overlooking the harbor, features 42 rooms and 3 suites (with kitchenettes) built around a freshwater swimming pool. Bedrooms are air conditioned and have cool terra cotta–tiled floors and rattan furnishings. Rooms on levels 3 and 4 offer the most spectacular views, for those who don't mind steep steps. Special features include use of the *Mariner Inn's* facilities, snorkeling trips, and transport to the island's best beaches. *The Verandah,* an open-air restaurant (see *Eating Out*), is a gathering spot for many yacht charterers. Road Town (phone: 42501; 800-334-2435 from the US).

VIRGIN GORDA

VERY EXPENSIVE

Bitter End Yacht Club This hideaway, at the east end of North Sound, is accessible only by boat. It's a sailor's haven, with more than 80 boats, including sailboats, powered skiffs, rowing sculls, and 10 live-aboard yachts. There are over 50 units in marina rooms, beachfront and hillside villas; another 50 rooms in separate chalets are considered more upscale. There's a stunning pool overlooking North Sound; scuba gear, snorkeling and sailing trips, and sailing instruction are available at the *Nick Trotter Sailing School. The English Carvery* features roasts and grilled meat; the popular *Clubhouse* downstairs draws boaters. All meals are included. North Sound (phone: 42746; 800-872-2392 from the US).

EXPENSIVE

Mango Bay One of Virgin Gorda's newer properties, it's on its own reef-protected beach lined with palms and mahogany, midway between the *Little Dix* resort and North Sound. The 12 two-unit white villas, each different from the others, are strung along the golden sand beach; all have attractive living rooms, full kitchens, and large outdoor porticoes with barbecue facilities. There's a boat jetty with a 34-foot boat available for charter, and good snorkeling off the reef; snorkeling and windsurfing equipment are complimentary. Mango Bay (phone: 55672 or 55673; 800-223-6510 from the US; fax: 55674).

MODERATE

Guavaberry Spring Bay Intriguingly clustered around, between, and atop giant boulders like those at the nearby Baths geological site, these small, attractive, hexagonal wooden cottages have 1 or 2 bedrooms, living areas, sun decks, and fully equipped kitchens. There's a commissary, but no restaurant. Spread across 20 hillside acres, the units are all about a 5-minute walk to the beach. Guavaberry Spring Bay (phone: 55227).

Olde Yard Inn A breezy gazebo and an extensive library with a piano are among the assets of this personable hideaway. With 14 small, neat, double rooms (4 with air conditioning), it's more retreat than resort. Good food and wines are served at the restaurant (see *Eating Out*). A 20-minute, strenuous walk from Savannah Beach; the Baths are 2 miles away. The Valley (phone: 55544; 800-74 CHARMS from the US; fax: 55986).

JOST VAN DYKE

VERY EXPENSIVE

Sandcastle at White Bay In this small, secluded colony, modern octagonal cottages are surrounded by hibiscus and bougainvillea. There's a pleasant outdoor restaurant and bar plus 200 feet of fine sandy beach (windsurfing available). This remote place seems designed for those who *really* want to get away from it all. The owner picks guests up at Red Hook, St. Thomas, US Virgin Islands (phone: VHF Ch. 16; 800-446-5963 from the US; fax: 237-8903).

EATING OUT

As in most of the British islands, the best food is simply prepared and straightforward, with seafood a major attraction. Expect to spend $70 and up for a meal for two, not including wine, tip, or drinks, in restaurants listed as expensive; $35 to $70 in those classified as moderate; and under $35 at places in the inexpensive category. When calling from a phone within the British Virgin Islands, use only the local numbers listed below. For information about dialing from elsewhere, see "Telephone" earlier in this chapter.

TORTOLA

EXPENSIVE

Brandywine Bay Dinner is served on the elegant garden patio of this charming old house at the water's edge. The Florentine-cum-continental menu includes cracked conch, linguine with scampi, and a dessert aptly called Chocolate Decadence. Open for dinner only; closed Sundays. Reservations necessary.

Major credit cards accepted. Brandywine Bay, just east of Road Town (phone: 52301 or VHF Ch. 16).

Captain's Table A French chef with much experience in the Caribbean has brought his skills to Tortola. The dinner menu features escargots in puff pastry, fettuccine with a spinach and garlic cream sauce, and a perfectly pink rack of lamb. Lunch is less elaborate, but all meals are enjoyed alfresco on a terrace overlooking the inner harbor in Road Town. Open for lunch and dinner; lunch only on Saturdays. Reservations necessary. MasterCard and Visa accepted. Wickhams Cay I (phone: 43885).

Cloud Room This outdoor, hilltop dining spot offers a panoramic view; in good weather, the roof opens to reveal the starry sky. The menu presents a combination of continental and island dishes, including filet mignon, curried shrimp, and stuffed breast of chicken. Transportation to and from your hotel in a canvas-topped vehicle is included. Open for dinner only; closed Sundays. Reservations essential. Major credit cards accepted. Ridge Rd. (phone: 42821).

Mariner Inn A pleasant open-air bar and restaurant overlooking the busy *Moorings Marina* and Drake's Channel. The ambience is casual from breakfast through happy hour; dinners are candlelit and more elegant, with such choices as West Indian grouper or filet mignon. Open daily. Reservations advised for dinner. Major credit cards accepted. Wickhams Cay II (phone: 42332).

Sugar Mill California food writers Jinx and Jeff Morgan have found the perfect vehicle for their culinary expertise at this 300-year-old sugar mill. Their menu, considered by many to be the island's best, features garden-fresh ingredients. Specials might include mulligatawny soup (rich beef or vegetable broth seasoned with curry and other spices) or pork medallions; steaks and fish are always offered. Dessert choices include amaretto soufflé and icebox cheesecake with strawberry sauce. Open daily for breakfast and dinner. Reservations necessary. Major credit cards accepted. Apple Bay (phone: 54355).

The Verandah Sailors and local businesspeople like to gather on this gingerbread open-air terrace. Grilled shrimp with aioli (garlic) sauce becomes island-oriented when served with steamed pumpkin flavored with cinnamon; walnut cake is the perfect choice for meal's end. On Saturday nights there's a Caribbean barbecue and Wednesday nights feature a cookout with steaks and chicken. Open daily for lunch and dinner. Reservations advised. Major credit cards accepted. At the *Treasure Isle Resort,* Road Town (phone: 42507).

MODERATE

The Apple Another find on Tortola's northwest coast is tucked into a little West Indian house on pretty Apple Bay. The house drink, "Virgin Souppy," is a must: It consists of soursop juice, Coco Lopez, and local Cruzan rum topped with a sprinkle of nutmeg. Try the pumpkin soup, conch fritters, or whelks. Open for dinner only; closed Mondays. Reservations essential. Major credit cards accepted. Apple Bay (phone: 54437).

Fish Trap Consistently good seafood is served on a candlelit patio surrounded by bougainvillea or in the air conditioned dining room. Try the conch fritters, salt fish cakes, soft shell crabs, or the daily buffet. Open for lunch and dinner; dinner only on Sundays. Reservations advised for groups of more than six people. Major credit cards accepted. Columbus Centre, Wickhams Cay I (phone: 43626).

Garden Continental and West Indian flavors merge in this restaurant at the *Long Bay Beach* decorated with flowers. The prix fixe dinner menu may include island-style red bean soup, grilled wahoo with passion-fruit sauce, or roast beef with Yorkshire pudding; there's always a vegetarian selection. A scratch band plays Tuesday and Thursday nights. Open daily for dinner. Reservations advised. Major credit cards accepted. Long Bay (phone: 54252).

Mrs. Scatliffe's Definitely a family affair, with Mrs. Scatliffe and one daughter in the kitchen, another daughter waiting tables, a son-in-law mixing drinks, and Mr. Scatliffe strumming the guitar. The food is home cooking, West Indian–style, using fresh vegetables from the garden and fish from the sea beneath the terrace restaurant. Favorite dishes include chicken in a coconut shell and curried goat. After dinner, the family jams on the ukulele, merengue box, or a handy gourd. Open daily for dinner only. Reservations essential. No credit cards accepted. Carrot Bay (phone: 54556).

Pusser's Landing This chain of salty dining spots offers English and American-style food, from meat pies to steaks. There are two other similar branches: *Pusser's Outpost,* also in Tortola, and *Pusser's* on Virgin Gorda. Open for lunch and dinner; no dinner on Saturdays at *Pusser's Outpost*. Reservations advised for dinner at *Pusser's.* Major credit cards accepted. Sopers Hole Wharf, West End (phone: 54554); Main St., Road Town (phone: 44199); and Leverick Bay, Virgin Gorda (phone: 57369).

Santa Maria At the *Village Cay* resort, this casual place lies an arm's length from luxury yachts at anchor. Seafood, steaks, a salad bar, and sandwiches are on the menu; twice a week, there's a barbecue. A buffet lunch is served Tuesdays and Thursdays; a buffet dinner, with steel band entertainment, on Friday nights. Open daily for lunch and dinner. Reservations essential in high season. Major credit cards accepted. Wickhams Cay I, Road Town (phone: 42771).

Sebastian's A beachfront dining room that dishes up fare ranging from barbecued chicken to filet mignon, with plenty of seafood. West Indian entertainment Sunday nights. Open daily. Reservations advised. Major credit cards accepted. Apple Bay (phone: 54212, ext. 1313).

Skyworld It's quite a drive up, but this place offers a spectacular view over all the Virgin Islands and fabulous sunsets. Bring a camera (and a sweater if the wind is blowing). Lunches are fairly simple; dinners are either à la carte or six-course affairs featuring local seafood dishes. The conch fritters are fabulous. Open daily for lunch and dinner. Reservations necessary for dinner. Major credit cards accepted. Ridge Rd. (phone: 43567 or VHF Ch. 16).

INEXPENSIVE

Paradise Pub Another typical English pub, this is Tortola's oldest nightclub (since 1967), very informal and popular with the yachting crowd. Steaks, seafood, and pasta are served until about 3 AM; there's nightly entertainment. Open for breakfast, lunch, and dinner; closed Sundays. Reservations advised. Major credit cards accepted. At *Fort Burt Marina,* next to the *BVI Yacht Club,* in Road Town (phone: 42608).

Other inexpensive and unpretentious eateries on Tortola include *Stanley's* (phone: 54520), *Rhymer's Beach Bar* (phone: 54639), and *Quito's Gazebo* (no phone), all on beautiful Cane Garden Bay; *Peg Leg Landing* at Nanny Cay (phone: 40028); and *Maria's* (phone: 42595), *Downstairs* at the *Prospect Reef* (phone: 43311), and *Bobby's Fast Food* (phone: 42189), in Road Town. *Marlene's Delicious Design* (Wickhams Cay I; phone: 44634) dishes out homemade pâtés, *rôtis,* sandwiches, cakes, and pastries that can be taken out or eaten in the air conditioned dining room; closed Sundays.

VIRGIN GORDA

EXPENSIVE

Biras Creek The elegant hilltop dining room at this exclusive resort offers one of the most romantic views around. The first-rate food emphasizes light cooking and fresh produce. A five-course set meal is served each night, with a choice of three entrées and lobster. The wine list, with more than 150 vintages from five countries, is one of the Caribbean's best. Open daily for breakfast, lunch, and dinner. Reservations necessary. Major credit cards accepted. North Sound (phone: 43555 or 53556).

Olde Yard Inn Small and special, this is the kind of cozy inn one dreams of coming home to after a long day. Exquisite meals are served alfresco on a terra cotta-floored gallery to soft classical music. Seafood in creole sauce or homemade fettuccine are terrific starters; breads are freshly baked on the premises; fresh local fish or veal served with shrimp, herbs, and cheese are perfect. There's also a small, well-chosen wine list. Open daily for breakfast, lunch, and dinner. Reservations necessary. Major credit cards accepted. The Valley (phone: 55544).

Other Virgin Gorda dining options are the exclusive resorts of *Little Dix Bay* or the *Bitter End Yacht Club,* both pricey. The first offers fine food; the latter has the *English Carvery* (serving steaks and roasts) and the less formal *Bitter End Clubhouse.* Still other eateries include *Chez Michelle* (in The Valley; phone: 55510) for continental choices (though a little short on ambience), the pub-type *Bath & Turtle* (at the Virgin Gorda Yacht Harbour; phone: 55239), *Fischer's Cove Beach* (St. Thomas Bay; phone: 55252), the *Crab Hole* (Spanish Town; phone: 55307), and *Teacher Ilma's* (next to the laundromat on Virgin Gorda; phone: 55355) for local food, local atmosphere, and often a local band.

OTHER ISLANDS

MODERATE

Last Resort On its own little islet in the middle of a circular bay, with great anchorage for yachtsmen, this popular port of call features a fairly routine British-style buffet (from 7:30 PM till it's gone), followed by a rather bawdy show by owner/entertainer Tony Snell, an amazing one-man band. Come over by dinghy, or call and they'll send one for you. Open for breakfast, lunch, and dinner; closed Sundays. Reservations essential. Major credit cards accepted. Bellamy Cay, Beef Island (phone: 52520).

Drake's Anchorage This delightful pavilion restaurant, caressed by sea breezes, features myriad seafood dishes, some West Indian fare, and other choices with a French flair. Dolphin with curry sauce and bananas is the most popular entrée, with grilled rack of lamb a close second. Close to Virgin Gorda; the inn sends a boat over to pick up guests. Open daily for breakfast, lunch, and dinner. Reservations essential. Major credit cards accepted. Mosquito Island (phone: 42254 or VHF Ch. 16).

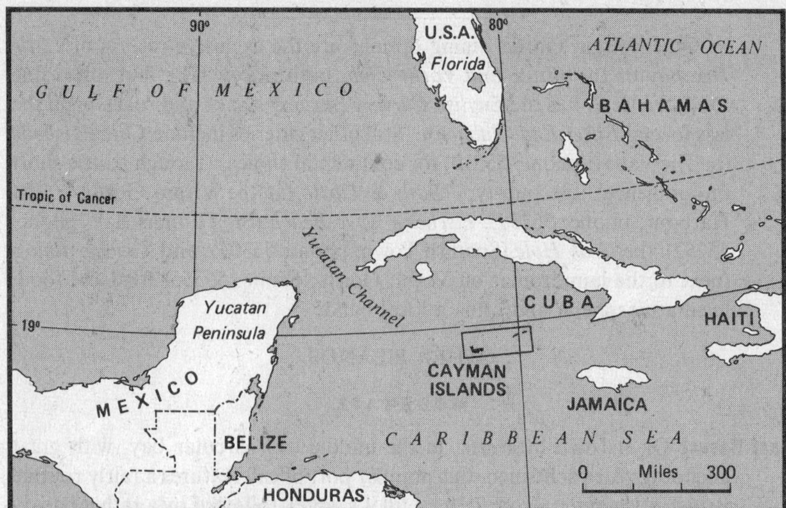

90°
80°
U.S.A.
Florida
ATLANTIC OCEAN
GULF OF MEXICO
BAHAMAS
Tropic of Cancer
Yucatan Channel
CUBA
HAITI
19°
Yucatan
Peninsula
MEXICO
CAYMAN
ISLANDS
JAMAICA
BELIZE
CARIBBEAN SEA
0 Miles 300
HONDURAS

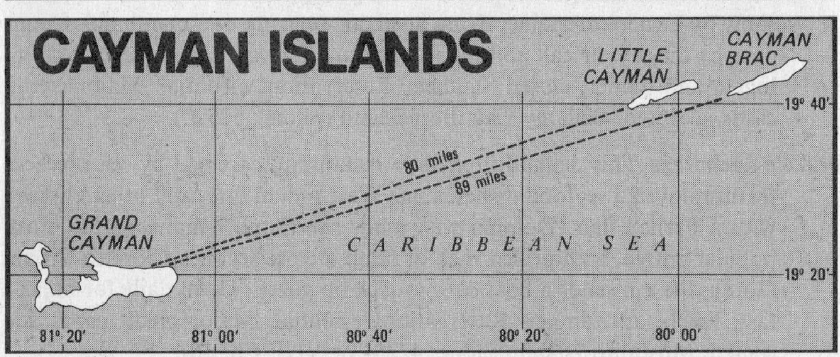

CAYMAN ISLANDS
LITTLE
CAYMAN
CAYMAN
BRAC
19° 40'
80 miles
89 miles
GRAND
CAYMAN
CARIBBEAN SEA
19° 20'
81° 20'
81° 00'
80° 40'
80° 20'
80° 00'

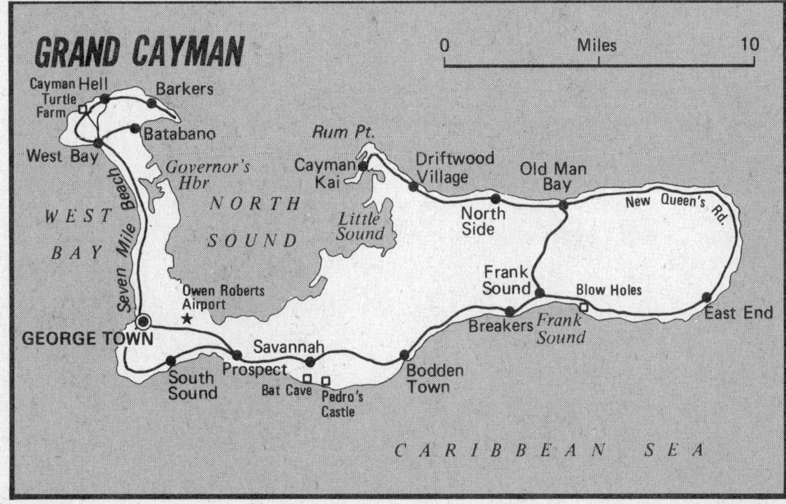

GRAND CAYMAN
0 Miles 10
Cayman Turtle Farm
Hell
Barkers
Batabano
West Bay
Rum Pt.
Governor's Hbr
Cayman Kai
Driftwood Village
Old Man Bay
NORTH SOUND
Little Sound
North Side
New Queen's Rd.
WEST BAY
Seven Mile Beach
Frank Sound
Blow Holes
Owen Roberts Airport
East End
GEORGE TOWN
Breakers
Frank Sound
Savannah
South Sound
Prospect
Bodden Town
Bat Cave
Pedro's Castle
CARIBBEAN SEA

Cayman Islands

Once upon a time, if you mentioned the Cayman Islands, the response was likely to be "Cayman who?" followed by "where?" and "why?" Today, however, Grand Cayman is considered the Caribbean's condominium and the offshore financial industry's capital, as well as one of its fastest-growing beach spots and most popular scuba diving destinations. Its two small sister isles also are being discovered by scuba enthusiasts and anglers who enjoy not only superlative sporting opportunities but also the islands' peaceful isolation.

The Cayman Islands are a trio of tiny coral dots poking out of the western Caribbean. Called Grand Cayman, Little Cayman, and Cayman Brac (Brac means "bluff" in Gaelic), they are outcroppings of the Cayman Ridge, a submarine mountain range extending from Cuba's Sierra Maestra to the Misteriosa and Rosario banks that point their underwater way southwest toward Belize. Grand Cayman, the largest and most developed, and Little Cayman are mostly flat — the highest point on Grand Cayman rises 60 feet above sea level. Mountainous by comparison, Cayman Brac has a bluff running up its spine that starts from sea level on the west end and rises 140 feet to a cliff at its easternmost point. Each Cayman is formed entirely of calcareous rock so porous that there are no streams. There are, however, freshwater wells throughout the islands and, on Grand Cayman, a large modern desalination plant that provides the bulk of the island's water supply. Many islanders still maintain cisterns that catch and store rainwater.

Columbus found the Caymans by accident when, en route from Panama to Hispaniola in 1503, he was blown off course. The islands' large turtle population led Columbus to call them Las Tortugas. The label didn't stick, however; the current name comes from *caymanas* (the Spanish-Carib word for "crocodiles"), although the *caymanas* referred to were probably iguanas.

In the 16th and 17th centuries, ships plying the Caribbean called at the islands for supplies of turtle meat and fresh water, but there was no rush to settle them. It was not until 1655 that the first colonists — deserters from Oliver Cromwell's army who, according to legend, sneaked off from Jamaica when England took it from the Spanish — arrived. Fifteen years later, the Treaty of Madrid made the Cayman Islands a British possession. This status has been a source of pride to loyal islanders ever since.

For a relatively quiet destination, these islands have had a rowdy history. Pirate tales abound, as do stories of buried treasure and sunken fortunes. But the sea story Caymanians love best (and support most vigorously, though historians can find no basis for it) is the "Wreck of the Ten Sails." On a dark November night in 1788, a convoy of merchant ships was passing east of Grand Cayman when the lead ship struck the reef. Her warning signal was misunderstood, and nine more vessels piled up with her. Residents of East End purportedly rescued many of the ships' passengers, including a royal personage, and King George III gratefully granted the Cayman Islands freedom from taxation or, according to other sources, freedom from wartime conscription — benefits that the islands still enjoy.

Despite the generous spirit shown to the shipwrecked travelers, Caymanians' reaction was less enthusiastic when the first tourists found their way here in the early 1950s. A request for travel information in those days brought a boat-mailed reply, mimeographed slightly off-center on a single legal-size sheet. It pointed out the disadvantages of potholed roads, disintegrating cars, a large number of insects, and an uncertain electrical supply. Its tone wasn't "Stay away," but, more candidly, "Don't say we didn't warn you."

But fishermen and beach nuts, undaunted, continued to arrive in increasing numbers. In the early 1960s, divers discovered the islands' spectacular underwater sites. In 1966, the Legislative Assembly passed a series of laws creating a variety of tax-haven investment opportunities on Grand Cayman favoring offshore banking, trust-company formation, and the registration of companies. These enticements spurred considerable outside interest, and there are now more than 500 banks on Grand Cayman. The Caymanian economy has been improving dramatically ever since, and tourism has come to stay.

Also in 1966, a tourist board was established to encourage and control the industry. It set up a system of hotel inspections that have raised standards — though there is still room for improvement, and it has ridden herd on tour operators and the quality of their offerings. Cayman accommodations may be attractive, clean, and well maintained, but only a few resorts can honestly be labeled "luxurious." Restaurants aren't inexpensive either — although the food is only occasionally first-rate (at *Lantana's* and *The Wharf,* for example). There are a few interesting historic sights and a handful of nightlife and dancing options on Grand Cayman.

There are, however, patches of loveliness — rows of royal palms, tall pines moving in soft breezes, and splashes of floral and faunal color. Cayman beaches, found primarily on Grand Cayman's west and north coasts, rank among the most beautiful in the Caribbean, including Seven Mile Beach (in reality, about 6 miles long) and the quiet and unspoiled area of the Cayman Kai Retreat section of the North Side.

But the coral gardens, dramatic sheer walls, and sloping drop-offs of these islands' undersea world are undoubtedly their most famous natural attractions. The variety of marine life, ideal diving conditions (calm seas, little current, superb visibility), and the largest number of professional dive services in the Caribbean combine to create an underwater nirvana.

Other water sports, from parasailing and sailboarding to glass-bottom boat rides and jet skis, beckon the non-amphibious vacationer. Would-be

Jules Vernes can voyage to the bottom of the sea aboard one of the island's 3 submarines. Last, but certainly not least, the islands offer superb sport fishing with year-round action from bonefish (particularly good on Cayman Brac, outstanding on Little Cayman), small tarpon, and further offshore, blue marlin, wahoo, yellowfin tuna, dolphin, and other game fish. Indeed, when it comes to things aquatic, these islands lack nothing except an underwater hotel.

Topside, there may be no spectacular land vistas, but even the smallest, humblest house on the Caymans is tidy and often brightened with flowers. The islands have one of the highest standards of living in the entire Caribbean, hospitable and courteous residents, and only a rare instance of panhandling. The squadrons of souvenir hawkers who stalk visitors on other shores are absent — a fact that makes Grand Cayman one of the top cruise ship ports in the Caribbean. The Caymans remain a safe, comfortable spot with a very North American atmosphere. Its pleasant people, stable government, and crime-free atmosphere keep many visitors returning each year. For those requiring only sun, sand, and sea — in a non-exotic wrapper — the Caymans might be paradise at any price.

Cayman Islands At-a-Glance

FROM THE AIR

The three Cayman Islands together have a total land area of about 96 square miles. Grand Cayman, looking vaguely like a sperm whale from the air, is 76 square miles, about 22 miles long and 8 miles wide at its broadest point. Some 80 miles east-northeast of Grand Cayman is Little Cayman, resembling a sea slug, with 10 square miles of land ringed by crystal white beaches. Eel-shaped Cayman Brac, just 5 miles due east of Little Cayman, has a total of only 10 square miles — it's 10 miles long and only 1 mile across at its widest point.

The hallmark of Grand Cayman is West Bay Beach (that's the official name; everybody calls it Seven Mile Beach), which runs in a gentle curve along the western shore and has the majority of the resort hotels. The western half of the island is sculpted by huge North Sound, whose entrance is entirely protected by a giant coral reef. North Sound digs into the body of the island and deprives it of what would be another 40 square miles of land. Grand Cayman, site of the islands' capital, George Town, has the bulk of the population, just over 26,000 of the 28,000 total. Of the remaining 1,700 or so, practically all live on Cayman Brac. Little Cayman is home to 33 permanent residents. Grand Cayman is almost precisely due south of Miami, some 480 miles and about an hour's plane ride away. Jamaica lies 180 miles east-southeast. Jets land at Owen Roberts International Airport, just outside George Town, in the southwest corner of the island, a few miles from Seven Mile Beach.

SPECIAL PLACES

There are no dazzlers on the islands, but you might like to take a day away from the beach to do some wandering.

GEORGE TOWN The small, clean, unpretentious capital, where building heights are limited to 5 stories, keeps the blue sky in sight at all times, and there seem to be sea views from everywhere. Sights include a clock monument to King George V, located at the corner of Fort and Edward Streets; the Legislative Assembly on Fort Street; the Courts Building opposite; the Government Administration Building on Elgin Avenue, called the Glass House by locals; the neat little library on Edward Street, which stocks English novels and magazines; and the General Post Office (also on Edward St.), near the town center, where you can buy popular stamps at cost in the Philatelic Bureau. The *Cayman Islands National Museum,* on the waterfront at Hog Sty Bay, has some 2,000 fascinating exhibits about the islands' history. The collection includes shipbuilding tools, weapons, coins, and books. Open Tuesdays through Fridays from 8:30 AM to 4:30 PM; Saturdays from 10 AM to 5 PM; and Sundays from 1 to 5 PM. Admission charge (phone: 949-8368).

ELSEWHERE ON GRAND CAYMAN

To see more than George Town on Grand Cayman, it's necessary to hire a cab or rent a car, motorbike, or bicycle. Some of the island's attractions can be seen by driving out along Seven Mile Beach, past the beachside residence of His Excellency the Governor to the vicinity of the settlement of West Bay. Noteworthy sights and stops include:

HELL Supposedly named by a former commissioner who said, after seeing its weird coral and rock formation for the first time, "This is what Hell must look like." To capitalize on the name, there is a post office nearby where the postmistress stamps all cards and letters "Hell, Grand Cayman." There is a ramp leading to a photo vantage point above the limestone fields, and two gift shops where visitors can buy Hell memorabilia and refreshments. The nearby *Club Inferno* bar is owned by the McDoom family!

BATABANO On North Sound, this is where local fishermen bring their catch, and where fresh fish, lobster (in season), conch, and turtle meat are sold. North Sound's reef is an outstanding site for divers and sport fishermen.

CAYMAN TURTLE FARM Established in 1968 by a private enterprise and now owned by the Cayman government, this is the only commercial green sea turtle farm in the world. The reptiles are hatched and raised through young adulthood on the premises. There are educational exhibits and a gift shop selling items with a turtle motif, souvenirs, and tortoiseshell crafts. *Warning:* Until the US Government's endangered species ban is lifted, "look but don't buy" are the watchwords for Americans where tortoiseshell jewelry and other turtle souvenirs are concerned. Open daily from 9 AM to 5 PM. Admission charge. West Ball St., just west of Hell (phone: 949-3894).

For the sights in the other direction, head east out of George Town to:

SOUTH SOUND ROAD On this pine-lined street, one of the most attractive on the island, are quaint old wooden Caymanian houses. Look for one on the seaward side painted with colorful abstract designs by the owner, a Caymanian lady who prefers to remain an obscure artist-in-residence and not a tourist attraction. Look, enjoy, and pass on, please.

BAT CAVE Cave buffs who don't mind exploring on their hands and knees can take the dirt road off the main road (to Bodden Town, heading east) on the seaside just beyond the speed restriction sign. Drive to the end of the road, then proceed on foot toward the sea, turn left, and walk along the cliff edge for about 30 yards until you're standing above a sandy beach. Climb down the 10-foot cliff, look away from the sea, and you'll see the low mouth of Bat Cave directly in front of you. There's a central domed cavity with a few side passages. The bats are not dangerous, but they squeak a lot when you enter. Watch for falling "deposits"!

PEDRO'S CASTLE Now a rustic bar and sometime restaurant in Newlands on the south shore, this spot is a restoration of the oldest building in the Cayman Islands, supposedly dating from the 1700s. It may or may not be a former pirate hangout.

BODDEN TOWN The islands' first capital, its chief claims to present fame are Gun Square (marked by two cannon, stuck muzzle-first into the ground, that were used to guard the reef channel in the 18th century), and Pirates' Caves, where human bones and cannonballs have been found, indicating (perhaps) that it was once a pirates' hideout. The caves, located on the edge of town, are privately owned; there's an admission charge.

CAYMAN ISLANDS NATIONAL PARK Only partially open at press time, the 60-acre facility offers a 1½-mile walking trail and a nearly finished "Heritage Garden"; several other additions are in progress. Off the cross-island road connecting the south shore with the north side. Call the National Trust for information about the park and other nature spots (phone: 949-0121).

CAYMAN'S "BLOW HOLES" These are the sprays of water that shoot into the air when waves hit the rocks on the picturesque stretch of old coral formations called "Ironshore."

EAST END Here, sticking out of the water, a fluke of an anchor said to be a relic of the "Wreck of the Ten Sails" is sometimes visible. It's not wise to wade or swim out for a closer look because the reef in that spot is alive with sea urchins. Around a bend, in the main channel through the reef at East End, is a visible wreck of modern times, the MV *Ridgefield.* East End boasts two hostelries: the scuba buff's small *Cayman Diving Lodge* (phone: 947-7555) and the *Morritt's Tortuga Club* complex (see *Checking In*).

NEW QUEEN'S ROAD Opened by Elizabeth II on February 16, 1983, it lines a tranquil stretch of totally undeveloped oceanfront between East End and the small settlement at Old Man Bay. From the settlement you can continue west to the *Cayman Kai* resort and the North Sound landing, or south on the cross-island road to Frank Sound through the lushest part of Grand Cayman. With royal palms and orchids growing wild, green Cayman parrots are sometimes spotted here, especially during spring mango season.

Sources and Resources

TOURIST INFORMATION

The Cayman Islands Department of Tourism has an office at Harbour Centre in George Town (phone: 949-0623). There are also tourist information booths at the airport and at the pier where cruise passengers land. For information about Cayman Islands tourist offices in the US, see GETTING READY TO GO.

LOCAL COVERAGE *Key to Cayman* magazine is in all hotel rooms. The *New Star,* a local lifestyle magazine, comes out monthly. For additional current information, the *Caymanian Compass,* the local newspaper, is published weekdays, and the *New Cayman,* a weekly paper, is published on Thursdays.

RADIO AND TELEVISION

Radio Cayman is the government-run AM/FM radio station. ZFZZ (99.9 FM) plays light rock music. Cayman also has its own television station.

TELEPHONE

When calling from the US, dial 809 (area code) + (local number). To call from another Caribbean island, the codes may vary, so call the local operator. When calling from a phone on the Cayman Islands, use only the local numbers unless otherwise indicated.

ENTRY REQUIREMENTS

For stays up to 6 months, visitors from the US and Canada need only a passport or other proof of citizenship (birth certificate or voter's registration card, plus a photo ID) and a return or ongoing ticket. There's a departure tax of $7.50 per person.

CLIMATE AND CLOTHES

Average winter temperature is 75F (24C); summer, 5 to 10 degrees warmer. May to October is the rainy season, and showers are intense and brief. The

Cayman Islands are informal and casual. Women wear bright blouses, skirts, slacks, and shorts (and, on beaches, the inevitable bikini), and men favor slacks, sport shirts, and swim trunks. Evenings, women sometimes dress up a bit in long cotton dresses (to which they might add a sweater or shawl); but jackets and ties are rarely required for men.

MONEY

The Cayman Islands have their own currency, the Cayman dollar, which is valued at a fixed ratio to the US dollar ($1 CI equals $1.25 US). Stores, restaurants, and hotels usually accept US dollars and credit cards (check to see if prices listed are CI or US dollars). Traveler's checks can be cashed at local banks (open from 9 AM to 2:30 PM, Mondays through Thursdays, from 9 AM to 4:30 PM on Fridays). All prices in this chapter are quoted in US dollars.

LANGUAGE

Caymanians speak a lovely English, flavored with bits of West Indian, Welsh, Irish, Scottish, and American. They pronounce the name of their largest island "Grahnd Cay-*mahn.*"

TIME

The Cayman Islands are on eastern standard time all year, so the hour is the same as it is in the eastern US during EST months. When daylight saving time is in effect, there's an hour's difference; when it's noon in New York EDT, it's 11 AM in the Cayman Islands.

CURRENT

The same as the US, with standard 110-volt, 60-cycle current. No need for converters or adapters.

TIPPING

There is no general rule about service charges. Some hotels add 10%, some 15%. At apartment/condominium complexes, several add 5%; a couple, 10%. To avoid double-tipping, check the service charge policy when you check in. If there is a service charge added, figure that it covers everything except extra special services. If not, give room maids $1 to $2 per room per day; bellboys about 50¢ per bag for carrying luggage, with a $1 minimum. There are airport porters, but your taxi driver will generally pick up your luggage and carry it to the car, and unless you're carrying an unusually large load, it is not necessary to tip him for the luggage lift or the ride since he probably owns his own cab.

GETTING AROUND

BUS Operating roughly once an hour from George Town and West Bay along Seven Mile Beach, buses stop at all hotels; fares depend on destination.

CAR RENTAL Easy to arrange and a good way to get about. Cars cannot be picked up at the airport on arrival, but can be left there on departure. Prices start at about $38 per day during winter (without insurance, which is $5 per day extra) and go up from there. *Coconut Car Rentals* (phone: 949-4037 or 949-4377) and *Cico/Avis* (phone: 949-2468) include unlimited mileage in their rates, but in summer there's a mileage charge on rentals of less than 3 days from *Budget* (phone: 949-5605), *Hertz* (phone: 949-2280), and *National* (phone: 949-4790). The newest option (and lots of fun) is to rent a four-wheel-drive vehicle from *Just Jeeps Ltd.* (phone: 949-7263), which costs about $40 a day. You can request a jeep with automatic transmission. Off-season rates are about 25% less than in winter. At the time of rental, the agency will issue a driving permit for $3 to renters who can prove that they're at least 21 years old and have a valid license from home, though some firms set a minimum age of 22. *Important:* This is a British world, and driving is on the left. Gasoline is measured by the imperial gallon, which is 25% larger than the US gallon.

MOTORCYCLE RENTAL Honda motorcycles are available for about $15 to $20 per day, unlimited mileage, at *Caribbean Motors* (phone: 949-8878); mopeds are about $13 per day, unlimited mileage at *Caribbean Motors, Cayman Cycle Rentals* (phone: 947-4021), or *Soto's Scooters* (phone: 947-4652).

SEA EXCURSIONS *Surfside Watersports* (phone: 949-7330), *Bob Soto's Diving* (phone: 949-2022), and *Aqua Delights* at the *Holiday Inn* have glass-bottom boat trips for about $15 per person. The following offer a variety of day sail and snorkeling trips: *Surfside Watersports, Aqua Delights, Cayman Diving Lodge* (phone: 947-7555), *Crosby Ebanks* (phone: 947-4049, days; 949-3372, nights), *Don Foster's Dive Grand Cayman* (phone: 949-5679), *Rivers Sports* (phone: 949-1181), *Treasure Island Divers* at the *Ramada Treasure Island* resort (phone: 949-4456), and *Sunset Divers* (phone: 949-7111). *The Spirit of Ppalu* (phone: 949-8745) is a 65-foot catamaran available for day sails and snorkeling trips, while *Captain Marvin's* (phone: 947-4590) and *Crosby Ebanks* have a variety of daily, half-day, and moonlight trips on power or sailboats. *Charter Boat Headquarters* (phone: 947-4340) also books all types of boating and water sport activities.

Grand Cayman is one of the few places in the world where visitors can take submarine trips to view the marine life of a tropical reef system. No diving experience or certification is necessary to ride in the 28-passenger *Atlantis,* which reaches depths of up to 150 feet in either day or night dives. The sub leaves the George Town harbor 12 times a day on the hour. Reservations are required on most dives (phone: 949-7700); cost is $69 for adults, half price for children under 12. For the more scientific-minded, *Research Submersibles Ltd.* (phone: 949-8296) has two 2-passenger Perry craft that stay submerged for as long as 3 hours and dive to 800 feet; cost is about $245 per person.

SIGHTSEEING BUS TOURS Regularly scheduled bus tours are operated by *Tropicana Tours* (phone: 949-4599); *Evco Tours* (phone: 949-2118); *Reid's Premier Tours* (phone: 949-6531); *Rudy's Travellers Transport* (phone: 949-3208); and *Majestic Tours* (phone: 949-7773). The latter offers hotel pickup, air conditioned buses, and friendly, animated guides who are half the fun.

SIGHTSEEING TAXI TOURS Arranged through the *Cayman Islands Cab & Transport Association* (phone: 947-4491), these cost about $25 per hour for up to five persons. West Bay tours (including a Turtle Farm stop) are about $20 per car; Pedro's Castle trips, about $20.

TAXI Taxis meet all arriving flights. Rates are fixed by the Cayman Island Taxi Cab Association and are published in the tourist department's *Rate Sheet and Fact Folder.* Typical one-way fares from the airport, per taxi, maximum four passengers: to George Town, about $8; to most hotels on Seven Mile Beach, about $9 to $15. The longest rides — from the airport to *Morritt's Tortuga Club* on the East End or the *Cayman Kai* resort and Rum Point on the North Shore — are about $47 plus about 10% tip. But, given advance notice, both *Morritt's Tortuga Club* and *Cayman Kai* will provide courtesy transport.

INTER-ISLAND FLIGHTS

Air Jamaica has service from Kingston, Jamaica, to Grand Cayman. *Cayman Airways* flies direct from Kingston, Jamaica, and connects Grand Cayman with Little Cayman and Cayman Brac. *Island Air* also flies among the Caymans; both firms offer special three-island fares plus a choice of daylong fishing excursions and longer vacation packages bound for all three islands.

SPECIAL EVENTS

The biggest annual events are *Batabano* and *Brachanal,* carnivals with parades, exhibits, and dances held in April; the *Queen's Birthday* celebration in June (on the Monday following the Saturday appointed as her official birthday), which is observed with a uniformed parade and the presentation of awards and honors; and the country's national festival, *Pirates Week,* an elaborate week-long celebration with costumes, parades, and swashbuckling special events in late October. On *Ash Wednesday,* there's an *Annual Agricultural Show,* and June is *Million Dollar Month,* featuring an international saltwater fishing tournament with cash prizes for record catches. Other holidays when banks, stores, and government offices are closed: *New Year's Day; Good Friday; Easter; Easter Monday; Discovery Day* (third Monday in May); *Constitution Day* (first Monday in July); *Remembrance Day* (Monday after *Remembrance Sunday* in November); *Christmas Day;* and *Boxing Day* (December 26).

SHOPPING

At one time very limited, the spectrum of merchandise has improved a lot in George Town with the expansion of existing duty-free shops, the opening of new ones, and a general upgrading. The road along Seven Mile Beach has experienced an explosive growth of mini-malls, with shops selling everything from scuba gear to frozen yogurt. Many famous international brand names are imported here with no sales tax added. But sellers are still free to set prices, so some bargains are better than others. Here, as elsewhere, the best protection is knowing US prices — including those at discount stores — especially on cameras and electronic equipment. *Note:* Processed black coral (such as jewelry) may be brought into the US only in small amounts, and tortoiseshell is prohibited completely.

To stock up on typical island products such as hats, baskets, and straw items, try *Heritage Crafts* (on the waterfront in George Town; phone: 949-7093). Here are some other places worth a stop:

CAYMANIA Large selection of European fragrances, cosmetics, and jewelry. Church St. (phone: 949-2405).

CHESTS OF GOLD Coral and gold jewelry and some interesting original creations. *Galleria Plaza West* (phone: 949-7833).

ENGLISH SHOPPE Crystal curios, pearls, and souvenirs. On the waterfront (phone: 949-2457).

JEWELS OF THE SEA Good pieces of lapis lazuli. *Seven Mile Shops* (phone: 949-8033).

KIRK FREEPORT The biggest selection of name crystal, china, and earthenware. Four locations in *Kirk Freeport Plaza* (one phone for all four: 949-7477).

MITZI Pink coral jewelry. Old Fort Bldg. (phone: 949-7805).

PIECES OF EIGHT Jewelry made from ancient coins, both designed and sold by Irvin Banks. Fort St. (phone: 949-7578).

PURE ART GALLERY Artist Debbie van der Bol sells paintings, prints, and sculptures by local talent. S. Church St. (phone: 949-4433).

RICHARD'S FINE JEWELRY Known as the "artist to the stars," Richard Barile's creations have been coveted by a galaxy of celebrities, including Larry Gatlin, Jonathan Winters, Conway Twitty, and Muhammad Ali. Church St. (phone: 949-7156).

SMITHS The ultimate in rare coins and ancient necklaces. Fort St. (phone: 949-7877).

VIKING Scandinavian items, plus Caribbean fashions, paintings, crafts. Located near the cruise passenger landing, it's hard to miss. Church St. (phone: 949-4090).

SPORTS

Since the sea is so warm and gentle, most sports activities take place in, on, or under the water.

BOATING *Surfside Watersports* (phone: 949-7330) rents Hobie Cats for $30 an hour. Small boats can be chartered from a number of water sports operators, including *Aqua Delights* (at the *Holiday Inn*); *Treasure Island Divers* (at the *Ramada Treasure Island* resort; phone: 949-4456); and *Red Sail Sports* (at the *Hyatt Beach Club;* phone: 949-8745). The cost ranges from $50 to $75 per day. Sunday sailing races are held off Seven Mile Beach; if you want to join in, contact Gerry Kirkconnell (phone: 949-2651 or 949-7477).

GOLF At the *Britannia* resort on Grand Cayman, next to the *Hyatt Regency Grand Cayman* hotel, there is a prototype course specially designed by Jack Nicklaus to accommodate the "short" ball. Because of its weight (about half that of a normal golf ball) and convex dimples (which create aerodynamic drag), the ball flies just about half the distance of a standard ball, thereby requiring a much shorter course, and making for a much faster game. It tends to equalize player ability, too. An 18-hole, par 72 course is created by playing the 9 holes twice, each time from different tees (the front 9 is 3,157 yards and the back 9 is 3,092 yards). This unique course is as challenging as it is fun. Greens fees are about $35; golf carts range from $10 to $18 (phone: 949-8020).

SNORKELING AND SCUBA Aficionados rate the Cayman Islands as one of the world's top dive areas, and Grand Cayman boasts at least 20 full-service dive operations. Coral reefs and the famous vertical coral walls teeming with marine life surround each island, so the underwater show is close enough to shore for snorkelers and novice divers to take it in easily. Some of the world's best dive sites can be found off Little Cayman and Cayman Brac. Little Cayman's Bloody Bay Wall, for example, has been called the third-best site in the world by no less an authority than Jacques Cousteau. Although experienced divers do not really need boats, guided trips are recommended for convenience and safety's sake. Among the brilliant, friendly fish found here are angelfish, butterfly fish, trumpet fish, grunts, squirrelfish, snapper, and grouper. At Stingray City, off Rum Point, stingrays come in to be hand-fed by divers. There are also shipwrecks, some close enough to the surface to be viewed by snorkelers. Most hotels have fins, face masks, and snorkels to rent for about $5 to $7 a day, and can arrange scuba trips for you. Typical rates: A two-tank diving trip including equipment is about $55 per person; a full day with three dives and lunch, about $80; night dives (one tank), $45 per person; a half-day snorkel trip, $25; a half-day scuba instruction course, $90 per person; complete *PADI* basic certification, including several dive trips, about $350 per person. A resort course (about $90) offers non-divers an introduction to scuba and has participants experiencing the underwater wonders (under close supervision) in 1 day. Many dive shops offer rental equipment (upon presentation of a national diving association certification card only), instruction, and arrange guided dive trips. The *Cayman Kai* resort, *Cayman Windsurfing* at *Morritt's Tortuga Club, Quabbin Dives* (phone: 949-5597), *Bob Soto's Diving* (phone: 949-2022), *Sunset Divers* (phone: 949-7111), *Surfside Watersports* (phone: 949-7330), *Don Foster's Dive Grand Cayman* (phone: 949-5679), *Red Sail Sports* (phone: 949-8745), *Eden Roc Diving Center* (phone: 949-7243), *Peter Milburn's Dive Cayman* (phone: 947-4341), *Fish Eye* (phone: 947-4209), *Parrot's Landing* (phone: 949-7884), and *Treasure Island Divers* (phone: 949-4456) are all first-rate. On Cayman Brac are *Brac Aquatics* (phone: 948-7429) and Peter Hughes's *Dive Tiara* (phone: 948-7553). The experienced diver can book a week-long dive expedition aboard the luxury live-aboard dive yacht *Cayman Aggressor I* or its sister ship, *Cayman Aggressor II.* Contact *Sea and See Inc.* (phone: 800-DIV-BOAT). For a list of firms offering snorkeling trips, see *Sea Excursions,* above.

SPORT FISHING Game fish abundant in Caymanian waters include bonefish, tarpon and, in deeper waters, marlin, yellowfin tuna, yellowtail, dolphin, and wahoo. Charter boats are available from a number of sources; your hotel can make arrangements. Typical rates: deep-sea fishing, $400 for a half day; $600 for a full day's outing; reef and bonefishing, about $200 for a half day; $400 for all day. Little Cayman's bone and tarpon fishing are tops. *Charter Boat Headquarters* (phone: 947-4340) has complete information and prices. Spearfishing is not an option for visitors, since spear guns can be used by licensed residents only.

SWIMMING AND SUNNING The most magnificent site is Seven Mile Beach; it is, incidentally, a public beach, and (not incidentally) the majority of the island's hotels and villa and apartment complexes are located along its length. But hotels and condos are small enough and far enough apart so that crowding is seldom a problem. In addition, there are coves, bays, and expanses of coastline all around Grand Cayman (and on the other Cayman Islands) that can be all yours for an hour or a day in the sun and sea.

TENNIS No big layouts, but more than 30 courts in all. On Grand Cayman: at the *Beach Club Resort, Caribbean Club, Cayman Kai, Holiday Inn, Morritt's Tortuga Club,* and *Treasure Island.* On Cayman Brac: at *Brac Reef, Beach Club,* and *Divi Tiara Beach.* On Seven Mile Beach, at the following cottages and condos: *Anchorage, Beach Bay, Casa Caribe, Cayman Islands Resorts, Christopher Columbus, Club Colonial, Coral Caymanian, Discovery Point Club, George Town Villas, Grand Bay Club, Grapetree/Cocoplum, Island Club, Lacovia, London House, Plantation Village, Silver Sands, Tamarind Bay,* and *Villas Pappagallo.* Non-guests can play at the *Caribbean Club, Morritt's Tortuga Club,* and the *Holiday Inn* for $5 to $12.50 an hour.

WATER SKIING AND WINDSURFING Water skiing is offered by several hotels at about $40 per hour, everything included; windsurfing boards run about $15 an hour; a 2-hour lesson costs about $32.50. Parasail rides go for about $30 each. There's a *Mistral Windsurfing School* at the *Treasure Island* resort.

NIGHTLIFE

Nobody comes to the Cayman Islands for after-dark action, but there is casual nightclubbing at *Faces* (near the *Cayman Islander* hotel off West Bay Rd.), with disco music nightly (except Sundays) and live bands (and occasionally special overseas performers) on Saturdays. The Barefoot Man, who mixes calypso with country-and-western and is Cayman's most popular entertainer, can be heard in the *Wreck of the Ten Sails* at the *Holiday Inn. Island Rock* (phone: 947-5366) is a disco upstairs at the *Falls Shopping Centre* near the *Holiday Inn.* Watch the stingrays and exotic tropical fish glide past in the underwater *BWI* nightclub at the *Radisson* resort (West Bay Rd; phone: 949-0088). It's open 6 nights a week. Grand Cayman's best and most frenetic nightspot is the 350-seat *Silver's Night Club* at the *Ramada Treasure Island* resort. Live music that includes 1950s and 1960s revues and occasional concerts by top country artists keep this place full 6 nights a week. Most nightspots charge admission and are open until 1 AM during the week, all close at midnight on Saturdays, and there is no music of any kind, anywhere, on Sundays.

Best on the Islands

CHECKING IN

In the conventional Caribbean sense, there are only a few complete resort hotels with all the eating and entertainment facilities built in: the *Holiday Inn,* the *Grand Pavilion, Radisson, Ramada Treasure Island,* and *Hyatt Regency.* Grand Cayman hotels, as well as condo, apartment, and villa complexes and guesthouses, charge top dollar. On the whole, apartment and villa rentals seem to be the best deal; fully furnished with kitchenettes, they not only allow you to be pleasantly independent, but to keep meal costs under control.

A word about that word "condo." On Grand Cayman, where no building may rise more than 5 stories, condominiums are not little congested boxes stuffed into a megastructure. Almost all properties are designed to offer spacious living and privacy. These condos offer what Europeans call a "self-catering holiday" — all the comforts of home without the housework. The condo manager often knows the best places to buy groceries and can arrange for a cook and/or maid to take care of everything from shopping to cleanup (for an extra fee). But be sure to arrange for transportation to and from your condo rental.

In listings below, rates of $220 and up for a double room or condo apartment without meals (EP) between December and April are considered expensive; between $150 and $210, moderate; and under $150, inexpensive. For breakfast and lunch or dinner on the Modified American Plan (MAP), where available, add $35 to $45 per person per day. Off-season rates, normally in effect from mid-April to mid-December, are approximately 30% to 40% less. Most hotels assess a service charge of between 10% and 15% on all bills in lieu of tipping, and in some places an "energy surcharge" is added for air conditioning. There's a 6% government tax on room rates, and a 10% resort tax. When calling from a phone within the Cayman Islands, use only the local numbers listed below. For information about dialing from elsewhere, see "Telephone" earlier in this chapter. The central, toll-free telephone number for hotel reservations on the Cayman Islands is 800-327-8777 from the US.

GRAND CAYMAN

SEVEN MILE BEACH

EXPENSIVE

Anchorage Fresh and good-looking, this Caymanian condominium resort encompasses 14 neatly laid-out 2-bedroom apartments with full kitchens; tennis, swimming pool, and Seven Mile Beach at the door (phone: 947-4088; fax: 947-5001).

Beach Club Style that enhances but never stifles the fun is its hallmark. Rooms with balconies or terraces have garden or sea views. There's chummy dining on the terrace. Also offered here are water sports (scuba, snorkeling, sailing), a smooth swath of beach, congenial gathering spots, and fine dining. Notable summer packages. About 2 miles from George Town on West Bay Rd. (phone: 949-8100; fax: 947-5167).

Caribbean Club At the beach's midpoint, it has 18 stylish villas grouped around a clubhouse with a lounge, and *Lantana's,* a first-rate restaurant (see *Eating Out*). There's also a good tennis court. Condominium rentals when owners are away. West Bay Rd. (phone: 947-4099; fax: 947-4433).

Casa Caribe Superb tropical decor in all 21 units and a casually elegant atmosphere attracts an upscale clientele. Tennis, a freshwater pool, a fine beach, a Jacuzzi, and attentive management and staff make this resort among the best on Grand Cayman. Its 2- and 3-bedroom units can be shared by four to six guests (phone: 947-4287).

Colonial Club A pastel pink property you'd expect to find in Bermuda. Although situated in the heart of the busy Seven Mile Beach strip, this condominium complex has a charming sense of seclusion and good taste. Twenty-four 2- and 3-bedroom units are tastefully furnished and have fully equipped kitchens; tennis, pool, Jacuzzi, and lots of beach (phone: 947-4660).

Holiday Inn Grand Cayman No surprises. With 215 air conditioned, carpeted rooms; on the beach and with all sorts of built-in beach action; sports facilities, including 4 lighted tennis courts, sailing, and snorkeling; diving arranged. There's poolside lunching, a coffee shop, a dining room, and *The Wreck of the Ten Sails* nightclub (phone: 947-4444; 800-421-9999 from the US; fax: 947-4213).

Hyatt Regency Grand Cayman A $41-million, 236-room resort; each room contains a mini-bar and spacious bath with robes and complimentary toiletries. Regency Club suites are in a separate wing. Set on lush landscaped grounds, there are 2 pools, tennis courts, a beach club, scuba facilities, and a golf course (see "Golf"). Other features include 3 restaurants, including the elegant *Garden Loggia Café* and the casual *Hemingway's* (see *Eating Out* for both); 4 lounges with nightly entertainment; and full conference facilities for meetings of up to 350. About 2½ miles from George Town on West Bay Rd. (phone: 949-1234; 800-527-7882 from the US).

Indies Suites Close to West Bay about 4 miles from George Town, it's worth the drive to reach this property, Grand Cayman's only all-suite hotel. Here are 40 sumptuous, Mediterranean-style suites (the spacious kitchens even have microwave ovens) in a 20-acre tropical setting, with a beautifully landscaped courtyard, pool, and Jacuzzi. A secluded part of Seven Mile Beach is a 5-minute walk away. Continental breakfast is complimentary (phone: 947-5025; 800-654-3130 from the US; fax: 947-5024).

London House Twenty appealing apartments, elegantly furnished in airy rattan and bright colors. All feature patios or balconies with sea views, air conditioning and ceiling fans, full kitchens, and daily maid service. Choice of 1 or 2 bedrooms. Pluses include a freshwater pool; helpful, accessible management; and a lovely, peaceful beach. Packages are available. At the quiet, northern end of Seven Mile Beach (phone: 947-4060; fax: 947-4087).

The Palms This beachfront condominium complex has 15 air conditioned 2- and 3-bedroom units, a pool, a hot tub, and a tennis court. On Seven Mile Beach (phone: 947-5291).

Radisson Grand Cayman This 315-room beachfront property just a half mile from George Town has a pool (open 24 hours); a health club; and a full range of water sports and activities, including the *Cayman Mermaid,* one of the largest glass-bottom boats in the world. There is good dining in the *Regency Grille,* a snack bar at the beach, and a lounge bar with dancing nightly. West Bay Rd. (phone: 949-0088; 800-333-3333 from the US; fax: 949-0288).

Ramada Treasure Island Several years back, a consortium of country-and-western stars and investors took over the derelict *Paradise Manor* hotel, long unfinished, to create this unusual 290-room resort. One of the island's larger hotels, it is also one of Cayman's most attractive properties, with its lavish open-air lobby and lush tropical landscaping. There are pools, tennis courts, a nightclub, and top-rated dining in the *Top of the Falls* restaurant (see *Eating Out*). On West Bay Rd. (phone: 949-7777; 800-228-9898; fax: 949-8489).

Villas of the Galleon A 75-condominium cluster next to the *Holiday Inn,* it has 1-, 2-, and 3-bedroom units with big air conditioned rooms, fully equipped kitchens, and patios or balconies (phone: 947-4433; 800-232-1034 from the US; fax: 949-7054).

West Indian Club Toward the middle of the beach, in a stately royal-palm setting, it's as posh as it gets hereabouts, with 9 comfortable 1- and 2-bedroom apartments and 1 efficiency, all with maid/cook in attendance from 8:30 AM to 2:30 PM (at $25 extra per day per person). Individually decorated, all apartments have sizable balconies. The minimum stay is 7 days. No bar, no lobby — presumably you'll set up your own socializing (phone: 947-5255; fax: 947-5204).

MODERATE

Beachcomber Here are 23 two- and three-bedroom apartments with kitchens in a 3-story condo on the beach, near shopping and restaurants. Amenities include air conditioning, ceiling fans, and a swimming pool (phone: 947-4470; fax: 947-5019).

Christopher Columbus With 25 two- and three-bedroom apartments, this complex at the northern end of Seven Mile Beach also includes a freshwater pool and 2 tournament-quality tennis courts. Some good package buys. On the beach (phone: 947-4354; fax: 947-5062).

Seagull Nicely decorated, these 32 carpeted 1-bedroom apartments are on the beach. No packages, but fishing and scuba excursions are easily arranged (phone: 949-5756; fax: 949-9040).

Victoria House Pleasantly decorated and well managed, this attractive apartment complex at the north end of the beach (you'll need a car) has everything from 1-room studios to a penthouse; all are fully furnished, with kitchenettes and air conditioning. There is a tennis court, shuffleboard, a barbecue area, snorkeling gear to rent. Fishing, scuba, and boat trips arranged (phone: 947-4233; fax: 947-5328).

INEXPENSIVE

Cayman Islander Though small and slightly motel-shaped, this recently remodeled 64-room property is friendly, presentable, and a great budget buy (one of the few) because it's across the road from, not right on, the beach (phone: 949-0990; fax: 949-7896).

Sleep Inn This Quality/Comfort Inn property is the closest establishment on Seven Mile Beach to downtown George Town. There are 116 rooms and

8 suites with queen-size beds, a pool, a poolside bar and grill, and an on-site dive facility operated by *Parrot's Landing* (phone: 949-9111; 800-4-CHOICE from the US).

ELSEWHERE ON GRAND CAYMAN

EXPENSIVE

Retreat at Rum Point Old friends of Grand Cayman will remember the *Rum Point Club.* The thatch-roofed, barefoot fun is gone, but the lovely beach and splendid solitude remain, now enhanced by one of the island's top resorts — great for those interested in Cayman's advantages without the Seven Mile Beach setting. Twenty-three well-decorated 1-, 2-, and 3-bedroom units on 1,300 feet of beach are protected by the north coast barrier reef. There's a pool, tennis, sauna, and a small, complete gym/exercise room — all complimentary. *Surfside Watersports* handles the scuba and aquatic fun with the same flair seen at their Seven Mile Beach facility. On the north shore of the island at Rum Point (phone: 947-9135; fax: 947-9058).

MODERATE

Cayman Kai Big, attractive condominium and resort complex, delightfully isolated on the north coast. North Wall diving is aided by a first class shop (rentals, lessons, photography, guided day and night trips). Also other water sports, deep-sea fishing, lighted tennis courts. Choice of 1- or 2-bedroom sea lodges, 2-bedroom townhouses, or 1- to 4-bedroom beach houses — all with living-dining areas, kitchens, and patios. Clubhouse with bars; indoor and outdoor dining. Rum Point (phone: 947-9266; 800-336-6008 from the US).

Coconut Harbor Located just south of George Town, this neat, efficient, 35-room property has air conditioning and kitchenettes. Balconies overlook sea and pool. Excellent shore diving. West Bay Rd. (phone: 949-7468; 800-552-6281 from the US; fax: 949-7117).

Morritt's Tortuga Club On the grounds of the old *Tortuga Club,* this property has 54 efficiency condominiums available. *Cayman Windsurfing* is on site, renting snorkeling and windsurfing equipment and sailboats. There's also a formal restaurant. West Bay Rd. (phone: 947-7449; fax: 947-7669).

INEXPENSIVE

Seaview One of the oldest properties on the island, this 15-room hostelry just south of George Town has a pool, dining room, piano bar, and diving facilities. West Bay Rd. (phone: 949-8804; fax: 949-8507).

Sunset House Advertised as a hotel for divers by divers, this small, award-winning resort is even more. South of George Town, on the Ironshore (the craggy limestone shoreline with a steel gray cast), the informal but well-managed property has 57 simple, comfortable rooms and one of the Caymans' best-run dive operations. The thatch-roofed, seaside *My Bar* is a great gathering place, day and night. If you can't stay here, at least stop in and toast the sunset. South Church St. (phone: 949-7111; fax: 949-7101).

CAYMAN BRAC

MODERATE

Divi Tiara Beach Fresh, friendly, and informal, this 70-room property has a white sand beach, fine diving, all levels of scuba instruction, fishing, tennis court, pool, and complete dive shop. There are 7 luxury apartments with ocean views, Jacuzzis, king-size beds, color TV sets, and telephones. There is also an 80-seat conference center, the *Divi Village,* with 18 deluxe rooms, pool, bar, and dining room. Good packages for divers, honeymooners, loafers. EP rates, MAP add-on available. On the southwest side of the island, 3 miles from the airport near West End (phone: 948-7553; 800-367-3484 from the US; fax: 948-7316).

INEXPENSIVE

Blackie's Sea View House Here are 9 guestrooms in a simple, rustic setting with good home cooking and a friendly atmosphere. All rooms have private bath, a TV set, an ocean view, and ceiling fans that work with the air conditioning to keep things cool. There's a pool and a snack bar that serves wonderful tropical-flavored homemade ice cream. Nine miles from the airport (phone: 948-8232).

Brac Reef Beach Designed and built by Bracker Linton Tibbetts — the Floridian considered the godfather of Cayman Brac tourism — this lovely 40-room resort has a private beach, freshwater pool, Jacuzzi, superb native and continental food, and a friendly, typically Bracker atmosphere that makes time seem irrelevant. A great place to relax and really get away without roughing it. All rooms are naturally air conditioned by breezes off the cool south coast. Excellent dive and vacation packages year-round (phone: 948-7323).

LITTLE CAYMAN

MODERATE

Pirate's Point Run by chef-hostess Gladys Howard, this small, very out-island, 12-room lodge offers scuba packages that include all meals (Howard has won awards for her cooking) and two dives daily. It's minutes from Bloody Bay Wall, a famous dive spot. Bonefishing and deep-sea fishing also are available (phone: 948-4210).

Sam McCoy's A 10-room diving lodge that is friendly and functional without many resort amenities. Local resident Mary McCoy runs the kitchen, her sons are dive guides, and there are separate rates for divers and non-divers. Rate includes all meals (phone: 948-2249; 800-843-2177 from the US).

Southern Cross Club A hospitable 10-unit sportsperson's enclave, it's casually comfortable from rooftop to terrace. Complete scuba programs, fishing setups with emphasis on fly fishing, guides, and inclusive packages are available (phone: 948-3255). Stateside address: 1005 E. Merchants Plaza, Indianapolis, IN 46204 (phone: 317-636-9501).

EATING OUT

Caymanian meals star fresh fish, turtle soup and steaks, codfish and *ackee* (a Jamaican specialty), conch stew, and native lobster in season (August through January). In George Town and along the beach, the choice ranges from informal hamburger places to an elegant old plantation house where dinner is served by candlelight on the verandah, and the tab, including wine and tip, runs to more than $50 per person. Although the sister islands' dining opportunities are mostly limited to hotel dining rooms, Grand Cayman has an eclectic and ever-changing array of ethnic culinary diversions. In places we call very expensive, expect to pay $50 and up per person; expensive, $40 to $50; moderate, $25 to $40; and inexpensive, $25 and under. When calling from a phone within the Cayman Islands, use only the local numbers listed below. For information about dialing from elsewhere, see "Telephone" earlier in this chapter.

GRAND CAYMAN

VERY EXPENSIVE

Chef Tell's Grand Old House Run by local television personality Tell Erhardt, this former plantation house is an extra special eating place. True, some dishes are superior to others, but it is the ambience of the picturesque old house on the seashore that is most memorable. Start with a drink in the *Clown Bar,* then move to the verandah for your meal. Marinated conch, escargot, Cayman land crab, and crêpes impérial serve as appetizers; entrées include fresh fish, Cayman lobster, veal cordon bleu, pepper steaks, and fondue *bourguignonne.* Open daily for lunch and dinner. Reservations necessary. Major credit cards accepted. S. Church St. (phone: 949-9333).

EXPENSIVE

Bella Capri Romantic ambience and excellent Italian cooking are the lures here. The *scaloppine alla piemontese* is recommended. Open daily for dinner only. Reservations unnecessary. Major credit cards accepted. Off Seven Mile Beach Rd., across from the *Holiday Inn* (phone: 947-4755).

Garden Loggia Café A unique and elegant café in an indoor and outdoor setting. Open daily for breakfast, lunch, and dinner; its lavish luncheon buffets are a must at least once, as is the superb Sunday champagne brunch. Dine and dance on Saturday evenings to a piano/string ensemble. Reservations necessary. Major credit cards accepted. At the *Hyatt Regency Hotel,* West Bay Rd. (phone: 949-1234).

Golden Pagoda Chinese fare Hakka-style, with West Indian overtones to some dishes. Buffet lunch Mondays through Fridays; dinner nightly, except Mondays. Takeout available. Reservations advised. MasterCard and Visa accepted. West Bay Rd. (phone: 949-5475).

Hemingway's This delightful white pavilion is at the center of the *Hyatt/Britannia Beach Club* overlooking the Caribbean. The open-air restaurant is casual, though decor and service are polished. Superior rum drinks are served at poolside or even on the beach. Inside, dine on black-peppercorn fettuccine in conch and clam sauce, or fresh grilled dolphin or tuna with lemon garlic sauce. There are even some low-fat choices on the menu. Open daily for lunch and dinner. Reservations advised. Major credit cards accepted. At the *Hyatt Regency Hotel,* West Bay Rd. (phone: 949-1234, ext. 3009).

Lantana's With a kicky blend of American Southwest and Caribbean dishes, chef Fred Schrock has created the most exciting new restaurant on the island. Housed in the *Caribbean Club,* this place is a visual delight, with its ethnic artifacts, soft lighting, and warm colors. Schrock's creative presentations include long, braided breadsticks served in stemware, frizzled tortilla soup, tortilla roll-ups, and fire-roasted quail glazed with honey-chipotle sauce. Open daily for lunch and dinner. Reservations essential. Major credit cards accepted. West Bay Rd. (phone: 947-5595).

Lobster Pot Overlooking the sea, this is an old favorite with visitors and residents, due to fine service and consistently fine seafood (lobster, conch chowder, and very fresh local fish), and also because of the legendary rum punches. A great place to watch the sunset. Open for lunch and dinner; closed Sundays. Reservations advised. Major credit cards accepted. N. Church St. (phone: 949-2736).

Ottmar's Owner/chef Ottmar Weber, a 23-year veteran of such fine island dining spots as the *Grand Old House* and *L'Escargot,* has opened his own showplace for his brand of classic cooking. Attractive and formal, the restaurant's continental dishes often come with rich sauces, and portions are generous. Try the baked gulf shrimp as a appetizer, then move on to chicken breast Oscar or the pan-fried catch of the day. Open daily for lunch and dinner. Reservations essential. In the *Transnational Conference Centre,* West Bay Rd. (phone: 947-5879).

Pappagallo One of the island's most unusual dining spots, this thatch-roofed waterfront building has an ambience that is both tropical and elegant — there are live parrots and waiters in black tie. It features a northern Italian menu, with seafood, veal, and pasta specialties. Smart casual dress only. Lunch and dinner served daily. Reservations advised. Major credit cards accepted. At *Villas Pappagallo* resort, about 15 minutes north of George Town at Barkers in West Bay (phone: 949-3479).

Periwinkle Cheerful spot with unique menu of island specialties (conch fritters, turtle steak medallions, lobster), Italian dishes (lasagna Morandini, pizza Periwinkle), good homemade soups, and desserts. Under the talented, experienced hand of chef/owner Johann Guschelbauer, this is another favorite place among locals. Open daily for lunch and dinner. Reservations advised. Major credit cards accepted. West Bay Rd. (phone: 947-5181).

Top of the Falls This elegant resort dining room features French delicacies, such as chateaubriand, veal, fine seafood (including escargots in numerous incarnations), and sinfully rich pastries. There's a fine Sunday brunch. Open daily for breakfast, lunch, and dinner. Reservations advised. Major credit cards accepted. *Ramada Treasure Island,* West Bay Rd. (phone: 949-9889).

Wharf Waterfront dining in one of the island's prettiest, most romantic settings. You can choose between indoor, deck, or terrace seating, all with a lovely sea view. Classic continental fare blends with Caribbean dishes to create an exciting mix, including blackened yellowfin tuna, lobster and shrimp "Port-au-Prince," and Key lime pie topped with golden, caramelized meringue. There's even a floor show provided by nature — the memorable spectacle of huge tarpon leaping around just off the edge of the wharf waiting to be fed at 9 PM. Open for lunch and dinner daily. Reservations necessary. Major credit cards accepted. Seven Mile Beach (phone: 949-2231).

MODERATE

Almond Tree Here, dinner is served island-style on an outdoor garden patio or inside the big, thatch-roofed restaurant. First-rate tropical punches and piña coladas, and good island food like baked turtle steaks are served. Open daily for dinner only. Reservations advised. Major credit cards accepted. N. Church St. (phone: 949-2893).

Biggie's Although this place bills itself as a steakhouse, the West Indian specialties are the most tasty. It's worth arriving a little early for the lunch specials, including oxtail stew, turtle soup, and anything with curry. Open daily for breakfast, lunch, and dinner. Reservations unnecessary. Major credit cards accepted. Located within walking distance of the airport. Airport Centre (phone: 949-7736).

Cracked Conch Conch — in chowder, fritters, stew, and even burgers — is king, but there are also all sorts of other seafood and island side dishes like *cho cho* and fried plantain; lime and coconut pies are star desserts. Good service, cute nautical decor. On Thursday and Saturday nights, local duo Chuck and Barrie play island music. Open for lunch and dinner; closed

Sundays. Reservations unnecessary. MasterCard and Visa accepted. West Bay Rd. (phone: 947-5217).

DJ's Café With its bistro atmosphere, good food, and fast service, this is a regular haunt of an interesting local clientele, from divers to bankers. Check the blackboard for entrées ranging from lobster to lasagna. Open daily for dinner only. Reservations unnecessary. Major credit cards accepted. Behind the *Coconut Place Shopping Centre* (phone: 947-4234).

Pirate's Den (PD's) One of the few spots that serves the local Buccaneer brew on tap; this is an upbeat pub with wood-beamed ambience and a snack menu featuring fish 'n' chips. Open daily for lunch and dinner. No reservations. Major credit cards accepted. In the *Galleria Shopping Centre* on West Bay Rd. (phone: 949-7144).

Santiago's Friendly atmosphere, colorful decor, and outstanding Mexican fare with margaritas by the jug at reasonable prices. Live entertainment every night except Sundays. Open daily for lunch and dinner. No reservations. Major credit cards accepted. On West Bay Rd. (phone: 949-8580).

West Bay Polo Club The chalkboard menu here features good bistro fare — from fresh fish to stir fries, soups, and steaks. It's a gathering place and watering hole for residents, too, so there's lots of camaraderie. Nearly 2 dozen varieties of beer to choose from. There's also a large sports bar with multiple TV screens showing US (and sometimes local) athletic events. Open daily for lunch and dinner. No reservations. Major credit cards accepted. In *Falls Shopping Centre* on West Bay Rd. (phone: 949-9890).

INEXPENSIVE

Crow's Nest, South Sound Dine inside or out, overlooking the sea, at this tiny, informal, family-style Caymanian eatery. Seafood, burgers, and West Indian specialties are served for lunch or dinner. One of the best buys on the island and worth finding. Open daily for lunch and dinner. No reservations. Major credit cards accepted. South of George Town on the seaside road (phone: 949-9366).

Liberty's, West Bay A great dollar-stretching place for those who really want to try West Indian food at its best; the menu includes such exotica as curried goat, codfish and ackee, oxtail, and seafood Cayman-style. Open daily for lunch and dinner. No reservations. Major credit cards accepted. Reverend Blackman St. (phone: 949-3226).

Lone Star The partying never stops at this large, noisy restaurant/bar. The food is Tex-Mex, and there's a lot of it; check out the regular daily specials such as "Fajita Rita" and "Cajun" dishes. Overhead TV screens continually show what's going on in the world of US and local sports. Open daily for lunch and dinner. Reservations unnecessary. Major credit cards accepted. Seven Mile Beach (phone: 947-5175).

Colombia's Caribbean Coast

The much-publicized violence caused by the drug cartels and other outlaw groups in Colombia, which make law and order in much of the country a sometime thing, has fostered an undeserved image of general lawlessness along the country's Caribbean coast.

Although the US State Department continues to urge caution when traveling in Colombia, it considers travel to the Caribbean port cities of Cartagena, Santa Marta, and Barranquilla relatively safe. Major cruise ships and charter flights once again serve the area. Still, while the falling exchange rate makes Colombia a bargain spot in the high-priced Caribbean, visitors should continue to exercise caution.

Topographically, little of Colombia's 1,000-mile Caribbean coast has changed since European ships first landed on its shores at the beginning of the 16th century. Those avid explorers claimed its sunbaked beaches and virgin forests for Spain. Today, while the coastal area ranks as one of the country's major agricultural and cattle raising regions, in addition to providing home ports for a substantial fishing industry, its population is still relatively small. Tiny fishing villages are scattered along stretches of beach and large deep-water bays and hidden coves front the jagged coastline from the desolate plains of the Guajira peninsula in the east to the dense jungles of the Gulf of Darién in the west.

Few travelers see these isolated fishing villages and almost uninhabited jungle. What lures contemporary travelers are the two major resort areas on the coast — the walled city of Cartagena and historic Santa Marta — as well as the isolated Caribbean free-port island of San Andrés, located almost 500 miles to the northwest in the Caribbean Sea. The gateway to Colombia's Caribbean coast is the city of Barranquilla, Colombia's largest port (pop. 1.7 million).

The first European to set eyes on Colombia's coast was the Spanish explorer Alonso de Ojeda, in 1500. The next year, Rodrigo de Bastidas, a wealthy notary from Seville, explored the entire coast, and almost 24 years later, he returned to set up the first permanent European settlement on the South American mainland in Santa Marta. In 1533, Don Pedro de Heredia landed at what was then the Carib fishing village of Calamari, in a natural harbor formed by a bay and a sand-spit breakwater. He promptly renamed it Cartagena de las Indias, and it soon became one of Spain's most prized New World possessions.

The growing Spanish Empire needed gold and silver to finance further

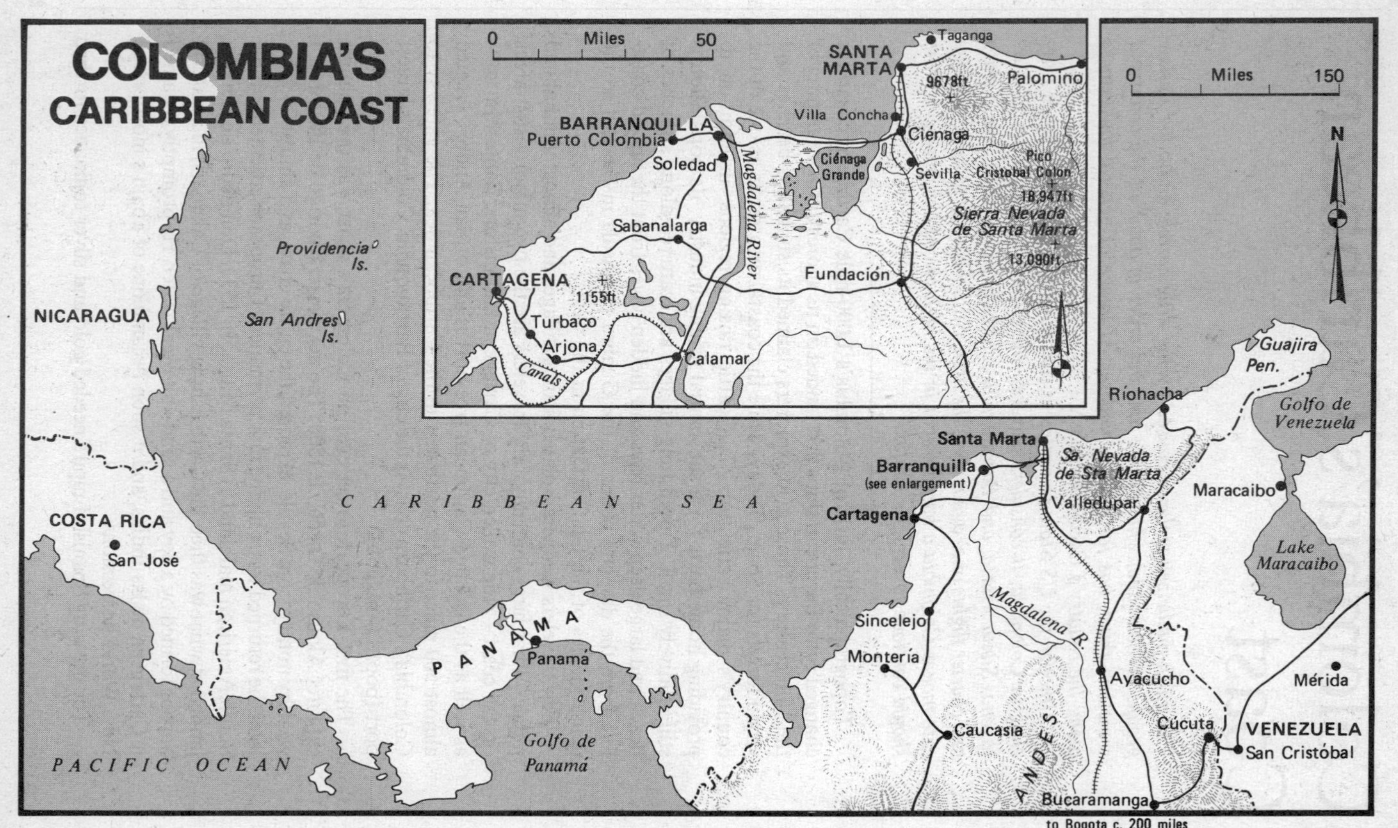

COLOMBIA'S
CARIBBEAN COAST
0 Miles 50
SANTA MARTA
Taganga
9678ft
Palomino
Villa Concha
BARRANQUILLA
Puerto Colombia
Ciénaga
Soledad
Ciénaga Grande
Sevilla
Pico Cristobal Colon
18,947ft
Sierra Nevada de Santa Marta
13,090ft
Magdalena River
Sabanalarga
Fundación
CARTAGENA
1155ft
Turbaco
Arjona
Calamar
Canals
0 Miles 150
N
Providencia Is.
San Andres Is.
NICARAGUA
COSTA RICA
San José
CARIBBEAN SEA
PANAMA
Panama
Golfo de Panamá
PACIFIC OCEAN
Ríohacha
Guajira Pen.
Golfo de Venezuela
Santa Marta
Sa. Nevada de Sta Marta
Barranquilla
(see enlargement)
Maracaibo
Valledupar
Cartagena
Lake Maracaibo
Magdalena R.
Sincelejo
Montería
Ayacucho
Mérida
Caucasia
ANDES
Cúcuta
VENEZUELA
San Cristóbal
Bucaramanga
to Bogota c. 200 miles

expeditions as well as to pay the military forces needed to protect these new possessions and their supply lines across the Atlantic and Caribbean. Cartagena became the principal storehouse, a formidable fortress, and the main transit point for the seemingly inexhaustible wealth that flowed to Spain from the New World; it also became a key target for attacks by English, French, and Dutch pirates. It was sacked time and again, only to be reestablished after each attack. Its location made it irreplaceable as a Caribbean port for Spanish galleons loaded with gold, emeralds, pearls, indigo, tobacco, and coffee.

Cartagena was captured and held for ransom by Sir Francis Drake in 1586; subsequently, for the next 2 centuries Spanish rulers spent a fortune fortifying the city. Philip II commissioned the top military engineer in Europe to plan the city's defenses, and 23 forts and 7 miles of walls were completed in 1796. Seven of the nine original forts still stand, and visitors marvel at the ingenious maze of underground passageways, strategic gun emplacements, cisterns for collecting rainwater, ventilation systems, dungeons, and large storage areas for ammunition and food — most of them 25 feet underground.

As part of the defense system, tons of rock were dropped at the wide western entrance to the bay, forming an underwater barrier that still prevents ship passage through this end of the bay. A causeway across the strait connects mainland Cartagena with Boca Grande, the newer sand-spit section where the city's major hotels are located. Today, visitors can take a cruise that provides a pirate's-eye view of the two forts guarding this passage into the inner harbor. You also can sail the Bay of Cartagena, so large that at one time it was said to be big enough to hold all the world's fleets. The beaches are so shallow that hostile ships could not come close enough to bombard the city. Although ships were well protected while they were inside the bay, they still would fall prey to pirates at certain times of the year when lakes and swamps between the Magdalena River and Cartagena dried up, forcing the ships to put to sea. In order to bring their rich cargoes from the interior of the country to the fortress safely, the Spaniards brought thousands of black slaves from Africa to build a 65-mile canal from the Magdalena River to Cartagena that is still in use.

Cartagena (pop. 800,000) remains Colombia's most popular tourist destination, and its appeal seems to be growing. The city drew approximately 500,000 Colombian and foreign tourists in 1992, more than twice the number of visitors in 1990. The city combines the colonial antiquity of the Old City, with its crooked narrow streets, impressive fortifications, and well-preserved early churches and palatial homes, with the Boca Grande area's modern, high-rise hotels and smart shops.

However, the beach resort of Santa Marta and the island of San Andrés are gaining in popularity, especially among foreign vacationers. Santa Marta is the oldest European-founded city on the continent, and the favored point of departure of early explorers venturing into an unknown continent in search of gold. Today, tourists bask on the sparkling beaches below the towering snow-covered Sierra Nevada.

On San Andrés, set in the Caribbean some 500 miles northwest of the northern coast of Colombia, descendants of English Pilgrims and African slaves still speak English and worship in Protestant churches. This tropical land of lush green hills and coconut groves has some of the finest weather, clearest waters, and loveliest beaches in the Caribbean. In addition, there is a duty-free port and two gambling casinos. Its tiny sister island, Providencia, some 60 miles farther northeast, is becoming increasingly popular with those seeking an off-the-beaten-path, non-touristy Caribbean destination.

Colombia's pride in its colonial heritage, combined with its *mañana* atmosphere, sometimes proves so pervasive that prospective visitors may choose to overlook its current turbulence. However, travelers in Colombia should follow common sense precautions: Be aware of current conditions in the country; don't carry large sums of money or wear expensive jewelry; and use hotel safes to store valuables — or better still, leave them at home. Road travel between Colombian cities can be dangerous because of robbers and leftist rebels, but the country does have a modern internal air transport system, and the best way to travel within the country is by plane. *Avianca,* though not immune to terrorism or accidents, is considered reliable. Bus travel between the country's Caribbean cities is also considered safe.

By 1991, a year after an infamous terrorist campaign by drug traffickers had subsided, tourism began to pick up on Colombia's Caribbean coast. The country's natural beauty and low prices drew many new visitors, especially from Canada and Western Europe. It is hoped that in the years ahead, conditions will allow even more travelers to discover and enjoy Colombia's wild and beautiful shoreline.

Colombia At-a-Glance

FROM THE AIR

Colombia's Caribbean coast stretches from Panama to Venezuela — 1,000 miles of the northernmost edge of South America — in a jagged line of bays, capes, and beaches broken here and there by dense jungle and towering mountains. Only 150 miles across at its widest point, this narrow strip of coastal lowlands occupies a delta-shaped alluvial area between the snow-capped Sierra Nevada and the central and western spurs of the Andes. When you look down from the plane as you approach Barranquilla, the gateway to Colombia's Caribbean resorts, the sparkling blue sea suddenly gives way to a lush green mat of tropical vegetation that shows scars of civilization. Gray asphalt roads stretch out in long lines toward red-tile rooftops, farmland, large estates, and the helter-skelter of buildings that make up this city.

Just 2½ hours by air from Miami, the busy city of Barranquilla sits at the midpoint of the Colombian coast, on the west bank of the Magdalena River, one of Colombia's principal waterways. A 1,500-meter bridge spans the river and leads to the four-lane Caribbean highway, a direct and sometimes scenic route along the coast that leads to Santa Marta; to the Sierra Nevada and Tairona National Park beyond; and farther still to the little-known beaches, deserts, and Indian country of the Guajira peninsula on the border of Venezuela. West of Barranquilla, in the opposite direction, lies Cartagena.

SPECIAL PLACES

CARTAGENA The city's "dangerous" reputation, though not as extreme as Bogotá's, is based on its popularity among drug traffickers and the existence of significant street crime. Thanks to a stepped-up police presence in the streets, the tourist areas of the Old City are now reasonably safe for walking. Remember, tourists should not wear expensive jewelry or carry large sums of money, and should avoid deserted streets at night. Cartagena's once impregnable fortifications are still formidable, blocking the Boca Grande entrance to the harbor (now a causeway to the city) and guarding the Boca Chica mouth of the bay in which the city is nestled. Walls 40 feet high and 50 to 60 feet wide encircle this "heroic city," and seven of its nine original forts — with ingeniously laid out underground passages, barracks, and storage areas — remain standing.

A good way to see the city and get a full appreciation of its strategic importance is to take a boat trip around the harbor. The Old City, with its crooked narrow streets, palm-filled plazas, and stately colonial mansions with wrought-iron gates and balconies, stands out in sharp contrast to the functional high-rise condominiums and hotels, fine restaurants, and fashionable shops in the Boca Grande strip between the bay and the Caribbean.

For a panoramic view of the city and harbor, drive or take a taxi (about $1.50 for the trip) to the 17th-century monastery at the top of La Popa Hill (admission charge). Just below is the city's most important fortification, San Felípe de Barajas (admission charge), which remains in almost perfect condition. Originally constructed in 1657, it was captured and destroyed in 1697 by a force of 650 French corsairs, pirates, and buccaneers. Between 1762 and 1769 it was transformed into the impressive fort that still guards the harbor.

A statue of an enormous pair of shoes stands in the plaza in front of San Felípe Fortress, honoring one of Cartagena's best-loved poets, Luis Carlos López. López praised the city in one of his poems, saying it inspired as much affection and comfort as an old pair of shoes.

On the western side of Cartagena, along the Caribbean, several early buildings have been restored by public-spirited citizens. The Church of San

Pedro Claver (on Av. San Juan de Dios) is named for the 17th-century Jesuit monk who dedicated his life to helping the African slaves imported by the Spaniards. The remains of this South American saint, canonized in 1888, repose in a chest under the main altar. On the Plaza Bolívar is the former Palace of the Inquisition, a splendid example of colonial architecture that now houses the city's tourist office and a museum documenting the horrors of the Inquisition. It also houses memorabilia of the city's past, including its receipt for the 10-million-peso ransom it paid to Sir Francis Drake for not burning the city. The museum is open weekdays from 8 to 11:30 AM and from 2 to 5:30 PM; admission charge.

The cathedral, which faces the Plaza Bolívar, was begun in a kind of Renaissance-Andalusian style in 1575 and completed in this century with a pink and white Moorish tower. Its original hand-carved altar has been restored with gold plating.

Diagonally across the Plaza Bolívar, a block north and a block west (toward the sea), is the oldest church in Cartagena, the Church of Santo Domingo, built at the end of the 16th century. You will recognize it by the tower, part of the original construction, which appears to lean slightly. Of special interest inside is the statue of the Virgin Mary, wearing a crown of gold and emeralds.

On the Calle de las Damas is a fine colonial residence where, according to legend, the patron saint of Cartagena appeared to Fray Alonso de la Cruz and ordered him to build the Church of La Popa on the highest hill in the area. The beautiful patio and elaborately decorated rooms are now the site of *Bodegón de la Candelaria,* a good seafood restaurant (see *Eating Out*). The house of the Marqués de Valdehoyos, a man who made a fortune trading in flour and slaves, is nearby (on Calle Factoria), only a block from the cathedral. Its vaulted Moorish ceilings, double balconies, spiral staircase, and lookout provide some outstanding examples of colonial art and architecture. The marques's home also houses the local offices of Corporación Nacional de Turismo (the Colombia National Tourist Corporation). The house of Don Benito, a 17th-century mansion once owned by a gentleman who fell afoul of the Inquisition for preaching Judaism, is a few blocks north of here, by the Parque Madrid. It is now a popular handicrafts shop.

The Parque Morillo, located opposite the Clock Tower, near the center of the Old City, is a symbol of Cartagena's indomitable spirit and love of liberty. On November 11, 1811, Cartagena became the first city in what are now Colombia and Venezuela to declare its independence from Spain. Freedom fighters expelled the Spanish in 1815 and held the city-state until Pablo Morillo retook it after a 3-month siege. Upon entering the city, Morillo offered the native freedom fighters "amnesty in the name of peace," and then proceeded to execute hundreds of people. Although the park bears the name of the Spanish "peacemaker," it commemorates the people he executed.

The Indiacatalina statue, another city landmark, commemorates the early Carib inhabitants of this area. A beautiful Indian princess, Catalina was taken prisoner by Spanish conquistadors when she was a child and returned as a young maiden with Don Pedro de Heredia to help establish Cartagena. Today, bronze replicas of her are given out as "Catalinas" — awards at the annual *International Film Festival* held at the Baluarte de Santa Catalina, just off the Plaza Bovedas.

Little remains of most of the old forts that once protected the city from marauding pirates. However, one of these forts, Castillo de San Fernando, has been restored and is well worth a visit. It is on Boca Chica Island, very reachable by boat from the city ($7 per person each way).

SANTA MARTA Set between two lovely beaches, Santa Marta is a notable port and commercial fishing center, as well as the capital of a sizable agricultural region where large banana plantations flourish. This 450-year-old city can be reached easily from Barranquilla, Bogotá, and other Colombian cities by plane or car.

Many of the visitors to Santa Marta are Colombians from other parts of the country who come here to sunbathe, scuba dive, and enjoy the scenic mountains, which rise 18,000 feet to their snowy crests only 30 miles from the Caribbean coastline. It is a low-key resort town, with some sightseeing and very little nightlife.

The two magnificent beaches, with the snow-capped Andes and Sierra Nevada in the background, are the reason most people visit Santa Marta. Rodadero Beach is more modern; it has newer hotels, restaurants, and the only nightlife to speak of in town. Irotama Beach has older (but not necessarily less expensive) accommodations; it is quieter and somewhat isolated.

The town's other main attractions are the Sierra Nevada, home of the reclusive Kogi Indians, and the site of the Ciudad Perdida (Lost City), accessible only by helicopter (see *Extra Special*). Also of interest are the quiet fishing villages of Taganga (about 10 miles north) and Villa Concha (15 miles to the south), and the banana plantations surrounding the area, most accessible from the village of Sevilla (32 miles south of Santa Marta). Tairona National Park, located 25 miles northeast of Santa Marta, has what are probably the most beautiful beaches in all of Colombia. Here you can camp or rent grass-roofed huts on a jungle hill overlooking a spectacular beach. For reservations and information, contact *Inderena,* Colombia's environmental agency, in Bogotá (phone: 1-286-8643, 1-284-1700, or 1-285-8029; fax: 1-283-3202).

The hacienda of San Pedro Alejandrino, about 3 miles southeast of the city, is an interesting side trip. The Great Liberator, Simón Bolívar, was exiled here, unfortunately without his beloved mistress Manuela Sáenz, who was forbidden to accompany him. Totally destitute, he accepted the hospitality of, ironically, a Spanish nobleman whose fortune had been considerably reduced by Bolívar's Wars of Independence. The final days of Bolívar's life inspired the 1990 novel, *The General in His Labyrinth,* by Colombia's Nobel Prize–winning author, Gabriel García Márquez. The Great Liberator died here, disillusioned, on December 17, 1830. His few possessions are on display in the hacienda. Although Bolívar's body was removed to the National Pantheon in Caracas, Venezuela, his heart remained (literally) in Santa Marta, kept in the cathedral in a leaden casket, which was lost after a fire in 1872. The stately main house is now a museum, and the entire estate is an attractive park with giant shade trees dating from Bolívar's time. Open daily from 9:30 AM to 4:30 PM; admission charge (phone: 54-236259).

SAN ANDRÉS Almost 500 miles northwest of Colombia, San Andrés is actually closer to Nicaragua. This tropical paradise is the largest island of a tiny archipelago that produces coconuts and other fruits. Its main attractions are its luxurious sandy beaches, warm sea, reliable sun, and an almost constant temperature of 80F (27C) 10 months of the year.

Unlike mainland Colombians, most San Andréans speak English. Originally discovered by the Spanish in 1527, the island was settled by English Pilgrims sailing on the *Seaflower,* sister ship to the *Mayflower,* who planted cotton and began importing African slaves to work their plantations. Later the island became a pirate refuge, and buccaneer Henry Morgan set up a base here for his raids on Spanish shipping.

Isolated from the continent, San Andrés has changed little since Morgan's time and is still untainted by Colombia's mainland violence. In fact, Morgan's treasure has never been found and is, according to history and rumor, still hidden in one of the many caves or one of the nearby cays.

In 1822, San Andrés became part of the Colombian province of Cartagena and lay quietly in the Caribbean until it was declared a free port in the 1950s. Although regular air service was established at that time, and the free-port status attracts a large number of bargain hunters (from the Colombian mainland as well as the rest of the world), the island has remained fairly primitive and underdeveloped. There are some good hotels and restaurants; however, tap water is undrinkable, hot water often is unavailable, there are occasional blackouts, and restaurant menus depend on ship arrivals.

There are only two towns on the island: San Luis and the self-named San Andrés. The airport is just a $2 taxi ride from San Andrés, or about a 15-minute walk. The free-port shops, for the most part, are clustered around Avenida La Playa, the main street of the resort section of San Andrés; most tourist hotels are also nearby. There are several good, paved roads, and with a rental car you can drive around the island along a scenic route that meanders through several coconut groves and passes what is reputed to be Morgan's Cave, as well as the Hoyo Soplador, or Blow Hole, which spouts sea water about 30 feet into the air. San Luis is home to most of the island's residents. A small, primitive fishing village of simple but special beauty, peace, and charm, it is an appealing stop on a San Andrés excursion.

The resort area of San Andrés features 600 or so free-port shops, but don't miss the older section of the town, centered around the Baptist church on La Loma Hill, which is the site of many old island mansions surrounded by oleander and banyan trees. From here there is an incredible seascape of pristine beaches and multihued waters. These beaches and warm waters are perfect for all water sports, and its coral reefs are filled with a variety of colorful fish.

There are several offshore keys; the two that attract most visitors are Johnny Key and Haines Key, accessible by launch (cost: $4 per person each way) from San Andrés. Both have picnic facilities and beautiful waters. Haines Key shelters a natural aquarium within its reefs, and a scuba mask, snorkel, and fins are all that's necessary to explore the colorful world beneath the waves.

PROVIDENCIA This pristine, mountainous island, 60 miles northeast of San Andrés and 900 miles south of Miami, hasn't yet been developed as a tourist destination. Unlike San Andrés, Providencia is mountainous and volcanic. It features sandy beaches, an extensive coral reef on its east side, a slow pace, and residents who are friendly and who (for the most part) speak English.

The island was settled in 1629 by passengers of the *Seaflower,* who began a slave trading enterprise known as the Providence Company. Today, most of the native residents of Providencia are descendants of the English and Dutch settlers and the many pirates who originally lived here.

Satena airlines (phone: 1-413-8158) has daily flights between San Andrés and Providencia, and arrangements can be made for the $50 round-trip flight through travel agencies. After arriving at Providencia's El Embrujo Airport, visitors are transported via taxi-trucks through Santa Isabel, the island's main town, and on to Sweet Water Bay, where most of the hotels are. All accommodations on the island are modest and small-scale. Stay at the 17-room *Royal Queen* in town, or at Bahía de Agua Dulce (Sweet Water Bay), where there are several choices of modest accommodations for visitors.

Things to do on Providencia: Visit the white sand beach at Southwest Bay, eat fresh fish, rent horses, and buy coral handicrafts (forget about tortoiseshell items — you can't bring them into the US). For an interesting inland journey, climb the Peak, the highest mountain on the island. Hire a guide by asking at the Bottom House, a village in the south part of the island, or contact the tourist information office at the airport. You also can hire a small boat at Sweet Water Bay and visit isolated Crab Cay, which is one of the best places for snorkeling. Or sail past Morgan's Head, a rock outcropping shaped like a human head, then on to the island of Santa Catalina, site of a fishing village.

EXTRA SPECIAL **The Ciudad Perdida (Lost City), containing pre-Columbian ruins of the Tairona Indians, was discovered in 1975 in the Sierra Nevada, just outside of Santa Marta. The Tairona built circular stone platforms, walls, and roads along the crests of the mountains. Their interconnected cities numbered more than 300, and Ciudad Perdida was their sacred center. There are no roads leading to the Lost City, but helicopter trips can be arranged through Federico Serrano at *Aviatur, Inc.* in Bogotá (phone: 1-282-7111). Reservations should be booked several weeks in advance; flight schedules are affected by guerilla violence in the region and weather conditions.**

Sources and Resources

TOURIST INFORMATION

Corporación Nacional de Turismo (the Colombia National Tourist Corporation) has offices in Barranquilla in the Edificio Arawak (74 Carrera 54; phone: 58-454458), and in Cartagena at the Casa de Marqués de Valdehoyos (Calle Factoria 36-37 Carsera 3; phone: 53-647015 or 53-647017; fax: 53-656076). In addition, there's a tourist office in Cartagena in the old Palace of the Inquisition on the Plaza Bolívar (no phone); in Santa Marta at El Rodadero (16-44 Carrera 2; phone: 54-235773 or 54-233418); and on San Andrés (9-50 Av. Colombia; phone: 811-3832 or 811-4230). For information on tourist offices in the US, see GETTING READY TO GO.

LOCAL COVERAGE *Cartagena: The Voice of the Spanish Main,* an English-language visitors' guide, provides an excellent introduction to the city, its history, and its better-known shops and restaurants. It is available at the national tourist office and at major hotels in Cartagena. On San Andrés, the local newspapers are printed in both English and Spanish.

RADIO AND TELEVISION

CNN is broadcast in most of the hotels that have satellite cable access. There are no English-language radio stations on the Caribbean coast.

TELEPHONE

When calling from the US, dial 011 (international access code) + 57 (country code) + (city code) + (local number). The city code for Cartagena is 53; for Santa Marta, 54; and for San Andrés, 811. When calling from Colombia or elsewhere in South America, dial 9 before the city code. To call from anywhere else, the access code may vary, so call the local operator. Note that city codes are included in the telephone numbers listed in this chapter. When calling within a Colombian city, use only the local number.

ENTRY REQUIREMENTS

US and Canadian citizens need valid passports and tourist cards or visas. The cards are immediately available free when you present a passport (which you should carry with you at all times) and a round-trip ticket (or a letter from your travel agent stating reservations for your trip have been made and outlining your itinerary) at the office of the air or cruise line on which you'll travel. Visas, which require presentation of a passport and round-trip or ongoing tickets, are obtainable at the Colombian consulates in Barranquilla (68-15 Calle 77; phone: 58-457088), and in the US (2118 Leroy Pl. NW, Washington, DC 20008; phone: 202-387-8338). Smallpox vaccinations and yellow fever or cholera inoculations are required only if you're coming from an infected area. If you stay for more than 24 hours, you must pay an $18 airport departure tax.

CLIMATE AND CLOTHES

Barranquilla is usually very hot and muggy, with the average temperature hovering at 85F (30C). Cartagena is about the same, but the evenings and nights are cooler, as are the beaches, where winds always blow. On San Andrés, the average temperature is 80F (27C) most of the year. The most popular months for a visit are from January through April and from July through September, when it is relatively dry. Spring and fall tend to be rainy and humid.

Daytime dress in the cities and seaside resorts is very casual and informal. Colombians like to dress up in the evenings, especially for dinner at a good restaurant; men will don their fancy *guayaberas* or sport shirts (but seldom a jacket), and women choose light cocktail dresses. Formal dress is not necessary in the casinos.

MONEY

Official currency is the Colombian peso, which has been slowly but steadily losing value against the dollar over the last few years. The current exchange rate is about 725 pesos to $1 US. Dollars are accepted enthusiastically in most hotels, restaurants, and shops, but most of the time you will lose money on the exchange, so change money at banks. Hotels and travel agencies offer a slightly less favorable exchange rate, but sometimes you can do better at shops at the time you make a purchase. *Warning:* Do not be tempted to change money with people offering you fantastic rates — even if they are operating within sight of a policeman. When you leave the country, you can exchange a maximum of $100 worth of pesos into US currency at the airport bank, but only if you can show a receipt indicating that the original dollar/peso exchange was effected legally. Banks are open from 9 AM to 3 PM on weekdays. All prices in this chapter are quoted in US dollars.

LANGUAGE

Spanish is the official language of Colombia, but visitors who don't speak Spanish will have little difficulty in the cities and resort areas of the Caribbean coast, as most hotels, restaurants, and stores cater to English-speaking tourists. On San Andrés, the natives speak English plus an English/Spanish dialect inscrutable to speakers of either. Most hotels and restaurants outside the tourist areas are operated by Spanish-speaking Colombians, many of whom speak very little English.

TIME

The coastal cities and San Andrés are on eastern standard time in winter and spring and on eastern daylight saving time in summer and fall, just like the US East Coast.

CURRENT

At 110 volts, 60 cycles, it's the same as the US.

TIPPING

Some hotels, restaurants, and bars add a 10% to 15% service charge to bills. If they don't, do so yourself. For special service, leave an additional 10%. Taxi drivers do not expect tips, but porters should get about $1 per piece of luggage. If you leave your car under the watchful eye of an attendant, he should get about $1, depending on how long it's been in his care.

GETTING AROUND

BUS In Cartagena, buses fall into two categories: large windowless types, which cost only 30¢ per person; and smaller buses with windows, which vary from 40¢ to 50¢ per person. The routes are a little complex, so check with the driver to be sure the bus goes where you want to go. Santa Marta has very little in the way of local bus service, since there are few roads within the town. Carrera 1, which runs along the beach, is the main line; and the bus, which runs from one end of town to the other, making stops throughout the shopping center, costs 30¢. There simply is not enough business (or space) to warrant the use of buses on San Andrés.

CAR RENTAL Available everywhere. In Cartagena, *Autocosta* (phone: 53-653259) has Chevrolet Sprints for $25 per day, plus 30¢ per kilometer. *Hertz* (phone: 53-652921), in the lobby of the *Capilla del Mar* hotel, has two- and four-door sedans available, as well as jeeps (for traveling outside the city).

In Santa Marta, *Hertz* (phone: 54-27046), which has offices at the airport and on Rodadero Beach, has Chevrolet Sprints available for about

$25 a day, plus 30¢ per kilometer. San Andrés has no public transportation system, so it's either taxis or rental cars. Since the rate for a mini-moke or a mini-jeep (Citröen) is only about $18 per day (unlimited mileage), we recommend renting one and exploring the island on your own. There are only a few vehicles — dune buggies and motorcycles among them — available for rent on the island, however. Check at the tourist office or your hotel desk to find out what is available.

SEA EXCURSIONS *Excursiones Roberto LeMaitre* (phone: 53-655622 or 53-652873; fax: 53-652872) in Cartagena offers a regularly scheduled trip to El Pirata Island for a fish or lobster lunch and swimming for $20. For a few dollars more, you can arrange to stay overnight at one of the *LeMaitre* cabañas, with three meals included. A castaway tour can be arranged through *Caribe Tours* in Cartagena (phone: 53-655221, 53-653352, or 53-652542). Given advance notice, they will set you adrift, on a raft equipped with whatever you request, headed toward your own private beach, where you remain, abandoned, until 4 PM, when a motor launch picks you up.

On San Andrés, excursions are available to Johnny Key and Aquario Haynes Key. Private excursions can be arranged through the *Aquarium Dive Shop* (phone: 811-23117 or 811-23120). If you go to Providencia, be sure to take a boat trip around the island. Ask around at Sweet Water Bay, or inquire at your hotel.

TAXI Plentiful in all the coastal cities and inexpensive by US standards, you'll find taxis at the airports, docksides, hotels, and tourist offices. Try to get a firm price before starting out; if you do not know the town, the choice of route (and the final fare) is the driver's. San Andrés is the exception — taxi fares are based on a mileage rate. Here, also, reach an agreement with the driver about the fare before starting the trip. In Cartagena's downtown area, there is a minimum fare of 500 pesos (75¢) for short trips to and around the Old City. You can bargain with a taxi driver for an hourly rate (usually about $5), and see the sights of the Old City in comfort.

Cartagena also has picturesque horse-drawn carriages, perfect for a romantic nighttime ride through the Old City. Rates are negotiable and the carriages are available near the large hotels, such as the *Caribe* and the *Cartagena Hilton.*

INTER-ISLAND FLIGHTS

Avianca flies between Cartagena, Bogotá, and other Colombian cities. There are also connecting flights between Santa Marta and Bogotá on *Avianca* and *SAM,* and San Andrés may be reached via *SAM* and *ACES* from Bogotá.

SPECIAL EVENTS

Cartagena celebrates its *Independence Day* on November 11, and the festival is wild. Complete with masks and costumes, dancing in the streets, and fireworks, this party can get a little rough. On the same day, the *Miss Colombia Contest* is celebrated here as if it were a royal coronation. The city also hosts the annual *Caribbean Music Festival* in mid-March. The big party in Santa Marta is the pre-*Lenten Carnaval.* Colombia's *Independence Day* is July 20; a *Festival of the Sea* is held during late July or early August along the coast. Offices, banks, stores, and museums also are closed on *Epiphany* (January 6); *St. Joseph's Day* (March 19); *Holy Thursday* and *Good Friday; Labor Day* (May 1); *Ascension Day;* the *Feast of Corpus Christi;* the *Feast of the Sacred Heart* (June 2); the *Feast of Saints Peter & Paul* (June 29); *Battle of Boyacá* (August 7); *Assumption Day* (August 15); *Columbus Day* (October 12); *All Saints' Day* (November 1); the *Feast of the Immaculate Conception* (December 8); *Christmas;* and *New Year's Day.* Banks close from December 24 to January 2. (*Note:* Religious feast days that fall on weekends are observed as holidays the following Monday. The same is true of Cartagena's *Independence Day,* Colombia's *Independence Day,* and *Labor Day.*)

SHOPPING

In Cartagena's Old City, keep an eye out for native handicrafts, especially in the 23 former dungeons known as Las Bóvedas located in the 45-foot-thick city walls. There is also a chain of government shops called *Artesanías de Colombia,* which carry a wide array of goods at favorable prices. The stores in this shopping district handle all types of merchandise, from handmade native items to fine leather goods and Colombian emeralds. The native crafts will probably be the best buy, but if you decide to purchase an emerald, make sure you do so only from a reputable dealer, never from a street peddler. Remember that the deeper the color and greater the sparkle, the more valuable the emerald. *Greenfire Emeralds* (phone: 53-650413) has a store in the *Pierino Gallo Centro Comercial* in Boca Grande.

On most other goods, get an idea of prices at home before you go; after paying duty on some items, you really don't save much over US discount prices. The exception is coffee, which at 30¢ to 35¢ a pound is well worth buying in quantity if you have the space in your suitcase. Buy it at a local market, not a tourist shop. Bargains may also be found in the duty-free shops on San Andrés. There are some 600 stores in the shopping area on the island, with goods from all over the world. This area does not cater to American buyers in particular, but rather to local Colombians and Central and South American travelers. There are Swiss watches, French perfume, cameras, and liquor available at, for the most part, similar prices to those in other duty-free areas. Coloma, a local coffee liqueur, costs about $4 for a 750-ml bottle. Except for a few stores offering inexpensive souvenirs and T-shirts, shopping in Santa Marta is poor. Most shops in Colombian cities are open from 9:30 AM to 7 PM daily except Sundays.

SPORTS

BOATING Most coastal resorts have small boats for rent or charter cruisers. In Cartagena, the *Caribe* hotel rents paddleboats and canoes and other craft for about $5 an hour; small boats and water skiing cost $20 an hour. In Santa Marta, check with Captain Ospina at his beachside stand on Rodadero Beach. Boats here rent for about $10 an hour, paddleboats and similar craft go for about $8 an hour. On San Andrés, small boats can be chartered for anywhere from $10 an hour to $110 per day (for a fully equipped fishing cruiser with captain). *Excursiones Roberto LeMaitre* in Cartagena (phone: 53-655622 or 53-652873; fax: 53-652872) allows modern-day Robinson Crusoes to rent their own boat (with or without crew) and their own island for about $150 a day. Some of the available islands, which are in the Rosario Archipelago, just 20 miles from Cartagena, are just tiny atolls and reefs, with just enough rock or coral for a small cabin.

SNORKELING AND SCUBA There are wrecks offshore around Cartagena that provide excellent diving. Jim Buttgen of *Caribe Tours* (phone: 53-655221, 53-653352, or 53-652542) runs excursions, rents equipment, and provides supplies. Bill Moore, a treasure hunter, also takes divers out in his boat; ask for him at the *Caribe* hotel. *Marina Todomar* (phone: 53-654477) arranges diving trips as well. On San Andrés, scuba gear rentals and trips on a 40-foot dive boat, the *Karina,* are available through the *Aquarium Dive Shop* (phone: 811-23117 or 811-23120), next to the *Aquarium* hotel. The *Sea Horse Inn* also has a well-equipped dive shop.

SPORT FISHING In Cartagena, the *Club de Pesca* (in the fortress of San Sebastian) can arrange charters (phone 53-661239 or 53-664104).

Santa Marta has excellent fishing, and Captain Ospina will be glad to charter a boat and point out the way. He operates from his stand on Rodadero Beach, and the rates vary, depending on the vessel, the weather, the time of year, and the captain's mood.

SWIMMING AND SUNNING The Boca Grande section of Cartagena has some decent beaches, though much of the shoreline is marred with trash and matted sands. It's worth taking a boat to the Rosario Islands near Cartegena for better beaches. Santa Marta has good beaches, as does the island of San Andrés.

TENNIS In Cartagena, the *Cartagena Real, Hilton,* and *Caribe* hotels have courts of their own, and there are 3 private clubs that have arrangements with various hotels. Let the hotel desk make the reservations for you; the fees are minimal. The *Irotama* hotel in Santa Marta also has courts. On San Andrés, there is a 4-court tennis club near the *Isleño* hotel (on Avenida de la Playa), with courts available to visitors for a modest fee.

NIGHTLIFE

The nightlife on the Colombian coast is found in its gambling casinos, bars, and discotheques. Although there are some live shows with local and imported talent, there are few lavish, spectacular floor shows. One exception is the *Cartagena Hilton,* which regularly features a local dance show. Also in Cartagena, the *Casino del Caribe* (*Pierino Gallo Centro Comercial*) has one room devoted to slot machines and another for roulette and blackjack. Minimum table bets are 700 pesos (about $1), so the place gets crowded. The casino remains open until 3 AM. Cartagena bars that are worth a visit include *Club Náutico los Veleros* (El Laguito; phone: 53-650406) and *Paco's* (at Plaza Santo Domingo; phone: 53-644294); both serve food.

For discotheques, your best bet is the Boca Grande hotel area. Stay along Avenida San Martín to find *Zorba* (phone: 53-645471); in the same neighborhood you'll find *La Escollera* (Calle 5; phone: 53-654462). They feature dancing to US rock or good Latin-American music. Drinks are inexpensive if you stay away from imported brands, including all wines, and drink local rums. Tres Esquinas is recommended, and often is mixed with ginger ale. There are three small, bohemian bars in the Old City worth visiting: *El Zorba* (at the Parque Fernández de Madrid; no phone), *La Vitrola* (Calle Baloco at Plaza Artilleria; phone: 53-648243), and, best of all, the tower bar in the *Bodegón de la Candelaria* (Calle de las Damas; phone: 53-647251), which features live piano music. A disco worth trying on Santa Marta is *La Escollera de la Marina* (in El Rodadero; phone: 54-228186), with an inviting, tropical ambience. On San Andrés, the *Reggae Nest* (Km 6 on Av. Circunvalación) is a popular discotheque, located outside of town, with a laser light show. The *Tiuna* hotel also has a discotheque.

There are also two casinos in town — *Casino Internacional* (phone: 811-25931) and *Casino El Dorado–Monte Carlo* (phone: 811-26964); both are at the corner of La Playa and Providencia Avenues. Stakes here start at 60¢, no jackets are required, and the hours are 9 PM to 3 AM at both casinos.

Best on the Coast

CHECKING IN

The Colombian coastal resort cities have more than 200 hotels and guesthouses, with a total of some 4,000 rooms. Key tourist areas such as Barranquilla, Cartagena, Santa Marta, and the island of San Andrés boast some first class properties. Expect to pay about $70 for a double room without meals in the places listed below as expensive (the *Hilton* is the exception; its rates start at more than twice that during high season); between $50 and $60 a day at hotels in the moderate range; and less than

$40 a day in an inexpensive place. The telephone numbers listed below include both the city code and the local number. When calling within a city, use only the local number.

CARTAGENA

EXPENSIVE

Capilla del Mar On the beach in the Boca Grande section, it has 198 rooms, 47 of which are suites. Carrera 1 and Calle 8 (phone: 53-651140 or 53-653866).

Caribe Built in 1939, it has 361 rooms. On the beach with an Olympic-size swimming pool, lush gardens, and shops. 2-87 Carrera 1 (phone: 53-650155, 53-637811, 53-650813, or 53-650973; fax: 53-653707).

Cartagena Hilton International The best in town, this property is in the El Laguito residential neighborhood at the tip of Boca Grande peninsula. It has a beach on three sides, swimming pools, lighted tennis courts, water sports, shops, restaurants, party evenings, and a bar/nightclub. All 289 rooms have balconies, air conditioning, and lagoon or sea views. El Laguito (phone: 53-650666 or 53-654657; 800-HILTONS from the US; fax: 53-652211).

MODERATE

Cartagena Real An attractive modern resort hotel catering to vacationers and businesspeople. Just across the street from the beach, it has 75 air conditioned rooms, a small pool, tennis, a restaurant, and a bar with music nightly. 10-150 Av. Malecón (phone: 53-655555 or 53-653766).

Decameron On the Boca Grande hotel strip between the bay and the sea, it has a good restaurant and a wide beachfront. 10-10 Carrera 1 (phone: 53-654400 or 53-654401).

Las Velas This establishments offers suites and apartments, as well as standard double hotel rooms, and a spectacular 18th-floor bar for sunset watching. On the beach in the Boca Grande section. 1-60 Calle Las Velas (phone: 53-650000 or 53-656866; fax: 53-650530).

INEXPENSIVE

El Dorado A high-rise, beachfront property favored by Colombians, it has 326 rooms in an older section, and another 250 in a new, separate annex. 4-41 Av. San Martín (phone: 53-650211, 53-650914, or 53-650752; fax: 53-650479).

Residencias Boca Grande A family hotel with apartments on the beach; the owners and staff will take very good care of you. 7-187 Calle 8 (phone: 53-654435).

SANTA MARTA AND ENVIRONS

EXPENSIVE

Irotama An old-fashioned resort hotel on a fine beach, offering 130 private, air conditioned cottages; rates include water sports, tennis, and meals. *La Barra Viva,* which serves French fare, is also open to non-registered guests (see *Eating Out*). Carretera Santa Marta at Km 14, Barranquilla (phone: 54-227643).

Santamar A resort/convention center complex located on a beautiful beach a mile out of town, it offers 105 air conditioned rooms, 3 pools, 2 restaurants, and 24-hour room service. Km 8 on Via Aeropuerto (phone: 54-228040 or 54-218486; 800-255-3050 from the US).

MODERATE

La Sierra Offers 75 air conditioned rooms plus a seafood restaurant and a bar. El Rodadero Beach (phone: 54-227965; fax: 54-227960).

INEXPENSIVE

TraveLodge Ballena Azul This small hotel is set in a sleepy fishing village. Its 40 rooms (some with air conditioning) overlook a picturesque bay. While it doesn't offer much in the way of luxury, it's fine for those seeking an authentic, non-touristy Colombian experience. In Taganga, about 15 minutes out of Santa Marta (phone: 54-234328; 2-178608 or 2-354542 in Bogotá; fax: 2-357911 in Bogotá).

SAN ANDRÉS

EXPENSIVE

Aquarium A total of 112 rooms are in several units built on pilings overlooking the water. 1-19 Av. Colombia (phone: 811-26923).

MODERATE

Casa Blanca Small (44 rooms, 14 cabañas) and friendly, it caters mostly to young couples and young families from the US and Latin America. Just across from the beach, it has its own pool and water sports. 1-40 Av. Costa Rica (phone: 811-25950).

Decameron Located on San Luis Beach and related to its namesake in Cartagena, it offers a package program that includes meals and activities. Reserve through the main office located in Cartagena (phone: 53-654400 or 53-654401).

Isleño Located on what is considered to be the best beach on the island, and within sight of Johnny Key, this place has 47 rooms; air conditioning isn't necessary, since the island is always cooled by the breeze. 5-117 Av. La Playa (phone: 811-23991 or 811-23992; fax: 811-23126).

Sea Horse Inn A small, simple place just outside town, it's known for its super scuba setup and congenially casual atmosphere. There are 20 rooms, a small pool, and a bar. Carretera San Luis (phone: 811-25529).

Tiuna The largest hotel on the island, it boasts 171 rooms, a restaurant, and a discotheque. 3-59 Av. Colombia (phone: 811-23235 or 811-23237).

PROVIDENCIA

INEXPENSIVE

Posada del Mar Although not located on the beach, the accommodations (only 8 rooms) are the best on the island. A-frame style structures are built around a courtyard restaurant. Make reservations at your hotel on San Andrés or try calling the restaurant. Posada del Mar (phone: 811-48168).

Royal Queen A 17-room hotel with modest facilities. In town (phone: 811-48138).

EATING OUT

The coastal resort cities are blessed with some of the finest seafood in the world. However, service on the laid-back Caribbean coast can be maddeningly slow. Choose a place with a pleasant atmosphere and be prepared to relax, enjoy a drink, and wait.

The most notable culinary choices are the Caribbean lobster (a form of crayfish) and a host of other "fruits of the sea," including squid, crab, oysters, mussels, scallops, jumbo shrimp, red snapper, and even barracuda, which is prepared with local herbs. *Viudo de pescado* (a spicy, baked fish stew), *ceviche de camarones* (shrimp marinated in lemon juice, peppers, and onions and served cold), and *escabeche* (pickled seafood) are specialties; soups are super; ditto *canasta de coco* (coconut custard in a meringue basket). Dinner for two is about $40 at the most expensive places, between $18 and $30 at moderate establishments, and $15 or less at inexpensive ones. Prices do not include wine, drinks, or tips. The telephone numbers listed below include both the city code and the local number. When calling within a city, use only the local number.

CARTAGENA

EXPENSIVE

Bodegón de la Candelaria Elegantly ensconced in a restored colonial mansion in the Old City, this is one of the country's finest restaurants. Before dinner, enjoy a drink at the balcony bar, amid cool breezes and a magnificent ocean view. Seafood and Colombian specialties are served. Open daily for lunch and dinner in June, July, December, and January; closed Sundays the rest of the year. Reservations advised for large groups. Major credit cards accepted. Calle de las Damas (phone: 53-647251).

Capilla del Mar A fine seafood restaurant with a French accent that specializes in lobster and shrimp dishes; also boasts a fine wine cellar. Open daily for lunch and dinner in high season; closed Mondays the rest of the year. Reservations advised. Major credit cards accepted. 8-59 Carrera 5, Boca Grande (phone: 53-655001).

Classic de Andrei Located in the walled Old City, this spot serves traditional Colombian dishes. Open daily for lunch and dinner. Reservations advised. Major credit cards accepted. Calle de las Damas (phone: 53-642663).

MODERATE

La Casa del Pescado All the dishes served here are prepared in authentic Caribbean style, with an emphasis on seafood. Open daily for lunch and dinner. Reservations necessary for large groups. Major credit cards accepted. El Pueblito, Boca Grande (phone: 53-653686).

Chef Julian Very good seafood, Spanish-style; *triumph de cocina* is a trio of lobster halves done three different ways (thermidor, American, and grilled); try to save room for the coconut pie. Open daily for lunch and dinner. Reservations advised. American Express accepted. 9-161 Carrera 2, Boca Grande (phone: 53-648220).

Club de Pesca This place offers dining on seafood specialties (including a fine paella) under the stars near the ramparts of an old fort, with a view of the lights of Cartagena shimmering on the bay. Open daily for lunch and dinner. Reservations advised. Major credit cards accepted. Within the Fortress del Pastelillo (phone: 53-661239 or 53-664104).

Doris If you're looking for an international menu, this is the place. Open daily for lunch and dinner. Reservations advised. American Express and MasterCard accepted. 9-73 Carrera 4a (phone: 53-653808).

La Escollera de la Marina Caribbean-style fare in an informal atmosphere. Live music on weekends. Open for lunch and dinner; dinner only on Fridays and weekends. Reservations advised. Major credit cards accepted. Calles San Juan de Dios and Ricaute (phone: 53-641337, 53-653168, or 53-642724).

La Fontana di Trevi First-rate Italian fare is served in an elegant (but relaxed) setting. The pasta is highly recommended. Open daily for lunch and dinner. Reservations unnecessary. Major credit cards accepted. 6-147 Av. San Martín (phone: 53-653814).

INEXPENSIVE

Nautilus A small, modern seafood eatery within the Old City, it serves only the freshest of fish (when the catch of the day is gone, they close) done in *tipico* Cartagena style — broiled, fried, or in an herb casserole. Open daily for lunch and dinner. Reservations unnecessary. Major credit cards accepted. Two locations: Calle San Pedro Martín, Boca Grande (phone: 53-653964), and in front of the Indiacatalina statue (phone: 53-644204).

SANTA MARTA AND ENVIRONS

MODERATE

La Barra Viva Probably the best dining spot in town, it serves both French and other European dishes as well as steaks from nearby cattle ranches. There's a fine wine cellar. Open for lunch and dinner; closed Thursdays. Reservations advised. Major credit cards accepted. In the *Irotama Hotel,* Carretera Santa Marta at Km 14, Barranquilla (phone: 54-227643).

El Karey One of the many places at which to try fresh seafood prepared in the traditional island way. Open daily for lunch and dinner. Reservations unnecessary. Major credit cards accepted. 1-19 Calle 9 (phone: 54-227250).

Pez Caribe This spot offers a varied international menu. Open daily for lunch and dinner. Reservations advised. Major credit cards accepted. 11-59 Carrera 4 (phone: 54-227001).

INEXPENSIVE

Pan American A delightful stop if you're downtown, this eatery features light meals and a very informal atmosphere. Open daily for lunch and dinner. Reservations unnecessary. No credit cards accepted. 16-10 Calle 18 (phone: 54-222900).

SAN ANDRÉS

EXPENSIVE

La Barracuda de los Ojos Verdes A fine selection of international dishes is served here. Open daily for breakfast, lunch, and dinner. Reservations unnecessary. Major credit cards accepted. 1-19 Av. Colombia (phone: 811-23120, 811-23117, or 811-25953).

MODERATE

La Fonda Antioquena This is the place to go for Colombian and local specialties like *viudo de pescado* (fish stew with plantains and yucca, in creole sauce), *lechón tolimense* (suckling pig), or *cabrito* (kid) with tamales and yucca. Open daily for breakfast, lunch, and dinner. Reservations unnecessary. No credit cards accepted. la-16 Av. Colombia (phone: 811-26885 or 811-26163).

INEXPENSIVE

Miss Bess Meals home-cooked, native fashion, and served in a Colombian atmosphere. Open daily for lunch and dinner. Reservations unnecessary. No credit cards accepted. La Loma (phone: 811-25747).

El Oasis Excellent seafood specialties are offered here. Try *cazuela de mariscos en coco* (seafood casserole in a coconut). The drinks, rum-based for the most part, introduce the meal nicely. Open daily for lunch and dinner. Reservations advised. Major credit cards accepted. Av. La Playa (phone: 811-23819).

Curaçao

From its very beginning, Curaçao has followed its own unpredictable plan of development. According to geologists, the volcanic isle was reimmersed several times, until its natural, protective coral reef rose permanently above the sea. The present exposed layers of lava and coral (which fringe the island) have been hewn and polished by trade winds to form an intricate filigree of caves and grottoes, interspersed with beaches of coral and volcanic sand, bleached by the Caribbean sun and sea.

By the time Curaçao was discovered by European explorers in 1499, it already was inhabited by the Caiquetio, a tribe closely related to the Arawak. They were natural seafarers who probably landed here during their own voyage of discovery, a journey motivated by a need to escape the fierce Carib Indians who dominated South America. The Caiquetio established the basic trade link with Venezuela, some 35 miles away, an economic relationship that remains the mainstay of the island's economy today; the island's name comes from their language, although there are several poetic tales that claim it is a corruption of the Portuguese word *coracão,* which means "heart."

The European colonizers and treasure hunters left the tiny island alone until 1527, when the Spanish returned to occupy it. A century later, as Spain's global power began to wane, Holland began to challenge the Spanish. In 1621, the Dutch West India Company was formed, both to promote trade and to encourage privateers to further hamper Spanish dominance. In 1634, Van Walbeeck, an officer of the company, claimed the island for the Dutch. They banished the Spanish governor and 400 assorted Spaniards and Indians to Venezuela, and the island became the main Dutch base for trading with the rest of the Caribbean and South America.

The island flourished under Dutch rule and became one of the most important trading centers along the former Spanish Main (the north and eastern coasts of South America originally dominated by the Spanish). Jews fleeing persecution in Portugal, Spain, Mexico, and Brazil found a far more tolerant atmosphere in Curaçao and established a sizable community on the island beginning in 1651. Their synagogue, Mikve Israel-Emanuel, is the oldest in the Western Hemisphere. Muslims found themselves welcome here, too, as did English Pilgrims. Simón Bolívar sought asylum here twice during South America's independence struggles. So Curaçao evolved into a peaceful, thriving international community, and as such became an attractive target for greedy pirates and ambitious European nations.

During this initial period, Curaçao's capital city, Willemstad, took on the storybook atmosphere that now characterizes the entire island. The Dutch took great pains to re-create the towns they had left behind. The

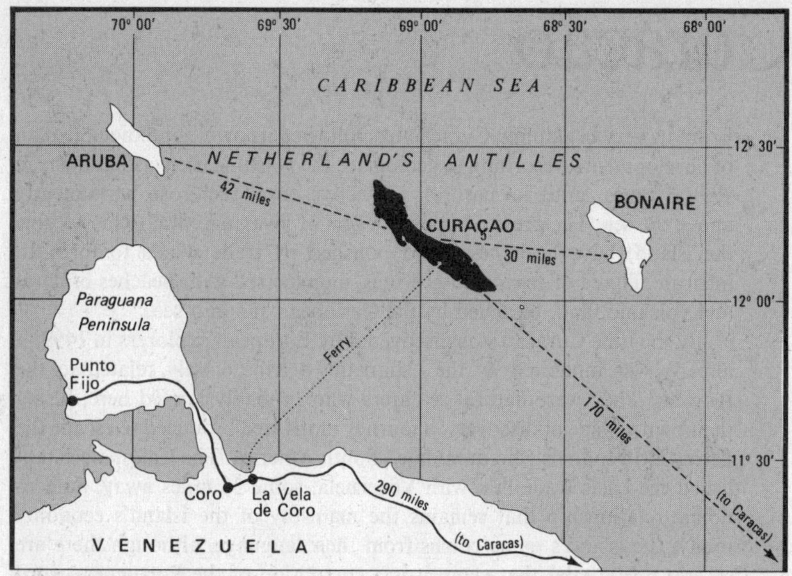

70° 00′
69° 30′
69° 00′
68° 30′
68° 00′
CARIBBEAN SEA
12° 30′
ARUBA
NETHERLAND'S ANTILLES
42 miles
BONAIRE
CURAÇAO
30 miles
12° 00′
Paraguana
Peninsula
Ferry
Punto
Fijo
170 miles
11° 30′
Coro
La Vela
de Coro
290 miles
(to Caracas)
(to Caracas)
VENEZUELA

North Point
CURAÇAO
Boca Tabla
Westpunt
Savonet
Knip
Estate
0
Miles
10
Knip
Bay
Mt. Christoffel
1239ft
Lagoen
Playa
Grandi
St. Kruis
Barber
Boca
Sta.
Cruz
Soto
Santa
Marta Bay
Hato Gulf
San Juan
Bay
486ft
St. Willibrordus
Kleine Berg
308ft
Hato International
(Dr. Albert Plesman)
Airport
Port Marie Bay
Daaibooi
Bay
Bullen
Bay
Grotto
of Hato
Santa Maria
Sta. Catharina
San Michiels
Bay
Isla
Refinery
Schottegat
St. Joris
Bay
Piscadera
Bay
Sta. Rosa
Groot St. Joris
St. Anna Bay
Montagne
Willemstad
Jan Thiel Bay
Tafelberg
636ft
Caracas Bay
CARIBBEAN SEA
Spanish Water
Nieuwport
Santa
Barbara Beach
East
Point

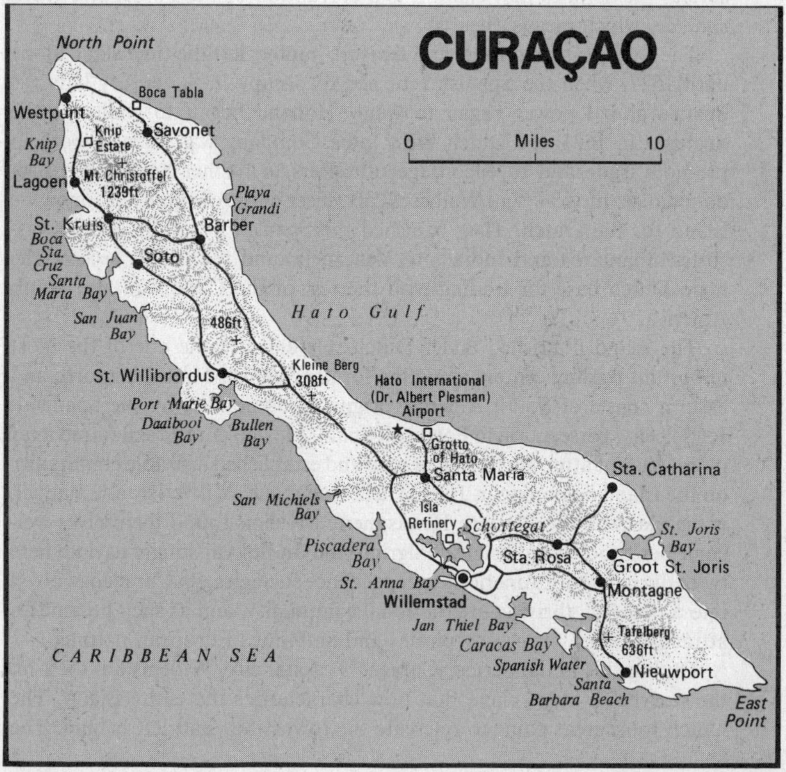

carefully laid out streets trimmed with neat, well-constructed homes, and the plantation mansions, called *landhuizen,* were patterned after buildings in Holland. One of the colonial governors, however, is said to have complained that the tropical sun reflecting on the white houses gave him severe headaches. According to the story, the obliging citizens painted the houses pink, yellow, purple, and almost every other tropical hue. To this day Willemstad retains an air of unreality, with its small, immaculate streets and 200-year-old pastel houses. Despite its fairy-tale appearance, the city has seen numerous engineering and technological advances, one of the earliest and most significant being the construction of the Queen Emma Pontoon Bridge across the harbor in 1888, connecting both sides of the city.

As wars raged through Europe, Curaçao and its neighboring islands of the West Indies changed hands several times. In 1800, after several attempts, Britain took the island and held it until 1803, when Curaçao-born Pedro Luis Brion, the 21-year-old chief of the island militia, defeated the occupation forces and freed the island. In 1807 the British again captured Curaçao and retained possession until the island was returned to the Dutch in 1816.

War and the resultant isolation from Europe had taken their toll on the islands' economy. Beet sugar had replaced cane sugar on the Continent, and by the mid-19th century, the slave trade had been abolished everywhere. Curaçao retired into a peaceful, isolated existence until 1914, when oil was discovered in Venezuela. Curaçao then emerged as a worldwide trading port.

Venezuelan oil comes to Curaçao for refining and storage, and is thereafter shipped to ports all over the world. The Royal Dutch Shell Company built one of the world's largest refineries on Curaçao, taking advantage of its stable government and the excellent deep-water port, just as the Dutch West India Company had centuries before. Today, it's the ISLA Oil Refinery, owned by Petroleos de Venesuela.

A $1.5-million port expansion was completed in 1987, making Curaçao's facilities among the Caribbean's finest. Willemstad is now the seventh-largest harbor in the world (and among the busiest), hosting ships of virtually every international flag. The oil-based prosperity has brought a tremendous influx of refinery and shipping workers, and, in turn, merchants and businesses from around the globe. In addition, Curaçao has developed a reputation as a financial center, and international corporations manage the distribution of their products to the Caribbean and South America from here. Today, some 79 nationalities are represented on Curaçao, including Dutch, English, Spanish, Chinese, Portuguese, East Indian, Venezuelan, and Caiquetio. The island also has a jetport, the Hato International Airport, with the longest runway (11,148 feet) in the Caribbean.

Curaçao is part of the kingdom of the Netherlands; the other Dutch island territories — Bonaire, Saba, St. Eustatius, and St. Maarten — are still administered through Willemstad, the capital city for the Netherlands Antilles. This status explains the city's many fine buildings, offices, and public spaces.

Curaçao, with its quaint towns, beautiful beaches, and its exceptional spots for diving, snorkeling, and other water activities, also is coming into its own as a popular tourism destination. Currently, the island has 1,656 rooms in large hotels and 270 rooms in smaller lodgings. In conjunction with major expansion and renovation projects at many hotels in recent years, the island has launched an aggressive tourism promotion campaign. By the turn of the century, tourism officials predict that there will be some 450,000-plus visitors to the island each year.

Curaçao At-a-Glance

FROM THE AIR

At 38 miles long, from 2 to 7½ miles wide, and pinched to a narrow "waist" near its middle, Curaçao looks a little like the wings of a bird in flight. Lying diagonally, northwest to southeast, 35 miles north of the Venezuelan coast, it is 42 miles east of Aruba, 30 miles west of Bonaire, and about 1,710 miles south of New York. It is the largest and most populous (150,000 inhabitants) of the five islands that make up the Netherlands Antilles.

The topography of Curaçao is similar to that of the American Southwest — fairly flat, arid, but not quite desolate. Instead of green Caribbean palms, the island's flora are an amalgam of browns and russet. Willemstad, the capital, is just to the southeast of the island's narrow center, occupying the southern shore. Half the residents of Curaçao live in Willemstad; the rest occupy the many small villages scattered along the shores and flatlands. The countryside, or *cunucu,* is flat and dotted with cacti rising as tall as 20 feet and divi-divi trees forever bent before the fierce trade winds. Mt. Christoffel, at the northwestern end of the island, is the highest point — 1,239 feet above the sea. The coast is ringed with coves, beaches, caves, and underwater grottoes — reminders of the island's volcanic origin.

SPECIAL PLACES

WILLEMSTAD

With St. Anna Bay facing Venezuela (just 35 miles away) and its long, narrow channel leading into a totally sheltered harbor, this was a natural berthing place for the Spanish and Dutch. Adding a couple of forts (on either side) to guard the entranceway made the capital of Curaçao a virtually impregnable trading port. The city grew on both sides of the channel, with the eastern side becoming known as the Punda and the west as the Otrobanda, literally "other side."

QUEEN EMMA BRIDGE (*KONINGIN EMMABRUG*) Originally, there were roads around the harbor and a ferry across the canal. In the late 1800s, however, American consul Leonard Burlington Smith suggested a means of providing transportation across the harbor that would not interfere with the shipping traffic in the canal: a pontoon bridge. Fixed on one end only, it could swing out of the way when ships passed through the canal. The bridge, completed in 1888, opens over 30 times a day to admit the 8,000 oceangoing ships that use the harbor canal each year; any tour of Willemstad must begin here. Spend half an hour beside the bridge, watching the supertankers pass. The contrast between the ultramodern ships and the 17th-century houses on either side is striking, as is the view of the Queen Emma, floating mere feet above the water, and the "new" Queen Juliana Bridge (completed in 1974), standing almost 200 feet high and spanning 1,625 feet.

WATERFORT AND FORT AMSTERDAM The Waterfort, which originally guarded the mouth of the canal on the Punda side, is now the site of the *Van der Valk Plaza* hotel; its task of standing guard has been left to Fort Amsterdam, just behind it and also overlooking the canal. The plaza between the two forts is dedicated to General Manuel Carlos Piar, a Curaçao native and member of the Great Liberator's (Simón Bolívar's) staff.

The far side of Fort Amsterdam is at the foot of the Queen Emma Bridge, and the yellow and white section of the fort facing the canal, along Handelskade, is now the Governor's Palace. A walk through its archway into the courtyard beyond is a bit like stepping back in time. The entire structure dates to the 18th century, and the old Dutch church directly opposite still has an English cannonball embedded in its walls (from 1804). The corner of the fort is at the intersection of Handelskade and Breedestraat, the beginning of Curaçao's main shopping district.

SHON SHA CAPRILES KADE At the north end of Handelskade, just a few minutes' walk from the bridge, is an inlet of St. Anna Bay known as Waaigat, and along this channel runs Shon Sha Capriles Kade, a street named after a well-known local composer and banker, Charles Maduro, who was also known as Shon Sha Capriles. Here Venezuelan schooners and sailboats still tie up, bringing a true floating market to Curaçao. This market continues a trading tradition begun by the Caiquetio well before Ojeda claimed this land for Spain. The South Americans mostly bring tropical fruits and vegetables to Curaçao, but also haul dried meat, fish, spices, and cloth. Cash is now the accepted medium, but in years past this was more a bartering and trading market; even now haggling is the norm. There is also an enclosed public market for those who prefer to do business indoors, but it's just not the same.

MIKVE ISRAEL-EMANUEL SYNAGOGUE Located on the corner of Columbusstraat and Kerkstraat, between Shon Sha Capriles Kade and the Fort, this is the oldest synagogue in the Western Hemisphere. Built in 1732, it is not only a historic house of worship but also an excellent example of colonial Dutch architecture. There is a central courtyard, and the interior of the building is carpeted with a layer of white sand, symbolic of the Jews' journey through the desert to the Promised Land. The Reader's Platform is set in the center, so the congregation surrounds it in much the same way as the tribes are presumed to have gathered in the desert. Four 24-candle brass chandeliers, three of which are over 250 years old, hang from the original mahogany ceiling; they are replicas of the candelabra in the Portuguese Synagogue in Amsterdam. Services are held every Sabbath at 10 AM and 6:30 PM and holidays at 6:30 PM.

JEWISH HISTORICAL AND CULTURAL MUSEUM Next door to the synagogue, this building, which dates to 1728, was once a rabbi's house and later a Chinese laundry, until a centuries-old *mikvah* (a communal bath used for ritual purifications) was uncovered in its courtyard. Since then, the building has undergone considerable restoration. On display here are utensils for kosher butchering, beautiful silverwork, various religious articles, scales, and a Torah said to date from 1492. Open from 9 to 11:45 AM and again from 2:30 to 5 PM weekdays; admission charge (phone: 611633). The museum is closed on all Jewish and public holidays.

BRIONPLEIN On the Otrobanda, at the foot of the Queen Emma Bridge, this plaza is the site of a statue of Curaçao's favorite son and best-known war hero, Pedro Luis Brion. Born in 1782, this fierce and clever fighter is credited with preventing several British invasion attempts. After they finally took the island in 1800, Brion, then chief of militia of Curaçao, led the island forces in their resistance against the invaders and forced the British withdrawal in 1803. The Riffort, once guardian of the canal on this side, now houses a bistro and a seafood restaurant.

WEST OF WILLEMSTAD

It's roughly 100 miles around the island of Curaçao, and since the roads vary only between good and excellent, the route can be driven easily in a matter of hours. Although Willemstad is the island's principal attraction, the *cunucu,* or countryside, should not be ignored. Some of the best examples of Dutch architecture, the *landhuizen* (mansion houses) of the old plantations, are here.

CURAÇAO MUSEUM A short distance from the Queen Emma Bridge, on Van Leeuwenhoekstraat, is the *Curaçao Museum.* Built in 1853 as a seamen's hospital and restored in 1942, it contains relics of the Caiquetio Indians, including a funeral urn, some pottery, beautiful bits of Caribbean coral, and cradles. The cockpit of the Fokker F-XVIII trimotor (the *Snipe,* or *Snip)*, which made the first commercial crossing of the southern Atlantic from Holland to Curaçao in 1934, is also on display. In addition, the museum has a replica of a colonial kitchen, painted brick red with white polka dots, either to ward off evil spirits or to conceal kitchen spatter and confuse the flies. The museum gardens contain specimens of all the island's plants and trees. Open from 9 AM to noon and 2 to 5 PM; Sundays from 10 AM to 4 PM; closed Mondays and the last Sunday of each month; admission charge (phone: 623873).

JAN KOCK HOUSE Traveling northwest along the highway that heads toward the tip of the island, you'll come to this yellow and white *landhuis.* Built in 1650, it's the oldest continually inhabited building in Curaçao. The plantation here originally produced salt, but it's now a private home owned by Jeannette Leito, who offers 1-hour tours through the antiques-filled rooms while regaling visitors with ghost stories. Tours are by appointment only (phone: 648087); there's an admission charge. On Sunday mornings, Ms. Leito opens the *Fungi Pot* restaurant behind her home and serves delicious homemade Dutch pancakes.

ASCENCION PLANTATION Continuing west along the north coast, the road leads to this stately 17th-century *landhuis,* now a rest and recreation center for the Dutch Marines. Open to the public on the first Sunday of each month, from 10 AM to 2 PM, with live music, folkloric dancing, local handicrafts, and food; no admission charge (phone: 641950).

MT. CHRISTOFFEL As you continue along the coast, this peak, the highest point in the Netherlands Antilles, rises 1,239 feet on the left. It's actually just about in the center of this end of the island, but on the flat *cunucu,* it can be seen for miles. Boca Tabla Grotto, on the coast to the right, is a good place to stop for a short rest. It is the best known of the hundreds of grottoes that dot the coastline of Curaçao, and most representative of the island's origins. The coral and limestone-pitted landscape — some of it smooth, other parts sharp — resembles a savage moonscape. Wear sturdy sneakers so that you can climb into the caves and listen to the waves outside. Some parts of these caves are below water, so be careful.

NORTH AND EAST OF WILLEMSTAD

ROOSEVELT HOUSE Beyond the business district, on the peninsula formed by the Waaigat and an inlet of the harbor, is the US Consulate, known as Roosevelt House. On Ararat Hill overlooking the city and the approach to the Queen Juliana Bridge, it was a gift from the Dutch in appreciation for the US's protection during World War II.

FORT NASSAU Located just northeast of the city, on the same peninsula as Roosevelt House, this fortress (ca. 1796) has an imposing view from 200 feet above the inner harbor. From here, Willemstad resembles a city of dollhouses, and the mammoth ISLA refinery looks like a toy.

BOLÍVAR MUSEUM On Penstraat, along the coast to the southeast of town near the *Avila Beach* hotel, is this odd little museum (126-8 Penstraat; phone: 612040), also known as the *Octagon House.* Bolívar visited his two sisters here during the wars of South American independence. The rooms of the mansion have been restored and furnished with period pieces. Open daily from 9 AM to noon and from 3 to 6 PM; admission charge.

AUTONOMY MONUMENT From the *Bolívar Museum* swing north, traveling along the east side of the harbor, to the intersection of Fokker Weg and Rijkseenheid Boulevard, where this modern monument stands. Dedicated to the stable, essentially self-governing island of Curaçao, the piece was created by native designer J. Fresco.

AMSTEL BEER BREWERY Turn left at the Autonomy Monument and go north on Rijikseenheid Boulevard until the smell of hops signals your arrival at the only brewery in the world to make beer from distilled seawater. (Since 1929, Curaçao has relied upon water produced in its own desalination plants, made by evaporating seawater and then condensing the vapor into virtually pure drinking water.) This modern facility takes 2 weeks to make a good brew, and 40,000 bottles are filled each hour. Tours, followed by complimentary beer tastings, are offered Tuesdays and Thursdays at 10 AM; no admission charge. The brewery is closed from June 15 to August 6.

CHOBOLOBO (CURAÇAO DISTILLERY) Continue east and north around the harbor for a treat — the home of the original Curaçao liqueur. This famed after-dinner drink is produced, from a secret family recipe, on the 17th-century estate of Senior & Co., called Chobolobo. Two hundred gallons of the liqueur, uniquely flavored by the sun-dried unripened peel of the Curaçao golden orange (called the *laraha*), are made each week in the 1-room distilling facility. The *laraha* grows only on Curaçao; when planted anywhere else, it simply grows into a regular-size orange. Tours of the distillery (phone: 378459) are held Mondays through Fridays from 9 AM to noon and 1 to 5 PM; no admission charge. There is a tasting session at the end of each tour.

OIL REFINERY The area of the island that extends across the north end of the harbor, along Schottegatweg Noord and Schottegatweg West, is the site of the Venezuelan oil refinery and other Shell-created facilities, including a golf club, a yacht club, and a country club.

EAST END

CURAÇAO SEAQUARIUM To get here, follow the coast road from Willemstad past the zoo and botanical gardens (neither is exceptional) about 2 miles to Jan Thiel Bay. The extraordinary *Seaquarium* occupies 6 acres next to the *Lion's Dive* hotel and the Underwater Marine Park. It's the world's only public aquarium that raises and cultivates sea creatures by completely natural methods, with 46 glass tanks that house over 400 species of marine creatures found in local waters. The best time to come is in the morning, when the fish are fed. Outside, a viewing platform overlooks the wreck of the steamship HMS *Oranje Nassau,* which sank in 1906 and now sits, coral-encrusted, in 10 feet of water. The complex also features a shark channel, 2 restaurants, an open-air bar, and glass-bottom boats that take visitors over the underwater park reefs immediately offshore. The nearby manmade beach is a perfect spot to relax or to engage in some sailing, fishing, or sailboarding. Changing rooms are available. Open daily from 9 AM to 10 PM; admission charge (phone: 616666).

FORT BEEKENBERG From the *Seaquarium,* head east along the coast to Caracas Bay, where this fort towers above the place where cruise ships dock. Across the neighboring bay, four yacht clubs line the shore at Spanish Water and fleets of sail and power boats do their Sunday cruising.

SANTA BARBARA PLANTATION South of Fort Beekenberg and past Tafelberg, a unique phosphate mountain, is this private plantation. Visitors can swim in the turquoise waters off Santa Barbara Beach (with changing rooms, toilet facilities, snack bar, Sunfish and windsurfer rentals; open daily until 5 PM).

ST. JORIS If you're still hungry for sights, detour north from the Santa Barbara Plantation to St. Joris to admire its plantation houses and watch the bay's teal waters rush through the north channel to the Caribbean.

WEST END

WESTPUNT AND WESTPUNT BAY On the far western tip of the island, this area contains some of Curaçao's best and most appealing small beaches, all apt to be crowded with residents on weekends. During the week, however, fishermen can be seen casting their nets and gutting their catch on the beach. It's only an hour's ride from Willemstad. After a swim, stop at one of Westpunt's restaurants for a tasty lunch (see *Eating Out*). There are no changing facilities, though each secluded sandy spot has its own little cove, and if things aren't too crowded, most restaurants will allow patrons to use their restrooms for changing.

CHRISTOFFEL NATURAL PARK After visiting Westpunt, nature fans may want to make a short western detour to visit this 4,450-acre preserve before hitting the south shore road for Willemstad. The park, with its centerpiece, Mt. Christoffel, is dedicated to the conservation of flora (rare palms, cacti, and the bent divi-divis) and fauna (iguanas, rabbits, deer, and a number of bird species). The visitors' center, housed in an outbuilding of the privately owned 18th-century *landhuis* Savonet, serves as park headquarters and sells a guide to the park. An eastern trail leads to four caves embellished with Indian signs and unusual rock formations; another trail winds through nature paths, passes stately ruins, and climbs into the hills. Hikers can follow yet another winding trail 1,239 feet up to the top of the mountain, where they'll be rewarded by stunning views of the island. Although the park is open daily (from 8 AM to 5 PM, Sundays from 6 AM to 3 PM), no one is admitted after 2 PM as the circuit takes approximately 3½ hours to complete. Admission charge except for children under 6 (phone: 640363).

Also in the park is the *Savonet Museum of Natural and Cultural History,* a former plantation house with remains and artifacts from Curaçao's pre-Columbian inhabitants, as well as exhibits highlighting some of the island's present-day natural environment. The museum also features a collection of cave drawings made over 500 years ago by the Caiquetio. It's open from 8 AM to 5 PM; Sundays from 6 AM to 3 PM. No admission charge to park visitors.

ELSEWHERE ON THE ISLAND

BETH HAIM CEMETERY On Schottegatweg West, northwest of town past the ISLA facilities, this is the oldest Caucasian burial ground still in use in the Western Hemisphere. It contains 2,500 graves on 3 acres of land, and was consecrated before 1659. Note the intricate stonework on the unusual 17th- and 18th-century tombstones.

HATO CAVES Located near the airport, these caves, opened in 1992 and operated by the *Holland* hotel, are the island's newest tourist attraction. Inside the large network of caverns, hidden lights illuminate the white limestone formations while gravel walkways lead through the tunnels. One-hour guided tours are offered Tuesdays through Sundays from 10 AM to 5 PM; admission charge (phone: 680379).

Sources and Resources

TOURIST INFORMATION

The Curaçao Tourist Board has offices in Willemstad at the *Waterfort Arches* (phone: 613397), at 19 Pietermaai (phone: 616000), and at the airport (phone: 686789). Maps, folders, and multilingual staff members are available at all three locations. Radio Paradise (phone: 636105) also has information on activities and events. For information about Curaçao tourist offices in the US, see GETTING READY TO GO.

LOCAL COVERAGE *Curaçao Holiday,* an island publication in English, carries useful information on special events, shopping hints, restaurants, and nightlife; it's free at the airport, tourist office, and hotels.

RADIO AND TELEVISION

Curaçao has some locally produced television and radio shows in Dutch, some in English, some in Papiamento, and some in Spanish. Radio Paradise broadcasts news in English every hour on the hour from 9 AM to 7 PM daily. Most hotels offer CNN.

TELEPHONE

When calling from the US, dial 011 (international access code) + 5999 (country code) + (local number). To call from another Caribbean island, the access code may vary, so call the local operator. When calling on Curaçao use only the six-digit local number unless otherwise indicated.

ENTRY REQUIREMENTS

US and Canadian citizens need a passport or other proof of citizenship (a birth certificate or voter's registration card, plus a photo ID), and a return or continuing ticket to a destination outside of the Netherlands Antilles.

CLIMATE AND CLOTHES

The average annual rainfall is only 21 inches, and the daytime temperatures remain constant in the low- to mid-80s F (60s C) on Curaçao. Because of the trade winds, it does get cool enough at night to make a light wrap useful for women. Casual clothes are fine during the day, but beach clothes and shorts are frowned upon in town. In the evening, ties are never required and men seldom wear jackets. If you plan on exploring the beaches and grottoes of the island, wear rubber-soled walking shoes or sturdy sneakers, since many of the access trails are rough.

MONEY

The coin of the realm is the Netherlands Antilles florin or guilder (the two names are interchangeable), written NAf ($1 US equals about 1.77 NAf). US dollars and all major credit cards are accepted virtually everywhere, so there is no need to convert any cash unless it benefits you; check prices beforehand. Banks are open on weekdays from 8 AM to 3:30 PM.. All prices in this chapter are quoted in US dollars.

LANGUAGE

The official tongue is Dutch, but English and Spanish are spoken widely. The native language is Papiamento, a blend of Spanish, Dutch, French, English, and Portuguese, plus some Caribbean and Indian dialects.

TIME

Curaçao is on atlantic standard time all year long. It is 1 hour later than eastern standard time but the same as daylight saving time on the US East Coast.

CURRENT

Local electricity is 110 to 130 volts AC, 50 cycles, with US-style outlets. This is fine for razors and most hair dryers. If you need a converter, your hotel will probably supply one.

TIPPING

Most restaurants add a 10% service charge while hotels add 12%, which covers bartenders, bellhops, chambermaids, and waiters; for special services, an additional 5% may be added at your discretion. Taxi drivers should be tipped only for special services such as helping with bags, and porters should be tipped on a per-bag rate (50¢ each).

GETTING AROUND

Most of the sights and shopping in Willemstad are within walking distance of one another, and hotels outside the town usually provide complimentary shuttle bus service. There also are public buses available from the downtown area to several island destinations (just check the front of the bus or ask the driver), with fares ranging from 40¢ to 80¢ (in local currency). Some private vans function as buses as well; they can be boarded at bus stops. They will list destinations on their windshields and show the word "Bus" on their license plates. The minimum fare is about 50¢.

CAR RENTAL Available from *Avis* (phone: 611255), *Budget* (phone: 683466 or 683198), *National* (phone: 680373), and *Dollar* (phone: 613144 or 290262), as well as *Caribe Rentals* (phone: 613089 or 615666). They all have offices at the airport and also will deliver cars to your hotel. The rates vary by company and vehicle, but range from about $28 to $50 a day depending on the size of the car, plus 14¢ a kilometer; unlimited mileage rates apply to rentals of 3 days or more and begin at about $26 a day. Weekly rates, including unlimited mileage, start at about $145. A valid US or Canadian driver's license is all that is required.

SIGHTSEEING BUS TOURS Choices offered by *Taber Tours* (phone: 376637 or 376713) and *Daltino Tours* (phone: 614888) range from a 2½-hour tour for about $10 per person to a full-day tour for about $16. *Casper Tours* (phone: 653010 or 616789) offers custom-tailored tours around the island in an air-conditioned van for about $25 per person.

TAXI Curaçao's taxis are easily identified by the signs on their roofs and the letters "TX" after the license number. There are taxi stands at the airport (phone: 681220) and all hotels. The going rate for a taxi tour is about $20 an hour. Cabs are not metered but there is an official tariff sheet, which drivers must carry. Ask to see the driver's copy, or ask the bell captain in your hotel for a copy. Always come to an agreement with the driver before starting, and be aware of whether the price stated is in dollars or florins (guilders). The run from the airport to town (or your hotel) should be about $12, but that can be split with other passengers. (It's your responsibility to put a group together; the driver will not do so.) If you want to take a taxi from town to your hotel, get in the cab on the same side of the canal as your hotel. It costs nothing to walk across Queen Emma Bridge, but your fare can double by crossing the Queen Juliana Bridge.

WALKING TOURS *Old City Tours* (53 DeRuyterkade; phone: 613554) offers fascinating walking tours of the old residential neighborhoods of the Otrobanda guided by local architect Anko van der Woude. The itineraries include some renowned plantation houses. Tours depart Tuesdays and Saturdays at 9 AM with pickup at your hotel. Special tours can be arranged for groups of four or more. Prices vary.

INTER-ISLAND FLIGHTS

Both *Air Aruba* and *ALM Antillean Airlines* offer daily flights from Curaçao to Aruba and Bonaire. *ALM* also has frequent flights to Caracas, Venezuela. Charter aircraft can be arranged through either the *Curaçao Aero Club* (phone: 681050) or *Oduber Agencies* (phone: 615011 or 615837). Day and overnight packages are available.

SPECIAL EVENTS

Curaçao's *Carnival* begins in January with costume parades, dancing in the streets, and pervasive partying with little restraint. Prime *Carnival* activity occurs the weekend immediately preceding *Ash Wednesday.* Also celebrated are *New Year's Day* (and *Eve*), the *Queen's Birthday* (April 30), *Good Friday, Easter Monday, Labor Day* (May 1), *Ascension Day* (May 19), *Flag Day* (July 2), *Christmas,* and *Boxing Day* (December 26). Stores and banks are generally closed on these holidays.

SHOPPING

Willemstad's 6 square blocks of luxury-stocked shops testify to the fact that shopping has ranked as a leading indoor/outdoor sport in Curaçao since the days of the first cruise ships. Facilities became even more attractive with the addition of the 32-shop *Waterfort Arches* in downtown Willemstad. The local import tax is still so low that prices are virtually duty-free, but be aware of US prices to help you choose the real bargains. There are excellent buys — at 20% to 25% below stateside prices — on many true luxury imports, especially fine English bone china, porcelain, crystal, Swiss watches, and precious jewelry. In these categories, as a rule, the higher the price tag, the greater the savings. And "closeout sale" shelves may save you as much as 50% over stateside prices. Since this is a prime cruise port, the best shopping hours are in the morning, before the ship passengers disembark. Although many shops close for lunch from noon till 2 PM, some stay open to accommodate the extra volume on heavy traffic days. The small plaza where Breedestraat and Heerenstraat intersect is the place to start.

Among others, these Willemstad shops are tops:

BERT KNUBBEN This beachfront boutique specializes in unique black coral jewelry, handcrafted on the island. Although collecting black coral from the sea is forbidden by law, Bert has been granted special permission by the

Curaçao government to gather his off the north coast, then bring it ashore to carve into exquisite jewelry, which is sold at reasonable prices. In the *Holiday Inn Crowne Plaza* (phone: 614944).

BOOLCHAND'S Now that electronics are duty-free on Curaçao, this is a good stop. 50 Breedestraat (phone: 616233).

D'ORSY'S A first-rate emporium for a wide variety of perfume and cosmetics. 23 Breedestraat (phone: 617462).

GALLERY 86 The place for original art, including oil paintings, watercolors, sculptures, and ceramics. 2-N Bloksceeg (phone: 613417).

GANDELMAN JEWELERS It specializes in intricate, uniquely Curaçaoan gold pieces, in a wide array of contemporary designs and settings. 35 P. Breedestraat (phone: 611854).

J. L. PENHA & SONS This shop in the city's oldest building (ca. 1708) stocks French perfume; European clothing; Delft and Hummel collectibles; leather goods from Italy, Spain, and South America; knits and cashmere items from the British Isles. At the corner of Heerenstraat and Breedestraat (phone: 612266).

LITTLE SWITZERLAND Featuring precious jewelry, Swiss watches, Rosenthal china, crystal, and flatware. 44 P. Breedestraat (phone: 612111).

SALAS Books, prints, and other reading matter. 50 Fokkerweg (phone: 612303).

SPRITZER & FUHRMANN The island staple for fine jewelry and gifts is still alive, well, and offering impressive savings. *Gomez Plaza,* Breedestraat (phone: 612600).

YELLOW HOUSE For perfume, cosmetics, boutique accessories. 46 P. Breedestraat (phone: 613222).

SPORTS

BOATING Call *Coral Cliff Diving* (phone: 642822) for 21-foot sailboat rentals. If you're a yacht club member at home, the *Curaçao Yacht Club* may be able to make some arrangement for you. The yacht club is at Spanish Water (toward the southeast end of the island; phone: 673038) and welcomes visitors who give advance notice. The *Top Watersports* facility at the *Lion's Dive* hotel has Sunfish and catamarans for rent. *Seascape Dive & Watersports* (at the *Curaçao Caribbean* hotel) runs deep-sea fishing charters, and rents pedal boats and Sunfish. One-hour morning, afternoon, and evening harbor cruises are available aboard the HMS *Hilda Veronica* (phone: 611257) at $7 for adults; $4 for children under 12.

FITNESS CENTERS Locals and visitors alike head to the *Rif Recreation Area,* locally known as the *Corredor,* the public oceanfront recreational area between the *Curaçao Caribbean* and *Holiday Beach* hotels. The *Corredor* has been upgraded to include a jogging track and a children's playground, plus barbecue and picnic areas. The *Sundance Health & Fitness Center* (J.F. Kennedy Blvd.; phone: 627740) offers saunas, Turkish baths, whirlpool baths, weight and fitness training, massage and beauty treatments, and rejuvenation therapies, all under the supervision of a professional medical and paramedical staff. The *Ooms Sports Institute,* at the *Lions Dive* hotel (phone: 657969), features state-of-the-art fitness equipment as well as exercise classes.

GOLF The *Curaçao Golf and Squash Club* (Schottegatweg Noord; phone: 373590), near the oil refinery, welcomes visitors to its 9-hole course, with oiled sand "greens." Open to the public by prior arrangement (call the day before you wish to play); the greens fee is $15.

HORSEBACK RIDING If you wish to ride, have your hotel contact Joe Pinedo (phone: 681181). Fees are about $12 an hour, including transportation. *Ashari's Ranch* (phone: 686254) offers horseback riding for $12 per hour.

SCUBA DIVING AND SNORKELING Curaçao is becoming better known as a scuba destination, and now has several topnotch dive and water sports operations. Snorkels, masks, and fins are available for rent at most hotels for about $10 a day. *Seascape Dive & Watersports* (at the *Curaçao Caribbean* hotel), offers beginning scuba diving courses, dive packages, certification courses, and snorkeling trips. *Underwater Curaçao* (phone: 618131), located at the *Lions Dive* hotel and marina just adjacent to the *Curaçao Seaquarium,* is a *PADI* 5-star training facility, with the largest air station in the Caribbean, a fully equipped dive shop and school, two modern dive boats, and a full range of diving and snorkeling activities, including daily single- and two-tank dives, underwater still and video photography, and certification courses. The *Top Watersports* facility (also affiliated with the *Lion's Dive* hotel) offers snorkel gear rentals and lessons. A *Peter Hughes* dive operation was being set up at press time at the enlarged *Holiday Inn Crowne Plaza*'s dive facility.

The island's most extensive snorkel and scuba environment, the Underwater Marine Park, starts at Jan Thiel Bay and stretches from the *Holiday Inn Crowne Plaza* along 12½ miles of shore to the island's eastern tip. It is fringed by a virtually untouched coral reef that starts only 150-feet offshore and slopes gently downward from a depth of 30 feet to a depth of 120 feet, where the drop-off occurs. The park boasts several sunken ships plus 16 mooring buoys that mark top dive and snorkel sites. Hook and line fishing is permitted throughout the park, but spearfishing and coral collecting are not. Also off Princess Beach is a unique manmade reef, created in 1968 when the government deep-sixed two huge barges and 30 wrecked cars and trucks; it's now a gathering place for fish and coral in all colors of the rainbow. In nearby Caracas Bay, wreck enthusiasts also can explore a 15-foot tugboat encrusted with stag, elkhorn, head, and flowering orange tube coral. *Note:* There is a fully equipped decompression chamber on Curaçao, available 24 hours a day, at Sint Elizabeth Hospital (phone: 624900).

SQUASH The *Curaçao Golf and Squash Club* (Schottegatweg Noord; phone: 373590) has courts available daily from 8 AM to 6 PM.

SWIMMING AND SUNNING Curaçao's public beaches — at Westpunt, Knip, Kline Knip, Daaibooi, and Santa Barbara — are among its very best. The island has a number of small cove beaches, many attached to hotels. What nature has not provided, man has, with artificial beaches near the *Curaçao Caribbean* and the *Holiday Inn Crowne Plaza* hotels. There's also swimming at most of the hotel beaches, where basic water sports equipment can be rented.

TENNIS Most of the hotels have courts; if yours doesn't, check with the activities desk to see if they have any arrangements for play elsewhere. If not, call the *Santa Catherina Sports and Country Club* (phone: 677028), home to the Bollittieri Salas Tennis Academy; courts are available for $7 per 45 minutes during the day; $10 per 45 minutes in the evening.

WINDSURFING The first *Pro-Am World Cup Windsurfing Championship* was held off Curaçao in 1986; now held here every June, it attracts much local and international talent. The *Top Watersports* facility at the *Lion's Dive* hotel and the *Seascape Dive & Watersports* at the *Curaçao Caribbean* hotel have windsurfers for rent and offer instruction, as does *Sail Curaçao* on Spanish Water Bay (phone: 676003).

NIGHTLIFE

Curaçao's nine casinos (in the *Curaçao Caribbean, Van der Valk Plaza, Holiday Beach, Holiday Inn Crowne Plaza, San Marco, Holland, Las Palmas, Sonesta Beach,* and *Otrobanda* hotels) start their action at 1 PM and remain open until 4 AM. The big hotels feature entertainment and dancing several nights a week. There are also regularly scheduled entertainment nights at some of the hotels, such as the *Curaçao Caribbean*'s Folkloric Evenings, Thursday Night Shipwreck (read: Rum) Parties, and beachside barbecues. The *Avila Beach* hotel has a show on Saturday night. The nightclubs *Infinity* at Fort Nassau (phone: 613450), and *L'Aristocrat* at Salina (phone: 614353) welcome tourists.

Best on the Island

CHECKING IN

Most hotels are in Willemstad or have shuttle bus service to and from town, so wherever you stay, you'll be able to get to town easily. Almost every hotel has a private (albeit small) beach, and there are beautiful public beaches all around the island. Since there is considerable international commercial trade going on continuously on the island, hotels can be crowded anytime. You can make reservations at several island hotels conveniently by calling the Curaçao Hotel and Tourism Association 24-hour hotline (phone: 800-328-7222). At hotels we describe as expensive, rates range from $160 to $250 per night, double occupancy, without meals in winter. Suites cost more, and most of the hotels are on European Plan (no meals), but have a Modified American Plan (including breakfast and dinner) for about $20 to $35 a day per person. Hotels listed below as moderate will cost between $120 and $160 a day, and those in the inexpensive category charge less than $120 a day. These prices can drop by 15% to 30% between April 15 and December 15. There is an additional 12% service charge and 7% tax.

Many hotels and restaurants do not bother with street names, which can complicate things if you choose to rent a car, but directions are easily obtained by calling ahead or asking any cab driver. When calling from a phone on Curaçao use only the six-digit local numbers listed below. For information about dialing from elsewhere, see "Telephone" earlier in this chapter.

EXPENSIVE

Curaçao Caribbean Owned and operated by the Golden Tulip group, this modern 200-room resort has a small beach, a pool, a complete water sports and dive center, and tennis. An exceptionally pleasant place, it's on Piscadera Bay and has a shuttle to downtown shopping; it also has its own shopping arcade. At night, there's dining, dancing, entertainment, and action at the casino. Renovation of the first four floors of guestrooms was planned at press time, as was the construction of a 50-room addition and a luxury condominium project. Be sure to ask for a room on the top floor, which already has been renovated. 2 St. Anna Blvd. (phone: 625000; 800-223-9815 from the US; fax: 625846).

Holiday Beach This property now features a remodeled lobby and a beach bar and restaurant. The 200 rooms have been tropically redecorated as well; all have 1 king- or 2 queen-size beds, sleek bleached wood and rattan furnishings, and balconies. A big pool is a center of daytime action, while a lovely half-moon, manmade beach protected by a manmade "reef" offers shallow swimming and water sports. There are also 2 lighted tennis courts and a dive shop. Beach barbecues and steel bands add to the festive atmosphere. There's considerable evening activity, especially in the casino — the largest on the island. Pascadera Bay (phone: 625400; 800-223-9815 from the US; fax: 624397).

Holiday Inn Crowne Plaza With 202 rooms, this fine hotel has its own beach and diving facilities, a big pool, a shopping arcade, excellent dining, and a lively nightspot and casino. One of the island's top resorts, it's popular with discriminating travelers seeking an upscale yet fun resort with an excellent mix of facilities, services, and amenities. 8 Dr. Martin Luther King Blvd. (phone: 614944; 800-HOLIDAY from the US; fax: 614131).

Kadushi Cliffs In the beautiful, lush, and hilly far western end of the island, this new complex offers 12 two-bedroom, two-bath modern villas filled with eye-pleasing furniture and luxury appointments. It's a true get-away-from-it-all place, with not much to do on premises except relax around the pool or on the tiny beach below the cliff. A rental car is a must. Westpunt (phone: 640200; 800-KADUSHI from the US; fax: 640282).

Sonesta Beach This $41-million, 238-room property has a beach, free-form pool with swim-up bar, wading pool, health spa and fitness center, tennis courts, water sports, a shopping arcade, and a 5,000-square-foot casino. Across the street from the Curaçao International Trade Center (phone: 368800; 800-SONESTA from the US; fax: 627502).

MODERATE

Avila Beach Right next door to the *Bolívar Museum* stands this stately yellow mansion dating to 1780. A recent expansion nearly doubled its previous capacity; there are now 90 rooms and 18 apartments. The older rooms are modest and pleasant, but the new rooms are more comfortable; all have air conditioning, mini-refrigerators, and terraces. The surrounding area is residential, and the well-managed hotel overlooks the ocean and its own beach. There is an outdoor bar, a restaurant, and a tennis court. Penstraat (phone: 614377; 800-448-8355 from the US; fax: 611493).

INEXPENSIVE

Coral Cliff A simple, low-rise retreat with 35 air conditioned apartments (each with its own kitchenette and phone); while there's no pool, it has its own beach, water sports, tennis, children's playground, and a restaurant and bar with slot machines. Its proximity to prime diving, plus a complete *PADI* dive shop, make this a popular site with underwater enthusiasts. On secluded Santa Maria Bay, 14 miles (23 km) west of Willemstad (phone: 641610; 800-223-9815 from the US; fax: 641781).

Lions Dive Adjacent to the *Curaçao Seaquarium,* it caters to the scuba crowd, Dutch business travelers, and an upscale young clientele in search of value and reasonable rates. It offers easy access to the island's underwater park and other premier dive sites. *Underwater Curaçao,* the island's largest dive facility, is located here. All 72 air conditioned rooms have ocean views, private balconies, and tiny bathrooms. *Rumours* restaurant (see *Eating Out*) is a plus, as is the state-of-the-art, air conditioned *Ooms* health club and fitness center. About 2 miles east of Willemstad on Jan Thiel Bay (phone: 618100; 800-223-9815 from the US; fax: 618200).

Otrobanda The only harborfront property in the Otrobanda, this 45-room hostelry has views of passing cruise ships and of the gabled Dutch architecture of Punda across the water. A casino, coffee shop, and open-air restaurant and bar with a panoramic view of the harbor entrance complete the offerings here. Popular with business travelers. Breedestraat, Oost (phone: 627400; fax: 627299).

EATING OUT

Curaçao dishes have been influenced by the cooking of some 40 countries, although everything is flavored by Dutch overtones. One of the most popular dishes is Indonesian: *rijsttafel,* a rice-based dish served with up to 24 different side dishes. Expect to pay $45 or more for dinner for two without drinks or wine at restaurants described as expensive; between $25 and $45 at a moderate place; and less than $25 at an inexpensive place. There is also an additional 10% service charge. Few restaurants require jackets in the evening. Keep an eye out for Amstel beer, brewed right on the island (see *Special Places*). When calling from a phone on Curaçao, use only the local numbers listed below. For information about dialing from elsewhere, see "Telephone" earlier in this chapter.

WILLEMSTAD AND ENVIRONS

EXPENSIVE

Baffo & Bretella An Italian bar and restaurant known for homemade pasta, fresh fish, and typical Italian fare. Open for dinner; closed Tuesdays. Reservations advised. Major credit cards accepted. At the *Seaquarium* (phone: 618700).

Fort Nassau Inside the old fortress, with a commanding view of the inner harbor and the town, this place has a varied menu for lunch and dinner. Generous portions of Dutch and continental specialties are served in a glass-enclosed, air conditioned dining room; you also can get drinks at the outdoor terrace-bar. The food is good, but it's overshadowed by the spectacular view. Open daily; no lunch on weekends. Reservations advised. Major credit cards accepted. Fort Nassau (phone: 613450 or 613086).

Landhuis Zeelandia Situated in a 150-year-old plantation house in the Salina area, this place offers beef, chicken, lamb, and fish prepared in continental style, as well as an extensive wine list. Open for dinner; closed Sundays. Reservations advised. Major credit cards accepted. Polarisweg (phone: 614688).

De Taveerne In the wine cellar of a remarkable, restored octagonal antique *landhuis,* once the residence of a Venezuelan president, the town's handsomest eating place features a cooked-to-order, à la carte menu that changes every 5 weeks. Sole meunière and filet steaks are first-rate. Open for lunch and dinner; closed Sundays. Reservations necessary. Major credit cards accepted. Landhuis Groot Davelaar (phone: 370669).

MODERATE

Bistro Le Clochard The French connection on the other bank — the Otrobanda. One of Curaçao's best bistros, it's housed in a renovated 18th-century harbor fortress. Specialties are fresh fish and steaks. Open for lunch and dinner; dinner only on Saturdays; closed Sundays. Reservations advised. Major credit cards accepted. Riffort (phone: 625666).

Bon Apetit This cozy Dutch coffeehouse in the heart of the shopping center serves great breakfasts (try the Dutch pancakes) and filling lunches and dinners, all easy on the wallet. Closed Sundays. Reservations unnecessary. Major credit cards accepted. 4 Hanchi Snoa (phone: 616916).

Grill King In the heart of town, this casual and popular waterfront eatery serves grilled seafood, steaks, and chicken. Live music on weekends. Open from noon to midnight; dinner only on Sundays. Reservations advised. Major credit cards accepted. At the *Waterfort Arches* (phone: 616870).

El Marinero Excellent seafood and Spanish specialties are served at this nautical restaurant. Try the sea bass, Caribbean lobster, or the seafood paella, and come hungry — the portions are large. Open daily for lunch and dinner. Reservations advised. Major credit cards accepted. 87-B Schottegatweg, east of Willemstad (phone: 379833).

La Pergola This Italian eatery with a good wine list offers both indoor and seaside dining, with northern Italian fare. Choose from homemade pasta, veal chops, and dishes prepared with local seafood. Open daily for lunch and dinner. Reservations advised. Major credit cards accepted. At the *Waterfort Arches* (phone: 613482).

Le Recif A refreshing find tucked in under three arches at the remains of the old fort in the Otrobanda. Nautical decor to match its specialties — fresh local seafood dishes. Open daily for lunch and dinner; on holidays, dinner only. Reservations advised. Major credit cards accepted. Riffort (phone: 623824).

Rijsttafel Restaurant Indonesia One of Curaçao's not-to-be-missed dining experiences, this place features lavish, authentic Javanese specialties, with the 20-course *rijsttafel* (the house specialty) served buffet-style. The bar is a popular local gathering place. Open for lunch and dinner; dinner only on Sundays. Reservations advised. Major credit cards accepted. 13 Mercuri-usstraat (phone: 612606 or 612999).

Rumours An open-air eatery that features salads, meat dishes, and fresh catch of the day. Open daily for lunch and dinner. Reservations advised. Major credit cards accepted. At the *Lions Dive* hotel, about 2 miles east of Willemstad on Jan Thiel Bay (phone: 617555).

Wine Cellar Wooden tables and candles add to the atmosphere at this intimate, award-winning little restaurant. Choose simple or elaborate fare; there's a superb wine list. Open for lunch and dinner; no lunch on weekends; closed Mondays. Only eight tables, so reservations advised. Major credit cards accepted. Concordiastraat (phone: 612178).

INEXPENSIVE

Fort Waakzaamheid This place with a friendly Dutch tavern atmosphere serves Dutch and island specialties (good fish), steaks, and sandwiches at lunch. Open daily. Reservations advised. Major credit cards accepted. On the Otrobanda in Seru di Domi (phone: 623633).

Golden Star Though very basic, this place has a friendly Curaçaoan atmosphere and superior Antillean fare. Open daily for lunch and dinner. Reservations unnecessary. Major credit cards accepted. 2 Socratesstraat (phone: 654795).

Great Wall The current wok-away winner in the island's Chinese restaurant sweepstakes, it offers savory selections in all columns. No atmosphere and no frills, just good food. Open for lunch and dinner daily. Reservations unnecessary. Major credit cards accepted. In *Centro Commercial Antilia* (phone: 377799).

WESTPUNT AREA

INEXPENSIVE

Jaanchie's Opened in 1930 by the present owner's father, this delightful alfresco place serves fine local food with the accent on seafood specialties. Open daily for lunch only. Reservations unnecessary. No credit cards accepted. Near Christoffel Natural Park (phone: 640126).

Playa Forti Offered here at no extra charge is one of the most scenic views on the island, overlooking Westpunt Bay. Specialties at this hilltop eatery include lamb, red snapper, and a native conch stew. Open daily for lunch and dinner. Reservations unnecessary. American Express and Diner's Club accepted. On Westpunt Bay (phone: 640273).

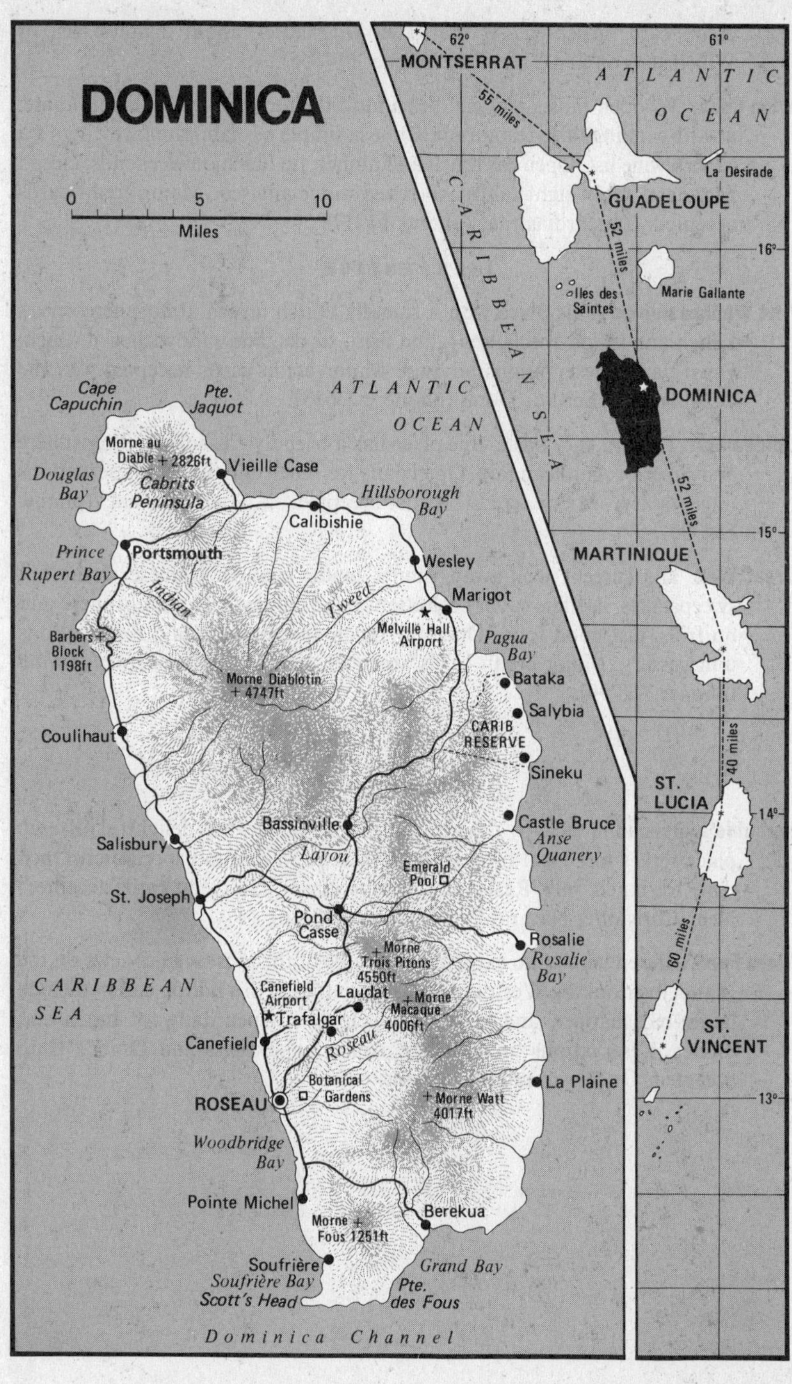
DOMINICA
0 5 10
Miles
ATLANTIC OCEAN
CARIBBEAN SEA
Dominica Channel
Cape Capuchin
Pte. Jaquot
Morne au Diable + 2826ft
Vieille Case
Douglas Bay
Cabrits Peninsula
Hillsborough Bay
Calibishie
Prince Rupert Bay
Portsmouth
Wesley
Marigot
Indian
Tweed
Melville Hall Airport
Pagua Bay
Barbers Block 1198ft
Morne Diablotin + 4747ft
Bataka
Salybia
CARIB RESERVE
Coulihaut
Sineku
Bassinville
Castle Bruce
Anse Quanery
Salisbury
Layou
Emerald Pool
St. Joseph
Pond Casse
Rosalie
Rosalie Bay
Morne Trois Pitons 4550ft
Canefield Airport
Laudat
Morne Macaque 4006ft
Trafalgar
Canefield
Roseau
La Plaine
Botanical Gardens
ROSEAU
Morne Watt 4017ft
Woodbridge Bay
Pointe Michel
Berekua
Morne Fous 1251ft
Soufrière
Soufrière Bay
Grand Bay
Scott's Head
Pte. des Fous
62°
61°
MONTSERRAT
55 miles
ATLANTIC OCEAN
La Desirade
GUADELOUPE
CARIBBEAN SEA
52 miles
16°
Marie Gallante
Iles des Saintes
DOMINICA
52 miles
15°
MARTINIQUE
40 miles
ST. LUCIA
14°
60 miles
ST. VINCENT
13°

Dominica

The island of Dominica (pronounced Dom-i-*nee*-ka) is still the primitive garden that Columbus first sighted in 1493 — filled with tropical rain forests, flowers of incredible beauty, and animals that exist nowhere else in the world. Also living on Dominica are the last remnants of the fierce Carib Indian tribe whose ancestors prevented European settlements on this island for years.

Not everyone wants to visit an island that has so few white sand beaches, no casinos, no duty-free shops, no glittering nightlife. Still, it appeals to travelers who want to immerse themselves in its mountain jungles — botanists, serious explorers, seekers after its special and uncompromising solitude.

On November 3, 1978, the 485th anniversary of its discovery by Columbus, Dominica became an independent nation within the British Commonwealth. The government pledged both to encourage tourism and to protect the island's enormous natural beauty. To date, this promise has been kept. Having quickly recovered from devastating hurricanes in 1979 and 1989, Dominica today remains an untamed, beautiful land. Its primary allures are its wild mountains; deep rain forests; and the splendor of the Emerald Pool, a grotto fed by a waterfall, lined with giant ferns, and home to darting lizards and tropical birds. The peak of Morne Diablotin, 4,747 feet above sea level, is usually swathed in a cloudy mist. The island's profuse plant life is fed by "liquid sunshine," a native term for mist so fine it can only be seen against a backlight of sunshine. Everything planted on this island grows well and quickly in the rich, volcanic soil; even power and phone lines are interwoven with blossoming vines.

When Columbus discovered Dominica (so named because he first glimpsed its shores on a Sunday), he found it inhabited by the fierce and determined Carib Indians, whose poisoned arrows frustrated his search for fresh water (a pity, because Dominica is filled with beautiful, deliciously clear streams). Although the might of the French, Spanish, and British fleets gave the Europeans control of most of the Indian lands, the Carib could not be forced to abandon Dominica. Its rain forest interior provided them with protected bases from which to raid the European settlements, as well as the villages of other Indians.

In 1748, the French and English signed the Treaty of Aix-la-Chapelle, agreeing that neither would attempt to settle the island. However, the agreement was a failure, and Dominica was awarded to the British in 1763, taken by the French in 1778, won back by the British in 1783, and finally, raided by the French in 1805, after which the British paid $60,000 to be left alone by the French. Through all this, both sides were harassed by the Carib. In 1903, the British forced the Carib to accept fixed boundaries.

About 1,000 pure-blooded Carib, along with another 1,500 people of mixed ancestry — Carib and descendants of African slaves — live in what is known today as the Carib Indian Territory on the northeast coast of the island. Visitors are welcome to tour this area.

The Carib presence prevented the island from being developed into plantations until just before the abolition of slavery in 1832. As a result, the island's population did not grow during the period of European colonization throughout the rest of the Caribbean. Though it is the largest of the Windward Islands, its population, at 73,000, is the smallest in the group.

This island is the only home of the sisserou, or imperial parrot (*Amazona imperialis*), a large, purple-breasted parrot facing extinction. The endangered jacquot, or red-necked parrot (*Amazona arausiaca*), is also a Dominican native. Both are protected. And only on Dominica will you hear the native solitaire, or siffleur, whose call sounds like the opening of Beethoven's *Fifth Symphony.* In the island's forests are gommier and châtaignier trees, some reaching 150 feet, not to mention mahogany, cedar, bamboo, giant tree ferns, and palms.

Bananas have replaced lime juice as the island's major export, and the government is looking for light industries to bolster its economy. Careful control over the growth of tourism — especially hotel building — still has top priority. The Dominican people's dependence on themselves, rather than on a jet airstrip, superhighways, and towering hotels, has enabled the island to restore itself quickly after being hit by two hurricanes in the past 15 years. The lack of such "improvements" is also more than part of the reason that the rush of rivers still drowns out traffic noise on island roads, and the scent of lime is still stronger than exhaust fumes along the shore near Roseau. Dominica remains an ideal island for vacationers looking to escape the "realities" of tourism for just a little while longer.

Dominica At-a-Glance

FROM THE AIR

Dominica lies south of Guadeloupe, just north of Martinique, and is separated from both neighbors by wide channels. It is 29 miles long and 16 miles wide at its widest point, with a total of 298 square miles of very rugged terrain culminating in the peaks of Morne Diablotin. (There are actually three mountain ranges on the island.)

Flying into Dominica is like arriving nowhere else in the world. Larger planes (44-seaters) still land at Melville Hall Airfield, at the island's northeastern edge. It was carved out of a coconut plantation, and planes make their approach over thick mountain jungles and hill after tree-covered hill. Twenty feet from the airport a broad river rushes by, nearly drowning out the sound of the propellers. The plane rolls down the runway to stop just before reaching the sea.

At first glance Dominica is like a terrarium, with giant ferns, feathery foliage, and mists that rise from the valleys and hover over palmy hillsides. It is said that there are 365 rivers on Dominica, one for each day of the year. The 1-hour (minimum) taxi drive to Roseau takes the visitor through some of the most spectacular mountain scenery in the tropics.

Smaller aircraft (up to 19 seats) land at Canefield Airport, only 15 minutes from Roseau. Crosswinds here often make for an exciting landing between the mountains and the deep blue sea. Served regularly by *LIAT, Air Guadeloupe,* and *Air Caraïbes,* Canefield brings the capital within day-trip range of Antigua, Guadeloupe, and other neighboring islands.

SPECIAL PLACES

ROSEAU At first glance, Dominica's capital city is a curious mixture — a few streets, a jumble of 2-story buildings ringed by several blocks of 1-story houses. The older buildings are wooden, and the 2-story structures have balconies overhanging the sidewalks, with shutters pinned back and wooden railings set in floral designs or starburst patterns. Newer buildings are concrete block or stucco, built in the same style as the earlier ones. Many buildings are painted in bright, contrasting colors. The new market is near the river. The old market, once a slave trading site, has been converted to a crafts market for tourists and houses a tourist information center. Roseau is dotted with local restaurants and "cool out" spots offering refreshing drinks and a break from shopping.

The peak of Morne Bruce stands behind the city and can be reached by car via the winding road past some of the nicer residences, or by the footpath from the nearby Botanical Gardens. There is a large cross at the top, several shade trees under which to rest, and an excellent view of Roseau. From here you can see the Roseau River as it meanders through town. The town of Roseau was named after the reeds that grow in profusion along the banks of the river. The Carib used them to make poison-tipped arrows; today they are woven into baskets.

A popular stop is Roseau's Botanical Gardens, filled with plants from all the surrounding islands, including beautiful flamboyant trees and luscious orchids, as well as Dominica's national flower, the *bwa kwaib,* or Carib wood. In 1990, the gardens — boasting some 500 species — celebrated their centennial.

The *Fort Young* hotel, located on the waterfront, has been rebuilt within sections of the 18th-century fortress, where the French and English battled over the island. Some of the earliest and most persistent visitors to the island were missionaries, and the results of their work are obvious. Catholicism dominates Dominica, and the island's cathedral, across the street from Fort Young, is suitably impressive. The nearby Anglican church, which Hurricane David reduced to rubble in 1979, has been rebuilt, and Anglicanism is still a tangible force in the country.

Currently under way is the restoration of the historic Roseau Bayfront. The project includes a complete replication of the original architecture of the buildings, and the creation of a lighted, tree-lined promenade facing the seawall. Future plans include building a berth for cruise ships.

SCOTT'S HEAD At the southern tip of the island, this point may be reached by taking a private boat or vehicle along the west coast past Pointe Michel and Soufrière, where there are sulfur springs.

The climb to the top of Scott's Head, along a road mostly of stones and dirt, is not difficult. The view at the crest is incredible — the Atlantic on one side, the Caribbean on the other, Martinique in the distance, and Dominica stretching out ahead with its valleys of trees and mountainous peaks capped with lush green vegetation. The Atlantic side of the island is lined with beaches, some covered with gray volcanic sands, others with smooth stones that tumble and make wonderful music as the waves splash against the shores.

MORNE TROIS PITONS NATIONAL PARK This is a primordial rain forest. Some of the trails through the park are marked and plants are identified, but even with this help, the sheer profusion of green life is staggering. No tree trunk is bare of some kind of vine or symbiotic growth; giant ferns flourish on the shady ground, and anthurium, *z'ailes mouches,* and bromeliads live on the limbs and trunks of trees. An easy 30-minute walk through lush forest leads to beautiful Emerald Pool, a grotto carved into black rock, filled by a waterfall, and surrounded by lovely ferns, orchids, and tropical vegetation. Among the park's other natural high points, figuratively and literally (bring a windbreaker up here): Fresh Water Lake, accessible by four-wheel-drive vehicle, affords an expansive view of the island's eastern coast; Boeri Lake, a short hike from its freshwater sister, is rimmed with volcanic rock; and Boiling Crater Lake, a rather arduous full-day hike, is the second-largest of its kind in all the world. The lake's water is kept bubbling by the volcanic heat of the crater in which it is cupped. It's best to explore the park with a guide; your hotel or the tourist office can make arrangements.

PORTSMOUTH Dominica's second town faces the Caribbean on the northern end of the island. A cruise ship berth opened at Prince Rupert's Bay in mid-1991; it's the best anchorage on the island, and several hotels and small restaurants now line the palm-fringed, gray sandy beach. The town, however, remains three streets parallel to the bay. It's filled with colorful houses, each with its own little garden, hibiscus plants growing in tin cans, and conch shells trimming neat paths. On the green behind the town, there's a cricket pitch where Saturday afternoon matches are played. Cabrits National Park, Portsmouth's most historic site, is also one of picturesque natural beauty, a forested peninsula north of town. Once called

Prince Rupert's Head, it is dominated by two steep hills covered by one of the Caribbean's few dry woodland areas. Its 18th-century Fort Shirley was the scene of a locally famous mutiny in 1802 and abandoned as a military post in 1854; some 50 structures survive. Restoration is currently under way, and there is a small museum. The marine section of the park, in Douglas Bay, has fascinating rock and coral formations under cliffs, great for snorkeling. To the south, emptying into Prince Rupert's Bay, is the mangrove-lined Indian River, a popular tourist attraction. Boat rides are best arranged through the local tour guide service on Boroughs Square in Portsmouth, as the jetty boys tend to be a bit aggressive. Insist on going by rowboat so as not to disrupt the peaceful atmosphere. Rides cost about $8 per person. The park is open weekdays from 8 AM to 4 PM; contact the Division of Forestry for weekend hours (phone: 82401, ext. 417).

TRAFALGAR FALLS In the south-central section of the island, 5 miles from Roseau, the road runs high along the walls of a valley, passing through the tiny village of Trafalgar. The final approach to the falls is by foot, about a 15-minute walk until the cascading water comes into view. There are two major falls (one hot, the other icy cold), which rush and tumble into rocky pools below. The third (often called the "baby" falls) only flows heavily during the rainy season. Visitors can splash in the pools among the rocks.

SULFUR SPRINGS Near the falls, also north and east of Roseau, are remnants of the island's volcanic existence — sulfur springs. They are hot pools of mud that bubble like a witch's cauldron, belching smelly sulfurous fumes. These leave little doubt that the island is alive and will likely erupt again.

OLD MILL CULTURAL CENTER Dominica's agricultural and industrial heritage is reflected at this site, an accurate reproduction of a 1774 sugar mill. Exhibits trace the development of the sugar and agricultural industries on the island. Open Mondays through Fridays from 8 AM to 4 PM; admission charge. Located near Canefield Airport (phone: 91032).

TITOU GORGE A deep narrow gorge where visitors can swim beneath a waterfall (depending on the seasonal rainfall), then warm up under a hot sulfur spring nearby. A guide is a must, however, as the swim can be dangerous when the falls are flowing heavily.

SYNDICATE This is a true bird watcher's paradise. About 200 acres of this area on the northwest part of the island have been designated as a home for both endangered species of Dominican parrot. Other birds that make their nests here include the pearly-eyed thrasher, the scaly-eyed thrasher, and the red-legged thrush. To see the parrots, it's advisable to start your hike before daybreak; a guide is recommended. For more details on the above attractions, check with your tour operator, the tourist board, or the Division of Forestry (phone: 82401, ext. 417).

EXTRA SPECIAL **The Carib Territory, a reserve created by the British at the turn of the century, consists of six villages: The largest are Salybia, where there's a church with an Indian canoe for an altar; Bataka, with the native school; and Sineku. There is much discussion about how many pure-blooded Carib are left, since women of other Indian tribes and black women have married into the tribe (the Carib will accept no non-Carib males into their community). Pure-blooded Carib have distinctive Asian features — almond-shaped eyes, high cheekbones, and straight black hair. Their territory is now accessible — whatever the weather — thanks to a paved road that crosses a wide river and passes through a swamp and over a small mountain, offering a spectacular view of the valleys and cliffs.**

The Carib formerly used two languages: Carib for the men and Arawak for the women; now they speak English and the patois of the island, a type of French creole. They still have a tribal chief and remain the independent race of people who once held their island home against the might of two of the 18th century's greatest nations. However, visitors will find them friendly, hospitable, and rather shy. Their simple homes have flower gardens in front and are flanked by fruit and vegetable patches. Several small shops sell the famed Carib baskets and straw mats; fresh fruit, vegetables, and flowers also are available for purchase — just ask. The enterprising and very charming Charles Williams offers overnight accommodations and local food (phone: 51256).

Sources and Resources

TOURIST INFORMATION

The Division of Tourism of the National Development Corporation has an office in Roseau at Valley Road. Mailing address: PO Box 73, Roseau, Dominica, WI (phone: 82351; fax: 85840). For information about Dominica tourist offices in the US, see GETTING READY TO GO.

LOCAL COVERAGE The *Dominica Chronicle* is published weekly. *The Dominica Story: A History of the Island, Isle of Adventure,* and *Our Island Culture,* all by Lennox Honychurch, are available at *Cee Bee's* (20 Cork St.; phone: 82379), *Paperbacks* (6 Cork St.; phone: 82370), and other bookstores. The Division of Forestry (Botanical Gardens, Roseau; phone: 82401, ext. 417) also sells a selection of good guidebooks.

RADIO AND TELEVISION

DBS Radio broadcasts mostly in English, but with some programs in a French patois or creole. There are two local TV stations, which air CNN and US news.

TELEPHONE

When calling from the US, dial 809 (area code) + 44 (country code) + (local number). To call from another Caribbean island, the access code may vary, so call the local operator. When calling from a phone on Dominica, use only the local number unless otherwise indicated.

ENTRY REQUIREMENTS

US and Canadian citizens need only a valid passport or other proof of citizenship (birth certificate or voter's registration card, along with a photo ID) and a return or ongoing ticket. Departure and security taxes add up to about $10.

CLIMATE AND CLOTHES

Daytime temperatures range from 70 to 90F (20 to 34C). However, they may drop to the mid-50s in the mountains. Rainfall on the coast averages 75 to 80 inches, but the interior rain forest receives some 250 to 400 inches per year. Some days it rains a dozen times, the sun and showers creating magnificent rainbows. February through July is the "dry" season, though in the mountains it seems to rain most of the year.

The island is very casual. In this climate, light, comfortable cotton clothes are all that are required: shorts, slacks, jeans, swimsuit, walking shoes, maybe a pair of deck shoes if you expect to do any boating. A waterproof windbreaker, long-sleeve shirt (perhaps a sweater), and good hiking shoes will be very useful for those who plan to go into the mountains. A waterproof bag for your camera is also advisable. Swimsuits are not worn in the streets. Evenings are informal, but conservative. Take along a light sweater for the cooler nights, especially if you plan to stay at a mountain resort.

MONEY

The Eastern Caribbean dollar is the official currency, at press time valued at about $2.68 EC to the US dollar. American currency is accepted throughout the island, but buying power can be increased a little by exchanging currency in a bank. Most banks are open Mondays through Thursdays from 8 AM to 3 PM and Fridays from 8 AM to 5 PM. Credit cards are accepted at most hotels and restaurants (some establishments charge an additional fee of up to 5%). All prices in this chapter are quoted in US dollars.

LANGUAGE

The official language is English, but most of the natives also speak a French creole patois.

TIME

In the winter Dominica is 1 hour ahead of eastern standard time; when it is 11 AM in Roseau, it is 10 AM in New York; in summer, when the US is on daylight saving time, the time is the same in both places.

CURRENT

Electricity is 220–240 volts, 50 cycles, AC, often with British three-square-pin outlets. American appliances must have a converter; it's a good idea to bring your own.

TIPPING

A 10% service charge is added by most hotels and some restaurants in lieu of tipping. For special services, an additional gratuity is left to your own discretion. Taxi drivers do not receive tips unless they perform a special service (such as unloading a lot of luggage).

GETTING AROUND

BUS Bus transport can be quite an adventure, considering the fact that they don't run on any set schedule or on Sundays. The trip from Roseau to Portsmouth costs about $3.

CAR RENTAL *Valley Rent-a-Car* (phone: 83233; fax: 86009), *Budget Car Rental* (phone: 92080; fax: 81111), *Wide Range Car Rentals* (phone: 82198; fax: 83600), *STL Car Rental* (phone: 82340 or 91339 after hours; fax: 86007), *Anslem's Car Rentals* (phone: 82730; fax: 87559), *Fiesta Car Rentals* (phone: 83221; fax: 83124), *Jerry's Car Rentals* (phone: 82559; fax: 92071), *Pierro Auto Rental and Nature Safari* (phone/fax: 85826), *Sag Motors* (phone: 91093; fax: 91098), and *Tropical Jeep Rentals* (phone: 84821) all have cars for rent. Costs average about $35 per day. Driving is officially on the left (however, local practice is the horn method — toot and then pull over to the side; but fight your instinct to veer to the right). Many of the better roads are only wide enough for one vehicle at a time. (A note of warning: Thursdays are banana days. Banana trucks don't — and sometimes can't — stop for anything.) A local driver's permit can be obtained for $8 at the Department of Motor Vehicles in Roseau or at either of the airports on arrival. Applicants must show a valid driver's license.

FERRY *Caribbean Express* links the islands from Guadeloupe in the north to Martinique in the south. The 200-seat catamaran is air conditioned and comfortable, and offers duty-free shopping and a snack bar, but the trip can be a bit rough (uneasy sailors beware). Check with the tourist office for details and a schedule or at the *Whitchurch Travel Agency* (phone: 82181).

MOTOR BIKES *De A's Bike R Around* (phone: 85075) and *Pierro Auto Rental and Nature Safari* (phone/fax: 85826) rent motor bikes for about $25 a day; driver's permit required (see "Car Rental" for details).

SIGHTSEEING TOURS There is a lot to see on Dominica, and many ways to travel; tours can be arranged on land or water. Taxi sightseeing can be arranged for about $20 per car an hour, for up to four people; ask any driver at the airport. *Emerald Safari Tours* (phone: 84545), *Dive Dominica Tours* (phone: 82188), *Paradise Tours* (phone: 85999), *Dominica Tours* (phone: 82638), *Mally's Tours* (phone: 83114), *Nature Island Taxi and Tour* (phone: 83397), and *Nature Tours* (phone: 83706) organize bus, car, four-wheel-drive, and hiking trips to the island's most famous spots. All of these tour operators will arrange drivers, guides, rentals, and whatever else is needed. For exploring the more remote regions, contact *Ken's Hinterland Adventure Tours* (phone: 84850), *Rainbow-Rover* (phone: 88650), *Antours* (phone: 86460), or *Roxy's Tours* (phone: 84845). *Whitchurch Travel Agency* (phone: 82181) handles charters as well as air reservations. For wildlife tours, contact the Division of Forestry at the Botanical Gardens near Roseau (phone: 82401, ext. 417; fax: 85200). Ask for the forestry director or park superintendent. The tourist office can be very helpful in arranging special-interest tours for groups and in locating naturalist guides.

TAXI Rates are set by law. The trip from Melville Hall Airport to Roseau (37 miles) is currently about $17 per passenger, with a minimum charge of about $45 per car. From Canefield Airport to Roseau (3 miles), the minimum charge is about $8 per car.

INTER-ISLAND FLIGHTS

LIAT has several flights daily from Antigua, Barbados, Guadeloupe, Martinique, San Juan, and St. Lucia. *Air Caraïbes* connects from St. Martin and Antigua; and *Air Guadeloupe* flies twice daily from Guadeloupe. Canefield can accommodate smaller planes (up to 19 seats), so only passengers on the larger *LIAT* aircraft have to trek across from Melville Hall. This is a good hour's taxi ride, but the drive, which passes through the tropical rain forest, is a good introduction to the island.

SPECIAL EVENTS

Carnival in Dominica is a big 10-day, pre-*Lenten* festival that ends on the Tuesday before *Ash Wednesday.* Festivities include nightly shows, band competitions, a parade of floats, and dancing in the streets. *National Day* (November 3) is preceded by a month of events celebrating Dominica's independence and culture with creole songs, dances (both the African-influenced belaire and the French quadrille), folk narratives or *contes,* and art and crafts displays — graced by island women in *wob dwiyet,* the madras-and-foulard-draped national dress. *National Day* ends with evening "jump-ups" (dancing in the streets). *Domfesta* (the *Dominica Festival of Arts*) is spread out over weeks, usually beginning in July and continuing through August, and features art exhibits, music and dance, literary workshops, readings, lectures, films, and street bazaars. On *Creole Day,* celebrated the last Friday in October, Dominicans all turn out for work or school attired in national dress, and restaurants feature local dishes. *New Year's Day, Merchant's Day* (Jan. 2), *Good Friday, Easter Monday, Labor*

Day (May 1), *Pentecost Monday, Emancipation Day* (first Monday in August), *Christmas,* and *Boxing Day* (December 26) are all public holidays.

SHOPPING

There is no duty-free shopping on the island; there are, however, some excellent buys on native products. The *Bello* company produces excellent jams from pineapple and passion fruit, guava jelly, fruit syrups, hot pepper sauce, and bay rum after-shave in gift packs and individual containers. *Coconut Products, Ltd.* produces soaps (some in the shape of the endangered sisserou parrot), hair care products, body lotions, and sunscreens. *Windward Processors* makes aloe vera products — including skin lotions and a sports tonic drink — from locally grown plants. *Jas Garraway & Co.,* the local tobacco company, produces cigarettes, cigars, and pipe tobacco (very strong) packaged in attractive gift boxes. A Carib straw basket, lined with colorful madras material and filled with assorted local products, makes a wonderful gift. Artwork is on display at restaurants including the *Orchard, Guiyave,* and *Cartwheel.* Pottery also is made locally and is available in a number of shops. Consider some of the following:

BLOOMS Tropical cut flowers, packed to go. They also provide a plant inspection certificate. Hanover St., Roseau (phone: 87402).

BLOWS TEA A good selection of tea, spices, and local herbs. Valley Rd., Roseau (phone: 86504).

BROTHER MATTHEW LUKE An arts and crafts studio and gallery selling lovely, colorful, hand-painted "rain forest creations" in Indian cotton. If you're driving near Emerald Pool, by all means stop off to see his handiwork at Pond Casse, off the Imperial Hwy. (phone: 91836).

CANDLE INDUSTRIES A factory near Canefield Industrial that produces a variety of candles decorated with, among other things, images of the popular Dominican parrot. Items are priced at about $5 to $10 apiece, and also can be found in some shops in town. Industrial site at the Canefield (phone: 91006).

CARIB TERRITORY CRAFTS CENTER The big scene-stealer here is a traditional bag made of two layers of reeds — that create an incredible 3-color effect thanks to a natural processing technique — with a layer of broad banana-type leaf between that makes it waterproof. A series of six little baskets that fit into one makes a nice gift at about $10. Carib Territory (no phone).

CEE BEE'S The best source of books about Dominica, past and present. 20 Cork St., Roseau (phone: 82379).

DOMINICA EXPORT/IMPORT AGENCY Fresh island-grown grapefruit can be purchased by the box here in season (approximately August through March).

The necessary agricultural papers for passing through customs are provided, but be sure to ask. Arrangements need to be made in a day or two in advance. On Bayfront, Roseau (phone: 83494).

FLORAL GARDENS This gift shop sells only high-quality local products, including handmade coconut and wooden jewelry, straw items, pottery, food products, and skin care items. Near Melville Airport at Concorde (phone: 57636; fax: 57636).

FRONT LINE COOPERATIVE An eclectic selection of books on local folklore and culture can be found here, including the complete line of works by famed native writer Jean Rhys. Queen Mary St., Roseau (phone: 88664).

LEATHERCRAFT Stop off to order handmade leather bags, shoes, and sandals. Elliot Ave., Roseau (phone: 83598).

TROPICRAFTS Locally produced straw mats are woven into intricate designs; placemats, handbags, and other souvenirs are available. Queen Mary St., Roseau (phone: 82747).

SPORTS

BOATING A motorboat for six people will cost about $50 per person for a 6-hour tour, including lunch; a 2-hour snorkeling trip for a minimum of six people runs $20 per person. A sailboat trip is $35 per person for 6 hours at the *Anchorage* (phone: 82638) or *Castaways* (phone: 96244) hotels, or through tour operators.

HUNTING Visitors are prohibited from hunting land crabs, *crapauds* (frogs, locally called mountain chickens), river fish, and other wildlife.

SCUBA AND SNORKELING The island has the fully equipped, *NAUI*-certified *Dive Dominica,* operated by Derek and Ginette Perryman (based at *Castle Comfort Lodge;* phone: 82188; fax: 86088). Perryman's expeditions explore virtually virgin southern and western coastal waters; rental equipment, night dives, and snorkel trips are available, too. *Dominica Dive* resort (phone: 82638; fax: 85680), a *PADI* dive center, also offers scuba diving and water sports. It caters to divers from the *Anchorage* hotel, and the *Portsmouth Beach* and *Picard Beach* resorts. *East Carib Dive* (at Salisbury Beach; phone: 96575; fax: 96603) and *Dive Castaways* (at the *Castaways* hotel; phone: 96244) offer a full line of water sports, including water skiing, sailing, diving, windsurfing, and snorkeling. Prices run about $70 for a two-tank dive and about $100 for a resort course, which includes one or two open-water dives. Dive packages are available.

SPORT FISHING Charters can be arranged through the *Anchorage, Castaways,* or *Coconut Beach* hotels for about $300 per day for up to six people.

SQUASH The only squash court available to visitors is at the *Anchorage* hotel.

TENNIS Both guests and non-guests can play at *Reigate Hall* and *Castaways.*

NIGHTLIFE

The best thing to say about activities after dark in Dominica is that it's a beautiful island, and the rum drinks are tasty, pleasantly relaxing, and inexpensive. Some of the hotel lounges stay open until 11 PM or so, and the bar at *Reigate Hall* often jumps until even later. There is music on weekends during the winter season at several of the hotels. *Fort Young* has a happy hour on Friday with live entertainment. For island barbecue and entertainment, reserve at *Sisserou* (in Castle Comfort Village; phone: 83111) on Wednesday nights. *Piña Colada* (Bath Rd.; phone: 86921) offers jazz on Friday nights. *Wykies Trends* (15 Old St.; phone: 88015), a popular local spot with a pub atmosphere, features music and darts nightly. The *Good Times Bar-b-que* (Canefield, about 3 miles from Roseau; phone: 91660) is a casual restaurant with a popular bar with music. It's open Wednesday through Sunday nights and stays open as long as there's something going on. On weekends there is music, mostly calypso and reggae, at the *Warehouse* (about 3 miles from Roseau; phone: 91303).

Best on the Island

CHECKING IN

Dominica hotels and guesthouses offer a wide range of accommodations, none of which can be considered expensive compared to those in most of the rest of the Caribbean. The most expensive room on the island is probably a VIP suite at the *Reigate Hall* hotel, which goes for about $190. The expensive hotels here charge $100 to $150 for a double room with breakfast; those in the moderate category run $60 to $100; and places listed as inexpensive charge under $60. Some places have slightly lower rates (10% to 30%) from April 15 through December 14, but most offer pretty much the same prices year-round. There is a 5% room tax, and some places charge an additional fee if you pay with a credit card. Hotels are divided into three categories: beachfront, country and mountain retreats, and within the city of Roseau. While prices stay pretty much the same, appeal varies greatly, so look around — you're sure to find one of the following to your liking. When calling from a phone on Dominica, use only the local numbers listed below. For information about dialing from elsewhere, see "Telephone" earlier in this chapter.

BEACHFRONT

EXPENSIVE

Castaways A longtime favorite, set on a gray beach, with 27 seaside rooms. There's also a popular alfresco bar and spacious dining room overlooking the beach. Nicely landscaped, clean, and friendly, pluses include a dive center, water sports, tennis, and tours. 11 miles north of Roseau (phone: 96244, or 800-476-6833 from the US; fax: 96246).

Fort Young This charming and historic hotel was built into the stone walls of the original 1770 fort. Its 50 bedrooms, some split-level with sitting areas, all have air conditioning, ceiling fans, hardwood decks, and private baths. There's also a swimming pool, restaurant (see *Eating Out*), bar, and boutique. On the waterfront (phone: 85000; fax: 85006).

Lauro Club Each of the 8 cottages at this Swiss-owned development has a panoramic view of the coast, and each is painted in a different, bright, tropical color. The restaurant offers fresh seafood dishes and continental fare (see *Eating Out*). There is also a swimming pool on the grounds. On the leeward coast of the island (phone: 96602; fax: 96603).

MODERATE

Anchorage Here are 32 simple but agreeable rooms, built around a pool that faces a curving bay where yachts anchor, a dock, and a small black beach. There is a steady stream of visiting yachtsmen in the cocktail lounge and restaurant at night. This is basically a family business, which offers the added benefits of water sports and the *Dominica Dive* resort on the grounds. On the water at Castle Comfort near Roseau (phone: 82638; fax: 85680).

Castle Comfort Lodge Only 10 rooms, completely renovated and overseen by the genial hostess. Mrs. Perryman runs a "family home," and you're soon a part of it. The restaurant features delicious creole food (see *Eating Out*). Operated in conjunction with *Dive Dominica.* Guests enjoy complimentary snorkeling gear. On the waterfront (phone: 82188; 800-525-3833 from the US; fax: 86088).

Coconut Beach Five cottages and 6 rooms at the end of Prince Rupert's Bay near Portsmouth, a stone's throw from Indian River. Safe anchorage for yachts, with dock facilities, water sports, and a beachside restaurant. One advantage of staying by the sea is that there is much less rain. A good jumping-off point for touring in the north. At Picard Beach (phone: 55393 or 55415; fax: 55693).

Evergreen A friendly, family-style establishment with 16 attractive rooms of stone and brick with modern baths. The 2 rooms on the seaside are somewhat larger, while 4 on the street in back have porches with mountain views. The dining room serves excellent food, and there is a swimming pool on the grounds. Diving facilities are shared with *Castle Comfort Lodge* next door. On the shores of Castle Comfort, 1 mile south of Roseau (phone: 83288; fax: 86800).

Picard Beach Here are 8 cottages; each have a full kitchen and sleep up to four people. Facilities are shared with the *Portsmouth Beach* next door. On Picard Beach (phone: 55131; fax: 55599).

Portsmouth Beach This is the sister hotel to the *Picard Beach* resort (they're managed by the same owners). A casual, 98-room property (popular with local medical students), it offers a beach, swimming pool, bar, and restaurant. Water sports also are available. On Picard Beach (phone: 55142, 55130, or 55131; fax: 55599).

COUNTRY AND MOUNTAIN RETREATS

VERY EXPENSIVE

Reigate Hall Nestled on the mountainside a mile above Roseau is one of Dominica's top (and most expensive) hotels. Local stonework and wooden finishings and floors handsomely contrast with white-walled interiors. The 17 rooms are tastefully appointed, and there are 2 VIP suites — each with a four-poster bed and private Jacuzzi. Facilities include a pool with a nice view, a meeting room, a tennis court, sauna, gym, and gameroom. The bar is a popular gathering spot. The restaurant features continental and local dishes (see *Eating Out*). On Mountain Rd., 10 minutes outside Roseau (phone: 84031; fax: 84034).

MODERATE

Chez Ophelia This family-owned and -operated small resort features 5 duplex self-catering cottages designed in traditional island style and set amidst lush vegetation. A casual restaurant specializes in fresh local foods and juices, and there is a small grocery on the premises. Located at Copthalla in the Roseau Valley near Trafalgar Falls, Sulfur Springs, and the Roseau River (phone/fax: 83061).

Floral Gardens Small, with just 10 rooms, this hotel is set in a tropical garden, where a small wildlife park houses indigenous animals. Located in the country on the northeast side of the island near the Carib Indian Territory (phone: 57636; fax: 57636).

Papillote Wilderness Retreat This is a very special place for nature lovers, dreamers, and children (who usually are both). Anne and Cuthbert Jon-Baptiste take a personal interest in the well-being of their guests, starting with a good orientation to the island's many offerings. Kids love the hotel's pets, jungle setting, birds, river bathing, hot mineral pools, and the 10-minute nature trail up to Trafalgar Falls. There are 7 comfortable rooms. The delightful garden restaurant is popular with weekend day-trippers (see *Eating Out*). A masseuse trained in shiatsu, reflexology, and acupressure conducts 3-week wave-massage sessions in hot mineral water twice yearly. In the foothills of Morne Macaque (phone: 82287; fax: 82285).

Sans Souci Manor Four tastefully appointed apartments with kitchens (meal service also available), pool, and free daily transportation to town. On a hillside 2 miles from Roseau (phone: 82306; fax: 86202).

Springfield Plantation Picturesque Victorian plantation house and outbuildings with 6 rooms plus 3 cottages, furnished mostly with antiques; rooms No. 11 and No. 15 are best. There are stunning views, a river-fed natural pool, and trail maps for hikers. It's often cool enough for a nighttime fire. High in the hills, 2 miles from the National Park entrance (phone: 91401 or 91224; fax: 92160).

ROSEAU

EXPENSIVE

Garraway Heritage The newest property in town, it is located along the newly developed Roseau Bayfront area (see *Special Places*) and has 31 tastefully appointed guestrooms. Facilities include an elegant restaurant and bar, hydraulic elevators and ramps to accommodate the disabled, and a fully equipped conference room. There is also a lovely terrace and courtyard. Bayfront (phone: 83247).

MODERATE

Ambassador's Formerly the *Excelsior,* it's the nearest hotel to Canefield Airport. Located in a largely residential area, it has undergone a recent renovation of its public areas and 13 guestrooms; its conference facilities make it popular with businessfolk. On the eastern side of the airport (phone: 91501; fax: 92304).

INEXPENSIVE

Continental Inn Located in the center of Roseau, it has 10 rooms, half with private bath. Good for bargain hunting businesspeople. 37 Queen Mary St. (phone: 82215; fax: 87022).

EATING OUT

Because of a restriction on hunting, some island specialties — land crab, *crapaud* ("mountain chicken" in local jargon, actually a large land frog), crayfish, and *manicou* (an animal similar to possum) — are unavailable from March through August. There are no restrictions, however, on the abundant seafood available year-round.

Island cooking styles include creole, continental, and North American, but the native dishes tend toward creole foods like fried *tee-tee-ree* (tiny freshly spawned fish), *lambi* (conch), callaloo or pumpkin soup, and crab backs (the backs of red and black land crabs stuffed with crabmeat seasoned creole-style). Bello Hot Pepper Sauce, made on Dominica, is served everywhere, with almost everything. The island fruit juices — pineapple, paw paw, guava, and lots more — are out of this world, as are the rum punches ("A day without rum punch is no day at all" is a common island saying). Bartenders also blend a terrific coconut rum punch, made fresh from coconut milk, sugar, rum, and bitters. Liquor, and local rum especially, is inexpensive; wine is not. Many brands of beer and lots of fresh juice are available.

Food prices on Dominica are consistently reasonable. Expect to spend $50 to $70 for two at places we call expensive (usually in hotel restaurants); $30 to $50 in moderate restaurants; and less than $30 at an inexpensive place. (Note that some restaurants add a surcharge if you pay with a credit card.) Prices do not include drinks, wine, or tips. When calling from a phone on Dominica, use only the local numbers listed below. For information about dialing from elsewhere, see "Telephone" earlier in this chapter.

EXPENSIVE

Castaways Pleasant service, fine sea view, good creole food. A Sunday brunch and evening beach barbecue, as well as special holiday events are highlights. Open daily for breakfast, lunch, and dinner. Reservations unnecessary. Major credit cards accepted. A half-hour drive north of Roseau (phone: 96244).

Coconut Beach Large portions of the usual Dominican fare, with daily lunch specials. Its location at Picard in Portsmouth makes it the place for lunch on a northern day tour. The candlelit dinners are served alfresco. Open daily for breakfast, lunch, and dinner. Reservations advised. Major credit cards accepted. Picard, Portsmouth (phone: 55393).

Fort Young The open-air setting enhances the atmosphere of this large dining room of the eponymous hotel. The à la carte menu features European and West Indian specialties, including crab backs, mountain chicken, lobsters, and steaks. Open daily for lunch and dinner. Reservations unnecessary. Major credit cards accepted. At the *Fort Young* hotel (phone: 85000).

Lauro Club European dishes and fresh conch and lobsters are served in an airy, attractive setting. Open daily for lunch and dinner. Reservations advised. Major credit cards accepted. At the *Lauro Club* (phone: 96602).

Reigate Hall More continental than creole; European versions of local dishes — such as mountain chicken in champagne sauce — are often interesting. Service is smooth and sweet, and the ambience, with candles and a splashing paddle wheel, is romantic. Popular bar. Open daily for breakfast, lunch, and dinner. Reservations advised. Major credit cards accepted. Mountain Rd., 10 minutes outside of Roseau (phone: 84031).

La Robe Créole Noted for its decor, ambience, and excellent, spicy creole cooking. The menu features creole lobster, freshwater shrimp and crayfish, mountain chicken, *lambi* (conch), grilled meat and fish, good soups (pumpkin, callaloo, crab), fruit punches, salads, and even hamburgers. Air conditioned. Popular with visitors and businessmen for lunch, as well as for dinner until 11 PM. Closed Sundays. Reservations advised. MasterCard accepted. Victoria St., Roseau (phone: 82896).

MODERATE

Castle Comfort Lodge Delicious fresh local creole food served right by the sea. Added attractions: a tropical garden and nautical decor. Open daily for breakfast and dinner. Reservations essential. Visa and MasterCard accepted. In the Castle Comfort area on the outskirts of Roseau (phone: 82188).

Floral Gardens Located just outside the Carib Indian Territory, it's a nice lunch stop after a tour. Local fruits and vegetables and freshwater crayfish are the specialties. Open daily for lunch and dinner. Reservations unnecessary. Visa and MasterCard accepted (phone: 57636).

Guiyave Specializes in island dishes such as curried beef, highly seasoned baked *crapaud,* and crayfish when available. Congenial atmosphere, popular for business lunches. Breakfast and lunch only; closed Sundays. Reservations advised. Major credit cards accepted. Cork St., Roseau (phone: 82930).

Orchard Filled with tropical plants, it offers a variety of chicken and beef pies and *rôtis* (chicken or beef with vegetables in pastry). Open for lunch and dinner; closed weekends. Reservations unnecessary. MasterCard and Visa accepted. King George V St., Roseau (phone: 83051).

Papillote Very popular outdoor hotel restaurant near Trafalgar Falls, a sort of oasis in the rain forest. After lunching on *bookh* (tiny river shrimp) or crayfish with delicate homegrown salads, ask proprietor Anne Jon-Baptiste to take you around her tropical gardens; then take the short hike to the falls, a swim in the cool mountain river, and a hot bath in the natural mineral pools. This is a place to spend the day. Open daily for lunch and dinner. Reservations necessary; make them well in advance. Major credit cards accepted. Near Trafalgar Falls (phone: 82287).

Wykies Trends Charming, rustic bamboo bar and restaurant specializing in local goodies such as *courbouillon* (boiled fish) and *cochan pafimé* (smoked pork soup). Don't miss the "jing ping" sessions — performances featuring local instruments such as the boom-boom and shak-shak — held every 2 weeks. Open daily for lunch and dinner. Reservations unnecessary. No credit cards accepted. 51 Old St., Roseau (phone: 88015).

INEXPENSIVE

Cartwheel Café A cozy corner for sandwiches and hot food, featuring a display of local art that attracts Dominicans and visitors alike. Breakfast and lunch only; closed Sundays. Reservations unnecessary. No credit cards accepted. Corner of Bay St. and John's La., Roseau (phone: 85353).

Continental Tasty local cookery featuring lobster, freshwater shrimp, and "mountain chicken." Open daily for lunch and dinner. Reservations advised. Major credit cards accepted. Queen Mary St., Roseau (phone: 82214).

Good Times Bar-b-que Not surprisingly, barbecued chicken, pork, steaks, fish, and lamb — served with salad and French fries — are the specialties here. Open for dinner Wednesdays through Sundays only. Reservations unnecessary. Major credit cards accepted. Canefield (phone: 91660).

Manjé Domnik A casual snack bar serving such local dishes as stuffed bakes (meat-filled pastry) and meat pies, with fresh juices always available. Open for breakfast and lunch; closed Sundays. Reservations unnecessary. No credit cards accepted. Two locations: Cork St. (no phone) and the Old Market Plaza (no phone).

World of Food Dominican specialties, including *rôti* and crab backs (in season). Lunch and dinner in the old house and courtyard of famed Dominican novelist Jean Rhys. Open daily. Reservations unnecessary. No credit cards accepted. In *Vena's Guest House,* 48 Cork St., Roseau (phone: 83286).

Dominican Republic

The Dominican Republic, sprawled over the eastern two-thirds of the big island of Hispaniola (the western third is Haiti), can claim more "oldests" than anywhere else in the Caribbean — indeed, in the Western Hemisphere: Its capital, Santo Domingo, is the New World's oldest city, with the New World's oldest street, oldest house, oldest cathedral, oldest university, and the ruins of its oldest hospital.

These historical distinctions are due in large part to the Columbus clan. It was Christopher who found the island on his first voyage in 1492, and his brother Bartolomeo founded Santo Domingo 4 years later. In 1509, Christopher's son, Don Diego, became the colony's governor, serving as viceroy when the Dominican Republic, then the colony of Santo Domingo, was the provisioning port and launching spot for Spain's greatest expeditions into (and out of) the Americas. From Santo Domingo, Velázquez sailed to settle Cuba; Juan Ponce de León to colonize Puerto Rico; and Cortés to conquer Mexico. Britain's Sir Francis Drake ended this golden age when he attacked, sacked, and set fire to the capital in 1586. The city took centuries to regain its lost grandeur.

In the interim, the colony was claimed in succession by France, Spain, itself (during the "Ephemeral Independence" proclaimed by José Nuñez de Cáceres in 1821), and, shortly thereafter, by Haiti, whose president, Pierre Boyer, declared it part of his country in 1822. It was not until February 27, 1844, that the country, under Juan Pablo Duarte's La Trinitaria movement, achieved its independence. Except for a brief episode in the early 1860s, when revolts led government leaders to place the island under Spanish control, the Dominican Republic has been an autonomous nation ever since. Visitors often are a bit surprised to see armed military and policemen stationed throughout the country. But far from threatening imminent revolution, these guards are posted to preserve peace and order, and thus their presence is curiously reassuring.

The Dominican Republic has only recently become a popular destination for the current generation of American island lovers. This is due to the influence of the strong man once known as El Benefactor, Generalissimo Rafael Leónidas Trujillo, who took power in 1930 and held fast until his assassination in 1961. Although he helped establish a degree of economic order in the country, Trujillo siphoned off enormous sums of money for himself and his friends during his increasingly oppressive dictatorship. When the populace objected, he simply tightened his grip. In spite of the capital's deluxe hotels and gambling casinos, Trujillo and tourism were incompatible. What once had been a steady stream of business and pleasure traffic slowed to a trickle and, in the late 1950s, almost stopped entirely.

DOMINICAN
REPUBLIC
ATLANTIC OCEAN
BAHAMA IS.
Turks & Caicos Is.
CUBA
Cayman Is.
CARIBBEAN SEA
JAMAICA
HAITI
DOMINICAN REPUBLIC
PUERTO RICO
20°
76°
72°
68°
Cap Haitïen
Montecristi
Bahía Isabela
Luperón
Isabela
Puerto Plata
Cabarete
Sosua
Amber
Grande
Coast
Cordillera
Septentrional
Valverde
N. Yaque
Dajabón
Santiago Rodriguez
Santiago de los Caballeros
Moca
San Francisco de Macoris
Nagua
Bahía Escocesa
Samaná
Sánchez
Bahía de Samaná
La Vega
Yuna
R.
Hinche
HAITI
CORDILLERA
Jarabacoa
Pico Duarte 10,382ft
Bánica
Artibonite
Cotui
Sabana de la Mar
Cordillera
Oriental
Miches
Yuma
Bonao
Constanza
CENTRAL
San Juan
Ozama
Hato Mayor
Bayaguana
Higüey
Punta Cana
Cul de Sac
L. Enriquillo
Neiba
Yaque S.
Azua
San Cristóbal
SANTO DOMINGO
Boca Chica
Las Americas Int. Airport
San Pedro de Macoris
La Romana
Altos de Chavon
Casa de Campo
Boca de Yuma
Bahía de Yuma
Mona Passage
PORT-AU-PRINCE
Massif de la Selle
Saltrou
Duverge
Baní
B. de Ocoa
Barahona
Bahía de Neiba
Sierra de Bohoruco
Saona I.
Pedernales
B. de Aguillas
Oviedo
Beata I.
CARIBBEAN SEA
0 Miles 60

The country did not really get back into the mainstream of the Caribbean travel picture until the early to mid-1970s, when the government invested many millions of dollars in the resort infrastructure and in hotel development. Tourism also received sizable support from the Gulf & Western conglomerate (now Paramount Communications), which built the super development complex called *Casa de Campo,* on the south coast (since sold), and two hotels in the capital. In the late 1970s, the first cabinet-level minister of tourism was appointed, and since then the government has remained steady in its promotion of tourism. For example, a concerted effort was made to draw visitors to the country in 1992 to commemorate the 500th anniversary of Columbus's discovery of the New World. Unfortunately, the festivities fizzled due to controversy surrounding the building of the $70-million Columbus Lighthouse Monument and the question of whether Columbus's activities were actually worth celebrating.

Nonetheless, from a meager 87,000 visitors in 1967, the volume of Dominican tourism has climbed to an average of more than 1 million people per year. The Dominican Republic offers the same sea, sand, and sun as many other Caribbean islands, and several superb resorts — at substantially lower costs.

The country does have problems — inflation and unemployment are soaring, electricity often is shut off for several hours daily, and gas stations are open only sporadically due to lack of fuel. However, hotels and resorts function more smoothly each season, the locals are friendly to Americans, and the number of hotel rooms continues to rise. In Santo Domingo, construction of several luxury hotels has kept up with the increase in demand, and new properties are under construction at Boca Chica, Juan Dolio, Samana, Sosúa, and Punta Cana. The nation recently has begun courting tourists more actively, rejoining the Caribbean Tourism Organization and hiring an advertising agency. It is now promoting itself with a new name: "Dominicana," an abbreviated version of *La Republica Dominicana,* its official Spanish name. No matter what the country is called, however, you'll find that its people seem genuinely delighted to greet American travelers.

Dominican Republic At-a-Glance

FROM THE AIR

The island is almost a primer in basic geography, illustrating many kinds of topography. Rugged peaks, rolling hills, rich valleys, lush sugarcane plantations, and fine white beaches are all part of the terrain. The Dominican Republic and Haiti share Hispaniola, the second-largest of the Greater Antilles islands (only Cuba is bigger), which is situated along the upper arch of the Caribbean archipelago. The country is washed by the Caribbean on the south, the Atlantic on the north, and the 75-mile-wide Mona

Passage, which separates it from Puerto Rico, on the east. It is also a neighbor of Jamaica (300 miles west) and Cuba (150 miles northwest).

The Dominican Republic is large compared to other Caribbean island countries — 19,120 square miles, with a population of 7.5 million. Its principal mountain range — the Cordillera Central—boasts the highest peak in the West Indies, Pico Duarte, rising 10,417 feet above sea level. Three other ranges run almost parallel, west to east, across the country, and four major rivers — of which the longest is the 125-mile Río Yaque del Norte — flow from the mountains to the ocean and the sea.

Santo Domingo, the capital, is at the mouth of the Ozama River in the center of the south coast. A wide, landscaped highway leads to Las Américas International Airport, about 20 miles east of the city on the edge of the Caribbean. It's about 3½ jet hours from New York, about 2 hours from Miami, and about 40 minutes from Puerto Rico.

Almost one-third of the coastline is edged with beaches. For visitors, the most appealing north coast seaside towns are Puerto Plata, around which a resort area has been developed and continues to grow; Sosúa, founded by Jewish refugees from Europe in the 1940s; and Samaná, a fishing village populated by the descendants of escaped American slaves who still speak English — though they've been loyal Dominicans for generations. The resorts at Punta Cana also boast a spectacular, 20-mile stretch of sand — the longest beach in the Caribbean. The best southeastern beaches are near Boca Chica and La Romana. The towns of Jarabacoa, Constanza, and Santiago (the Dominican Republic's second city), nestled in the central mountains, are a cool change from the tropical sea scene.

SPECIAL PLACES

When it comes to sightseeing, the Dominican Republic is really two places: Santo Domingo and everywhere else. In Santo Domingo, a combination of foot and taxi is probably the best way to get around. In the colonial area, parking can be a problem, but everything there is within walking distance. Otherwise, driving is comparatively easy (though road signs are few and often confusing), and Dominicans are usually happy to offer directions to those who get lost. Within the colonial district, non-Spanish–speaking visitors are advised to join an organized tour with an English-speaking guide; few locals, aside from staff in the major hotels and restaurants, speak English. Guides for walking tours can be hired at the plaza in front of the Cathedral of Santa María la Menor. The cost is about $16 for 2 to 3 hours.

COLONIAL SANTO DOMINGO

Seeing the sights — modern and historical — in Santo Domingo can fill several days, especially for those who take the time to trace all the city's roots. But the major points can be covered in a day if you move fast.

CHRISTOPHER COLUMBUS LIGHTHOUSE MONUMENT Across the Ozama River, this complex was inaugurated in 1992 in honor of the Columbus quincentenary. A longtime dream of President Joaquín Balaguer, it nevertheless caused a firestorm of protest because of its expense (about $70 million), the scarcity of available electricity to light the beacon, and controversy about Columbus himself. The 7-story monument sits on a bluff in the area's southeastern corner. (There are no elevators; visitors must climb the stairs for the panoramic view.) At the center of the cross-shaped building, which is nearly 700 feet long and 132 feet wide at its widest point, is an impressive marble sarcophagus that supposedly contains the remains of the island's discoverer. (The true identity of the body is uncertain, however, as at least two other countries also claim to be Columbus's final resting place.) Emanating from this point are numerous collections and exhibits, including a library of publications relating to Columbus's voyages; a cartography display, including the first map of the New World drawn by Columbus; an exhibit on the explorer; and a display of ceramic pieces from the 15th century to the present, many unearthed at archaeological digs throughout the country. Restaurants and shops line the periphery of the 2,500-acre park, where parking is available. Admission charge (no phone).

COLUMBUS SQUARE A large bronze statue of the discoverer stands watch at this square. On the south side of the square is the Cathedral of Santa María la Menor on Calle Arzobispo Meriño, a classic example of Spanish Renaissance architecture. Completed in 1523, it is the oldest cathedral in the Western Hemisphere, and it was in the 450-year-old nave that what are said to be the mortal remains of Christopher Columbus resided before being moved to the Columbus Lighthouse Monument. Be sure to take a tour with one of the expert guides, who speak English and Spanish. The guide will point out details of the cathedral — the gold and silver treasures, delicate carvings, elaborate altars and shrines — that visitors might otherwise overlook. (Tip guides about $1 for the half-hour go-round.)

Other square landmarks: Old Santo Domingo City Hall (now a bank) to the west and, on the east, the Palace of Borgella, headquarters of the Haitian governor from 1822 to 1844 during the Haitian occupation. Nearby, at the corner of Calles Padre Billini and Arzobispo Meriño, the *Museum of the Dominican Family* (Tostado House) exhibits mementos of a well-to-do Dominican family of the Victorian era. Guided tours in English are available. Open Tuesdays through Fridays 9 AM to 5:30 PM, Saturdays, Sundays, and holidays 9 AM to 4 PM; admission charge (phone: 687-3622).

Turn left on Calle Padre Billini, then left again on Calle Las Damas, where you'll see the restored walls of the Ozama Fortress and the 1503 Tower of Homage, a massive structure where guards stood watch and condemned prisoners awaited their fate.

CALLE LAS DAMAS (LADIES STREET) The oldest and one of the most beautiful streets in the New World, Calle Las Damas (named for the ladies of the viceregal court who once lived here and promenaded in the evenings) offers a number of excellent examples of 16th-century colonial architecture. One is the *Bastidas House* (admission charge; phone: 682-4672), now the site of national museum workshops, and small exhibits. Another is the house of Governor Nicolás de Ovando, who planned and presided over the building of the city in the early 16th century; it is now the *Hostal Nicolás de Ovando,* a small, charming hotel and restaurant (see *Checking In* and *Eating Out*).

The National Pantheon, just across the street, is a must for buffs of both history and art. Once a Jesuit monastery (1714), its austere lines and massive size contrast with the graceful, smaller-scale colonial houses that surround it. Inside, note the commemorative ceiling mural above the altar and the massive bronze and onyx chandelier, a gift of Spain's Generalissimo Franco, and the grills bearing swastikas, from the German government. Many national heroes are buried within its walls. Its operating hours are irregular; no admission charge. You can get a local guide to show you around for a $1 tip. Also along Calle Las Damas are the Chapel of Our Lady of Remedies, where the first colonists attended mass, and an antique sun clock.

MUSEO DE LAS CASAS REALES (MUSEUM OF THE ROYAL HOUSES) Opened during the state visit of King Juan Carlos of Spain in 1976, the museum is housed in a number of colonial buildings on Calle Las Damas. Its handsome displays include models of Columbus's original three ships, and a map that traces with lights his four voyages of discovery. Also on display are a re-created courtroom, pharmacy, and sugar mill, plus an excellent display of tapestries. Antique artifacts tell the story of local life and government during Santo Domingo's glory days. Upstairs are Trujillo's offices, which resemble throne rooms, with crystal chandeliers and paintings of 16th- to 18th-century Spanish kings. If you have time to see only one museum in the city, make it this one. Open Wednesdays through Mondays and holidays, 9 AM to noon and 2 to 5 PM, but call ahead to be sure; admission charge (phone: 682-4202).

ALCÁZAR DE COLÓN Also called the Columbus Palace, this castle at the foot of Calle Las Damas was built in 1510 for Christopher's son, Don Diego Colón, who ruled as first Spanish viceroy from 1509 to 1516. It was so painstakingly and authentically restored in 1957 that Don Diego would probably feel completely at home today among the black-and-white terrazzo floors and hand-carved wooden beds. On view are the dining room, several bedrooms, the kitchen, reception rooms, and the private chapel. The statue on the plaza is of Columbus's patroness, Queen Isabella. Tours with an English-speaking guide are available. Open 9 AM to noon and 2:30 to 5:30 PM; closed Tuesdays; no admission charge (phone: 689-5946).

Directly across the street from the Alcázar are the gleaming white walls of La Atarazana, once a colonial arsenal that housed the city's first customs office. It dates from 1507 and has been restored to house shops, restaurants, and galleries (see *Shopping* below).

CASA DEL CORDÓN Located near the Alcázar, at the corner of Calles Emiliano Tejera and Isabel la Católica, this is where Diego Colón and his wife, María de Toledo, lived while they waited for the Alcázar to be completed. Somehow it has survived hurricanes, earthquakes, and the ravages of Sir Francis Drake to remain standing as the oldest house in the New World. It is now the executive office of the Banco Popular, which offers free guided tours in English during business hours. Open Mondays through Fridays, 8 AM to 4 PM (phone: 544-5600).

SAN FRANCISCO MONASTERY Built early in the 16th century, this structure was plagued by earthquakes, pillaged by Sir Francis Drake, and bombarded by French artillery. Amazingly, much of it still stands. On Calle Emiliano Tejera at Calle Hostos; an old stone paving leads to the site.

ST. NICOLÁS DE BARI HOSPITAL This was the first hospital in the New World, founded by Governor Nicolás de Ovando in 1503. Visitors may walk among the ruins, located on Calle Hostos (at Luperón).

MODERN SANTO DOMINGO

Santo Domingo has many interesting attractions outside the colonial area.

INDEPENDENCE PARK This large city square, where independence was proclaimed in 1844, marks the beginning of modern Santo Domingo. A shrine to the three fathers of the country (Duarte, Sánchez, and Mella) dominates the square.

PLAZA DE LA CULTURA North of Avenida Bolívar, on Avenida Máximo Gómez, this complex of modern buildings stands on the site of Trujillo's mansion. It houses the *Gallery of Modern Art,* the National Library, the *Museum of Natural History,* the *Museum of History and Geography,* and the large and impressive *National Theater* (phone: 682-7255 for performance information). The anthropological *Museum of the Dominican Man* boasts a notable collection of pre-Columbian pieces and other interesting exhibits, but all the signs are in Spanish. Open from 10:30 AM to 5:30 PM, Tuesdays through Sundays; admission charge (phone: 682-9111).

NATIONAL ZOO This free-space zoological park also deserves a visit. The animals roam around natural landscapes surrounded by a moat. Open daily, from 9 AM to noon and 2 to 6 PM; admission charge. The nearby Botanical Gardens feature carriage rides through several sections — an English garden, a Spanish garden, and so on. Open Tuesdays through Sundays, 9 AM to noon and 2 to 6 PM; admission charge. The zoo and the gardens are in the Arroyo Hondo neighborhood, on the Avenida de los Próceres.

LOS TRES OJOS (THE THREE EYES) Ten minutes from Santo Domingo on Las Américas Highway, these three subterranean lagoons of fresh, salt, and sulfur water are fed by an underground river and surrounded by rock formations and lush vegetation. Cool, beautiful, and worth a trip.

ELSEWHERE ON THE ISLAND

Outside Santo Domingo, driving is the best way to get around. Most roads are adequate to good, and gas stations are reasonably spaced. Dominicans are more than happy to help with directions, but if you don't speak Spanish, it's a good idea to carry a Spanish phrase book; by all means pick up a road map from the tourist office or a gas station.

LA ROMANA One of the most enjoyable day trips (or, better yet, an excursion of several days) is the *Casa de Campo* complex at La Romana, on the southeast coast. This beautifully situated resort offers a broad range of sports facilities, including tennis, golf, skeet shooting, hunting, sailing, and sport fishing (see *A Regal Resort* in *Checking In*). On the way, stop and sample the beaches at Boca Chica or the rum at the Pedro Justo Carrion distillery in San Pedro de Macorís. From downtown Santo Domingo, driving time is about 2 hours.

EXTRA SPECIAL

Altos de Chavón is a re-creation of a 15th-century village created about a decade ago by an Italian set designer near *Casa de Campo.* Designed to be part living museum, part artisans' colony, part tourist diversion, it now comprises a small, ornate stone church (St. Stanislaus), a Grecian-style amphitheater, a museum exhibiting artifacts of the extinct Taíno Indians, and workshops, studios, and galleries where visitors may not only buy but learn to make jewelry, macramé items, art prints, and more. There are also continental, Italian, and Mexican restaurants, a terrace café, and a cozy inn. Adding to the appeal is the village's site above the winding green Chavón River.

NORTH COAST The country's most ambitious tourist developments are located on the north coast, where the mountains of the Cordillera Central meet long, white sand beaches along the Atlantic Ocean. This area is also known as Costambar (the Amber Coast) because of the large deposits of the substance in the nearby hills.

PUERTO PLATA (PORT OF SILVER) This town is 130 miles northwest of Santo Domingo on a crescent-shaped bay. The local airport has seen an increasing number of international arrivals in recent years, as the resort development boom here continues. Take the funicular, if it's running, to the top of Isabela de Torres peak for a spectacular view of the countryside and the ocean. Outside town, new tourist resorts have materialized. At Playa Dorada, a number of resort hotels have opened around the Robert Trent

Jones, Sr. golf course. Another ambitious development, farther east at Playa Grande, currently is under way, but progress is slow. At the moment, Playa Grande beach remains one of the most beautiful, unspoiled stretches of sand in the Caribbean.

SOSÚA Ten miles east of Puerto Plata, following a strip of beautiful beaches, Sosúa Beach is a veritable tourist bazaar; vendors emerge from the shacks lining the beach, hawking imitation Lime ceramic figures, Haitian art, and inexpensive, made-to-order jewelry, while "secretaries" mob tourists, offering their services as gofers. Many small resort hotels, restaurants, and clubs have opened here in recent years, offering a striking counterpoint to Puerto Plata. In addition to being a charming vacation spot, Sosúa has an interesting history. It served as a haven for Jews fleeing the Nazis at the start of World War II. While some of the refugees left their Caribbean refuge at the end of the war, many more remained. Sosúa has become a popular spot for Canadian and European package tours. Most Americans, however, have yet to discover this bargain destination.

CABARETE This windsurfing town past Sosúa resembles Malibu before it was built up. Its lovely beach is under development — hotels are popping up, houses are available for rent, and restaurants are opening here and there. The *Punta Goleta* resort is popular with French Canadians (see *Checking In*).

SAMANÁ In the 1820s, thousands of escaped American slaves settled in this remote fishing village on a peninsula jutting out of the northeast coast, establishing an English-speaking, Protestant community in a Spanish-speaking, Catholic country. Selected by the government as a potential tourism center, today this small, peaceful town combines isolation with development. There are a variety of accommodations available here, from simple guesthouses to luxury resorts such as the *Gran Bahía* (see *Checking In*) and the *El Portillo Beach Club.*

Sources and Resources

TOURIST INFORMATION

In Santo Domingo, the Dominican Tourist Information Center (at the corner of Av. México and 30 de Marzo; phone: 687-8038 or 800-752-1151) can answer questions. For information about Dominican Republic tourist offices in the US, see GETTING READY TO GO.

LOCAL COVERAGE The *Santo Domingo News,* distributed free at hotels and shops, carries a current entertainment section that is directed more toward English-speaking residents than to tourists. The bilingual *Bohío,* a free tourist magazine, is obviously ad-oriented, but helpful.

La Cotica: National Tourism Guide to the Dominican Republic, the most complete and available guidebook, is $2 to $3 at hotel newsstands and sundry shops, or can be obtained free from the tourist offices. It offers, in addition to a comprehensive view of the country, valuable addresses and phone numbers. *Viejo Santo Domingo* is an excellent free guide with a map and a bit of history published by the Dominican-American Cultural Institute.

Listin Diario, El Caribe, El Siglo, Nuevo Diario, Hoy, El Nacional, La Notíca, and *Ultima Hora* are the daily local Spanish-language newspapers. The English-language *San Juan Star* and day-old Miami and New York papers are available in hotels.

RADIO AND TELEVISION

Although local radio and TV stations broadcast only in Spanish, many of the larger hotels offer cable TV from the US.

TELEPHONE

The area code for the Dominican Republic is 809.

ENTRY REQUIREMENTS

A $10 tourist card, valid for approximately 90 days, is required, and can be obtained by presenting a valid passport or other proof of citizenship (a birth certificate or voter's registration card along with photo ID) to a consulate, carrier, or — on arrival — an immigration official. An ongoing or return ticket also is needed. The departure tax is $10.

CLIMATE AND CLOTHES

The island of Hispaniola lies on the same latitude as Hawaii. Sweeping trade winds and the warm Caribbean help keep temperatures pleasant year-round. Daytime winter temperatures range between 75F (24C) and 80F (27C), with cooler breezes at night. Summer temperatures run from about 80F (27C) to 90F (32C); August is the warmest month. May and June, October and November are the rainiest, but rainfall often comes in short downpours followed by clear skies and fresh, clean air.

In general, daytime dress is casual and comfortable. Lightweight sportswear — slacks and shirts, skirts and dresses in natural fabrics or wash-and-wear blends — are fine for sightseeing; active sports clothes (for beach, tennis, golf, and so on) are right for resorts and the pools and courts of hotels in town. Pack a light sweater or jacket for cooler winter evenings or air conditioned restaurants and clubs. Evenings tend to be a touch dressier with jackets (but not necessarily ties) suggested at better restaurants and hotels. Santo Domingo also has some spots (for example, the *Alcázar* dining room of the *Santo Domingo* hotel and *Mesón de la Cava*) for those who like to get decked out for a night on the town.

MONEY

At banks and exchange houses, $1 US buys about 12.50 Dominican pesos; the exchange rate at shops and restaurants may be somewhat lower. Try not to have a surplus of pesos at departure time; it's difficult and time-consuming to exchange them.

Shops and hotels happily accept US dollars, but often won't take Canadian currency. Many larger stores accept major US credit cards, as do most hotels and restaurants. Traveler's checks are welcome everywhere, but no discounts are given for payment in either cash dollars or traveler's checks. All prices in this chapter are quoted in US dollars.

LANGUAGE

Spanish is the Dominican Republic's official language, but most Dominicans in tourist-related businesses speak some English. Outside of the prime tourist areas, visitors who don't speak Spanish may run into some language problems, but Dominicans are friendly, helpful people who will find a way to communicate.

TIME

The Dominican Republic runs on atlantic standard time. In late fall, winter, and early spring, noon in New York is 1 PM in Santo Domingo; when daylight saving time is in effect in the US, noon in New York is noon in Santo Domingo.

CURRENT

Same as in the US and Canada — 110 volts, 60 cycles.

TIPPING

Local law requires that hotel bills and restaurant checks include a 10% service charge, which is supposed to cover all tips. For especially good service, however, it's customary to add 5% to 10% more — especially in restaurants not connected with hotels. Tip hotel maids $1 to $2 per day per room, bellboys and airport porters 50¢ per bag (but never less than $1 overall). Give taxi drivers 10% to 15% of the fare.

GETTING AROUND

BUS In Santo Domingo they are sometimes crowded, but also inexpensive and efficient, and they cover the entire city. From the airport, bus service is available into Santo Domingo at about 55¢ per person, though only infrequently (six daily trips to and from the airport). Call *Expressos Dominicanos* (phone: 682-6610) to find out when the next one is due. Air conditioned bus service from Santo Domingo to other towns — Bonao, Jarabacoa, La Romana, La Vega, Puerto Plata, San Pedro de Macorís, Santiago, and Punta Cana — is comfortable and offers travelers the chance to meet local people and see the country. Check the number of stops, however; some routes offer a bit more local color than you'll want. For schedule and route information, call *Compañía Nacional* (phone: 565-6681) or *Metro Tourist Services* (phone: 566-7126). A cool bargain: the 3-hour air conditioned ride to Puerto Plata for about $2.40.

CAR RENTAL There are international and Dominican car rental agencies at the airport and in several cities. Rates range from $50 to $75 a day (according to the size and type of car and terms of rental), with unlimited mileage (you buy gas), plus mandatory $14-per-day collision insurance.

Hertz, Avis, and *Budget* will make reservations through their mainland toll-free phone numbers or the following local numbers: *Hertz* (phone: 688-2277), *Budget* (phone: 549-0177), *National* (phone: 562-1444), *Avis* (phone: 532-9295). They all have desks at the airports in Santo Domingo and Puerto Plata, and at some hotels; as does *Nelly Rent-A-Car,* one of the best local firms (phone: 549-0232; 688-3366 in Santo Domingo; 586-4888 in Puerto Plata). *Pueblo* (phone: 689-2000), and other Dominican Republic companies often have representatives in the better hotels. All companies listed above have drop-off centers at the airport in Puerto Plata. A special license is not necessary to drive in the Dominican Republic; a valid US license is good for 90 days.

Note that Dominican drivers tend to use their horns instead of their brakes. In Old Santo Domingo, the streets are narrow, with blind corners, so be alert. In the countryside, limit your driving to daylight hours; the roads aren't lit, and a meandering mule could wipe out more than your damage waiver.

LIMOUSINE Share-the-ride car lines travel from the capital to towns throughout the country. There are set fares and schedules. The number to call for information varies according to the direction in which you're traveling; check the *Official Guide,* or call the *Centro Dominicano* (phone: 685-3282).

SIGHTSEEING BUS TOURS Excursions on air conditioned buses, with English-speaking guides, are offered by a number of local companies. *Prieto Tours* (phone: 688-5715) is one of the best. *Metro Tours* (phone: 544-4580 in Santo Domingo, 587-4611 in Santiago) and *Terrabus* (phone: 567-9715) also are good; others to check out are *Palm Tours* (phone: 682-3407 or 682-3284), *Vimenca Tours* (phone: 533-2318), and *Santo Domingo Tours* (phone: 567-6818). In Puerto Plata, try *Puerto Plata Tours* (phone: 586-3858 or 586-2770) or *Apollo Tours* (phone: 586-2019). On the south coast, *Tropical Tours* at *Casa de Campo* is a topnotch operator (phone: 556-5801). Tour options include beach trips, city and country sightseeing, shopping, sports packages, and visits to the mountain towns of Jarabacoa, Constanza, and Santiago. Prices run from about $23 for a half-day city sightseeing trip to about $56 for a full-day, out-of-town tour with lunch included.

SIGHTSEEING TAXI TOURS These cost more than bus tours, but are a great way to see the country, provided you can find a driver who speaks your language, knows his Dominican history and sights, and has good springs in his car. Consult your hotel travel desk for specific names. Otherwise, you're better off on a bus tour with an English-speaking guide.

TAXI There are plenty of cabs at the airport and in town. But they aren't metered, so make sure the fare (and the number of passengers for which it pays) is understood and agreed upon beforehand. There's a minimum in-town fare of 10 pesos (about 80¢) per ride. The fare from Las Américas Airport to Santo Domingo's central tourist hotels runs about $20; a taxi ride from the airport in Puerto Plata to resorts at Playa Dorada costs about $8. Numerous *conchos* — small taxis following a set route, with passengers getting in and out along the way — serve Santo Domingo. Other transportation alternatives include hopping onto a *moto-concho,* a rickshaw-type cart powered by a man and his motorcycle, or paying a few pesos for a lift on the back seat of a motor scooter.

INTER-ISLAND FLIGHTS

American Eagle has daily flights to La Union International Airport, which is near Puerto Plata and the north coast, from San Juan, Puerto Rico. There also are frequent charter arrivals in Puerto Plata and charter flights out of Santo Domingo. *ALM* (*Antilles Airlines*) links Curaçao, Aruba, and Bonaire with Santo Domingo; *Dominair* flies between San Juan and Santo Domingo; and *VIASA* connects Santo Domingo and Caracas.

SPECIAL EVENTS

The Dominican Republic's big festival time is *Merengue Week,* celebrated in Santo Domingo during the last part of July. Rum flows freely and everyone takes to the dance floor — or the street or the nearest tabletop — to do the rhythmic national dance. If your merengue is a little rusty (or nonexistent), don't worry; there'll be more than enough volunteer instructors around to help. *Carnaval,* another traditional celebration, is held on *Independence Day* (February 27).

Legal holidays — when banks, businesses, and most government offices are closed — are *New Year's Day, Epiphany Day* (January 6), the *Day of Our Lady of Altagracia* (January 21), *Duarte's Day* (January 26), *Independence Day* (February 27), *Good Friday* and *Easter, Labor Day* (May 1), *Corpus Christi Day* (60 days after *Easter*), *Restoration Day* (August 16), *Feast of Our Lady of Mercy* (September 24), *Columbus Day* (October 12), and *Christmas.*

SHOPPING

Among the best buys in the Dominican Republic are jewelry and decorative pieces made from amber. Some pieces encase insects, leaves, or dew drops, which make them more valuable. Color can range from crystal clear to almost black; gold is most common. But buy amber only in established shops; that nice amber piece that a street vendor offers may actually be plastic.

Larimar, or "Dominican turquoise," is another popular local stone. Milky blue and perhaps even prettier than turquoise, it's often mounted with wild boars' teeth or silver. Polished pink pieces of conch shell also are crafted into striking jewelry.

Other worthwhile take-home items include rocking chairs — very popular in the Dominican Republic, sold knocked down and boxed for easy transporting — woodcarvings, macramé, baskets, and leather goods. Lime figurines, the Dominican Republic's answer to Spain's Lladró, are also very popular; less expensive replicas are sold at roadside and beachside stands. Be sure to haggle with the seller — about half the asking price is usually fair.

Some of the most attractive jewelry and gift items sold in the Dominican Republic are made from tortoiseshell. Be aware, however, that many species of tortoise are on the US endangered list, so any tortoiseshell item that a US customs officer finds in your luggage will be confiscated. La Atarazana (the Terrace), a winding street across from the Alcázar and near the river, is lined with gift shops and galleries. Savvy shoppers browse here, then move on to Calle El Conde, the oldest and most traditional shopping area in the city, to do their buying.

The *Mercado Modelo,* Santo Domingo's model native marketplace (on Av. Mella), is full of stalls that offer all kinds of craft items. If you don't speak Spanish, you may want to have your cab driver come along as interpreter, or give one of the small boys at the gate $1 to lead you through and fend off some of the more eager merchants. With or without escort, you won't be hassled, but you should bargain before you settle on a final buying price. Also look for Dominican coffee — sold unground, it's good, strong, and less expensive than special roasts back home.

Duty-free shops at the Centro de los Héroes, La Atarazana, and the *Santo Domingo, Sheraton,* and *Embajador* hotels in town carry the usual range of French perfume, liquor, camera equipment, watches, and jewelry. Travelers choose items from the stock on hand; duplicates of the selected merchandise are delivered to their planes or ships. The principle is the same as at airport duty-free shops, but the selection in La Zona Franca (Santo Domingo's duty-free zone) is greater. You must pay in dollar-denomination traveler's checks or cash dollars. The *Plaza Criolla* downtown (Av. 27 de Febrero) is a center for fine jewelry shops and other boutiques. Excellent amber items are sold there, as are silver pieces from some of the oldest wrecks sunk off the island.

Generally, shops open daily from 8:30 or 9 AM to noon, close for siesta, then reopen from 2:30 until about 6:30 PM. Here are some places where the time (and money) might be well spent:

AMBAR MALDO Besides the standard amber, larimar, and coral items, this store carries pottery and masks. 782 Atarazana, Santo Domingo (phone: 688-0639).

AMBAR MARIE One of the best and most extensive amber collections, from tiny drop earrings to museum pieces. 19 Calle Rosa Duarte, Santo Domingo (no phone).

ARAWAK GALERÍA DE ARTE The native art lures collectors here. 104 Av. Pasteur, Santo Domingo (phone: 685-1661).

EL CONDE GIFT SHOP The place to find rocking chairs, along with other Dominican wares. 25 Calle El Conde, Santo Domingo (phone: 682-5909).

GALERÍA DE ARTE NADER Lots of artwork, including oils and wooden sculptures, from the Dominican Republic, Haiti, and Latin America, displayed in what is reputedly the capital's oldest gallery. 9 Atarazana, Santo Domingo (phone: 688-0969 or 682-7726).

HARRISON'S Fine jewelry and hand-crafted gift items made from local amber, larimar, and coral are this establishment's stocks in trade. Plaza Isabela near the Playa Dorada complex in Puerto Plata (phone: 586-3933).

LAR GIFT SHOP A large selection of Lime figures, but penny-watchers beware — the amber jewelry gets pricey. 15 Av. John F. Kennedy, Santo Domingo (phone: 586-2751).

MACALUSO'S An inviting boutique specializing in fine jewelry primarily made of local stones, and crafts. 32 Duarte St., Puerto Plata (phone: 586-3433).

MÉNDEZ Among the best buying and browsing shops — particularly for distinctive jewelry. Sr. Méndez claims to have discovered larimar and has done some handsome things with it. Calle Arzobispo Noel, corner José Reyes, Santo Domingo (phone: 685-6469).

***MUSEO DEL AMBAR* (AMBER MUSEUM)** Boasting both jewelry and crafts that are reasonably priced, this tiny museum is worth a visit for its amber displays alone. Calle Emilio Prudhomme at Duarte, Puerto Plata (phone: 586-2848).

NOVEAU Paintings, sculpture, and silk screens are featured at this gallery. 354 Av. Independencia, Santo Domingo (phone: 689-6869).

SALA DE ARTE ROSAMARIA Good local paintings in a lovely patio setting. 7 Atarazana, Santo Domingo (phone: 688-2744).

SPORTS

Fine weather year-round, lots of unspoiled land, and beautiful water — as yet not overpublicized — make the Dominican Republic a great place to feel the sun and sea, meet the challenge of a tough par 4 hole, or fight it out with a blue marlin. The country's sporting facilities are top quality now, and — with the further development of resort areas like those at Puerto Plata — they'll be expanding.

BASEBALL A national obsession. At any given time, 50 Dominican Republic–born players are in the US majors (current and previous players include former MVP George Bell, All-Star shortstop Tony Fernández, and Pedro Guerrero). Major league coaches frequently arrive to scout potential players. The professional winter season runs from October to the end of January; the summer season is April to September. Check local papers for schedules at five stadiums, or ask any Dominican for the location of the nearest game.

BOATING Small sailboats are available through hotels in Santo Domingo and on the north coast; *Club Med* and the *Punta Cana Beach* resort at Punta Cana and *Casa de Campo* at La Romana have their own fleets of day sailers. Large-boat charters aren't always easy to arrange; hotels and the tourist offices may have information on boats available in the Santo Domingo area. Try the *Andrés Boca Chica Club* (phone: 685-4940) or the *Santo Domingo Nautical Club* (phone: 566-1684). Better still, arrange ahead by corresponding through your home yacht club or marina. The *Punta Cana Beach and Golf Club* can accommodate yachts up to 85 feet at its 80-slip marina.

COCKFIGHTING The violence and bloodshed may turn some off, but there's no denying it's part of the Latino scene. Cockfights are regularly held at *Coliseo Gallistico,* Av. Luperón, Herrera (phone: 566-3844).

DOG RACES Greyhound races are held year-round at *Canodromo El Coco,* about 15 minutes north of the capital (phone: 565-8333 or 567-4461). Races are held Wednesdays through Sundays, starting at 7 PM (4 PM on Sundays). General admission is about 15¢; about 65¢ gets you into the clubhouse. Minimum bet: 1 peso (about 8¢).

FISHING Flatboats, with guides, can be hired for about $35 for a half-day river fishing for snook and tarpon at La Romana, Boca de Yuma, and on the north coast around Samaná. Inquire at your hotel.

Offshore waters are home to marlin, sailfish, dorado, bonito, and other game fish. Best spots are Cumayasa, La Romana, Boca de Yuma on the east; Palmar de Ocoa and Barahona on the south; Monte Cristi and Samaná on the north. Charter fishing boats are available for about $100 for a half day for up to six people. Have your hotel make arrangements, or try the *Santo Domingo Nautical Club* (phone: 566-1684), *Andrés Boca Chica* (phone: 685-4940), *Haina Nautical Club* (phone: 533-3961), *Mundo Submarino* (phone: 566-0340), or *Actividades Acua'ticas* (phone: 688-5838 in Santo Domingo; 586-3988 in Puerto Plata).

GOLF In addition to several other good layouts, Santo Domingo boasts two of the world's finest championship courses.

TOP TEE-OFF SPOTS

Casa de Campo The two greats are right here, but if it were necessary to choose just one island course on which to play, it would have to be the one known — for good reason — as "The Teeth of the Dog." Unquestionably Pete Dye's finest island work, this seaside course presents more excitement, interest, and sheer brawny challenge than any other golf course we've ever seen. Seven holes play directly along the seaside, and they are unlike any other such water holes you have heretofore experienced. Just standing on one of the championship tees can be an exercise in sheer terror, as the terrain between tee and green occasionally looks as if it might be inhabited by the Loch Ness Monster. In this instance, said monster would be a welcome relief from the rigors that Dye has wrought.

In addition to the superb seaside stretch, the other 11 holes are scarcely less challenging. Dye's unique inclination to enclose terrain within wooden retaining walls and to create traps that look like the Sahara are only part of the picture that greets each golfer from the outset. And lest you think the second course at *Casa de Campo* is any real respite, "The Links" is thought by many to be even more difficult. Greens fees are $62.50 at the "Teeth of the Dog," and $47.50 at "The Links." There is a third course, *La Romana Golf Club,* but to play here you must make contact with a member. If a member accompanies you while playing, it's $30 for 18 holes; if you are introduced by a member but play on your own, it's $60. The real bonus from the third course is that its members — mostly local Dominicans — no longer clog up the fairways at *Casa de Campo's* 2 resort courses (phone: 523-3333, ext. 3187; 305-856-5405 from Florida; 800-223-6620 from elsewhere in the US).

There is also a handsome Robert Trent Jones, Sr. course at the Playa Dorada complex, near Puerto Plata, and visitors can play the *Santo Domingo Country Club* course, but only on a members-first basis — which practically rules out weekend play for visitors. In addition, 18 holes of a Robert Trent Jones, Sr.–designed golf course have been completed at Punta Cana. The course eventually will encompass 36 holes on 2,000 acres.

HORSE RACES Held year-round on Tuesdays, Thursdays, and Sundays at the *Hipodromo Perla Antillana,* Av. San Martin, Santo Domingo (phone: 567-4407).

HORSEBACK RIDING Dominicans love riding, and their country offers some of the best in the Caribbean. Rarely do you find an animal that even remotely resembles the stereotypical tired hack horse. To ride in Santo Domingo, call the *International Horseback Riding Club* (phone: 533-6321), *Rancho School* (phone: 682-5482), or the *National Horseback Riding School* (phone: 682-5482). The resorts at La Romana raise their own horses, and about 400 homegrown steeds are available to ride at *Casa de Campo's*

Rancho Centro Romana, where you can arrange to ride with a guide (required) for up to 8 hours (about $4 per person per hour) on a horse suited to your skill. Or take private or group lessons in riding or polo through the Activities Office at *Casa de Campo* (phone: 523-3333, ext. 2249). Horseback riding is also featured at the *Punta Cana Beach* resort; trail rides lead to a working cattle ranch, past some Arawak ruins, and along the beach (about $16 per person for a 3-hour guided tour).

PARASAILING *Actividades Acua'ticas* (phone: 688-5838 in Santo Domingo; 586-3988 in Puerto Plata) provides the island's only outlet for this sky-high sport.

POLO The polo season runs from October through May, and there are regular games at *Sierra Prieta* in Santo Domingo and at *Casa de Campo* near La Romana. Guests may join the twice-a-week competition, as long as they've brought their handicap from a home club. Mallets are appreciated, too, but they can be provided in a pinch. Call *Casa de Campo* (phone: 523-3333, ext. 2249). This is the place to learn to play polo, or to improve your game if you already play, in a glorious setting with patient instructors and over 100 polo ponies from which to choose. Private lessons run $30 per hour.

SNORKELING AND SCUBA *Dominican Divers* (phone: 567-0346) takes certified divers on half-day ($30) and daylong ($60) trips. *Actividades Acua'ticas* (phone: 688-5838 in Santo Domingo; 586-3988 in Puerto Plata) offers lessons and tours. Some of the most spectacular underwater scenery is at La Caleta, near the entrance to Las Américas International Airport, where there are miles of coral reefs, caves, and fissures more than 40 feet deep. Snorkel gear is loaned or rented for a small fee by resort hotels. Near La Romana, the *Dominicus Beach* resort offers a full water sports program. *Casa de Campo* guests can sail to nearby Catalina Island aboard the 52-foot schooner *Merengue* for a day's snorkeling. The $30-per-person trip includes a guided snorkeling tour, lunch, and some beach time. Reserve a day ahead. Twice-daily snorkeling sails (including equipment) are free to guests of the *Punta Cana Beach* resort. The waters off the shores of *Club Med* are filled with spiny urchins, snails, and tropical fish, as well as huge quantities of brain coral. Snorkeling equipment is free to guests; scuba diving also is available, though not free.

SWIMMING AND SUNNING The country's most beautiful strands are those on the north coast, where resort development has grown up around the town of Puerto Plata, about a 3-hour drive north of Santo Domingo on a fast, relatively new highway. Beach addicts drive up, lunch in the hills at Santiago, the Dominican Republic's second city, and stay for 2 or 3 days to sample the pleasures of the miles of sandy beach that line the calmer coast of the Atlantic. Here are a couple of the best.

DREAM BEACHES

Playa Grande, a nearly deserted sweep of poster-perfect sand on the north shore, is a great place to spend a long, lazy day (bring a picnic, playthings, and maybe a beach umbrella). Next door, Sosúa offers a tranquil alternative, a semicircle of beach flanked by the town, whose cafés, shops, hotels, and friendly atmosphere have made it popular with Canadians, Europeans, and most recently, Americans.

Also on the north shore, Playa Dorada offers great sunning, swimming, snorkeling, and beachcombing.

The coast is craggy at Santo Domingo with no sand beaches. The nearest good ones are Boca Chica, just beyond the airport, and Juan Dolio, about 40 to 45 minutes east of town. About 2 hours out, guests at *Casa de Campo* swim at pretty Las Minitas or Bayahibe. The *Punta Cana Beach* resort and *Club Med* are situated on a magnificent stretch of beach at Punta Cana on the island's far eastern tip.

TENNIS Santo Domingo offers an impressive number of courts for racketeers — from rank beginners to pros.

CHOICE COURTS

Casa de Campo The tennis segment of this 7,000-acre complex is first class; everything works, and everything is in absolutely mint condition. Facilities: 13 clay-composition courts (2 are stadium courts, 6 are lighted) at *La Terraza Tennis Village* (a 5-minute jitney ride from the main building); and 4 additional all-weather, lighted Laykold courts near the main administrative building. There is a resident pro; lessons are about $33.50 per hour with the pro, $26.50 with the assistant pro, $20 with the junior assistant pro. Eight to 12 people can also set up their own daily clinic at rates that vary according to the season. There's also a ball machine and a pro shop. Court fees are $17 per hour of day play; $20 per hour at night. Tennis packages are offered year-round. A roster of terrific ballboys, including some very fine players, makes it possible to guarantee guests games at all levels of skill (phone: 523-3333, ext. 2940; 305-856-5405 from Florida; 800-223-6620 from elsewhere in the US).

The *Embajador, Dominican Fiesta, Santo Domingo,* and the *Sheraton* hotels also have courts (some lighted), pro shops, and teaching pros. The *Ramada Renaissance Jaragua* boasts an 800-seat tennis stadium and usually has a highly ranked tennis pro. The *Gran Hotel Lina* and *Ramada Renaissance Jaragua* have courts, too. At Puerto Plata, there are good courts at the *Jack Tar Village, Playa Dorada, Playa Dorada Princess,* and *Villas Doradas;* those at the *Montemar* in Puerta Plata, the *Cofresí* hotel in Costambar, and the *Villas del Mar* in San Pedro de Macorís, are on the rustic side. At Punta Cana, courts at the *Punta Cana Beach* resort, *Bavaro Beach,* and *Club Med* are first-rate.

TRAP AND SKEET SHOOTING You can perfect your aim at *Casa de Campo.* Basic shooting orientation is free for beginners; clinics and lessons are available for experienced marksmen.

NIGHTLIFE

Take your pick — a Vegas-style review, a lounge with a cabaret singer or show tunes played on a piano, New York–style disco dancing, a wild night of merengue, casinos where you can play until dawn, or a quiet drink in a café by the ocean — Santo Domingo has them all.

Hotels offer traditional, small-scale shows most evenings. A current smart spot is *Las Palmas* in the *Santo Domingo* hotel, with live music Monday through Thursday nights. *L'Azotea,* the lounge atop the *Dominican Fiesta,* and *El Yarey* at the *Sheraton* are catching on with the tourist crowd, while the *Embassy Club* at the *Embajador* is still a favorite with both Dominicans and visitors. The *Merengue Lounge* at the *Ramada Renaissance Jaragua; Mesón de la Cava* (see *Eating Out*), with folkloric music; *Lina's Salon La Mancha, Maunaloa, La Taverna de María Castoña,* and *El Castillo* in the *San Gerónimo* hotel are the places for Latin music. The *Ramada Renaissance Jaragua* features Vegas-style shows in its 1,600-seat *La Fiesta* showroom about twice monthly. Livelier types make for *Raffles* or the *Village Pub* downtown for music (CDs, tapes, or live depending on the day of the week) and sociability, or *Drake's Pub* for drinks and 16th-century Dominican ambience. There's also the *Blues Bar* for jazz and drinks, and *Le Café* and the *Golden Club* for cocktails and conversation. More down-to-earth types may want to try the *Petit Chateau* (Av. Mirador del Sur) just west of town.

You can relieve disco fever at the *Sheraton's* slick *Omni* or *Opus. La Belle Blu* (Av. George Washington) is a must for the see-and-be-seen scene; *Alexander's* (Av. Pasteur) draws discoing Dominican preppies. Later, move on to *El Viniedo* for wine, cheese, and a game of backgammon. *Mesón de Barri,* in the colonial district, is popular with artists and writers for drinks. Or, if you're still ready to roll, there's *Neon* at the *Hispaniola* hotel. The *Embajador, Sheraton, Dominican Fiesta, Hispaniola, Lina,* and *San Gerónimo* hotels have casinos; so does *Maunaloa,* a nightclub at the Centro de los Héroes. The *Ramada Renaissance Jaragua* boasts the Caribbean's largest gambling facility. At most places in town with entertainment, there's an admission charge.

Out of town, at *Casa de Campo,* options are limited but pleasant, with eight different dining spots at the resort and at the artisans' village of Altos de Chavón; Altos is also the site of the supersound disco called *Genesis.* A special spot for drinks is *La Caná,* the thatch-roofed bar perched over a swimming pool. At Puerto Plata, the *Castilla* hotel bar is the favorite gathering place in town; the *Montemar* has a small disco; and the *Playa Dorada* has the hottest nightspot on the beach. The discos at *Heavens* and *Paradise Resort* are also popular, but the disco *Casa del Sol* in Sosúa is purported to have the best sound system in the Caribbean. Casinos buzz at *Jack Tar Village,* the *Puerta Plata Beach* resort, the *Playa Dorada,* and at the *Punta Cana Beach* and *Bavaro Beach* resorts, both in Punta Cana. Other casinos on the island are at the *Matun* hotel in Santiago and *De Cameron Club* in Juan Dolio. Casinos throughout the Dominican Republic are open from 4 PM to 4 AM Mondays through Thursdays and 4 PM to 6 AM Fridays and Saturdays.

Merengue music and folkloric shows are often featured poolside at the *Punta Cana Beach* resort. The resort's *La Tortuga Beach Club* (with the largest thatch-roofed building on the island) has disco dancing nightly.

Best on the Island

CHECKING IN

The Dominican Republic has about 23,000 hotel rooms, with choices in all price categories. Santo Domingo hotels cater to a fairly sophisticated crowd of history buffs, shoppers, nightlife lovers, businesspeople, gamblers, and some quickie divorcers. La Romana offers a tops-in-class sports resort. Puerta Plata, on the north coast, features luxury beach hotels, including the Playa Dorada complex, which includes 12 resort properties (for information, call 809-586-3132). Sosúa, popular with Canadians and Europeans, is also a rapidly developing area, and further hotel plans are on the drawing boards for neighboring North Shore coastal areas, which one day will be connected to the resort development on the east coast near Punta Cana.

In Santo Dominigo, rates stay about the same year-round because of steady business traffic. At resort hotels, the situation is different: Winter prices are steep — La Romana's *Casa de Campo* (see *A Regal Resort,* below) costs about $230 a day for a casita room for two without meals. In summer, prices drop 40% to 50%, and there are attractively priced packages. Hotels beyond Santo Domingo, La Romana, and Puerto Plata are considerably less expensive, whatever the season.

With the exchange rate favoring the dollar, food and beverage costs at even the finest restaurants can be attractive, so it's a good idea to book your room EP and sample some of the country's many interesting restaurants. However, the Modified American Plan (MAP) may be the best option at *Casa de Campo* resort at La Romana, since there are few good restaurants outside the complex.

In the listings below, hotels classed as expensive charge $100 and up per night for a double without meals; hotels in the moderate category charge in the $50 to $100 range; at inexpensive places, the rate is under $50. At some places, the Modified American Plan (MAP), which includes breakfast and dinner, is available for an additional $20 to $25 per person. Additional costs include a 5% room tax and a 10% service charge. All telephone numbers are in the 809 area code unless otherwise indicated.

For an unforgettable island experience, we begin with our favorite, followed by our recommendations of cost and quality choices of hotels large and small, listed by area and price category.

A REGAL RESORT

Casa de Campo The aim was — quite simply — to build the perfect sports resort. The result was this big complex built on 7,000 acres near the old sugar mill town of La Romana. Guests are met at the airport by a hostess and shown to an air conditioned courtesy suite where they can wait comfortably until all the guests have assembled. Folks with private planes can land at the resort's airstrip. There's just about everything here: 2 great Pete Dye golf courses, a terrific 13-court tennis layout called *La Terraza* (there are 4 more all-weather courts elsewhere on the property), stables (both English- and Western-style riding), 2 polo fields (with coach in attendance), guides and boats for deep-sea and river fishing, and trap- and skeet-shooting ranges. All this plus villa rooms that Oscar de la Renta had a hand in decorating. An improved sandy beach — Las Minitas — is a short golf-cart ride from the main complex; its pleasures include swaying palms, showers, changing facilities, and a snack bar where the hamburgers are super. The place to be at sunset is *La Caña,* an imaginative, thatch pavilion with a 360° view. There's dinner in the main dining room (grilled meat, local lobster are specialties). Other appetizing options: country inn–like *La Piazzetta* (elegant Italian), *La Bahía* (seafood), *Casa del Río* (continental, with a spectacular view), and *Café de Sol* (pizza and ice cream) built into Altos de Chavón, the evocation of a 15th-century artisans' village atop a nearby hill. For merengue and dance-mood music, there's *La Caña;* for discoing, *Genesis* in Altos de Chavón (phone: 523-3333; 305-856-5405 from Florida; 800-223-6620 from elsewhere in the US).

SANTO DOMINGO

EXPENSIVE

Ramada Renaissance Jaragua The grande dame of Santo Domingo hotels, this 355-room complex occupies 14 acres on the *malecón.* It boasts 4 lighted clay tennis courts (plus tennis pro and an 800-seat tennis stadium), a pool, a European-style spa, and a 20,000-square-foot casino, touted as the largest in the Caribbean. Other drawing cards: 5 restaurants, including the *Manhattan Grill* and *Figaro* (see *Eating Out*); Las Vegas–style entertainment in *La Fiesta Showroom;* a lounge for dancing; and a disco. 367 Av. George Washington (phone: 221-2222; 212-545-7688 from New York; 800-331-3542 from elsewhere in the US; fax: 686-0528).

Santo Domingo Facing the sea, this luxurious 220-room city hostelry, with interiors by Oscar de la Renta (himself a native Dominican), is a top choice. The decor features lots of elegant latticework, tall potted palms, and locally made furnishings; some rooms face the ocean. The Premier Club, a concierge floor, has beautifully decorated rooms and a most accommodating staff. The hotel offers a large pool and a sun deck with a bar, a sauna, and 3 tennis courts. There are 2 restaurants, including the excellent *El Alcázar* dining room (see *Eating Out*). *Las Palmas* is the nightspot, a pianist plays in the lobby bar every afternoon, and there's another most agreeable breeze-conditioned bar. Av. Independencia and Av. Abraham Lincoln (phone: 221-1511; 305-856-7083 from Florida; 800-223-6620 from elsewhere in the US; fax: 535-4050).

Sheraton Santo Domingo Most of the 260 rooms (except those on the third floor) have a sea view; suites have terraces. Basically a business hotel in a convenient location, it has a good-looking modern design with lush green potted plants, and management that's skilled and thoughtful. There are 3 restaurants, including *Antoine,* a Chaîne des Rôtisseurs selection, which serves luncheon buffets only, and the less formal *La Terraza,* which serves lunch and dinner. Other amenities include a lounge, a nightclub, a pool, a health club with sauna and massage, 2 lighted tennis courts, a Jacuzzi, a stylish casino, and a top-flight disco. 365 Av. George Washington (phone: 221-6666; 800-325-3535 from the US; fax: 687-8150).

V Centennario Named in honor of the quincentennial of Columbus's discovery of the island, this newest addition to the hotel scene is right on the *malecón.* It has 201 luxurious rooms with fabulous sea views; amenities include a concierge, a tennis court, a squash court, a pool, water sports, an 18-hole golf course, a gym and spa, 2 bars, a casino, and the country's first underground parking garage. Guests can enjoy a choice of Spanish, French, and local fare at the hotel's 3 dining rooms. 218 Av. George Washington (phone: 686-0000; 800-223-5652 from the US; fax: 686-3287).

MODERATE

El Embajador On a slight hill in the western part of town, this property has 300 rooms, with those facing south overlooking the sea. Club Miguel Angel is an executive floor. There's a nice Olympic-size pool, 4 tennis courts (1 clay), basketball and volleyball courts, 3 bars, a disco, a coffee shop, a casino, evening entertainment at the *Embassy* nightclub (a smart-set favorite), and 2 very good restaurants — one elegant continental (the *Grill Embassy Club*) and one Chinese (*El Jardín de Jade* — see *Eating Out*). Av. Sarasota (phone: 221-2131; 212-838-3322 from New York; 800-457-0067 from elsewhere in the US; fax: 532-5306).

Gran Hotel Lina The reincarnation of a longtime Latino favorite, it has 220 air conditioned rooms, a pool, tennis courts, an exercise room, a casino, and

Lina, one of the capital's best Spanish restaurants (see *Eating Out*). Rooms are simple but attractively furnished. Av. Máximo Gómez and Av. 27 de Febrero (phone: 563-5000; 305-374-0045 from Florida; 800-336-6612 from elsewhere in the US; fax: 686-5521).

Hispaniola This is the well-liked but less sumptuous sister of the luxurious *Santo Domingo* across the street (see above). Actually, it's a pleasant, modest, but comfortable place, very popular with Dominicans and business travelers; the staff is most hospitable. Some of the 165 rooms on the south side have sea views. Guests may use of all the facilities at its sister hotel (all the play for less pay). Facilities include a pool and sunning space, an outdoor coffee shop, and a pool bar. There's also *El Vivero* dining room; *La Piazzetta,* an Italian restaurant (see *Eating Out*); the swinging *Neon* disco; and a casino. Av. Independencia and Av. Abraham Lincoln (phone: 221-7111; 800-223-6620 from the US; fax: 535-4050).

INEXPENSIVE

Comodoro Centrally located in the newer section of town, this place has only 90 rooms, but there's a pool and a restaurant. Clean and efficient, it's a good value. 193 Av. Bolívar (phone: 541-2277; fax: 562-4486).

Nicolás de Ovando In the heart of Old Santo Domingo, overlooking the Ozama River, it's called "the oldest hotel in the New World." It's the restored colonial home of Nicolás de Ovanda, who supervised the building of the city; the reigning King and Queen of Spain have stayed here. The 50 high-ceilinged, beamed rooms boast charming windows, modern air conditioning, and 16th-century–style furniture. This is the place for you if you love atmosphere and history and don't care about sports. There's a small pool, a piano bar on weekends, and the *Midomodo* restaurant (see *Eating Out*). 53 Calle Las Damas (phone: 687-3101; 800-448-8687 from the US; fax: 688-5170).

PUERTO PLATA

EXPENSIVE

Dorado Naco This first luxury component in the Playa Dorada complex has 141 air conditioned 1- and 2-bedroom and penthouse condominium apartments (each with full kitchen), rentable when owners are away; interiors have attractive Dominican furnishings, though some are a bit the worse for wear. Features include the *Flamingo* restaurant (see *Eating Out*), a coffee shop, a cocktail lounge, live entertainment, laundry, and a small supermarket, as well as a swimming pool, super beach, and horseback riding; golf is on the adjoining Robert Trent Jones, Sr. course. Playa Dorada (phone: 586-2019; 305-284-9900 from Florida; 800-322-2388 from elsewhere in the US; fax: 586-3608).

Flamenco Beach Adjacent to its sister hotel, *Villas Doradas* (see below), this resort is larger (310 air conditioned rooms) and offers greater variety (horseback riding, bicycling, several water sports, tennis on 2 courts, and a daily activities program are complimentary). Also on the premises: a golf course, a children's pool, 2 restaurants and a bar, and live shows nightly. Playa Dorada (phone: 586-3660; 800-332-4872 from the US; fax: 586-4790).

Jack Tar Village A club-like, all-inclusive complex, with 240 rooms and suites, catering to all — singles, couples, and families — in a lush setting on the sands at Playa Dorada. There are all kinds of activities — sailing, snorkeling, horseback riding, golf, tennis (2 courts, 1 night-lit), and bicycling. The casino is open to the public. Playa Dorada (phone: 586-3800; 800-999-9182 from the US; fax: 586-4161).

Playa Dorada Promoted as "a luxury beach resort," it has 254 deluxe air conditioned rooms with terraces, balconies, and contemporary furnishings. The public areas have an island-Victorian decor. With 3 restaurants, pool with swim-up bar, full water sports center, lighted tennis courts, golf on its Robert Trent Jones, Sr. course ($36 for 18 holes), horseback riding, piano bar, disco, casino, and nightly entertainment. Request an ocean-view room. 102 Av. 12 de Julio (phone: 586-3988; 305-266-7701 from Florida; 800-423-6902 from elsewhere in the US; fax: 586-1190).

Playa Dorada Princess The 336 rooms and suites are set in clusters of 2-level casitas, designed in island-Victorian style. Each air conditioned unit has a kitchenette and a terrace; many overlook the Robert Trent Jones, Sr. golf course. There are 3 good restaurants, including the elegant *La Condesa* (see *Eating Out*), a pool with a swim-up juice bar, a gym and sauna, 7 tennis courts, and constant activity poolside: aerobics, volleyball, Spanish lessons, chicken races, and merengue dancing to local bands. The beach is within walking distance, where *La Tortuga Loca* offers drinks and snack lunches, and snorkeling and sailing equipment is provided at no charge to hotel guests. Guests may choose accommodations only or the all-inclusive plan, featuring three meals daily and a plethora of activities. Playa Dorada (phone: 586-5350; 305-261-4455 from Florida; 800-852-4523 from elsewhere in the US; fax: 586-5386).

Villas Doradas A first class resort with 207 rooms and suites, it has a pool and kiddie pool, tennis, 3 restaurants (one features Chinese food), and 3 bars. There's a beach, water sports (many of which are included in the rate), a jogging track, bicycles, horseback riding, and golf available within the complex. Playa Dorada (phone: 586-3000; 212-838-3322 from New York; 800-332-4872 from elsewhere in the US; fax: 586-4790).

MODERATE

Costambar Beach On Puerto Plata Bay with 3 miles of bright, white beach, this condominium complex offers a choice of 70 one-, two-, and three-bedroom cottages and apartments, with ocean and mountain views. Each unit sleeps two to six, has its own terrace, living/dining area, and fully equipped kitchen. Each building houses 6 units and has its own pool. Daily rental includes maid and linen service. There's a restaurant, a bar, and a disco; golf and volleyball are available nearby. 17 El Peñón (phone: 586-3828; 718-507-6770 in New York; fax: 586-5451).

Victoria With 121 rooms and suites, this resort within the Playa Dorada complex has a restaurant, piano bar, and pool. Complimentary tennis is available at a nearby hotel. Golf course and private beach are within walking distance. Rates include water sports, horseback riding, and bicycling. Playa Dorada (phone: 586-5145; 800-223-6510 from the US; fax: 809-586-4862).

SOSÚA

EXPENSIVE

Sand Castle Perched atop a cliff above the water, this 240-room pink Moorish wonderland resort includes 2 pools, 4 restaurants, plus a disco and meeting facilities. A full program of water sports is available. Puerto Chiquito Beach (phone: 571-2420; 800-446-5963 from the US; fax: 571-2000).

Sosúa Caribbean Fantasy This Grecian-inspired, coral-colored property is on the main road to Sosúa. There are 5 stories, with no elevator, but the view from the penthouse terrace is worth the climb. The 68 rooms and suites have air conditioning, balconies, and marble bathrooms. The especially attractive lobby and bar are decorated with interesting local handicrafts, paintings, and sculpture. A lovely outdoor restaurant, a pool, Jacuzzi, conference room, and disco complete the picture. Carr. Sosúa (phone: 571-2534).

MODERATE

Los Coralillos Overlooking Sosúa Bay, this establishment offers great views, a charming Spanish atmosphere, and direct access to the beach. Individual guestrooms and 1- and 2-bedroom tile-roofed villas (27 in all) are set amid gardens. There's also a pool, an outdoor dining terrace, and a restaurant. Mella (phone: 571-2645; fax: 571-2095).

La Esplanada This lovely resort is located in Pedro Clisante, a seacoast town near Sosúa that may become the next Puerto Plata. There are 210 rooms, more than half of which are junior suites. Activities include windsurfing, tennis, and volleyball; there's a playground, and baby-sitting services are offered. The atmosphere is less crowded and more relaxed than at most of the other resorts. Pedro Clisante (phone: 571-3333; 800-332-4872 from the US; fax: 571-3922).

Lora Unique and charming, this 32-room inn features a hand-crafted decor in a natural setting. It has stained glass windows, and a spiral staircase embedded with colored-glass mosaics leads up to 2 penthouse apartments with terraces. All rooms have kitchens, and there's also a restaurant, a small pool, and Jacuzzi. Av. Dr. A. Martínez (phone: 571-3939).

CABARETE

MODERATE

Punta Goleta This distinctive property is a complete resort across from the beach. Its 126 large, attractive rooms have terraces and are decorated with local contemporary art. Facilities include horseback riding, a pool, a restaurant, beach and pool bars, and even a lagoon for rowboating. Windsurfing, Cabarete's main attraction, is available, as are 2 lighted tennis courts, 3 racquetball courts, and a disco (phone: 571-0700; 305-361-8885 from Florida; 800-874-4637 from elsewhere in the US; fax: 571-0707).

NORTH COAST (COSTAMBAR)

EXPENSIVE

Cofresí In a most spectacular setting by the sea, this all-inclusive resort offers 192 rooms, 2 pools, 2 tennis courts, 1 hour of horseback riding on the beach, all meals and drinks at the restaurant, a bar, a disco, and nightly shows. Rooms are basic — go for the sports and pools or visit the property with a daily pass that costs about $45, and includes meals, drinks, and facilities. This place fills up with Europeans and Canadians in winter, so book early (phone: 586-8165; fax: 586-1511, ext. 7424).

Villas Marlena An apartment hotel offering 33 immaculate studios and 1-, 2-, and 3-bedroom units with kitchenettes, but without air conditioning. There's a pool, a restaurant, and a bar. A 5-minute walk from the beach (phone: 586-5393; 212-545-8469 from New York; 800-223-9815 from elsewhere in the US).

ELSEWHERE IN THE COUNTRY

EXPENSIVE

Bavaro Beach An isolated, low-rise resort with 1,360 superior rooms, a pool, water sports, 3 lighted tennis courts, 9 restaurants, a disco, and a casino. Rates include buffet breakfast and dinner; 7-night packages include all water sports as well. Punta Cana (phone: 682-2162/2168; 305-374-0045 from Florida; 800-336-6612 from elsewhere in the US; fax: 682-2169).

De Cameron This all-inclusive resort next door to the *Talanquera* (see below) offers rooms with kitchenettes, a good beach across the street, a variety of beach activities, a pool, and 3 tennis courts. There's also a casino, a restaurant, a nightclub, and a disco. Juan Dolio, about 45 minutes from Santo Domingo (phone: 526-2307; 212-689-9694 from New York; 800-223-9815 from elsewhere in the US; fax: 686-6741).

Gran Bahía Perched on a bluff on the Samaná Peninsula, this Victorian-style hostelry boasts two sand beaches. There are 96 rooms and suites; 2 all-weather, lighted tennis courts; a pool; horseback riding; croquet; a gym; and a private dock with a boat for fishing. Most water sports are complimentary. An unusual activity is watching whales mate in the bay. Pluses include a dining room serving continental fare, a café for dining alfresco, and a piano lounge. No children under age 5 permitted. Samaná (phone: 538-3111; 203-655-4200 from Connecticut; 800-372-1323 from elsewhere in the US; fax: 538-2764).

Metro Set in 3 buildings amid tropical gardens on the beach at Juan Dolio, this property is managed by Occidental hotels, which also handles the *Embajador* in Santo Domingo, and the *Flamenco Beach, Montemar,* and *Villas Doradas* in Puerto Plata. The 180 air conditioned rooms face either the sea or the pool and have telephones. Facilities include 2 restaurants, a beach bar, 2 lighted clay tennis courts, a pool and kiddie pool. Lessons in Spanish and the merengue are offered. Juan Dolio (phone: 526-1706; 212-838-3322 from New York; 800-843-6664 from elsewhere in the US; fax: 526-1808).

Punta Cana Beach The beauty of this resort is its location — on 2,200 feet of white sand beach dotted with coconut palms. Each building is designed in an eclectic mix of island-Victorian architectures, thatch roofs, and Greek columns. The 350 studio rooms, suites, and villas have a tropical decor, with Dominican marble tiles and wicker furniture, kitchenettes, and balconies. All-inclusive rates are for breakfast and dinner daily, plus a roster of activities such as tennis, boat rides, theme parties, and bicycling. Also available are snorkeling trips, deep-sea fishing excursions, and horseback riding nearby. Guests can dine either outdoors (at lobster barbecues and Dominican pig roasts), or more formally at the *Mama Venezia* restaurant. There are evening performances by folkloric groups, a piano bar, and merengue and disco dancing until the wee hours. Other facilities include an 18-hole golf course, a marina, 4 tennis courts, a huge pool with a swim-up bar, a shopping center, a health club, and a casino. Punta Cana (phone: 541-2714; 212-545-8469 from New York; 800-223-9815 from elsewhere in the US; fax: 541-2286).

MODERATE

Club Med A 600-bed village of 3-story bungalows facing long, white, thickly palm-studded beaches. There's a central entertainment complex, a fresh-water pool, a restaurant, and a disco. Tennis (10 courts), water sports, a circus workshop (trapeze, tightrope, clowning), group games (including soccer), a highly regarded Mini-Club for children (those under 5 stay free), nightly entertainment, all meals (with wine or beer; alcoholic drinks outside of meals additional) included. Optional local excursions cost extra. Punta Cana (phone: 567-5228/5229; 800-CLUB-MED from the US; fax: 565-2558).

Hamaca Beach At Boca Chica, the closest beach to Santo Domingo, this new 256-room resort offers its guests both the cosmopolitan attractions of a major city and the natural pleasures of the beach. The well-appointed rooms, good restaurant, hot, jazzy nightlife, and land and water sports combine to make this a fun place to stay. Boca Chica Beach (phone: 562-7475; 800-545-8087 from the US; fax: 566-2354).

El Portillo This property is still charmingly rustic, even though it has been converted to an all-inclusive resort. On a beautiful beach called Las Terrenas, there are 99 rooms, sailing, windsurfing, 2 tennis courts, and volleyball. Liquor and food are available to guests throughout the day. Samaná (phone: 688-5715; fax: 685-0457).

Talanquera Located on the sunny south coast, this is a contemporary enclave of 250 rooms and 1- and 2-bedroom villas. There are 2 tennis courts, horseback riding, biking, a solarium, a pool, water sports on a private beach, a bar, a cafeteria, and a restaurant. Linked in combination packages with *El Embajador* in town. Juan Dolio (phone: 541-6834; fax: 541-1292).

INEXPENSIVE

Punta Garza A cluster of small beachfront cottages with 151 rooms, it's clean and pleasant, with a market and nice beach nearby. A restaurant, bar, and disco complete the picture. Juan Dolio (phone: 526-3506; fax: 526-3814).

EATING OUT

Native Dominican cooking is appealing rather than wildly tempting. Beef can be expensive (Dominicans raise fine cattle, but export most of the meat); there's lots of very fresh fish and seafood, however. Island-grown tomatoes, lettuce, papaya, mangoes, passion fruit, and citrus are delicious. Roast pork and goat are big local favorites, as are *chicharrones* (crisp pork rinds), *chicharrones de pollo* (small pieces of fried chicken), fried *yuca* (cassava), and *moro de habicuelas* (rice and beans). Dominicans are also fond of *sopa criolla dominicana,* a native soup of meat and vegetables; *pastelon,* a baked vegetable cake; *sancocho,* a stew made with anywhere from 7 to 18 ingredients; *mero* (bass) done in half a dozen delicious ways; and such Latin American standbys as *arroz con pollo* (chicken with rice) and *pastilitos* (meat pies). Two desserts are stellar: *cocoyuca,* a yuca flan with chunks of coconut; and *majarete,* a delicious corn pudding. (*Note:* Dominicans like their coffee strong, so decaffeinated is sometimes hard to find.)

Dominican Presidente, Quisqueya, and Bohemia beers are first-rate; so are rum drinks (Brugal and Bermúdez are the Dominican brand names to remember); rum añejo — dark and aged — on the rocks makes a good after-dinner drink.

Dress is often informal, although better restaurants discourage shorts. It's best to check ahead to find out if a jacket is required. At places we list as expensive, expect to pay $40 and up for two, including tip, wine, and drink; at moderate places, $20 to $40; and at inexpensive places, $20 and under. By law, a 10% service charge is added to all bills; extra-special service may be rewarded with an additional tip. There's also an 8% food-and-beverage tax. Still, dining out is surprisingly inexpensive. All telephone numbers are in the 809 area code unless otherwise indicated.

SANTO DOMINGO

EXPENSIVE

El Alcázar In the *Santo Domingo* hotel, this dining spot is a treat for the eyes and the palate. Designed by Oscar de la Renta in a Moorish motif, it sparkles with tiny mirrors and antique mother-of-pearl; yards and yards of tenting fabric are overhead. A different elaborate international lunch buffet is served each day; elegant continental dinners each evening. Reservations advised. Major credit cards accepted. Av. Independencia and Av. Abraham Lincoln (phone: 221-1511).

De Armando A branch of the award-winning restaurant of the same name in Puerto Plata, with the same delicious soups, steaks, lobster and other seafood, and its two famous desserts — *cocoyuca* (coconut chunks in a yuca flan) and *majarete* (corn pudding). Open daily for lunch and dinner. Reservations advised in high season. Major credit cards accepted. Santiago at the corner of José Joaquín Pérez (phone: 689-3534).

Il Buco At Pucci Estorniollo's small, congenial *ristorante,* the antipasto is fabulous, the pasta is homemade, and the seafood fresh as can be. Open daily for dinner only. Reservations advised. MasterCard and Visa accepted. 152-A Arzobispo Meriño (phone: 685-0884).

Café St. Michel First class French and continental food and ambience are found here. The escargots and steak tartare are excellent. Open daily for lunch and dinner. Reservations advised on weekends. Major credit cards accepted. 24 Lope de Vega (phone: 562-4141).

Figaro Italian food, prepared in an open kitchen, is served at this trattoria-type dining spot in the *Ramada Renaissance Jaragua* complex. Choices range from eggplant parmigiana to tournedos Rossini. The delicious vegetable lasagna appears on the regular menu or, on specified nights, is prepared according to the requirements of the spa menu. Try the creamy corn pudding for dessert. Open daily for dinner only. Reservations advised.

Major credit cards accepted. 367 Av. George Washington (phone: 221-2222).

Jai-Alai This eatery is both Peruvian and Dominican. Delicious seafood (try the Peruvian ceviche) is served in a simple setting with tables outdoors and in. Evenings, there's guitar music, sometimes with a Spanish sing-along. Open daily for lunch and dinner. Reservations unnecessary. Major credit cards accepted. 411 Av. Independencia (phone: 685-2409).

Lina Lina herself came from Spain, was once Trujillo's personal chef, and left to open her own place in the *Gran Hotel Lina.* International fare with a strong Spanish accent is featured; everyone talks about the paella. The decor is contemporary, the food, great — especially shrimp dishes and *mero* (bass) done in several ways, including *à la zarzuela* in a casserole faintly flavored with Pernod. Open daily for lunch and dinner. Reservations advised. Major credit cards accepted. Av. Máximo Gómez and Av. 27 de Febrero (phone: 563-5000).

Manhattan Grill The *Ramada Renaissance Jaragua*'s premier eatery, overlooking the casino, offers steaks, lamb, and lobster prepared in an open kitchen. The service is attentive. Member of the Chaîne des Rôtisseurs. Open daily for lunch and dinner. Reservations advised. Major credit cards accepted. 367 Av. George Washington (phone: 221-2222).

La Piazzetta Italian choices served in a gaily decorated dining room, featuring comfortable wicker chairs and murals of tropical plants. Antipasto is served all day. Try the *penne Cavour* — pasta with ham and mushrooms in a cream sauce. Open daily for dinner only. Reservations unnecessary. Major credit cards accepted. At the *Hispaniola Hotel,* Av. Independencia and Av. Abraham Lincoln (phone: 535-7111).

Reina de España A highly praised restaurant featuring international fare, with creole and Spanish specialties. The mixed seafood grill and paella are extremely popular. Open daily for lunch and dinner. Reservations necessary on weekends. Major credit cards accepted. 103 Calle Cervantes (phone: 685-2588).

Vesuvio I One of the best Italian restaurants this side of Italy. The irresistible — and always fresh — fare includes everything from seafood, pasta, homemade cheese, meat, and a feast of antipasto to a dessert tray that will dissolve even the firmest diet resolve. Open daily for lunch and dinner. Reservations advised on weekends. Major credit cards accepted. 521 Av. George Washington (phone: 689-2141).

MODERATE

Crucero del Mar This 71-year-old restaurant at the far east end of the *malécon* is a true find. The location is ideal — close to the colonial district, but far from the crowds — but it's the food that will bring you back. All the local seafood dishes are delicious, and the grouper stuffed with shrimp or lobster and covered with just enough hot sauce is out of this world. If a waiter recommends something, try it. Open daily for breakfast, lunch, and dinner. Reservations unnecessary. MasterCard and Visa accepted. 27 Av. George Washington (phone: 682-1368 or 686-4382).

Fonda de la Atarazana In a restored colonial building across from the Alcázar, this is the ideal lunch spot on a shopping/sightseeing day. It's highly regarded for its native menu (try the pork dishes). At night, musicians perform on the back terrace. Open daily for lunch and dinner. No reservations. Major credit cards accepted. 5 La Atarazana (phone: 689-2900).

El Jardín de Jade Elegant, spacious, leisurely, authentically Oriental — and less expensive than you'd think from the atmosphere. The chef woks his way expertly through five-, seven-, and ten-course meals. Open daily for lunch and dinner. Reservations advised. Major credit cards accepted. In the *Embajador Hotel,* Av. Sarasota (phone: 221-2131).

Mesón de la Cava This have-to-see-it-to-believe-it restaurant is in a natural cave complete with stalagmites and stalactites. The chef's meat dishes are his pride. It's a popular hangout, with good merengue and disco music nightly. From 8 to 10:30 PM, there's folkloric entertainment. Open daily for dinner only. Reservations necessary. Major credit cards accepted. 1 Av. Mirador del Sur (phone: 533-2818).

Vesuvio II Known as *Vesuvito,* the little brother of *Vesuvio I* (see above) serves pasta, pizza, and shrimp that are just as toothsome. Open daily for lunch and dinner; especially popular at lunch. No reservations. Major credit cards accepted. 17 Av. Tiradentes (phone: 562-6060).

INEXPENSIVE

La Fromagerie A popular spot for French fondue and creole cooking in a modern atmosphere. Open daily for lunch and dinner. Reservations advised. Major credit cards accepted. In *Plaza Criolla,* Av. 27 de Febrero at the corner of Máximo Gómez in front of Olympic Park (phone: 567-8606).

Grand Café Adjacent to and owned by the same people as *Café St. Michel* (see above), this establishment features light café fare with a DJ nightly and live jazz and rock on Wednesday nights. Open daily for lunch and dinner. Reservations unnecessary. Major credit cards accepted. Lope de Vega (phone: 562-4141).

Midomodo Spanish and Dominican dishes are specialties at this dining room in the *Hostal Nicolás de Ovando.* The colonial atmosphere makes up for the rather slow service. Try the *fileta fortaleza* and the fried plantains. Open daily from 6 AM to 3 AM. Reservations advised. Major credit cards accepted. 53 Calle Las Damas (phone: 687-3101).

EXPENSIVE

De Armando Guests at Armando Rodríguez Pelegrin's award-winning restaurant feel as though they're dining in an elegant home. The service is topnotch, and the food is splendid. The menu features nine soups (try the delicious pumpkin), super ceviche, steaks, and heavenly lobster Atlántica in a special house sauce. Two of the desserts are themselves worth the visit: *cocoyuca* (a yuca flan with chunks of coconut) and *majarete* (a traditional corn pudding). A guitar trio serenades nightly except on *All Souls' Day* (Nov. 1). Open daily for dinner only. Reservations advised in high season. Major credit cards accepted. 23 Av. Mota (phone: 586-3418).

La Condesa The *Playa Dorada Princess* hotel's elegant dining room features the tenderest local beef and the freshest fish and seafood on its continental menu. The wine list, which is quite lengthy, includes some excellent Chilean vintages. Jacket required. Open daily for breakfast, lunch, and dinner. Reservations advised during holiday seasons. Major credit cards accepted. Playa Dorada (phone: 586-5350).

Flamingo At the *Dorado Naco,* this is one of the best eating spots in Puerto Plata. Try the medallions of beef, veal, and chicken in a medley of three different sauces. Open daily for dinner only. Reservations advised. Major credit cards accepted. Playa Dorada (phone: 586-2019).

Jimmy's One of the two best places in town for continental and Dominican dishes (the other is *De Armando*). Seafood is cooked as the customer chooses; favorite desserts include caramel flan and bread pudding. A very popular spot. Open daily for lunch and dinner. Reservations advised. Major credit cards accepted. 72 Calle Beller (phone: 586-4325).

Neptune With the waves crashing against the windows and a statue of the God of the Sea in plain view, this is the ideal place to dine on seafood, although the chicken pâté appetizer and the shish kebab are also excellent. Open daily for lunch and dinner. Reservations advised. Major credit cards accepted. This *Puerto Plata Beach* resort's restaurant is right on the beach, just across the *malecón* from the hotel (phone: 586-4243).

Los Pinos The finest, freshest local steaks, seafood, vegetables, fruit, and lobster are given the tender, loving culinary care they deserve. This eatery is especially known for its chicken, shrimp, and beef fondue. Open daily for breakfast, lunch, and dinner. Reservations advised. Major credit cards accepted. Av. Hermanas Mirabal (phone: 586-3222).

Valter's Dine in an altogether beautiful setting — a Victorian house with gingerbread trim and a wide porch overlooking a lush jungle of a garden. The menu features soups, salads, pasta, seafood, and meat. Open daily for lunch and dinner. Reservations unnecessary. MasterCard and Visa accepted. Av. Hermanas Mirabal (phone: 586-2329).

INEXPENSIVE

Adolfo's Wienerwald One of several beachside cafés that are great for snacks. This one, with just a few tables and some palm-stump stools at the counter, is also the best breakfast place in town. Go for Adolfo's Austrian omelette, homemade strawberry jam, and the friendly staff. Open daily until 2 AM. Reservations advised. No credit cards accepted. Long Beach (no phone).

Porto Fino An Italian eatery with casual indoor/outdoor dining in a fluorescent-green setting. Try the heavenly lasagna or some of the Dominican dishes. Crab creole with French fries is a bargain. Open daily for lunch and dinner. Reservations unnecessary. Major credit cards accepted. Av. Hermanas Mirabal (phone: 586-2858).

SOSÚA

MODERATE

Marco Polo Club The most scenic spot in Sosúa for drinking and dining, with a fabulous view of Sosúa Bay. Open daily for lunch and dinner. Reservations advised. Major credit cards accepted. 2 Av. Martínez (phone: 571-2757).

INEXPENSIVE

Tree Top Lounge An airy, upstairs meeting place for drinks and backgammon. The decor is tropical, with rattan, ceiling fans, and lots of greenery. Order a pizza from the pizzeria downstairs (15 varieties from which to choose) and relax with a piña-banana colada, the house specialty. Open daily from 4 PM to 3 AM. Reservations unnecessary. Visa and MasterCard accepted. Pedro Clisante (phone: 571-2141).

ELSEWHERE IN THE COUNTRY

EXPENSIVE

Casa del Río Perched on a cliff, with breathtaking views of river and valley, this *Casa de Campo* eatery provides a rustic setting for nicely done fresh fish and seafood dishes. Open daily for lunch and dinner. Reservations necessary. Major credit cards accepted. Altos de Chavón (phone: 523-3333, ext. 2345).

La Fonda Dominican specialties — seafood, beans, rice — are served at this dining spot in the stylized historic village that is part of the *Casa de Campo* resort. Open daily for lunch and dinner. Reservations advised. Major credit cards accepted. Altos de Chavón (phone: 523-3333).

La Piazzetta Ensconced in *Casa de Campo*'s re-created 15th-century village above the winding green Chavón River, this *ristorante* supplies a romantic change of scene. Mood and food are elegant Italian, with excellent pasta, carpaccio, seafood, and a good wine list, plus violin music and candlelight. Open daily for dinner. Reservations necessary. Major credit cards accepted. Altos de Chavón (phone: 523-3333, ext. 2339).

MODERATE

Las Américas Generous portions of fresh and beautifully prepared seafood, creole dishes, and international fare are served in a charming atmosphere (local art, paddle fans). Popular with the locals, this place also has great margaritas, good service. Open daily for lunch and dinner. Reservations necessary. Major credit cards accepted. 52 Calle Castillo Marqués, La Romana (phone: 556-4582).

Shish Kebab What's a nice Lebanese restaurant like this doing in a small eastern Caribbean sugar-mill town? Well, a Lebanese chef married a Dominican woman, and now they make beautiful *kebbehs* (Middle Eastern meatballs rolled in wheat and fried) and *pasteles en hojas* (Dominican spiced ground meat wrapped in plantain dough and cooked in a plantain leaf) together. They also do great shakes (banana, pineapple, papaya, orange) and a luscious concoction of orange juice, milk, sugar, and vanilla called *morir soñando* (literally, "to die dreaming"). Open daily. No reservations. Major credit cards accepted. 32 Calle Castillo Marqués, La Romana (no phone).

INEXPENSIVE

Café de Sol An open-air place for pizza and ice-cream extravaganzas. Open daily for lunch and dinner. No reservations. No credit cards. Altos de Chavón (phone: 523-3333).

WORTH A DETOUR **The picturesque fishing village of Bayahibe, about 20 miles from *Casa de Campo*, has two good, simple restaurants — *Bayahibe* and *La Bahía* — that serve locally caught fish and lobster (and great French fries) — in an open-air setting. Prices at both are expensive to moderate; both accept major credit cards.**

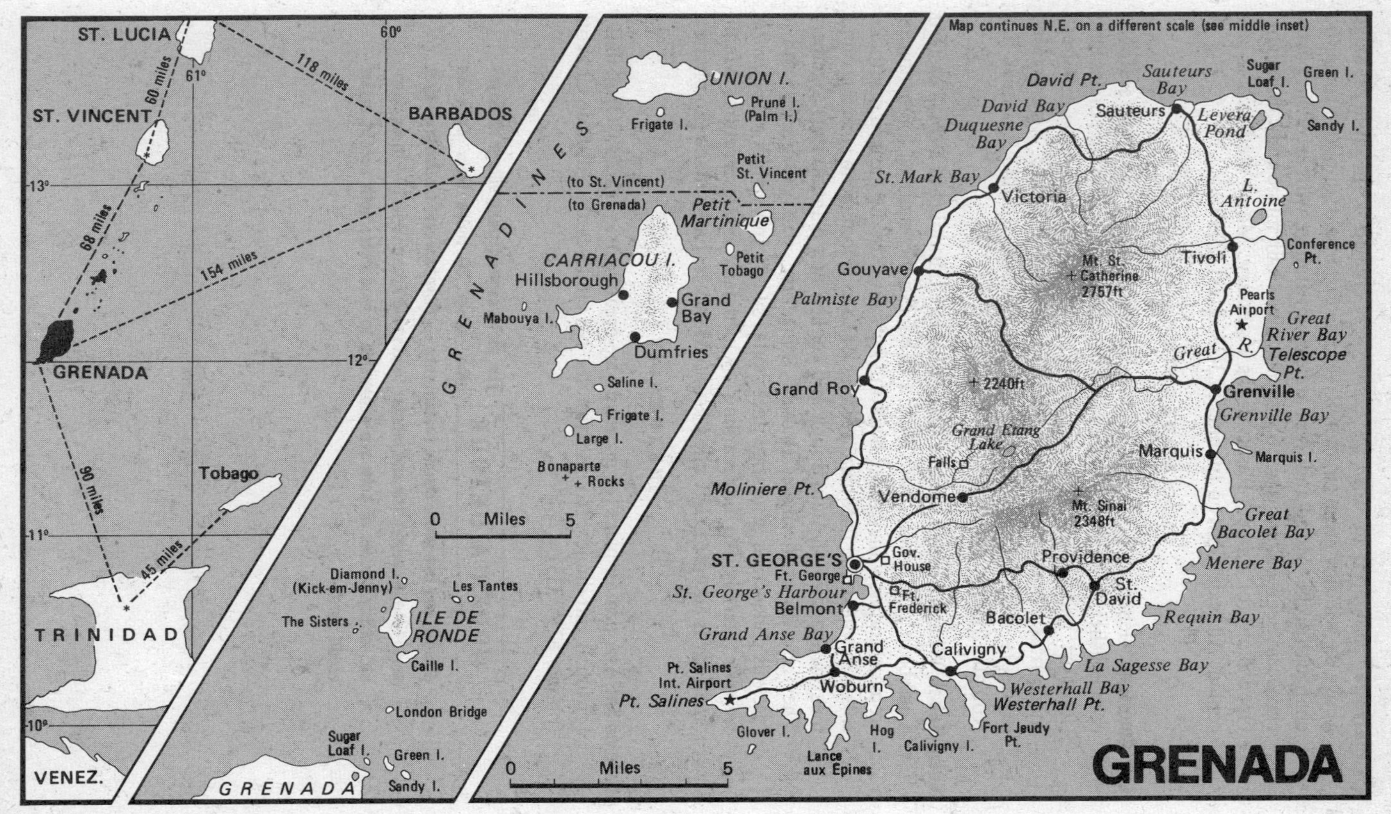
GRENADA
Map continues N.E. on a different scale (see middle inset)
ST. LUCIA
ST. VINCENT
BARBADOS
GRENADA
TOBAGO
TRINIDAD
VENEZ.
60 miles
68 miles
118 miles
154 miles
90 miles
45 miles
61°
60°
13°
12°
11°
10°
GRENADINES
UNION I.
Prune I. (Palm I.)
Frigate I.
Petit St. Vincent
(to St. Vincent)
(to Grenada)
Petit Martinique
Petit Tobago
CARRIACOU I.
Hillsborough
Grand Bay
Dumfries
Mabouya I.
Saline I.
Frigate I.
Large I.
Bonaparte Rocks
0 Miles 5
Diamond I. (Kick-em-Jenny)
Les Tantes
The Sisters
ILE DE RONDE
Caille I.
London Bridge
Sugar Loaf I.
Green I.
Sandy I.
GRENADA
David Pt.
Sauteurs Bay
Sugar Loaf I.
Green I.
Sandy I.
David Bay
Sauteurs
Levera Pond
Duquesne Bay
St. Mark Bay
Victoria
L. Antoine
Conference Pt.
Tivoli
Gouyave
Mt. St. Catherine 2757ft
Palmiste Bay
Pearls Airport
Great River Bay
Great R.
Telescope Pt.
Grand Roy
2240ft
Grenville
Grenville Bay
Grand Etang Lake
Falls
Marquis
Marquis I.
Moliniere Pt.
Vendome
Mt. Sinai 2348ft
Great Bacolet Bay
Menere Bay
ST. GEORGE'S
Gov. House
Providence
Ft. George
St. George's Harbour
Ft. Frederick
St. David
Belmont
Bacolet
Requin Bay
Grand Anse Bay
Grand Anse
Calivigny
La Sagesse Bay
Pt. Salines Int. Airport
Woburn
Westerhall Bay
Westerhall Pt.
Pt. Salines
Glover I.
Hog I.
Calivigny I.
Fort Jeudy Pt.
Lance aux Epines
0 Miles 5

Grenada

Grenada has been called "all the Caribbean islands in miniature" for good reason. Like so many of its neighbors, it is of volcanic origin, it is endowed with lush green mountains and beautiful beaches, it was discovered by Columbus, and it has had a dramatic history, from the seesawing French-English struggles of the 17th and 18th centuries to its own 20th-century quest for identity and independence.

Columbus found Conception Bay — now called Levera Beach — at the island's northern tip in 1498. Though whether he actually came ashore is open to debate, it is certain that he never explored the island in depth. (That failure is ironic in that of all the islands he was to visit, Grenada came closest to meeting his original goal — a source of spices accessible by sailing west from Europe instead of east.) Spanish sailors dubbed the island Granada because its hills reminded them of home. The French, in their turn, referred to it as Grenade; and the British made the final adjustment to Grenada (pronounced Gren-*ay*-da).

In the century and a half that followed its discovery by Columbus, neither the British nor the French were able to establish settlements on the island. It was not until 1650 that a party of 200 Frenchmen sailed from Martinique and succeeded in purchasing land from the chief of the Carib people living there — literally for some glass beads and a selection of metal knives and hatchets. Soon the Carib, realizing their chief's mistake, began a futile struggle to retake the island from the French. After a series of battles, the 40 remaining Carib men threw the tribe's women and children over the northern precipice (now called Morne des Sauteurs, or Carib's Leap) and followed them to their deaths on the jagged rocks below.

But this bloody event did not give the French undisputed possession of the island. The familiar French-British conflict began anew on Grenada. Amassing troops at opposite ends of the island, the two nations built substantial fortifications and battled stubbornly for decades. The capital city of St. George's is flanked by two impressive historic landmarks: Fort George, built by the French in 1705, is on a promontory overlooking the harbor, and overlooking the town on the southern part of the island is Fort Frederick, begun by the French and completed by the British after they took control of the island as a result of the 1783 Treaty of Versailles. Grenada became a Crown Colony in 1877. After an abortive attempt to form a federation with nine other UK-associated islands, Grenada was declared a British Associated State in 1967.

During the 1960s, Grenada emerged as one of the eastern Caribbean's first tourist destinations. St. George's, with a superb natural harbor, is perhaps the most beautiful Caribbean town. In addition, there are lovely mountains, waterfalls, colorful flowers, fine white and black sand beaches, and the sea.

But the early 1970s brought the issue of independence, and with it an identity crisis that split island politics right down the middle. In late 1973 and early 1974, a general strike actually closed the island down, but in February 1974, independence was at last proclaimed, and the island slowly started to recover. Unfortunately, Prime Minister Sir Eric Gairy proved a less than inspiring administrator, seemingly more interested in black magic and UFOs than in island economics. When his dictatorial regime was ousted in March 1979 by Maurice Bishop's New Jewel Movement, hopes rose. But they fell abruptly once Prime Minister Bishop, a protégé of Cuban President Fidel Castro, invited Cuban military advisers to Grenada. Visitors began staying away.

On October 25, 1983, units of the US Marines and Army landed on Grenada to spearhead the rout of a combined Grenadian/Cuban defense force. Along with forces from Barbados, Dominica, Jamaica, St. Lucia, and St. Vincent, the US troops deposed the former colleagues of Maurice Bishop, who had had Bishop assassinated a week earlier for not being radical enough. The lessons of its turmoil have been deeply impressed on the country, especially a keen shock at Grenadians having killed Grenadians (many died with Bishop prior to the intervention). More than one American tourist has been told, "You rescued us."

Grenada's civil authority is now on its own; the US and eastern Caribbean troops — supplemental police, really — have departed. Political stability appears assured. Since March 1990, Nicholas Brathwaite of the National Democratic Congress has been Prime Minister; his plan is to keep the flow of visitors rising without making major changes to the island.

Bolstered by US aid, substantial improvements in basic services and island infrastructure have been made, and the outlook is for steady, moderate tourism growth. Touch-tone telephones and cable TV are no longer curiosities, and paved roads have halved travel times to most parts of the island. The once controversial, Cuban-constructed airport runway at Point Salines now lies next to a full-fledged, comfortable, modern international terminal building, complete with duty-free shopping. It is not surprising that Grenada's tourism numbers have been growing steadily each year; recently, an increasing number of European visitors have contributed to the growth.

For visitors who have come to love the island as it was (and still mostly is), perhaps slow change is best. Grenada retains a lush, unspoiled character that any neighbor nation might covet.

Grenada At-a-Glance

FROM THE AIR

Grenada, the southernmost island of the Windward Antilles, 90 miles north of Trinidad, looks like an oval fish swimming northeast with its mouth open as though to swallow the tiny islands of the Grenadines strung between it and the island of St. Vincent 68 miles northeast. The "mouth" of the fish is Sauteurs Bay; its tail is the beach-bordered peninsula called Point Salines, extending below the capital of St. George's (pop. 11,000) and forming the island's southeastern tip.

The island is only 21 miles long and 12 miles wide at its widest point; its 120 square miles encompass green jungle-covered mountains, racing rivers and streams, waterfalls and lakes, and a ring of beaches of extraordinary beauty. The central mountain range, reaching heights of over 2,000 feet, divides the island diagonally in half, with stretches of desert and cactus to the southwest and cane fields, coconut groves, and banana and spice plantations stretching from the southeast to the northwest.

The highest, wettest, coolest, most densely forested areas of the island are found near the city of Grenville, halfway up the eastern coast. The route from there to the southwest, where most of the hotels are located, passes through the island's driest section. The drive from Point Salines International Airport to the hotel district takes 10 minutes.

Fifteen miles off Grenada's northern tip lie the nation's major dependencies, Carriacou and Petit Martinique, which are part of the island group known as the Grenadines.

SPECIAL PLACES

ST. GEORGE'S Grenada's capital is one of the Caribbean's most picturesque ports. Its landlocked inner harbor is actually the crater of a dead volcano. The waterfront, known as the Carenage, is lined with pink, ocher, and brick-red commercial buildings and warehouses, many of which date from the 18th century. Behind them, narrow streets climb green hills dotted with neat red- and green-roofed houses. The Esplanade (or Outer Harbour) area of the city is on St. George's Bay; it's connected to the Carenage area via Sendall Tunnel, a one-way traffic and pedestrian passage cut through St. George's Point, which divides the harbor and the bay.

The French built St. George's in 1732, and French architecture — like the wrought-iron work along the Esplanade and Market Square — survives among the British Georgian–West Indian buildings in a charming blend of European and tropical island styles. Wood has been a forbidden building material since a number of disastrous fires in the island's earliest days, so most buildings are built of brick brought over as ballast on British trading ships.

The most appealing sights in St. George's are vistas of the city and harbor from high points around the town. If you're sightseeing by taxi, let the driver know you'd like to stop wherever the view is especially fine, such as the lookout point built at the Ft. George Cultural Landmark downtown. Better still, take a good hour to walk and climb around the city (it's not very big), sampling the view whenever you please.

Make your first stop the Grenada Board of Tourism on the Carenage to pick up maps and sightseeing information. Then stroll a little farther east to the Botanical Gardens and Zoo (open daily), with tropical trees and flowers, and rare Caribbean birds and animals. Walk westward along the edge of the Carenage, where schooners, sailboats, yachts, and dinghies are tied up to concrete posts containing old spiked cannon. Call at the *Grenada National Museum* (Young St.) which offers both historic exhibits and a cool refuge on a too sunny day. The museum is open weekdays from 9 AM to 3 PM; admission charge. Above, on the hill, stands the town's dominant structure, Fort George, built by the French as Fort Royal in 1705; it is now the headquarters of the Grenada police force. On its ramparts, ancient cannon, still used for official salutes, are aimed out across the water.

From the fort, go back down the hill, turn right, and follow Young Street to the Carenage, then go right, right again, and left through Sendall Tunnel, built by the French in the 18th century. This is the west side of town, where the principal shops run along the waterfront Esplanade and up Granby Street. Follow Granby 1 block east to Market Square, where on Saturday mornings Grenadian women in bright cotton dresses, aprons, and wide straw hats pile their produce — mangoes, coconuts, spices, pineapples and paw paws (papayas), among others — on rough cloths and flour bags for sale. Also on the square, the *Straw Mart* offers crafts made of straw and coconut. (There are also tortoiseshell items here, but don't buy them; they cannot be imported into the US.)

From Market Square head east on Granby, which turns into Lucas, to Fort Frederick on Richmond Hill. Construction of the fort was started by the French in 1779 and completed by the British in 1783; its battlements command a magnificent view of the city and its harbors. Nearby is Government House, the residence of the queen's official representative, the governor-general. It was built in the late 18th century; later additions — particularly the 1887 façade — are not all considered architectural triumphs. But the view of the port, the harbor, and the town is indisputably beautiful.

Turn back down Lucas Street. At the Church Street intersection, turn right up the hill to visit the Roman Catholic cathedral, where dark plaster saints oversee both petitioners and their prayers. Also on Church Street, left of Lucas, is the 166-year-old Anglican church. It's pink with heavy stained glass windows, frescoes, and stone memorial tablets carved in England and dedicated to British soldiers who fought against the French. Farther along Church Street, St. Andrew's Presbyterian Church, built in 1830, is crowned with the square-spired clock tower that's a trademark of the town skyline. After a visit (or an admiring glance in its direction), head back down the hill to the Carenage for lunch or a rum punch at *Rudolf's* or the *Nutmeg* (try a Nutmeg Special), two nearby restaurants popular with locals and visitors alike (see *Eating Out*).

Two lush spots not far from St. George's are worth visiting for their lavish landscapes. Bay Gardens, about a 20-minute drive east of town in the suburb of St. Paul, encompasses 6 dense acres of tropical flora and mostly feathered fauna (you may not see the island's favorite pripri birds, but you'll certainly hear them). For about $1, a guided tour will introduce you to an abundance of exotic fruits and spices in their natural state. The feeling is a little like strolling through a primitive island painting. The gardens are open daily from 7 AM to sunset.

Annandale Falls are a 20-minute drive northeast of St. George's, just off Grand Etang Road. Here, young boys eagerly climb the surrounding tall trees to pluck orchids for visiting ladies, and show off for tips by diving off the top of the falls into the placid pool 50 feet below.

NORTH OF ST. GEORGE'S

To explore the spice country, coastal beaches, and villages of the island's northern reaches, head north out of St. George's along the western coastal road. You'll pass curving bays, small seaside settlements, and shores where fishermen with small boats and big nets bring in their catches.

A NOTE OF PERSPECTIVE **Most of Grenada's limited wealth flows to the southwest corner of the island, where tourism is concentrated. Grenadians are among the friendliest, most courteous people in the Caribbean, and a vast majority favored the US–East Caribbean intervention. But in the many small settlements in parishes north and east of St. George's, where most people are poor and have few immediate prospects for significant advancement, they are likely to be less outgoing and to resent being photographed without permission.**

CONCORDE FALLS Not far off the western coastal road, a turnoff leads to the falls, a wildly beautiful yet accessible picnic destination. Spread out your lunch (most hotels will be happy to pack one; order the night before) in a hideaway setting festooned with liana vines, feathery rock plants, giant elephant ears, and other greenery, while water cascades down a 50-foot fall into a blue-green pool. Afterward, you can swim beneath the waterfall, then hike along the river through the tropical forest to the more remote second fall.

GOUYAVE Back on the western coastal road, head farther north to the village of Gouyave, which looks like an island painting, with weathered red-roofed houses along the sea wall dwarfed by the Anglican and Catholic churches behind them. Gouyave is a center of the nutmeg and mace industry (both are produced from a single fruit). The nutmeg processing plant is open to visitors on weekdays from 8 AM to 4 PM, and on Saturdays from 8 AM to noon. Just inland, on the Dougaldston Estate, you can see most of the island's spices growing naturally, and being sun-dried and sorted. The estate is open to the public weekdays from 9 AM to 3:30 PM and Saturdays from 9 AM to noon (phone: 444-8213).

SAUTEURS From Gouyave proceed along the coast to Sauteurs, at the north end of the island. Behind St. Patrick's Roman Catholic church are the cliffs called Carib's Leap, where, in the 17th century, the last of the Carib Indians are said to have jumped to their death rather than submit to slavery under the French. East of Sauteurs is pretty, palm-edged Levera Beach, an ideal spot for a picnic and a swim (if the Atlantic is not in one of its occasionally rough moods). Nearby is the Levera National Park and Bird Sanctuary, with bird watching lookouts, and marked nature trails that lead around Levera Pond. The sulfurous Chambord Boiling Springs are also in this area. Not far south is the River Antoine Rum Distillery (phone: 442-7109), an amazing establishment dating from the 18th century and one of the last agro-industrial enterprises in the hemisphere still powered by a waterwheel. The foreman is happy to provide guided tours on weekdays between 8 AM and 3 PM, and to explain the process of turning sugarcane into potent rum. Plans for building a new bridge to make this attraction more accessible have been stalled for several years; check with the tourist office. If the bridge is not ready, your driver will know whether the river is low enough to ford safely.

EXTRA SPECIAL **Lunch at Betty Mascoll's *Morne Fendue* in St. Patrick's Parish near Sauteurs, a 90-minute drive from St. George's, is an ideal stop on any island tour. This plantation house, home to three generations of Betty's family, is worth a visit as much for her stories and pleasant presence as for the food, which is island fare, handsomely served and delicious. The menu might include *callaloo,* ginger chicken, savory pepper pot, vegetables from the garden, and homemade guava ice cream. A meal will cost about $18 per person; reservations are necessary (phone: 442-9330).**

GRENVILLE From Sauteurs, head south along the east coast to Grenville, Grenada's second city. There are two lively markets here: the waterfront fish market, which does a brisk business every day except Sunday; and Saturday's fruit and vegetable market. Visitors are welcome at the spice factory at the edge of town, where spice baskets and aromatic souvenirs are sold.

INLAND ROAD From Grenville, turn inland toward the heart of the island along a road that passes small spice farms, girls sorting nutmegs, and cacao plantations with trays of chocolate brown pods drying in the sun. Follow the road as it winds up and up into the mountains, with each hairpin curve bringing a surprise view of lush, fern-covered hillsides, nutmeg trees brimming with yellow fruit, cacao and banana groves, and mountain streams tumbling toward the sea. The road reaches its peak at Grand Etang

National Park (phone: 440-7425), a national reserve filled with giant ferns, towering trees, and tropical flowers in a profusion of colors. If you are quiet — and lucky — you may also see luminescent blue butterflies, mona monkeys, mongooses, and the emerald-throated hummingbird. Hikers can follow the path through the rain forest to Grand Etang Lake, a shimmering cobalt lake that fills the crater of Grenada's extinct volcano. The park also has a nature-oriented interpretation center, a snack bar, and a souvenir shop. The return trip down the same road offers tantalizing glimpses of blue-and-white-coved shoreline all the way to St. George's.

SOUTH OF ST. GEORGE'S

South of St. George's lie the superb beaches and rambling resorts of the Grand Anse and L'Anse aux Epines districts. To tour this end of the island, follow the Royal Drive, so named because it's the route along which Elizabeth II was escorted during her 1966 visit. Leaving St. George's, past Government House and the panoramic overlook at Richmond Hill, the drive proceeds down to Westerhall Point, a beautifully landscaped residential development on the southern coast, through the fishing village of Woburn, and the cane fields of Woodlands. At La Sagesse Nature Center (phone: 444-6458), there are plenty of trails, wild birds, a banana plantation with guided nature walks, and a lovely beach for relaxing. Past the nature center, closer to the eastern side of the island, is Marquis Village, renowned for its expert straw weavers. Here artisans weave wild palm leaves into sturdy hats, baskets, handbags, and placemats.

GRENADINES

CARRIACOU One of Grenada's island dependencies, it lies 23 miles northeast of St. George's, a 13-square-mile retreat where Grenadians "get away from it all." It is a special favorite with yachtsmen. In winter, the chain of hills extending down its center is fresh and green; in summer, the land dries to pale beige, and islanders declare "leggo" season — when goats, cows, and sheep are let go to forage for themselves and gardeners guard their flowers with their lives. Whatever the season, Carriacou's attractions include excellent beaches and natural harbors (Tyrell Bay is especially beautiful), plus the prospect of relaxed living among people who seem genuinely to enjoy having visitors.

Ruins of greathouses in the hills testify to Grenada's once-thriving sugar industry; now cotton, peanuts, and limes are grown on the island. Its strongest surviving heritages are African (most black islanders can trace their ancestry to a particular tribe) and Scottish. The McLarens, MacLaurences, McQuilkins, MacFarlands, and Comptons of Windward on the east side of the island still hand-build some of the Caribbean's finest sailing workboats. The sprinkling of goat's blood and holy water at launchings recognizes both cultural influences.

Excepting the annual August regatta — when 2,000 people have been known to squeeze themselves onto the island and 300 or 400 manage to dance all night — launchings are Carriacou's biggest parties, sometimes lasting for days. Otherwise, things are pretty quiet here. Visitors laze, swim, sail, snorkel, and dive (nearby Sandy Island has some interesting reef formations), search for seashells, poke about the ruins, and gather at dusk in Hillsborough, the island's only town. From his Hillsborough office, a senior executive officer, supervised by a parliamentary secretary, administers the affairs of both Carriacou and Petit Martinique, the island 3 miles due east.

PETIT MARTINIQUE The residents of this island have a reputation as master seamen (each year they carry off the lion's share of prizes from the regatta) and — some say — smugglers. Whether or not the latter is true, it has inspired some wonderful stories, such as this one, told by Frances Kay in *This — Is Carriacou:* "A very strict customs official from Grenada was sent to Petit Martinique to make a thorough check. When he arrived, he found the entire population standing mournfully around an open grave. 'Who died?' he asked. 'Nobody,' came the matter-of-fact reply. 'We dug it for you.' "

These days, Petit Martinique's approximately 600 French-descended inhabitants are polite, even pleasant, to sailors who drop anchor overnight in their harbor. But there are few accommodations for visitors on this 3-square-mile island. Privacy is still an important commodity.

Grenada's other island dependencies — Ile de Ronde, Kick-em-Jenny (possibly from *caye qui gene,* or "troublesome shoal"), Green Bird, and Conference among them — are small, picturesque land dots, important only as landmarks for cruising yachtsmen. Other Grenadine islands are administered by St. Vincent, which serves as the administrative center for the entire chain.

EXTRA SPECIAL **Grenada's People-to-People program puts travelers in touch with Grenadians who have similar jobs, hobbies, and interests. Visitors may play a round of golf, go to a church service, have a traditional island meal, or simply see the sights with a local resident. People who have participated in this program have found it to be both enlightening and a lot of fun. There's no charge, though you might want to pick up part of the tab for any excursion. To make arrangements before arriving, contact *New Trends Tours,* PO Box 438, St. George's, Grenada, West Indies (phone: 444-1236; fax: 444-4836).**

Sources and Resources

TOURIST INFORMATION

The Grenada Board of Tourism on the Carenage in St. George's (phone: 440-2279, 440-3377, or 440-2001) can supply information, maps, literature, and answers to visitors' questions. They can brief you on excursions to and lodging on Carriacou and Petit Martinique too. Office hours are from 9 AM until 4 PM. For information on Grenada tourist offices in the US, see GETTING READY TO GO.

LOCAL COVERAGE Consult the *Grenada Voice* or the *Informer,* the island's two weekly newspapers, for sports schedules and special events information, or buy the *Griot* ($6), an arts and entertainment magazine published every 2 months. Books about Grenada and the West Indies can be found at *Sea 'Change* on the Carenage, and at *St. George's Bookshop* on Halifax Street.

RADIO AND TELEVISION

There is one television station and two radio stations.

TELEPHONE

The area code for Grenada is 809.

ENTRY REQUIREMENTS

Visitors to Grenada must present a valid passport or proof of citizenship (a birth certificate or voter's registration card *plus* a photo ID), and an ongoing or return ticket. A departure tax of $10 is collected at the airport.

CLIMATE AND CLOTHES

At the beach, the daytime temperatures stay close to 80F (27C) year-round, with cooling trade winds. In the mountains (around Grand Etang Lake, for example), it can be as much as 10 degrees cooler; you may even be glad you brought a light sweater along. During the rainy season (June to December), there's a shower for about an hour or so almost every day, and the countryside is at its greenest. Casual, lightweight resort clothes are most comfortable and appropriate for both men and women. Though bathing suits and short shorts are fine on the beach, they are frowned on in St. George's. In the evenings — especially during the winter season — people tend to dress up a bit for dinner in the better hotels and restaurants. But men can leave sports coats at home, and women should skip high heels. If you plan to hike around the Grand Etang Lake, bring some sturdy sneakers.

MONEY

Grenada's official currency is the Eastern Caribbean dollar (EC); $1 US equals approximately $2.68 EC. On the islands, prices are usually quoted in EC dollars, but sometimes shopkeepers will quote them in US dollars to US citizens in an effort to be helpful. Know which dollars are being quoted before committing to a purchase or a cab ride. Banking hours are 8 AM to noon Mondays through Thursdays; 8 AM to noon and 2:30 to 5 PM on Fridays. Traveler's checks are accepted by stores, restaurants, and hotels; most honor major credit cards as well. No shops offer discounts for payment in US dollars. All prices in this chapter are quoted in US dollars unless noted otherwise.

LANGUAGE

Grenada is a former British Crown Colony, and English is spoken everywhere with a Caribbean lilt. You occasionally may hear islanders speaking among themselves in their own patois — mostly French with some African words and rhythms mixed in.

TIME

Grenada is on atlantic standard time, 1 hour ahead of eastern standard time (when it's noon in New York, it's 1 PM in Grenada); during daylight saving time, Grenada and New York are in sync.

CURRENT

It's 230 volts, 50 cycles AC, so an adapter is needed for American appliances. Some hotels supply them, but it wouldn't hurt to bring one along.

TIPPING

Hotels add a 10% service charge to your bill, which takes care of bellhops, waiters and waitresses, bartenders, and maids. If you visit a dining room at a hotel you're not staying at, or at non-hotel restaurants, tip 10% to 15% of the check. Taxi drivers do not expect tips unless they help you with your baggage at the airport (give $1 or so unless your load is very heavy).

GETTING AROUND

BUS The older models, painted kindergarten colors, take off from the Market Square in St. George's for all parts of the island, but since seats are boards, springs are hard to come by, and schedules are erratic, they aren't recommended for anything except photographs. Many visitors have taken to the minibuses that travel between island points and charge from $1.25 to $4.50 EC, depending on your destination.

CAR RENTAL A good idea if you enjoy exploring on your own. Rates run from about $50 to $60 a day, $275 a week with unlimited mileage in winter; they are somewhat lower in summer. Gas — at about $2.50 per gallon — is extra. Reliable agencies include *Royston's* (phone: 444-4316), *McIntyre Bros.* (phone: 440-2044 or 440-2045), and *Spice Isle/Avis Rentals* (phone: 440-3936). All will deliver cars to the airport and pick them up at the end of your stay. Visitors must obtain a local driving permit, which costs about $11. They can be purchased from most car rental companies and at the fire station on the Carenage. Remember: Driving is on the *left,* British-style.

SEA EXCURSIONS The glass-bottom boat *Rhum Runner* (phone: 440-2198) sails from St. George's Harbour Saturdays at 7 PM for a 2½-hour sunset cocktail cruise; the fare — about $12 per person — includes rum punches and steel band and limbo music to watch fish by. Reef trips may be scheduled on the days when cruise ships are in port; call to check.

Five times a week, freighters sail from Grenada to Carriacou, leaving anytime between 7 and 10 AM for the 3- to 4-hour trip; fare is about $8 per person one way, $12 round-trip. The steamship M/V *Eastward* (phone: 440-3422) travels between Grenada and Carriacou and can be chartered. Check with the tourist board for current details.

TAXI While taxi rates are fixed, the cabs are unmetered, so be sure to establish the price of the trip with the driver before getting into the cab (at night, add a $4 surcharge). From the airport, the ride to hotels in L'Anse aux Epines costs about $10; to Grand Anse, about $10; to St. George's, about $12. From St. George's to most hotels at the southern end of the island, fixed rates run from $6 to $10 per cabload plus a 10% tip. Although not specially trained as such, island taxi drivers are good guides and can tell you lots about the island. Hotels can arrange all-day, around-the-island cab tours for about $15 per hour. Usually, the cabs are shared by two or three people, depending on the size of the car and how cozy you like to be. Water taxis will whisk you from the beach at Grand Anse to town and back for $2 per person each way — it's cheaper than a land taxi, but you might get your feet wet.

TOURS *Henry's Tours, Ltd.* (phone: 444-5313) and *Arnold's Tours* (phone: 444-1167) arrange custom excursions for adventurous and fit tourists who wish to hike into the interior for a picnic, to swim by a jungle waterfall that few Grenadians even see, or to visit lakes and other natural wonders. Hiking segments range from 1 hour to a half day. On Carriacou, Bryan White of *Carriacou Tours and Travel* (phone: 443-7134) is a friendly, knowledgeable guide offering 90-minute tours of the island; the cost is $24 for up to four people.

INTER-ISLAND FLIGHTS

BWIA and *LIAT* both have flights to Grenada from Trinidad and Barbados; *LIAT* also flies between Antigua and Grenada (with as many as 7 stops en route) and has daily flights to Carriacou. *New Trends Tours* (phone: 444-1236) offers flights to Union Island in the Grenadines with a return trip by schooner, and day trips to Margarita Island and Venezuela. *Grenair* (phone: 444-4845) provides air taxi service to nearby islands, as well as St. Lucia, St. Vincent, and Barbados.

SPECIAL EVENTS

Carnival is Grenada's national festival, celebrated for 4 days and nights in early August with lots of steel band and calypso music, processions, pageants, and beauty contests, and climaxing in a "jump-up" parade of massed bands, floats, and street dancers. Carriacouans prefer their own smaller but equally festive "old-fashioned" pre-*Lenten Carnival;* they really cut loose at their early August *Regatta.* Other holidays when banks and businesses are closed: *New Year's Day, Independence Day* (February 7), *Good Friday, Easter Monday, Labour Day* (first Monday in May), *Whitmonday, Corpus Christi, Emancipation Day* (first Monday and Tuesday in August), *Thanksgiving Day* (commemorating the intervention of US and other military forces against the Communist-backed People's Revolutionary Government, on October 25), *Christmas,* and *Boxing Day* (December 26).

SHOPPING

The big-tag items are luxury imports (especially British) at prices that aren't literally duty-free, but close. The little-tag buys are uniquely Grenadian, such as the woven "spice baskets" full of fresh island-grown nutmeg, mace, cinnamon, cloves, and more. Roughly a thousand times more aromatic than those fading on the supermarket shelves back home, they make great souvenirs for yourself, or gifts for favorite cooks. *Straw Mart* (on Granby and Young Sts.; no phone) and market ladies have big supplies; *Sea 'Change* (on the Carenage; phone: 440-3402) has individually packed spices; and the *Grand Anse Shopping Centre* has strolling spice vendors every day. As for imported buys, brand names like Liberty, Pringle, Waterford, Wedgwood, Bing & Grøndahl, and Dior — at 40% to 60% below stateside prices — will tempt you.

Of the three main shopping areas, the largest is on the Esplanade side of Fort George around Market Square and in the shops facing the harbor along Melville Street; the second is on the Carenage side along the waterfront and on Young Street; and the third, and fastest-growing, is in and near the *Grand Anse Shopping Centre,* handiest to hotels. Some good places include the following:

BEST LITTLE LIQUOR STORE Good selection of local rum, vodka, and gin, as well as imported wines and spirits. Two locations: the Carenage (phone: 440-2198) and Point Salines Airport (phone: 440-3422).

BON VOYAGE Duty-free crystal, china, watches, and jewelry. Located both on the Carenage (phone: 440-4217), and at the airport (phone: 444-4165).

CREATION ARTS AND CRAFTS Craftwork by artisans from Grenada and other Caribbean islands, as well as Africa. Also features leather shoes and handbags, batik, and jewelry. The Carenage (phone: 440-0570).

FRANGIPANI Tie-dyed batik, patchwork apparel, and watercolors by local artists. The Carenage (no phone).

GIFT SHOP Well known for its duty-free crystal by Waterford, Orrefors, Lalique, and Daum; it also has Coalport and Wedgwood china, watches, and jewelry. In the *Grand Anse Shopping Centre* (phone: 444-4408).

GIFTS REMEMBERED Locally made handicrafts, straw work, and jewelry. Cross St. (phone: 440-2482).

GITTEN'S DUTY FREE Name-brand cosmetics and perfumes, including Clinique, Estée Lauder, Calvin Klein, Christian Dior, Oscar de la Renta, and Ralph Lauren. Located in the Carenage (phone: 440-3174) and in the departure lounge at the airport (phone: 444-4101).

GRAND BAZAAR One-of-a-kind, hand-painted play and party clothes. Considering the designs are originals, the prices are very reasonable. Halifax St. (phone: 440-3065).

IMAGINE High-quality gift items, crafts, and resortwear from Grenada and other islands. In the *Grand Anse Shopping Centre* (phone: 444-4028).

SPICE ISLAND PERFUMES Makes and sells scents and potpourris concocted from island flowers and spices. A real treat for the nose, and a great place to buy locally made perfumes, colognes, lotions, and even sunscreens. The Carenage (phone: 440-2006).

ST. GEORGE'S BOOKSHOP Wide selection of news magazines and works by Caribbean writers. Halifax St. (phone: 440-2309).

TIKAL Cheerfully stocked with straw bags, hats, baskets, mats, rugs, crafted mobiles, shell jewelry, local pottery, and batik, plus some imported porcelain and glass. Easily the best shop in town for browsing. Young St. (phone: 440-2310).

YELLOW POUI Run by Jim Rudin, formerly of the New York *Museum of Modern Art,* this gallery displays the best artwork — be it paintings, sculpture, prints, or maps — from Grenada and neighboring Caribbean islands as well as from North America. Above *Gifts Remembered* on Cross St. (phone: 440-3001).

SPORTS

Not surprisingly, considering the splendid white and black sand beaches and calm blue sea that surround it, Grenada's active sports life is centered on the shoreline and in the water.

BOATING Sailors rate the sailing conditions from Grenada north through the Grenadines to St. Vincent as some of the best in the world. There are about 80 miles of coastline and about 65 bays. On a small scale, there are Sunfish, Sailfish, and Hobie Cats to rent for just-offshore fun (at about $8 and up an hour) on hotel beaches. Farther out, yachtsmen rate the island cruising from Grenada north through the Grenadines to St. Vincent as world class. Not only does St. George's have first-rate marina facilities, but Grenada is headquarters for a number of charter operations who can arrange skippered or bareboat charters for a week or longer. Among them: *Grenada Yacht Services* (St. George's; phone: 440-2508); *The Moorings* (Secret

Harbour; phone: 444-4548); *Go Vacations* (Prickly Bay; phone: 444-4942); and *Spice Island Marine Services* (L'Anse aux Epines; phone: 444-4257). Prices vary enormously according to size and style of boat, provisioning, crew, and so on, but fall by about 20% in summer.

The *Rhum Runner* (phone: 440-2198), a twin-decked catamaran, offers reef snorkeling, sailing, and glass-bottom boat tours, moonlight cruises, and rum punch cruises. *World Wide Watersports* (phone: 444-1339) offers glass-bottom boat tours, sunset cruises, and a popular calypso cruise. The steamship M/V *Eastward* (phone: 440-3422) sails to Carriacou and can be chartered for parties.

CRICKET This cousin of US baseball is played from January to May on pitches (fields) ranging from exquisitely manicured greens like *Queen's Park* to vacant lots. Cricket is a spectator sport that is also a social event. For a schedule of upcoming matches, check with the tourist board or consult the sports section of the island newspaper.

GOLF The two-way view of the Atlantic and the Caribbean is the most noteworthy thing about the 9 holes at the *Grenada Golf Club* (phone: 444-4128).

HIKING A favorite islanders' pastime, accessible to visitors thanks to government encouragement and a supportive system of national parks. The tourist board will brief you on location of trails and level of expertise required, and — with a day's notice — can put you in touch with expert guides. The Grand Etang National Park has maps of marked nature trails. Climbing Mt. Qua Qua along a well-marked footpath is a challenging afternoon's hike, and affords stunning views of the surrounding vistas. The Morne LaBaye Trail, which begins behind the national park, is a scenic journey through ferns, palms, and lush flowery vegetation. Several adventures involving hiking are offered by *Henry's Tours, Ltd.* (phone: 444-5313).

SCUBA AND SNORKELING Along the submerged reef that parallels most of the island's west coast, you can see and photograph a fascinating underwater world of coral formations, submarine "gardens," and friendly schools of exotic fish (blue-headed wrasse, gobies, French angelfish). Experienced divers can also explore the 594-foot-long wreck of the sunken ocean liner *Bianca C,* just offshore. Snorkeling and dive trips can be arranged through *Grand Anse Aquatics* at their *Coyaba* location (phone: 444-4219, ext. 144), or the *Dive Grenada* water sports concession (phone: 444-4371). Per-person rates are about $20 for an hour's snorkel trip, $40 for a one-tank dive, and $65 for a two-tank dive. *Grenada Yacht Services* (phone: 440-2883 or 440-2508) offers snorkeling day trips on the 40-foot *Flamingo,* $30 per person for a group of eight.

SPORT FISHING Best in Grenadian waters from November to May, when the catch includes sailfish, blue and white marlin, yellowfin tuna, dorado, kingfish, and wahoo. Fishing charters can be arranged through hotel water sports desks. A fully equipped high-speed Bertram charters for about $75 per hour for a party of four. Jason Fletcher (phone: 440-4961 or 444-1422) offers charters on his 28-foot Grady-White fishing boat, while Bob Evans (phone: 444-4422 or 444-4217) runs deep-sea charters on his 35-foot Bertram. Rates for both are $500 per day and include crew, bait, tackle, and drinks. *Captain Peters* offers a 4-hour fishing trip for two people at $155 (phone: 440-1349), including crew, bait, and tackle. The annual *International Game Fishing Tournament* takes place sometime in January, depending on the moon.

SWIMMING AND SUNNING Grenada has 45 beaches, many with fine white sand, and all free and open to the public. Grand Anse Beach is the long, beautiful, famous one. A number of hotels and guesthouses are on or just across the road from it, so chances are the place you stay will border a piece of it too. (You can visit strips along hotels you're not staying at, too, though they are likely to charge a small fee for the use of changing facilities and chaise longues.) The beaches at Calabash and Horseshoe bays are other southern beauties. At the other end of the island, Levera Beach on the northeastern shore, where the Atlantic and the Caribbean meet, is palm-lined, uncrowded, and a favorite picnic place. Carriacou's most seductive sands line Paradise Beach and small Sandy Island offshore.

TENNIS The *Grenada Renaissance, Secret Harbour, Coyaba, Calabash, Coral Cove, Twelve Degrees North,* and *Holiday Haven Cottages* all have facilities, and non-guests can play (if courts are available) for a nominal fee (up to $5; sometimes for free). The *Richmond Hill Tennis Club* will arrange temporary memberships (1 month) for $15. Contact Richard Hughes (phone: 440-2751). Visiting non-members can play for a nominal per-person, per-hour charge. The Grand Anse tennis courts are open to the public.

WINDSURFING Equipment is available for rent at hotels for about $15 to $20 per hour.

NIGHTLIFE

For visitors, it's centered at hotels, each of which holds buffets, barbecues, island shows, and dancing (a combo one night, steel band the next) several nights a week in season, less often in summer. (The *Grenada Renaissance* hotel is the most active in this department.) You can hotel-hop, but most people are content to sit, sip, and talk on their own terraces after dinner. On weekends, islanders and visitors alike dance into the wee hours at the *Fantasia 2001* disco on Morne Rouge Beach (phone: 444-1189) and at *Le Sucrier* in the sugar mill on the Grand Anse roundabout (phone: 444-1068).

Best on the Island

CHECKING IN

Grenada has a total of about 1,200 rooms. The *Grenada Hotel Association* (phone: 800-322-1753; fax: 809-444-4847) provides room availability and rates information, and a free reservations services. In the US and Canada, reservations also may be made by calling 800-223-9815.

Grenada's better hotels offer a more casual, understated style of elegance than found elsewhere in the Caribbean. Don't be surprised if a hotel advertised as "deluxe" turns out to be somewhat shy of services — what you're paying for here are some of the most charmingly situated resort hideaways anywhere in the Caribbean, not marble and mirrors. All hotels are low-rise — the rule in Grenada is that no building may be taller than the tallest palm tree.

In-season rates are very reasonable compared to those on a number of neighboring islands, and most establishments deliver comparatively good value in quality of accommodations, food, and pleasantly rendered service; use of water and land sports equipment is generally included. Expect to pay $200 or more for a double room without meals during the winter season in hotels we list below as expensive, from $125 to $200 in moderate places, and $125 or less at inexpensive properties. The cost of adding breakfasts and dinners (Modified American Plan) varies from $30 to $45 extra per person, per day. Note that rates do not include the 8% government hotel tax or the 10% service charge automatically added to your bill. Hotel rates generally drop 20% to 30% in the off-season. All telephone numbers are in the 809 area code unless otherwise indicated.

GRAND ANSE BEACH

EXPENSIVE

Grenada Renaissance The island's largest resort, complete with 19 acres of beachfront property, and 184 rooms, each with a patio or balcony, hair dryer, air conditioning, and direct-dial phone. There are lots of shady palms, a lounge bar, 2 synthetic-surface tennis courts, a pool, and 4 shops. Also offered: all water sports, including diving excursions via a concessionaire. Dining is alfresco or indoors with air conditioning in the *Greenery* (open in the winter season only), and there's nightly entertainment (phone: 444-4371; 800-228-9898 from the US; fax: 444-4800).

MODERATE

Blue Horizons Spruced up and landscaped, its 32 cottage suites (all with kitchenettes, air conditioning, ceiling fans, hair dryers, telephones, and clock radios) are reasonably priced even at the height of the season. There's a pool, whirlpool, small playground, and an outstanding restaurant, *La*

Belle Creole (see *Eating Out*). For those who prefer to eat in, cooks are available. Grand Anse is 200 yards down the road, and guests can use the beach and water sports concessions at the nearby *Spice Island Inn.* Genuine island atmosphere and thoughtful service are right here. Children under 12 may stay free in their parents' room (phone: 444-4316; 800-223-9815 from the US; fax: 444-2815).

Coyaba This resort occupies a lovely 2½-acre site on Grand Anse Beach. The central pavilion, which houses the reception area, bar, lounge, boutique, and 2 open-air restaurants, is surrounded by three 2-story lodges, with 40 air conditioned rooms. All accommodations feature private verandahs with views of the sea or St. George's Harbour (sometimes both) and phones. Facilities include a pool with swim-up bar, the *Grand Anse Aquatics* dive operation, volleyball, tennis courts, and a playground (phone: 444-4129; 800-223-9815 from the US; fax: 444-4808).

INEXPENSIVE

Flamboyant On the hillside at the end of Grand Anse Beach, the 39 units (studios, 1- and 2-bedroom apartments, and 2-bedroom cottages) have fabulous views of St. George's and the harbor. The apartments and cottages have full kitchens; all accommodations are air conditioned. There's also a pool, a good restaurant, and a bar (phone: 444-4247; fax: 444-1234).

L'ANSE AUX EPINES

EXPENSIVE

Calabash Twenty-eight complete suites (6 have private Jacuzzis; another 8 have private swimming pools) are set in 10 buildings spread over 8 landscaped acres fronting the beach. Each has a full kitchen (a maid comes in to prepare breakfast), and a verandah just steps from the water's edge. (If money is no object, try to book the pool suite 11A.) Other pluses are a pretty beach, a large pool with poolside café, Sunfish, a lighted tennis court, billiard room, and one of the island's best restaurants (see *Eating Out*). There's some nighttime entertainment. The place draws a lot of repeat business, so book early (phone: 444-4234; 800-223-9815 from the US; fax: 444-4804).

Secret Harbour A marvelous Spanish-Moorish design, complete with tiled roofs, terraces, arches, and opulent finishing touches (stained glass, sunken tubs, and 2 big four-poster beds per room), sets the ambience here. About half the 20 units have a small fridge wedged into the dressing area; it's a draw, primarily for long-term visitors, but does nothing for the otherwise charming atmosphere. Pluses include a sandy beach, a tile-framed swimming pool, a tennis court, and an extensive water sports concession, including a 50-slip marina under the aegis of *The Moorings.* Evenings are very quiet (phone: 444-4548; fax: 444-4819).

MODERATE

Horse Shoe Beach This lushly landscaped property has 12 elegant Mediterranean cottage suites that recently have been spruced up (including hand-carved four-poster beds), plus 6 newer and more modern suites. All are air conditioned, with a patio, TV set, and telephone. The view from the dining room is marvelous. There's a small beach, but also a pool, a complete water sports center, table tennis, billiards, and croquet (phone: 444-4410; 800-223-9815 from the US; fax: 444-4844).

Twelve Degrees North Tastefully done, these 20 one- and two-bedroom cottages are designed for island housekeeping the easy way. Maids, on duty from 8 AM until 3 PM, clean, launder, and cook. (If you ask, they'll prepare dinner ahead of time for you.) Beach equipment includes a dock, a float, Sunfish, a Boston Whaler, plus a thatch bar and barbecue setup. There's also a pool and a tennis court. You're on your own for dinner (cook in, eat out), and groceries are on you. It's all very relaxing. No children under age 12 (phone: 444-4580; 800-223-9815 from the US; fax: 444-4580).

INEXPENSIVE

Coral Cove Here are 18 guestrooms, including 1- or 2-bedroom units overlooking a white beach suitable for some water sports (the water is very shallow in this area). A pool and tennis court round out the facilities. Full maid and laundry service; car rentals and charter fishing can be arranged (phone: 444-4422; 800-223-9815 from the US; fax: 444-4847).

No Problem Apartment Hotel A 20-suite complex less than a mile from the airport, the rooms here are pleasant, with twin beds, a sofa bed, air conditioning, a TV set, a radio, and a fully equipped kitchen. There's a pool, a bar, a casual restaurant, and free bicycle use. A free shuttle provides transport to the airport, town, and Grand Anse Beach. Children under 12 may stay for free in their parents' room (phone: 444-4634 or 444-4635; 800-223-9815 from the US; fax: 444-2803).

ELSEWHERE ON THE ISLAND

EXPENSIVE

La Source The first all-inclusive resort on Grenada, this sister of *Le Sport* on St. Lucia is scheduled to open at press time. The upscale property, nestled on 40 acres near the island's southwest tip, has 100 rooms and suites decorated with bright fabrics and marble touches and featuring seaview balconies, air conditioning, direct-dial phones, and radios (but no TV sets). There are 2 lovely beaches, a free-form pool with a waterfall, 2 restaurants, and 2 bars. Meals, snacks, land and water sports (including scuba), spa services, tips, and airport-to-hotel transfers are all included in the rate. Pink Gin Beach (phone: 444-2556; 800-544-2883 from the US; fax: 444-2561).

CARRIACOU

INEXPENSIVE

Caribbee Inn A refuge for writers, poets, and quiet souls in which 6 bedrooms, 1 apartment, and 1 cottage grace a lush hillside. Home cooking is supervised by its British owners, and is prepared with a creole touch. There's a small library, several bicycles are available, and water sports are nearby. Swimming is at 2 secluded beaches. Near Bogles Village (phone: 443-7380; fax: 443-7999).

Silver Beach Located smack on Beausejour Beach, this property has 18 simply (but fully) furnished units ranging from basic rooms to self-contained apartments with kitchenettes — all with patios and either a sea or garden view. *Dive Paradise,* a water sports and scuba diving operation, is on site. Beausejour Bay (phone: 443-7337; 800-223-9815 from the US; fax: 443-7165).

EATING OUT

Grenadian food owes its special flavor to good island cooks and very fresh ingredients: just-caught fish, lobster, crab, and conch (called *lambi*), just-picked garden vegetables, and tropical fruits in great variety. Island dishes to try: pumpkin soup; *callaloo,* with greens and crab, ranging in thickness from soup to stew; conch (in conch and onion pie, or curried); turtle steaks; and soursop ice cream. "Oil Down," virtually the national dish, consists of breadfruit and salt pork covered with dasheen leaves and steamed in coconut milk. The national drink is rum punch, *always* with freshly grated Grenadian nutmeg on top; local Carib beer is quite good.

Food at Grenadian hotels is generally excellent. Most have continental chefs and menus that feature continental specialties, plus a few West Indian choices. Since most dining rooms are small, with only limited space for outside guests, it is essential to call ahead for reservations if you want to sample the food at another hotel. Expect to pay $40 to $50 for a dinner for two at any of the places listed below as expensive; $22 to $35 at spots described as moderate; and under $22 in any of the places we list as inexpensive. Prices don't include drinks, wine, the 8% tax, or tips. Most hotel restaurants fall into the expensive range, which means the MAP accommodation prices make sense. All telephone numbers are in the 809 area code unless otherwise indicated.

ST. GEORGE'S AND ENVIRONS

MODERATE

Mamma's A friendly, homelike atmosphere prevails at this informal eatery. No menu, just a profusion of truly memorable West Indian offerings (up to 25 courses, served family-style, are the rule for large parties) that have made this place a must-stop for authentic island cooking. Always ask if there's any turtle available and be sure to try the sea moss ice cream. Any cab driver can find it, but make reservations well in advance, as there are only a few tables on the back-to-basics patio and inside. Open daily for lunch and dinner. No credit cards accepted. Old Lagoon Rd., Belmont (phone: 440-1459).

Rudolf's A Swiss-owned spot for lunch or dinner in a pub-like setting. The menu is international, including fish and chips, and lobster-as-you-like-it; there are also a few local specialties and potent rum punches. Try the crab back and homemade soursop ice cream. Closed Sundays. Reservations necessary for dinner. No credit cards accepted. North corner of the Carenage (phone: 440-2241).

INEXPENSIVE

Nutmeg Overlooking the Carenage, this is the most popular noontime spot in town, and a good place for drinks, snacks, or a full meal almost anytime. Chatty and easygoing, it's popular with visiting yachtspeople. Have a rum punch, *callaloo,* lobster, or *lambi.* Opcn daily; dinner only on Sundays (unless a cruise ship is in port). Reservations unnecessary. MasterCard and Visa accepted. The Carenage (phone: 440-2539).

GRAND ANSE

EXPENSIVE

La Belle Creole For the real island McCoy, this small and cordial balcony dining room is the scene of some highly imaginative West Indian meals in the Hopkins family tradition. One of the island's best. Open daily for lunch and dinner. Reservations necessary. Major credit cards accepted. In the *Blue Horizons Cottage* hotel, 200 yards down the road from Grand Anse Beach (phone: 444-4316).

Canboulay Definitely in the "don't miss" category, it sits on the hillside above Grand Anse Beach and features fantastic views of the entire town. Traditional ingredients are served in such dishes as "moko jumbies" (jumbo shrimp served on skewers), "parang poulet" (chicken in orange-ginger sauce), and red snapper steamed in banana leaves. Good starters are the coconut buns stuffed with salt fish *souse,* and breadfruit with pickled cucumber. Open for lunch and dinner; closed Mondays. Reservations necessary for dinner. Major credit cards accepted. Morne Rouge (phone: 444-4401).

L'ANSE AUX EPINES

EXPENSIVE

Calabash This prize-winning restaurant in the hotel of the same name offers the handiwork of chef Cecily Roberts. Fresh seafood and island-grown fruits and vegetables are prepared in Grenadian style and served on a flower-draped terrace. Open daily for lunch and dinner. Reservations necessary. Major credit cards accepted. L'Anse aux Epines (phone: 444-4234).

Red Crab Upscale dining in a relaxed atmosphere is the attraction here. Seafood dishes such as shrimp crêpes are specialties. Open for lunch and dinner; dinner only Sundays. Reservations advised. Major credit cards accepted. L'Anse aux Epines (phone: 444-4424).

MODERATE

Boatyard A convivial eatery featuring fish and chips and burgers for lunch and seafood dishes for dinner. Famous for their crowded happy hours. Open for lunch and dinner; closed Mondays. Reservations unnecessary. Major credit cards accepted. In the *Spice Island Marina* compound at Prickly Bay, L'Anse aux Epines (phone: 444-4662).

Casa Blanca West Indian specialties such as pumpkin soup and fish creole are served in this open-air dining room. The sinful homemade desserts include nutmeg mousse and rum raisin ice cream. Open daily for lunch and dinner. Reservations unnecessary. Major credit cards accepted. At the *Horse Shoe Beach Hotel,* L'Anse aux Epines (phone: 444-4410).

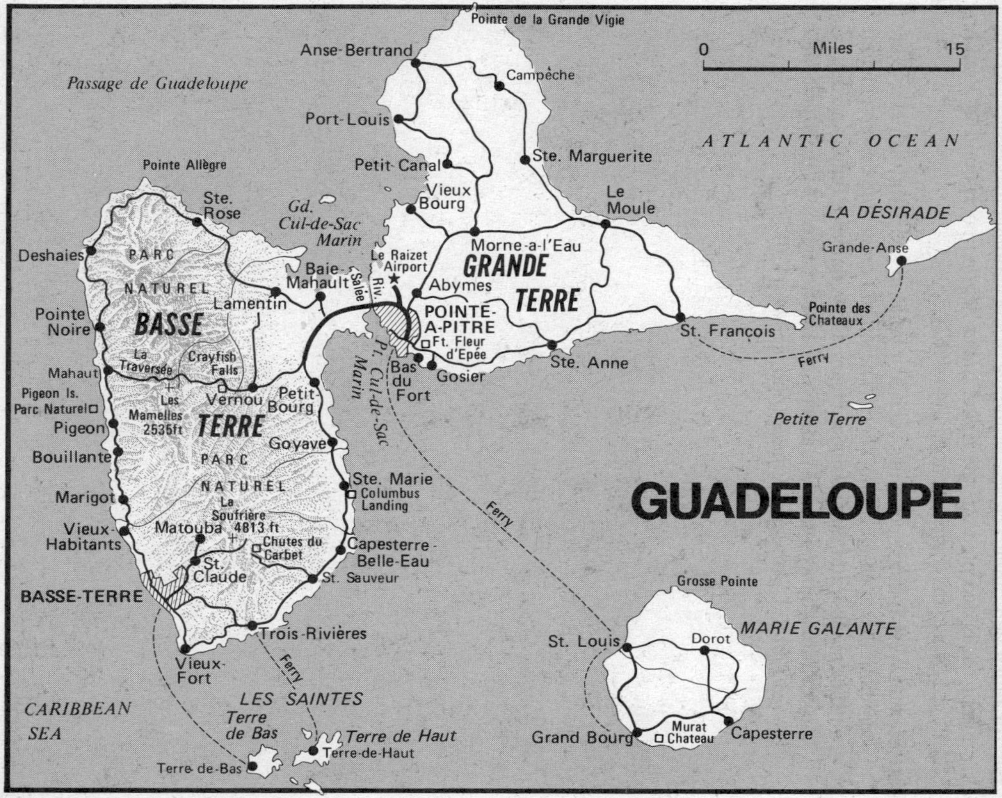

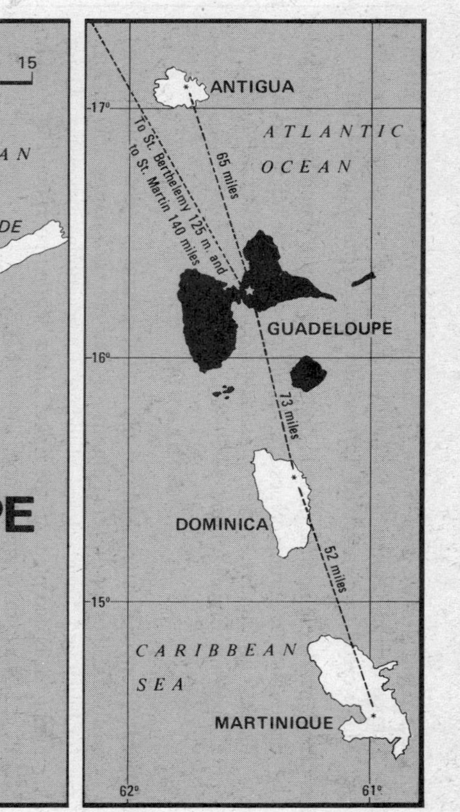

GUADELOUPE
Passage de Guadeloupe
Pointe de la Grande Vigie
Anse-Bertrand
Campêche
Port-Louis
Petit-Canal
Vieux Bourg
Ste. Marguerite
Le Moule
Morne-a-l'Eau
GRANDE TERRE
Abymes
POINTE-A-PITRE
Ft. Fleur d'Epée
Bas du Fort
Gosier
Ste. Anne
St. François
Pointe des Chateaux
LA DÉSIRADE
Grande-Anse
ATLANTIC OCEAN
0 Miles 15
Petite Terre
Ferry
Pointe Allègre
Ste. Rose
Deshaies
Gd. Cul-de-Sac Marin
Le Raizet Airport
Riv. Salée
Baie-Mahault
Lamentin
Pointe Noire
BASSE TERRE
PARC NATUREL
La Traversée
Crayfish Falls
Mahaut
Pigeon Is. Parc Naturel
Les Mamelles 2535ft
Vernou
Petit-Bourg
Pigeon
Bouillante
Goyave
Pt. Cul-de-Sac Marin
Ste. Marie
Columbus Landing
Marigot
La Soufrière 4813 ft
Matouba
Chutes du Carbet
Vieux-Habitants
St. Claude
Capesterre-Belle-Eau
St. Sauveur
BASSE-TERRE
Trois-Rivières
Vieux-Fort
CARIBBEAN SEA
LES SAINTES
Terre de Bas
Terre-de-Bas
Terre de Haut
Terre-de-Haut
Grosse Pointe
MARIE GALANTE
St. Louis
Dorot
Grand Bourg
Murat Chateau
Capesterre
ANTIGUA
17°
16°
15°
62°
61°
ATLANTIC OCEAN
65 miles
To St. Berthelemy 125 m. and to St. Martin 140 miles
GUADELOUPE
73 miles
DOMINICA
52 miles
CARIBBEAN SEA
MARTINIQUE

Guadeloupe

Like its sister island, Martinique, Guadeloupe has its own dormant (more or less) volcano, tropically forested mountains, an impressive Parc Naturel, cane fields, banana plantations and pineapple stands, a surf-pounded Atlantic coast and calmer leeward bathing beaches, creole cooking, and the beguine. Each island has *région* status and is governed as if it were physically attached to France. The people are French citizens, vote in French national elections, are entitled to French social benefits, and are bound by France's compulsory educational requirements.

But there are significant differences. Guadeloupe is actually two islands linked by a drawbridge over the Rivière-Salée. In addition, Guadeloupe has a number of dependencies: the nearby islands of La Désirade, Marie Galante, and Iles des Saintes (also called Les Saintes), plus the French half of the island of St. Martin and tiny St. Barthélemy. It offers not only the stunning scenery of its own two islands to explore, but day or overnight trips to its intriguing, unspoiled, dependent islands as well.

In 1493, 9 years before he found Martinique, Christopher Columbus happened upon Guadeloupe, christening it Santa María de Guadalupe de Estremadura to fulfill a promise made to the monks of the Spanish monastery of the same name. The French landed on both islands in 1635. But while Martinique flourished, Guadeloupe foundered — thanks to the ineptitude of its leaders and the lack of farming skill among its volunteer settlers, all of whom were indentured to work 3 years without pay in exchange for their passage from France.

The French Revolution goaded Guadeloupe into asserting itself: Infuriated by the Declaration of the Rights of Man and the abolition of slavery (which doomed their cane fields), the islanders declared themselves autonomous, inviting the enemy English to invade and stay awhile. In 1794, the Committee of Public Safety in Paris dispatched a force of 1,150 men to discipline the islanders. They ousted the English, set up guillotines in the main squares of Basse-Terre and Pointe-à-Pitre, and beheaded 4,000 Guadeloupeans before being removed to Guiana. Slavery was reestablished under Napoleon. The British reconquered Guadeloupe in 1810, surrendered it to Louis XVIII during the Restoration, reoccupied the island when Napoleon staged his 100-day comeback, and gave it up for good when the Little Emperor was permanently exiled to St. Helena in 1815. Guadeloupe has been French ever since, but it has developed its own character — a unique blend of France and the West Indies.

Guadeloupe's hotels generally follow the large, luxurious, made-in-France pattern, with *tous* sports built in, or the small, French-speaking hostel-on-the-beach design. Its capital is a small port city called Basse-Terre, which could be described as dull in comparison to its working heart, bustling Pointe-à-Pitre. Despite its high-rise housing and burgeoning industry, Pointe-à-Pitre moves to a distinctly Caribbean beat. To feel it, stroll down to the waterfront, lined with chunky island boats, where blue-eyed Iles des Saintes fishermen hawk their morning catch, or pay an early morning visit to market stalls piled with fruits and spices dear to the soul of its creole cooks.

This creole fare — vying with traditional French specialties — fires the Guadeloupean spirit. Classic French restaurants like *La Plantation* (see *Eating Out*) are respected and admired, but the real heroines of this island's kitchens are Prudence, Félicité, Violetta, Trésor, among others, who conjure up their magic *blaffs, boudins,* and *crabes farcis* in plain places in the hills and along the shores. The whole island celebrates their art with a grand parade, a cathedral blessing, music, dancing, and a 5-hour feast at the annual August *Fête des Cuisinières* (Women Chefs' Festival). At any time of year, though, lunch or dinner is an adventure and — when your eye and palate have become acclimated to the spices and surprises — a special delight.

If you're looking for a place with fine beaches that's a bit offbeat, and if you can say "Vive la différence" with feeling, Guadeloupe is for you.

Guadeloupe At-a-Glance

FROM THE AIR

Guadeloupe is a butterfly-shaped formation of two islands, Grande-Terre (218 square miles) and Basse-Terre (312 square miles), separated by a narrow strait called the Rivière-Salée (Salt River) and connected by a drawbridge. It has a total area of 582 square miles and a population of 340,000. One of the Leeward Islands, its nearest neighbors are Antigua (65 miles northwest), Dominica (73 miles south), and Martinique (121 miles south and slightly east).

Guadeloupe's two islands are quite different topographically. Basse-Terre has mountainous terrain inland and a rugged coastline with few (but good) beaches suited to daylong basking. Grande-Terre consists of flat cane fields and low, chalky hills rimmed by a number of appealing beaches. The city of Basse-Terre (population just over 15,000), on the southwest edge of the island of the same name, is the capital of the *région;* but the larger city of Pointe-à-Pitre (population 100,000), on the southwest coast of Grande-Terre, near the point where the Rivière-Salée separates the two islands, is its commercial center.

SPECIAL PLACES

Most island visitors stay on Grande-Terre at the shore hotels of Bas du Fort, Gosier, Ste. Anne, and St. François, or at any of the 20-odd small hotels and inns conforming to the high standards of service and comfort that are required of members of the Relais Créoles group. Visitors typically spend half a day shopping and strolling around Pointe-à-Pitre, and make a day-tour visit to Basse-Terre's Parc Naturel and the city of Basse-Terre. Some travelers rent cars to explore on their own, but since Basse-Terre's roads tend to be mountainous inland and sharply curved along the shore, most visitors sign up for organized bus tours at hotel travel desks. Athletic types can arrange a guided climb to the top of Soufrière, the island's dormant volcano. Day trips via ferry or plane to Iles des Saintes and Marie Galante combine sightseeing with a chance to laze on pleasant, secluded beaches (Petite Anse, a long, golden stretch of sand on Marie Galante, is one of the best).

POINTE-À-PITRE Guadeloupe's port and chief city, on Grande-Terre, likes to call itself the "Paris of the Antilles," but it looks more like a Riviera port than the city on the Seine. Apartments and condominiums form a high-rise backdrop for its 19th-century cathedral, tree-planted squares, and boat-lined harbor. It is busy, but not so bustling or big that you can't see it all and get in your shopping, too, in half a day — preferably morning, when the waterfront and outdoor market are liveliest.

Start by picking up brochures and a map of Guadeloupe (including a street map of Pointe-à-Pitre) at the tourist office, housed in a white colonial building across from the Place de la Victoire. The park-like area is shaded by flamboyants and palms as well as antique sandbox trees planted by Victor Hugues, whose victory over the British in 1794 gave the square its name. It was here that Hugues, Guadeloupe's first dictator, erected a guillotine to execute enemies of the Revolution.

A short walk from the tourist office is the *Centre St. Jean Perse,* a $20-million waterfront complex. The huge structure includes the headquarters of Guadeloupe's Port Authority, as well as 80 stores, including duty-free shops selling local rum and French perfume; three restaurants, most notably *La Canne à Sucre* (see *Eating Out*); and the *St. John Anchorage* hotel (see *Checking In*).

Rue Duplessis, at the Place de la Victoire's southern edge, runs along La Darse, the old port where inter-island ferries leave for Marie Galante and Les Saintes, schooners tie up, and where, farther out, cruise ships drop anchor. West of the harbor, the shopping district's narrow streets are crowded with shops that range from sidewalk stalls to boutiques full of French perfumes and sportswear. Chief shopping streets are Rue de Nozières and Rue Frébault (both of which run north and south) and Rue Achille René-Boisneuf (usually referred to by its hyphenated name alone), running east and west. At 54 Rue René-Boisneuf, a plaque marks the birthplace of St. Jean Perse, the French poet who won the Nobel Prize for Literature in 1960, and nearby on the same street is the *Musée St. Jean Perse* (phone: 909228). It's open from 8:30 AM to noon and from 2:30 to 5:30 PM; closed Saturday mornings and Sundays; there's an admission charge. A block north, bounded by Rues Schoelcher, Peynier, Frébault, and Thiers, the open-air market hums with the give-and-take of housewives and women vendors — some straw-hatted, some wearing traditional madras turbans — bargaining across stacks of fire-red pimientos, paw paws, pineapples, mangoes, and spices. Behind the market is the *Musée Schoelcher* (24 Rue Peynier; phone: 820804), dedicated to Victor Schoelcher, the man credited with abolishing slavery here. It's open the same hours as the *Musée St. Jean Perse* (above); there's also an admission charge. A short walk north and east brings you to the peaceful Place de l'Eglise, where you can rest and sip a punch or a *café filtre* across from the yellow and white Cathédrale de St. Pierre et St. Paul, nicknamed "the Iron Cathedral" because of its skeleton of bolted iron ribs, designed to keep the church standing through hurricanes and earthquakes.

ELSEWHERE ON GRANDE-TERRE

Most points of interest are along the shores east of Pointe-à-Pitre. As you drive east from town, they are:

FORT FLEUR D'EPÉE The well-preserved battlements and dungeons of this 18th-century fortress are located 3 miles east of Pointe-à-Pitre. They command a view of the city, the nearby islands of Marie Galante and the Iles des Saintes, and in the distance the mountains of Basse-Terre and the island of Dominica. On the shore below, Bas du Fort is the site of several late-model resort hotels and vacation condominiums. Not far from the marina at Bas Du Fort is the large *Aquarium de la Guadeloupe* (phone: 909238), with over 150 species of fish and tropical plants.

GOSIER Four and a half miles east of Pointe-à-Pitre, this shoreside center has an extensive beach, site of many of the island's major resort hotels.

STE. ANNE The most quaint of Guadeloupe's villages, it features a pastel Town Hall, a pretty church, and a main square dominated by a statue of emancipationist Victor Schoelcher, erected by the island's citizens to commemorate the end of slavery in 1848. *Club Med,* six small Relais Créoles inns, and extensive beaches are nearby.

ST. FRANÇOIS This fishing village has long, white sand beaches, many good creole and French restaurants, and an expanding resort complex (marina, casino, golf course).

POINTE DES CHÂTEAUX The easternmost tip of Grande-Terre, the Atlantic and the Caribbean meet here. There's a towering castle-like rock formation, crowned by a rugged cross that has survived more than a century. Despite the crashing waves, the tranquil, coved beaches make this a fine picnic destination.

LE MOULE There's a long crescent beach at this small coastal fishing village and antique sugar port northeast of Pointe-à-Pitre. The fascinating and attractively designed historical and archaeological *Musée Edgar Clerc* (phone: 235757) is here, and just north of town at Morel, archaeologists have unearthed a pre-Columbian Arawak village. At the Beach of Skulls and

Bones, the ocean has uncovered graves and petrified remains, macabre relics of once savage warfare between the Carib and the French and British invaders.

Interesting places along the coastal road north of Pointe-à-Pitre include:

PORT-LOUIS AND ANSE-BERTRAND These fishing villages have good beaches nearby.

POINTE DE LA GRANDE VIGIE At the northernmost tip of the island, it is named for the sweeping Atlantic view from the top of its rocky cliffs.

BASSE-TERRE

To see Basse-Terre, which is west of Pointe-à-Pitre, across the drawbridge over the Rivière-Salée (the river that connects the Caribbean and the Atlantic), head west on La Traversée, the highway that crosses Basse-Terre through the lush highlands of the Parc Naturel of Guadeloupe, then go south along the west coast to the capital city of Basse-Terre and return via the island's east coast. Alternatively, you can take the coastal roads first and return on La Traversée, traveling west to east. If you follow the latter route, you'll encounter:

STE. MARIE Columbus landed on this spot during his second voyage in 1493; he left in a hurry, however, when the Carib started peppering his crew with arrows. Today, a statue of Columbus stands in the town square, and the area is largely populated by East Indian descendants of the laborers imported to work plantations after the 1848 emancipation of black slaves. Just south of town is much-photographed Allée Dumanoir, a half-mile stretch of road lined on both sides with tall palms planted in the last century by Pinel Dumanoir, whose major claim to fame was — surprisingly — his French dramatization of *Uncle Tom's Cabin.*

LES CHUTES DU CARBET This trio of waterfalls impressed Columbus's crew, who — when they sighted them from the sea — thought they were "avalanches of white stones." For a closer look, take the road inland from the coastal town of St. Sauveur past the round mountain lake called Grand Etang and up Soufrière mountain to a cleared viewing point near the three cascades. The lowest is between 60 and 70 feet high; the second and top falls are over 300 feet each. A 20-minute walk brings you to the pool at the foot of the lowest waterfall.

TROIS-RIVIÈRES A seaside settlement with a modern Town Hall, but the older sights here are much more interesting: Near the harbor where ferries depart for Iles des Saintes, rocks in a small park bear pre-Columbian inscriptions, and for a few francs one of the local boys will show you the portrait of a chieftain on the wall of a nearby grotto.

BASSE-TERRE Guadeloupe's capital is a small, neat city of narrow streets and palm-filled parks set between the sea and the green heights of La Soufrière.

Chief points of interest: the nicely designed administrative buildings that make up the old Carmel quarter; the 17th-century Cathedral of Our Lady of Guadeloupe in the Saint-François section; and Fort St. Charles, which has stood guard over the city since its founding in 1643.

VIEUX-HABITANTS Just a few miles north of Basse-Terre, this small fishing village is where the first French settlers landed in 1635. *La Maison du Café* (phone: 984842) is a restored coffee plantation with a museum devoted to the story of local coffee production, and a restaurant. It's closed Mondays.

LA SOUFRIÈRE This tenuously dormant volcano has given Guadeloupeans some anxious moments recently, often breathing steam from its fumaroles (steam holes) and burping sulfurous fumes from its pits and mud cauldrons. The foot of the crater can be reached by car; there, at the Savane-à-Mulets parking lot, spectators feel the heat of the subterranean lava and enjoy a magnificent view of Basse-Terre, the sea, Iles des Saintes, and Dominica. Adventurous types can climb one of four marked trails to the edge of the crater to view its 5-acre center of bubbling lava and eerie rock formations. The *Guide to the Natural Park,* available from the tourist office, grades trails by difficulty: the blue is rated 1 (easy walk); the yellow and green, 2 (some difficulty); and the red, 3 (for the experienced hiker only). The round-trip trek takes from 1 to 3 hours, depending on your stamina; guides are strongly recommended because of sudden mountain mists and shifting paths (due to fast-growing vegetation).

LA TRAVERSÉE The well-maintained Transcoastal Highway provides a convenient way to see the Parc Naturel en route from Basse-Terre to Pointe-à-Pitre. You reach its western end by driving north along the coast past black sand beaches; the small town of Vieux-Habitants (see above); Bouillante, boiling with hot springs and geysers; and the spot where dive trips and glass-bottom boat rides leave for Pigeon Island and the nearby underwater reserve. La Traversée starts just north of Pigeon at Mahaut and travels 10½ miles east through a pass between mountains graphically referred to as Les Deux Mamelles (the Two Breasts). The road offers a broad view of the hills, valleys, and coasts of Basse-Terre, and the bays called Grand and Petit Cul-de-Sac, plus the park's forests, lakes, and waterfalls. On the way, you can stroll in the Zoological and Botanical Park at Bouillante or perhaps swim in the pool at the bottom of the Cascade aux Ecrevisses (Crayfish Falls). The eastern end of La Traversée joins the road that crosses the drawbridge back to Pointe-à-Pitre.

EXTRA SPECIAL

Iles des Saintes and Marie Galante are two unspoiled offshore island destinations that are perfect for daylong getaway plane trips or ferry crossings that can be organized by tour operators or arranged on your own. Marie Galante offers a bit of sightseeing (the sunny little town of Grand-Bourg, sugar mills, pastoral landscapes, architecturally splendid Murat Château), and fine white

beaches. Pack a picnic, or lunch on creole fare at *Touloulou* or *lambi* at *Békéké;* both eateries are on the sand near Capesterre. Visitors who want to skip the sightseeing can take jitneys or buses to Capesterre Beach from the market or bus depot a couple of blocks away (cost is about $1 per person). When you've had enough sun, just stand on the highway and hail a bus headed back toward town. Most Iles des Saintes trips land breathtakingly (it's a very short runway with a mountain-pass approach) on Terre-de-Haut island. There are minibus "taxis de l'île," but it's a very short walk past the cemetery, with its white tombs, hand-carved crucifix, and conch shell–framed grave sites, and over the hill to the town, which is one of the Caribbean's prettiest. There's a quaint, tiny town square, rows of miniature, uniquely painted houses, and flowers everywhere. There are a number of good places for lunch: In Pointe Coquelet eat at the terrace café at the *Kanaoa* hotel (see *Checking In*), the appealing restaurant *Le Foyal* (see *Eating Out*), or *Le Mouillage* near the pier and bask on a beach nearby; or take the launch from the town pier or taxi out to the *Bois Joli* hotel (see *Checking In*) for lunch and a choice of clothed, topless, or bare beaching. There are a number of good hotels if you'd like to stay overnight (see *Checking In*). Big round salako straw hats (like those worn by Chinese coolies), unique to these islands, make super souvenirs — when you can find them.

Sources and Resources

TOURIST INFORMATION

The Guadeloupe Office of Tourism, near the waterfront in Pointe-à-Pitre (5 Place de la Banque; phone: 820930), is open from 8 AM to 5 PM on weekdays and from 8 AM to noon on Saturdays, and supplies maps, information, and advice. The staff also will answer phone queries in English. For French West Indies tourist offices in the US, see GETTING READY TO GO.

LOCAL COVERAGE *Guadeloupe Bonjour,* the island's official tourist booklet, published periodically in both French and English, is distributed free at the tourist office, at the airport, and in hotels. It is full of useful information, plus up-to-date specifics on excursions, restaurants, and nightlife. A booklet called *Guadeloupe Excursions* details six excellent itineraries for touring the islands by car; it is available from the tourist office in Pointe-à-Pitre.

The *Librairie Antillaise* (41 *bis* Rue Schoelcher; phone: 821996 or 832515) is the place for fiction and nonfiction books on island history and legend.

Guadeloupe, a book of color photographs collected by Hans W. Hannau, is available at large bookstores. *A Woman Named Solitude,* a novel by André Schwarz-Bart (Atheneum, 1973), incorporates much Guadeloupean history and atmosphere, as does *Between Two Worlds* (Harper &

Row, 1981) by Schwarz-Bart's wife, Simone. (The latter is out of print, but check your local library.)

RADIO AND TELEVISION

Television is in French, but radio, which is locally produced or picked up from neighboring islands, broadcasts in several languages, including English. Most hotels have satellite-dish facilities.

TELEPHONE

When calling from the US, dial 011 (international access code) + 590 (country code) + (local number). From another Caribbean island, the access code may vary, so call the local operator. When dialing on Guadeloupe, use only the local number unless otherwise indicated.

ENTRY REQUIREMENTS

For stays of up to 3 weeks, a current or expired passport (not more than 5 years old) or proof of citizenship in the form of a voter's registration card or birth certificate with raised seal accompanied by an official photo ID (such as a driver's license) is necessary. A return or ongoing ticket also is required. For longer stays, a valid passport is necessary. US or Canadian citizens need no vaccination certificates.

CLIMATE AND CLOTHES

The weather is tropical, tempered by trade winds and with thermometer readings varying considerably between sea level and the mountains. At beach resorts on the southern coast of Grande-Terre, temperatures range from an average low of 75F (24C) to an average high of 86F (30C). In the higher, cooler inland regions, the averages run from 66 to 81F (19 to 27C). September and October are the wettest months — not immune to hurricanes; November to May, the driest. But even in the residential suburb of St. Claude, where it's said the climate is perfect — sunny, cool, and breezy year round — it showers almost every day. Most tourist accommodations are air conditioned.

Topless sunning is taken for granted just about everywhere. There are officially designated nude beaches on Guadeloupe proper and Iles des Saintes. Off the beach, lightweight sportswear is most comfortable. Both men and women should pack some sort of cover-up — long-sleeve shirts or beach caftans — to slip on for lunch or when you've simply had enough sun. Slacks and sport shirts for men and slacks or skirts for women are right for downtown shopping, lunching, or excursions. For the Parc Naturel, wear sturdy, crepe-soled shoes or sneakers, and take along a light jacket (preferably waterproof) or sweater in case of a chilly spell or shower. At night, especially in the large hotels, women wear casual dresses or nice slacks; men wear slacks and open-neck shirts. Ties are seldom, if ever, required, but you might pack one just in case.

MONEY

Guadeloupe's currency is the French franc, whose value in US dollars is quoted in the business sections of most major daily US metropolitan newspapers; at press time it was about 5 francs to $1 US. Though most hotels will exchange a limited amount of dollars for francs, banks offer the most favorable exchange rates. (French francs can be reconverted to dollars only at banks.) Like most Guadeloupean businesses, banks are closed for lunch between noon and 2:30 PM. You'll get more for your shopping money if you pay for your purchases in dollar-denomination traveler's checks; some tourist-oriented Pointe-à-Pitre merchants discount prices an extra 20% when paid in traveler's checks or with a major credit card. Some shops accept payment in dollars, but don't give the additional discount when they do. All prices in this chapter are quoted in US dollars.

LANGUAGE

Guadeloupe's official language is French, with creole (African words and rhythms grafted onto French stems) a virtual second tongue. You can count on English-speaking tour guides (if you've specified beforehand) and on some personnel in hotels and tourist-frequented shops who understand English. But if your French is rusty to nonexistent, carry a dictionary or phrase book. The French West Indies Tourist Board's free *Helpful Hints for Visitors* includes a glossary of useful phrases.

TIME

Guadeloupe time is 1 hour later than eastern standard time (when it's noon in New York, it's 1 PM in Pointe-à-Pitre); or the same as eastern daylight saving time. Local time is also measured on a 24-hour clock, so that 1 PM is 13 *heures*.

CURRENT

Local electricity is 220 volts AC, 50 cycles. Large hotels sometimes have adapters to lend, but if your travel kit includes essential electric gadgets, better bring your own adapter plugs.

TIPPING

French law requires that a 15% service charge be automatically added to all restaurant and bar bills. Tip room maids about $1 or $2 a day. Porters should be tipped about 85¢ per bag. Most taxi drivers own their own cars and do not expect tips.

GETTING AROUND

BUS The least expensive and most colorful way to go land roving is by bus — if your French and hang-loose spirit are up to it. Small, late-model jitney vans leave from two stations in downtown Pointe-à-Pitre: the Gare Routière de Bergevin for Basse-Terre destinations; the Gare Routière de la

Darse for Grande-Terre hotels and resorts. They depart every 10 to 20 minutes, depending on the importance of the route. A one-way trip between St. Anne and Pointe-à-Pitre is about $2 by bus; the same trip by cab is about $25 to $27.

CAR RENTAL Rental car agents are reluctant to rent for just 1 day, even in off-season. Also, rates are higher at hotel locations than at the airport or in town. Major international agencies — *Avis* (phone: 823347), *Budget* (phone: 829558), *Hertz* (phone: 820014), *EuropRent* (phone: 914216), and *National-Europcar* (phone: 825051) — have offices in the arrival area of Le Raizet Airport. Local firms — also with airport offices — include *Guadeloupe Cars* (phone: 832288), *Jumbo Car* (phone: 914217), and *Agence Azur* (phone: 843056). *Avis, Budget, Hertz, Jumbo, National-Europcar,* and *Agence Azur* also have desks at the larger hotels.

Rates start at about $50 to $60 a day, including insurance and mileage. Cars with automatic transmission are in short supply. A valid driver's license is required; minimum renting age varies from 21 to 25 (depending on the agency), and you must have had at least 1 year's experience as a licensed driver.

Using government-designed self-drive tours and the tourist board's big, clear map, it's easy to plot your own trip. *One caution:* Driving on Grande-Terre, where roads are good and the land rolls gently, is easy going. Basse-Terre's mountain roads — with their steep ascents, descents, and switchbacks — are different; if you're nervous about driving, it's probably wiser to go by bus.

FERRY SERVICES Guadeloupe can be reached by ferries operated by *Caribbean Express* (phone: 601238), which make several trips a week to and from Dominica, Martinique, and St. Lucia. In winter, an expanded schedule includes the islands of St. Martin, St. Barts, Antigua, St. Kitts, and St. Vincent. Several ferries run between these five destinations: Pointe-à-Pitre, Basse-Terre, Trois-Rivières, Iles des Saintes, and Marie Galante. There is also ferry service from St. François to Les Saintes, Marie Galante, and La Désirade.

SEA EXCURSIONS Day sails to nearby islands or to secluded beaches from docks convenient to your hotel can be arranged through hotels or local tour operators. Sailboats up to 50 feet and catamarans can be rented, and the long-established glass-bottom boat *Papyrus* is available for day, twilight, or moonlight sails for about $28 an hour, per person (phone: 909298). For travelers who'd like to indulge in a bit of island-hopping, a small ship called *Le Ponant,* leaving from Pointe-à-Pitre on Grande-Terre, offers 7-day cruises to other Caribbean ports. The ship, a class of luxury sailboat called a sail cruiser, carries 64 passengers and features an open-air disco and a platform in the stern for swimming and water sports. Two cruises are available — the northern route goes to St. Martin, Antigua, and Dominica; and the southern route makes stops in Martinique, St. Lucia, and the Grenadines. For information and reservations, contact *Elite Custom Travel,* 208 E. 58th St., New York, NY 10022 (phone: 212-752-5440 from New York; 800-662-4474 from elsewhere in the US).

SIGHTSEEING BUS TOURS Organized by local operators, these range from a half day of Grande-Terre sightseeing with shopping in Pointe-à-Pitre to a whole day's exploration of Basse-Terre. Among the best and most personalized are the tours put together by Georges Marie-Gabrielle, who has his headquarters at the airport (phone: 820538). It's a very good idea to check tour offerings for special features; when lunch is included, ask where before making reservations. Your concierge or hotel travel desk will have current details and rates on available tours and can make arrangements that include pickup at your hotel.

SIGHTSEEING TAXI TOURS These are reasonable if you can put a group together to share the fare. Ask your concierge or desk clerk to get you a driver-guide and to determine the rates — standardized by the government. Samples: from Pointe-à-Pitre or Gosier to Pointe des Châteaux (half day), about $70; to the Soufrière volcano (6 hours), about $95.

TAXI It will cost about $14 (not inexpensive, but a Mercedes often arrives) for the under-10-minute trip from the airport to your Gosier hotel; at night and on Sundays the rates are at least 40% higher. Since there is no airport limousine service, and buses are provided only for groups, you'll have to take a taxi from the airport unless you rent a car.

INTER-ISLAND FLIGHTS

American has regular flights from San Juan, Puerto Rico. *Air Guadeloupe* serves Iles des Saintes, Marie Galante, La Désirade, St. Barthélemy, and St. Martin, as well as Dominica and Antigua. Several local operators provide the same service for groups of four or more: *Carib Jet* (phone: 822644), *Georges Marie-Gabrielle* (phone: 820538), *Petrelluzzi* (phone: 828230), and *Safari* (phone: 843073). *LIAT* provides air links with several neighboring islands, and *WINAIR* flies directly from Dutch St. Maarten. *Air St. Barthélemy* also has small charter planes. Since the outer islands are popular destinations for Guadeloupeans, book as early as possible.

SPECIAL EVENTS

Carnaval on Guadeloupe is more than a few days' revelry — it's a season that stretches from the first Sunday in January through *Ash Wednesday,* the first day of *Lent,* with all sorts of celebrations (masked parades, beguine contests, a beauty pageant, song competitions) scheduled each Sunday and a 5-day super-gala that begins the Saturday before *Mardi Gras* and doesn't quit till King Vaval goes up in smoke *Ash Wednesday* evening. On that climactic weekend, everyone heads into town for nonstop partying; no islander thinks about much else for the next week. From a tourist's point of view, the Sunday events can be great fun; they also can be ignored if you're so inclined. Not so, the last bash. So if crowd scenes and slightly distracted service would spoil your fun, schedule your visit for another time. Other special occasions: *Mi-Carême,* a mid-*Lenten* break with processions and the funeral of King Vaval; *La Fête des Cuisinières* (the Women Chefs' Festival) held in early August with a parade and much feasting (your hotel can arrange for tickets to the banquet); the *Tour de la Guadeloupe* (mid-August), a 10-day international cycling race; *Festival of the Sea* (celebrated August 15, along with the *Feast of the Assumption,* on Iles des Saintes); *All Saints' Day* (November 1), observed with candle lighting in cemeteries; *St. Cecilia's Day* (November 22), celebrated with musical fetes in cities and towns; and *Young Saints' Day* (December 28), marked with a special mass and children's parade. *Easter Monday, Ascension Day, Pentecost Monday, Bastille Day* (July 14), *Schoelcher Day* (July 21), *Assumption Day* (August 15), *Armistice Day* (November 11), *Christmas,* and *New Year's Day* are also public holidays.

SHOPPING

Most of the shops in Pointe-à-Pitre are centered around Rue de Nozières, Rue Frébault, and Rue Schoelcher. Stores are open from 9 AM to 1 PM and 3 to 6 PM on weekdays, and 9 AM to 1 PM on Saturdays. If there's a cruise ship in port, shop hours often are extended. Some merchants offer 20% discounts to those paying with US dollar denomination traveler's checks or credit cards. Chanel perfume, Orlane and Dior cosmetics, Hermès scarves, Baccarat and Lalique crystal, and the other standard imports are all here, but stocks are smaller and not so enticingly displayed as in Martinique's Fort-de-France, and the language barrier is harder to surmount. If you've a choice of islands and a long French-import shopping list, you'll probably do better faster on Martinique.

Local products? The best are coffee and rums that range from new and fiery white to 12-year-old and mahogany-colored — a take-home most North Americans sip and savor like a liqueur. Other souvenirs include some nicely made baskets, straw hats (both the wide-brimmed bakoua and flat coolie salako shapes), hammocks, shell items, and creole dolls. Shops to seek out:

A LA RECHERCHE DU PASSÉ Bibelots, antique books, and nautical items. At the marina, Bas du Fort (phone: 909739 or 908415).

L'ARTISAN CARAÏBE Lots of locally crafted items of wood, cloth, and other local materials, including unique chess sets, toy buses painted in colorful island style, wall hangings, and painted wood carvings. Sister shop to *Galerie Ayti* and the *Little Gallery,* all in *La Coursive Shopping Center,* St. François (phone: 886938).

AU CARAÏBE Souvenirs, some nicely made baskets, straw hats, hammocks, and creole dolls. 4 Rue Frébault, Pointe-à-Pitre (no phone).

AUTHENTIQUE Sports- and casualwear for men and women fashioned by Chipie and Chevignon in France. Also belts, totes, and accessories. 3 Rue Henri IV, Pointe-à-Pitre (phone: 829362).

LE BAMBOU Island-made madras sportswear in both adult and children's sizes, dashikis, island souvenirs. Rue de la Liberté, St. François (phone: 884561).

CENTRE D'ART HAÏTIEN Paintings, painted metal cutouts, textiles, and wall hangings by Haitian artists. 69 Montauban, Gosier (phone: 840484).

DISQUES CELINI All sorts of recordings — both French and island. Three locations: 53 Rue Schoelcher and 31 Boulevard Chanzy in Pointe-à-Pitre, and Le Raizet Airport (no phone).

FLORAL ANTILLES Experts in packing island flowers for your trip home. Two locations, both in Pointe-à-Pitre: 50 Rue Schoelcher (phone: 829765) and 80 Rue Schoelcher (phone: 821863).

GRAIN D'OR Local branch of a Paris shop offering stylish gold jewelry. 84 Rue de Nozières, Pointe-à-Pitre (phone: 821173).

HAIKEL An eclectic assortment of Val St. Lambert crystal, porcelain, perfume, some ready-to-wear, and Moroccan leather accessories. Rue Frébault, Pointe-à-Pitre (phone: 820093).

K-DIS Worth a stop for French kitchen gadgets and fine food items (pâté, mustard, and the like). In the *Galerie du Port* at the foot of Rue Frébault, Pointe-à-Pitre (phone: 820906).

OCEAN'S Shells and shell-decorated boxes, frames, and the like, plus madras dresses, dolls, and other crafts items. 25 *bis* Rue Lamartine, Pointe-à-Pitre (no phone).

PHOENICIA Brand-name perfume and cosmetics (20% off if paid in US dollars). Three locations: 8 Rue Frébault, Pointe-à-Pitre (phone: 835036); 121 Rue Frébault, Pointe-à-Pitre (phone 822575); and Grande Escale, Gosier (phone: 908556).

ROSÉBLEU Offers the largest stock and widest choice of French cosmetics, fashion accessories, and crystal. At several locations: 5 Rue Frébault, Pointe-à-Pitre (phone: 834284); 25 Rue A. René-Boisneuf, Pointe-à-Pitre; 18 Rue du Dr. Cabre, Basse-Terre (no phone); plus a duty-free shop at Le Raizet Airport.

SEVEN SINS Fine selection of French wines, but no great bargains on the "duty-free" hard liquor. 6 Rue Frébault, Pointe-à-Pitre (phone: 828839).

TIM TIM A worthwhile antiques shop run by the well-known French author, André Schwarz-Bart, and his Guadeloupean wife, Simone, also a writer. 15 Rue Jean-Jaurès, Pointe-à-Pitre (phone: 834871).

VENDÔME Imported fashions (dresses, shirts, swimwear, accessories) for men and women; also Cardin watches, jewelry, and Orlane cosmetics. English is spoken here. 8-10 Rue Frébault, Pointe-à-Pitre (phone: 834284).

LA VERANDA An attractive place to shop for island-made antiques, reproductions, paintings, and decorative accessories. Place Créole, Bas du Fort (no phone).

SPORTS

Guadeloupe's action is largely land-based on Basse-Terre (hiking in the Parc Naturel and the climb to the top of 4,813-foot La Soufrière) and sea-linked on Grande-Terre, where the best beaches are, although the beach at Deshaies on Basse-Terre is excellent. If your French isn't fluent, ask your hotel to help you make sports arrangements.

BICYCLING An inexpensive way to get around, but not recommended for long hauls or on Basse-Terre's mountain roads. Rentals are available at *Dingo Location* in Pointe-à-Pitre (phone: 838119) or in St. François at *MM* (phone: 885912), *Easy Rent* (phone: 887627), and *Rent-a-Bike* (phone: 885100). For mountain biking on an 18-speed *velo tout terrain* (all-terrain bike), contact *Association Guadeloupéenne de VTT* (phone: 828267).

BOATING Sailing, on a small scale, is as easy as walking out to the hotel beach and renting a Sail- or Sunfish. Yacht charters — both crewed and bareboat — can be arranged through *The Moorings* (phone: 908181; 800-535-7289 from the US), *ATM Yachts* (phone: 909202; 800-634-8822 from the US), *Jet Sea Yachting* (phone: 908295; 800-262-5382 from the US), or *Massif Marine Antilles* (phone: 908280), which offers a fleet of cruising sailboats.

Visiting yachts dock at either of two Grande-Terre marinas: the *Carénage* in Pointe-à-Pitre and the fully equipped, 700-berth *Port de Plaisance* at Bas du Fort. Smaller marinas include *Marina de la Grand Saline* (phone: 844728), a 140-berth installation at St. François, and the 160-berth *Marina de Rivière-Sens* (phone: 817761), at Gourbeyre near Basse-Terre, within touring distance of La Soufrière volcano. Marie Galante and Iles des Saintes — both within easy cruising distance — offer protected anchorages, too.

GOLF There's only one major course on Guadeloupe, but it's a beauty.

TOP TEE-OFF SPOT

Golf International de St. François For a long time, this course provided a source of comedy for the entire French Caribbean, as its opening took what seemed to be eons. But all that wait turned out to be worthwhile, since the 6,755-yard, par 71 course has been praised as one of the best in the eastern Caribbean. Designed by Robert Trent Jones, Sr., its operation is under the aegis of the St. François municipality. Players pay about $45 for 18 holes, about $240 for a week's play in high season. Electric carts rent for about $45 for 18 holes, pullcarts for about $10. The pro is multilingual.

Maintenance has improved steadily, and there appears to be a real will to keep the course the centerpiece of the effort to lure golfers to the southeastern corner of the island (phone: 884187).

There's also a 9-hole course at *Plantation Ste. Marthe.*

HIKING Basse-Terre's Parc Naturel is possibly the best in the Caribbean. Well-marked trails lead through deep green rain forests past waterfalls, mountain pools, and steaming fumaroles to the edge of La Citerne crater. The Guadeloupe Tourist Office provides hiking brochures; guided hikes can be arranged through the *Organisation des Guides de Montagne* (Maison Forestière, Matouba; phone: 810579). Other contacts are M. Livain at the *Club des Montagnards* (PO Box 1085, Pointe-à-Pitre 97181; no phone), and *Habitation Beausoleil* (Monteran, Saint-Claude; phone: 802425; fax: 800546).

HORSEBACK RIDING Can be arranged at *Le Criolo* in St. Félix (phone: 843890); lessons are about $8.50 per hour. Trail rides are available at *La Ferme de Campêche* (phone: 821154), *Poney Club* in Le Moule (phone: 240374), and *La Martingale* in Baie-Mahault (phone: 262839).

SNORKELING AND SCUBA Especially rewarding in waters off the western and southern coasts of Basse-Terre. Most hotels rent snorkeling equipment and can arrange guided snorkelers' excursions. Jacques Cousteau has spent considerable time under the local waters and described those around Pigeon Island as one of the world's ten best areas. US divers should be aware that most instructors and guides are certified under the French *CMAS* rather than *PADI* or *NAUI,* which may make a difference in the type and amount of gear you want to bring along. Complete rental outfits are available, but all components are French. *Chez Guy* (phone: 988172) and *Les Heures Saines* (phone: 988663), which face Pigeon Island across from the beach at Malendure, specialize in diving excursions to the island. But wherever you stay, lessons for beginners and excursions for experienced divers are easily arranged through the *Aqua-Fari Plongée* at *La Créole Beach* hotel. Michel Ané's *Centre Nautique* at Terre-de-Haut on Iles des Saintes (phone: 995949) also has good facilities. For any serious diving, a license and certification book, doctor's certificate, and insurance coverage are required. Equipment can be rented at *Scuba Pro* in Abymes (phone: 823355) or *SOGIG* in Bergevin (phone: 823335). Single-tank dives range from $45 to $70 depending on site; multiple dives and week-long packages are available.

SPECTATOR SPORTS Cockfighting is in season from November to April; if you're interested, check with your hotel. There are periodic horse racing meets at the *St. Jacques Hippodrome* at Anse-Bertrand (phone: 221108). Check with the tourist board for a schedule.

SPORT FISHING For barracuda and kingfish (January–May), and tuna, dolphin, and bonito (December–March), the fishing is best off the leeward coast of Basse-Terre. *Fishing Club Antilles* on Route de Birloton (phone: 907010) has day and weekly charters with bungalows for rent. Your hotel can arrange half- or full-day charters for up to six people. Other operators include *Le Rocher de Malendre* near Pigeon Island (phone: 988345) and *Caraïbe Pêche* at the *Bas du Fort Marina* (phone: 909751).

SWIMMING AND SUNNING These are major preoccupations, and Guadeloupe rises to the occasion in style.

DREAM BEACHES

Pointe des Châteaux On the east-pointing tip of Guadeloupe's Grande-Terre "wing," there are several sand beaches from which to choose: one of them, Pointe Tarare, is dedicated to *au naturel* bathing, and another (and more traditional) one is in nearby St. François. The rocky cliffs also shelter several sandy coves, all of which are fine for a picnic and a dip. There's a nature trail that rambles among signposted native trees and other vegetation, eventually leading to a spectacular viewpoint atop a promontory.

Petite Anse, Marie Galante, near Guadeloupe On the cookie-shaped island, which is a 10-minute flight from Guadeloupe's Le Raizet Airport, this beach is where the Guadeloupais — who consider it their secret — go for their weekend picnics. It's long and golden, with no improvements or facilities except for a simple restaurant called *Touloulou* that serves creole lunches and lobster in season. No excitement, but true beach buffs will find it worth the trip.

Beaches on the island vary in texture and color. On rugged Basse-Terre, west coast beaches are surf-combed, usually gray or black sand in the south and orange sand in the north. Grande-Terre has long stretches of white sand along its shores — extensive artificial beaches on the southern coast between Bas du Fort and Gosier; beautifully natural stretches from Ste. Anne to the tip of Pointe des Châteaux; and sandy strands along the northeastern coast at Le Moule and northwest at Anse-Bertrand and Port-Louis.

Chances are you'll spend most of your sand-and-sea time on your own hotel's beach, but if you want to visit others, most hotels will welcome you (there's usually a small fee for changing facilities, chaises, towels). On Guadeloupe's public beaches, there's no charge or only a small fee for parking. They're fine for picnicking, but most also have small seafood restaurants where you can pick up an inexpensive creole lunch. Public beach names to know: Ste. Anne, Raisins Clairs at St. François, Anse Laborde and Anse-Bertrand on the northeast coast, Anse du Souffleur near Port-Louis. In addition to Pointe Tarare, other nudist beaches include: those on Ilet Gosier, a tiny offshore land dot to which several Gosier hotels provide boat transportation (it's clothed on Sundays); at the *Club Med* enclave; and behind the *Bois Joli* hotel, on Iles des Saintes.

TENNIS There are floodlit courts at many island hotels; day play is free all around, but some hotels charge for night games. Hotels with courts include the *Anchorage Anse des Rochers, Auberge de la Vieille Tour,* the *Club Med* resort, *Méridien, PLM Azur Marissol, Relais du Moulin, Salako, Hamak, Résidence Karukéra, Golf Marine Club, Fleur d'Epée–Novotel, Toubana, Canella Beach, Golf Village, Plantation Ste. Marthe, Arawak,* and *La Créole Beach.* Visitors may also be able to arrange to play at the private *Marina Club* at Pointe-à-Pitre (phone: 908408) and *Centre Lamby Lambert* in Gosier (phone: 909097).

WATER SKIING AND WINDSURFING Water skiing is offered by most seaside hotels for about $20 to $25 per half hour. Windsurfing is so good that major international events are held here. Rentals average $13 to $15 per hour, lessons about $20 per hour. *The Union des Centres de Plein Air (UCPA)* in St. François offers week-long packages with daily lessons (phone: 886480).

NIGHTLIFE

No matter where the beguine began (Guadeloupeans swear it was here), they dance it with gusto throughout the island. Guadeloupeans love to dance; hang a bit loose and they'll have you swinging right along in no time. The island's folk company, on stage 1 or 2 nights a week at hotels, performs the old-fashioned dances (don't miss them). Dinner dancing clubs and hotel discos (all very intimate, oozing trendiness, and favored by as many islanders as tourists) update the movements, and play into the small hours. Current favorites in Gosier include *PLM Azur Marissol*'s *Fou Fou*, *Le Caraïbe* at *Le Salako,* the *New Land* (Rte. Riveria; phone: 843791), and the very popular *Mandingo* in the *Domaine Caribéen* (phone: 842785), which also has a restaurant. *La Victoria* (phone: 909776) and *Elysées Matignon* (phone: 908905) are hot at Bas du Fort. More casual clubs include the *Jardin Brésilien* (phone: 909931) and *La Chaîne* (no phone) at the marina in Bas du Fort.

Elsewhere, *Club Med* prides itself on new shows nightly (lots of staff participation). At St. François there's a small discotheque called *Acapulco* (no phone), and the *Blue Sea* (no phone), a music bar where things always seem to be stirred up. There are also two casinos: one at St. François called *Casino de la Marina* (closed Sundays), and one at Gosier on the grounds of the *Arawak* called *Gosier-les-Bains* (closed Mondays). Gambling hours are from about 9 PM to 3 AM; minimum age is 21. Proofs of age and identity — with photo — are required. Admission is about $14. No slots, but roulette, blackjack, baccarat.

None of the island's late-night entertainment is inexpensive. Count on $10 and up for admission at clubs and discos (usually with one free drink), about $6 a drink for gin or whiskey, a bit less for rum or local beer.

Best on the Island

CHECKING IN

Guadeloupe offers a wide range of hotels in terms of size, location, ambience, and price. The smaller ones are more intimate and service-oriented; the larger resorts attract an active, sports-minded clientele. The approach is much more continental than Caribbean, since so many of Guadeloupe's visitors are Europeans. Hotels have relatively high standards of service, and offer a broad range of on-site activities and food that's good even in coffee shops.

Where to stay? If you like hotel hopping, the answer is the Gosier strip of three- and four-star resort hotels along the beach, or Bas du Fort, just down the shoreline, with more three-star establishments. Farther out at Ste. Anne and St. François on Grande-Terre, there's a choice of self-contained, multi-activity resorts. Other choice places include more modest resort hotels and country inns, many of which now belong to an association called Relais Créoles. In the list that follows, very expensive is defined as $250 or more per night for two including continental breakfast in winter; expensive is $200 to $250; moderate, $125 to $200; and inexpensive, below $125. Summer rates are from 25% to 35% less. As a rule, hotel room rates quoted in dollars are guaranteed for the whole season — winter or summer — whatever the franc's fluctuations. Virtually all hotels, large and small, accept US credit cards. When calling from a phone on Guadeloupe, use only the local numbers listed below. For information about dialing from elsewhere, see "Telephone" earlier in this chapter.

GOSIER

VERY EXPENSIVE

Auberge de la Vieille Tour The sugar mill tower in front, dating from 1835, was the inspiration for the French colonial architecture here. The 80 guestrooms have ocean-view balconies, and there is a bar, a good dining room (see *Eating Out*), and a poolside restaurant. The steep, stone steps everywhere will ensure you get enough exercise even if you don't use the lighted tennis courts, volleyball court, or pool. The property is now being operated by Pullman, the French hotel chain. On its own small beach (phone: 842323; 800-223-9862 from the US).

Le Salako French-speaking and modern, this property has 120 stylish rooms, 2 restaurants, a disco, 2 tennis courts, and all water sports. The casino is right next door. On the beach (phone: 842222; 800-366-1510 from the US).

EXPENSIVE

Arawak With 160 trim rooms and 6 penthouse suites, this 8-story property offers a big pool, a beach, all sorts of sports, and plenty of services. There's also a popular terrace-bar and the *Gosier-les-Bains* casino. On the beach (phone: 842424; 800-223-6510 from the US).

Canella Beach Residences There are 148 studios (some of them duplexes), junior suites, and duplex suites here, set in 3-story, Caribbean-style buildings. All units are air conditioned with a kitchenette and a balcony or terrace. Four tennis courts, all water sports, and a fine restaurant (see *Eating Out*) are on the premises. On Gosier Beach (phone: 904400; 800-223-9815 from the US).

La Créole Beach Part of the locally run Leader Hotel group, this is definitely one of Gosier's best. It's a bustling and cheerful place with 156 rooms, 8 duplex apartments, a pool, a large beach, and top water sports. The restaurant has French and creole chefs. On the beach (phone: 904646; 800-366-1510 from the US).

MODERATE

Cap Sud Caraïbes A very charming Relais Créole property in a tranquil setting, it offers 12 air conditioned rooms with sea-view balconies. Chemin de la Plage, near Petit-Havre Beach (phone: 859602).

Ecotel Guadeloupe Small and relaxed, it's staffed by hotel school students. All 44 rooms are on one garden level overlooking a big, freshwater swimming pool. The staff is friendly, and there's a fine restaurant, *Le Jardin Gourmand* (see *Eating Out*), and complimentary transportation to the beach. In Gosier (phone: 906000; 800-528-1234 from the US).

PLM Azur Callinago Beach Right on the beach, this small, modern European hostelry has 40 simply furnished rooms with mini-bars. On Gosier Beach (phone: 842525; 800-223-9862 from the US).

PLM Azur Callinago Village A simple, attractive complex of apartments (93 studios, 22 duplexes), it's adjacent to the hotel of the same name and has use of its facilities. A good buy for families, all units have complete kitchenettes, balconies, baths; there's a small supermarket on the premises. Overlooking Gosier Beach (phone: 842525; 800-223-9862 from the US).

INEXPENSIVE

Carmelita's Village Caraïbe Just outside Gosier, this 16-bungalow enclave overlooks the beach and mountains. The units have kitchenettes and balconies. There's horseback riding at *Le Criolo* nearby. St. Félix (phone: 842828).

BAS DU FORT

VERY EXPENSIVE

Fleur d'Epée–Novotel Here are 190 attractive rooms (most with balconies) in a waterfront hotel with three Y-angled 3-story wings. There are landscaped gardens, and lots of sports options (phone: 904000; 800-221-4542 from the US).

MODERATE

PLM Azur Marissol These two rambling 2- and 3-story buildings house 200 cheerful rooms. There's a marina nearby, all water sports, 2 tennis courts, a disco *(Fou Fou),* and weekly folkloric shows. The informal staff makes guests feel welcome. Beachfront (phone: 908444; 800-223-9862 from the US).

Relais Bleus du Gosier An attractive condominium/hotel on the lagoon, it has 20 studios and 10 apartments, grouped around a pool and garden. All have air conditioning, kitchenettes, and balconies or patios. Rates include maid service. There's a car rental agent on site. Guests may use the nearby *PLM Azur Marissol*'s beach and sports facilities (phone: 908146).

Sprimhotel This 17-unit studio and 1-bedroom apartment complex features kitchenettes and daily maid service. A beach, sports facilities, shopping, and restaurants are nearby (phone: 908290; 800-223-9815 from the US).

Sun Village The 82 hilltop units at the *Village Soleil* (its French name) include studios with kitchenettes and 1-bedroom suites designed for self-catering stays. Among the facilities are a pool, a snack bar, a restaurant, and a small market. It's a short drive to the beach; Port de Plaisance restaurants and entertainment are a walk away (phone: 908576).

STE. ANNE

EXPENSIVE

La Toubana These 32 bungalows — each with garden, terrace, and kitchenette — offer a super view from atop a high cliff. There's a tennis court, a pool, and a small beach. The staff is happy to assist with car rentals and excursions. The dining room serves French and creole specialties. Overlooking Ste. Anne Beach (phone: 882578; 800-366-1510 from the US).

MODERATE

Caravelle Club Méditerranée The 3-unit, all-inclusive establishment (300 rooms) feels vast, with a beach to match (nude bathing area included). Lots happening always; there's a staff-produced show several nights a week. The clientele includes lots of singles over 30, as well as quite a few couples. On the beach (phone: 882100; 800-CLUB-MED from the US).

Relais du Moulin This country retreat consists of 40 cottages (20 are newer) around an antique sugar mill. The emphasis is on peaceful, casual relaxation, with water sports available on a nearby beach. Pool, tennis, car rental, and riding stables on premises; "adventure" activities organized for more active guests. There's also a very good restaurant serving casual creole lunches and more formal French fare at night. Châteaubrun, between Ste. Anne and St. François (phone: 882396; 800-366-1510 from the US).

Le Rotabas Relaxed and cordial, this place has 44 air conditioned rooms right on the water. There's a good French/creole restaurant; water sports and beach are nearby. Management is very helpful with excursion arrangements. Beachfront (phone: 882560).

ST. FRANÇOIS AND ENVIRONS

VERY EXPENSIVE

Hamak Elegant, peaceful, and very private, this retreat offers 56 stylish bungalows in a tropical garden setting, each with a patio and terrace. There's no swimming pool; all water sports take place on a private artificial beach. A good restaurant serving a buffet breakfast overlooks the sea, and other restaurants and nightlife are within walking distance. There's also a private airstrip, and the Robert Trent Jones, Sr. golf course is next door. St. François (phone: 885999; 800-372-1323 from the US).

Méridien Just about what you'd expect from one of this chain's Caribbean outposts; this property is well equipped for sports — especially tennis (4 courts), and water sports on a fine beach. It's adjacent to Robert Trent Jones, Sr. golf course; a marina is nearby. Activities include rentals of ULMs, low-power seaplanes you can operate yourself. The 265 rooms are undistinguished, though comfortable. The nightlife is fairly active. Near the casino, St. François (phone: 885100; 800-543-4300 from the US).

EXPENSIVE

Golf Marine Club Located opposite the golf course, this modern, 68-unit (rooms and suites) complex features a restaurant, bar, and lovely pool; the club will arrange transport to the nearby beach. St. François (phone: 886060; 800-223-6510 from the US).

Golf Village Here are 52 pretty 1- and 2-bedroom bungalows on 10 garden-filled acres. Each unit has a kitchenette, a living room, a terrace, an outside shower, and a direct-dial telephone. There's also a pool, tennis courts, a putting green, and a gameroom. The property looks over the sea and the island's golf course; the beach is about 900 yards away. The restaurant serves creole fare. Breakfast is included in the rate, and MAP rates are available. Ste. Marthe, above St. François (phone: 887373; fax: 886170).

MODERATE

Les Marines de St. François This 10-acre enclave of 230 sleek, contemporary studios, apartments, and duplexes borders the marina. Each units has air conditioning and a fully equipped kitchenette; maid service available. Many of the units are occupied by long-term residents. There are 2 swimming pools, with water sports at the nearby *Méridien,* and sailing from the adjacent marina. Golf, restaurants, and a casino are at its doorstep. Minimum 3-day stay. St. François (phone: 885955).

Plantation Ste. Marthe This retreat exudes tropical elegance. Built on the site of a former sugar plantation, the 15-acre property is set in the hills above the St. François resort area, near the golf course and some of the island's best beaches. The 240 rooms are decorated in traditional style, with mahogany furniture, French fabrics, and a wrought-iron balcony offering a lovely countryside view; each has such modern amenities as cable TV and hair dryers. Facilities include the largest pool on the island, 4 lighted tennis courts, a health club, horseback riding, a 9-hole golf course, and water sports. There's also a French restaurant (see *Eating Out*). Ste. Marthe (phone: 887246; 800-223-9815 from the US; fax: 887247).

ELSEWHERE ON THE ISLAND

MODERATE

Auberge de la Distillerie This small, tile-roofed country inn is surrounded by fields of cane and pineapple, with 16 comfortably rustic rooms and 1 bungalow. There's a dining room by a small garden pool; continental breakfast is included. Route de Versailles at Tabanon, Petit-Bourg on Basse-Terre (phone: 942591).

Relais Bleus du Raizet Guadeloupe's only good hotel near the airport, it's a modern motel-style building with 62 well-equipped, comfortable units and a pool. Le Raizet on Grande-Terre (phone: 900303).

Relais de la Grande Soufrière Housed in a hillside manse, these 21 rooms mark a reincarnation of the once very popular *Relais de la Grande Soufrière.* The mountain views are wonderful. Saint Claude on Basse-Terre (phone: 800127).

St. John Anchorage On the waterfront at Pointe-à-Pitre, this hostelry has 44 rooms furnished with locally crafted mahogany furniture. Some rooms have private terraces; all have spectacular views of the harborfront and the bay. Conveniently located in the *Centre St. Jean Perse,* with its many shops and restaurants. Pointe-à-Pitre (phone: 825157).

La Sucrerie du Comté Guadeloupe's newest hotel sits on the grounds of a former rum distillery by the sea. The 26 guestrooms are air conditioned and feature terraces and creole decor. Amenities include a pool, tennis, a restaurant, and a cocktail bar set into a natural volcanic rock structure. Comté de Lohéac, Ste. Rose on Basse-Terre (phone: 286017).

Tropical Club Nestled in a coconut grove just off the beach on the northeastern coast, this new property has 72 guestrooms with terraces and ocean views, a pool, and a restaurant. Each unit can accommodate up to four people, which makes the hotel an economical seaside choice. Just outside Le Moule on Grande-Terre (phone: 939797; fax: 939700).

OFFSHORE — TERRE-DE-HAUT, ILES DES SAINTES

MODERATE

Auberge les Petits Saints aux Anacardiers With its charming village atmosphere and 10 comfortable, hillside rooms, this place is a good value. The units, distributed between the main house and a newer bungalow, are furnished with antiques but have such modern amenities as mini-bars. There's a pool, a sauna, and a boat to take guests on excursions. The excellent restaurant, *Les Anacardiers* (see *Eating Out*), features French and creole dishes and has a view of Baie des Saintes. La Savane, Terre-de-Haut (phone: 995099).

Bois Joli On this tranquil hilltop setting, with a great view, there are 5 beach bungalows and 21 small, neat rooms (13 air conditioned), all of which have private baths or showers. Features include 2 pretty beaches (Crawen Beach is nearby for bathing *au naturel*); water sports and boat trips are available. Good creole food is served. There's a bus and boat shuttle to town. Anse à Cointe (phone: 995038; 800-366-1510 from the US).

Village Créole The best-appointed of Les Saintes' accommodations, its 22 duplex apartments have kitchenettes. Take a moped ride to the good beach and other attractions (scuba diving, boating, museums, forts) nearby. Pointe Coquelet, Terre-de-Haut (phone: 995383; 800-476-5849 from the US).

INEXPENSIVE

Kanaoa On the water at Pointe Coquelet, with 14 pleasant air conditioned rooms (request Anse Mire cove view), its amenities include all water sports, snack bar, and an inviting restaurant. Rates include breakfast. Anse Mire, Terre-de-Haut (phone: 995136; 800-366-1510 from the US).

EATING OUT

Guadeloupe's favorite food is creole — probably because its cooks are great at it. Specialties: *crabes farcis* (stuffed crabs), *accras* (hot, puffed, cod fritters), *boudin* (blood sausage) for appetizers; lots of fresh fish and seafood — especially red snapper, *lambi* (conch), and langouste (lobster); spicy fish stews and curries zinged with turmeric, mustard, and seven kinds of hot peppers; native vegetables like *christophine,* breadfruit, and fried plantain. For dessert: island-grown guava, pineapple, papaya, coconut, and mango ice cream. But there are classic French restaurants, too. A three-course meal with wine for two will cost $150 and up at restaurants we describe as very expensive, $90 to $140 at expensive places, $60 to $90 at places in the moderate category, and under $60 at eateries listed as inexpensive. A 15% service charge is added to the bill.

Meals, whether creole or *cuisine française,* are usually accompanied by French wine, which is plentiful and reasonably priced. But before and after, Guadeloupeans most often order a punch in one of several dynamite variations: 'ti-punch, a fiery rum in a small glass that packs a large wallop; plain punch, white rum with lemon; and after the meal, a *vieux* punch of dark rum, cane syrup, and lime. Restaurants tend to be small; some close on Sundays. Unless otherwise noted, reservations are always a good idea, particularly during high season and on weekends. When making a call from a phone on Guadeloupe, use only the local numbers listed below. For information about dialing from elsewhere, see "Telephone" earlier in this chapter.

GOSIER

VERY EXPENSIVE

L'Habitation Among the best restaurants on the island, this dining room at *Canella Beach* is owned and run by author Francis Delage, host of a local French cooking show. The creole/French-influenced menu features fresh crabmeat mousse, smoked marlin, lobster bisque served with crayfish ravioli, and imported caviar. Open daily for lunch and dinner. Major credit cards accepted. *Canella Beach Residences,* Gosier Beach (phone: 904400).

EXPENSIVE

Auberge de la Vieille Tour This place is as charming as ever, serving such delicacies as *velouté* of fresh fennel, ravioli stuffed with scallops in saffron sauce, red snapper in sea urchin sauce, pork steaks in coconut milk, and *langouste maison.* Extensive wine list. Open daily. Major credit cards accepted. Off Rte. de Gosier (phone: 842323).

Le Boukarou A cozy, air conditioned dining room, it offers fine traditional French fare at lunch and dinner, but the real treat is the French-style pizza cooked in a wood-fired oven (evenings only). Closed Sundays; no lunch on Saturdays. Major credit cards accepted. On the Montauban west of town (phone: 841037).

Le Jardinet Near the casino and all the big beach hotels at Pointe de la Verdure, this place specializes in lobster cooked over an open wood fire. Open daily for lunch and dinner. Major credit cards accepted. Located on the beach in Gosier (phone: 843555).

MODERATE

Le Bananier Cornélia, formerly head of the *Auberge de la Vieille Tour* dining room, runs this place, which serves excellent creole fare. Open for lunch and dinner; closed Mondays. Major credit cards accepted. Rte. de Gosier (phone: 843485).

La Chaubette A small, friendly spot offering baby clam soup, langouste, and coconut ice cream. Open for lunch and dinner; closed Sundays. Major credit cards accepted. Rte. de Ste. Anne (phone: 841429).

La Créole–Chez Violetta Home stove of one of the island's best cooks and the president of the Women Chefs' Association. From the excellent selection of creole specialties, try *crabes farcis* and/or *court bouillon* — not broth, but a savory fish and tomato dish. Open daily for lunch and dinner. Major credit cards accepted. Gosier Village (phone: 841034).

Le Jardin Gourmand Straightforward continental preparations such as seafood cassoulet, steaks, and *navarins* of lobster, and an occasional local dish such as curried goat, are served at this hotel dining room. Open daily. Major credit cards accepted. At the *Ecotel Guadeloupe* (phone: 906000).

INEXPENSIVE

Paradise A late-night spot that doesn't open until 8 PM and gets going some time after that. The small menu includes hamburgers, salads, and daily specials with fish, chops, or steaks. Plenty of music, mostly jazz and standards. Open daily. Reservations for large groups only. No credit cards accepted. 73 Montauban (phone: 840569).

BAS DU FORT

VERY EXPENSIVE

La Plantation One of the finest classic French restaurants in the Caribbean, this chic, popular spot features Bordeaux specialties, as well as dishes with a creole touch. The *ouassous* (crayfish) is *extraordinaire.* Open for lunch and dinner; closed Sundays. Major credit cards accepted. *Galerie Marina* (phone: 908483).

EXPENSIVE

Le Barbazar An attractive French and creole dining place with a friendly staff. Specialties include conch and other seafood dishes, *maracudja* and grapefruit desserts. Open for lunch and dinner; closed Sundays. Major credit cards accepted. At the marina (phone: 908349).

MODERATE

Rosini The Rosini family goes to great lengths to serve classic, authentic Italian dishes in a warm, welcoming setting. Try the mixed homemade pasta (in

Italian-flag colors — red, white, and green), local river shrimp *fra diavolo,* and homemade desserts. Open daily for lunch and dinner. Major credit cards accepted. Bas du Fort (phone: 908781).

POINTE-À-PITRE

EXPENSIVE

La Canne à Sucre Arguably the best kitchen in the Caribbean, it's on the waterfront, with a brasserie on the street level and a quieter, 60-seat dining room upstairs. Chef Gérard Viginius turns out the nouvelle creole specialties that have gained him fame throughout the islands. His creations include *beignets* (fritters) of pumpkin and malanga, savory *crabes farcis,* parrot fish prepared with anise seeds, and the *coupe Canne à Sucre* (crème chantilly and coconut sherbet with banana caramel, aged rum, and a bit of cinnamon) — *c'est merveilleux!* Fine wines, too. Closed Saturday afternoons and Sundays. Major credit cards accepted. *Centre St. Jean Perse* (phone: 821019).

MODERATE

Le Big Indian and The Big Two restaurants, one much larger (*Le Big Indian*) and oriented toward faster eating and snacks, the other (*The Big*) next door, geared toward business lunches. Both are air conditioned and offer similar menus emphasizing steaks — entrecôtes, tournedos, rib steaks, you name it — all with your choice of five different sauces: shallot, chive butter, green peppercorn, roquefort, and mustard. Music Thursday through Saturday evenings. Open for lunch and dinner; closed Sundays. Reservations advised at *The Big* for lunch. Major credit cards accepted. 2 Rue Delgres at the Quai Lardenoy (phone: 821244).

Normandie A pleasant spot on the main square, with either alfresco service or indoor seating. The menu features salads, pasta, pizza, grilled meat, and fish; there's a daily 3-course special for less than $15. Most of the youthful, energetic staff, speak at least some English — as well as Italian, Spanish, and Dutch. Open daily for lunch and dinner. Major credit cards accepted. 14 Place de la Victoire (phone: 823715).

ST. FRANÇOIS

VERY EXPENSIVE

Vallée d'Or The fare at the elegant *Plantation Ste. Marthe* dining room consists of light, contemporary versions of French dishes. French cheeses and wines round out the meal. Open daily; dinner only. Major credit cards accepted. Ste. Marthe, near St. François (phone: 887246).

EXPENSIVE

La Louisiane A charming, colonial house where traditional French fare with creole influences is served. Among the superb offerings: pâté of sea urchin, and lean duck slices with lychees flambéed in old rum. Open for lunch and dinner; closed Thursdays. Major credit cards accepted. Quartier Ste. Marthe, just outside St. François (phone: 834434).

MODERATE

Café Gourmand The ambience is typically French and the food is very good at this tiny sidewalk bistro, the best in town for salads, pizza, or ice cream sundaes. Closed Mondays. Major credit cards accepted. In the *Gulf Marine Club* hotel (phone: 886939).

Chez Honoré This homey, unpretentious place serves very good fresh fish and seafood dishes (caught by *le patron*). Open daily for lunch and dinner. Major credit cards accepted. 5 Place du Marché (phone: 884061).

La Langouste Casual beach spot; not surprisingly, grilled lobster is its specialty. The quality is consistent with owner's other restaurant, *Chez Honoré* (see above). Open daily for lunch. Reservations unnecessary. Major credit cards accepted. Anse à la Gourde (phone: 884061).

Zig Zag André Rojchouze, the owner, has upgraded the place both physically and gastronomically. Choices range from creole (fricassee of octopus and curried goat) to continental (veal scaloppine Milanese, entrêcote in green peppercorn sauce). Open for breakfast, lunch, and dinner; closed Mondays. Reservations advised for dinner. Major credit cards accepted. Port de Pêche (phone: 884273).

INEXPENSIVE

Le Mareyeur The fixed price lunch at this open-air creole dining spot — Antillean salad, grilled fish, and *glace* for dessert — is a rare and tasty bargain at about $12 per person. Open for lunch and dinner; closed Tuesdays. Major credit cards accepted. Rue de la République, overlooking the waterfront (phone: 884424).

ELSEWHERE ON GRANDE-TERRE

EXPENSIVE

Les Oiseaux In a pastoral setting, with stone walls and open windows, this friendly eatery delivers first-rate creole cooking, with a welcome touch of country French. Highlights include fish fondue, gratinéed lobster steaks, marinated conch. Closed Thursdays; no dinner on Sundays. Reservations advised for dinner. Major credit cards accepted. Anse des Rochers (phone: 889256).

MODERATE

Château de Feuilles A delightful terrace on an old country estate, it offers such unusual specialties as Tahitian fish soup, seafood sauerkraut with green papaya, and tropical fruit charlotte. Open daily for lunch and dinner. Major credit cards accepted. Near Anse-Bertrand, Campêche (phone: 221910).

INEXPENSIVE

L'Amour en Fleurs A very small roadside place with very good creole food. Try tender conch and octopus mixed with rice and beans, *boudin, blaff* (a savory fish stew), langouste, *court bouillon,* homemade ice cream. Open daily. Reservations unnecessary. No credit cards accepted. Across from the cemetery, Ste. Anne (phone: 881202).

Chez Odette A popular *patronne* oversees the presentation of pumpkin fritters, *crabes farcis,* goat curry, and creole chicken with *christophine gratinée.* Open for lunch and dinner; closed Sunday nights. No credit cards accepted. On Rue Charles Cagnet, Port-Louis (phone: 849240).

BASSE-TERRE

MODERATE

Chez Paul Located in an East Indian Basse-Terre neighborhood; the specialties here are curries and creole dishes. The menu changes daily; when you call for reservations, check what's on. Open for lunch and dinner; closed Mondays. Major credit cards accepted. Matouba (phone: 802920).

La Goyave Rose Hearty home-style cooking featuring ragouts (stews) and *colombos* (curries). Best starter is a salad mixed with local black pudding called *Antilles boudin.* Open daily for lunch and dinner. No credit cards accepted. La Rose, Goyave (phone: 955176).

Karacoli, Grande Anse One of the best for such creole specialties as *colombos* (island curries), and *coquilles Karacoli* (coquilles Saint Jacques with creole spices), served indoors or on a tree-shaded terrace by the beach. English-speaking staff. Open for lunch and dinner; closed Fridays. Major credit cards accepted. Plage Grande, Anse Deshaies (phone: 284117).

INEXPENSIVE

Chez LouLouse Cheerful and rustic, it's a favorite spot for divers returning from Pigeon Island. Menu *touristique* features salad, fresh grilled fish, curried chicken, rice, wine, and fruit. No extra charge for spontaneous song accompaniment. Open daily for lunch and dinner. Reservations unnecessary. No credit cards accepted. On the beach, Malendure (phone: 987034).

La Touna There's always a warm welcome at this open-air spot, which is also the *Fishing Club Antilles.* The menu depends on what the boat brings in. Closed Sunday evenings and Mondays. Reservations advised for dinner. No credit cards accepted. Pigeon Galet in Bouillante (phone: 867010).

OFFSHORE — TERRE-DE-HAUT, ILES DES SAINTES

EXPENSIVE

Le Relais des Iles A 10-table dining room in the home of chef Bernard Mathieu and his gracious wife. There's a fresh lobster tank on the terrace. Seafood specialties on the menu include pâté of fish and creamy scallops Florentine; try the lemon sherbet with vodka for dessert. Open daily for lunch and dinner. Reservations advised for dinner. Major credit cards accepted. Route de Pompière, Terre-de-Haut (phone: 995304).

MODERATE

Les Anacardiers The terraced hotel dining room is well known for its fine seafood, especially the local smoked kingfish, as well as stuffed squid and sea urchin *blaff* (stew). It's poolside, so take a dip before dining. Open daily for lunch and dinner. Major credit cards accepted. In *Auberge les Petits Saints aux Anacardiers,* La Savane, Terre-de-Haut (phone: 995099).

Le Foyal Just outside Terre-de-Haut, this restaurant offers dining on a balcony overlooking the harbor. The open kitchen, specializing in seafood, serves wonderful lunches and candlelit dinners. Open daily. Reservations advised for dinner. Major credit cards accepted. Anse Mire, Terre-de-Haut (phone: 995092).

Pizzeria le Genois Cozy waterfront spot with all kinds of — you guessed it — pizza. Try the Santoise, topped with cheese and minced conch. There's also a Buccaneer's Platter of smoked marlin, tuna, and marinated local fish. Open daily for lunch and dinner. Reservations unnecessary. Major credit cards accepted. Terre-de-Haut (phone: 955301).

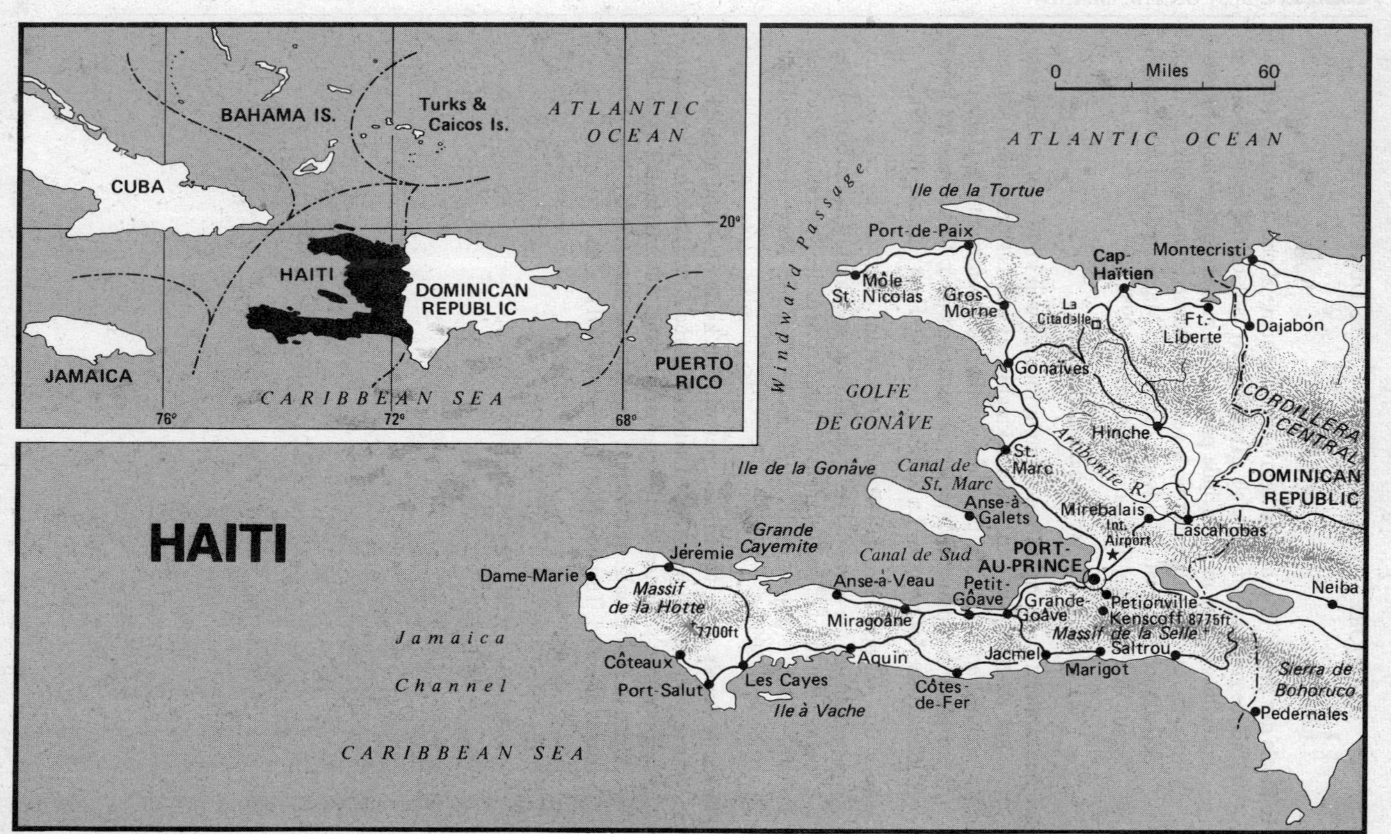
HAITI
BAHAMA IS.
Turks &
Caicos Is.
ATLANTIC
OCEAN
CUBA
HAITI
DOMINICAN
REPUBLIC
JAMAICA
PUERTO
RICO
CARIBBEAN SEA
20°
76°
72°
68°
0
Miles
60
ATLANTIC OCEAN
Windward Passage
Ile de la Tortue
Port-de-Paix
Môle
St. Nicolas
Gros-
Morne
La
Citadelle
Cap-
Haïtien
Montecristi
Ft.
Liberté
Dajabón
Gonaïves
GOLFE
DE GONÂVE
Hinche
CORDILLERA
CENTRAL
St.
Marc
Artibonite R.
DOMINICAN
REPUBLIC
Ile de la Gonâve
Canal de
St. Marc
Anse-à-
Galets
Mirebalais
Int.
Airport
Lascahobas
Grande
Cayemite
Jérémie
Canal de Sud
PORT-
AU-PRINCE
Dame-Marie
Massif
de la Hotte
7700ft
Anse-à-Veau
Petit-
Goâve
Grande-
Goâve
Pétionville
Kenscoff 8775ft
Massif de la Selle
Neiba
Miragoâne
Jamaica
Channel
Côteaux
Aquin
Jacmel
Saltrou
Marigot
Les Cayes
Port-Salut
Côtes-
de-Fer
Ile à Vache
Sierra de
Bohoruco
Pedernales
CARIBBEAN SEA

Haiti

The political situation in Haiti at the moment is unstable, to say the least, with no guarantee of safety for visitors. As we went to press, the US State Department had issued a warning advising US citizens to defer all travel to Haiti, and by and large travelers have been discouraged from visiting the country by everything from erratic flight schedules to the specter of internal upheaval. Prospective travelers should check with the US State Department's Citizen's Emergency Center (phone: 202-647-5225) prior to departure. The US State Department recommends that those US citizens who do travel to Haiti avoid large crowds and areas of unrest while visiting, and register upon arrival with the American Consulate in Port-au-Prince (phone: 220200, 220354, 220368, or 220612). We offer the following in the hope that Haiti's turmoil will end sometime soon, and that it will once again become a desirable place to visit.

There is only one generalization true of every first visit to Haiti: It is not a neutral trip. This is a country where voodoo and voodoo gods (*loa*) are taken quite seriously by many, where the highest infant mortality rate and the second-lowest life expectancy rate exist in the Western Hemisphere, where four out of five cannot read or write, where poverty has struck the hardest in the Western Hemisphere, and where the country's first freely elected president was ousted by a military coup less than a year after his inauguration. If and when you visit Haiti you may be appalled, intrigued, astonished, even delighted. But you won't remain blasé or unaffected.

Haiti shares the island of Hispaniola (just 50 miles east of Cuba) with the Dominican Republic. The culture of the Dominican Republic is essentially Spanish; that of Haiti, essentially French. This cultural and political bifurcation is the result of a past as unique as any in the Caribbean, and more dramatic than most. Haiti's lurid 20th-century history — the gunboat diplomacy of the US during and after World War I; the rise to power of the Duvalier family under ruthless Papa Doc, succeeded by his less fearsome (though nearly as corrupt) son Jean-Claude, now in exile; and the political turmoil that followed the family's reign — has tended to obscure the country's truly heroic past.

Haiti was the world's first black republic, a distinction it wrested from Napoleon's armies in 1804, after 12 years of fighting and 300 years of colonial exploitation, first by the Spanish and then the French. The island of Hispaniola was claimed for Spain by Christopher Columbus on his first voyage in 1492. Within a century the Spanish had decimated the indigenous Indian tribe that inhabited the island, and had established the beginnings of a plantation culture heavily dependent on slaves. At the same time, France was threatening Spain's dominance of the Caribbean, and

French settlers, who moved onto the island's west end, mixed with slaves to sow the seeds of a creole culture. At the end of the 17th century, Spain and France struck a bargain — called the Treaty of Ryswick — which, among other things, gave the west end of Hispaniola to France.

The creole plantation culture depended solely on the ruthless exploitation of slaves brought from Africa. In 1791 the slaves revolted, burning plantations and murdering plantation owners. The French governor was forced to come quickly to terms with the slaves because of the imminent threat of invasion by Spanish and English forces. Slavery was abolished in 1793, and one of the leaders of the black revolt, François Toussaint (known as Toussaint L'Ouverture), led a black army against the encroaching Spanish and English. Having secured Saint Domingue (as Haiti was then called) for the French, Toussaint was named governor-general, but he then reorganized his army for a final battle for independence against the French themselves. Napoleon's forces initially defeated Toussaint (who ended his days in a French prison), but the battle was carried on by Toussaint's generals Henri Christophe, Alexandre Pétion, and Jean-Jacques Dessalines; in 1803, the local forces prevailed. When independence was declared, the country's name was changed to Haiti, a name that means "mountainous land."

After an initial political arrangement failed, the country was divided more or less into halves, with Christophe the emperor of the north (he was the prototype of Eugene O'Neill's *Emperor Jones*) and Pétion controlling the south. Although considered a tyrant by many, Christophe was also truly committed to building schools, roads, irrigation works, fortresses, and palaces for the betterment of the black republic. He spent his career overseeing mammoth building projects, the culminating triumph of which was the Citadelle (see *Special Places*). The world's first black republic was also the second country in the Americas to make a Declaration of Independence, and was an early supporter of Simón Bolívar in South America. This libertarian tradition was lost in the 20th century, however, with the election of François "Papa Doc" Duvalier, who brought with him the *tontons macoute,* his dreaded secret police. Papa Doc was made president on September 22, 1957; the corrupt and violent tone he set for ruling the people of Haiti is still felt throughout the land.

After Papa Doc's death in April 1971, his son, Jean-Claude "Baby Doc" Duvalier, succeeded him. Among other atrocities, Baby Doc stole millions of dollars from a country whose commerce, educational system, and agriculture were faltering severely, as they still are. In 1986, Baby Doc was overthrown (with significant assistance from the US State Department), and he and his wife fled into exile in the south of France.

A caretaker government took charge until elections could be held. The first attempt at elections, in November 1987, begat extraordinary violence and terrible bloodshed, with some voters killed at the polls. After the bloody massacre in 1987, Haiti saw a succession of four presidents — all apparently with connections to the military, and none of them freely elected by Haiti's people.

The peaceful and democratic elections of December 1990 were a modern-day first for Haiti. Jean-Bertrand Aristide, a liberal priest with no previous political experience, was elected president. In January 1991, just a month before Aristide's scheduled inauguration, die-hard supporters of Duvalier led an unsuccessful coup attempt. Then, on September 30, 1991 — less than a year after taking office — Aristide was ousted by a second coup led by General Raôul Cedras.

As this book went to press, Haiti remained under a stringent economic embargo imposed by the Organization of American States and the US in protest of Aristide's overthrow. The country's political turmoil and economic deprivation have spurred thousands of Haitians to leave in small and often unseaworthy boats, hoping to reach the US or neighboring islands. Of the more than 40,000 Haitians who set out for the US, the great majority were returned to Haiti because the US government did not consider them political refugees requiring asylum. Last year, Haiti reached an agreement with the United Nations that would restore Aristide to the presidency, but at press time, it had not yet been implemented.

The latest political unrest has dealt a stunning blow to the country's tourism industry, which was already suffering in recent years due to fears associated with AIDS (acquired immune deficiency syndrome). Tourists shunned Haiti when reports pointed to Haitians as among the groups most susceptible to the dread virus. Recent research, however, indicates visitors run no risk from simply vacationing here. (A more relevant medical concern to travelers in Haiti is the periodic instances of malaria, a disease found in many Third World countries with poor sanitation. Prospective travelers can counter the threat of malaria by taking medical precautions before leaving home.)

Despite all the negatives, the experience of seeing Haiti firsthand is illuminating and compelling. It's strangely easy to fall in love with this mysterious, complex, troubled, and beautiful country. For all of its turmoil and tortured history, Haiti remains very much an aristocrat of the Caribbean. The spirit of its people is indomitable. Haitians, it's said, don't smile; they laugh. They don't walk; they dance.

Haiti At-a-Glance

FROM THE AIR

Haiti is a country of dramatic contrasts in appearance and feeling, with steep mountains and deep valleys tempered by the soothing blues of the seas that wash her shores. Occupying the mountainous western third of the island of Hispaniola, the country is shaped like giant jaws, with northern and southern peninsulas closing around the western Gulf of Gonâve and the big, peanut-shaped Ile de la Gonâve that floats in its center. To the north is the Atlantic Ocean; to the south, the Caribbean Sea; and across the eastern border, the Dominican Republic. The eastern tip of Cuba is only 50 miles away, as is the island of Inagua in the Bahamas.

In land area, Haiti is about the size of Maryland (10,714 square miles) and has a population of more than 6 million. Although all its major cities are seaports, more than 80% of the people live in the rural interior. Of Haiti's land total of nearly 6 million acres, an estimated 4.3 million are on a slope of 10 degrees or more, and only 2 million acres of this mountainous land is arable. The capital city of Port-au-Prince lies on the west coast where the jaws meet at the deepest point of the Bay of Port-au-Prince. The mountain suburb of Pétionville, where some of the finer hotels are located, is due east of the capital, about 20 to 25 minutes from the international airport at Mais Jata. The airport is a 10- to 15-minute ride northeast of Port-au-Prince. From there, New York is 1,550 miles and 3½ hours away; Miami is 716 miles and 1¾ hours; Santo Domingo, capital of the Dominican Republic, is 161 miles and 40 minutes by air, a full day by car. The airport at Cap-Haïtien recently has been expanded and upgraded to receive international flights. At press time, however, the schedule of daily departures and arrivals was yet to be set.

SPECIAL PLACES

In order of priority, the sites to see are Port-au-Prince; Jacmel and/or the beaches; and Kenscoff in the mountains. If you can give it the 2 or 3 days it deserves, an excursion to Cap-Haïtien is recommended in addition to or as an alternative to the Jacmel and Kenscoff trips.

A word about driving: Haiti is difficult to explore by car. Except for the roads to Jacmel, the beaches, and Cap-Haïtien — all of which are in good shape and offer a pleasant look at local landscapes — country roads are rough. Driving in Port-au-Prince is confusing, tangled, noisy, and not suggested if you want to sightsee at the same time. A better idea is to ask your hotel to put you in touch with an English-speaking driver who's pleasant and informed. Hire him for a day of shopping and sightseeing in Port-au-Prince, then arrange for longer excursions if you get along well.

PORT-AU-PRINCE From villages and towns in the hills, people come here to sell their wares on the sidewalk or in the market. The obvious poverty of so many people is difficult for some tourists to take. On the other hand, the hostility shown on some islands toward Americans doesn't exist here.

The *Iron Market* — so called because the building is wrought of the stuff — is likely to be your first stop. It is huge and teeming, but the jostle is amazingly good-natured. From all sides, it's "You come my shop next," with everything from primitive paintings and hand-carved mahogany to antique Hula-Hoops, peanuts, and ladies' underwear on sale. Terrific bargains can be found here, but browsing inside is definitely a body-contact sport. There are beggars, and they will approach you. Your best bet is to accept if your driver offers to go along with you. Or pick one of the young boys who will offer himself as a guide; with him to carry your packages and fend off the others, you'll find the going lots easier. He's well worth his 50¢ to $1 tip. Remember, too, that bargaining is part of the game. Listen to the seller's price, offer half, and carry on from there; paying two-thirds to three-quarters of the original asking price is considered par for the course.

Port-au-Prince's more serene sightseeing is centered around the downtown Champs de Mars (the Square of the Heroes of Independence), a landscaped park with an impressive statue of Jean-Jacques Dessalines, who became Haiti's first emperor in 1804. There is also the famous bronze statue of the Unknown Marron (short for "cimarron," meaning wild or savage; it's a tribute to the world's fugitive slaves) sounding a call to liberty on his conch shell. No longer in evidence are the letters that once spelled out "Duvalier — President A Vie," ripped out after Baby Doc fled.

Across the street, the National Palace looks like a cross between Washington's White House and Paris's Petit Palais. Inside is a Hall of Busts (former presidents) and, nearby, a mausoleum where Dessalines and Pétion rest.

The Episcopal Cathedral of Ste. Trinité and the Catholic cathedral — both within walking distance of the palace — are must-sees: The first has stunning murals by such Haitian masters as Obin, Bottex, and Bigaud, with a biblical perspective you may not recognize from your Sunday schooling (Judas has the white face); the second has a handsome rose window. The city's original 200-year-old Catholic cathedral was destroyed in January 1991, following a failed coup attempt. The murals can be viewed by the public from 8:30 AM to 3 PM weekdays.

Last stop in the park area is the *Musée d'Art Haïtien* (Museum of Haitian Art; phone: 222510), which displays some of the finest examples of Haitian primitive art, including some works by Hector Hippolite, whose paintings have sold for up to $44,000 at *Sotheby's* in New York. In back is a shop where you can buy original paintings, prints, and handicrafts. If you're planning to shop for paintings or sculpture later, this is a good place to learn more about local art. The *Café du Musée* is a pleasant place for lunch (see *Eating Out*). The museum is open from 9 AM to 2 PM daily except Sundays (a donation of $1 is suggested). If you're in Haiti during the *Christmas* holidays, be sure to stop by the museum to see the annual competition and exhibition of "fanals" — cardboard and paper churches and houses lit by candles. Some of these wonderful creations are 3 feet high and are marvels of workmanship by local artists. History buffs should also make it to the *Musée du Panthéon National,* on the Champs de Mars, which tells the story of Haiti from its discovery to the present through both historic artifacts and an impressive art collection. The museum is open from 10 AM to 2:30 PM weekdays, 10 AM to noon Saturdays. English-speaking guides are available from 10 AM to 12:45 PM Tuesdays through

Fridays and from 10 AM to noon Saturdays; admission charge (phone: 224560 or 228337).

Tours of Port-au-Prince's gingerbread houses can be arranged through *Agence Citadelle,* near the statue of the Unknown Marron (phone: 225900 or 235900). Visiting these private homes and meeting their owners is a good way to see another side of Haiti.

JACMEL On the southern coast, a 2-hour drive from Pétionville (via the hilly, corkscrew turns along La Route de L'Amitiée), this is a pretty, old, colonial coffee port with a choice of beaches suitable for picnics (Raymond les Bains and Ti-Mouillage are the most beautiful, if somewhat primitive; Congo, with gray volcanic sand and palms, is at Jacmel's front door), and a few pleasant hotels and guesthouses of a certain age in case you decide to stay over. The entire town is a marvelous French antique, with its miniature *Iron Market,* colorful tap-taps (pickup trucks that serve as public transportation), burros, and teeming streets. Sixty years ago, Haiti's wealthy French, enjoying a thriving coffee economy, built elegant homes here amid a bustling business district. But with World War II, the town died like a boomtown of the American Old West. A modern highway (a gift from the French government in 1981) has done much to revive the town. Congo Beach, which is public, is rife from morning until night with a rich tableau of Haitian life — fruit and souvenir peddlers, fishermen launching their boats, women with bolts of cloth on their heads, children tumbling into the surf.

KENSCOFF Many well-to-do Haitians flee the city's heat for summer homes here, high in the mountains south of Port-au-Prince. The road is winding (and at times, treacherous); the views, magnificent. On Tuesdays and Fridays, you'll pass women balancing huge baskets of vegetables on their heads on their way to the village's open-air market. On the way from Port-au-Prince to Kenscoff, you'll find Fort Jacques, with a crafts shop and snack bar; at Furcy, a bit farther on, you can ride horseback into the hills or picnic under the pines. Also on the way is the Jane Barbancourt Distillery; be sure to stop for a tour and free samples of rum liqueurs flavored with — among other exotica — hibiscus, mango, papaya, nougat, and spice. Connoisseurs consider Barbancourt's three-, four-, and five-star rums among the best in the world.

CAP-HAÏTIEN A 40-minute plane ride via *Caribintair* (phone: 460737) or a 4½-hour drive from Port-au-Prince, Cap-Haïtien is headquarters for seeing the country's two most spectacular manmade sites: the ruins of the elegant Palais de Sans Souci and the spectacular Citadelle La Ferriere, with its 12-foot-thick walls and bristling cannon, perched on a mountaintop more than 3,000 feet above the sea. Both are near the small inland town of Milot at Cap-Haïtien. A national park and tropical gardens also are nearby.

The usual procedure for seeing these sites is to tour the skeletal Palais de Sans Souci (picture its tapestries, paneling, chandeliers, its silk-and-velvet-clad courtiers), then board a jeep for the rocky trip to the parking lot halfway up the mountain and transfer to a bony horse or mule for the half-hour ride to the Citadelle on the mountaintop. You don't need equestrian skills for the trip, but an iron bottom wouldn't hurt. But even if it does mean eating standing up for a day or so, don't miss this. (The athletic may opt for the vigorous, 30-minute hike to the top.)

The fortress, built by 200,000 conscripted former slaves who dragged its thousands of tons of rock and cannon and other munitions up the tortuous road, was designed to protect Henri Christophe and 9,999 companions from an attack by Napoleon, who never set foot on the island. Day tours by land or air from Port-au-Prince are available but exhausting, with hotel departures scheduled for 6:15 or 6:30 AM; prices range from about $150 and up per person, including transport and sightseeing. It's a better idea to stay in Cap-Haïtien for a night or two. Rent a car and take a Haitian guide with you; the tourist office in Port-au-Prince can recommend one (phone: 235633; ask for Director-General Pierrot Delienne or Director-General Ernest Belande). It's important to agree with your tour guide on all charges before leaving. Two people will end up paying $80 to $100 for the trip, but it is spectacular and unique. There also are 3- and 4-hour tours originating in Cap-Haïtien, available through hotels for about $50 per vehicle, plus $6 per person for horses. Wear sturdy shoes and comfortable clothes, and bring change to buy sodas and to tip the roadside musicians, as well as the two men who push-pull your mule to the top and back. Cap-Haïtien itself is a gingerbread-trimmed colonial capital of considerable charm. It was near here at La Navidad that Columbus is said to have landed on *Christmas Day* in 1492 and where his ship *Santa María* sank over five centuries ago. The ship is the subject of a number of salvage studies that, it is hoped, will one day raise her from her watery grave. Something of an artists' colony is forming at "Le Cap" these days, and there are several comfortable hotels. Labadie village, with its beach, is a favorite destination for all-day picnics. In less turbulent political times, the *Royal Caribbean Cruise Line* ships *Song of Norway* and *Nordic Prince* land here Mondays and Fridays; on days that a cruise ship is not in, there's a $3 charge to use the beach.

Those who want to break up the 4½-hour drive to Cap-Haïtien can stop at Gonaïves, which is 2½ hours from Port-au-Prince on Route 1. This dry, extremely poor city hasn't much — but it does have a gas station, and *Chez Frantz* (on the right side of the street as you head out of town) serves cold drinks and sandwiches.

ELSEWHERE ON THE ISLAND

If you have the time, a four-wheel-drive vehicle, a tolerance for potholes and crazy driving, and a sense of daring, there's lots of beautiful countryside to explore. Be forewarned, however: These spots have only great scenery and a bit of adventure to recommend them. Be prepared for small local restaurants that come nowhere near American health standards — though they serve delicious traditional meals — and near-deserted small hotels and pensions whose room amenities consist of a bucket of water and (if you are lucky) a fan.

FORT LIBERTÉ There is no beach, no shopping, not even a phone in this sleepy town, but the hour and a half drive east from Cap-Haïtien (toward the Dominican border) offers a spectacular view of the North Plain of Haiti, scene of the slave revolts that led to Haiti's independence in 1804. Fort Liberté has one good waterfront lunch spot, *Chez Calixte,* which also has decent sleeping accommodations.

LES CAYES The 3½-hour drive from Port-au-Prince to Les Cayes (once you have survived the congested Carrefour Road) is gorgeous, especially the portion that runs alongside the Caribbean Sea. The third-largest city on Haiti, Les Cayes is on the southern tip of the southern peninsula, and the road from the capital runs past all matter of beautiful sights — forts, brightly colored towns, lush vegetation, and scenery in myriad hues of blue and green — that make you feel as if you're driving through a Haitian painting. There is not much to see in the city itself, but an hour farther west is Port Salut, a truly spectacular beach. There are no overnight accommodations at Port Salut, however, so plan on returning to Les Cayes. There, the *Ideal Guesthouse* (ask for directions) offers clean, modest rooms at reasonable rates. If you are visiting during one of the rainy seasons (March through May and August through November), hire a guide to take you to the breathtaking falls of Saut Mathurine, 1 hour north of Les Cayes.

Sources and Resources

TOURIST INFORMATION

The main tourist office is near the center of Port-au-Prince (on Av. Marie-Jeanne; phone: 221729). There also is an information booth at Port-au-Prince International Airport and branch offices in Jacmel and Cap-Haïtien. Hotels also have some material on tours and entertainment. Note: At the moment, there are no Haitian tourist offices in the US or Canada.

LOCAL COVERAGE There are no English-language dailies. However, the *Miami Herald* and *USA Today* are available at *Asterisks,* a stationery store opposite Place St. Pierre in Pétionville, and at major hotels. *Le Nouvelliste, Le Matin, L'Observateur,* and *L'Union* are the largest French-language dailies.

For background reading, try *Best Nightmare on Earth* by Herbert Gold (Prentice Hall Press; 1991); *The Rainy Season: Haiti Since Duvalier* by Amy Wilentz (Simon and Schuster, 1990); *Where Art Is Joy: Forty Years of Haitian Popular Art* by Selden Rodman (Ruggles Delateur, 1988); *The Haitian People* by James Leyburn (Yale University Press, 1941); or *Divine*

Horseman: The Living Gods of Haiti by Maya Deren (Thames & Hudson, 1953), about the voodoo religion. Most are available in paperback. *The Comedians,* Graham Greene's novel set in the bad old Papa Doc days, offers more insight into Haiti's past than its present. Buy it before or after your trip — you won't find it in Haiti.

RADIO AND TELEVISION

Most of the media broadcast in French and creole. Tele-Haiti (Channel 4) has English programming. A cable TV station, subscribed to by a number of hotels, also broadcasts in English, as does CNN. Metropole, Radio Caraibe, Superstar, and Haiti Inter are the major radio stations.

TELEPHONE

When calling from the US, dial 011 (international access code) + 509 (country code) + (local number). To call from another Caribbean island, the code may vary, so call the local operator. When calling from within the same city, simply dial the local number. When calling from one city to another within Haiti, operator assistance may be required. Check with the hotel operator to find out if you have a direct-dial line. Note that many publications may still list old (now useless) numbers.

ENTRY REQUIREMENTS

US and Canadian tourists are required to show an onward or return ticket, plus a valid passport. A tourist card is issued on arrival; you'll be asked to turn it in and pay a $25 departure fee when you leave.

CLIMATE AND CLOTHES

Haiti's climate is consistently Caribbean: warm days, sometimes cooler evenings, showers in the late afternoons. In coastal areas, temperatures range from 70F (21C) to 90F (32C); in the mountains, they range anywhere from 50F (10C) to 70F (21C). The driest months are December through March, but even in the wetter months, rainfall rarely lasts longer than an hour or so. Most hotels are air conditioned.

For day, bring comfortable, lightweight, informal clothes. Leave your new resort clothes in the closet when you go sightseeing; even a shopping session kicks up some dust. In the evenings the better hotels and restaurants require a well-groomed, put-together kind of dressing; occasionally during the winter season that can mean a jacket and tie for men.

For a trip to the mountains, Cap-Haïtien, or the backcountry, you'll need heavier things: a sweater (just in case), good walking shoes, and sturdy pants.

MONEY

Although the official rate remains at $1 US to 5 gourdes (Haiti's official currency), since July 1990 a legal parallel market has existed. US dollars can be exchanged at numerous banks at the floating rate, currently $1 US to 10 gourdes. US dollars and traveler's checks are accepted everywhere, though Canadian dollars generally are not. Most prices that tourists will come across in Haiti, including those on menus, are quoted in Haitian dollars, though dollars are not the country's actual currency (a "Haitian dollar" is equivalent to 5 gourdes). Banking hours are 9 AM to 1 PM on weekdays. Do not rely on the airport banking facility; it is seldom staffed. All prices in this chapter are quoted in US dollars.

LANGUAGE

The official language is French. Haitian creole, the local tongue, is a combination of African grammar and a vocabulary rooted in French. Unlike either French or English, every letter in creole is pronounced.

TIME

Haiti matches its time to New York's year-round through both eastern standard and daylight saving times.

CURRENT

It's 110 volts, 60 cycles, so American appliances don't need adapters or converters. Be aware that Haiti suffers from frequent major blackouts. Travelers are advised to pack a flashlight and carry it with them at night.

TIPPING

Most hotels and restaurants add a 10% service charge to your bill. Hotel employees and waiters rarely receive this money, however, so tip waiters 10% to 15%; hotel maids, $1 per room per day; bellboys and porters 50¢ per bag. But, to quote the tourism office, "Nobody — not even the Haitians — tips taxi, *publique,* minibus, or tap-tap drivers."

GETTING AROUND

BUS TOURS Individual sightseers usually tour the country by limo or minibus, and the per-person price of the tour is the charge for the vehicle divided by the number of passengers (usually one to ten). Routes are fairly standardized. Half-day trips include a morning in Kenscoff (about $40 per car), and a city sightseeing and shopping tour (about $30). All-day trips to Jacmel or the beaches are about $60 (lunches extra). Your hotel will arrange things. Or contact *Reno Travel* (phone: 220343), *San Souci* (phone: 224652), *Hemisphere Tours* (phone: 221332), *Agence Martine* (phone: 222141), *Magic Island Tours* (phone: 222025), or *Southerland Tours* (phone: 221500) in Port-au-Prince. Most tour companies also offer 3-hour cockfight tours (price negotiable).

CAR RENTAL Driving in Haiti is not recommended. Country roads are rough, and in Port-au-Prince it's easy to get lost because streets and houses aren't numbered. That said, *Avis* (phone: 462696), *Budget* (phone: 455813), *Hertz* (phone: 460700), *National* (phone: 220611), and *B&B* (phone: 220181) have representatives at the airport. Rates generally include insurance and unlimited mileage, but not gasoline or the 10% tax. Rates start at about $45 per day for compacts, and go up to $90 for 4-wheel-drive vehicles. Weekly rentals are also available. Smaller local car rental agencies in Port-au-Prince and Pétionville will take phone orders and deliver a car to the hotel. *Secom* (phone: 871913) is reliable, with plenty of cars and frequent special deals. Two others are *Transauto* (phone: 464359) and *Zenith* (phone 221986). It takes at least 36 hours to confirm a reservation. Most firms accept credit cards. Drivers need a valid US, Canadian, or international license.

PUBLIQUES, MINIBUSES, AND TAP-TAPS Haitian alternatives to high-priced taxis — recommended only if you are strong of heart, flexible of spine, and/or addicted to high-density, offbeat transport — include *publiques* (public cars), minibuses, and tap-taps (pickup trucks equipped for passengers). For 50¢, a *publique* will take you anywhere within Port-au-Prince (slightly higher at night), provided the driver doesn't enter your hotel grounds; the bad news is that the driver can pick up as many people as he wants, stop as often as he likes, and rarely speaks English. You can recognize *publiques* by the red ribbon attached to the rearview mirror. For about 35¢ you also can hop one of the minibuses or small station wagons that travel between Pétionville Square and downtown Port-au-Prince. Or become part of a movable Haitian art form — the tap-tap, named for the sound of their engines as they climb the hilly roads that surround the capital. These brightly muraled, titled pickup trucks often sport tailgate mottoes. A beauty: "You love me so you will forgive me for Saturday Night." For that same 35¢, a tap-tap will take you the length of Carrefour Road to downtown Port-au-Prince, but the bad news above goes double — and their wooden seats have no springs.

SEA EXCURSIONS José Roy, an independent operator on Caçique Island (Ibo Beach, north of Port-au-Prince), offers a variety of boat excursions, including deep-sea fishing charters, and 3-day trips to Gonâve and Tortuga islands for fishing, snorkeling, and exploring old pirate coves. Roy's 46-foot catamaran, the *Pegasus,* can accommodate up to 40 people and the price for a full day includes drinks and food (even lobster). Call for individual and group prices (phone: 482471). Another good contact is the *Scuba Nautic Club* (phone: 257773); boat trips also are offered at the *Kaliko* and *Moulin Sur Mer* beach resorts.

SIGHTSEEING TAXI TOURS The best way to see Port-au-Prince for the first time. Your hotel can arrange for an English-speaking driver who qualifies as a tour guide. If you like him, ask for his card or phone number so you can contact him for other expeditions. But when it comes to shopping tips, beware. Even good drivers sometimes take commissions from local store owners.

TAXI Plentiful at the airport and near hotels and tourist spots. Check the cost of the trip before you start. Cabs aren't metered, but drivers are required to carry a card that spells out rates set by the government. The ride from the airport to hotels in Port-au-Prince is about $12; to Pétionville, about $14; and to beach hotels anywhere from $25 to $55. Fares within Port-au-Prince and Pétionville are generally about $1.50 per person. You also can rent a taxi (one to five passengers) for approximately $10 an hour, $35 for 3 hours, and $60 for an 8-hour day, depending upon itinerary. But rates are subject to frequent review and change, so check first and/or ask your hotel to make arrangements. *Nick's Radio Taxi* (phone: 557777) provides reliable taxis with good drivers that can be contacted by phone.

INTER-ISLAND FLIGHTS

Air Jamaica has connecting flights from San Juan. There are also connections from Santo Domingo in the Dominican Republic via *Air France.* Luggage is all-too-frequently lost, so keep prescription medications, toiletries, a bathing suit, and other essentials with you, just in case.

SPECIAL EVENTS

For Haitians, the big day is *Independence Day* (January 1), a time for parades, speeches, and fireworks that carry over to *Forefathers' Day* (January 2), which celebrates such national heroes as Dessalines, Pétion, Christophe, and Toussaint L'Ouverture. But the tourists' favorite is *Mardi Gras,* or *Carnival,* which takes place throughout the country during the 3 days before *Ash Wednesday;* there's parading, with floats and costumes, dancing in the streets, and the sound of drums through the night.

Other national holidays observed by banks, government offices, and most businesses include *Pan American Day* (April 14), *Labor Day* (May 1), *Flag and University Day* (May 18), *Corpus Christi Day* (June 3), *All Saints' Day* (November 1), *Armed Forces Day* (November 18), *Discovery Day* (December 5), and *Christmas.* As one official says, "Haitians love a good party."

SHOPPING

Crafts — paintings, mahogany carvings, metal sculptures, baskets, leatherwork, antique furniture and tableware, printed fabrics, handmade and embroidered fashions — are Haiti's best buys, and they're sold everywhere. The moment you leave your hotel or step out of your car, some entrepreneur will be there with something to sell. (If it isn't exactly what you had in mind, say *"Non, merci"* and keep walking.) In most shops, bargaining is *de rigeur*. Paintings, especially Haitian primitives (or naïfs, as New York galleries now refer to them), are the country's most notable prospective buy. You'll find them hanging on country fences and stacked in *Iron Market* stalls, as well as on display in recognized galleries. And though prices aren't as low as they once were, you can still make excellent buys. If you're a serious buyer, browse through the *Museum of Haitian Art* (see *Special Places*) and several galleries to familiarize yourself with styles and prices before you make a decision.

At any given time, there'll be two or three basic pictures — a particular crowd scene, animal scene, bird-in-tree design — so successful you'll find them mass-produced by the dozens. Avoid the current best sellers unless you fall desperately in love with one; if you do, be doubly tough about the price. Don't pay original prices for a knock-off. Be sure, too, to double-check both (first and last) of the artist's names before you invest: Prefete Duffaut's works sell for several thousand dollars each; Prego Duffaut's, though amazingly similar, may go for less.

Antiques also are great items to buy in Haiti. An array of collectibles — colonial mahogany desks, beds, tables and chairs, armoires, silverware, coins, and earthen pots — are to be found in great shape and at reasonable prices. Ask the store owner to help you arrange shipping.

Wood and metal sculptures — also good buys here — are sold at many of the same spots as paintings, as well as along the roadside, in the *Iron Market,* and at your hotel door. The metal sculptures, primarily cutout designs made from sheets of flattened steel oil drums, are particularly prized. The metal sculptures of George Liautaud have been exhibited worldwide. Mahogany isn't as plentiful or inexpensive as it once was, but it's still a bargain.

NOTE **A few important crafts precautions: If you buy a woodcarving, put it in the freezer for a few days when you get home; this will take care of any wood-craving beasties. Consider fumigating baskets as well. Finally, beware of the patched goatskin rugs sold along the roadside; the US Public Health Service often will confiscate them since they may carry anthrax.**

The following are some of the best spots to buy art and crafts in Haiti:

AMBIANCE A good stop for Haitian-made items, as well as imports from the Caribbean, Africa, and far-flung islands. 17 Av. M, Port-au-Prince (no phone).

L'ART HAITIEN GALERIE NADER One of the country's leading galleries. Georges Nader, the owner, has been instrumental in exposing the works of Haitian artists to a worldwide audience. 258 Rue du Magasin de l'Etat, Port-au-Prince (phone: 220069 or 220033). A Pétionville branch of the gallery, *L'Atelier Galerie Nader,* displays an extensive collection of Haiti primitive art and high-quality wooden frames. 48-50 Rue Gregoire, Pétionville (phone: 570855 or 575602).

ATELIER CÉCILE G Features handmade traditional and modern quilts of all sizes, and custom-made cotton and silk jackets. 4 Rue Pacot, Port-au-Prince (phone: 450655).

LE CENTRE D'ART Housed in a gracious 18th-century residence, the gallery sells selected works by "undiscovered" artists at modest prices. Works by early primitive painters can be purchased by appointment. 58 Rue 22 Septembre 1957, Port-au-Prince (phone: 222118).

CLAIRE'S Aubelin Jolicoeur, a well-known Haitian journalist, has turned his large home into an art gallery. Jolicoeur was the inspiration for the character Petit Pierre in Graham Greene's novel *The Comedians.* There are no prices on his paintings and Jolicoeur has been known to present them free to anyone insulting enough to offer too little. Behind the *Oloffson Hotel,* Port-au-Prince (phone: 224752).

COHAN A nonprofit artists cooperative, where works of up-and-coming artists go for good prices. 155 Av. John Brown, Port-au-Prince (phone: 456158).

COLLECTION FLAMBOYANT A wide selection of paintings from the cream of the emerging crop of Haitian artists, including Stivenson Magloire and Julién Valery. Fine European paintings can be found here, too. 9 Rue Darguin, Pétionville (phone: 571374).

DECORALYS A fascinating collection of antique furniture, silverware, old coins, tapestries, and colonial artifacts. 4 Rue Faubert, Pétionville (phone: 572466).

EDNER PIERRE PIERRE Complete selection of Haitian arts and crafts. More like a warehouse than a gift shop. Be prepared to dig through boxes and to bargain. Between 4 and 5 Rte. de Delmas, Port-au-Prince; look for the large wooden lions out front (no phone).

GALERIE BOURBON-LALLY The country's newest art gallery features paintings by Le Saint Soleil, a group of five artists whose haunting, spiritual work is inspired by voodoo and Haitian country life. There's also a good selection of *drapeaux voodoo* (voodoo flags). Rues Lamarre and Villate, Pétionville (phone: 576321).

GALERIE DR. CARLOS JARA Jara, the former director of *Galerie Mapou,* is regarded as one of the most knowledgeable gallery owners in Haiti. At his shop, you can find the work of Lafortune Félix, an artist and voodoo priest, and Prosper Pierre-Louis, the dominant figure of the Le Saint Soleil group of artists. 25 Rue Armand Holly, Port-au-Prince (phone: 457164).

GALERIE MAPOU Superior-quality paintings and sculpture. Rue Pan Américaine, Pétionville (phone: 576430).

GALERIE MONNIN Internationally known among art lovers. Although it displays some paintings of such Haitian grand masters as Hippolite and Philome

Obin, the gallery specializes in emerging talent like Jean-Louis Sénatus, Simil, and Saint-Louis Blaise. Two locations: 19 Rue Lamarre in Pétionville (no phone), and 17 Rte. Laboule de Kenscoff, LaBoule (phone: 574430). The latter location is open only sporadically; be sure to call ahead.

GAY POTTERY A prince of a shop in Port-au-Prince, specializing in ceramics and earthenware. Must-sees include desk bells, masks, angels, and Nativity sets. Prices are reasonable. 8 Rte. de Delmas, Port-au-Prince (no phone).

ISSA'S One-of-a-kind gallery located in a mountain mansion behind the *Oloffson* hotel; selections number in the hundreds. The price marked is the price charged — no bargains here — but the tags are fair. There are quite a few metal pieces, as well as paintings. On your way out, peer through the lattice below; there's often an artist working in the studio under the gallery. Av. Chile, Port-au-Prince (phone: 223287).

LA MAISON DEFLY This pink gingerbread house located next to the *Museum of Haitian Art* carries antique furniture and colonial artifacts. One section is also a museum featuring turn-of-the-century furnishings. Champs de Mars, Port-au-Prince (no phone).

MOUNTAIN MAID L'ARTISANE Quality crafts are key at this shop. But in addition to getting good value on everything from unusual hand-carved bull's horn pieces to seed bead necklaces, you'll want to see the place itself, which is on the site of the Baptist Mission. The pleasant ride up into the hills offers sweeping views of broad mountain valleys and glimpses of Haiti's most elegant homes. Closed Sundays. In Fermathe, about 30 minutes from Port-au-Prince on the road to Kenscoff (no phone).

LE MUSÉE GALERIE D'ART DE LA FAMILLE NADER D'HAITI This link in the well-known chain of art galleries displays and sells paintings from Georges Nader's extensive collection of primitive Haitian art. Every month, it presents a show featuring the work of a different island artist. 18 Rue Bouvreuil Croix Desprez, Port-au-Prince (phone: 450565).

ZIN D'ART Choice selection of pottery, paintings, carvings, baskets, macramé, wall hangings, and many other crafts. Two locations: 86 Av. John Brown, Port-au-Prince (no phone), and Rue Clerveau, at the corner of Rue Chavanne, Pétionville (no phone).

Note: A number of small shops and individual women in both Pétionville and Port-au-Prince will hand-make and embroider a dress or a shirt for as little as $18 to $20 and have it ready before you leave or mail it to your home; ask at your hotel for recommendations, and shop early, to allow time for fittings.

In Jacmel, many unnamed artisans' ateliers sell brightly painted wooden boxes and papier-mâché animals (also found in Port-au-Prince at higher prices). You will happen upon these small shops as you stroll through town.

SPORTS

Haiti is no place for you if great sport facilities are essential to your vacation happiness. A pool and maybe a tennis court are about all you can expect from your hotel, since most are inland; you'll have to rely on the person in charge of tours and sightseeing to advise you and arrange any off-premises sport expeditions. Bring your own equipment for tennis, scuba, and snorkeling — if you plan to do more than the 3-hour package trip on which masks and fins are provided. But don't bother with golf clubs — the 9-hole *Pétionville Club* course isn't worth it.

BIRD WATCHING There is an amazing variety of birdlife to observe, especially in the lake area. Flamingos nest from December through March, and there also are egrets and herons. The drive to the lake area takes approximately 2 hours. Head from Port-au-Prince toward Hinche, turn off at Thomazeau, and then out to Nan Tête source. Four-wheel-drive and high clearance are necessary. Make arrangements through your hotel desk.

BOATING The *Kaliko Beach* hotel at La Gonâve Bay has Sunfish-scale boats and a boat for snorkeling and dive trips. The *Moulin Sur Mer* resort in Montrouis, an hour north of Port-au-Prince, also offers boat trips. Rental fees are moderate. At most beaches, there will be someone willing to take you out in a local boat for sailing and snorkeling. Rates are negotiated with the individual, but usually are about $5 per person for a 4-hour outing.

HORSEBACK RIDING There is beach riding at the *Kaliko Beach* hotel and in the hills at Furcy, near Kenscoff (for information, call Romy Roy at 482471). In addition, there is an Italian couple in Jacmel who have a stable of finely bred and well-trained horses. They can arrange wonderful day excursions in the mountains around Jacmel (about $13 for 6 hours), as well as overnight trips to the village of Sequin, located a day's ride north of Jacmel. Ask your hotel in Jacmel to make arrangements.

HUNTING Not recommended. It's not advisable for tourists to carry guns during these volatile times.

SNORKELING AND SCUBA Best around Les Arcadins, La Gonâve, and coastal reefs. Visibility around Les Arcadins island is 80 to 100 feet. The coral reef at Amaniy Beach, the northernmost of the series of beaches along the coast north of Port-au-Prince, is the most spectacular for underwater swimming. Consult your hotel travel desk about day trip arrangements. *Cormier Plage* (phone: 221000; if no answer, try calling the *Mont Jolly* resort at 227764) and the *Kaliko Dive Center* (a *PADI* Training Association) at the *Kaliko Beach* hotel have the diving setups with gear, reef excursions, and instruction for certification (also the only air for diving tanks in the country). The *Scuba Nautic Club* (phone: 257773) offers snorkeling and dive trips, but does not have scuba gear available.

SPECTATOR SPORTS Haitians are crazy about soccer; matches are held at the *Sylvio Cator Stadium* in Port-au-Prince (see newspapers or consult your hotel desk for schedules). Cockfights are held Saturdays and Sundays; the *Arène des Coqs* (on Rue de Frères, Pétionville) is the scene of the most action, but there are also numerous floating matches. Be forewarned, it's not a pretty sight. Ask your hotel to set it up with a driver, or contact *Southerland Tours* (phone: 221500).

SWIMMING AND SUNNING Mostly practiced around hotel pools. Though there are some good-looking beaches (at the *Kyona Beach, Kalikò Beach,* and *Moulin Sur Mer* resorts near Port-au-Prince; *Wahoo Beach* in Montrouis; *Raymond les Bains* near Jacmel; *Coco Beach, Cormier Plage,* and *La Badie* near Cap-Haïtien), Haitian seaside resorts, on the whole, are not up to the standards of those in the rest of the Caribbean, either in terms of comfort or built-in equipment. *Kyona Beach* and *Kaliko Beach* north of the city come closest. Sunday is the big beach day for Haitians. All beaches charge a $2 to $4 entrance fee, and have waiters on the beach to take lunch and drink orders (at moderate prices).

The *Kyona Beach* resort is the best for small children, with its gentle slope and sandy area. Labadie is the "tropical paradise beach" developed by *Royal Caribbean Cruise Line.* There is a $20 admission charge on days when cruise ships are in port (other days the admission is $3). The beach offers a variety of restaurants and souvenir/handicrafts shops. Bring your own picnic or order fresh lobster and cold beer from the local villagers who will paddle across the bay to seek you out.

With the influx of European visitors in recent years, the sight of women bathing topless has become quite common at the beaches, but waiters are still apt to drop a tray of drinks when encountering this sight around hotel swimming pools.

TENNIS Courts are available at *El Rancho, Villa Créole, Royal Haitian, Montana, Moulin Sur Mer, Wahoo Beach,* and *Kaliko Beach* hotels. In Cap-Haïtien, there's tennis at the *Mont Joli* and *Cormier Plage.*

WATER SKIING AND WINDSURFING *Scuba Nautic* (phone: 259993) offers water skiing off a number of beaches. Skis and tows are available at the *Wahoo Beach* and *Kyona Beach* hotels. Charges vary, but they're not high. The *Kyona Beach* and *Kaliko Beach* hotels have windsurfing boards to go.

NIGHTLIFE

There are no gala reviews or big names. Nightlife is centered around dining out, going to a casino, and visiting three or four local nightspots. The *Oloffson* hotel has dancing Friday and Monday nights and a concert featuring *RAM,* a jazz/rock band whose music is influenced by voodoo rhythms, and Haitian dancers on Saturday nights. Dinner and entertainment run approximately $25 to $30 per person.

Discos aren't the rage here that they are in other parts of the world, but there is enough activity to keep you from forgetting all your dance floor moves. The most popular dance clubs are in Pétionville. *Regis* (Rue L'Ouverture) is the current "in place." *Faces,* a nightclub in the *El Rancho* hotel, offers a wide variety of music; the *Ibo Lélé* hotel and the *Djumbala Night Club* (Rue de Frères) often feature local bands on weekends. Have a desk clerk at your hotel call ahead. Local artists play in restaurants around Pétionville on Friday and Saturday nights; again, ask your hotel clerk for details. Cover charges run from $5 to $15 on weekends only; drinks, about $3 to $5. There also are two casinos in Pétionville, one at the *Christophe* hotel and a larger one at the *El Rancho* hotel. Vegas they're not, but worth a whirl for roulette, craps, blackjack; slot machines, too.

You won't see authentic voodoo, but you can get a sense of it at the nightly ritual staged for patrons of a unique place called *Le Péristyle* near Mariani on the Carrefour Road. The approach is respectful and the effect sometimes stunning. Go with a few other people, and then talk with Max Beauvoir, the impressive *houngan* (priest) who presides. He'll do his best to explain things to you. Admission is about $10 per person, plus drinks. (At press time, because of the political climate, most voodoo shows had been suspended. Call Mr. Beauvoir at 242818 to see if any are scheduled.)

Best on the Island

CHECKING IN

It's no ad-copy cliché: Haitian hotels are different — from hotels in the rest of the Caribbean and from each other. No mass-produced decor, no sprawling resort complexes with something-for-everyone atmosphere (or lack of it). The hotels display an individuality that is as much a part of Haiti's ambience as zebras and giraffes are a part of the landscape of local art. All in all, Haitian hotels are an excellent buy unless you need a beautiful beach to make you happy; with some exceptions, most tend to be long on atmosphere, short on sand.

In the Port-au-Prince area, there's a geographic choice: Hotels right in town tend to be most intensely Haitian, and the handiest to sightseeing, but when it's hot they are very hot. (Air conditioning — essential to sleeping comfort here, especially in summer — is found in hotel bedrooms, but not in restaurants, lobbies, and other common areas.) Hotels above town in the Pétionville hills are naturally cooler, breezier, with more of a resort feeling. Beach hotels are particularly popular. Week-long packages that combine 3-night stays at Port-au-Prince hotels with stays in Cap-Haïtien or at a choice of beach resorts can be arranged; check with your travel agent.

Rates tend to be very reasonable — particularly when compared with winter prices elsewhere in the Caribbean. In the listings below, expensive means $100 and up for a double room, including breakfast, during the winter season (mid-December to mid-April); about $75 and up for two, EP (without meals), in summer. Moderate ranges from $55 to $95 for two, EP, in winter; about $50 to $75 double, EP, in summer. Anything below that is considered inexpensive. There's a 10% tax on hotel bills. When calling from within the same city in Haiti, use only the numbers listed below. For information when calling from elsewhere, see "Telephone" earlier in this chapter.

WORTH NOTING **At press time, several of the hotels in Port-au-Prince were temporarily closed due to the lack of tourism resulting from the continuing political instability and the OAS and US economic embargo. Call ahead to check the status of these establishments.**

PORT-AU-PRINCE

EXPENSIVE

Oloffson Richard Morse, who has operated this place since 1987, has put lots of time, paint, sweat, and enthusiasm into fixing ceilings, floors, and rooms. A piano has been shipped in from Connecticut and painted by Haitian artist Ra-Ra; all other furnishings were made in Haiti, some by Morse himself. The rooms, suites, and cottages are all comfortable and air conditioned; planned structural renovations are on hold, though. The hotel served as a marine hospital during the American occupation (1915–24), and later as a gathering spot for famous visitors such as Graham Greene (who used it as the model for the hotel in *The Comedians*). These days, it's the preferred haunt of European journalists. Leader of the locally popular band *RAM* (which performs at the hotel on Saturday nights), Morse hopes to attract a new wave of artists, writers, and others to Haiti. On Rue Capois (phone: 230919 or 234000).

MODERATE

Plaza Holiday Inn An 80-room oasis in the middle of Port-au-Prince. A typical bedroom at this affiliate of the American chain offers two double beds, a TV set, a radio, and air conditioning, as well as a small balcony overlooking the pool and central courtyard. Good weekly creole buffet (see *Eating Out*). Convenient downtown location across from a park and the *Museum of Haitian Art,* Rue Capois (phone: 239800). Moderate.

Villa St. Louis Where Port-au-Prince meets Pétionville, very convenient to the airport, with 50 comfortable air conditioned rooms, a pool, and a dining room featuring wonderful creole cuisine. Rue Louissant (phone: 456241).

PÉTIONVILLE

EXPENSIVE

El Rancho Somewhat down-at-the-heels, but this former private mansion offers appealing splashes of Haitian color and a 1930s Hollywood style. There are 115 guestrooms ranging from clean and simple to a bit more luxurious (the fancier rooms are in the newer wings). Some rooms have red porcelain bathtubs with gold-plated fixtures. Other features include twin swimming pools, a lighted tennis court, a badminton court, a whirlpool bath, a gym, a masseur, an indoor-outdoor dining room, a poolside bar with entertainment several nights a week, the *Faces* nightclub, and a casino that sparkles and glitters after a recent renovation. Av. Pan-Américaine (phone: 572080 to 572084).

MODERATE

Ibo Lélé Once visited by the rich and famous, it sits on a spectacular site overlooking city and countryside. There's a terraced pool surrounded by sun decks plus a whirlpool bath and a gameroom. Standard rooms feature exceptional woodcarving; superior rooms have terraces with city, mountain, and sea views. Great value. Rue Ibo Lélé, Montagne Noire (phone: 575668 or 571695).

Kinam Conveniently located opposite Place St. Pierre in Pétionville, this is the choice lodging of US businesspeople. There are 30 modern and adequately appointed rooms in this quaint, authentic gingerbread-style house with a pool. The restaurant serves breakfast, lunch, and dinner in pleasant surroundings; in addition to standard fare, creole dishes are offered. Rue Lamarre, Place St. Pierre (phone: 570462)

Montana In a lovely, tranquil setting neatly balanced on a hillside between Pétionville and Port-au-Prince, with fabulous views of the capital city, this is the hotel of choice for American journalists and film crews. The corner rooms of this 70-room place are the best — they have good-size balconies with views of the mountains in one direction, the sea in the other. Amenities include air conditioning, tennis courts, a super swimming pool, a restaurant, a boutique, and a conference room. Go for lunch to enjoy the views even if you don't stay here. Rue F. Cardozo (phone: 571920 or 574020).

Villa Créole This restored and gracefully expanded mansion in the hills is a top choice — pretty, serene, relaxed, with 70 air conditioned rooms with TV sets and marble bathrooms. There's also a large pool, tennis, a restaurant, and patio dining; breakfast under the almond tree is particularly delightful. Known for its friendly atmosphere and the congenial hospitality of its manager, Roger Sunwell, and the staff. 95 Rue Bourdon (phone: 571570 or 571571).

JACMEL

MODERATE

La Jacmélienne This 2-story beachfront property is big and modern for Jacmel, with 30 large rooms, all with terraces opening onto the sea, Haitian furnishings, and ceiling fans. There's also a swimming pool, 2 bars, and a restaurant that features outdoor eating during the day; indoor (but open-air) dining at night; and very good food at all times. Situated on Congo Beach, Jacmel Bay (phone: 224899).

CAP-HAÏTIEN

MODERATE

Beck This fortress-like 23-room hostelry is built on a hill overlooking the city. Everything here seems oversize, including the large terraces, the two verandah swimming pools, and the deck area. Beautifully furnished with antiques and mahogany pieces built by staff carpenters. Delicious continental cooking is served in the dining room (phone: 620001).

Cormier Plage A beautiful 32-unit property on a lovely beach, this is the perfect place to relax, enjoy a lobster lunch in the open-air restaurant, play tennis, swim, snorkel, or scuba dive. Just west of Cap-Haïtien (phone: 621000 or 621069).

Mont Joli Very pleasant, relaxed, with 40 rooms (some overlooking the sea), a large pool, tennis, and a good Haitian dining room; also a nightclub with Haitian music and folkloric shows. Sans Souci–Citadelle tours can be arranged (phone: 227764).

Roi Christophe Built in 1724 as the residence of the French Governor of Saint Domingue, this cozy 18-room inn has retained its lovely original arched doorways, beamed ceilings, interior courtyards, and colonial wood furniture. Service is gracious and the dining room is excellent. There are gardens, an outdoor bar, and a pool. Downtown (phone: 620414).

ELSEWHERE ON THE ISLAND

EXPENSIVE

Moulin Sur Mer An establishment with a little of everything Haiti has to offer: sandy beach (perfect for sunset cocktails), a waterwheel fed by a 200-year-old aqueduct, a colonial sugar mill converted into a museum dedicated to Haitian independence, a greathouse dining room decorated in a most eclectic manner, and a salon devoted to billiards. There are 2 suites, 26 rooms, and 8 beach cabañas. Other features include tennis, racquetball, badminton, miniature golf, and water sports, plus a saltwater swimming pool. Dinner in the greathouse is French/continental; lunch is at *Les Boucaniers,* a beachfront barbecue restaurant. The 42 acres are liberally sprinkled with gardens and gazebos, plus a duck-filled pond. In Montrouis, 46 miles north of Port-au-Prince on National Hwy. 1 (phone: 221844 or 221918; call local operator).

Relais de l'Empereur Located in a small town where visitors can see how real Haitians live. Owner Olivier Coquelin has restored "a mansion of Emperor Faustin I of Haiti" to witty (or quirky) elegance (or flamboyance). Its high-ceilinged, artifacts- and antiques-dazzled lounges, dining room, and 10 suites — all with hyper-opulent bathing arrangements — serve as a home and party base for guests who spend days lolling on the stunning pooled and pavilioned beach at Plantation Cocoyer, a short boat ride away. In Petit-Goâve, about 40 miles west of Port-au-Prince along the coast of the southern peninsula (phone: 456027; call local operator).

MODERATE

Kaliko Beach Adjacent to the *Kaliko Dive Shop,* it offers a smiling attitude and lots of sports — snorkeling equipment, sailing, horseback riding, and tennis are included. Also on the premises of this 39-room establishment: a waterfall pool, deck, bar, disco, and *Le Triton* restaurant, which features Haitian and continental fare. The ideal destination when you're feeling *très sportif.* La Gonâve Bay, about 50 miles north of Port-au-Prince on National Hwy. 1 (phone: 228040 or 226530).

Kyona Beach The 12 cottages in the palms along the shore beside a long white beach are nothing splashy, but pleasantly decorated. Should you feel like snorkeling or horseback riding, it's here. Charcoal-grilled lobster and creole specialties are served in a big thatch-topped outdoor dining room. Montrouis (phone: 226788; call local operator).

Wahoo Beach In a spectacular location on the Gulf of Gonâve, at the base of the Chaîne de Matheux mountains, this 22-room resort gives the feeling of being on a private estate, with rolling lawns, magnificent mountain views, and a pool that seems suspended above the beach. Water sports, tennis courts, horseback riding, and a restaurant are available. Montrouis (phone: 239653 or 451336).

EATING OUT

Sampling Haitian cooking — from the French-inspired dishes of the best restaurants to the native street food — is one of the special pleasures of the country. Creole is the local style — not too spicy, not too far-out, but far from anything at home. One specialty: *tassot,* made from beef, turkey, or pork, dried on a hot tin roof for 24 hours, marinated, then grilled. *Lambi* (conch) is served many ways, but is especially good cooked with onions, garlic, and tomato sauce and served over rice. *Homard* and langouste — both in the lobster family — are delicious flamed in brandy or simmered in creole sauce; lobster ragout is made with cooked lobster meat, cubed, sautéed in butter, and flamed with rum, native vegetables, and spices. Other favorites are *griots,* pork marinated in lemon and salt, fried, and served with hot, spicy sauce; bananas *pesées,* or fried green bananas; *poisson grossel,* white fish (usually snapper) steamed with onions, shallots, and garlic; *riz et pois rouges collés,* rice and red kidney beans; and *manba,* a spicy peanut butter. *Tablette,* a peanut and cane syrup confection similar to peanut brittle, is best purchased from the roadside vendors along the highway between Port-au-Prince and the beaches to the north.

Dining out in Haiti can be expensive, moderate, or downright cheap. At places we call expensive, expect to pay $80 or more for two, including cocktail or wine and tip; at places in the moderate category, $50 to $80; inexpensive, under $50. If you have a strong stomach, for less than a dollar in country markets you can try fried bananas and goat served on a piece of brown paper, which is best enjoyed while strolling the market or cruising along the highway. Most restaurants accept MasterCard and Visa (not American Express), but travelers will get a much better exchange rate if they pay with Haitian gourdes. (If you insist on using credit cards, it's a good idea to call ahead to make sure they will be accepted.) Haitians dine late; restaurants start to fill up around 9:30 to 10:30 PM. The majority of places are closed either Saturdays or Sundays, although at press time restaurants were closing additional days to save fuel; ask at your hotel or call ahead to check. Most places don't require reservations, and there is usually a bar where you can sip cocktails while waiting for a table. When calling from within the same city, use only the numbers listed below. For information about calling from elsewhere, see "Telephone" earlier in this chapter.

PORT-AU-PRINCE

MODERATE

Plaza Holiday Inn Reasonably priced food in a convenient location, although the coffee shop ambience might be a bit of a comedown for exotic Port-au-Prince. The real treat is the weekly creole buffet, very popular with local businesspeople. Open daily for lunch and dinner. Reservations advised. Rue Capois (phone: 239800 or 238494).

Le Tiffany A downtown spot with tasty food and a friendly atmosphere; a popular place for business lunches. Try the *tassot creole* or steak *au poivre,* and finish with the luscious *marquis de chocolat* (rich, French-style chocolate mousse cake). Open for lunch only. No reservations. Av. Marie Jeanne, near the American Embassy (phone: 223506).

INEXPENSIVE

Café du Musée Located at the back of the *Museum of Haitian Art,* this eatery serves freshly prepared French/Vietnamese dishes. There's outdoor seating on a terrace with a view of a lovely garden. Take a stroll through the museum while you wait for your meal. Open for lunch Mondays through Fridays. Reservations unnecessary. Champs de Mars (phone: 222510).

Café Terrasse A terrific lunch spot where you can sit indoors or out and enjoy fresh salads, tasty quiche, full lunches, fresh juices, and delectable cheesecake. Friendly ambience, with a crowd of mostly young professionals. Open for lunch only. Reservations unnecessary. 11 Rue Capois at Champs Mars (phone: 225648).

PÉTIONVILLE

EXPENSIVE

La Belle Epoque An old house and garden provide an evocative setting for very good French-Haitian lunches and dinners. Open daily. Reservations unnecessary. 23 Rue Grégoire (phone: 571530).

La Cascade An "in" place at the moment, especially with diplomats and well-to-do locals. The menu features outstanding French fare, including steak *au poivre* and chicken creole, and the atmosphere hints of Paris with its modern elegance and crisp, white tablecloths. Open for dinner only. Reservations necessary. Rue Gregoire (phone: 570724 or 576704).

Chez Gérard Elegant and leisurely French dining in an old Haitian house off the square. Highly popular and romantic setting, with colored lights strung through fig tree branches. Ask Gérard Balthazar, who has been serving diners here for 23 years, for a table on the porch and take your time. The *djon* (a black mushroom found in the mountains here) and *escargot gris* are good choices. Open for dinner only. Reservations advised. 17 Rue Pinchinat (phone: 571949).

La Plantation A local favorite, with first-rate continental fare and a distinct "California" decor: Customers sit in salmon-colored directors' chairs surrounded by potted palms that have been lit by oversize lamps. Open for dinner only. No reservations. 41 Rue Borno (no phone).

La Souvenance Some of the best French food around, in an atmosphere that mixes Provence and Haiti. Edwige and Jean Guy Barme's beautifully presented specialties include a heavenly squash pie with a light green sauce of mint, parsley, and whipped cream; lamb ribs with almonds; steak *au poivre;* and a great chicken curry from a recipe handed down by the owners' mother. The wine list has the most extensive choice of French wines in the country. Open for dinner only (parties of 12 or more can make special reservations for lunch). Reservations necessary. Rue Lambert (phone: 577688).

Le Steak Inn Charcoal-broiled steaks served in a garden setting or in the main dining room. Live music nightly. Open for dinner nightly. No reservations. 31 Rue Magny (phone: 572153).

La Voile Seafood with a French accent — and a nautical theme. Seating is on two levels under a canvas roof for an "all hands on deck" atmosphere. The French couple who own the place are on hand to take orders and explain the specials. Open for dinner only. No reservations. Rue Clerveaux (phone: 574562).

MODERATE

Bolero Antoine, the owner of this eatery that's reminiscent of a French pizzeria, makes patrons feel immediately at home. His impeccable service, wonderful menu, and great taste in wines are guaranteed to charm. Most seating is outdoors by candlelight. Open for dinner only. Reservations advised. Rue L'Ouverture (phone: 571131).

Magritte The owner, Luc Cosyns, is from the same Belgian town as artist René Magritte, and this is his homage to him. A pleasant spot for dinner if garden dining, seafood, and surrealism appeal. There are 10 seafood dishes, all of them grilled. Open for dinner only. No reservations. Rue Geffrard; look for the *Magritte* sign (phone: 570841).

Le Pote Where French cuisine meets Haitian creole cooking. Selections include tournedos, chicken in a sauce made with the black *djon-djon* mushrooms, and shrimp in a zesty garlic sauce. Small, informal, and favored by a younger crowd. Open for dinner only. No reservations. 43 Rue Magny (no phone).

BEACH AREA

MODERATE

Moulin Sur Mer Set in an old sugar mill on a meticulously restored 36-acre sugar plantation, this resort's beachside gazebo grill is perfect for lunch. Continental and creole specialties are served. A must if you are in the beach area. Open daily for lunch and dinner. No reservations. At the *Moulin Sur Mer Hotel,* Montrouis (phone: 221844, 221918, or 227652; call local operator).

ELSEWHERE

MODERATE

Altitude 1300 Perched on the Kenscoff mountainside, this eatery serves meals beneath the trees, on the verandah, or inside. This is the perfect lunch spot after a Sunday stroll or hike through Kenscoff or a horseback ride in Furcy. Grilled meat and creole cooking are their specialties. Home cooking with hefty portions. Open for lunch on Sundays only. Reservations unnecessary. Ask for directions in Kenscoff (no phone).

INEXPENSIVE

Mountain Maid This is a reputable snack bar with real hamburgers. It's part of the Baptist Mission crafts shop. In Fermathe, about 30 minutes from Port-au-Prince on the road to Kenscoff (no phone).

Jamaica

Jamaica is one of the most provocative Caribbean islands, tempting visitors with a diversity of dramatic landscapes and seascapes, more variety of flora and fauna than any of its Greater Antillean neighbors, and a rich culture that has seduced even the most seasoned traveler. The real Jamaica is found in the Jamaicans themselves, 2.5 million people whose features may be African, European, Arabic, Chinese, or East Indian, and who embody the country's national motto, so similar to our own: "Out of many, one people."

The third-largest Caribbean island, Jamaica has an area of 4,411 square miles (slightly smaller than Connecticut). On the southeastern coast is the busy capital of Kingston, one of the commercial hubs of the West Indies. On the north coast are the fine powdery beaches of Montego Bay and Ocho Rios. Negril's 7-mile expanse of white sand beaches at the island's northwestern tip — a fast-growing resort area for those who truly want to get away from it all — adds yet another dimension. And the broad selection of hotels, luxury villas, evocative guesthouses, and charming small inns sprinkled throughout the island makes Jamaica one of the Caribbean's most interesting destinations.

Rugged highlands and mountains dominate the landscape: More than half of Jamaica rises 1,000 feet above the sea. The highest point, Blue Mountain Peak, provides the stunning backdrop for Kingston, towering over the capital at 7,402 feet. From the plunging waterfalls and languorous Rio Grande of Port Antonio to the surrealist moonscape of Cockpit Country in the northwest, Jamaica is a study in dramatic contrasts.

With the hypnotic, haunting rhythms of reggae and the breeze-cooled, hidden beaches of elegant resorts, Jamaica offers both stimulation and relaxation. Water sports aplenty can be pursued under and upon the turquoise waves, and Jamaica has nine championship golf courses, hundreds of tennis courts, and a first-rate equestrian center near Ocho Rios.

The Jamaican people create memories as vivid as the varied landscape of their country. Proud, resourceful, and extremely creative in many artistic fields, from literature and music to arts and crafts, their unrelenting good humor, ingenuity, and natural hospitality make them among the most accessible of all Caribbean peoples. While some visitors are taken aback by this gregariousness, most find it engaging.

Many have described Jamaica as seductive, and it has cast its spell over adventurers and rogues, as well as some of the most civilized bon vivants of the last century. Ian Fleming wrote his 007 series at his house in Orcabessa, while Noël Coward produced some of his finest works at Firefly, his hilltop retreat at Port Maria, once dear to the infamous pirate Henry Morgan.

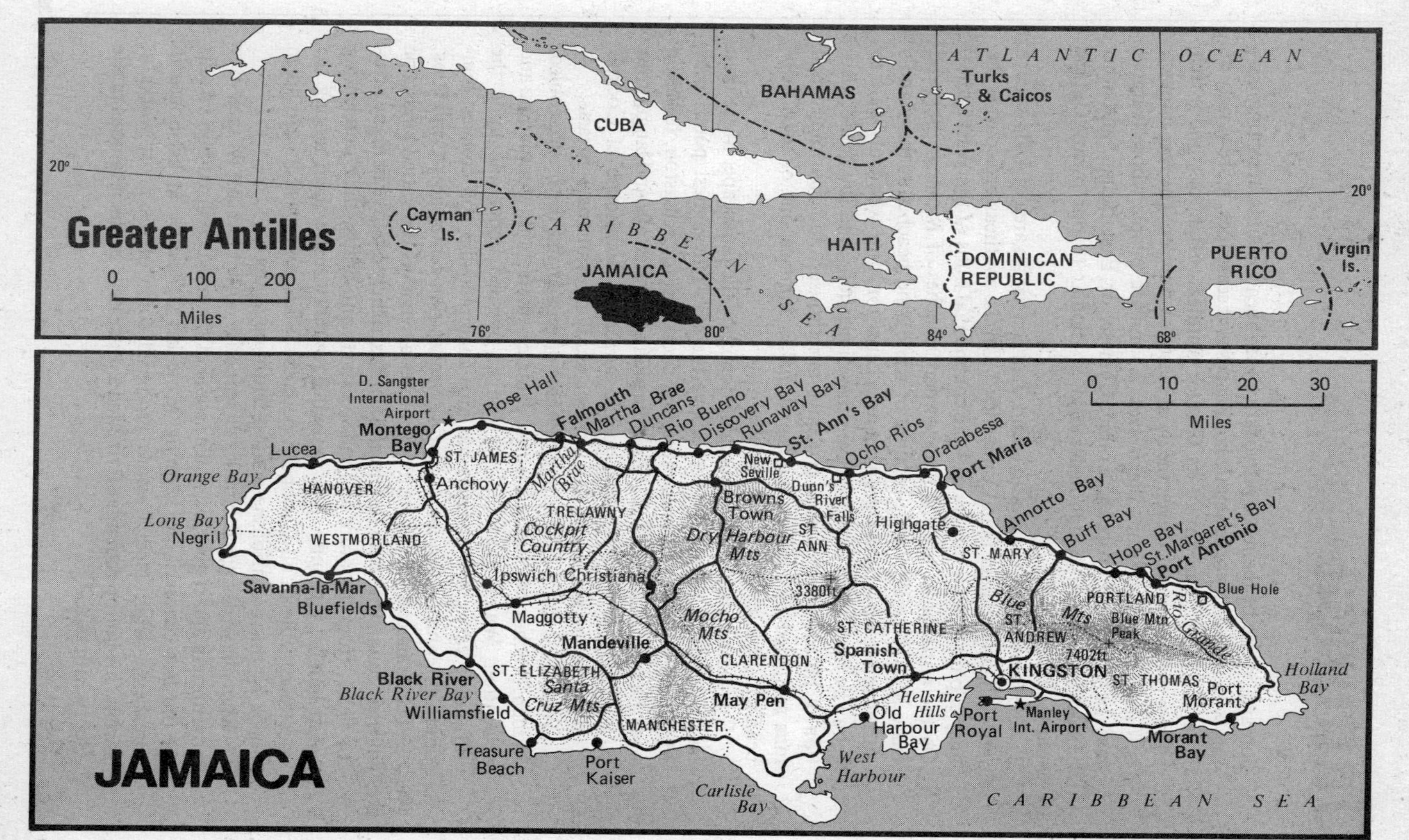
Greater Antilles
0
100
200
Miles
ATLANTIC OCEAN
CARIBBEAN SEA
BAHAMAS
Turks & Caicos
CUBA
Cayman Is.
JAMAICA
HAITI
DOMINICAN REPUBLIC
PUERTO RICO
Virgin Is.
20°
76°
80°
84°
68°
JAMAICA
0
10
20
30
Miles
D. Sangster International Airport
Montego Bay
Rose Hall
Falmouth
Martha Brae
Duncans
Rio Bueno
Discovery Bay
Runaway Bay
St. Ann's Bay
Ocho Rios
Oracabessa
Port Maria
Annotto Bay
Buff Bay
Hope Bay
St. Margaret's Bay
Port Antonio
Blue Hole
Lucea
Orange Bay
Long Bay
Negril
HANOVER
WESTMORLAND
ST. JAMES
Anchovy
Martha Brae
TRELAWNY
Cockpit Country
New Seville
Dunn's River Falls
Browns Town
ST ANN
Dry Harbour Mts
3380ft
Highgate
ST. MARY
Blue Mts
PORTLAND
Blue Mtn Peak
7402ft
Rio Grande
ST. ANDREW
KINGSTON
ST. THOMAS
Port Morant
Holland Bay
Morant Bay
Savanna-la-Mar
Bluefields
Ipswich
Christiana
Maggotty
Mandeville
Mocho Mts
ST. CATHERINE
Spanish Town
CLARENDON
May Pen
Black River
Black River Bay
Williamsfield
ST. ELIZABETH
Santa Cruz Mts
MANCHESTER
Treasure Beach
Port Kaiser
Carlisle Bay
West Harbour
Old Harbour Bay
Hellshire Hills
Port Royal
Manley Int. Airport
CARIBBEAN SEA

Jamaica has inspired visitors ever since Christopher Columbus first sighted its north coast in May 1494. His first visit was relatively uneventful; after sighting land in the neighborhood of Rio Bueno, he sailed to Montego Bay before returning to Cuba. His second call, in 1503, was stormier; foul weather and two crippled ships forced him to put in at St. Ann's Bay, where he and his crew were marooned until the jealous Governor of Hispaniola saw fit to send a ship to rescue them a year later.

In 1510, after his father's death, Christopher's son Don Diego, then Governor of all the West Indies and based in Santo Domingo, sent Don Juan de Esquivel to found a permanent Spanish settlement in Jamaica. Twenty-four years later, the town called New Seville was abandoned in favor of a new capital at Villa de la Vega, the Town on the Plain, now called Spanish Town.

In 1655, Britain's Oliver Cromwell dispatched 6,000 men to counter Spain's claim to Jamaica. They successfully drove out the 500 Spaniards then residing on the island and almost immediately set up privateering headquarters at Port Royal, across the harbor from what is now Kingston. The settlement soon earned the reputation as "the wickedest city on earth." Henry Morgan, the notorious buccaneer, took charge and carried out a series of raids that climaxed with his sacking of the Spanish colony at Panama and Spain's final recognition of England's claim to Jamaica. The end of Port Royal's era of outrageous fun and profit came in 1692 with the literal fall of the city — during a severe earthquake, more than half the town slid into the harbor.

Meanwhile, agriculture became the colony's chief concern. After unprofitable attempts at the commercial growing of indigo, tobacco, and cotton, the planters settled on sugarcane as their main crop. And sugar meant slaves. By the end of the 18th century, Jamaica's population consisted of roughly 300,000 African slaves and 20,000 whites. The situation was complicated by "free coloureds," the offspring of white men and slave women, and by Maroons (from the Spanish *cimarrón,* meaning "untamed"), descendants of freed slaves. (Descendants of the Maroons still live in the hilly Cockpit Country to the west and at Moore Town in the hills of Portland to the east.) Plantation owners were constantly harassed by guerrilla-style raids — so much so that the government signed a formal treaty with the Maroons, guaranteeing them freedom within specified tax-free boundaries in return for their help against "enemies of the government," and the return of runaway slaves. Though this last provision was rarely honored, the Maroon threat was lessened.

Revolts by the slaves themselves began during the mid-1700s. The most serious of these broke out in 1760 and continued on and off until December 1831, when a bloody clash took place in Montego Bay. Sparked by now-hero "Daddy" Sam Sharpe, a Baptist deacon and slave (who was hanged in the square that today bears his name), the confrontation hastened the end of slavery in Jamaica, which came 7 years later.

For a number of reasons — including abolition and increased competition from Cuba — sugarcane became less and less profitable. In 1865, drought struck and, pushed beyond endurance, the impoverished and desperate free Negroes of Morant Bay rioted, killing a government official. The uprising was summarily put down, but in the process the Jamaican Assembly, which had previously exercised considerable control over island affairs, surrendered much of its power to the governor. As a result, in 1866, Jamaica was designated a Crown Colony, which it remained until 1944, when full adult suffrage was granted.

The emergence of bananas as a major crop, the very profitable discovery of bauxite, and the rise of year-round tourism shored up the economy. Eighteen years later, Jamaica became fully independent within the British Commonwealth. But autonomy does not ensure stability, and since its independence ceremony on August 6, 1962, Jamaica has had its share of traumatic ups and downs.

The basic problems were both economic and political. During the mid-1970s, unemployment and the cost of living were up, incomes down. Further, the left-leaning statements of Prime Minister Michael Manley — and rumors of his government's romance with Cuba — gave rise to worldwide belief that the island was about to go Communist. Stories of violence — many true, all dramatically reported — were repeated often. Visitors began staying away in droves. To try to set the economy right, the government declared a massive austerity program and devalued the Jamaican dollar several times.

Devaluation boosted the tourist trade by keeping hotel and package prices low, and the island's natural beauty made it one of the most appealing tropical destinations. Tourism began a slow, steady recovery. The number of visitors rose to nearly 600,000 in 1979, only to plunge again in 1980 with news of pre-election strife between supporters of Manley and his more conservative Jamaica Labour Party opponent, Edward P. G. Seaga. Seaga's victory inspired new hope around the world for Jamaica's economic recovery and reassured its Caribbean neighbors — including the US. It also gave tourism an immediate and enormous emotional lift that led, ultimately, to an all-time high of over a million visitors in 1991. At the same time, resort projects built largely by foreign investors added more than 3,000 rooms, and introduced significant vitality and vivacity.

New elections — Seaga vs. Manley again — were held early in 1989, and a more moderate Manley regained power. In contrast to his fiery rhetoric of more than a decade before, Manley vowed to pay Jamaica's debt and to encourage tourism, by then Jamaica's largest industry. Manley retired in 1992 at the age of 67; his successor, P. J. Patterson, chairman of the People's National Party and a former Deputy Prime Minister, also supports tourism. And Patterson's re-election last year (though marred by violence during the campaign and at the polls) indicates that the country is willing to continue moving in a positive direction.

Should you grab your bathing suit and sunblock and take off for Jamaica? The answer is an equivocal "yes," as long as you exercise the same common sense that you would at home: Don't leave your wallet unattended at the beach, or your camera on the front seat of your rental car, and don't go strolling down dark, deserted streets alone. There are police foot patrols in all major tourist areas, and both major political parties have made a sincere commitment to "encourage decorum and law and order." In terms of political unrest, even the most fervent demonstrations are generally protests directed at government policies, not hostilities directed toward visitors. It's significant that none of the victims of any recent violent incident was a tourist.

One thing to watch out for, however, is the over-exuberance of some islanders. In Jamaica, it doesn't matter that you just told four taxi drivers that you don't need a cab, the fifth will solicit you anyway. Ditto the craft vendor trying to sell you wares. Do beware of the young men who want to guide you around town. They expect a tip for their service. In Jamaica, your "no" needs to be polite but very firm. In terms of cost and comfort, the overall picture in Jamaica has been steadily brightening. No longer must villa renters tote in staples and foodstuffs that are unavailable on the island, although savvy sportspersons still bring their own equipment. The rising cost of imported food and oil has sent restaurant, taxi, and car rental prices up, but no more so than on other Caribbean islands. On the other hand, hotel prices remain reasonable. Winter occupancies have climbed back to the 80% to 90% range, due in no small part to Jamaica's pioneering of all-inclusive resorts. From Negril to Port Antonio, more and more vacationers are lolling on Jamaica's beaches, splashing in its sea, seeking its pleasures — and finding them.

Jamaica At-a-Glance

FROM THE AIR

Jamaica is shaped something like a swimming sea turtle, and measures 146 miles from east to west and 51 miles from north to south at its broadest point, with a total land area of 4,411 square miles and a population of 2.5 million. Dark green mountains rise from foothills in the west, stretch the length of the island, and reach their highest point at Blue Mountain Peak (7,402 feet) in the east. The island's best-known resort areas — Montego Bay, Negril, Runaway Bay, Ocho Rios, and Port Antonio — lie along the gently curved north coast. In contrast, the long southern shoreline forms a deeper curve irregularly notched by coves, bays, and harbors, the most important of which is the eastern harbor on which Kingston (pop. 750,-000), Jamaica's capital and chief port, is located.

The island is about 90 miles due south of Cuba and approximately the same distance from its two other near neighbors, Haiti to the northeast and the Cayman Islands to the northwest. Its gateway airports are Norman Manley International, about 20 minutes from downtown Kingston, and Sir Donald Sangster International (where most vacationers deplane), about a 10-minute drive from Montego Bay. International flights stop at both airports. Flight time from Miami (about 590 air miles) is about 1½ hours; from New York (about 1,450 air miles), less than 4 hours.

SPECIAL PLACES

Jamaican sightseeing isn't an obligation; it's a delightful diversion. Each of the island's vacation areas, as well as its capital, has sights worth seeing, and there are also old Georgian towns and plantation greathouses to explore.

NEGRIL In the northwesternmost corner of Jamaica, this area was one of the island's last secret places until recently. But sleepy, bohemian Negril has developed rapidly, and today there are many hotels, villas, and cottages — including several luxurious all-inclusive resorts. There are also campsites at *Roots Bamboo* and the Negril Lighthouse Park.

There's little sightseeing to be done here, save to watch the few over-imbibing divers who regularly jump off the cliffs into a deep pool below *Rick's Café.* Instead, Negril is for those who love water sports and prefer to explore the local countryside. Negril is famous for its laid-back village atmosphere, its 7 miles of sea grape– and coconut palm–dotted beaches, its tranquil turquoise seas, superb scuba diving, and unforgettable sunsets that set the clouds afire with color. According to law, no buildings may be taller than the tallest palm tree, so no ultramodern high-rises mar the skyline.

Among possible activities on Negril is an excursion to Booby Cay, a small island across from Rutland Point that is popular with nude sunbathers. You can also take a sunset cruise on the *Sunsplash,* a 55-foot catamaran (book through your hotel). The outdoor *Craft Market* is a good place to pass an afternoon bargaining for souvenirs. If you rent a car, head for the Roaring River Caves, located in Savanna-la-Mar; a soft-spoken Rastafarian named Shaper will guide you through the underwater caverns.

Negril is not recommended for children, but it is great for singles, couples, sports enthusiasts, and those who want to get away from it all. The beach resorts along Norman Manley Boulevard are where most people stay, but there's also a thriving nightlife, several good eateries, and a number of popular watering holes along West End Road.

MONTEGO BAY This second-largest city in Jamaica (and the capital of Jamaican tourism) offers enough attractions, excellent beaches, restaurants, and nightlife to make it a desirable spot, especially for those who like to sightsee (though it's rather short on picturesque views).

The city's center is the Parade (also known as Sam Sharpe Square), with its Old Courthouse (1804). Also worth visiting is the Cage, an 18th-century jail that was used for slaves and runaway seamen. St. James Parish Church, at St. Claver and Church Streets, is a faithful restoration (after severe damage by a 1957 earthquake) of the Georgian original (1775–1782). Regarded as one of the finest churches on Jamaica, it is surrounded by tropical gardens and is full of fascinating monuments. Church Street itself boasts some handsomely restored Georgian homes. The *Town House,* a Georgian red brick structure at 16 Church Street, was built in 1765 as the town residence of a wealthy sugar planter. Today it houses a restaurant (see *Eating Out*). Fort Montego, on Fort Street, still has two old cannon turned toward the sea.

An excellent excursion that begins in Montego Bay is a trip on the *Appleton Estate Express;* another is the Mountain Valley Rafting Tour (see *Getting Around* for details about both). Birders flock to *Rocklands Feeding Station* (phone: 952-2009) in Anchovy (turn left onto Rte. B8 south of town); established by artist-writer-naturalist Lisa Salmon, the sanctuary is the home of some 100 species, a number of which arrive to be fed promptly at 4 PM. Many birds, including the Doctor Bird hummingbird, will eat right out of your hand. Bring a camera and arrive at 3 PM. There's an admission charge; no children under 5 allowed.

In the early 17th century, some Maroons hid on the Cockpit Mountains and warded off all attempts by the British to return them to slavery. The *Maroon Tourist Attraction Co.* (phone: 952-4546) offers guided historical tours from Montego Bay to Accompong Town, a Maroon village high up in the mountains.

Water sports enthusiasts will enjoy the Montego Bay Marine Park, a national underwater preserve. The 6,000-acre park stretches from the airport to the Great Rivers. Ask at your hotel tour desk for information on tours and water sports packages.

Montego Bay was once a major port for sugar and bananas. Today, the main remnants of this industry are the magnificent houses of the sugar barons, such as Greenwood Great House and Rose Hall. The Greenwood Great House, which belonged to members of Elizabeth Barrett Browning's family, is very close to the Trelawny–St. James Parish line, outside of Montego Bay on the way to Falmouth. Open daily from 9 AM to 6 PM (admission charge), its original books, letters, musical instruments, furniture, and other household items dating back over 200 years give a truer picture of plantation life than Rose Hall. However, Rose Hall, about 10 miles east of Montego Bay, is Jamaica's best-known greathouse, partly due to the legend of its second mistress, Anne Palmer, the infamous voodoo-practicing White Witch, who disposed of husbands and lovers by murdering them. The tour guide's tale of love, lust, and unbridled passion is in itself worth the price of admission. Afterward, you can sit in *Annie's Pub* (where the dungeons were located) and sip a drink called "the Witch's Brew." Open daily from 9:30 AM to 6 PM; admission charge (phone: 953-2323).

Closer to Falmouth (follow the signs) is the Jamaica Safari Village (phone: 952-4415 or 954-3065). Kids will love this bird sanctuary, petting zoo, and crocodile exhibit and farm. It's located on the film set of the James Bond movie *Live and Let Die.* There's an admission charge.

FALMOUTH This small 18th-century port town on the north coast, about 23 miles east of Montego Bay, is an interesting destination for a drive. Park on or near Water Square and take half an hour to explore on foot. Among the noteworthy sites in the town center are the courthouse, a reconstruction of the 1817 building; the customs office; the 1796 parish church; and William Knibb Memorial Church at George and King Streets (the present church building is new, but ask about its predecessors' stories).

As you leave town, turn south (away from the water); at the town of Martha Brae, the road forks. If greathouses intrigue you, take the right, then — almost immediately, when the road divides again — the left fork to visit Good Hope, the 18th-century home of one of the wealthiest planters in Jamaican history, John Thorpe. The main house and several outbuildings have been impeccably restored, but tours are by appointment only (phone: 954-3289). There are stables, and horseback riding is offered daily on trails through the estate's 6,000 acres. If you bear left at Martha Brae town (following the signs), you arrive at Rafters' Village, where visitors can take a raft ride on the Martha Brae River (see "River Rafting" in *Getting Around*), enjoy a dip in the pool, then have lunch in the thatch restaurant (Jamaican food at reasonable prices).

Before returning to Montego Bay, drive 2 miles east of Falmouth on the main road to the *Caribatik* factory (see *Shopping*). Nearby, owner Muriel Chandler has an open-air studio with batik items for sale, and a gallery displaying many of her paintings. Just east of *Caribatik,* stop at *Glistening Waters Marina* (phone: 954-3229 or 954-3138; see *Eating Out*) for a cool drink or some seafood and a look at the beautiful Oyster Bay, which glows with bioluminescence caused by microorganisms in the water. Boat rides depart from the main dock Mondays through Saturdays at 6:30 PM in winter, 7 PM in summer (cost: $6 per person, call in advance for reservations).

NORTH SHORE DRIVE The trip from Montego Bay to Ocho Rios (a 67-mile drive) can be done as a day's excursion (to Dunn's River Falls for lunch and back) or as a link between stays in Montego Bay and Ocho Rios or Port Antonio. The sea is on your left as you drive east, and to your right is Jamaican plantation country. Some of the land is devoted to sugarcane, some to pimiento, and some is now pastureland. Detours along any one of a dozen narrow roads will reveal antique greathouses and little old settlements. Going from west to east on the main road (A1), beyond Falmouth, you'll come to:

RIO BUENO A tiny fishing village with old stone houses, a photogenic church, a fort, and Joe James's art gallery (sample pepper pot soup and seafood in his adjoining restaurant). The historian Samuel Eliot Morison believed that Columbus did not find Discovery Bay until his fourth and final voyage, and that he actually landed here first, in 1494.

RUNAWAY BAY Once a touristic satellite of Ocho Rios, it is now a resort in its own right, with several hotels. The area is named for escaped slaves, who hid in nearby caverns. Not far away is the *Chukka Cove Farm* (phone: 972-2506), an equestrian center where polo matches are often held. A few miles farther east, past the ruined church at Priory, is the Columbus Monument at the entrance of Seville Estate. It commemorates the explorer's year-long stay here as well as the site of Jamaica's first Spanish settlement, nearby Sevilla la Nueva, founded in 1510 by Christopher's son Don Diego.

DUNN'S RIVER FALLS Located in Ocho Rios, these famous, stair-stepped cascading falls splash wonderfully down the mountainside on the right, rush under the road, and join the sea by the white sand beach on the left. This is must-see attraction, even if you decide not to participate in the popular (and quite safe) get-wet climbing tour up the falls. Wear sneakers and bring your camera for some unforgettable pictures. There are changing facilities, lockers, and a snack bar; admission charge.

OCHO RIOS On the northern coastline, midway between Montego Bay and Port Antonio, this spot is ideal for tourists who want upscale resort pampering plus some of the island's best scenery. The town has maintained its charm in spite of extensive building and the cruise ships calling at its port.

In addition to Dunn's River Falls, another local attraction is Fern Gully, a 3-mile-long dry riverbed surrounded by giant ferns that grow along the steep hillside and intertwine in spots to form a natural roof over sections of the gully. Naturalists also can head over to the 34-acre *Shaw Park Botanical Gardens* (phone: 974-2723). Located on a hill above town, the gardens offer a spectacular view.

Several working plantations in the vicinity offer jitney or horseback tours of their grounds. The most interesting of these (and the one closest to town) is Prospect Plantation (phone: 974-2058). The $10 entrance fee (no charge for children under 12) includes a jitney tour ride of the plantation. They also offer 1½-hour horseback tours along trails that lead through groves of citrus and coffee trees, past impressive stands of mahogany, and along the banks of the White River; the cost is $35 per person.

Harmony Hall, built toward the end of the 19th century as the great-house of a small pimiento estate, is a few miles east of Ocho Rios. Now an art gallery, it has an excellent selection of Jamaica artwork and handicrafts for sale (see *Shopping*). Rafting trips on the White River are also available (see "River Rafting" in *Getting Around*).

From Ocho Rios, the North Shore Road wends east through Oracabessa, a small banana port. Beyond Oracabessa is the modest villa, Goldeneye, in which the late Ian Fleming wrote the original James Bond books; it is private property and cannot be visited. Port Maria is 3 miles farther east, but drive slowly so you won't miss the right turn to Firefly Hill, the tiny home high on the hill where British playwright Noël Coward lived and wrote from 1950 until his death in 1973. This place is open to the public. The simplicity of the house and its mementos (Coward's paintings and clothes are just where he left them) is immensely touching; the view of the curved harbor below is breathtaking (admission charge). The road briefly takes to the hills in the coconut and banana country beyond, then passes Llanrumney Estate, once the property of Henry Morgan, the buccaneer who became lieutenant governor, before it is joined by the railroad right of way at Albany. Nearby are signs for Marsh Farms (phone: 975-4352), a 19-acre attraction for horticulture buffs featuring flowers and fruits indigenous to Jamaica and numerous species of birds. There's a fabulous view of Rio Nuevo, too. Open daily; admission charge. From here, the road continues on to Annotto Bay. Watch closely for signs to Crystal Springs, a 350-acre natural garden with rivers, waterfalls, birds, hundreds of orchids, and a restaurant. The main road then goes through Buff Bay, Hope Bay, and St. Margaret's Bay, where it crosses the Rio Grande — Jamaica's original rafting river — then goes into Port Antonio.

PORT ANTONIO A miniature island port built around two picture-book harbors, it is 67 miles east of Ocho Rios and 134 miles east of Montego Bay. Its quaint buildings extend onto the peninsula between the two harbors and up into the hills behind. It is famous for quiet beauty, deep-sea fishing, and river rafting, which Hollywood legend Errol Flynn invented as a tourist attraction when he saw the skinny bamboo craft islanders used to ferry bananas down to the port for shipping. Another Flynn landmark is Navy Island, in Port Antonio Harbor. Once his private hideaway, this 64-acre retreat now comprises the *Navy Island* resort (see *Checking In*). It can be reached by ferry (about $4 round-trip) from the Navy Island land base in Port Antonio.

Port Antonio itself boasts two intriguing architectural sites. The first is the Folly, the crumbled ruins of a splendid concrete mansion built on an eastern headland by millionaire Connecticut Yankee Alfred Mitchell in 1906. The second building, a turreted fantasy castle designed by architect Earl Levy, commands the rockbound shoreline east of the *Trident* hotel. History buffs also may want to take a short detour to Fort George Street, where the remains of Fort George, built in 1865 by the British, can be seen on the grounds of Titchfield High School. Neighboring natural wonders include the Blue Hole, a 282-foot-deep lagoon; Somerset Falls, in the gorge of the Daniel River above Hope Bay, where visitors can take a gondola ride to the hidden falls; the Caves of Nonsuch, unique for their fossilized sea life; and the Gardens of Athenry, 3 acres of well-tended native trees, flowers, and plants with a spectacular shore view. Fabulous vistas also can be seen from the Blue Mountains — a tropical version of the soaring peaks of Switzerland. Tours, including hiking and bicycling excursions, are also available. (Bring a sweater, as the temperature drops about 20 degrees at higher elevations.) Reach Falls, at Machioneal, offers a lovely view of what many consider Jamaica's finest waterfalls, but it's a steep climb even for hardy souls.

KINGSTON Jamaica's capital is a 2-hour drive from either Ocho Rios or Port Antonio. Like Port Antonio, it is a good base for day trip explorations into the Blue Mountains. While far from being a resort area, Kingston is undergoing something of a cultural and architectural renaissance, particularly close to the harbor, where the Convention Centre, *National Gallery,* Bank of Jamaica (which houses the *Museum of Coins and Notes*), and other modern buildings are located, and in the New Kingston business district farther north. Kingston is the seat of government and a major port. It's also Jamaica's business, political, commercial, and industrial center. Businesspeople and West Indies scholars and enthusiasts will enjoy its schools, its museums, and Port Royal. Briefly, here's what's where.

DOWNTOWN

INSTITUTE OF JAMAICA Founded in 1870, it has one of the most extensive and scholarly collections of West Indian and Jamaican books, prints, and historical documents in the world. It contains both a *Natural History Museum* and a *Historical Gallery,* and its West Indian Research Library is the best of its kind outside Great Britain. Open Mondays through Thursdays from 8:30 AM to 5 PM. No admission charge. 12 East St. (phone: 922-0620).

KINGSTON CRAFTS MARKET The stalls are laden with Jamaica's largest assortment of handmade straw and wood items. On the waterfront, at the end of Harbour St.

NATIONAL GALLERY OF JAMAICA In its own building near the waterfront in Kingston, it features Jamaican art from the 17th century to the present. Although it contains portraits of planters and their families, the gallery concentrates largely on the period from the 1920s to the present. Impressionist paintings, colorful portrayals of all aspects of Jamaican life, and abstracts are included in the impressive collection. Among the most interesting painters represented are Barrington Watson, Karl Parboosingh, and Albert Huie. Sculptures and drawings by Edna Manley also are exhibited. Open 10 AM to 5 PM; closed Sundays. Admission charge. Roy West Building, Orange St. and Ocean Blvd. (phone: 922-1561).

NATIONAL HEROES PARK Formerly George VI Memorial Park and a racecourse (not at the same time), there are now 74 acres of playing fields, gardens, and memorials to Jamaica's national heroes. Government buildings line the eastern edge. At the north end of East St.

THE PARADE Where King and Queen Streets meet. There is a public park, the historic *Ward Theatre,* and the Kingston Parish Church.

NORTH AND EAST OF NEW KINGSTON

DEVON HOUSE This is the handsomely restored 19th-century home of George Stiebel, one of the Caribbean's first black millionaires. It boasts several elegant rooms with period furnishings, china, and other decorative items. In addition to the restored rooms, there are the pleasant *Grog Shoppe, Devonshire,* and *Coffee Terrace* restaurants for patio or verandah dining (see *Eating Out*), and the handsome *Things Jamaican* shops, which offer the nation's best collection of island-crafted furniture and gifts (see *Shopping*). The museum is open from 9:30 AM to 5 PM Tuesdays through Saturdays. Admission charge. Hope and Waterloo Rds. (phone: 929-7029).

BOB MARLEY MUSEUM Opened in 1986 to mark the 5th anniversary of the death of the reggae music legend, this stately 19th-century home is where Marley lived with his wife, Rita, and their five children. It features the most comprehensive collection of Marley memorabilia anywhere. Open from 9 AM to 4:40 PM Mondays, Tuesdays, Thursdays, and Fridays. Admission charge includes a tour. 56 Hope Rd. (phone: 927-9152).

JAMAICA HOUSE AND KINGS HOUSE In a large park where East Kings House Road meets Hope Road, these are the official residences of the prime minister and the governor general (the queen's representative), respectively. Kings House is open from 9 AM to 5 PM Mondays through Saturdays; Jamaica House by appointment only (phone: 927-9941).

HOPE BOTANICAL GARDENS AND ZOO A small zoo, but the lawns and ornamental gardens are big and beautiful. Open daily from 8:30 AM to 6:30 PM. Admission charge to the zoo. Old Hope Rd.

SANGSTER'S LIQUORS In the hills of the Blue Mountains is World's End, named by Dr. Ian Sangster, a former chemistry teacher from Scotland turned master liqueur maker. Guided tours (no charge, but you must make an appointment) are followed by tastings of 15 liqueurs. The rum creams are ambrosial. Stock up, as their prices are less expensive than at the airport. Garden Town Rd., World's End (phone: 926-8888 or 926-8211).

THE GAP Ecotourists and hikers will enjoy a day at this Blue Mountain retreat 4,200 feet above sea level. There are several marked nature trails in the nearby Hollywell National Park, a restaurant swathed in clouds that serves memorable soups and lunches, and a gift shop. Open Tuesdays through Sundays (phone: 923-5617 or 923-7055); no admission charge.

ACROSS THE HARBOR

PORT ROYAL These are the remains of what was once Jamaica's number one city and the wealthiest stronghold of 17th-century buccaneers. It was the headquarters of Henry Morgan (sometimes called pirate, sometimes — more respectably — privateer) and his Brethren of the Coast. A large chunk of the city, which is located at the tip of the long, skinny, natural breakwater called the Palisadoes, was toppled into the harbor by an earthquake and subsequent tidal wave in 1692. Surviving are St. Peter's Church; Fort Charles, where British naval hero Admiral Horatio Nelson once served; the tipsy Giddy House, an old artillery store, permanently tilted by the 1907 earthquake; and the old Naval Hospital, now an archaeological museum. All are open from 9 AM to 5 PM daily; admission charge. A Committee of Friends of Port Royal and the Jamaica National Trust are planning new tours, further reconstruction, and expanded attractions. There's also a small, pub-style restaurant, as well as a full-service bar, restaurant, and small hotel at *Morgan's Harbour Marina.*

WEST OF KINGSTON

SPANISH TOWN Jamaica's old capital (1534–1872), 13 miles due west of Kingston on Routes A1 (confusingly, two A1s lead out of the city, then they converge into a single highway, also called A1). Its chief architectural monument is much-photographed Antique Square, which might have been designed by a Georgian wedding cake baker. The cupolaed monument celebrates Admiral Rodney and his 1782 victory over the French navy near Iles des Saintes. Though no Spanish buildings remain, several historical sites still stand around Antique Square: the old British House of Assembly, the façade of the Old King's House (the governor's residence, now an archaeological museum), the Old King's House stables (now the *Jamaican People's Museum of Crafts and Technology*, housing crafts rooted in Africa, Europe, Asia, and Central America), the Cathedral Church of St. James, and a number of other 18th-century buildings. Museums are open weekdays, 10 AM to 4 PM; admission charge.

At White Marl, on the way to Spanish Town, there is an *Arawak Museum* with displays from Jamaica's pre-Columbian past. Open from 10 AM to 5 PM daily; admission charge.

MANDEVILLE AND THE SOUTH COAST Here visitors will find a quieter, simpler Jamaica. On Friday and Saturday mornings, stop in at the market on Manchester Road in the center of Mandeville to dicker over crafts, clothes, fruits, and vegetables. Book a tour to the *High Mountain Coffee Plantation* (Williamsfield, phone: 962-1072 or 962-3265) to see how coffee is processed, ground, and packaged. At the same time, arrange a visit to the *Pioneer Chocolate Factory* (Williamsfield, phone: 962-1072) as well, where cocoa beans are turned into fine chocolates. Bird lovers will want to tour Marshall's Pen, an 18th-century greathouse set on a 300-acre wildlife sanctuary (by appointment only, phone: 962-2260). Owner Robert Sutton is one of Jamaica's leading ornithologists. Other highlights include Lover's Leap, a cliff that plunges 1,700 feet to the sea and a spot where the sunsets are truly breathtaking; Bamboo Avenue, a scenic stretch of highway in St.

Elizabeth shaded by a natural arch of tall, intertwining bamboo; and a boat tour on the Black River — one of Jamaica's largest and longest rivers. *South Coast Safaris* offers a 1 ½-hour excursion covering 10 miles round-trip; participants can see and photograph a wide variety of birds, as well as the American crocodile, indigenous to Jamaica (despite its name). Special tours can be arranged for botanists, and for wildlife and fishing enthusiasts. The cost is $15; $7.50 for children under 12 (phone: 965-2513; 962-0220 after 7 PM.)

South Coast Safaris also offers whole-day tours, including lunch and a boat trip, to the uncommercialized YS Falls (the name is pronounced one letter at a time). Located 40 miles south of Montego Bay and about 25 miles west of Mandeville, these wonderfully scenic tiered cascades have far fewer tourists than the falls at Dunn's River. Nature lovers also will want to visit *Apple Valley Farms,* located in St. Elizabeth. This 418-acre property is built around a former greathouse that now accommodates overnight guests (phone: 997-6895).

EXTRA SPECIAL **Jamaica's "Meet the People" program puts visitors in touch with Jamaicans who have similar jobs, hobbies, and interests. A call to the "Meet the People" officer at any tourist office in Jamaica (see addresses and phone numbers below) can result in a shared excursion or a meal or drinks with a local family. There's no charge, though you might want to pick up part of the tab. Judging by recent reports, the experience is usually not only enlightening but fun. You also can make arrangements before arriving on Jamaica by contacting any Jamaica Tourist Board office in the US or Canada. Call 800-JAMAICA for more information.**

Sources and Resources

TOURIST INFORMATION

The Jamaica Tourist Board's head office on the island is at the Tourism Centre in Kingston (21 Dominica Dr.; phone: 929-9200 or 929-9219). There are regional offices in Montego Bay (at Cornwall Beach; phone: 952-4425), Ocho Rios (in the *Ocean Village Shopping Centre;* phone: 974-2570 or 974-2583), Port Antonio (at City Centre; phone: 993-3051), Mandeville (21 Ward Ave.; phone: 962-1072), Black River (1 High St.; phone: 965-2076), and Negril (Adrija Plaza; phone: 957-4243). These offices will supply maps and brochures and answer questions about facilities, events, and sightseeing. Due to the occasional harassment of tourists, Jamaica has set up several security/information kiosks to complement the tourist board's main offices. These kiosks can be found in Ocho Rios,

Montego Bay, and Negril. For information on Jamaica tourist offices in the US, see GETTING READY TO GO).

LOCAL COVERAGE The *Visitor,* published twice weekly, tells tourists what's going on where. It's free at hotels, airports, tourist board offices. Also free, the *Daily Gleaner*'s widely distributed tourist guide updates shopping, dining, and nightlife every other week. Another useful tourism newspaper is the *Vacationer,* which is published in Montego Bay. Look for the *Vacation Jamaica* guide in your hotel room, and for the free *Destination Jamaica* magazine, put out by the Jamaica Hotel & Tourist Association; it's available at the tourist board and at hotels. The local newspapers include the *Daily Gleaner,* the *Jamaica Herald,* the *Star,* and the bi-weekly *Western Mirror. The New York Times* is available at hotel newsstands on the afternoon of the day it is published.

RADIO AND TELEVISION

Jamaica Broadcasting Corporation (JBC) produces radio and television programs; Radio Jamaica (RJR) broadcasts music, news, and features. There also are five FM stations: FAME, JBC Radio 2, IRIE, KLAS, and Radio Waves.

TELEPHONE

The area code for Jamaica is 809.

ENTRY REQUIREMENTS

Proof of citizenship (either a passport, or a birth certificate plus a laminated photo ID) and a return or ongoing ticket are the only documents required of US and Canadian citizens for stays of up to 6 months. There is a departure tax of $200 JDS (about $9).

CLIMATE AND CLOTHES

In winter, daytime temperatures range from the high 70s to the mid-80s F (25 to 30C), and in Kingston, about 90F (33C), but these temperatures are moderated by the prevailing trade winds blowing from the northeast. During October and early November and again in May and early June, there are usually brief showers every day, but the sun returns quickly. Lightweight resortwear is right for daytime, plus a jacket or sweater if you're going into the cooler mountains. Short shorts and swimsuits are for beaches, not city streets. Be cautious about sunning, and keep protection (long-sleeve shirt, pants, hat, sunscreen) handy if you're going to be exposed to the sun for a long time — sailing or rafting, for example.

Evening dress varies from barefoot-casual in Negril to quite formal in season in other resort areas, where a few hotels and restaurants still require men to wear jackets and ties at dinner. A rule of thumb: If the restaurant is labeled "expensive" in our listings, then in the winter season, women should wear a dress and men a sport jacket (and possibly a tie). Summer is less dressed up everywhere, although a few places still require a jacket (no tie required in summer, except perhaps in Kingston). On the whole, the dress for most restaurants is Caribbean casual, which means a skirt or slacks and a cotton shirt, worn with casual shoes or sandals. In Negril, where the term "casual" is taken more literally, a clean pair of shorts and a T-shirt will suffice at any restaurant in the cliffs, and at most others as well.

MONEY

Jamaica's currency, the Jamaican dollar (JDS), is subject to frequent revaluation. At press time the exchange rate was $22 JDS to $1 US. Visitors can use almost any currency here, but be aware that most prices in tourist areas are quoted in US dollars (as are all the prices quoted in this chapter). Some shops and restaurants offer better exchange rates than others, so it's smart to check the official rate at a bank. There's also an exchange bureau at every airport. Traveler's checks are generally accepted, and most hotels and many restaurants and shops honor major credit cards. Banking hours generally are 9 AM to 2 PM Mondays through Thursdays; 9 AM to noon and 2:30 to 5 PM on Fridays. Some banks are open Saturday mornings; all are closed Sundays and holidays.

LANGUAGE

The official language is English. There is also a Jamaican patois, an intriguing British-accented mixture of English, African, and island words and rhythms — plus, some say, a bit of Welsh.

TIME

Jamaica is on eastern standard time year-round, so during daylight saving time East Coast US cities are 1 hour ahead.

CURRENT

Electricity varies from hotel to hotel; 110 volts in some, 220 in others. Where it's necessary, most hotels will supply converters or adapters for electric shavers or hair dryers; but check with your travel agent to be sure.

TIPPING

Most Jamaican hotels and restaurants add a service charge of 10%; check to see if it's included in your bill. If not, tip waiters 10% to 15%; leave $1 to $2 per person per day for hotel chambermaids. Airport porters and hotel bellhops should be tipped 50¢ per bag. It's not necessary to tip taxi drivers, although it's appreciated.

GETTING AROUND

AIRPORT TRANSFERS If transfers are included in your package, you'll be given a voucher with the name of the operator, and a company representative will meet you at the airport. If your arrangements are being made independently, have your agent reserve transfer space in advance. Fares in *JUTA* (*Jamaica Union of Travellers Association*) taxis that hold up to five people run about $7 to $12 per car from Sangster Airport to Montego Bay hotels; $80 to hotels in Negril or Ocho Rios. The ride from Norman Manley International Airport to Kingston area hotels costs $14; to Port Antonio, $80. Your best bet if you are headed outside of Montego Bay (and if you're not in a rush) is to purchase a seat on *Tropical Tours* (phone: 952-1111) at their desk just outside the luggage area of the airport. They run air conditioned minibuses to Ocho Rios and Negril and charge about $20 per person. The only drawback is that they usually don't make the trip until the bus is at least half full.

BUS An inexpensive way to get around the Kingston and Montego Bay areas, but they run infrequently and are often crowded and uncomfortable. Bus service covers the rest of the island as well, but again, buses are often crowded — not only with people, but also with chickens and produce going to market. Unscheduled, but quite frequent, minibus jitneys serving the same routes are more comfortable. Still, most visitors rent a car or call a cab.

CAR RENTAL Good roads make most Jamaican attractions accessible to visiting motorists, so renting a car is a good idea if you like driving and sightseeing at your own pace and can handle driving "British-style" — on the left side of the road. There are a couple of dozen agencies on the island, many of which have desks at the Montego Bay and Kingston airports as well as branches throughout the island. The major operators are *Avis* (phone: 926-1560 in Kingston; 952-4541 in Montego Bay; 952-4543, Montego Bay airport); *Budget* (phone: 926-8411 in Kingston; 924-8762, Kingston airport; 974-5617 in Ocho Rio); and *National* (phone: 929-9190 in Kingston; 952-2769 in Montego Bay). *United Car Rentals,* based in Montego Bay, offers very reasonable rates on good-quality cars (phone: 952-3077 or 952-1781). In Ocho Rios, there's also *Sunshine Jamaica Ltd.* (phone: 974-5025) and *Caribbean Car Rental* (phone: 974-2123 or 974-2513). In Port Antonio, there's *Eastern Car Rental* (phone: 993-3624) and *Don Car Rental* (phone: 993-2241). Major international chains accept bookings through stateside toll-free (800) numbers; be sure to request written confirmation and bring it along.

Although there are some 2,800 rental cars on the island, it's still wise to reserve well ahead because cars are in short supply sometimes. Rates run from about $65 to $100 a day, with unlimited mileage. The renter pays for gas at the current price of about $2 an imperial gallon (one-fifth larger than the US gallon). There's also a 10% government tax. Valid US and Canadian driver's licenses are good on Jamaica, but many agencies require drivers to be over 25. *A word of warning:* Many Jamaican drivers have their "cowboy" moments. The easiest way to deal with the occasional challenge — at a one-lane bridge, for example — is to yield.

A reasonably priced alternative to straight car rental is the 7-day "Fly-

Drive Jamaica/The Great Escape" package, which combines a rental car with air transportation and overnight accommodations. Offered by *Vacation Network* (1501 W. Fullerton, Chicago, IL 60614; phone: 312-883-1020 or 800-423-4095 in the US or Canada), the package includes prepaid accommodations vouchers that are redeemable at any of 45 participating Jamaican small hotels and inns, a guidebook specifically geared for drivers, and road maps.

RIVER RAFTING An only-in-Jamaica experience, it's best on Jamaica's original rafting river, the Rio Grande, starting at Rafter's Rest in St. Margaret's Bay, 15 minutes west of Port Antonio; but there are shorter trips available on the Great River west of Montego Bay, on the Martha Brae River in Falmouth, and on the White River in Ocho Rios. A bamboo raft for two, poled by a skilled guide, takes you on a ride through jungles of vines and guango trees (where the blue heron live) down to the sea. Wear a bathing suit and swim from the raft. The leisurely 2½-hour Rio Grande trip (phone: 993-2778) is about $35 for two. The 1-hour Martha Brae trip (phone: 952-0889) operates daily from 9 AM to 4 PM and is about $40 for two. The 1-hour Mountain Valley Rafting Tour (phone: 952-0527), an expedition on the Great River, begins at the historic village of Lethe, south of Montego Bay, and wends its way through Jamaica's beautiful mountainous interior, ending at a recreational area where there are complimentary donkey rides for the kids and hammocks to laze in. There's also an optional hayride. The cost is about $45 for two. *Calypso Rafting* (phone: 974-2527) offers 45-minute White River excursions at about $30 for two. The trips operate from 9 AM to 5 PM daily. Arrangements also can be made at hotel tour desks.

SEA EXCURSIONS In Montego Bay, snorkel and sail cruises are offered on the *Calico* (phone: 952-5860) and the *Rhapsody* (phone: 979-0104). Glass-bottom boat rides are offered by most Ocho Rios and north coast hotels at about $10 per person for an hour's trip. Yacht excursions to Dunn's River Falls, with drinks and dancing on the beach, are offered by *Water Sports Enterprises* of Ocho Rios (phone: 974-2244) and range in price from $10 to $55 per person. Out of Port Antonio, the catamaran *Lady Jamaica* (phone: 993-3318) makes hour-long harbor cruises for about $6.50; 2½-hour cocktail sails cost about $12.50 per person, including snacks and drinks. At *Morgan's Harbour* hotel outside Kingston, you can arrange a boat ride to Lime Cay for swimming and/or a picnic for a nominal fee. From Kingston, you can take the ferry to Port Royal; it leaves every 2 hours from the *Craft Centre,* on the harbor; the 30-minute trip costs about 45¢. A number of day sailers and motor yachts offer daylong snorkel and party cruises with lunch, all the drinks you can handle, entertainment, and use of snorkeling equipment included in the price. Many also offer sunset and evening cruises. In Ocho Rios, contact the *Red Stripe* (phone: 974-2446) or the *Dreamweaver* (*Heave-Ho Charters;* phone: 974-5367). In

Montego Bay, there's the *Mary-Ann* (phone: 953-2231; ask for the tour desk) or the *Montrose II* (phone: 952-1760 or 952-5484). In Negril, try the *Lollypop* (phone: 952-4121 or 952-5133) or the *Eclipse* (*Aqua Nova Water Sports;* phone: 957-4323).

SIGHTSEEING TOURS Tours are run by *Jamaica Tours* (phone: 952-2887), *Blue Danube Tours* (phone: 952-0886 in Montego Bay; 974-2031 in Ocho Rios), *Greenlight Tours* (phone: 952-2200 in Montego Bay; 974-2266 in Ocho Rios; 929-9190 in Kingston), *Holiday Service* (phone: 974-5377 in Ocho Rios), and *Sun Holiday Tours* (phone: 952-5629 or 952-4585), operating out of various resort areas. In Port Antonio, contact *JUTA* (phone: 993-2684) or your hotel desk. Prices range from $20 for a few hours of around-the-town orientation and shopping to a more comprehensive $25 to $55 for a daylong trip with a specialty theme (history, nature, sports). The most worthwhile excursions from Montego Bay include the greathouse tour (3 hours), the coast tour to Ocho Rios and Dunn's River Falls (7 hours), and the Negril Beach circle tour (all day). The Hilton High Day Tour, out of Montego Bay, includes an optional tethered hot-air balloon ride, as well as breakfast, a plantation tour, a suckling pig luncheon feast, and a drive home through the Cockpit Country (see your hotel tour desk or call 952-3343). Excursions available from Ocho Rios include the plantation tour of Brimmer Hall (3½ hours), hour-long helicopter tours offered by *Helitours* (phone: 974-2495), and an inland tour to Kingston and Spanish Town (7 hours). There are also several excellent train and local airplane tours (see below). For tours focusing on Jamaican folk art, birds, gardens, or greathouses, contact the *Touring Society of Jamaica* (phone: 952-9188).

TAXI Recommended for short trips between island points. *JUTA* taxis and coaches are readily available at airports and at most resorts, but if you're going to an out-of-the-way spot, like a restaurant in the hills, arrange with the driver to return to pick you up. Most taxis are unmetered, so be sure to agree on the rate with the driver before you get into his cab, or ask the doorman at your hotel to make the arrangements. If in doubt, ask to see the rate sheet, which all cabs should have. From midnight to 5 AM, a 25% surcharge (frequently negotiable) is additional.

Many Jamaican cab drivers also make good guides, but only use those recommended by your hotel or *JUTA*. Hotel travel desks can make the arrangements; rates run from about $20 to $25 an hour for up to four people.

TRAIN The *Jamaica Railway Corporation* (phone: 922-6620) runs a diesel train twice daily between Kingston and Montego Bay; the 5½-hour trip is a good way to see a lot of the country; it's about $18 per person first class, about $10 coach. In addition, Jamaica has a sightseeing rail tour that is popular with visitors to Montego Bay, the departure point. The *Appleton Estate Express* (phone: 952-3692 or 952-6606) chugs high into the hills, through tiny villages on its way to the Appleton Rum Distillery, where tour participants are treated to a hearty Jamaican lunch, a tour of the distillery, and rum tastings. This all-day excursion by air conditioned train features a visit to the Ipswich Caves, where nature has created a breathtaking cathedral, with limestone stalagmites and stalactites, and a short stop at the Catadupa cloth market, where seamstresses measure you for a garment (you pick the material) in the morning and have it ready by the time the train returns later the same day. The train only runs four times a week and reservations are essential; book early, as it's very popular. Price is $60 per person and includes lunch, all the rum and soft drinks you can handle, entertainment, and transportation to and from your hotel.

INTER- AND INTRA-ISLAND FLIGHTS

Flights to the island land in either Montego Bay or Kingston. *Air Jamaica* (phone: 800-523-5585), the island's national carrier, flies in from Grand Cayman, Haiti, and Puerto Rico.

Air taxis save time and aggravation on long transfer runs — between Kingston or Montego Bay and Ocho Rios or Port Antonio, for example. The surest and least expensive way to use them is to book in advance through your travel agent. Local intra-island service is provided by *Trans Jamaican Airlines* (phone: 952-5401 or 952-5403), connecting the various resort centers and providing a bit of island-seeing between points. The Kingston–Montego Bay fare is about $64 round-trip. A good local charter service, *TIM-AIR* (phone: 952-2516), based at Montego Bay's airport, offers three tours, as well as local transportation; the tours require a minimum of two people and range in price from $35 to $120 per person. *Helitours Jamaica* (phone: 974-2495 in Ocho Rios; 929-8150 in Kingston) offers helicopter tours of the scenic areas of Ocho Rios and Kingston.

Montego Bay airport has been a frequent scene of frustration for both arriving and departing passengers. We recommend having your hotel reconfirm your return flight 3 days in advance. Then arrive at the airport for your flight home *at least* 2 hours before scheduled departure — and after calling the airline to find out when the flight is actually departing.

SPECIAL EVENTS

Twice a year, the Jamaica Tourist Board publishes a detailed calendar of events, available from their offices in the US and Jamaica. "Junkanoo" is a *Christmastime* celebration throughout the island. Fantastically costumed and masked dancers parade and perform in village and city streets, and there is much feasting and rum punch partying. *Bruckins,* the *LTM* (*Little Theatre Movement*) *Pantomime,* is an annual Jamaican folk musical with original songs, dances, and stories performed from December 26 to April. *Jamaica Carnival,* which takes place in April, is an island-wide celebration with *soca* parties, fetes, calypso and reggae bands, street dancing, and spectacular costumed road marches. *Reggae Sunsplash,* a week-long, mid-

July music fest, held at the *Bob Marley Center* in Montego Bay, draws reggae's (and rock's) top artists (and huge crowds). *Jamaican Independence Day* (first Monday in August) celebrates the establishment (on August 6, 1962) of Jamaica as a sovereign country; it's also an occasion for parades, music, dancing, and an arts festival. August is also when Port Antonio celebrates its 10-day *Portland Jamboree* with colorful parades, beach parties, cultural shows, and sporting events. Other holidays, when banks and most stores are closed, are *New Year's Day, Ash Wednesday, Good Friday, Easter Monday, Labour Day* (May 23), *National Heroes Day* (third Monday in October), *Christmas,* and *Boxing Day* (December 26). With the exception of *Good Friday,* all public holidays feature numerous island-wide celebrations, including reggae festivals, balls, sporting events, and the like.

SHOPPING

Things to bring home from Jamaica fall into two categories — art and crafts produced on the island, and imports at duty-free prices that are often a good deal lower than what you'd pay in the US. (Note, however, that a new 10% General Consumption Tax has been added to the prices of all goods and services.) Duty-free shops tend to cluster in shopping centers and arcades in each major tourist area. They offer all the classic luxury items: cameras and electronic equipment, Swiss watches, gold jewelry, French perfume, British woolens, liquor, cigarettes, fine European crystal, bone china, and porcelain. Stores specialize in different kinds of merchandise, and each has its exclusive brands and patterns, but prices are roughly standard. Most shops keep regular hours: 8:30 or 9 AM to 5 PM on weekdays, to 6 PM on Saturdays. Stores also are open on Sundays when ships are in port.

Visitors (with proof of identity) pay in Jamaican dollars, traveler's checks, or a wide range of credit cards and may carry away all duty-free purchases except consumables. Liquor (including Jamaican rums, coffee-flavored Tia Maria, and Rumona, the unique rum liqueur), cigarettes, and those good Jamaican cigars (Royal Jamaica is the top brand) may be picked up at the pier or the airport. With a firm grasp of US prices to help sort out the bargains and a well-planned shopping list, a morning or an afternoon should be enough to cover all the tempting duty-free buying.

Shopping for island-made things is more serendipitous. Some handcrafted items are not much different from those found in the rest of the Caribbean; others, such as original art by Jamaican artists in a variety of media, Jamaican fashions, and island-mined gemstone jewelry, are unique. Locally produced straw work, baskets, clothing, and wood items have improved tremendously in the past several years; and colorful, attractive, *and* reasonably priced goods are available. Craft outlets are everywhere. Besides shops selling the finest handmade goods, less sophisticated items line the stalls in government-sponsored craft markets such as the *Kingston Crafts Market* at the end of Harbour Street, the *Montego Bay Crafts Market* in downtown Montego Bay, the *Port Antonio Craft Market* at the intersection of Harbour and West Streets, and the *Negril Crafts Market* across from the tourist board office. Ocho Rios has several craft markets: the *Ocho Rios Craft Market* (off Main St. in the center of town), the *Olde Market Craft Shoppes* (next to the *Seow Supermarket*), the *Pineapple Craft Circle* (adjacent to the *Pineapple Shopping Centre*), the *Coconut Grove Craft Market* (adjacent to the *Coconut Grove Shopping Centre*), and the *Fern Gully Craft Centre* (at Fern Gully). At all these outdoor sources, asking prices vary and bargaining (or haggling) is okay, even expected. And be sure to try some of Jamaica's finest brew: its rich, aromatic Blue Mountain coffee (try the *Coffee Mill* shop in the MoBay Airport in Montego Bay for a good selection).

Straw things — hats, baskets, woven table and beach mats — run the style and workmanship gamut from terrific to tacky. The best show up in boutiques at non-negotiable fashion prices. But generally, a bit of market-stall research can unearth very similar merchandise for less. If you see something that's almost but not exactly what you want, ask; often the proprietor will alter to suit or make just what you're looking for at no extra cost. Carvings — statues, bookends, and other crafts — of lignum vitae, a rosy native hardwood, are also found in crafts markets and in a concentration of roadside stands along the north shore between Montego Bay and Falmouth.

Art is a source of considerable, justifiable Jamaican pride. Individuality and quality are high; so are prices, but not necessarily out of sight. The most revered names are those of the painters John Dunkley and Henry Daley, both of whom worked during the 1930s and 1940s, and the late Edna Manley (wife of one former prime minister and mother of another), a major sculptor and a founder of the Jamaica School of Art, renamed the Edna Manley School of Art in her honor. More contemporary are Karl Parboosingh, Carl Abrahams, Eugene Hyde, Albert Huie, Barrington Watson, Ralph Campbell, Rhoda Jackson, and Gloria Escoffery. The works of renowned primitive painter and sculptor Kapo (given name: Mallica Reynolds) are in Kingston's *National Gallery* and other island museums. Besides the shops and galleries listed below, other capital places to browse and buy include the Edna Manley School of Art (at the Cultural Training Centre, Arthur Wint Dr.); the *Bolivar Gallery* (Grove Rd. off Half Way Tree Rd.); the *Contemporary Arts Centre* (1 Liguanea Ave.); and the *Frame Centre Gallery* (10 Tangerine Pl.). The latter two have some fine old Jamaican prints and maps at more modest prices.

Island fashion designers have erased all trace of loving-hands-at-home amateurishness; their present clothes are clever, stylish, and great fun to wear. Most are made up in colorful fabrics silk-screened on the island. Shopping centers and arcades, both downtown and in the hotels of the four major tourist areas, are the places to look for island-designed resort fashions, as well as duty-free bargains. In Negril, there's the *Sunshine Village Shopping Centre.* In Montego Bay, there's the *Montego Freeport;* the *City Centre Arcade,* not far from the Parade; and the *Holiday Village Shopping Centre,* across from the *Holiday Inn.* In Ocho Rios, *Pineapple Place,* on the main road about a mile east of town, is an interesting collection of duty-free shops and boutiques, with an adjacent crafts market. A little farther east are *Coconut Grove Shopping Centre,* opposite *Plantation Inn; Ocean Village Shopping Centre* on Ocho Rios Bay, next to *Turtle Beach Towers;* the *Little Pub Yard,* with a few small shops adjoining the *Little Pub* restaurant; and the *Taj Mahal Shopping Centre,* a duty-free complex on Main Street close to the *Ruins* restaurant. In Port Antonio, there's the *City Centre Shopping Plaza* and *Goebal Shopping Complex,* both on Harbour Street. Kingston has the most shopping plazas in Jamaica. Some of the best are the *New Kingston Shopping Centre,* an enclosed mall on Dominica Drive; the *Sovereign Centre* mall (in Liguanea at the corner of Liguanea Ave. and Hope Rd.); and Mall Row, which features the smaller *Pavillion, Premier, The Mall, Village,* and *The Springs* shopping centers one after the other (located in the Half Way Tree area). The activities desk at most hotels can arrange shopping tours of the capital, including a few hours at the downtown crafts market.

BLUE MOUNTAIN GEMS Unusual gemstone jewelry — coral agate from Jamaican riverbeds, black coral, and other semi-precious finds in original handwrought settings. You can watch the polishing and casting. *Holiday Village Shopping Centre,* Montego Bay (phone: 953-2338).

CARIBATIK The outlet produces fine batik men's and women's resortwear, paintings, and wall hangings in rainbow-colored hand-dyed silks and cottons. Open 10 AM to 3 PM, Tuesdays through Saturdays, and closed September 16 to November 15. Located 2 miles east of Falmouth (phone: 954-3314).

CARIBBEAN CAMERA CENTRE Among the best-known duty-free stores for photography fanatics. *Pineapple Place,* Ocho Rios (phone: 974-2421).

CASA DE ORO A duty-free shop specializing in perfume, watches, and fine jewelry. *Holiday Village Shopping Centre,* Montego Bay (phone: 953-2600); and at *Pineapple Place,* Ocho Rios (phone: 974-2577).

FAREL'S One of the island's best menswear stores. Three locations: 4 South Odeon Ave. (phone: 926-7711) and *Twin Gates Plaza* (phone: 926-4169 in Kingston; and 10 Church St., Montego Bay (phone: 952-3784).

GALLERY OF WEST INDIAN ART Whimsically painted, hand-carved wooden fish, parrots, chickens, pigs, and alligators from top Jamaican artisans vie for floor and shelf space at this incredible shop, while Jamaican and Haitian paintings line the walls. 1 Orange La., at the corner of Church St., Montego Bay (phone: 952-4547).

HARMONY HALL GALLERY A good selection of artwork and superior-quality crafts — an excellent place to view the works of some of Jamaica's best known and some of its undiscovered artists; the coveted, locally made Annabella boxes are for sale here, too. Open daily from 10AM to 6 PM. About 4 miles east of Ocho Rios (phone: 974-4222).

INSTITUTE OF JAMAICA A good source of color facsimiles of antique Jamaican scenic prints and books about Jamaica. Open Mondays through Thursdays, 8:30 AM to 5 PM. 12 East St., Kingston (phone: 922-0620).

MOTTA'S Carries Sony, among other electronic names, duty-free. At three Kingston addresses: 27 King St. (phone: 922-8640); *Jamaica Pegasus* hotel (phone: 929-8147); and Norman Manley International Airport (phone: 924-8023).

NATIVE SHOP Woodcarvings, with special emphasis on the works of Lester Clarke; also has hand-turned salad bowls, plates, cups and saucers, masks, and pineapple lamps. *Beachview Shopping Plaza,* Montego Bay (phone: 974-2348).

PINEAPPLE SHOP Island clothes in island prints, ready-to-wear or custom-made at quite attractive prices, also fabrics by the yard. At the *Montego Freeport, Fantasy Resort,* and *Holiday Inn* (central phone: 952-2750), Montego Bay.

PRESITA Fine stereo names (like Sansui) and camera equipment. *Montego Freeport* (phone: 952-2744) and *City Centre Arcade* (phone: 952-3261), Montego Bay.

RUTH CLARAGE Women's day and evening wear in original prints and designs, with accessories and costume jewelry, too. Branches at *Montego Freeport* (phone: 952-3278) and *Half Moon Club* hotel (Gloucester Ave.; phone: 953-2211) in Montego Bay; *Pineapple Place* (phone: 974-2658) and the *Ocean Village Shopping Centre* (phone: 974-2874) in Ocho Rios; and at the *Wyndham New Kingston* hotel, Kingston (phone: 926-5430).

SWISS STORES Not only famous watches (Patek Philippe, Piaget, Rolex, Omega, Tissot, Juvenia, and more), but exquisitely hand-crafted jewelry, duty-free. *Half Moon Club* hotel, Montego Bay (phone: 953-2520); *Ocean Village Shopping Centre,* Ocho Rios (phone: 974-2519); *Jamaica Pegasus* hotel, Kingston (phone: 929-8147); corner of Harbour and Church Sts., Kingston (phone: 922-8050); and Norman Manley International Airport (phone: 924-8023).

THINGS JAMAICAN The cream of the hand-crafted crop — from four-poster beds to figurines, appliquéd quilts to antique spoons. Devon House, 26 Hope Rd., Kingston (phone: 929-6602); and at 44 Fort St., Montego Bay (phone: 952-5605), with branches at Norman Manley International Airport and Sangster Airport.

SPORTS

BOATING Most beach hotels have Sunfish, Sailfish, and/or windsurfers for rent at $10 per hour. To charter larger boats, contact the *Royal Jamaica Yacht Club* (phone: 924-8685/8686), the *Montego Bay Yacht Club* (phone: 952-3028), or *Morgan's Harbour Marina* (Port Royal; phone: 924-8464), which also has facilities for visiting yachts. Every February, March, or April, the *Montego Bay Pineapple Cup Yacht Race* draws some of the sport's top teams from the US, Canada, and Great Britain to compete in a grueling contest, which ends at the *Montego Bay Yacht Club.* Spring brings *Jamaica Sail Week,* with a full roster of races, regattas, and parties on the north coast or in Kingston. Call the Jamaica Tourist Board for details.

CYCLING Although Jamaican distances and the terrain are daunting except to seasoned bikers, the very active Cycling Association organizes races and tours throughout the year. Check with the local Jamaica Tourist Board office for details of activities during your stay. *Blue Mountain Tours, Ltd.* (West Palm Ave., Port Antonio; phone: 993-2242) takes cyclists by van to the Blue Mountains, where experienced guides lead the bicycling group downhill.

FISHING Both fresh- and saltwater fishing are very popular. Jamaica's rivers yield such freshwater game as mountain mullet, hognose mullet, drummer, and small snook. There's also snook and tarpon fishing in the Black River and its tributaries. Deep-sea fishing charters can be arranged through hotels in Port Antonio (one of the outstanding deep-sea fishing centers in the Caribbean), Montego Bay, Ocho Rios, and Kingston. Rates run about $250 to $350 for a half day, $400 to $600 for a full day, including crew, bait, and tackle. The captain keeps half the catch; the rest you can arrange to have prepared by the chef at your hotel. Billfish run through Jamaica's north coast waters year-round, although local anglers say September to April is the hottest time for blue marlin. The proximity (and proliferation) of billfish in this area has sparked international attention. Other game fish include Allison tuna (March–June), wahoo (October–April), kingfish (October–April), dolphin (April–October), bonito and barracuda (September–April). Each September to October, Jamaica hosts three international blue marlin and game fish tournaments, in Montego Bay, Ocho Rios, and Port Antonio. Foreign anglers are not only welcomed but actively recruited to participate in these events and in the *Big Game Angling Club*'s *Blue Marlin Tournament* in May and the *Falmouth Yacht Club*'s *Fishing Tournament,* held during the annual *Trelawney Carnival,* the third week of May. There is also an annual *Port Antonio Spring Tournament* in March. Exact dates and information are available from all Jamaica Tourist Board offices.

GOLF Over the years, Jamaica has developed some of the Caribbean's most beautiful and challenging courses, and it now offers nine championship links. Jamaica also is an official PGA golf destination. Montego Bay is the place for dedicated golfers to stay; there are four courses in the area, and it's not necessary to be a guest at a hotel to play its course.

TOP TEE-OFF SPOT

Tryall About 12 miles due west of Montego Bay, the *Tryall* resort course is without question the finest on Jamaica. Where the other courses on this island seem somehow restricted by their flat terrain and rather repetitious hole configuration, *Tryall* (par 71) exults in its 6,680 yards of hills and dales, and no cost seems to have been spared to create the most interesting course possible. These grounds were once one of the island's most productive sugar plantations. All that remains of those earlier days is a rusty old waterwheel and some ruins along the course boundaries, but they do provide a context in which to survey the surrounding landscape.

Don't take too much time to reflect on history, however, for the course itself is sufficient challenge for any player. The constantly changing direction of the wind off the nearby sea restructures each hole virtually every day, so there are fresh problems each time you set your ball on a *Tryall* tee. The course is closed to non-guests during winter season. In the summer the greens fee is $38, and the mandatory caddie is $8 to $15 (phone: 952-5110/1; 800-237-3237 from the US; fax: 952-0401).

Other MoBay courses include the 18-hole layouts at the *Half Moon Golf Club* (7,115 yards, par 72; phone: 953-2560), *Wyndham Rose Hall* (6,598 yards, par 72; phone: 953-2650), and *Ironshore Golf and Country Club* (6,663 yards, par 72; phone: 953-2800). Elsewhere on the island, there are 18-hole courses at *SuperClubs' Runaway Bay Golf Club* (6,884 yards, par 72; phone: 973-2561), the *Upton Golf Club* near Ocho Rios (6,600 yards, par 71; phone: 974-2528), the *Constant Spring Golf Club* (6,196 yards, par 70; phone: 924-1610), and the *Caymanas Golf Club* (6,844 yards, par 72; phone: 926-8144 or 926-8146) in the Kingston vicinity. Mandeville has a 9-hole course, *Manchester Club* (2,865 yards, par 35; phone: 962-2403), but its 18 tees allow each green to serve as 2 different holes. Greens fees range from $30 to $50 in winter, $18 to $38 in summer. The greens fee at *Manchester*'s course is about $8 per round. Caddies get about $5 for 9 holes, $10 to $15 for 18; club rental runs $5 to $17; cart rentals, $15 to $30 a round. There's also a miniature golf course at *Prospect Plantation* (phone: 974-2058) in Ocho Rios.

HIKING The hills above the resort areas of the north coast are a scenic area for walking tours. An especially popular journey on foot in Ocho Rios is the climb (600 feet) to the top of Dunn's River Falls — do it in your swimsuit; it's a wonderfully damp trip. Serious mountain climbers scale the Blue Mountains in the southeastern part of the island, where the Forest Department manages mountain retreats: Chinchona, Clydesdale Forest Camp,

Clydesdale Rest House, and Hollywell Recreation Centre; for information contact the tourist board in Kingston. The nature-oriented *Jamaica Alternative Tourism, Camping & Hiking Association* (*JACHA,* PO Box 216, Kingston 7; phone: 927-2097) arranges hiking, climbing, and backpacking tours as well as river canoeing, biking, and low-cost camping and guesthouse accommodations. Special arrangements for the strenuous climb up 7,402-foot Blue Mountain Peak can also be made with John Allgrove (8 Armon Jones Crescent, Kingston 6; phone: 927-0986 after 5 PM) or Peter Bentley of the *Maya Lodge* (Peter Rock Rd., Jacks Hill, Kingston 6; phone: 927-2097). Bentley also offers camping trips and occasional whitewater rafting and cycling tours.

HORSEBACK RIDING A beautiful way to explore Jamaica's backcountry of plantation lands and hills, pine forests, shaded streams, and waterfalls. Some stables are open all year; others take summer vacations on a varying schedule; it's best to ask your hotel to set things up. The top outfit is *Chukka Cove Farm* (for reservations: Box 160, Ocho Rios, St. Ann, Jamaica; phone: 972-2506) on the old Llandovery estate west of Ocho Rios. A complete equestrian operation, it offers trail, picnic, and moonlight rides at about $20 per person per hour; it also sets up 3- and 5-day Horseman's Holiday packages that include trail and picnic rides, lessons, and bus trips to thoroughbred stud farms. Elsewhere, guided rides cost between $15 and $25 per hour. In the Montego Bay area, *Rocky Point Stables* (phone: 953-2286), just east of the *Half Moon Club,* offers excellent instruction, as well as beach and trail rides, and *White Witch Stables* (phone: 953-2746), near the Rose Hall Great House, offers daily trail rides in the hills. In the Ocho Rios area, try *Prospect Plantation* (phone: 974-2373), and in Negril, *Hedonism II* (phone: 957-4200), *Negril Rhodes Hall Plantation* (phone: 957-4258), or *Horseman Riding Stables* (phone: 957-4474). Kingston has the *Polo Club* (phone: 922-8060); Mandeville, the *Riding Stables* (phone: 962-2822). In Port Antonio, contact the *Bonnie View* hotel (phone: 993-2752).

HORSE RACING Races are run at *Caymanas Race Track,* Kingston, on Wednesdays, Saturdays, and some public holidays. Consult your hotel desk and the newspapers for specific times.

SCUBA AND SNORKELING Reefs, formed of 50 varieties of coral and populated by brightly colored fish, anemones, lavender fans, and other marine flora and fauna, are accessible within 100 yards of the beach at a number of places along the north coast. Farther out — at about 200 yards — are drop-offs to depths where more seasoned divers can venture down in the clear waters to see and photograph larger fish and explore giant sponge forests, caves, and shipwrecks. Most of the all-inclusive resorts and large hotels have certified on-premises dive shops, fully equipped dive boats, and licensed instructors who run the daily dives and teach the get-in-the-water-in-one-day resort courses. The best diving on the island is found at Montego Bay, famous for its wall diving, coral caves, tunnels, and canyons; and at Negril, where the reefs are unspoiled. Dive shops that offer rentals and guided snorkel and scuba trips in Montego Bay include *Jamaica Rose Divers* (29 Gloucester Ave.; phone: 979-0104); *Sea World* at the *Cariblue* hotel (phone: 953-2180), with branches at the *Holiday Inn* and *Wyndham Rose Hall Beach* hotels; *Sandals Beach Resort Watersports* (phone: 952-5510); and *Poseidon Nemrod Divers Ltd.* at the *Chalet Caribe* hotel (phone: 952-1364 or 952-1365) and at *Marguerite's by the Sea* (phone: 952-3624). The Ocho Rios area has *Sun Divers* (phone: 973-2346), *Garfield Dive Station* (phone: 974-5749), and Paul Dadd's *Fantasea Divers* (phone: 974-5344 or 800-522-DIVE from the US). In Negril, there's *Village Resorts* (phone: 952-4200); *Sun Divers* at the *Poinciana Beach* hotel (phone: 957-4069), the *Negril Scuba Centre* at the *Negril Beach Club* (phone: 957-4425), and *Blue Whale Divers* (Norman Manley Blvd.; phone: 957-4438). Port Antonio has *Aqua Action* (San San beach; phone: 993-3318). Scuba trips cost about $40 (1 tank) to $50 (2 tanks) including all equipment, $10 less if you bring your own; snorkel trips are $15 per person, which includes boat ride and equipment. Most of these shops also offer instruction.

SPECTATOR SPORTS Jamaica's British colonial past is evident today in its spectator sports. Cricket is the national pastime, and matches are played from January through August in Sabina Park, Kingston, and at other locations throughout the island; check with the tourist board for schedules. The second most popular sport is football (soccer, that is), played in the fall and winter. Polo has over a century of tradition in Jamaica, and matches are played year-round in Kingston (Thursdays and Sundays, Caymanas Park, 7 miles west of the New Kingston area) and at Ocho Rios (Saturdays at Drax Hall, 5 miles west of town). Captain Mark Phillips, ex-husband of Britain's Princess Anne and an *Olympic* equestrian, conducts an annual clinic at *Chukka Cove Farm* (phone: 972-2506), near Ocho Rios.

SURFING The finest is on the north coast east of Port Antonio, where the longest and best breakers roll into Boston Bay. Since no lifeguards are present, surfing by novices is not recommended.

SWIMMING AND SUNNING Most of Jamaica's best beaches are on the northern coast, from secluded coves to broad stretches of white sand. Your hotel will have its own — or privileges at one nearby — and there are a number of public beaches you can visit, too. Most famous is Doctor's Cave Beach on Montego Bay, the 5-acre strand that helped lure the first tourists to this part of the world; it has changing rooms and snack bars. Doctor's Cave has attracted so many people that the tourist board decided to develop the 300-yard Cornwall Beach, adjacent and to the east; both charge small entry fees. For beachcombers who want more sand to themselves, Negril, at the western tip of the island, 50 miles from Montego Bay, has 7 shining white miles of it. New resorts are being developed in this area, but the beach's northern segment is still far from crowded and worth a special trip. *Hedonism II,* a young, high-energy resort, has nudist beaches onshore. Nudist areas are also found on sections of Long Bay Beach and on Booby Island, a small island just offshore. The *Navy Island* resort on Navy Island, Port Antonio, has a good beach and a small nude cove. Jamaica's southern coast has a few good beaches, notably at Hellshire near Kingston and Treasure Beach in St. Elizabeth. Other good beaches for sunning and swimming: Puerto Seco Beach in Discovery Bay; Rio Bueno and Turtle Beach in Ocho Rios; and San San, Boston Beach, and Long Beach in Port Antonio.

TENNIS Plenty of places to play — and many courts are lighted for cooler nighttime play.

CHOICE COURTS

Half Moon Club This island's most extensive complex, it has 15 tennis courts (4 lighted), 4 international squash courts occasionally co-opted by the racquetball crowd (Byron Bernard is the pro). Year-round, ex–*Davis Cup/Wimbledon* player Richard Russell, the head pro, sets up clinics according to guest interest, with video playback. No charge to hotel guests for day or night play; court reservations necessary only in peak season (phone: 953-2211; fax: 953-2731).

In addition, most hotels without courts have access to those of nearby properties; court use is usually free to guests; fees for non-guests run $10 to $12 per court per hour. Many resort hotels have resident pros; a number offer tennis packages. The *Sans Souci* hotel has a special Tennis Week package each January, featuring tournaments, clinics, and celebrity pros. The *Jamaica, Jamaica* resort offers an ongoing intensive instruction program at its Tennis Academy.

WATER SKIING The Blue Lagoon in Port Antonio and Doctor's Cave Beach in Montego Bay are ideal locations. Water skiing also is part of the water sports program at most beach hotels; rates run about $15 per quarter hour. Jet skiing is also available at Cornwall Beach in Montego Bay, on Turtle Bay in Ocho Rios, and at the *Negril Tree House* in Negril; rates, about $25 to $30 per hour.

NIGHTLIFE

At the larger resort hotels, after-dark entertainment is a lot like that on most of the islands north of Trinidad. Besides small combos and occasional guitar-carrying calypso singers, at least once a week there's a torchlit Jamaican folkloric show complete with steel band, amazing contortionists, limbo dancers, and masochistic types who eat fire and stomp barefoot on broken bottles for a living. First-timers shouldn't miss it; old island hands, who've seen it a dozen times before, can make for the nearest sound-shielded bar and wait for the commercialization to go away.

But Jamaica does offer something different. "Boonoonoonoos" — which means something special, a delight, in local patois — is the name of and theme for a series of year-round weekly special events and gala parties uniquely Jamaican in setting, food, and — in the case of the river nights — even transport (by dugout canoe). The drinks are rum-based and free-flowing; the entertainment, less stereotyped and with more folk feeling than most hotel productions. Each island area has its own events, which are included in the price of week-long "Boonoonoonoos" tour packages or available to guests on an individual basis. In Negril, there's a weekly Jamaica Night with Jamaican food, music, dancing, and entertainment at *Hedonism II.* In Montego Bay, every Monday evening is *MoBay Nite Out,* a festive street fair. Gloucester Avenue is turned into a pedestrian mall from *Jack Tar Village* to the *Pelican Grill* restaurant and the street comes alive with mento and steel bands, dancing, mingling, and curbside food and drink vendors. This weekly cultural festival is sponsored by the tourist board. It's free, begins around 6 PM, and runs until midnight. An "Evening on the Great River" is another entertaining option. It begins with a torch-lit canoe ride, and ends with drinks, dinner, a show, and dancing in a re-created Arawak village (about $50 per person; phone: 952-5097 or 952-5047). In Montego Bay, there's also a weekly beach party at Cornwall Beach and a Friday night bash held on Walter Fletcher Beach — both with buffet, open bar, limbo show, and beach games ($34 per person). In Ocho Rios, a "Night on the White River" includes a canoe ride, open bar, floor show, and starlit dancing (adults, about $40; children, about $20; phone: 974-2619). *Rock Cliff* hotel in Negril is famous for its Sunday night lobster barbecue and roasted suckling pig. The feast is topped off with fire eaters, limbo dancers, and a rocking reggae band.

In Negril, *Rick's* (phone: 957-4335) is literally and figuratively the way-out place to be for sunset and after. Live reggae concerts can be found most evenings at *Kaiser's Café* (on the cliffs at Negril; phone: 957-4070) and in the west end of town at *Sam Sara* (phone: 957-4395), *MX III* (phone: 957-4818), or the *Compulsion Disco* (phone: 957-4416). The *Negril Tree House* (Norman Manley Blvd.; phone: 957-4287), on the beach, is also popular. MoBay's latest popular watering holes are *Hemingway's* (phone: 952-8606) and *Walter's* (phone: 952-9391), next door to each other on Gloucester Avenue. MoBay's liveliest discos are *Pier 1* (Howard Cooke Blvd. opposite the craft market; phone: 952-2452), which is open on Friday nights after 10 PM; the *Cave* (at the *Sea Wind Beach;* phone: 952-4070); *Disco Inferno* (at *Holiday Village;* phone: 953-2113); *Hell Fire* (at the *Wyndham Rose Hall Beach*), and *Thriller* (at the *Holiday Inn*). *Sir Winston's Reggae Club* (on Gloucester Ave. in downtown Montego Bay; phone: 952-2084) features live music several times a week and attracts a good local crowd. Ocho Rios's favorite night places are the *Little Pub* in the *Little Pub* shopping complex (phone: 974-2324); the *Safari* dance club (at the *Ambiance* hotel; phone: 973-4705); *Silks* (at the *Shaw Park Beach* hotel); *The Roof* (James Ave., phone: 974-1042), an open-air disco and nightclub; and the *Acropolis* (70 Main St.; phone: 974-2633) for disco action. Port Antonio comes alive at the popular *Roof Club* (11 West St.; no phone), the *Taurus Fan Club* (phone: 993-2161), and at *Shadows* (40 West St.; phone: 993-3823). The *Fern Hill Club* has a Monday-night beach party, fashion show, and buffet barbecue; on Friday nights, there is a Jamaican buffet. Both events feature live entertainment. Aimless late-night roving in Kingston is not recommended, so hop a cab over to the *Godfather,* a disco (Knutsford Blvd.; phone: 929-5459) or to *Epiphany* (St. Lucia Ave., off Trafalgar Rd.; phone: 929-1130) on Thursday nights to hear the newest reggae bands. For oldies music, stop in at *The Rock* (on Redhill Rd.; phone: 925-8261) on Wednesdays. Wednesday is also the night for jazz in the basement of the *Mutual Life Centre* (on Oxford and Hope Rds.; no phone). There's also the *Wyndham New Kingston's Junkanoo* disco (phone: 929-3390), *Mingles* (at the *Courtleigh* hotel; phone: 929-5321), and *Illusions* (Lane Plaza on South Ave.; phone: 929-2125). For dancing and casual socializing, try *Disco 1692* (at *Morgan's Harbour),* and *Peppers* (Upper Waterloo Rd., phone: 925-2219).

Best on the Island

CHECKING IN

It's no secret that Jamaica's accommodations are now among the best buys in the Caribbean. Even the country's four Elegant Resorts, an association of the local crème de la crème, are surprisingly reasonable for the value and ambience they offer. They are Montego Bay's *Round Hill* hotel, the *Tryall Golf, Tennis & Beach Club,* the *Half Moon Golf, Tennis & Beach Club,* and Port Antonio's *Trident* hotel. The group's all-inclusive Platinum Plan is noteworthy; it includes accommodations, welcoming champagne, flowers, a fruit basket, three meals daily, all bar drinks, afternoon tea, nightly entertainment, airport transfers, taxes, and tips, plus limited land and water sports. Guests on the plan can take advantage of the Dine Around/Sleep Around option, which allows them to experience more than one Elegant Resort during the same week.

In addition, a fair number of Jamaica's hotels are operated entirely as all-inclusive resorts, in the *Club Med* fashion (though there is no *Club Med* here). Jamaica has been a Caribbean pioneer of the all-inclusive idea. While most all-inclusive resorts here are for couples only, more and more are welcoming singles and families. These club-style holidays, which usually are sold as 3-, 4-, 5-, or 7-night packages, represent some of the best value-for-the-money vacations in the entire Caribbean. The price covers all expenses — accommodations, three meals daily plus snacks, wine, beer, and all bar and soft drinks, nightly entertainment (and sometimes theme parties), all water and land sports plus instruction and equipment, airport transfers, taxes, and tips. In fact, airfare, telephone calls, and souvenirs are the only extras likely to be incurred by most people, although a close reading of the literature may reveal slight variations in the all-inclusive idea from resort to resort. (For instance, some resorts include drinks while others do not. Also, some include only non-motorized water sports.)

Friends and families planning to travel together can benefit from Jamaica's vacation villa and apartment rental system. Several hundred properties — some 1-bedroom models but most with 2 to 6 bedrooms, with private pools or near the beach — are available for about $550 and up a week in summer, about $650 and up in winter. The price includes staff to take care of you and the place; rental cars and minibuses also can be reserved. Even counting the cost of food, it's a scheme that cuts costs way down for a group of compatible couples or a family. The *Jamaica Association of Villas and Apartments* (*JAVA,* 1501 W. Fullerton, Chicago, IL 60614; phone: 312-883-3485 from Chicago; 800-221-8830 or 800-VILLAS6 from elsewhere in the US) represents more than 300 properties of all sizes and degrees of luxury in all resort areas. *Villas and Apartments Abroad* (420 Madison Ave., New York, NY 10017; phone: 212-759-1025 from New York; 800-433-3020 from elsewhere in the US) lists about 200 select Jamaican properties. Another unique outfit, *Jamaica Alternative Tourism, Camping & Hiking Association* (*JACHA,* PO Box 216, Kingston 7; phone: 927-2097), arranges low-cost camping and informal guesthouse accommodations, as well as nature- and outdoor-oriented tours of the island.

In the listings that follow, hotels classed as expensive ask about $250 and up a day for a double room, including breakfast and dinner in season (MAP); about $160 and up without meals (EP). Rates at moderate places run about $160 to $250 for two MAP; about $100 to $150 EP. Places in the inexpensive category charge as little as $50 to $100 for two without meals. Between April 15 and December 15, prices all over the island — including those for villa rentals — drop from 25% to 40%. Check with your hotel to see if its rates include the new 10% GCT (General Consumption Tax). All telephone numbers are in the 809 area code unless otherwise indicated.

For an unforgettable island experience, we begin with our favorites, followed by our recommendations of cost and quality choices of hotels large and small, listed by area and price category.

REGAL RESORTS AND SPECIAL HAVENS

Ciboney Ocho Rios Nestled in the hills overlooking the sea, this all-inclusive, Radisson-run resort boasts 264 luxurious 1-, 2-, and 3-bedroom villas plus 36 rooms in the resort's greathouse. Privacy and pampering are the key words here. Each tropically decorated villa has an attendant who does everything from unpacking and light ironing to preparing a scrumptious breakfast. The villas also feature spacious bathrooms, stocked refrigerators and bars, living rooms with remote-control TV sets and VCRs (movies may be borrowed at the concierge desk), private balconies or patios for dining, and private swimming pools. Open-air jitneys shuttle guests between their villas and the rest of the resort, which is spread over 45 acres. The Grecian-looking but ultramodern spa is a big draw here. All guests receive a complimentary Swedish massage, foot, back and neck rubs, manicure, and pedicure. There are also air conditioned squash and racquetball courts, 6 tennis courts (plus free clinics), a fitness/weight room, aerobics room, steam room, sauna, hot tubs, and cold plunges, plus a beach and a private beach club. Greens fees and transportation to two nearby golf courses are included in the rate. There is also a daily low-key activities program, croquet, scuba, water sports, 4 restaurants, 2 pools (both with swim-up bars), a jogging track, and nightly entertainment in an intimate club. Congenial and plush, it's geared towards luxury-loving singles, couples, and families traveling with children over the age of 16. Ocho Rios (phone: 974-1027 or 974-5600; 800-333-3333 from the US).

Round Hill Actually set in a quiet cove several miles west of the clamor of Montego Bay, this is the sort of traditional resort that harkens back to the days of colonial Jamaica. It was once so exclusive that there was a popular impression that guest privileges were restricted to members of the peerage. Things are a little more accessible nowadays, though not much, for this is where the so-called society tends to congregate when visiting Jamaica. The protected atmosphere is accentuated by the fact that many "guests" actually own the villas in which they are staying. The total facilities include 36 extremely stylish rooms in the very comfortable Pineapple House, plus 60 suites in the surrounding 27 villas, which are available when their owners are not in residence. The hotel operation (including the restaurants) is open year-round. This is by far the snazziest address on Jamaica, with prices to match, and if you like to keep your upper lip stiff while sunning and swimming, this is the place for you. Hopewell, Hanover (phone: 952-5150; 305-666-3566 from Florida; 800-237-3237 from elsewhere in the US).

Trident It's impossibly romantic even in the morning, when the sun finds rainbows in the spray of the waves crashing on the rocks below your terrace and a peacock trails across the lawn to join you for breakfast. The current hotel re-creates the country house charm of its predecessor (destroyed twice by hurricanes). Each villa and tower suite is individually decorated, full of pastels, pleasing prints, and comforting touches (a cushioned window seat, an antique desk). Service is individual too — from breakfast (brought one course at a time to your terrace or balcony) right through the day. There's a small beach, pool, tennis; the not overfamiliar pleasures of

Port Antonio and green-hilled Portland (surf beaches, river rafting, plantation visits, picnics by waterfalls and blue lagoons) are invitingly accessible. Afternoon tea is a tradition; dinner is a formal, superb six-course event, complete with white-gloved, silver-domed service in the stately dining room. Like all the rest, it's done with great style and personal attention, but utterly (and this is the special delight) without self-conscious pretension (phone: 993-2602 or 993-2705; 305-666-3566 from Florida; 800-237-3237 from elsewhere in the US; fax: 993-2590).

NEGRIL

EXPENSIVE

Grand Lido Quieter, more elegant, and more luxurious than its Negril counterparts, this all-inclusive sanctuary caters to adults (no guests under the age of 16). The 200 suites are comfortable, with entertainment centers, patios or balconies, and 24-hour room service. The crowd is international, there's a section of the beach reserved for nude sunbathing, and all guests receive complimentary manicures and pedicures. Organized activities and sports, 4 restaurants, a nightly knock-out midnight buffet, a fitness center, and sunset cocktail cruises on a 147-foot yacht previously owned by Prince Rainier of Monaco complete the picture at this architecturally dramatic resort. Bring nice resortwear even though it's Negril. Make reservations early at the fine dining room, *Placere,* then dance the calories off at the modern discotheque. Bloody Bay (phone: 957-4013; 516-868-6924 from New York; 800-858-8009 from elsewhere in the US; fax: 957-4317).

Hedonism II This all-inclusive resort attracts pleasure-seeking singles and couples of all ages (children under 16 excluded, however). There's plenty of action and activity — everything from scuba diving to horseback riding; toga parties to reggae. On 22 acres, with 280 large rooms (plus another 70 scheduled for completion at press time), 6 lighted tennis courts, lots of land and water sports, a famous clothing-optional beach, a fitness center, and a continuous fun-and-games atmosphere. Rutland Point (phone: 957-4200; 516-868-6924 from New York; 800-858-8009 from elsewhere in the US and Canada; fax: 957-4289).

Sandals Negril The byword is casual at this all-inclusive, couples-only resort set amidst lush foliage on Jamaica's largest stretch of private beach. The mix of privacy, group activities, and fun is perfect for couples seeking a luxurious and sportive getaway. Accommodations range from garden or beachfront rooms to 1-bedroom loft suites; amenities include an offshore island, swim-up pool bar, 3 restaurants, a fitness center, Jacuzzi, 2 freshwater pools, tennis, squash and racquetball courts, croquet lawn, disco, daily activities program, and just about every type of water sport imaginable. Scuba divers will love this place, as will those wanting to learn. Health-conscious eaters should head to the *4-C* beach restaurant, where low-calorie vegetables, seafood, and poultry are stir-fried. Rutland Point (phone: 957-4216; 800-SANDALS from the US and Canada; fax: 957-4338).

Swept Away This all-inclusive, couples-only oasis is the place for fitness-loving duos. The 10-acre sports complex features 8 lighted tennis courts (plus clinics, tournaments, and classes), 2 air conditioned squash courts, 2 racquetball courts, a lap pool, an open-air gymnasium, and a spa. Just across the road, overlooking the beach and sea, are 26 two-story villas housing 130 Caribbean-style suites. There's a poolside juice and veggie bar; a restaurant featuring spa fare with a Jamaican flair; and an *haute* pizza and pasta eatery. Water enthusiasts can scuba, snorkel, sail, and windsurf. There's also a daily exercise program and dining under the stars. Norman Manley Blvd. (phone: 957-4040; 800-526-2422 from the US; fax: 957-4060).

MODERATE

Charela Inn Here are 39 neat, nicely appointed, air conditioned rooms, with their own sunny slice of beach, a small bar, a good French and Jamaican restaurant with an informal atmosphere, and friendly management. A water sports facility is located just up the beach. Norman Manley Blvd. (phone: 957-4277; 800-423-4095 from the US; fax: 957-4414).

Negril Beach Club This beachfront hostelry has 113 rooms, including 20 one- and two-bedroom suites with kitchens. Amenities include 2 tennis courts, a large pool, a restaurant, a bar, and an on-premises water sports facility. Horseback riding can be arranged. Optional food plan. Norman Manley Blvd. (phone: 957-4221; 800-JAMAICA from the US and Canada; fax: 957-4364).

Negril Gardens About half of this hotel's 54 rooms are on the beach. The rest are nestled around the pool across the street. Highlights include a restaurant, bar, gift shop, and discotheque. A water sports facility is nearby. Norman Manley Blvd. (phone: 957-4408; 800-243-9420 from the US; fax: 957-4374).

Negril Tree House This pleasant property is on the 7-mile Negril beach. Only 48 of the 68 rooms are air conditioned; 20 have received a recent refurbishing. There is an on-premises water sports facility, as well as a gift shop, restaurant, and bar. Stop in for the Monday night Beach Barbecue Party. Norman Manley Blvd. (phone: 957-4287; 800-NEGRIL-1 from the US; fax: 957-4386).

Poinciana Beach A relatively intimate resort on Negril's famous 7-mile beach. The 130 units include 2 blocks of 22 villas, 8 one-bedroom suites, and 6 studio apartments. All units feature kitchenettes and ocean views. This low-key, family-oriented property features complimentary daily toddler and children's programs. Facilities include a swimming pool, a children's pool, a Jacuzzi, a restaurant, beach and pool bars, water sports, gift shops, and satellite TV. Children under 12 stay for free. Meal plans are available. Norman Manley Blvd. (phone: 957-4256; 800-468-6728 or 800-771-1700 from the US; fax: 957-4229).

Rock Cliff On the Negril cliffs high above the sea, this resort with 33 rooms features first-rate accommodations, an excellent restaurant, a pool, ocean access for swimming and snorkeling, and a disco for evening revelry. West End Rd. (phone: 957-4331; 312-883-1020 from Chicago; 800-423-4095 from elsewhere in the US; fax: 957-4331).

T-Water Beach An informal complex of 70 neatly done, air conditioned rooms and suites on Negril's magnificent long beach. All water sports can be arranged. Children are welcome. There's a beach bar, a restaurant featuring home-style cooking, and entertainment; breakfast and lunch included. Norman Manley Blvd. (phone: 957-4270 or 957-4271; 212-519-0634 from New York City; 800-654-1592 from elsewhere in the US; fax: 957-4334).

MONTEGO BAY AREA

EXPENSIVE

Half Moon Here is a luxurious country club–like 400-acre layout, with 208 rooms. It offers 2 restaurants, 15 lighted tennis courts (with resident pro); an 18-hole championship golf course and clubhouse; full beach facilities for sailing, swimming, and water sports (including scuba); a big freshwater pool; a fitness center; and 4 squash courts. The elegant suites in the main house are choice; ditto the Royal Suites, 23 spacious, stylishly private beachfront accommodations, though a long hike from main house doings. Some opulent villa suites have private pools. The week-long Platinum Plan package is an affordable option. On the shore 7 miles east of Montego Bay (phone: 953-2211; 305-666-3566 from Miami; 800-237-3237 from elsewhere in the US or Canada; fax: 953-2731).

Sandals Montego Bay Romance was built into this lushly tropical property: There are hidden alcoves, several Jacuzzis surrounded by tall shrubs, and hammocks large enough for two strung between palm trees. One of the island's most popular and spirited couples-only, all-inclusive resorts, this lively 243-room creation has become the model for the other Sandals properties in Jamaica. The upscale rooms all feature king-size beds, private balconies or patios, telephones, and hair dryers. Packages cover all water and land sports (including equipment and instruction), all meals, snacks, and alcoholic beverages, taxes, tips, airport transfers, nightly entertainment, and theme parties. Pluses are a swim-up pool bar, first-rate fitness club, popular piano bar, and 3 restaurants. Its beach is the largest private stretch of sand in Montego Bay. Recent additions include glass-bottom boat rides, a miniature golf course, and a special lounge to serve all of the Sandals resorts departing guests. Reserve early. On the beach. Kent Ave. (phone: 952-5510; 800-327-1991 or 800-SANDALS from the US or Canada; fax: 952-0816).

Sandals Royal Another all-inclusive, couples-only resort, it has 190 rooms in British colonial-style buildings that, in a previous incarnation, hosted Queen Elizabeth. All meals (served at 3 restaurants), drinks, water sports, tennis, daily activities, nightly entertainment, taxes, tips, and airport transfers are included. The property has a genteel atmosphere, a garden setting, and a nice-size crescent of beach. Peacocks stroll onto your terrace, there's a swim-up pool bar, and a private island offers sunbathing during the day and the *Bali Hai* restaurant serves Indonesian fare at night. Complimentary transportation to the nearby 18-hole, par 72 *Ironshore Golf and Country Club* (no greens fees for *Sandals Royal* guests), is also available. Mahoe Bay (phone: 953-2231; 800-SANDALS from the US and Canada; fax: 953-2788).

Tryall This exclusive 2,200-acre resort includes the 156-year-old, totally refurbished greathouse, with 52 rooms, and 42 luxury villas with 2, 3, 4, or 5 bedrooms. On a hill overlooking a fine curve of beach, it offers quietly elegant country-estate atmosphere, with a beach club, pool, and a perfect terrace and bar for sea and sunset watching. It also has the best golfing on the island (see *Top Tee-Off Spot* in *Golf* in this chapter). There are 9 tennis courts, with resident pro and free court time during shoulder seasons. The food is good; nights are peaceful. The all-inclusive Platinum Plan is an attractive option. Twelve miles west of town. Sandy Bay, Hanover (phone: 952-5110 or 952-5111; 305-666-3566 from Miami; 800-237-3237 from elsewhere in the US; fax: 952-0401).

Wyndham Rose Hall Beach With an 18-hole championship golf course, 6 lighted tennis courts (resident pro, too), all kinds of beach and water sports, sea, and swimming pools, this property is popular with all types of folk, from golfers to mature honeymooners, to large groups. It has 489 good-looking rooms and 36 suites. There's a choice of the *Great House Verandah* or *Brasserie and Terrace* restaurants, or exclusive dining at *Ambrosia,* featuring excellent northern Italian cuisine; refined entertainment in the *Palmer Hall Lounge* or late-dancing at the *Junkanoo* disco. An all-inclusive package is available. Nine miles (15 minutes) east of the airport. Rose Hall (phone: 953-2650; 800-822-4200 from the US; fax: 953-2617).

MODERATE

Gloucestershire Located in downtown Montego Bay, the 85 rooms are just steps away from the public Doctor's Cave Beach. Amenities include a restaurant, tour desk, room service, pool, and Jacuzzi. A daily meal plan is available. Gloucester Ave. (phone: 952-4420; 800-742-4276 from the US; fax: 952-8088).

Holiday Inn The on-premises beach, shopping complex just across the street, lively disco, and reasonable rates make this 516-room resort popular with singles and groups. Facilities include 3 restaurants, a huge pool, 4 tennis courts, and a disco. 480 Rose Hall (phone: 953-2485; 800-HOLIDAY from the US; fax: 953-2840).

Sandals Inn One of six Sandals resorts on Jamaica, it's tailor-made for fun-loving twosomes who like the intimacy of a small hotel and don't mind their beaches small and across the road. (True beach lovers who don't mind the inconvenience can just hop the complimentary hourly shuttle over to *Sandals Montego Bay.*) It features 52 guestrooms, some with terraces, and an all-inclusive rate that covers all meals, drinks, water sports (including scuba and water skiing), tennis, a fitness room, daily activities, nightly entertainment, taxes, airport transfers, and tips. There's a pool, an award-winning dining room, and room service for breakfast, cocktails, and late-night snacks. Handy location near town. Kent Ave. (phone: 952-4140; 800-327-1991 or 800-SANDALS from the US and Canada; fax: 952-6913).

Sea Wind Beach A high-rise with excellent views, set on a private white sand beach, with 468 standard rooms, suites, and apartments. Its amenities include 2 swimming pools, 4 tennis courts, 3 restaurants, 5 bars, a water sports center, and the popular *Cave* discotheque. An all-around good value with lots of activities; the beautiful beach is the main draw. Across from the *Montego Bay Yacht Club.* Montego Bay, Freeport (phone: 952-4874 or 952-4875; 800-223-6510 from the US; fax: 952-1839).

INEXPENSIVE

Lifestyles This 100-room property is set on historic Miranda Hill, overlooking Walter Fletcher Beach, 5 miles out of the downtown area. High garden walls create a feeling of seclusion without obscuring a magnificent view of the bay. Facilities include the *Victoria Terrace* restaurant, 2 bars, 2 pools, a Jacuzzi, tennis courts, a basketball court, and the *Scruples* disco. There's nightly entertainment and free transportation to public beaches. Gloucester Ave. (phone: 952-4703; 800-JAMAICA from the US; fax: 952-6810).

Richmond Hill A former greathouse with considerable style and grace, it's best known for its restaurant (see *Eating Out*). The 20 guestrooms are small but impeccably decorated, and there's a big pool, an extraordinary view of Montego Bay and the Caribbean, and a sociable bar. Union St., on Richmond Hill above town (phone: 952-3859; fax: 952-6106).

FALMOUTH

EXPENSIVE

Trelawney Beach The fresh look and friendly spirit of this 350-room (all air conditioned) property and its semi-inclusive activity policy make up for its somewhat isolated location. Guests can choose a cottage room (with its own patio) near the pool, beach, and garden, a superior room with an ocean view, or the standard room with a garden or mountain view. Tennis clinics and 4 lighted Laykold courts, water sports (including a daily 1-tank scuba dive), a shuttle to Montego Bay, nightly live entertainment, and a daily supervised children's activities program, are included. There's also a disco and a nude beach area. The *Jamaican Room* offers buffet or four-course dinners every evening; Tuesday night is Jamaican night with a poolside buffet. Two meal plans are available. Children 14 and under stay for free in their parents' room during the summer. Ten minutes from Falmouth and Martha Brae rafting (phone: 954-2450; 212-545-2222 from New York City; 800-223-0888 or 800-JAMAICA from elsewhere in the US; fax: 954-2173).

RUNAWAY BAY

MODERATE

Club Caribbean All 128 rooms are in cottages in a tropical garden setting. This semi-inclusive resort offers a special daily activities program for children, tennis, snorkeling, windsurfing, water skiing, and sailing. An on-premises *PADI* 5-star international scuba diving training facility offers a range of dive packages. There's a private beach, a pool, a disco, a bar, and a restaurant. Price includes breakfast and dinner, taxes and tips. Special rates for children under 12. On the beach (phone: 973-3507; 212-545-8469 from New York City; 800-223-9815 from elsewhere in the US; fax: 973-3509;).

FDR This upscale all-inclusive property is ideal for families. The 67 one-, two-, and three-bedroom apartment suites are spacious, and each one has a pullout sleep sofa in the living room. In addition, every suite comes with a "Girl Friday" who acts as a nanny, cook, housekeeper, and kitchen stocker. For a small extra charge, she'll even baby-sit in the evening. Rates include all meals, transfers, a shopping trip to nearby Ocho Rios, a glass-bottom boat tour, scuba diving, land and water sports, nightly entertainment, and greens fees at *Runaway Bay Golf Club.* For children and teens there are special supervised activities; there's also a petting zoo and a playground. Other features include an open-air restaurant and beach grill, a piano bar, and a discotheque. Across from the beach (phone: 973-3067; 800-654-1FDR from the US; fax: 973-3071).

Jamaica, Jamaica An exuberant 238-room member of the SuperClubs group, this place is notable for its Jamaican decor and dining. Its chefs have won gold medals from the Jamaican Cultural Commission for their innovative cooking. The rates cover everything — horse-and-buggy rides, music, parties, all sports (excellent scuba facilities), meals, all drinks, shopping shuttle, cruise, transfers, taxes, tips, and entertainment. Special complimentary sports clinics include the Tennis Academy (morning and afternoon lectures, video, and sessions with visiting pros) and the Golf Academy (driving range, putting green, and intensive instruction at the nearby championship *Runaway Bay Golf Club*). There's a separate nude beach. Adults (over 16) only. On the beach (phone: 973-2436 or 973-2437; 516-868-6924 from New York; 800-858-8009 from elsewhere in the US; fax: 973-2352).

INEXPENSIVE

Silver Spray Small, serviceable, quiet and basic, this property has 13 rooms on a cliff overlooking the sea. There's a saltwater pool, and a nearby water sports facility offering diving, fishing, and Waverunners. The food is good, and a meal plan is optional (phone: 973-3413 or 973-2006; 800-526-2422 from the US).

OCHO RIOS AREA

EXPENSIVE

Boscobel Beach This SuperClubs member is a lively 228-room, all-inclusive resort. Fourteen 2-bedroom suites are in a building next door to the main building. There are 3 restaurants, 2 pools, golf, aerobics classes, scuba, a fitness center, tennis, and a fine beach. Best of all, while the adults play, the kids are kept happy in supervised activity programs. There's even a separate program for teenagers, plus a Mini Club with a computer classroom, movie theater, mini-farm, video games, donkey rides, picnics, arts and crafts classes, disco, and activities room. About 10 miles east of Ocho Rios (phone: 975-3330; 516-868-6924 from New York; 800-858-8009 from elsewhere in the US; fax: 975-3270).

Couples The emphasis on romance and relaxed fun at this 172-room couples-only resort draws lots of repeaters, and lots of weddings. Weekly rates include everything — room, airport transport, tips, taxes, all meals, all sports (water skiing, scuba, kayaking, tennis, squash, and horseback riding), entertainment, wine, bar drinks, even cigarettes. There's a gym overlooking the ocean, 4 restaurants, golf nearby, and a nude beach on a small, private island. In St. Mary, about 5 miles east of Ocho Rios (phone: 975-4271; 516-868-6924 from New York; 800-858-8009 from elsewhere in the US; fax: 974-4439).

Enchanted Garden Built on the grounds of Carinosa Gardens, this all-inclusive resort is surrounded by 20 acres of tropical flowers, cascading waterfalls, and exotic birds. The 112 deluxe 1-, 2-, and 3-bedroom villas all have private patios with magnificent views of Ocho Rios Bay, while 40 feature a private indoor plunge pool. The price includes all meals, wine and bar drinks, nightly entertainment, tennis, horseback riding, plus a facial, massage, manicure, and pedicure. Free shuttles are provided to the beach, golf courses, and in-town shopping areas. In the hills above Ocho Rios (phone: 974-5346; 800-323-5655 from the US or Canada; fax: 974-5823).

Jamaica Grande This property is the result of the marriage between the neighboring *Ramada Mallards Beach* and the *Americana Beach* resorts. About $23 million went into renovating the two properties and merging them under the Ramada Renaissance banner as Jamaica's largest resort (720 rooms). The island's largest and most extensive convention and meeting facilities are here, so expect large groups of business types. Other amenities include 4 lighted tennis courts; a pool complex with waterfalls, swim-through grottos, a swim-up bar, and a children's wading pool; a beach; water sports; fitness center with daily exercise classes; a video room; a disco; 5 restaurants; bars; and a tour desk. There is also Club Mongoose, a supervised children's activity and day-care program; 24-hour room service; and an impressive open-air reception area. This high-rise resort offers varying rate plans that range from room and breakfast only to an all-inclusive package. An ID card on an elastic bracelet differentiates between guests on the various plans. Ocho Rios (phone: 974-2201; 800-228-9898 from the US; 800-268-8998 from Canada; fax: 974-5378).

Jamaica Inn A small (45 rooms), classic island inn offering gentle luxuries — comfortable rooms, thoughtful service, good food (with an orchestra every evening in winter), and relaxed life on a beautiful private beach. Tennis facilities are around the corner at the *Shaw Park Beach* hotel; riding and golf can be found at *Upton Country Club,* a short drive away. The place draws lots of repeaters, so book early. About 2 miles east of Ocho Rios (phone: 974-2514; 800-243-9420 from the US; fax: 974-2449).

Plantation Inn One of the island's most inviting properties, it features a lush garden setting overlooking twin crescent beaches and genteel service. Here are 76 lovely rooms with private ocean-view balconies where breakfast is served each morning. Water sports, tennis, and a health club with sauna are on the premises; riding and golf are nearby; and there's elegant dining and nightly entertainment. About 2 miles east of Ocho Rios (phone: 974-5601; 800-742-4276 from the US; fax: 974-5912).

Sandals Dunn's River Another all-inclusive, couples-only resort, it won enthusiastic reviews even before its acquisition by the Sandals group. Its façades and interiors have an Italianate/Mediterranean cast. There are 257 rooms in a 6-story main building, a 5-story west wing, and 2 lanai buildings; 4 restaurants; a disco; 2 freshwater swimming pools (one is the largest in Jamaica); 3 Jacuzzis; 2 whirlpool baths; an upgraded beach bar; a fitness center; tennis courts; a jogging course; and a pitch and putt golf course. The 3- to 7-night package price includes all land and water sports and other activities featured at their sister resorts (including a Dunn's River Falls tour), plus complimentary massages and an hourly shuttle to *Sandals Ocho Rios*. Located a few miles west of Ocho Rios (phone: 972-1610; 800-SANDALS from the US or Canada; fax: 972-1611).

Sandals Ocho Rios Like the other Sandals resorts on the island, it's an all-inclusive, couples-only haven. It occupies 9 acres of beachfront, offering 237 rooms in the balconied, multistory main building (ocean or mountain view) or in garden cottages. Three freshwater pools complement the deep blue sea; 2 restaurants and 4 bars (among them a swim-up pool bar), a piano lounge, and a discotheque provide ample entertainment opportunities. Packages are for 3 to 7 nights and rates include — besides the room and three squares — unlimited cocktails, wine, and beer; a full roster of water sports (including scuba diving) and land sports; nightly parties with live music and entertainment; an excursion to Dunn's River Falls; airport transfers, taxes, and tips. About 1½ miles east of Ocho Rios center (phone: 974-5691; 800-SANDALS from the US or Canada; fax: 974-5700).

Sans Souci This charming and truly classy enclave has 74 freshly and stylishly decorated rooms and suites terraced down a lush, gardened hillside above a small private bay. Most have wide balcony views; all are sumptuous and spacious. In addition, there are 36 beachfront 1-bedroom suites. There are 2 pools (1 freshwater, 1 fed by a mineral spring), and 4 tennis courts. Guests have privileges at a nearby golf course; riding and polo can be arranged. *Charlie's Spa* offers a full range of beauty and body treatments, aerobics, aquacize programs, and fitness holiday packages that include spa cuisine. Complete water sports facilities are on the beach. There's the very attractive and unusual *Balloon Bar* and the outstanding *Casanova* restaurant (see *Eating Out*). All-inclusive L'esprit Plan available. About 4 miles east of Ocho Rios center (phone: 974-2353 or 974-2354; 800-654-1FDR from the US; fax: 974-2544).

MODERATE

Shaw Park Beach An appealing place with 118 rooms on a lovely stretch of pure white sand with the feel of a private beach, its atmosphere is active but not frantic. Once so-so, it's now an affordable, upscale, beach resort. Features include water sports (including scuba), a pool, tennis, and a helpful tour desk. After dark there's fine dining, entertainment, and *Silks* disco for night owls. About 2½ miles east of Ocho Rios center (phone: 974-2552 or 974-2554; 800-243-9420 from the US; fax: 974-5042).

INEXPENSIVE

Hibiscus Lodge This neat little hotel (26 well-kept rooms, 9 of which are air conditioned) is very personally, personably run. Activities are limited (tennis, pool, sunning, swimming, snorkeling from a reef-protected beach, golf privileges at the *Upton Country Club*). But it's near the center of town, within walking distance of restaurants and shopping. Good home-style Jamaican food is served at the *Almond Tree* (see *Eating Out*). Ocho Rios (phone: 974-2676 or 974-2813; 800-JAMAICA from the US and Canada).

Hummingbird Haven In a garden setting with a sea view, this camping ground is where backpackers and those on an austere budget can literally pitch their tents. Several spartan cabins also can be rented. Located 2 miles east of the Ocho Rios clock tower, on Main Hwy. (phone: 974-5188; fax: 974-2559).

PORT ANTONIO

EXPENSIVE

Jamaica Palace An international resort richly deserving of its name. This romantic, beautifully appointed hotel offers 63 refurbished rooms filled with genuine antiques, crystal chandeliers, and oriental rugs. There's a shuttle to the beach; guests also can take a swim "around the island" in the 114-foot-long Jamaica-shaped pool. There are also 2 bars, a restaurant serving island and continental fare, gamerooms, and numerous sun decks (phone: 993-2020; fax: 993-3459).

MODERATE

Fern Hill Club Port Antonio's only all-inclusive property, it has 32 air conditioned rooms and suites. Rates include all meals, wine, beer, or local bar drinks, most sports, nightly entertainment, transfers from Kingston, taxes, and tips. Scuba diving and horseback riding, offered nearby, are extra. Located on 40 acres of land in the hills above San San Beach (phone: 993-3222; 800-263-4354 from the US; fax: 993-2257).

Goblin Hill Villas To the delight of its many longtime guests, this legendary property has reclaimed its original name, after an assortment of monikers. The fresh, airy, 1- and 2-bedroom apartments are in 28 townhouse-like villas on the grounds of a former private home on a 700-acre hilltop estate. There are tennis courts, a pool; snorkeling and swimming at San San Bay; water skiing, scuba, and horseback riding nearby. No dining room or bar, but each apartment has a butler and a maid who shops and cooks. One of the island's most gracious and cherished refuges — the essence of the villa vacation lifestyle. East of Port Antonio at San San Beach (phone: 993-3286 or 993-3049; fax: 925-6248 in Kingston).

Navy Island The renamed *Admiralty Club* is a private 64-acre island, once Errol Flynn's hideaway. This lovely, unspoiled spot — with a small 8-slip marina — is reached by a short ferry ride from the Port Antonio marina. It has 7 studio cottages, 2 guestrooms, and 3 villas (cook/housekeeper optional), all cooled by ceiling fans and tropical breezes. The accommodations are basic: no TV sets and no telephones. The main building boasts an attractive nautical decor with native wood embellishments plus a waterfront dining room, *Chuups* (see *Eating Out*), with magnificent views of Port Antonio and the Blue Mountains. There's also a fine swimming beach, the secluded Trembly Knees Cove for nude sunbathing, and a tennis court. Some water sports are on the premises; others can be arranged. There's an Errol Flynn room with posters and memorabilia. Every Saturday night, there's a reggae party at Crusoe's Beach. Navy Island, Port Antonio Harbour (phone: 993-2667; fax: 993-2041).

KINGSTON

EXPENSIVE

Jamaica Pegasus Consistently topnotch service is found at this well-run city hotel with the feel of an upscale resort. A 17-story high-rise in the New Kingston business district, favored by business and pleasure travelers, its 350 rooms, deluxe suites, and amenity-laden, extra-service Knutsford Club executive floor rooms are large, comfortable, and clean. Room and valet service are prompt and high quality. The pool and bars are popular after-hours meeting places. A pianist entertains at the afternoon tea in the lobby weekdays from 3:30 to 6:30 PM. There is a Sunday night poolside barbecue with live entertainment, the elegant *Pavillon* restaurant, and a less formal *Country Kitchen* restaurant. There's also a children's pool, a small fitness center, a jogging trail and tennis court, plus a tennis club across the road. Other amenities include 24-hour room service, duty-free shops, a hair salon, pharmacy, car rental desk, and tour desk. 81 Knutsford Blvd. (phone: 926-3691 or 926-3699; 800-225-5843 from the US or Canada; fax: 929-5855).

INEXPENSIVE

Morgan's Harbour The yacht club–like lodging alternative to downtown Kingston, this is across the harbor, at the end of the Palisadoes Peninsula. Life centers on the harborside pool complex; recreational possibilities include swimming, snorkeling, boat trips to the cays, deep-sea fishing trips, working out in the small gym, or dancing in the new *Disco 1692.* The breezy open-air bar and roof-shaded restaurant have a handsome view of Kingston across the bay. The 66 rooms are neat but smallish; ask for one in the new wing. At press time, 10 rooms in the beach block were undergoing a complete renovation. Service is friendly. Ten minutes from Norman Manley Airport, near Port Royal (phone: 924-8464; 800-526-2422 in the US; fax: 924-8562). Moderate.

Courtleigh Located across the street from the Japanese Embassy, this 40-room, elegant hotel is especially popular with Japanese businessmen. The *Courtleigh House,* a medium-rise building adjacent to the hotel, features 42 additional 1-, 2-, and 3-bedroom suites. There also are 2 restaurants, a pool with bar, and the *Mingles* cocktail lounge, one of New Kingston's more popular nightspots on Wednesday and Friday nights. Shops and recreational facilities are also nearby. 31 Trafalgar Rd. (phone: 926-8174, 926-8178, or 929-5320; 800-JAMAICA from the US; fax: 926-7801).

Four Seasons A beautifully converted Edwardian greathouse, with 39 air conditioned rooms, all individually decorated. Run by two German sisters, the property is set in a walled tropical garden, its restaurant is well regarded, and it's close to all New Kingston business, sports, and entertainment. 18 Ruthven Rd. (phone: 926-8805; 800-742-4276 from the US; fax: 929-5964).

Terra Nova What was once a graceful private home is now an inn with 33 air conditioned rooms, well-tended gardens, and a pool. The restaurant is a favorite of government officials and Kingston's high society. 17 Waterloo Rd. (phone: 926-2211 or 926-9334; fax: 929-4933).

MANDEVILLE AND THE SOUTH COAST

INEXPENSIVE

Astra Cool off at this inn in the Mandeville hills, 2,000 feet above sea level in the island interior. The restaurant and bar serve excellent Jamaican dishes in a Caribbean country inn setting. There's a pool and sauna; tennis and golf are available, as are horseback tours of nearby plantations. Its 22 rooms are popular with Jamaicans who want to go rural for a weekend, ecotourists, and bird watchers. 62 Ward Ave., Mandeville (phone: 962-3265 or 962-3377; 800-JAMAICA from the US; fax: 962-1461).

Mandeville A small, informal, and friendly 62-room resort with hints of the Victorian era in its decor, set in tropical gardens. The restaurant and bar follow this motif. Another cool, country refuge much different from north coast resorts. None of the rooms have air conditioning, and only the more expensive rooms have TV sets. The Wednesday night poolside barbecue is popular with guests, as is the new disco, *Chester's.* Guests have golf privileges at the nearby *Manchester Club.* 4 Hotel St., Mandeville (phone: 962-2460 or 962-2138; 800-742-4276 from the US; fax: 962-0700).

Treasure Beach This oasis on Jamaica's sunny, palm-shaded south coast features 20 air conditioned rooms with TV sets and telephones, set in several cottages. Among the amenities are a freshwater swimming pool, poolside bar, and 2 restaurants. Located about 65 miles south of Montego Bay, southeast of Black River, at Treasure Beach (phone: 965-2305; 800-742-4276; fax: 965-2544).

EATING OUT

The trend toward EP (European Plan; without meals) hotel rates is made more tempting by the number of good restaurants, most offering some island dishes as well as continental choices. Jamaican soups are superior — including meaty pepper pot, spicy *callaloo,* red pea, and pumpkin. The island's most famous concoction is salt fish and *ackee,* a mixture of cod and a bland local fruit, which tastes something like flavorful scrambled eggs. Another traditional dish is jerk pork or jerk chicken — the meat is highly seasoned and grilled or smoked for hours over pimiento (allspice) wood and leaves (especially good at the *Pork Pit* in MoBay — see below). Most visitors enjoy the spicy Jamaican patties, which are pastry shells filled with beef or vegetables; stamp & go (codfish fritters) or *akkra* (vegetable fritters); and rice and peas served as a main or side dish, along with *christophine* (a squash-like vegetable) and yams. Roast suckling pig and curried goat are also favorite main dishes; Jamaican mango chutney is fine with the latter and to take home. Native fruits — mango, sweetsop, soursop, paw paw (papaya), bananas, and the rest — are delicious fresh or made into tarts or ice cream. And Jamaicans are almost as proud of their rich Blue Mountain coffee, first-rate Red Stripe beer, and liqueurs (coffee-flavored Tia Maria, rummy Rumona, and a pimiento liqueur made from ripe, red allspice berries) as they are of their famous rums.

Expect to pay over $40 for dinner for two (without drinks and tip) at places described below as expensive; from $22 to $40 at restaurants in the moderate category; and less than $22 at places listed as inexpensive. Generally lunch prices are lower than those for dinner. The 10% General Consumption Tax may not be included in the listed menu prices; be sure to ask. In the Montego Bay area, many restaurants offer complimentary pick-up and drop-off car service to and from hotels. Just request this service when you call to make reservations. All telephone numbers are in the 809 area code unless otherwise indicated.

NEGRIL

MODERATE

Charela Inn Features à la carte and five-course French and West Indian fare, a good wine list, a nice atmosphere, and good service. Open daily for breakfast, lunch, and dinner. Reservations necessary. Major credit cards accepted. Norman Manley Blvd. (phone: 957-4277).

Cosmo's Casual waterside location just east of town. Soup, fish, lobster, Jamaican dishes, and good cracked conch are served. Open daily for lunch and dinner. Reservations unnecessary. No credit cards accepted. Norman Manley Blvd. (phone: 957-4330).

Hungry Lion A very casual alfresco eatery in the cliffs, specializing in excellent vegetarian and seafood dishes. Open daily for dinner only. Reservations advised. No credit cards accepted. West End Rd. (phone: 957-4486).

Negril Tree House Club Good island fare, especially lobster, is featured, along with a lovely view and live reggae music at sunset. Serves all three meals daily, plus an all-you-can-eat barbecue with live entertainment on Monday nights. Reservations unnecessary. Major credit cards accepted. Norman Manley Blvd. (phone: 957-4287).

Rick's Café Very casual and all outdoors. Young folks staying in nearby cottages, homes, and small hotels head here as soon as they unpack. Favorite brunch item: eggs Benedict Caribe (with filet of lobster where the ham or Canadian bacon would usually be), good soups, and omelettes. Sunset is witching (and drinking) hour. Fresh fish and lobster are dinner specialties. Open daily for lunch and dinner. Reservations advised. Major credit cards accepted. Lighthouse Rd. (phone: 957-4335).

INEXPENSIVE

Negril Jerk Centre Serving up jerk chicken, pork, and fish, by the quarter-, half-, or whole pound. Beware the hot sauce — its nickname is Jamaican Hellfire. Wash it all down with coconut water, homemade ginger beer, or a Red Stripe. Open daily for breakfast, lunch, and dinner. Reservations unnecessary. No credit cards accepted. West End Rd., just past the *Sunshine Village Shopping Centre* (phone: 957-4847).

MONTEGO BAY AREA

EXPENSIVE

Calabash A dining spot with a super view and a first-rate Jamaican menu; seafood, too. Open daily for breakfast, lunch, and dinner. Reservations advised. Major credit cards accepted. Queen's Dr. (phone: 952-3891).

Georgian House This beautifully restored 18th-century house, a historic landmark, offers lots of romantic charm. The downstairs dining room has the atmosphere of an old English pub, and opens onto a restored courtyard. There is also an elegant dining room upstairs. Try the lobster Newburg, prepared with secret seasonings, or the Jamaican specialties. Open daily for dinner only. Reservations advised. Major credit cards accepted. 2 Orange St. (phone: 952-0632).

Julia's A covered outdoor dining area with a spectacular view of the surrounding town and bay; excellent Italian menu, with prix fixe dinner that includes soup, pasta, main course, and dessert. Open daily for dinner only. Reservations advised. Major credit cards accepted. Bogue Hill (phone: 952-1772).

Marguerite's by the Sea A romantic seaside setting, attentive service, and reliable food make this small, appealing place a favorite with islanders as well as visitors. Lobster dishes, fresh local shrimp, and the catch of the day are recommended; there's a good wine list, too. Open daily for lunch and dinner. Reservations advised. Major credit cards accepted. Gloucester Ave. (phone: 952-4777).

Pelican For breakfast, lunch, and dinner, this casual place — one of MoBay's most popular eateries for more than 25 years — serves local soups and Jamaican dishes. The adjacent *Cascade Room,* open for dinner only, is more formal, with exotic lobster and seafood, pricier but still reasonable. Open daily. Reservations advised for the *Cascade Room.* Major credit cards accepted. Gloucester Ave. (phone: 952-3171).

Pier 1 On the waterfront, a casual but classy gathering place for both the yachting set and businesspeople. Great lobster and shrimp creations, soups, and tropical drinks, with a nice view of the marina. Open daily for lunch and dinner; late Friday nights it becomes one of MoBay's most popular nightspots. Reservations unnecessary. Major credit cards accepted. Howard Cooke Blvd. (phone: 952-2452).

Richmond Hill More romance at a hilltop restaurant on the terrace and around the pool of a mansion turned small hotel. The view is splendid, the setting elegant. Excellent lobster, seafood, steaks. Open daily for dinner only. Reservations advised. Major credit cards accepted. Union St., on Richmond Hill above town (phone: 952-3859).

Town House A colonial atmosphere prevails in the brick-lined basement of a handsomely restored 18th-century home. It's a cool lunch retreat, and quietly stylish at night. Very good soups (pepper pot, pumpkin), stuffed lobster, and shrimp or red snapper papillote (baked in a paper bag) are offered. Open daily for lunch and dinner. Reservations advised. Major credit cards accepted. Church St. (phone: 952-2660).

Wexford Court Grille Good local dishes and continental fare are presented in a clean, simple setting. It's popular with the local crowd and businesspeople at lunch. Open for breakfast, lunch, and dinner. Reservations advised. No credit cards accepted. Gloucester Ave. (phone: 952-2854).

INEXPENSIVE

Le Chalet A Chinese eatery with a French name, this no-frills spot is clean, offers good service, and serves good sweet and sour chicken, *choy fan* (mixed vegetables and roast pork), and fried wontons. Popular with the local business crowd at lunch and with tourists at dinner. Open daily. Reservations unnecessary. No credit cards accepted. Next to the *Wexford Court Hotel* (phone: 952-5240).

Pork Pit A small open-air gazebo on the beach strip, it serves the best jerk pork, chicken, and ribs we've found. Well worth finding, if you thrive on spicy local fare. Open daily for lunch and dinner. No reservations. No credit cards accepted. Off Gloucester Ave. (no phone).

FALMOUTH

MODERATE

Glistening Waters A friendly, informal spot for fresh fish and seafood on the edge of Oyster Bay — brilliantly "phosphorescent" on moonless nights. Angler and raconteur Pat Hastings and his wife, Patty, who is the kitchen wizard, run it, serving great soups, fresh fish, lobster, conch, and Jamaican dishes. It's worth the trip from MoBay for a lazy day by the water. Open for lunch and dinner; lunch only on Sundays. Reservations unnecessary. Major credit cards accepted. Located a couple of miles east of Falmouth (phone: 954-3229 or 954-3138).

OCHO RIOS

EXPENSIVE

Almond Tree Attractively set on the *Hibiscus Lodge*'s gingerbread-trimmed back porch, this spot is popular for Jamaican lunch dishes — pepper pot, pumpkin soup, and fish sautéed with lime, onion, herbs, and butter — as well as delectable seafood and continental dinners with an island flavor, such as Caribbean bouillabaisse and Jamaican beef tenderloin. The setting is intimate, and the service is good. Open daily for lunch and dinner. Reservations advised. Major credit cards accepted. Main St. (phone: 974-2813).

Casanova Based on the quality of its food and service, this is one of Jamaica's finest. Executive Chef Deta Plunkett has won many awards in national and Caribbean culinary competitions for her innovative Jamaican dishes, which rely heavily on seafood. A special low-calorie spa menu is featured. Jackets are required in season. Open daily for lunch and dinner. Reservations essential. Major credit cards accepted. At the *Sans Souci* hotel, about 4 miles east of town (phone: 974-2353 or 974-2535).

MODERATE

Carib Inn Imaginative local and seafood dishes are served in a garden setting. Good service and an almost elegant atmosphere make this place worth several visits. Open daily for lunch and dinner. Reservations advised. American Express and Visa accepted. Main St. (phone: 974-2445).

Evita's A top-flight Italian dining spot, specializing in pasta dishes and seafood. Located in an authentic 1860 gingerbread house with an incredible view of Ocho Rios Bay. Open for lunch and dinner. Reservations advised. Major credit cards accepted. Located next to Carinosa Gardens. Eden Bower Rd. (phone: 974-2333).

Parkway Good, simple soups, seafood, and Jamaican dishes in a coffee shop setting. Fast service, and a break from high prices. Open for breakfast, lunch, and dinner daily. Reservations unnecessary. No credit cards accepted. Off Main St. (phone: 974-2667).

INEXPENSIVE

Double V A friendly hangout with some of the best jerk chicken and pork in town. Open daily for lunch and dinner. Reservations unnecessary. No credit cards accepted. On East Main St. (phone: 974-5998).

Little Pub This thatch-topped, casual spot is a good choice for lunch (hamburgers or other snacks) and dinner (lobster and Jamaican dishes). It's also a popular gathering place, with music and dancing most nights. Open daily. Reservations unnecessary. Major credit cards accepted. West of the Ocho Rios roundabout (phone: 974-2324).

PORT ANTONIO

VERY EXPENSIVE

Trident A very formal dining room (polished woods, gleaming silver, crystal, proper 5-course place settings), attended by tuxedoed, white-gloved waiters who, as a matter of course, take their time to serve you. At the *Trident* hotel, one of Jamaica's four Elegant Resorts, it deserves its top rating. From the excellent wine list to the exquisite pastries, this is a memorable dining experience, whether for a casual garden luncheon or a $49.50 per person prix fixe formal dinner. Men are required to wear jackets in the dining room after 7 PM. Open daily. Dinner reservations are essential year-round. Major credit cards accepted. East of Port Antonio on Rte. A4 (phone: 993-2602).

EXPENSIVE

Chuups at Navy Island Its name means "a kiss" in Jamaican patois. Formerly the *Admiralty Club,* this casual and relaxing place on a private island offers good seafood, authentic Jamaican dishes, daily specials, and great atmosphere — the island once belonged to Errol Flynn. Sip a cocktail and drink in the scenery of Port Antonio from the bar. There's a fixed-price, 5-course dinner for $24 to $30, depending on the entrée. Ferry service to the island is provided. Open daily for lunch and dinner. Reservations advised for dinner. Major credit cards accepted. Navy Island, Port Antonio Harbour (phone: 993-2667).

MODERATE

DeMontevin Lodge A gingerbread-trimmed family hotel that serves delicious Jamaican dinners by appointment. Call a day ahead. American Express only accepted. Musgrave and George Sts. (phone: 993-2604).

INEXPENSIVE

Bonnie View This small, cordial hostelry serves a traditional afternoon tea and informal Jamaican dinners. Located above town, with a panoramic view of Port Antonio. Open daily. Reservations unnecessary. Major credit cards accepted. Bonnie View Rd. (phone: 993-2752).

EXPENSIVE

Norma's Elegant innovative Jamaican fare served with flair in the courtyard of an old Spanish-style building with Mediterranean tile floors and clay pots overflowing with plants. The portions are large, the sauces light, and the presentation mouthwatering. This is the "in" spot for lunch. Norma recently opened a second branch near Montego Bay. Lunch and dinner served daily. Reservations necessary for dinner. MasterCard and Visa accepted. 78-80 Harbour St., Kingston (no phone) and in Reading, just west of Montego Bay (phone: 979-2745).

Le Pavillon Hushed tones prevail within this soft cocoon of pink, mauve, and white. Guests sit upon silk-upholstered chairs and scallop-backed couches, the lighting is low, the service unobtrusive, and the presentation of the creative continental fare *très* elegant. Come for a splurge, a romantic evening, or for the all-you-can-eat Sunday brunch. Open for dinner daily and Sunday brunch. Reservations necessary for dinner. Major credit cards accepted. 81 Knutsford Blvd., in the *Pegasus Hotel* (phone: 926-3690).

Raphael's This casually elegant northern Italian eatery specializes in homemade pasta and wonderful veal, fish, and chicken dishes. Try the ravioli stuffed with beef, the fettuccine in lime sauce, or the red snapper with lemon and capers. Dining is alfresco, either on the patio beneath the leaves of a huge lignum vitae tree or on the terrace, with romantic music playing in the background. Leave room for dessert — the gelato bar offers homemade Italian ice cream: mango, coconut, banana, and tamarind. Open for lunch and dinner; dinner only on Saturdays; closed Sundays. Reservations advised. Major credit cards accepted. 7 Hillcrest Ave. (phone: 978-2983).

MODERATE

Devon House Kingston's government-owned showplace mansion offers two dining options. The elegant *Devonshire,* on the verandah, is a fine restaurant in an intimate garden setting, serving continental fare for lunch and dinner (dinner reservations advised). The *Coffee Terrace,* another verandah-style eatery, serves light lunches, teas, and a Sunday Jamaican brunch (reservations advised). Closed Sundays, except the *Coffee Terrace.* Major credit cards accepted. Hope and Waterloo Rds. (phone: 929-7046 for the *Devonshire;* 929-7063 for the *Coffee Terrace*).

Terra Nova A fashionable favorite with Jamaicans as well as visitors, this eatery features a classic continental menu. There's a popular Wednesday seafood lunch buffet. Open daily for full American and Jamaican breakfast, lunch, and dinner. Reservations advised for dinner. Major credit cards accepted. 17 Waterloo Rd. (phone: 926-2211 or 926-9334).

INEXPENSIVE

Chelsea Jerk Centre One of Kingston's most popular casual eateries for jerk pork and chicken, and roasted fish. Open for lunch and dinner; closed Sundays. Reservations unnecessary. No credit cards accepted. 7 Chelsea Ave. (phone: 926-6322).

OUTSIDE KINGSTON

EXPENSIVE

Blue Mountain Inn This dining spot, located on the grounds of a former coffee plantation set alongside the Hope River, offers an exceptionally attractive setting. The late 19th-century, wood-shingled building is delightfully decorated with English colonial antiques, mahogany tables, and a working fireplace. Guests begin with drinks on the terrace outside, then eat indoors in cozy intimacy. The service is attentive, the mood romantic, the wine cellar well stocked, and the fare a blend of continental and seafood specialties topped by baked Alaska and other hedonistic desserts. It is well worth the special trip out of Kingston. Jackets are required for men. Open for dinner only; closed Sundays. Reservations necessary. Major credit cards accepted. Gordon Town Rd., 20 minutes from New Kingston (phone: 927-1700 or 927-2606).

Martinique

"A bit of France in the Caribbean." As clichés often are, this one is largely true. Not that wild, tropical Martinique looks like *la mère patrie.* Unlike France's snow-topped Alps, Martinique's mountains are blanketed with green jungle; thick stands of bamboo and giant breadfruit trees thrive in the island's rain forests, and there's even a patch of desert in the south.

Despite all appearances, though, Martinique is indeed France. It is a *région,* whose citizens exercise the same rights and privileges accorded citizens of France. They are eligible for French social security benefits, health programs, and free compulsory education. (The literacy rate in the French West Indies is over 95%.) In addition to having a local government, island residents vote in French national elections. Few people in Martinique speak of island independence; the majority can't imagine what they would have to gain.

Martinique has a distinctly French *air.* Boutiques are full of Baccarat crystal, Chanel perfume, and Hermès scarves; *pâtisseries* sell fresh-baked croissants and display cheeses just off the boat from Marseilles; the streets are filled with honking Peugeots and buzzing *bicyclettes;* and French is heard everywhere.

But Martinique has its own personality, too, born of its sensuous climate, its lush landscapes, and its proud people. The island has its own distinctive musical heritage, including mazurkas and valses from plantation days, the hot sounds of zouk (danceable music with an African/beguine/West Indian sound), and the timeless, sexy beguine. Martinique's food is also distinctive — creole cooking combining native sea creatures, tropical fruit, and feisty spices.

Martinique's recorded history dates to 1493, when Columbus discovered the island but didn't land here. More than a century later — in 1635 — a party of Frenchmen arrived to claim the island for France and begin permanent settlement. The British conquered the island in 1762, only to give it up again a year later under the 1763 Treaty of Paris in exchange for France's relinquishing her claim to Canada. Martinique has been French ever since.

The island's story is sprinkled with the names of interesting people, such as Victor Schoelcher, a Parisian-born deputy from Alsace who was instrumental in helping to free the island's slaves in 1848. A statue of Schoelcher with a slave child stands in front of the island's Palais de Justice, and a Fort-de-France street, a suburb, and the capital's library bear his name. Painter Paul Gauguin lived and worked in Carbet for about 5 months in 1887. And then there's Marie-Josèphe Rose Tascher de la Pagerie, who became Napoleon's Empress Josephine. Her birthplace in Les Trois-Ilets is now a national museum, and her name is on the tongue

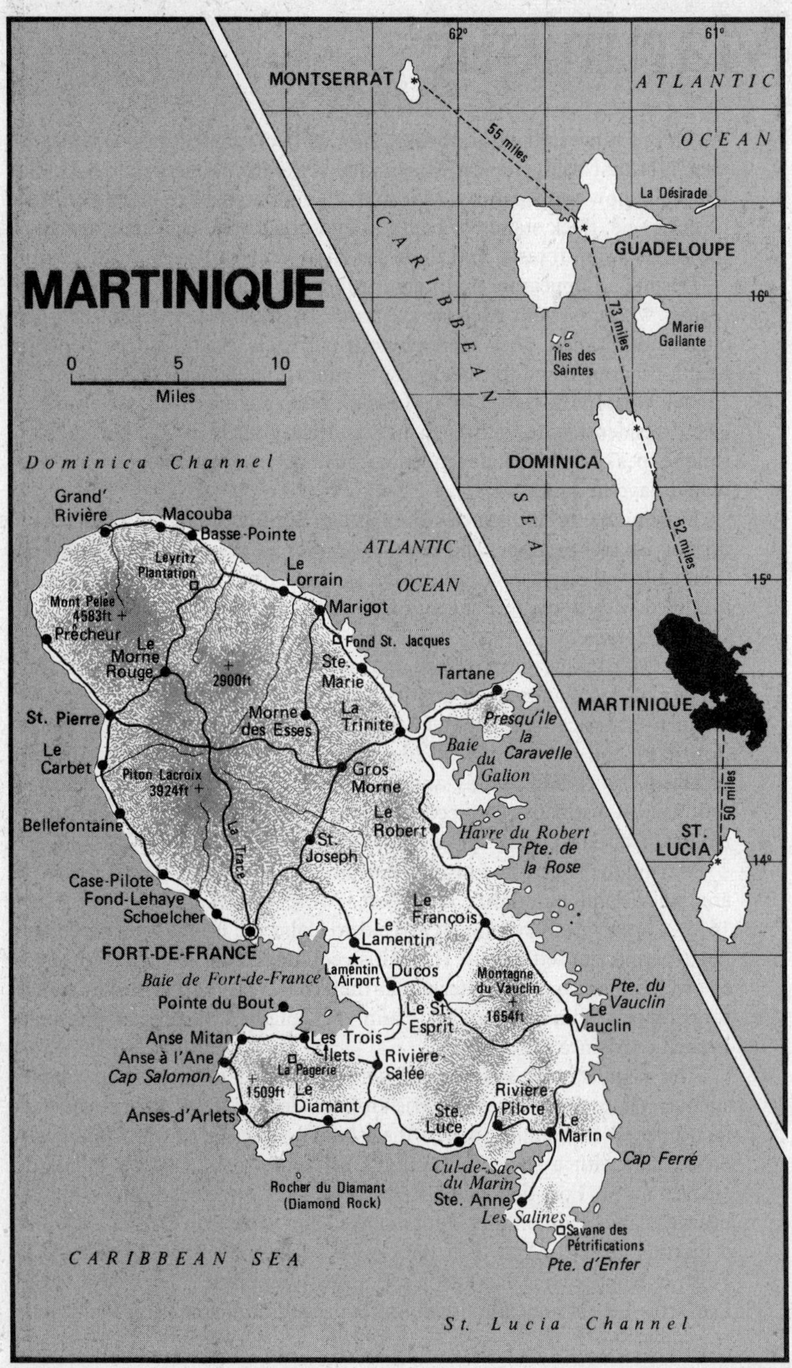

MARTINIQUE
0 5 10
Miles
Dominica Channel
ATLANTIC OCEAN
CARIBBEAN SEA
St. Lucia Channel
MONTSERRAT
55 miles
La Désirade
GUADELOUPE
73 miles
Marie Gallante
Îles des Saintes
DOMINICA
52 miles
MARTINIQUE
50 miles
ST. LUCIA
62°
61°
16°
15°
14°
Grand' Rivière
Macouba
Basse-Pointe
Leyritz Plantation
Le Lorrain
Marigot
Mont Pelée 4583ft
Prêcheur
Le Morne Rouge
2900ft
Fond St. Jacques
Ste. Marie
Tartane
St. Pierre
Morne des Esses
La Trinité
Presqu'île la Caravelle
Baie du Galion
Le Carbet
Piton Lacroix 3924ft
Gros-Morne
Bellefontaine
La Trace
Le Robert
Havre du Robert
Pte. de la Rose
St. Joseph
Case-Pilote
Fond-Lehaye
Schoelcher
Le François
FORT-DE-FRANCE
Le Lamentin
Lamentin Airport
Ducos
Montagne du Vauclin 1654ft
Baie de Fort-de-France
Pointe du Bout
Le St. Esprit
Pte. du Vauclin
Le Vauclin
Anse Mitan
Les Trois Ilets
Anse à l'Ane
La Pagerie
Rivière Salée
Cap Salomon
1509ft
Le Diamant
Anses-d'Arlets
Rivière-Pilote
Ste. Luce
Le Marin
Cap Ferré
Cul-de-Sac du Marin
Rocher du Diamant (Diamond Rock)
Ste. Anne
Les Salines
Savane des Pétrifications
Pte. d'Enfer

of every tour guide. (Her memory is not exactly revered by local people, however. The reason: In the late 1700s, slavery was outlawed in France and all its island properties, but Josephine asked Napoleon to reinstate it in Martinique because her family's sugar plantation had many slaves. As a result, slavery continued on the island for another 75 years.)

In Josephine's day and until the late 19th century, Martinique lived well on its production of sugar and rum. Elegant plantations with large houses, cane processing factories, and round-towered windmills dotted the country. Except for the steepest mountainsides, the island was quilted with green fields of cane. Sugar — and the rum made from it — is still an important crop on Martinique. But growing it requires hard labor. For this reason and because of the gradual decline in sugar prices, crops have been diversified in recent years. More and more banana plantations and bristly fields of pineapple are appearing. Fish, shellfish, and livestock remain important sources of food.

And then there's tourism. If there's any Francophile in you, the combination of Gallic culture, gentle climate, and natural beauty will be irresistible. The sports facilities are good and varied — visitors can enjoy biking, fishing, golf, tennis, hiking, boating, boardsailing, water skiing, and scuba diving — and there's also a choice of interesting historic sites.

But can you enjoy Martinique's charms if you don't speak French? That depends on you. In small, out-of-the-way hotels and restaurants, you'll probably have difficulty making yourself understood. One day you might find yourself in front of a shop counter miming a waterproof watch for a puzzled salesgirl who doesn't speak English. If such things bother you, forget about Martinique.

On the other hand, staff members of most tourist hotels, popular shops, and restaurants speak fair-to-excellent English; tours in English are available; and islanders usually are much more willing to bridge the language gap than are their Parisian counterparts. With a good phrase book, a little patience, and a sense of humor, you'll find your room, order a meal, shop, see the sights, and even lose your limit at the casino. If you don't mind occasionally communicating by gestures, and if intriguing foreign places appeal to you, you'll love this "little bit of France in the Caribbean."

Martinique At-a-Glance

FROM THE AIR

The island of Martinique is 50 miles long and 22 miles wide with a land area of 425 square miles and a population of 360,000. It is about halfway down the arc formed by the Windward (eastern) islands of the Lesser Antilles. Its nearest neighbors are Dominica (52 miles north), Guadeloupe (125 miles north), and St. Lucia (50 miles south).

Martinique is shaped somewhat like an elongated right-hand mitten with the space between its west coast thumb-and-forefinger edge forming an admirable deep-water harbor. On the tip of the thumb sits Pointe du Bout, the island's principal resort area, with its highest concentration of medium-rise hotels and condominium apartments surrounding a handsome marina. Directly north of the point — a 20-minute ferry ride across the harbor — is Martinique's only real city, its capital and chief commercial port, Fort-de-France (pop. 105,000).

Lamentin International Airport is just inland of the harbor's eastern edge, about 20 minutes from Fort-de-France and about 30 minutes from Pointe du Bout. The distance from New York is 1,965 miles, from Miami about 1,470 miles, and from San Juan, 425 miles.

Martinique's east coast, pounded by Atlantic surf, combines rugged shoreline, occasional wave-combed beaches, and a few small fishing towns: Vauclin, François, Le Robert, Tartane (on the peninsula called Presqu'île de la Caravelle, which is mostly nature preserve), Ste. Marie, and Grand' Rivière. The western and southern coasts are washed by the gentler Caribbean. Lining the shore south of Pointe du Bout are some of the island's best bathing beaches: Anses d'Arlets, Le Diamant, Plage des Salines, and Ste. Anne.

Much of the northern half of the island is covered with rain forests and tall, green mountains. Most famous of these is Mt. Pelée, a now-dormant (but still alive) volcano whose 1902 eruption destroyed the city of St. Pierre. St. Pierre never recovered; the ghost town is a chief sightseeing destination here.

SPECIAL PLACES

FORT-DE-FRANCE Martinique's capital is a small-scale combination of New Orleans and Nice — with narrow streets and iron grille balconies, blue-capped *flics* (cops) marshaling traffic, and a fleet of trim-hulled yachts riding at anchor in its Baie des Flamands. It's where the banks, the shops, and some of the best restaurants are, the place everyone visits at least once.

The heart of the city is La Savane, the big green park handsomely restored and landscaped with benches, walks, and playing fields. Located here is the once-beautiful statue of Josephine, dedicated in 1859 and mysteriously beheaded in 1991. The beheading, some Martiniquais say, was long overdue because Josephine championed the slavery that cursed their forefathers. On the park's edge, near the harbor, a roofed market shades craftswomen and their stacks of baskets, straw hats, woodcarvings, beads, bangles, and shells for sale. Just across the street is the ferry dock, and on the strategic hilltop to the east looms Fort St. Louis.

Walk west along Boulevard Alfassa following the harbor's edge, and you'll find the tourist information center and the government-sponsored Caribbean Arts Center, where the work of local artisans is displayed and sold. Along the savannah's western edge runs the main street, Rue de la

Liberté. It's lined with "les quick-snack" vans on the park side and, on the other, the town's chief hotels, the frenetic post office, the *Musée Départemental,* and the city's library and architectural *chef d'oeuvre,* La Bibliothèque Schoelcher, imported lock, stock, and trompe l'oeil from Paris after the *Exposition of 1889.* Installed in a gracefully restored and air conditioned townhouse, the *musée*'s collections include relics of prehistoric Arawak and Carib civilizations as well as some pretty pieces of antique furniture. The museum is open weekdays from 8:30 AM to noon and from 2:30 to 6 PM, and Saturdays from 8:30 AM to noon; it's closed Sundays. There's an admission charge (phone: 724555). Streets leading off Rue de la Liberté to the left (west) shelter Fort-de-France's best-stocked shops full of perfume, crystal, porcelain, handbags, scarves, and other elegant imports — mostly from France, but from Switzerland, Germany, Japan, and the rest of the world as well. One block west on the Rue Schoelcher and opposite its own small square stands the *cathédrale.*

Just outside the Centre Ville, or City Center, is the *Aquarium de Martinique* (Bd. de la Marne; phone: 730229; fax: 730222), home to 2,000 sea creatures. It offers an enlightening glimpse into Caribbean sea life, including its kaleidoscopic coral reefs. There's a huge den of sharks, as well as an impressive re-creation of a tropical rain forest and river. Even if you plan an ocean dive or a trip into Martinique's rain forest, this place is worth a look. Open daily from 9 AM to 7 PM; admission charge.

NORTH OF FORT-DE-FRANCE

ST. PIERRE Once the Paris of the West Indies and now its Pompeii, the remains of this city are Martinique's top day-trip destination. Only the ruins of the theater, the cathedral, and the broken gray walls remain of what were once homes, gardens, and stately villas before the eruption of Mt. Pelée in May 1902. A small volcanological museum named for its American founder, Dr. Franck A. Perret, displays pictures and relics — fused coins, a charred sewing machine, petrified spaghetti, a melted bottle with perfume still inside. It's a featured stop on a number of half-day and daylong bus tours departing from Fort-de-France and major tourist hotels. About an hour north of Fort-de-France, it's an easy drive-yourself destination, too. The museum is open from 9 AM to 5:30 PM; closed Mondays; admission charge (phone: 781516).

BALATA CHURCH Perched in the hills above Fort-de-France, the church, which resembles Paris's Sacré-Coeur, is visible from a distance. Day tours headed for St. Pierre and Leyritz give you a closer look. Or drive up and see for yourself — especially on Sunday, when families promenade in their brightest and best.

BALATA BOTANICAL PARK On Route de Balata, about a 10-minute drive from Balata Church, this idyllic spot is a veritable feast for the senses. Waves of brilliant hibiscus, orchids, anthuriums (the island's official flower), flaming red torch lilies, and thousands of other tropical beauties bloom across the hillside. Open daily from 9 AM to 5 PM; admission charge (phone: 644873).

CARBET Columbus landed here in 1502; Gauguin lived here for 5 months in 1887. Today it's a small fishing village with a photogenic shoreline and Martinique's only Olympic-size swimming pool built into the hills (admission charge). There's also a little Gauguin museum, with several reproductions but, unfortunately, no originals; admission charge (phone: 772266).

FOND ST. JACQUES Dominican fathers established a community here in the hills above the Atlantic in 1658. The most famous of them, Père Labat, lived here from 1693 to 1705. His *Voyages to the American Islands* could be considered the first Caribbean guidebook. The chapel, rebuilt in 1769, still stands, as do the partially restored buildings of a sugar estate. Most impressive: the vast purgery — the room where sugar was dried — with its great, arched, beamed ceiling. This is a stop on the all-day Leyritz tour.

LA TRACE A serpentine road through Martinique's rain forest, it scales the heights from Fort-de-France to towering Morne Rouge and offers great views.

LEYRITZ The best-restored plantation on the island, it's now an inn (see *Checking In*), a restaurant, a working banana concern, and a doll museum housing miniatures of celebrated women, each doll made of plant materials. Open daily from 8 AM to 6 PM; there's an admission charge for the gardens and the main house (phone: 693477). This is the final destination of some day tours; a swim-and-lunch stop on others.

CERON PLANTATION This magnificent old estate, located near Le Prêcheur on the northwest Caribbean coast of the island, makes for an out-of-the-ordinary daylong excursion. Lovingly restored, the estate, which dates from 1670, includes a main house (now the owners' residence), a sugar refinery (now a restaurant), an immense garden, and a number of well-preserved ruins of other structures. Visitors may stroll about the grounds and the nearby forest, or swim in the estate's river. Trips to the beach and boating may also be included in the excursion. Open during daylight hours; no admission charge. For tour information, call 529453.

SOUTH AND EAST OF FORT-DE-FRANCE

LA PAGERIE This ruin evokes another era. Its crumbled stones outline the plantation house, the sugar factory with its tall chimney, and the grounds that Marie-Josèphe Rose Tascher de la Pagerie (later Napoleon's Empress Josephine) called home. The cottage that was the plantation kitchen is a government-operated museum whose displays include paintings, a white net stocking (monogrammed and mended) and other bits of clothing, Josephine's childhood bed, and a smoldering love letter from Napoleon (with an English translation) that is worth the trip in itself. Some southbound tours combine this with a beach outing and lunch at Le Diamant. If you're staying at Pointe du Bout, it's a reasonable destination for a moped ride, or stop on the way to the golf course at Les Trois-Ilets. There's a refreshment stand. Open 9 AM to 5 PM; closed Mondays; admission charge (phone: 683455).

DIAMOND ROCK Looming out of the Caribbean off the south-coast beach at Le Diamant, it is the only rock ever commissioned as a ship in the British navy. For 18 months between 1804 and 1805, it was — officially — the HMS *Diamond Rock,* manned by the British and bombarded by the French, who were in firm possession of the rest of Martinique. The siege failed miserably until (legend says) the French smuggled some rum within striking distance of the British, then re-took the rock while the British crew was under the influence.

PRESQU'ÎLE DE LA CARAVELLE Embellished with the ruins of Château Dubuc, ancestral home of the Sultana Validé, this peninsula juts dramatically into the Atlantic. A nature preserve with good campsites, it's part of the big Parc Naturel, which also encompasses the tropical mountains in the north and the highlands as far south as Les Salines.

EXTRA SPECIAL **Much of Martinique's sugarcane ends up at one of the 14 *rhumeries* sprinkled across the island, where the juice is squeezed from the cane, boiled into syrup, and distilled into a knock-your-socks-off potion. Free rum tasting and distillery tours are offered at each *rhumerie;* arrive during rum season (August until about December) and you can watch the machines in action. The St. James Distillery, in Sainte-Marie (phone: 753002), has a small but interesting museum with 200 years of rum making artifacts. Set in a lovely creole house, the museum is open from 9 AM to 5 PM Mondays through Fridays and 9 AM to 1 PM Saturdays and Sundays. For a list of additional distilleries, contact the Martinique Tourist Office (phone: 637960).**

Sources and Resources

TOURIST INFORMATION

The tourist office information center along the waterfront in Fort-de-France (Bd. Alfassa; phone: 637960) is open from 7:30 AM to 5:30 PM Mondays through Thursdays (to 5:00 PM on Fridays), 8 AM to noon on Saturdays. The tourist office's airport information desk is open until after the last flight of the day arrives. For information on Martinique tourist offices in the US, see GETTING READY TO GO.

LOCAL COVERAGE *Une Histoire d'Amour Entre Ciel and Mer,* published seasonally by the tourist office in French and English, is available free at the airport, hotels, and the Fort-de-France center, and gives up-to-date information on hotel facilities, sightseeing, restaurants, shopping, and entertainment. It includes a map of Fort-de-France, as well as briefings on culture and history. The tourist office also publishes a helpful monthly bilingual newspaper called *Bienvenue en Martinique.* The privately published English-language *Choubouloute* — also free — covers much of the same material and includes a clear color map of the island. *Ti Gourmet* is a handy guide to Martinique restaurants that features color photographs and sample menus as well as a section on nightlife. It's available free from many hotels and shops.

The daily French-language newspaper, *France-Antilles,* is well written, and carries easily understood (even for those who don't speak French) entertainment ads. Parisian papers flown in from France and the English-language *International Herald Tribune* normally arrive on the island the day after publication.

In hotels, bulletin boards often carry descriptions and schedules of tour offerings (scuba trips, cocktail sails, and so on).

The deluxe picture book — one of a number for sale locally — called *Martinique* (Editions Exbrayat, about $30) is worth having for its short, readable essays by local experts on island history and culture, as well as for its dramatic photographs.

RADIO AND TELEVISION

Television is in French, but radio (which is produced locally or picked up from neighboring islands) broadcasts in several languages, including a nightly English news program on Martinique-Inter. Most hotels have satellite-dish facilities.

TELEPHONE

When calling from the US, dial 011 (international access code) + 596 (country code) + (local number). To call from another Caribbean island, the access code may vary, so call the local operator. When calling from a phone on Martinique, use only the local number unless otherwise indicated.

ENTRY REQUIREMENTS

In addition to an ongoing or return ticket, a current passport (or a passport expired not more than 5 years) or other proof of citizenship (voter's registration card or birth certificate with raised seal, plus official photo ID, such as a driver's license) is required for stays of up to 3 months. A visa is needed for longer visits.

CLIMATE AND CLOTHES

The average year-round temperature is 79F (26C). The weather is tropical and tends to be humid at sea level during the day, but can be 5 to 10F cooler — and breezy — in the hills. Even summer days are tempered by trade winds; expect high 60s or low 70s (20 to 23C) at night. November through April are the driest months; July to November, the wettest; but it doesn't rain every day even in the wet season, and more than a few dry season days have a shower or two — especially in the rain forest areas around Morne-Rouge and La Trace.

For daytime, wear lightweight sports clothes, bikinis or monokinis (female) and bikini trunks (male) on the beach. Caftans and djellabas make popular beach robes for both men and women. For touring and shopping, slacks and tops, cool cotton dresses or separates for women; slacks and knit or cotton-blend sport shirts for men. Shorts are less well received. Nights are dressier — especially in season. For women, that could mean a cocktail dress or fancy pants and top; for men, a long-sleeved, open-neck shirt and slacks. Jacket and tie are seldom, if ever, required. Women might want a light sweater or shawl for breezy nights and air conditioned restaurants and discos.

MONEY

Martinique's official currency is the French franc, whose day-to-day dollar value is quoted in the business sections of major metropolitan US newspapers; at press time it was about 5 francs to $1 US. Banks pay a little more for US currency than for traveler's checks. However, several tourist-oriented shops offer an additional 20% discount when shoppers use traveler's checks or credit cards (but not cash dollars) to pay for purchases. Francs are best for restaurant meals, taxi fares, and other day-to-day expenses.

Banks (at the airport and in Fort-de-France) offer the best rate of exchange. Hours are approximately 7:30 AM to 4 PM, but they close for lunch between about noon and 2:30 PM, and in the afternoon preceding a public holiday. Hotels will usually cash traveler's checks at a slightly lower francs-per-dollar rate. French francs can be reconverted to dollars only at the banks (including the one at the airport), not at hotels. Your home bank will charge an unconscionable amount for the reconversion service (and only exchange paper bills), so allow enough time to reconvert leftover francs at the airport before you leave. All prices in this chapter are quoted in US dollars.

LANGUAGE

Most native-born Martiniquais speak both French and creole — a mélange of French with African words and rhythms. Some employees at major tourist hotels and popular shops speak English, but country people are less likely to. If you're not fluent in French, carry a dictionary or phrase book.

TIME

Martinique time is 1 hour later than eastern standard time. When it's 7 PM EST in New York, it's 8 PM on Martinique. When New York is on daylight saving time, the Martinique hour is the same. Like France, a 24-hour clock is used, so 1 PM becomes 1300 hours, 2 PM, 1400 hours, and so on.

CURRENT

Local electricity is 220 volts AC, 50 cycles, so you'll need a converter and an adapter. Several large hotels lend them; but to be sure, bring your own.

TIPPING

A French law requires the automatic addition of a 15% service charge to all restaurant and bar bills. If you decide to tip extra in a restaurant or nightclub, be sure to leave cash. Credit card gratuities go directly to the establishment, not to the individual server. Give bellboys and porters about 5 francs per bag. Most cab drivers own their cars and do not expect tips.

GETTING AROUND

BUS There are a few point-to-point buses on the island. The system is pretty informal; you can hail them on the street. For more information, contact the tourist office. Taxis Collectifs, or TCs, are eight-seat limos or vans that provide most of Martinique's public transport for rates that run from about $1.50 to about $8, depending on the distance. Fort-de-France departure point for most TCs is Pointe Simon on the waterfront. They operate from early morning until around 6 PM. To travel on them confidently, you should be able to speak a little French or know exactly where you want to go. Check with the tourist office, a short distance from Pointe Simon on the waterfront Boulevard Alfassa, for schedules and fares.

CAR RENTAL Easy to arrange, and rates aren't exorbitant: from $40 to $50 a day plus 40¢ a kilometer to about $75 a day with unlimited mileage. Many companies offer a choice of day rate plus mileage or unlimited-mileage rate — whichever computes more favorably for the renter at turn-in time. Weekly rentals offer a 10% discount. The renter pays for gas, insurance, and 14% local tax; if you don't have a credit card, you will have to put down a cash deposit of about $300 to $350. Your own driver's license is good in Martinique for up to 20 days; if you stay longer, you'll need an international driver's permit, obtainable from a local *American Automobile Association* chapter for about $20 before you leave home (you don't have to be a member). Minimum renter age is 21 to 25, depending on the rental company; you must also have had at least 1 year's experience as a licensed driver. *Avis, Budget, Dollar, Europcar, Hertz,* and *Thrifty* have branches through which you can make advance reservations; you can also arrange rentals at the airport or through your hotel travel desk after you arrive. Local firms include *Tropicar* (phone: 582681), *Citer–LAM* (2 locations in Fort-de-France, phone: 726648 and 714737; and at the airport, phone: 516575), *Pop's Car* (phone: 510272), *Europcar* (phone: 733313), and *Safari-Car* (phone: 660626); their rates are occasionally lower than the international companies' (by about $3 to $5 a day). The major rental agencies and many of the local companies accept one or more credit cards, although some smaller ones may operate on a cash-only basis.

Martinique has more than 175 miles of well-paved but sometimes zigzagging main roads. Driving is on the right. The tourist office has outlined six self-guided driving tours that take a half to a full day to cover. But if strange, sometimes steep and curving roads make you nervous, opt for the bus.

FERRY SERVICE Runs from early morning until after midnight between Fort-de-France and Pointe du Bout, where a number of the best-known tourist hotels are; fare is about $2.25 one way, about $4 round-trip. A ferry links Fort-de-France with Anse Mitan and Anse à l'Ane from morning until late afternoon. For information, call 730553 or 713168.

SEA EXCURSIONS Several excursion boats operate out of the *Pointe du Bout Marina,* the *Méridien* and *La Batelière* hotels, and other docks for daylong trips to St. Pierre in the north and Diamond Rock in the south. These include the catamaran *Micaline* and the schooner *Toumelin* (phone: 660285 for both). The *Captain Cap* schooner (phone: 660000) offers beach trips with swimming, snorkeling, and picnic lunch for about $60 per person. The catamaran *Emeraude Express* (phone: 601238; fax: 705075) makes several trips a week from Guadeloupe and Dominica. Day trips on a catamaran or converted tuna boat cost about $70 per person, including lunch. The glass-bottom *Aquarium* operated by geologist Jacques Meneau docks at *La Batelière* hotel (phone: 520631). The *Seaquarium* (phone: 615577), another glass-bottom boat, can take up to 100 passengers for evening cruises on the bay, with a bar, a buffet, steel band entertainment, and an impressive, illuminated underwater show. Hour-long undersea excursions in Aquascopes — odd, bug-shaped metal pods that poke around the ocean floor and allow passengers to view the scenery through big glass windows — are offered several times a day in Ste. Anne (phone: 767106 or 767345) and at the *Pointe du Bout Marina* in Les Trois-Ilets (phone: 748741).

SIGHTSEEING BUS TOURS Local operators offer day and half-day tours along five key routes; each combines historical sites, scenery, and — often — a sample of good creole cooking. The standard itineraries (with departures from La Savane in Fort-de-France and some tourist hotels): north to St. Pierre or *Leyritz Plantation* or both; east to the Atlantic coast; south to the village of Ste. Anne and the beach at Les Salines, or to La Pagerie and Le Diamant with its white sand beach and landmark rock. Among the best operators: *Caribtours* of Pointe du Bout (phone: 660256), *Madinina Tours* of Fort-de-France (phone: 706525), *Jet Tours* at the *Pointe du Bout Marina* (phone: 660507 or 660305), and *S.T.T. Voyage* in Fort-de-France (23 Rue

Blénac; phone: 716812 or 733200). Guides are pleasant and speak English well. Buses are air conditioned. You can book tours directly or through your travel agent, your hotel, or the tourist office.

SIGHTSEEING TAXI TOURS These are a good choice when several passengers share the ride and split the cost. Typical itineraries: a half-day trip from Fort-de-France to Les Trois-Ilets and Le Diamant beach (about $75) or to St. Pierre via the Caribbean coast, then on to Morne Rouge and La Trace (about $90). Be sure the cost of the ride is agreed upon before you start. Drivers speak some English, but it's a good idea to take along your own good map and a sightseeing guide. One excellent tour guide is Bernadette Ducteil (phone: 513187). A lover of Martinique history, folklore, and flora, she speaks fluent English and often works for the tourist office.

TAXI Travel by taxi is expensive. The fare for two people and their luggage from Lamentin Airport, where all international flights land, to Pointe du Bout hotels is about $28 during the day, about $45 at night. From Fort-de-France to Pointe du Bout, the day fare is about $35; between 8 PM and 6 AM there's a 40% surcharge.

INTER-ISLAND FLIGHTS

American leaves from San Juan, Puerto Rico, daily, but arrival time is close to midnight; return flights depart in the early morning. *Air Martinique* flies to and from St. Martin, Antigua, Dominica, St. Lucia, Barbados, St. Vincent, Montserrat, St. Kitts, St. Croix, St. Thomas, Grenada, and Trinidad. There are frequent daily flights to and from Guadeloupe on *Réseau Aerien Français des Caraïbes,* a French airline consortium that includes *Air Martinique, Air Guadeloupe,* and *Air France. LIAT* also flies to and from neighboring islands. *Antilles Aero Service* (phone: 516688) at Lamentin rents small planes, with or without pilot, by the day or the hour.

SPECIAL EVENTS

The most festive time of the year is *Carnaval.* Just before *Lent,* it involves days of parading, masquerading, and celebrating. But before that there are weeks of dancing and gala goings-on to get everyone in condition for the main event. It comes to a wild climax on *Ash Wednesday* eve when Vaval, the spirit of *Carnaval,* is burned in effigy on a giant bonfire off La Savane. During July, the *Cultural Festival* of Fort-de-France takes place, and during the first 2 weeks in December the biennial *Guitar Festival* (to be held this year) and the *Jazz and Popular Music Festival* alternate. Martinique calls a halt to fasting with *Mi-Carême* (mid-*Lent*); May 1 is *Labor Day* with workers' parades; the *Tour de la Martinique,* a thrilling week-long bike race, takes place in mid-July; and the *Tour des Yoles Rondes,* a week-long yawling contest, is in late July. *Easter Monday, Ascension Day* (a Thursday, 40 days after *Easter*), *Pentecost Monday, Slavery Abolition Day* (May 22), *Bastille Day* (July 14), *Assumption Day* (August 15), *All*

Saints' Day (November 1), *Armistice Day* (November 11), *Christmas*, and *New Year's Day* are also public holidays.

SHOPPING

The brightest bargains around are French imports — Lalique crystal, Limoges dinnerware, fashions and fragrances from the best-known Paris houses — all at prices 25% to 40% below US, with an additional 20% discount if you pay in traveler's checks (some shops extend the extra discount to purchases made with major credit cards). The prices not only beat those in many of the world's so-called free ports, but those in Paris boutiques as well. Finds include cosmetics made in France, French food (truffled pâté, quail eggs, *moutarde*), kitchen gadgets (graters, food mills, crêpe pans), and liqueurs and brandies. Martinique's own favorite rum comes in shades from Vieux Acajou (dark, mellow Old Mahogany) to Jeune Acajou (newer, paler Young Mahogany) to clear white (fiery, 100 proof). The connoisseur's buy: deep brown, liqueur-like, 12-year-old rums bottled by St. James, Bally, and Clément.

On the whole, Martinique's crafts are not remarkable. By far the most fun are big, bright, appliquéd hangings depicting island folks and folkways. The ubiquitous Martiniquais doll, in her *madras et foulard* national dress, is available in every size. There are also some nicely woven straw hats (the pointed *bakoua* is the island's official topper), baskets, and placemats. Best for browsing: The open-air market at La Savane, and the *Centre des Métiers d'Art* (see below).

A Caribbean shopping survival tip: Try to avoid cruise ship crowds. Check with your hotel desk or the tourist office downtown so you can plan to shop when the fleet's not in. Shopping hours are from 9 AM to 12:30 PM and 2:30 to 6 PM; some shops, like *Roger Albert*, stay open during lunchtime as well. Stores are closed Saturday afternoons, Sundays, and holidays,

Some notable shops in Fort-de-France:

AGATIS A very small, very up-to-date boutique specializing in French couture, mostly for women, some men's clothes, too. 51 Rue Victor Hugo (phone: 730983).

ALBERT VENUTOLO Moderately priced gold and silver jewelry, tea services, crystal; 20% off for payment with US dollar traveler's checks or a credit card. Four locations: 13 Rue Victor Hugo (phone: 725744); 17 Rue St. Louis (phone: 714334); *Centre Commercial* in Cluny (phone: 702682), and Rue Ernest André in Lamentin (phone: 511158).

BOUTIQUE MOUNIA High-style Parisian fashions. 26 Rue Perrinon (phone: 737727).

CADET-DANIEL The place to look for gold and silver chains and other real jewelry at prices well below those back home. Rue Antoine Siger (phone: 714148).

CARAMBOLE A cut above typical tourist souvenirs, with arts and crafts by local, Haitian, and other Antillean artisans, jewelry, books on Martinique, swimwear. Four locations: Nos. 3 and 17 Rue Victor Hugo (phone: 700212, 734651, respectively); 20 Rue Ernest DeProge (phone: 639363); and Lamentin Airport (phone: 514503).

CENTRE DES MÉTIERS D'ART (CARIBBEAN ARTS CENTER) Offering patchwork, textile prints, pottery, shellwork, creole dolls, paintings, books, maps, and local rums. Two locations: 38 Rue Ernest DeProge, facing the tourist information center on the waterfront (phone: 702501) and Ste. Anne (on the main road; no phone).

CLEOPATRE The place for exotic island jewelry and colorful pareos (sarongs). 72 Rue Victor Hugo (phone: 738088).

GEORGIA Small, but chic, it showcases the latest in avant-garde fashions for women. 56 Rue Victor Hugo (phone: 638163).

HIT PARADE Featuring the latest island discs, as well as recorded folk songs, beguines, zouk, and mazurkas. 55 Rue Lamartine (phone: 700151).

MERLANDE Smaller and not as crowded as *Roger Albert,* but still offering 20% off purchases made with US dollar traveler's checks or a credit card. Good selection of fragrances and cosmetics; also sunglasses, hats, and pocketbooks. Corner of Rues Schoelcher and Siger (phone: 718950).

MONTACLAIR Gold and silver jewelry at good prices. 37 Rue Victor Hugo (phone: 630911).

NEW BORSALINO A boutique selling men's clothing. 27 Rue Blénac (phone: 719709).

OTHELLO A real men's haberdashery, with suits, jackets, slacks, shirts, and ties. 43 Rue Blénac (phone: 713838).

ROGER ALBERT Just off the Savane, Fort-de-France's best-known and biggest specialty shop stocks just about everything, including chic watches and Limoges place-card holders. The shop offers an extra discount on purchases made with major credit cards. 7 Rue Victor Hugo (phone: 717171) and a branch at the *Méridien Trois-Ilets* hotel.

THOMAS DE ROGATIS For gold and silver chains, watches, crystal, and other fine jewelry at discount prices. 22-24 Rue St. Louis (phone: 702911).

VALENTINO What the well-dressed man is wearing is on display. 46 Rue Perrinon (phone: 739592).

The following shops, located outside of the capital, are also recommended:

ELLA Purveying an intriguing assortment of homemade tropical jams, purées, preserves, and liqueurs, as well as island-grown spices, this *boutique gourmande* is in the village of Bézaudin near Ste. Marie (no phone).

LA PAILLE CARAÏBE Outside the little town of Morne-des-Esses, island-famous for its basketry (*vannerie*), with small shops and stands selling all styles and sizes. In the village of Bézaudin near Ste. Marie (no phone).

SPORTS

The Martiniquais attitude is that sports are to play, not to work at. So you won't find super pro golf clinics, tennis camps, or any of the popular American sweat-and-learn setups. But you will find plenty of opportunity for activity and better-than-adequate equipment.

BOATING Sail on your own one- or two-seater Sunfish, Sailfish, Hobie Cat, or other small craft. They're rented by the hour (about $11 and up) from kiosks on most hotel beaches. Yacht charters, both bareboat and skippered, are available from numerous sources. The capital city of Fort-de-France boasts two yacht clubs: *Club de la Voile de Fort-de-France* at Pointe Simon (phone: 702663) and the *Yacht Club de la Martinique* (phone: 632676). A number of places offer yacht charters or boat rentals, including the following at the *Pointe du Bout Marina* in Les Trois-Ilets: *Tropic Yachting* (phone: 660385); *Star Voyages* (phone: 660072); *Soleil et Voile,* now affiliated with *The Moorings* (phone: 660914); *Caraïbes Evasion* (phone: 660285); and *Cat Club* (phone: 660301). *ATM* in Port de Plaisance du Marin in Le Marin (phone: 749817) has the largest fleet on the island. Also in Le Marin with an all-catamaran fleet is *Bambou Yachting* (phone: 624657), and specializing in motor boats is *Ecole Nautisme Accastillage* (Cité Mansarde in Le Robert; phone: 651818). The *Affaires Maritimes* (phone: 719005) is a good source of nautical information. In addition, the 140-page, French and English *Guide Trois Rivières: A Cruising Guide to Martinique* is a highly regarded boating manual, available for about $25 in island bookstores or from the publisher: *Editions Trois Rivières,* BP 566, 97242 Fort-de-France (phone: 750707 or 751747).

CYCLING Mopeds may just be the best way to take a jaunt to La Pagerie or to get yourself to the golf course at Les Trois-Ilets. Rates are about $15 a day for Vespas, on which two can ride comfortably. Reserve a day ahead; you'll need a credit card or a cash deposit of about $225. In Fort-de-France, *Funny* (phone: 633305) and *T. S. Autos* (phone: 634282) rent Vespas, mopeds, and bicycles. Rentals in Pointe du Bout can be made at *Discount* (phone: 665437). All-terrain bikes can be rented at *VT Tilt* in Anse Mitan (phone: 660101) and *Basalt* in Bellefontaine (phone: 550184). Park authorities have developed some unusual itineraries for cyclists (phone: 731930).

GOLF The *Golf de l'Impératrice Joséphine* in Les Trois-Ilets (phone: 683281) is a good, sporty Robert Trent Jones, Sr. course (6,640 yards, par 71). It has a well-stocked pro shop, English-speaking pro, rental clubs, carts, caddies, and *Le Country* bar/restaurant. Its greens adjoin *La Pagerie*'s premises. Greens fees are about $40 per person, carts are $45 for 18 holes, hand carts about $9. Lessons cost about $22 for a half hour. Ask your hotel to telephone for a starting time.

HIKING It's best in the nature preserve of Presqu'île de la Caravelle, where, in addition to trails that explore the ruins of the Château Dubuc and exotic, tropical landscapes (some stamina but no special skills required), you'll find safe surf beaches (this is the Atlantic side of the island) and a fishing village called Tartane. For more serious trekking, contact the Parc Régional de la Martinique (Quartier Bouillé, Fort-de-France; phone: 731930) to make reservations with a guide for the 2-hour Mt. Pelée climb (as trails are often overgrown with dense foliage, a guide is essential; because of cloud cover, the view from the top can't be guaranteed) or a trek through the Gorges de la Falaise (moderate length, not too difficult) or the rain forest between Grand' Rivière and Le Prêcheur (choice of trails, several degrees of difficulty). *Cariballad* (phone: 545188) offers some off-the-beaten-track treks for about $70, including bus departure, lunch, and guides.

HORSEBACK RIDING Rides along scenic hillside and banana country trails are offered at *Ranch-Jack* (phone: 686397) in Anses-d'Arlets, 20 minutes from Pointe du Bout; the ranch also runs group rides through nearby mountains, cane fields, and around sea coves (rates from $18 to $20 per person for a 2½-hour ride; a half-day trail ride with guide costs about $45 to $50 per person. Also offering riding excursions are *Black Horse* in Les Trois-Ilets (near *La Pagerie* hotel; phone: 660346), *Ranche Val d'Or* in Ste. Anne (phone: 767059), and *La Cavale* (near the *Diamant-Novotel;* phone: 762294).

SCUBA AND SNORKELING The best diving spots are off Ste. Anne, Anses-d'Arlets, Ilet Ramier, Cap Saloman, and the shipwrecks at St. Pierre. The following operations offer a variety of packages, with single-tank dives ranging from $30 to $50: the *Union Centre de Plein Air* (*UCPA*), located behind the *Christophe Colombe* hotel in Carbet (phone: 781913); the *Club Subaquatique* (phone: 787375) in Case-Pilote, halfway between Carbet and Fort-de-France; *Tropicasub,* on the beach in St. Pierre (phone: 783803) and at *La Batelière;* and, at Pointe du Bout, *Bathys Club* at the *Méridien Trois-Ilets,* and the dive boat *Planete Bleue* at the marina (phone: 660879 or 660622). *Diamant-Novotel*'s *Sub Diamond Rock Club* has daily excursions around Diamond Rock and offers packages at sea. Also in the area are *Bleue Marine* at the *Marine* hotel (phone: 764600) and the *Okeonos Club* in Diamant (phone: 762176).

Snorkeling fins and masks are available at many hotels, including *Le Bakoua, Bambou, Club Med, Frantour, PLM Azur Carayou, Diamant-Novotel, Marine, Méridien,* and *La Batelière.* A variety of snorkeling excursions sail from the Pointe du Bout hotels as well as *La Batelière* and *Diamant-Novotel* hotels.

SPECTATOR SPORTS Cockfighting is the big spectator sport for Martiniquais. Mainlanders may call it cruel or revolting, but it is far and away the

Sunday favorite from December to July. The place and time of the action shifts from week to week. If you'd like to see what it's all about, ask at the tourist office or at the travel desk of your hotel; they may be getting a group together. Try to find a taxi driver or guide who'll stick with you and explain the action and the betting. Note: For the blood-sport enthusiast, snake and mongoose matches also are staged, but on irregular schedules.

There's also a good deal of island soccer playing, and it draws sizable crowds; local papers and hotel desks can fill you in on schedules. If there's a yawling regatta in town, don't miss it. It's a great thrill to see skilled seamen hanging from the rigging of a yawl (a fishing boat) with its huge, colorful sails, while racing at daredevil speeds.

SPORT FISHING Captain René Alaric and his 37-foot *Rayon Vert* at the *Auberge du Varé* at Case Pointe offer full-day excursions for up to six people (phone: 788056), including lunch, drinks, tackle, and everything else the serious angler needs; the cost is $2,400 per day. *Bathys Club* at the *Méridien* offers half-day trips aboard *La Mauny* at $250 per person for 3½ hours.

SWIMMING AND SUNNING Fine, if not fantastic. Martinique possesses no unending miles of beach. However, with 6½ miles of bright sand facing the landmark HMS *Diamond Rock,* Le Diamant is a favorite swim-and-picnic destination. Bring snorkel equipment (rented from your hotel), beach towels, and a picnic — maybe langouste with white wine. Also, most hotels have their own beaches — natural, or helped along with imported sand and groin-jetties to keep it in place. As a result of such assistance, Pointe du Bout beaches have never been better. The natural beach at Anse Mitan just down the shore serves small, mostly French-speaking hotels such as *Bambou* and *Auberge de l'Anse Mitan.* Beaches north of Fort-de-France tend to be soft, volcanic gray; those to the south are whiter, and all are public, though hotels charge non-guests a small fee for lockers and changing cabañas. Many hotels that are not on or near the beach have swimming pools. To escape the hotel scene, plan a day's picnic trip to the pretty, palm-treed shores at Ste. Anne, Les Salines, Le Diamant (see above), or Anses-d'Arlets. (Topless sunbathing is okay on beaches and at poolside, but tops are *de rigueur* at beach bars and restaurants.)

TENNIS Courts are part of the big-hotel scene. Most are free for guests during the day and cost about $5 to $10 after dark; for non-guests, the cost is about $17 per half hour. Court time should be reserved in advance. *Le Bakoua, Club Med, PLM Azur Carayou, Diamant-Novotel, Habitation LaGrange, Leyritz Plantation, Méridien,* and *La Batelière* hotels have tennis courts on their grounds; all except the *Plantation*'s have lights. *Buccaneer's Creek, Club Med,* and *La Batelière* have teaching pros, as does the *Golf de l'Impératrice Joséphine* (phone: 683281) with its 3 lighted courts. Serious players also can arrange temporary memberships at private clubs like the *Tennis Club of Fort-de-France* or *Tennis Club du Vieux Moulin* — and games with local players — via hotels, the tourist office, or La Ligue Régionale de Tennis (phone: 510800).

WATER SKIING AND WINDSURFING Available at Le Diamant, Ste. Anne, *La Batelière, Club Med,* and *Bathys Club* at the *Méridien* beach, within easy reach of Pointe du Bout and Anse Mitan hotels. Water skiing costs about $18 to $22 per half hour. Windsurfing costs $15 to $20 for a half-hour lesson or an hour's use of the board only. The best windsurfing site away from hotels is Cap Michel, near Cap Chevalier in the south. There is no rental equipment here, however. *Passeport pour la Mer* (phone: 640448) offers classes in scuba, parasailing, jet skiing, and various other watersports from its catamaran *D'Lo.*

NIGHTLIFE

Wherever you stay, don't miss *Les Grands Ballets de Martinique,* performances by a bouncy young troupe of teenage singers, dancers, and musicians playing weekly at larger hotels (*Le Bakoua, PLM Azur Carayou, Diamant-Novotel, La Batelière, Méridien,* and *Caritan Beach*) as well as on visiting cruise ships. By combining stories of plantation days with choreographed valses, beguines, and mazurkas, they give you a special feeling for island history and seem to have a terrific time doing it.

Small hotels have dance music 1 or 2 nights a week, sometimes more often during high season; the larger places tune up most evenings — more or less sedately during dinner, fairly frenetically in their discos later on. The *Méridien*'s *Cocot-Raie* is small, dark, and loud; *La Paillote* at the *PLM Azur Carayou* has live entertainment, including steel band dinner-dances on Sundays and Mondays, and fabulous views across the bay to Fort-de-France. *Le Bakoua* has dinner dancing, limbo shows, ballet performances, steel bands — something different every night; *La Queens* at *La Batelière* is perched on the water's edge offering dance music that mixes some hustle, updated beguine, a few Latin beats, and zouk, the most popular style on the island.

For something a bit more native, try the downtown clubs in Fort-de-France: There's dancing and song at *Le New Hippo* (Bd. Allègre; phone: 602022); dancing at *L'Elysée Matignon* (Rue Ernest DeProge; phone: 631706); entertainment at the open-air and tropical *Coco Loco* (on the corner of Rue Ernest DeProge; phone: 636377); and jazz at *La Carafe* (phone: 631616). A short cab ride from downtown is the *Palace Club* (at Palmiste near Lamentin Airport; phone: 505638), and *Le Manoir* (Rte. des Religieuses; phone: 702823), a popular weekend spot for dancing to local rhythms. In La Trinité, *Le Top 50* (Rue du Boc Beausejour; phone: 586-6143) is a sizzling discotheque. Nightclubs and discos exist in the smaller towns and resort areas as well, but finding them after dark is sometimes difficult, so ask for directions from your hotel social desk.

Caution: Disco drinks, especially scotch and whiskey, are expensive —

starting at about $8 each when you add taxes and service charge. Rum drinks and local Lorraine beer (quite good) cost less.

There are casinos at the *Méridien Trois-Ilets* and *La Batelière.* Games are American and French roulette and blackjack. Jackets and ties are not required. Croupiers are European-trained islanders; minimum bet is about $5. Hours are 9 PM to 3 AM nightly; admission fee is about $12. *Note:* The legal gambling age is 21; casinos require photo ID.

Best on the Island

CHECKING IN

Martinique hotels range from charming Relais Créole country inns and seaside cottages to sprawling 300-room high-rise resorts. Food, even in very small places, tends to be quite good.

Martinique hotel choices hinge on location. Choose Pointe du Bout if you want to be where the other tourists are, make the most of sports, dine around, and take in all the nightlife. For a quieter time, pick a self-contained resort or a country inn farther out (*Leyritz Plantation* or *St. Aubin,* for example). By far, the best beaches are found in the southeastern part of the island. Most large tourist hotels are air conditioned, but some are not — especially smaller ones in the *relais* or *pension* category. In this listing, very expensive is defined as $225 and up for two, including breakfast; expensive is $175 to $225; moderate, from $100 to $175; and inexpensive, under $100 for two without meals. Prices run about 25% to 35% less in summer. As a rule, hotel room rates quoted in dollars are guaranteed for the whole season — winter or summer — whatever the franc's fluctuations. When calling from a phone on Martinique, use only the local numbers listed below. For information about dialing from elsewhere, see "Telephone" earlier in this chapter.

POINTE DU BOUT

VERY EXPENSIVE

Le Bakoua A Sofitel resort affiliated with the prestigious Accor Loisir group, this 139-room facility is perhaps the island's best. Public areas are decorated in Caribbean colors and native woods, and there's a squash court, workout room, small library, and gameroom. All guestrooms are air conditioned, have patios or balconies, and feature amenities such as hair dryers. There also are 2 good restaurants, 2 bars (including one that floats in the lagoon), a big pool, water sports, and 2 tennis courts. On the beach (phone: 660202; 800-221-4542 from the US; fax: 660041).

Méridien Trois-Ilets This property has 300 small, but bright, air conditioned rooms with balconies and wonderful views. There's still a strong chain-hotel feeling, but it's hardly a major deterrent with the pleasant indoor-outdoor lobby with restaurant, attractive and busy cocktail bar, and *Roger Albert* boutique. There are facilities for most water sports, and a spacious pool. The well-run activities center offers scuba and deep-sea fishing excursions. Two tennis courts are available. There's evening entertainment, a disco, and good food, especially beachside dinners at *La Case Créole*. Convenient location on the beach near the ferry dock and marina (phone: 660000; 800-221-4542 from the US; fax: 660074).

EXPENSIVE

PLM Azur Carayou The informal atmosphere makes this a good choice for families. The 200 rooms have summer cottage decor (rattan chairs and tables, striped fabrics) and air conditioning. Located on a nice but small beach; there's also a pool and tennis courts, archery, golf practice areas, and water sports equipment. Scuba, fishing, and boat trips can be arranged; water skiing, golf, and horseback riding are nearby. On the beach (phone: 660404; 800-223-9862 from the US; fax: 660057).

MODERATE

PLM Azur La Pagerie A good spot for do-it-yourselfers, this place features balconied studios — 64 with kitchenettes, 28 with refrigerators. A nice choice of restaurants and beaches are within walking distance, and the ferry is nearby. There's a swimming pool; guests may use the facilities at the nearby *PLM Azur Carayou.* The lobby bar is a congenial gathering place. Convenient to a small supermarket. Near the marina (phone: 660530; 800-223-9862 from the US; fax: 660099).

INEXPENSIVE

La Karacoli Hidden along a hill overlooking the bay, this charming family-owned inn has 18 modern rooms and 8 one-bedroom apartments. Each has a terrace, kitchenette or full kitchen, and telephone. No air conditioning, but trade winds create a nice breeze, even in the heat of the day. A little beach rims the water out back, though bigger beaches are within walking distance. A swimming pool and solarium are also featured. Full breakfast included, and guests are invited to join the host family for dinner. In the hotel area near the *PLM Azur La Pagerie* (phone: 660267).

ANSE MITAN

MODERATE

Bambou A casual beach hotel, it has 118 rooms in 60 rustic, tile-roofed chalets, all air conditioned. The decor is simple but functional. There's a pool and a busy terrace restaurant with a panoramic view of the bay. On the beach (phone: 660139; fax: 660505).

Rivage A stone's throw from the beach, this cheerful little property has 17 garden studios with kitchenettes and air conditioning. There's a pool, barbecue pit, snack bar, and an English-speaking staff. A good buy. On the beach (phone: 660053; fax: 660656).

ANSE À L'ANE

MODERATE

Frantour With peach buildings sitting right on the beach, this pretty place has 38 newer rooms and 36 renovated units. The grounds are palmy and the pool is lovely. The staff is extra friendly, and a delicious daily breakfast is included. On the beach (phone: 623167; fax: 683765).

Le Panoramic Located on the hillside above the *Frantour,* here are 36 large, balconied rooms that can accommodate up to four people. Each room has a kitchenette, and there's a swimming pool on the premises. Short walk to the beach (phone: 683434; fax: 500195).

FORT-DE-FRANCE AND ENVIRONS

EXPENSIVE

La Batelière About a 10-minute drive north of Fort-de-France on the sea, this place has 200 large, recently refurbished and air conditioned rooms, each with a balcony and fine water views. There also are 6 lighted tennis courts, water sports, a nice small beach, a sun deck, a sauna, a pier, 3 dining rooms (including a seaside restaurant and bar), and a disco. In Schoelcher on the beach (phone: 614949; 800-223-6510 from the US; fax: 617057).

MODERATE

Squash Three squash courts are the main attraction of this 58-room hostelry. It also boasts a fitness center, a Jacuzzi, and a small outdoor pool, but there is no restaurant. Overlooking the harbor just outside Fort-de-France (phone: 630001; 800-223-9862 from the US; fax: 630074).

INEXPENSIVE

Impératrice A dependable old standby, it's attractively set on Place de la Savane, with an Art Deco façade and 24 air conditioned rooms with creole decor. There's a busy sidewalk café and a dining room serving creole fare. On Rue de la Liberté, Fort-de-France (phone: 630682).

Martinique Cottages Handsomely landscaped, well-managed, and 15 minutes from town, this property has 8 modern bungalows set in a flowery hillside; each unit has a kitchenette, private verandah, and telephone. Facilities include a pool, Jacuzzi, and *La Plantation* restaurant (see *Eating Out*). Pays Mélé Jeanne d'Arc (phone: 501608; fax: 502683).

STE. ANNE

Note: All hotels in this small village are located along the main road.

EXPENSIVE

Caritan Beach Very casual and relaxed, this is an ideal place for families. It has 96 rooms with kitchenettes and air conditioning, a tiny beach, pool, water sports, and a restaurant (phone: 767412; 800-366-1510 from the US; fax: 767259).

MODERATE

Buccaneer's Creek/Club Med A sprawling property with 300 small, spartan (but air conditioned) rooms in a beach and garden setting. Activities offered include water sports, tennis (7 courts), aerobics, basketball, and more. There's a lovely dining room, along with a theater, bar, marina café, late-night restaurant, and disco. As with every Club Med village, the draw here is that all activities and meals are included in one weekly package price. However, when it comes to island congeniality and plushness, the facilities can't compare with Martinique's primo resorts. On the beach (phone: 767452; 800-CLUB-MED from the US).

La Dunette Here are 18 air conditioned rooms, most with sea views and terraces, and a good seafood restaurant (phone: 767390; fax: 767605).

Hameau de Beauregard This residential hotel, run by the Groupe Archipel, features 90 apartment-style units with fully equipped kitchenettes; each unit can accommodate three guests. Located very near the beach, there's also a large pool and lovely aquatic gardens. Concierges assist with excursions and offer recommendations (phone: 631372; fax: 732075).

DIAMANT

VERY EXPENSIVE

Diamant-Novotel Set on a jutting peninsula, offering a postcard-perfect panorama of Diamond Rock, this 5-acre, 181-room resort is dotted with well-manicured tropical gardens and boasts a freshwater pool with a dramatic footbridge. Three small white sand beaches, 2 tennis courts, and *beaucoup de* water sports are among the many amenities. There's a riding stable nearby. The restaurant offers superb wining and dining, and there's a bit of nightlife and some English-speaking staff members. Honeymooners love this spot. Just outside Diamant, about 20 minutes south of the airport via the highway (phone: 764242; 800-221-4542 from the US; fax: 762287).

MODERATE

Diamant les Bains This hotel creates a very homey atmosphere. There are 24 air conditioned units, including a few bungalows on the beach. Amenities include a flower-rimmed swimming pool, bar, and a terrace restaurant serving fine creole fare. Dining room closed Wednesdays; the whole inn closes for September. In the village, with a great view of Diamond Rock offshore (phone: 764014; fax: 762700).

Marine This establishment offers 150 rooms with balconies, kitchenettes, and fabulous views. There's a large pool, a water slide, 2 lighted tennis courts, and a boat pier. On a hillside overlooking the sea and Diamond Rock (phone: 764600; 800-221-4542 from the US; fax: 762599).

Plein Sud Another residential hotel run by the Groupe Archipel. Like the *Hameau de Beauregard* (see above), this 52-unit property features apartment-style accommodations for up to three people, equipped with complete kitchenettes. Concierge service is provided by a local couple. There's also a large pool and a shopping arcade. Located across the road from Diamant Beach and a short stroll to the center of town (phone: 762609; fax: 762607).

Relais Caraïbes Just down the street from the *Diamant-Novotel,* these 16 bungalows are neat, clean, and comfortable. The hillside location offers great sea views, and a lush garden provides plenty of privacy. All rooms are air conditioned and include modern bath and direct-dial phones. Guests may use the *Novotel*'s beach. Just outside Diamant (phone: 764465; 800-223-9815 from the US; fax: 762130).

THE NORTH

VERY EXPENSIVE

Habitation LaGrange This luxurious establishment is set on the 7½-acre grounds of a former sugar plantation and rum distillery. Seventeen rooms are located in an 18th-century creole mansion and in 3 newer cottages built around a pool. An 18th-century ambience prevails — a horse-drawn carriage transports guests from the entrance to the manor house, staff members wear period costumes, and the rooms are furnished with antiques and four-poster beds (they're also equipped with TV sets, VCRs, and minibars). There's a restaurant and bar, and a lighted tennis court. Guided hikes, sailboat excursions, and other activities can be arranged. The best beach for swimming is about 20 minutes away. Marigot (phone: 536060; 800-633-7411 from the US; fax: 535058).

MODERATE

Bel Air Village Located in the Morne Vert hills, just a short drive to the beach, this place features 4 studios and 12 one-bedroom apartments, decorated in creole style and equipped with kitchenettes. Guests have the choice of hiking in the nearby mountains and rain forests, or relaxing on the beach at Carbet, just 1½ miles away. There's also a swimming pool. Quartier Bout Barrière, Morne Vert (phone: 555294; fax: 555297).

Leyritz Plantation In the idyllic landscape of Martinique's lush north, this 50-room inn is set among lawns and tropical gardens. Surrounding the beautiful property is a 25-acre banana and pineapple plantation. The focal point is a restored 18th-century manor furnished with antiques. Traditional island furnishings decorate the remaining accommodations, all in rebuilt dwellings and equipped with modern plumbing and air conditioning. There is a tennis court and swimming pool. The nearest beaches are about 30 minutes away (the hotel provides transportation). Near Basse-Pointe (phone: 785392; fax: 789244).

Primerêve With 111 units, it's one of the largest properties on the island's northeastern coast. Perfect for families, there are 25 single and double rooms and 86 suites that accommodate up to four people, all in sea-view bungalows. There's a secluded beach, a large pool, 2 lighted tennis courts, a variety of water sports facilities, a restaurant, a bar, and a beachside snack bar. Anse Azerot (phone: 644975; fax: 644973).

St. Aubin This impressive French colonial *maison de campagne* is set in sugarcane country, above the Atlantic coast. The 17 guestrooms, surprisingly spartan, are all air conditioned; the gardens and pool are lovely. The beaches and water sports of the Caravelle Peninsula are just 15 minutes by car from this very quiet retreat. Dining (for guests only) is a big draw. In Trinité near the Caravelle Peninsula (phone: 693477).

INEXPENSIVE

L'Auberge de la Montagne Pelée Perched on top of Mt. Pelée, 4,500 feet up, these 8 modest bungalows provide the ultimate retreat. Located in a remote jungle setting that's often masked in mist and clouds, the sunsets here are spectacular. Dining in the inn's creole restaurant is an exceptional experience. Located near Morne Rouge, about an hour's drive from Fort-de-France (phone: 523209; fax: 732075).

OFFSHORE ISLANDS

VERY EXPENSIVE

Les Ilets de l'Imperatrice These two private islands under the same ownership as *Habitation LaGrange* (above) offer a luxurious, secluded getaway. Each island has a rustic creole-style guesthouse staffed with a maid, cook, and boatman, as well as having a beach and boat dock. The house on Ilet Oscar has 5 bedrooms with private baths. The house on Ilet Thierry features 6 bedrooms, each with private toilet and sink; showers are shared. Rates include airport transportation, all meals, drinks, water sports, and use of a motorboat. Off the windward coast of the island (contact through *Habitation LaGrange;* phone: 536060; 800-633-7411 from the US).

EATING OUT

Two things are true of the French West Indies that aren't true anyplace else in the Caribbean: Local people eat much the same food as visitors, and the local food is exceptionally good. Restaurants range from casual to elegant; the only big restaurants on the island are in hotels, but all care a great deal about their food.

The fare falls into two categories — French haute and island creole — with most restaurants serving a combination of the two. Steaks are available, but delicious fish and seafood (sometimes exotic) are staples. Most common fowl are pigeon and peacock, as well as chicken and duck *à l'orange.* Roast suckling pig often appears on buffets.

Favorite appetizers include *accra* (delicately flavored cod cakes), *crabes farcis* (deviled crab with bread crumbs and seasoning, served in its own shell), *soudons* (small, sweet clams), and *coquille de lambi* (minced conch in a creamy sauce served in a shell). Entrée specialties are red snapper, *cribiches* (large river shrimp), langouste (clawless rock lobster), *lambi* (conch), *oursins* (sea urchins), and *chatrou* (octopus). *Colombo* is the creole version of curry (usually chicken, mutton, or goat); *pâté en pot* is a thick creole mutton soup. *Blaff* is an aromatic, spicy creole stew whose name — they say — comes from the sound the poor fish makes when it's plopped into the kettle. For dessert: tropical fruit served fresh with imported French cheeses, or in somewhat more elaborate form, such as coconut cake or rum-fired banana flambé.

With dinner, the Martiniquais serve French wines that are good to great, and priced accordingly. Before and after, the drink of choice is local rum — in several different forms. Tourists tend to opt for *les planteurs* — the familiar planter's punch with a sweet fruit juice base. Islanders prefer a *décollage* — a blast-off of aged, herbed rum with a fruit juice chaser — or a white *ti punch* (*ti* means small) of rum, sugar syrup, and lime. For an after-dinner *digestif,* try 12-year-old Bally or Clément rum.

Dinner for two, including wine and service charge, will cost over $100 at restaurants described as expensive below; from $50 to $100 at moderate places; and less than $50 at inexpensive places. If you're having language difficulties, ask the hotel desk to make reservations for you. When calling from Martinique, use only the local numbers listed below. For information about dialing from elsewhere, see "Telephone" earlier in this chapter.

FORT-DE-FRANCE AND ENVIRONS

VERY EXPENSIVE

Le Lafayette Overlooking La Savane, this place is in a class by itself. The menu ranges from nouvelle cuisine to classic French fare flavored with a touch of creole. The result is fresh, savory, and irresistible. Impeccable service, exquisite decor. Open for lunch and dinner; closed Sundays. Reservations necessary. Major credit cards accepted. 5 Rue de la Liberté, Fort-de-France (phone: 632409).

La Plantation The award-winning dining room of *Martinique Cottages.* The seafood ratatouille alone is worth the drive. Fish, fowl, beef, and lamb are prepared in delicious, inventive ways, and the owners love discussing their culinary art. Closed Saturday afternoons and Sundays. Reservations necessary. Major credit cards accepted. Pays Mélé Jeanne d'Arc, Lamentin (phone: 501608).

EXPENSIVE

La Belle Epoque With a well-deserved reputation for fine food, this spot serves haute cuisine in a turn-of-the-century setting befitting its name. Closed Sundays, Mondays, and Saturday afternoons. Major credit cards accepted. In the suburb of Didier, 97 Rte. de Didier (phone: 644798).

La Biguine A small, simple, and select place, here the menu includes both French (salmon mousse with sauce) and creole (prawn kebabs flambéed with *pastis*) classics. The seasoning is not as hot as at other local restaurants, but it's close enough for those palates not accustomed to creole food. Excellent service. Open for lunch and dinner; no dinner on Sundays. Reservations necessary. Major credit cards accepted. 11 Rte. de la Folie, Fort-de-France (phone: 714775).

La Fontane This private home has a very elegant, tranquil ambience and a most imaginative menu featuring French and creole fare. Open for lunch and dinner; closed Sunday evenings and Mondays. Reservations necessary. Major credit cards accepted. Km 4, Rte. de Balata (phone: 642870).

La Grand' Voile Seafood and classic French provincial specialties are served at this spot on the second floor of the town's yacht club. There's a fine wine cellar. Open daily for lunch and dinner. Reservations necessary. Major credit cards accepted. Pointe Simon (phone: 702929).

Le Mareyeur Seafood specialties include all the creole favorites — *lambis, soudons, palourdes,* and *oursins* — carefully prepared and beautifully presented. Try *blaff de poisson* (steamed fish in local spices), shark in coconut milk, or, better yet, order the *assiette* for a smorgasbord-like taste of all the house specialties. Closed Saturday afternoons and Sundays. Reservations advised. Major credit cards accepted. Rte. du Littoral, Pointe des Nègres (phone: 617470).

La Mouina A delightful old colonial villa above the town. Impeccably prepared creole and French dishes (bonito *en papillote,* avocado sherbet) are served on the villa's terrace. Presidents George Bush and François Mitterrand dined here in 1991. Open for lunch and dinner; closed weekends. Reservations necessary. Major credit cards accepted. 3, Rte. de la Redoute, Fort-de-France (phone: 793457).

Palais Créole The dining room of the eponymous hotel, with bistro-style specials such as *coq au vin* at lunch and French- or creole-style seafood preparations for candlelit dinners. Closed Sundays. Reservations usually unnecessary. Major credit cards accepted. 26 Rue Perrinon, Fort-de-France (phone: 638333).

Le Verger Enjoy lunch or dinner on the terrace of a big country house set in a fruit orchard. This is gracious dining, with many specialties from Périgord (foie gras, confit of duck, cassoulet, pheasant, and more). There's also a variety of local creole dishes. Closed Sundays. Reservations advised. Major credit cards accepted. Place d'Armes, Fort-de-France (phone: 514302).

INEXPENSIVE

Le Vieux Milan Bright and bustling, this Italian eatery serves up generous portions of pasta, including gnocchi with gorgonzola and tagliatelle with salmon. Other specialties include thin-crusted pizza, carpaccio, and *tiramisù.* Closed Saturday afternoons and Sundays. Reservations advised. Major credit cards accepted. Located along La Savane, 60 Av. du Caraïbes, Fort-de-France (phone: 603531).

POINTE DU BOUT

INEXPENSIVE

La Marine This spacious dockside patio restaurant is popular with local boaters and tourists. The atmosphere is upbeat, the food good to very good. Brick-oven pizza, chicken, and creole dishes are the bill of fare. The adjoining bar is a good place to have a beer or a *planteur* punch. Open daily for lunch and dinner. Reservations unnecessary. Major credit cards accepted. At the marina (phone: 660232).

ANSE MITAN

MODERATE

L'Amphore Guy Dawson's second spot in Anse Mitan (see *La Villa Créole,* below), with lobster as the prime drawing card, prepared in any number of delicious ways. Fish, curries, and *entrecôte* (steak) are also on the menu. Pretty seaside location. Good guitarist. Closed Mondays; no lunch on Tuesdays. Reservations advised. Major credit cards accepted (phone: 660309).

Le Matadore One of Anse Mitan's best creole spots — François Crico's bouillabaisse, red snapper in court bouillon, and *colombo* of goat have been winning plaudits for years. Closed Wednesdays; no lunch on Thursdays. Reservations advised. Major credit cards accepted (phone: 660536).

La Villa Créole Guy Dawson's perfect combination of soft lights, music, and excellent food served in a romantic garden has made this a most popular spot in Anse Mitan. Predominantly creole dishes include *blaff* of sea urchins, court bouillon, conch tart, terrine of local red fish, curried chicken, pork, and lamb. Closed Sundays; no lunch on Mondays. Reservations necessary. Major credit cards accepted (phone: 660553).

GRAND' ANSE

EXPENSIVE

Le Flamboyant des Isles Named for the gorgeous flamboyant trees that speckle the property, this romantic place features candlelight dining on a deck that extends over the sea. The view of the ragged crescent coastline is stunning. The fare is creole *et gastronomique,* with specialties such as octopus salad, shrimp fritters, conch fricassee, and flambéed bananas. Closed Sunday nights and Tuesdays. Reservations advised. Major credit cards accepted. Anse d'Arlet (phone: 686775).

MODERATE

Ti' Sable Set in a typical creole-style house, with verandahs and an adjoining canopied terrace, this laid-back place offers traditional island dishes — rich seafood, grilled meats, and curries. The beach site is accessible by car or boat. Closed Mondays; lunch only on Sundays. Reservations advised. Major credit cards accepted. Anse d'Arlet (phone: 686244).

STE. ANNE

MODERATE

Poï et Virginie A waterfront spot with lots of character: bamboo walls, ceiling fans, and drinks garnished with big flowers. Seafood platters, curries, and steaks are quite good, but the menu highlight is the luscious lobster and crab salad. A fine choice for lunch and dinner. Closed Mondays and from mid-September through mid-October. Reservations unnecessary. Major credit cards accepted. On the waterfront (phone: 767686).

INEXPENSIVE

L'Arbre à Pain Favored by locals, it's set in a little brick courtyard beneath *l'arbre à pain,* a breadfruit tree. Choose from creole creations such as sea urchin tart and avocado stuffed with crab, or opt for the brick oven–baked pizza. Open daily for dinner only. Reservations unnecessary. Major credit cards accepted. On the main road away from the beach (phone: 767293).

Le Touloulou Among the many shacks on Ste. Anne Beach offering tasty fare, this one stands out. The breezy dining room is decorated with island posters and sits right on the sand. The *colombo* (curry-style) preparations are delicious, as are the grilled *lambi* (conch) and *poulet* (chicken). Closed Sundays and Tuesdays during low season. Reservations unnecessary. Major credit cards accepted. Ste. Anne Beach (phone: 767327).

DIAMANT

MODERATE

Chez Lucie On the waterfront, two distinct menus are available here: One offers Vietnamese and Chinese specialties such as stir fry, satays, and curries; the other features creole preparations including *blaff* of seafood or sea urchins, turtle steaks, and shrimp. Almost every seat faces the ocean; service is slow. Open daily for lunch and dinner. Reservations advised for lunch. Major credit cards accepted (phone: 764010).

Un Coin Tranquille Creole cooking is featured at this country inn. A family operation — mom and dad greet guests and daughter serves. Closed Wednesdays; no lunch on Thursdays. Reservations advised. No credit cards accepted. Bitaille (phone: 764112 or 762282).

THE NORTH

EXPENSIVE

L'Ami Fritz A bit of Alsace in the Antilles: Perfect *choucroute garnie* and the best of Alsatian wines and cheeses are served along with local dishes in a manor house on gorgeous grounds. Open daily for lunch and dinner. Reservations advised. Major credit cards accepted. Brin d'Amour, near Trinité (phone: 582018; fax: 912121).

Le Colibri Diners have a wonderful hillside view and are given royal treatment at the home of Mme. Palladino, whose sea urchin *tarte,* roast suckling pig, stuffed pigeon, and crab *callaloo* are scrumptious. Closed Mondays. Reservations necessary. Major credit cards accepted. Morne des Esses (phone: 699195).

Le Madras A lively place, especially on weekends when islanders come to hear local bands play rousing music. Specialties include medallions of beef with goat cheese and the catch of the day. Open daily for lunch and dinner. Reservations advised. Major credit cards accepted. Overlooking the beach in the tiny town of Tartane (phone: 583395; fax: 583363).

MODERATE

La Belle Capresse This is a worthwhile place to stop for lunch while on a northern tour. Original creole creations such as shark pâté, fried sea urchins, crab soufflé, pork flambéed in aged rum, and chicken in coconut milk are specialties. Open daily for lunch and dinner. Reservations necessary for dinner. Major credit cards accepted. Prêcheur (phone: 529623).

Chez Mally Edjam A 70-year-old virtuosa cook serves seafood and creole meals in her modest home at the island's northernmost tip. Open daily for lunch and dinner. Reservations necessary. No credit cards accepted. Rte. de la Côte Atlantique in Basse-Pointe (phone: 755118).

Mexico's Caribbean Coast

CANCÚN, COZUMEL, AND ISLA MUJERES

For many years, small groups of divers and determined sun worshipers had the lagoons, beaches, and islands of Mexico's Caribbean coast along the Yucatán Peninsula almost to themselves. People planning a trip to the Yucatán had to choose among the Maya ruins at Chichén Itzá, Uxmal, and Tulum; sun and sea sports along the coast of Quintana Roo, including Xel-Ha (pronounced Shell-*ha*) and Akumal; or the islands of Isla Mujeres, Cancún, or Cozumel. Transportation was too difficult to make all sides of the vacation coin easily accessible. In those days, Mexico's largest island, Cozumel, was the preferred Caribbean destination of less well-heeled travelers, and Cancún was an undeveloped spit of land off the coast to the north.

All that changed when FONATUR, the government agency charged with improving Mexico's tourist facilities, chose Cancún as its first multimillion-dollar experiment in resort development. Cancún had all the natural attributes of a resort area — beautiful sea and some of the best diving in the world, adequate space and facilities, and proximity to the ruins. So new it wasn't even marked on road maps in 1970, Cancún has blossomed into one of the world's most bustling — and some feel overdeveloped — resorts. It has become Mexico's main tourist destination, attracting 19% of the country's visitors.

One of the major dividends of Cancún's development is that travelers no longer have to choose between culture and carousal. Part of the Cancún master plan is a system of roads, transportation, and communications that connects the resort area to the major ruins and Mérida. Both Cancún and Cozumel benefit from a beeline road from the sea to Chichén Itzá, along which tour buses roll daily. And both are helped by the improvement of the shoreline road to Xel-Ha and the small but interesting ruins at Tulum and Cobá.

But the sea is still the major attraction. The crystalline Caribbean offers visibility to 100 feet, and the stretch of sea along the peninsula and into Belize is world-famous as an area rich in fish, wrecks, and coral. Unruffled Nichupté Lagoon, which separates Cancún from the mainland, has been cleaned up over the past few years. Protected from the open sea, it offers a tranquil place for sailing or water skiing. In addition, the government has poured some $100 million into the area to assure a complete resort infrastructure — recreational facilities like the 18-hole Robert Trent Jones, Jr. golf course, a panoply of hotels, ships for touring, and boats for sailing — to augment the area's natural attributes.

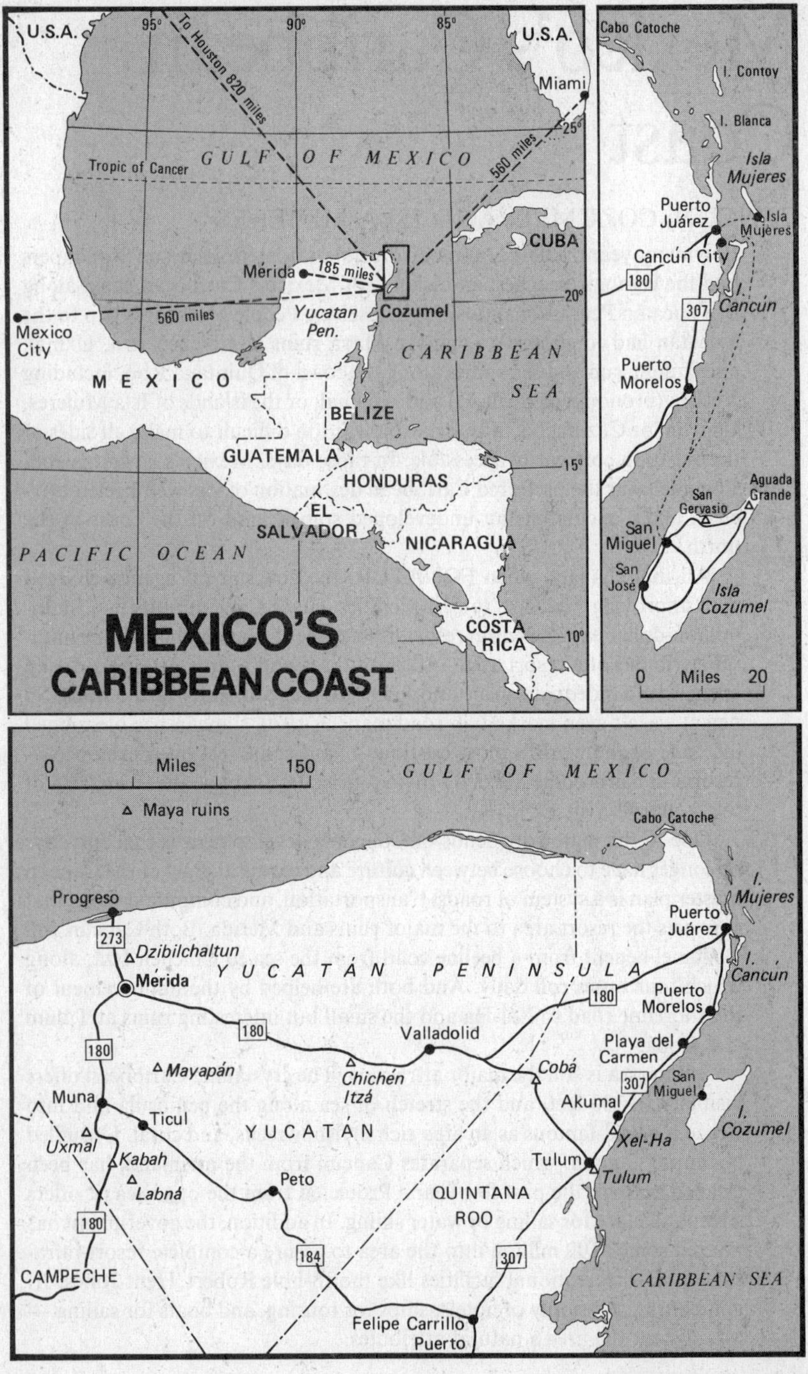

MEXICO'S CARIBBEAN COAST

U.S.A.
95°
To Houston 820 miles
90°
85°
U.S.A.
Miami
25°
560 miles
Tropic of Cancer
GULF OF MEXICO
CUBA
Mérida
185 miles
20°
560 miles
Mexico City
Yucatan Pen.
Cozumel
CARIBBEAN SEA
MEXICO
BELIZE
GUATEMALA
15°
HONDURAS
EL SALVADOR
NICARAGUA
PACIFIC OCEAN
COSTA RICA
10°

Cabo Catoche
I. Contoy
I. Blanca
Isla Mujeres
Puerto Juárez
Isla Mujeres
Cancún City
180
I. Cancún
307
Puerto Morelos
Aguada Grande
San Gervasio
San Miguel
San José
Isla Cozumel
0 Miles 20

0 Miles 150
GULF OF MEXICO
△ Maya ruins
Cabo Catoche
I. Mujeres
Progreso
Puerto Juárez
273
Dzibilchaltun
I. Cancún
YUCATÁN PENINSULA
Mérida
180
Puerto Morelos
180
Valladolid
Playa del Carmen
180
Mayapán
Chichén Itzá
Cobá
307
San Miguel
Muna
Akumal
I. Cozumel
Ticul
YUCATÁN
Uxmal
Xel-Ha
Kabah
Tulum
Tulum
Labná
Peto
QUINTANA ROO
180
184
307
CAMPECHE
CARIBBEAN SEA
Felipe Carrillo Puerto

In addition to the construction necessitated by Hurricane Gilbert, which hit the area in 1988, lots of new hotels and support facilities have been built in the past several years. Paseo Kukulcán, the boulevard running from one end of Cancún to the other, also has been expanded from two lanes to four, and the 12,000-seat Convention Center has been renovated to handle the increasing onslaught of tourists. There are now over 80 hotels, plus condominium buildings, shopping centers, restaurants, and marinas scattered along the Kukulcán. The weather and facilities of Mexico's Caribbean coast are tempting, but this is no longer the place for those who prize peace and privacy.

Although Cozumel was the first island in the area to be developed, it has grown at a much slower pace than Cancún, and tends to attract visitors who are more interested in fabulous skin diving and fishing than in glitz and glamour. Plans for several new hotels were dropped for fear of damaging the island's ecological system.

Isla Mujeres, with a few charming but fairly simple hotels and wide expanses of beaches, has a small but loyal following of snorkelers, divers, and loafers. Guests here must be willing to give up certain luxuries (such as air conditioning) for lower prices and access to El Garrafón, an underwater national park famous for its coral reef and tropical fish.

The Quintana Roo area on the mainland known as the "Cancún-Tulum Corridor" is peppered with delightful hotels and restaurants set at the edge of the sea. It's hard to tell how many more years of peace and tranquillity remain for this area, however, as two large resort development projects, Puerto Aventuras and Playacar, are well under way.

Mexican Caribbean At-a-Glance

FROM THE AIR

Mexico's Caribbean islands are grouped around the northeastern corner of the Yucatán, the chunky peninsula that divides the Gulf of Mexico from the Caribbean Sea. They are flat, sunbaked, and sea-washed bits of land. Their centers are dense green brush and coconut palms rimmed by white limestone sand beaches. Cancún is flanked to the south by Cozumel and to the north by Isla Mujeres.

The islands are about 560 miles southwest of Miami (about 1½ hours by jet), about 640 miles (1½ hours) east of Mexico City, and about 185 miles (35 minutes) east of Mérida, capital of the Mexican state of Yucatán.

Cancún (pronounced Can-*koon*), 14 miles long and one-quarter mile wide, is shaped like an emaciated sea horse, connected by a causeway at its nose to Cancún City — the support city on the mainland where most of the resort's 300,000 residents live. (Cancún's jetport is 12 miles southwest of the city.) For most of the rest of its length, Cancún is separated from the mainland by Nichupté Lagoon. Most of the island's resort hotels are set along the skinny east-west sand spit that forms the sea horse's head. And along its back, the Caribbean surf rolls in along 12 miles of intermittent beaches and hotel sea walls.

Already prosperous, Cancún City has an even brighter future. Slated for development in the next few years is the $600-million Malecón Cancún, a 330-acre project that will include homes, shops, restaurants, and a park overlooking the lagoon and Cancún's Hotel Zone.

Cozumel (Ko-sue-*mehl*), 30 miles long and 9 miles wide, lies about 50 miles south of Cancún and about 2 miles off the Yucatán coast. Its almost straight eastern shoreline is pounded by rough, windward seas; on its leeward western side, the waters off its resort beaches are calm, the shore notched with sandy coves. The coral reefs that surround it — especially the sunken mountains of the Palancar reef chain — make it a prime skin divers' destination. Most of the island's resort hotels are just north of its only town, San Miguel (pop. 60,000), on the northwest coast. The jet airport is between the hotels and town.

Isla Mujeres (*Ees*-lah Moo-*hair*-res), 5 miles long and a half mile wide, is 6 miles north of Cancún and 6 miles off Puerto Juárez at the tip of the Yucatán Peninsula. It has a tiny town, beautiful beaches, lagoons, reefs, and transparent waters that make it a super retreat for snorkelers, skin divers, and loafers. There's a lovely lookout point and a Maya "lighthouse" at the southern end of the island. It's no longer a sleepy little island; most places have phones; the few roads are paved; and there are even several discos.

SPECIAL PLACES

There's little sightseeing on Mexico's Caribbean islands. Each has a town with restaurants and at least a few shops.

There are, however, a number of interesting excursions from the resort areas, including some of the Yucatán mainland's most intriguing archaeological sites. Fascinating Chichén Itzá and the ruins of the coast city of Tulum are both easy to reach. You really should see at least one of the two, preferably Chichén Itzá, although Tulum's cliffside setting is spectacular.

CANCÚN

CONVENTION CENTER Completely rebuilt at a cost of $90 million, it accommodates up to 12,000 people and has facilities for theater performances, concerts, and expositions as well as conferences. The center also has a large shopping center, an observation deck, a disco, and a revolving restaurant atop a 50-story "needle" tower.

EL CASTILLO A small reproduction of El Castillo pyramid (the original is in Chichén Itzá) has been erected in front of *Plaza Caracol.* Every night, except Tuesdays, the phenomenon of the spring and fall equinox, when the movement of the sun across El Castillo produces the illusion of a serpent creeping down the staircase, is reproduced. The show in English begins at 8 and 9 PM; in Spanish at 7 PM. There's an admission charge.

CANCÚN CITY On the mainland, Cancún City, like the resort itself, did not evolve but was built from scratch as part of a FONATUR master plan. It didn't exist at all in 1970; now it's home to about 300,000 people — many of them native Yucatecans — almost all of whom work on the resort island. There are a number of restaurants and shops, most located along the main thoroughfare, Tulum Avenue, and Yaxchilán Avenue, which is 2 blocks west and parallel to Tulum.

EL REY These modest Maya ruins on the lagoon at the southern end of the island are hardly impressive compared with those at Tulum or Cobá, let alone Chichén Itzá, but they are worth a visit. When these ruins were first excavated in the 1950s, the skeleton of a human male was discovered, as well as scattered remains of other bodies, apparently human sacrifices. Some anthropologists suggest that the main skeleton was that of a chieftain (hence the name "rey," king in Spanish). Unfortunately, because the site had been sacked by looters before archaeologists found it, there is little evidence of just what purpose this temple served in ancient Maya times.

SOUTH OF CANCÚN

DR. ALFREDO BARRERA MARÍN BOTANICAL GARDENS Located 2 miles (3 km) south of Puerto Morelos, about 24 miles (38 km) south of Cancún, this nature preserve covers 150 acres. Trails wind through the semi-evergreen tropical forests that border a mangrove swamp. The gardens are closed Mondays.

PUERTO AVENTURAS About 54 miles (86 km) south of Cancún is one of the newest resort areas — and one of the most exclusive enclaves — on Mexico's Caribbean coast. Puerto Aventuras is nestled in the natural beauty of the region and enhanced with Asian palms and orchids brought in from the Brazilian Amazon. There's a 250-slip marina set in a crystal-clear cove fed by underground springs, an 18-hole golf course, and outdoor tennis courts (see *Sports*). A glimpse of the area's maritime history can be seen at the *Pablo Bush Romero CEDAM* (Center of Exploration of Marine Archaeology; no phone), a museum that displays 18th-century silver goblets, gold coins, medallions, cannons, and other relics salvaged from the *Matanceros,* a Spanish merchant ship that sank off the coast of Akumal in 1741 (no admission charge). Still in the early stages of development, the area has several hotels (see *Checking In*), and many villas and condominiums are currently under construction.

AKUMAL About 5 miles (8 km) south of Puerto Aventuras, this town — founded as the headquarters of the private *Mexican Underwater Explorers Club* — has one of the loveliest beaches in the area, with excellent snorkeling. For an adventure right out of *The Deep,* minus the hazards, the *Explorers Club* has an offshore, underwater museum whose collection includes sunken treasure from a Spanish galleon. Here you also can view anchors and guns encrusted in coral among the rocks. There's a dive shop and restaurant. The *Club Akumal* hotel is a great spot for lunch.

CHEMUYIL About 6 miles (10 km) south of Akumal, a sign welcomes visitors to "the most beautiful beach in the world." The *Chemuyil* hotel is charming (see *Checking In*).

XEL-HA Another 4 miles (6 km) farther south, this is the site of a national park where a lagoon forms a natural aquarium for snorkeling.

TULUM Once a thriving Maya city-fort built on a cliff above the sea, this ancient city about 80 miles (128 km) south of Cancún lacks the magnitude of earlier cities such as Chichén Itzá and Uxmal, but its beautiful setting makes it a compelling destination nonetheless. There are 25 major structures, including the city wall, a large pyramid overlooking the sea, a number of temples with brightly colored frescoes and relief carvings, and several platforms that were used for dances and ceremonies. Tulum commands a magnificent view of the Caribbean, and the small beach below the main pyramid is the perfect place to cool off after a hot day among the ruins.

For lunch or a snack, stop in at *El Faison y El Venado,* a simple, rustic eatery located where the Coastal Highway intersects with the road to the Tulum ruins (it's next to the tiny *Nuevo* hotel). The menu features all manner of well-prepared regional dishes at reasonable prices.

Tulum is connected to Cancún by daily bus service (plan on a 1½-hour ride each way). The ruins are open daily from 8 AM to 5 PM; there's an admission charge. A number of tour companies offer excursions to Tulum — with stops at Akumal and at Xel-Ha for snorkeling. Half- or full-day trips are offered, but we recommend the latter — with its more leisurely pace and the beach lunch at Akumal — for about $40 per person. Ask at your hotel's activities desk for details.

COBÁ Archaeology buffs won't want to miss this, one of the most recent (in terms of excavation date) and potentially most intriguing of Maya ruins. A half-hour away from Tulum, and about 2 hours from Cancún, this jungle-bound site was discovered in 1897 by Teobert Maler, but exploration and excavation did not begin until 1974 and is still far from complete. The city is believed to have been a major trade center, connected by a network of highways with other major Maya cities such as Chichén Itzá and Uxmal. The painstaking process of reclaiming the ancient ruins from the jungle (archaeologists believe some 6,500 structures once stood here) has only just begun; Cobá presents travelers with the rare chance to see an archaeological site before it is completely uncovered and understood. A tour of the main sites involves a 2-mile walk along jungle paths (bring insect repellent). The ruins are not labeled, but informational booklets in English are sold at the small gift shop at the entrance to the site, and guides are available for a small fee. Among the ruins are several large pyramids, including the tallest Maya pyramid in the Yucatán (130 feet); visitors may climb its 120 steps for a sweeping view of the jungle. The site is open daily from 8 AM to 5 PM; admission charge. Cobá is easily reached by car: Turn inland at the marked road just south of Tulum; it's 26 miles (42 km) straight ahead. *Club Med's Villa Arqueológica* (phone: 203-3833 or 203-3086 in Mexico City) is nearby for lunch and/or overnight lodging.

SIAN KA'AN Stretching south of Tulum to Punta Allen is a 1.3-million-acre nature reserve, containing tropical forests, mangrove swamps, salt marshes, palm-rimmed beaches, archaeological ruins, and coral reefs. Pronounced Shahn *Can,* it's a paradise for bird watchers and crocodile and butterfly lovers. If you venture far enough into the jungle (not recommended as a solo journey), you're likely to come across a jaguar or some other large cat. There are two fine hotels on the reserve geared especially toward sportspeople who come here for the bonefishing: the pricey *Club de Pesca Boca Paila* represented by *Turismo Boca Paila* (AP 59, Cozumel, QR; phone: 20053 or 800-245-1950 from the US), and *Pez Maya* (phone: 800-336-3542 from the US; fax: on Cozumel, 20072). The *Club de Pesca Boca Paila* is a hotel in the summer only; during the rest of the year, it runs fishing expeditions. Considerably more rustic accommodations are available at *El Retiro* at Punta Xamach (clean cabins, but no private baths), or at *Posada Cuzan* at Punta Allen (thatch palm tepees); for reservations, call the Isla Mujeres tourist office (phone: 70316; ask for Cuauhtémoc Sunta). In Punta Allen, Sonia López will provide a good meal if you ask nicely, and arrangements can be made with one of the fishermen to visit *los cayos* (the keys). For guided visits, contact the *Association of Friends of Sian Ka'an* (Plaza Américas, Suite 50, Cancún, QR; phone: 849583; fax: 873080).

COZUMEL

PLAZA The heart of Cozumel is a wide plaza near where the ferry docks. Long regarded as unique in its ugliness, it has been transformed into an inviting place for strolling, sitting, and people watching. Most of the shops and restaurants are found here. There's an esplanade on the sea side, and the *malecón,* the road that follows the shore north and south, is lined with relaxed cafés and tourist shops.

COZUMEL MUSEUM Impressive three-dimensional models of underwater caves in the offshore reefs, and historical and ethnographical exhibits are displayed. There's also a library, a restaurant, and a crafts shop. Open from 10 AM to 6 PM, Sundays through Fridays. No admission charge. Located on Rafael Melgar between Calles 4 and 6 (phone: 21545).

CHANKANAB LAGOON AND BOTANICAL GARDENS About five miles (8 km) south of town, this place features a natural aquarium with an array of multicolored tropical fish. Since suntan lotion collects in the water and harms the fish, swimming and snorkeling are sometimes prohibited in the lagoon. More than 400 species of tropical plants live in the botanical gardens. Open daily from 7 AM to 5 PM. Small admission charge to the lagoon.

SAN FRANCISCO BEACH The island's best beach, it can be reached via paved road, but it's also fun getting there on the *El Zorro* cruise (phone: 20831).

PUNTA MORENA BEACH On the open Caribbean side of the island, the surf here is rough and swimming can be dangerous. *Mezcalito's* is a good place to stop for some grilled fish and a beer (see *Eating Out*).

A NOTE ON COZUMEL RUINS **There are archeological ruins in the island's interior, but they're mostly overgrown and not worth the buggy, sweaty, dusty trip unless you're an archaeological zealot. On a day's drive around the southern end of the island, a sandy detour off the main paved road leads to "The Tomb of the Snail," but if you're planning on an excursion to Tulum or Chichén Itzá, don't bother. Day trips to Tulum and Xel-Ha (by boat and bus, about $50 per person, including lunch) are available from Cozumel.**

ELSEWHERE ON THE COAST

ISLA MUJERES The name means Isle of Women; the Spanish so dubbed it because they found many sculptures of females here. A dot 5 miles long and one-half mile wide, it is 6 miles north of Cancún and 6 miles off Puerto Juárez on the Yucatán Peninsula. The island's tiny town, beautiful beaches, lagoons, reefs, and transparent waters make it a pleasant retreat for snorkelers and skin divers. Hotels and restaurants are moderate to inexpensive. Ferries run regularly from Puerto Juárez and Punta Sam on Cancún. By day, try the *Tropical Cruiser* (phone: 831488) or *La Bamba* (phone: 833011) which include an open-air bar and lunch; by night, the *Noche Pirata.* There are also full-day snorkeling cruises from Cancún to Isla Mujeres (about $40 per person).

CONTOY ISLAND Declared a National Wildlife Reserve in 1961, this tiny, uninhabited coral island is 25 miles (40 km) north of Cancún. A favorite destination for bird watchers, it is home to over 100 species, although their numbers are, unfortunately, diminishing. It's also an important migratory point for other birds, and an egg-laying spot for sea turtles. Daily boat excursions to the island are offered by *Barracuda* (phone: 844551) and *Cooperativa Transporte Turística Isla Mujeres* (phone: 70274) for about $40, including lunch. The trip is not for landlubbers — it's a 2½-hour sail each way, and the actual time spent on shore is short (about 3½ hours), but very sweet. The island is completely undeveloped and beautiful; the afternoon can be pleasantly spent lying on the narrow and nearly deserted beach on the island's leeward shore; swimming and snorkeling (though the visibility is not great here) in the warm water; taking a boat ride (there's an additional fee) into the island's interior lagoons, where bird nesting areas are visible; or doing a bit of exploring. Contoy Island is not for thrill seekers, but it is perfect for those who seek a soothing cruise, a pristine beach, an untouched landscape — and a respite from the crowds of Cancún.

EXTRA SPECIAL **A trip to the ruins at Chichén Itzá (which date to the early 11th century) is the best way to experience the buildings of the Maya civilization. The most famous and complete of the ancient Maya cities, this site is a testament to their engineering genius. Here are temples, sacrificial wells, sacred ball courts, reclining idols, and the great El Castillo pyramid. The ruins are located in the interior of the Yucatán Peninsula, about a 2½-hour drive from Cancún. All hotel travel desks book the daylong, air conditioned bus trip, or it may be included in your basic Mexico travel package. Price, including guided tours of the site and lunch at a nearby resort hotel, is about $46 to $66 per person.**

Sources and Resources

TOURIST INFORMATION

The Mexican Ministry of Tourism is the best source of brochures and background material on all of Mexico. Information can be obtained by contacting any of their US offices (see GETTING READY TO GO).

The sources and quality of information available through the local tourist offices, however, are very limited. In Cancún, there's a modern information center (on Av. Tulum near the *Ki-Huic Market*) and a tourist office (Av. Cobá and Nader; phone: 848073). On Cozumel, the tourist office is upstairs in the Plaza del Sol building (phone: 20972). Information is also available at your hotel activities or travel desk or at the desk of *Cozumel Holidays* (a reliable tour operator) at the *Cabañas del Caribe* hotel. On Isla Mujeres, there's a tourist office (6 Hidalgo; phone: 70316), but the staff there is uninformed and can be rude. You can, however, get information from the English-speaking personnel in charge of the activities desk at *Mexico Divers* (phone: 70274), or from Doña María Mendes at *Maria's Kan Kin* restaurant south of town (don't eat there, just ask questions).

LOCAL COVERAGE In Cancún, two periodicals — the comprehensive quarterly *Cancún Tips* and the affiliated bimonthly *Cancún Tips Magazine* — contain good background information, ads, and some handy listings of happenings, hotels, restaurants, shops, night places, and tour operators. Two similar publications, *Cozumel in One Day* and the *Blue Guide to Cozumel,* are distributed on Cozumel. On Isla Mujeres, *The Islander* lists current events.

There's also a national English-language daily paper called the *News.* Newspapers from Mexico City arrive on Cozumel and Cancún on the day they're published, as do the *Miami Herald,* the *Houston Chronicle,* and *USA Today.* Local newspapers (in Spanish) include *Quintana Roo, Novedades de Quintana Roo, El Tiempo de Cozumel,* and *Diario de Quintana Roo.* They're available on all three islands.

For background or take-along reading: *Incidents of Travel in the Yucatán,* the fascinating two-volume journal of John L. Stephens, the New Englander who explored some 44 Maya sites in 1841, 85 years before the Mexican government took an interest in them (Dover; $9). Also, pick up a copy of our own *Birnbaum's Cancún, Cozumel, & Isla Mujeres 94* (HarperCollins; $11).

RADIO AND TELEVISION

There are no local English-language radio or television stations. Most hotels have satellite access to CNN and other English-language stations.

TELEPHONE

When calling from the US to Cancún, Isla Mujeres, or Cozumel, dial 011 + 52 (country code) + (city code) + (local number); when calling from the Caribbean, dial 52 (country code) + (city code) + (local number). The city code for Cancún is 98; for Isla Mujeres and Cozumel, 987. When calling from a phone among the three islands, use only the local number unless otherwise indicated.

ENTRY REQUIREMENTS

US citizens must have proof of citizenship (either a current passport or a birth certificate, voter's registration card, naturalization certificate, or Armed Forces ID card, along with a photo ID); Canadian citizens need a current passport or birth certificate. Both must have a tourist card, obtainable free at Mexican embassies and consulates, airlines and travel agencies booking trips to Mexico, Mexican Ministry of Tourism offices, *Greyhound Bus Line* offices, or *American Automobile Association* offices. Carry the card with you at all times. There's also a $12 airport departure tax.

CLIMATE AND CLOTHES

Year-round temperatures average in the low 80s F (about 27C). From October through April, sunny days prevail; in July, August, and September there are brief showers, usually in the afternoons. At the resorts, most of the days you'll wear beach clothes, with cover-ups or caftans for protection from too much sun. You're requested to wear tennis clothes (though not necessarily all white) and tennis shoes on the courts. For sightseeing trips, light dresses, tops and skirts, or pants are most comfortable for women; slacks and shirts for men. Mexicans generally do not wear shorts outside of beach areas, so you shouldn't either. Nights also are casual but neat (for the most part, discos bar T-shirts and sneakers). Neither coats nor ties are required for men, but many women tend to dress up a bit — dresses or dressy pants and tops — at Cancún's posher hotels. The same, on a slightly more casual level, goes for Cancún's smaller hotels and Cozumel. On Isla Mujeres, a fresh shirt and a pair of slacks are as dressy as evening attire ever gets.

MONEY

In January 1993, Mexico introduced the *nuevo* (new) *peso.* The old currency, however, was *not* devalued. Three zeros were dropped from the old peso, and the new currency is distinguished by the symbol N plus a dollar sign, as well as new colors and designs (note, too, that some new peso coins have replaced certain denominations of old peso bills). The *nuevo peso* is valued at about 3N$ to $1 US. Be aware that both old and new pesos may still be in circulation, so be sure to check when exchanging money or making a purchase. Credit cards and traveler's checks are widely accepted in Mexico, but paying in cash sometimes means avoiding the 15% value added tax (VAT), at least on retail store purchases. All prices in this chapter are quoted in US dollars.

LANGUAGE

Spanish is the official language, but some English is usually understood and spoken in tourist areas of Cancún, Cozumel, and Chichén Itzá. Its use is somewhat rarer on Isla Mujeres, but with a little patience and a phrase book, non-Spanish speakers usually manage fine.

TIME

Mexico's Caribbean islands lie in the central standard time zone. When it's noon on Cozumel, Cancún, and Isla Mujeres, it's noon CST in Chicago and 1 PM eastern standard time in New York. From spring through fall, when it's noon on these islands, it's 1 PM central daylight saving time in Chicago and 2 PM eastern daylight saving time in New York.

CURRENT

Electricity on Cancún, Cozumel, and Isla Mujeres is 110 volts, 60 cycles. However, the safety feature on most US plugs — a fatter prong — makes it impossible to use most of the outlets without an adapter.

TIPPING

No service charge is added to hotel bills, so give the room maid $1 to $2 per person per day; the bellboys get $1 to $2 for two to three bags and $1 for calls that require a trip to your room. Give the doorman 50¢ when he calls a cab for you; taxi drivers get 10% of the tab, if they seem to charge a fair price. Airport porters get the same amount as bellboys. In Cancún, you don't have to leave any additional sum when a 15% service charge is added to your food or drink bill; on Cozumel and on Isla Mujeres, where there is seldom a service charge, tip 10% to 15%. Also, tip gas station attendants about 35¢ for service.

GETTING AROUND

BUS In Cancún, transfers between the airport and local hotels are handled by a fleet of minibuses that depart promptly, handle all luggage, and charge about $5 per person. From 6 AM until midnight, another bus fleet covers the distance between Cancún City and the Tourist Zone's hotels and shopping area; fare is about 75¢. On Cozumel, the minibus fare from the airport to island hotels runs about $1 per person.

CAR RENTAL In Cancún, several agencies offer rental cars from $35 to $165 a day (most include mileage): *Avis* (phone: 830803 or 830004); *Budget* (phone: 840204); *Econorent* (phone: 841826); *Thrifty* (phone: 842699); *Dollar* (phone: 841709), which also rents jeeps for about $80 per day, including 120 free miles (200 km), insurance, and tax; and *Rentoautos Kancun* (phone: 841175). Agencies on Cozumel include *Avis* (phone: 20099) and *Hertz* (phone: 22136); car rental on Cozumel starts at about $60 per day (including mileage).

FERRY There's ferry service from Playa del Carmen on the mainland near Cancún to Cozumel (about 45 minutes; $7 one-way). The ferry to Isla Mujeres from Punta Sam on the mainland carries vehicles and people for about $6 per trip per car. Most visitors, however, take the passenger boat from Puerto Juárez (on the mainland north of Cancún City); the trip takes an hour, and costs about $1.50 per person one way.

FLIGHTSEEING *Pelican Pier Avioturismo* (phone: 830315 or 831935), across the street from *Casa Maya* in Cancún, has a Cessna 206 that can transport up to five passengers. The approximate cost per planeload for a trip to Cozumel is $240; to Tulum, $360; to Chichén Itzá, $540; to Mérida, $840; to Chetumal, $900. Flights to other destinations are available. Each trips includes a 2-hour stopover. The company also has a one-passenger ultralight seaplane that makes a 15-minute tour of the Hotel Zone for about $45. In Cozumel, *Aviomar* (phone: 20477) has plane tours to Chichén Itzá.

MOPEDS Small motorbikes, an easy way to get around, are available at many Cancún hotels. *Casa Maya* and *Franky's* at the *Krystal* rent mopeds for about $35 per day. On Cozumel, *Rentadora Cozumel* (phone: 21120 or 21503) charges $25 for a 24-hour rental. They also rent bicycles for $3 a day. Mopeds are available at the *Plaza las Glorias* (phone: 22000) at the southern end of town. On Isla Mujeres, motorbikes — available from *Ciro's* (phone: 70351) or *Moto Rent Cárdenas* (phone: 70079) for about $25 a day — are the only way to go. Slower, but considerably less expensive, are sport bikes that rent for about $5 from *Rent Me* at Juárez and Morelos.

SEA EXCURSIONS *The Columbus* (phone: 831021), a 62-foot motor-sailing vessel, takes off from Cancún for Isla Mujeres at 8 AM on Mondays, Wednesdays, and Fridays; lunch is included. The *Carnival Cancún* — a tri-level open-air boat — makes trips from the Playa Linda Pier to Isla Mujeres; a light breakfast, beverages, lunch, live entertainment, and games are included (phone: 846433 or 846742). The trimaran *Aqua-Quin* (phone: 831883 or 830100) sails daily to Isla Mujeres from Cancún for snorkeling at El Garrafón, with lunch and open bar included. It leaves at 11 AM and returns around 5 PM. Also available are the *Fiesta Maya* glass-bottom boat excursion, which includes lunch, open bar, and snorkeling for $35 per person (phone: 830389), and the *Noche Pirata* on the *Tropical,* an evening cruise to Isla Mujeres, with dinner and open bar, for about the same price (phone: 831488). The *Nautibus* (phone: 833552 or 832119), a catamaran with seats and windows in the keel, provides a panoramic view of sea life. The *México,* billed as the world's largest water jet, makes a round trip daily from Cozumel to Playa del Carmen (phone: on Cozumel, 21508; in Cancún, 846656). Cozumel's *El Zorro* cruise (phone: 20831) stops for snorkeling at three reefs and for a buffet on the beach and is good fun. On Isla Mujeres, *Mexico Divers* (phone: 70274) and the *Cooperativa Transporte Turística Isla Mujeres* (phone: 70274) take visitors to Contoy Island for fishing and some time on the beach for $35, including drinks and lunch.

SIGHTSEEING BUS TOURS A number of Cancún agencies operate bus tours to sites on the mainland; chances are one has a desk in your hotel lobby. If not, contact *American Express* (Plaza Américan; phone: 841999), *Viajes Parmarc* (at the *Plaza del Sol* hotel; phone: 841934), or *Wagon-lits* (at the *Camino Real;* phone: 832891 or 833165).

SIGHTSEEING TAXI TOURS Some taxi drivers on Cancún are guides (your hotel activities person will know several) and will drive you to Tulum and Xel-Ha for about $50 for the half day. For two or more people, it's the least expensive, most pleasant way to go. Private, air conditioned cars with English-speaking drivers are available from *Mayaland Tours* for $225 (considerably more if you make arrangements through a travel agency) for up to 5 passengers for the trip to Tulum, Xel-Ha, and Akumal (phone: 45255 or 43694). On Isla Mujeres, similar trips can be arranged from the taxi stand next to the pier (phone: 70066).

TAXI Small green-and-white cabs are available at reasonable fares, according to zone, in the Cancún area (fare from the most distant hotel to the city is about $12). On Cozumel, meterless island taxis operate by arrangement; i.e., you and the driver agree on a price for the proposed trip before you get into the cab. The average ride comes to about $5. When you talk pesos, make sure you and your driver are speaking the same language (see *Money*).

INTER-ISLAND FLIGHTS

Aero Cozumel and *Aero Caribe* make connections between Cancún and Cozumel, as well as several other cities on the mainland of Mexico.

SPECIAL EVENTS

The annual *Cancún Fair* takes place in November, with cockfights, dances, and shows. Isla Mujeres hosts regattas from St. Petersburg, Florida, and Galveston, Texas, between April and June. A unique attraction on the first day of spring or fall is the Chichén Itzá phenomenon, when light and shadow strike the Castillo pyramid in such a manner that the snake god Kukulcán appears to be crawling along the side of the monument.

Mexicans enjoy celebrating so much that they often take off the day before and the day after a holiday, as well as the big day itself. Most banks, businesses, and government offices are closed on the following days: *New Year's Day* (January 1), *Constitution Day* (February 5), *Juárez's Birthday* (March 21), *Easter* (and often much of the preceding week), *Labor Day* (May 1), *Anniversary of the Battle of Puebla* (May 5), *Independence Day* (September 15–16), *Columbus Day* (October 12), President's State of the Nation address (November 1), *All Saints' Day* and the *Day of the Dead* (November 1–2), *Anniversary of the Mexican Revolution* (November 20), *Feast of the Virgin of Guadalupe* (December 12), and *Christmas* (December 25).

SHOPPING

In addition to traditional Mexican crafts (silver, ceramics, papier-mâché, alabaster, leather, and straw goods), there are boutiques stocked with imported perfumes, fashions (especially accessories), crystal, china, and more. Mexican resortwear (embroidered and lace-trimmed caftans, beach cover-ups, and shirts) is brightly colored, fun, and remarkably reasonable in price, considering the amount of handwork involved. But before you buy, be sure to try on those classic Yucatecan take-homes — *huipils* (loose white dresses embroidered at neck and hem) and *guayabera* shirts (dressy-casual with tucked fronts, sometimes embroidery) — they can look either terrific or very tacky. Sisal mats, hats, rugs, and bags are other local specialties.

Downtown Cancún's tourist shops are along Avenida Tulum, between Avenidas Uxmal and Cobá, and range from superior to so-so. On Cozumel, shop along Calle Hidalgo and the *malecón.* On Isla Mujeres, head for the beach instead.

The booklet *GSP & the Traveler,* available free from the US Customs Service (PO Box 7118, Washington, DC 20044), has information about items that may be available duty-free.

DOWNTOWN CANCÚN

LA CASITA Arts, crafts, decorative items, leather, jewelry, and Mexican-inspired clothing are sold in a delightful setting. 115 Av. Tulum (phone: 841468).

SYBELE High-quality imports from around the world, ranging from men's suits and women's lingerie to leather briefcases and fine perfume. Downtown at 109 Av. Tulum (phone: 841181) and *Plaza Caracol* (phone: 831738).

HOTEL ZONE

The most elegant shops in the *zona turística* generally are located in *El Parián, Plaza Caracol, Mayfair, La Mansión-Costa Blanca, Plaza Flamingo, Plaza Nautilus,* and *Plaza Terramar* shopping centers on Paseo Kukulcán.

ARTLAND Maya art, rubbings, batiks, paintings, and jewelry, all inspired by Maya designs. *Plaza Flamingo* (phone: 832663).

CAROLI Jewelry and art objects crafted from sterling silver and semi-precious stones. *Plaza Flamingo* (phone: 850985).

LOS CASTILLO AND LILY CASTILLO Branches of one of Taxco's finest silversmiths, both carrying the beautifully designed and crafted jewelry and art objects. *Los Castillo* is known for its "wedded" metals, a union of silver, copper, and brass. They also do exceptional work in stoneware with silver inlays. *Plaza Caracol* (phone: 831084).

CENTRO CULTURAL COSTA BLANCA Paintings, sculptures, and lithographs by some of Mexico's best contemporary artists. *La Mansion, Costa Blanca Shopping Center* (no phone).

CHANTAL Select pieces of hand-crafted silver and black coral (note: it is legal to bring a small number of black coral finished pieces, such as jewelry, into the US, as long as they are for personal use). The shop has a stunning African motif complete with two live parrots to greet visitors. *Plaza Caracol* (phone: 830450).

GALERÍAS COLONIAL Tableware with beautifully painted patterns, carved marble knickknacks, and chess sets. *Plaza Caracol* (phone: 830914).

ONYX AND HANDICRAFTS Good quality and prices in onyx and other handicrafts. *Plaza Nautilus* (phone: 830699).

RONAY One of Mexico's most prestigious jewelers, specializing in gold. *Plaza Caracol* (phone: 831261).

SEBASTIAN The very finest in designer silver jewelry. *Plaza Caracol* (phone: 831815) and *Plaza Nautilus* (phone: 831949).

TANE Silver and vermeil jewelry, tableware, and art objects, many using traditional pre-Hispanic designs. Others are copies of antiques. Two locations: *Camino Real* (phone: 830200) and *Hyatt Regency* (phone: 831349).

XCARET An unusual and varied selection of some of the very best of Mexico's handicrafts — ceramics, textiles, papier-mâché — at reasonable prices. *Plaza Flamingo* (phone: 833256).

COZUMEL

BAZAR COZUMEL The work of some 200 first-rate Mexican artisans is offered here, including silver items, tapestries with modern art motifs, weavings, pottery, and lots more, at fair prices. Av. Juárez (no phone).

LA CASITA Smashing Mexican resort clothes as well as Sergio Bustamante's imaginative animal and bird sculptures. Av. Rafael E. Melgar (phone: 20198).

PAMA High-quality duty-free imports ranging from jewelry and perfume to silk ties and ladies' fashions. 9 Av. Rafael E. Melgar (no phone).

PLAZA DEL SOL A nest of nearly a dozen art, crafts, jewelry, and import boutiques; of particular note is *Cinco Soles,* which offers handicrafts from all over Mexico. Rafael E. Melgar at Calle 8 (phone: 20685, in *Orbi*).

ISLA MUJERES

RACHAT & ROMÉ Outstanding jewelry designed and crafted by the friendly Cuban who owns this wonderful place. In the flamingo-colored building just a few steps from the ferry dock (phone: 70250).

BEACH (AND STREET) VENDORS **Although "legally" outlawed in this part of Mexico, these ambulant salespeople materialize on almost every beach. They can be persistent, but unless you are interested in their wares, make your feelings understood with a firm "no."**

SPORTS

As on most islands, water activities come first, and they're most of what it's all about on Cozumel and Isla Mujeres. But on all the islands, especially Cancún, the possibilities don't end there.

BOATING Craft large and small, power and sail, crewed and uncrewed, are available in Cancún. Make arrangements at *Aqua-Quin* (phone: 831883) or the *Royal Yacht Club* (phone: 850391); at the *Marina Stouffer Presidente, Club Lagoon,* or *Marina Camino Real*; or at any hotel travel desk. The *Regata* *del Sol al Sol,* from St. Petersburg, Florida, ends at Isla Mujeres. It's held yearly sometime between April and June, and is followed by the *Amigos* regatta around the island.

BULLFIGHTS Bullfights are held on Wednesdays, beginning at 3:30 PM, at the *Plaza de Torres* ring in Cancún City. Tickets cost $30 for general admission and are available through hotel travel desks. The modern 3-tiered arena seats 6,000, and there is ample parking.

CYCLING There's a 6-mile serpentine path of pink brick bordered by garden plants and the seashore on Cancún, with *palapa*-topped rest stops along the way.

GOLF In Cancún, *Pok-Ta-Pok* (phone: 831230), the Robert Trent Jones, Jr. golf course (par 73), offers gently rolling fairways bordered by palms. The *Puerto Aventuras Golf Club* (phone: 987-22300), about 54 miles (86 km) south of Cancún, has an 18-hole course that was built around several pre-Columbian structures and incorporates ancient *cenotes* (sinkholes). The greens fee for both courses is about $50; cart rental is about $30 per round.

HORSEBACK RIDING *Hacienda San José de las Vegas* (at Km 11.5 on the road to Tulum; phone: 845178) runs escorted horseback tours to a hacienda in the jungle; two trips daily, Mondays through Saturdays. On Sundays they rent horses by the hour.

JET SKIING Cancún's lagoon is great for this activity, which requires a minimum of learning time. Available at the *Royal Yacht Club* (phone: 850391); *Marina Aqua Ray,* in front of the *Continental Villas Plaza* (phone: 833007); or, a bit farther afield, the *Marina del Rey* opposite the *Oasis* hotel (phone: 831748).

SCUBA AND SNORKELING The variety of the reefs and the clarity of the water (average undersea visibility, year-round, is 100 feet, but you can often see much farther) make Mexico's Caribbean a top area for underwater exploring. Cozumel takes the diving honors. Its prime attractions are the reefs 500 yards off the island's leeward shore along El Cantil (the Drop-Off), the edge of the shelf that borders the Yucatán Channel to the south. Famous 6-mile-long Palancar Reef has — in addition to forests of black, staghorn, and other species of live coral and friendly swarms of Day-Glo–colored fish — a number of antique wrecks in which to poke around. You can dive to look and take pictures, but removing flora or fauna is strictly forbidden. Several dive shops on the *malecón* in San Miguel — including *Aqua Safari* (phone: 20101); *the Big Blue* (phone: 20396); and *Del Mar Aquatics* in *La Ceiba* (phone: 20816), at *Casa del Mar* (phone: 21944), and at *Plaza las Glorias* (phone: 22000) — offer rental equipment, instruction, and dive trips. Most hotels also offer facilities (at higher rates), but the on-site convenience is worth it. Scuba pool instruction (about 3 hours) costs about

$55 per person. A 4- to 5-day seminar with a certified instructor (including diving theory, pool instruction, shallow shore dives, full-day dives, and certification) is about $350 per person. A full day's guided diving tour from Cozumel to Palancar — including equipment — is about $40. Equipment rentals run about $6 for tank and weights, $6 for a regulator, and $5 for fins, mask, and snorkel. An underwater camera rents for about $25 at *Del Mar Aquatics* at the *Casa del Mar* hotel (phone: 21944).

Though great for scuba diving, Cozumel seems short on good snorkeling spots; best are the shallow reefs to the south, where depths range from 5 to 35 feet. Although some of the beach was lost to Hurricane Gilbert in 1988, Chankanab Lagoon, midway down the leeward coast, with its underwater grottoes and fairly large fish population, is still a good place for beginners to get their fins wet. (However, since suntan lotion collects in the water and harms the fish, swimming and snorkeling are not always permitted.)

Cancún's best scuba diving and snorkeling are found in the reef-filled waters off its southern point. Dive trips and equipment rental can be arranged through your hotel. Guided scuba trips, including equipment, cost approximately $50; gear can be rented for about $5 per person per day. Two hours of morning scuba instruction in the lagoon and an afternoon dive trip cost $50.

Isla Mujeres is surrounded by reefs, so snorkeling is fairly good along its shores. Scuba divers can rent equipment from *La Bahía,* across from the ferry dock (no phone), and *Cooperativa Transporte Turística Isla Mujeres* and *Mexico Divers* (in the same office on Av. Rueda Medina, phone: 70274) for about $30 per day. These operations also arrange dive trips for about $45, including equipment and two dives.

SPORT FISHING Strong men and women do battle on the deep sea with sailfish, bonito, and dolphin fish (in season from March through August), white marlin (April through August), wahoo and kingfish (May to September), and barracuda, red snapper, bluefin, grouper, and mackerel (year-round). Closer to shore, light tackle anglers attempt to hook the elusive permit (tour operators can help you get one). Boats, both large and small, are available at *Marina Aqua Ray* (phone: 833007), *Royal Yacht Club* (phone: 850391), and *Aqua Tours* (phone: 830227 or 831137). Here again, hotels can make all the arrangements. Firms charge about $80 per person per day or $240 to $310 for a half day for groups. On Isla Mujeres, *Cooperativa Transporte Turística* and *Mexico Divers* (Av. Rueda Medina; phone: 70274) arrange trips for four people for about $400 a day.

SWIMMING AND SUNNING The texture and whiteness of Cancún's sand are so distinctive they inspired special studies by geologists, who found that many of the sand's individual grains contain microscopic, star-shaped fossils of an organism called Discoaster, extinct for 70 million years. Through the ages, the sea has ground and polished these grains till they've become brilliant and powder soft. What's more, their limestone composition has a cooling effect that makes the island's sand — even under the noonday sun — feel comfortable to bare feet. Unless you stay right in Cancún City, chances are your hotel will have its own beach as well as a pool, but there are also several public strands — Playa Tortugas and Playa Chac-Mool are just two examples.

Cozumel's beaches — shaped into distinctive coves — are mostly on the island's leeward side, north and south of San Miguel. The majority of hotels are there, too, and you'll probably spend most of your sun and sea time beside your own hotel or on nearby sands. You can visit other beaches, including the lengthy one about 10 miles (16 km) south of San Miguel at San Francisco (a bit crowded these days, particularly on weekends); the more secluded shore of Passion Island, cupped in its north coast bay; and Punta Morena, on the rough side with a sheltered lagoon nearby. Because the undertow can be tricky, it's a good idea to observe the currents before you take the plunge (plan to enter the water at one point, exit at another), and never swim alone.

On Isla Mujeres, the southern beach called El Garrafón, with its undersea formations and its intriguing fish, is the target of many day trips from Cancún. Sand seekers tend to congregate on the manmade beaches that have been built on platforms against the hill that leads up to the shops and restaurants. Tortuga's and María's beaches are less crowded.

TENNIS On Cancún there are courts at the *Fiesta Americana Condesa, Continental Villas Plaza, Oasis, Fiesta Americana Coral Beach, Westin Regina, Marriott Casa Magna, Ritz-Carlton Cancún, Meliá Turquesa, Meliá Cancún, Calinda Cancún Beach, Sheraton, Camino Real, Hyatt Cancún Caribe, Krystal, Casa Maya,* and *Aristos* resorts, and the *Pok-Ta-Pok Golf Club* (phone: 830871). On Cozumel there are tennis courts at the *Cozumel Caribe,* the *Meliá Mayan Cozumel, El Cozumeleño, Villablanca, Fiesta Americana Sol Caribe, Fiesta Inn, Stouffer Presidente, Holiday Inn Cozumel Reef,* and *La Ceiba.* The *Puerto Aventuras Golf Club* (phone: 22300) has 2 public outdoor tennis courts.

WATER SKIING The lagoon behind the island of Cancún is the ideal place to learn or perfect this exhilarating sport. Make arrangements at any island hotel, or at the *Royal Yacht Club* (phone: 850391), *Marina Aqua Ray* (phone: 833007), *Marina del Rey* (phone: 831748), or the *Club Lagoon* hotel. Boat time costs about $60 an hour.

WINDSURFING Once you've learned to stand on a surfboard, 2 or 3 hours of instruction are all you need. On Cancún lessons are available at several hotels, including the *Camino Real.* Boards rent for about $10 an hour. Lessons cost $25 per hour, and several places offer weekly rates that include lessons.

NIGHTLIFE

Reigning Cancún dance clubs are easily discernible by the crowds gathering outside before opening time (around 10 PM.) Current hot spots are *Christine's* at the *Krystal* (phone: 831205), *Cat's Reggae Bar,* downtown (at 12 Yaxchilán), *La Boom* (on Paseo Kukulcán; phone: 831458), and *Dady'O* (near the *Convention Center*). The *Hard Rock Café* (at *Plaza Lagunas;* phone: 832024) and *Carlos 'n' Charlie's Cancún* (at the marina; phone: 831304) are good places for food, drink, dancing, and meeting people. *Daphny's* at the *Sheraton* is a popular video bar with live and taped dance music. At *Sixties,* in the *Marriott* hotel, there's dancing to music from the 1950s to 1990s. *Azúcar* at the *Camino Real* features a nightly cabaret of Caribbean music and dance. *Batachá Tropical,* the newest disco, offers a combination of tropical and Latino sounds in its live salsa music (in the Hotel Zone; no phone).

For lots of silly fun, there's the Pirate's Night Adventure cruise, available in both Cancún and Cozumel (phone: 831021). Not to be missed is the *Ballet Folklórico,* which is presented nightly at the *Continental Plaza* hotel; the show includes dinner and drinks. There is a flamenco dinner show at *Gypsy's* (phone: 832015 or 832120) with after-dinner dancing by the pier. A torchlit beach, a delicious buffet, and exotic drinks make for a romantic evening at the *Hyatt*'s Mexican Night, Mondays, Wednesdays, Fridays, and Saturdays at 7 PM; a similar event goes on at the *Sheraton* Wednesdays at 7:30 PM. Another show is held at *Plaza las Glorias* on Tuesdays; for information, call the tourist office (phone: 848073).

On Cozumel, *Scaramouche* (Av. Melgar near R. Salas) is lively and attempts sophistication. The other possibility is *Neptuno* (phone: 21537), next to the *Acuario* restaurant. No matter where you go, it's mostly a young crowd.

On Isla Mujeres, there's *Buho's Disco Bar, Calypso, Tequila Video Disco,* and *Casablanca,* as well as beach parties and night cruises.

Best on the Coast

CHECKING IN

All the hotels on Cancún are relatively new, aspire to be lavish, and boast some of the highest prices along Mexico's Caribbean coast. Travelers on a budget, however, can find less costly accommodations away from the beaches. During high season (December to May), expect to pay $180 to $270 or more per day for a double room in those places we call very expensive; about $110 to $175 in places listed as expensive; $75 to $100 in establishments labeled moderate; $60 or less in those in the inexpensive category. Prices drop as much as 50% during the summer months. There is an additional 15% value added tax on hotel rooms. Cancún's hotel space can't keep up with the demand during the winter, so it is best to go only with a confirmed reservation. Many of the hotels fall within an area along Paseo Kukulcán referred to as the Hotel Zone.

The more luxurious Cozumel hotels are either in the North Zone or South Zone, above and below the town. The in-town hotels (most of which have neither beach nor pool) appeal most to budget travelers. Hotel prices on Cozumel are similar to those in Cancún; it is best to arrive with a confirmed reservation. In general, accommodations on Isla Mujeres are a bit less expensive.

When calling on Cancún, Isla Mujeres, or Cozumel, use only the local numbers listed below; for information about calling from elsewhere, see "Telephone" earlier in this chapter.

NOTE **Parking can be a problem at some hotels.**

MOTELS NO! **There is a very different connotation given to the word *motel* in Mexico. While a Mexican *hotel* is generally comparable to the US version, a *motel* serves one purpose: to rent by the hour. These *auto-hoteles,* as they are also advertised, have curtained garages to ensure the privacy of any "guests" who might not like their license plates seen. Many an unsuspecting tourist has pulled into a *motel* hoping to enjoy a relaxing evening, only to discover that there is no furniture (other than the rather dominant bed), no closet, and no phone in the room.**

CANCÚN AND THE MAINLAND

HOTEL ZONE

VERY EXPENSIVE

Camino Real Located at the northeast tip of Cancún and surrounded on three sides by water, the Westin Hotels' pleasure palace features 2 beaches, an enclosed saltwater swimming lagoon, a pool with swim-up bar, 3 tennis courts, a marked running path, and all the usual water sports. The 381 rooms are in two buildings. The older, main building has a distinctive architecture that was inspired by Maya pyramids. The newer, high-rise *Royal Beach Club,* a luxury hotel-within-a-hotel, has 67 deluxe guest rooms and 18 suites, and features additional services and amenities. All rooms have balconies or terraces with ocean views, and feature a simple Mexican decor. There are 3 restaurants, including *Calypso,* a fancy dinner spot, and the casual open-air *La Brisa* (see *Eating Out* for more on both), and 2 bars, including *Azúcar,* which features Caribbean music. On the northern tip of the island (phone: 830100; 800-228-3000 from the US; fax: 831730).

Continental Villas Plaza Splendid is the only way to describe this 638-suite coral-toned complex that sprawls over 7 blocks of oceanfront. Among the amenities are 7 restaurants, 3 swimming pools, 2 tennis courts, and private Jacuzzis in most rooms. Km 11 on Paseo Kukulcán (phone: 831022 or 851444; 800-88-CONTI from the US; fax: 832270).

Fiesta Americana Each of the 280 rooms has rattan furnishings and a balcony overlooking the water. The pool area is nicely laid out with thatch-roofed, open-air restaurant and bars overlooking the aqua blue bay. Snorkeling gear is available poolside. The fountain-filled lobby is a pretty place for before-dinner cocktails. Km 8, Paseo Kukulcán (phone: 831400; 800-FIESTA-1 from the US; fax: 832502).

Fiesta Americana Condesa A Grand Tourism hotel (Mexico's 5-star rating), it has 3 towers, each with its own atrium lounge covered by a glass, *palapa*-shaped roof. The decor is mostly rattan complemented by fresh, vivid colors. There are 500 rooms (including 27 suites with Jacuzzis on private terraces), a split-level pool with a 66-foot waterfall, 5 restaurants, 3 indoor, air conditioned tennis courts, a jogging track, a spa, and a lobby bar where live music is played in the evenings. The beach, most of which was swept away by Hurricane Gilbert, is finally returning, but it is still small. Km 15, Paseo Kukulcán (phone: 851000; 800-FIESTA-1 from the US; fax: 851800).

Fiesta Americana Coral Beach This 602-suite hotel is comprised of 2 post-modern peach-colored towers. There are several restaurants and bars, a nightclub, a huge pool, 3 lighted tennis courts, and a health club and spa. Km 8.5, Paseo Kukulcán (phone: 832900; 800-FIESTA-1 from the US; fax: 833084).

Hyatt Cancún Caribe A graceful white arc a short walk from the *Convention Center,* this 200-room resort has 39 villas, 4 restaurants, 3 lighted tennis courts, 3 pools, a Jacuzzi, water sports, and an art gallery in the lobby. There are also gardens spread out over 10 acres. Km 8.5, Paseo Kukulcán (phone: 830044; 800-233-1234 from the US; fax: 831514).

Hyatt Regency Beautifully housed under a glass atrium, all 300 rooms have ocean views. There's a pool, 3 bars, and 3 restaurants. On the northern tip of the island (phone: 830966; 800-233-1234 from the US; fax: 831349).

Krystal Cancún Lush and thick, with greenery outside and in, it offers 270 rooms and suites, tennis, and 5 fine restaurants, including a good breakfast buffet. On the northern tip of the island (phone: 831133; 800-213-9860 from the US; fax: 831790).

Marriott Casa Magna A 6-story building of contemporary design, stunningly decorated in Mexican textures and colors. All 452 rooms have balconies and a view of either the Caribbean or the lagoon. There are also 4 restaurants, including a Japanese steakhouse; a nightclub; a pool; a Jacuzzi; and 2 lighted tennis courts. Paseo Kukulcán (phone: 852000; 800-228-9290 from the US; fax: 851731).

Meliá Cancún A marble and glass extravaganza, with a waterfall that cascades over the entrance and a huge central atrium that looks and feels like a tropical jungle. Beautifully decorated with bright tiles, and bentwood and wicker furniture. There are 450 rooms and suites, 4 restaurants, 5 bars, 3 tennis courts, and an 18-hole golf course. Km 15, Paseo Kukulcán (phone: 851114; 800-336-3542 from the US; fax: 851260).

Oasis Built in the tradition of an ancient Maya city, this 1,000-room complex of angled structures offers 7 restaurants, 9 bars, satellite TV, and the longest swimming pool (nearly a third of a mile) in the Caribbean, plus 4 tennis courts, and a 9-hole golf course. It is far from town, though; unless you plan *never* to leave the hotel grounds or the huge beach, transportation may be a problem. Km 47, Paseo Kukulcán (phone: 850867; 800-44-OASIS from the US; fax: 833486).

Radisson Sierra Plaza The 261 air conditioned rooms are elegantly decorated with a Southwestern flair. The oceanfront property features 2 restaurants, 3 lounges, 2 snack bars, an outdoor pool, a fitness center, 2 tennis courts, and plenty of water sports. Paseo Kukulcán (phone: 832444; 800-333-3333 from the US; fax: 833486).

Ritz-Carlton Cancún This brand-new, super-luxurious resort features 370 guest-rooms (including 54 suites), all with private seaview balconies, mini-bars, 2 bathrooms, and remote-control TV sets. On the premises are a health club, 2 pools, 3 lighted tennis courts, and 3 restaurants. 36 Retorno del Rey, in the Hotel Zone (phone: 851212; 305-446-0776 from Florida; 800-241-3333 from elsewhere in the US).

Stouffer Presidente On the golf links and boasting 1 tennis court, fishing, and water skiing, this stately, 295-room hostelry is a favorite of sports enthusiasts. Its beach and location are among the best on Cancún. Km 7, Paseo Kukulcán (phone: 830200, 830202, or 830414; 800-HOTELS-1 from the US; fax: 832515).

Villas Tacul A colony of 23 Spanish-style 2- to 5-bedroom villas with gardens, patios, and kitchens. Guests can set up luxurious housekeeping, eat out at the *palapa,* cook for themselves, arrange for someone to come in — or combine all of the above. There's a narrow but pleasant beach. Good for families and congenial two- or three-couple groups. Km 5.5, Paseo Kukulcán (phone: 830000; 800-842-0193 from the US; fax: 830349).

EXPENSIVE

Calinda Beach Cancún Located on the best beach on the island, between the Nichupté Lagoon and Bahía Mujeres, this popular property isn't as lavish as many of the others hereabouts, but it's the kind of place people return to year after year. All 460 guestrooms have great views of the ocean; facilities include a restaurant, bars, pool, tennis, and gym. Km 4, Paseo Kukulcán (phone: 831600; 800-228-5151 from the US; fax: 831857).

Casa Maya Originally built as condominiums, the 350 rooms and suites here are large, with immense walk-in closets, sinks the size of bathtubs, and tubs the size of swimming pools. Among the pluses are moped rentals, 2 lighted tennis courts, a swimming pool, a restaurant, and cordial service. The place is especially popular with families. Km 5, Paseo Kukulcán (phone: 830555; 800-44-UTELL from the US; fax: 831188).

Club Med With one of the widest beaches on the island, it's among the best places to stay in all of Cancún. The 410 rooms, each with 2 wide single beds and traditional Mexican decor, are in 3-story bungalows facing either the ocean or the lagoon. Windsurfing, sailing, snorkeling, scuba diving and instruction are included in the rates, as are all meals. There's nightly entertainment. At Punta Nizuc, at the southern end of the island (phone: 842090; 800-CLUB-MED from the US).

Meliá Turquesa A giant white pyramid that slopes down to the beach, this property has 446 rooms decorated in soft colors and equipped with satellite TV, mini-bars, and safe deposit boxes. There are several restaurants and bars, tennis courts, and a pool that seems to float over the sea. Km 12, Paseo Kukulcán (phone: 832544; 800-336-3542 from the US; fax: 851241).

Omni Here are 334 rooms, each with a large terrace, as well as 35 suites and 27 villas. Facilities include 2 lighted tennis courts, 8 restaurants, bars, a gameroom, and a health center. The beach was all but washed away by Hurricane Gilbert, but there are hammocks strung up on the grounds for lounging and sipping tropical drinks by the sea. Four of the rooms are equipped for disabled guests, and there are access ramps to all public areas. Km 16.5, Paseo Kukulcán (phone: 850714; 800-THE-OMNI from the US; fax: 850184).

Royal Solaris A Maya pyramid-like structure, it has 280 rooms (including 13 suites), an Olympic-size pool, a pleasant beach, a health club, and social programs. Km 23, Paseo Kukulcán (phone: 850100; 800-368-9779 from the US; fax: 850354).

Sheraton This 748-room property — self-contained and as big as a village — is set apart on its own beach, which it shares with a small Maya temple. Facilities include 6 tennis courts, 6 pools, and *Daphny's* bar with live music; there are also aerobics classes and scuba lessons. Km 12.5, Paseo Kukulcán (phone: 831988; 800-325-3535 from the US; fax: 850202).

Westin Regina Formerly the *Conrad,* this resort complex has 385 units, including 12 deluxe rooms and 4 one- or two-bedroom suites in a 6-story building, and a presidential suite in a separate tower. All rooms view the ocean or lagoon, and many have balconies. Facilities include 5 outdoor pools, 2 lighted tennis courts, 6 whirlpools, a health club/recreation center, and a water sports center; a dock provides access to scuba diving, snorkeling, boating, evening cruises, and water skiing. There are 2 restaurants, a bar, and a lobby lounge. Baby-sitting service is available. Km 20, Paseo Kukulcán, at Punta Nizuc at the southern end of the island (phone: 850086 or 850537; 800-228-3000 from the US; fax: 850074).

MODERATE

Aristos The friendly scale and Mexican hospitality make for easy comfort here. Features 244 smallish but pleasant rooms, an inviting pool area, a beach, 2 lighted tennis courts, and a restaurant. Km 9.5, Paseo Kukulcán (phone: 830011; 800-5-ARISTO from the US; fax: 830078).

Club Lagoon This secluded collection of adobe-type dwellings on quiet Laguna Nichupté is a real find. There are 89 rooms and 2-level suites; one picturesque courtyard opens onto another, with flowers playing colorfully against the white cottages. The best units face the lagoon. It also has 2 restaurants, 2 bars, and a nautical center. Km 5.5, Paseo Kukulcán (phone: 831111; 800-388-8354 from the US; fax: 831808).

Fiesta Inn Golf Cancún Located at the edge of the *Pok-Ta-Pok* golf course, its 120 rooms are decorated in quiet pastel shades. Guests get a 50% discount on greens fees, and may use the facilities and services at other local Fiesta hotels. Free transportation is provided to the hotel's beach club. Paseo Kukulcán (phone: 832200; 800-FIESTA-1 from the US; fax: 832532).

Playa Blanca A pioneer among the Cancún hotels, it opened in 1974 on a small beachfront and is now part of the Best Western chain. It has 161 rooms, a pool, and every water sport imaginable. Since it's next door to the marina, the boating facilities are excellent. Km 3, Paseo Kukulcán (phone: 830344; 800-528-1234 from the US; fax: 830904).

CANCÚN CITY

MODERATE

America There are 180 large rooms, each with its own terrace, at this pleasant place. Though not right on the beach, it does provide free shuttle service to its own beach club. There's also a pool, a restaurant, a bar, and a coffee shop. Av. Tulum (phone: 847500; fax: 841953).

INEXPENSIVE

Plaza Caribe A good budget bet downtown, across from the bus station. The 140 air conditioned rooms fill up fast (phone: 841377; 800-334-7234 from the US; fax: 846352).

Plaza del Sol Half-moon-shaped, with two stylized canoes over its portals, it has 87 rooms, a pool, a restaurant, a bar, and free transportation to the beach (phone: 843888; fax: 844393).

ELSEWHERE ON THE MAINLAND

EXPENSIVE

Chemuyil This charming place on a stunning beach has 10 suites with kitchenettes, a few guestrooms, and 12 double or family-size tents with maid service for those who want to rough it in style. Showers and restrooms are nearby. In Chemuyil, about 6 miles (10 km) south of Akumal and 65 miles (104 km) south of Cancún. For reservations, write well in advance to Don Lalo Román Chemoir, Fidecomiso Xel-Ha, Tulum, QR, Mexico (no phone).

Oasis Club de Playa Part of the beautiful new Puerto Aventuras resort area, located 54 miles (86 km) south of Cancún, this beachfront property has 36 rooms, a restaurant, a bar, a spa, and a *PADI* dive center. Puerto Aventuras (phone: 987-23376 or 987-2387).

Oasis Marina Mar Another Puerto Aventuras resort, this establishment has 309 rooms, all with kitchenettes. Located next to the marina, it has a pool and a restaurant. Puerto Aventuras (phone: 987-23376 or 987-2387).

La Posada del Capitán Lafitte Located in Punta Beté, about 21 miles (38 km) south of Cancún Airport, this beachfront bungalow complex features reefs just 100 yards offshore. Reservations may be made through *Turquoise Reef Resorts,* Box 2664, Evergreen, CO 80439 (phone: 800-538-6802 from the US).

COZUMEL

VERY EXPENSIVE

Club Cozumel Caribe A twisting, palm-canopied drive leads to this expansive 260-room property with attractive grounds. It offers tennis, a small pool, and a restaurant. Rate includes all meals, drinks, water sports, sightseeing, and a moonlight cruise. San Juan Beach (phone: 20100; 800-327-2254 from the US).

EXPENSIVE

Coral Princess Club One of the newest additions to Cozumel's hotel scene, this posh establishment has 70 units with kitchenettes and private terraces, a pool, a restaurant, and a bar. On the north end of the island (phone: 23200 or 23323; 800-272-3243 from the US; fax: 20016).

El Cozumeleño This property has 80 large rooms, 3 restaurants, a bar, a tennis court, and a free-form pool. Santa Pilar Beach (phone: 20050; 800-437-3923 from the US; fax: 20381).

Fiesta Americana Sol Caribe A beautiful 322-room resort (102 rooms are in a new tower) 'twixt beach and jungle, it has 3 tennis courts, good diving facilities, and a fine dining room. South Zone (phone: 20466; 800-FIESTA-1 from the US; fax: 21301).

Holiday Inn Cozumel Reef This 165-room hotel is located 4½ miles (7 km) south of San Miguel. There are 3 restaurants, a coffee shop, 2 bars, a spa, a variety of water sports, 2 lighted tennis courts, a dock, and a gym. Km 7.5 on Carr. Chankanab (phone: 22622; 800-HOLIDAY from the US; fax: 22666).

Meliá Mayan Cozumel Set on the isolated north end of the coast, this 12-story high-rise on the beach has 200 rooms and suites, an abundance of terraces, 2 tennis courts, a restaurant, a Fiesta Mexicana on Thursdays, and a Caribbean Fiesta on Fridays. Playa Santa Pilar (phone: 20411; 800-336-3542 from the US; fax: 21599).

Plaza Las Glorias Set on the southern end of San Miguel, this 170-room complex offers king-size beds, satellite TV, and mini-refrigerators in each room. There is also a private marina, 2 restaurants, 2 bars, a scuba diving school, a pool, and facilities for the disabled. South Zone (phone: 22000; 800-342-AMIGO from the US; fax: 21937).

Stouffer Presidente Cozumel The original upscale establishment on the island and still one of the best. There are 253 rooms, a pleasant beach, a nice pool, tennis, and an excellent dining room. South Zone (phone: 20322; 800-HOTELS-1 from the US; fax: 21360).

MODERATE

La Ceiba The best equipped and located establishment for scuba divers, this 115-room hostelry has satellite TV, a spa, tennis, a restaurant, and a cocktail lounge. Paradise Point (phone: 20844; 800-777-5873 from the US; fax: 20065).

Fiesta Inn A 3-story, colonial-style hostelry surrounded by beautiful gardens and connected to the beach by a tunnel. Its 178 rooms and 2 suites have satellite TV, and there's a large pool, tennis court, motorcycle rental, dive shop, restaurant, bar, and coffee shop. Km 1.7 Costera Sur (phone: 22899; 800-FIESTA-1 from the US; fax: 22154).

Mara Most of the 48 rooms face the lovely beach. Facilities include a pleasant pool, restaurant, and dive shop. North Zone (phone: 20300; 800-221-6509 from the US; fax: 20105).

La Perla Quiet, comfortable, and right on the beach, this 4-story, 22-room hotel has its own swimming cove and a pier for private yachts. There's also a pool and deli-bar; dive packages are available. 2 Av. Francisco I. Madero (phone: 20188; 800-852-6404 from the US; fax: 22611).

Playa Azul A family favorite, it has 60 rooms and suites, a restaurant, a bar, and water sports facilities. North of San Miguel, at Km 4 on Carr. San Juan (phone: 20033; 800-528-1234 from the US; fax: 20110).

Sol Cabañas del Caribe This friendly, informal semitropical hideaway is on one of the island's best beaches. It has 50 rooms, 9 cabañas, and a small pool. North Zone (phone: 20017 or 20072; 800-336-3542 from the US; fax: 21599).

INEXPENSIVE

Villablanca Though its facilities resemble those of a large resort hotel — tennis court, pool, dive shop, boat for up to 60 divers, classes in all water sports — this property has only 50 rooms and suites, some with Jacuzzis and all with air conditioning and fans. Across the street, on the water's edge, is its restaurant-bar-beach club, *Amadeus.* Km 2.9 on Playa Paraíso (phone: 20730 or 20865; 800-780-3949 from the US; fax: 20865).

ISLA MUJERES

EXPENSIVE

Cristalmar Tucked away on the coast facing the mainland, this new 38-suite hotel has 1-, 2-, and 3-bedroom studios with kitchenettes and air conditioning. Other amenities include a pool, a restaurant and bar, and an on-premises dive shop. Lote 16, Fraccionamiento Paraíso Laguna (phone: 800-441-0472 from the US; no local phone at press time).

MODERATE

Costa Club A budget-conscious *Club Med,* this all-inclusive resort has 100 rooms plus 63 villas. Well equipped for family-style fun, it offers water sports and games for kids. There's a nice beach with huge *palapa* canopies for lazing in the sun. At the far end of the North Beach (phone: 70015; 800-969-3222 from the US; fax: 70187).

INEXPENSIVE

Cabañas María del Mar Forty-eight units (including 10 cabañas) in front of *El Presidente* hotel, with a restaurant and a full-service 20-slip marina. The proprietors make everyone feel at home. Av. Carlos Lazo (phone: 70179; fax: 70156).

Posada del Mar One of the best hotels on the island, and one of the best values as well. There are 42 pleasant, air conditioned rooms, palm-shaded grounds, a restaurant, a bar, a pool, and a laundromat. Across from the beach. 15 Av. Rueda Medina (phone: 70300 or 70044; 800-451-8891 from the US; fax: 70266).

Roca Mar Thirty-four basic but pleasant rooms, all with a view. Av. Nicolás Bravo y Guerrero (phone: 70101).

EATING OUT

Hotel food in Cancún is better than average because the hoteliers want to keep the money spent on food in the house; this means that the non-hotel restaurants must work extra hard to lure customers. Be sure to try Yucatecan specialties, which are quite different from standard Mexican fare. Start the day with eggs *moltuleños* — fried eggs on a tortilla — black beans, and a spicy sauce. Don't miss delicious and filling Yucatecan lime soup, which also contains chicken, vegetables, and tortillas. All restaurants listed below accept MasterCard and Visa; a few also accept American Express and/or Diners Club. Expect to pay $40 to $60 for two at restaurants we describe as expensive, about $30 at places in the moderate category, and under $25 at spots listed as inexpensive. Prices do not include wine, tips, or drinks. Note that there is a 15% tax on restaurant meals; calculate the tip on the bill before tax.

Almost all the restaurants on Cozumel are in town, although a few, open only for lunch, are out on the beaches. Restaurant prices here, as well as on Isla Mujeres, are more moderate than those on Cancún. When calling among the three islands, use only the local numbers listed below; for information when dialing from elsewhere, see "Telephone" in this chapter.

CANCÚN AND THE MAINLAND

HOTEL ZONE

EXPENSIVE

Augustus Caesar Seafood and traditional Italian dishes are served with flair in ultramodern surroundings. Live music is featured from 8:30 PM to midnight. No shorts or T-shirts. Open daily for lunch and dinner. Reservations advised. At *La Mansion–Costa Blanca* shopping center (phone: 833384).

Blue Bayou Cajun and creole fare and specialty drinks are served in a multilevel suspended dining area amid waterfalls and lush tropical greenery. Live jazz nightly. Open daily for dinner. Reservations necessary. In the *Hyatt Cancún Caribe* hotel (phone: 830044, ext. 54).

Bogart's International dishes are served with quiet elegance in exotic Moroccan surroundings. No shorts or T-shirts. Seatings at 7 and 9:30 PM daily. Reservations advised. At the *Krystal* hotel (phone: 831133).

Calypso The decor here mixes elegance with tropical exuberance. The color scheme echoes that of the scene outside — the soft white of the sand and the brilliant turquoise of the sea. Fountains and pools enhance the seaside ambience. The menu features Caribbean fare, with a strong emphasis on seafood — try the braided fish (snapper and salmon) with lobster medallions and scallion sauce. There's live reggae music nightly. Open daily for dinner. Reservations advised. At the *Camino Real* hotel (phone: 830100, ext. 8060).

Grimond's Formerly *Maxime,* this elegant dining place set in what used to be the mayor's home has European furniture, Oriental rugs, English china, and French crystal — not to mention 4 sitting rooms, 1 dining room, and an upstairs piano bar. The French chef recommends the shrimp sautéed in cherry-wine sauce. Jackets are not required, but shorts and sandals are not permitted. Open daily for dinner only. Reservations advised (phone: 830438).

Gypsy's A touch of Spain in the Mexican Caribbean, this rustic-looking eatery specializes in Iberian cooking (the paella is exceptional). Flamenco dancers entertain nightly. Open daily for dinner only. No reservations. On the Nichupté Lagoon, across from the *Villas Plaza* hotel (phone: 832015 or 832120).

Hacienda el Mortero An authentic copy of a hacienda in Súchil, Durango, it specializes in steaks and Mexican haute cuisine. Open daily for dinner. Reservations advised. In the *Krystal* hotel (phone: 831133).

Iguana Wana This trendy spot — which bills itself as "a contemporary Mexican café and bar" — offers live jazz and a varied menu including Tex-Mex chili and buckets of peel-your-own shrimp. Open daily for lunch and dinner. No reservations. *Plaza Caracol* shopping center (phone: 830829).

Jaguari's This is the place to sink your teeth into a thick, juicy steak. Run by a Brazilian, it offers premium beef cuts served with a South American *churrasquería* sauce. Open daily for dinner. Reservations advised. Gaviota Azul Beach on the island (phone: 832939).

Lorenzillo's Named after a French pirate who came to Mexico in 1683, this outdoor eatery specializes in seafood dishes such as soft-shell shrimp and lobster. Overhead, a giant *palapa* extends over Nichupte Lagoon. Jackets are not required, but shorts and T-shirts are not allowed. Open daily for lunch and dinner. Reservations unnecessary. Paseo Kukulcán (phone: 831254).

Scampi Superb northern Italian fare — delicious pasta, meat, and seafood — is featured at this beautiful dining spot. Open daily. Reservations advised. At the *Hyatt Regency* hotel (phone: 830966).

Seryna This pretty place offers Japanese specialties such as sushi, teppanyaki, sukiyaki, shabu-shabu, and tempura. Open daily for lunch and dinner. Reservations advised. At the *Plaza Flamingo* shopping center (phone: 851155 or 832995).

MODERATE

Bombay Bicycle Club Casual and comfortable, the menu is strictly US-style fare — good hamburgers, barbecued ribs, and calorie-filled desserts. Excellent, friendly service. Open daily for lunch and dinner. No reservations. Paseo Kukulcán, across from Playa Tortuga (no phone).

La Brisa This casual, open-air eatery features a well-stocked salad bar and specializes in grilled seafood (the red snapper is quite good) and steaks. Be sure to save room for dessert — the coconut mousse is luscious. Open daily for breakfast, lunch, and dinner. Reservations advised for dinner. At the *Camino Real* hotel (phone: 830100).

Johnny Rocket's Rock 'n' roll with a 1950s theme is the draw of this hamburger eatery–video bar. The music is hot, and the food even hotter. Definitely not a place for easy listening. Open daily for lunch and dinner. No reservations. *Plaza Terramar Shopping Center* (phone: 833092).

INEXPENSIVE

100% Natural The menu consists of fresh fruit drinks, salads, sandwiches, and fruit and vegetable platters; there's live jazz music nightly. No reservations. At the *Plaza Terramar Shopping Center* (phone: 831180); also at 6 Av. Sunyaxchen, Cancún City (phone: 843617).

CANCÚN CITY

EXPENSIVE

La Dolce Vita Modern decor is the backdrop to intimate dining at this spot, where the sweet life is manifested in tasty pasta and seafood dishes. Locals consider this one of the best places in town. Open daily for dinner only. Reservations advised. 87 Av. Cobá (phone: 841384).

La Habichuela The place locals go for a night out and for *mar y tierra* (surf and turf) in a Maya garden replete with ruins. Open daily for lunch and dinner. Reservations advised. 25 Margaritas (phone: 843158).

El Pescador Perhaps the best seafood eatery in Cancún, it serves fresh lobster, shrimp, and red snapper on Mexican pottery. Don't miss the Yucatecan lime soup or the hot rolls; try for a table outside, on the fan-cooled terrace. Open for lunch and dinner; closed Mondays. Reservations unnecessary. 5 Tulipanes (phone: 842673).

MODERATE

Pizza Rolandi All kinds of Italian dishes are served in an informal, outdoor setting. Open daily for lunch and dinner. Reservations unnecessary. 12 Av. Cobá (phone: 844047).

Torremolinos Paella, crayfish, and crab done the Spanish way. Open daily for lunch and dinner. No reservations. Tulum and Xcaret Aves. (phone: 843639).

INEXPENSIVE

Los Alemendros Authentic Yucatecan food and the same management as its famous Mérida namesake. Open daily for lunch and dinner. Reservations unnecessary. Av. Bonampak and Sayíl (phone: 840807).

Café Amsterdam Reasonably priced European dishes are served in this intimate bistro. The delicious bread is baked on the premises, and there is a huge salad and fresh fruit bar. Open daily for lunch and dinner; closed Mondays. Reservations unnecessary. 70 Av. Yaxchilán (phone: 844098).

COZUMEL

EXPENSIVE

Acuario Once an aquarium, it's now an elegant seafood restaurant, with entertainment provided by an immense tankful of exotic tropical fish in the middle of the room. Open daily for dinner. Reservations advised. On the *malecón,* San Miguel (phone: 21097).

Donatello A premier Italian dining place with a New Orleans French Quarter ambience, it serves superb fresh pasta and offers a beautiful ocean view. Open daily for dinner only. Reservations advised. 131 Av. Melgar Sur, San Miguel (phone: 22586 or 20090).

Morgan's Lobster and special coffees are favorites at this very comfortable, popular wood cabin serving good steaks and seafood. Open daily for lunch and dinner. Reservations advised. On the main plaza, San Miguel (phone: 20584).

Pepe's Grill This romantic spot by the waterfront serves excellent seafood and steaks. Live music nightly. Open daily for lunch and dinner. Reservations advised. Av. Rafael Melgar, San Miguel (phone: 20213).

MODERATE

Casa Denis An ever-changing variety of Yucatecan dishes are served under a mamey tree in a courtyard. Open daily for lunch and dinner. Reservations unnecessary. On the main plaza, San Miguel (phone: 20067).

Mezcalito's Set on the surf-pounded Caribbean side of Cozumel, this large open-air *palapa* serves up some of the tastiest shrimp and fish on the island. The atmosphere — white sand, ocean breezes, and friendly chatter — is unbeatable. A good spot just to stop for a cold beer or a piña colada. Open daily for lunch and dinner. No reservations. Punta Morena (no phone).

Las Palmeras Opposite the ferry dock, it's a great meeting place offering a varied menu for every meal. The homemade biscuits and French toast are a great way to start the day. Open daily for breakfast, lunch, and dinner. Reservations unnecessary. On the *malecón,* San Miguel (phone: 20532).

Pancho's Backyard A delightful place with modern Mexican decor, this popular spot is housed in a gracious old building. The classical Mexican fare is served on hand-crafted ceramic pottery. Strolling mariachis give this place a certain *sabor mexicano.* Open for breakfast, lunch, and dinner; dinner only on Saturdays; closed Sundays. Reservations advised in season. On the *malecón* and Calle 8, San Miguel (phone: 22142).

Plaza Leza A sidewalk café serving good Mexican snacks, charcoal-broiled steaks, and seafood. Open daily for lunch and dinner. Reservations advised. On the main plaza, San Miguel (phone: 21041).

INEXPENSIVE

San Francisco The fare is — what else? — seafood, and a band plays in the afternoons. Open daily for lunch only. Reservations unnecessary. Located a quarter of a mile from San Francisco beach and about 9 miles from town (no phone).

Sports Page If you can't survive without the *Super Bowl* or the *World Series,* stop in and watch the games on TV while munching on a burger and fries. Open daily for lunch and dinner. No reservations. Av. 5, San Miguel (no phone).

ISLA MUJERES

EXPENSIVE

Ciro's Lobster House A wide selection of Mexican wines accompanies the lobster and red snapper served here. Open daily for lunch and dinner. Reservations advised. 11 Matamoros (phone: 70102).

MODERATE

Gomar Lobster and fresh fish are best enjoyed on the romantic terrace, where tables sport bright red Mexican cloths at night; white during the day. You can also dine indoors. Upstairs, the *Sombrero de Gomar* serves steaks and hamburgers. Open daily for lunch and dinner. Reservations unnecessary. Hidalgo and Madero (phone: 70142).

Hacienda Gomar Known for its good seafood buffet and exotic drinks. Open daily for lunch and dinner. No reservations. On the west side of the island on the road to El Garrafón (no phone).

Los Pájaros A *palapa*-style eatery at the north end of town, facing the island's best beach. Open daily for lunch and dinner. Reservations unnecessary. At the *Posada del Mar* hotel (phone: 70044).

INEXPENSIVE

Buho's Paradise Great for late snacks. Open daily. Reservations unnecessary. Next to *Cabañas María del Mar,* Av. Carlos Lazo (phone: 70179).

Pizza Rolandi Pizza cooked in a wood-burning oven and other Italian dishes. Open daily. Reservations unnecessary. Hidalgo between Madero and Abasolo (phone: 70430).

MOBILE FOOD STANDS

One international public health specialist we know refers to these movable feasts as "epidemics on wheels." Food at these less-than-sanitary open-air stands is usually left unrefrigerated for long periods of time and exposed to the street soot, gasoline fumes, and heat. Do yourself and your health insurance company a favor and eat only in clean, good-quality restaurants, or at your hotel.

Montserrat

There may not be leprechauns on this verdant, idyllic island, but there is a feeling of Irish magic. The Irish who settled on Montserrat in the early 1600s nicknamed it the Emerald Isle because of the greenery that grew beyond its gray and black volcanic beaches.

The tiny island, which sits between Antigua and Guadeloupe in the Leeward Islands, was initially sighted by Columbus during his second visit to the Caribbean. It was later settled by the British, held on two occasions by the French (after bitter fighting), used as a deportation colony by the British, and finally became a British Crown Colony. Named by Columbus for the quiet hills surrounding the Abbey of Montserrat in Spain, this serene haven — the epitome of peace today — knew little tranquillity for almost 250 years.

The British decision to settle Montserrat was based primarily on their occupation of neighboring St. Kitts and Nevis. About 20 years after the initial English settlement, a large contingent of Irish were sent to the island; whether these people had been deported directly from Ireland as a result of their involvement in the rebellions suppressed by Oliver Cromwell or whether they left (or were forced to leave) St. Kitts is an unresolved historical question. The island's Irish heritage is reflected in the number of red-haired islanders who even have a hint of brogue. Nevertheless, this is one of the most West Indian of all the Caribbean islands, intensely uncommercial and very proud of its culture and customs.

Shortly after the Irish settled Montserrat, the French became interested in the island. In 1664 the British governor ordered a new fort to be built. It was considered impregnable because of its position on a steep hill, yet was taken a year later by a French and Carib force. After 4 years, the island again came under British control. Then, in 1783, the French took Montserrat again. It was returned to Britain by treaty shortly after the American Revolution, and it has remained British ever since.

Both the British and the Irish worked to make Montserrat into a farm and plantation island. Slaves were imported to develop sugar and lime plantations, and crops of potatoes, tomatoes, and other vegetables were planted. But however perfect for semitropical wild growth, the terrain was simply too rugged for the kind of agriculture planned by the colonists.

The island remained an undisputed English possession for the next 100 years, but its plantations never did turn the island into the boomtown and trading port the British had envisioned. The limes and sugar produced attracted only the occasional trading vessel, and the Sea Island cotton was unable to compete with other fiber sources. With the abolition of slavery in the mid-1800s, profitable agriculture was finished on the island for good.

Since that time, Montserrat has been more or less dependent on Britain

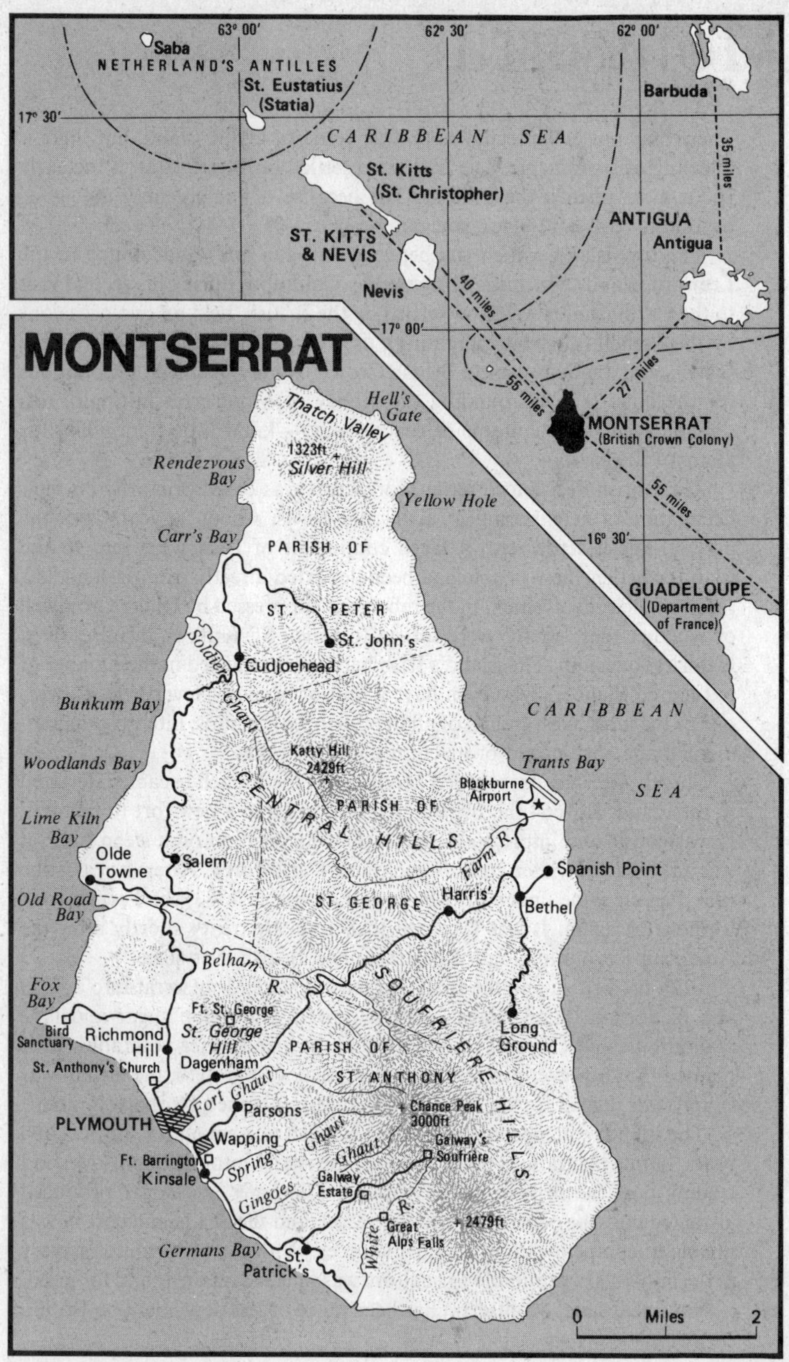
MONTSERRAT
Saba
NETHERLAND'S ANTILLES
St. Eustatius
(Statia)
CARIBBEAN SEA
St. Kitts
(St. Christopher)
ST. KITTS
& NEVIS
Nevis
Barbuda
ANTIGUA
Antigua
35 miles
40 miles
55 miles
27 miles
55 miles
MONTSERRAT
(British Crown Colony)
GUADELOUPE
(Department
of France)
63° 00′
62° 30′
62° 00′
17° 30′
17° 00′
16° 30′
Hell's Gate
Thatch Valley
1323ft
Silver Hill
Rendezvous Bay
Yellow Hole
Carr's Bay
PARISH OF
ST. PETER
St. John's
Cudjoehead
Soldier Ghaut
Bunkum Bay
Woodlands Bay
Katty Hill
2429ft
CENTRAL HILLS
PARISH OF
ST. GEORGE
CARIBBEAN
SEA
Trants Bay
Blackburne
Airport
Farm R.
Lime Kiln
Bay
Olde
Towne
Salem
Old Road
Bay
Spanish Point
Harris'
Bethel
Belham
R.
SOUFRIERE HILLS
Fox
Bay
Bird
Sanctuary
Richmond
Hill
Ft. St. George
St. George
Hill
Long
Ground
St. Anthony's Church
Dagenham
PARISH OF
ST. ANTHONY
PLYMOUTH
Fort Ghaut
Parsons
Chance Peak
3000ft
Wapping
Ft. Barrington
Kinsale
Spring
Ghaut
Ghaut
Galway's
Soufrière
Gingoes
Galway
Estate
White R.
Great
Alps Falls
2479ft
Germans Bay
St.
Patrick's
0
Miles
2

for its economic livelihood. Though it produces enough fruit and vegetables for its own needs — and even exports bumper crops like tomatoes — the island essentially remains undeveloped. Offered associate statehood by the British in 1966, Montserrat chose to remain a Crown Colony.

In recent years, tourists began to discover this tiny isle. Montserrat's mystique was enhanced by Air Studios, a state-of-the-art recording studio built in the lush northern hills. For several years, Stevie Wonder, Paul McCartney, Sting, Elton John, and other artists came to Montserrat to cut albums and to relax in the tranquil beauty. As word spread, the hills were soon literally alive with music. Unfortunately, Hurricane Hugo pulled the plug in 1989. Air Studios suffered major damage and is still up for sale.

Today, Montserrat offers visitors luxury villas, several first class hotels and restaurants, and a welcoming atmosphere. And a new $30 million seaport is being built in the town of Plymouth so that cruise ships may once again dock here. Montserrat is unhurried, uncommercialized, and for the most part, undiscovered. But then, peace and privacy are a large part of this island hideaway's appeal.

Montserrat At-a-Glance

FROM THE AIR

Montserrat is a pear-shaped island about 27 miles southwest of Antigua, and 275 miles southeast of Puerto Rico. Only about 11 miles long and 7 miles across at its widest point, almost a third of its 39 square miles is either virgin forest or unsuitable for any agricultural purpose. Half of what is left is devoted to tree crops or is otherwise cultivated. The remainder is developed or urban land. The island is volcanic, and active sulfur vents may be found in the mountain region. It is renowned for its black sand beaches and thick tropical vegetation. The majestic Chance Peak, the tallest point on the island, rises 3,002 feet above sea level.

SPECIAL PLACES

PLYMOUTH This colorful, charming port is marvelously West Indian in flavor, although a touch of the British influence remains. It's an easy town to explore on foot, but dress properly; residents here don't appreciate bathing suits or other such ultra-informal dress. A small town of 3,500 people, Plymouth stretches along the Caribbean without a real harbor — there's just a jetty to serve as a tie-up place for visiting yachtsmen. The streets are quiet and clean; the entire town is very proper, neat, and serene. Touring Plymouth takes about an hour and a half, and it's best to start with Government House (on Peebles St.). This delightful Victorian structure, with its well-maintained lawns and gardens of flowering poincianas, evokes the illusion that 18th-century Britain still exists. The gardens are open from 10 AM to noon weekdays except Wednesdays. Signing the visitors' book is a must. In honor of the Irish who settled and cultivated the island, the building is decorated with a shamrock.

Fridays and Saturdays are market days, and starting early on those mornings rural islanders bring their produce into Plymouth and city merchants prepare for a big day of shopping. Vegetables, fruit, fresh fish, and tidbits of gossip are rapidly exchanged, and villagers and farmers discuss island politics, the weather, and prices in an age-old island ritual.

While in town, ask directions to the Philatelic Bureau (phone: 2996), 1 block from Government House, where there are displays of current and past stamp issues, prized by collectors and souvenir seekers alike.

Also of interest is St. Anthony's Church, on Church Street just a few steps north of Government House toward the outskirts of town. Originally constructed in 1636, the church was destroyed and rebuilt five times. Displayed inside the church are two silver chalices, gifts from emancipated slaves. On Richmond Hill, the tiny *Montserrat Museum,* ensconced in an antique sugar mill, displays a collection of artifacts, some of which date back to Carib and Arawak times. It's open Sundays and Wednesdays from 2:30 to 5 PM and at other times for special groups (phone: 5443).

On another hill, about 1,200 feet above the town, is the old fort. Never named, it was built in 1664 under the orders of Governor Anthony Briskett, Jr. He considered it impregnable, but the French overran it a year later.

Fort Barrington, on the cliff above the banana pier, was built in the 18th century but saw little action. Fort St. George, in the hills overlooking Plymouth, about a 15-minute drive from town, was thrown together in 1782 as a defense against an oncoming force of French and Carib invaders. These forts did not prevent the French from taking the island a second time.

ELSEWHERE ON THE ISLAND

CHANCE PEAK The tallest point on Montserrat offers an incredible panorama. There are two ways to get to the top. The easiest route is to climb the 2,003 steps built into the side of the mountain (bring a canteen and wear sneakers or sturdy shoes). The other option is to hike up the mountain itself, which can be difficult and hazardous without a guide, so arrange for one at any hotel before setting out. The mountain is in the southern section of the island.

FOXES BAY BIRD SANCTUARY Fifteen acres of mangrove swamp at Bransby Point on the northwest side of the island have been turned into a preserve for nesting colonies of Caribbean coots, green herons, the rare little blue herons, ringed kingfishers, and numerous other avian species. There are no organized tours, but marked trails lead to the circular pond.

GALWAY'S PLANTATION On the way south to Galway's Soufrière, this historic sugar plantation is the site of picturesque ruins and annual summer archaeological digs.

GALWAY'S SOUFRIÈRE In the south-central region of Montserrat, this small (about 4 feet across), open crater bubbling with grayish-yellow molten sulfur is a vivid reminder that the volcano beneath the island's surface still lives. In addition to giving off sulfur fumes, this crater also allows experts to monitor volcanic activity under the island.

GREAT ALPS WATERFALL At the end of a healthy 1-mile hike (which takes about 45 minutes) through dense rain forest, this small waterfall drops 70 feet into a pool of clear water just deep enough to splash (but not swim) in. It's best to hike in the cool morning air; be sure to wear sturdy shoes. The roadway from which to start is about a 15-minute drive south of Plymouth. At noon, the overhead sun turns the mist over the pool into rainbows.

MONTSERRAT SPRINGS THERMAL BATHS The *Montserrat Springs* hotel has tapped into an underground molten sulfur rivulet flowing from Galway's Soufrière to create baths purported to have therapeutic properties. Guests of the hotel can use the baths for free; non-guests pay $4. The hotel is in Richmond Hill, north of Plymouth (see *Checking In*).

RENDEZVOUS BEACH On the far northwest coast is the island's only white sand strand, a popular swimming, sunning, and picnic destination. The easiest way to get there is by boat; otherwise it's a half hour hike over the hills from Little Bay.

RUNAWAY GHAUT In 1712, this *ghaut* (the Indian word for "river" or "ravine") in the hills near the north end of the island was the site of a valiant effort by an English captain and the few men under his command to hold off French invaders while the unprepared island forces gathered themselves.

Sources and Resources

TOURIST INFORMATION

There's a small tourist office in Plymouth (Church Rd.; phone: 2230). Since it's a friendly town, don't hesitate to ask questions of passersby. You also might contact *Best Foot Forward,* a free local tourist assistance program run in conjunction with *Caribbean Connection Plus,* the booking agent for the island. Ask for Miss Daley; she runs the program and will be glad to answer any questions (phone: 5872). For information about Montserrat tourist offices in the US, see GETTING READY TO GO.

LOCAL COVERAGE Maps and guides are periodically available through the tourist office in Plymouth. The *Montserrat Reporter* and *Montserrat News* are the island's weekly newspapers.

RADIO AND TELEVISION

There are radio broadcasts in English, as well as some English-language television programs.

TELEPHONE

When calling from the US, dial 809 (area code) + 491 (country code) + (local number). When calling on Montserrat, dial only the four-digit local number unless otherwise indicated.

ENTRY REQUIREMENTS

British, US, and Canadian citizens need only proof of citizenship — a current passport, or an original or certified birth certificate plus an official photo ID such as a driver's license — and a return or ongoing ticket.

CLIMATE AND CLOTHES

Temperatures in Montserrat vary between the mid-70s F (20s C) and about 90F (35C), and the humidity is quite low. Rainfall averages about 60 inches per year, but it is irregular, and there is no predictable wet season. Dress tends to be more formal here than on other islands, so don't wear short shorts or swimsuit cover-ups in town. Evenings call for something slightly dressy, such as casual resortwear. A sweater or jacket is recommended for evenings in December and January. Bring deck shoes or sneakers for boating; sturdy, comfortable shoes for walking.

MONEY

Montserrat currency is the Eastern Caribbean dollar (EC), called the "BeeWee" by most local people. The current exchange rate is about $2.70 EC to $1 US. US dollars are accepted at most places in Montserrat; Canadian dollars are not. Banking hours are from 8 AM to 3 PM on Mondays through Thursdays; 8 AM to 5 PM on Fridays. The Bank of Montserrat is open from 8 AM to 12:30 PM on Saturdays. All prices in this chapter are quoted in US dollars.

LANGUAGE

English is spoken with the usual West Indian dialect and an occasional hint of Irish brogue.

TIME

Montserrat is on atlantic standard time. When it is 11 AM in Plymouth, it is 10 AM in New York. During daylight saving time, island and US East Coast time are the same.

CURRENT

Most hotel outlets are 220 volts, 60 cycles, AC. A converter is needed for all US appliances here; some hotels will provide one.

TIPPING

Hotels add a 10% service charge to bills, which takes care of room maids and other staff. Airport porters should get about $1 per bag. Taxi drivers and providers of other services should be tipped 10%.

GETTING AROUND

CAR RENTAL There are 115 miles of well-paved roads on Montserrat. Your hotel desk or the tourist board can arrange for a rental car, or contact *Pauline Car Rentals* (at the airport; phone: 3846), *Neville Bradshaw* (phone: 5270), *Budget Rent-A-Car* (phone: 6065), or *Jefferson's Car Rental* (phone: 2126). Standard rates are about $40 per day for a car with automatic transmission and unlimited mileage (you pay for gas). Mini-vans, which hold up to 14 people, are $65 per day per vehicle. Mini-moke rentals are available at *Reliable Car Rental* (Marine Drive; phone: 6990).

A temporary island driver's license is required. They cost about $12 and are available at Blackbourne Airport or at the Traffic Department on Strand Street in Plymouth. Driving is on the left, British-style.

TAXI Rates are standardized by law — and rather expensive. From the airport, the trip to Plymouth is about $12; to the *Vue Point* hotel, $18; to the *Montserrat Springs* hotel, $14. Taxi tours around the island run about $12 an hour. If you need a taxi and one's not around, call the *Taxi Stand* (phone: 2261) in Plymouth.

INTER-ISLAND FLIGHTS

LIAT offers regular service between Antigua and Blackbourne Airport on Montserrat. The flight takes 15 minutes and costs $66 round-trip. *Montserrat Air Services (MAS;* phone: 2533 or 2713) runs nine-seater charters and sometimes sells individual tickets. There is a $6 departure tax (save your ticket receipt and boarding pass, as in-transit passengers do not need to pay Antigua's departure tax).

SPECIAL EVENTS

Christmastime, which lasts from December 16 to January 1, is celebrated throughout the island with parades, masquerades, parties, dinners, and dances, all accompanied by singing and steel and string bands. Businesses are closed on *Christmas Day, New Year's Eve,* and *New Year's Day.* Other official holidays include *St. Patrick's Day,* (March 17, with all sorts of festivities held in the village of St. Patrick's), *Good Friday, Easter Monday, Labor Day* (May 1), the *Queen's Birthday* (early June), *Whitmonday* (day after the seventh Sunday after *Easter*), the *August Bank Holiday* (first Monday in August), and *Boxing Day* (December 26).

SHOPPING

Not a major preoccupation, since there are few duty-free imports to consider, but local crafts grow more interesting by the season. The best buys are pottery, china, hand-screened prints, anything made from Sea Island cotton, leather sandals, local jams and jellies, and Perk's Rum Punch. Worth looking into:

ARROW'S MAN SHOP Owned by Alphonsus "Arrow" Cassell, king of soca music and famous for the song "Hot! Hot! Hot!" This boutique specializes in clothing, shoes, bags, and luggage for men. 6 Marine Dr., Plymouth (phone: 2993).

DUTCHERS STUDIO Intriguing decorative pieces made from salvaged bottles, tile, glass, and other materials. Olveston (phone: 5253).

ISLAND HOUSE This art gallery specializes in Haitian paintings, as well as crafts, pottery, and glassware. John St., Plymouth (phone: 3938).

LEATHERCRAFT CENTER Hand-tooled leather shoes, sandals, belts, bags, key rings, and bookmarks are sold here. Groves (phone: 4934).

MONTSERRAT SEA ISLAND COTTON COMPANY Features useful and wearable items, including blouses, sundresses, and piles of table linen, much of it handwoven from locally grown fiber. George St., on the bayfront, Plymouth (phone: 7009).

RED CROSS HUT Hand-crafted straw items plus rag rugs, hand-painted ceramic ornaments, and cards at low prices. Dagenham (phone: 2699).

TAPESTRIES OF MONTSERRAT Don't miss the island-made rugs,. wall hangings, totes, and mats displayed here. They also create custom designs and stock duty-free crystal, watches, and jewelry. In the *John Bull Shop,* Parliament St., Plymouth (phone: 2520).

SPORTS

BOATING The *Vue Point* hotel can arrange for day cruises around the island for up to 12 people. Several other yachts and some small craft also may be available for rent from individual owners. There are no formal rental facilities at this time, but check the bulletin board at the tourist office or at your hotel.

CYCLING *Island Bikes* (phone: 4696) rents mountain bikes.

GOLF The *Montserrat Golf Club* (phone: 5220) maintains a challenging year-round 11-hole course that can be played a number of ways. Greens fees for visitors are $23 per day; clubs and pullcarts can be rented for $4.50 per day. Local members can arrange permission for guests to use the clubhouse, and visitors are welcome to enter the island's major tournament, the *Montserrat Open,* in March. Other less formal tournaments are held as well.

HIKING AND MOUNTAIN CLIMBING The 3,002-foot Chance Peak affords spectacular views of nearly the entire island (see *Special Places*).

SAILING CRUISES Day cruises around Montserrat on Captain Martin Haseby's trimaran, the *John Willie* (phone: 5738), provide access to the island's beaches and cost $45 per person, including open bar and snorkeling gear. Arrangements also can be made through the *Vue Point* hotel.

SCUBA DIVING Montserrat's unspoiled reefs boast a variety of corals and sponges. *Dive Montserrat* is a *PADI*-certified dive shop offering one- and two-tank dives and resort courses. Contact Chris Mason (phone: 8812). *Sea Wolf Diving School* (phone: 6859) also offers one- and two-tank dives as well as certification courses.

SNORKELING The *Vue Point* hotel lends equipment to its guests at no charge. *Danny's Watersports* (phone: 5645) rents equipment and offers lessons in snorkeling, windsurfing, sailing, and water skiing. Otherwise, you'll need to bring your own equipment or take one of the sailing cruises offered (above). Woodlands and Lime Kiln are the most popular beach choices for snorkeling and diving.

SPORT FISHING The fish are out there, but special arrangements must be made. The tourist board or your hotel can set up something with a local fisherman. Bringing your own tackle will facilitate matters. Both Chris Mason (phone: 8812) and *Danny's Watersports* (phone: 5645) offer half- and full-day charters. For spearfishing, Foxes Bay and Little Bay are best.

SWIMMING AND SUNNING The most popular and crowded beach for sunning is Old Road Bay Beach. There are volcanic sand beaches on both coasts, which are easily reached by car or are within walking distance of most hotels. The island's only stretch of white sand, Rendezvous Beach, can be reached either by boat or by a 30-minute hike from Little Bay. Most of the hotels and villas have pools and lounging areas.

TENNIS The *Vue Point* hotel has 2 lighted, hard-surface courts on which non-guests can arrange to play for a small fee. The *Montserrat Springs* hotel also has 2 lighted courts (1 hard surface and 1 grass court). Rates average $4 per hour for daytime play, $6 for night use.

NIGHTLIFE

Nights, which tend toward the quiet, cognac-and-conversation side, are occasionally enlivened by island entertainment (dance bands, singers) at local clubs or at the main hotels. The island has a disco — *La Cave* (Evergreen Dr., Plymouth; no phone) — where the locals dress to the teeth and dance until dawn. Other favorite "liming," or watering, holes are the *Plantation* in Wapping (phone: 2892); the *Village Place* in Salem (phone: 5202); and the *Las' Call Beach Bar* in the *Montserrat Springs* hotel (phone: 6738). Hotel parties — such as the Wednesday evening barbecues and the Friday night dinner dances at the *Vue Point* — feature steel band music, occasional crab races, and relaxed fun.

Best on the Island

CHECKING IN

Montserrat has six hotels — the largest with fewer than 50 rooms — and a fine selection of rental villas and resort condominium apartments. Air conditioning is rare, but hardly necessary, since the island is naturally cooled by trade winds. In the winter season, expect to pay from $210 to $250 for a double room with breakfast and dinner at hotels we've listed as expensive. A double without meals will cost $85 to $100 at moderate places and less than $75 at inexpensive lodgings. Rates are reduced by about a third during the off-season. A 10% service charge and 7% government tax are in effect year-round.

Private villa rentals are an established part of tourism on Montserrat, and the primary choice of residence among island visitors. Properties range from 1-bedroom cottages to 5-bedroom private homes complete with pools and sunset views. There is usually a 1-week minimum stay, but occasionally bookings for 5 nights are accepted. Weekly rates run from about $900 to $3,000 in high season, and about $600 to $2,000 during the summer months. Prices generally include maid service, gardeners, round-trip transfers to the airport, an orientation tour of the island, and refrigerators stocked with groceries; cooks and baby-sitters are available on request. Cribs, rollaway beds, and rental cars are also available at daily rates. Villa rentals can be booked through *Caribbean Connection Plus* (PO Box 261, Trumbull, CT 06611; phone: 203-261-8603), or on the island through the *Neville Bradshaw Agencies* (PO Box 270, Plymouth, Montserrat, BWI; phone: 5270). *Caribbean Connection Plus* will also handle hotel reservations, and staff members of their offshoot service, *Best Foot Forward,* greet all incoming guests and help them find their way around the island. When calling from a phone on Montserrat use only the local numbers listed below. For information about dialing from elsewhere, see "Telephone" earlier in this chapter.

PLYMOUTH

EXPENSIVE

Villas of Montserrat Together, these 3 villas offer some of the most deluxe accommodations on the island. Each 3-bedroom home features 3 bathrooms, rattan furniture, daily maid service, a private pool, a well-equipped kitchen, a dining room, and a large living room with a stereo system and cable TV. The villas overlook Isle Bay, the Caribbean Sea, and the *Montserrat Golf Club.* Bookings are made either on the island (phone: 5513) or through *Caribbean Connection Plus* (see above).

MODERATE

Flora Fountain A circular-shaped, contemporary establishment in town with 18 air conditioned rooms that open onto a patio with a fountain. It's island-basic, with no sport facilities, but there is a bar and a dining room featuring Caribbean, Indian, and international dishes. Convenient location on Church Rd. (phone: 6092; fax: 2586).

INEXPENSIVE

Oriole Plaza In the heart of Plymouth, this 12-room property offers no-frills, basic (and very tiny) accommodations. All rooms have ceiling fans and cable TV. The central location offers easy access to beaches and shopping, and the dining room serves truly authentic local dishes. There's also a lounge. Parliament St. (phone: 6982; fax: 6690).

ELSEWHERE ON THE ISLAND

EXPENSIVE

Montserrat Springs This property, with its sweeping views of the mountainside, is within walking distance to town. There are 34 garden rooms plus 6 two-bedroom suites, all air conditioned and with modern decor. Amenities include hot tubs, 2 lighted tennis courts, a beach bar, a 70-foot pool, a restaurant, and room service. The Friday-night barbecues held in the winter are quite popular. In Richmond Hill, overlooking Emerald Isle Beach, to the north of the city (phone: 2481; 800-253-2134 from the US; fax: 4070).

Vue Point Overlooking the Caribbean, this charming, truly first class hotel has 28 individual cottages, 12 double bedrooms in connected units, a pool, a small putting green, 2 lighted tennis courts, and the island's most complete water sports setup. The dining room is one of the best on the island, with a very popular Wednesday night West Indian buffet/barbecue (see *Eating Out*). The *Michael Osborne Complex* is a multipurpose conference center and venue for theater productions. The hotel is closed from September through October. Olde Towne (phone: 5210; 800-235-0709 from the US; fax: 4813).

INEXPENSIVE

Shamrock Villas Features 50 fully furnished 1- and 2-bedroom apartment-villas with kitchens, white tiled floors, pastel color schemes and ceiling fans. The accommodations lack both air conditioning and TV sets, but they're a good value. Some have views of the sea, and the complex is 400 yards from the beach. Other pluses: a freshwater pool; twice weekly maid service for about $20 a week extra. Richmond Hill (phone: 3736; fax: 2434).

EATING OUT

"Goat water," a rich, meaty stew laden with fresh vegetables, is the island's unofficial national dish and should be one of your gustatory objectives while you're on the island. Try a bowl of it at *Anne Morgan's* (see below). Another local delicacy is mountain chicken, actually legs of the large frog native only to this island and nearby Dominica. Rum punches are the island's real specialties — each hotel and bar seems to have its own recipe. The most powerful belongs to JWR Perkins, who bottles Perk's Punch, a rum-based brew with the kick of an island mule (it makes a great gift for the folks back home). Expect to pay $50 and up for dinner for two at a restaurant we've listed as expensive; from $20 to $40 at a place described as moderate; and under $20 at any of the restaurants we've listed as inexpensive. Prices do not include drinks, wine, or tips, although restaurants do include a 10% service charge. When calling from a phone on Montserrat, use only the local numbers listed below. For information about dialing from elsewhere, see "Telephone" earlier in this chapter.

EXPENSIVE

Belham Valley A stylish establishment with a romantic setting and a view of Old Road Bay, this was once a private home. Island drinks and continental dishes are served with piano accompaniment. Open daily for lunch and dinner. Reservations necessary for dinner. Major credit cards accepted. Olde Towne, not far from the *Vue Point* hotel (phone: 5553).

Vue Point A five-course table d'hôte, as well as an à la carte dinner menu, is offered at this dining room overlooking the sea. Especially good are the West Indian curried chicken, Bessie's beautiful lime pie, and the guava cheesecake. Don't miss the Wednesday night barbecue; it's a real feast, with steel band music. Open daily for dinner only; closed September through October. Reservations essential for dinner. Major credit cards accepted. At the *Vue Point Hotel,* Olde Towne (phone: 5210).

MODERATE

Blue Dolphin With an eye-catching view of the town and the harbor, this eatery is plain, but it has the best local food on the island. Fresh fish dishes are the specialty of its fisherman owner. Open daily for dinner only. Reservations unnecessary. Major credit cards accepted. In Parsons on the outskirts of Plymouth (phone: 3263).

Emerald Café Set beneath a canopy of blooming hibiscus, this garden restaurant features seafood and sandwiches. Try the huge, tasty swordfish steaks. Open daily for lunch and dinner. Reservations unnecessary. Major credit cards accepted. Wapping (phone: 3821).

Niggy's A small, intimate eatery serving continental breakfast, inexpensive lunches, and Italian dinners. Try the pasta, chicken cacciatore, or the shrimp scampi. Open daily. Reservations advised for dinner. No credit cards accepted. Located a 15-minute walk from Plymouth in Kinsale (phone: 7489).

Oasis This casual, British-run spot is housed in a 200-year-old stone building. Fish and chips and other international specialties are featured. Serves lunch and dinner; dinner only Sundays; closed Wednesdays. Reservations advised. No credit cards accepted. Just across the street from Plymouth in Wapping (phone: 2328).

Village Place The closest thing to a soul food restaurant on Montserrat, it was once the favorite local haunt of superstar musicians Elton John, Sting, Mick Jagger, and others who used to record their albums at the now-defunct Air Studios. "Goat water" and fried chicken are the most popular dishes. Open for dinner only; closed Tuesdays. Reservations unnecessary. No credit cards accepted. Salem (phone: 5202).

INEXPENSIVE

Anne Morgan's This is the place to try the local stew called "goat water," a big favorite among the islanders. Anne serves it on Fridays and Saturdays. Open for lunch on Fridays and Saturdays; dinner on Fridays and Saturdays by advance request. Reservations unnecessary for lunch. No credit cards accepted. St. Johns (phone: 5419).

Golden Apple No-frills, authentic West Indian dishes are offered here; the chef's version of "goat water" is served every weekend. Open daily for lunch and dinner. Reservations advised. Major credit cards accepted. Cork Hill (phone: 2187).

Hangout Bar & Restaurant Homemade island fast food, from hamburgers to fish burgers, is served here. On Friday and Saturday evenings, the specialties of the house are "goat water" and *souse* (a soup made with the head and feet of a pig). Open daily. Reservations unnecessary. No credit cards accepted. Wapping (phone: 3945).

Ziggy's Casual, relaxed drinking and dining at the *Montserrat Yacht Club.* Local dishes and potent rum punches are specialties. Open daily for lunch and dinner. Reservations unnecessary. No credit cards accepted. Wapping (phone: 2237).

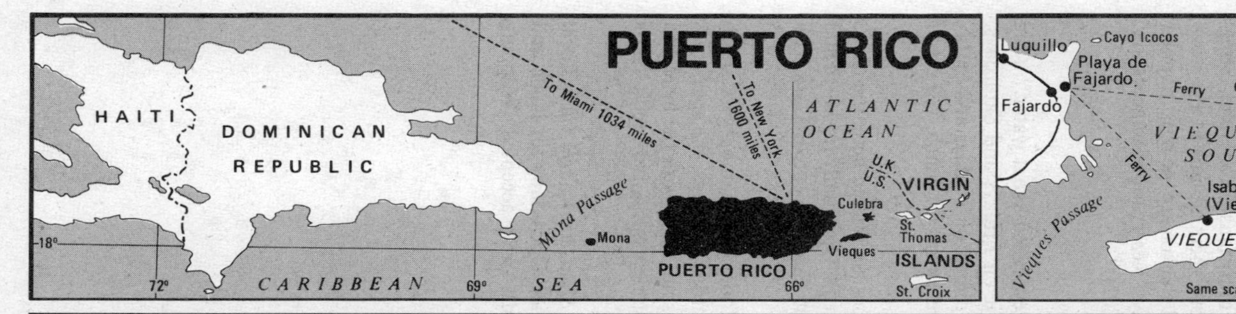
PUERTO RICO
HAITI
DOMINICAN REPUBLIC
To Miami 1034 miles
To New York 1600 miles
ATLANTIC OCEAN
U.K.
U.S.
VIRGIN ISLANDS
Culebra
St. Thomas
Vieques
St. Croix
Mona Passage
Mona
PUERTO RICO
CARIBBEAN SEA
18°
72°
69°
66°
Luquillo
Cayo Icocos
Playa de Fajardo
Fajardo
CULEBRA
Culebra
Ferry
VIEQUES SOUND
Isabel Segunda (Vieques)
VIEQUES
Vieques Passage
Same scale as the main map

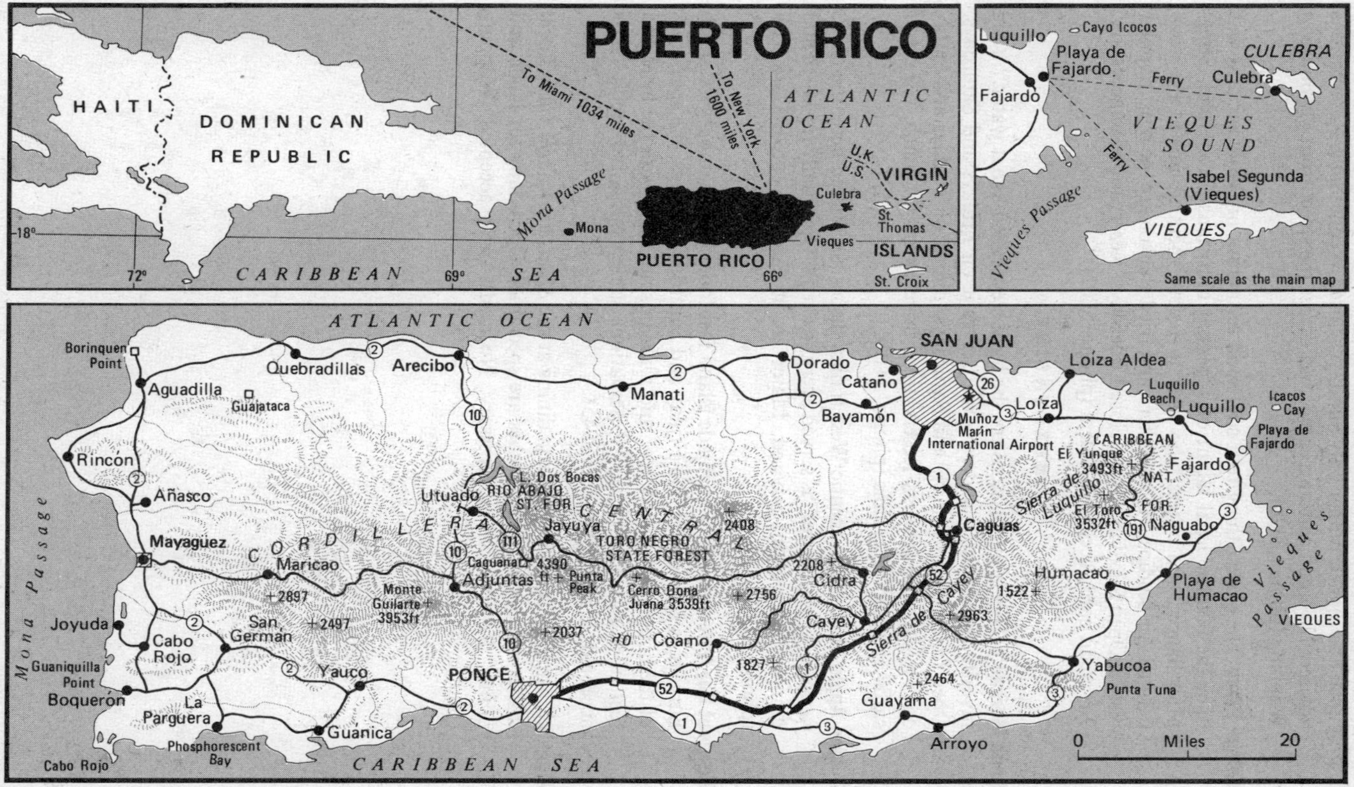

ATLANTIC OCEAN
SAN JUAN
Borinquen Point
Aguadilla
Quebradillas
Arecibo
Guajataca
Manati
Dorado
Cataño
Bayamón
Loíza Aldea
Luquillo Beach
Luquillo
Icacos Cay
Playa de Fajardo
Loíza
Muñoz Marín International Airport
CARIBBEAN NAT. FOR.
El Yunque 3493ft
Fajardo
Sierra de Luquillo
El Toro 3532ft
Naguabo
Rincón
Añasco
Mayagüez
CORDILLERA CENTRAL
L. Dos Bocas
RIO ABAJO ST. FOR
Utuado
Jayuya
2408
TORO NEGRO STATE FOREST
Caguas
Caguana
4390 ft Punta Peak
Maricao
Adjuntas
Cerro Dona Juana 3539ft
2208
Cidra
2756
2897
Monte Guilarte 3953ft
2497
2037
Cayey
Humacao
1522
Playa de Humacao
Sierra de Cayey
2963
Vieques Passage
VIEQUES
Joyuda
Cabo Rojo
San German
Coamo
1827
Yabucoa
Mona Passage
Guaniquilla Point
Yauco
PONCE
2464
Punta Tuna
Boquerón
La Parguera
Guayama
Guanica
Phosphorescent Bay
Arroyo
Cabo Rojo
CARIBBEAN SEA
0 Miles 20

Puerto Rico

Puerto Rico is finally overcoming its image problem. In the past, if you asked most mainland Americans, "Quick, name three things you expect to find on Puerto Rico," without hesitation they'd usually list glitzy hotels, Vegas-style gambling and nightlife, and wrenching poverty. All of these still exist, but they are just part of the picture. To a certain extent, they describe the city of San Juan, which is too often mistaken for the whole 3,435-square-mile commonwealth (more than a third of Puerto Rico's 3.5 million people live in the metropolitan area). So tropical travelers in search of great sports, escapist resorts, and lush island atmosphere have looked to other islands, even though they all can be found less than an hour's drive from Luis Muñoz Marín International Airport. Puerto Rico offers extraordinary vacation variety, but in the past its potential often was overlooked. Today, however, more and more travelers are finding that Puerto Rico is — as it's described on local license plates — an "Island of Enchantment."

Though Puerto Rico may take up the smallest area of the Greater Antilles (behind Cuba, Hispaniola, and Jamaica), it leads the pack in action, excitement, and the variety of visitor attractions. Recognition of the island's quality is expanding, and today tourism is again booming, with visitor arrivals rising to 3.7 million in 1992.

Evidence of the tourism turnaround has appeared all over the island — more than $100 million has been spent to spruce up San Juan's old buildings and construct new plazas, with much of the work unveiled in 1992 during the island's commemoration of Columbus's discovery of the Americas. On the drawing board are plans to upgrade Marina Street, which parallels the cruise ship piers, and to build the 450-room *Wyndham* hotel on the waterfront. In the southern coast city of Ponce, $450 million has been invested in refurbishing historical sites, and another $70 million has been spent on renovation projects in 79 smaller towns and cities across the island. The number of *paradores* (country inns) has risen to 15, and several major mainland airlines use San Juan as their prime Caribbean hub, so the island is assured of an increasing flow of visitors.

Ecotourism continues to grow as well; in the spirit of renewed interest in nature and the environment, many travelers are taking day trips from San Juan to visit Las Cabezas de San Juan Nature Reserve near Fajardo, the Río Camuy Cave Park south of Arecibo (one of the largest underground river systems in the world), and Mona Island, home of rare, 3-foot-long iguanas, among other exotic creatures. For astronomy fans, the Arecibo Observatory houses the world's largest radar/radio telescope.

Puerto Rico offers accommodations in a wide range of styles and price categories, located throughout the island. San Juan does have some luxury properties as tall and determined to dazzle as those along the Atlantic City boardwalk, but it also offers alternatives: A number of smaller hotels (originally geared to business travelers) make up for what they lack in resort frills with reasonable rates and the sort of personal service few bigger places ever manage. Some are only steps from the beach, and they can be ideal for vacationers looking for a home base from which to explore, rather than a hotel that's a destination in itself. Condominiums often offer all the resort facilities, plus kitchenettes, which are especially useful for families. In addition, there are more than a dozen small, well-run guesthouses, each with its own personality, scattered through residential neighborhoods, like Ocean Park and Punta Las Marías, as well as in San Juan's Condado and Isla Verde resort sections. They line the beaches, yet their highest in-season rates are less than half the minimum charged at big-name beachfront hotels.

There are more choices outside San Juan. You won't find many better golf or tennis layouts than those at such resorts as the *Hyatt Dorado Beach–Cerromar* complex and at *Palmas del Mar,* with its sports-oriented villa villages. Seaside resort towns like Rincón and Guánica and La Parguera (the fishermen's favorite) offer a casual life at low prices, as well as a chance to meet Puerto Rican families. And hotels like the *Mayagüez Hilton International* and Ponce's *Meliá* reflect the pride and Spanish heritage of cities *en la isla* ("out on the island," meaning beyond San Juan). Finally, there are Puerto Rico's unique *paradores,* inns that have been awarded government sponsorship because of their unique atmosphere, interesting sites, fine food, and high standards of service and cleanliness.

San Juan's nightlife, while not so lavish in scale, often outstrips that of Las Vegas in variety and local color. The big hotels split their year's billings between imported stars and the best Puerto Rican performers, and they downplay their casinos, which are basically low-key and carefully regulated. In addition to some outstanding hotel dining rooms, there are good Chinese, French, German, Mexican, Italian, Argentine, Spanish, US–style, and Puerto Rican restaurants. There are also San Juan's flamenco shows and cafés — plus a number of late-playing discos.

As for poverty, Puerto Rico — like every other island in the Caribbean — has its share, although Puerto Rico boasts one of the Caribbean's highest per capita incomes. But the progress that started with 1949's "Operation Bootstrap" — a program offering tax exemptions and other incentives to lure industry and new jobs to the island — has continued, though with a new orientation. More Puerto Ricans now seem to be returning from the continental US to live on the island than are leaving to find jobs on the mainland, and the island has become the tenth-largest overseas market for products manufactured on the mainland United States.

Operation Bootstrap was the first in a series of self-help programs that have changed the face and future of Puerto Rico. In its early days, the

7-block-square area within the Old City walls of San Juan was declared a historic zone, and 10 years' tax exemption was offered to anyone who would buy and restore one of its buildings. The result was the salvation of what is now known as Old San Juan, the city founded by Juan Ponce de León, who was with Columbus when he discovered the island in 1493. The land that the native Taíno Indians called Borinquen — a name still used by Puerto Ricans in a mood of affection and pride — was christened San Juan by the Great Discoverer.

After he became governor of the island, the first settlement Ponce de León established, in 1509, was at Caparra, south of San Juan Bay. Eleven years later, the Spaniards' hopes for gold had dwindled, but the island's strategic importance had increased. So in 1521 the settlement moved to the more defensible peninsula on which it now stands. Since the name of his patron saint, San Juan, already belonged to the island, Ponce had no choice but to pick another for the city. Optimistically, he called it Puerto Rico, "rich port." Later, the city and island swapped names.

Building began on fortifications; later a cathedral, a convent, and homes were erected. One of the prettiest of the latter, the *Casa Blanca,* was built in 1521 as Ponce's residence. But Ponce de León took off on his fatal search for the fountain of youth and never lived there. Today the building houses two museums: the *Juan Ponce de León Museum* and the *Taíno Indian Ethno-Historic Museum.* Its recent restoration, along with that of numerous other irreplaceable Old San Juan landmarks, has been accomplished under the caring eye of the Institute of Puerto Rican Culture, created in 1955 and dedicated to fostering the arts and an appreciation of Puerto Rico's heritage and folklore.

After a prolonged struggle, the island achieved autonomy under Spanish rule in 1897. It had barely begun to enjoy it when, in the course of the Spanish-American War, American troops landed at Guánica on July 25, 1898. With the signing of the Treaty of Paris in April of 1899, Puerto Ricans took a giant step backward and again became subjects ruled by a foreign power — this time, the US. It was not until 1917 that Congress granted them full American citizenship, and not till 1952 that the island, as a one-of-a-kind commonwealth under the US flag, again was given its own constitution and government. Since then, Operation Bootstrap and similar programs have helped Puerto Ricans devise creative solutions to their problems.

Maintaining Puerto Rico's share of a very volatile tourism market has taken some doing. During the 1970s, overbooking, overpricing, overbuilding, and incessant union demands sent Puerto Rico's reputation plummeting. The government's tourism company stepped in to try to turn things around. After a taste of the hardships caused by hotel closings, rates have steadied, and authorities have come down hard on consistent overbookers.

One battle the government and residents are still fighting is a high incidence of crime, especially in San Juan. Visitors should take the same common-sense precautions here that they would in any large city: Keep a close watch on personal belongings, avoid wearing jewelry in the streets and on the beaches, and be sure not to walk around deserted areas after dark. Another recent problem has been the occurrence of several cases of dengue fever. This disease is carried by local mosquitoes, so remember to bring a good supply of bug repellent with you.

On a more personal basis, it is easy to see why Puerto Rico is the Caribbean's most popular tourist destination, far ahead of any other island in the region. Puerto Ricans buy (and sell) American products, crack American jokes, watch reruns on American cable TV, and like most of the same things mainlanders like; at the same time, they maintain a strong sense of traditional identity and relish being able to impress it on visitors. "I know this is a great place to live," said the owner of a Humacao Exxon station, chatting as he pumped gas into a rental car. "So . . . I guess it's a great place to visit, right?" No arguments here.

Puerto Rico At-a-Glance

FROM THE AIR

Puerto Rico is the smallest and the easternmost of the group of islands known as the Greater Antilles, which also includes Cuba, Jamaica, and Hispaniola (the island shared by Haiti and the Dominican Republic). With a landmass of over 3,400 square miles (measuring 110 miles from east to west and 35 miles from north to south), it is roughly three-fourths the size of Jamaica, and about as rectangular as an island can get. The commonwealth's nearest neighbors are the Dominican Republic, about 54 miles west, and the US Virgin Island of St. Thomas, 40 miles east.

Its capital, San Juan (pop. 1.5 million), is on the north coast; Ponce, its second city, overlooks a bay in the center of the southern coast; and Mayagüez, the third-largest metropolis, is at the middle of the western shoreline.

Puerto Rico's 272-mile coastline is rimmed with beaches, but its mid-island spine of mountains — the Cordillera Central, plus the northeastern Luquillo and southeastern Cayey Ranges — creates a lush interior, a green northern sector, and a drier southern coastal strip, with a desert-like west end complete with cactus and arid soil. The commonwealth also has several offshore islands. Vieques and Culebra (to the east) are basically dry with some hills and uncrowded beaches; with 8,708 and 1,515 inhabitants respectively, both serve as getaway vacation places for islanders as well as for a few peace-seeking visitors from the north. Icacos, a sandy spit a few miles northeast of Las Croabas at Puerto Rico's northeastern corner and easily visited from *El Conquistador* resort, is uninhabited, but a favorite snorkel-trip destination; and little, round Mona Island, plunked down in the western sea passage of the same name, is barren plateau and cliffs.

From flight height, it is not difficult to spot several of the island's most distinctive geographical features: El Yunque rain forest in the northeast; La Parguera's Phosphorescent Bay in the southwest; the central island's mountain lakes, waterfalls, and teak forests; and the dramatic karst area, limestone earth pocked with deep, conical sinkholes and dotted with small haystack hills, north of the Cordillera Central. You also will see evidence of farming: sugarcane in the northern coastal plains; tobacco and plantains in the foothills; and pineapple in the center of the northern plain.

Luis Muñoz Marín International Airport on the eastern outskirts of San Juan, now a modern, cosmopolitan, air conditioned facility, is 1,000 miles (2½ hours' flying time) southeast of Miami; 1,500 miles (3½ hours) south of New York City. Flying times from Chicago and Los Angeles are 4½ and 6 hours, respectively. Service also has expanded at the Rafael Hernández Airport in Aguadilla and the Mercedita Airport in Ponce.

SPECIAL PLACES

As they are in most old cities, the capital's streets are narrow and teeming with traffic. But exploring the 7-block-square Old San Juan Historic Zone on foot is pleasant and rewarding; pick up a map at the tourist office by the docks or use the one in *Qué Pasa,* the official visitors' guide. You'll spot more than 400 restored buildings, some almost 500 years old, with charming Spanish architecture of iron or carved wood balconies clinging to pastel-painted buildings.

Depending on your interests, you could easily spend 2 days exploring the nooks and crannies of Old San Juan, or spend a half day visiting the historic highlights and a half day browsing in the stores. The next most popular site after the historic district is undoubtedly El Yunque, the island's exotic rain forest. Tour companies offer dozens of guided half-day and all-day trips to El Yunque, and you can easily book one through your hotel travel desk. If you aren't all that interested in flora, you may want to substitute a day's snorkeling trip (see *Sea Excursions* below). Better still, rent a car, and combine an El Yunque visit with a drive across the island. There's much that's surprising and pleasing — including genuine charm and beautiful countryside — about the vast area beyond San Juan.

With first-rate roads circling the island and a superhighway from San Juan to Ponce, driving here isn't the bumpy adventure it once was. However, if you're visiting out-of-the-way places, factor in some getting-lost time, as many side roads aren't marked clearly. Also, new roads haven't eliminated traffic jams — especially during traditional commuting hours and on weekends. Avoid Route 26 to the airport, which joins Route 3 to El Yunque and Route 2 through Bayamón to Dorado between 8 and 10 AM and 4 and 6 PM. And plan to do as much of your touring as you can on weekdays. Or make the most of your time by flying to a point out on the island (like Ponce, Mayagüez, or Aguadilla), picking up a car there, and taking a slow, meandering route back to San Juan. Wherever you stay on the island, you should see something of the following:

OLD SAN JUAN

The 7-block-square area on the tip of the peninsula that forms the westernmost part of the city, Old San Juan was once completely encircled by the city wall — part of which still stands — and guarded by Forts San Cristóbal and El Morro. Administered by the US National Park Service, which provides tours of each, the forts are massively impressive, well preserved, and open to the public from 9:15 AM to 5:45 PM each day. Begin your explorations with a visit to El Morro. (Unfortunately, the *San Juan Museum of History and Art,* which used to be the best place to begin an Old San Juan tour, is still closed after being damaged by Hurricane Hugo. The restoration process is under way, but at press time there was no projected completion date.)

Two parking garages can be found on Recinto Sur Street; all-day parking will cost about $5. If they are full, try the parking lot at La Puntilla, the waterfront district, which is located past the pink colonial customs house. Buses from the Isla Verde and Condado sections of San Juan leave passengers at the Covadonga parking facility or Plaza de Colón. Free open-air buses and trolleys run through some parts of the area, including a route between Plaza Las Armas and Covadonga, but you will still have to walk to catch all of the sites. Walking along Old San Juan's hilly streets can be tiring, especially in the midday sun; bring a hat and wear comfortable walking shoes.

Start your tour at Paseo de la Princesa (Princess Promenade), a tree-lined walkway that skirts the city wall. About halfway down the promenade, stop in at La Princesa, built as a prison in 1837. Now headquarters for the Puerto Rico Tourism Company, the building has been renovated as part of a major Old San Juan Waterfront renewal project. Three cells have been reconstructed, and there's a newly restored courtyard, with fountains and royal palms. The 15-foot-high brick ceilings, massive mahogany doors, and brass accents provide a showcase for works by Puerto Rican artists. The gallery is open weekdays from 8 AM to 4:30 PM; no admission charge (phone: 721-1862). Continue along the promenade, which curves behind the seawalls and leads to the San Juan Gate, built in 1639 and formerly the principal entry into the walled city. Turn left onto Recinto de Oeste and left again at Caleta de Las Monjas. A shady path here leads to El Morro.

FUERTE SAN FELIPE DEL MORRO (EL MORRO FORT) Though smaller than the fortress of San Cristóbal, this fort is more dramatic. Recently refurbished, it houses a museum with artifacts from early Puerto Rican times within its gray, 18-foot-thick walls. The main battlements were built in 1591 on a foundation of earlier defense works that dated back to 1539. In 1595, El Morro was credited with preventing Sir Francis Drake from entering San Juan Harbor. It was attacked many times — mostly unsuccessfully. Since 1783 the fort has been a single, compact unit with 6 levels looming 140 feet above the sea and its large land area laced with many tunnels. It's open 9:15 AM to 5:45 PM. Guided tours are at 10 and 11 AM, 2, 3, and 4 PM; no admission charge (phone: 729-6960). If you arrive by taxi, have the driver take you all the way into the fort; you'll get all the exercise you need on the long walk out.

FUERTE SAN CRISTÓBAL (SAN CRISTÓBAL FORT) From El Morro, follow Calle Norzagaray along the ocean until you reach San Cristóbal Fort. Rising 150 feet above the sea on 27 acres of land and consisting of five independent units connected by tunnels and dry moats, it walls the north side of Avenida Muñoz Rivera, the route that brings you from the Condado hotel strip to the old sector. The fort was built from 1766 to 1772 to supplement El Morro and defend the land side of the city. Open 9:15 AM to 5:45 PM. Tours are at 10 and 11 AM, 2, 3, and 4 PM; no admission charge (phone: 729-6960).

PLAZA DEL QUINTO CENTENARIO (QUINCENTENNIAL PLAZA) Head back toward El Morro and cross the street to find the newest plaza in the Old City. Opened in 1992 during the island's festivities to commemorate Columbus's discovery of the Americas, this controversial square created from a parking lot has been criticized by local residents because its modern touches clash with the surrounding architecture. The most intriguing sight here is a 40-foot-high sculpture covered with black granite and ceramic fragments which its creator, Jaime Suárez, used to symbolize the earth and clay of America. The plaza also has a fountain with 100 streams that symbolize the first 100 years after America's discovery and three flights of stairs to represent the next 300 years. Two needle-shaped columns point to the North Star, the explorers' guiding light.

IGLESIA DE SAN JOSÉ (CHURCH OF SAN JOSÉ) On the east side of Quincentennial Plaza facing Plaza de San José, this is the church of Juan Ponce de León's descendants and the second-oldest church in the Western Hemisphere. The statue on the square is that of Juan Ponce himself. The famous conquistador's body was buried in this church from 1559 until 1908, when it was moved to the cathedral. His coat of arms still hangs above the San José altar. The vaulted Gothic ceilings are reminiscent of 16th-century Spain. Open 8:30 AM to 4 PM Mondays through Saturdays, with Sunday mass at 12:15 PM (phone: 725-7501).

MUSEO DE PABLO CASALS (PABLO CASALS MUSEUM) At the corner of Plaza de San José, adjacent to the church, this museum houses memorabilia — including manuscripts and the late maestro's cello — left to the people of

Puerto Rico. It's open from 9:30 AM to 5:30 PM, Tuesdays through Saturdays, and on Sundays from 1 to 5 PM; no admission charge (phone: 723-9185).

CASA DE LOS CONTRAFUERTES (HOUSE OF BUTTRESSES) Around the corner from Plaza de San José, on the Calle San Sebastián, this is thought to be the oldest building designed as a private residence on the island. Built in the early 18th century, it now houses the tiny *Museo del Grabado Latinamericano* (Museum of Latin American Graphics) on the second floor, where periodic exhibitions are held, and the one-room *Pharmacy Museum,* with a collection of porcelain and glass jars displayed in a replica of an old apothecary's shop. Both museums are open from 9 AM to noon and 1 to 4:30 PM, Wednesdays through Sundays; no admission charge (phone: 724-5998 or 724-5949).

MUSEO DE LAS AMÉRICAS (MUSEUM OF THE AMERICAS) On the west side of the Quincentennial Plaza, this museum was opened during the 1992 quincentennial festivities. Formerly a hospital, the 1854 structure now contains anthropological exhibits from Puerto Rico and several countries in Latin America. Open Tuesdays through Sundays, 10 AM to 4 PM; no admission charge (no phone).

EL ASILO DE BENEFICIENCIA (WELFARE HOUSE) Just across the street from *Museum of the Americas* is this handsomely restored 19th century building, which was once used as a mental hospital. Today it is the headquarters of the Institute of Puerto Rican Culture and displays rotating exhibits of Puerto Rican and Latin American art. Open Wednesdays through Sundays, 9 AM to 4:30 PM; no admission charge (phone: 724-0700).

CASA BLANCA On Calle San Sebastián next to the Welfare House is a serene white house that was built for, but never lived in by, Ponce de León. After his death, his son-in-law, Juan García Troche, had the original frame house replaced with the present masonry one, where his descendants lived for 250 years; it was later a residence for both Spanish and US military commanders. The house is now the site of two museums: the *Juan Ponce de León Museum,* whose exhibits illustrate 16th- and 17th-century Puerto Rican life, and the *Taíno Indian Ethno-Historic Museum.* Open Wednesdays through Sundays from 9 AM to noon and 1 to 4 PM; admission charge (phone: 724-4102).

Exit the museum on Calle del Sol past "step streets" on either side, and turn right — downhill again — on Cristo. A block's walk brings you to a shaded square. Facing it, on the east side of Cristo, is the city's main cathedral.

CATEDRAL DE SAN JUAN (SAN JUAN CATHEDRAL) First built in 1540, and extensively restored in 1977, the circular staircase and four nearby rooms with vaulted Gothic ceilings are all that remain of the original structure; the rest is predominantly early 19th century. The body of Ponce de León now rests in a marble tomb near the transept; a relic of the Roman martyr San Pío is enshrined near it. Open daily from 8:30 AM to 4 PM; guided tours Mondays through Fridays by appointment; mass daily (phone: 722-0861).

EL CONVENTO The imposing building with great wooden doors on your right facing the square as you leave the cathedral, this was built as a Carmelite convent in the 17th century. Nowadays it's a hotel with a patio that's convenient for lunch or a refreshing drink.

At this point, those who've had enough sightseeing can continue down Calle Cristo, where they'll find some of the city's most enticing boutiques; to explore a bit more history, follow the Caleta las Monjas (Little Street of the Nuns) from *El Convento* downhill to the Plazuela de la Rogativa at the city wall. Turn left on Calle Recinto Oueste, and walk downhill to the San Juan Gate.

LA FORTALEZA (THE FORTRESS) Just past the San Juan Gate, this is the Western Hemisphere's oldest executive mansion, home to more than 200 Puerto Rican governors. Its original single tower and patio were built in 1540; its more palatial elements were 19th-century additions. Note especially the polished reception rooms, stately mahogany staircase, the mosaic-lined chapel, and the gardens. Open from 9 AM to 4 PM weekdays, except holidays; free guided tours (phone: 721-7000 for schedule). Leaving La Fortaleza, walk east (toward the city's center) on Calle Fortaleza and turn right on Cristo. At the end of the street on your right is a small park.

PARQUE DE LAS PALMAS (PIGEON PARK) Named for its resident birds, this is a good place to rest and admire the surrounding cluster of antique buildings. Notice tiny Cristo Chapel, with its silver altar visible through glass doors. It's open Tuesdays from 10 AM to 3:30 PM. Also nearby is *La Casa del Libro* (House of Books), a scholarly book and bookmaking museum set in an 18th-century house. The collection of 4,000 volumes includes original letters from Ferdinand and Isabella; special exhibitions are held on the first floor. Open Tuesdays through Saturdays, except holidays, from 11 AM to 4:30 PM (phone: 723-0354).

BASTIÓN DE LAS PALMAS Follow the wall east 1 block to reach this defense emplacement–turned–park with a great view of the bay and the mountains beyond. Then turn north on Calle San José and walk 2 short blocks.

PLAZA DE ARMAS The former heart of the city, this plaza is faced on the west by the neo-classical Intendencia, which houses some Justice Department offices, and on the north by the City Hall (don't wait for tours, but stock up on tourist information at the center near the main entrance).

ARSENAL A few blocks south, in the waterfront section known as La Puntilla, this restored 19th-century arsenal features handsome fountains; periodic exhibitions are held in its three galleries. Open Wednesdays through Sundays, 9 AM to noon and 1 to 4:30 PM (phone: 724-5949).

PLAZA DE COLÓN (COLUMBUS PLAZA) Located five traffic-filled blocks east whichever *calle* you take (San Francisco and Fortaleza are both major tourist shopping streets), this plaza is the site of the graceful *Tapia Theater* (phone: 722-0407), now restored to its 19th-century elegance and presenting ballet, concerts, and dramatic performances. A few steps away, *La Tasca del Callejón* (phone: 721-1689) serves tasty Puerto Rican lunches and cold beer.

EAST OF SAN JUAN

EL YUNQUE Follow Route 3 east about 25 miles, and turn right (south) onto Route 191, which climbs up into the forest surrounding El Yunque's 3,493-foot peak and that of its taller brother, El Toro (3,523 feet). The trip will take about 45 minutes from downtown San Juan. Officially called the Caribbean National Forest, it was set aside by the Spanish Crown in 1876; later designated a forest reserve by Theodore Roosevelt, its 28,000 acres make up the only tropical forest in the US national system. El Yunque boasts 240 different species of trees, only 6 of which are indigenous to the continental US; it is also a bird sanctuary, and one of the few places where you can hear the call of Puerto Rico's national mascot — the tiny tree frog called *coquí* — in the daytime. It is almost certain to shower while you're there (100 billion gallons fall here each year), but don't worry: Rains are brief, and there are lots of shelters. The Sierra Palm Visitors Center on Route 191, open daily from 9:30 AM till 5 PM, gives free nature talks and slide shows (phone: 887-2875 or 766-5335). There's also a waterfall-fed swimming hole (picturesque, but cold) and a rustic restaurant. Then make your way back to Route 3 and travel 5 miles farther east to:

LUQUILLO BEACH About 30 miles east of the capital, it is certainly the most famous of the 12 major island beaches with government-built *balneario* facilities (lockers, showers, parking). Open Tuesdays through Sundays 9 AM to 5 PM in winter, 8 AM to 5PM in summer. It's gorgeous, too — long, white, and lined with leggy palms, but apt to be crowded on weekends. Bring your own towels and lunch (or snack on coconut milk, *pionoños,* and *pasteles* at stands near the entrance). Fees: 25¢ per person for locker, shower, and changing space; $1 per car for parking. (Tent sites also are available.) Then back to Route 3 and keep an eye on the signs until you come to:

LAS CABEZAS DE SAN JUAN NATURE RESERVE This 316-acre nature reserve opened in 1991 and includes forest land, mangroves, lagoons, cliffs, beaches, coral reefs, offshore cays, and a 19th-century lighthouse. The reserve is better known as "El Faro," or "The Lighthouse," and is surrounded on three sides by the Atlantic Ocean. Open Wednesdays through

Sundays by reservation only; guided tours are given at 9:30 AM, 10:30 AM, and 1:30 PM (be sure to call well in advance, especially on weekends, when the tours fill up quickly); admission charge (phone: 722-5882).

FAJARDO A small east coast seaport, bustling but relaxed. Ferries leave from here every morning and afternoon for Vieques; the one-way fare is about $2 for adults, $1 for children under 12 for the less-than-1-hour trip. There are also ferries to Culebra; the 1-hour ride each way costs $2.25 for adults, $1 for children under 12. At the small harbor at Las Croabas, you can hire a native sloop (capacity: six passengers) to take you out to Icacos for a swim (half-day price: $50 or so, depending on the boat and your bargaining power; bring masks and flippers if you want to snorkel). An ocean of water-based activities is available at the Puerto del Ray marina (see *Boating*), including deep-sea fishing and day sails. Carry on along Route 3, until you reach:

HUMACAO Not a tourist town, but it has a splendid *balneario*-equipped beach (25¢ per person for locker, changing room; $1 to park your car); casual snack stands, too. Detour south to the beautiful 2,750-acre sports resort called *Palmas del Mar* (see *Checking In*). Have a swim and a rum punch (at the beach, not the pool — which tends to get overcrowded), and stay over in comfort. Or travel along Route 3 to Arroyo (another public beach — Punta Guilarte — is just east of town) and Guayama, where you turn right (north) on Route 15 to join Las Américas Expressway 52 to speed back to San Juan.

SOUTH OF SAN JUAN

PONCE About 75 miles south and west as the Las Américas Expressway flies (take Route 1, then 52), Ponce is the island's second-largest city. Founded in 1692 by Ponce de León's great-grandson, it runs the architectural gamut from handsomely historic (the dignified Cathedral of Our Lady of Guadalupe, dominating the central plaza) and notably modern (the small *Museum of Art* designed by Edward Durell Stone, famed architect of the *Museum of Modern Art* in New York City) to just plain kooky (the combustibly christened *Parque de Bombas* — i.e., firehouse — is red-and-black-striped with green and yellow fanlights; it houses fire-fighting memorabilia). The marketplace at Atocha and Castillo Streets is almost as colorful.

Not to be missed is the *Ponce Museum of Art* (on Las Américas Ave.), the best in the Caribbean, with a 1,500-piece collection. Its exhibitions feature the works of contemporary Latin American artists and European greats such as Rubens and Rodin, though it is best known for its pre-Raphaelite paintings and its baroque paintings and sculpture from Italy, Spain, and France. Included in the museum's permanent collection are several works by Puerto Rican artists Miguel Pou and Francisco Oller. Open daily; admission charge (phone: 848-0505).

A 40-by-80-block area of the city has been designated a National Historic Site and Treasure; walk around and see some of the 1,000 colonial buildings and lovely Victorian houses and banks (almost half of these were restored by the US government for the 1992 celebration of the city's founding 500 years earlier). Streets are again edged with pink marble and illuminated by replicas of 19th-century gas lamps. For tourist information, stop at the Institute of Puerto Rican Culture (Casa Armstrong-Poventud; phone: 844-8240); it's open weekdays from 8 AM to noon and 1 to 4:30 PM. If you're in the mood for a cool drink or a bite to eat, stop at the *Meliá* hotel off the main plaza.

Then follow narrow Bertoly Street until you see a huge pink palace perched on a hill overlooking the city. This is *Castillo Serrallés,* a restored 19th-century landmark and home of the Serrallés family (makers of Don Q rum). The 15-room Spanish Revival house has been refurbished to look as it did during the 1930s. Most impressive are the huge windows that make the landscape — the Caribbean Sea to the south and the Cordillera Central to the north — seem like part of the building itself. There's also a display on rum production and a café. It's open daily except Mondays from 10 AM to 5:30 PM; tours in English and Spanish are offered. There's an admission charge (phone: 259-1774). Next to *Castillo Serrallés* is the 100-foot-tall El Vigía observation tower, which offers the best view of the surrounding area. It's open Tuesdays and Wednesdays from 9 AM to 5:30 PM and Thursdays through Sundays from 10 AM to 10 PM; admission charge (phone: 840-4141).

Just north of town, at the *Tibes Indian Ceremonial Center,* pre-Taíno ruins from AD 700 — restored to include a re-created village, a museum, and seven intact ceremonial ball courts — are well worth a visit. The museum is closed Mondays; admission charge (phone: 840-2255). On Route 10, Hacienda Buena Vista is a restored coffee plantation featuring re-creations of mechanical mills, slave quarters, a coffee husker, and photographs from the plantation as it was in 1870. Open Fridays through Sundays; reservations necessary; admission charge (phone: 722-5882).

COAMO A mineral springs resort in the hills northeast of Ponce, it's been rediscovered and rejuvenated. The spa *parador, Baños de Coamo* (Rte. 546; phone: 721-2884 or 825-2186), with pools, air conditioned rooms and restaurant, makes it a pleasant detour or overnight spot.

TORO NEGRO STATE FOREST In the central mountains north of Ponce, the 7,000-acre preserve has woods, waterfalls, picnic tables, barbecue pits, a spring-fed swimming pool, and an observation tower. With an early start it could be a day trip from San Juan, but it's easier from Ponce.

WEST OF SAN JUAN

DORADO This town is off Route 693, which turns north off the main Route 2 a few miles west of Bayamón. There are a few interesting gift and crafts shops on the main drag and a shopping center as you exit town to the north. It's the nearest town to the sister resorts of *Hyatt Cerromar Beach* and *Hyatt Dorado Beach.* Drive through the resorts' grounds, stay for lunch or a drink, and then return to Route 2 and continue west to:

ARECIBO A commercial town by the sea known for its lighthouse, its beaches, its rum distillery (Ron Rico), and its goat cheese. It's also a tour turning point. To the south, Route 10 leads to a mixed bag of sites:

RÍO ABAJO STATE FOREST A 5,800-acre woodland (predominantly teak) with ranger's office, sawmill, recreation area (very pretty for picnicking), and a big, blue, manmade lake called Dos Bocas on which there are launch trips (no swimming).

CAGUANA INDIAN CEREMONIAL PARK Several miles farther south on Route 111 off Route 10 near the coffee town of Utuado, this is a 13-acre landscaped park with paved walks and plazas, and monoliths put here by the Taíno Indians 800 years ago. Open daily 9 AM to 4:30 PM; no admission charge (phone: 894-7325). Route 140 is the scenic road back to San Juan.

ARECIBO OBSERVATORY A special place with special visiting hours: between 1 and 4:30 PM on Sundays, and between 2 and 3 PM Tuesdays through Fridays. It has the world's largest radio telescope, with a 20-acre curved reflector installed over a natural karst sinkhole 1,300 feet wide by 300 feet deep. If astronomy fascinates you, it may be worth the 35-minute drive from Arecibo, via Rtes. 129, 134, 635, and 625 (phone: 878-2612).

RÍO CAMUY CAVES Southwest of Arecibo Observatory (via Routes 635 and 455), this 250-acre park features the island's natural vegetation. The most interesting part of the park is a series of limestone caves with stalactites and stalagmites, accessible by trolley cars. Guides lead visitors (45-minute tours are offered in English as well as Spanish) through the very cool caves that are 200 feet underground. There are also sinkholes (depressions in the earth made from the river eroding the land) that are open to visitors. The caves are 2 hours from San Juan, and are open from 8 AM to 4 PM Wednesdays through Sundays and holidays; admission charge (phone: 756-5555 or 898-3100).

JAYUYA (PRONOUNCED HA-*JU*-JA) West and a little south of Utuado, this is the site of a former coffee plantation house, *Parador Hacienda Gripiñas,* which is now a most appealing inn. Nothing to do but enjoy the view, the peace, the good food, the pool, and the mountain air (see *Checking In* for details).

You may, however, want to skip this detour and from Arecibo keep moving west along Route 2 for Quebradillas, site of the island's first *parador, Guajataca* (stop for turtle steaks, smashing views of the sea, and/or an overnight — see *Checking In*); Aguadilla, site of *Arenas del Mar,* a moderately priced club-type resort catering largely to charter groups (phone: 890-4560); Rincón, the beach resort with several small, casual hotels that's a favorite with surfers (the *World Championships* were held here in 1968 and 1988); and finally on to any of the following scenic highpoints:

MAYAGÜEZ Halfway down the west coast, this is Puerto Rico's third-largest city. A friendly, busy port that is architecturally unremarkable, it still shines as a headquarters for exploring the western and southwestern sections of the island. Mayagüez once was considered the needlework capital of Puerto Rico, and intrepid shoppers may still be able to unearth fine embroidery and drawn-thread work in the older shops downtown. The western campus of the University of Puerto Rico and the Federal Agricultural Experimental Station (phone: 831-3435) — the latter with the Western Hemisphere's largest collection of tropical plants — both have grounds worth seeing. And the zoo, which is open daily except Mondays 9 AM to 5 PM, is super; admission charge (phone: 834-8110)). Mayagüez is also the home of *Fido's Beer Garden,* little more than a corner deli (at Berisario del Valle and Dulievre Sts.), where Fido sells his locally famous, and quite potent, sangria for $5 a bottle or $10 a gallon, complete with orange-and-cherry-trimmed plastic cups.

MONA ISLAND About 50 miles west of Mayagüez, this rugged island is inhabited by colonies of sea birds and yard-long iguanas. Its breathtaking, 200-foot cliffs have caves said to have been hiding places for pirate booty, and beautiful white-sand beaches line the shore. The island is protected by the National Park Service and the Puerto Rico Natural Resources Department. Overnight camping is allowed (permits cost $2 per day) and there are also some cabins available for lodging. For more information or to apply for a camping permit, contact the Puerto Rico Natural Resources Department, located next to *Club Naútico de San Juan* in Miramar (phone: 722-1726); or write to the department at PO Box 5887, San Juan, PR 00907.

BOQUERÓN BEACH The government has installed small cottages at this mile-long west coast gem of a beach that's as beautiful as any in the Caribbean, and the prices for overnight accommodations are very low (about $15 a night), provided an application is mailed 4 months in advance to the Recreation and Sports Department (Box 2923, San Juan, PR 00903; phone: 722-1551, ext. 225, or 721-2800, ext. 275). Swimming is less complicated: 25¢ per person for a locker and changing space, $1 for parking. *Note:* Weekends attract lots of local families and teens with boom boxes. A little to the north of here are Guaniquilla Point, with a lagoon filled with spikey limestone boulders; tiny Buyé Beach; and a proliferation of seafood restaurants at Joyuda Beach.

CABO ROJO LIGHTHOUSE At the island's southwesternmost corner (and not to be confused with the town of the same name farther north), the century-old Spanish lighthouse is worth seeing.

SAN GERMÁN The island's second-oldest city (pronounced San Her-*mahn*) has a couple of pretty plazas, a colonial atmosphere, interesting architecture (shops and homes with turrets and gingerbread trim), and a winsome church that may be the New World's oldest (Porta Coeli, dating from 1606), now a museum of religious art with some pieces dating from the late 16th century. Open Wednesdays through Sundays 8:30AM to noon and 1 to 4:30 PM; no admission charge (phone: 892-5845). A charmingly restored hotel, the *Parador Oasis* (see *Checking In*), is here.

LA PARGUERA This tiny fishing village on the south coast, headquarters for deep-sea charter boats, has a casual, friendly inn, the *Villa Parguera* (see *Checking In*), and the famous Phosphorescent Bay, which glows in the dark.

GUÁNICA A small beach resort, also on the south coast, it's got lots of sand, space, and an informal hotel, the *Copamarina* (phone: 821-0505).

EXTRA SPECIAL **The Ruta Panorámica meanders across the Cordillera Central and the Cayey Range from Mayagüez on the west coast to Yabucoa and Punta Tuna Lighthouse at the southeast corner of the island. Built for scenery, not speed, it comprises 40 roads over 165 miles which offer stunning vistas all the way, often with rain forest on both sides. It intersects with principal north-south routes so even if you can't spare 12 hours to drive from one end to the other, you can enjoy random samples. Several inns and *paradores* lie a few miles north or south if you want to take it really easy.**

Sources and Resources

TOURIST INFORMATION

The Puerto Rico Tourism Company operates several US offices (for information, see GETTING READY TO GO). They also maintain information centers at two key tourist points in San Juan: at the International Airport (phone: 791-1014 or 791-2551) and La Casita (near Pier One) in Old San Juan (phone: 722-1709 or 724-4788). Elsewhere on the island, tourist information is available in the city halls of Adjuntas, Añasco, Bayamón, Cabo Rojo, Culebra, Dorado, Guánica, Jayuya, Luquillo, Maricao, Mayagüez, Naguabo, Ponce, Rincón, and Vieques.

LOCAL COVERAGE The *San Juan Star,* Puerto Rico's English-language newspaper, is published every morning. *El Vocero* and *El Día* are Spanish-language dailies. New York City and Miami newspapers usually are available on the day of publication in hotels and at the *Book Store,* at 257 San José in Old San Juan (phone: 724-1815).

Qué Pasa, the free official visitors' guide published monthly by the tourist office, is the best of its kind in the Caribbean, with information on special events, sports, sights, lodging, restaurants, transportation, and shopping in San Juan and out on the island. Get one at your hotel desk or at any information center. Ask at the tourist office for maps of historic sites and material on galleries and craft studios. A magazine/guide available only in Puerto Rico, *Walking Tours of Old San Juan* ($2.50), packs in lots of visitors' information. *A Short History of Puerto Rico,* by Morton J. Golding, and *The Forts of Old San Juan,* by Albert Manucy and Ricardo Torres-Reyes, are good reading for history buffs.

RADIO AND TELEVISION

WOSO-AM broadcasts in English, and Puerto Rico Cable TV carries local English programming.

TELEPHONE

The area code for Puerto Rico is 809.

ENTRY REQUIREMENTS

Neither passports nor visas are required of US or Canadian citizens, but Canadians must carry some form of identification (such as a birth certificate).

CLIMATE AND CLOTHES

It's warm and sunny year-round on the island's resort coasts, always 5 to 10F cooler in the mountains. Winter temperatures in San Juan range from the low 70s F (about 22C) to the low 80s F (27 to 29C). In summer, the spread edges up about 5F. The wettest months are May to December; you're least likely to need an umbrella in March and April. As a general rule, however, there's more rain on the north coast than in the south.

In San Juan, clothing needs range from daytime beachwear to nighttime casino attire. But keep in mind that beyond the hotel strip, San Juan is both a city and Spanish in its heritage. That means no short shorts downtown, in churches, or in public buildings. And it means nights are dressier — especially in casinos, nightclubs, and the tonier restaurants. Women should carry sweaters or light wraps to foil air conditioning drafts.

At the larger sports resorts out on the island (*Hyatt Dorado Beach, Hyatt Cerromar Beach,* and to a somewhat lesser extent, *Palmas del Mar*), days call for classic sports clothes (tennis togs are required on the courts); nights go tieless but call for a certain sense of style, with blazers or jackets preferred for men, casual resort evening wear for women.

Both in cities and out on the island, dress is generally more casual at smaller hotels and guesthouses.

MONEY

Only the Yankee dollar is official in Puerto Rico, though some places will — reluctantly — accept Canadian currency. Major credit cards (MasterCard, Visa, American Express, Diners Club) are widely accepted in Puerto Rican hotels, restaurants, and shops. Banking hours are from 9 AM to 2:30 PM on weekdays, except holidays. The big US banks all have branches on the island.

LANGUAGE

In cities and major tourist resorts, English is always understood, usually spoken. With islanders, however, Spanish — though not of the pure Castilian idiom — is still *número uno.*

TIME

Clocks keep atlantic standard time — that's 1 hour ahead of eastern standard time, the same as eastern daylight saving time. So in winter, when it's noon in New York it's 1 PM in San Juan. From April until late October, noon in the eastern US is noon in Puerto Rico.

CURRENT

It's 110 volts, 60 cycles — the same as in the continental US and Canada.

TIPPING

The commonwealth's system is like that in the continental US. Airport porters expect $1 per bag; and taxi drivers, 15% of the fare. Leave $1 to $2 per room per day for the hotel chambermaid; give the doorman 50¢ to $1 for calling a cab. The standard tip in hotel dining rooms and supper clubs is 15%; and, unless the package tour you bought specifically states otherwise, remember that package-trip meal coupons usually do not cover tips, so leave 15% of your estimate of the cost of the meal.

GETTING AROUND

AIRPORT LIMOUSINES These are the least expensive way to get from Isla Verde's Luis Muñoz Marín International Airport to your hotel. Rates are between $1 and $1.75 from the airport to most of San Juan's hotel areas and $12 to Dorado. Unless the driver does you some very special favor, you needn't tip. (Don't count on limousine service to the airport, however; limos aren't allowed to pick up at hotels.)

BUS Neat, handy, and inexpensive, they run day and night for a fare of 25¢ or 40¢, depending on the route. There are two models: a conventional bus (painted brown), and a blue and white air conditioned model. City terminals are at the Plaza de Colón and the Covadonga parking garage; elsewhere, bus stops are marked by yellow posts or metal standards reading "Parada" or "Parada de Guaguas." Routes to note: No. 1, marked "Río Piedras," which goes through the banking district in Hato Rey to the University of Puerto Rico; and Nos. T1, A7, and 2, which run from Old San Juan to Condado and Isla Verde and pass many of the hotels. Bus lanes run against traffic on main thoroughfares. For additional information, call 767-7979.

CAR RENTAL Rental cars are easy to come by. Rates start at about $37 a day, $210 a week (plus insurance), for a compact with automatic shift. Mileage is unlimited, and the rate includes oil, maintenance, and standard insurance; you pay for gas. *Avis* (phone: 791-5212; 800-221-1084 from the US), *Budget* (phone: 791-3685 or 725-1182; 800-468-5822 from the US), *Hertz* (phone: 791-0844; 800-654-3001 from the US), *National* (phone: 791-1805 or 791-5063), and *Thrifty* (phone: 791-4241; 800-367-2277 from the US) are all represented in downtown San Juan, some Condado and Isla Verde hotels, Isla Verde Airport, and in Ponce and Mayagüez as well. Local firms like *Afro* (phone: 724-3720 or 723-8287), *Atlantic* (phone: 721-3811 or 721-3813), *L&M* (phone: 725-8416 or 725-8307; 800-666-0807 from the US), and *Target* (phone: 728-1447 or 728-1684) offer special low cash deals; they do take credit cards, but don't have reassuring offices out on the island. For a day trip out of San Juan, they're okay. For longer tours, the internationals are probably a wiser choice. Always opt for air conditioning.

Puerto Rican speed limits are given in miles per hour, but road signs show distances in kilometers. (A kilometer equals roughly .6 of a mile.) Also, the car horn remains a basic Puerto Rican driving tool. On twisting roads out on the island, it's imperative that you honk when approaching blind curves to warn oncoming cars to keep right. Finally, if you plan to return a rental car to the airport (Isla Verde, that is), allow plenty of time, drive slowly, and follow your car company's signs very carefully; it's confusing out there. Better still, turn in your car in town and take a cab to catch your plane.

FERRY SERVICE Boats sail every half hour from the small pier next to Pier One for the little town of Cataño across the bay; it's a neat $1 (round-trip) way to cool off any day, but in July, when the population stages a fiesta in honor of its patron saint, it's a ticket to a party with parades, booths, rides, dancing, and all sorts of fun in the streets. From Fajardo, at the eastern end of the island, a Port Authority launch makes daily morning and afternoon trips carrying passengers only to the islands of Vieques and Culebra. There is service between Culebra and Vieques on Mondays, weekends, and holidays. One-way fare: about $2 per person. Weekdays, a ferry carrying cars makes a round trip. If you want to take your car (a good idea if you want to visit all the hidden beaches on these islands), call 863-0705 or 800-223-6530, Mondays through Fridays, for reservations and current schedule; the round-trip fare is $25.

PÚBLICOS Cars or minibuses whose license plate numbers are followed by the letters PD or P provide point-to-point transport all over the island for reasonable rates. Basic routes run from Town A plaza to Town B plaza, with drivers stopping to pick up or drop passengers anywhere along the route. They are insured, and the Public Service Commission sets the prices. If your Spanish is in working order and your schedule is flexible, you might give them a whirl.

SEA EXCURSIONS A 2½-hour sunset cruise around San Juan Harbor is offered by *Caribe Aquatic Adventures* (phone: 724-1882); the $50 cost includes beer and refreshments. The *Condado Plaza* (phone: 721-1000) has dinner cruises for groups of 10 or more for $75 per person. The sailboat *La Esperanza* leaves twice a day (at 3 and 7 PM,) except Tuesdays, from Plaza Darsenas in Old San Juan for a 2-hour jaunt around the bay. The cost is $10 for adults, $5 for children under 9 (phone: 724-5590 or 721-8037). From Fajardo, several tour operators go to the numerous cays and islands off the coast for a day of snorkeling and swimming. Try *Sea Ventures* (phone: 863-3483) or *Spread Eagle* (phone: 863-1905). Rates, which include lunch, are about $45. On Saturdays, Sundays, and holidays, a ferry departs from Malecón Avenue (Route 10) in Ponce to Caja de Muerto Island (Coffin Island), where visitors can swim or snorkel (bring your own equipment). The cost is $5.50 for adults and $3.50 for children under 11. The same company that runs the ferry also offers bay cruises and private tours (phone: 848-4575).

The *Palmas del Mar* marina, near Humacao, arranges skippered charters for a day or longer (phone: 852-6000). And from La Parguera (the *Villa Parguera* pier), boats depart from 7:30 PM through 12:30 AM (depending on demand) on moonless nights for a firsthand look at the luminous wonders of Phosphorescent Bay. Even on evenings when the moon is out, you can witness the sparkling phenomenon on early trips; best are the glass-bottom boats (fare, about $3 for the 1-hour ride).

SIGHTSEEING BUS TOURS A number of firms offer daily rain forest tours (at about $25 per person for the half-day trip to El Yunque, including a swim at Luquillo Beach) plus assorted trips to the Bacardi rum distillery, *El Comandante* racetrack, and Ponce. Principal companies are *Borinquen Tours* (phone: 722-1745), *Gray Line* (phone: 727-8080), *Fuentes Bus Line* (phone: 780-7070), *United Tour Guides* (phone: 725-7605 or 723-5578), and *Rico Suntours* (phone: 722-2080 or 722-6090). Offerings change, so consult *Qué Pasa* or your hotel travel desk about current best values.

TAXI Cabs are found at the airport, near the cruise piers, and in lines outside major San Juan hotels. All cabs authorized by the Public Service Commission are metered (although the meter is not used on trips outside normal taxi zones; for these, you and the driver should agree on a price in advance). The fare from the airport to an Isla Verde hotel runs about $7 including tip; it's about $12 to Condado, and about $17 to downtown San Juan plus an additional 50¢ per bag. The fare from an Isla Verde or Condado hotel to Old San Juan runs $7 to $9 plus luggage charge. San Juan drivers don't do much taxi touring.

INTER-ISLAND FLIGHTS

In Puerto Rico, *American Airlines' American Eagle* flies from San Juan to Ponce and Mayagüez. *Vieques Air-Link* (phone: 722-3736) offers frequent daily flights (in small 8-seaters) from San Juan's Isla Grande Airport to

Vieques. The airline also offers flights from Vieques to St. Croix. *Flamenco* (phone: 724-7110) flies to Culebra from Isla Grande Airport, next to the downtown area and handy to Old San Juan and close-in Condado hotels. Numerous flights (95 daily) connect Puerto Rico and other Caribbean islands. St. Thomas is a short 30 minutes away, and St. Croix, 45 minutes. *American Eagle* has daily service to St. Thomas and to La Romana in the Dominican Republic. Charters are available to the Greater and Lesser Antilles (phone: 791-8181).

SPECIAL EVENTS

Puerto Rico has more celebrations than any other Caribbean island. Every town has its patron saint, and holds a 1- to 3-day fiesta marking his or her feast day each year. On June 24, San Juan celebrates the *Feast of St. John the Baptist,* when resort hotels often sponsor beachside barbecues that culminate in the traditional mass midnight dunking — for good luck — in the surf; the 8-day observance in honor of *Santiago Apostal* (St. James the Apostle), one of the island's most festive celebrations, starts on July 25 in Loíza, 15 miles east of San Juan; and there are 75 to 80 others. The last week of July, Vieques holds its *Carnaval,* featuring calypso music.

The *Casals Festival,* begun in 1957 by the late cellist-conductor-composer Pablo Casals, takes place at the *Performing Arts Center* in San Juan, usually during the first 2 weeks in June. Tickets are very hard to come by; for details, write as far in advance as possible to *Corporación de las Artes Escénico-Musicales* (Apto. 41227, Minillas Station, Santurce, PR 00940-1227). More than 130 Puerto Rican craftspersons participate in the 30-year-old *Barranquitas Artisans Fair* in mid-July in Barranquitas. Colorful masks and folk music characterize the *Hatillo Festival of the Masks* in late December in Hatillo. Bacardi also holds an annual arts and crafts festival in December on the grounds of its rum plant in Cataño. Numerous *Carnaval* festivities take place in February; the city of Ponce holds one of the most exciting, with masqueraders, live music, and lots of street parties.

Puerto Rico also seems to have more than its share of public holidays. Official national holidays include *New Year's Day, Three Kings' Day* (January 6), *Martin Luther King Day, Washington's Birthday, Good Friday, Easter Sunday, Memorial Day, Fourth of July, Labor Day, Veterans' Day, Thanksgiving, Christmas,* and *Election Day.* The island also celebrates its own *Constitution Day* (July 25), *José Celso Barbosa's Birthday* (July 27), *Columbus Day* (October 12), and *Discovery Day* (November 19). On these days, banks, businesses, government offices, and schools are closed.

But there are also half holidays, when banks and businesses remain open but government offices and schools close. These include educator and patriot *Eugenio María de Hostos's Birthday* (January 11), *Emancipation Day* (March 22), and poet and statesman *Luis Muñoz Rivera's Birthday* (July 17).

LeLoLai, a musical expression borrowed from the song of the Puerto

Rican *jíbaro* (freely translated as "hillbilly"), is the name of a year-round festival of weekly events sponsored by the Puerto Rico Tourism Company, which features native dance, music, and foods. The events are included free in many tour packages. You can also buy tickets for individual events from information centers and hotel travel desks for about $2 to $30 each. The Puerto Rico Tourism Company recently expanded the *LeLoLai* program to include a wider selection of shows and discounts on guided tours, restaurants, and car rentals. For details, contact the company's New York office at 575 Fifth Ave., 23rd Floor, New York, NY 10017 (phone: 800-223-6530).

SHOPPING

The good news is that you pay no duty on anything you take home to the continental United States from Puerto Rico. That's because US import taxes have already been paid. Which brings us to the bad news: Since the island is not a duty-free port, you'll find no ultra-low-price imported bargains. What you will find is a number of specialized stores and boutiques staffed with helpful people and stocked with island crafts that aren't for sale at home.

Island crafts take many forms: predictable (straw work, ceramics); useful (hammocks, men's *guayabera* shirts, *mundillo* or handmade bobbin lace fashioned into collars and tablecloths); surprising (weird Loíza masks, cheery papier-mâché fruit); and unique (guitar-like *cuatros,* hand-carved *santos* figures).

Crafts centers include *Galería Epoca en Tourismo* (at La Casita Information Center), *Iquitos* (103 Calle Cristo), and the *National Center of Popular Arts and Crafts* (253 Calle Cristo). In addition, *Mercado de Artesanía Carabali* (Sixto Escobar Park) and *Mercado de Artesanía Puertorriqueña–Hermandad de Artesanos* (Muñoz Rivera Park) are open on weekends; both are in Puerta de Tierra, between Old San Juan and the Condado strip.

To visit artisans' shops "out on the island" — *santeros* (*santos* makers) and mask makers in Ponce, basket weavers in Jayuya, or hammock makers in San Sebastián — visitors can contact the government-sponsored *Centro de Artes Populares* (phone: 724-6250), or the Tourism Artisan office (phone: 721-2400, ext. 248) to find out which artisans welcome visitors. Other excellent sources for authentic handicrafts are the craft festivals held annually throughout the island. They include Ponce's *Crafts Festival* (March); the *Puerto Rico Weaving Festival,* held in Isabela (May); the *Artisans Fair* in Barranquitas (mid-July); San Juan's *Summer Arts Festival* in Muñoz Rivera Park (August); Mayagüez's *Crafts Fair* (November); and the *Bacardi Arts Festival* (December).

The art scene on the island is alive and exciting, with contemporary Puerto Ricans working in every medium. Jan d'Esopo is a well-known local painter whose images of island life are sold in the *Galería San*

Jerónimo in the *Condado Plaza* (phone: 722-1808). Luis Hernández Cruz, Myrna Báez, Francisco Rodon, Rafael Tufino, and Julio Rosado del Valle are among the island's best-known graphic artists.

Rum, another source of Puerto Rican pride, sells for about half its stateside price, and there's no limit to the tax-free bottles you can bring home. Ask at your hotel for a nearby shop that sells stamped bottles (the average Puerto Rican liquor store does not), where you'll have a bigger selection than at the airport shop. Most Puerto Rican rums are fine and light, but the connoisseurs' choice is aged añejo, which has the smoothness and power of a good brandy. An excellent one, Ron del Barrilito, sells for under $10 on the island, just a little more than half its typical stateside price.

For a tasty further education in the history and art of making rum, visit the Bacardi rum distillery in Cataño (take the ferry from Old San Juan and then a *público* to the distillery). Free guided tours and samples are given daily except Sundays and holidays from 9:30 AM to 3 PM (phone: 788-1500).

Puerto Rican coffee, which is grown in the central mountain range and is noted for its rich and aromatic flavor, can be purchased in all grocery stores. Look for such brands as Café Crema, Café Rico, Rioja, and Yaucono, which each sell for about $3.60 per pound.

Along Calle Fortaleza are the majority of Old San Juan's good jewelry shops, including *N. Barquet* (No. 104), *Letran* (No. 201), and *Yas Mar* (No. 205). Travelers looking for wearable souvenirs can browse along Calle Cristo between Calles Fortaleza and San Francisco, the main shopping street for apparel in Old San Juan. For couture of an haute-er order, stroll along Ashford Avenue in Condado, where boutiques feature the originals of such locally known designers as Nono Maldonado, Fernando Peña, Annie Lago, and Milli Arango.

Most major hotels have shops that are branches of downtown establishments. In these, as well as in downtown stores and at most places on the island, price tags mean what they say. There's no haggling. Stores are generally open from 9 AM to 6 PM, Mondays through Saturdays; in Old San Juan, shops may extend their hours during high season if several cruise ships are in town; at *Plaza Las Américas* (with 250 stores) shops are open until 9 PM on Fridays and from noon to 5 PM on Sundays. Major credit cards are accepted, except where noted. Among the many places where you might want to part with your money (all are in San Juan, unless otherwise noted):

BARED AND SONS Fine imported china and crystal, which the staff claims are 30% to 35% below US mainland prices. There are three stores in Old San Juan: at Fortaleza and San Justo (phone: 724-4815), Fortaleza and Tanca (phone: 724-4816), and Fortaleza at Cristo (phone: 724-4811).

CASA CAVANAGH High-priced chic resortwear for both men and women. *Condado Plaza,* Ashford Ave. (phone: 723-1125).

GALERÍA BOTELLO Among the best galleries on the island, it showcases the work of Botello and other Latin American artists, and has a fine *santos* collection. 208 Calle Cristo (phone: 723-2879 or 723-9987).

GILLIES & WOODWARD Stop off for cigars made of island tobacco, hand-rolled while you watch, and selling for $24 to $37 per box. 253 San Justo (phone: 725-5280).

LEATHER & PEARLS Majolica pearls and Gucci, Fendi, and Mark Cross products at a slight discount. 202 Calle Cristo (phone: 724-8185).

LONDON FOG FACTORY OUTLET More than just rain gear, here are men's, women's, and children's fashions — all at substantial discounts. 156 Calle Cristo, Old San Juan (phone: 722-4334).

M. RIVERA Miniature Spanish-style houses (*casitas*), starting at $15, make unique gifts. 107 Calle Cristo (phone: 724-1004) and 3 Calle Marina (phone: 722-2388).

MATT BAGS A wide selection of high-quality leather handbags at reasonable prices, plus interesting jewelry. 301 Calle Tanca (phone: 721-3483).

NONO MALDONADO Trendy fashions for *GQ* readers. Two locations: 1051 Ashford Ave., Condado (phone: 721-0456) and at *El San Juan* hotel (phone: 791-7550).

OLÉ The place for crafts, including hand-painted watercolors and prints by island artists, leather sandals, and gourd masks. Antiques are sold at the back of the shop; the most interesting items are the *santos* from Puerto Rico and Latin America. 105 Calle Fortaleza (phone: 724-2445).

POLO/RALPH LAUREN Men's, women's, and children's clothing, including jeans, at discounts of 30% to 50%. Calles Cristo and San Francisco (phone: 722-2136).

PUERTO RICAN ART & CRAFTS The finest in artisanry from all over the island, including choice ceramics, sculpture, leather goods, and costume jewelry. 204 Calle Fortaleza (phone: 725-5596).

RIVIERA A must-see for anyone in the market for jewelry set with fine stones. 205 Calle Cruz (phone: 725-4000).

SPICY CARIBBEE An offbeat shop offering Caribbean spices, top-quality Puerto Rican coffee beans (selling around $10 per pound), and cookbooks featuring local recipes. 154 Calle Cristo (phone: 725-4690).

SPORTS

The hotels along the San Juan–Condado–Isla Verde coastline naturally concentrate on beach and water sports, plus some tennis and spectator sports. San Juan's marina is a major departure point for deep-sea fishing boats. If you're really serious about your sporting life, head for one of the four extraordinary playing places out on the island: Dorado with its *Hyatt Dorado Beach* and *Hyatt Cerromar Beach* hotels, the *El Conquistador* at the island's northeast end, and *Palmas del Mar* near Humacao. Baseball is big here, and soccer (called *fútbol*) is quite popular, too. Occasionally San Juan is the scene of title boxing bouts.

BASEBALL As beloved on the island as on the mainland. Games are played in stadiums in San Juan, Mayagüez, Ponce, Arecibo, Caguas, and Santurce from October to mid-April. Nascent North American stars often play with Puerto Rico's six teams during the winter season.

BOATING From San Juan, up to six people may sail on the 35-foot sloop *Airborne* for $390 a half day, with drinks and lunch included, through *Caribbean School of Aquatics* (phone: 723-4740). At *Palmas del Mar*'s *Marina de Palmas* near Humacao, you can sign up for a full-day or half-day sail on a captained yacht to offshore Vieques or Monkey Island through *Riviera Yacht Charters* (phone: 850-2084), or take sailing instruction. *Villa Marina Yacht Harbor* in Fajardo also rents and charters boats (phone: 863-5131 or 728-2450). A massive marine complex has developed at the upscale *Marina Puerto del Ray* in Fajardo (phone: 860-1000), where the hurricane-proof harbor has 740 wet slips to handle boats up to 200 feet long and haul-out and repair facilities for vessels up to 90 feet long. The 600-acre *Marina Puerto del Ray* project is also home to *Club Naútico International Powerboat Rentals,* which rents powerboats (phone: 860-2400); a dive shop with dive boats; and a restaurant. Hotels offering rentals on a very-small-boat scale (Sunfish, Sailfish) include the *Condado Plaza, Palmas del Mar* in Humacao, and the *Hyatt Dorado Beach* (kayaks) near Dorado. Row-boats can be rented at the Condado Lagoon pier for about $5 an hour. Boating equipment is also available at *San Juan Bay Marina, Isleta Marina* and *Puerto Chico* in Fajardo, and *Marina de Salinas* in Salinas.

COCKFIGHTING Here, the "sport" is as civilized as it ever gets (which is not very) in the *Coliseo Gallistico* (air conditioned, with comfortable seating, restaurant, bar, and a fake-grass-carpeted pit) in Isla Verde. The feathers fly Saturdays from 1 to 7 PM (phone: 791-1557 to confirm).

CYCLING The *Hyatt Dorado Beach* rents bicycles for $4.50 an hour. Morning group bike rides are led by the activities coordinator assistant, who points out trees and tells tales of the plantation house.

GOLF Out on the island, 10 championship courses lie waiting for the golf aficionado.

TOP TEE-OFF SPOTS

El Conquistador The 18-hole, 6,700-yard, par 72 championship course created by Robert Von Hagge that opened here in 1967 has been redesigned by Arthur Hills & Associates. The original course has been greatly altered, with 16 holes in completely different configurations. While the course features undulating fairways and greens, the severe rolling hills of the old course — never popular with amateur duffers — have been trimmed away. Nonetheless, the elevation and the winds combine to make this a real challenge. The location is as stunning as ever — atop a cliff at the northeast corner of the island, where the Atlantic and Caribbean converge, with spectacular views of the water and the El Yunque rain forest in the distance (phone: 863-1000; 800-468-5228 from the US).

Hyatt Dorado Beach Although the opulent *Dorado Beach* resort complex is no longer operated under the aegis of the original Rockresort management, few golfers will be able to tell the difference. The two topflight courses that wind their way through this former grapefruit and coconut plantation are sufficiently difficult to make players regularly wish the land had been left in citrus cultivation. But that is only for those for whom the final score is everything. In fact, these are as good a pair of golfing tests that exist side by side on any island, and among the liveliest arguments heard around the 19th hole here are the discussions about which course is best (record one vote here for the East).

And if even these two fine layouts are not enough to satisfy your desire for assorted golfing venues, there is the added attraction of the two sister courses just down the road at the *Hyatt Cerromar Beach* hotel. Having all four of these to choose from permits the playing of your own private Dorado Open, and that has got to be bliss for anyone. The greens fee is $75 and a cart is $36 for 2 people. Lessons with the head pro cost $35 per half hour (phone: 796-1600; 800-233-1234 from the US for reservations only).

Palmas del Mar This resort near Humacao has what are considered by many the toughest 18 holes on Puerto Rico. Designed by Gary Player, its 6,600-yard, par 72 layout is a magnet for top tee-ers. Resident pro Seth Bull is the one to go to for advise on the course's most challenging holes — 11 through 15. He might also warn you about the par 5 18th, as tricky as they come hereabouts. Greens fees are $34 for guests, $54 for non-guests and a golf cart is $32 for two. Golf packages are available at either of *Palmas del Mar's* hotels — the *Palmas Inn* or the *Candelero* (phone: 852-6000, ext. 54).

Other island greens: there's an 18-hole course at the *Ponce Hilton.* The former Ramey Air Force Base site that's now *Punta Borinquen* in Aguadilla (phone: 890-2987) has an 18-hole course, and although there are no public courses per se, tourists can play at the highly regarded *Berwind Country Club* (phone: 876-3056) and *Club Riomar* (phone: 887-3964 or 887-3064), each with 18 holes, in Río Grande, and also at *Dorado del Mar Country Club,* with 9 holes, in Dorado (phone: 796-2030). The *Mayagüez*

Hilton International arranges for guests to play at the private *Club Deportivo del Oeste*'s 9-hole course. Greens fees vary widely — up to $75 for 18 holes. No caddies, but golf carts cost about $35 for 18 holes; some courses rent clubs and shoes.

Major tournaments include the *New York Life Champions Senior PGA Tournament* at the *Hyatt Dorado Beach* in December, and the *Rums of Puerto Rico National Pro Am* at the *Hyatt Regency Cerromar Beach* in November.

HIKING The Caribbean National Forest has three verdant and well-maintained trails: El Yunque (from an easy 15 minutes to a more difficult 2 hours), Mt. Britton (1¼ hours), and El Toro (most ambitious, at 8 hours). The Sierra Palm Visitors Center is near the park entrance.

HORSEBACK RIDING *Palmas del Mar* has its own equestrian center and scenic paths that wind through a pine-laden nature preserve; trail rides, as well as jumping and riding instruction, are available. *Le Petit Chalet Mountain Inn* offers rides on the beach at Luquillo or in El Yunque rain forest. You also can arrange to ride at the *Hacienda Carabali* at Mameyes near Luquillo Beach (by reservation only; phone: 889-5820 or 887-4954), or the *Caribbean School of Aquatics* (phone: 723-4740); a half day, including transportation and a snack, costs $55 per person.

HORSE RACING *El Comandante* racetrack in Canovanas, east of San Juan, is cheerful, colorful, and fun. Post time is 2:30 PM on Wednesdays, Fridays, Sundays, and holidays; admission charge. The 900-seat, air conditioned restaurant opens at 12:30 PM on race days (for reservations, call 724-6060.) Check with your hotel about packages including transport and entrance fee. Also ask at tourism information centers about *paso fino* meets (races between horses with a high-stepping, tiny gait) and rodeos.

RUNNING The annual *San Blas Half Marathon* draws international competitors each February in Coamo.

SNORKELING AND SCUBA Available through water sports desks at several major San Juan hotels. The *Caribe Hilton,* the *Condado Plaza Watersports Center,* and the *Hyatt Dorado Beach* offer instruction and equipment rental. Coral reefs, cays, and mangrove clumps along the coast make for interesting snorkeling. So do day-long picnic excursions to Icacos Island (see *Fajardo,* in *Special Places*). The best dive sites are off the *Caribe Hilton*'s beach (outside the reef there's a 33-foot drop with underwater caves) and a considerable distance out to sea. The *Caribbean School of Aquatics* (phone: 723-4740) offers daily scuba trips for $94 for a one-tank dive, a snorkeling trip with lunch for $69, and a five-day package in scuba instruction for $325. Or try *Caribe Aquatic Adventures* (phone: 724-1882). *Sea Ventures* (phone: 863-3483) offers swimming, snorkeling, and diving trips to Fajardo's offshore islands and diving certification courses.

Elsewhere on the island, *Coral Head Divers* (phone: 850-7208 or 800-635-4529 from the US), at the *Palmas del Mar* resort near Humacao, operates Puerto Rico's largest diving fleet. You also can rent equipment in La Parguera, Vieques, and Culebra.

SPORT FISHING More than 30 world-record fish have been taken in these waters. The catch: blue marlin (April through November); white marlin (April through June, October, November); sailfish (October through June); also wahoo, Allison tuna, dolphin, mackerel, tarpon, and snook, plus fighting bonefish in the shallows. José Castillo operates half- and full-day trips aboard his 38- and 48-foot yachts at the *ESJ Towers* in Isla Verde (phone: 791-6195, or 726-5752 evenings). *Marina de Palmas* at *Palmas del Mar* offers half-day and overnight trips from *Karolett Fishing Charters* (phone: 850-7442) and *Maragata Charters* (phone: 850-7548). Rates run about $390 for a half day, about $365 for a full day for up to four people including bait, tackle, beer, and soft drinks. The priciest trips are aboard Captain Mike Benítez's island-famous yachts, the 45-foot *Sea Born* and 61-foot *Sea Born II*, which are berthed at the private *Club Naútico de San Juan* (phone: 723-2292); day rate is about $625 to $1,200 for up to 6 people. This is also the site of the *International Billfish Tournament.*

SURFING A north and west coast pursuit. Pine Grove Beach in Isla Verde (north) and Punta Higüero, near Rincón (west), are the most popular surfing beaches. Rincón, site of the *World Surfing Championships* in 1968 and 1988, has been called the "Hawaii of the Caribbean." Within 10 miles, favorite surf spots include Tres Palmas, Steps, Indicators, Dogman's, and Dome's, possibly the most crowded. The best time to hit the waves is from October through February, at 6 AM. Punta Borinquen, near Aguadilla (west), is a good beach for body-surfing, especially at Wilderness, Surfers, and Crashboat beaches. Other popular areas include Los Turbos in Vega Baja, Pine Grove in Isla Verde, and La Pared in Luquillo. Travel agencies that can arrange specific surfing tours include *Surf Express* (phone: 407-783-7184) for custom arrangements and *Par Avion Travel* (phone: 800-927-3327 from the US) for professional surfing groups.

SWIMMING AND SUNNING On the beach or by the pool, both are only an amble away from your room at the big strip hotels. But all San Juan hotel beaches are not created equal — check the hotel's setup before you make reservations. The *Caribe Hilton* and the *Condado Plaza* are among the best in the Condado section. In San Juan, the Isla Verde section has the best beaches by far. One caution: Rough sea conditions can sometimes create local rip currents or undertow off the Condado–Isla Verde hotel beaches, some of which do not provide full-time lifeguards. Puerto Rico's nicest beaches are away from the city. Out on the island, the *Hyatt Dorado Beach* and *Hyatt Cerromar Beach* resorts have especially fine sandy shores. By law, all Puerto Rican beaches are open to the public. But the government has installed special *balneario* facilities (lockers, showers, and changing rooms plus parking, at about 25¢ a day for a locker, $1 for parking) at a dozen of the island's most beautiful, now referred to as "public," beaches. They're open from 9 AM to 5 PM in winter, 8 AM to 5 PM in summer; closed Mondays. Luquillo, on the north coast about 30 miles east of San Juan, is most famous (although not as clean as it was pre-Hugo) and most popular (too much so on weekends) with islanders as well as tourists. Another public beach is Escambrón in San Juan. On the east coast, there's Humacao. Along the south coast, there are three beaches: Punta Guilarte, near Arroyo; Caña Gorda, near Guánica; and Rosada, near La Parguera. On the western shore there's Boquerón and Añasco (not highly recommended). Along the north coast west of San Juan: Cerro Gordo, about 25 miles from the city; La Sardinera near Dorado; and Punta Salinas between Dorado and Cataño. Sombé Beach (called "Sun Bay" by locals) is on the offshore island of Vieques. With all the public *balneario* accoutrements, but with a special sense of faraway privacy, it is very beautiful. Although it has no *balneario* facilities, Flamenco Beach on Culebra ranks among the best in the Caribbean.

TENNIS It's big stuff throughout Puerto Rico with about 100 courts in and beyond the city limits.

CHOICE COURTS

El Conquistador This sprawling resort offers 9 Har-Tru courts, 4 are night-lighted. There's also a pro, a complete instruction program, and a clubhouse. They're also happy to find a tennis partner for guests (phone: 863-1000; 800-468-8365 from the US).

Hyatt Cerromar Beach/Hyatt Dorado Beach Courts are scattered all around this two-resort complex; if tennis is your consuming interest, be sure your room is near one of them. Both resorts host tennis weeks and offer special packages. At *Cerromar* there are 14 Laykold courts — 1 is a stadium court; 2 are lighted. At *Dorado,* there are 5 Laykold courts by the pro shop, 2 courts at the west end of the property; 2 are lighted. *Peter Burwash International* handles instruction at both hotels; private lessons cost $50 an hour, $25 a half hour; tennis clinics are $15 an hour. Given notice, they'll arrange videotaping and tournaments for groups. Court time runs about $15 a daylight hour, $18 at night in winter (phone: 796-1234; 800-233-7674 from the US).

Palmas del Mar A complex of condominiums at Humacao, where you should be sure to stay in the tennis village. Facilities are excellent; 20 courts, of which 5 are Har-Tru (more like clay), 15 Tenneflex (harder surface), 7 lighted. Private lessons with the pro are $45 an hour. Package costs $200 for 5 hours of lessons (phone: 852-6000, ext. 51; for reservations only, 800-468-3331 from the US).

Another major complex is located at *Club Riomar* in Río Grande with 13 courts, lessons, and a pro shop (phone: 887-3964 or 887-3064).

In the San Juan area, the *Carib-Inn* hotel (formerly the *Racquet Club*) has 4 clay and 4 Laykold (and lighted) courts available at $8 per hour; instruction may be arranged (phone: 791-3535). The *Condado Plaza* also offers tennis, while the *Caribe Hilton* has a topnotch setup — 6 lighted courts, a pro shop, instruction, and a "match making" program, whereby guests may be matched with a local player of equal talent. You can also play on 17 public courts (with lights) in San Juan Central Park (phone: 721-0303) for about $1 per hour daily. Out on the island, there are courts at *Punta Borinquen* in Aguadilla; the *Mayagüez Hilton, Ponce Hilton, Parador El Guajataca* and *Parador Vistamar* in Quebradillas; *Parador Villa Antonio* in Rincón; *Hacienda Juanita* in Maricao; and *Parador Baños de Coamo* in Coamo. Visitors can also use courts at *Dorado del Mar Country Club* at Dorado (phone: 796-2030).

WATER SKIING Practiced to a limited extent on San Juan's Condado Lagoon and out on the island at Boquerón Bay and *El Conquistador.* Rent equipment at the *Condado Plaza*'s water sports center.

WINDSURFING Best setups are at *Palmas del Mar,* the *Condado Plaza,* and the *Hyatt Dorado Beach,* where rentals and instruction are available. Ocean Park in San Juan and Boquerón Bay are popular windsurfing spots.

NIGHTLIFE

Dining, going to the theater, dancing, gaming, and *LeLoLai* happenings are the options for a night out on Puerto Rico. The *Centro de Bellas Artes* (Av. Ponce de León; phone: 724-5949) is the island's fine arts center, presenting a full range of concerts, theater, opera, and dance performances. More than a dozen casinos — where games range from baccarat to blackjack — are among the island's big draws. By law, all are in hotels with 100 or more rooms: among them, the *Caribe Hilton, Condado Plaza, Ambassador, Holiday Inn Crowne Plaza, Dutch Inn, Clarion, Sands,* and *El San Juan* hotels in the San Juan area and, out on the island, *Palmas del Mar, Hyatt Regency Cerromar Beach, Hyatt Dorado Beach, El Conquistador, Ponce Hilton, Mayagüez Holiday Inn,* and *Mayagüez Hilton.* The atmosphere at the casinos is a bit formal and somewhat subdued. No drinking is permitted at the tables (you may order free coffee or soft drinks and sandwiches). Dressy (but not black-tie) attire for women and jackets and ties for men are firmly suggested after dark (especially at the *Caribe Hilton, Condado Plaza,* and *Sands*). Casinos are open from noon until 4 AM; you must be at least 18 to enter.

The *Chart House* (see *Eating Out*) remains the best spot to kick off the evening with drinks in a congenial atmosphere. All the big hotels have nightclubs; in season, the *Caribe Hilton*'s classy *Caribar* (phone: 721-0303, ext. 1587) spotlights the best Latin talent; the *Condado Plaza*'s *Fiesta*

Lobby Lounge features a Latin revue, and its piano bar draws a crowd. At the big hotels, a dinner-and-show evening may easily run $75 and up for two, which underscores *LeLoLai's* bargain-level evening prices.

Other, less expensive alternatives are hotel lounges with combos for dancing and a minimum but no cover charge. *The Patio* at *El Convento* hotel provides piano serenades; the piano bar at the *Regency* hotel in Condado is popular with the business set; and the *Player's Lounge* at the *Sands* in Isla Verde features live music, noon to 4 AM. All of the flamenco shows are mild compared to the real, moaning Madrid thing. *El San Juan's Club Tropicaro* and *La Concha* are some places to watch dancers click their heels. Of the current crop of discos, the most popular are *Amadeus* at *El San Juan* and *Isadora's* in the *Condado Plaza. Neon* (203 Tanca; phone: 725-7581) and *Lazer* (251 Cruz; phone: 723-6448), both in Old San Juan, are video-theques attracting the teen crowd. *Peggy Sue's* (Ashford Ave; phone: 725-4664) features 1950s and 1960s rock 'n' roll. For live jazz, try *Café San Juan Bistro* (152 Calle Cruz; phone: 724-1198). *Shannon's Irish Pub* (1503 Loíza St., Santurce; phone: 728-6103) also features rock 'n' roll bands. If you want to belly up to a bar, try *El Batey* (101 Calle Cristo; no phone) where graffiti-covered walls provide a colorful atmosphere for late night conversations. After dancing, snack on burgers and omelettes at *The Green House* on Condado (1200 Ashford Ave; phone: 725-4036) till 4:30 AM (see *Eating Out*).

Out on the island, all's relatively quiet with the exception of the *Hyatt Cerromar Beach,* site of *El Coquí Sports Bar* with video music. The *Bacchus Music Club* at the *Mayagüez Hilton* also does its share of swinging, and there's live music at the *Vista Terrace Lounge.* The new *El Conquistador* lures late-nighters with live entertainment and a disco.

Best on the Island

CHECKING IN

In San Juan, accommodations range from very expensive, full-service resort hotels to small, cheerful guesthouses. Their counterparts out on the island are low-slung luxury hotel and villa complexes and the island's unique network of simple country inns called *paradores* (double rooms from $38 to $90), which can be booked in the US by calling 800-443-0266 or the Puerto Rico Tourism Company (phone: 800-223-6530). For information on individually run hotels, small to large, contact the Caribbean Hotel Association (phone: 800-74CHARM). With Puerto Rican tourism gaining strength, there is increased development outside of San Juan, including plans for the *Dorado del Mar,* a resort on 300 acres in Dorado, with a 600-room hotel and 200 condominiums. At press time, the completion date for the project was uncertain.

Whatever the season — but especially in summer — check out package deals offered by airlines, tour operators, or travel agents. At the very least, they can mean free *LeLoLai* parties, special perks (free greens fees for a round of golf, a San Juan bay cruise), and souvenirs.

For families, Puerto Rico's hundreds of rental and/or resort condominiums and hotel suites equipped with kitchens not only mean substantial savings on food costs, but added scheduling flexibility. Be aware, however, that the word *motel* in Puerto Rico usually means a place that caters to illicit lovers.

Hotels listed here as very expensive ask more than $300 (EP — no meals) per night for a double room, in season; expensive, $200 to $300; moderate, $100 to $200; inexpensive, $75 to $100. Modified American Plan (MAP) arrangements — including breakfast and dinner — are often available for an extra charge of about $50 per person per day. Expect to pay 25% to 50% less during the off-season. There is a 7% room tax at hotels without casinos, 9% at hotels with casinos. It's a good idea to reconfirm your reservation before leaving home, and double-check with your agent or airline tour desk about operative guarantees and what to do just in case there's a problem. Most places a tourist is likely to stay, both in San Juan and out on the island, are air conditioned. The area code for Puerto Rico is 809.

For an unforgettable island experience, we begin with our favorites, followed by our recommendations of cost and quality choices of hotels large and small, listed by area and price category.

A REGAL RESORT AND A SPECIAL HAVEN

El Conquistador A massive development of 926 rooms in five "environments," this resort overlooks the Atlantic and the Caribbean from a 300-foot cliff. The property incorporates some of the former hostelry's structures, while introducing such innovations as glass funiculars that transport beach-loving guests down to the sand below. Sports-minded visitors have their choice of activities — there are 36 great holes of golf (see *Top Tee-Off Spots* in *Golf* in this chapter), 9 tennis courts (including a stadium court), 5 pools, a health club and spa, a private marina with fishing and sailboats available for charter, and a private 100-acre island set aside for water sports. There are 16 restaurants and lounges, including fine dining at *Isabela's* (continental), *Blossom's* (Oriental), and *Otello's* (Italian). A casino, evening entertainment, a children's camp, and a large conference center complete the enormous picture. This resort is like a separate, self-contained country whose only purpose is your enjoyment. Las Croabas (phone: 863-1000; 800-468-8365 from the US; fax: 791-7500).

Horned Dorset Primavera This hostelry with the unusual name is often described as Puerto Rico's most exclusive resort (and now it is the island's only Relais & Châteaux member as well). Located on the west coast near Rincón's great surfing beaches, the property has 22 small, elegant suites, some with balconies overhanging the sea. Each room has a four-poster bed, there are painted tiles on the floors, and flowers can be seen just about everywhere. There's also a swimming pool and a spectacular beach. The hotel is run by a twosome who have an inn in upstate New York — also called *Horned Dorset* — and the pervasive feeling is that of tranquillity and serenity. Visitors feel as if they're staying in a luxurious private hacienda (with stunning appointments) rather than a public hotel. The food is also first class (see *Eating Out*); there are six-course dinners with fine wines and excellent service. Breakfast and lunch are served on a lovely outdoor patio. Apartado 1132, Rincón (phone: 823-4030 or 823-4050; fax: 823-5580).

SAN JUAN–CONDADO–ISLA VERDE AREA

VERY EXPENSIVE

Caribe Hilton International On many counts still the best in town, this place has 668 well-tended rooms and suites, including the deluxe executive floor, plus landscaped grounds complete with an antique fort. The service is smooth more than 90% of the time — good by any island standard. Other features include a casino, beach, excellent tennis facilities, air conditioned racquetball and squash courts, 2 pools, children's summer and holiday day camp, a health club, 3 restaurants, and the *Caribar* outdoor café. The poolside bar is yacht-size. Modified American Plan available in winter. Old San Juan is a short cab ride away. San Gerónimo St., San Juan (phone: 721-0303; 800-445-8667 from the US; fax: 809-725-8849).

El San Juan The centerpiece of this landmark is its Palm Court lobby — with a massive chandelier, rose marble floor, and hand-carved mahogany ceiling — where guests can enjoy afternoon tea and chamber music. Near the airport, it has 392 rooms, including guesthouses with private patios, one of San Juan's largest casinos, a nightclub, 24-hour café, lounge, the *Amadeus* disco, and the island's only *cruvinet* wine bar. There are 5 restaurants, including *Back Street Hong Kong,* which is housed in the actual set from the Hong Kong pavilion at the *1962 Brussels World's Fair* (see *Eating Out*). There also are 2 swimming pools, extensive water sports facilities, a fitness center, and 3 lighted tennis courts. 187 Isla Verde Rd., Isla Verde (phone: 791-1000; 800-468-2818 from the US; fax: 800-253-0178).

EXPENSIVE

La Concha This property features a pleasant, large (but heavily populated) pool surrounded by fountains. There's a lovely beachfront with lanais, 2 tennis courts, water sports (including scuba), a restaurant, a lobby lounge with flamenco shows, and a poolside bar. All 235 air conditioned, terraced rooms have ocean views and direct-dial telephones. Ashford Ave., San Juan (phone: 721-6090; 800-468-2822 from the US; fax: 722-3200).

Condado Beach Pretty though not plush, this Art Deco–style hostelry, the former *Condado Vanderbilt,* was built in 1919. It has fine service, 245 rooms (half with ocean view), the international *El Gobernador* restaurant, pool, and use of the tennis courts at *La Concha* next door. A dine-around plan for MAP guests is offered. VIP guests have a club floor, honor bar, and other privileges. 999 Ashford Ave., Condado (phone: 721-6888; 800-468-2775 from the US; fax: 722-5062).

Condado Plaza A best seller for good reason: good looks, good service, 3 pools, new fitness and conference centers, lots of daytime action, and varied nightlife, with several winning restaurants (notably the darkly elegant *L. K. Sweeney & Son Ltd.;* see *Eating Out*), a disco, and a big casino. The Plaza Club floor offers on-floor concierge service, key-only elevator access, a private lounge, and complimentary breakfast and snacks. The 559-room, two-hotel complex includes the original beachfront property, plus the Laguna section, linked by a walkway across Ashford Ave., Condado (phone: 721-1000; 800-624-0420 from the US; fax: 722-7955).

Radisson Normandie Built in 1941 to resemble the celebrated French ocean liner, it lay in ruins for years — little more than an Art Deco hulk opposite the *Caribe Hilton.* Now beautifully restored, and a National Historic Landmark, this gem boasts 177 rooms (more than half are suites), and all the amenities for upscale leisure and business travelers, small groups, and conventions. Features include the handsome *Atrium Café,* the *Normandie,* which serves French fare (see *Eating Out*), a beachfront pool, and a jogging track. Muñoz Rivera Rosales corner of Puerto de Tierra, San Juan (phone: 729-2929; 800-333-3333 from the US; fax: 729-3083).

Sands Formerly the *Palace* hotel (next to *El San Juan* in the Isla Verde section), this property offers 418 air conditioned rooms (including 51 suites), all with private balconies. Situated on 5 acres along a stunning crescent beach, it features a huge casino, an enormous swimming pool with waterfalls and a swim-up sandwich bar, 4 restaurants, a nightclub/disco, gift shops and boutiques, 24-hour room service, baby-sitting, and a sophisticated sports and recreation program. The property offers an all-inclusive option; 90 rooms of the hotel comprise the "Diamond Club," where guests pay one rate for accommodations, all meals and liquor, shows, casino game lessons, non-motorized water sports, and more. Rte. 37, Isla Verde (phone: 791-6100; 800-443-2009 from the US; fax: 791-8525).

San Juan Marriott Almost 8 years after the former *Dupont Plaza* was devastated by fire in 1986, the Marriott hotel group is set to reopen the property early this year. About $131 million have been spent on rebuilding and refurbishing the 516-room luxury getaway, which will feature 406 guestrooms and 110 cabañas. Other amenities will include 2 restaurants, a pool, 2 tennis courts, a casino, a health club, and a business center. There will also be a parking garage. Ashford Ave., Condado (phone: 800-228-9290).

MODERATE

Casa San José This charming property, fashioned from a 4-story 17th-century mansion, has 10 rooms and suites with old marble floors and antique furnishings, an interior patio, and a large and comfortable upstairs salon, where afternoon tea and cocktails are served. Rates include continental breakfast and evening drinks. No children under age 12 allowed. 159 San José, Old San Juan (phone: 723-1212; fax: 723-7620).

El Convento Once a 17th-century Carmelite convent in Old San Juan, it is now a low-key Ramada hotel. The 99 air conditioned rooms and suites with private baths and TV sets are smallish, and the hotel in general could stand a major sprucing up, but antique touches add style. An ideal base for seeing the city or for pre- and post-cruise stays, it's the only large hotel in the historic district. Except for a small pool and sun decks, there are no sports facilities on the premises, but the desk will arrange tennis, golf, or fishing. *El Patio* is a favorite in-town lunch spot. 100 Cristo St., San Juan (phone: 723-9020; 800-468-2779 from the US; fax: 721-2877).

Galería San Juan Formerly the quarters for the Spanish artillery in the 18th century and now a charming bed and breakfast establishment, it has the ambience of a private home and art studio. The building has been restored, and its public areas are filled with paintings, drawings, and sculptures by owners Jan D'Esopo and Hector Gandia, as well as other artists. The 8 rooms and suites (7 air conditioned) are individually decorated and feature private baths and lovely views of the harbor, the ocean, or the area's historic forts. A simple breakfast buffet is included in the rate, and several restaurants are nearby. It's a special place. 204 Calle Norzagaray, Old San Juan (phone: 722-1808 or 725-3829; fax: 724-7360).

INEXPENSIVE

El Canario Inn Located in the heart of the Condado Strip, this delightful 25-room guesthouse is San Juan's most famous and attractive small hotel. It is near, but not on, the beach. Rooms are air conditioned and have cable TV. Continental breakfast is included. 1317 Ashford, San Juan (phone: 722-3861; 800-223-0888 from the US; fax: 722-0391).

La Playa A gem of a guesthouse located right on Isla Verde, this 15-room inn has air conditioning, a restaurant and bar overlooking the ocean, and a patio full of lush plants and colorful birds. 6 Amapola St., Isla Verde (phone: 791-1115).

DORADO

VERY EXPENSIVE

HYATT DORADO BEACH Lushly landscaped, this 2-level, 298-room former Rock-resort boasts a casino, super golf (two Robert Trent Jones, Sr. layouts), top tennis (7 courts, pro clinics, lessons), 2 pools, a Jacuzzi, long sweeps of beach, snorkeling, and miles of bike paths and weekly nature walks. The intimate *Su Casa* restaurant, in a separate colonial mansion, provides evocative island dining (see *Eating Out*). The main building houses the glass-walled *Surf Room,* serving continental food with a spotlighted view of the ocean, as well as an inviting lobby. There's also the *Ocean Terrace,* an open-air (breakfast and lunch) dining area, where netting has solved the problem of annoying blackbirds. Hyatt earns high marks for the refurbished rooms, especially the waterfront casitas, which are attractive and comfortable. Ground-floor units have patios. A convention center and ballroom, in a separate building, continue the resort's tradition of buildings no higher than the palm trees. The "Caribbean Sports Academy" offers golf, tennis, or windsurfing instruction for adults and children. There also are excellent summer sport packages, a free summer and holiday camp for kids, and activity programs for teenagers. Rte. 693, Dorado (phone: 796-1234; 800-233-1234 from the US; fax: 796-6065).

Hyatt Regency Cerromar Beach Far less lush and more commercial than the *Hyatt Dorado Beach,* it's a renovated former Rockresort high-rise with 504 rooms, 2 Robert Trent Jones, Sr. golf courses (not as good as *Dorado*'s), 14 tennis courts (pro clinics, lessons), a health club with sauna and exercise classes, a pool, a small beach, and a gigantic lawn. Eateries include *Medici's,* serving northern Italian fare, *Sushi Wong's* for Far Eastern food, and the tri-level outdoor *Swan Café.* What some claim is either the world's largest swimming pool (Guinness doesn't agree) or a "water complex," is actually an artificial river, a third of a mile long, with currents, a waterfall, peripheral hydromassages, and other diversions. *El Coquí* sports bar, a nightclub, and a casino enliven nights; *Camp Hyatt* is a weekend, summer, and holiday day camp for kids ages 3 to 15. The "Caribbean Sports Academy" offers instruction in a wide variety of sports. Summer sport packages are excellent buys. Rte. 693, Dorado (phone: 796-1234; 800-233-1234 from the US; fax: 796-6065).

PONCE

EXPENSIVE

Ponce Hilton Set on 80 acres overlooking the Caribbean, there are 156 rooms and suites, a beach, a pool with cascading waterfall, an 18-hole golf course, a jogging trail, a bicycle path, 2 night-lighted tennis courts, a casino, 2 restaurants, a disco, and a lounge. A convention center that accommodates 1,000 and an executive business center are aimed at attracting the briefcase crowd. On the outskirts of Ponce in the La Guancha area (phone: 259-7777; 800-HILTONS from the US; fax: 259-7674).

MODERATE

Meliá Popular with business travelers, it's a first choice for a night or two in town because of its setting (facing the plaza) and Spanish-accented atmosphere.

The 1908 architecture is interesting, but the 80 rooms are disappointing. There are swimming and golf privileges, but no pool. Continental breakfast included. 2 Cristina St., Ponce (phone: 842-0260; fax: 841-3602).

ELSEWHERE ON THE ISLAND

EXPENSIVE

Mayagüez Hilton This place features 145 big rooms, personal service, an Olympic-size pool, a bar, 2 restaurants, a disco, 3 tennis courts (2 lighted), a casino, a parcourse fitness circuit, a walking trail, a mini-gym, and landscaped grounds with a pond and outdoor Jacuzzi. Rte. 104, Km 0.3, Mayagüez (phone: 831-7575; 800-223-1146 from the US; fax: 834-3475).

Palmas del Mar A 2,700-acre Mediterranean-style resort composed of the luxury 23-room *Palmas Inn,* the 102-room *Candelero* hotel (group and family oriented, slightly less pricey), and 400 stylish villas (about 150 available for rent) grouped around a marina, a championship golf course, and a 20-court tennis complex with a pro. Other features include children's programs and teen activities, a miniature golf course, nature and bike trails, an equestrian center, a palm-lined beach, deep-sea fishing, water sports, a fitness center, a casino, and 7 restaurants. Hotel and villa accommodations have been gradually renovated and updated over the past few years. Dine-around plan for MAP guests includes theme-night parties and choice of nearby island restaurants. Rte. 3, Km 86.4, Buena Vista, Humacao (phone: 852-6000; 800-468-3331 from the US; fax: 850-4448).

MODERATE

Parador Guajataca Set on a dramatic sweep of beach, this *parador* has 38 basic air conditioned rooms with balconies, 2 pools, tennis, golf nearby, a restaurant (buffets on Sundays and Wednesdays), and an informal ambience. During your stay, visit the roadside *La Granja de Guajataca* and sample the *queso do hoya,* white layered cheese, and the *tembleque,* a gelatinous sweet. Rte. 2, Km 103.8, Quebradillas (phone: 895-3070; fax: 895-3589).

INEXPENSIVE

Baños de Coamo A modest government *parador;* the 48 rooms are clean and air conditioned. The grounds in the mountain foothills — with thermal and freshwater pools where water-therapy programs are offered — are pleasant. There's also a swimming pool and tennis court. The charming, old-fashioned dining room serves generous portions of simple Puerto Rican fare. It's a favorite weekend retreat for locals, and FDR and Frank Lloyd Wright once "took the waters" here. Rte. 546, Coamo (phone: 721-2884 or 825-2186; fax: 825-4739).

Beside the Pointe For serious surfers and their families, with beachfront buildings that hold 12 simply furnished efficiency apartments with kitchenettes and a café. Rte. 413, Rincón (phone: 823-8550).

Parador Casa Grande One of the latest additions to the country's list of 15 country inns, this *parador* in the central mountains offers 20 suites with balconies, a swimming pool, and a restaurant with a lounge. It's close to the Arecibo Observatory and Río Camuy Cave Park. Rte. 612, Utuado (phone: 894-3939).

Parador Hacienda Gripiñas Edgardo and Milagros Dedos's genuine pleasure in pleasing guests makes this place special. On the grounds of a former coffee plantation, it's a 200-year-old house set in lush foliage; its 19 rooms vary in size (some are rather small) but are pin-neat and cheery. There's a chilly mountain pool and excellent, reasonably priced Puerto Rican food. But the chance to relax in a rocker or loll in a hammock on the verandah sipping a piña colada is what it's really about. In Jayuya; no matter what the map says, heading south on the Ponce Speedway, then north at Juana Díaz, is the fastest route from San Juan (phone: 828-1717; fax: 828-1719).

Parador Martorell For beach nuts only, it offers 9 super-neat rooms in a former private house; there is a patio but no surrounding grounds, pool, or dining room. The famous beach is only half a block away. Buffet breakfasts on the patio are included in the room rate. 6A Ocean Dr., Luquillo (phone: 889-2710; fax: 889-2710).

Parador Oasis A 200-year-old family mansion and winery, now a hospitable inn, it has 52 air conditioned rooms and a pretty courtyard dining area, a pool and gym. It's within walking distance of the town's historic sites. 72 Calle Luna, San Germán (phone: 892-1175; fax: 892-1175).

Le Petit Chalet Mountain Inn This guesthouse in the rain forest has long been a secret favorite of bird watchers and scientists visiting El Yunque. There are 10 rooms with private baths; breakfast is included in the room rate, although some cottages have kitchens. A highly regarded restaurant is also on the premises (see *Eating Out*). Activities include hiking in the rain forest, horseback riding on the beach and in the rain forest, and trips to Arecibo Observatory. A children's sleepaway camp is also located here. Advance reservations are required. Near El Yunque (phone: 887-5802 or 887-5807; fax: 887-7926).

Posada Guayama Jag Mehta, who also owns *Casa San José,* has created a 20-room inn in this small, historical town on the island's south side. Rooms are air conditioned and have TV sets and verandahs. There's a restaurant and bar, a pool, and night-lighted tennis and basketball courts, which can keep you amused after you've seen the town, with its steepled churches and *Museo Cautino,* featuring turn-of-the-century furnishings. Rte. 3, Km 138.5, Guayama (phone: 866-1515).

Villa Parguera A classic fishermen's inn, rustic but comfortable; the dining room specializes in fresh seafood. With 61 rooms and a pool, it's adjacent to Phosphorescent Bay. Rte. 304, La Parguera (phone: 889-3975).

MODERATE

Club Seabourne Recently expanded, the laid-back property on Culebra now has 4 rooms, 8 villas, 2 cottages, and 1 room in a crow's nest. It boasts the only pool on the island and also has air conditioning and a bar and restaurant. Continental breakfast is included in the rate. Located just outside of Dewey on Culebra (phone: 742-3169; fax: 742-3176).

INEXPENSIVE

Casa del Francés This turn-of-the-century sugarcane plantation house on Isla de Vieques (it resembles Tara in *Gone With the Wind*) is a delightful, 18-room guesthouse run by an informal, convivial owner/manager team. It's only a 15-minute walk to spectacular Sombé Beach, or a 10-minute stroll to the lively, funky fishing village of Esperanza, with its harborside restaurants and bars. Delicious, imaginative meals (including "theme dinners") are served at *La Casa* on the attractive back patio, and the popular poolside bar is a local favorite. A perfect refuge from television, telephone, and tension. Carr. 996, Esperanza, Isla de Vieques (phone: 741-3751).

Trade Winds Even less expensive than *Casa del Francés,* this guesthouse offers 10 no-frills rooms and a restaurant and bar overlooking the ocean. It's close to *Bananas,* the popular nighttime bar, and within walking distance of Sombé Beach. Esperanza, Vieques (phone: 741-8666).

EATING OUT

San Juan is a city with a predictably citified selection of continental restaurants and steakhouses, with many European-trained chefs. In addition, there are several restaurants dedicated to the Puerto Rican way of cooking (somewhat similar to, but not as olive oil–based, as Spanish fare, nor as fiery as Mexican food). Lately, there has been a trend toward including island dishes on more hotel menus. Worth sampling: black bean soup, very rich, often served with chopped raw onion; *bacalaitos* (codfish fritters); *morcillas* (spicy blood sausages); *piononos* (spicy ground beef enclosed in strips of ripe plantains); *tostones* (deep-fried plantain slices, often served as a side dish); *pescado* (any fresh fish, especially good in seaside restaurants out on the island); *asopao* (a soupy but generally delicious concoction of chicken or seafood with rice); *arroz con pollo* (chicken and rice); *jueyes* (land crabs, often deviled and served in the shell); *lechón asado* (roast suckling pig); and, for dessert, Puerto Rican pineapple or guava (preserved halves or squares of "paste") served with white cheese. To drink: Puerto Rican coffee (which is the dark, strong stuff you get when you order a "small" cup), light Puerto Rican rum, and island-brewed Medalla and India beer.

Lunch is generally served from noon to 2:30 PM; 8 to 10 PM is the most popular dinnertime for vacationers, though Puerto Ricans usually eat earlier, between 5:30 and 7:30 PM. Outstanding independent restaurants are often found in hotels. A three-course dinner for two including tip, but no drinks, will cost over $70 at a restaurant we describe as expensive; from $40 to $65 at a place in the moderate category; and under $30 at spots listed as inexpensive. Lunches run a couple of dollars lower. The area code for Puerto Rico is 809.

EXPENSIVE

Augusto's This impressive place specializes in continental dishes combined with local ingredients, such as venison medallions with polenta and fresh foie gras. Closed Sundays; dinner only on Mondays and Saturdays. Reservations necessary. Major credit cards accepted. 801 Ponce de León Ave., Miramar (phone: 725-7700 or 721-7400).

Back Street Hong Kong The Chinese food is authentic, priced higher than its New York equivalent, and the decor is mysterious and unique — it's the set from the Hong Kong pavilion at the *1962 World's Fair* in Brussels. Open daily for dinner only. Reservations advised. Major credit cards accepted. In *El San Juan Hotel,* Isla Verde (phone: 791-1000).

Horned Dorset Primavera The dining room of this beautiful inn of the same name overlooks the beach. It offers a semi-formal, six-course, $40 prix fixe dinner (although special dietary requests are honored). Excellent French fare with a tropical accent (try the smoked dorado and the chocolate mousse cake), wine list, and service. Open daily for dinner only. Reservations advised. Major credit cards accepted. Bo Barrero, Rte. 429, Km 3, Rincón (phone: 823-4030).

L. K. Sweeney & Son Ltd. Richly decorated with green leather, dark wood, and crystal chandeliers, this dining spot specializes in the freshest of seafood. The almond pudding with Fra Angelica sauce is a heavenly experience, and the oyster bar is the largest in the Caribbean. Open daily for dinner only. Reservations advised. Major credit cards accepted. In the *Condado Plaza Hotel,* Condado (phone: 723-5551).

Normandie This Art Deco eatery housed in the 1940s *Radisson Normandie* hotel provides noteworthy French dining. Regulars love the pâté and mussel saffron cream soup, not to mention the delicate pastries. Open daily for dinner only. Reservations advised on weekends. Major credit cards accepted. Puerto de Tierra (phone: 723-5588).

Ramiro's Formerly *Reina de España,* this highly regarded restaurant serves creole and Spanish food in a graceful old Condado townhouse. Open daily; no lunch on weekends. Reservations advised. Major credit cards accepted. 1106 Magdalena, just off Ashford, Condado (phone: 721-9049).

Su Casa International delicacies served in one of the most romantic settings possible, in an original 1928 oceanfront plantation mansion complete with iron grillwork, tinkling fountains, and strolling musicians. Try the grilled rack of lamb with roasted garlic, with a side order of *tostones* (fried plantain). Dietetic choices also are available. Open for dinner only; closed Sundays and Mondays. Reservations necessary. Major credit cards accepted. *Hyatt Dorado Beach,* Dorado (phone: 796-1234).

La Zaragozana Longtime favorite for its Spanish–Cuban–Puerto Rican menu, and the dim, romantic atmosphere. Black bean soup and the chicken Andaluza are top choices. Strolling musicians on weekends; nightly in season. Open daily. Reservations necessary in season. Major credit cards accepted. 356 Calle San Francisco, Old San Juan (phone: 723-5103).

MODERATE

Chart House This graceful, verandah-enclosed townhouse surrounded by well-kept gardens is the pride of the Condado strip. Extremely handsome, with dark polished woodwork and excellent artwork (both traditional and modern), it serves flawless steaks, lobsters, rack of lamb, and the freshest salads in a variety of rooms: a bar room, up- and downstairs parlors — even a treehouse. The piña coladas are the best in town. Open daily for dinner only. Reservations advised. Major credit cards accepted. 1214 Ashford Ave., Condado (phone: 728-0110).

Che's Popular with locals, this restaurant specializes in Argentine fare. The steaks are hard to resist, but make sure you're hungry when you come — the portions are *big.* Open daily for lunch and dinner. Reservations unnecessary. Major credit cards accepted. 35 Caoba St., Punta Las Marías, Santurce (phone: 726-7202).

La Mallorquina In the heart of Old San Juan, this popular and venerable spot (established in 1848) is perfect for lunch or dinner following a shopping tour. Puerto Rican and Spanish specialties (black bean soup, *asopao,* beans, and rice) are served. Closed Sundays. Reservations advised for dinner. Major credit cards accepted. 207 Calle San Justo (phone: 722-3261).

La Monserrate Sea Port Diners are served inside or on the terrace overlooking the water. Seafood with a Spanish flavor is the specialty here; the *empanadillas* and corn sticks are wonderful. Open daily for lunch and dinner. Reservations necessary for large groups. Major credit cards accepted. Rte. 2, Ponce (phone: 841-2740).

Los Naborias One of the *mesones gastronomicos* (gastronomic inns recognized by the government for serving excellent Puerto Rican food at moderate prices), here is a fine place to try traditional dishes, such as black bean soup and coconut flan. Open daily for dinner only. Reservations advised for large groups. Major credit cards accepted. Rte. 690, Vega Alta (phone: 883-4885).

El Patio de Sam A casual, congenial oasis in Old San Juan, it has an imaginative menu (savory black bean soup, seafood crêpes Mornay, and daily specials, plus great burgers). It's also known for its fruit drinks, served both with and without rum, and its Sunday brunch. Open daily for lunch and dinner. Reservations unnecessary. Major credit cards accepted. 102 Calle San Sebastián, Old San Juan (phone: 723-1149).

Le Petit Chalet Rarely found by tourists, this little gem is in a private home, where the dining room seats no more than 40 people. Specialties include leg of lamb and grilled red snapper. Open for lunch and dinner daily except Mondays, when it will open only for a group. Reservations (essential) should be made 1 or 2 nights in advance. Major credit cards accepted. Near El Yunque (phone: 887-5802 or 887-5807).

La Tasca del Callejón Traditional Spanish dishes (best known recently for its hot and cold *tapas*) are served in this charming, restored colonial home. The waiters also sing and entertain. *Tapas* and sandwiches are served during the day; a full menu is available for dinner. Closed Sundays. Reservations advised. Major credit cards accepted. 317 Calle Fortaleza, Old San Juan (phone: 721-1689).

INEXPENSIVE

Amanda's Café A delightful hideaway facing the sea, this tiny French/Mexican café specializes in drinks that are close cousins to desserts (Amanda Robles inherited her know-how from her dad, who was bar manager at the old *Lindy's* in New York and invented the Black Russian). Black bean soup, gazpacho, guacamole, enchiladas, French-Mexican fish soup, and frappés are among the innovative recipes. This is a late-night spot, staying open until 2 AM during the week and until 4 AM Fridays through Sundays. Reservations advised for groups. Major credit cards accepted. To get here, follow the road uphill by San Cristóbal Fort (phone: 722-1682).

Butterfly People Both an unusual gallery (exotic butterflies mounted in plastic cases) and an extremely pleasant lunch stop in Old San Juan. Soups, salads, local grilled specialties, and sandwiches are served on the upstairs balcony surrounding the atrium. Open for breakfast, lunch, and dinner; closed Sundays. Reservations necessary for large parties (restaurant seats 42). Major credit cards accepted. 152 Calle Fortaleza, Old San Juan (phone: 723-2432).

Criollíssimo Puerto Rican dishes are served at this hot spot, including stuffed mofongo (fried, mashed plantains shaped into a bowl and filled with beef, chicken, pork, or seafood) and homemade soups for lunch and dinner. Open daily. Reservations unnecessary. Major credit cards accepted. 300 F.D. Roosevelt Ave., Hato Rey (phone: 767-3344).

Green House What it lacks in atmosphere, it more than makes up in good food, cordial service, and reasonable prices. Stop in for burgers, omelettes, daily specials, and divine desserts. Popular with residents. Open daily until 4:30 AM. Reservations advised on weekends. Major credit cards accepted. 1200 Ashford Ave., Condado (phone: 725-4036).

Metropol This chain of eateries serves perhaps the best Cuban food on the island. The menu is basically the same at each location: stuffed Cornish hen, red snapper, steaks, and even liver — all prepared Cuban-style. All locations are open daily for lunch and dinner, except the Santurce branch, which is closed Mondays. Reservations unnecessary. Major credit cards accepted. 105 De Diego, Santurce (phone: 724-7567); 124 F.D. Roosevelt Ave., Hato Rey (phone: 751-4022); Isla Verde Rd., Isla Verde (phone: 791-4046).

Saba

For years there was a shakily handwritten sign just outside the 2-room airport at the edge of the tiny airstrip: "Welcome to Saba, the Storybook Island." The sign is gone, but the fairy-tale appeal remains.

Saba (pronounced *Say*-bah) is mite-size, beachless, and mountainous. Most of the island's 5 square miles seem to go either straight up or straight down, and The Road — Saba's only major thoroughfare — switches back and forth like a dragon's tail, but it never stops ascending or descending. Everything looks doll-size: the gingerbread-trimmed houses of Hell's Gate clinging to the mountain; English Quarter, with its picture-book church; and Windwardside, where the island's only museum is an antique home just a bit larger than a child's playhouse. Seen from The Road above, even The Bottom, Saba's capital, looks like a Christmas-tree miniature.

Grouped with St. Maarten and St. Eustatius in the Windward Islands of the Netherlands Antilles, Saba has been Dutch since 1812. Its prime spoken language, however, is English — the legacy of the Shetland Islanders who were its first residents.

For centuries, the steep hillsides kept Saba isolated from the rest of the Caribbean. Its men became expert seamen, fishermen, and longshoremen. They learned to unload vital cargo offshore, wrestle the stuff through the surf, and haul it up the cliff no matter what the object's size or shape.

Perhaps because of its isolation, minor events anywhere else are major historical landmarks for Saba — including the opening of Windwardside's first supermarket (1963), the arrival of Saba's first cruise ship (the *Argonaut,* in 1966), and the arrival of a jeep in 1947. Lashed to two rowboats, the island's first car narrowly missed being swamped as 50 men lifted it ashore. Decades later, there are still fewer than 300 automobiles on Saba.

Saba is an island scaled to individuals (there are only 1,200 residents), and if you're lucky, you'll meet its memorable ones, such as Will Johnson, a former chairman of the Saba Tourist Board, who edits and publishes the monthly mimeographed *Saba Herald* (which he began in 1968) and serves as Senator of Saba; and ESP-clued Pauline Paul, who gives piano lessons to young and old, and invariably arrives in her wobble-brimmed straw hat to interview visitors for her nightly radio show.

Of all Dutch subjects, only Sabans — because of the extreme ups and downs of their island's topography — are permitted to bury their dead in their own yards. Although the burial custom is fading with rising property values, almost every old house has its flower garden grave site, and the effect is more cheerfully practical than gloomy. Sabans are self-reliant and kind, to each other and to visitors. It's an unwritten rule of The Road that anyone with wheels who's going your way will stop and offer a ride.

There is some development in process on Saba, but on a very modest

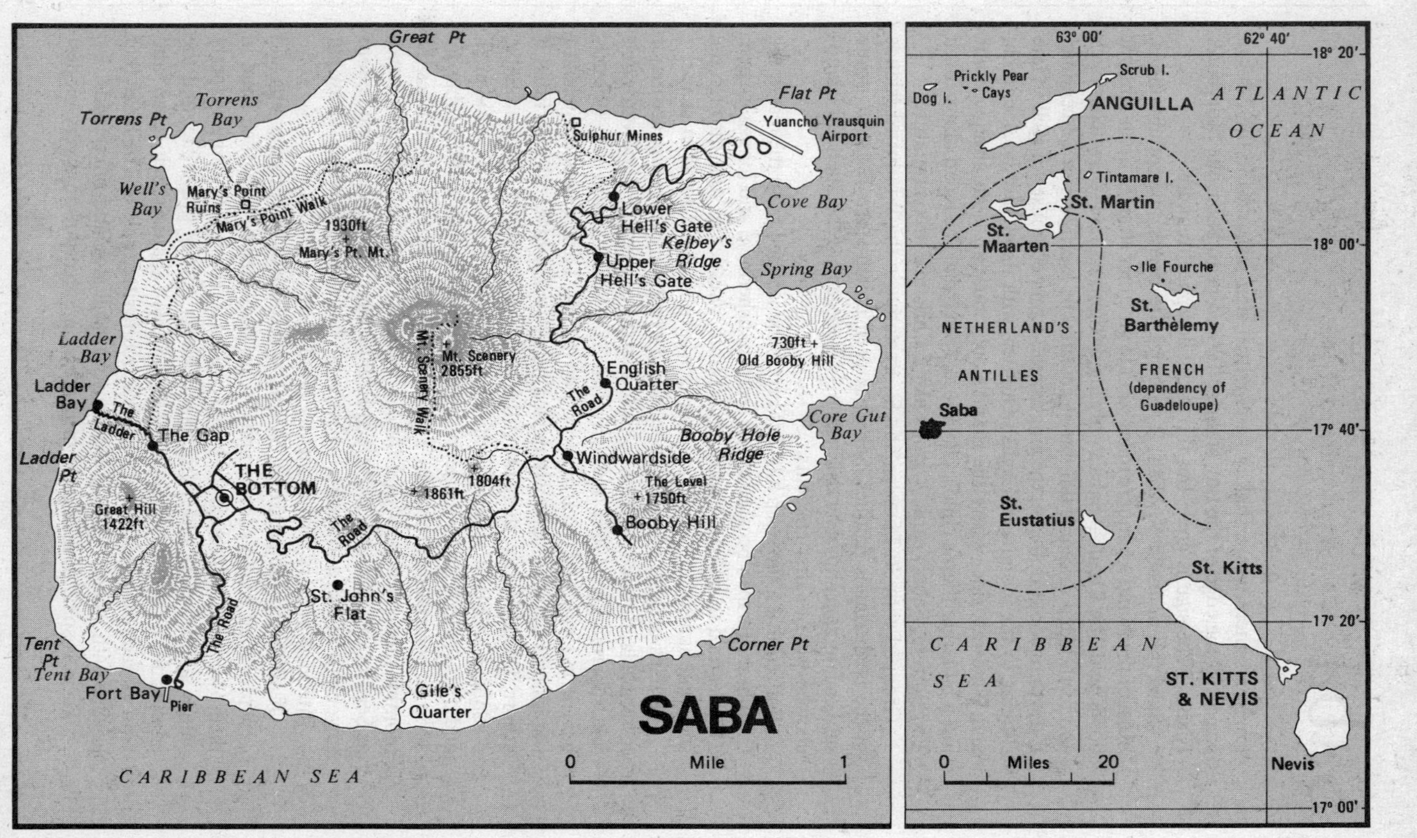

SABA
Great Pt
Torrens Pt
Torrens Bay
Well's Bay
Mary's Point Ruins
Mary's Point Walk
1930ft
Mary's Pt. Mt.
Sulphur Mines
Flat Pt
Yuancho Yrausquin Airport
Cove Bay
Lower Hell's Gate
Kelbey's Ridge
Upper Hell's Gate
Spring Bay
730ft
Old Booby Hill
Ladder Bay
Ladder Bay
The Ladder
The Gap
Ladder Pt
Mt. Scenery 2855ft
Mt. Scenery Walk
English Quarter
The Road
Core Gut Bay
Booby Hole Ridge
Windwardside
THE BOTTOM
1804ft
1861ft
The Level 1750ft
Booby Hill
Great Hill 1422ft
The Road
St. John's Flat
The Road
Tent Pt
Tent Bay
Fort Bay
Pier
Gile's Quarter
Corner Pt
CARIBBEAN SEA
0 Mile 1
63° 00'
62° 40'
18° 20'
18° 00'
17° 40'
17° 20'
17° 00'
Prickly Pear Cays
Dog I.
Scrub I.
ANGUILLA
ATLANTIC OCEAN
Tintamare I.
St. Martin
St. Maarten
Ile Fourche
St. Barthèlemy
NETHERLAND'S ANTILLES
FRENCH (dependency of Guadeloupe)
Saba
St. Eustatius
St. Kitts
CARIBBEAN SEA
ST. KITTS & NEVIS
Nevis
0 Miles 20

scale. In 1989, the island added a fiber optic phone system for clearer reception and better intra-island access. The following year, it acquired a decompression chamber from the Royal Dutch Navy, making it the only Eastern Caribbean island with this diving equipment. Recently, Vernon Hassell, a local businessman, built a new resort, the *Queens Gardens* (see *Checking In*). Hassell also plans to build 15 two- and three-bedroom cottages with private swimming pools. Two Dutch investment firms are also building *Saba Villas,* which will consist of 50 luxury villas, each with a price tag of $1 million.

Friday and Saturday night dances are as exciting as Saba ever gets. If you are not a mountain climber, botanist, or scuba diver, there's a limited amount to see and do. After you've taken the 2-hour all-island tour, there are still two "step roads" (steep, narrow paths traveled via hand-hewn stone stairs) to explore: one leads to the top of Mt. Scenery, the other down to Ladder Bay. There are also 7 marked hiking trails, mostly footpaths trod by farmers for centuries.

Otherwise there are several small hotel pools, three small dive operations, and a quasi-tennis court at The Bottom. However, there are no casinos, no beaches, no golf courses, no marinas, and no big glitzy resorts. You can read or snooze in the sun, walk around a bit, meet a few people, and take pictures. You can hike, bird watch, take naturalist tours or marine ecology seminars, or join the Wednesday morning social breakfast at *Scout's Place,* where "the purpose is just to come together and have interesting talks." After the day's inactivity, you can return to *Scout's* for more conversation. The slow pace would drive some people crazy. For others, it's addictive — the perfect escape.

Saba At-a-Glance

FROM THE AIR

Saba is green, round, and tiny — only 5.1 square miles. At 2,855 feet above sea level, about 28 miles (15 minutes' flying time) south of the Dutch/French island of St. Maarten/St. Martin and 150 miles east of Puerto Rico, it looks like a mountain up to its shoulders in sea — which is exactly what it is. Eons ago its highest peak — 2,855-foot Mt. Scenery — was an active volcano. Now its crater is dead, and a rain forest grows on its sides. Mt. Scenery and surrounding high points (variously and whimsically christened The Level, St. John's Flat, Bunker, Booby, and Old Booby Hills), which range from just over 1,000 to just under 1,700 feet, produce Saba's extreme vertical topography. So suddenly does the island rise out of the Caribbean that for years not a road, but a series of steps called The Ladder, climbing up its western cliffs, provided the only access to its capital town, The Bottom. Landing at Juancho E. Yrausquin Airport on northeastern Flat Point is akin to putting down on an aircraft carrier: the

1,312-foot airstrip, one of the world's shortest, is 130 feet above sea level, with cliffs at either end. Visitors are then taxied through Lower Hell's Gate and Upper Hell's Gate, southwest across the island to English Quarter and Windwardside, then down again via St. John's to The Bottom. The impossible Road, which divides the island diagonally, ends at Fort Bay on the southwestern edge, where there's a pier.

Saba has no beaches. In 1989, Hurricane Hugo washed a tiny sand patch ashore at Fort Bay and, with great optimism, Sabans named it the "Wandering Beach." Unfortunately, it wandered off later that year, never to return.

SPECIAL PLACES

The Road, which climbs, hairpin curving back and forth, from the airport up the steep side of the island to reach Saba's interior, is the island's first special sight. After every expert pooh-poohed the idea, Josephus Lambert Hassell took a correspondence course in engineering and designed The Road, which he and his fellow Sabans built by hand over the next 20 years — thus demonstrating the Saban will and spirit. Reconstruction of The Road has been completed from Windwardside to The Bottom, and at press time was in progress from Windwardside to the airport.

HELL'S GATE, UPPER HELL'S GATE, AND ENGLISH QUARTER These neighborhoods, which consist of clusters of houses, neatly painted in white with contrasting shutters, bright red roofs, and jigsaw-cut gingerbread trim, line the way to the island's top settlement.

WINDWARDSIDE At the top of The Road, slightly east of the island's midpoint, at 1,804 feet, is Saba's second-largest settlement, site of a number of tourist shops and the greater part of the island's guestrooms. Windwardside is also the site of the *Harry L. Johnson Memorial Museum* (phone: 82288). The former home of a Dutch sea captain, the museum is filled with a growing collection of antique Saban furnishings, a lovely rock oven, crisp curtains of Spanish lace, a few pre-Columbian stone tools, and touching mementos of the severe hurricane of 1772 (don't miss the letter Sabans sent to the Dutch government soliciting its help). Also be sure to check out the guestbook — the sixth signature is that of Jacqueline Kennedy Onassis. The museum is open weekdays from 10 AM to 3 PM; admission charge. In the grassy meadow just above the museum is a bust of Simón Bolívar, commemorating his 1816 visit to recruit help for his struggle to free South America from its colonizers. A little beyond Windwardside, a set of 1,064 hand-hewn steps scales the side of Mt. Scenery through a rain forest where some wild orchids still bloom (look, don't pick) and ferns grow taller than Saban children.

THE BOTTOM Saba's capital town lies in a round valley 820 feet above sea level. It takes its name from the fact that the valley is bowl-shaped (*botte* is Dutch for bowl). Actually, its official name is not The Bottom at all. In the late 19th century, the local council voted to change it to Leverock City in honor of Moses Leverock, a patriarchal Saban who had done much for his native island. His memory is still revered, though the name never took hold. Among The Bottom's top sites: the governor's official residence, painted sunny yellow and white, and the small garden park adjoining it; *Heleen's Art Gallery,* with lovely watercolors and an old fireplace (open weekdays 8 AM to 6 PM or by appointment; phone: 63348); and *Cranston's Antique Inn* (phone: 63203), once the government's guesthouse, now a private hotel and late-afternoon watering spot. Northwest of town, restoration has been completed on the steps of The Ladder, a set of concrete and stone steps that lead to a rocky beach and the sea.

FORT BAY At the end of the 9-mile cross-island Road is the island's power plant, its only gas station, the *Saba Deep Dive Shop, Wilson's Dive Shop,* the Saba Marine Park, and the 250-foot pier where imports and some visitors are landed. Sabans and visitors often swim here, making their way to the water via the remaining steps from the old pier.

Sources and Resources

TOURIST INFORMATION

The Saba Tourist Bureau Office is in Windwardside, in the renovated Lambert Hassell Building (phone: 62231; fax: 62350). It is normally open from 8 AM till noon and from 1 to 5 PM. For information on Saba tourist offices in the US, see GETTING READY TO GO.

LOCAL COVERAGE For a little island, Saba is covered with newsprint. The *Saba Herald* is a lively, mimeographed roundup of island news and political opinion that comes out on the 24th of every month. *New Age,* the *Chronicle,* the *Clarion,* and *Windward Island News Day* — all printed on St. Maarten — are delivered to Saba subscribers the day they are published. Somewhat surprisingly, the *San Juan Star* sometimes reaches Saba on the afternoon of the day of publication. A free *Travel & Sports Guide* is available at the tourist office.

Two delightful books worth investigating are *Saban Lore — Tales from My Grandmother's Pipe* by Will Johnson and *Saba — The First Guidebook* by Natalie and Paul Pfanstiehl. In St. Maarten you might be able to find historian Dr. J. Hartog's *St. Maarten, Saba, St. Eustatius* and his *History of Saba* in the paperback English translation. Divers will want the *Guide to the Saba Marine Park* by Tom van't Hof (available at the park office and at most island bookstores). Heleen Cornet's *Saban Cottages* features reproductions of her watercolor paintings and information on local architecture.

RADIO AND TELEVISION

There are several English-language radio and television programs. Major hotels have cable access and receive CNN.

TELEPHONE

When calling from the US, dial 011 (international access code) + 5994 (country code) + (local number). To call from another Caribbean island, the access code may vary, so check with the local operator. When calling from a phone on Saba, use only the local number listed, unless otherwise indicated.

ENTRY REQUIREMENTS

All that is required of US or Canadian citizens is a current passport, or one that expired less than 5 years earlier, or other proof of citizenship (an original or certified birth certificate or a voter's registration card, plus a photo ID) and a ticket for return or ongoing transportation.

CLIMATE AND CLOTHES

Temperatures range from a high of about 85F (about 30C) on a sunny day in Hell's Gate to about 65F (around 19C) on a cool night in Windwardside. Take cottons and polyester blends that can easily be laundered; there are no dry cleaners. Dress is informal. You'll probably need rubber-soled hiking shoes and a sweater for cool evenings.

MONEY

Official currency is the Netherlands Antilles florin, also known as a guilder, and abbreviated NAf, currently exchanged at about 1.77 NAf to the US dollar, but US dollars are accepted throughout the island; Canadians should change their money for florins before departing from St. Maarten, or at either the Banco Barclays Antilliano or the Commercial Bank in Windwardside, both open from 8:30 AM to noon weekdays. Some credit cards are now accepted at *Captain's Quarters, Saba Deep, Sea Saba,* and some island gift shops. All prices in this chapter are quoted in US dollars.

LANGUAGE

Though all of the public signs are written in Dutch, the island's official language, everybody on the island speaks English, the native tongue of Saba's original Scottish-English-Irish settlers. The national greeting exchanged by Sabans passing on steps or road is "Howzzit? Howzzit?" delivered with a very slight raised-hand salute.

TIME

Saba operates on atlantic standard time, 1 hour ahead of eastern standard and the same as eastern daylight saving time. In winter, when it's noon in New York, it's 1 PM on Saba; during daylight saving time, when it's noon in New York, it's noon in Saba.

CURRENT

Electricity is 110 volts, 60 cycles — no problem for North American travel appliances.

TIPPING

A 10% to 15% service charge is usually added to restaurant, bar, or hotel bills. If not, that's the right amount to leave. Give cab drivers $1 or $2. Travel light to Saba, as there are no airport porters.

GETTING AROUND

CAR RENTAL The going rate for the use of a car from the island's fleet of nine is about $35 to $40 a day from *Scout's Place* (phone: 62205), *Johnson's Rent-A-Car* (phone: 62269), or *Doc's Car Rental* (phone: 62271), including a tank of gas and unlimited mileage. Your hotel can make arrangements, but considering the precipitous Road and difficult parking, hitchhiking is both friendlier and easier.

HITCHHIKING An approved way of getting around. Just start walking, and in minutes a Saban will stop and give you a lift as far as he's going in your direction. Wherever he drops you, someone else is sure to pick you up. It's a great way to get to know the people and the island.

TAXI Several taxis meet every arriving flight and ship; they serve both as point-to-point transport and tour vehicles. Taxi drivers are not only proficient in negotiating the zigs, zags, ups, and downs of The Road, but they will be glad to fill you in on island lore. An island tour for one to four people will run about $30; afterward you can be dropped off at *Scout's Place* or *Captain's Quarters* for lunch. The driver will also pick you up after lunch in time to make an afternoon flight.

WALKING Can be a challenge — even within a limited area such as the lanes of Windwardside. Inclines are steep, and the concrete slippery. Sturdy, ground-gripping shoes are a must.

INTER-ISLAND FLIGHTS

Windward Island Airways (WINAIR; phone: 5995-54237 or 5995-54210 in St. Maarten) flies STOL (short takeoff and landing) craft from St. Maarten's Juliana Airport to Saba 5 times daily. In the past, such flights were thought to be impossible — like The Road — until aviation pioneer Rémy de Haenen (former Mayor of St. Barts) built the amazing 1,312-foot airstrip, little more than half as long as the much-maligned strip on St. Barts. The 15-minute flight costs $50 round-trip. Flight schedules permit visitors to spend most of the day sightseeing and lunching on the island before catching the afternoon flight out, or to plan longer stays. Organized full-day tours leave St. Maarten every Thursday and include air transport, sightseeing, and lunch at *Captain's Quarters* for $85.

SPECIAL EVENTS

The Queen's Birthday, April 30, honors Beatrix of Holland with sports events, parades, and fireworks. Ten days in late July are dedicated to *Saba*

Carnival, with shows, games, contests, steel bands, and dancing. During *Saba Days* in early December, there are greased-pole and spearfishing contests, swimming and donkey races, games of all sorts, maypole dances, and lots of partying. Legal holidays include *New Year's Day, Good Friday, Easter* and *Easter Monday, Labor Day* (May 1), *Ascension Day* (40 days after *Easter*), *Saba Day* (the first Friday in December), *Christmas,* and *Boxing Day* (December 26).

SHOPPING

It's more like stepping into someone's parlor. The shops to see are in Windwardside and easy to handle in an after-lunch stroll; store hours are from approximately 9 AM to noon and 2 to 6 PM. Crafts are the most interesting items for sale here.

For almost 125 years, Saban women have been famous for their drawn-thread work called Saba lace. Introduced on the island in 1870 by Mary Gertrude Johnson, who learned it from nuns in her convent school in Caracas, it's a form of needlecraft that involves drawing and tying selected threads in a piece of linen to produce an ornamental pattern. Though the number of women skilled in it has dwindled, the *Island Craft Shop* in Windwardside (phone: 62229) still offers fairly extensive collections of lace-worked blouses, sheets, pillowcases, tablecloths and napkins, and handkerchiefs. The work, remarkably delicate, can be beautiful, but it does require careful laundering and can be expensive. Marguerite Hassell, one of the island's "tatters," sells her own Saba lace from her Windwardside home (phone: 62261).

Today's most visible island craft is silk-screen printing on cotton, handsomely practiced by the *Saba Artisans Foundation* (phone: 63260), whose designs are adapted from Spanish-work details photographed and enlarged, as well as the shapes of palm fronds, leaves, and flowers. At their main shop and workroom in The Bottom you'll find everything from silk-screened head scarves, T-shirts, and placemats to full-length dresses; items are priced from a few dollars to about $40. They also show leatherwork and dolls from Curaçao, black coral jewelry from Bonaire, and woodwork from Statia (St. Eustatius).

Another local specialty is "Saba Spice" — an aromatic blend of 151-proof cask rum, brown sugar, anise seed, cinnamon, nutmeg, and secret ingredients — home-brewed by Patsy Hassell of Hell's Gate and a number of other locals. While no two bottles are exactly alike (each brewer uses his or her own recipe) they all are sweet, spicy, and pack quite a wallop.

Other spots, all in Windwardside: *Breadfruit Gallery* (in the Lambert Hassell Building; phone: 62509) for a large selection of original paintings, prints, and other fine art by local artists; *Saba Tropical Arts* (in the same building; phone: 62201), for a little bit of everything the island produces; and the *Belle Isle Boutique* (phone: 62208) for clothing.

SPORTS

CROQUET At noon on the first Sunday of each month on the grounds of the *Harry L. Johnson Memorial Museum* in Windwardside, Sabans gather, dressed in their best croquet whites, to play this venerable British game. Wear white, bring a smile, and watch your language — each profanity carries a guilder fine!

HIKING Allow 3 to 4 hours for the trek up the 2,855-foot extinct volcano Mt. Scenery, but if a cloud hovers at the peak, wait until the morning mist burns off or go another day. Try to start out as early as possible. Wear good walking shoes and sunscreen; bring a camera and a canteen. Begin the climb either from Windwardside at the road sign "Mt. Scenery" or midway up at the end of Mountain Road, where a 1,064-step concrete stairway leads to the top. (This can be slippery, but is well worth any scrambling.) A tropical paradise of giant elephant ears and ferns, palms, banana and mango trees, heliconias, and 17 species of wild orchids prepare you for the spectacular view from the summit. If you're uneasy going it alone, Glenn Holm at the tourist bureau may be able to provide a guide, or to accompany you himself. He has catalogued a list of over 16 island trails, of which 7 are mapped out, complete with instructions, trail hazards, and a description of the sights en route. Bernard Johnson (phone: 62432) offers a 4-hour hike from the sulphur mine to Well's Bay for $50 per person (the price drops if there are more than three people) and fills the hours with historical information, island trivia, and ecological insights.

SCUBA AND SNORKELING Saba has become one of the premier diving locations in the Caribbean, and it has 38 officially designated dive sites around the island. The three diving operations on Saba — *Wilson's, Sea Saba,* and *Saba Deep* — offer single-tank, two-tank, and night dives, as well as longer term packages. *Saba Deep* is based at Fort Bay (phone: 63347), and its US representative is *Surfside* (in Scranton, PA; phone: 717-346-6382); *Sea Saba* is owned by Louis and Joan Bourque, both *PADI* instructors (phone: 62246); and *Wilson's* (phone: 63410) also has an office at Fort Bay. Special arrangements can be made for marine ecology seminars, slide presentations, underwater photography instruction, and fishing excursions to Saba Bank. *Sea Saba* and *Saba Deep* also offer 5-day Open Water certification courses. Snorkeling trips and equipment rental can be arranged through *Wilson's* for about $20 a day. Two boats that offer dive trips also moor around the island: the *Caribbean Explorer* (phone: 800-322-3577 from the US) and *Coral Star* (no phone).

A 1-day package from St. Maarten, including two dives, all equipment, transport, lunch, and sightseeing, is available for about $175. Contact *Rising Sun Tours* on St. Maarten (phone: 5995-42855 or 5995-52055). Arrangements for other packages can be made through *Maho Watersports* on St. Maarten (phone: 5995-52801, ext. 1871 or 5995-54387).

You can dive very close to shore. Underwater visibility, normally in excess of 100 feet, can reach up to 200 feet. There are both shallow and very deep dives: Some of the reef structures include lava flows, towering vertical walls, underwater caverns and caves, and even underwater mountains. The black-sand bottom accents the striking colors of large purple sponges, breathtakingly huge stands of black coral, and abundant fish. Even the most seasoned diver will be stunned by the site called Outer Limits, which features a huge mountaintop under 90 feet of water.

In 1987, Saba established the Saba Marine Park (SMP) to protect its still virgin marine life. The park encircles the island and includes the waters and seabed from the high-water mark down to 200 feet. The SMP's new Edward S. Arnold Snorkel Trail at Torrens Point is well thought out, informative, and fun. For $5, you can get a laminated trail map that can be read underwater; it's useful as you follow the arrows leading to the 11 sites. Arrangements can be made with any of the three island dive shops (see above).

The SMP also maintains a system of 38 permanent mooring buoys (including 4 overnight yacht moorings) to facilitate diving and to prevent anchor damage to coral. An information office is located at Fort Bay (phone: 63295), and complimentary slide shows are offered to all visiting dive groups. A diving decompression chamber is housed at the *Saba Marine Park Hyperbaric Facility* (phone: 63295) in Fort Bay.

SPORT FISHING Contact Robbie Hassell (phone: 62367), who will motor you in his 32-foot vessel to Saba Bank, 3 miles offshore and known for its excellent catches. Arrindell Hassell (phone: 62261) also offers deep-sea fishing charters. Saba Bank is 32 miles long and 20 miles wide, mostly 6 to 20 fathoms deep, and in some areas the bottom can be seen clearly.

SWIMMING Seasonal swimming is possible at Well's Bay, but it's an hour's hike down the mountain to get there. Otherwise, there is a lovely pool clinging to the top of the mountain at *Captain's Quarters,* and smaller pools at *Scout's Place, Queens Gardens, Juliana's,* and *Cranston's Antique Inn.* You don't need to be a hotel guest to use the pools.

TENNIS Few people take advantage of the cement tennis court at The Bottom (free and open to all). If the net isn't up, ask around (no phone). A new court was being built at press time at *Queens Gardens.*

NIGHTLIFE

The weekly Friday and Saturday night dances — to which everyone is invited and just about everyone goes — are held at *Guido's* (in Windwardside; phone: 62230). Other action can be found at *Lime Time* (phone: 63256 or 63351) and at *Birds of Paradise* (phone: 62240), both in The Bottom. If there is a party, most everyone on the island will know. Ask at your hotel. Movies also are shown every weekend at the *Royal Theater* (phone: 63263). That's it — although people have been known to sit up late and swap yarns and philosophical observations around the bar at — guess where — *Scout's Place* or the *Captain's Quarters.*

Best on the Island

CHECKING IN

Saba has several hotels, plus a fine selection of less expensive vacation apartments and guesthouses, including some traditional Saban wood cottages that rent on a daily, weekly, or monthly basis. Apartments usually cost about $45 a day, $240 to $290 a week in winter; $30 a day, $195 a week in summer. Most are completely equipped. Contact the Saba Tourist Bureau in the US or on Saba for a full listing. Several large, fully furnished villas with private pools are also available for rent through *Saba Real Estate* (phone: 62299; fax: 62415). Weekly rates range from $700 to $1,900 for two to six people.

At hotels listed here as very expensive, expect to pay $240 or more for a double in peak season; at expensive places, $125 to $240; moderate, $75 to $110; inexpensive, $65 or less. A 5% room tax and a 10% to 15% service charge are additional. Since nights tend to be cool, most Saban hotels are not air conditioned. When calling from a phone on Saba, use only the local numbers listed below. For information about dialing from elsewhere, see "Telephone" earlier in this chapter.

VERY EXPENSIVE

Queens Gardens Saba's first luxury resort was built by local businessman Vernon Hassell on 8 acres of tropical gardens on the slopes of Troy Hill. It has 12 studios and suites, all with living rooms and kitchens. There's also a restaurant, bar, swimming pool, and a small library. A tennis court, small fitness center, and conference room were still under construction at press time. Troy Hill (phone: 62236; fax: 62450).

EXPENSIVE

Captain's Quarters Long on old-fashioned charm (its two houses are 100 and 175 years old, with much furniture to match), its 10 rooms are big, airy, and island-stylish (fresh colors, four-poster beds, sisal rugs, antique touches). While the rooms do not have TV sets or telephones, the view, the terrace, dining room, bar, and swimming pool are all mighty attractive, and the fare has greatly improved in recent years (see *Eating Out*). Rates include continental breakfast. Windwardside (phone: 62201; 800-223-9815 from the US or Canada; fax: 62377).

MODERATE

Juliana's Here are 10 no-frills, but functional, units — 8 double rooms, 1 one-bedroom apartment, and 1 two-bedroom cottage. The double rooms have small refrigerators and private balconies, and the apartment and cottage have full kitchens and patios. There's also a pool and a restaurant that serves breakfast and lunch. Windwardside (phone: 62269; 800-223-9815 from the US or Canada; fax: 62309).

Scout's Place It describes itself as "Bed 'n' Board, Cheap 'n' Cheerful." In addition to the older 4 doubles, there are 10 sparkling double rooms in the newer section, all with four-poster beds, private baths, and balconies. There is a small pool, and the view is great, but its special appeal is the feeling it has of being right at the heart of it all — everybody stops by late in the day to drink a cold beer and discuss life. Scout has turned the business over to Dianna and Harold Medero, his former cook and barman, but he takes all his meals here and still holds court. Rates include breakfast. Windwardside (phone: 62205; fax: 62388).

INEXPENSIVE

Cranston's Antique Inn A small guesthouse where Queen Juliana slept during her 1955 visit (ask for Room 1). The 6 rooms have four-poster beds and patios. There's a pool, and the restaurant serves West Indian dishes. The Bottom (phone: 63203; 800-223-9815 from the US or Canada).

EATING OUT

Most visitors to Saba eat at their guesthouse restaurant, but there are a few other options. Expect to pay about $50 for dinner for two at a restaurant we list as expensive, $30 to $40 at places in the moderate category, and less than $25 at inexpensive places. When calling from Saba use only the local numbers listed below. For information about dialing from elsewhere, see "Telephone" earlier in this chapter.

MODERATE

Brigadoon Saban-born chef Greg Johnson serves a delightful array of Caribbean and continental dishes ranging from fresh fish to succulent steaks. He also has the only live lobster tank on the island. Leave room for his homemade desserts. Open daily for dinner. Reservations unnecessary. Major credit cards accepted. Windwardside (phone: 62380).

Captain's Quarters The alfresco setting is enchanting, and the West Indian and American dishes are prepared with imagination and care. Open daily. Reservations necessary by mid-morning. MasterCard and Visa accepted. Windwardside (phone: 62201).

Scout's Place The island's most popular eatery, it serves a mixture of Caribbean dishes and standard favorites, including stewed goat and mutton, and well-prepared fish dishes. The open-air dining room has a sweeping view of the sea. After dinner, stick around for some conversation or join in a card game. Open daily for lunch and dinner. Reservations advised. MasterCard and Visa accepted. Windwardside (phone: 62205).

INEXPENSIVE

Guido's The island's combination rec room and pizza place, it offers decent pizza, subs, and standard rib-sticking Italian favorites. Part of the draw here is the large-screen TV set, the dart boards, and the loud stereo, which sometimes prompts dancing at night. Open daily for lunch and dinner. Reservations unnecessary. No credit cards accepted. Windwardside (phone: 62230).

Queenie's Serving Spoon Authentic and plentiful family-style West Indian food, served in an 8-table appendage to Queenie's home. Chicken with peanut sauce, pumpkin fritters, and homemade soursop ice cream are all specialties. Open daily. Reservations necessary by about noon. No credit cards accepted. The Bottom (phone: 63225).

Saba Chinese A 100-plus item menu features Chinese and a few Indonesian dishes. With good food and a funky decor, it's one of Saba's weekend hot spots. Open daily for lunch and dinner. Reservations unnecessary. No credit cards accepted. Windwardside (phone: 62268).

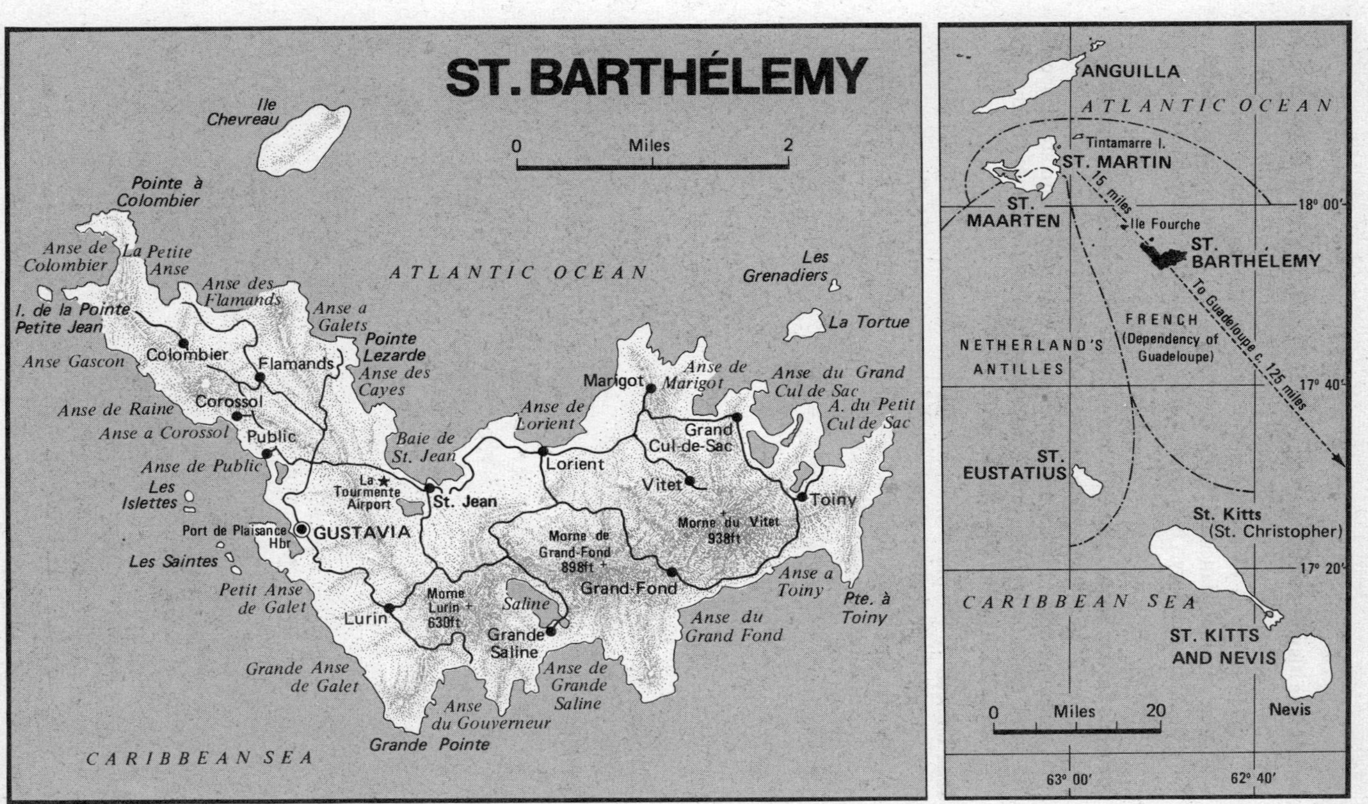
ST. BARTHÉLEMY
0
Miles
2
Ile Chevreau
Pointe à Colombier
Anse de Colombier
La Petite Anse
Anse des Flamands
I. de la Pointe Petite Jean
Anse Gascon
Colombier
Flamands
Anse a Galets
Pointe Lezarde
Anse des Cayes
ATLANTIC OCEAN
Les Grenadiers
La Tortue
Anse de Raine
Corossol
Anse a Corossol
Public
Anse de Public
Les Islettes
Baie de St. Jean
La Tourmente Airport
St. Jean
Port de Plaisance Hbr
GUSTAVIA
Les Saintes
Petit Anse de Galet
Lurin
Morne Lurin 630ft
Saline
Grande Saline
Grande Anse de Galet
Anse du Gouverneur
Grande Pointe
Anse de Grande Saline
CARIBBEAN SEA
Marigot
Anse de Marigot
Anse de Lorient
Lorient
Grand Cul-de-Sac
Vitet
Morne de Grand-Fond 898ft
Grand-Fond
Morne du Vitet 938ft
Anse du Grand Cul de Sac
A. du Petit Cul de Sac
Toiny
Anse a Toiny
Pte. à Toiny
Anse du Grand Fond
ANGUILLA
ATLANTIC OCEAN
Tintamarre I.
ST. MARTIN
ST. MAARTEN
15 miles
18° 00′
Ile Fourche
ST. BARTHÉLEMY
FRENCH (Dependency of Guadeloupe)
NETHERLAND'S ANTILLES
To Guadeloupe c. 125 miles
17° 40′
ST. EUSTATIUS
St. Kitts (St. Christopher)
17° 20′
CARIBBEAN SEA
ST. KITTS AND NEVIS
Nevis
0
Miles
20
63° 00′
62° 40′

St. Barthélemy

People tend to be protective about St. Barts — both for the island's sake and their own. It is tiny — only 8 square miles — and beautiful, endowed with small green mountains, coral sand coves and beaches, a dollhouse-size capital port, and a free-and-easy pace. Its vacation life is unprogrammed, its sands uncrowded, and its denizens — including wealthy Americans and European aristocrats — want it to stay that way. Over the past 10 years or so, St. Barts has been discovered, but with fewer than 700 hotel rooms, an airstrip accommodating nothing larger than a 19-seat short takeoff and landing (STOL) plane, and (for the most part) astronomic prices, most visitors still come from among the privileged. The masses are limited to a few hours off a cruise ship or a day trip from nearby St. Martin/St. Maarten.

Discovered by Columbus in 1493 and named for his brother Bartolomeo, the island received its first French settlers in 1648. Except for a minor takeover by the British in 1758 (during which its French-speaking inhabitants temporarily fled to neighboring islands), it remained firmly Gallic until 1784, when St. Barts' citizens awoke to the astounding news that one of Louis XVI's ministers had traded the island — lock, stock, and citizens — to Sweden for trading rights in Göteborg.

While the permanent population continued to eke out a living from the stone-walled fields and sea, the Swedes took over, rechristened the island's capital Gustavia in honor of their king, declared it a free port, and began trading — and prospering. In 1878, when St. Barts became French again, the free-port status remained — along with such Viking legacies as neat-lined buildings, a few street signs, and the town name.

St. Barts' residents look like few other Caribbean islanders. About 90% of the population of 4,000 are descendants of the island's first settlers — from the Normandy, Brittany, and Poitou regions of France — and are white-skinned and blue-eyed. They're a sober-looking group, whose *anciennes dames* pad about the village of Corossol barefoot; wear big, white, kiss-me-not sunbonnets; and weave straw hats, placemats, and baskets to sell to tourists.

But St. Barts is also St-Tropez French — a world of monokinis and beach café lunches with lots of wine and laughter. And after the beach day is over, the evening is for small, fine restaurants where cuisine is spelled with a capital "C" and the wine cellars are well stocked. Late-night activity might include a leisurely stroll along the boat-filled waterfront, where the occasional strains of a visiting jazz group can be heard, or lingering over a cognac on a *Castelets* terrace, basking in the moonlight and picking out lights on the yachts anchored in the St. Jean Bay far below. There's no big-city hustle and bustle here — just a laid-back atmosphere and small-gem perfection. You'll either be bored to tears or you'll love it. If the latter is the case, after a couple of days of leisurely island existence you're sure to find yourself feeling protective about St. Barts, too.

St. Barts At-a-Glance

FROM THE AIR

St. Barts is vaguely V-shaped. Its bottom point aims south, and its northwest arm is slightly narrower than its northeastern one. It lies 125 miles northwest of Guadeloupe, of which it is a dependency, but only 15 miles (a 10-minute flight) southeast of St. Martin/St. Maarten. Notable geographic features include steep, green, once actively volcanic hills, deep valleys, and white-gold beaches with bays scooped into the shoreline on every side. Its capital, Gustavia, is built around a harbor 13 to 16 feet deep, which cuts into the island's southwest coast. The town is home to less than 15% of St. Barts' population. Gustav III Airport, at La Tourmente — which could have been named for the emotion first-timers feel when they contemplate its short runway — lies north of town on the road to St. Jean. The beach at Baie de St. Jean is the most famous strand on the island, with a number of small hotels, restaurants, bistros, and a shopping plaza nearby. It is washed with gentle waves, as are most north-facing shores. The surf is sometimes quite strong along the Anse du Gouverneur, Anse de Grande Saline, Anse du Grand Fond, and Anse à Toiny on the southern coast. Roads are, for the most part, well paved and easy to cope with in the lowlands and valleys, but often they scale hills at an angle only a chamois could love.

SPECIAL PLACES

GUSTAVIA St. Barts' toy-scaled capital lines the three protective sides of the harbor or *port de plaisance.* Too small for most cruise ships, it's a favorite layover for sailing yachts. When a liner or large windjammer does anchor offshore, tenders ferry passengers to the principal quay on the east edge of the port. Focal point of a good deal of town activity, the quay is surrounded by tourist-oriented boutiques offering duty-free French imports. The town, with its cafés and restaurants in old houses and its architectural mix of Swedish colonial (the Town Hall, the former yacht club, the old Clock Tower at the foot of Morne Lurin) and French creole (almost everything else), is quaint, pretty, and pin-neat. There are only a few historic monuments, and although pirates hid out here in the 18th century, they left no souvenirs.

A stroll around the whole town takes only an hour or two, depending on your café-resistance threshold. Park at the quay, then browse down the Rue de la République and/or the Rue Général de Gaulle; turn right and follow Rue du Centenaire along the harborside, past the old 10-ton English anchor (marked "Liverpool Wood–London," the type used by 18th-century warships) perched over the harbor opposite the Anglican church; then, if you still feel like walking, turn right and take Rue Jeanne d'Arc along the harbor's third side. Here you may want to stop at the terrace of *La Marine,* the popular *L'Escale* restaurant next door (see *Eating Out* for details on both), or *Café Caraïbes.* Or reverse direction and continue strolling, ending your tour with a stop (or stops) at *Chez Joe, Le Sélect Bar,* or the *Bar de l'Oubli* back in the center of town.

ELSEWHERE ON THE ISLAND

GRAND FOND ROUTE Drive east past the Baie de St. Jean and a succession of stunning beaches (Anse de Lorient, Anse de Marigot, Anse du Grand Cul de Sac, and Petit Cul de Sac). Picnic or stop for a seafront lunch at *Chez Francine* or *Le Pélican* (see *Eating Out* for both) or at the peaceful *Marigot Bay Club,* where the snorkeling is fine between fresh fish courses. Then turn south and swing along the surf-pounded shore of the pastoral Grand Fond district, a miniature otherworld of stone-fenced farms and small, tile-roofed houses with hills for backdrop and waves breaking at their feet. Finally, return through the mountains to rejoin the north shore road. The circuit takes more than an hour and a half, depending on lunch and swim time.

COROSSOL ROUTE This second, somewhat shorter drive explores the northwest end of the island. Take a sharp left at the crossroads between town and the airport, and drive parallel to the Anse de Public past the cemetery to the "straw village" of Corossol. Here live the descendants of the earliest French settlers. Old, barefoot women wearing starched, white Breton poke bonnets sell fine straw hats, placemats, and similar items made in small home-parlor shops. (They are shy about being photographed, so ask before you snap.) Colorful fishing boats line the beach at the end of the road. The small *Inter-Oceans Museum* (phone: 276297) houses an exhibit of shells from the world over. Open Mondays through Saturdays from 10 AM to 4 PM; admission charge. Return to the main road and turn left toward the Quartier du Colombier, where you can stop for a drink at the gracious *François Plantation,* a handsome little hotel with a good restaurant (see *Eating Out*). After a detour to the long, sandy Anse des Flamands (site of four small hotels) or the Petite Anse beyond for a swim, head back over the hills for "home."

Sources and Resources

TOURIST INFORMATION

The tourist information bureau in Gustavia is located in a new building on the Quai Général de Gaulle, across from the Capitainerie (phone: 278727; fax: 277447). Open Mondays through Thursdays from 10:30 AM to 12:30

PM and 3 to 5 PM. On Fridays, hours are 10:30 AM to 12:30 PM. Appointments are available weekdays from 8:30 to 10:30 AM. The information booth at the airport is open during arrival and departure hours. Hotel people are also happy to suggest restaurants and beaches and to tell you how to get where you want to go. There are also French West Indies tourist offices in the US (see GETTING READY TO GO).

LOCAL COVERAGE Both *Bonjour St. Barth!,* a detailed French-English guide with attractive illustrations, good maps, practical information, and charming tales about the island's history and traditions, and Georges Bourdin's more scholarly *History of St. Barthélemy* are usually available at *Le Colibri* (Rue de la République; phone: 278708) in Gustavia. *St. Barth Magazine,* published regularly during high season, is free and distributed all over the island. Seasonal publications include *Tropical St. Barth* and the *Guide Saint Barth,* published by the hotel association.

RADIO AND TELEVISION

Radio St. Barts broadcasts a news and variety program in English daily from 1 to 4 PM; programming is in French the rest of the time. Most large hotels have satellite access to US television programming.

TELEPHONE

When calling from the US, dial 011 (international access code) + 590 (country code) + (local number). To call St. Barts from the Dutch side of St. Maarten, dial 6 plus the local six-digit number. When calling from other islands in the Caribbean, codes may vary; call an operator for assistance. When dialing from a phone on St. Barts, use only the six-digit local number unless otherwise indicated. To make a call from a pay phone, callers must first purchase a credit card at the post office for 50 francs (about $10) or 85 francs (about $17). There are no coin-operated phones on the island.

ENTRY REQUIREMENTS

For stays up to 3 weeks, travelers must present proof of citizenship (a current passport or one that has expired within the past 5 years, or a birth certificate with raised seal or voter's registration card accompanied by a government-authorized photo ID such as a driver's license) in addition to a return or ongoing ticket. For longer periods, a valid passport is required.

CLIMATE AND CLOTHES

Year-round average daytime temperatures of 72 to 84F (about 22 to 29C) make the climate right for light cotton and cotton-blend sports clothes — especially with a French casual chic. That means T-shirts, tight jeans, shorts, pareos, or loose cotton shirts; on the beach, bikinis or monokinis are worn by literally everybody. Nighttime dress is slightly spruced up, but basically just as informal and comfortable, except possibly at *Castelets,*

François Plantation, the *Manapany,* the *Guanahani,* or *La Toque Lyonnaise* at *El Sereno Beach,* which call for something a shade dressier; ties and jackets are never required.

MONEY

The official monetary unit is the French franc. Stores and restaurants freely accept US dollars and traveler's checks (but offer no discount for them); Canadian currency is accepted a bit less frequently. The current exchange rate is 5 francs to $1 US; exchange rates are pretty standard, so there's little need to rush to the bank to change dollars to francs. Banking hours in Gustavia are 8 AM to noon and 2 to 3:30 or 4 PM weekdays; closed weekends, holidays, and afternoons preceding holidays. Credit cards are not honored everywhere, so before checking into your hotel or ordering at a restaurant, determine which cards (if any) they accept. All prices in this chapter are quoted in US dollars.

LANGUAGE

Pervasively French — you'll feel at home faster if you can *parlez* a little. But language needn't be a barrier. In most shops, hotels, and restaurants, there's someone who speaks some English; and with a phrase book and patience, you'll be okay. St. Barts' second language — one you probably won't hear much — is the Norman dialect spoken by the old ladies of Corossol and the inhabitants of the northern part of the island.

TIME

St. Barts runs on atlantic standard time all year — the same as eastern North America's daylight saving time; an hour ahead of eastern standard time (e.g., when it is noon EST in New York, it is 1 PM AST in Gustavia).

CURRENT

Electricity is 220 volts, 50 cycles; French plug adapters and a converter kit are needed to use American appliances. It's best to bring your own.

TIPPING

A 10% to 15% service charge normally is added to both hotel bills and restaurant checks and is adequate except in the case of some extra special service. If no service charge has been added, give the waiter 10% of the check. In the more expensive restaurants, a small additional gratuity (about 5% of the check), called a *pourboire,* is customary. For an errand above and beyond the call of duty, tip 5 francs or $1 (American coins are hard for islanders to exchange). Taxi drivers, most of whom own their own cars, don't expect a tip.

GETTING AROUND

CAR RENTAL More fun and more freedom than using taxis, car rentals are easy to arrange (except during peak season, when advance reservations are strongly advised), providing you're of legal driving age and have at least 1 year's licensed driving experience. A mini-moke or a Suzuki Samarai can be picked up minutes after landing at the airport with a minimum of red tape. Considering the hilly terrain, they're the only cars that make sense, but you must be able to operate a stick shift capably and comfortably. Rates are standard: about $225 to $285 a week or $38 to $45 a day in season for 2 to 6 days, on a sliding scale thereafter, with unlimited mileage, one full tank of gas (but be sure to check the tank, as they often arrive nearer to empty!), and free delivery (if you don't pick up your car at the airport). Collision damage insurance runs an extra $7 or $8 a day. *Mathieu Aubin Car Rental* (phone: 276238) is one of several agencies at the airport. Aubin maintains his cars well, and is as knowledgeable as anyone about island happenings. Others at the airport include *Hertz,* represented by *Henri's* (phone: 277114); *Avis,* by *St. Barth Car* (phone: 277143); *National,* by *Europcar Caraïbes* (phone: 277333); *Budget,* by *Jean-Marc Gréaux* (phone: 276743); *Maurice Questel* (phone: 277322 or 276405); *Guy Turbé* (phone: 277142); *USA* (phone: 277001); and *Soleil Caraïbe* (phone: 276718 or 276506). In St. Jean, there's *Edmond Gumbs* (phone: 276193) and *Robert Magras* (phone: 276312); in Terre Neuve, *Odette Brin* (phone: 276399); in Gustavia, *Charles Gréaux* (phone: 277001); in Colombier, *Ernest Lédée* (phone: 276163); and in Flamands, *Solange Gréaux* (phone: 276485).

Check the car's brakes carefully before charging off into the countryside. And when the man says to use first gear to climb Morne Lurin, the hill on which *Castelets* is perched, PAY ATTENTION! He means first gear and full throttle all the way — at least from the point where you turn off the main road. If you're lucky enough to be staying at *Castelets,* try to get a taxi to drive you from the airport and take advantage of free rental car delivery service *after* you've settled in. If you plan to have dinner there after dark, arrange for a cab to take you and call for you afterward.

Motorbikes, mopeds, and scooters are plentiful. French law requires that you wear a helmet and have a motorbike or driver's license. Rentals average about $35 a day, with a $100 deposit. Check with Denis Dufau's *Rent Some Fun* (phone: 277059), near the two churches in Gustavia; *Ernest Lédée* (phone: 276163); or *Frederic Supligeau* (phone: 276789).

There are two gas stations. The one near the airport is open Mondays through Saturdays from 7:30 AM to noon and 2 to 5 PM, and sells debit cards for self-service use when closed. The one in Lorient is open from 7:30 AM to 5 PM; it's closed Thursday and Saturday afternoons and all day Sunday.

FERRY SERVICES Several boats ferry passengers between St. Martin/St. Maarten and St. Barts for about $25 to $30 one-way or $45 to $50 round-trip per person. Days of operation and departure/arrival times vary with the season, so be sure to check well in advance. Some boats, such as *St. Barth Express* (phone: 277724), leave from Marigot on St. Martin's French side;

others, such as *White Octopus* (phone: 23170 on St. Maarten; 24096 or 23170 on St. Barts), leave from Philipsburg on the Dutch side, where there is a $5 departure tax. Reservations on some of the boats making the crossing can be made through *Yacht Charter Agency* in Gustavia (phone: 276238). For help with travel plans, *Saint-Barth Voyages* (Rue Duquesne, Gustavia; phone: 277979), a full-service travel agency, is good and reliable.

SIGHTSEEING BUS TOURS The tourist office (phone: 278727) offers three tours of the island, all in VW minibuses that depart from the pier in front of the office on Quai Général de Gaulle in Gustavia. The trips last from 45 minutes to 1½ hours, are moderately priced, and are designed for small groups. There are numerous tour operators on St. Barts, including *Céline Gréaux* (phone: 276598), *Bruno Béal* (phone: 276005), *Emile Gréaux* (phone: 276601), and *Robert Magras* (phone: 276312).

TAXI It seems all 3 dozen drivers meet the morning arrival of catamarans full of day visitors from St. Martin, but only five or six are on call in the evenings. The taxi stand phone number is 276631. If you do manage to arrange for a cab after dark, note that there is a 50% surcharge at night, as well as on Sundays and holidays.

INTER-ISLAND FLIGHTS

From St. Maarten's Juliana Airport (where most international flights land), *Windward Island Airways* (*WINAIR;* phone: 44230 or 44237 on St. Maarten) and *Air St. Barthélemy* (phone: 277190) make the 10-minute flight to St. Barts for about $35 one-way. There is a $5 departure tax from the Dutch side. *Air Guadeloupe* (phone: 276190) makes the flight out of St. Martin's Espérance Airport, near Grand Case on the French side, for about $55 round-trip. *Air Guadeloupe* also flies in from the island of Guadeloupe (about a 1-hour flight), as well as from St. Thomas on Mondays, Wednesdays, and Fridays. *Virgin Air* (phone: 277176) serves St. Barts from San Juan, Puerto Rico, and St. Thomas.

SPECIAL EVENTS

The *Festival of St. Barthélemy,* celebrated every August 24, is like a French country fair gone tropical. Booths line the tiny streets; there are sport competitions and wining, dining, fireworks, and partying after dark. The next day, in Corossol, the sea is blessed to ensure the safety of fishermen; Lorient celebrates with similar activities during the last weekend in August. St. Barts also has its small *Carnaval,* climaxing with *Mardi Gras* and *Ash Wednesday*'s black-and-white parades and parties. In December, the annual *La Route du Rosé Regatta* reaches St. Barts from St. Tropez, some 4,000 miles away. The tall ships carry a cargo of rosé wines from France, in keeping with the long-established tradition of trade between free harbors. In January or February, St. Barts stages its *Annual Music Festival,* featuring classical and jazz music and ballet. Legal holidays include *New*

Year's Day, Labor Day (May 1), *Mi-Carême* (mid-*Lent*), *Easter Monday, Bastille Day* (July 14 — more fun and fireworks), *Schoelcher Day* (July 21), *Assumption Day* and *St. Barts/Pitea Day* — Pitea is the island's Swedish sister town — (August 15), *All Saints' Day* (November 1), *All Souls' Day* (November 2), *Armistice Day* (November 11), and *Christmas*.

SHOPPING

Duty-free prices are good on imported liquor, watches, crystal, porcelain, and other luxuries — especially French perfume, cosmetics, and name-brand sportswear. Among island crafts, traditional straw work (especially peaked and broad-brimmed beach hats and fine-worked baskets), block-printed cotton resort clothes, shellwork (jewelry, boxes, frames, mobiles), and island paintings are most likely to please you as much when you get them home as they do here. Should you feel an irrational craving for one of those white sunbonnets (called *calèche* or *quichenotte*) the ladies of Corossol wear, they will make one to order in 3 to 5 days for about $35. Works by local artists Arden Rose and Jean-Paul Sorel are available in several island shops. Among St. Barts' most beautiful buys are the brilliantly colored, hand-blocked cotton and silk fabrics created by Jean-Yves Froment, either sold by the meter or transformed into everything from skirts to bikinis. Check with the tourist office or your hotel desk about where they're sold. In St. Jean, the best shopping is at the *Centre Commercial* and the *Villa Créole Shopping Center* right next to it. Though a tad pricier than those in town, these shops are open later (until 7 or 8 PM), and the best boutiques have branches here. If you still haven't had enough, there's the attractive *La Savane Centre Commercial,* opposite the airport, with more chic shops. Remember many shops follow the French tradition of closing for several hours at lunchtime. Some of our favorite places:

ALMA Crocheted and embroidered linens, Baccarat crystal, Limoges china, and more, all remarkably priced by US standards. Rue de la République, Gustavia (phone: 276494).

BLEU MARIN Resortwear for men and women. *Villa Créole Shopping Center,* St. Jean (phone: 276128).

CARAT A treasure trove of jewelry, precious gems, fine china and other tableware. Rue de la République (phone: 276722).

LA CAVE Amazing collection of France's top vintages, scrupulously stored in climate-controlled buildings. Rue Marigot, Marigot (phone: 276321). A branch in town is called *La Cave du Port Franc,* Quai de la République, Gustavia (phone: 278629).

CITRON VERT Located near the Sous-Préfecture, a real find for luxurious, sexy lingerie, as well as Paris fashions. Rue Toiny, Publicité (phone: 278017).

HERMÈS Synonymous with the ultimate in luxury: handbags, linen, scarves, jewelry. *Not* for the budget-minded. Quai de la République, Gustavia (phone: 276615).

KOKONUTS Exotic clothing and jewelry; trendy sportswear and beachwear. At two locations: Rue de Roi Oscar II, Gustavia (phone: 278343), and *Villa Créole,* St. Jean (phone: 277948).

KORÉRUPINE Resident gemologist–jewelry designer Dominique Elie sells his own creations and those of other top jewelers; he also buys and sells gems and gold, and does engraving and repairs. *Villa Créole,* St. Jean (phone: 276811).

LITTLE SWITZERLAND Fine 18K gold jewelry, precious stones, crystal, and china at the island branch of the well-known Caribbean retailer. Rue de la France, Gustavia (phone: 276466).

LOULOU'S MARINE An island institution, *the* place for fishing and snorkeling gear, marine equipment, and nautical sportswear. Its bulletin board offers local yachting information. Rue de la France, Gustavia (phone: 276274).

MANUEL CANOVAS A full range of home furnishings from the very high fashion, expensive designers: fabric, bath and table linen, coordinated china/linen breakfast services, beach towels, totes, luggage, and even bathing suits. Quai de la République, Gustavia (phone: 278278).

OPTIQUE CARAÏBE Stop here for chic sunglasses and prescription lenses set into top European designer frames, plus a great food shop, a pharmacy, and a snack bar/café. Rue St. Jean, St. Jean (phone: 276910).

PRIVILÈGE Duty-free perfume, cosmetics, and other beauty indispensables. At two locations: Rue Général de Gaulle, Gustavia (phone: 276743), and *Centre Commercial,* Rue St. Jean, St. Jean (phone: 277208).

LA RÔTISSERIE The long-established deli that provides hors d'oeuvres, pâtés, French sausages, roast chicken, salads, and fine wines for an elegant picnic. Open daily 8 AM to 1 PM and 4 to 7 PM. At two locations: Rue Lafayette and Rue du Roi Oscar II, Gustavia (phone: 276313), and Rue St. Jean, St. Jean (phone: 277346).

SAMSON An eclectic array of Balinese handicrafts and clothing. Quai de la République, Gustavia (phone: 276046).

SOPHIE LAURENT One of the newer shops featuring men's and women's fashionable casual sportswear. They will, if you wish, imprint their tasteful logo on whatever you buy. Rue Général de Gaulle, Gustavia (phone: 276757).

STÉPHANE & BERNARD Carrying women's international designer collections. At two locations: Rue de la France, Gustavia (phone: 276569); and *La Savane Centre Commercial* at the airport (phone: 276913).

THALASSA Fabulous lingerie and swimwear. Two locations: *La Savane Centre Commercial,* St. Jean (no phone) and Quai de la République, Gustavia (phone: 276911).

SPORTS

The new *St. Barth Sports Agency* (phone: 277725 or 276806) will arrange everything from windsurfing and water skiing to hiking, horseback riding, and tennis.

BOATING Sunfish and small boats can be rented at most beaches near hotels for a nominal hourly fee. Most hotels also arrange day sails to offshore islands aboard 38-, 40-, or 42-foot sailing yachts through either *La Marine Service Boat Rental and Diving Center* (phone: 277034) or the nearby *Maison de la Mer* (phone: 278100). Cost is about $80 per person for up to 8 passengers for a day's swimming, snorkeling, cocktails, and buffet on an uninhabited isle, such as Ile Fourchue, with a final swim stop at lovely, isolated Colombier Beach; a sunset cruise with booze goes for $30 per person. Both itineraries also are available on the *Ne Me Quitte Pas* from the *Quai de Yacht Club* (phone: 277034). Skippered charters to Anguilla, St. Maarten, Saba, and St. Kitts can be arranged through *Sibarth* (phone: 276238). In winter, a half-dozen yachts moored in Gustavia Harbor are usually available for half-day, full-day, and longer charters. Since their status changes from tide to tide, ask your hotel to investigate; or check at *Loulou's Marine* (phone: 276274), the two agencies mentioned above, or the tourism office.

St. Barts can accommodate 500 yachts, most at anchor. Gustavia Harbor, 13 to 16 feet deep, has mooring and docking facilities for about 40 yachts. There are also good anchorages at Public, Corossol, and Colombier.

HORSEBACK RIDING Laure Nicolas's *Ranch des Flamands* is located at Anse des Flamands (phone: 278072). A 2-hour trip costs $35 per person.

SNORKELING AND SCUBA Good off some beaches. Several of the beachside hotels have equipment for rent, such as *Le Pélican,* on St. Jean. Otherwise bring your own equipment or buy it downtown. For snorkeling trips, see "Boating," above. For scuba diving trips, gear rental, and instruction, contact Guy Blateau at *La Marine Service* (phone: 277034), *Dive With Dan* at the *Emeraude Plage* hotel (phone: 276478), or *Scuba Club La Bulle* (phone: 276893).

SPORT FISHING Tuna, marlin, bonito, wahoo, dorado, and barracuda are found in the waters north of Lorient, Flamands, and Corossol. *La Marine Service*'s 32-foot *Merry Fisher* costs about $800 for a full day of fishing (food and beverages included) or about $500 for a half day (phone: 277034). *La Maison de la Mer* operates the 36-foot *Rampage* and the 31-foot *Ocean Master* at similar rates (phone: 278100). Trips with fishermen can be arranged by your hotel, given a day's notice. Bring your own tackle.

Warning: As is often true in tropical waters, many fish caught around St. Barts are very toxic. Get an expert opinion before consuming your catch.

SWIMMING AND SUNNING Unquestionably the reason most visitors seek out St. Barts. The island's combination of gleaming stretches of sand and unique isolation make it irresistible to unwinders.

DREAM BEACH

St. Jean Two adjoining curves of gold sand beach, not wide, slope into water that is beautifully clear and buoyant. In spite of its French-Swedish heritage, this is one island where nude bathing is not only discouraged, it is grounds for arrest or at least a summons. On the other hand, bikinis get very brief. Don't bring a picnic. Instead have lunch at *Chez Francine* right at the edge of the sand — as much for the people watching as for the good steaks and red wine. Unless you make arrangements with a nearby hotel to use its changing facilities, come wearing bathing suits and cover-ups; there are no dressing rooms on the beach itself.

Pools — where they exist — are incidental. Other super strands: quiet Marigot and Lorient, favored by island families on Sundays; Colombier, the least accessible; Shell Beach, the most accessible; Grand Cul de Sac, site of *El Sereno Beach, Le Grand Cul de Sac,* and *St. Barths Beach* hotels; long, surfy, and isolated Anse de Grande Saline; Anse des Flamands, with the *Baie des Flamands* hotel and the *Taiwana Club,* but room for independents, too; and small, secluded Anse du Gouverneur, tucked behind Morne Lurin near the island's southern tip. No hotel really owns a beach, but some collect a small fee for the use of their facilities.

TENNIS The *Guanahani* hotel has 2 illuminated, artificial grass courts. There are 2 lighted courts at the *Sports Center of Colombier* (phone: 276107 or 276238) and 2 courts at *Le Flamboyant Tennis Club* (phone: 276982). *St. Barths Beach* hotel has 1 court, as do the *Manipany* hotel (phone: 276655) and the *Youth Association of Lorient,* located off the main road in Lorient (no phone). The *Taiwana Club* (phone: 276501) has 1 unlighted court, as does *Les Islets de la Plage* (phone: 276238).

WATER SKIING Allowed only in Colombier Bay and only between 8:30 AM and 3 PM. For information on equipment and instruction, contact *La Marine Service* (phone: 277034), which charges about $45 an hour.

WINDSURFING Especially popular at such beaches as St. Jean, Grand Cul de Sac, Flamands, and Lorient. Certified instructor Jean-Michel Marot operates *St. Barth Wind School* on St. Jean Bay near the *Tom Beach* hotel (phone: 277122), where he also rents windsurfers, Sunfish, Suncats, and snorkeling gear. Also check out *Wind Wave Power* (phone: 276273) at the *St. Barths Beach* hotel at Grand Cul de Sac. Rentals are available at the *Filao Beach* hotel in St. Jean; at *Ouanalao* in Gustavia (phone: 278127); and on the beach at Marigot Bay. Rentals are about $20 an hour; lessons, about $35 for one person ($60 for two), including equipment.

NIGHTLIFE

Anyone who cares about food and ambience should savor a whole evening — from aperitifs through dinner — at *Castelets,* with its breathtaking view of St. Jean Bay and offshore islands; at suave *El Sereno Beach,* where *La Toque Lyonnaise* has been gathering garlands; at *L'Hibiscus,* the fine restaurant at *L'Hibiscus* hotel (see *Eating Out* for details on these three places); or at the *Café Caraïbes* with its grand view of Gustavia Harbor. The bar at the *Carl Gustaf* hotel, with its harbor view, is also a popular spot. All evening long, locals and visiting crews gather at *Le Sélect* downtown (phone: 278687) for dominoes, beer, and talk, or across the street at the slightly more St. Tropez–like *Bar de l'Oubli* (no phone).

La Licorne, at Lorient (open weekends only; phone: 276074), is a popular dance club that attracts a young crowd. There is usually live music and an uproarious atmosphere at *Le Pélican* (see *Eating Out*) and the *Manapany* hotel. Quieter late spots are *El Sereno* and the *Guanahani* on the beach at Grand Cul de Sac, and the mountaintop *François Plantation* in Colombier.

Best on the Island

CHECKING IN

The largest hotel on St. Barts (80 rooms) would be small on most other islands. The very special charm of this island is still reflected in the intimacy of its tiny, often luxurious hotels, many of which are actually a string of cottages or chalets built up a hill or strung among sea grapes along a beach. The island has become so fashionable that prices have skyrocketed. Our expensive category starts at $200 a day for a double without meals (*Le Toiny* and *Manapany* are very expensive, with rates as high as $1,000 a day). The moderate range is $130 to $200, and anything under $130 is considered inexpensive (and you won't find a room under $75 in high season). Continental breakfasts often are included.

A number of furnished hillside and beach villas are rented by the week or month. *Sibarth Rental and Real Estate* has some 200 listings (PO Box 55, St. Barts, FWI; phone: 276238; 401-849-8012 from Rhode Island; 800-932-3222 from elsewhere in the US). *Villas St. Barth* (PO Box 158, St. Barts, FWI; phone: 277429; 800-648-3940 from the US) and *St. Barth's Properties* (phone: 508-528-7727 from Massachusetts; 800-421-3396 from elsewhere in the US) have fewer listings but some very special properties. Rates vary depending upon the number of bedrooms, location, access to beach or pool, maid service, and the like, with winter weekly rents starting at about $800 for a 1-bedroom house. Summer rates are 30% to 45% lower. Because of the island's growing number of good restaurants, CP (Continental Plan, continental breakfast only) rather than MAP (Modified American Plan, breakfast and dinner included) rates are now the norm. Almost all the resort hotels accept major credit cards. When calling from St. Barts, use only the local number. For information about dialing from elsewhere, see "Telephone" earlier in this chapter.

For an unforgettable island experience, we begin with our favorites, followed by our recommendations of cost and quality choices of hotels large and small, listed by area and price category.

SPECIAL HAVENS

Castelets It's as though a small, very elegant part of France had been transplanted to an island mountaintop. Formerly *Sapore di Mare,* this *très chic* resort is now back under its original ownership after a 2-year hiatus. French provincial antiques, handsome fabrics, and tasteful prints decorate its 10 rooms and villas, each with its own full-length balcony from which to enjoy the views of the neat little port city of Gustavia and the sea, beaches, hills, and valleys below. Meals are superb (see *Eating Out*). There's a tiny pool, though no other sports facilities, and there's a nice small beach down a rugged road on the other side of the mountain. If you're an adventurous driver, rent a car; otherwise, the hotel will call an island car to take you wherever you'd like to go. Breakfast is included in the rates. A beautiful retreat. Closed September. Morne Lurin (phone: 276173; 800-223-1108 from the US; fax: 278527).

Guanahani St. Barts' largest hotel, with a total of 80 rooms, includes 1- and 2-bedroom suites, junior suites, and deluxe rooms in West Indian–style cottages trimmed in gingerbread and sprawled across a spectacular beachfront site adjoining Rothschild property. All rooms have sea-view patios or decks, air conditioning, ceiling fans, radios, TV sets, and VCRs. Most have either kitchenettes or full kitchen facilities; many have their own private pools. All rooms differ in size and layout and may be interestingly combined to form family or friendly enclaves. Amenities include a freshwater pool and Jacuzzi overlooking the beach, 2 lighted tennis courts, and 2 restaurants — the small *Bartolomeo,* serving French cuisine with a Provençal touch, and the informal poolside *L'Indigo* (see *Eating Out*). Full water sports facilities and free airport transfers are included. The hotel also offers a week-long cooking school that features classes in French cuisine, and plenty of free time for exploration and relaxation. Grand Cul de Sac (phone: 276660; 800-628-8929 from the US; fax: 277070).

Le Toiny Opened in late 1992, this sumptuous retreat rests on a secluded hill in a glorious crest of palm trees, mountains, and rocky pastures that tumble down to the sea. Each of the 12 cottages — with its own luxuriant garden, picket fence, and swimming pool — gives the feeling of a private, very luxurious home. Gleaming hardwood floors, four-poster beds, designer draperies and plush fabrics, and sunken tubs provide a sense of comfortable elegance. Delicious, complimentary breakfast is served on your terrace, and the splendid *Le Gaiac* restaurant features the best in *gastronomique* dining (see *Eating Out*). Service is world class, with prices to match, but this is definitely the premier new resort on the island. Closed from September through mid-October. Anse Toiny (phone: 278888; 800-346-8480 from the US; fax: 278930).

GRAND CUL DE SAC — MARIGOT — VITET — ANSE TOINY

EXPENSIVE

El Sereno Beach A group of 20 invitingly private rooms, each distinctively decorated and facing a patio, private garden or the ocean. Rooms have refrigerators, phones, wall safes, and TV sets with closed-circuit video. Most recent additions are 9 one-bedroom villas, situated near the hotel on a hillside, each with a living room, bedroom, kitchenette, and spacious terrace. Top flight in every respect, with a pool, a bar, and one of St. Barts' most acclaimed restaurants, *La Toque Lyonnaise* (see *Eating Out*). Grand Cul de Sac (phone: 276480; 800-223-9815 from the US; fax: 277547).

St. Barths Beach and Grand Cul de Sac Beach Next door to each other and under the same ownership, these pretty properties share a calm stretch of beach on one side, a quiet lagoon on the other. Tour groups and families like them for the full range of water sports, tennis, and saltwater pool. At the *St. Barths Beach* hotel, there are 36 very pleasant rooms, all with private baths and balconies. The *Grand Cul de Sac* has more private bungalows, 16 airy rooms with kitchenettes, and use of all *St. Barths Beach* facilities. Grand Cul de Sac (phone: 276070 or 276273; 800-223-6510 from the US; fax: 277557).

MODERATE

Hostellerie des Trois Forces Here is a peacefully remote mountainside cluster of rustic bungalows, each designed for a different zodiac sign. French astrologer–owner Hubert Delamotte conducts early-morning yoga classes by the pool, mountain hikes, and astrology lessons in low season. Swim-up bar; the attractive poolside restaurant features fish and meat grilled in French and creole style. Closed July and sporadically throughout the off-season if business is slow. Vitet (phone: 276125; fax: 278138).

Marigot Bay Club A charming sea-view hotel, with 6 studios, it's always in great demand. On the beach, all units have kitchens, terraces, living rooms, and air conditioning. The owner fishes daily for the specials served at the restaurant. Marigot (phone: 277545; fax: 279004).

Sea Horse Club Tucked into a tropical garden surrounding a pool are 12 large suites, each with twin beds, a bath, living room, kitchenette, terrace, and an exceptional view of the sea. Attractively decorated and comfortable, this spot is within walking distance of the beach, water sports, and several good restaurants. A week-long cooking school is occasionally offered. Marigot (phone: 277536; 800-932-3222 from the US).

LORIENT

EXPENSIVE

La Banane This unforgettable gem, in a tropical setting with banana trees, offers 9 traditional cottages, some air conditioned, with nontraditional interiors; one has a tub and shower near the four-poster bed and live plants and trees throughout; bungalows No. 2 and No. 3 can be rented together; and No. 4 has a very private terrace. There's a bar, a table d'hôte dinner nightly, and 2 freshwater pools. Breakfast included. Near Lorient Beach (phone: 276825; 800-223-6510 from the US; fax: 276844).

Le Manoir de Lorient This is one of the island's most unusual hideaways. The lobby and public areas are the focal point of this 17th-century Normandy country house; around it are 4 one- to three-bedroom villas, grounds rich with mango, lime, and papaya trees, and a small waterfall, which feeds the all-natural swimming pool (ecologically balanced by aquatic plants and tropical fish). It's all very, very relaxed (hammocks, huge cushions, and macramé sculptures everywhere) and a lot of fun. Across the road from the beach (phone: 277927).

Le Village de Lorient Just as much fun (and as unusual) as *Le Manoir de Lorient,* these 8 rustic stone and wooden cottages are decorated with a highly original flair. Set in an enclosed tropical compound, it's a very private spot — in fact, half the townsfolk don't even know it exists. On the beach at Lorient (phone: 277518; fax: 276575).

MODERATE

Blue Marlin The first hotel at Pointe Milou, long favored as a villa vacation area, it has 2 suites with kitchenettes, a pool, Jacuzzi, and a restaurant. There also are several bungalows, each with double room and bath, in a tropical garden setting. Pointe Milou (phone: 277650).

Les Islets Fleuris On a mountaintop, with a panoramic view of the offshore islands, this tranquil spot has 6 large studios and 1 suite in a garden setting with a pool. Several units have sea views; all are attractively furnished and have ceiling fans. Above Lorient (phone: 276422; 800-223-9815 from the US).

INEXPENSIVE

Les Mouettes Overlooking the water, this lovely place has 7 air conditioned rooms in 4 bungalows with kitchenettes and patios. It's a short walk to the beach, which is family-oriented on weekends, and always popular with surfers (phone: 276074; fax: 276819).

La Normandie This very hospitable *petit hôtel* has 8 modest but neat rooms decorated in pretty floral fabrics. There's a small pool, garden, and bar/restaurant. Just a few minutes' walk from the beach, the town church, and the many activities of Lorient (phone: 276166).

ST. JEAN

EXPENSIVE

Emeraude Plage Grouped around a green lawn and tropical garden right on the beach are 24 bungalows, 3 suites, and 1 villa. All are air conditioned, with kitchenettes, showers, and porches. Quiet and well managed, this place is a good value. Restaurants are nearby (phone: 276478; 800-932-3222 from the US; fax: 278308).

Filao Beach Forming a crescent above St. Jean Beach and the pool are 30 very comfortable rooms, most with sea-view terraces, and each with a sitting area, refrigerator, double and single beds, a direct-dial telephone, a radio, and bath with built-in hair dryer. Sunning, swimming, water sports, and boat charters are all on site. The informal poolside restaurant is popular with locals and French expatriates (see *Eating Out*). Breakfast is served on your terrace or by the pool. The service is good. On the beach (phone: 276484 or 276424; 800-372-1323 from the US; fax: 276224).

MODERATE

Eden Rock St. Barts' first inn was built on a great crag of quartzite jutting into St. Jean Beach. The traditionally furnished red-roofed cottages house 6 rooms, 2 of which have been nicely restored; the others are scheduled for a face-lift. Several units are air conditioned; the rest are cooled by sea breezes. St. Jean Beach (phone: 277294; fax: 278837).

Jean Bart Part of the PLM Azur chain, this hotel overlooks Baie St. Jean. Its 50 terraced, balconied rooms have air conditioning; half have kitchenettes. All are relatively small and comfortable, fostering considerable privacy. There's a freshwater pool and poolside bar; boat excursions can be arranged. St. Jean Beach, the island's most famous, is just down the road (phone: 276337; 800-223-9862 from the US; fax: 276327).

St. Jean Gardens Studios and apartments here are in varying sizes (16 units in all), with kitchenettes, large terraces, great views of St. Jean Bay, and a big pool with sun deck. The staff couldn't be more accommodating (phone: 277019; 800-366-1510 from the US; fax: 278440).

Tropical Gingerbread flounces make this place look especially inviting. Its 20 neat, twin-bedded rooms, each with either a verandah or a sea-view balcony, lie in a U-formation around a flowered garden. There is a small pool, a music and reading room with a TV set and videos in English and French, a bar, a breakfast terrace, and a snack bar. Handy to the beach, water sports, nearby restaurants. On a hillside only 50 yards above the bay (phone: 876487; 800-223-6510 from the US; fax: 278174).

Village St. Jean There are lovely bay views from this 24-room "village." Accommodations include rooms with terraces and twin beds; deluxe cottages with kitchenettes (some with full kitchens next to the terrace); 1- and 2-bedroom villas; and a deluxe suite with a Jacuzzi. A pool in a hillside setting provides panoramic views. The beach is a 5-minute walk. There's a commissary, a library/listening room, and the *Patio* restaurant (phone: 276139; 800-633-7411 from the US; fax: 277796).

MORNE LURIN — GUSTAVIA

EXPENSIVE

Carl Gustaf A truly deluxe hotel with 14 light-housekeeping suites in a hillside location overlooking Gustavia Harbor (the popular bar has a wonderful view). There's a pool and a fitness center on the premises. Less than a quarter mile from Shell Beach — close to town and the marina. Gustavia (phone: 278283; 800-932-3222 from the US; fax: 278237).

L'Hibiscus This intimate hillside inn (11 cottages) overlooking the harbor is one of the island's prettiest, with a fabulous view, great decor, and a cloak of bougainvillea, oleander, and rubber plants. The comfortable rooms all have air conditioning, ceiling fans, showers, and balconies. There's a small pool and *L'Hibiscus,* an alfresco restaurant with fine French cuisine and live music (see *Eating Out*). Under the Clock Tower, Gustavia (phone: 276482; 800-932-3222 from the US; fax: 277304).

INEXPENSIVE

Sunset The upper floors of a lovely old building have been turned into a 7-room hotel; the 3 rooms facing the harbor have great views of boating life. All are simple but comfortable, and have air conditioning, a mini-bar, and telephone. Rue de la République, Gustavia (phone: 277721; 800-366-1510 from the US; fax: 278344).

ANSE DES CAYES — COLOMBIER — ANSE DES FLAMANDS

VERY EXPENSIVE

Manapany A posh colony of 32 luxury units in island-style red-roofed gingerbread cottages sprawled along a beach or tiered on the flowered hillside above. Best are the extravagant beachfront Club Suites — each with a large marble bath, full kitchen, bar, open-air living room/dining area — and the balconied cottages. The other accommodations consist of rather small double rooms and adjoining suites with bedrooms, kitchenettes, and large living room/dining terraces, which can be rented together. Amenities include a good-size pool (for St. Barts), a lighted tennis court, closed-circuit TV, Jacuzzi, water sports, a fun bar, and 2 good restaurants, *Le Ballahou* and *Ouanalao* (see *Eating Out*). Anse des Cayes (phone: 276655; 800-847-4249 from the US; fax: 278714).

EXPENSIVE

François Plantation Quiet and elegant, this establishment consists of 12 good-size rooms (4 with garden views; 8 with sea views) in delightful, pastel bungalows on a hillside. The queen-size four-poster beds and furnishings are excellent antique reproductions; the fabrics are paisley prints from Provence; the marble-floored, spacious bathrooms are furnished with oversize towels. All rooms have air conditioning and ceiling fans, refrigerator/bars, wall safes, multisystem TV sets with American and French programs, and telephones. Breakfast is beautifully served on the bungalow terraces; dinner is French and fabulous (see *Eating Out*). The pool, which sits at the top of the property, gives guests an unforgettable view of the sea surrounding the countryside. Colombier (phone: 277882; 800-366-1510 from the US; fax: 276126).

Isle de France This *très chic* establishment is quickly becoming one of the island's finest addresses. Twelve bungalows, 9 bedrooms, and 3 suites are richly adorned with marble floors, rattan furniture, showers and sunken tubs, and wide terraces with smashing views of the beach and sea. There's also a fitness center, a tennis court, and the island's only squash court. Closed mid-September through October. On Anse des Flamands (phone: 276181; fax: 278683).

MODERATE

Baie des Anges A beachside bungalow complex built on a diagonal, with all 9 units facing the sea. Best are the two that have terraces right on the beach and full kitchens; the others have kitchenettes. All are cozy, simply furnished, and comfortable. On Anse des Flamands (phone: 276361; 800-223-6510; fax: 278344).

Baie des Flamands A 2-story, motel-style inn popular with families, it's on the truly magnificent beach of the same name. One of St. Barts' older properties, its 24 air conditioned rooms are good-size, half with kitchenettes, half with just refrigerators. There is a large saltwater pool, a terrace bar, and a restaurant with creole food. Free airport transfers and mini-mokes for rent. On Anse des Flamands (phone: 276485; 800-223-1588 from the US; fax: 278398).

White Sand Beach Cottages On the peaceful white sands of Anse des Flamands sit 4 bungalows, all with kitchenettes, terrace/living rooms, sun decks, gardens, and air conditioning. Perfect for quiet beach living. On Anse des Flammands (phone: 277099; 800-932-3222; fax: 277069).

INEXPENSIVE

Auberge de la Petite Anse Mother Nature lends the beautiful decor to this serene get-away-from-it-all collection of bungalows, set on a hillock above the sea, at the far end of Anse des Flamands, and connected by path to the beach. There are 16 air conditioned rooms in 8 balconied houses, all immaculate, though spartanly furnished. Petite Anse (phone: 276460; 800-223-6510 from the US; fax: 277230).

Le P'tit Morne In a stunning setting, this casual and friendly mountaintop retreat has 14 pleasantly decorated studio apartments, each with a full kitchen. All units have air conditioning, though it's seldom needed with the cool Atlantic breezes here. There's a swimming pool with snack bar for breakfast and lunch. Colombier (phone: 266264; fax: 278463).

EATING OUT

St. Barts offers a variety of options — snack places and town bistros, informal beachside cafés featuring charcoal-grilled steaks and fresh lobster, a couple of spots for creole-spiced island cooking, and many restaurants serving truly haute cuisine. Only a select few can really be considered inexpensive. St. Barts has few native dishes — except for fresh fish and lobster, which, unfortunately, are no longer inexpensive, either. The cost of a three-course dinner for two, not including wine, ranges from "inexpensive" (under $50), to moderate ($50 to $100), to expensive ($100 and up, up, up!). Unless stated otherwise, dinner reservations are advised — especially in season and on weekends. When calling from St. Barts, use only the local numbers listed below. For information about dialing from elsewhere, see "Telephone" earlier in this chapter.

GUSTAVIA

EXPENSIVE

L'Ananas In an elegant old house with a terrace overlooking the harbor, this place is set apart by its pleasing decor and very creative menu, which features delights such as colombo of lamb, cassoulette of lobster, and red snapper steamed and served with passion-fruit sauce. Extra special desserts include a delicate coconut soufflé and cookies layered with black and white chocolate mousse in a *Cointreau* sauce. Open daily for dinner only. Major credit cards accepted. Rue Thiers (phone: 276377).

Au Port One of St. Barts' oldest and most reliable restaurants serves a French-creole menu. The *filet de boeuf* is superb, as are the duck, snapper, and other house specialties. Open for dinner only; closed Sundays. Major credit cards accepted. Rue du Centenaire (phone: 276236).

L'Hibiscus Besides a great view of the harbor and the old Swedish belfry, *L'Hibiscus* hotel's appealing poolside restaurant/piano bar features such specialties as smoked island fish in puff pastry, beef tenderloin sautéed with foie gras, duck served with oranges and grapefruit, grilled salmon with sea urchin butter sauce, banana flambé, and passion-fruit mousse. The service is friendly and the ambience a delight. Open daily for dinner only. Major credit cards accepted. Under the old Clock Tower, Rue Thiers (phone: 276482).

La Langouste Near the *Sunset* hotel, this is a perfect place for those wanting authentic creole cooking in the most tranquil of settings — a friendly, very comfortable, pink and white dining room. Lunch or dinner might consist of creole cod fritters, stuffed land crabs, fresh fish with *christophine* (a squash-like vegetable), and *flan au coco.* Or try *boudin,* the spicy creole blood sausage, *soupe de poisson,* or — the big draw — lobster and more lobster. Open for lunch and dinner; closed Thursdays. MasterCard and Visa accepted. August Nyman (phone: 276947).

Le Sapotillier Across from the quay and next to the alley leading to *L'Ananas,* this place accommodates guests in a cozy indoor dining room and outside under the old sapotilla tree for which it's named. The menu lists such entrées as duck filet with raspberries and apple, and stuffed back of rabbit with pasta and basil. Appetizers include salmon marinated in dill and lime, and fish mousse in gazpacho sauce. The dessert selection stars a rich white and black chocolate mousse. *Note:* Even with a reservation, you may have to wait a while for a table. Open daily for dinner only. Major credit cards accepted. Rue du Centenaire (phone: 276028).

Wall House Jean-Pierre DeLage's attractive eatery at La Pointe is, naturally enough, across from historic Wall House. It offers such preparations as duck breast on a bed of *paillasson* potatoes and red currants, and fricassee of shrimps and scallops in saffron sauce. Open daily for dinner only. No credit cards accepted. La Pointe (phone: 277183).

MODERATE

Asia French-Vietnamese food is served at this eatery. Some dishes are familiar — sweet-and-sour pork, Cantonese-style roast duck, fried wontons — while others are more exotic — chicken sautéed with lemon grass, pork with Vietnamese mushrooms, curried fish with coconut milk. Open for lunch and dinner; closed Tuesdays in the summer. MasterCard and Visa accepted. Rue du Roi Oscar II (phone: 278137).

Eddy's Ghetto You'll never know what you'll find on the menu, but choices may include *soupe de giraumon* (pumpkin soup), chicken curry, grilled shark, and locally raised goat. Open daily for dinner in season (November to March). No reservations. No credit cards accepted. Rue Général de Gaulle (no phone).

L'Escale On the wharf, next to *La Marine,* this popular spot features exotic salads and well-prepared pasta and pizza, as well as chicken, beef, and seafood grilled over a wood fire. The casual alfresco waterfront ambience is fun in good weather. Open for lunch and dinner daily. No reservations. Major credit cards accepted. On the far side of the harbor (phone: 278106).

La Marine Picnic-style tables and benches on a waterside terrace make up this tiny, popular spot offering succulent seafood, as well as pizza and hamburgers. Islanders-in-the-know (and savvy visitors) come on Monday and Thursday nights to enjoy fresh mussels flown in from France. Unusual offerings include *raie au buerre noir* (skate with black butter) and *dorade aux blanc de poireaux* (dolphin fish with leeks). Open daily for lunch and dinner. Reservations unnecessary. Visa and American Express accepted. Rue Jeanne d'Arc (phone: 277013).

Le Repaire Gustavia's newest harborfront café is also its most stylish: a whitewashed alfresco setting with polished woods, spinning fans, a pretty fish pond, and recorded reggae music. The fare — pastries, fancy salads, sandwiches and fish — is very good, though second to the surroundings. Open daily for lunch and dinner. Reservations unnecessary. Major credit cards accepted. Quai de la République. (phone: 277248).

INEXPENSIVE

Les Lauriers The place to go for authentic island food, prepared by a Gustavia woman who really knows how to cook. The modest setting is a colorful little frame house on a hill; the fare includes *crabes farcis* (creole stuffed crabs), *boudin creole* (sausage stuffed with blood pudding), *ragout de lambis* (conch stew), and, for dessert, flaming bananas or chocolate *gâteau.* Open for dinner only; closed Mondays. No credit cards accepted. Rue Thiers (phone: 276412).

ST. JEAN

EXPENSIVE

La Louisiane This eatery is set on the terrace of a large St. Bartian house. Among the specialties are smoked salmon, foie gras, and lobster salad with ginger honey. Open for dinner nightly from December through April. Major credit cards accepted. On the main road, near the *Jean Bart* hotel (phone: 277136).

Le Pélican Dinner unfolds in a seaside dining room decorated in gentle green colors, with lamp-lighted tables, pink napkins, and floral fabrics. The *pièce de résistance,* however, is the remarkable food, which includes fresh fish, lobster, and shish kebab. Light midday meals of shrimp brochettes, grilled meat or fish, and salads are served on the terrace. Open daily for lunch and dinner. Reservations advised for dinner. Major credit cards accepted. On the beach (phone: 276464).

MODERATE

Brasserie La Créole This attractive spot offers open-air tables and begins serving in the early morning; breakfast features excellent omelettes, warm croissants, and freshly squeezed juices. Tasty salads, simple grilled meat and fish, sandwiches, and desserts are available day and night. Open daily. No reservations. Major credit cards accepted. *Centre Commercial* (phone: 276809).

Chez Francine The attractions of this beach café are many: The view over the turquoise St. Jean Bay, the carefree, good-looking clientele, and the delicious food. Highly recommended are the fresh langouste; the shish kebab with crisp *pommes frites;* the chicken, fish, or steak platters; and the freshly baked exotic island fruit from Guadeloupe and Martinique. Open daily for lunch and Fridays through Sundays for dinner. No reservations. No credit cards accepted. On the beach (phone: 276049).

Filao Beach Tempting light meals — salads, omelettes, stuffed land crabs, and the like — are served in the café bar or around the pool of this perennially popular hotel. Light, crisp *accras* (salt cod fritters) can be enjoyed as appetizers at lunch or as an accompaniment to a tall rum drink. Lobster and swordfish are often on the menu, as are fresh coconut tarts. A buffet dinner is prepared a few days a week for hotel guests. Open daily for lunch only; closed September to mid-October. Reservations unnecessary. Major credit cards accepted. On the beach (phone: 276484).

Topolino Attractive and lively, this terraced spot serves salads, barbecued fish and steaks, as well as Italian dishes — pizza and pasta, sliced tomatoes and mozzarella. A good place for family dining; children love it. Open for lunch and dinner; closed Mondays. No reservations. MasterCard and Visa accepted. On the main road (phone: 277092).

ANSE DES CAYES — COLOMBIER

EXPENSIVE

Le Ballahou Filled with greenery and overlooking the sea, this dining room at the *Manapany* hotel is the perfect romantic setting. There are flowers and candlelight, and French music performed on the piano and guitar. The menu combines selections from classic and nouvelle French and continental dishes, including *assiette norvégienne* (smoked salmon with dilled whipped cream), and escargot turnovers. Homemade pastries and tropical fruit are among the choices for dessert. In an adjacent bar, colorful, exotic drinks are served in huge glasses topped with paper parasols and fresh flowers. Open daily for dinner only; closed mid-April to mid-November. Major credit cards accepted. Seaside at Anse des Cayes (phone: 276655).

François Plantation The entrance to this sophisticated, elegant establishment — under a long, beautifully designed arbor covered with blooming vines — hints at the gentility of the experience to come. The attractive, terraced dining room seats 50, chefs Thierry Alix and Eric Brenot, from Paris's *Olympe* and *Jamin,* prepare the classic French haute cuisine. Featured appetizers include *Plantation François* fish soup, orange-flavored mussel soup, and home-smoked trout; main dishes include scallops St. Jacques, medallions of lobster with mushrooms, duck breast with smoked salmon roe and foie gras, and *gambas* (small lobsters) *à la créole.* Desserts are light, such as a trio of sorbets or tropical fruit salad with ginger. Open daily for dinner only. Major credit cards accepted. Set on a hill at Colombier (phone: 277882).

Ouanalao A bright and breezy spot under a pavilion at the *Manapany* hotel, near the pool. Specialties include fresh pasta dishes, veal scaloppine with ham and cheese, lobster in Mornay sauce au gratin, and fresh island fish. Pasta is also served. Open daily for lunch and dinner. Major credit cards accepted. Seaside at Anse des Cayes (phone: 276655).

INEXPENSIVE

New Born This little dining room has become popular for its authentic creole dishes, offered at reasonable prices. No fancy decor, but pleasant surroundings, just a stone's throw from the beach where fresh seafood is hooked and netted regularly. Typical local dishes, such as blood pudding, lamb kebabs, wood-fire grilled fish and lobster, and *callaloo* are served. Open for dinner only; closed Sundays. Major credit cards accepted. On the road to the *Manapany* hotel, marked by a sign with a nursing baby. Quartier, Anse des Cayes (phone: 276707).

GRAND CUL DE SAC — MARIGOT — VITET

EXPENSIVE

Le Bartolomeo An elegant dinner place at the *Guanahani* hotel, serving French cuisine of a very high order made with interesting Caribbean ingredients: *colombo* of chicken breasts with ratatouille, lobster fritters West Indian style, and lamb sautéed with rosemary served with a flan of spring vegetables. Desserts include *crème brûlée* and pineapple-chocolate *mille feuilles.* Half the room is a bar-salon with piano entertainment. Open daily for dinner only. Major credit cards accepted. In Lieu dit Marigot, Grand Cul de Sac (phone: 276660).

Club Lafayette Year after year this dining spot packs in an attractive crowd whose noonday ritual is a quick swim before lunch (choice of the sea or small pool), drying off in the shade of a coco palm or sea grape tree while sipping a tall rum *planteur,* feasting on barbecued lobster, crispy duck, or grilled fish with hot pepper sauce, and then topping it all off with pecan pie or the scrumptiously dense chocolate marquise. Fun fashion shows from the restaurant's own boutique are part of the daily lunchtime entertainment. Open daily for lunch in season; closed May through October. Reservations advised. No credit cards accepted. Seaside, Grand Cul de Sac (phone: 276251).

Le Gaiac Located in the main house at the elegant new *Le Toiny* hotel, this dining spot offers exemplary Gallic gastronomy in a romantic hillside setting. There's indoor or outdoor dining with a view across a shimmering pool and the sound of waves crashing on the seashore below. Every dish is a work of art, and tastes as good as it looks. Specialties might include filet of roasted stuffed rabbit with figs and pine nuts, breast of chicken with foie gras, and lamb filets with wild mushrooms. Open daily for dinner; closed from September through mid-October. Major credit cards accepted. At *Le Toiny,* Anse Toiny (phone: 278888).

Hostellerie des Trois Forces The attractions here include shrimp, lobster in basil sauce, lobster flambéed with cognac and cream and served inside a light pancake, fish mousse with hollandaise sauce, and a variety of excellent meat dishes — all prepared in a wood-burning fireplace; potatoes are baked in the ashes. There's also a fine vegetarian menu and exquisite desserts (the swan-shaped profiteroles are almost too graceful to eat). The atmosphere is relaxed and friendly, and the young proprietor makes some of the best rum drinks on the island. Open daily for lunch and dinner. Major credit cards accepted. Vitet (phone: 276125).

L'Indigo With a poolside café and bar, this is a wonderful place for casual daytime dining at the *Guanahani* hotel. Typical French lunches — light, but with three courses — as well as some sandwiches are served. The service is very professional, and there is an air of relaxed sophistication. Open daily for lunch. Reservations unnecessary. Major credit cards accepted. In Lieu dit Marigot, Anse de Grand Cul de Sac (phone: 276660).

La Toque Lyonnaise Marc and Christine Llepez make an outstanding contribution to an island that receives much gastronomic praise. The menu changes every 2 or 3 months; in addition to the à la carte menu, there is a "carte gastronomique" (about $60 per person) offering a three- or five-course sampling from the main menu. Two delicious starters are monkfish salad with Chinese cucumbers, and lobster ravioli. Other enticing offerings: steamed lobster in a light creamy sauce, filet of duck in a creamed lemon and saffron sauce, and chicken breast and hot scallop of foie gras in a potato cake. The foie gras is made right here, as are the excellent pastries, which are wheeled to each table despite noble protests. The wine list, like everything else, is superb. Open daily for dinner in season; closed June through October. Reservations necessary. Major credit cards accepted. At *El Sereno Beach Hotel,* Grand Cul de Sac (phone: 276480).

MODERATE

Chez Pompi Pompi is Louis Ledec, restaurateur, bulldozer operator, and artist naïf, whose place is as much a gallery of his paintings as it is a restaurant. The menu is creole. Open for lunch only; closed Sundays. No credit cards accepted. Grand Cul de Sac (phone: 277567).

La Lagon Bleu This beachside spot next to *El Sereno* hotel serves Provençal barbecued fish, seafood, and meat. The Lyon-trained chef also turns out crab salad, leek pie, red pepper salad dressed in an oil and herb marinade, and eggplant Provençal. Open for lunch only May through October; lunch and dinner November through April. No reservations. No credit cards accepted. Grand Cul de Sac (phone: 276480).

Marigot Bay Club An extremely popular seaside spot swathed in greenery and palm trees atwitter with bananaquits. Swim or snorkel between courses of *christophine farcis* with lobster, *accra* (fresh codfish and lobster in pastry), fresh fish brochette, or grilled fish with excellent sauces (aïoli, fennel, or creole — ask for a taste of all three). The filet mignon, which is imported, is tops, as is the smiling service. Open for lunch and dinner; closed Mondays; dinner only on Sundays. MasterCard and Visa accepted. Hillside above Marigot Bay (phone: 277545).

Le Rivage Nestled right on the beach between the *St. Barths Beach* hotel and the *Grand Cul de Sac* hotel, this eatery serves a wide variety of good food. Try the chicken or fish pâté for an appetizer, or as an entrée, the grilled lobster and flame-broiled steaks with tomatoes Provençal and French fries. Also tasty: blood sausage, kebab shrimp with curry sauce, and creole crab. Open for lunch and dinner; dinner only Thursdays. Major credit cards accepted. Grand Cul de Sac (phone: 278242).

INEXPENSIVE

Le Flamboyant Good, reasonably priced home cooking is the draw here. Set in Albert Balayn's little stucco house on a hill overlooking Grand Cul de Sac, this eatery's French menu is not extensive, but it's rounded out by a creole *plat du jour. Cassoulet de langouste* is the house specialty. Open for dinner only; closed Mondays. No credit cards accepted. Hillside on Grand Cul de Sac (phone: 277565).

LORIENT

EXPENSIVE

La Banane This small and charming tropical paradise offers a table d'hôte dinner created to be savored leisurely. Nightly cabarets by the pool make the evening extra special. Open for dinner only; closed Wednesdays and the months of May, June, September, and October. Major credit cards accepted. On the outskirts of Lorient (phone: 276825).

INEXPENSIVE

Au Bon Coin Creole cooking and fresh grilled fish — nicely prepared, simply served, and modestly priced — ensure that the eight tables here are always booked. Open for dinner only; closed Wednesdays. No credit cards accepted. To find this tiny hillside restaurant, go down a long, rough road that skirts the sea at Lorient, then climbs up to the little house (phone: 276138).

ELSEWHERE ON THE ISLAND

EXPENSIVE

Castelets This elegant eatery (formerly *Sapore di Mare*) is owned by restaurateur Pino Luongo, owner of restaurants in Manhattan, Dallas, Houston, and East Hampton (New York), and his partner, restaurateur Cesare Dell'Aguzzo. The charming Dell'Aguzzo invites diners to sample inventive new dishes as well as the same Italian coastal dishes that made the original *Sapore di Mare* in East Hampton such a success. The location atop one of the island's highest peaks offers breathtaking views. Dining is indoors and on a covered outdoor terrace. Open daily for dinner and Thursdays through Mondays for lunch; closed September. Reservations advised for dinner. Major credit cards accepted. Morne Lurin (phone: 276173).

MODERATE

Maya's Fresh seafood, lobster, hamburgers, and creole dishes are featured at this small waterfront terrace. The *accras de giraumon* (pumpkin fritters), *salade de patate douce au buerre de cari* (curried sweet potato salad), and *ragoût de lambi* (a fiery conch stew) are favorites. The sherbets and pies are all homemade and fresh. Open for lunch and dinner; closed Sundays and from June through October. Reservations unnecessary. No credit cards accepted. On the northwest end of Public's Beach (phone: 277361).

Le Tamarin This very informal, very "in" place is in a bucolic setting just off the bumpy road to the Plage de Saline. Excellent grilled chops, sardines and other fish, and honey and prune chicken are featured; daily specials might include *tabouli,* smoked swordfish salad, and ceviche with lime and coconut. For dessert, try the delightful *tarte tatin* or a chocolate *gâteau.* Dining is either on a porch or on the surrounding grass. While waiting to be seated, guests can hone their archery skills or sip drinks under the huge centuries-old tamarind tree after which the restaurant is named. Watching over the comings and goings is a brilliantly plumed parrot. Open daily for lunch only. Major credit cards accepted. Plage de Saline (phone: 277212).

St. Eustatius

Today, St. Eustatius, the small Dutch island everybody calls Statia, is very quiet. But around 1650, Oranjestad harbor was a pivotal point in international trade, with the Lower Town buzzing with activity from merchant ships. Not only Dutch but French and Spanish merchants sold everything from sailors' pants and iron pots to silver plates, painted silks, and Portuguese wines. Unlike its neighboring islands, whose fortunes were tied to agriculture, Statia's prosperity was due to its importance as a transshipment location for sugar, cotton, and other commodities smuggled out of their nearby home islands by the British and French in protest against monopolies and taxes imposed by their governments. It also specialized in selling arms — at a goodly profit — to the North American rebels for use in their revolt against the British. During the 1770s, the island was known throughout the Caribbean as the "Golden Rock."

In subsequent centuries, however, a variety of circumstances changed Statia from a bustling commercial center to a sleepy vacation spot. The first, on December 20, 1780, was Britain's declaration of war on the Dutch. The second came less than 2 months later, when Admiral George Brydges Rodney led an army onto St. Eustatius, confiscated everything on the island, and began selling off goods at considerable profit. Not satisfied with found riches, he kept the Dutch flag flying from Fort Oranje for a month, entrapping a total of 150 ships. Six months later, in August 1781, he left the island considerably poorer, but virtually undamaged. In November, the French, under the Marquis de Bouillé, Governor of Martinique, drove the British out. Three years later, the French also left, returning Statia to the Dutch.

By 1786, the island seemed as bustling and prosperous as ever, but appearances were deceiving. Island life was elegant, but wealth had made Statia's merchants corrupt and lazy. So eager were they to make money for themselves that there was little left for the Dutch West Indies Company, which had bankrolled the island's original settlement and which had headquarters there. It foundered and, in 1791, left the island. From that point, the island experienced a steady decline.

Statia's fortifications, which had never amounted to much anyway, had deteriorated to the point of uselessness. In 1780, a Dutch ship's officer reported that Fort de Windt's four cannon were manned by a constable, a small boy, and a maid. Fort Oranje's big guns could not be used because chunks of the supporting cliff dropped away every time the cannon fired. But people were too busy making money to pay attention, and the French easily reconquered the island in 1795. When the British took over in April 1801, all trade stopped.

Statia finally was returned to Dutch hands in 1816, but the island never

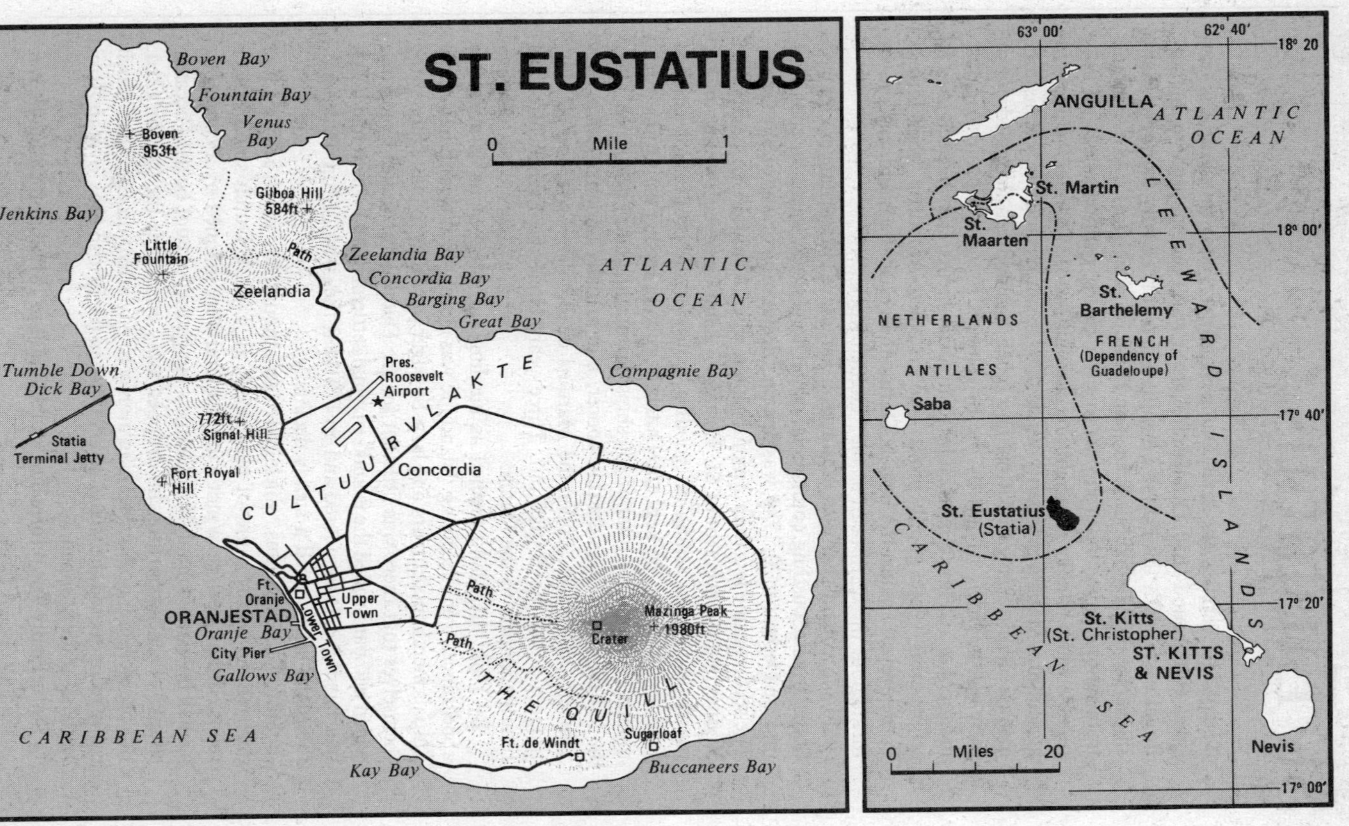
ST. EUSTATIUS
0
Mile
1
Boven Bay
Fountain Bay
Venus Bay
Jenkins Bay
Boven 953ft
Gilboa Hill 584ft
Little Fountain
Path
Zeelandia
Zeelandia Bay
Concordia Bay
Barging Bay
Great Bay
ATLANTIC OCEAN
Compagnie Bay
Tumble Down Dick Bay
Statia Terminal Jetty
772ft Signal Hill
Fort Royal Hill
Pres. Roosevelt Airport
CULTUURVLAKTE
Concordia
Ft. Oranje
ORANJESTAD
Oranje Bay
City Pier
Gallows Bay
Lower Town
Upper Town
Path
Crater
Mazinga Peak 1980ft
THE QUILL
Ft. de Windt
Sugarloaf
CARIBBEAN SEA
Kay Bay
Buccaneers Bay
63° 00′
62° 40′
18° 20
18° 00′
17° 40′
17° 20′
17° 00′
ANGUILLA
ATLANTIC OCEAN
St. Martin
St. Maarten
LEEWARD ISLANDS
St. Barthelemy
FRENCH (Dependency of Guadeloupe)
NETHERLANDS ANTILLES
Saba
St. Eustatius (Statia)
CARIBBEAN SEA
St. Kitts (St. Christopher)
ST. KITTS & NEVIS
Nevis
0
Miles
20

recovered its former economic strength. Plantations had long since been allowed to go to seed in favor of the island's more profitable, less troublesome trade, and now empty warehouses also were left to crumble into ruins, or to be pushed over by hurricanes. When storms ruptured the seawall, built — in Dutch fashion — to reclaim land from the sea, no one bothered to repair it. Eventually the water returned and foundations disappeared under it. On land, the old Customs House (now the island's electrical station), two brick warehouses, and a network of ruined walls survive. A number of old buildings and substantial ruins are clustered near Fort Oranje in the Upper Town, and the St. Eustatius Historical Foundation is doing its best to shore them up and save them.

The island's population — officially counted at 7,830 in 1790 — has dwindled to some 2,080. About 25 of these residents are retired North Americans who've built villas in the hills overlooking the sea. Two Americans provided Statia with its first real spark of tourist life. About 20 years ago they built a small inn called the *Old Gin House* (that's "gin" as in "cotton"), on the foundations of an old building in the Lower Town. These days, its patio is a gathering place for islanders and visitors alike.

Today, tourists trickle through Statia at the rate of about 18,000 a year. Many are attracted by the unique diving possibilities opened up by *Dive Statia,* a full-service dive operation located next to the *Old Gin House.* Others do the standard sightseeing tour — which holds few thrills — and wonder why they bothered. But a few become so addicted to the island's relaxed, unstructured life and the easy friendliness that they return again and again, join the historical foundation, and become a part of the place.

Statia is still very quiet — perhaps too quiet for most people. But it may be just the retreat you've been looking for.

St. Eustatius At-a-Glance

FROM THE AIR

Little 11.8-square-mile St. Eustatius looks like a lozenge-shaped table, slightly above sea level, with a sawed-off volcano at its southern end and a pile of lower hills pointing northwest at its other tip. Lying diagonally southeast to northwest, Statia forms a 2½-by-5-mile barrier between the Atlantic Ocean and the Caribbean. It is about 35 miles south of St. Maarten, about 17 miles southeast of its sister island of Saba, and about 11 miles northwest of the British Leeward Island of St. Kitts. The volcano, known as the Quill (a corruption of the Dutch word *kuil,* meaning pit, presumably referring to its crater), is almost symmetrical. You can climb up the mountain and look down into the dense green rain forest cupped in its burnt-out top.

But what strikes most visitors first is the utter flatness of Statia's central plain, De Cultuurvlakte, with the 1,900-foot Franklin D. Roosevelt airstrip at the center. About a mile south of the airport, the island's capital, Oranjestad, occupies land on top of and beneath the pink-gray coastal cliffs. Soft gray volcanic beaches dot the leeward (Caribbean) side of the island from just south of Gallows Bay below Oranjestad to the base of Fort Royal hill northwest. (Unfortunately, hurricanes have claimed some of them.) Beaches also line the shore of Tumble Down Dick Bay a bit farther north (where an oil storage facility has been installed with the hope of boosting the island economy). On the northeast-facing windward side, surf from the deep blue Atlantic rolls in along the island's most picturesque gold sand beaches at Zeelandia, Concordia, Barging, and Great bays — good spots for experienced surfers, but not advisable for swimming because of the fierce undertow.

SPECIAL PLACES

A list of Statia's monuments has a way of sounding more impressive than the collection actually looks. Before booking an extended stay, remember that when Statians talk about *ruins,* they mean just that. But the remains are nevertheless arresting, and history buffs will feel right in their element.

ORANJESTAD St. Eustatius's capital is, in a sense, a ghost town, only now coming out of the coma into which it lapsed in the early 19th century. Your first stop should be Fort Oranje, where, at the tourist office, you can pick up the historical foundation's *Walking Tour Guide* ($1.50 per copy, at the museum or the tourist office) or pay 55¢ for the booklet *Get to Know St. Eustatius.* This spot also offers a fine view of the Lower Town. It is difficult to believe that the skeletal stone walls below are the vestiges of what was once the immensely rich port known as the Golden Rock.

Fort Oranje, with its three bastions, is in the best shape of any Statian landmark, having been extensively restored in honor of the US bicentennial celebration of 1976. Now its ramparts bristle with shiny black cannon, and it houses the post office and several other government offices. Further rebuilding, including museum space, is still in progress. A plaque commemorates the return of the salute fired by the US brig *Andrew Doria* on November 16, 1776, by which "sovereignty of the United States of America was first formally acknowledged" by a foreign government (though Fort Frederik on St. Croix, then owned by the Dutch, claims to have made a similar acknowledgement a few weeks earlier). Since Fort Oranje's act helped to bring on war with the British, it is one that islanders may have regretted later.

Leaving the fort, turn right on Fort Oranjestraat and, following the *Walking Tour Guide* map, visit the Upper Town's other sights, many of which are part of a $20 million restoration project: the Gertrude Judson Memorial Library; the renovated barracks-like Government Guesthouse (it now houses government offices, the tourist office, a pre-Columbian museum containing artifacts and an Amerindian skeleton or two, a handicraft center, and a snack bar), near which the remains of four old buildings were found; the gingerbread-frilled house at 4 Fort Oranjestraat, a 20th-century building constructed in keeping with the surrounding 18th-century architecture; and behind it, the remains of the 18th-century house called Three Widows Corner with its restored cookhouse, patio, and herb garden.

The beautifully restored Simon Doncker House (at Wilhelminaweg in the center of Oranjestad), once the home of a wealthy merchant, became Admiral Rodney's headquarters after he captured the island in 1781. The house is now the *St. Eustatius Historical Foundation Museum,* housing relics from the golden era of the island, including 18th-century period furniture and engraved glassware. It is open 9 AM to 5 PM weekdays; check with the tourist office for weekend hours. There's a small admission charge. The aforementioned booklets, a few souvenirs, and postcards are sold here. The Town House on the corner of the continuation of Fort Oranjestraat and Bredeweg is on the verge of tumbling down but still provides a glimpse of classic Statian stone and wood construction. Just behind it, on Synagogpad, stand the ruins of the Honen Dalim ("Charity to the Poor"), the second-oldest synagogue in the Western Hemisphere (begun around 1740). On the outskirts of town on Princessweg, there is a tiny, lovingly tended Jewish cemetery with 21 legible tombstones dating from 1742. Next to it is a ruin of what some believe was a *mikvah* (Jewish ritual bath); although other, less spiritual folks speculate that it was part of an old rum factory.

ELSEWHERE ON THE ISLAND

If you're touring by car or taxi, be sure to stop at the stately ruins of the Dutch Reformed Church (c. 1755) as you head out of town toward Fort de Windt. The church's tower and choir loft have been restored by the historical foundation and the churchyard is full of fascinating stones — a find if stone rubbing is your hobby. Other places to explore are the ruins of the old sisal factory and sugar mill just beyond the church, Fort Nassau, and tiny Fort de Windt, with newly rebuilt walls, part of a 16-emplacement chain of defenses spotted around the island's periphery.

The strong of lung and limb can climb the slopes of the Quill. Since this mountain gave up smoking some centuries back, a lush rain forest has grown in its tip; the views from the trail and the flora within the crater make the effort worthwhile. It's a half-day trip that takes more energy than skill, and there are rest spots along the way. Guides go along for about $20, but they're not essential — even for the novice. In all, the tourist office has 12 mapped nature trails, from the Crater Track down into the Quill, to the easy White Bird Track along Oranjestad Beach beneath Powder Hill, where "white birds" or tropic birds rest and nest. Contact the tourist office (phone: 2433) or the *Old Gin House* to arrange for a guide.

At this point, unless you've brought a picnic, head back for the terrace of the *Old Gin House* and lunch. Then — to get the real feel of the island — change into a bathing suit and a pair of expendable sneakers and go exploring among the ruins and along the shore in either direction. Shards of pottery and glass, coins, buttons, bones, and other remnants of Statia's rich past are still found all over the island, above *and* below the water. Another option is just to sit in the sun and absorb the peace.

Sources and Resources

TOURIST INFORMATION

If you're flying in from St. Maarten (you probably will be) and have a chance to visit Philipsburg before taking off for Statia, stop in at the tourist office at the head of the Little Pier for brochures about Statia. Also look in a St. Maarten bookstore for Dr. J. Hartog's *St. Maarten, Saba, St. Eustatius.* The St. Eustatius Tourist Office (phone: 2433), located in Oranjestad's 200-year-old Government Guesthouse, and the historical museum also distribute printed information (although they occasionally run out). In addition, the friendly people at the Gertrude Judson Library and at the historical foundation's headquarters on Prinsestraat will do all they can to help you. For information on tourist offices in the US, see GETTING READY TO GO.

> **NOTE** **When sending mail to St. Eustatius's capital, leave the name of the city out of postal addresses to avoid having your letter detoured to the other Oranjestad, capital of the better-known island of Aruba, hundreds of miles to the south.**

LOCAL COVERAGE The *San Juan Star* turns up every couple of days, and the *Chronicle,* an English daily published on St. Maarten, arrives late each morning.

An invaluable resource is *Ypie Attema's St. Eustatius, A Short History,* found at the tourist office and almost always at the historical foundation, the museum, and the *Mazinga Gift Shop. St. Maarten Holiday* offers only a few squibs of information about Statia.

RADIO AND TELEVISION

Radio broadcasts and television programs in English are readily available throughout the island. Most hotels have cable access.

TELEPHONE

When calling from the US, dial 011 (international access code) + 599 (country code) + 38 (city code) + (4-digit local number). To call from another Caribbean island, the access code may vary, so contact the local operator. When calling from a phone on St. Eustatius, use only the local number unless otherwise indicated.

ENTRY REQUIREMENTS

US and Canadian citizens need only proof of citizenship (a current passport or one that expired less than 5 years ago; or a voter's registration card or birth certificate with raised seal *and* a photo ID), plus a return ticket. There's a departure tax of $3 if you're going to the US; $4 if you're heading for any other Caribbean island.

CLIMATE AND CLOTHES

The climate is comparatively dry (only 45 inches of rain a year) with daytime temperatures in the mid-80s F (29 to 30C) and nights in the 70s F (23C) all year. The word "casual" is a shade overstated to describe the island's mode of dress. People are neat, but style couldn't matter less. Bring some old sneakers for walking through the ruins along the shoreline. You might put on a fresh shirt and pants or a light dress for dinner, but whether or not you do is up to you. There are no real dress-up occasions on Statia.

MONEY

Official currency is the Netherlands Antilles florin (abbreviated NAf), also called the guilder, valued at about 1.77 NAf to $1 US. US dollars are as acceptable for all tourist purposes, but Canadians should change their money for florins before departing from St. Maarten or at the Banco Barclays Antilliano on Statia, which is open from 8:30 AM to 2 PM on weekdays and also from 4 PM to 5 PM on Friday afternoons; it's closed weekends and holidays. Credit cards are generally not accepted except in hotels and some restaurants. All prices in this chapter are quoted in US dollars.

LANGUAGE

Most public signs are written in Dutch, the island's official language, but everybody speaks English. The common greeting is, "Awright, ok-a-a-y."

TIME

Statia is on atlantic standard time — which is 1 hour ahead of eastern standard time — year-round. In winter, when it's noon in New York, it's 1 PM on Statia; in summer, when daylight saving time is in effect in the US, the time's the same in both places.

CURRENT

Electricity is 110 volts, 60 cycles AC — which means no trouble for American travel appliances.

TIPPING

A 15% service charge is added to restaurant, bar, and hotel bills, and that takes care of waiters, maids, bartenders, et al. Don't worry about bellhops and porters; there aren't any. Tip taxi drivers $1 to $2.

GETTING AROUND

CAR RENTAL Rental cars are available from several sources, a list of which is available at the tourist office. *Avis* now has offices in town and at the airport (phone: 2421; 800-331-1084 from the US). You'll be asked to show your license; other formalities are minimal. Cost is $50 daily or $300 weekly, with unlimited mileage.

FERRY SERVICES At press time, a ferry service between Statia and St. Maarten was in the works. Contact the tourism office for information.

TAXI Cabs meet incoming flights and will take you to your hotel in town — an average distance of 2 miles — for $3.50 per person. A 2-hour taxi tour is also available; ask for amiable Josser Daniel (phone: 2358). The tour price ($35 per carload) includes a cassette-taped commentary, produced by the historical foundation, in your choice of English, French, Dutch, Spanish, or German. A couple of hours' touring will cover the Upper and Lower Towns, plus a ride out the southwestern coast road to Fort de Windt, below the side of the Quill they call White Wall, where there's a spectacular view of St. Kitts. When you get back to the Upper Town, ask to be dropped at the tourist office or the museum, where you can pick up a guidebook with a map and continue on your own. But if you're not staying overnight, set a time with the driver to be taken to the airport. Taxis also meet the small cruise ships that call in, and charge about $2 from the pier to town.

INTER-ISLAND FLIGHTS

Windward Island Airways (WINAIR) flies STOL (short takeoff and landing) planes from St. Maarten's Juliana Airport to Statia five times daily. Both *WINAIR* and *LIAT* fly between Statia, St. Kitts, and Nevis. Air transport between St. Maarten and Statia runs about $62 round-trip; from St. Kitts, $60; from Nevis, $80. Private charters can be arranged from St. Croix or St. Thomas. There are also day tours from St. Maarten, Mondays through Saturdays; cost is $75, including airfare and lunch (phone: 5995-322700, ext. 82, on St. Maarten).

SPECIAL EVENTS

Statia-America Day (November 16), commemorating the first salute to the American flag by a foreign government, in 1776, and *Statia Carnival,* concluding with *Carnival Monday,* in July are the year's big celebrations, with sunup to way-past-sunset parading, partying, and the like. The *Queen's Coronation Day* (April 30) is also a day for fireworks, sports events, music, and dancing. Other legal holidays include *New Year's Day, Good Friday, Easter* and *Easter Monday, Labor Day* (May 1), *Ascension Day* (40 days after *Easter*), *Christmas,* and *Boxing Day* (December 26).

SHOPPING

There's not much. Visitors can find a few imported Dutch items, jewelry, toiletries, liquors, cigarettes, magazines, and books among the general stock at the *Mazinga Gift Shop* in Upper Town (phone: 2245); T-shirts, island wear, and the local exportable elixir, Mazinga Mist (soursop schnapps) at *Dive Statia's* boutique next to the *Old Gin House* (phone: 2348 or 2435); and a limited selection of postcards and books at the museum.

SPORTS

The scale is small, but the hiking and water sports potential is considerable and unique.

HIKING Trekking up the side of the Quill, a former volcano now endowed with rain forest and spectacular scenery, is a rewarding and fairly easy hike (see *Special Places*).

SNORKELING AND SCUBA Most fun is found among the underwater ruins in Oranje Bay; contrary to off-island legend, you won't find a whole city buried intact, but there are enough submerged masonry, cannon, old coins, wine bottles, and coral to make it interesting. Historians believe there are more than 200 old ships sunk in this untouched bay. Visibility isn't the greatest, but it is worth an underwater visit. *Dive Statia* (phone: 2348 or 2435), a dive shop in the warehouse next to the *Old Gin House,* offers a full range of instructional programs, and occasionally a shared 1-week plan with Saba, Statia's equally unspoiled neighbor. It also rents snorkel equipment for about $10 a day per person.

SWIMMING AND SUNNING Pleasant areas for quick dips or leisurely swims are on all the small volcanic beaches on the southwest shore. The northeast, or windward beaches, such as Zeelandia and Lynch, are beautiful for walking or sunning but very dangerous for swimming due to the strong undertow.

TENNIS The single concrete court at the Community Center on Madam Estate is rudimentary, but it's open daily and lighted for night play for about $3.50 an hour.

NIGHTLIFE

The biggest show is an occasional Saturday concert by the *Statia Steel Band,* the *Killy-Killy String Band,* the *Re-creation Roots Patience* combo, or local reggae/calypso groups such as the *J-B Beat Band.* Check out *Franky's* (in Ruyterweg; phone: 2575), *The Golden Era* (Lower Town, Oranjestad; phone: 2345), *Charlie's Bar* (no phone), or *Talk of the Town* (on the airport road; phone: 2236) for weekend music. Otherwise, evenings consist of sipping brandy, talking, and early to bed.

Best on the Island

CHECKING IN

Statia's 130 hotel rooms are a mixed bag. Roughly half, overlooking your choice of Oranje Bay or the Atlantic, are in three proper hotels; their in-season rates range from about $150 (expensive — of which the *Old Gin House,* see below, is the only one) to $80 (moderate) for two without meals; breakfast and dinner will add another $30 to $40 per person a day. Additional hotel charges usually add up to another 20% or so for service, utilities, and a 7% government tax.

Guesthouses offer basic, inexpensive accommodations costing the bargain-hunter anywhere from a rock-bottom $7 to about $35 per day for a double room. A list of guesthouses is available at the tourist office. When calling from a phone on St. Eustatius, use only the local numbers listed below. For information about dialing from elsewhere, see "Telephone" earlier in this chapter.

For an unforgettable island experience, we begin with our favorite, followed by our recommendations of cost and quality choices of accommodations, listed by price category.

A SPECIAL HAVEN

Old Gin House Set on the land side of the street, this restored 18th-century warehouse — the Mooshay Bay Publick House — is fitted out with a snug pub; a cool, high-ceilinged dining room; a terraced outdoor restaurant; and 20 antiques–filled guestrooms. The air is nostalgic and casual; the decor is relaxed and elegant. And the road is the main street of what was once the richest port in the Caribbean. Today, much of what remains of the Lower Town lies under the water of the bay (great for scuba exploring). On land, not much happens — though the Upper Town has some ruins and an old fort. There's plenty of time for reading, swimming, and strolls down the historic ruin–lined shore. Dive packages also are available. The seaside *Terrace* restaurant serves breakfast and lunch. Dinner at the *Mooshay Bay Dining Room* (see *Eating Out*) is beautifully served — Delftware and pewter, candles in tall crystal chimneys — and tastes even better. If you ask what else there is to do, you probably shouldn't be here. On the other hand, if you have too much to do everyplace else in your world, this could be your spot to unwind. Children under 10 are not permitted.

MODERATE

Golden Era Simple but comfortable, this establishment overlooking Oranje Bay offers 20 air conditioned harborfront rooms (although the balconies face concrete walls). Rooms are neat and clean, with private baths and international-access telephones. The beach is a tenth of a mile away, and there's a pool on the property. The restaurant's decor won't win any awards, but the food is good, reasonably priced island fare. Lower Town, Oranjestad (phone: 2345 or 800-365-8484 from the US; fax: 2445).

La Maison sûr la Plage The 10-room establishment overlooks an isolated but lovely 2-mile stretch of beach on the dramatic ocean side of the island. The rooms are clean, fresh, and simple. There's a pool, and breakfast is included. The restaurant is known for its fine French fare (see *Eating Out*). Zeelandia Beach (phone: 2256).

Talk of the Town This place, above one of Statia's finest restaurants (see *Eating Out*), is considered one of the island's best lodging choices. The 17 modern rooms (1 with kitchenette) are air conditioned and have baths, cable TV, and phones. New additions include a pool and a boutique. Buffet breakfast is included. L. E. Saddlerweg (phone/fax: 2236).

INEXPENSIVE

Airport View Apartments Formerly the *Henriquez Apartments,* here are 9 comfortable units next to (you guessed it) the airport, each with either a king-size bed or 2 double beds, bath, refrigerator, coffee maker, fan, and TV set. There's a bar/restaurant and an outdoor patio with barbecue. Carine Henríquez sometimes comes over from *L'Etoile* restaurant (see *Eating Out*) to cook, depending on where the demand is. Oranjestad (phone: 2299).

Recommended guesthouses include *Cherry Tree Villas* (phone: 2478; 314-569-2501 from the US), *Country Inn* (phone: 2484), *Daniel's Guest House* (phone: 2358), *Princess Weg* (phone: 2424), and *Richardson Guesthouse* (phone: 2378).

EATING OUT

For a meal for two, expect to pay about $65 in a restaurant listed as expensive, between $35 and $60 in places in the moderate category, and less than $35 in inexpensive spots. Prices do not include drinks or service charge. When calling from a phone on St. Eustatius, use only the local numbers listed below. For information about dialing from anywhere else, see "Telephone" earlier in this chapter.

EXPENSIVE

Mooshay Bay Dining Room A la carte or prix fixe dinners ($25 per person, including two wines) might begin with grapefruit soup or a salad of freshly smoked local red snapper in mousseline sauce, followed by chateaubriand in *dijonnaise* sauce or lobster sautéed with garlic, butter, and chives; homemade snow orange or Key lime pie rounds out the meal. The candlelit rustic dining room next to the illuminated pool draws guests back year after year. Dinner only; closed Sundays. Reservations necessary; make them early — preferably before lunchtime. Major credit cards accepted. At the *Old Gin House*, Lower Town (phone: 2319).

MODERATE

La Maison sûr la Plage Notable French food is served at this trellised restaurant with Atlantic views. Popular dishes include escargots, steak with roquefort or green peppercorn sauce, and *crêpes à l'orange* or profiteroles for dessert. Open daily for dinner. No reservations. MasterCard and Visa accepted. Zeelandia Beach (phone: 2256).

INEXPENSIVE

L'Etoile A simple upstairs snack bar/restaurant where Carine Henríquez prepares West Indian dishes such as salt fish and spareribs (when she's not cooking for guests at the *Airport View Apartments*). You'll also find hamburgers, hot dogs, and drinks. A great place to stop for lunch. Open daily. Reservations advised. Major credit cards accepted. Upper Town, Oranjestad (phone: 2299).

Stone Oven This pleasant, rustic spot is a good place to try such local fare as stewed conch, goat, and salt fish with johnnycakes. Guests may eat indoors or out, under the huge almond tree and coconut palms on the patio. There's sometimes live music on Friday nights. Open daily for lunch and early dinner. Let them know *hours* before you're coming, lest you find no one there to cook, or only a couple of the many menu items available. No credit cards accepted. Upper Town, Oranjestad (phone: 2543).

Talk of the Town Definitely the best choice for local fare. Be sure to ask for a table on the sea-view sun terrace. The menu beams with the best available ingredients; choices include chicken, seafood, steaks prepared Statian-style, and sandwiches. Open daily for breakfast, lunch, and dinner. Reservations unnecessary. Major credit cards accepted. L. E. Saddlerweg (phone: 2236).

Statia also has two Chinese restaurants: the *Chinese Bar and Restaurant* (phone: 2389) and *Statia's Bar and Restaurant* (phone: 2218). Lighter meals are usually available at the *Old Gin House Terrace* (phone: 2319), *Franky's* (in Ruyterweg; phone: 2575), *Sunny's Place* (phone: 2609), and *Kool Corner* (no phone) in Upper Town.

St. Kitts and Nevis

They call themselves "the secret Caribbean" in tourism promotions, and to most of the world, they are. The intimate islands of St. Kitts and Nevis are gorgeous, green, and volcanic; they offer some of the Caribbean's most dramatic panoramas — as well as one of its warmest welcomes. But their strongest attraction is their "Old West Indies" charm and their small, gracious hotels and inns, in which visitors can savor a vanishing way of life.

Despite very British roots and lingering traditions (as in most of the West Indies, cricket is a national passion, driving is on the left, and English is spelled, honourably, the Queen's way), the islands are now determined, in a peaceful and stable way, to establish their own identity as the Caribbean's newest independent country. The Federation of St. Kitts–Nevis was established as a nation within the British Commonwealth in September 1983.

For the past several decades, the whimsical politics of these islands has seemed to be the only thing of interest to the press. Few people heard about the lush cane fields, the volcanic vistas, the rain forests, and the black and blonde sand beaches that make St. Kitts a visual jewel; the superb, palm-cloaked, beige sand beaches of Pinney's Bay and the secluded coves on Nevis; or the charming, centuries-old inns and rare serenity awaiting visitors to either island. They did hear about bizarre tales of sibling rivalry and petty political diatribes exchanged with the distant triplet, Anguilla (a coral isle 60 miles north, with little in common with St. Kitts and Nevis other than British rule). The skirmishes were part of the ongoing familial flap that got its start back in 1825, when the British made a single Crown Colony of the three. It was a union that just didn't work.

When Anguilla declared itself independent of the St. Kitts–Nevis association in 1967, the press portrayed the event as a West Indian version of *The Mouse That Roared.* Plans of an invasion of Anguilla by the hostile twins to the south, and of a private kingdom set up by foreigners, hit the wire services. But then the islands again fell into relative obscurity, except for an occasional rumor that the two remaining siblings, St. Kitts and Nevis, had a violent rivalry and planned to ask for separate independence decrees.

There is a small grain of truth in that gossip, although the *real* rivalry is more a matter of pride than prejudice. Kittitians are more business-minded, tense, and anxious for development — or so the Nevisians claim. Kittitians, on the other hand, refer to their neighbors as "lazy and sometimes snooty, taking too much advantage of the special easygoing atmosphere of Nevis." They are merely jealous, Nevisians insist, pointing out that every weekend and public holiday, their pristine beaches are a magnet

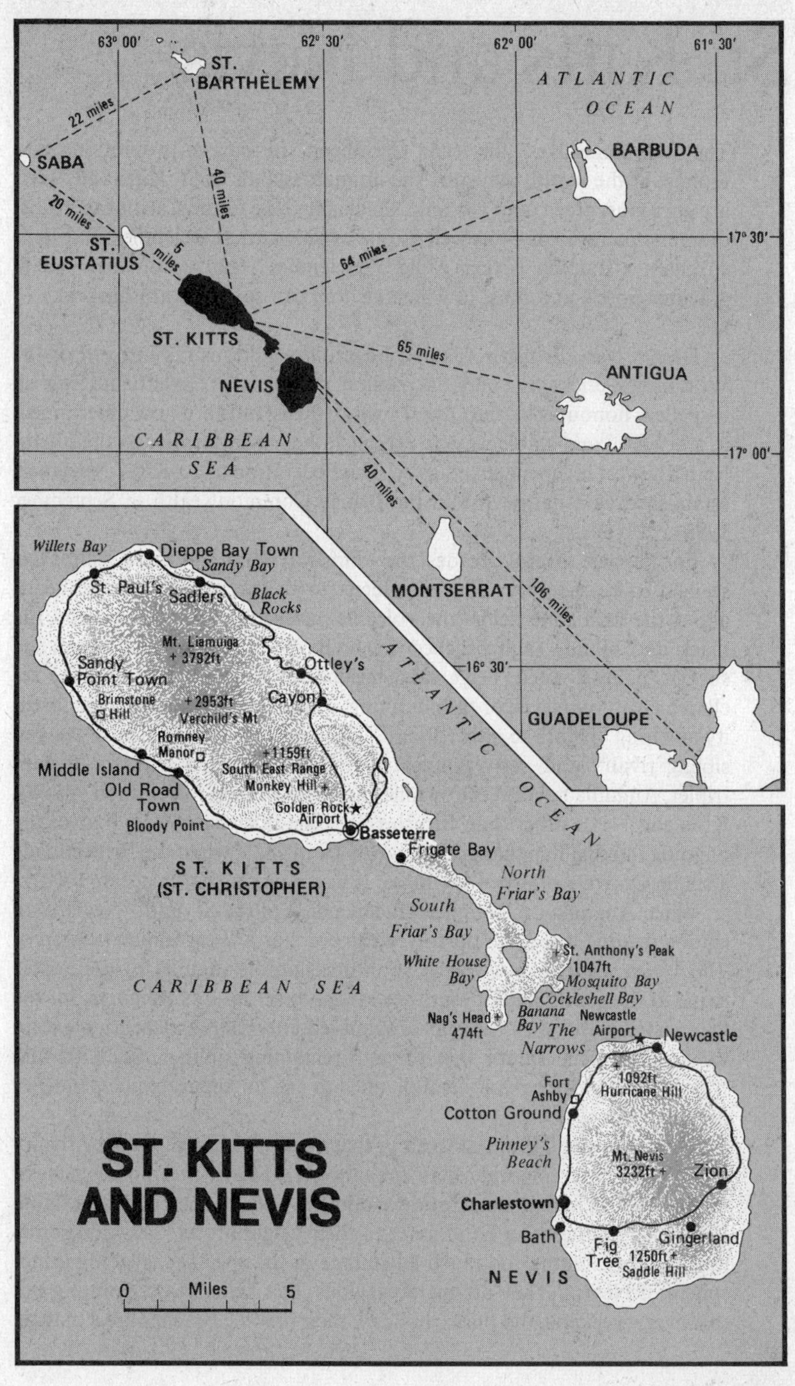

63° 00′
62° 30′
62° 00′
61° 30′
ST.
BARTHÈLEMY
ATLANTIC
OCEAN
22 miles
SABA
40 miles
BARBUDA
20 miles
17° 30′
ST.
EUSTATIUS
5
miles
64 miles
ST. KITTS
65 miles
NEVIS
ANTIGUA
CARIBBEAN
SEA
17° 00′
40 miles
MONTSERRAT
106 miles
16° 30′
GUADELOUPE
Willets Bay
Dieppe Bay Town
Sandy Bay
St. Paul's
Sadlers
Black
Rocks
Mt. Liamuiga
3792ft
Sandy
Point Town
Ottley's
Cayon
Brimstone
Hill
2953ft
Verchild's Mt
Romney
Manor
1159ft
Middle Island
South East Range
Monkey Hill
Old Road
Town
Golden Rock
Airport
Bloody Point
Basseterre
ATLANTIC
OCEAN
Frigate Bay
ST. KITTS
(ST. CHRISTOPHER)
North
Friar's Bay
South
Friar's Bay
White House
Bay
St. Anthony's Peak
1047ft
Mosquito Bay
CARIBBEAN SEA
Cockleshell Bay
Nag's Head
474ft
Banana
Bay
The
Narrows
Newcastle
Airport
Newcastle
1092ft
Hurricane Hill
Fort
Ashby
Cotton Ground
Pinney's
Beach
Mt. Nevis
3232ft
Zion
ST. KITTS
AND NEVIS
Charlestown
Bath
Fig
Tree
Gingerland
1250ft
Saddle Hill
NEVIS
0
Miles
5

for weary Kittitians, who make the swift 2-mile crossing as quickly as they can to unwind from life in "the big city." It's a very amusing story — especially to anyone who has visited both islands and knows how beautiful and slow-moving each actually is.

Sugar and cotton, once sources of tremendous wealth for both islands, are no longer cash crops for Nevis, which makes tourism its primary industry. St. Kitts continues to raise cane commercially, but here, too, tourism is first. The southeast peninsula road, opened in 1990, is spurring development that eventually will result in over 300 additional hotel rooms at the island's southernmost tip.

The country is a model of stability in the Caribbean. Peace and quiet and congenial, caring people are the trademarks of St. Kitts and Nevis, and the islands are so far from being a tropical trouble spot that it's difficult to imagine their turbulent history. Columbus sighted them during his second voyage in 1493, and it was he who named them: St. Christopher — for either himself or the patron saint of travelers (the British gave the island its nickname, St. Kitts); and Nevis — originally Las Nieves, Spanish for "the snows" — because of the snow-white cloud clinging to its peak. Then Columbus sailed on, leaving the islands and their resident Carib Indians undisturbed.

More than a century passed before the British settled at Old Road Town on St. Kitts in 1623. In 1625, they were joined by the crew of a French ship seeking refuge after a skirmish with a Spanish warship. The two groups wiped out the Carib and then divided the island strangely, but peaceably — the French took both ends and the English, the midsection. In 1629, the two groups again joined forces to resist a Spanish attack, then turned their attention to the many islands around them. During the next decades, the British, from their St. Kitts base, fanned out to colonize Antigua, Barbuda, Tortuga, and Montserrat. The French sent landing parties to claim Martinique and Guadeloupe. St. Kitts earned its credentials as "Cradle of the Caribbean" in two languages. Then intra-island friction sparked a seesaw struggle: By 1664, the French managed to squeeze the British off the island. The British retook it in 1689. And in 1782, the French returned to lay siege to the British fort on Brimstone Hill. It eventually fell, despite a brave defense. In 1783, the Treaty of Versailles restored both fort and island to Britain once and for all, leaving the islanders free to concentrate on sugarcane crops and business.

At one time, Nevis's sugar trade made the island even more prosperous than St. Kitts; it was nicknamed "the Queen of the Caribbees." By the late 18th century, the elegant *Bath* hotel that Thomas Huggins built just outside Charlestown, the capital of Nevis, was attracting 4,000 tourists each year (a remarkable number for those times, although small compared to the more than 88,000 per annum who visit St. Kitts and Nevis today).

In 1834, the abolition of slavery meant the beginning of the end of the sugar culture, and with it the eventual decline of Nevis's fortunes. St. Kitts, still deeply involved in cane production, fell into a partial slumber as the world demand for its sugar decreased.

Throughout much of the history of St. Kitts and Nevis, no one on the two islands thought much about Anguilla, the third member of the tripartite Crown Colony. During the 1950s, that island became restless to break away from its southern sisters; at last, on February 27, 1967, Anguilla declared itself independent of the St. Kitts–Nevis association. Islands all over the Caribbean took sides. There even was talk of invasion to bring the recalcitrant island back into line. To forestall any such local moves, a British "peacekeeping force" landed on Anguilla's beaches in 1969, and in 1971, the Mother Country reassumed full responsibility for the island — much to its citizens' delight.

Since then, St. Kitts and Nevis have been relatively quiet in terms of politics, but much busier as far as tourism is concerned. St. Kitts now has an 18-hole and a 9-hole golf course, many hotels, a casino, a deep-water port, and an airport with both nonstop and direct jet service from the US and Canada. Most recently, Nevis added its first major hotel, the *Four Seasons* resort, with 196 rooms and an 18-hole golf course (see *Checking In*).

Today, only the impressive fortress of Brimstone Hill, overlooking the south coast of St. Kitts from an imposing perch at 800 feet, lingers as a reminder of these islands' uneasy history. Little disturbs the order and tranquillity of these tiny islands. But the islands are attracting more and more visitors each year; if you want to beat the crowds, you'd better hurry.

St. Kitts and Nevis At-a-Glance

FROM THE AIR

St. Kitts is a 68-square-mile island shaped (as Kittitians insist) like a cricket bat, with the wide end pointing northwest toward the Dutch island of St. Eustatius, about 5 miles away, and the handle pointing toward Nevis, the 40-square-mile "ball" that lies to the southeast across a 2-mile channel called The Narrows. St. Kitts is only 5 miles across at its widest and 23 miles long from tip to handle. St. Kitts has a population of only 35,000; Nevis, about 9,000.

Basseterre, the capital of St. Kitts, is tucked into a harbor on the southern shore. Golden Rock Airport is a mile from town, 70 minutes by air from San Juan, and 30 minutes from Antigua or St. Maarten. The route to most of the island's resorts leads through Basseterre. Bay Road, the capital's main street, connects with the principal circle road that follows the shoreline all the way around the island. All of St. Kitts' principal settlements lie along it.

At the island's northwest end, Mt. Liamuiga (3,792 feet), its highest peak, is surrounded by sugarcane fields. Pronounced Lee-*a*-mwee-ga, the dormant volcano's name means "the fertile land" in the Carib language. On the coast south of the peak, on top of 800-foot cliffs, sits Brimstone Hill's impressive fortress, the landmark that made St. Kitts "the Gibraltar of the West Indies." Among other scenic assets are a crater lake — Dos d'Anse Pond — caught in the top of Verchild's Mountain (2,953 feet), virgin tropical forests, tall palms, and innumerable poincianas, the flame-bloomed tree now found throughout the Caribbean but nurtured and developed here.

Nevis, lush, green, and ringed with beaches, lies south of the Dutch islands of Saba and St. Eustatius and due west of Antigua. From the air it looks like a cone, with cloud-capped Nevis Peak its 3,232-foot central apex; it is bracketed by Saddle Hill (1,250 feet) to the south and Round Hill (1,014 feet) to the north.

Like several other British islands, Nevis is divided into parishes: St. Thomas Lowland, St. James Windward, St. Paul Charlestown, St. George Gingerland, and St. John Figtree. On the island's west side, massed rows of palm trees form a coconut forest, while single palms bend in the breeze along the windward eastern coast. The "black" (actually dark gray) sand beaches at Jones and Mosquito bays in the northwest rank high as sightseeing attractions, but the white sand beaches to the north and west are more appealing for swimming.

SPECIAL PLACES

ST. KITTS This island is ideal for leisurely touring, discovering bays and beaches, exploring small fishing villages, and meeting people. The action, such as it is, centers around Basseterre, a quaint, friendly, and very photogenic West Indian port with a colorful harbor. Small craft and, about twice a week, a large cruise liner, lie at anchor in the waters offshore; ferryboats chug off to Nevis across the way.

BASSETERRE The town has looked as it does (West Indian with British overtones) for centuries, but it is punctuated with modern accents. An easy and safe place for a walking tour early in the morning or later in the afternoon (to avoid the heat), it boasts what have been called some of the most perfect examples of West Indian architecture in the islands. The black and white Treasury Building on the waterfront is a fine specimen; others are the 2-story buildings surrounding the Circus, which forms the hub of the city.

The Circus won't remind you much of Piccadilly, but its centerpiece is the island's "Big Ben," an ornate, cast iron Victorian clock tower with four faces, columns, coats of arms, and a fountain in its base. A few blocks away is Independence Square (formerly Pall Mall), where a park has taken the place of the old slave market. Nearby Government House is properly Georgian, as are several antique townhouses surrounding the Circus; they have small, fenced gardens in front, first stories of cut volcanic stone, second stories of shingled cedar wood bordered by arched galleries, wide terraces trimmed with gingerbread, and steep roofs. Other town landmarks include the Anglican Church of St. George (Cayon St.), plagued by disasters, including an earthquake, since its first incarnation in 1670; its churchyard, where graves date back to the early 18th century; and the post office and its philatelic bureau (Bay Rd.), where you can buy St. Kitts and Nevis stamps, outranked in popularity only by those of the BVI in the world of Caribbean philately.

THE CIRCLE ROAD

Taxi drivers on both islands are some of the best guides in the eastern Caribbean, well-known for their running commentary of island life and lore. While it's safe and easy to drive yourself, it's much more fun to sit back and listen to the amazing history and island gossip a reliable taxi driver can provide. Whether you travel by taxi or in your own rental car, take the Circle Road tour. You can make it all the way around the island in a little over 3½ hours, but do it more slowly. Pack a picnic, or call ahead to make lunch reservations at *Rawlins Plantation* (phone: 465-6221) or at the *Golden Lemon* (phone: 465-7260), near Dieppe Bay. Traveling clockwise, starting north from Basseterre, you'll see:

ST. KITTS SUGAR FACTORY Located at the edge of Basseterre, the factory provides a look into the island's history. The best months to visit are February to July, when cane is ground and you can see the entire sugar-making process from raw cane to bulk sugar. Tours are available at no charge, but you must call ahead to make an appointment (phone: 465-8157).

CARIB BEER BREWERY Near the sugar factory, the brewery offers a tour and a complimentary tasting by appointment only (phone: 465-2309).

FOUNTAIN ESTATE High on a hill north of town, it was the home of Philippe de Longvilliers de Poincy, who was for 20 years governor of the French Antilles and for whom the royal poinciana (or flamboyant) tree was named. Though a landmark, the estate is private property; no tours are offered.

BLOODY POINT Here the British and French massacred the Carib Indians in 1626.

ROMNEY MANOR After a scenic drive through a tropical rain forest, visitors will reach the home of *Caribelle Batik,* a 19th-century house surrounded by 5 acres of well-tended gardens, with a huge saman tree ("rain tree") said to be over 350 years old. Visitors are invited inside the factory to watch craftsmen make the colorful cloth. There is a fine selection for sale here, and shoppers can custom order clothing and wall hangings. Open weekdays 8:30 AM to 4 PM; no admission charge (phone: 465-6609 or 465-6253).

OLD ROAD TOWN This was the first permanent British settlement in the West Indies and the early capital of the island. There are Carib petroglyphs —

a small cluster of boulders with carvings — on Wingfield Estate nearby. Ask your driver to point them out, or ask directions at Romney Manor.

MIDDLE ISLAND VILLAGE Here Sir Thomas Warner, leader of the original British landing party, is entombed under a cracked marble slab — with a weighty epitaph written in Old English — in the yard of St. Thomas Church.

HALF-WAY TREE VILLAGE A giant sandbox tree here marks the midpoint of Britain's holdings when the French shared the island.

SANDY POINT The first British settlers landed at this spot in 1623, in the shadow of Mt. Liamuiga.

DIEPPE BAY This is a pleasant spot for swimming and picnicking. Gibson's Pasture estate, which overlooks it, was once a combined sugar mill and fort; two cannon have been found on the reef below. The sands of Dieppe Bay are volcanic gray to black. In fact, from here around the northeast coast of St. Kitts to Black Rocks, the beaches are of black sand. While not every beach lover's ideal (you'll find it hard to remove from your skin when dry), black sand has its own startling beauty, especially under bright sunlight.

BLACK ROCKS On the island's windward (Atlantic) side, these are eerie lava formations deposited over the years by the now dormant Mt. Liamuiga. Every November 5, Kittitians stage their *Guy Fawkes Day* picnic here.

MONKEY HILL A green, 1,319-foot knoll west of Basseterre, named for the local population of black-faced vervet monkeys, originally imported by the French and left behind when their masters moved on. Lucky shutterbugs will sight a few in their camera viewfinders. In any case, the view from the top is worth the trip. On the way up, you'll pass the ruins of a picturesque 2-story greathouse called the Glen, now tangled in green overgrowth.

FRIGATE BAY Near the beginning of the skinny handle of land that extends east from Basseterre, this area boasts two beaches — a surf-pounded one on North Frigate Bay on the Atlantic (or windward) side, and a calmer strand on South Frigate Bay on the Caribbean (or leeward) side. Designated a tourist zone by the government in order to preserve the rest of the island in a more pristine state, Frigate Bay is the site of a number of hotel and condominium projects, including the *Jack Tar* resort and the island's 18-hole golf course. North Friar's Bay and South Friar's Bay are farther to the southeast.

ELSEWHERE ON ST. KITTS

SOUTHEAST PENINSULA Before the opening in 1989 of Dr. Kennedy Simmonds Highway — a 6-mile road that starts from the Frigate Bay area and stretches across the island — a boat was necessary to get here. The roadside has some of the island's most beautiful scenery, including 9 unspoiled beaches, lagoon-like coves, pastures of tall guinea grass, and the Salt Pond (which looks pink because of the millions of tiny red krill shrimp inhabiting it). The peninsula is largely uninhabited except by black-faced vervet monkeys, white-tailed deer, and tropical birds. Two major hotels, however, are scheduled to open here this year: the 88-suite *Casablanca* and *Sandals,* a 250-room, all-inclusive, couples-only resort. Camping is permitted, though you must bring everything you need with you. The *Turtle Beach Bar & Grill* (no phone) is a good choice for lunch.

BRIMSTONE HILL FORTRESS No trip to St. Kitts is complete without a day spent at Brimstone Hill. Named for the faint fume of sulfur that lingers around it, the fort (800 feet above the Caribbean) commands a spectacular six-island (Nevis, Montserrat, Saba, Statia, St. Martin, and St. Barts) view. Because of its site and size, it took 105 years to build. Its massive volcanic stone walls, 7 to 12 feet thick, link a number of bastions and enclose the remnants of extensive life-sustaining installations (hospital, storerooms, cookhouses, asylum, cemetery, and freshwater cistern system) as well as the predictable parade, barracks, officers' quarters, and mess. There has been meticulous restoration of the Prince of Wales Bastion; it includes a visitors' center and souvenir shop. The fortress was attacked only twice. In 1782, before it was completed, 8,000 French troops under the Marquis de Bouillé mounted a siege that finally exhausted the British. They surrendered and were permitted — as a tribute to their bravery — to march out in uniform with drums beating and colors flying. A year later, the British retook the fort under the terms of the Treaty of Versailles and accorded the French the same honor. An information sheet is available for about 40¢ from the guard at the bottom of the steps. Open 9:30 AM to 5:30 PM Mondays through Saturdays; 2 to 5:30 PM Sundays; admission charge. Pack a picnic to spread on a grassy hilltop after or midway through your explorations. (A small bar and restaurant offers supplementary drinks and snacks.)

SPECIAL PLACES

NEVIS The island's capital, Charlestown (pop. 1,200), is a miniature West Indian port whose life revolves around the arrival of the ferries from St. Kitts. Since almost everything Nevisians want or need has to be imported, a small crowd gathers when a ferry docks to wait for wares to be unloaded and transferred to the open market on the waterfront.

CHARLESTOWN A walking tour of the town needn't take more than an hour, but it often does. You can go on your own or take the historical society's walking tour, given weekly in winter. The 1-hour trek costs $10 per person, and the schedule varies, so call ahead to make a reservation (phone: 469-5786). Leave the pier, turn right at the old Cotton House and Ginnery, and stroll through the marketplace. At the dead end, turn left on Prince William Street and follow it along to Memorial Square, a cordoned-off area dedicated to the dead of World Wars I and II. The coral stone building with the box-shaped clock tower overlooking the square is the court house (downstairs) and public library (upstairs). Visitors who are planning to drive on the island and haven't yet gotten their local driver's license should detour right on Main Street to call at the police station. Otherwise, turn left for the heart of town, which is roughly 3 blocks long. Turn into Happy Hill Alley and follow your nose to the *Nevis Bakery* for bread, coconut tarts, and cookies warm from the oven. Then head back toward Main Street and cross to the tourist office (handsome wall maps are for sale here) and the *Nevis Philatelic Bureau,* where stamps are one of the island's popular souvenir buys. Farther along on Main Street, note the customs house and the post office (stamps for sale here, too, but not first covers). Past Chapel Street, on Low Street, is the site of Alexander Hamilton's birthplace, the town's most interesting stop for most Americans. The original is gone, but a replica on the spot houses the *Alexander Hamilton Museum* (phone: 469-1424) downstairs and meeting quarters of the Nevisian House of Assembly upstairs. The museum has exhibits on Hamilton and island history and culture, and the gift shop sells various guides to the island; a useful *Walking and Riding Guide of Nevis,* a leaflet with maps, also is available for a small fee. Farther down Main Street stands St. Paul's Church, first built in the 17th century and rebuilt several times since. There's also an old Jewish cemetery at the corner of Jews Street and Government Road.

About 1½ miles north of town lies St. Thomas Church (ca. 1640), the oldest on the island, which has been reincarnated several times after several natural disasters, including earthquakes and hurricanes.

ELSEWHERE ON NEVIS

The tricky, rutted roads climbing inland up the sides of Mt. Nevis are best left to intrepid island drivers. The best route is the good (relatively) main road that circles the island. Virtually all Nevis's remaining landmarks lie along it; more important, so do vistas and ruins that offer a sense of the days when Nevis was the Queen of the Caribbees. Plan to stop for lunch or a picnic and a swim at Pinney's Beach or *Nisbet Plantation.* If you do drive, be alert. Even on the main drag you're likely to round a curve and suddenly find yourself tailgating a flock of goats, a sauntering donkey, or a slow-rolling cart.

Heading north from Charlestown and proceeding clockwise, you'll come to:

PINNEY'S BEACH This is still one of the island's best beaches. The reef-protected waters here are clear and fine for swimming and snorkeling, and there are several miles of sand near the *Four Seasons* resort. Don't leave without discovering the sleepy lagoon (very *South Pacific*) that lies through the palms at the beach's windward edge.

COTTON GROUND A village whose chief claim to fame is Nelson's Spring, with its lagoon, where Horatio Nelson is said to have replenished the freshwater supply of his flagship *Boreas.*

FORT ASHBY This overlooks what is thought to be the site of Jamestown, a settlement that slid into the sea — the victim of an earthquake and tidal wave — around 1640.

ROUND HILL The view from the top of this hill takes in St. Kitts and Booby Island, named after the brown pelican, Nevis's national bird.

NEWCASTLE A tumbled old village near the airport, it's known for its fishing fleet and as one of the best places to buy (in the morning) fresh lobster, conch, and fish.

NISBET PLANTATION A restored greathouse-hotel that serves good island lunches, it overlooks a gorgeous beach and an elegant, formal sea vista lined with grass lawns and tall palms. As at all Nevis beaches and restored greathouses, you're welcome to stop, sup, and swim (phone: 469-9325).

EDEN BROWN ESTATE Now a gaunt, gray ruin, this estate was built and elegantly furnished by a wealthy planter for his daughter, but was abandoned after her fiancé and his best man killed each other in a drunken duel on the eve of the wedding.

NEW RIVER ESTATE Nevis's last operating sugar mill ceased operation in 1956, but you still can wander through the stone ruins at your leisure.

MONTPELIER ESTATE Now a hotel site (the original gateposts stand), this was the scene of the marriage of "Horatio Nelson, Esquire, Captain of his Majesty's Ship, the *Boreas,* to Frances Herbert Nisbet, Widow," on March 11, 1787. So reads the entry on a tattered page of the register displayed in St. John's Church, Figtree Village. The scrawled signature below is that of the Duke of Clarence — later William IV of England — who witnessed the ceremony. The church sexton can be coaxed to say a few words about the Nelson-Nisbet nuptials; but he'd rather talk about Sunday's hymns, or the church itself, or the mossy old graveyard where stones date back to 1682. The estate is closed from mid-August to October.

LORD NELSON MUSEUM An astonishingly complete collection of mementos of the great admiral, as well as 18th-century period clothing are displayed here. Open Mondays through Fridays from 10 AM to 4 PM and Saturdays in winter from 9 AM to 1 PM; admission charge. Located next to the Government House (phone: 469-0408).

BATH HOUSE The remains of an 18th-century watering place that put Nevis on the map as "the West Indian spa" for more than 100 years. Its social life was the talk of the islands, and its guest list included not only British gentry from all over the Caribbean but European nobility as well. Although they are very basic, five mineral-steeped spa baths have been restored and are now open for visitors' use; there is speculation that the massive hotel, which is still standing, may be restored as well. Open 8 AM to 4 PM weekdays; 8 AM to noon Saturdays; admission charge.

Sources and Resources

TOURIST INFORMATION

The local St. Kitts Tourist Board (*Pelican Shopping Mall,* Bay Rd., Basseterre; phone: 465-4040 or 465-2620; fax: 465-8794) is close to the center of things. The staff is pleasant and helpful, although sometimes short on printed information. There's also a desk at Golden Rock Airport (phone: 465-8970). The Nevis Tourist Office (Main St., Charlestown; phone: 469-5521, ext. 2049; fax: 469-1806) has brochures and current rate sheets on the island's hotels. For information on tourist offices in the US, see GETTING READY TO GO.

LOCAL COVERAGE *A Motoring Guide to St. Kitts* (about $4) is published locally and is available at *Wall's Deluxe Record and Book Shop* in Basseterre (Fort St.; phone: 465-2159), as is the locally published *Discover St. Kitts* by Amalia Stone and Frank Sharman. Your hotel also may have copies for sale. A tourist map, indicating hotels and points of interest on both St. Kitts and Nevis, is available free at the tourist office and sells for about $1 at local shops. The tourist board also makes available, at no charge, *The Traveller Tourist Guide,* with information on sightseeing, dining, shopping, and entertainment. The *Democrat* and the *Labor Spokesman* are the St. Kitts newspapers, published Mondays through Fridays. Stateside papers generally aren't available, and nobody minds much.

No newspapers or tourist periodicals are published on Nevis. Island papers occasionally are ferried over from St. Kitts, but on no regular schedule. If you're going to do any exploring, *A Motoring Guide to Nevis,* available at the tourist office, is worth its price (about $6). Also invaluable is the *Walking and Riding Guide of Nevis,* available free from the tourist board or for $1 at the *Alexander Hamilton Museum.* For background reading, try *Nelson,* Carola Oman's biography, and *Nevis, Queen of the Caribees,* by Joyce Gordon; both books can be found at the gift shop at the *Four Seasons.*

RADIO AND TELEVISION

There are two radio stations, ZIZ Radio (555 AM and 96 FM) and Voice of Nevis (VON; 895-AM). The local television station, ZIZ-TV, broadcasts from 3 to 11:30 PM daily. All carry local programs plus US and BBC pickups. The Trinity Broadcasting Network (TBN) broadcasts religious television programs via satellite and also airs some local programs. Satellite TV is available at most hotels.

TELEPHONE

The area code for St. Kitts and Nevis is 809.

ENTRY REQUIREMENTS

A passport or other proof of citizenship (a voter's registration card or birth certificate *and* an official photo ID such as a valid driver's license) and a ticket for return or ongoing transportation are all that's required of citizens of the US or Canada on short visits to either island. There's an $8 departure tax, payable at the airport when you check in to leave (*not* when going from one island to visit thc other).

CLIMATE AND CLOTHES

The temperature on St. Kitts ranges from about 78 to 85F (25 to 30C) during the day all year long; at night, it sometimes drops to 68F (20C). Nevis, with about the same temperatures, can be uncomfortably humid during the summer, even though it is cooled by trade winds. During the rainy season (mid-June to mid-November), it can shower heavily, but the downpour lasts only an hour or two.

On St. Kitts, dress is for casual comfort, not for fashion; cotton and cotton-blend sports clothes are fine for daytime and touring whatever the season. Be sure to pack sturdy walking shoes or sneakers for Brimstone Hill and other places, plus several swimming changes. Even for May to November showers, you probably won't need a raincoat. Evenings, wear what you please; but the northeast trade winds keep it cool enough for a light wrap on winter evenings.

Daytime dress is similar on Nevis, but swim clothes are worn only at the beach or pool; you'll want a shirt or a cover-up at lunchtime or when you've had enough sun. At night, jackets and ties never are required for men, but something about the greathouse atmosphere makes many women enjoy dressing up a bit in long (but casual) skirts or summer evening dresses.

MONEY

Currency on both islands is the Eastern Caribbean dollar (EC) valued at about $2.70 EC to $1 US. Except at hotels, most prices in the islands are quoted in $EC. US and Canadian bills generally are accepted, but foreign coins are not welcome because they're difficult for islanders to exchange. It's a good idea to have some EC currency handy for small purchases. Most banks are open from 8 AM to 3 PM Mondays through Thursdays and from 8 AM to 5 PM on Fridays. The St. Kitts–Nevis National Bank in

Basseterre also is open on Saturday mornings from 8:30 to 11 AM, and the Bank of Nevis and the St. Kitts–Nevis-Anguilla National Bank are open Saturdays from 8 to 11 AM. In general, the exchange rate at hotels and shops is the same as the bank rate. All prices in this chapter are quoted in US dollars.

LANGUAGE

English has been the official language on St. Kitts for more than 350 years, although there's also a local patois. On Nevis, you'll hear English spoken with an island lilt.

TIME

St. Kitts and Nevis clocks are set to atlantic standard time throughout the year. So, in winter when it's noon in New York or Washington, it's 1 PM in Basseterre and Charlestown. When the US is on daylight saving time, there is no time difference.

CURRENT

Here 230 volts predominate, though a number of hotels are now wired for 110 volts (standard in the US and Canada). Check, or bring a converter just in case.

TIPPING

Hotels add a 10% service charge, which really covers everybody. If you're eating out and no service charge is included, tip 10% to 15%; the same goes for taxi rides. On St. Kitts, give an airport porter 50¢ per bag, with a $1 minimum (there are no porters on Nevis).

GETTING AROUND

ST. KITTS — Bicycle Rental Mountain bikes are available for rent at *Tropical Surf Watersports* at the *Turtle Beach Bar & Grill* on the Southeast Peninsula (phone: 465-9086 or 465-2380).

BUS These run between island villages, but tourists seldom use them because taxis are always handy and provide round-trip transportation (not always easy to plot using bus schedules) to exactly the place you want to go.

CAR RENTAL Easy to arrange, car rental costs are about $38 and up per day, including unlimited mileage; gas is on you. A local driver's license, available at the police station in Basseterre for about $12, is required; you'll need to present your driver's license from home. *Delisle Walwyn & Co.* (Liverpool Row; phone: 465-2631 or 465-8449), *Sunshine* (11 Cayon St.; phone: 465-2193), *TDC* (W. Independence Sq. St.; phone: 465-2991), *Holiday* (S. Independence Sq. St.; phone: 465-6507), *Caine's* (Princes St.; phone: 465-2366), and *Island Car Rental* (12 W. Independence Sq. St.; phone: 465-

3000) are good firms in Basseterre. Shop around; some companies offer free pickup and drop-off. Don't forget to drive on the left!

FERRY SERVICES The government-operated ferry makes one or two trips between St. Kitts and Nevis daily except Thursdays and Sundays. The 45-minute crossing is generally calm and pleasant, and costs about $8 per person round-trip. The *Spirit of Mt. Nevis,* a private ferry run by the *Mt. Nevis* hotel, makes one or two runs per day Thursdays through Sundays between Charlestown and Basseterre; the round-trip fare is about $12 (phone: 465-7474).

SEA EXCURSIONS Trips to neighboring islands, sunset cruises, and deep-sea fishing and scuba trips are arranged through hotels or directly with *Kantours* (phone: 465-2040 or 465-3128) and *Tropical Tours* (phone: 465-4039 or 465-4167). *Kenneth's Dive Centre* (phone: 465-7043); *Tropical Dreamer,* a sailing catamaran (phone: 465-8224); *Loose Mongoose,* a cruise ship that does half-day snorkeling and sailing excursions and sunset cruises (phone: 465-2754 or 465-2380); and *Spirit of St. Kitts,* another catamaran (phone: 465-7474), also offer sea excursions. A day trip to Nevis is a must if time permits; take the government ferry (see *Ferry Services,* above).

SIGHTSEEING TOURS *Kantours* (phone: 465-2040 or 465-3128) and *Tropical Tours* (phone: 465-4039 or 465-4167) both offer 3½-hour historic and sightseeing tours for $15 per person. Taxi tours are also popular because hotels try to team visitors with a driver who'll make the trip pleasant (although if dates and statistics matter to you, take your guidebook along). Rates run about $48 for a 4-hour island tour for up to 4 people. If you'd like extra stops or time, negotiate — or ask your hotel to — before you take off.

TAXI The transportation mainstay here, taxis are found waiting at the airport and at the Circus in Basseterre, and each hotel has its coterie of loyal drivers waiting outside in the shade or at the other end of a phone call. You also can call for a taxi (phone: 465-2050). Cabs are not metered, but the Taxi Association (phone: 465-4253) publishes a list of point-to-point rates (look for it in local tourist guides, or ask for a copy). Even so, the price should be settled before you start off (establish whether the rate quoted is in EC or US dollars). The ride from the airport to town generally runs about $7; it's about $10 and up to out-of-town hotels. There are no airport buses.

GETTING AROUND

NEVIS — Bus There's bus service between villages, but there's no set schedule; taxis are much easier.

CAR RENTAL Japanese and American cars, and a few open-air mini-mokes are available. Rentals are easily arranged — ask your hotel to set it up. The going rate is about $38 to $60 a day with unlimited mileage and a full tank of gas to start you off (generally you won't need a refill). You'll need a

Nevis driver's license, available at the police station in Charlestown for about $12 (bring your driver's license from home). Remember — keep left!

FERRY SERVICES See listings for St. Kitts above.

SEA EXCURSIONS Strictly plan-it-yourself, using the local ferry services (see listings for St. Kitts).

SIGHTSEEING TAXI TOURS Simple to negotiate. Your hotel will find you a driver. Rates are about $50 for a 3-hour tour (which includes time for a lunch stop) for up to four people. There are no sightseeing bus companies.

TAXI Unlike the yellow honk-and-hack metropolitan cabs on St. Kitts, the system here is individual car-and-driver. Rates are fixed and published in the tourist guides available at the airport and at the tourist office. The trip from the airport to the most distant hotel should be no more than $18. Before taking any trip, confirm whether the fare is quoted in EC or US dollars. Also remember that fares increase 50% between 10 PM and 6 AM.

INTER-ISLAND FLIGHTS

LIAT has flights to St. Kitts from Nevis, Antigua, San Juan, St. Thomas, St. Croix, and St. Martin/St. Maarten. *American Eagle* has service from San Juan, Puerto Rico, and St. Thomas to St. Kitts; the regional flight from St. Kitts to Nevis can be booked through on the same ticket. *Carib Aviation* (phone: 465-3055 or 469-9295) and *Air St. Kitts Nevis* (phone: 465-8571 or 469-9241) offer charters between St. Kitts and Nevis, and to other islands as well.

SPECIAL EVENTS

Carnival — December 24 to January 2 — is the big party on St. Kitts, complete with parades, music, and dancing. Summer's *Culturama* (late July, early August) brings calypso shows, dances, parties, and festive events to Nevis. Legal holidays on both islands include *New Year's Day, Carnival Day, Good Friday, Easter Monday, Labour Day* (first Monday in May), *Whitmonday,* the *Queen's Birthday* (early June), *August Monday* (first Monday in August), *Independence Day* (September 19), *Christmas,* and *Boxing Day* (December 26).

SHOPPING

Duty-free shopping is relatively new to St. Kitts, but liberalized licensing legislation has resulted in an increasing number of shops that feature imported merchandise — perfume, jewelry, watches, china, and crystal. There is some rather good local crafts work, interesting local jewelry, and island casual wear. Be sure to sample (and take home) a bottle of CSR (Cane Spirits Rothschild), a St. Kitts–made cane spirit delicious in mixed drinks. Two shopping plazas in the center of town, *Palms Arcade* and *TDC Mall,* are worth a visit. The newest venue is the *Pelican Shopping Mall* on

Bay Road, near the pier in Basseterre; it opened in 1992 to provide more shopping possibilities for cruise-ship passengers. It features 26 shops, a covered bandstand, 2 lounges, and a restaurant in an Old World setting. The selection of goods on Nevis has increased in recent years, with many new shops offering island fashions in addition to the predictable souvenirs, T-shirts, and some fairly routine island craft work (shell and straw, mostly). Almost all the shops are in Charlestown, along Main Street and one or two side streets.

ST. KITTS

CARIBELLE BATIK Dresses, skirts, blouses, shirts, pareos (sarongs), and wall hangings made from batik, tie-dyed, and hand-painted Sea Island cotton fabrics are made and sold here. All are brightly colored, in island-inspired designs, and guaranteed colorfast and washable. Romney Manor near Old Road Town (phone: 465-6453 or 465-6253).

ISLAND STYLE Locally made baskets, coconut tree products, and clothing. *Palms Arcade,* Basseterre (phone: 465-7488).

OBJECTS OF ART Jewelry handmade locally from black volcanic rock, conch shells, whelk shells, the seeds of the sandbox tree, and imported amber and larimar stone. *TDC Mall,* Basseterre (phone: 465-2705).

PALMCRAFTS Resortwear designed by Canadian John Warden and made in St. Kitts; also Sunny Caribbee brand spices and teas, tropical costume jewelry, and scarves. *Palms Arcade,* Basseterre (phone: 465-2599).

A SLICE OF THE LEMON French perfume, imported jewelry, watches, china, crystal — the largest selection and the best brands and buys, all duty-free. *Palms Arcade,* Basseterre (phone: 465-2889).

SPENCER CAMERON ART GALLERY Locally produced silk-screened fabrics, watercolors, and other paintings. Cayon St., Basseterre (phone: 465-4047).

SPLASH T-shirts, jazzy island clothing, batik cotton sportswear, bathing suits, and woodwork. *Pelican Shopping Mall,* Basseterre (phone: 465-9640 or 465-9279).

WALL'S DELUXE RECORD AND BOOK SHOP Good selection of books about the area, works by West Indian authors, and records of calypso, reggae, and steel band music. Fort St., Basseterre (phone: 465-2159).

NEVIS

AMANDA FASHIONS Hand-painted T-shirts and cotton clothes for men, women, and children. Prince William St., near the Court House, Charlestown (phone: 469-5774).

AVENUE GIFT SHOP Local art, spices, jams, jellies, and shell jewelry, as well as cotton men's and women's sportswear. Main St., Charlestown (phone: 469-5784).

BATIK BY CARVELLE Formerly the *Nevis Craft Studio* (in fact, its sign still says so), this is a good source for batik fashions. Main St., Charlestown (no phone).

CARIBBEAN CONFECTIONS Baskets of jams, jellies, and candies to take home, plus fresh tropical fruit ice cream for immediate consumption. Main St., Charlestown (phone: 469-5685).

GALLERY OF NEVIS ART Local artwork is featured. Main St., Charlestown (phone: 469-1381).

THE ISLAND HOPPER Batik cloth and tie-dyed and hand-painted cotton clothing and wall hangings made at *Caribelle Batik* on St. Kitts. The *Arcade Gardens.* Off Main St., Charlestown (phone: 469-1491).

NEVIS HANDICRAFT CO-OPERATIVE A wide selection of crafts. Next to the tourist office, Main St., Charlestown (phone: 469-1746).

NEVIS PHILATELIC BUREAU Magnificent, colorful island stamps. The postcards already come with the prettiest stamps available. Just off Main St., Charlestown (phone: 469-5535).

NEWCASTLE POTTERY Gift items and cooking pots; visitors may watch the merchandise being made and fired over burning coconut shells. Just east of the airport, Newcastle (phone: 469-9746).

SANDBOX TREE Gifts, souvenirs, and clothing for men, women, and children, including embroidered placemats, hand-carved wooden fish, and an entire room full of toys and books. *Evelyn's Villa,* Cedar Trees, Charlestown (phone: 469-5662).

WILLIAMS EULALIE MAIN STREET GROCERY Nevis hot pepper sauce, among the Caribbean's best, is a good souvenir or gift. CSR, the St. Kitts–made cane spirit, is also available here. Main St., Charlestown (phone: 469-5226).

SPORTS

ST. KITTS — Boating Day sails to Nevis, moonlight cruises, and coastal cruises are offered by a number of outfits, including *Tropical Tours* (phone: 465-4039), *Kenneth's Dive Centre* (phone: 465-7043), and *Leeward Island Charters* (phone: 465-7474), in Basseterre; and at *Fisherman's Wharf,* which is part of the *Ocean Terrace Inn* complex in Basseterre (phone: 465-2754 or 465-2380).

GOLF Jack Tar Village has the *Royal St. Kitts* golf course, an 18-hole championship layout at Frigate Bay (phone: 465-8339). The par 72, 160-acre course incorporates seven lakes and is bounded by the Caribbean and the Atlantic. Greens fees are included for *Jack Tar Village* guests, who must, however, pay for a cart — $25 for 9 holes, $30 for 18. Others pay greens fees of $20 for 9 holes, $30 for 18 holes, plus the cart fee. Caddies are not available, but lessons are. There is also a 9-hole course at Golden Rock (phone: 465-8651).

HIKING AND MOUNTAIN CLIMBING No fully marked trails exist on St. Kitts, so either hire a local guide through your hotel or take a tour. Monkey Hill is rated an easy climb, but it's hard to find the trail. The 2½-hour hike to the crater rim of dormant volcano Mt. Liamuiga is moderately strenuous. A spectacular vista of steaming sulphur and lush greenery can be seen from the top of the 1,600-foot crater. The full-day hike up Verchild's Mountain and back is more difficult; make sure you're in good enough physical shape before you go. Another possibility is a rain forest hike up hidden mountain trails and past waterfalls and dense vegetation where monkeys, mongooses, and hummingbirds often are seen. *Greg's Safari Tours* (phone: 465-4121) and *Kris Tours* (phone: 465-4042) offer half-day rain forest tours ($35 to $40 per person), as well as full-day tours to Mt. Liamuiga ($40 to $45 per person, including lunch and drinks).

HORSEBACK RIDING *Trinity Stables* (phone: 465-3226 or 465-9603) offers 1-hour beach rides for $15 per person, and *Royal Stables* (phone: 465-2222 or 465-2945) runs half-day riding trips to the rain forest for $35 per person.

SNORKELING AND SCUBA Instruction, equipment, dive and snorkeling trips are offered by *Pro Diver* at *Fisherman's Wharf* and Turtle Beach (phone: 465-3223 or 465-2380); and *Kenneth's Dive Centre* (phone: 465-7043). A one-tank dive will cost about $40; a two-tank dive, $60; a snorkeling trip, about $30.

SPORT FISHING St. Kitts's waters abound with fish, including dorado, kingfish, wahoo, and tuna. Charter boats for deep-sea fishing at *Fisherman's Wharf* (phone: 465-2754 or 465-2380), *Kenneth's Dive Centre* (phone: 465-7043), *Jeffers M. C. Enterprises* (phone: 465-1900), *Tropical Tours* (phone: 465-4039), and *Sam Lake* (phone: 465-8225). The cost is $50 per person for a 3-hour trip and includes tackle, bait, and drinks on board. If you make a catch, *Fisherman's Wharf* (phone: 465-2754) will prepare it for dinner that night with their compliments.

SWIMMING AND SUNNING The widest and whitest sands are at the southern end of the island. Frigate Bay and Friar's Bay have beaches on both the Atlantic and Caribbean. White House Bay is just south of Friar's Bay; Banana Bay and Cockleshell Bay, on the island's southernmost shore, beyond Great Salt Pond, are other good names to know. Unusual black sand beaches rim the northeast coast of St. Kitts from Dieppe Bay to Black Rocks. There's also surf on the windward side of Frigate Bay. Few hotels are directly on the beach, though most aren't far away and will arrange transportation; most also have swimming pools. The best beach is the Sand Bank Bay on the Southeast Peninsula.

TENNIS If you're addicted, stay at the *Jack Tar Village,* which has 4 courts, 2 lighted, and a pro; non-guests can use the courts by purchasing a day pass ($50) that entitles them to use all the resort's facilities. There is 1 court at the *St. Kitts Bridge and Tennis Club* (at Fortlands in Basseterre; phone: 465-2938), 1 court at the *Golden Lemon* (for guests only), 2 courts at *Bird Rock Beach* (for guests only), 2 courts at *Sun 'n' Sand* (phone: 465-8037), and a grass court at *Rawlins Plantation* (for guests only). *St. Kitts Lawn Tennis Club* (phone: 465-2051) will grant temporary membership to visitors.

WATER SKIING Go to *Roy Gumbs Watersports* (phone: 465-8050), on the Caribbean beach at Frigate Bay; about $15 per circuit.

WINDSURFING For lessons and board rental, *Roy Gumbs Watersports* (phone: 465-8050) or *Tropical Surf* at Turtle Beach (phone: 465-2380). Rentals run from $10 to $13 per hour.

SPORTS

NEVIS — Golf There's only one, but it's tops.

TOP TEE-OFF SPOT

Four Seasons This is Nevis's first course, and it's a real gem: 18 holes designed by Robert Trent Jones, Jr., the course begins at sea level, slopes toward 3,232-foot Mt. Nevis, and ends up on the beach. The 15th hole, which features a ravine and a 600-yard drop to the green, is the most challenging. With its beautiful layout, uncrowded fairways, stunning views, and crew of staff members who patrol the course with refreshments, a round here is bound to be memorable, regardless of your score. Greens fees are $60 (phone: 469-1111; 800-332-3442 from the US).

HIKING AND MOUNTAIN CLIMBING The *Nevis Academy* (phone: 469-2091) offers three different ecological hiking tours of the island. The 3-hour treks cost $20 per person. Climbing to the top of Nevis Peak, the dormant volcano, is not difficult, though the dirt path can be muddy from April to November. Wear sturdy climbing shoes or sneakers and hardy, easily washed clothes. The climb takes about 6 hours round-trip, and most hotels will pack a lunch. A guide (recommended) will ask about $25 for two people; your hotel can make arrangements.

HORSEBACK RIDING Hotels can arrange for guests to ride through Garner's Estate by calling Ira Dore (phone: 469-5528). The charge, including a guide, is about $35 per person for a 1½-hour ride. At the *Hermitage*

Plantation (phone: 469-3477), a 1-hour ride costs $25, and a 1-hour horse-drawn carriage ride runs about $25 per person.

HORSE RACING There are races six times a year at the *Indian Castle Race Track: New Year's Day, Easter Monday, Labor Day* (the first Monday in May), *August Monday* (the first Monday in August), *Independence Day* (September 19), and *Boxing Day* (December 26). Ask anywhere for details.

SPORT FISHING Barracuda, shark, kingfish, wahoo, and snapper can all be caught in local waters. The going rate for sport fishing is about $50 per hour (3 hours minimum); contact *Sea Nevis* (phone: 469-1997) or your hotel desk to arrange for an outing with a reputable guide.

SWIMMING All beaches are public. Pinney's Beach on the Caribbean side is the longest and the best. Of the island's hotels and inns, only the *Nisbet Plantation,* the *Oualie Beach Club, Pinney's Beach,* and the *Four Seasons* are on beaches. Other hotels have large swimming pools, usually well placed for views, and offer free transportation to private cabañas on Pinney's Beach.

TENNIS For such a small island, Nevis offers excellent racketeering for both novices and more experienced players.

CHOICE COURTS

Four Seasons This complete resort offers 10 courts — 3 lighted, 6 with all-weather surfaces, and 4 of red clay (a rare treat in the Caribbean). There's also topflight instruction and round-robin tournaments (phone: 469-1111; 800-332-3442 from the US).

Other tennis options: There is 1 court each at the *Nisbet Plantation, Golden Rock, Montpelier, Pinney's Beach,* and *Rest Haven* hotels.

WATER SPORTS The *Oualie Beach Club* (phone: 469-9735) rents Sunfish; *Scuba Safaris* (phone: 469-9518), located at the hotel, offers a full range of snorkeling, scuba diving, and instruction (*NAUI*). A one-tank dive costs around $50; a two-tank dive, $80. Glass-bottom boat trips are also available.

NIGHTLIFE

Low voltage. Most hotels have string or steel band performances on regular schedules in season. On St. Kitts, *Ocean Terrace Inn* has entertainment twice a week (a steel band, plus a show of batik fashions on Wednesdays; a steel band accompanied by either a West Indian buffet or a barbecue on Fridays); call ahead for reservations (phone: 465-2754 or 465-2380). A night pass, available with or without dinner, will get you into *Jack Tar Village* (phone: 465-8651) for the evening's show. The *Royal St. Kitts Casino* — the only one on the island — is also here. Admission is free to hotel guests; non-guests must purchase a day pass; gamblers receive complimentary drinks. The casino offers slot machines, roulette, craps, blackjack tables, and a disco. Late-late nightspots include *Reflexions* at *Flexes Fitness Centre* (Frigate Bay Rd.; phone: 465-7616) and the *Cotton Club* disco at *Canada Estate* (phone: 465-5855). *Fisherman's Wharf* at the *Ocean Terrace Inn* serves food and drinks late and features a steel band and dancing every Friday night into the wee hours.

On Nevis, there's some local music and dancing on Saturday nights at *Dick's Bar* (phone: 469-9182), at Brick Kiln in the northeastern part of the island. *Fort Ashby,* on Canes Bay (phone: 469-0135), is a popular spot for conversation and local music.

Best on the Island

CHECKING IN

Hotels on St. Kitts tend to be small, low-profile, charming resorts, with lots of personality (island law decrees that no building can be higher than the tallest palm tree). But few qualify as luxurious. New construction in the Frigate Bay area, including several large-scale projects, has added to the island's supply of 840 guestrooms, and further development is proceeding farther to the south. *Sandals,* an all-inclusive resort for couples only, is scheduled to open at the southernmost tip of St. Kitts in the middle of this year (phone for information: 800-SANDALS from the US). Also under construction in the same area is *Casablanca,* an 88-suite hotel slated for completion early this year (phone for information: 800-231-1945 from the US).

Accommodations on Nevis consist mainly of inns and condo complexes that range from small to tiny — except for the luxurious *Four Seasons,* with its 196 rooms; most innkeepers describe their places as "more of a house party, really." Guests who meet for the first time over after-dinner drinks often end up planning an outing together for the next day, and by the end of the week they may plan to vacation together the following year. Much of the attraction of these inns lies in their origins as sugar plantations. While more and more places are adding air conditioning, others still rely on sea breezes and ceiling fans to keep things cool and comfortable.

Many of the hotels listed below operate on a Modified American Plan (MAP), which means that breakfast and dinner are included in the room rate. Most of the others generally offer a MAP at an additional $30 to $60 per person, per day. At hotels on Nevis, beach transportation and sports facilities are generally included, too. Properties described below as expensive charge $275 and up a day for a double room with meals. Hotels listed as moderate charge between $125 and $200 a day for a double room without meals (EP); inexpensive places charge under $100 a day for a double without meals. A 7% tax is added to hotel bills. Prices drop by about 35% in summer. Rental cottages, a less expensive option, go for about $175 and up a week; addresses can be obtained from the islands' tourist offices. A few hotels do not accept credit cards, so check ahead. All telephone numbers are in the 809 area code unless otherwise indicated.

For an unforgettable island experience, we begin with our favorite, followed by our recommendations of cost and quality choices of hotels large and small, listed by area and price category.

A SPECIAL HAVEN

Four Seasons, Nevis Nestled within a former coconut palm tree grove is this island's largest and most luxurious resort, with 196 rooms situated in 12 cottages that overlook either the pristine sands of Pinney's Beach or the scenic rolling hills of the first-rate 18-hole Robert Trent Jones, Jr. golf course. The quiet center of this complex is the plantation-style greathouse, which contains 3 excellent restaurants (see *Eating Out*), library, main bar, and nightclub. A marble staircase leads to the pool pavilion, the beach, and the dock. Flowering yellow bells, hibiscus, and bougainvillea line the walkways. Each air conditioned guestroom is a tropical oasis, with either king-size bed or full-size beds, a stocked mini-bar, large closets, mahogany armoire with color TV set and VCR, huge tile-and-marble bathroom, and either a private patio or screened-in balcony. For children, there's the "Kids for All Seasons" supervised daily activities program. Other pluses include a complete health club and fitness center, a spa, 10 tennis courts, 24-hour room service, and an attentive, pleasant staff. This well-run resort is easy on the mind and the body, making it a topnotch getaway for guests who want pampering and relaxation. Pinney's Beach (phone: 469-1111; 800-332-3442 from the US; fax: 469-1040).

ST. KITTS

BASSETERRE

MODERATE

Ocean Terrace Inn One of St. Kitts' best, on a hilltop at the far west hook of Basseterre harbor, this place has many appealing qualities. The air conditioned rooms have tiled floors, a tropical decor, breezy terraces from which to watch the harbor life, and satellite TV. The grounds are charming, and the restaurant and bars have a lively, congenial atmosphere. The 54 rooms include 8 attractive 1- and 2-bedroom apartments. Both EP and MAP rates are available — guests can eat in the hotel's dining room (indoors or outdoors with an ocean view) or at the hotel-owned *Fisherman's Wharf* restaurant (see *Eating Out*), a 5-minute walk away, where there is also a boating and scuba facility. Other pluses: 2 swimming pools and free shuttle twice daily to Frigate Bay's Caribbean beach and to *Turtle Beach Bar &*

Grill. Fortlands (phone: 465-2754 or 465-2380; 800-524-0512 from the US; fax: 465-1057).

FRIGATE BAY

MODERATE

Colony Timothy Beach Now managed by the Colony hotel group, this 61-unit property is at the foot of Sir Timothy's Hill, on a golden-sand beach. Rooms are air conditioned and feature a patio or balcony; studios and suites also have full kitchens. Water sports, as well as use of the golf course at *Jack Tar Village,* are available. The hotel's beachside restaurant, the *Coconut Café,* specializes in seafood, cooked on an open grill. About 3 miles from Basseterre (phone: 465-8597; 800-777-1700 from the US; fax: 465-7723).

Island Paradise Beach Village The first condominium development in Frigate Bay, with 36 one-bedroom, 18 two-bedroom, and 4 three-bedroom apartments, all with fully equipped kitchens. Freshwater pool and Atlantic beach; conveniences on the premises include a pizza and snack restaurant, a food shop, a liquor store, and a small souvenir shop. No credit cards accepted. Across from the golf course (phone: 465-8035; 800-828-2956 from the US; fax: 465-8236).

Jack Tar Village This 242-room establishment is patterned after the other resorts in the Jack Tar chain, and offers reasonable all-inclusive rates covering everything from meals and cocktails to water sports, tennis, horseback riding, nightly entertainment, and tips. The combination of the adjoining 18-hole golf course and a casino makes this the place for those seeking an active vacation at a typically modern resort. Closer to the Atlantic than the Caribbean beach, with free shuttle service to the latter. No minimum stay is required; in fact, those not staying here can buy a day pass ($50) permitting use of all facilities except a room. On Frigate Bay (phone: 465-8651; 214-987-4909 from Dallas; 800-999-9182 from elsewhere in the US; fax: 465-1031).

Leeward Cove A small condominium hotel opposite the *Jack Tar Village* golf course, with only 38 spacious and comfortably furnished 1- and 2-bedroom units, with access to the Atlantic beach. Pool, tennis court, plus waived greens fees at the golf course. There's a 3-night minimum stay in winter. On 5 acres; within walking distance of restaurants (phone: 465-8030; 800-223-5695 from the US; fax: 465-3476).

St. Christopher Club This 30-room condominium development faces the Atlantic Ocean. Air conditioned, well-appointed studio apartments (all with complete kitchens) are located next to the *Jack Tar Village,* and overlook its 18-hole golf course. There's also a freshwater pool (phone: 465-4854; fax: 465-6466).

Sun 'n' Sand Beach Village Just off the wild Atlantic and behind a hedge of sea grape bushes, with 18 cottages and 32 studio apartments. The 2-bedroom, 2-bath cottages are simple, but pleasant, with high ceilings, fully equipped kitchens, and air conditioned bedrooms. There's a small grocery and drugstore on the premises, as well as a casual beachside pub, 2 tennis courts, and a swimming pool. Continental breakfast is included; attractive weekly rates make it a good choice for families traveling on a budget (phone: 465-8037; 800-223-6510 from the US; fax: 465-6745).

INEXPENSIVE

Frigate Bay Beach It isn't exactly on a beach, but rather a 5-minute stroll from the Caribbean side of the bay. The 64 one- and two-bedroom apartments are in low-rise, vaguely Mediterranean-style buildings clustered around a big, handsome swimming pool. The good-size accommodations are undergoing a renovation that will add new furnishings and private terraces. The top units, with peaked roofs and ceiling fans, are the pick of the crop. There's a restaurant, too. Rates are EP only (phone: 465-8935 or 465-8936; 800-223-9815 from the US; fax: 465-7050).

ELSEWHERE ON ST. KITTS

EXPENSIVE

Golden Lemon "For the discriminating few who like to do nothing, in grand style" is how the brochure puts it. An old, beautifully refurbished greathouse, this is one of the few inns where as much attention has been lavished on sleeping rooms as public areas. Nine guestrooms are in the greathouse itself and there are 18 more rooms in 10 stylish villas at the water's edge. The inn has lovely gardens and courtyards, a tennis court, a freshwater pool, a small black sand beach, superb food (see *Eating Out*), and *Lemonaid,* an exclusive boutique. Rates include breakfast, dinner, afternoon tea, and laundry. At Dieppe Bay, on the island's northwest coast (phone: 465-7260; 800-223-5581 from the US; fax: 465-4019).

Ottley's Plantation Inn A hostelry on an old sugar plantation, it's near the foot of Mt. Liamuiga. It is high enough to offer scenic views from its 35 acres. The 15 air conditioned rooms are either in the restored, verandah-girded greathouse, where an English country look prevails, or in independent stone cottages within walking distance of the rain forest. There's a spring-fed swimming pool, as well as shuttle service to beach, golf, tennis, and shopping. The inn's *Royal Palm* restaurant is at the edge of the rain forest. Ottley's Estate, north of Basseterre (phone: 465-7234; 800-772-3039 from the US; fax: 465-4760).

Rawlins Plantation This owner-operated country estate of a dozen acres, a one-time sugar plantation, has beautiful gardens and arresting views. The main house, built on the foundations of the 17-century greathouse, houses the dining room; the 16 guestrooms are in cottages and other buildings scattered around the breezy hillside site. There's a pretty swimming pool, and a grass tennis court. Rates include breakfast, dinner, afternoon tea, and laundry. No credit cards accepted. At Mt. Pleasant, near Dieppe Bay on the north coast (phone: 465-6221; 800-621-1270 from the US; fax: 809-469-4954).

White House A restored 18th-century greathouse, decorated with antiques and mahogany, this establishment has only 10 guestrooms — 1 in the converted stable, 4 in the old carriage house, and 5 in new, but traditionally built stone cottages. The main house has 2 dining rooms (see *Eating Out*), one is the original, with its original antique dining table. There's also a pool and a tennis court. In St. Peter's, at the foot of Monkey Hill, about 3 miles north of Basseterre (phone: 465-8162; fax: 465-8275).

MODERATE

Bird Rock Beach The 40 rooms here are set in 2-story cottages on the waterfront. Each room has air conditioning, a color TV set, tile floors, and an ocean-front patio or balcony. There is a restaurant on the premises and another 5 minutes away, run by the same owner. In addition, there are 2 tennis courts and a pool with swim-up bar. Scuba gear is available for rent. Centrally located; the capital is nearby (phone: 465-8914; 800-621-1270 from the US; fax: 465-1675).

NEVIS

EXPENSIVE

Montpelier Plantation Inn Prettiest of the old estate inns, it's full of brick walkways through lovely gardens. At the center is a truly elegant old greathouse with 17 rooms. The inn raises its own lambs and chickens and turns out bountiful meals. It has its own windsurfer and a speedboat for water skiing, fishing, and snorkeling trips. There's an attractive pool and a tennis court, and transportation is provided to a private cabaña on Pinney's Beach. MAP plans offered only in winter. In the hills east of Charlestown, in St. John Figtree (phone: 469-3462; 800-255-9684 from the US; fax: 469-2932).

Nisbet Plantation Inn This establishment is on the site of an 18th-century plantation. A long alley of coconut palms runs from the manor house to the inn's white sand beach, and on either side are the 38 cottages with attractive bedrooms and small screened-in sitting areas. The manor house is where everybody congregates — in the bar, the sunny, comfortable lounge, or the antiques-filled dining room, where excellent West Indian and continental fare is served at dinner. There's a casual beachside pool and restaurant for breakfast and lunch; horseback riding, a tennis court, lawn croquet. Newcastle (phone: 469-9325; 301-321-1231 from Maryland; 800-344-2049 from elsewhere in the US; fax: 469-9864).

MODERATE

Croney's Old Manor Estate The main house and stone outbuildings of a restored 17th-century sugar plantation contain 14 spacious rooms and suites endowed with four-poster beds, high ceilings, hardwood floors, and huge windows for constant breezes. The *Cooperage* dining room (see *Eating Out*) is one of the best on the island. The swimming pool, lined with cut stone, is one of the most unusual around; it was the plantation's former cistern. Both MAP and EP rates available. In the hills east of Charlestown, in St. George Gingerland (phone: 469-3445; 800-255-9684 from the US; fax: 469-5388).

Golden Rock Estate Old plantation buildings form the core of this inn. There's enough left of the old plant to get a good idea of plantation life, and the innkeeper is more than happy to fill in the gaps. The 16 pleasant guestrooms, in cottages around the estate and in an old stone sugar estate windmill, are large and pleasant; the bamboo used to make the distinctive four-poster beds comes right off the property. Nature walks are arranged to observe monkeys living wild on the grounds. The inn has a tennis court, a swimming pool (open from *Christmas Day* through June), and beaches on leeward and windward sides, with free shuttle service for guests. Both MAP and EP rates available; the hotel sometimes gives special dinners that welcome non-guests (see *Eating Out*). In the hills east of Charlestown, in St. George Gingerland (phone: 469-3346; 800-223-9815 from the US; fax: 469-2113).

Mt. Nevis Hotel and Beach Club A spanking modern condominium hotel with 16 deluxe rooms and another 16 suites (sleeping up to 4 people), all with air conditioning, color TV sets and VCRs, plus private balconies from which to view the southern shore of St. Kitts. Units with kitchens are available. There's a freshwater pool on the property. The beach — where the hotel maintains a restaurant (the only place you'll find pizza) and water sports facilities — is a quarter mile away, but complimentary shuttle service is provided. Other features include a 110-passenger launch that ferries between Nevis and St. Kitts and is used for luncheon and sunset cruises when off duty. Newcastle (phone: 469-9373; 800-75-NEVIS from the US; fax: 469-9375).

INEXPENSIVE

Pinney's Beach A comfortable establishment in a convenient location on one of the island's nicest beaches. It's a 15-minute drive to the airport; a 7-minute walk to Charlestown. The 48 spacious, air conditioned rooms all have patios with beach or ocean views, coffee makers, and TV sets. There's a dining room, a pool, and a tennis court; fishing, sailing, and horseback riding can be arranged. Pinney's Beach (phone: 469-5207; 800-742-4276 from the US; fax: 469-1088).

EATING OUT

All kinds of dishes — from roast suckling pig, turtle stew, and crab backs to mutton stew, turtle steaks, and creole fried fish — appear on the menus of island restaurants, which cater to all tastes. Expect to pay $60 and up for two, excluding wine, drink, and tips, in the restaurants we list as expensive; between $30 and $50 at places in the moderate category; and less than $30 at inexpensive spots. All telephone numbers are in the 809 area code unless otherwise indicated.

ST. KITTS

EXPENSIVE

Georgian House This restored manor house offers intimate indoor or casual outdoor dining. The menu features Mediterranean and West Indian fare, plus fresh pasta and nightly specials. Open for lunch and dinner; dinner only Sundays; closed Mondays. Reservations advised. MasterCard and Visa accepted. South Independence Sq., Basseterre (phone: 465-4049).

Golden Lemon With an innovative menu, charming atmosphere, and grand service, this spot is a must for all island visitors. Open for breakfast, lunch and dinner daily. Dinner reservations essential. Major credit cards accepted. Dieppe Bay (phone: 465-7260).

Ocean Terrace Inn Centrally located, with a sweeping view of the harbor, the dining room here serves continental and island dishes in a tropical setting, indoors or outdoors. On Fridays, the menu alternates between a West Indian buffet and a barbecue with steaks, lobsters, and Cornish game hens; on Wednesdays and Fridays, there's steel band entertainment. Open daily for breakfast, lunch, and dinner. Dinner reservations necessary for those not staying at the hotel. Major credit cards accepted. Fortlands, Basseterre (phone: 465-2754; fax: 465-1057).

Rawlins Plantation With its panoramic view and cool country setting, this lovely dining room is where savvy Kittitian professionals entertain luncheon guests. It's located in the main house of a country estate that was built on the foundations of an old sugar works. Lunch is a West Indian buffet, dinner a fixed-price four-course meal from a set menu. Open daily for lunch and dinner. Reservations essential by noon. No credit cards accepted. Mt. Pleasant (phone: 465-6221).

White House Dine outdoors or in an exquisite room that was the original dining room of this 18th-century greathouse. The atmosphere is sophisticated. Lunch and a multi-course, fixed-price dinner are served daily, as is afternoon tea. Jackets are required for men. Reservations essential. Major credit cards accepted. St. Peter's, about 3 miles north of Basseterre (phone: 465-8162).

MODERATE

Blue Horizon Perched on the cliffs of Bird Rock, the menu here features top-flight dishes from the chef's native Austria, often featuring seafood and chicken. The late-night noshes are fantastic, as is the Sunday brunch. There's both indoor and outdoor seating, and the place stays open until the wee hours on weekends. Open daily for lunch and dinner. Reservations necessary for dinner during the winter season. American Express and Visa accepted. Bird Rock (phone: 465-5863).

J's Place In the foothills of the Brimstone Hill Fortress, it's a good spot for lunching on local fare. Open for lunch and dinner; closed Mondays. Reservations unnecessary. No credit cards accepted. Main Rd., Sandy Point (phone: 465-6264).

Lighthouse Good food, fine service, and a sophisticated atmosphere prevail. The place is air conditioned and centrally located, with panoramic views over Basseterre from the east side of town. Open for dinner only; closed Sundays and Mondays. Reservations advised. American Express and Visa accepted. Bird Rock, Basseterre (phone: 465-8914).

INEXPENSIVE

Ballahoo In the heart of Basseterre, this is a charming, cozy, upstairs eatery with tables on a balcony overlooking the hustle and bustle below. Open daily for breakfast, lunch, and dinner. Reservations unnecessary. Major credit cards accepted. On the Circus, Basseterre (phone: 465-4197).

Chef's Place West Indian dishes are served in a casual atmosphere. Open for breakfast, lunch, and dinner; closed Sundays. Reservations unnecessary. No credit cards accepted. Church St. (phone: 465-6176).

Fisherman's Wharf Seafood, plus chicken and ribs, are served at the picnic tables here. A very casual place at the water's edge, it belongs to the *Ocean Terrace Inn* and is only a short walk down from the hotel. Conch chowder is a house specialty. Open daily for dinner only. Reservations advised on Friday nights, when a steel band plays. Major credit cards accepted. Fortlands, Basseterre (phone: 465-2754).

NEVIS

While Nevis has virtually no restaurants other than inn dining rooms, this still is a place to unbuckle your belt and enjoy things culinary. Nevis grows much of its own food; consequently, the fruits and vegetables are plentiful and very fresh. The papaya you have for breakfast is likely to have come from a tree outside your door. Likewise, the fish is of the just-caught variety. Good ingredients inspire good cooking — whether at an inn or a casual beachside pub, the quality of the food here is unusually high.

Most of the inns are MAP only, which means breakfast and dinner are included in the daily rate. Most visitors will do just fine if they stay put, but those who want to sample fare at other inns may join them for lunch or for special dinners, such as *Golden Rock*'s lobster and fish special (charcoal grilled). Most of the inns host cookouts or West Indian buffets. Call and find out when and where. Don't miss the *Cooperage* at *Croney's Old Manor Estate* (phone: 469-3445). The fare there any night is likely to be memorable — green pepper soup, light and creamy cheesecake, fruit sorbets and ice creams — but the Friday night steak and lobster cookout, accompanied by a buffet of several kinds of vegetables and salads, is a real treat, as is the Sunday champagne brunch (reservations advised). In Charlestown, *Muriel's Cuisine* (Upper Happy Hill Dr.; phone: 469-5920) and *Unella's* (on the waterfront; phone: 469-5574), are local favorites. *Caribbean Confections* is good for a light snack. All three restaurants at the *Four Seasons* offer good fare, from snacks to formal dining; reservations and proper dress are advised for the excellent main dining room (phone: 469-1111). *CLA-CHA-DEL* (Shaws Rd., Newcastle; phone: 469-9640) offers the best in a "local scene" setting; the food is West Indian, with such dishes as "goat water," conch water, turtle, fish, and lobster.

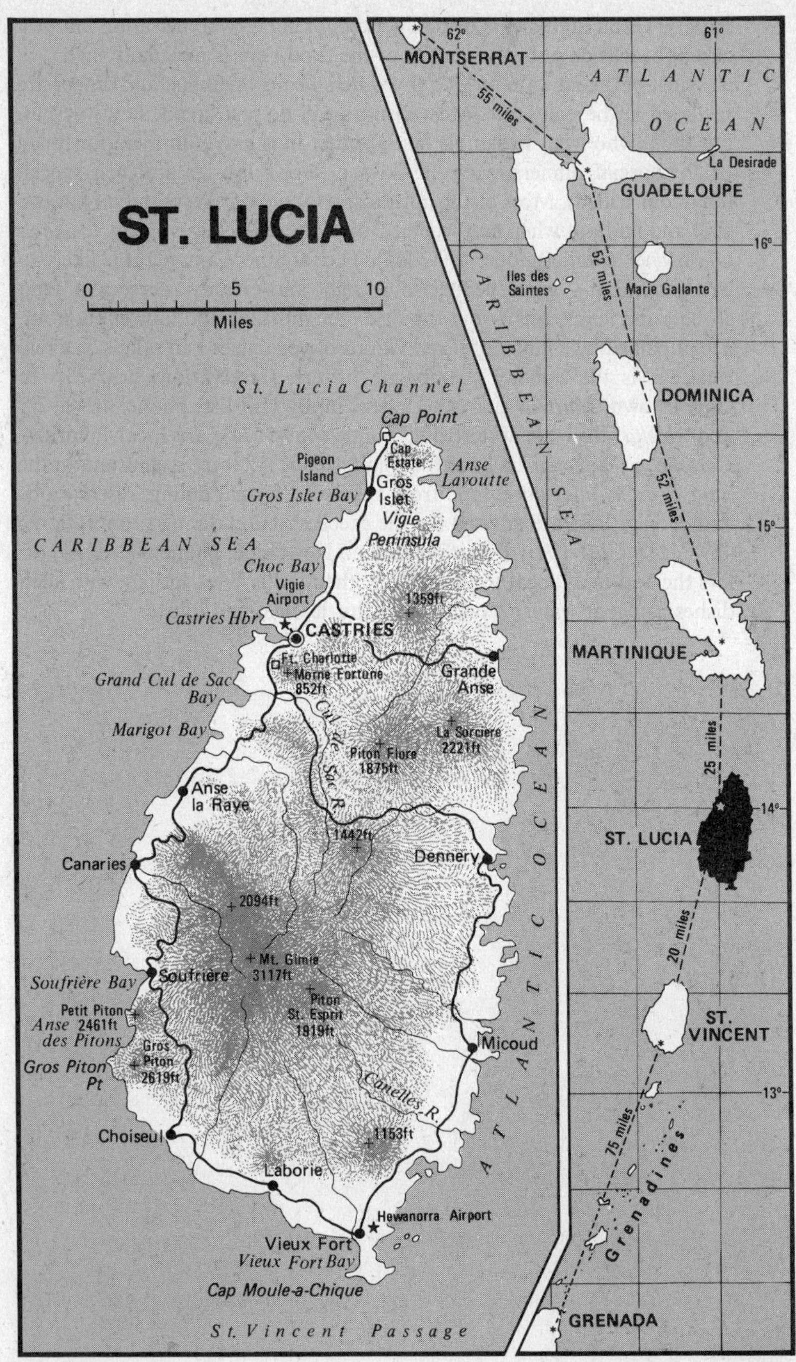

ST. LUCIA
0
5
10
Miles
St. Lucia Channel
Cap Point
Cap Estate
Pigeon Island
Anse Lavoutte
Gros Islet
Gros Islet Bay
Vigie Peninsula
CARIBBEAN SEA
Choc Bay
Vigie Airport
1359ft
Castries Hbr
CASTRIES
Ft. Charlotte
Morne Fortune 852ft
Grand Cul de Sac Bay
Grande Anse
Cul de Sac R.
Marigot Bay
La Sorciere 2221ft
Piton Flore 1875ft
Anse la Raye
1442ft
Dennery
Canaries
2094ft
Mt. Gimie 3117ft
Soufrière
Soufrière Bay
Piton St. Esprit 1919ft
Petit Piton 2461ft
Anse des Pitons
Gros Piton 2619ft
Gros Piton Pt
Micoud
Canelles R.
1153ft
Choiseul
Laborie
Hewanorra Airport
Vieux Fort
Vieux Fort Bay
Cap Moule-a-Chique
St. Vincent Passage
ATLANTIC OCEAN
62°
61°
MONTSERRAT
55 miles
ATLANTIC OCEAN
La Desirade
GUADELOUPE
16°
Iles des Saintes
52 miles
Marie Gallante
CARIBBEAN SEA
DOMINICA
52 miles
15°
MARTINIQUE
25 miles
14°
ST. LUCIA
20 miles
ST. VINCENT
13°
75 miles
Grenadines
GRENADA

St. Lucia

St. Lucia's location hints at its tempestuous past. Midway between French Martinique and British St. Vincent, the island has spent a good part of the last 300 years bouncing between Britain and France as those two countries fought over control of the West Indies.

Focusing *only* on St. Lucia's location, however, is to ignore the island's intoxicating beauty. Shaped like a fat tear sliding down the face of the Caribbean, it has some of the most magnificent shoreline in the entire island chain; remote Marigot Bay, as beautiful a sea cove as exists in the world; and inland jungles with two lushly forested mountains, the Pitons. It even has a quiescent (but still bubbling) volcano, Mt. Soufrière, where tourists can amble among smoking sulfur pits and gurgling mudholes.

The peaceful Arawak Indians apparently arrived on the island hundreds of years ago to escape the fierce Carib Indians. Remains of their villages have been found on Pigeon Island, just off St. Lucia's northern tip (today joined to St. Lucia by a causeway). Soon enough the Carib arrived on St. Lucia, however, and it was that tribe — not the Arawak — whom the Spanish found when they discovered the island. (Just when that was is open to debate. The island celebrates December 13, 1502, as its discovery day; but the French have a counterclaim based on a colony of shipwrecked French sailors who found their way to the island at about the same time.)

During the next 200 years, the island changed hands between the French and the English more than ten times. During the French Revolution, the British took possession of the small island but, finding that French republican terrorists made it too difficult to control, abandoned it. In May 1706, a force of 12,000 British troops retook St. Lucia. The Treaty of Amiens, in March 1802, awarded St. Lucia to the French, but a year later the two countries were at war again, and an invading English force stormed the fortifications on Morne Fortune with fixed bayonets and recaptured the island.

The island remained under British control until 1967, when St. Lucia became a self-governing state in association with Great Britain; on February 22, 1979, it was granted full sovereignty and became a full-fledged member of the British Commonwealth.

But what draws visitors from all over the world is not this active and colorful history, but rather the remarkable beauty of the island. St. Lucia is endowed with stands of towering bamboo trees, and tropical rain forests filled with giant ferns, colorful parrots, and hummingbirds; it also offers the drama of the open-pit volcano of Mt. Soufrière and the solitude of Marigot Bay and Anse Chastanet.

St. Lucia is now undergoing the development it missed during its violent earlier years. The growth of tourist facilities and immigration are proceeding at a controlled rate, and there has been some industrial expansion to support the new economy. And the island received international attention in late 1992, when native poet and playwright Derek Walcott was awarded the Nobel Prize for Literature. Yet, in spite of "progress," St. Lucia retains a unique sense of simplicity and pride that have earned it its deserved reputation as one of the "still unspoiled" islands surviving in the Caribbean today.

St. Lucia At-a-Glance

FROM THE AIR

St. Lucia is shaped almost like a leaf, the stem at its base being the peninsula of Moule-à-Chique. Its Barre de l'Isle ridge of mountains divides the island horizontally, with a network of rivers carrying water down the slopes, like the veins of a leaf. The island's mountainous terrain is softened in appearance by a gentle covering of tropical trees and flowering plants. The highest peak is Mt. Gimie, 3,145 feet, but more prominent are the twin half-mile-tall volcanic cones called the Pitons. To the left, Petit Piton stands straight up from the Caribbean to a height of 2,460 feet; on the right, Gros Piton rises to 2,619 feet. In between is Jalousie Bay and the stretch of land known as Anse des Pitons.

St. Lucia is 25 miles south of Martinique and 20 miles north of St. Vincent. From New York it is about 2,020 miles to St. Lucia.

SPECIAL PLACES

CASTRIES This is the island's capital, with its major port, a natural harbor. Its architecture is basically bland and modern, the result of severe fires in 1948 and 1951 that swept through the older buildings. Still, it's a lively West Indian town. The morning market is very active, especially on Saturdays. It fills up with small farmers and home industry workers, and everybody is selling or bartering. Fresh fish, plantain, mango, and paw paw (papaya) are among the foodstuffs traded and sold here.

Just behind the city rises Morne Fortune, from whose heights the French and the British alternately defended the island and its port and whose slopes they in turn charged in hopes of final victory. At the crest of the hill stands Fort Charlotte, an 18th-century fortress that changed hands about a dozen times during the years of English-French colonial warfare. The stone buildings of the French occupation forces contrast with those of the British, who built their structures of brick. Constant change of ownership resulted in a hodgepodge of materials and styles, and many buildings started by one side were completed or repaired by the other. But even more attractive to visitors than Morne Fortune's history is the view from its peak — north to Pigeon Island, south to the Pitons, and a panorama of the harbor at Castries and of the Vigie Peninsula. Vigie itself was the site of two major battles — both of them victories for the British.

ELSEWHERE ON THE ISLAND

PIGEON POINT North of Castries, off the west coast, this was formerly a separate island, but now is linked by a causeway to the town of Gros Islet. The ruins of Rodney Fort are here, and it was from this island that the fleet commanded by British admiral George Rodney sailed to intercept the French in the Dominica Passage, resulting in the Battle of the Saintes. The fort has been designated as a historic site. (The island, by the way, gets its name from Rodney's hobby of breeding pigeons.) Guided tours of the island are available, or you may explore on your own. A small museum (open daily) displays exhibits on the area's history; admission charge. A short distance north of Pigeon Point, at the very tip of St. Lucia, is Cap Estate, the site of a land development. On a clear day, it is possible to see Martinique from the gentle hills of the Cap area. On the island is *Les Pigeon,* a casual restaurant serving good food.

MARIGOT BAY On the west coast, south of Castries, is a yachtsman's haven. Most of the palm-lined shore remains primitive, but some sections are being developed with shops. It is still one of the most beautiful coves in the entire Caribbean. Just a few miles south along the coast is the little fishing village of Anse La Raye, where fishermen repair their nets and gut their catch on the beach and workmen still build canoes in much the same manner as Carib warriors 400 years ago. A little farther south, just below the midpoint of the island, the village of Canaries lies where one of the island's many rivers meets the sea. Here native women can be seen washing their clothing in the river.

Just inland from Marigot Bay itself are two large banana plantations. Cul-de-Sac is slightly north of the bay, the Roseau Estate just to the south. Visitors are welcome at both plantations; no appointment is needed. Two other working plantations on the island, Marquis Plantation, on the northeast, and Errard Plantation, in the south, offer tours. Nutmeg, sugarcane, coffee, and citrus fruits are grown at both plantations. For tour information, contact the *St. Lucia Representative Service* (phone: 452-3762) or your hotel's tour desk.

SOUFRIÈRE On the west coast of the island, about a third of the way from the southern tip, is the village of Soufrière, St. Lucia's second-largest community. From here, too, fishermen still put out to sea in the same kind of narrow dugout canoe used in this area for generations, and cast with homemade nets. Beyond the town, past the hill of green vines and trees that helped to hide the town from attackers, the Pitons stand over half a mile high, stretching from the shore of the Caribbean. The remains of the island's once-active volcanoes, they are formed from lava and rock, coated with fertile volcanic topsoil and tropical forest.

MT. SOUFRIÈRE The dormant volcano near Soufrière is a rocky moonscape of pits and open craters of boiling sulfur, bubbling grayish-yellow mud. A walk through the area, with its clouds of sulfur-reeking mist and intense earth-born heat, is like a visit to Dante's *Inferno.* Here are also some natural, spring-fed pools of heated waters containing traces of sulfur and other minerals. A sample sent to King Louis XVI was found to have a mineral content similar to the waters at the baths of Aix-la-Chapelle. The natural baths at neighboring Diamond Falls are cooler and sweeter smelling. The privately owned Diamond Mineral Baths (phone: 459-7250) are located on the Soufrière Estate; visitors can bathe in the waters from natural springs (admission charge).

MOULE-À-CHIQUE From this mountain peak you can see the Caribbean's distinct blue-green waters as they mix with the Atlantic's very different blue, or look southward, slightly west, toward the nearby island of St. Vincent.

FRIGATE ISLAND A rocky offshore spur off the east coast of St. Lucia, it is home to the rare frigate bird (called "scisseau" or "scissors" by islanders). The area, until recently almost inaccessible from the mainland, is one of the few remaining places the bird can be observed nesting and roosting. The St. Lucia National Trust now manages the island and arranges tours (phone: 452-1654 or 452-5005; ask for Barbara Jacobs).

Sources and Resources

TOURIST INFORMATION

On St. Lucia, the tourist board office is at Pointe Seraphine (Box 221, Castries, St. Lucia; phone: 453-0053, 452-4094, or 452-5968; fax: 453-1121). There are also visitor information centers at Vigie and Hewanorra airports, and on Bay Street in Soufrière. All the offices can provide brochures and maps (most are free). Hotels also provide information for tourists. For information about St. Lucia tourist offices in the US, see GETTING READY TO GO.

LOCAL COVERAGE There are three local daily papers — the *Crusader,* the *Voice of St. Lucia,* and the *Star;* regionally, *Caribbean Week* is of interest; *The New York Times* is also available, usually 2 days late.

RADIO AND TELEVISION

Radio St. Lucia and Radio Caribbean International broadcast local and regional programming, and TV stations HTS and DBS carry local as well as some US programs.

TELEPHONE

When calling from the US, dial 809 (area code) + (local number). To call from another Caribbean island, the code may vary, so call the local operator. When dialing on St. Lucia, use only the local number unless otherwise indicated.

ENTRY REQUIREMENTS

US and Canadian citizens need only a passport or proof of citizenship (birth certificate or voter's registration card, plus photo ID), and a return or ongoing ticket. There is an airport departure tax of about $10.

CLIMATE AND CLOTHES

In winter, temperatures range between 65 and 85F (19 to 30C); in summer, between 75 and 95F (24 to 35C). Summers tend to be a little rainy, but winters are dry. Summer clothing is worn all year; cottons are prevalent. Casual resortwear is fine for both men and women during the day, although shorts and bathing suits should not be worn into town. In the evening, women wear dresses, or dressy pants or skirts and tops; for men, jackets and occasionally ties are required only at the larger hotels and a few restaurants during the winter season.

MONEY

St. Lucia uses the Eastern Caribbean dollar, which is valued at the rate of $1 US to about $2.68 EC ($2.50 EC in hotels and stores). In general, banking hours are from 8 AM to 3 PM Mondays through Thursdays; on Fridays 8 AM to 5 PM. Banks are closed on Sundays and holidays. US and Canadian dollars are accepted by stores, restaurants, and hotels, as are traveler's checks and most major credit cards (check when making reservations for meals or accommodations). All prices in this chapter are quoted in US dollars.

LANGUAGE

English is the official tongue of St. Lucia, and it is spoken by almost all the inhabitants. A French-creole patois, similar to that of Guadeloupe and Martinique, is also spoken.

TIME

St. Lucia is on atlantic standard time all year: When it's noon in New York, it's 1 PM in St. Lucia. During daylight saving time, it is the same time in both places.

CURRENT

Electricity is 220–230 volts, 50 cycles, AC. Most hotels have provisions for electric shavers; however, converters are needed for hair dryers and other small appliances.

TIPPING

A 10% service charge is included on hotel bills; it covers room maids and so on. There also is an 8% government tax added to the bill. Extra tipping is called for only if some special service is rendered. Restaurants add a 10% service charge to the check; it covers the waiter's tip. Cab drivers should be tipped about 10% of the fare. Airport porters depend on tips for a substantial portion of their income; tip 50¢ per bag, with a $1 minimum.

GETTING AROUND

CAR RENTAL Costs run about $60 to $70 per day, plus mileage (the first 30 to 50 miles are usually free). Rates drop slightly during the off-season (April 15 through December 15). Agencies with desks at the airport for pickup and drop-off include *Avis* (phone: 452-2700 or 452-2202; fax: 453-1536), *National* (phone: 450-8721; fax: 450-8577), and *Dollar* (phone: 452-0994; fax: 452-0102). Other agencies are located elsewhere, but most offer free drop-off and pickup. Check *Hertz* (phone: 452-0742), *St. Lucia Yacht Service Car Rentals* (phone: 452-5057), *Budget* (phone: 452-0233), or *CTL Rent-A-Car* (phone: 452-0732). Several agencies also have desks at resorts. All take MasterCard; a few accept other credit cards. An international or St. Lucia driver's license is required. Those with international licenses must have them endorsed; most car rental agencies will do it (there's no charge). If you don't have an international license, a St. Lucia license can be obtained through most rental agencies on the island for about $14; you must present a valid US, Canadian, or UK license.

SEA EXCURSIONS Most popular is the daylong sail to the Pitons with a shore trip to Soufrière's Sulphur Springs. Lunch, drinks, swim and snorkeling stop, plus steel band music en route are included for about $75 per person. The square-rigged brig *Unicorn* (phone: 452-8232) sails twice a week. *Motor Vessel Vigie* (phone: 452-2333), *Endless Summer* (phone: 452-3762), and *Surf Queen* (phone: 452-8351) also offer day sails from Castries. Tour operators also book sea excursions.

SIGHTSEEING TOURS There are tours to suit almost any desire: all-inclusive day trips to other islands (Martinique, about $185; Grenadine Islands, about $210), half- or full-day island tours, land and sea excursions, rain forest walks, and shopping tours. For details, contact *Barnard's Travel* (phone: 452-2214; fax: 453-1394), *St. Lucia Representative Service* (phone: 452-3762), or *Sunlink International* (phone: 452-8232; fax: 452-0459). A complete list of other tour operators is available from the tourist office. The travel desk at any hotel also can help with arrangements for excursions.

TAXI Unmetered rates are fixed by the government and the Taxi Association. A list of point-to-point fares is available from the tourist office. However, rates may vary from driver to driver, so confirm them in advance and also establish whether the fare is in US or EC dollars. Some sample fares: Vigie Airport to the *Sandals St. Lucia* resort, about $8; to the main shopping center, about $6; from Hewanorra Airport, the island's international airport, to the hotels in the Castries area (an hour's drive), about $60 for up to four people.

INTER-ISLAND FLIGHTS

American Eagle flies between St. Lucia and San Juan, Puerto Rico. For connections to other islands, small plane charters can be arranged with *Air Martinique* (phone: 452-2463), *Eagle Air* (phone: 452-1900), and *Helenair* (phone: 452-7196; fax: 452-7112). *St. Lucia Helicopters, Ltd.* (phone: 453-6950) charters helicopters.

SPECIAL EVENTS

On *New Year's Day* and January 2, a festival in Vigie Field is part of the traditional French celebration of *Le Jour de l'An;* there are dances, picnics, and partying throughout the island as well. *Carnival,* usually in late February, is the year's big festival, with the crowning of a Carnival Queen, dancing, costumed parades, steel band music, and calypso singing. The *St. Lucia Jazz Festival,* with performances by such internationally acclaimed musicians as Wynton Marsalis, Vanessa Rubin, McCoy Tyner, and the *Kenny Barron Trio,* is held in mid-May. Other holidays when most stores and businesses close are *Independence* (February 22), *Good Friday, Easter Monday, Labor Day* (May 1), *Whitsuntide* (late May or early June), *Corpus Christi, Emancipation Day* (first Monday in August), *Thanksgiving Day* (first Monday in October), *National Day* (December 13), *Christmas,* and *Boxing Day* (December 26).

SHOPPING

Castries's big department stores are *J. Q. Charles, Ltd.* (on Bridge St.), and *Cox's* (on Wm. Peter Blvd.) — both are worth browsing. The outdoor market on Jeremie Street sells fresh produce, and also has a wide array of handmade goods such as pottery and small straw baskets filled with local spices and herbs (nutmeg, cinnamon, and bay leaves). The entire area is undergoing a major face-lift, and improved facilities are being added.

Pointe Seraphine offers duty-free and late-evening shopping for the convenience of cruise ship passengers.

ARTSIBITS GALLERY Features paintings, pottery, and woodcarvings, all by the finest local artists. On the corner of Brazil and Mongiraud Sts., Castries (phone: 452-7865).

BAGSHAWS STUDIOS A must stop for unique hand-screened fabrics and fashions. La Toc Rd., Castries with branches at Pointe Seraphine and Marigot Bay (phone: 452-2139).

CARIBELLE BATIK A fine fabric emporium with a selection of island prints. Old Victoria Rd., Castries (phone: 452-3785).

CHOISEUL ARTS AND CRAFTS Locally crafted baskets, woodwork, and straw articles such as hats and placemats. In the LaFargue area of Choiseul (phone: 459-3226).

NOAH'S ARKADE The place to shop for high-quality West Indian gift items. Three locations: Bridge St., Castries (phone: 452-2523); Rodney Bay (phone: 452-8831); and Soufrière (phone: 454-7514).

PHILATELIC BUREAU Colorful island stamps. At Point Seraphine (phone: 452-7894).

WINDJAMMER CLOTHING COMPANY Tropical clothing for men, women, and children. Vigie Cove (phone: 452-1041).

SPORTS

BOATING St. Lucia, with excellent anchorages at Marigot Bay and Rodney Bay and in Castries Harbour, is rapidly growing in popularity with yachtsmen. In 1992, the *Atlantic Rally for Cruisers* (*ARC*), the largest annual transoceanic sailing rally in the world, selected St. Lucia as its finishing point for over 150 yachts. Yachts start arriving in November and continue to show up through the end of December. For information, contact the St. Lucia Tourist Board in London (phone: 71-937-1969; fax: 71-937-3611). Most hotels have Sunfish and windsurfers for loan or rent (rates about $8 to $12 per hour). Yachts can be chartered through *Sunsail* (Rodney Bay; phone: 452-8648; fax: 452-0839; US address: 3347 NW 55th St., Ft. Lauderdale, FL 33309; phone: 305-484-5246 or 800-327-2276 in the US; fax: 305-485-5072) the *Moorings* (Marigot Bay; phone: 451-4357; fax: 451-4353; US address: 1305 US 19S, Suite 402, Clearwater, FL 33346; phone: 800-334-2435 in the US; fax: 813-530-9747); and *Trade Wind Yacht Charters* (Rodney Bay; phone: 452-8424; fax: 452-8442; US address: 1186 Cot Circle, Gloucester, VA 23061; phone: 804-694-0881 or 800-825-7245 in the US; fax: 804-693-7245). Rates depend on the craft and the season and on whether the boats are crewed or you sail them yourself. The companies listed above also have yachts that can be chartered, with or without a skipper, to sail to the nearby Grenadine Islands.

GOLF *Cap Estate* (phone: 450-8523), at the northern tip of the island, has a 9-hole course, though it is not very challenging; the greens fee is about $20. The course also rents clubs for about $8 per day and pull carts for about $3; caddies get about $5.

HIKING Organized hiking is limited, but there are trails all over the island, and the Pitons are a time-honored climbers' challenge. Petit Piton (Little Piton) has been officially closed until 1996 due to a fire caused by climbers that greatly damaged the area, but Gros Piton (Big Piton) is still open to hikers. The St. Lucia National Trust (phone: 452-5005) and the Forestry Division (phone: 452-3231) have developed several nature walks, as well as more advanced climbs, and can provide details and arrange guides for a small fee. None of the island's peaks should be attempted without a guide, because of frequent — and sudden — mists and rains.

HORSEBACK RIDING *Trim Stables* (phone: 450-8273) offers all levels of riding from Cap Estate and Cas-En-Bas. Also try *North Point Riding Stables* in Cap Estate (phone: 450-8853). Rides lasting 1¼ hours are about $25; transportation from your hotel is included. Horse-and-buggy rides are also available.

SNORKELING AND SCUBA St. Lucia's reefs are beautiful to explore, and the Anse Chastanet area — where there's good diving right off the beach — is the most popular. For snorkeling and scuba equipment, reef and wreck trips, and instruction, contact *Scuba St. Lucia* at the *Anse Chastanet Beach* hotel (phone: 459-7000; fax: 459-7700) or at the *St. Lucian* (phone: 452-8009); the *Moorings Scuba Centre* at Marigot Bay (phone: 451-4357); *Dolphin Divers* at Rodney Bay (phone: 452-9922; fax: 452-8524); or *Buddies Scuba* at Vigie Marina (phone/fax: 452-5288). *Couples* resort (phone: 452-4211; fax: 452-7419) offers guests a resort package price that includes unlimited diving. *Windjammer Diving,* a *PADI* dive shop (located at the Windjammer Landing at Brelotte Bay; phone: 452-1311; fax: 452-0907), also offers diving instruction and excursions. Snorkeling equipment rents for about $4; the going rate for a snorkeling trip is about $25. Chances are, however, that your hotel will provide snorkeling gear gratis. A one-tank dive costs between $45 and $60; a 3-hour introductory course, including a shallow-water dive, $75; a full certification course, about $400.

SPECTATOR SPORTS The cricket season runs from January through June. Football — we call it soccer — is played from July through January. Both sports are played at sites throughout the island.

SPORT FISHING Game fish in these waters include barracuda, mackerel, kingfish, tuna, wahoo, swordfish, sailfish, and cavalla. Fishing charters, fully equipped with fighting chairs, run about $260 and up for a half day, and $520 and up for a full day, for a party of six. If your hotel doesn't have boats of its own, it can make the arrangements for you. Or contact *Barnard's Travel* (phone: 452-1615) or *Captain Mike* (phone: 452-7044).

SQUASH Courts are available at *Club St. Lucia,* the *St. Lucia Yacht Club* (phone: 452-8350), and *Cap Estate* (phone: 450-8523).

SWIMMING Beautiful white beaches edge the calm, leeward side of the island. These are the best swimming beaches; the eastern, windward side is rugged and often has rough surf that makes swimming unsafe and sometimes simply impossible. Outstanding beaches include Vigie Beach, just north of Castries Harbor; Choc Bay, in the same area; Reduit Bay, well north along the coast from Castries; and Pigeon Island off the northern shore. To the south of the island are La Toc Bay, the black volcanic sand beach at Soufrière, and the reef-protected beaches of the Vieux Fort area. Most St. Lucia hotels are on a beach.

TENNIS *Club St. Lucia* has 7 lighted courts and offers temporary memberships at its tennis club. *Windjammer Landing* has 2 lighted courts. The *St. Lucian,* with 2 courts, also has a pro. Most hotels have at least 1 court or will arrange for guests to play at a nearby resort.

WATER SKIING Most hotels have the equipment available, or will make arrangements for guests.

WINDSURFING The *St. Lucian,* the local affiliate of Windsurfing International, a Mistral school, offers a certification course of three 1-hour lessons for $45. Most beach hotels will rent windsurfers to non-guests for about $15 an hour.

NIGHTLIFE

Most of the island's nightlife is confined to the hotels; they have entertainment on a regular basis during the season and sometimes during the off-season. Friday night is "jump-up" (party) night and everyone at the north end of the island heads for Gros Islet for a big street party. A steel band usually performs, while residents and visitors dance together in the street. At Marigot Bay they head for *Hurricane Hole* (phone: 451-4357). *Rain* (Columbus Sq., Castries; phone: 452-3022) stays open late some evenings; the *"A" Pub* at Rodney Bay features *karaoke* nightly (phone: 452-8725); and there are shows and live entertainment several times a week at the *Green Parrot* (Red Tape La., Morne Fortune; phone: 452-3399). Other popular nightspots include *The Lime* at Rodney Bay (phone: 452-0761); *Fisherman's Wharf Disco* at the *Sandals Halcyon,* with live music and disco on a covered jetty over the water; and *Splash,* the disco at the *St. Lucian.*

Best on the Island

CHECKING IN

St. Lucia offers two types of accommodations: relatively expensive luxury hotels (including several all-inclusive properties) and less costly "self-catering" setups in apartment or villa complexes. Most places offer Modified American Plan (MAP) arrangements, which add between $50 and $60 per person to the daily room rate. In winter, two people should expect to pay from $260 up to $600 a day, excluding meals, at the places we list as very expensive; $200 to $260 at establishments in the expensive category; $130 to $200 at places we call moderate; and under $130 at places listed as inexpensive. Rates drop 30% to 50% during the summer season. Many hotels will add a 10% service charge to these rates, and there is an 8% government tax. When calling on St. Lucia, use only the local numbers listed below. For information about dialing from elsewhere, see "Telephone" earlier in this chapter.

For an unforgettable island experience, we begin with our favorite, followed by our recommendations of cost and quality choices of accommodations, listed by area and price category.

A SPECIAL HAVEN

Anse Chastanet Beach One of the great small island retreats, it's not really a hotel in the usual sense but a cluster of octagonal cottages perched on cool green hillsides above the Caribbean. Most of the 25 hillside rooms have wraparound views of St. Lucia's twin trademark mountains — the jolly green Pitons — their lush valley, and the sun-glinted sea beyond; there are also 23 beachside units. The view is beautiful and so is the privacy — ideal for reading, writing, loving, sleeping, or just watching the bougainvillea ruffle in the breeze. When you're ready, the beach is down 125 steps, a trip you aren't likely to make more than once a day. Happily, the fine gray sands below are equipped with a life-sustaining snack bar, chaises, Sunfish, and snorkel and dive gear. At the end of the day, to reward your upward climb, the main building (another stack of octagons) offers a congenial bar, good company, and food to match. Soufrière, a truly unspoiled West Indian town, is only a short drive away. Soufrière (phone: 459-7000; 800-223-1108 from the US; fax: 459-7097 or 914-763-5362 from the US).

CASTRIES AND NORTH

VERY EXPENSIVE

Royal St. Lucia A luxury resort, located on Reduit Beach, with 98 suites (some with their own swimming pools), complete water sports facilities, a swimming pool, restaurant, and nightly entertainment. Reduit Beach (phone: 452-9999; 800-225-5859 from the US; fax: 452-9639).

Le Sport Facing the sea on Anse de Cap Beach, at the northernmost tip of the island, is this 102-room all-inclusive property which recently has completed an extensive renovation. An active beach vacation is combined with "thalassotherapy" (seawater massages, jet baths, toning) and a healthy diet, *"cuisine légère."* Cariblue Beach (phone: 450-8551; 800-544-2883 from the US; fax: 450-0368).

Windjammer Landing Here are 211 rooms, each with a fully equipped kitchenette, living room, balcony, and plunge pool. There's also *Jammer's* bar and grill, a pool, tennis courts, a bar on the beach, and facilities for most water sports. Labrelotte Bay, Castries (phone: 452-1311; 800-243-1166 from the US; fax: 452-9454).

EXPENSIVE

Club St. Lucia This 312-bungalow, all-inclusive resort has a panoramic view of the curved bay, plus a free-form pool and casual bar. There also are 7 lighted tennis courts, 1 squash court, a gym, and a children's mini-club; all water sports, except scuba diving, are available. Castries (phone: 450-0551; 800-223-1588 from the US; fax: 450-0281).

Rendezvous Formerly *Couples St. Lucia,* this resort is now under the same management as *Le Sport* (above). Couples only (defined as "any two mutually interested people"); no singles, no children. Everything is included: meals and drinks, all sports (including unlimited scuba diving) and instruction, 2-day excursions, nightly entertainment, even cigarettes. This 100-room resort sits on Malabar Beach, among lushly landscaped grounds. Accommodations are in beachside cottages or in the hotel section, all with plenty of water to gaze at. Recent additions and renovations include a pool with a swim-up bar and 2 dining rooms. Malabar Beach (phone: 452-4211; 800-544-2883 from the US; fax: 452-7419).

St. Lucian There are 222 rooms in pastel-colored buildings along Reduit Beach; facilities include a pool, tennis courts, and equipment for all water sports (which, except for diving, are included in the room rate). There's also *Flamingo,* a fine restaurant specializing in dolphin fish (see *Eating Out*), and evening entertainment at *Splash,* the hotel's disco. Reduit Beach (phone: 452-8351; fax: 452-8331).

Wyndham Morgan Bay Located on a 3½-acre nature preserve, this recently opened property features 240 rooms decorated with floral pastels and wicker, 2 restaurants, and a lounge. The all-inclusive price includes meals and beverages (except champagne), airport transfers, choice of 25 sports activities, and 2 island sightseeing trips. Five miles from Castries (phone: 453-2511; fax: 453-6214).

MODERATE

Harmony Apartel Family-run, family-welcoming cluster of 21 two-bedroom apartments, each with living/dining room, 1 or 2 baths, kitchen, and a sizable balcony; air conditioning is optional. There's a freshwater pool and a restaurant. On Rodney Bay Lagoon (phone: 452-0336; fax: 452-8677).

Sandals Halcyon On Choc Bay and recently acquired by the Sandals chain of all-inclusive resorts, it has 180 air conditioned, cabaña-style rooms with patios, most with ocean or garden views; there also are 2 pools, 2 tennis courts, full water sports facilities, and a children's playground. Dining is at a popular casual wharfside eatery and a more formal à la carte restaurant. The wharfside disco has shows Mondays, Wednesdays, and Fridays. Three miles from Castries (phone: 452-5331; 800-SANDALS from the US; fax: 452-5434).

INEXPENSIVE

Bois d'Orange Small colony of 8 one- and 3 two-bedroom, air conditioned cottages with living rooms and kitchenettes — all immaculately kept — overlooking the island's northern tip and Reduit Bay. The view is spectacular. There's a pool, and once-a-day transport to Reduit Beach. The restaurant features local dishes. Castries (phone: 452-8213; fax: 452-4115).

SOUTH OF CASTRIES

VERY EXPENSIVE

Jalousie Plantation One of St. Lucia's newer resorts, this 115-room property (including suites and 1- and 2-bedroom cottages) is located near Soufrière between the beautiful Pitons. The all-inclusive rate really does include everything — meals, drinks, sports facilities, even cigarettes! Amenities include 3 good restaurants and a fully equipped spa. Near Soufrière (phone: 459-7666; 800-877-3643 from the US; fax: 459-7667).

EXPENSIVE

Club Med Set on 90 acres on the southern tip of the island, this property has 256 rooms, and a well-equipped sports facility with 8 tennis courts, horseback riding, volleyball, soccer, archery, basketball, softball, and a workout center — all for the free use of guests. Its sailing center has 2 large boats for up to 24 people. There's also a circus school and "Mini-Club" for children. All rooms are air conditioned with a view of the sea. On Savannes Bay, just 5 minutes from Hewanorra Airport (phone: 454-6546; 800-CLUB-MED from the US; fax: 454-6017).

Ladera This resort (formerly the *Dashene Villas*) is composed of 7 West Indian-style villas and 9 suites sandwiched between Gros Piton and Petit Piton on the western shore of the island. The villas are like luxurious tree houses — each is furnished with antiques and has an open verandah with an exceptional sea view. Each unit has 2 or 3 bedrooms, 2 baths, a full kitchen, and a spacious living room; a maid, cook, laundress, and gardener take care of your needs. Some units have a private swimming pool with a Jacuzzi. Between Gros and Petit Piton (phone: 459-7323 or 800-841-4145; fax: 459-5156).

Marigot Bay Situated along one of the Caribbean's most beautiful anchorages, this complex has an inn, villas, and a hotel, plus boutiques, restaurants and bars, a full water sports center, and yacht berths. The 32 one-, two-, and three-bedroom villas have full kitchens; the open-air, casual, West Indian–style inn has guestrooms with kitchenettes and balconies overlooking the yacht basin. The more rustic *Hurricane Hole,* the resort's hotel, is the only one in the area with a pool. On Marigot Bay, 9 miles from Castries (phone: 451-4357; 800-334-2435 from the US; fax: 451-4353).

Sandals St. Lucia Formerly the *Cunard La Toc* and *La Toc Suites,* it's now part of the Sandals chain of all-inclusive, couples-only resorts. At press time, an extensive renovation was under way, including refurbishing the 255 rooms and suites, enlarging the pool and health club, and adding a swim-up bar and 3 dining rooms. Three miles from Castries (phone: 305-284-1300 from Florida; 800-SANDALS from elsewhere in the US; fax: 305-284-1336).

EATING OUT

American, Chinese, and European dishes are all available on St. Lucia, but island specialties are really excellent. Be sure to try the fresh produce and distinctive island dishes: callaloo soup, stuffed breadfruit, banana bread, fried plantain, pumpkin soup, fried flying fish, crab backs stuffed with spiced crab and lobster meat, and baked lobster. Those places where dinner for two, with tip and drinks, can be expected to cost $80 and over are considered expensive; restaurants in which dinners fall into the $55 to $80 range are listed as moderate; and establishments where dinner for two can be had for less than $55 are listed as inexpensive. When calling on St. Lucia, use only the local numbers listed below. For information about dialing from elsewhere, see "Telephone" earlier in this chapter.

CASTRIES

EXPENSIVE

Bon Appétit This tiny, charming eatery is perched on top of Morne Fortune, offering diners a spectacular view over Castries and the harbor, Pigeon Island, and Martinique beyond. Specialties include rib steaks, lamb shanks, and shrimp creole. Open daily for lunch and dinner. Reservations advised. Major credit cards accepted. Red Tape La., Morne Fortune (phone: 452-2757).

Green Parrot Trained at *Claridge's* in London, this spot's St. Lucia–born owner and chef is an inventive interpreter of French and creole dishes, with a distinctly English bent. Try soup *oh-la-la,* a spicy pumpkin mixture that earned its sobriquet from a French patron's instant appreciation; the mixed grill; or the steaks. On Morne Fortune with fabulous views of Castries, this is a fun spot, popular with visitors and locals. A live show is presented on Mondays and Wednesdays; Friday is jazz night. Monday night is also Ladies' Night; if a woman wears a flower in her hair and is accompanied by a man wearing a jacket and tie, her meal is on the house. Open daily for lunch and dinner. Reservations advised. Major credit cards accepted. Red Tape La., Morne Fortune (phone: 452-3399).

Rain A green-and-white building, with decor inspired by the sultry old movie *Rain,* is in true Somerset Maugham–South Seas style from its tin roof on down. Specialties include powerful rum drinks, salads, and local dishes done with real flair, including the Champagne Banquet, a 7-course dinner featuring red snapper mousse and pepper pot. Best "meet me at" place in town. Open daily for lunch and dinner. Reservations advised. Major credit cards accepted. Columbus Sq. (phone: 452-3022).

San Antoine Overlooking Castries harbor, one of St. Lucia's most elegant dining spots serves fine continental fare in a century-old building rebuilt after a fire in 1970. Specialties include filet mignon stuffed with crayfish, and breast of chicken in puff pastry with spinach. Open for lunch and dinner; dinner only on Sundays. Reservations advised. Major credit cards accepted. On the Morne (phone: 452-4660).

MODERATE

Jimmie's At Vigie Cove Marina, it has a superb view of the harbor. Local fare is served; fish, octopus, and *lambi* (conch) dishes usually are available. Open for lunch and dinner; no lunch on Sundays. Reservations advised. Major credit cards accepted. Vigie Cove Marina (phone: 452-5142).

SOUFRIÈRE

EXPENSIVE

Hummingbird A lovely place for a lingering lunch featuring a glorious Piton view, a pool to cool off in, and a creole menu with lobster, shrimp, and fish prepared lots of ways. But the real treat is freshwater crayfish in lime or garlic butter (when available). Open daily for lunch and dinner. Reservations advised. MasterCard and Visa accepted. Soufrière (phone: 459-7232).

MODERATE

The Still An old rum distillery, now an excellent eatery. Much of what is served is grown or produced on the owners' plantation. The creole buffet at lunch is a real treat. Dinner is a relaxed affair, with lots of island favorites on the menu. Open daily for lunch and dinner. Reservations advised. Major credit cards accepted. On the south end of the island between the Pitons (phone: 459-7224).

NORTH

EXPENSIVE

Capone's Southern Italian dishes are featured here; there's also pizza, and a complete ice cream parlor for dessert choices. The interior decor combines a Jazz Age 1920s motif with Art Deco touches from the 1930s. Open for lunch and dinner; closed Mondays. Reservations advised. Major credit cards accepted. Rodney Bay (phone: 452-0284).

Charthouse Wood paneled, full of plants, and open to the breezes from the yacht harbor it overlooks, this is a handsome steak and lobster house. Open daily for happy hour and dinner. Reservations necessary. Major credit cards accepted. Rodney Bay (phone: 452-8115).

Flamingo Specialties in this hotel dining room include crab callaloo soup and poached egg *soufrière* (poached egg topped with spinach). Open daily for dinner. Reservations advised. Major credit cards accepted. At the *St. Lucian* hotel (phone: 452-8351, ext. 403).

Mortar & Pestle On the waterfront, with a wonderful variety of Caribbean specialties: *ackee* (a fruit) and salt fish from Jamaica, flying fish from Barbados, Guyana pepper pot, and stuffed jack fish from Grenada. Open daily for lunch and dinner. Reservations necessary, well in advance. Major credit cards accepted. Rodney Bay (phone: 452-8756).

MODERATE

"A" Pub Another dining spot on Rodney Bay, facing the waterfront, it has a friendly pub atmosphere, with a local following and happy hour every evening. Selections include local *rôti* (pastry stuffed with a stew-like filling of chicken, vegetable, or beef) and Mexican dishes. Open daily; dinner only on Sundays. Reservations unnecessary. American Express and Visa accepted. Rodney Bay (phone: 452-8725).

Banana Split Sitting right on the beach in the town of Gros Islet, it's open-air and casual, the kind of place to linger over a long lunch. The menu offers creole dishes, West Indian curries, conch, plain boiled lobster, grilled steaks, and — what else? — banana splits. Go on Friday night, when the whole town is something like a carnival and the restaurant stays open until the band packs up. Open daily for lunch and dinner. Reservations advised. No credit cards accepted. Gros Islet (phone: 452-8125).

Lime A nice little spot for a quick lunch, with eight tables inside, five alfresco. Lunch here is very inexpensive; you'll have a tough time spending $5 per person for *rôti,* sandwiches, or dishes like fish lasagna, and steak and kidney pie. Dinner runs the gamut from seafood and chicken to chops and steaks. Closed Tuesdays. Reservations unnecessary. MasterCard and Visa accepted. Rodney Bay (phone: 452-0761).

Marina Steak House A great view of the waterfront and air conditioning enhance this place, which specializes in steaks and seafood. Open for lunch and dinner; closed Sundays. Reservations advised. Major credit cards accepted. Near Rodney Bay (phone: 452-9800).

INEXPENSIVE

Bread Basket Fresh baked bread and pastries; also light snacks. Open daily for breakfast, lunch, and tea. Reservations unnecessary. No credit cards accepted. Rodney Bay (phone: 452-0647).

ELSEWHERE

MODERATE

Chak Chak This spot features West Indian creole cooking as well as some continental dishes. There are 2 bars and a large courtyard where there is frequent entertainment. Open daily from 9 AM to midnight. Reservations unnecessary. Major credit cards accepted. Near Vieux Fort, close to the airport (phone: 454-6260).

Dolittle's Simple island foods pleasantly presented in a special waterside setting. Open daily for breakfast and lunch. Reservations unnecessary. Major credit cards accepted. At *Marigot des Roseaux* on Marigot Bay (phone: 451-4246).

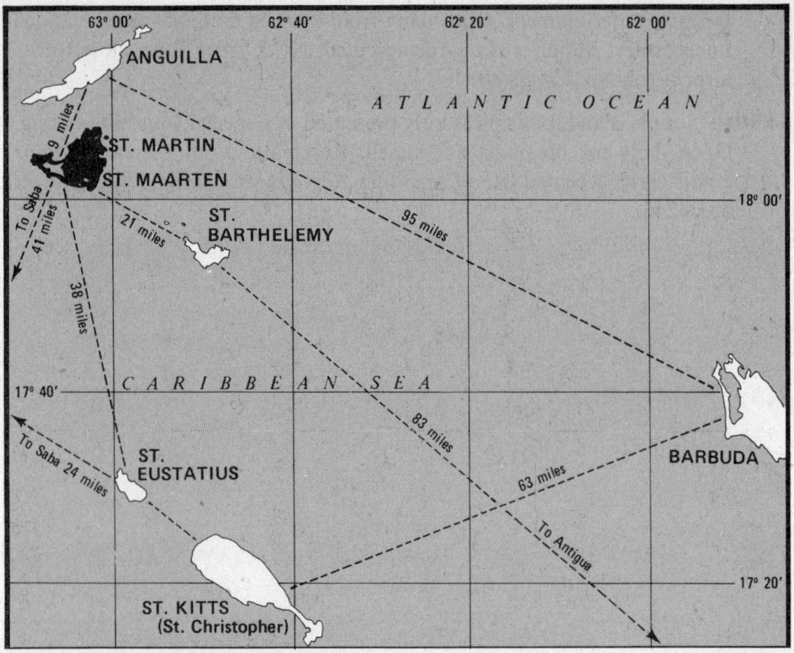

63° 00'
62° 40'
62° 20'
62° 00'
ANGUILLA
ATLANTIC OCEAN
9 miles
ST. MARTIN
ST. MAARTEN
18° 00'
To Saba 41 miles
21 miles
ST. BARTHELEMY
95 miles
38 miles
17° 40'
CARIBBEAN SEA
83 miles
To Saba 24 miles
ST. EUSTATIUS
BARBUDA
63 miles
To Antigua
17° 20'
ST. KITTS (St. Christopher)

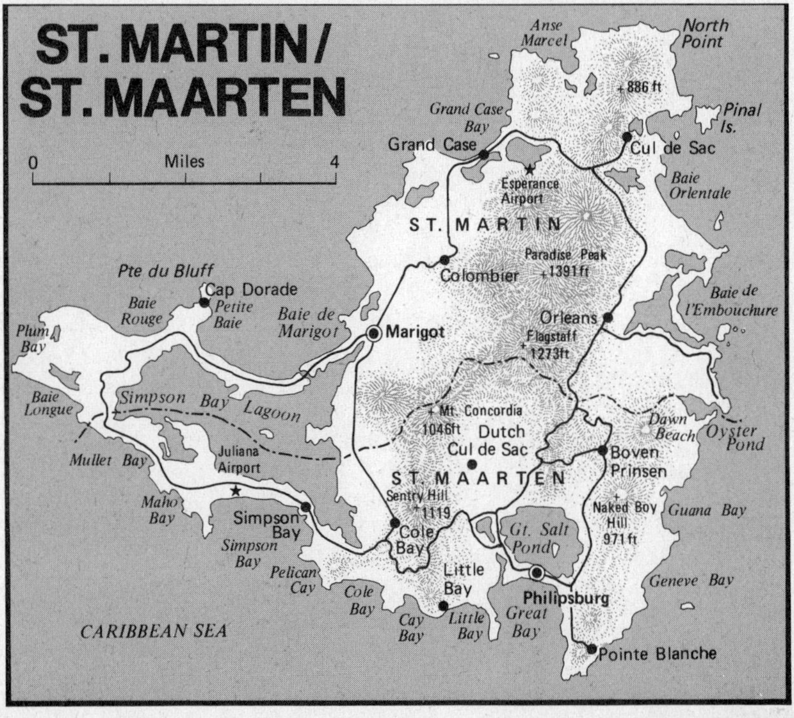

ST. MARTIN / ST. MAARTEN

0 Miles 4

Anse Marcel
North Point
+886 ft
Grand Case Bay
Pinal Is.
Grand Case
Cul de Sac
Esperance Airport
Baie Orientale
ST. MARTIN
Paradise Peak +1391 ft
Pte du Bluff
Colombier
Baie de l'Embouchure
Cap Dorade
Baie Rouge
Petite Baie
Baie de Marigot
Orleans
Plum Bay
Marigot
Flagstaff +1273 ft
Baie Longue
Simpson Bay Lagoon
+Mt. Concordia 1046 ft
Dawn Beach
Oyster Pond
Dutch Cul de Sac
Mullet Bay
Juliana Airport
Boven Prinsen
ST. MAARTEN
Sentry Hill +1119
Maho Bay
Simpson Bay
Naked Boy Hill 971 ft
Guana Bay
Gt. Salt Pond
Cole Bay
Simpson Bay
Pelican Cay
Little Bay
Geneve Bay
Cole Bay
Philipsburg
CARIBBEAN SEA
Cay Bay
Little Bay
Great Bay
Pointe Blanche

St. Martin/St. Maarten

People have all kinds of ways of picking a particular vacation spot in the Caribbean. Some go for super sports facilities or health spas. Others look for culture, historical and archaeological remains, social cachet, or nightlife. Still others seek that rare 20th-century commodity — total relaxation on memorable beaches.

St. Martin/St. Maarten (the island is divided into French and Dutch territories) offers only modest quantities of the above features, with the exception of its abundant beaches. Its sports facilities are good, but not spectacular; culturally, it can't compete with Puerto Rico, Jamaica, or Haiti; and as an archaeological site it is still largely unexamined, although recent research and restorations are turning up interesting data and on the Dutch side there's a museum featuring finds from excavations in the area. Socialites and celebrities who visit the island tend to keep to themselves; they own or lease villas, or else they take a secluded suite at *La Samanna* or *La Belle Créole.* Nightlife here is equally subdued, although there are casinos on the Dutch side, one or two "shows," and a handful of discos.

Nevertheless, St. Martin has boomed enormously in the past few years. The secret of the island's considerable success with tourists is simple. People can relax here. Its sun is dependable, and its sea and beaches are beautiful. There are plenty of activities to amuse you (though sightseeing isn't one of them). Favorite diversions include golf, tennis, and sea excursions to Saba, St. Barts, Anguilla, or uninhabited Ilet Pinel. You can scuba under the sea, water-ski across it, or catch the end of a spinnaker and fly over it. Visitors feel at home very quickly, because St. Martin remains "the Friendly Island," in spite of its ever-increasing popularity and large-scale development. (With development, however, has come an increase in crime, particularly theft. Although you may feel as if you're in paradise, you should take the same precautions you would in any urban location: check the security arrangements provided at your hotel, be careful with your possessions, and avoid walking in deserted areas at night.)

The French and the Dutch have shared this small island for more than 150 years. The original French and Dutch settlements signaled the end of the island's Carib Indian civilization in the early 1630s. The Spanish pushed out the Dutch in the 1640s, but they surrendered the island to them peacefully a few years later. St. Martin/St. Maarten was divided in 1648, when (according to local legend) a Frenchman and a Dutchman (the former fueled by wine, the latter by gin) started out back to back and walked in opposite directions around the periphery of the island until they met on the other side, each claiming the land they had paced off for their country. A border marker by the side of the Philipsburg-Marigot road commemorates the first Dutch-French treaty of friendship, signed that same year. Actually, island land changed hands at least 16 times after that, but a final settlement was reached in 1816, and relations between the two countries have been serene ever since.

If it weren't for the monument and the sign that reads *"Bienvenue Partie Française,"* you probably wouldn't know that you were crossing the border. There are no guards, no customs officials. Differences between Dutch and French portions of the island are a matter of style. The island's biggest hotels traditionally have been on the Dutch side, which, on the whole, has been more developed than the French. But building activity has been on the upswing on the French side, too. Many new hotels have opened, the harbor area has been expanded, and with the *Port la Royale* complex, Marigot now boasts well over 250 chic shops.

Philipsburg, the Dutch capital, is a charming, but bustling, town three streets wide. In midday or late afternoon traffic, it can take almost as long to drive from one end of Front Street to the other as to cross Manhattan. Shops full of duty-free luxuries from all over the world are prosperous, especially on a busy cruise ship day (there can be as many as eight ships in port at once), when Front Street is literally crammed with shoppers and (mercifully) closed to traffic. Last year, between cruise ship passengers and overnight vacationers, the island hosted just over a million visitors. The primary language is English (Dutch is seen mainly on street signs), but the mobs can be heard comparing prices in every language from Japanese to Papiamento, the Dutch Caribbean patois.

The French side is basically bucolic; even on cruise ship days, there's a slightly calmer (though busy) air about Marigot, the French capital. Boutique windows display the finest crystal, porcelain, and perfume, along with the latest styles in jewelry, bikinis, and clothing of French and Italian design. Shops are busy, but not overcrowded, with vacationers staying at the low-key French-side resorts, yachtspeople, and a smattering of cruise passengers. French — some pure, some patois — is most often heard in shops, hotels, and restaurants, although English is widely spoken and understood.

The border is so invisible that visitors forget it and move about as mood and mission dictate: to the French side in search of a secluded beach; to the Dutch to catch the boat or plane for Saba or to play a round of golf; to either side to shop, depending on the kind of bargain they're after. At night, Dutch-side guests cross over for a drink at one of the pleasant outdoor cafés and dinner. French-side guests reciprocate with a visit to one of the casinos on the Dutch side, finishing with a disco stop on the way home.

Visitors are welcomed on either the Dutch or the French side of the island at any time, which makes a trip to St. Martin/St. Maarten a bit like having two vacations in one.

St. Martin/St. Maarten At-a-Glance

FROM THE AIR

With a coastline of beaches notched by large and small bays, St. Martin/St. Maarten looks like an island jigsawed by a Victorian gingerbread addict. This is especially true of its southwestern section, where a curlicued framework of land surrounds a large body of blue water known as Simpson Bay Lagoon (also spelled Simson, Simpson's, and Simson's — but most often Simpson). Juliana Airport, now the second-busiest in the Caribbean (after San Juan's), occupies a slender strip of land on the south side of the lagoon. To the north is the town of Marigot, the capital of French St. Martin. Southeast, where the horseshoe of Great Bay curves into the coast, is Philipsburg, the capital of Dutch St. Maarten, occupying a narrow isthmus between the sea and Great Salt Pond.

St. Martin/St. Maarten, with an area of 37 square miles and a population of about 60,000 (28,000 on the French side; 32,000 on the Dutch), is the world's smallest island divided between two sovereignties. St. Maarten in the south (16 square miles) is part of the Netherlands Antilles, along with the neighbor islands of Saba and St. Eustatius and the larger Curaçao and Bonaire off the coast of South America. Like St. Barthélemy, the St. Martin half (21 square miles), is a dependency of Guadeloupe, 140 miles to the southeast, and is part of the French West Indies. The island's nearest unrelated neighbors are Anguilla, 9 miles north, and St. Kitts, some 50 miles south. Puerto Rico is a 30-minute, 144-mile flight west. Miami lies 1,223 miles (roughly 2½ hours flying time) northwest, and the 1,460-mile flight from New York takes about 3½ hours. Its position in the midst of so many small islands, and the frequency of landings at Juliana Airport make it one of the Caribbean's crossroads.

SPECIAL PLACES

If you love poking around in little out-of-the-way places, this is the island for you. St. Martin's pleasures lie in the unexpected discoveries you make on your own: an empty beach, a seascape, old houses, and sugar mill towers moldering away in nameless valleys. Rent a car and take off *ex tempore.* For visitors who hate to drive, there are guided tours by small bus or taxi. Roads are simply laid out, though some — especially on the Dutch side — are in pretty bad shape. Watch out for animals in the road, especially at night.

PHILIPSBURG Take an hour or two to stroll through the Dutch capital. Its central square (renamed Cyrus W. Wathey Square, but still De Ruyterplein to most), a long, narrow rectangle located few blocks east of the midpoint of Front Street, is usually so jammed with islanders, taxis, and visitors toting shopping bags that at first you're likely to mistake it for an impossibly clogged intersection. At the southern edge of the square, the Little Pier, from which several excursion boats depart and where cruise passengers land, juts into the harbor. Across Front Street, opposite the tourist office and Little Pier, stands one of the town's two notable buildings: the 1793 courthouse (now the post office and Town Hall), restored to its 1826 post-hurricane incarnation. At the other end of Front Street is the *St. Maarten Museum,* a restored 18th-century West Indian house operated by the St. Maarten Museum Foundation; it displays exhibits on St. Maarten's history and archaeological finds on the island. It's open Mondays through Fridays from 10 AM to 4 PM and Saturdays from 10 AM to 1 PM. There's a small admission charge.

Once there were only Front and Back Streets; now a third street — built on land reclaimed from the Old Salt Pond and generally called Pond Fill Road — has been added to relieve congestion. But Front Street still is clogged with traffic struggling east, except on major cruise ship days, when people rather than vehicles cause the congestion. Turning east from the square and creeping along with the traffic, you pass a jumble of shops, restaurants, and business places — a few in modern buildings, some in old Dutch West Indian–style arcades and courtyards, still others in old, pastel-painted houses with porches in front. One such building on the beach, once the official government guesthouse, forms the central section — lobby, bar, and dining terrace — of the *Pasanggrahan Royal Guesthouse* (see *Checking In*). A bit farther, behind an old house on the north side of the street, are brick ruins reputed to be the remains of a 17th- or 18th-century synagogue. Facing the head of Front Street is the Buncamper House, a handsomely proportioned structure with a front staircase and wraparound verandah. Built by an old island family, it is one of the island's purest examples of upper class West Indian architecture.

MARIGOT The French capital is a good distance from the cruise ships, and is somewhat less crowded and easier to explore, with expanded parking at the waterfront. The bustling harbor, busy with Anguilla-bound traffic, is alive with tropical sounds and colors, and fragrant with West Indian spices and French croissants, especially on Saturday mornings, when the waterfront market is liveliest. Old West Indian buildings line the quay, many now gracious restaurants and elegant shops. On the main corner, opposite *La Vie en Rose* restaurant, is the tiny tourist office with a few brochures (and public washrooms). The two main shopping streets are Rue de la République and Rue de la Liberté, while the *Port la Royale* complex at the southern end of town has an impressive marina and an array of chic boutiques, cafés, and bistros, which come alive at sunset with live music and beautiful people.

ELSEWHERE ON THE ISLAND

A circle tour of the island might start at Philipsburg and travel clockwise past the old cemetery at the foot of Front Street, then toward the 17th-century Fort Amsterdam (currently being excavated for planned reconstruction) and past Cay Bay, where Peter Stuyvesant — later governor of New Amsterdam — lost his leg in a skirmish with the Spanish. Just over Cole Bay Hill, turn right and take the most direct route to Marigot, passing the obelisk Border Monument and Mt. Concordia, where the original Dutch-French treaty of peaceful coexistence was signed. For a longer, more scenic route, turn left and follow the road that loops around Simpson Bay Lagoon and passes the airport; the green, sprawling *Mullet Bay* resort complex and nearby *Maho Beach* resort; gleaming, white *La Samanna;* and Pointe des Pierres à Chaux, on which stands the brainchild of the late Claude Philippe of the *Waldorf-Astoria: La Belle Créole* luxury resort. Drive on to Marigot, with its satellite, St. Tropez–style *Port la Royale Marina,* and to the small picturesque French settlements of Grand Case and Orléans; make a stop at landlocked Oyster Pond Harbor; then continue around Naked Boy Hill and along the road that skirts the Great Salt Pond and returns to Philipsburg. Feel free to stray from the route any time a beach or a picnic spot beckons (*Café Royal* in Philipsburg's *Royal Palm Plaza* dispenses excellent picnic baskets) or when lunch — especially at Marigot or Grand Case — seems like a good idea.

Sources and Resources

TOURIST INFORMATION

The St. Maarten Tourist Bureau (phone: 22337; fax: 24884), with maps of the island and literature, is on Cyrus W. Wathey Square, formerly called De Ruyterplein, Philipsburg's small, crowded main square at the head of the Little Pier. The office is open weekdays 8 AM to noon and 2 to 5 PM. There is also a tourist office on the French side, in its own building near the taxi stand at the corner of the harbor in Marigot (phone: 875721; fax: 875643). It's generally open weekdays from 8:30 AM to 12:30 PM and from 2:30 to 5:30 PM. For information on St. Maarten/St. Martin tourist offices in North America, see GETTING READY TO GO.

LOCAL COVERAGE *St. Maarten Holiday,* a Dutch-side monthly guide in English, is available free at the airport, the tourist bureau, and hotels, and contains much useful, up-to-date information on shopping, restaurants (including a few on the French side), hotels, nightlife, special events, and religious services; maps of Philipsburg and the island are included. The St. Maarten Chamber of Commerce publishes a handy and informative guide, updated twice yearly, called *What to Do.* Other free publications include *St. Maarten Events; St. Maarten Nights; Focus St. Maarten/St. Martin; Today; Discover St. Martin;* and *St. Martin's Week.* The *Flash Carson Guide,* available at the airports and bookstores, is also quite helpful — especially on the French side.

The New York Times, New York Daily News, New York Post, USA

Today, and *San Juan Star* arrive on St. Maarten newsstands the day they are published. Many hotels provide a free *New York Times Fax Sheet,* a daily fax compilation of the front page, the business page, and other important pages from the newspaper. The *International Herald Tribune* also is available.

The paperback *St. Maarten, Saba, St. Eustatius* by Dr. J. Hartog, published by the Netherlands Antilles Department of Education, is an interesting, illustrated survey of the history of the islands; you may be able to find it at island bookstores.

RADIO AND TELEVISION

Radio and television broadcasting in English is available in most hotels on the island.

TELEPHONE

When calling the Dutch side of the island from the US, dial 011 (international access code) + 5995 + (5-digit local number). When calling the French side dial 011 (international access code) + 590 + (6-digit local number). To call from another Caribbean island, the access code may vary, so call the local operator. When calling the Dutch side from the French, dial 5995 + (local number); when calling the French side from the Dutch, dial 6 + (local number). When dialing within one side of St. Martin/St. Maarten, use only the local number unless otherwise indicated.

ENTRY REQUIREMENTS

A current passport or an expired one less than 5 years old or other proof of citizenship (either a birth certificate with raised seal or photocopy with notary seal, or a voter's registration card, *plus* a driver's license or other government-approved photo ID) and an ongoing or return ticket are the only documents required of US and Canadian citizens for indefinite stays on the Dutch side. On the French side, the same documentation (without the ongoing or return ticket) is needed for stays of up to 3 months; for longer periods a visa is required, plus an ongoing or return ticket. There is a $10 departure tax at Dutch side Juliana Airport; from the French side, the departure tax is included in the airfare.

CLIMATE AND CLOTHES

The island is sunny and warm year-round, and constant trade winds take the edge off the heat. Average daytime temperature during winter is about 80F (27C); summer's a few degrees warmer and more humid. Average annual rainfall is about 45 inches, which means more air cooling thanks to occasional showers, especially in late summer and early fall. Daytime dress for both men and women is neat but comfortably casual. Proper tennis attire — not necessarily all white — is requested on most courts. Take two swimsuits, minimum, plus some sort of cover-up to wear for lunch or when you've had enough sun but don't want to leave the beach; you'll also want a beach hat. Both the French and the Dutch are easygoing about beachwear (although nudism is not allowed on Dutch beaches), but swimsuits are for beaches only — not hotel lobbies or downtown streets. Evenings are informal, although men may want to have a jacket and women a shawl or sweater to wear in the air conditioned casinos and some of the restaurants and hotels.

MONEY

Currency on the Dutch side is the Netherlands Antilles florin (or guilder), but most transactions are made in US dollars. Currency in French St. Martin is the French franc. Since US currency is accepted everywhere, there is no reason to exchange US dollars for local money, but Canadian dollars are not as readily accepted and should be exchanged for florins or francs. In some shops and restaurants, prices are given in both local currency and US dollars, sometimes only in US dollars. A few shops offer discounts for payment in US cash, but not in traveler's checks. Banking hours on the Dutch side are normally 8:30 AM to 3:30 PM Mondays through Thursdays and 8:30 AM to 4:30 PM on Fridays. Some banks may open Saturdays 8:30 AM until noon. On the French side, banks are open 8:30 AM to 1:30 PM weekdays. All banks are closed on weekends and holidays. The American Express representative is on the Dutch side: *S. E. L. Maduro & Sons* (Philipsburg; phone: 23407, 23408, or 22678). All prices in this chapter are quoted in US dollars.

LANGUAGE

Dutch is the official language of St. Maarten, and French is the official language of St. Martin, but English is spoken nearly everywhere. Some of the natives on the Dutch side speak Papiamento, the patois unique to the Netherlands Antilles.

TIME

The island is on atlantic standard time; in fall and winter when it's noon in Philipsburg and Marigot, it's 11 AM in New York. When the US East Coast is on daylight saving time, the hour is the same there as it is on the island.

CURRENT

Most hotels on the Dutch side are wired for 110 volts, as are the US and Canada; but on the French side, all run on 220-volt, 60-cycle current. If you depend on travel appliances, bring a converter and adapter plugs.

TIPPING

Hotels add a 10% to 15% service charge to bills, which is supposed to take care of room maids and other staff members. In some establishments, however, personnel see little, if any, of this sum, so a small gratuity for good service always is appreciated. Most restaurants on the French side include at least a 10% service charge on the check; on the Dutch side some do, some don't; always make sure, so you won't double-tip (or zero-tip). The customary tip to taxi drivers is 50¢ or $1; the expected tip for tours is bigger. For airport porters, $1 per bag is about right.

GETTING AROUND

BUS Buses run infrequently, so most visitors do not rely on them as a primary source of transportation. There is bus service to main points throughout the island, however, in addition to the Philipsburg — Marigot–Grand Case round trip. Flag buses down anywhere on the road; fares are $1 to $1.50, depending upon destination.

CAR RENTAL Enthusiastically recommended for those who want to sample several of the island's beaches, restaurants, and shops, rather than just stay put at a hotel (at some resorts, such as the 172-acre *Mullet Bay* — your own wheels are handy for getting from cottage to beach or golf course or restaurant). Unlimited mileage rates start at about $25 a day, depending on the size and type of car. Gas — at well over $2 per gallon — is extra, and tanks aren't likely to be full. If you don't use a credit card, a deposit of $350 to $1,500 normally is required. There is an extra daily charge of $9 or so for the optional Collision Damage Waiver, which may be advisable here because you may be liable for damages even if an accident is not your fault. A US or Canadian driver's license is valid for island driving. *Note:* The number of car thefts and burglaries (stealing batteries is common) has increased in recent months. *Never* leave anything in your car (especially the trunk) that you would mind losing, and always be sure to lock it.

On the Dutch side, car rental agencies share a building near the terminal at Juliana Airport, and many have offices in Philipsburg or at major hotels: *Avis* (phone: 54265), *Budget* (phone: 54030), *Caribbean* (phone: 45211), *Hertz* (phone: 54314), *Lucky Car Rental/National* (phone: 54268), *Risdon Car Rentals* (phone: 54239), *Roy Rogers* (phone: 52702), and *Thrifty* (phone: 52706). On the French side, car rentals are available at *Hertz* (phone: 877301), *Caribbean* (phone: 875122 or 873385), *Babi Richardson* (phone: 875111), *Dan's* (phone: 873408), *Sandig* (phone: 878825), *Espérance* (phone: 875109), and *St. Martin Auto* (phone: 875086). All will deliver cars to your hotel (cars rented on the Dutch side *must* be delivered to your hotel); on departure day you can drive to Juliana Airport and leave the car there.

MOPEDS AND MOTORCYCLES These can be rented from several firms, including *Carter's Cycle Center* (phone: 54251 or 22621), across from Juliana Airport on the Dutch side and *Gar Rent-a-Scoot* in Marigot (phone: 877947);

rates are about $20 per day. However, we strongly discourage this mode of transport here; the roads are often pockmarked, crowded, and dangerous.

SEA EXCURSIONS Several day sails are available from *Bobby's Marina* (phone: 22366), *Great Bay Marina* (phone: 22167), and Little Pier in Philipsburg. A number of catamarans offer trips to St. Barts, including the *White Octopus* (phone: 23170), which sails from *Bobby's*, and *Quicksilver* (phone: 22167), which leaves from *Great Bay Marina*. The crossing takes about 90 minutes and costs $50, plus the $10 departure tax. *El Tigre* (phone: 44309 or 22167) sails from Philipsburg to St. Barts ($45) or Anguilla ($60) with lunch included. Several boats at the Philipsburg marinas offer excursions to the Dutch island of Saba for about $55 round-trip. The *Cheshire Cat* (phone: 23170) sails to the uninhabited French island of Tintamarre, where you can swim, snorkel, and picnic. For information on other dive boats and snorkel trips to Tintamarre or Pinel Island and sunset cruises out of Philipsburg either look in *St. Maarten Holiday* magazine or ask at your hotel travel desk. *Lagoon Cruises and Watersports* at Mullet Bay (phone: 52801) also offers a number of sailing or cruising options. On the French side, check with *Port la Royale Marina* and the marina at Anse Marcel for day trips to neighboring cays. Ferries headed for Anguilla operate on regular schedules from the waterfront in Marigot for about $7 each way. In general, rates run about $50 for 4-hour sails, $65 to $70 for 6 to 8 hours, depending on whether lunch is included (there are almost always snacks, soft drinks, beer, and rum punch). There are also sunset sails and dinner cruises available on both sides of the island. Check with your hotel activities desk. Be sure to ask if the boat you choose is a member of the Charter Boat Association to ensure reliability and safety.

There are a number of yacht charter operators, particularly on the French side. These include *The Moorings* at Oyster Bay (phone: 873255); *ATM Yachts* at Port Lonvilliers (phone: 874030), and *Dynasty Yachts* at *Port la Royale Marina* (phone: 878521). In addition, the *Star Flyer*, the first clipper ship to be launched in 125 years, has cruises out of Philipsburg. The world's tallest sailing ship, with four masts that tower 220 feet above the deck, the 360-foot vessel can accommodate 180 passengers in 90 staterooms. The ship makes 7-day cruises, alternating between the Leeward Islands and the British and US Virgin Islands. The cost of a week-long cruise ranges from $1,000 to $2,500, not including airfare. For information, contact *Star Clippers* (4101 Salzedo Ave., Coral Gables, FL 33146; phone: 800-442-0551 from the US).

SIGHTSEEING BUS TOURS Principally designed for cruise passengers, 8- to 40-passenger buses are operated by *St. Maarten Sightseeing Tours* (Philipsburg; phone: 22753), and *Calypso Tours* (Cole Bay; phone: 23514), with representatives at eight of the larger hotels. Half-day tours are about $12 per person, and a 6-hour trip including lunch and swimming, about $25.

Other outfits, including *St. Maarten Taxi Association* (Cole Bay; phone: 55329), *Rising Sun Tours* (Philipsburg; phone: 45334), and *S. E. L. Maduro & Sons* (Philipsburg; phone: 23407), will arrange similar excursions.

SIGHTSEEING TAXI TOURS This is the way to see the island if you don't want to drive. Your hotel activities or travel desk will arrange for a car with a driver-guide; a 2½-hour tour around the island is about $35 for one person, with an additional charge of $10 for each extra passenger.

TAXI They are ready and waiting at the airport and hotels. Since there are no limos and rental car companies aren't allowed to garage cars on airport property, cabs provide the best transport to your hotel when you land. Car rental agencies do, however, have airport booths, where cars can be picked up if you arrive on a daytime flight and are staying on the French side.

Cabs are unmetered, but drivers are required to carry booklets listing rates for destinations throughout the island. The trip from Juliana Airport to Philipsburg currently runs $7; to Marigot hotels, $7; to Mullet Bay, $4; to Grand Case, $14; to Oyster Pond, $15; the trip from Philipsburg to Grand Case is about $14 — for one or two persons, plus $1 per additional person and more again for baggage. Rates go up 25% after 10 PM and 50% from midnight to 6 AM. For late-night service on the Dutch side, call the taxi stand in town (phone: 22359) or at the airport (phone: 54317); on the French side, call 875654.

INTER-ISLAND FLIGHTS

American Airlines connects the island to San Juan, Puerto Rico. *Air Guadeloupe* makes the 15-minute flight to St. Barts several times a day from Espérance Airport on the French side ($60 round-trip). *WINAIR* also flies between St. Maarten and Guadeloupe. *Air St. Barthélemy* runs a regular shuttle between Juliana Airport and St. Barts until dusk, as does *WINAIR* ($60 round-trip). *WINAIR* also schedules daily flights from Juliana Airport to Saba ($50 round-trip), St. Eustatius ($50 round-trip), Anguilla ($35 round-trip), St. Kitts ($90 round-trip), and St. Thomas ($125 round-trip), and several times weekly to Nevis ($115 round- trip).

SPECIAL EVENTS

A Dutch national holiday, the *Queen's Birthday* (April 30), and a French one, *Bastille Day* (July 14), are celebrated on both sides of the island with fireworks, dancing, and sports events. The annual *St. Maarten's Trade Winds Regatta* takes place in March. On *Schoelcher Day* (July 21), French St. Martin celebrates the end of slavery in the French West Indies with music, African dances, and feasting. At the end of May, the annual *St. Martin Food Festival* is held on the French side. On *St. Martin's* or *Concordia Day* (November 11), Dutch-French friendship is celebrated with parades and ceremonies at the border. Other holidays when banks and stores close include *New Year's Day, Carnival* (pre-*Lent* on the French side, in mid- to late April on the Dutch), *Good Friday, Easter* and *Easter Monday, Labor Day* (May 1), *Ascension Day* (40 days after *Easter*), *All Saints' Day* (French side, November 1), *Christmas,* and — on the Dutch side — *Boxing Day* (December 26).

SHOPPING

St. Martin/St. Maarten is that rarity — a truly duty-free island. No tax is paid on imports arriving on either side of the border. But that fact alone does not guarantee that all that glitters in either Dutch- or French-side shop windows is a bargain worth bringing home; individual merchants are free to set their own prices. In addition, certain manufacturers — especially of world-marketed items like calculators, cameras, and electronic equipment — work hard to fix prices across the international board; you often can do as well or better at your local discount store. Check prices before you leave home, and if you can, shop twice — first to research, and second, after a cooling-off period, to buy.

On the Dutch side, shopping hours are normally 9 or 9:30 AM to 1 PM and 2 or 2:30 to 6 PM. Some shops remain open at lunchtime; many also open for a few hours on Sundays or holidays when cruise ships are in port. Most take credit cards. Philipsburg's Front Street is lined with shops offering everything from Delftware, Swiss watches, French perfume, and British cashmeres to Chinese embroidery, Japanese cameras and electronics, Indonesian batiks, Italian leather goods, fine jewelry, crystal, linens, porcelain, liquor, and more. Try to avoid shopping on Front Street on cruise ship days, particularly Tuesdays, when you are better off taking a taxi to the French side, to the *New Amsterdam Mall,* not far from Philipsburg, or to the shopping arcades at the major resort hotels.

On the French side, there are no cruise crowds, but there are also fewer bargains. Small, elegant boutiques — a number with island exclusives on French and Italian fashion names — are featured here. Though priced below US levels, many are still very expensive — but the same clothing may not be available back home. You can save on French perfume, cosmetics, fashion accessories, porcelains, and crystal at Marigot's duty-free shops along Rues de la Liberté and de la République. The city's other top shopping centers are *Galerie Périgourdine, Palais Caraïbe,* and the St. Tropez–style *Port la Royale Marina,* a most attractive area for strolling and watching yachts or people from the many cafés and bistros along the wharf. Major US credit cards are accepted almost everywhere, but sometimes paying cash with US dollars can make for a better bargain. Some shops are open from 9 AM to noon or 12:30 PM and 2 to 6 PM, but many now keep the later hours set by the chic *Port la Royale* arcades (10 AM to 1 PM and 3 to 7 PM).

In addition, there are a number of galleries to visit in Marigot, and outside of town, in Rambaud, the French painter Alexandre Minguet has a studio (no phone). In Orléans, visit artist Roland Richardson at his lovely home. His watercolors, etchings, woodcut prints, and charcoal and oil paintings of island life and architecture make beautiful gifts. He receives visitors on Thursdays from 10 AM to 6 PM, or by appointment (phone: 873224).

ON BOTH SIDES OF THE ISLAND

ANIMALE Elegant French fashions, leather, and furs for the woman who wants to buy the very best — and spend the most for it. *Old Street Shopping Center,* Philipsburg (phone: 26082) and *Port la Royale,* Marigot (phone: 875703).

COLOMBIAN EMERALDS Designer jewelry, all of which comes with guarantees honored by their Miami service office. At two locations in Philipsburg: Front St. (phone: 22438) and *Old Street Shopping Center* (phone: 23933); and Rue de la République, Marigot (phone: 878605).

DALILA Exotic batik at an exotic boutique. Old St., Philipsburg (phone: 24623) and *Port la Royale,* Marigot (no phone).

D'ORSY'S International scents, cosmetics, and other grooming aids. At two locations along Front St., Philipsburg (phone: 24912 and 23017), at Juliana Airport (phone: 32063), and at *Port la Royale,* Marigot (no phone).

GUCCI The one and only. Designer creations, still expensive, but duty-free. 83 Front St., Philipsburg (phone: 23537) and Rue Charles de Gaulle, Marigot (phone: 878424).

LITTLE SWITZERLAND Luxury merchandise: English bone china, French crystal, and, of course, Swiss clocks and watches. *Hint:* Resist seemingly sensational buys in waterproof, shockproof, what-have-you-proof watches with unfamiliar names, no matter how glowing the guarantees that come with them, unless the salesperson can give you the name of a stateside organization that will make good on the claims. 42 Front St., Philipsburg (phone: 22523), and Rue de la République, Marigot (phone: 878914 or 875003).

SPRITZER & FUHRMANN An island staple for fine jewelry and gifts, it continues to offer golden (literally) opportunities. Juliana Airport (phone: 54217) and Rue de la République, Marigot (phone: 875962).

THE DUTCH SIDE

ARTISTIC Fine gold jewelry, Mikimoto cultured pearls. 55 Front St., Philipsburg (phone: 23453 or 23456).

BUTANI JEWELERS Unusual jewelry created in its own workshops. 86 Front St., Philipsburg (phone: 32118).

EMILE'S PLACE Wines, cigars, chocolates, imported snacks, and Edams and Goudas — a good pre-picnic stop. *Mullet Bay Resort* (no phone).

GOLDFINGER For 14K and 18K finery and Swiss watches. 109 *Old Street Shopping Center,* Philipsburg (phone: 24661).

GREENWITH GALLERIES Features the work of more than 40 local artists. At two locations: 20 Front St., Philipsburg (phone: 23842) and at the *Simpson Bay Yacht Club,* Simpson Bay (no phone).

H. STERN The reputable firm, whose elegant jewelry comes with ironclad (or should we say, platinum-clad) guarantees. 56 Front St., Philipsburg (phone: 23328).

JAVA WRAPS Exotic batiks to slip around head, shoulders, or waist. *Old Street Shopping Center,* Philipsburg (phone: 24605).

L'IL SHOPPE Everything from swimwear to eel-skin wallets and handbags to pearls and perfumes. Just off the Little Pier, Philipsburg (phone: 22177).

LITTLE EUROPE Movado, Piaget, Corum watches; precious stones and jewelry; 18K and 24K jewelry. Front St., Philipsburg (phone: 24371).

MAXIMOFLORENCE Italian leather shoes and bags, plus elegant sportswear. The Promenade, Front St., Philipsburg (phone: 22608).

MILLE FLEURS Fairly sparkles with exquisite crystal; china; jewelry; and unset, cut, and polished stones. Front St., Philipsburg (phone: 22473).

NEW AMSTERDAM For anyone on the lookout for jewelry, linen, Naf-Naf sportswear, and good buys on Swatch watches, with prices starting at about $5. Front St., Philipsburg (phone: 22787 or 22788).

THE FRENCH SIDE

BASTRINGUE Prêt-à-porter by Gaultier, Hamnett, Cyclopo Loco, Carbur. *Port la Royale,* Marigot (phone: 875820).

BEAUTY AND SCENTS Cosmetics and fragrances from international perfume houses. Rue Charles de Gaulle, Marigot (phone: 875877).

CARAT Lots of them, mainly the 14- and 18- kinds. Two Marigot locations: *Port la Royale* and Rue de la République (phone: 877340).

CARTIER Very elegant jewelry, watches, pens, and fragrances. Rue de la République, Marigot (phone: 878914 or 875003).

GINGERBREAD GALLERY Haitian art and handicrafts, as well as works by other Antillean naïfs. *Port la Royale,* Marigot (phone: 877321).

JET SET Menswear for the island hopper . . . and shopper. Rue Charles de Gaulle, Marigot (phone: 878706).

LIPSTICK Offering massages and all sorts of salon treatments, plus French cosmetics and other *attendrissements.* Two Marigot locations: *Port la Royale* and Rue de la République (phone: 875392).

MARITHÉ AND FRANÇOIS GIRBAUD Same owners as *Bastringue.* Designer clothing for men and women that can only be found in Paris, Tokyo, and, at 10% less, here. Rue de la Liberté, Marigot (phone: 879458).

ORO DE SOL Offering Ebel watches; Pratesi linens; fine china and crystal by Villeroy & Boch, Lalique, and Baccarat; and exquisite jewelry, among other luxury goods. Rue de la République, Marigot (phone: 875651).

PARIS 7 Mini-conglomerate of fine art run by Christine Pelletier. At two locations: 10 La Fregate, *Port la Royale,* Marigot (phone: 878503) and *Acacias* at Anse Marcel (phone: 873487).

SPORTS

BOATING Most hotels have Sunfish or Sailfish for loan or rent, and there are larger boats available for charter; ask your hotel travel desk. Sailing instruction and sailboat rental are available from *Caribbean Watersports* at *Mullet Bay Marina* (phone: 52801, ext. 337; or 54363). The big annual regatta is the *St. Maarten Trade Winds Race,* which takes place every year in early March.

FITNESS CENTERS AND SPAS *L'Aqualigne* (phone: 42426), the health spa–beauty clinic at the Dutch side's *Pelican* resort, isn't flashy, but it does offer a full range of treatments and equipment for men and women, including exercise machines; sauna, steamrooms, and whirlpool baths; dance, aerobics, and yoga classes; health bar; Swedish and shiatsu massages; cellulite treatments, waxings, and facials; and cosmetics and health foods. "Body sculpting," weight loss programs, and even cosmetic surgery are available, with weekly, monthly, and daily programs. Sports facilities at *Le Privilège* (phone: 873737), the French side's chic complex at Anse Marcel, include a pool, tennis, squash, jogging, weightlifting, yoga, archery, racquetball, shooting, and *pétanque,* a version of bowling played in France.

GOLF The windy, Joseph Lee–designed layout at *Mullet Bay* (phone: 42015) is a bit too gimmicky to please purists, but has good views of the water at 14 of its 18 holes. It extends along the palm-lined shores of the bay on one side and the lagoon on the other. The course is open only to hotel guests, island residents, and cruise ship passengers who purchase a golf package. Greens fee: $95 for 18 holes ($50 for hotel guests), $65 for 9 holes ($35 for hotel guests), cart included; rental clubs ($15) are also available.

HORSEBACK RIDING *Crazy Acres Riding Center,* on the Wathey Estate in Cole Bay (phone: 22061), offers 2-hour beach rides on weekdays for $45; book 2 days in advance. Private beach picnics can also be arranged, and riding instruction is available. On the French side, the *Coralita Beach* resort (phone: 873181) at Baie Lucas has a small stable.

JOGGING Several hotels have jogging on the beach, as does *Le Privilège* spa at Anse Marcel (phone: 873737). The *Road Runners* club meets Wednesdays at 5:30 PM and Sundays at 7 AM in the main parking lot of the *Pelican* resort for 5- or 10-kilometer runs. Races usually are held once a month. Visitors are welcome. For information, contact Dr. Fritz Bus of the *Back Street Clinic* (phone: 22467) or Malcolm Maidwell of *El Tigre* (phone: 44309 or 22167).

PARASAILING Rides are offered for about $25 by *Caribbean Watersports* at *Mullet Bay Marina* (phone: 52801, ext. 337; or 54363), the *St. Maarten Watersports and Waterski Club* on Simpson Bay Lagoon (phone: 54387), and *Lagoon Cruises & Watersports N.V.* (phone: 52801).

SNORKELING AND SCUBA Island water sports centers that offer equipment rental, instruction, and dive and snorkel trips include: *Maho Watersports* (which also offers dive packages to Saba), based at *Mullet Bay* (phone: 54387, ext. 379); *Ocean Explorers,* Simpson Bay (phone: 55252); *Red Ensign Watersports,* Dawn Beach (phone: 22929); *Little Bay Watersports* at *Little Bay Beach* hotel (phone: 22333/4); and *St. Maarten Divers & Watersports,* Great Bay (phone: 22446). On the French side, operators include *Lou Couture's Scuba Club* at Laguna Beach (phone: 872258); *Blue Ocean* at *Le Pirate,* Marigot (phone: 878973); *L'Habitation de Lonvilliers Diving* at Anse Marcel (phone: 873333); and *PLM Azur Royal Beach* at Baie Nettle (phone: 878989). *St. Maarten Watersports and Waterski Club* on Simpson Bay Lagoon (phone: 54387) offers snorkeling trips to Anguilla. The waters around the island are clear (75- to 125-foot visibility), and there is a fair amount of reef life to explore. Pinel Island, just offshore, also offers good snorkeling and shallow diving, and 1 mile off the coast there's a sunken 1801 British man-of-war, the *Proselyte,* replete with cannon and anchors, as well as a variety of coral and fish. Another way to see the aquatic world is offered by *Underwater Adventures,* c/o *Maho Watersports,* at *Mullet Bay* (phone: 54387): Walk underwater wearing a specially constructed bronze diving helmet. A cruise on the *Glass-Bottom Boat* (phone: 52115, ext. 4240) is another option.

SPORT FISHING Marlin, barracuda, tuna, kingfish, and dolphin are the best catches in the nearby fishing grounds. Tuna is fished year-round; dolphin, kingfish, and barracuda from December to April. Plenty of boats are available for hire on the Dutch side at *Bobby's Marina* (phone: 22366) and the *Great Bay Marina* (phone: 22167) in Philipsburg, as well as at Simpson Bay; arrangements can be made through your hotel. *Blue Water Charters* (phone: 52801 or 54363) also runs fishing trips. On the French side, check *Sailfish Caraïbes* based at Port Lonvilliers (phone: 873194) or *Mullet Bay* resort. The 35-foot *Sushi* is based at *Captain Morgan's Dock* across from *Port la Royale Marina* (phone: 879854). Charters usually include tackle, bait, food, and drink, and average $700 for a full day.

SQUASH There are 2 courts at *Le Privilège* (phone: 873737).

SWIMMING AND SUNNING The 37 beaches around the island are top attractions. Your hotel will likely have its own stretch of sand, and you'll want to see some of the others, for there is a great variety of wide, white expanses and secluded, shady coves to enjoy. Non-guests can use changing facilities at most hotels for a small fee; at many beaches, you won't need any facilities because nobody else will be there. You'll find very few people on the hideaway sands of Long Bay, north of *La Samanna,* and at Plum and Rouge bays on the French side, north of Long Bay. It's not a good idea to leave belongings unattended at these secluded spots. There is one designated nudist beach, on — *naturellement* — the French side, at Orient Bay, where there's also a simple nudist resort. But even on other French-side beaches, the general attitude toward bikinis, monokinis, and *sans* 'kinis is pretty relaxed.

TENNIS Very popular. At last count there were more than 40 courts on the island, 14 of them at the *Mullet Bay* resort (3 lighted). Most of the larger hotels have at least 1 court; *Grand Case Beach Club* has 1 lighted "omnisport" court; *Oyster Bay, Simpson Beach, Oyster Beach, Treasure Island, Esmeralda, Caravanserai,* and *Mont Vernon* have 2 each, and courts at the last two resorts are lighted; *Belair Beach* and *Laguna Beach* have 3 each, as do *Nettle Bay Beach Club* and *La Samanna* (all unlighted); *Maho Beach, Pelican Beach, and Dawn Beach* each have 4, as does *La Belle Créole* (all lighted); *Le Privilège* has 6 courts (4 lighted) and a practice wall. Fees for non-guests run about $5 per hour. Some hotels have instructional programs and pro shops. In the Dutch Cul-de-Sac, the new *Tennis and Fitness Center* (phone: 23685) is operated by tennis pro Michael Sprott. Lessons and clinics are available at the center, or Sprott will visit your hotel.

WATER SKIING Available at most beachside hotels and on calm Simpson Bay Lagoon. Contact *St. Maarten Watersports & Waterski Club* on Simpson Bay (phone: 54387) or *Caribbean Watersports* at *Mullet Bay* (phone: 52801, ext. 337; or 54363).

WINDSURFING Available at many Dutch-side beachfront hotels, including *Mullet Bay* resort, *Little Bay Beach, Dawn Beach* (serving Oyster Pond), and *St. Maarten Beach Club,* and on Simpson Bay Lagoon. Most French-side beach hotels are also equipped or will make arrangements. Lessons average about $25 to $30 per hour.

NIGHTLIFE

With some 300 restaurants on the island, dining out is the most popular pastime. On the Dutch side, nautical types usually begin their evenings at *Berrymore's* (Front St.; no phone). Later, many hotels on both sides have "West Indian nights," dancing under the stars, or discos — a current favorite dance club on the Dutch side is *Mullet Bay*'s *Studio 7. Cheri's Café* (phone: 53361), next to the *Maho Beach* resort, draws big crowds with live reggae and Latin music nightly, while *Coconut's Comedy Club* at Maho Beach (phone: 52115; closed Saturdays) hosts local and international comedians. Great Bay's *Chrysalis* has international entertainers. There's crowded late-night activity in Philipsburg at the *Greenhouse* at *Bobby's Marina* (phone: 22941). Hotel casinos include *Maho Beach, Pelican* resort, the *Belair Beach* hotel, *Atlantis* at the *Treasure Island* resort, *Mullet Bay* resort, *Great Bay Beach* and the *Seaview* in town. Most are Vegas-style: craps, roulette, blackjack, slot machines. Before playing, check the house rules, for they vary slightly from one casino to another; minimum playing age is 18. Some casinos have nightclubs that feature live entertainment; all serve complimentary drinks, and most open at lunchtime. Several French-side hotels provide free casino transport for their guests.

On the French side, dining begins with an aperitif at one of the lively café-bars or bistros of the chic *Port la Royale Marina,* where live music often fills the air as the temperature cools down. French-side nocturnal types also are found at *L'Atmosphère,* the *très chic* disco at *Port la Royale Marina* (phone: 875024), or at *Le Privilège,* at Anse Marcel (phone: 873737), where restaurants serve food all night. A more local flavor can be savored at *Night Fever* near Colombier (take the road from Marigot toward Grand Case, and turn right where marked). You can party till the wee hours at *La Bar de la Mer* on the beach in Marigot (phone: 878179).

Best on the Island

CHECKING IN

The Dutch side has more than 3,000 rooms and efficiency apartments with kitchenettes. Accommodations range from modest guesthouse rooms to big hotels by the sea. But, unlike the French side, the Dutch side offers no truly luxurious resorts. In fact, many of the bigger resorts have become more interested in selling timeshare slots than in providing good service to hotel guests. Other hotels rely heavily on back-to-back charter bookings, and their beaches and facilities are always crowded.

There are somewhat fewer rooms on the French side (though they number over 2,500) and options range from small efficiency apartments to lavish (and astronomically priced) resorts.

A number of fully staffed private homes are rented by the week or month on each side of the border. Prices start at about $800 a week in winter and range *way* up from there. Best contacts: Ms. Judy Shepherd at *St. Maarten Rentals* (Pelican House, Beacon Hill, St. Maarten, NA; phone: 44330), *Ambria International Realty* (180 Front St., St. Maarten, NA; phone: 22711), *Carimo* (Rue Charles de Gaulle, PO Box 220, Marigot 97150, St. Martin, FWI; phone: 875758); or *International Immobilier* (Marigot 97150, St. Martin, FWI; phone: 877900).

Best reservations advice: Shop carefully to make sure what you want is what you get (especially in the atmosphere department), and book early because there are many winter weeks when the island is almost sold out.

Among our recommendations below, expensive translates to $225 and up (way up) for a double without meals in winter; moderate, from $150 to $225; inexpensive, $150 and under. In summer, rates drop as much as 60% on the Dutch side; by about a third on the French side. On the Dutch side, there's a 5% tax on hotel rooms and usually a 15% service (or 10% service and 5% "energy") charge. French hotels add a 15% service charge, and a 2- to 7-franc government tax per person per night, which is sometimes incorporated into the room rate. When calling from a phone within one side of St. Martin/St. Maarten, use only the local numbers listed below. When calling the Dutch side from the French, dial 5995 + (local number); when calling the French side from the Dutch, dial 6 + (local number). For information about dialing from anywhere else, see "Telephone" earlier in this chapter.

For an unforgettable island experience, we begin with our favorites, followed by our recommendations of cost and quality choices of hotels large and small, listed by area and price category.

REGAL RESORTS AND SPECIAL HAVENS

La Belle Crêole Conceived by the late Claude Philippe (of New York's *Waldorf-Astoria*), this 156-room luxury resort is modeled after a typical fishing village on the French Riviera. Its 27 one- to three-story villas are linked by cobblestone streets, sidewalks, and courtyards, all surrounding a village square. All units are decorated in a Provençal motif and have air conditioning, mini-bars, cable TV, and phones. Some have beamed ceilings, and most have private terraces overlooking Marigot Bay or the lagoon. There are 44 connecting rooms, 2 of which are equipped for the disabled. Amenities include 3 beaches, a freshwater pool, 4 tennis courts and pro shop, and a full range of water sports. Boutiques, secretarial services, a drugstore, car rental agency, and concierge are also on the premises. The resort's excellent *La Provence* restaurant (see *Eating Out*) features international and creole cuisine; a café-bar at poolside serves light meals and snacks; a beach bar and a main bar offer regular entertainment. Children under 12 stay with their parents free of charge. Pte. des Pierres à Chaux (phone: 875866; 800-445-8667 from the US).

Le Méridien L'Habitation and Le Domaine Tucked under Pigeon Pea Hill on one of St. Martin's most beautiful beaches, this place sprawls over 150 of the island's choicest acres. Now a member of the French Méridien group, the property has a large freshwater pool, 4 restaurants, nightly entertainment, water sports, a 100-slip marina, and *Le Privilège* sports complex nearby. *Le Domaine,* a $45-million luxury wing, recently opened as well. This complex consists of 125 rooms and 20 suites in 5 two- and three-level buildings, as well as a pool, a bar, and an open-air restaurant. Each air conditioned room has a round bathtub with an ocean view, and a terrace or patio, as well as a direct-dial telephone, TV set, mini-bar, and safe. *Le*

Domaine buildings feature traditional creole architecture and are set in tropical gardens. The original *L'Habitation* complex, designed in pure West Indian style, is made up of 5 two-story buildings (overlooking a lagoon) and 3 three-story structures that make up the main building, which houses the deluxe rooms and suites, 3 restaurants, including the elegant *La Belle France* (see *Eating Out*), and entertainment facilities. There are 189 rooms and 73 one- and two-bedroom suites, each containing spacious, well-appointed baths. All rooms are air conditioned, with private balconies or terraces, direct-dial phones, TV sets, VCRs, and mini-fridges; some have kitchenettes. Each of the 1-bedroom marina suites includes a private patio (with a hammock, table, and chairs) and a fully equipped kitchen. A $1-million landscaping project has enhanced the gardens and grounds. Although large and rambling (for St. Martin), this property has a lot of charm and a professional, efficient management. Anse Marcel (phone: 873333; 800-543-4300 from the US; fax: 873038).

Oyster Pond In spite of its rustic name, it's actually a small Moorish structure on the far side of the Dutch portion of the island. Beautifully secluded on a remote point of land, it's cut off from the rest of the world by sudden hills on one side and a blue lagoon and the sea on the other. The ride down to the hotel can be slightly hair-raising, but this retreat is still the choice of many high-powered financial types, including at least one former head of the New York Stock Exchange. Beyond the breezy lobby, furnished in white wicker with Pierre Deux fabrics and lush with tropical plants and flowers, lies a sun-dappled patio and stairs that lead up to some of the best-looking rooms in the Caribbean. All 40, including the tower suites, are pastel-coordinated, naturally air conditioned by *Casablanca*-style ceiling fans, and completed with their own terraces and smashing views of the sea. The beach (called Dawn) is perfect for swimming and picnicking, and for a quick dip there's a choice: the wood-decked swimming pool or the coral-protected sea beside the hotel. Scuba is available by arrangement, other water sports are nearby; so is deep-sea fishing, and a charter boat is at the ready to cruise to offshore islands. French cuisine is served in the candelit dining room (see *Eating Out*). There's never a crowd: perhaps 60 guests at most, plus a few drop-in yachtsmen. Regrettably, the *Dawn Beach* condo and hotel crowd next door has meaningfully increased the area's population. Near the French-Dutch border (phone: 22206 or 23206; 800-223-6510 from the US; fax: 25695).

La Samanna This spot, recently purchased by the prestigious *Rosewood* hotels and renovated from top to bottom, is where the likes of Redford and Cavett come to soak up some rays as anonymously as possible. The quarter-mile crescent of white sand beach is merely perfect, and the Mediterranean-cum-Moorish design enhances the Arabian nights mystique. The resort is sleek, chic, more than slightly sexy, and *très* expensive. All 80 air conditioned villas (with 1, 2, or 3 bedrooms) are designed with tropical elegance, featuring bamboo furnishings and shades of coral, blue, and green. All have spectacular sea views, full kitchens, living rooms, and terraces, and many open onto the silky sand. The most popular is the Terrace Suite, which (befitting its name) has myriad balconies, including one with a thatched roof. Elaborate, complimentary (at their rates, they should be) breakfasts are delivered to your terrace each morning; and the dining room, candlelit and cooled by sea breezes, offers some of the haute-est French cuisine on the island (see *Eating Out*). Closed September and October. On Baie Longue (phone: 875122; 800-854-2252 from the US; fax: 878786).

THE DUTCH SIDE

NEAR THE AIRPORT

EXPENSIVE

Maho Beach The largest property in St. Maarten, this place on Mullet Bay has over 700 rooms and many amenities, including a beach, 3 pools, 4 tennis courts, and full water sports facilities. There are also several restaurants, a casino, a medical clinic, and *Coconuts Comedy Club* (phone: 52115 or 52119; 800-223-0757 from the US; fax: 53604).

Mullet Bay A multimillion-dollar refurbishment has restored some lost luster to this sprawling 172-acre condominium-cum-resort hotel, with 600 spacious, air conditioned rooms and suites, and just about everything in the way of facilities: water sports center, 18 holes of golf, 14 tennis courts, 1 freshwater and 1 saltwater pool, casino, disco, 6 restaurants, grocery store, clinic, shopping plaza, a branch of Chase Manhattan Bank, and regular shuttle service (although a car helps a lot). It's all remarkably self-sufficient. On Mullet Bay, about 4½ miles from Juliana Airport (phone: 52801; 800-325-0446 from the US; fax: 54355).

La Plage Maho's attractive time-sharing arrangement at the *Royal Islander* condominium and hotel complex offers 1- and 2-bedroom apartments, each with full kitchen, direct-dial phone, and air conditioning, as well as access to neighbor *Maho Beach*'s facilities (phone: 52388; 800-223-0757 from the US; fax: 53495).

MODERATE

Horny Toad A onetime governor's house on Simpson Bay beach, it now holds 8 bright apartments — each with a big balcony or porch overlooking the sea, kitchenette, generous bath, special charms (unit No. 1 has a step-down bedroom; studio No. 3 has a hanging basket chair). Caring management (phone: 54323; 800-365-8484 from the US; fax: 53316).

Mary's Boon The service is excellent at this hotel, which has 12 rooms, each with bath, kitchenette, and seaside patio. Decorated with a blend of antiques and tropical wicker, sisal, and bamboo, the rooms are breezy, but there's no air conditioning. Highlights include a great beach, an honor bar, and an unregimented atmosphere. Pets are welcome; children under 16 aren't. Delicious French cuisine with an American accent is served in the dining room. No one seems bothered by its location next to the Juliana Airport runway (phone: 54235; 800-223-9815 from the US; fax: 53316).

Summit One of St. Maarten's older properties, this informal place has a faithful following and an Italian restaurant (under a French chef). The pleasant 1- and 2-story chalets have porches (often looking onto the neighboring chalet); there's also a large pool. A shuttle bus transports guests to beaches and casinos (phone: 52150 or 54227; 800-622-7836 from the US; fax: 52150).

PHILIPSBURG

EXPENSIVE

Great Bay One of Philipsburg's oldest hotels, it has 285 spacious rooms, each with a king-size bed or 2 double beds, full tub, and shower. Amenities include a casino, beach, 2 pools, tennis, water sports, and seemingly endless activities. Popular with package tours. All-inclusive rates are also available. There's a Saturday night Caribbean party with a steel band. At the western end of Great Bay Beach (phone: 22446 or 22447; 800-223-6510 from the US; fax: 23859).

MODERATE

Horizon View Beach Conveniently located in the heart of Philipsburg, this pleasant beachfront hostelry has 30 air conditioned units — studios, 1-bedroom suites with living rooms and beach views, and 2-bedroom penthouse suites with patios and Jacuzzis. All units have kitchenettes and direct-dial phones. There's a Chinese restaurant and store on the premises. On Front St. and the beach (phone: 32120 or 32121; fax: 32123).

Town House Villas These 10 extremely attractive townhouses (each with 2 air conditioned bedrooms, 1½ baths, 2 patios, complete kitchen, and living and dining area) are located on the edge of town. On Great Bay Beach (phone: 22898; 800-223-9815 from the US).

INEXPENSIVE

Pasanggrahan Royal Guesthouse Formerly the *Government Guest House,* this historic West Indian building is St. Maarten's oldest inn and a favorite of many repeat visitors from statesmen to salesmen. There are 26 charming (but small) rooms, plenty of greenery, afternoon tea, and pleasant seaside bar and restaurant. No credit cards are accepted. On the beach (phone: 23588; 800-223-9815 from the US; fax: 22885).

ALSO ON THE DUTCH SIDE

EXPENSIVE

Dawn Beach Here are 155 spacious, air conditioned rooms, each with full kitchenette and terrace on one of the island's most beautiful reef-protected beaches (the surf can be choppy on windy days). The units on the beach are by far the most desirable. The attractive open-air dining room and bar are raised to catch the view and sea breezes. Other highlights: a freshwater pool with waterfall, 2 lighted tennis courts, water sports, and a popular Sunday brunch. On Dawn Beach, near the border (phone: 22929; 800-351-5656 from the US; fax: 24421).

THE FRENCH SIDE

MARIGOT

MODERATE

Le Grand St. Martin This hillside resort features 140 units, including 25 studios, 20 well-appointed rooms in the main complex, and fully equipped 1-bedroom apartments. Units have interesting split-level architecture, with some wooden beams, also terraces, air conditioning, and phones. Other features include a freshwater pool, fine beach, water sports, and 2 restaurants. Rue de Galisbay (phone: 875791; 800-727-7388 from the US; fax: 878034).

Le Pirate A gleaming white replacement for the former tiny property of the same name. Within walking distance of Marigot, it has 55 large studios (with kitchenettes and terraces) and 11 duplexes. Other features include a small pool, a beach within strolling distance, an informal waterfront snack bar, and a restaurant. Near Sandy Ground (phone: 877837; 800-666-5756 from the US).

INEXPENSIVE

Parapel A few minutes east of Marigot's center, this economical apartment hotel has 21 units set on a hill; all have kitchenettes (phone: 878604; 800-366-1510 from the US).

La Résidence A charming hotel in the heart of Marigot, it's set between the town center and the booming *Port la Royale Marina.* The 20 rooms, studios, and apartments, each with phone and refrigerator, encircle the quaint courtyard bar and restaurant. Rue Charles de Gaulle (phone: 877037; 800-932-3222 from the US).

Le Royal Louisiane Another "city" hostelry attractively built around a central patio where breakfasts, light lunches, and ice cream are served. The 68 rooms, including 13 duplexes, are cheery, and have air conditioning. Good value. Rue Charles de Gaulle (phone: 878651).

GRAND CASE

EXPENSIVE

Grand Case Beach Club On one of St. Martin's most splendid beaches, this property features fresh, airy, attractive studios, 1- and 2-bedroom apartments (76 in all) with full baths, kitchens, and private terraces. Swimming, sailing, water sports, tennis, *pétanque* (the Provençal equivalent of *bocce*), a bar, a panoramic restaurant, and friendly and gracious management. On Grand Case Bay (phone: 875187; 212-661-4540 from New York City; 800-223-1588 from elsewhere in the US).

INEXPENSIVE

Hévéa This pretty 8-room guesthouse is perhaps best known for its intimate, *soigné* 10-table dining room with unmistakably French food (see *Eating Out*). Located right in the heart of Grand Case (phone: 875685; 800-932-3222 from the US; fax: 878388).

NETTLE BAY

EXPENSIVE

Anse Margot In a lush tropical garden, the 95 rooms in the tri-level buildings are equipped with outdoor refrigerators and stoves. On the beach, there are also 2 moderate-size swimming pools, a bar, and a first class restaurant. Just west of Marigot (phone: 879201; fax: 879213).

Flamboyant Bounty This 270-room establishment, formerly the *Radisson Flamboyant,* is now an all-inclusive resort. Meals, drinks, entertainment, water sports, fitness classes, and sightseeing excursions are all included in the rate. Among the pluses are 2 freshwater pools, a restaurant with panoramic views, and a brasserie on the beach level. At the marina on Simpson Bay Lagoon next to the *Nettle Bay* resort (phone: 876000; 800-462-6868 from the US; fax: 879957).

Laguna Beach A somewhat smaller and less posh sister of the *Anse Margot,* this 64-room hostelry has 2 beachside 2-level buildings overlooking a swimming pool. The rooms are spacious and have terraces. Amenities include a restaurant, 2 bars, shops, and 3 tennis courts. Just west of Marigot (phone: 879175; 800-223-9815 from the US; fax: 878165).

Nettle Bay Two formerly separate resorts that have been consolidated — with much remodeling and landscaping — and now offer modern and comfortable accommodations in a variety of buildings: the inn (123 rooms), the gardens (35 rooms), and the villas (140 units). On the beach (phone: 879191; 800-223-9815 from the US).

MODERATE

Royal Beach For the budget-minded, this is a modest but comfortable hotel with its own restaurant and row of shops. The 108 rooms are small but bright, and the 33 three-story rooms in the new wing are cheerful. Freshwater pool. Overlooks Nettle Bay (phone: 878989).

Simson Beach Marine Featuring creole architecture, with wooden balconied loggia and stylish wicker furniture in the lounges, the hotel also boasts 128 studios and 48 duplex apartments, a pool, bar, and restaurant. In the Nettle Bay area (phone: 875454; 800-221-4542 from the US).

ATLANTIC COAST

EXPENSIVE

Belvedere Here are 132 air conditioned studio apartments (all with full kitchenettes and telephones) facing an excellent crescent beach on the Atlantic. Cul-de-Sac (phone: 873789; fax: 873052).

Captain Oliver Straddling the Dutch/French border is this French luxury complex. Each of the 35 air conditioned bungalows offers a kitchenette, terrace, direct-dial phone, radio, and room service from the eponymous waterfront restaurant. Many rooms have sea views. Oyster Pond (phone: 874026; 800-223-1588 from the US).

Esmeralda This delightful property on 100 secluded acres near Orient Bay has 14 villa-like structures with a total of 54 rooms designed in a mix of Antillean creole and Spanish mission architecture. Most villas have 3 air conditioned rooms plus a large luxury suite. All units have private entrances, sitting areas, large bathrooms, kitchenettes, and terraces. There are 14 pools, 2 tennis courts, complete water sports facilities, and a main pool area with an extensive deck overlooking the ocean. The restaurant offers French, creole, and continental dishes, and there is also a beachfront grill and bar. Orient Bay (phone: 873636; 800-622-7836 from the US; fax: 873518).

Green Cay Village Here are 16 cottages offering luxury and privacy on picturesque, secluded Baie Orientale. The spacious accommodations are air conditioned; each has 3 bedrooms, a full kitchen, and a private pool. There's no restaurant, but guests can arrange catered meals or even a private chef. Orient Beach is within strolling distance. Minimum 1-week stay. Baie Orientale (phone: 873863; 800-476-5849 from the US).

Mont Vernon One of the island's newer properties, the 394 units in junior and 2-room suites have terraces with sea views. There is also a large swimming pool, 2 lighted tennis courts, a water sports center, 3 restaurants, and a lounge with nightly entertainment. Bilingual staff (phone: 874222; 800-223-0888 from the US).

MODERATE

Club Orient A "clothing optional" naturist resort on a lovely, windswept 1½-mile-long beach. Accommodations are in 77 prefabricated red pine chalets imported from Finland; 25 have kitchens and living rooms; others have kitchenettes. Some accommodate up to 4 people. A beach bar/restaurant, water sports facilities, a boutique, and a basic grocery store are on the premises. No frills — but getting back to nature is what this place is all about. Baie Orientale (phone: 873385; 800-828-9356 from the US).

Jardins de Chevrise This property has 29 studios and duplexes in West Indian–style bungalows around the pool. Each room is air conditioned, with a kitchenette and patio or terrace. The beach is a 5-minute walk away. On the hillside at Mont Vernon overlooking a lagoon (phone: 873779).

Sol Ambiance Set higher on the hill than *Captain Oliver* (above), this cozy property has only 8 rooms, but it's cheerful and nicely appointed, with a pool and friendly management. Overlooking Oyster Pond (phone: 873810; 800-366-1510 from the US; fax: 873223).

INEXPENSIVE

Orient Bay Across the road from *Jardins de Chevrise,* this place has 31 studios and apartments, all air conditioned, with kitchenettes, phones, and terraces. There are 2 pools and a restaurant that serves native fare. Mont Vernon (phone: 873110; 800-223-5695 from the US; fax: 873766).

EATING OUT

St. Martin/St. Maarten offers a wealth of dining options. French cuisine, in both its classic version (escargots, frogs' legs, langouste flambé) and its creole variations (the savory fish stew called *blaff, crabes farcis,* curried conch, and chicken *colombos*) is prepared very well on both sides of the island. But if you're smitten with a sudden craving for bagels and lox, prime ribs, or a chocolate soda, these are available here, too. For lobster lovers, this island comes close to heaven (although most of the restaurant supply is now shipped over from nearby Anguilla). The meat is sweet and tender, and the price — compared to stateside levels — is palatable. There's also lots of good fish, but beware — sometimes it is "fresh frozen," that is, caught on the island but frozen instead of being served immediately. There's also plenty of good French wine (served by the carafe or bottle), and lots of tasty Dutch beer.

At lunch, nobody bothers about reservations; for dinner, they're usually a good idea. Most restaurants add a 10% to 15% service charge in lieu of tip, but neither government taxes meals. Expect to pay over $160 for dinner for two at restaurants described below as very expensive; from $100 to $160 at expensive places; from $60 to $100 at places in the moderate category; and less than $60 at eateries listed as inexpensive. When calling from a phone within one side of the island, use only the local numbers listed below. When calling the Dutch side from the French, dial 5995 + (local number); when calling the French side from the Dutch, dial 6 + (local number). For information about dialing from anywhere else, see "Telephone" earlier in this chapter.

THE DUTCH SIDE

PHILIPSBURG

EXPENSIVE

Le Bec Fin This long-established gastronomic address proffers elegant dining in a lovely 18th-century courtyard. The French chef offers a fairly traditional menu, albeit with some tempting deviations, such as chilled tomato soufflé, lobster salad, and marinated salmon. Definitely worth checking out. Open daily for lunch and dinner. Reservations advised. Major credit cards accepted. Front St. (phone: 22976).

Dario's On the water across from the *Caribbean* hotel, it features outstanding northern Italian fare, just like its sister restaurant of the same name on New York's Long Island. The grilled red snapper with garlic and oil, and the *veal chop dario* (lightly breaded, sauteed in white wine, and smothered in fontina cheese) are specialties. All meat is imported from the United States. Open daily for lunch and dinner. Reservations advised. Major credit cards accepted. 103 Front St. (phone: 23834).

L'Escargot In an old townhouse, this is one of the island's oldest restaurants (celebrating its 22nd anniversary this year). True to its name, the restaurant's snails are memorable; try them in puff pastry, *à la provençale, de bourgogne,* or in fresh mushroom caps. Other items include crisp duck in guavaberry sauce and lobster thermidor. A cabaret is included every Sunday with dinner. Open daily for lunch and dinner. Reservations advised. Major credit cards accepted. Front St. (phone: 22483). Expensive to moderate.

Da Livio The island's best Italian restaurant enjoys a seafront setting that's perfect for alfresco lunches on the terrace or elegant candlelight dinners. The menu features a myriad of pasta, veal, chicken, and seafood dishes. A few that are extra special: manicotti with spinach and ricotta cheese, scampi in garlic butter, saltimbocca (veal in wine sauce with ham and sage), and ricotta cheesecake with pine nuts. The owner, Livio, could not be more gracious. Open for lunch and dinner; closed Sundays. Reservations advised. Major credit cards accepted. Front St. (phone: 22690).

MODERATE

Café Royal This is the perfect place to stop during a busy shopping day in the *Royal Palm Plaza.* A cool, shaded garden where American (and Dutch) breakfasts, light lunches (including great salads), and dinners (during high season) are served. Try the traditional Dutch seafood: smoked eel, salmon, trout, or herring. The deli in the back prepares fancy *pique-niques* of French bread, cheese, and wine or, for the more demanding palate, lobster salad, pâté, pastries, and caviar. You can even get a map, insect repellent, suntan lotion, or rent an ice bucket and beach umbrella here. Open daily. Reservations advised. Major credit cards accepted. *Royal Palm Plaza,* Front St. (phone: 23443).

Callaloo A gathering place for locals and tuned-in tourists, with gazebo bar, snacks, as well as a menu featuring hamburgers, steaks, salads, pizza — just about everything except, inexplicably, *callaloo.* Open for lunch and dinner until 2 AM; closed Sundays. Reservations unnecessary. No credit cards accepted. Promenade Arcade (no phone).

La Rosa, Too The traditional Italian menu features several of Giuseppe La Rosa's own Sicilian recipes, such as *ziti alla Norma,* with fried eggplant and plenty of parmesan, as well as classic pasta, meat, and seafood dishes. Open for dinner only; closed Tuesdays. Reservations advised. Major credit cards accepted. In the *Maho Reef Shopping Mall* (phone: 53470).

Seafood Galley and Raw Bar Fresh oysters, mussels, clams, and other seafood landed locally or imported from New England and served *au naturel* (unless unavailable, when guests are advised of "fresh frozen" backups). Chicken and steaks are available for landlubbers. Right on the dock at *Bobby's Marina,* it's a pleasant breezy bar and boat watching site. Open daily for lunch and dinner, with a happy hour from 5 to 6 PM. Reservations advised. Major credit cards accepted (phone: 23253).

Wajang Doll Popular spot for authentic Indonesian feasting on *rijsttafel* of either 14 or 19 different exotic dishes. Highly acclaimed by Dutch expatriates who know their *rijsttafel* well. Open for dinner only; closed Sundays. Reservations advised. Major credit cards accepted. Front St. (phone: 22687).

INEXPENSIVE

Café Rembrandt For those who feel adventurous, or who want to experience the Caribbean version of a typical Amsterdam pub. There's a long lineup of such Dutch delights as *kroket* (crusty egg batter roll with ragout of mildly spiced meat), *bami* (spicy fried rice or noodles with chopped vegetables in an egg batter crust) and *satay* (grilled chunks of pork or chicken on a skewer with hot peanut sauce). Reproductions of the Old Master's works hang on the walls. Open daily for lunch and dinner. Reservations unnecessary. Major credit cards accepted. (phone: 25437).

EXPENSIVE

Oyster Pond Lunch or dinner at this retreat is special. Whether dining in the elegant, breezy, candlelit dining room with fine linens, Rosenthal china, and fresh flowers, or lunching informally under the umbrellas of the quiet courtyard, the ambience alone rates 5 stars. To that, add the superb cuisine of award-winning chef Paul Souchette. Before overdosing on minted cold cucumber soup, fresh asparagus in puff pastry with chervil butter, medallions of lobster with truffles, tomato, and basil, or sliced breast of duck in green peppercorn sauce, remember to save room for the banana, chocolate, or raspberry soufflé for dessert. Open daily. Reservations advised. Major credit cards accepted. Oyster Pond (phone: 22206 or 23206).

Le Perroquet Named after Chicago's original bastion of French cuisine, this tropical version overlooking the quiet waters of Simpson Bay Lagoon, not far from the airport, is another Dutch-side favorite. The West Indian–style house offers breezy dining on a lush garden porch. The menu features such unusual fare as breast of ostrich and fresh salmon, which is lightly smoked in herbs at your table (a truly memorable dish). Also good are fresh mussels with leeks in muscadet sauce. Charming ambience, smiling service, and a good wine list add to the experience. Open for dinner only; closed Mondays and during June and September. Reservations advised. Major credit cards accepted. Airport Rd. (phone: 54339).

Spartaco Since its smashing debut 8 years ago, this excellent Italian restaurant just seems to get better and better. It's an early-19th-century West Indian plantation house, where the late afternoon sun shines through a louvered verandah onto black Alessi *sottopiatti* and sparkling crystal, and mock Roman statuary lines the long stairs leading through the gardens to a flowered pool area with a view of the lagoon. Service is superb, the ambience quietly romantic, and the food excellent. Rich in snob appeal, yet friendly. Open for dinner only; closed Mondays in low season. Reservations advised. Major credit cards accepted. Almond Grove, Cole Bay (phone: 45379).

MODERATE

Café Juliana The lunch menu of steaks, chicken, seafood, burgers, sandwiches, salads, and quiches is designed for travelers newly arrived or about to depart. Nevertheless, the ingredients are first-rate and everything is well-prepared. In the evenings, when there are few flights and no jumbo jets, the café offers dining that is reasonably priced and only a short taxi ride away from the resorts at Mullet and Maho bays. Specialties include a very popular seafood lasagna, live Maine lobster from the lobster tank, and chicken bonzai in a soya wine sauce. Open daily. No reservations. No credit cards accepted. At Queen Juliana Airport (no phone).

Lynnette's This is the place everyone's talking about. It features local fare such as fried fish creole, curried goat, and stuffed crab backs, as well as fancier dishes like rack of lamb *bouquettière* (baked in mustard) and tomatoes stuffed with snails and mushrooms in a creamy Pernod sauce. Both indoor and outdoor dining is available. Open daily for lunch and dinner. Reservations advised for dinner. Major credit cards accepted. Simpson Bay Blvd., near Queen Juliana Airport (phone: 52865).

INEXPENSIVE

Paradise Café If you get a hankering for Mexican or Tex-Mex, this is the place for such traditional fare as burritos, tacos, and nachos, along with beef, chicken, and seafood specialties grilled over mesquite coals at the outdoor barbecue. Informal alfresco dining at tables overlooking a swimming pool, which guests are encouraged to use. Open for lunch and dinner; dinner only Mondays. Reservations unnecessary. Major credit cards accepted. Across from *Maho Beach* resort (phone: 52842).

Turtle Pier Bar There's a sun deck with lounge chairs for lazing around this relaxed, comfortable watering hole, which also has its own boat dock and mini-zoo with monkeys and parrots. The day begins with continental breakfast, and a sandwich menu is offered throughout the day and evening. Showers are available for boaters. Open daily. Reservations unnecessary. MasterCard and Visa accepted. Simpson Bay Lagoon (phone: 52230).

THE FRENCH SIDE

MARIGOT AND ENVIRONS

VERY EXPENSIVE

Le Poisson d'Or Small and select, this dining spot on the seaside terrace of a restored stone warehouse is one of Marigot's best. Start with the house aperitif — passion fruit, Armagnac, and champagne — before you choose from an exciting menu, which might include fresh lobster bisque, cassoulet of snails, or home-smoked spiny lobster in champagne butter. Try the chocolate cake; it's just this side of paradise. There is also a charming art gallery in the historic building. Open daily for lunch (in high season) and dinner; no lunch on Sundays. Reservations advised. Major credit cards accepted. A short walk from the port off Rue d'Anguille (phone: 877245).

Le Santal Housed in a splendid seaside villa just outside Marigot, this is one of the island's most refined dining rooms. The blue-and-white decor of the scalloped terrace matches the spectacular sea scenery reflected in cleverly placed mirrors. The enticing menu, in French and English, is pricey, but neither the food nor the service will disappoint. Very special are the fried rack of lamb with thyme and caramelized tomatoes, and the broiled red snapper with fennel, which is flambéed with Pernod. Open for lunch and dinner, but check hours — they change frequently. Reservations advised. Major credit cards accepted. Seaside, west of Marigot Bridge (phone: 875348).

La Vie en Rose Overlooking Marigot's picturesque waterfront, this popular restaurant is as gastronomically appealing as it is astronomical in price. If you would like a table on the small seaside balcony, say so when you reserve. There are young geniuses in the kitchen, preparing a rather modified nouvelle cuisine, with menus that change daily with the availability of ingredients. Generally, the seafood is fresh and local and most meat imported, as are many vegetables and fruits. Certain seafood much loved by the French (scallops, shrimp, and fish such as lotte or salmon) also are imported — at great expense. Enjoy — if you can — and catch your breath in the pleasant tearoom downstairs. Open daily for lunch and dinner; closed Sundays during off-season. Reservations necessary. Major credit cards accepted. Marigot Harbor (phone: 875442).

EXPENSIVE

La Calanque Marigot's landmark harborside restaurant for more than 25 years. In keeping with the French tradition, the menu changes frequently, but duck is always featured in one or more variations, as are such French classics as chateaubriand, rack of lamb, and steak *au poivre.* Upstairs is an open terrace with a pretty view of the bay. Open daily for lunch and dinner; closed June through mid-November. Reservations advised. Major credit cards accepted. Blvd. de France (phone: 875082).

La Casa Creole In a little tin-roofed building, this eatery presents top-quality island fare; sample menu items are stuffed chayote squash, black pudding, sea snails with ravioli, curried chicken, and octopus. Open for dinner only; closed Mondays. Reservations advised. Major credit cards accepted. Sandy Ground (phone: 872533).

Jean Dupont *Le Santal*'s less formal, but still elegant, brother (named after the owner of both restaurants) has been a smashing success. Its food is of the same top caliber — but at about one-half the price. Here are rich and inventive treatments of lobster, fish, veal, and chicken. Open daily for lunch and dinner. Reservations necessary. Major credit cards accepted. *Port la Royale Marina* (phone: 877113).

Messalina Lunch features light antipasti of carpaccio, salads, and pasta; dinners combine traditional northern Italian fare — pasta *al pesto, al Alfredo, alla bolognese, alle vongole* (with clams) — with exciting innovations such as chilled ginger soup with fresh beets or veal in a sweet and sour sauce with dates. Open for lunch and dinner; dinner only Sundays. Reserve well ahead for a table on the tiny terrace. Major credit cards accepted. Marigot Harbor (phone: 878039).

Le Nadaillac Another pricey Marigot terrace, this one with a Périgord touch. Specialties include *confit d'oie* (preserved goose), giblet salad, and chive-flavored snails in puff pastry. Also try the baked goose or filet of red snapper with spinach and champagne sauce. Reliably good, pleasant, and pretty. Open for lunch and dinner; no lunch on Sundays. Reservations advised. Major credit cards accepted. *Galerie Périgourdine,* Rue d'Anguille (phone: 875377 or 875616).

MODERATE

Cas' Anny *Colombos, crabes farcis, boudin, accras,* fish soup, and some French dishes are all served under the trees in a bamboo-fenced garden. Recently renovated, this place is popular with local political figures. Open for lunch and dinner; dinner only Sundays. Reservations advised. Major credit cards accepted. Rue de la Liberté (phone: 875338).

Davids The spinnaker in the rafters signals that two yachtsmen, both Englishmen named David, created this plain and very pleasant place that serves conch fritters and beef Wellington as well as good, hearty steaks, poultry, and fish. A "courtyard" at the back puts you under the stars. The two bars are popular with jolly expats. Open daily; no lunch on weekends. Reservations advised. Major credit cards accepted. Rue d'Anguille (phone: 875158).

Le Mini Club One of Marigot's oldest terrace restaurants, still under its original ownership, it is known especially for its big French/creole buffet (more than 35 dishes and "endless carafes of French wine"), usually offered Wednesday and Saturday evenings. The *court bouillon* (fish soup, creole-style), stuffed land crab, and dessert soufflés are all excellent. Open daily for dinner. Reservations advised. Major credit cards accepted. Rue de la Liberté (phone: 875069).

NOTABLE NIBBLES

In the *Port la Royale* complex, there are a dozen or so small, attractive places for lunch, dinner, and *le snack.* These include the above-mentioned *Jean Dupont;* others are somewhat simpler and often a good value, especially if your main goal is people watching rather than an elaborate meal. Choices include: *Café de Paris,* for a basic French menu at reasonable prices (phone: 875632); *Les Cocotiers* (no phone), for fresh seafood, French pastries, and a lively happy hour, often with live music; *La Vie Parisienne* (phone: 875870) for more French fare; *Café San Martino* (phone: 878271) for pizza; *La Croissanterie* (no phone) for (surprise!) croissants; *La Main à la Pâté* (no phone) for both pizza and croissants; *Don Camillo* (phone: 875288 or 875920) for Italian food; and *Etna* (no phone), the rage of St. Martin for fresh sorbets and ice cream (especially maracuja or passion fruit).

EXPENSIVE

Auberge Gourmande This homey-chic country inn (lanterns, crystal, louvered windows, beams) serves such fine French fare as rolled sole filets with spinach, beef tenderloins with olives and peppers, and chicken with mango and port wine sauce. There's also a delicious scallops and raspberry salad. Open daily for dinner; closed June and July. Reservations necessary. MasterCard and Visa accepted (phone: 877224).

Deep Blue One of Grand Case's more recent additions is this lovely seaside spot serving up ocean-fresh specialties such as red snapper, yellowtail, grouper, and local lobster prepared in your choice of several ways. There's a nightly three-course special dinner, usually for under $50. Open daily for lunch and dinner. Reservations advised. Major credit cards accepted (phone: 878620).

L'Escapade This eatery is in a pretty house with 2 softly lit and appealing dining rooms. The seafood is first-rate, with red snapper and lobster among the more popular main dishes, or duck breast with raspberry sauce for poultry fanciers. The escargots are as good as you will find on the island, while dessert favorites include lemon pie and a creamy chocolate mousse cake. Two seatings, 7 PM and 9 PM. Closed Mondays from April through December. Reservations advised. Major credit cards accepted. Seaside (phone: 877504).

Hévéa French cuisine with Niçoise accents is served in a tiny (10 tables) dining room decorated with china and island antiques. Specialties include duck liver pâté, red snapper *en papillote, noisettes d'agneau* (those little lamb riblets the French adore) in thyme and garlic sauce, and seafood and fish steamed in morel sauce. Open for dinner only; closed Mondays from mid-April through mid-December. Reservations necessary. MasterCard and Visa accepted. At the *Hévéa* guesthouse (phone: 875685).

Rainbow A very pretty, very exclusive terraced dining room overlooking the beginning of Grand Case beach serves "New American, freestyle" fare. The menu changes frequently but might include sushi of salmon with smoked salmon tartar, or shrimp and scallops with island chutney and beef chips. One of the more exquisite desserts is a strawberry, chocolate, and vanilla soup in a puff pastry. No pets, cigars, pipes, or children under 16! Two seatings, 7 PM and 9:30 PM. Closed Sundays and late June through October. Reservations advised. Major credit cards accepted (phone: 875580).

Sebastiano's An old-fashioned Italian welcome, homemade pasta, and northern dishes such as *piccatina* and osso buco keep regulars coming back to this modern, terraced dining room at the edge of town. Open for dinner nightly; lunch on Sundays only; closed Sunday evenings from April through November. Reservations advised. MasterCard accepted (phone: 875886).

Le Tastevin On an attractive seaside terrace, this establishment serves topnotch traditional French fare. The seafood salad appetizer, snapper with vanilla sauce, and the salmon steaks with leeks are excellent choices. Good wine list. Open for lunch and dinner; closed Wednesdays and September. Reservations advised. MasterCard and Visa accepted (phone: 875545).

MODERATE

Café Panoramique This place is strikingly situated on a promontory between two beaches. The menu includes shrimp, broiled stuffed lobster tail, veal *milanese* or marsala, steaks, pasta, and more. Open daily for lunch and dinner. Reservations advised. Major credit cards accepted. Far end of Grand Case Beach (phone: 875187).

Chez Martine This intimate guesthouse dining room is warm pink, with a gingerbread terrace overlooking the beach. The menu includes winners like raw salmon and scallops marinated in lime juice, olive oil, and basil; snails in pastry with garlic and parsley sauce; quail and goose liver *en gelée de porko;* red snapper soufflé in two sauces; chicken breast stuffed with mushrooms and cranberries; and a wonderful tournedos in Roquefort sauce. Open daily for lunch and dinner. Reservations advised in season and on weekends. Major credit cards accepted. On the beach (phone: 875159).

Daisy's A relative newcomer to the ever-less-affordable Grand Case "Restaurant Row," this spot offers traditional French fare with a bargain "dinner for two" that includes Caesar salad, escargots, rack of lamb, and a memorable *marquise au chocolat* at about $40. In a pretty old house, facing, unfortunately, the wrong way: The roadside terrace can be quite noisy from the traffic, but inside it's most agreeable, decorated with etchings of handsome local houses. Open daily for dinner only. Reservations advised. Major credit cards accepted. After the bridge (phone: 877662).

Ile Flottant and Porto This combination *boulangerie,* pâtisserie, restaurant, and pizzeria in an open and breezy multilevel location. Ideal for lunch or a snack, or take-away ice cream cones. The fare is moderately priced (for Grand Case). Open daily. Reservations unnecessary. MasterCard and Visa accepted. At the end of town where the road east divides into Front and Back Sts. (phone: 878946).

ELSEWHERE ON THE FRENCH SIDE

VERY EXPENSIVE

La Samanna This justifiably well-regarded restaurant is part of the hotel of the same name. Elegant and formal, it has an airy arched terrace overlooking

Baie Longue and is fragrant with tropical flowers and West Indian spices. Ask for a table at the outer edge, under the thatch roof. The food is prepared by a chef from the south of France, and the menu changes regularly according to the availability of fresh ingredients. Specials might include roasted rack of lamb or rock lobster *millefeuille,* layered with mashed potatoes and shredded black truffles. There's caviar — beluga, sevruga, and oscietra — for those who care to indulge. The ambience is romantic, and there's also a very respectable selection of French wines. Open daily for breakfast and dinner; closed September and October. Reservations necessary. Major credit cards accepted. Baie Longue (phone: 875122).

EXPENSIVE

La Belle France Breezy West Indian–style restaurant at *Le Méridien L'Habitation* resort, where the house cocktail combines blue curaçao, amaretto, lemon juice, and champagne in a drink that promises to make your tastebuds sit up and take notice. Presentation is everything, whether it's the puff pastry crown on a small *marmite* or a Maine lobster that looks almost too good to eat. The filet mignon of veal with morel cream sauce is another aesthetic adventure, and desserts are nothing but sinful, including *blancmange* with pears and pear liqueur, and mint mousse with bitter chocolate. Open daily for dinner. Reservations advised. Major credit cards accepted. Anse Marcel (phone: 873333).

Captain Oliver's Right on the border between the French and the Dutch sides, the seaside terrace here faces St. Barthélemy. The menu includes creamed crayfish soup, tuna tartare, grilled lobster flambéed in cognac, chicken *colombo,* and steak *frites.* Open daily for lunch and dinner. Reservations advised. Major credit cards accepted. Oyster Pond (phone: 873000).

Le Privilège The *Le Privilège* complex (with its marina/shopping plaza behind *L'Habitation* and sports complex/disco on the cliff above) boasts 2 restaurants: *Le Privilège Grill,* featuring vichyssoise, *grillades* of fish, and salads; and the main dining room, which offers both a conventional menu (fresh salmon stew with truffle juice; chicken breast with shrimp and ginger) as well as a low-calorie haute cuisine menu. Open daily for lunch and dinner. Reservations advised. Major credit cards accepted. Anse Marcel (phone: 873737).

La Provence This is the main restaurant of the deluxe *La Belle Créole* hotel, featuring fine French and creole specialties. With an expansive view of the lagoon and ocean, the posh atmosphere extends from a formal indoor dining room to seating out on the terrace. Open daily for breakfast and dinner. Reservations advised. Major credit cards accepted. At Pointe des Pierres à Chaux (phone: 875866).

La Rhumerie If it's authentic creole cooking you're after, this restaurant in a private house won't disappoint. Specialties include *poulet boucanne créole* (home-smoked chicken with baked green papayas and steamed, buttered cabbage hearts), herbed conch, curried goat, salad of *poisson coffre* (a local fish), and flavorfully spiced vegetables. There's also French fare, such as escargots, frogs' legs, and duck *à l'orange.* Open daily for lunch and dinner. Reservations advised. MasterCard and Visa accepted. Off the Marigot–Grand Case road near Colombier (phone: 875698).

MODERATE

Mark's Place Rather out of the way (unless you're staying at *L'Habitation* or planning to hit the *Privilège* disco at Anse Marcel), in a country setting, this extremely popular informal restaurant specializes in very fresh lobster and seafood, plus good creole dishes. Daily specials are listed on a blackboard and might include octopus or goat *colombo* (curried), while the *assiette créole* (*accra, boudin,* crab and *christophine farci*) is an interesting menu staple. Huge portions of very good food at very reasonable prices, and the rustic atmosphere, with open sides looking over the surrounding countryside and bay, has contributed to the restaurant's overwhelming success. Open for lunch and dinner; closed Mondays. Major credit cards accepted. French Cul-de-Sac (phone: 873450).

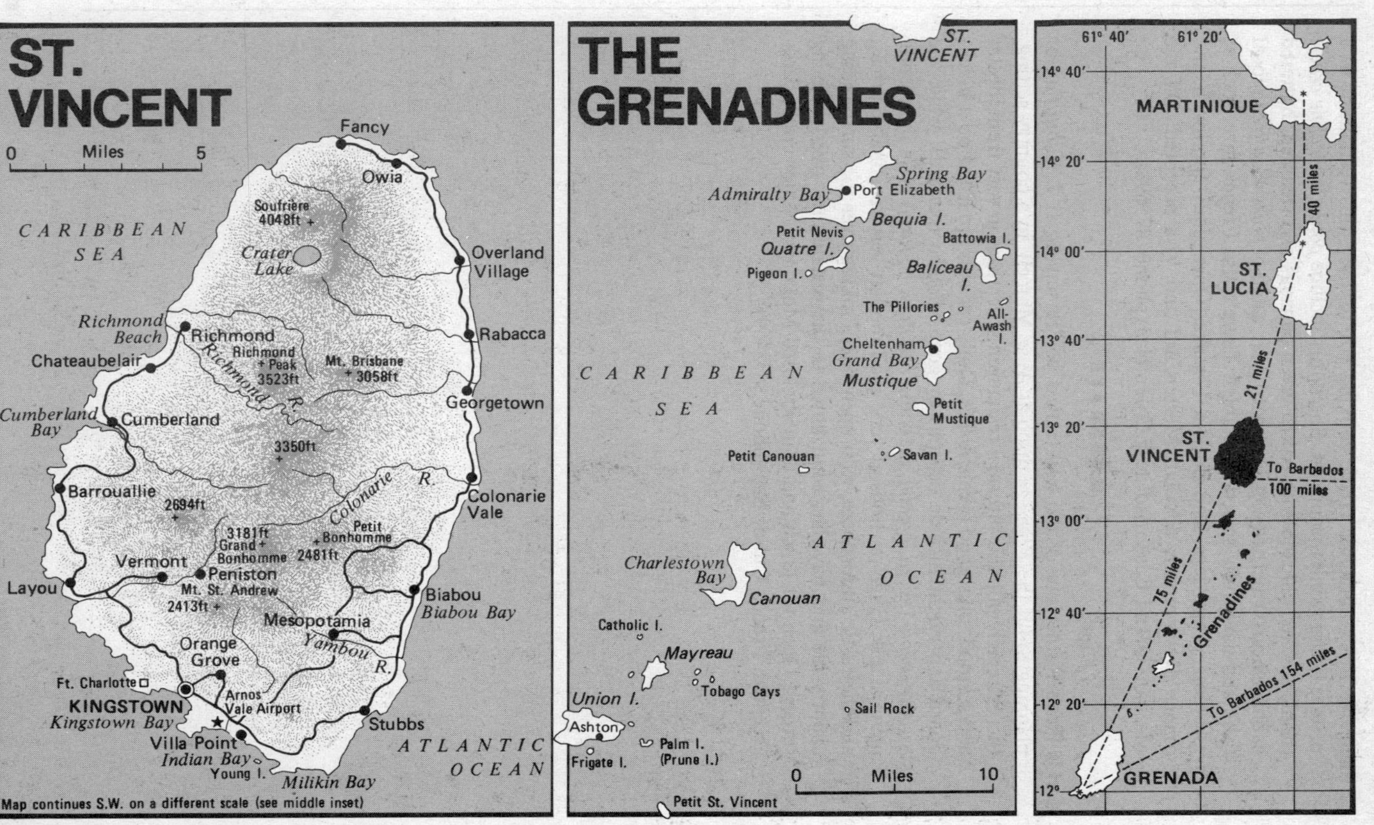
ST. VINCENT
0 Miles 5
CARIBBEAN SEA
Fancy
Owia
Soufrière 4048ft
Crater Lake
Overland Village
Richmond Beach
Richmond
Richmond Peak 3523ft
Mt. Brisbane 3058ft
Richmond R.
Rabacca
Chateaubelair
Georgetown
Cumberland Bay
Cumberland
3350ft
Colonarie R.
Colonarie Vale
Barrouallie
2694ft
3181ft Grand Bonhomme
Petit Bonhomme 2481ft
Vermont
Peniston
Layou
Mt. St. Andrew 2413ft
Biabou
Biabou Bay
Mesopotamia
Yambou R.
Orange Grove
Ft. Charlotte
KINGSTOWN
Kingstown Bay
Arnos Vale Airport
Stubbs
Villa Point
Indian Bay
Young I.
Milikin Bay
ATLANTIC OCEAN
Map continues S.W. on a different scale (see middle inset)
THE GRENADINES
ST. VINCENT
Spring Bay
Admiralty Bay
Port Elizabeth
Bequia I.
Petit Nevis
Quatre I.
Battowia I.
Pigeon I.
Baliceau I.
The Pillories
All-Awash I.
Cheltenham
Grand Bay
Mustique
CARIBBEAN SEA
Petit Mustique
Petit Canouan
Savan I.
ATLANTIC OCEAN
Charlestown Bay
Canouan
Catholic I.
Mayreau
Tobago Cays
Union I.
Sail Rock
Ashton
Palm I. (Prune I.)
Frigate I.
0 Miles 10
Petit St. Vincent
61° 40′
61° 20′
14° 40′
14° 20′
14° 00′
13° 40′
13° 20′
13° 00′
12° 40′
12° 20′
12°
MARTINIQUE
40 miles
ST. LUCIA
21 miles
ST. VINCENT
To Barbados 100 miles
75 miles
Grenadines
To Barbados 154 miles
GRENADA

St. Vincent and the Grenadines

St. Vincent and the Grenadine chain, more than 32 islands and cays anchored in the East Caribbean between St. Lucia and Grenada, have long been known to sailors and yachtsmen for their many quiet bays, beautiful beaches, pristine water, and coral reefs. The island of St. Vincent, known locally as "the mainland," has a largely unexplored interior alive with rushing rivers and waterfalls. The Grenadines offer all the luxury and charm of the Caribbean, with none of the commercial clamor of its so-called "glamour" destinations.

Kingstown, the major port and capital of St. Vincent, is a pleasantly bustling center of inter-island sea traffic and trade. The island's uncluttered volcanic beaches and tropically forested, mountainous landscapes make it a joy to explore — both for the hundreds of yachtsmen who make it a regular stop on their annual voyages around the Caribbean and for land-based visitors who fly in from Barbados and the surrounding small islands to relax in its verdant hills or along its unspoiled shores. A steady breeze provided by the northeast trade winds tempers the Caribbean's tropical warmth and creates a climate that stays within a shade of 78F all year. This, plus its healthy supply of rain and fertile terrain, has made St. Vincent one of the most cultivated isles of the West Indies, producing an abundance of fruit, vegetables, and arrowroot.

St. Vincent was one of the last strongholds of the Carib Indians; they managed to retard European colonization for almost 2 centuries after Columbus discovered the island and claimed it for Spain. However, by the 18th century, the French and the English were engaged in a bitter struggle for control of the Caribbean, and St. Vincent and the Grenadines were as much embroiled in the ongoing hostilities as any of the other islands. St. Vincent was passed between Britain and France three times during the 18th century, but in 1789 it became a British Crown Colony. It remained so until 1969, when it became a British Associated State. On October 27, 1979, the island, together with the Grenadines, proclaimed its complete independence. Still, emotional and economic ties with Great Britain remain strong, though unofficial.

Though essentially British, the islands reflect delightful traces of French culture. English is the official language, but some of the islets and cays have as much a sense of kinship with Martinique or Guadeloupe as with nearby, steadfastly British possessions. Nor do the influences stop with Europe. During the 18th century, while the Carib Indians were fighting off shiploads of Europeans, they were welcoming stranded black slaves from a ship wrecked off the coast. As a result of their hospitality, a new race of black Carib developed, which soon outnumbered the original tribe. During the mid-18th century, an influx of East Indian laborers and Portuguese settlers added new strains to the multiracial population (which currently numbers about 111,000) that still exists today. But the lasting influence of the French and the English can still be observed in both language and local architecture.

The Grenadines have served as safe harbors and prime ports-of-call for yachts for years. The islands and cays are beautiful — with exquisitely clear water and white powder beaches — but economically poor. To sustain themselves, most Grenadinians turn to boat building, to seasonal labor on other islands, and according to legend and local lore, to smuggling.

Life on St. Vincent and in the Grenadines is slow, simple, and relaxing. Tourists are welcomed with warmth and hospitality, but Tourism — with a capital T — is not. In fact, the unobtrusive form that tourism takes on these islands probably contributes to the overwhelming friendliness that all visitors sense as soon as they arrive. Several of the Grenadines have become the exclusive retreats of extremely well-off travelers. The rich have not taken over completely, however, and there are still many spots on the islands that are inexpensive or moderately priced and very comfortable. If you don't mind occasional interruptions in electric service, unannounced changes in inter-island boat schedules, and planes that may not arrive on time, and if you really want to do nothing but relax and enjoy the sea and some very nice people, St. Vincent and the Grenadines might be just the perfect group of hideaway islands for you.

St. Vincent and the Grenadines At-a-Glance

FROM THE AIR

St. Vincent looks like an imperfectly shaped oval kite with the Grenadine Islands trailing behind as its tail. Although it is only 18 miles long and 11 miles wide, St. Vincent has a richly varied terrain: many sand beaches washed by calm waters on the west (Caribbean) coast; breakers rushing against steep cliffs and rocks on the east (Atlantic) coast; plantations, fertile valleys, rolling hills, winding rivers, forests, and a 4,048-foot volcanic mountain, Soufrière, inland. The island's capital, Kingstown, sits on a scenic harbor on the southwest corner of the island. Two miles from Kingstown is Arnos Vale Airport, where flights land from Barbados and St. Lucia (the connecting point for flights from North America to St. Vincent and the Grenadines). St. Vincent lies 100 miles due west of Barbados, 21 miles south of St. Lucia, and 75 miles north of Grenada; it's about 1,600 miles from Miami and 2,100 miles from New York.

Although there are over 100 bodies of land in the Grenadine chain, the major islands running southward from St. Vincent are Bequia, Mustique, Canouan, Mayreau, Union, Palm (officially Prune Island), Petit St. Vincent, Carriacou, and Petit Martinique. The latter two are administered by Grenada, while the others are governed by St. Vincent.

SPECIAL PLACES

ST. VINCENT — Kingstown St. Vincent's capital and commercial center, with a population of roughly 10,000, is a lively, busy port. The waterfront, with island schooners unloading their cargoes and transatlantic freighters loading bananas and other island produce, is fascinating to watch. On Saturday mornings, the marketplace at the south end of town bursts with color and buzzes with activity when small farmers, fishermen, and merchants from all over the island come to town to sell yams, breadfruit, mangoes, papayas, soursop, and other produce as well as colorful fish. In the center of town, on Grenville Street, you will notice St. Mary's Catholic Church, a mishmash of architectural styles designed in the 1930s by a Flemish monk whose grasp of Romanesque, Gothic, and Moorish architecture was fanciful but flawed. On the north side of town, Fort Charlotte sits at the end of a winding road, on a promontory rising 636 feet above sea level. Named after the wife of King George III, the fort was built by the English to defend the island against the French. Three of the original cannon remain in place, and the living quarters of the military personnel have been turned into a museum containing a series of murals that depict black Carib history. The biggest attraction of Fort Charlotte, however, is the magnificent view of St. Vincent and the Grenadine Islands beyond. Access routes to the fort are in good condition; it's open daily from 6 AM to 6 PM (phone: 456-1165). East of the fort, on the north side of Kingstown, are the Botanical Gardens, the oldest of their kind in the Western Hemisphere (founded in 1765). The gardens cover 20 acres and encompass a formidable display of tropical plants (including a breadfruit tree grown from the original plant brought to St. Vincent from Tahiti by Captain Bligh in 1793). The gardens are also the site of the small, artifact-filled *National Museum,* which is open Wednesday mornings, Saturday afternoons, and when a cruise ship docks. There's an admission charge. For additional information, contact the museum curator (phone: 456-1787).

ELSEWHERE ON THE ISLAND

LEEWARD HIGHWAY North from Kingstown, the road climbs a series of steep hills with magnificent views all along the way before descending close to the sea and leading to the village of Layou. Ask any one of the villagers to show you the picture rock, which is one of several petroglyphs carved by Carib Indians over 13 centuries ago. Farther north is the whaling village of Barrouallie, where fishermen still set out with harpoons in small, brightly painted boats to hunt pilot whales, just as they did in the 18th century. Barrouallie and the nearby Grenadine island of Bequia are two of the few places left in the world where this type of whaling is still done. Off Bequia, huge humpback whales are harpooned from open boats. The tourist board is careful to inform visitors that "whaling here presents no danger to the extinction of the species, since so few are caught each year." (It is likely that the whalers will become extinct here before the whales — in recent years, catches have consisted of only a few.) When a whale is brought in, the occasion is cause for a big celebration. To finish your excursion with a swim, continue on the Leeward Highway to Richmond Beach before returning to Kingstown.

WINDWARD SIDE HIGHWAY A drive along St. Vincent's eastern Atlantic coast from Kingstown features the coastal surf pounding against rocky shores, banana and coconut plantations, arrowroot fields, and gently sloping hills set in a peaceful landscape. However, things here aren't always so peaceful; tropical storms and the occasional hurricane seriously damage St. Vincent's banana and coconut crops. Although the roads have improved in recent years, to venture past Rabacca Dry River to the northern tip of the island, you may need a four-wheel-drive vehicle. Check with the tourist board before setting out.

MARRIAQUA VALLEY (ALSO CALLED THE MESOPOTAMIA VALLEY) Another area worth visiting on St. Vincent. The journey begins at the Vigie Highway, just east of the Arnos Vale Airport runway, and continues northeast, then north, to the town of Mesopotamia. The route passes freshwater streams, boys on donkeys, terraced farms, winding rivers, and deep forests before heading north to Montreal Gardens (about 12 miles from Kingstown), where there are natural mineral springs, as well as tropical flowers and plants.

QUEEN'S DRIVE This trip loops into the high hills and steep ridges east of Kingstown. Begin at Sion Hill, just southeast of Kingstown, halfway to the Arnos Vale Airport. After turning northeast and driving a very short distance (about a city block), veer sharply right and climb Dorsetshire Hill to Millers Ridge, where the road will turn south and then head back toward the airport, with breathtaking views of the Grenadines and Kingstown along the way.

SPECIAL PLACES

THE GRENADINES Most of the 100 or more islands and islets that make up the Grenadines appear as mere dots on yachtsmen's charts. Stretching southward from St. Vincent, the major islands administered by St. Vincent are described below.

BEQUIA Northernmost of the Grenadines and 9 miles south of St. Vincent, Bequia (pronounced *Beck*-way), a picturesque island, is home to boat builders and sailors, and is one of the last whaling stations in the world where humpback whales are still captured by hand-hurled harpoons. This tradition will soon die out, as only one harpooner is still alive. Bequia's largest town, Port Elizabeth, sits at the edge of sheltered Admiralty Bay. The Bequia Tourist Bureau (phone: 458-3286), near the dock, dispenses information, sells postcards and stamps, and will recommend a driver to take visitors around the island ($15 to $20 per hour for four people; settle on the price in advance). Be sure to see several sites: the fort, which offers a sweeping view of the harbor; Industry Bay, where you can stop for a swim and a curry lunch; lovely Lower Bay with its popular *De Reef* restaurant (see *Eating Out*); the beaches of Princess Margaret and Friendship Bay; Paget Farm, the last whalers' village, opposite Petit Nevis; the steep vista point, which offers a 360° view of St. Vincent and the islands south; and Moon Hole, a remarkable American community built into the cliffs at the southern end of the island (the cave homes are private; visitors must make advance arrangements through the tourist bureau). In town, stop by *Mauvin's* or the *Sargeant Brothers* shops, where artisans craft beautifully accurate sailboat and ship models. But save time to browse along the line of souvenir and craft shops (*Crab Hole,* with its silk-screening studio, is a standout; see *Shopping*), small restaurants, and snack bars south of town on the beach between the *Frangipani* and the *Plantation House,* formerly called and still often referred to as the *Sunny Caribee.*

MUSTIQUE Princess Margaret, David Bowie, and Mick Jagger are only the most famous of the wealthy and celebrated people who own homes on this carefully manicured private island, 15 miles south of St. Vincent. About half of the mansions can be rented when the owners are not in residence; high-season prices, which include staff and car, range from about $2,500 a week for a 2-bedroom villa to $15,000 for a 6-bedroom house (Princess Margaret's place goes for a mere $6,500 in high season, and Mick Jagger's Japanese-style house rents for $6,500 off-season, $8,000 in-season). Rentals are handled by the *Mustique Company* (phone: 458-4621). Among the other lodging possibilities here are *Cotton House,* an exquisitely restored cotton estate; and *Firefly House* (see *Checking In* for more information on both places). Cars and motor-scooters are expensive to rent here, and a driver's license is required. Besides the magnificent mansions, don't miss Macaroni Beach, a lovely stretch of powder-white sand flanked by clear turquoise water, or the calmer waters of Gelliceaux Bay. *Basil's Bar,* one of the many enterprises run by successful entrepreneur Basil Charles, is where the yachting crowd gathers to drink and socialize (see *Eating Out*).

CANOUAN This sunny, offbeat isle, 25 miles south of St. Vincent, is visited mostly by yachtspeople. It's a little crescent-shaped haven surrounded by wide shallows and coral. Although it now has a paved airstrip and three hotels — including the *Canouan Beach* hotel, which is bringing development to the southern part of the island — it remains unspoiled. The small population of fishermen and farmers is friendly, and the white sand beaches are excellent.

UNION ISLAND The southernmost of the Grenadines, Union is a mountainous island and a well-known port of call for yachts. It has a small but busy airstrip, a few small inns, and a popular boaters' hangout with a French touch, the *Anchorage Yacht Club* (see *Checking In*). It's also a connecting point for launch access to nearby Petit St. Vincent and Palm Island, as well as the secluded islands of Mayreau and the national "water park" that surrounds the uninhabited Tobago Cays.

TOBAGO CAYS Four tiny islets, protected as a national park; though uninhabited, they have camping and picnic sites, handsomely protected anchorages for overnighting yachts, and incredibly beautiful snorkeling reefs. A must stop on any cruise.

MAYREAU Long a favorite yacht anchorage and occasionally visited by cruise ships now, this 1½-square-mile island boasts a tropical-gardened South Seas–style hotel, the *Salt Whistle Bay Club,* with villas, outdoor dining, a boutique, and some yacht charter and cruising facilities (see *Checking In*). The resort is a 20-minute walk along a pleasant bush trail from the tiny village (pop. 170) at the top of the hill. The island's beaches are among the world's best.

YOUNG ISLAND, PETIT ST. VINCENT, AND PALM ISLAND These three private islands in the Grenadines are essentially resorts whose guests constitute the majority of the population. Young Island, 200 yards south of St. Vincent, is known for its South Seas atmosphere. The other two, about 40 miles south of Kingstown, are reached by flying to Union Island (20 minutes on *LIAT* or *Mustique Airways; Air Martinique* flies in from Fort-de-France) and then there's a resort-launch pickup.

Sources and Resources

TOURIST INFORMATION

The St. Vincent Department of Tourism (Administrative Centre, Bay St. in Kingstown; phone: 457-1502) has information on accommodations and sightseeing and also carries the *St. Vincent and the Grenadines Visitor's Guide* booklet, which is especially helpful in providing facts, background information, and travel advice. There is a St. Vincent and the Grenadines information desk in the arrivals area of Grantley Adams International Airport in Barbados, open from 1 PM until the last flight to St. Vincent has gone. There is also a tourist information office on the island of Bequia (on the waterfront in Port Elizabeth) and at Clifton on Union Island. For information about St. Vincent tourist offices in the US, see GETTING READY TO GO.

A lovely coffee-table book is available in shops and some hotels: *St. Vincent and the Grenadines — A Plural Country,* by Dana Jinkins and Jill Bobrow (Concepts Publishing; $20).

LOCAL COVERAGE Two weekly newspapers are published on St. Vincent: the *Vincentian* and the *News;* both come out on Fridays.

RADIO AND TELEVISION

In addition to the local government-owned AM radio (705) and TV stations, there is cable TV and television programming beamed in from Barbados by BTS.

TELEPHONE

The area code for St. Vincent and the Grenadines is 809.

ENTRY REQUIREMENTS

Proof of citizenship (a passport is preferred, but a birth certificate or voter's registration card, accompanied by a photo ID, will do) and a return or ongoing ticket are the only documents required of US or Canadian citizens. St. Vincent charges an airport departure tax of about $7.50 ($20 EC).

CLIMATE AND CLOTHES

The thermometer hovers around 78 to 80F (25 to 26C) all year in St. Vincent and the Grenadines, and the northeast trade winds bring a gentle breeze that tempers the tropical heat. The mountains of St. Vincent attract more rain than the flatter atolls of the Grenadines. Summers are stiller and more humid; fall is hurricane season. Dress on the islands is very casual: Women wear bright blouses, skirts, slacks, jeans, and modest shorts; bikinis on the beach but not in town. (Topless and nude sunbathing is illegal.) Men wear slacks, shorts, and sport shirts; neither jacket nor tie is needed, as evenings are informal.

MONEY

The Eastern Caribbean dollar is the official currency of the islands. The rate of exchange is currently about $2.68 EC to $1 US. When shopping, always be certain which dollars — EC or US — are being quoted. US and Canadian dollars are accepted in most restaurants, hotels, and stores, as are traveler's checks. Some hotels and restaurants honor major US credit cards. Banking hours on St. Vincent are 8 AM to noon or 1 PM on weekdays and also 2 or 3 to 5 PM on Fridays; *Barclays Bank*'s hours on Fridays are 8 AM to 5 PM. All prices in this chapter are quoted in US dollars.

LANGUAGE

English is the language of this former British colony, and it is spoken with a touch of a Scottish lilt, with West Indian expressions.

TIME

St. Vincent and the Grenadines are in the atlantic standard time zone: When it's noon in New York, it's 1 PM in St. Vincent. During daylight saving time, the hour is the same in both places.

CURRENT

Except for Petit St. Vincent, where the current is 110 volts, 60 cycles, electricity generally operates at 220–240 volts, 50 cycles. American appliances must have converters. Some hotels can supply them, but it's more prudent to bring one along. Young Island and Mustique's *Cotton House* use British-style three-prong plugs.

TIPPING

Most hotels add a 10% to 15% service charge to the bill, and that takes care of room maids and other staff members. If a service charge is not added, tip bellboys 50¢ to $1 per bag, depending on the amount of luggage, $1 minimum; room maids $1 to $2 per person per day; and ask the manager what is customary for waiters. Tip taxi drivers 10% of the fare. Restaurants usually include a 10% service charge in the tab; if not, give the waiter a 10% tip, 15% if you're especially pleased with the service.

GETTING AROUND

BUS Small, colorfully painted vans set out from the market square in Kingstown and run along all the main roads. They are inexpensive, efficient, and fun. Just stick your hand out anywhere along the road and they'll stop for you. You pay when you disembark; rates run from about 40¢ to $1.90. Van owners love music, so be prepared to listen to some maximum-volume calypso.

CAR RENTAL *Avis* has a branch in Kingstown (phone: 456-5610). Other car rental firms in Kingstown include *Car Rentals* (phone: 456-1862 or 457-1614), *David's Auto Clinic* (phone: 457-1116), *Kim's Rentals* (Grenville St.; phone: 456-1884), and *De Freitas* (phone: 456-1862). Rates run about $35 per day. Car rental is more expensive on Mustique. The *Cotton House* (phone: 456-4777) charges up to $85 per day, and *Mustique Co. Ltd.* (phone: 458-4621; 457-1531 on St. Vincent) charges $75 to $85 a day. Shop around. The tourist department's *Car Rental Services* booklet contains helpful data on rental firms, plus other useful driver information. A temporary driver's license is required and may be obtained at the airport, the police station on Bay Street, or the Licensing Authority on Halifax Street. A valid US, Canadian, or international driver's license must be presented; there's a small fee (about $7.50). Remember that driving is on the *left.* And be very careful; there are lots of curves and sharp turns in the roads — sound your horn beforehand and be certain you're still on the left after the turn.

FERRY SERVICES A variety of boats offer island-to-island transportation or ferry service. The mailboat runs three times a week through the Grenadines (from St. Vincent to Union Island and back), and there is regular service (twice daily on weekdays and Sundays, and once on Saturdays) from Kingstown to Bequia. For information about ferry schedules and services, check with the tourist office in Kingstown or your hotel. Currently, there is service daily on the MV *Admiral I* and *Admiral II* to Bequia; there are also trips to Union via Bequia, to Canouan, and to Mayreau every other day. The island schooners *Friendship Rose* and *Maxann O* sail every weekday to Bequia. The *Snapper* makes the circuit from St. Vincent to Bequia, Canouan, Mayreau, and Union every other weekday and from St. Vincent to Canouan, Mayreau, and Union on Saturdays. All vessels take 1 to 1½ hours to travel between St. Vincent and Bequia and charge the same fare. A one-way trip to Bequia is $3.75, $4.50 on Sundays; to Union, about $7.50; to Canouan, about $4.90; and to Mayreau, about $5.65. The *Petit St. Vincent* and *Palm Island* resorts arrange launch pickups at Union Island for arriving guests.

MOTORBIKES Motorbikes are available on Mustique from *Mustique Co. Ltd.* (phone: 458-4621) for $35 per day.

SIGHTSEEING TOURS Minibus or taxi tours are best arranged through the tourist office, which has a trained Tour Guide Unit, or through the Taxi Drivers Association (phone: 457-1807). Tour operators in Kingstown include *Barefoot Holidays* (phone: 456-9334), *Global Travel* (phone: 456-1601), *Grenadine Tours* (phone: 458-4818), and *Emerald Travel* (phone: 457-1996).

TAXI Plentiful, unmetered, with rates set by the government. A listing of fares between island points is available from the tourist office. Agree on the rate with the driver — or ask someone at your hotel to do so — before getting into any cab. The fare from St. Vincent's Arnos Vale Airport to most hotels is about $10, plus a 10% tip. On Bequia, there are water taxis to the beaches from the *Frangipani* and *Plantation House* hotels.

Many of the taxi drivers provide good, well-informed guided tours. Your hotel can recommend one and negotiate the rate, about $15 per car per hour.

INTER-ISLAND FLIGHTS

LIAT has daily scheduled flights from Barbados to Mustique and Union Island via St. Vincent, and between St. Vincent and St. Lucia and all the way down the chain to Caracas, Venezuela. *Air Martinique* operates twice daily service to St. Vincent and Union Island from Martinique, via St. Lucia and Barbados. If your destination is one of the other Grenadines, you must take another short flight from St. Vincent or board a boat in Kingstown. *Mustique Airways* has frequent and efficient charter service to

Mustique and a shuttle between St. Vincent and Bequia (now more accessible than ever due to its new 3,600-foot airstrip). *SVG Air* also handles local charters, including direct Barbados-Mustique and Barbados–Union Island flights. Ask your hotel to book a connecting flight when you make your room reservations, and don't forget to confirm your return flight 72 hours before departure.

SPECIAL EVENTS

The St. Vincent *Carnival,* held in late June through early July (moved from the traditional pre-*Lenten* time in February), is a week-long celebration with traditional parades, dancing, music, steel band and calypso competitions, and feasting. Other holidays, when stores and businesses close, are *New Year's Day, St. Vincent and the Grenadines* (or *Discovery*) *Day* (January 22), *Good Friday, Easter Monday, Labour Day* (May 5), *Whitmonday, Caricom Day* (first Monday in July), *Carnival Day* (Tuesday after *Caricom Day*), *Emancipation Day* (first Monday in August), *Independence Day* (October 27), *Christmas,* and *Boxing Day* (December 26). In December, Mustique entrepreneur Basil Charles and local homeowners David Bowie and Mick Jagger co-host a barbecue on the beach to benefit the tiny island school. But you don't have to pull any strings to get in; just pull out your wallet and pay the hefty admission charge, and you're more than welcome. Details are available at *Basil's Bar* (phone: 458-4621).

SHOPPING

Although St. Vincent and the Grenadines aren't shoppers' paradises, a number of stores offer batik and tie-dyed fabrics, and various handicrafts. The Saturday marketplace in Kingstown is the liveliest shopping "center," although the bill of fare is fresh produce and staples, not items that you can carry home, except, perhaps, a bottle of locally made hot sauce — pure fire if taken in heavy doses, but delicious when used sparingly. Other stops worth including in your shopping itinerary include the following:

BASIL'S BOUTIQUE Owned by local businessman Basil Charles, this shop offers unusual Balinese batik items, including resortwear, as well as hand-painted T-shirts, and curiosities. Mustique (phone: 458-4621).

CRAB HOLE Nestled on the beach by the *Plantation House,* it features unique clothing and accessories for men, women, and kids. The sports clothes, hats, totes, bikinis, and pareos are all hand-sewn in original silk-screened cottons that you can watch them print in the workshop out back. Belmont, Bequia (phone: 458-3290).

ELLEN SCHWARZ A scrimshander, she works and sells from her boat, the *Praña,* tied up by the *Frangipani* hotel in town. Bequia (phone: 458-3244).

GARDEN BOUTIQUE Exquisite hand-dyed blouses, locally made batik dresses, and jewelry. Port Elizabeth, Bequia (phone: 458-3892).

GIGGLES Fine designer clothes for women. *Cobblestone Arcade.* Kingstown, St. Vincent (phone: 457-1174).

HIBISCUS Well-made, well-designed Caribbean grass rugs, mahogany carvings, and bowls. James St., Kingstown, St. Vincent (no phone).

ISLAND THINGS Hand-crocheted cotton sweaters, locally made dolls, woodcarvings, and jams. Port Elizabeth, Bequia (phone: 458-3903).

LOCAL COLOR T-shirts, hand-painted bathing suits, jewelry. Port Elizabeth, Bequia (phone: 458-3202).

MADE IN DE SHADE Imported women's fashions plus the work of local artists. Bay St., Kingstown, St. Vincent (phone: 457-2364) and at the *Gingerbread* complex, Port Elizabeth, Bequia (phone: 458-3001).

MAUVIN'S MODEL BOAT SHOP Beautifully hand-crafted model boats (including a copy of your own yacht if you so order). Port Elizabeth, Bequia (phone: 458-3669).

MELINDA'S One-of-a-kind hand-painted T-shirts. Port Elizabeth, Bequia (phone: 458-3895).

NOAH'S ARKADE A must-see for crafts — local and imported — this place also specializes in locally made tropical clothing, herbal teas, and spices. At two locations: on St. Vincent at Bay St., Kingstown (phone: 457-1513); and on Bequia at the *Frangipani* hotel, Port Elizabeth (phone: 458-3424).

ST. VINCENT CRAFTSMEN CENTER Noted specialists in local and imported crafts. Frenches St., Kingstown, St. Vincent (phone: 457-2516).

SAM MCDOWELL Locally crafted scrimshaw. Paget Farm, Bequia (phone: 458-3865).

SARGEANT BROTHERS Handcrafted model boats. Port Elizabeth, Bequia (phone: 458-3344).

SOLANA'S A crafts shop featuring the work of Caribbean artisans. Port Elizabeth, Bequia (phone: 458-3554).

SPROTTIES Original hand-painted and silk-screen designs. Port Elizabeth, Bequia (phone: 458-3904).

TREASURE A fine selection of gifts, including local crafts and upscale beachwear in the pink cottage across from *Basil's Bar.* Mustique (phone: 456-3521).

Y. DE LIMA Offers a fine selection of high-quality jewelry. Bay St., St. Vincent (phone: 477-1681).

SPORTS

Basically it's the sea — swimming, snorkeling, scuba diving, fishing, yachting, and sailing — that brings sportspeople to St. Vincent and the Grenadines.

BOATING It's a way of life in these islands — the most outstanding sailing grounds of the entire Caribbean. Various types of craft are available: Sunfish or Sailfish can be borrowed or rented from some hotels (*Young Island* and *Sunset Shores* on St. Vincent). Check the *Sunsports* facilities on Bequia, as well as the hotels at Friendship Bay. Day sails are extremely popular in the Grenadines and easily arranged; check with your hotel. *Young Island, Palm Island,* and *Petit St. Vincent* hotels offer regular day sails, as do *Canouan* and *Cotton House* on Mustique. On Bequia, day charters on the *S/Y Pelangi* (phone: 458-3255), *Toien* (phone: 458-3605), and *Passion* (phone: 458-3884) run about $50 to $65 per person. On Union Island, a sail on the *Scaramouche* (phone: 458-8418), with a fine lunch and open bar, costs about $40 per person.

Bareboat and skippered yacht charters are also available through *Barefoot Yacht Charters* on St. Vincent (phone: 456-9334 or 456-9526), the Lagoon Marina (phone: 458-4308), or the *Young Island* resort. On Union Island, Captain Yannis at the *Anchorage Yacht Club* (phone: 458-8244) usually knows which yachts are currently offering charters in the Grenadines. On Bequia, check with the *Frangipani* resort (phone: 458-3255). *Dive St. Vincent* (phone: 457-4714), on Villa, a stretch of land opposite Young Island, offers speedboat trips along the west coast to the Falls of Baleine and Wallilabou. For a slower, quieter experience, the *Sea Breeze* guesthouse (phone: 458-4969) sponsors a sailing trip to the falls on a 36-foot sloop.

HORSEBACK RIDING Arrange through Mustique's *Cotton House*. Rates are $30 per hour.

MOUNTAIN CLIMBING The Soufrière climb takes the better part of a day and should only be attempted in good weather and with a reliable guide. Make arrangements through the tourist board. The cost of a guide and jeep runs about $28 per person. A lovely, easier tour is the Buccament Valley Nature Trail along two marked paths through tropical rain forest. There are pre-Columbian stone writings at Buccament Cave. Book through the tourist board.

SNORKELING AND SCUBA There's plenty of marine life to observe under the sea here: coral formations, plants, brightly colored fish. Especially rewarding spots for diving are in the waters surrounding Young Island, Palm Island, Mayreau, Petit Canouan, Petit Nevis and Pigeon Island off Bequia, Pillory Rocks near Mustique, and the Tobago Cays. Off the island of Mayreau there is a sunken World War I gunboat 55 feet down. *Dive St. Vincent* (phone: 457-4714), opposite Young Island, offers complete diving services, including rentals, guided dive trips, night dives, and resort courses. Full scuba certification courses are also available on Bequia at *Dive Bequia* (phone: 458-3504), on Mustique at *Mustique Watersports* (phone: 456-3522), and on Union Island through the *Anchorage Yacht Club* (phone:

458-8244) or *Dive Anchorage* (phone: 458-8647). All of them also offer "certification vacations" — learn while exploring the Grenadines. There are also dive shops and other water sports facilities on Bequia at the *Frangipani, Friendship Bay,* and *Bequia Beach* hotels. Snorkeling equipment is available at most major hotels, at *Basil's Bar* on Mustique, *De Reef* at Lower Bay on Bequia, and the dive shops listed above.

SPORT FISHING Not formally organized, but most hotels and dive shops will arrange a fishing boat. Bring your own rod and reel. Some charter yachts are equipped with deep-sea fishing gear. The catch includes sailfish, marlin, snapper, dolphin, kingfish, tuna, bonito, blue runner, mackerel, jack, grouper, and pompano. Note that spearfishing is not allowed here except by special permission.

SQUASH *Cecil Cyrus Squash Complex* (phone: 456-1805) has 4 courts, the *Prospect Racquet Club* (in Prospect, 4 miles outside Kingstown; phone: 458-4866) has 2 courts, and the *Grand View Beach* hotel has 1 court.

SWIMMING AND SUNNING There are dozens of superb beaches on the shores of these islands. Most hotels are located on beaches, and you can visit as many others as you want on St. Vincent, where all beaches are public. The sands of the volcanic island of St. Vincent vary in color from the black of the north to the golden and white coral beaches of the south (where most of the resorts are located). The waters on the leeward side and in the lagoons are best for swimming; on the windward side the sea is rough. Swimmers are warned not to go very far out and not to swim alone.

TENNIS On St. Vincent, courts are at the *Prospect Racquet Club* (in Prospect; phone: 458-4866), the *Emerald Valley* hotel, *Young Island* resort, and the *Grand View Beach* hotel; on Bequia at the *Plantation House, Spring on Bequia, Friendship Bay,* and *Frangipani;* they're also at the *PSV* and *Palm Island* resorts; and on Mustique at the *Cotton House.*

WINDSURFING Available on St. Vincent at the *Young Island* resort (phone: 458-4826, ask for Irwyn Cumberbatch), where $20 will buy resort guests all the lessons they need. On Mustique, the *Cotton House* hotel (phone: 456-4777) has windsurfing equipment available, but no instruction. Windsurfing boards are also available on Bequia at the *Frangipani, Friendship Bay, Plantation House,* and *Bequia Beach* hotels, and at *De Reef* restaurant at Lower Bay.

NIGHTLIFE

The *Emerald Valley* hotel casino (with blackjack, roulette, and slot machines) is open nightly (phone: 456-7140). *Young Island* resort has music 4 nights a week. Most of the action is over well before midnight. On Thursday nights, flaming torches light the stone staircase of 18th-century Fort Duvernette on a satellite island a few yards from Young, and the hotel's guests are shuttled over by boat for a memorable cocktail party. Non-guests must reserve, as space on the rock is limited. *Basil's Too* (Indian Bay, St. Vincent; phone: 458-4205), next to the Young Island landing pier and under the same ownership as Mustique's *Basil's Bar* (see below), is a popular disco. It has a live band 2 to 3 nights a week, followed by disco music until the last guest leaves; Saturday night sees big action here. Otherwise, most after-dark diversion is provided by the hotels.

In the Grenadines, most resort hotels have a beach barbecue or some sort of "jump-up" 1 night a week. On Bequia, *Frangipani's* has a great "jump-up," especially on Thursday nights. *Friendship Bay* hotel (10 minutes from Port Elizabeth) really cooks on Saturday nights. On Mustique, *Basil's Bar* (phone: 458-4621) has a "jump-up" every Wednesday night and whenever one of the small, posh cruise ships calls in. *Basil's* is extremely popular with yachtspeople, jet set execs, titled homeowners, and even with the snooty celebs, so most of the island turns up here sooner or later.

Best on the Islands

CHECKING IN

The best hotels on these islands are worlds unto themselves, offering casual, pampered luxury and seclusion. They can be expensive, but in most cases they are worth it, if you can afford from about $220 to over $500 for two per day in winter (with all meals). There are accommodations that offer island ambience and amenities at more moderate prices: $100 to $220 for two per day in winter, breakfast and dinner included; it's also possible to get a basic room without meals for less than $60 — such places are listed here as inexpensive. Prices drop by about 30% in summer. A tax of 5% is added to all hotel bills, and most hotels also add a 10% to 15% service charge in lieu of tipping.

About half of the mansions on Mustique can be rented when their owners aren't around; prices range from about $2,500 a week for a 2-bedroom villa to $15,000 for a 6-bedroom house, in high season, including staff and car. Contact *Mustique Co. Ltd.* (phone: 458-4621). All telephone numbers are in the 809 area code unless otherwise indicated.

For an unforgettable island experience, we begin with our favorites, followed by our recommendations of cost and quality choices of accommodations, listed by price category.

ENCHANTED PRIVATE ISLANDS

Mustique: Cotton House and Mustique Villas With 1,350 practically deserted acres to explore, this exclusive — and until recently little known — isle is Princess Margaret's personal playground (she has a house here), and the people with whom you share it are apt to be peers in stylish cutoffs or barefoot but well-heeled Americans. Once part of a working plantation, *Cotton House* was superbly refurbished and decorated by the late Oliver Messel with intriguing English and Caribbean antiques — sea chests, silver, brasses, and a marvelous secretary's desk covered with cockle shells. The main building is ringed with wide breezy verandahs. Guest accommodations are in several pretty, comfortable cottages, some old and restored, other newer ones near the pool. There are 24 rooms (including 3 poolside cottages and 3 suites). Daytime is apt to be casual. There are beaches to sun on and swim from, water sports (Macaroni Beach has some surf), a tennis court, horseback riding, and an elegant hilltop swimming pool; and if you care to have a quiet read, there are even books in several languages. Nights are somewhat dressier, especially if the princess is in residence. Perhaps because the hotel has so few guests, the welcome seems especially pleasant and personal. Free transportation by van driven by ever-smiling Snakey, who manages all pickups with un-island-like punctuality. Mustique (phone and fax: 456-4777; 914-763-5526 from New York; 800-223-1108 from elsewhere in the US). *Mustique Villas* offers 41 luxurious 2- to 6-room fully staffed villas for weekly rental (phone: 458-4621).

Palm Island Beach Club John and Mary Caldwell discovered Prune Island (its legal name) when it was a bald, 110-acre islet. They planted its palms, opened its resort in 1967, and have been expanding and improving ever since. Now lining stunning Casuarina Beach are 12 cottages, 6 apartments, and 12 houses with 1 to 4 bedrooms, connected by a narrow stone path that winds among the lush palms, sea grapes, casuarinas, and almond trees. A lively alfresco bar at the main beach (there are 5 beaches in all) attracts the bareboat yachting crowd, and there is a variety of water sports, including windsurfing, snorkeling, and scuba diving. In addition, 3 yachts are available for fishing trips and catered day sails. The tennis courts are nearby, and there is a health club on the premises. The island is reached via a 45-minute flight from Barbados to nearby Union Island and a 20-minute launch ride from there. Palm (Prune) Island (phone: 458-8824; 800-776-7256 from the US; fax: 458-8804).

Petit St. Vincent You feel as if the world is yours around here — because it really is. The entire 113-acre island is a single resort, and it all belongs to you. You live in one of 22 airy villas that have been discreetly placed for maximum privacy (the hilltop ones have shielded terraces designed to allow nude sunbathing), plus the best of all possible views. Some are set right on the beaches, others on the small breezy hills overlooking the sea. The management is nonviolently antihassle. You won't be bothered by anyone or anything until you say the word or raise the flag by the door to summon room service — which arrives by jeep. The idea is that the best of everything should be right there when you want it. And it works. For sports: swimming, sailing, snorkeling, tennis, volleyball, croquet, and a health trail. At night: sometime music and good talk with visiting yacht folk. Rates include all meals (the island's meat is flown in from Julia Child's butcher in Massachusetts, lobster is really fresh, and nothing is overcooked) and all sports except those involving charter boats or scuba. Lower rates from mid-April until just before *Christmas.* Closed in September and October. Petit St. Vincent (phone: 458-8801; fax: 458-8428).

Young Island If Gauguin had lingered in the Caribbean, he might have found barefoot happiness on this 25-acre tropical paradise, with its central indoor-outdoor buildings surrounded by gardens and its individual Tahitian cottages with bamboo and *khuskhus* decor, ceiling fans, and outdoor showers. The king-size retreats in local stone and South American hardwood are naturally air conditioned by adjustable jalousies and louvers, entire glass-screened walls that slide away, and ceiling fans. Tiled baths lead to sexy outdoor showers secluded by ferns and luxuriant flowers, though in some of the beach cottages you may find yourself bathing back-to-back with a neighbor. The thatch-roofed *Coconut Bar* floats in waist-high water just offshore, and another bar operates on the beach. Meals are savored under beach gazebos or in a Polynesian pavilion built into the rocks above. There's a pretty beach, a small, free-form pool, water sports (including full diving facilities and instruction and windsurfers), 2 yachts that make regular day trips to Bequia and Mustique, tennis courts, and lots of relaxing (with lots of hammocks to do it in). Several times a week small bands of islanders ferry over to make music in the evening. Otherwise, it's sociable talk over brandy and a short stroll down the garden path to bed. Reached by ferry from Villa Beach dock on St. Vincent (phone: 458-4826; 800-223-1108 from the US; fax: 457-4567).

ST. VINCENT AND JUST OFFSHORE

EXPENSIVE

Grand View Beach Caring family management, smiling efficient service, beautifully landscaped grounds, and a truly grand view await guests at this elegant converted house. There are 20 homey double rooms (including 8 built only 2 years ago), each with bath. All are spacious and breezy; some also have air conditioning. The photogenic swimming pool sits out on the point, and trails lead down to the beach. A fitness center is the most recent addition. Other pluses: tennis and squash courts; summer packages; West Indian fare in a simple dining room with an excellent view. Villa Point (phone: 458-4811; fax: 457-4174).

MODERATE

Browne's on Villa Beach *Young Island* resort manager Vidal Browne's newest hotel caters to the business traveler with telephones, fax machines, a business center, and a valet service. But the 28 rooms still have West Indian flair and a tropical decor at a reasonable price; there's also a restaurant that serves West Indian and international fare. Villa Beach (phone: 457-4000; fax: 457-4040).

Emerald Valley Nestled among verdant hills, 7 miles from Kingstown, this pretty property has 12 rooms in 2-unit chalets, all with kitchenettes and balconies. Guests enjoy 2 freshwater pools, 2 tennis courts, horseback riding and horseshoes. There is also a small gaming room with craps, roulette, blackjack, and slot machines. For walks, there are nature trails in the surrounding hills; there's also a courtesy van for trips to town. Penniston Valley (phone: 456-7140; fax: 456-7145).

Lagoon Formerly *CSY,* this bright, modern hotel has 19 rooms overlooking a marina. Guests have access to the beach and 2 freshwater pools; sailing trips and charters are easily arranged. There's also a fun restaurant and bar with the same great view of the marina. Blue Lagoon (phone: 458-4308; fax: 457-4716).

Petit Byahaut This unusual retreat sits on a horseshoe-shaped bay in a 50-acre private valley accessible only by boat (guests are picked up at docks throughout the island). The accommodations are very basic — 6 open wooden decks with a roofed and netted sleeping area, a queen-size bed, a table and chairs, a propane lamp, and a hammock. These "tents" overlook the sea and are secluded from each other by lush foliage. There are outdoor flush toilets, some "solar showers" (essentially big bags of water warmed by the sun), and some conventional showers. Near the 500-foot sandy beach is an open-air patio, where simple, wholesome meals are served. There's equipment for all water sports, and superb snorkeling and scuba diving right off the beach. Inter-island excursions also can be arranged. The rate includes everything but drinks and snorkel equipment. For nature lovers who don't mind roughing it a bit, this is close to paradise. Located 4½ miles north of Kingston on the leeward coast (phone: 457-7008, leave a message; fax: 457-7008).

Villa Lodge Ten spacious, air conditioned rooms (with extra beds available for children), each with full tub bath, terrace, and TV set, some with a lovely sea view, 5 minutes from the beach. Shares a swimming pool with next-door *Breezeville Apartments.* Another pleasant amenity is the open-air bar with a view of the harbor. Villa Point (phone: 458-4641; fax: 457-4468).

INEXPENSIVE

Cobblestone Inn A converted 200-year-old sugar warehouse in the middle of town, it has 19 rooms; *Basil's,* a popular restaurant and bar (see *Eating Out*); and a pleasant rooftop snack bar. A favorite Vincentian business travelers' and boaters' stopover. Kingstown (phone: 456-1937).

Coconut Beach Inn Friendly, small place on the beach with 10 rooms in a simple but charming island style. There's a pool, piers, and a dock, as well as an open-air bar and restaurant serving Vincentian food and drinks. Indian Bay (phone: 458-4231).

Indian Bay Beach Very simple, but conveniently located, self-catering 12-unit complex on the beach. All rooms are air conditioned. The *A La Mer* alfresco restaurant is popular for its West Indian cuisine and weekly barbecues. Indian Bay Beach (phone: 458-4001; fax: 457-4777).

Umbrella Beach Nine simple but comfortable efficiency apartments, owned by the next-door *French* restaurant — perfect for vacationers and business-folks who'd rather spend money on good food and wine than on posh accommodations. Front rooms have patios on the beach directly opposite Young Island. Villa Beach (phone: 458-4651; fax: 457-4930).

THE GRENADINES

EXPENSIVE

Anchorage Yacht Club This French-owned inn has a certain raffish charm and is popular with yachtspeople and other mostly French-speaking passersby on their way to the other Grenadines. Not nearly so grand as its name, it offers 10 rooms and bungalows, bar, and restaurant with a French chef; also yachting provisions, water sports, day charters, boutique with newspapers from everywhere. Best meeting spot around, great for boating tips and gossip. Clifton, Union (phone: 458-8244; fax: 458-8365).

Canouan Beach The remote island's latest inn, it's on a narrow isthmus in the western part, near the airstrip. On one side is a sandy beach, on the other lies Charlestown Bay, anchorage for passing yachtspeople. Some good snorkeling is found off the reefs at Friendship Point (equipment is available). There's a dive shop and a certified instructor. Other activities include windsurfing, table tennis, volleyball, and day sails. There are 24 superior bungalows and 8 standard bungalows with bright spacious verandahs, while the 11 standard rooms in the main building are adequate and comfortable. All units are air conditioned. The management is French. So-so West Indian food is served in a charming restaurant/bar with friendly service; a steel band plays Mondays and Thursdays. Canouan (phone: 458-8888; fax: 458-8875).

Friendship Bay New owners Lars and Marget Abrahamsson reopened this handsome property after giving it a beach-to-hilltop refurbishing (much needed after a substandard previous remodeling). There are now 27 bright and cheery rooms, a lovely beach with charming beach bar, a restaurant serving local seafood, water sports (including parasailing, windsurfing, and full diving facilities and instruction), a yacht for charter and day cruising to Mustique, tennis courts, and a popular Saturday night barbecue with live reggae, calypso, and rock music. Friendship Bay, Bequia, 10 minutes from Port Elizabeth (phone: 458-3222; fax: 458-3840).

Salt Whistle Bay Club Another charming property on one of the world's most magnificent beaches. A stay here is a total getaway; there are no roads, no cars (just two vans), and no phones. Stone bungalows are hidden among the papaya and palm trees. Most water sports are free to guests; table tennis, darts, volleyball, backgammon, chess, and fishing poles also are available. Diving and boat excursions can be arranged. Alfresco beach bar/restaurant, with live entertainment in season. Delightfully informal and fun. Mayreau (no phone; telex: 06-218309 or radio VHF Ch. 16; reservations: 493-9609; 613-634-1963 in Canada; fax: 613-384-6300 in Canada).

Spring on Bequia Secluded on a 200-year-old working plantation, this place features 10 units in cool stone cottages with purple-heart wood and natural rock showers, perched above Spring Bay. There's an inviting Main House dining room and bar (try the popular Sunday curry lunch buffet). Tennis, pool, and beach (good for snorkeling) are a stroll away. Quiet, contemplative. Spring, Bequia (phone: 458-3414; 612-823-1202 from the US).

MODERATE

Blue Tropic Apartments Nine spacious apartments, all with kitchens and balconies overlooking Friendship Bay. The popular *Flame Tree* restaurant features a Wednesday night barbecue that draws locals from all over the island. Bequia (phone: 458-3573).

Firefly House "You don't have to be rich and famous to enjoy Mustique," says owner Billy Mitchell, who sailed the world for 19 years before building one of the island's first houses. She now rents 4 delightful rooms with private baths and terraces overlooking Britannia Bay. Breakfast and honor bar. Mustique (phone: 458-4621, ext. 414).

Frangipani Friendly and fun; favorite gathering place for visiting yachtspeople and locals even before its owner, James "Son" Mitchell, became Prime Minister of St. Vincent and the Grenadines. There's an open-air bar and popular restaurant (with a Thursday night "jump-up"); a second restaurant is down the beach at the club. The inn has 5 simple rooms in the main house with shared bathrooms and cold water only; the 8 garden units have private baths and hot and cold water. There's a tennis court, windsurfing center, dive shop and water sports center nearby. In addition, the hotel has a phone and fax center for yachters. Port Elizabeth, Bequia (phone: 458-3255; fax: 458-3824).

Old Fort Bequia's most charming hideaway is the dream-come-true of Otmar Schaedle, a well-traveled history and music professor from Germany who found the ruins of an old French fort and rebuilt it in local stone and hardwood for himself and his family. Guests share this special retreat in 6 breezy, rustic apartments, each with private bath and panoramic views from fragrant gardens. Perched on the lofty heights of Mt. Pleasant, this place is a world away from the bustle of the boating crowds below — on a clear day, you can see beyond the glittering lights of Mustique to distant Grenada. Breakfast, lunch, and dinner available. A gem. Bequia (phone: 458-3440; fax: 458-3824).

Plantation House A hospitable place with a wraparound porch, 5 guestrooms, and a dining room overlooking the beach at Admiralty Bay. Seventeen 1- and 2-bedroom cottages and a 3-bedroom beachfront cottage, each with private bath and verandah, are nestled on the grounds. Other features: a small pool; a lighted tennis court; a seaside drink and snack bar; one of Bequia's best restaurants (see *Eating Out*); and most water sports, including full diving facilities. Belmont, Bequia (phone: 458-3425; fax: 458-3612).

INEXPENSIVE

Villa Le Bijou This charming 6-room guesthouse is built of local stone and pebbles, with a large terrace and spectacular views. It's run by a transplanted Frenchwoman in love with the island and all its flavors. There are no private baths. Canouan (phone: 458-8025). Moderate to inexpensive.

Julie's and Isola's Guest House For the budget-minded, this 19-room property is clean and friendly, with excellent and inexpensive West Indian food. Breakfast and dinner are included in the rate. Port Elizabeth, Bequia (phone: 458-3304; fax: 458-3812).

EATING OUT

With very few exceptions, dining is limited to hotel restaurants. Most offer West Indian food (pumpkin and callaloo soup, local fish or lobster prepared creole style, and local specialties) and what they believe tourists like to eat (usually overcooked steaks, imported frozen shrimp, French fries, and so on). Bartenders pride themselves on variations of rum punch — which are always stronger than they seem. Compared to most Caribbean holiday islands, St. Vincent's prices — outside the luxury hotels — are not bad. Dinner for two (excluding wine and tip) at restaurants we list as expensive will run $60 to $80; at places in the moderate category, $30 to $60; at inexpensive places, $30 or less. Note that wine does not come cheap. Normally a 10% service charge and 5% government tax are added to the bill. For boaters, most restaurants take reservations via VHF channel 68. The following are the few recommendable dining spots beyond the hotel scene, as well as the outstanding hotel dining rooms. All telephone numbers are in the 809 area code unless otherwise indicated.

ST. VINCENT

EXPENSIVE

Basil's Basil Charles, of Mustique fame, took over the popular ground-floor restaurant of the *Cobblestone Inn.* The lunchtime buffet, served Mondays through Fridays, has proved a grand success. Other offerings include lobster salad, grilled snapper, omelettes, burgers, sandwiches, escargots, and grilled lobster, with several reasonably priced French wines. Closed Sundays. Reservations advised. Major credit cards accepted. Bay St., Kingstown (phone: 457-2713).

French Restaurant The chef is from Orléans, and the cuisine an admirable marriage of Gallic savoir faire with island ingredients and the few available imports. Starters include a luscious lobster crêpe, delicate quenelles, frogs' legs, and escargots. A live lobster pool guarantees freshness, and snapper is nicely prepared in a gratinéed basil sauce. With its delightful alfresco setting opposite Young Island, next to the dock, this is unquestionably the island's best choice for lunch or dinner out. Open daily for breakfast, lunch, and dinner. Reservations advised. Major credit cards accepted. Villa Beach (phone: 458-4972).

MODERATE

Aggie's A clean, brightly painted upstairs café with banners of English football (our soccer) teams hanging over the bar. The menu features such authentic West Indian fare as codfish and breadfruit, as well as continental dishes like shrimp creole. Open daily; dinner only on Sundays. Reservations unnecessary. No credit cards accepted. Grenville St., Kingstown (phone: 456-2110).

Basil's Too Thanks to the enterprising spirit of Basil Charles (see *Basil's,* above), the former *Aquatic Club* near Young Island Jetty now is an airy eatery (filled with striking artwork) that serves up sumptuous food. The disco rocks into the wee hours of the morning. The courtyard has lush plants and a fountain resembling a giant hibiscus blossom. Live music on Saturday nights. Don't miss it! Open daily for lunch and dinner. Reservations advised. Major credit cards accepted. Indian Bay, St. Vincent (phone: 458-4205).

Jana's Dolphin This open-air restaurant and bar owned and run by Jana Forde, a friendly young German woman, has a nightly barbecue featuring seafood and beef, and a menu of continental treats such as Hungarian goulash, shrimp cocktail, and sesame chicken wings. Open daily for dinner. Reservations unnecessary. No credit cards accepted. Villa Beach (phone: 457-4301).

Lime 'n' Pub A lively English-style pub serving local specialties across from Young Island. To get there, you have to walk the rocky ledge over the beach. Open daily for lunch and dinner. Reservations unnecessary. Major credit cards accepted. Villa Beach (phone: 458-4227).

THE GRENADINES

EXPENSIVE

Basil's Bar Even if it were not the only place to go on Mustique (besides the *Cotton House*), it still would be the *only* place to go (see *Nightlife*). This appealing alfresco wicker and wood complex opens early and closes late. Menu ranges from full breakfasts to sandwiches, salads, seafood, lobster, and homemade ice cream. Sailors and homeowners — viscounts and movie stars, princesses and jet set execs — mingle when the band plays (currently Wednesdays). Don't miss the chance to see and be seen. Open daily for lunch and dinner. Reservations advised. Major credit cards accepted. Mustique (phone: 458-4621).

Le Petit Jardin This upscale eatery features an extensive wine list to complement fine food and elegant surroundings. Owner/chef Owen Belmar trained at the *Culinary Institute of America,* and his food is sophisticated West Indian. Seafood is a specialty. Open daily for lunch and dinner. Reservations advised. Major credit cards accepted. Bequia (phone: 458-3318).

Plantation House Bequia's best dining spot serves fine presentations of standard island dishes with fresh local seafood, either on the breezy estate verandah or at *Coco's* beach bar and restaurant on Tuesdays and Fridays for a buffet accompanied by a steel band. Open daily for breakfast, lunch, afternoon tea, and dinner. Reservations advised for dinner. Major credit cards accepted. Bequia (phone: 458-3425).

MODERATE

Daphne Cooks It There's no set menu here; Daphne simply cooks whatever ingredients were acquired that day, using old family recipes. Open daily for lunch and dinner. Reservations advised for dinner. No credit cards accepted. Port Elizabeth, Bequia, across from the vegetable market (phone: 458-3271).

Gingerbread Café The breezy upstairs restaurant in the *Gingerbread* complex features local fish, curries, good salads, and sandwiches. Open daily for breakfast, lunch, and dinner. Reservations unnecessary. Major credit cards accepted. Admiralty Bay, Bequia (phone: 458-3800).

Mac's Pizzeria and Bakeshop On a lovely terrace overlooking the beach on Admiralty Bay, it's renowned for its lobster, pizza, pita bread sandwiches, quiche, banana bread, pineapple rolls, and chocolate chip cookies — all fresh. Yachtspeople love the take-out service. Open daily for lunch and dinner. Reservations unnecessary. MasterCard and Visa accepted. Near Port Elizabeth, Bequia (phone: 458-3474).

De Reef Popular beach bar and day spot, with a restaurant serving good local food — on island time (order, then have a swim). Showers and lockers are available, as well as windsurfing and snorkeling equipment. Some Saturday nights feature a seafood buffet and live entertainment. Special Sunday lunch. Open daily for lunch and dinner. Reservations advised for dinner. No credit cards accepted. Lower Bay, Bequia (phone: 458-3484).

INEXPENSIVE

Old Fig Tree A guesthouse serving a set dinner menu (conch is recommended) and pizza, local-style. Open daily for breakfast, lunch, and dinner. Reservations advised. MasterCard and Visa accepted. Port Elizabeth, Bequia (phone: 458-3201).

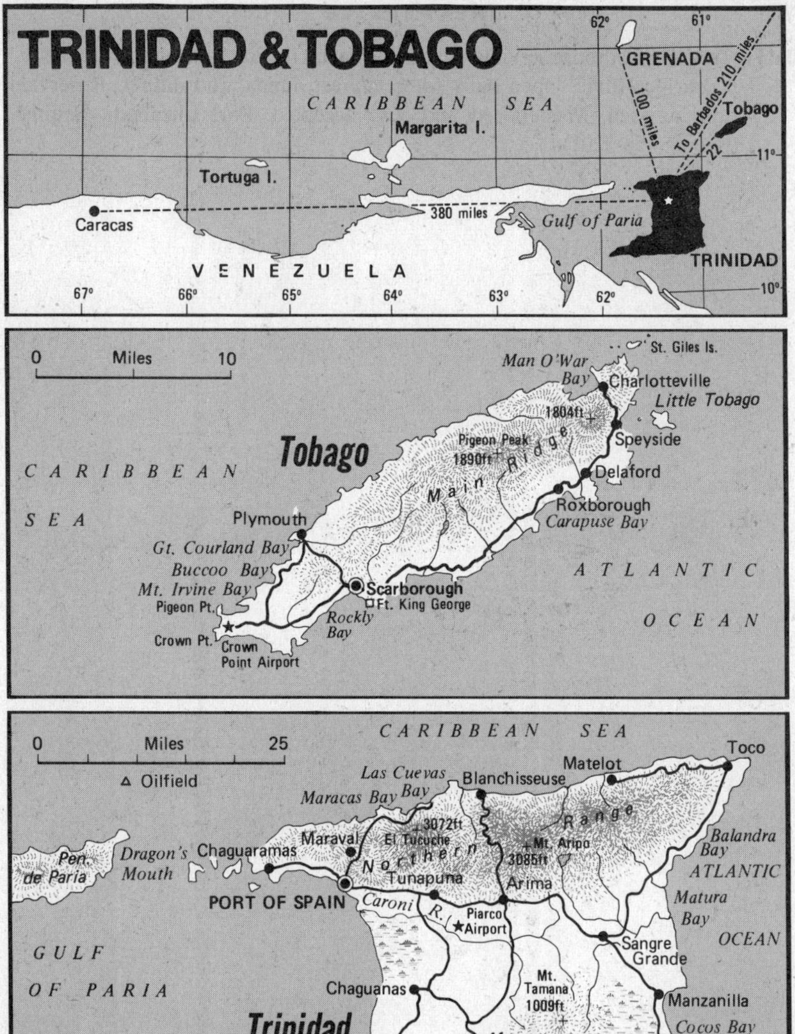

TRINIDAD & TOBAGO

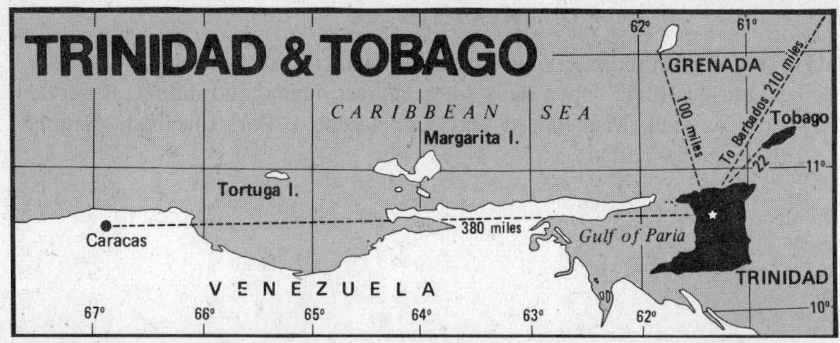

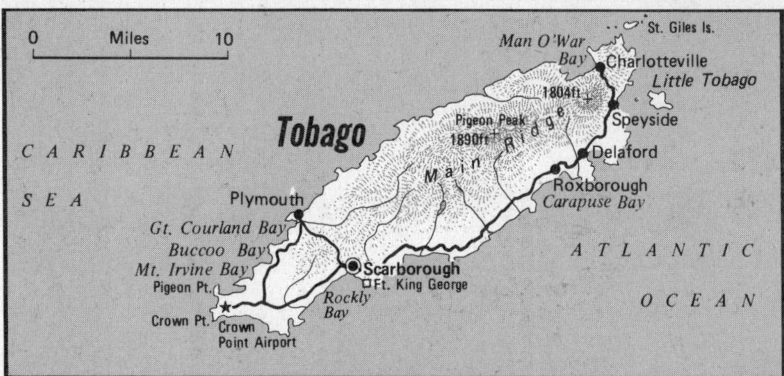

0 Miles 25
△ Oilfield
CARIBBEAN SEA
Toco
Matelot
Blanchisseuse
Las Cuevas Bay
Maracas Bay
3072ft
El Tucuche
Northern Range
Mt. Aripo 3085ft
Balandra Bay
ATLANTIC OCEAN
Pen. de Paria
Dragon's Mouth
Chaguaramas
Maraval
Tunapuna
Arima
PORT OF SPAIN
Caroni R.
Piarco Airport
Matura Bay
Sangre Grande
GULF OF PARIA
Chaguanas
Mt. Tamana 1009ft
Manzanilla
Cocos Bay
Trinidad
Montserrat Hills
Mariva Swamp
California
918ft
Point Radix
Rio Claro
Princes Town
San Fernando
St. Joseph
La Brea
Pitch Lake
Mayaro Bay
Point Fortin
Siparia
Trinity Hills
997ft
Guayaguayare
Bonasse
Moruga
Erin Bay
Erin Point
Serpent's Mouth

Trinidad and Tobago

The twin-island nation of Trinidad and Tobago is a study in contrasts. Call it the Caribbean's yin and yang: Trinidad is large and densely populated with several large cities and towns; Tobago is small and sparsely populated with settlements spread out all over the island. Trinidad is South American; Tobago is Caribbean. Trinidad and its capital, Port of Spain, are vibrant, industrial, and cosmopolitan; Tobago and its capital, Scarborough, are unhurried, tranquil, and Old West Indian. But these opposite islands do share an abundance of wildlife sanctuaries and natural reserves.

Originally inhabited by Amerindians, then settled by the Spanish, Trinidad became a British colony in 1797, when His Majesty's fleet captured the islands from the Spanish. Tobago has a more turbulent past. Besieged and occasionally occupied by the Dutch, the Spanish, the British, the French — even Courlanders from Latvia — it changed hands no fewer than 31 times in the course of 3 centuries of raids, counterattacks, and violent rebellions. It was not until 1803, when the British won a bloodless victory over the French and marched in to take their place in Scarborough, that the island found itself at peace.

During most of the 19th century, Tobago enjoyed tremendous prosperity due to its monopoly of the sugar industry. But in 1884, the London firm that had monopolized the island's financial dealings declared itself bankrupt, and the sugar industry folded. With the collapse of Gillespie & Company went the island's entire economy. Suddenly a poor relation, little Tobago became — somewhat reluctantly — a ward of larger, more economically secure Trinidad.

On August 31, 1962, the twin-island nation became an independent member of the British Commonwealth. In 1976, Trinidad and Tobago became a republic, with the president replacing the British monarch as head of state. The People's National Movement, founded by Dr. Eric Williams, was an early force in the drive for independence, and Dr. Williams was the nation's prime minister for 25 years, until his death in 1981.

Throughout its short life, the republic of Trinidad and Tobago has steadfastly shown its commitment to democracy. This was evident in 1986, when there was a smooth change of power from the political party that had governed since independence to the National Alliance for Reconstruction, led by A.N.R. Robinson. In 1990, however, Libyan-inspired black Muslims attempted a coup, and Prime Minister Robinson and other government officials were held hostage for several days before the rebels surrendered. A little more than a year later, the nation held peaceful elections and a democratic form of government continued under a new prime minister, Patrick Manning, and the People's National Movement. Manning had promised voters that he would ease hardships caused by the economic austerity program instituted by Robinson. So far, however, the faltering global economy has hindered Manning's progress.

Major industries in Trinidad and Tobago today include steel, natural gas, methanol, agriculture, and tourism. It is oil, however, to which this country has owed much of its prosperity and, more recently, its economic malaise (due to erratic world prices and supply). As the third-largest oil exporter in the Western Hemisphere, Trinidad has long been one of the richest and most industrialized countries in the West Indies. In addition to its oil supply, it possesses the world's largest pitch lake, which provides enough bitumen to pave the highways of the world — and even replenishes itself.

Natural gas sources, discovered off Trinidad's east coast, promise other possibilities for industrial expansion, as do the more standard Caribbean products: sugar, cocoa, coffee, citrus fruits, and coconuts. Trinidad must also be credited with giving mixed drinks that added special touch, as Angostura Bitters has for years been produced exclusively on the island.

Trinidad's mineral wealth represents a mixed blessing for tourists. While the profusion of birds (over 400 species), butterflies (600-plus species), orchids (700 species), reptiles, and other flora and fauna delight and dazzle, visitors may find themselves traveling through an oil refinery to reach a bird sanctuary or a jungle. Because of the island's oil reserves, gas prices are among the lowest in the Caribbean. On the other hand, the island's prosperity has, in the past, caused it to pay scant attention to visitors. Recently, however, there has been a push to increase tourism with some attractive packages from major hotels and airlines. Clearly, the welcome mat is out.

The expressions of welcome on Trinidad and Tobago are as varied as the islands' peoples. In addition to the heritage of the Amerindians, who are believed to have first settled the islands in about 5000 BC, there are strong African and East Indian influences, flavored with Carib, Creole, and Portuguese. Add British, Spanish, French, German, Chinese, Lebanese, Syrian, and North American peoples and you can understand Trinidad's unique personality — one that is reflected in the architectural mix in Port of Spain as well as in the mélange of spices in island food. The number of languages heard throughout the country — including Hindi, Urdu, Spanish, Chinese, English, and a local patois — is surpassed only by the spectrum of cooking styles. Over half the population is East Indian — Hindu and Muslim. Try *rôti* (a large flat bread made with split peas and filled with curried vegetables or meat) at a roadside stand, and consider visiting during the Indian religious holidays. This is as close as you'll get to visiting India without flying to Calcutta.

The varied character and hustle-bustle of life on Trinidad in no way disturbs the calm of nearby Tobago. Trinidad's nightlife, good restaurants, sightseeing, and exciting *Carnival* are ideally complemented by

Tobago's dreamlike sands. It would be almost impossible to find a better combination for a Caribbean visit. Tobago soothes where Trinidad titillates. To visit one without the other is certainly possible, but not wise; the two islands are halves of a perfect vacation whole.

Trinidad and Tobago At-a-Glance

FROM THE AIR

The 1.2 million inhabitants of Trinidad occupy what is roughly a rectangle, 37 miles by 50 miles. From above, the island looks like a jigsaw puzzle piece, ready to be moved into place next to neighboring Venezuela 8 miles away. Geologists theorize that Trinidad was, in fact, once part of South America and became an island about 10,000 BC.

The flora and fauna of the island closely resemble Venezuela's, and the northern range of mountains, which stretch from east to west, is actually a continuation of the South American Cordillera. The two highest peaks on Trinidad are El Cerro del Aripo (3,085 feet) and El Tucuche (3,072 feet). The rest of the island is fairly flat, except for the central Montserrat Hills and the Trinity Hills to the southeast.

The fish-shaped island of Tobago, 26 miles long by 7 miles wide, is one-sixteenth the size of its neighbor, and has a population of 100,000. With its mountainous terrain, Tobago differs more in topography from Trinidad than Trinidad does from Venezuela (which supports the notion that Tobago separated from Trinidad thousands of years before Trinidad broke from Venezuela). Tobago somewhat resembles the Windward Islands to the north, with its 1,500-foot hills rolling to white, sandy beaches and clear blue water.

SPECIAL PLACES

TRINIDAD — Port of Spain A good starting place for a walking tour is the huge, green Queen's Park Savannah. Locally known as "the Savannah," this 200-acre lawn has a racecourse, cricket fields, and an abundance of joggers, amateur football and soccer players, and vendors hawking everything from coconut water to oyster cocktails. The area was originally a sugar plantation, but a disastrous fire swept through the capital in 1808 and destroyed over 400 homes, the first Trinity Church, and more.

On the Maraval Road side of the Savannah are seven townhouses known as the Magnificent Seven. They are as grand and unified as any group of turn-of-the-century terraced houses, yet as flamboyant and varied as the rest of Trinidadian life. For example, the Queen's Royal College building, today a school, was built in German Renaissance style; the pink and blue structure has palms in front, a lighted clock tower, and a chiming clock. The Roodal Residence, called the gingerbread house, is typical of the baroque architecture of the French Second Empire. Stollmeyer Castle, built in 1904, is a copy of a German castle, although its stone turrets and archways make it resemble a Scottish baronial mansion. Whitehall — formerly the residence and now the office of the prime minister — looks like a cross between a wedding cake and a Moorish palace.

If you walk southwest from Maraval Road to Queen's Park West, you'll reach the *Queen's Park* hotel (it remains closed while its owners consider its future), and nearby, the *National Museum and Art Gallery* (closed Sundays and Mondays; phone: 623-5941). In addition to an ornately carved Spanish cannon, some Amerindian relics, representative island art, and an exhibit of snakebite cures, the museum houses a colorful display of *Carnival* costumes from past years. The care and presentation of some of the museum's collections leave a little to be desired, but admission is free and it's a pleasant diversion.

Turn down Frederick Street, the narrow, bustling main avenue of Port of Spain's shopping district. The jumble of merchandise, cramped quarters, and olfactory confusion of coconut oil, roasting corn on the cob (served with West Indian spices), peppers, and sausage are part of what Trinidad is all about. Look for local woodcarvings, jewelry, and the latest calypso discs.

Halfway down Frederick Street lies Woodford Square. Across the square on St. Vincent Street stands the Red House, a red, neo-Renaissance building that is the seat of the Trinidad and Tobago Parliament. Perpendicular to the Red House on Hart Street is the Holy Trinity Cathedral (ca. 1823), a beautiful Gothic structure with distinctive altar carvings and choir stalls, and interesting marble monuments to prominent citizens. Set apart from all the activity of downtown Frederick Street, a short distance from the Savannah, are the Royal Botanic Gardens, one of Port of Spain's major attractions. Covering some 70 acres of a former sugar plantation, the gardens are brimming with tropical flowers. A guided walk will initiate you into the world of orchids, frangipani, sausage trees, and lipstick plants. Keep an eye out for the raw beef tree, named because an incision in its bark resembles rare roast beef. There are also lotus lilies — sacred to the Egyptians — and the type of holy peepul (fig) tree under which Buddha is purported to have attained Nirvana. The gardens are open from 9 AM to dusk daily (phone: 667-4655).

ELSEWHERE ON TRINIDAD

ASA WRIGHT NATURE CENTRE, SPRING HILL ESTATE Twenty miles from Port of Spain via car or taxi (about $35 round-trip), in Blanchisseuse, near the city of Arima in the mountains of the northern range, the Asa Wright Nature Centre offers accommodations (see *Checking In*) on acreage devoted to tufted coquettes, squirrel cuckoos, toucans, and other exotic birds. A special attraction is a breeding colony of the nocturnal oilbird, or guacharo, that resides in Dunston Cave at the center. This is the only accessible colony of the species known, and the not-so-easy trek to the Guacharo

Gorge is quite an adventure; wear old, comfortable clothes. Staying overnight enables visitors to take advantage of both sunset and sunrise bird watching, but the center can also be an enjoyable day trip, complete with afternoon tea on a porch with a view of the flora and fauna. Field trips on the reservation are $30 per person; make arrangements 2 days in advance (phone: 667-4655).

WILDFOWL TRUST This 60-acre oasis of flowering lotus and manmade lakes on the Trintoc oil-refinery property is the site of protected breeding grounds for endangered native species of waterfowl. There is also an educational center with Amerindian artifacts and Tobago burial group artifacts. Visitors must reserve in advance to view the preserve Mondays through Fridays from 9 AM to 5 PM and on weekends from 10 AM to 6 PM (phone: 637-5145 or 662-4040). Wear good hiking shoes for the walks through the forest and the Fairy Woods. Admission is about $1, but larger donations are always welcomed by this nonprofit, volunteer-run organization.

LOPINOT HISTORICAL COMPLEX In the Arouca Valley, 1 hour's drive east of Port of Spain, this lushly gardened home of a 19th-century French count is now a plantation museum. The house features period furniture, pottery, and artifacts; there's also a cocoa drying house and a park. A quaint Anglican church is nearby. The complex is also a center for parang (rustic music with Spanish roots) concerts, particularly at *Christmastime.* For additional information, contact the tourist board, which supervises tours.

CLEAVER WOODS PARK A mile west of Arima, an hour's drive east of Port of Spain, this 31-acre nature preserve serves as a showcase for both ethnic and natural history. Habitat for dozens of species of indigenous birds, butterflies, and flowers, it also encompasses an Amerindian museum, a pine plantation, and picnic sites.

FORT GEORGE Built in 1804, the fort, on a 1,500-foot peak, is only 10 miles from Port of Spain on a good hardtop road. The drive affords uninterrupted vistas in all directions.

KNOLLY'S TUNNEL Near Tabaquite and the geographic center of the island, this quarter-mile-long tunnel was built between 1896 and 1898 for the railroad that hauled sugar, cocoa, and passengers to Port of Spain. Last used in 1965, it was reopened in 1991 as the first phase of a project developing the 62-acre reserve that surrounds it. Plans include the construction of three thatch-roofed cabins for overnight stays, a picnic area, and hiking trails. At present, horse-drawn carriage rides through the tunnel are offered. *Note:* Stay inside the carriage, since the bats inside are disturbed by daytime visitors. Entrance fee is about 50¢ and parking is another 50¢ (phone: 622-5146 or 628-6087).

NORTH COAST BEACHES The 34-mile drive from "the Saddle" — a pass dividing the Santa Cruz and Maraval valleys — across the northern range and down to Maracas Bay is a popular excursion. The view from 1,000 feet up — a 100-mile sweep from Tobago to Venezuela — is in itself worth the trip.

Enclosed by mountains, with white sand, clear water, and swaying coconut palms, Maracas Beach has changing facilities, snack bars, and other amenities. *Grace Offord* (phone: 628-2983), one of Trinidad's best caterers of local fare, will prepare a personal picnic for you. Las Cuevas Beach, with full facilities including changing rooms, a lifeguard, and snack bar, is a little farther along the north coast road, and farther still is Blanchisseuse Beach, another magnificent swimming spot that is seldom crowded (there are no showers or changing rooms, however). *Surf's Country Inn* (Blanchisseuse St.; phone: 669-2475), a day resort, serves excellent local food.

CARONI BIRD SANCTUARY Trinidad's national bird, the scarlet ibis, can be seen here. Hundreds of these bright red birds swoop in to nest on the mangrove islands that fill this 450-acre sanctuary. The sight of the mangrove trees appearing to burst into blood-red flames is exquisite, and the boat ride through the canals and waterways is a soothing way to spend a late afternoon.

The sanctuary is about 7 miles south of Port of Spain. Boatsmen leave the roadside dock at 4:30 AM and 4 PM; needless to say, the afternoon departure has more takers. Several tour operators also offer excursions. The best and most reliable is *Caroni Tours* (phone: 645-1305), which offers the trip for about $25 per person including pickup at your hotel. Other operators charge about $50 for one or two people sharing a cab or van; the price covers both the boat trip and hotel transfers. It's a 4-hour excursion, with daily departures from the *Hilton International* and other hotels at about 3 PM. Reservations are essential. The inner sanctuary, where the birds nest, is open to the public May to October, but the rest stays open all year.

SPECIAL PLACES

TOBAGO — Scarborough Tobago's tiny capital has few sights. Island life moves slowly; gossip is exchanged in the doorways of old-fashioned drapers' stores; and conversations in a distinctive creole patois fill the square, where there's a lively native market.

For an excellent view of the island as well as a taste of Tobago's history, drive or walk up to Fort King George, 430 feet above the town. A site for spectacular sunset viewing, the fort testifies to the endless struggles between the French and the British that characterized Tobago's past. Much of what's here, from old polished cannon to major buildings, has been restored. Enlist a knowledgeable guide such as Horris Job, who may be found at the fort, or ask the tourist board to arrange a guided tour.

Visitors also can look at the tombstone inscriptions in Plymouth churchyard nearby, some dating from the 1700s. For a scenic stroll, try the tiny, well-groomed Botanic Gardens beneath the fort.

NATIONAL FINE ARTS CENTER For those interested in Tobago art, this gallery is an absolute must. The knowledgeable and congenial director, Wilcox Morris, an accomplished artist in his own right, exhibits some excellent local art and refers interested buyers directly to the artists. Just 10 minutes from Scarborough on Orange Hill Rd. (phone: 639-6897).

PIGEON POINT As meager as Tobago is on sightseeing spots, it is rich in beautiful sands. Pigeon Point on the northwest coast is probably its most renowned bathing area, where the long coral beach has thatch shelters for changing, tables, benches, and lavatories. The clear, green water is inviting, although on weekends and holidays the beach can seem as busy as Coney Island.

MAN O' WAR BAY At the eastern end of the island, this is one of the finest natural harbors in the Caribbean. There's a long sandy beach on the bay's south shore, and a government rest house that's perfect for picnics.

CHARLOTTEVILLE Combine your visit to Man O' War with a stop at this nearby pretty little fishing village set above the bay on a hillside. Pigeon Peak, Tobago's highest mountain (1,890 feet), rises just behind it.

SPEYSIDE Set on the crescent of Speyside Bay along the Atlantic Coast, this lovely little fishing village offers the luxury of nothing to do except admire the views, enjoy the drive along the Windward Road, and see the bay. Otherwise, swimming places are better at Mt. Irvine and Bacolet bays.

BIRD OF PARADISE SANCTUARY Bird watching is a top Tobago activity, second only to sunbathing. This sanctuary, on the island of Little Tobago, is the place to go. A 450-acre isle off the coast near Speyside, it attracts serious ornithologists, eager to catch a glimpse of the area's golden-feathered namesake. Some 50 birds of paradise were brought to the island from New Guinea in the early part of the century (when extinction threatened them), but sadly, since then, their numbers have decreased; you can write ahead to the warden (Speyside Post Office, Tobago), and ask for the latest beak count before you go. But there are plenty of other exotic birds on Little Tobago — best sighting times are early morning or late afternoon.

BUCCOO REEF For a truly spectacular underwater show, complete with yellow angelfish, purple damsels, blue parrot fish, and extensive coral, don't miss Buccoo Reef. It lies about a mile offshore from Pigeon Point: The tourist crowds may seem overwhelming, but they don't bother the marine life and won't bother you once you've donned your mask. Departure times for boat trips to the reef vary, so ask when you buy your ticket at your hotel. Pickup is at the beach, Buccoo Point, and Store Bay.

Sources and Resources

TOURIST INFORMATION

On Trinidad, the tourism division has an information center at Piarco Airport (phone: 664-5196); on Tobago, there are offices in Scarborough (phone: 639-2125) and at Crown Point Airport (phone: 639-0509). The Trinidad and Tobago Tourist Development Authority headquarters are in Port of Spain (134-138 Frederick St.; phone: 623-1932 or 623-1934; fax: 623-3848). For information on tourist offices in the US, see GETTING READY TO GO.

LOCAL COVERAGE Trinidad's newspapers are a source of information on goings-on: the *Trinidad Guardian,* the *Trinidad Express,* and the *Evening News,* all dailies, are three to read.

RADIO AND TELEVISION

Trinidad and Tobago Television has local shows, as well as a broader range of programming in English. The National Broadcasting Company and Trinidad Broadcasting Company run the local radio stations.

TELEPHONE

The area code for Trinidad and Tobago is 809.

ENTRY REQUIREMENTS

Visitors must show a valid passport and will be asked to complete two separate entry forms. You will also have to pay a departure tax of $50 TT (about $12) in Trinidadian currency, so don't change all your TT dollars back into US currency.

CLIMATE AND CLOTHES

Cool trade winds tend to temper the tropical warmth of Trinidad and Tobago, where 8 hours of sunshine per day is the average. The rainy season generally hits late in May and lasts until November. Average year-round temperatures are 74F (23C) at night, 84F (29C) during the day, so lightweight clothing is a must, although a light wrap may be useful in winter months, particularly at higher elevations. Cocktail dresses and jackets and ties are often worn at night in Trinidad, while daytime Trinidad and anytime Tobago are casual.

MONEY

Local currency is the Trinidadian dollar (TT), which is exchanged at the official rate of approximately $4.25 TT to $1 US. However, US currency is universally accepted, and the single advantage of dealing in local currency is that purchases will occasionally prove less expensive. Although some banks have earlier openings, most are open from 9 AM to 2 PM Mondays through Thursdays and 9 AM to 1 PM and 3 to 5 PM Fridays. All prices in this chapter are quoted in US dollars.

LANGUAGE

English is spoken on both islands.

TIME

The islands are on atlantic standard time, 1 hour ahead of eastern standard time and the same as eastern daylight saving time.

CURRENT

Electricity is 110 or 230 volts, 60 cycles AC. At hotels, check with the management before plugging in appliances. Most of the better hotels provide electrical adapters for their guests.

TIPPING

Most of the larger hotels and restaurants charge a 10% service fee. Elsewhere, tip between 10% and 15%, depending on the service.

GETTING AROUND

BUS On Trinidad, buses run regularly from Port of Spain, linking the various cities on the island. Tobago's public buses are fairly modern and cheap. They make the trip from one end of the island to the other, and while they take longer than a taxi, they afford a good view of island life. Fares on both islands run about $1 and up, depending on the distance traveled.

CAR RENTAL Cars are probably the best transportation choice, if you don't have a problem driving on the left-hand side of the road with a right-hand mounted wheel. Gas usually costs less than back home. Most hotels can make arrangements for you, or you can contact one of the following companies. On Trinidad there's *Auto Rentals* at Piarco Airport (phone: 669-2244), *Singh's* (7-9 Wrightson Rd., Port of Spain; phone: 625-4247), *Budget* (22 Boissiere Rd., Maraval; phone: 622-6573), *Hertz* (68-72 Maraval Rd., Maraval; phone: 622-2093), *Tragarete* (75 Tragarete Rd., Port of Spain; phone: 622-3025), *Wong's* (114 Belmont Circular Rd., Port of Spain; phone: 624-5385), *Premier* (at the *Normandie* hotel, St. Ann's; phone: 624-7265), and *R. Pimento* in Diego Martin (11 La Croix Ave.; phone: 632-0558). On Tobago there's *Toyota Rent-a-Car* (Milford; phone: 639-7495), *Peter Gremli* (Crown Point; phone: 639-8400), *Maharaj* (Main St. and Rose Hill, Scarborough; phone: 639-3554), and *Auto Rentals* (Northside Rd., Scarborough; phone: 639-2496). Rates start at about $50 per day with unlimited mileage; you pay for gas. An international driver's license is useful, but not needed. A valid US driver's license is acceptable for stays of up to 2 months.

FERRY SERVICES The luxury coastal ferry M.F. *Panorama* that travels between the two islands accommodates 720 passengers; a first class one-way ticket costs $25 to $30; the one-way economy fare runs $12 to $15. There's also a no-frills ferry that costs about $20 round-trip.

TAXI Not a bad way to get around for a short stay, and many drivers will double as guides for a little extra. On Trinidad, cabs with an H as the first letter on their license plate tend to hover around the airport and big hotels, and cruise through Port of Spain. Cabs on both islands are unmetered; the fares for some common trips are regulated, based on route distances. The taxi ride from Trinidad's Piarco Airport to town, for example, usually runs about $25. From Tobago's airport to most hotels, it's $5 to $18 per person. Other fares are negotiable; agree on a price — and in what currency — before starting.

When it comes to touring, however, current wisdom has it that you're better off hiring a car and driver through a tour operator rather than hiring a taxi; you'll get a better car and a better deal. One of the best, *Trinidad and Tobago Sightseeing Tours* (phone: 628-6552), will provide a car and driver for about $80 a day. This is the only tour company to receive the Hospitality Award from the tourist board.

INTER-ISLAND FLIGHTS

American flies nonstop from San Juan, Puerto Rico, to Trinidad. In addition, *LIAT* flies between Barbados and the two islands. At present, no major airlines fly into Tobago, but Tobago's airport runway was recently extended to accommodate larger planes, and additional upgrading efforts are under way. *BWIA's Airbridge* flights link the two islands with a number of daily 20-minute flights; when booked as part of some excursion and tour fares, the inter-island flights may be included at no extra charge.

SPECIAL EVENTS

The event of the year is *Carnival* — where calypso singing and dancing are *everywhere.* The celebration, called "jump-up" on Trinidad, takes place in Port of Spain (the best place to be), San Fernando, and Arima on Trinidad, and in Scarborough on Tobago.

Carnival officially lasts from the dawn of the Monday before *Ash Wednesday* through midnight Tuesday. But from the previous Saturday on, the fantastically costumed citizens of the island dance through the streets to the lively rhythms of steel drums and the musical lyrics of topnotch calypsonians. If you plan to visit Trinidad during *Carnival,* make reservations at least a year in advance, and expect to pay double at some hotels.

Hosein (pronounced *Ho-say*), another major festival on Trinidad, is a

3-day Muslim celebration in the fall. It includes parades of elaborately designed miniature mosques (called *tadjahs*), music, colorful costumes, stick fighting, chanting, and tassa drumming. Check with the tourist board for details.

Since 1987, the *Natural History Festival* has been held the first 2 weeks of October; it spotlights Trinidad and Tobago's natural resources. Activities include the Orchid Society's annual show, bird watching, butterfly collecting, lectures, and slide presentations. One tour operator who knows the territory is explorer, plant enthusiast, and tropical-fruit expert Tom Economo at *Follow Nature Trail* (Box 450662, Miami, FL 33145; phone: 305-285-7173). The tourist office in Port of Spain can provide additional information.

The Hindu *Festival of Lights,* called *Devali,* takes place in October or November. At that time, celebrants place lights around their homes, gardens, and temples, transforming parts of the islands into glowing spectacles. Also in October or November, a ceremony of purification, *Katik-Nannan,* is performed on Trinidad's Atlantic coast at Manzanilla, to which hundreds of Hindus travel to bathe in the sea. An increasingly popular island event is the annual *Pan Jazz Festival,* held in mid-November, which features steel-pan music and the beats of black America, the Caribbean, Latin America, and Europe. Though only 6 years old, it is attracting musicians and music lovers from around the world.

The *Tobago Heritage Festival* takes place during the last 2 weeks of July and features goat and crab races, folk dancing, and other traditional activities (even a reenactment of a Tobago wedding). Goat and crab races also are held on *Easter* Tuesday at Buccoo Village.

Official holidays when banks and businesses on both islands are closed include *New Year's Day, Good Friday, Easter Sunday* and *Monday, Whitmonday, Corpus Christi* (late spring), *Labor Day* (in June), *Emancipation Day* (August 1), *Independence Day* (August 31), *Republic Day* (September 24), *Christmas,* and *Boxing Day* (December 26).

SHOPPING

The shops and merchandise here are not quite up to the level of those on some of the more sophisticated Caribbean islands. The *West Mall* in Port of Spain and the *Longcircular Mall* in St. James have attracted many of the more exclusive shops from downtown, although good merchandise and bargains can still be found along Frederick Street and Independence Square, where goods are sold in everything from plush shops to rickety pushcarts. Downtown shopping hours are 8 AM to 4 or 5 PM Mondays through Fridays, 8 AM to noon on Saturdays. At malls outside of town, regular shopping hours are 10 AM to 7 PM.

There is also fine shopping on Trinidad at *St. Ann's Village,* the shopping center in the *Normandie* hotel, where jewelry, clothing, crafts, and even delicious homemade ice cream are all available in an attractive arcade. The island's most exciting clothing designer, *Meiling,* has an outpost on Ariapita Avenue in Woodbrook (phone: 627-0367). The *Hilton International* hotel also houses an attractive cluster of air conditioned shops for easy browsing.

Shops and pushcarts offer soft Venezuelan leather loafers for women (about $20 per pair) in a wide array of styles and colors.

Don't miss Port of Spain's *Central Market* on Saturday mornings. The vendors here bring their goods — fruit, vegetables, baskets, and vetiver (a wonderful sachet) — in from the countryside. For more formal boutiques and shops, try any of the following:

TRINIDAD

ABERCROMBY BOOKSHOP Full of interesting choices, including works by native son V.S. Naipal, *Some Trinidad Yesterdays* by P.E.T. O'Conner, and *Voices in the Street* by Olga Mavro Gadato. 22 Abercromby St., Port of Spain (phone: 623-7752).

EL ALLIGATOR Handbags, belts, jackets, wallets, small accessories — everything in leather except shoes. *Longcircular Mall,* St. James (no phone).

ART CREATORS & SUPPLIERS The gallery that represents both Geoffrey and Boscoe Holder as well as other fine Trinidadian artists. In Aldegonda Park at 7 St. Ann's Rd., Port of Spain (phone: 624-4369).

THE BATIQUE A boutique filled with original batik garments and gift items. 43 Sydenham Ave., St. Ann's (phone: 624-3274).

BOUTIQUE CYBÈLE A local favorite for women's batik clothing. At the *Hilton International* hotel, Port of Spain (phone: 624-4669).

THE COLLECTION Jewelry, china, collectibles of all sorts. Two locations: *Town Centre Mall* on Frederick St., Port of Spain (phone: 623-1357) and *Longcircular Mall,* St. James (phone: 623-1351).

CROSBY'S Calypso recordings and other musical treats make sound waves in this records shop. 54 Western Main Rd., St. James (phone: 622-3814).

FABI COSMETIQUE ET PARFUM French and local fragrances and cosmetics. *West Mall,* Port of Spain (phone: 633-4364).

KACAL'S Fine art, woodcarvings by local artists. At the *Hilton International* hotel, Port of Spain (phone: 628-3473).

KAMS Local and international music on records, tapes, and compact discs. *Longcircular Mall,* St. James (phone: 622-8570).

LAKHAN'S BAZAAR If you're looking for Indian goods, stop here for saris, embroidered purses, and rugs. Bombay St. and Western Main Rd., Port of Spain (no phone).

LITTLE GOOSE STORE Giftware including cameras, clocks, and ceramics. Corner of Prince and Henry Sts., Port of Spain (phone: 623-8555).

PATRICK'S Imported and locally designed fabrics are sold by the yard. Queen and Henry Sts., Port of Spain (phone: 627-8467).

PEOPLE'S MALL Tiny stalls and shops line footpaths with such monikers as Zimbabwe Lane, Freedom Street, and Mandela Way. Many of the items featured have African or black motifs; most shops accept only cash. Entrances on Frederick St. and Henry St. near Queen St., Port of Spain (no phone).

SAN ANTONIO NURSERY A must for orchid fans. In upper Santa Cruz (phone: 676-8742).

STECHER'S Trinidad's most distinctive establishment: a stunning array of crystal, china, watches, jewelry, and other imported luxuries. It also carries duty-free goods, delivered, if you wish, to the airport. 27 Frederick St., Port of Spain (phone: 623-5912) and a half-dozen other locations, including a store on Tobago on Carrington St., Scarborough (phone: 639-2377).

TRINIDAD AND TOBAGO BLIND WELFARE ASSOCIATION Your best bet for rattan and grass weavings — everything from furniture to fruit baskets. 121 Henry St., Port of Spain (phone: 624-3356).

Y. DE LIMA High-quality gold and silver jewelry, duty-free cameras, watches, and a wide selection of crystal and china. There are 15 locations around town and the island, with the main store at 23A Frederick St., Port of Spain (phone: 623-1364).

TOBAGO

FOOTPRINT Arts and crafts made by local artisans; also swim and beach attire. *Turtle Beach* hotel (phone: 639-2851).

IDEAL BOOKSTORE Books on local lore, magazines, cards, and stationery supplies. *Scarborough Mall* (phone: 639-3366).

ISLAND CONCEPTS Tropical fashions, artwork, and handicrafts. Jerningham St., Scarborough (phone: 639-5058).

KHOURY'S *The* place to go for African goods, dolls made of shells, and native woodcarvings. On Burnett St., Scarborough (phone: 639-2273).

SPORTS

BIRD WATCHING David Rooks, a naturalist, conducts half-day tours to St. Giles Island on Trinidad to observe frigate birds and other species; cost is $25 per person (phone: 639-4276).

CRICKET This cousin of US baseball is played on pitches (fields) ranging from manicured greens to vacant lots. This spectator sport is a social event, much like *Carnival.* For upcoming matches, check with the tourist board of the island you plan to visit or consult the island newspaper.

GOLF Tobago has only one golf course, but it's tops.

TOP TEE-OFF SPOT

Mount Irvine Golf Club, Tobago It may seem unusual for such a small island to have such a superb golf course, but here it is, the very incarnation of the palm-shaded island links. The 18 holes run along the Caribbean coastline, where the most common hazards are falling coconuts. The best-known hole here is No. 9, famed for its minuscule green set at a devilishly rakish angle. The gentle terrain belies the difficulties of the taxing 6,800 yards, and it is small solace to be able to look out at the famous Buccoo Reef after an afternoon of soaring scores. The greens fee is about $50. *Mount Irvine Bay Hotel,* Tobago (phone: 639-8871; 800-223-6510 from the US).

The best course on Trinidad is *St. Andrews* at the private 18-hole *Moka Golf Club* (phone: 629-2314) in Maraval, 3 miles from Port of Spain. There is a public course at Chaguaramas (no phone), just outside Port of Spain.

HORSE RACING A popular year-round sport with plenty of betting. The big races are held on holidays — *Christmas, New Year's Day, Carnival, Easter,* and *Discovery, Republic,* and *Independence* days. The *Trinidad Derby* is run on *Republic Day* in September. There's racing at *Union Park* in San Fernando, *Queen's Park* in Port of Spain, and *Santa Rosa* in Arima. For information contact the *Trinidad Turf Club* (phone: 625-4122).

HUNTING Don't even think about it. Regulations prohibit firearms from being brought onto the islands; to buy firearms on Trinidad or Tobago you must obtain a gun permit (difficult), and then hunt certain animals only during specific seasons (listed with the forestry department). Fines for violating these rules can be stiff.

SAILING There are several possibilities on Tobago. Just $30 will carry you away on the *Sail with Chloe* (phone: 639-2851), a 36-foot sloop that accommodates up to 10 passengers. It makes 4-hour trips up the coast for sightseeing and snorkeling, departing at 2 PM and returning at sunset. No alcohol is served. The *Loafer* (phone: 639-8555) is a 50-foot catamaran; a daylong sail along the coast costs $50 and includes free pickup at your hotel, fruit platter, drinks, and lunch, as well as swimming, shelling on the beach, and snorkeling at the reef (equipment provided).

SKYDIVING These islands may well be the only places to pursue this sport in the Caribbean. Contact Derek Zegarchuk at the *T & T Sport Parachute Association* (phone: 632-1152) on Trinidad.

SNORKELING AND SCUBA Buccoo Reef on Tobago is *the* place for snorkeling. The best scuba diving is at Flying Reef on the island's west side (certification required); there also are some 2 dozen dive sites (10 rated for experts only) around Man O' War Bay. *Sean Robinson's Tobago Dive Experience* (phone: 639-1279) has operations at *Blue Waters* (phone: 660-4341), *Crown Point* (phone: 639-8781), and *Grafton Beach* (phone: 639-0191). *Tobago Marine Sports* (phone: 639-8571) also runs a dive shop. Winston Nanan of *Caroni Tours* conducts scuba tours for divers of all levels of expertise (phone: 645-1305).

SOCCER Called football here, it's the national sport. The two major leagues battle it out year-round at the *National Stadium.* The Trinidad & Tobago Football Association can provide schedule information (phone: 627-7661).

SPORT FISHING Good catches can be had all year. For kingfish and Spanish mackerel, try the north coast, June through October. Spearfishing for snapper, barracuda, and grouper takes place closer to shore, while trolling for bluefish is popular around the east and south coasts during winter months. Naturalist David Rooks will take up to six fishermen out in his 28-foot fiberglass boat for blue marlin, wahoo, billfish, sailfish, king mackerel, barracuda, and shark (phone: 639-4276); the trips cost $30 an hour. Winston Nanan, of *Caroni Tours* (phone: 645-1305), runs fishing trips on the Caroni River and its estuaries; charge, including hotel pickup and return, is about $150 per person for a 6-hour expedition in search of grouper, tarpon, snook, yellowtail, and snapper. See your hotel tour desk for help with arrangements.

SWIMMING AND SUNNING On Trinidad, visitors can choose from the beaches at Maracas and Las Cuevas in the north, Balandra and Toco to the northeast, and Manzanilla and Mayaro in the east. All beaches are accessible by car or bus. Surfing is possible at many beaches, particularly during winter months. Tobago's Back Bay, just west of the *Mount Irvine Bay* hotel, is picture-postcard-perfect, with palm trees, sea grapes, and usually complete privacy.

TENNIS Best bet on Trinidad is to try the *Hilton International* hotel, the *Trinidad Country Club* (phone: 622-3470), or the *Tranquillity Square Lawn Tennis Club* (phone: 625-4182) where non-guests are charged an hourly rate. There are public courts in Port of Spain on the grounds of the Princess Building off Frederick Street. On Tobago, the condition of the courts at the *Mount Irvine Bay* hotel is usually good; the courts at *Turtle Beach* are excellent.

WINDSURFING Available at the *Turtle Beach, Grafton Beach,* and *Mount Irvine Bay* hotels on Tobago.

NIGHTLIFE

On Trinidad, steel band music and shows dominate the entertainment scene, but local theater troupes as well as cultural and folkloric dance and music groups perform at several sites around town and, occasionally, at hotels. There are concerts at *Queen's Hall* on the grounds of the President's House off St. Ann's Road. For dancing, there are about a dozen discos plus the lounges at the major hotels. The *Aviary* at the *Hilton International* is particularly popular Thursday, Friday, and Saturday nights, when there is a live band. Monday evenings, the poolside "Pot Pourri Night" at the *Hilton International* also draws a crowd. Other nightspots include the *Pelican* in Cascade (2-4 Coblentz Ave.; phone: 624-7486), the *Attic* at the *Maraval Shopping Centre* (phone: 622-8123), and *Genesis* at the *Starlite Shopping Plaza* in Diego Martin (phone: 622-8074). Try *Chez Moi* (*West Mall,* Port of Spain; phone: 637-4533) for jazz, blues, and calypso. Other jazz and calypso clubs include the *Mas Camp Pub* in Port of Spain (19-23 French St.; phone: 627-8449), *Cricket Wicket* (149 Tragarete Rd., Port of Spain; phone: 622-1808), and *Moon Over Bourbon St.* (at the *Southern Landing, West Mall;* phone: 637-3448).

Tobago's nightlife is quiet. There are steel bands and limbo dancers at some hotels, where Saturday night fetes usually include a barbecue and music. The *Cellar Pub Disco* at the *Mount Irvine Bay* hotel tends to attract the most sophisticated crowd with nonstop entertainment from calypso, limbo, and steel bands. In Scarborough, the alfresco slide show and conviviality of the *Old Donkey Cart House* (phone: 639-3551) attract after-dinner drop-ins. *La Tropicale* at the *Della Mira Guest House* is a favorite with islanders for its Saturday night floor show, live band, and authentic Tobagonian dances. Watch for billboards advertising moonlit beach barbecues. These local events, often fund-raisers for churches, feature bands, plenty of chicken or fish, and rum punch, for about $5 to $10, and can go on until 1 or 2 in the morning. Beyond that, there are moonlit walks and late swims.

Best on the Islands

CHECKING IN

Accommodations on Trinidad run the gamut from deluxe, pool-oriented, multiroom complexes to smaller, less luxurious hostelries with a truer island flavor. There are also cottages for rent — a good idea for those planning an extended stay — and guesthouses for those seeking very inexpensive accommodations.

Many of the bigger, popular hotels are near Port of Spain, an advantage for those with sightseeing, shopping, or business on their agendas, but inconvenient for the avid beachcomber. Check whether your hotel arranges transportation to the beach. Otherwise, you probably can hook up with fellow hotel guests and share the cost of a taxi ride.

Expect to pay $100 to $170 (or more) a night for a double room, without meals, during the winter season at hotels we place in the expensive category; between $75 and $100 at places in the moderate range; and less than $75 a night for inexpensive accommodations. Rates are subject to a 15% value added tax (VAT) and some places also tack on a 10% or 15% service charge. Many hotels offer the Modified American Plan (MAP), which includes breakfast and dinner, at an additional $20 to $35 per person per day. A number of rental villas are also available. Summer rates on Trinidad are somewhat lower — about 10% to 20% less. Special rates (sometimes twice the regular rates) are often in effect during *Carnival* time, and multiple-night stays may be required. Those who want to enjoy true Trinidadian hospitality, especially during *Carnival* when most hotels are full, should contact Victor Peterson of the *Bed and Breakfast Association* (phone: 637-9329; fax: 627-0856). Some members offer a swimming pool and home cooking, and rates are reasonable, starting at $30 per night. All telephone numbers are in the 809 area code unless otherwise indicated.

TRINIDAD

PORT OF SPAIN AND ENVIRONS

EXPENSIVE

Holiday Inn Modern, comfortable, and air conditioned, this place has 225 rooms, nightly entertainment, and *La Ronde,* a revolving restaurant (see *Eating Out*) with a superb view. Located in the heart of the city's business and commercial section. Amenities include a large pool and 2 all-weather tennis courts. Wrightson Rd., Port of Spain (phone: 625-3361; 800-465-4329 from the US; fax: 625-4166).

Trinidad Hilton International This hilltop, upside-down hotel (with the lobby on top and resident floors below) is the top choice for businesspeople. It's luxurious and air conditioned, with all amenities, including 3 premium-rate, super-service executive floors with airport meeting service, daily newspapers, complimentary continental breakfast, and a special lounge with an open bar and hot hors d'oeuvres. In addition to 412 rooms with spectacular views, it boasts the largest convention facilities of any hotel in the southern Caribbean. Two restaurants, *La Boucan* (see *Eating Out*) and the *Pool Terrace,* are supplemented by pool buffets. Every Monday is "Pot Pourri Night," featuring folkloric music, entertainment, and a feast of roast pig on a spit, beef, chicken, and such island favorites as *callaloo* and *souse.* There are 2 lighted tennis courts, a large pool, a health club with sauna, and a 2-level shopping arcade. Lady Young Rd., Port of Spain (phone: 624-3211; 800-445-8667 from the US; fax: 624-3211, ext. 6133).

MODERATE

Chaconia Inn This suburban inn is popular with Trinidadians as well as visitors. There are 35 rooms and apartments, some with cooking facilities. A freshwater pool, sun deck, restaurant, and a popular pub with dancing in the evening are among its attractions; so is its proximity to the *Moka* golf course. 106 Saddle Rd., Maraval (phone: 628-8603; 800-223-6310 from the US; fax: 628-3214).

Normandie Anna and Fred Chin Lee have recently remodeled the 53 units here, building on the charm of the original turn-of-the-century structure to create a distinctive California/Mexico feel. Nestled on Nook Avenue, within easy walking distance of the Savannah and the *Hilton,* it has 16 rooms with sleeping lofts and one suite plus easy access to the conference center and gallery of shops. There are 37 older rooms, clustered around the swimming pool in its garden setting. All rooms are air conditioned. Be sure to dine at *La Fantasie* (see *Eating Out*). 10 Nook Ave., St. Ann's (phone: 624-1181; 800-223-8815 from the US; fax: 624-1181, ext. 2315).

Valley Vue This hotel has 68 rooms, including 12 suites. There are squash and tennis courts, a pool, a fitness room, and a sauna. Shops, a disco, a restaurant, and a bar are also on the premises. 67 Ariapita Ave., Woodbrook (phone: 623-3511; fax: 627-8040).

INEXPENSIVE

La Maison Rustique A delightful bed and breakfast establishment, with 2 units in the main building (which houses a charming tea shop, open during daylight hours) and 2 freestanding apartments, usually reserved for long-term tenants. Rooms are clean, service is attentive, and breakfast is a great introduction to Trinidadian fare. 16 Rust St., Port of Spain (phone: 622-1512).

Monique's Guest House A lovely inn with 11 large, immaculate, air conditioned rooms. One room on the lower level is equipped for handicapped guests. This engagingly informal establishment is the place to experience true Trinidadian hospitality; guests return again and again. It's located in suburban Maraval, only 8 minutes from the *Moka* golf course. 114 Saddle Rd., Maraval (phone: 628-3344; fax: 628-2351).

ELSEWHERE ON TRINIDAD

MODERATE

Asa Wright Nature Centre and Lodge Even if you're not a bird watcher, you'll enjoy waking up to the sounds of birds outside your window at this gracious 16-room establishment. Try to reserve room number 5 or 6 in the main building, both of which are large, charming, and high-ceilinged; the other rooms are best suited to those out bird watching all day. Rates include all meals, afternoon tea (a treat in itself), and rum punch each evening. Blanchisseuse, 20 miles from Port of Spain (phone: 677-4655; 800-426-7781 from the US).

Timberline Resort and Nature Centre Here are 12 units in converted cocoa houses in an idyllic setting on Trinidad's north coast. Nature lovers can enjoy ocean views, stroll the beach, or follow bird watching trails. Rates include breakfast and dinner. In Mount Lambert (phone: 638-2263).

INEXPENSIVE

Pax Guest House For something completely different, the 14 rooms here are part of a monastery at Mount St. Benedict in the hills of Tunapuna, about 20 minutes from Port of Spain. Accommodations are neat, clean, and spartan. Go for the spectacular view and the peace and quiet as well as for the homemade bread and honey served at teatime (phone: 662-4084; 212-727-0780 from the US).

TOBAGO

Tobago's hotels are more subdued than those of Trinidad, although that is changing rapidly as new establishments spring up; many more are in the works. Note, too, that hotel prices sometimes are higher here than on Trinidad. Winter rates at expensive hotels will run about $175 and up per night for a double room; a moderate place will charge $100 to $160; an inexpensive establishment will cost from $50 to $100. Tobago's rates are considerably lower (40% or so) in summer. Most hotels offer a Modified American Plan (including breakfast and dinner). Food at the hotels tends to be quite good, and given the dearth of restaurants, the MAP option makes sense.

The Tobago branch of the *T&T Bed & Breakfast Association* represents some 15 properties, most on the western end of the island, with rates ranging from $15 to $60 a night. For further information, contact Lloyd Anthony (phone: 639-8836). The *Tobago Villas Agency* (phone: 639-8737; fax: 639-8800) lists several attractive villas for rent on the Mount Irvine Bay estate; some are right on the beach. Telephone numbers are in the 809 area code unless otherwise indicated.

CROWN POINT — STORE BAY — AIRPORT AREA

MODERATE

Golden Thistle A 10- to 15-minute walk from Store Bay Beach, this property has 26 clean rooms (the 12 in the pool wing are the most popular); all are air conditioned and have full kitchens. There's a freshwater pool and a restaurant. Store Bay Rd. (phone: 639-8521).

Kariwak Village Air conditioned cottages containing a total of 18 rooms are clustered around a pool house. There's first-rate island food and entertainment (see *Eating Out*). Minutes from the airport, a 5-minute walk from the beach (phone: 639-8545; fax: 639-8441).

Sandy Point Beach This resort/village complex includes some condos, some time-share properties, and about 45 hotel units. The newer units in the village are spacious and air conditioned, with kitchenettes; the upper-level rooms have sleeping lofts. Features include 2 pools, the *Steak Hut* restaurant (see *Eating Out*), and free shuttle to Pigeon Point. Sandy Point (phone: 639-8533; 800-223-6510 from the US; fax: 639-8485).

INEXPENSIVE

James Holiday Resort Fourteen 1-bedroom efficiency apartments are tucked in between *Sandy Point Beach* and the *Tropikist* hotel. All units are air conditioned and have small furnished kitchens, ceiling fans, and balconies or patios. Bed linen is provided, but bring your own towels. Free pickup at the airport. Crown Point (phone: 639-8084).

NORTH SHORE

EXPENSIVE

Arnos Vale Club All 30 rooms face the Caribbean at this secluded hillside property, once a 400-acre plantation. There's a beach and a pool, plus lush gardens. Rooms are large and handsomely furnished European-style. The food is first-rate. Arnos Vale (phone: 639-2881; fax: 639-4629).

Grafton Beach This 114-room, 3-story hotel is located flush on the beach. All the rooms are air conditioned and have mini-bars. Additional attractions: lighted tennis courts, 2 squash courts, a restaurant, and a pool with swim-up bar. Near the Grafton Bird Sanctuary, and not far from *Mount Irvine* golf, with special greens fee arranged (phone: 639-0191; 800-223-6510 from the US; fax: 639-0030).

Mount Irvine Bay If you're a golfer, this is the place (see *Top Tee-Off Spot* in *Golf* in this chapter). The course is dazzling, and guests are entitled to reduced greens fees and use of the golf clubhouse. There are 23 air conditioned cottages, each with 2 rooms, patio, and views of the fairways or the sea; the main building has 52 additional rooms — all air conditioned and extremely comfortable — that wrap around a swimming pool. There are 2 floodlit tennis courts and equipment rentals, and a beach. The *Sugar Mill* restaurant (see *Eating Out*) is a fine dining choice (phone: 639-8871; 800-223-6510 from the US; fax: 639-8800).

MODERATE

Cocrico Inn This well-maintained motel-style property has 16 rooms, a pool, and a popular restaurant (see *Eating Out*). A 5-minute walk to the beach and a good base from which to experience village life and Tobagonian culture. Be sure to note the fine paintings by local artist Anthony Lewis. In the village of Plymouth (phone: 639-2961; 800-223-9815 from the US; fax: 639-6565).

SOUTH SHORE — SCARBOROUGH

EXPENSIVE

Palm Tree Village Here are 20 two- or four-bedroom villa-like units with full kitchens, air conditioned bedrooms, large living rooms, and patios. Cooks are available upon request. On the windward side of the island at Little Rockly Bay (phone: 639-4347; fax: 639-4180).

INEXPENSIVE

Della Mira Guest House The simple 14 rooms (all with private bath, half with air conditioning) are among the best low-budget deals on the island. The manager here also runs *La Tropicale* nightclub next door, which has entertainment and dancing. The property's location (only a short pace from Scarborough) makes it a popular choice. In Bacolet, just outside Scarborough (phone: 639-2531).

EAST END

MODERATE

Blue Waters A divers' haven at the eastern end of the island, this place has 29 rooms, all with kitchenettes. On the beach, it's close to great diving, snorkeling, and windsurfing. The Little Tobago Island Bird Sanctuary is nearby. Batteaux Bay, Speyside (phone: 660-4341; fax: 660-5195).

Richmond Great House One of Tobago's oldest greathouses, this is the perfect place for those who seek peace and quiet. The 5 simply appointed rooms have great sea views; the main rooms are filled with African art from the collection of the owner, a professor of African history at Columbia University in New York. There's also a pool and good home cooking — an interesting find, though a bit off the beaten track. Belle Garden (phone: 660-4467).

EATING OUT

A wide variety of dishes — Chinese, Indian, creole, Spanish, French, and West Indian — is available in Port of Spain. There are far fewer choices in Tobago.

The islands' gustatory exotica includes *manicou* (opossum) stew, and *tatou* (armadillo) stew, although some of these delicacies are no longer served legally, due to the current ban on hunting. But no matter, there are still plenty of delicious stuffed crabs, tiny clam-like shellfish (called *chip-chip*), and Indian-spiced *rôtis* stuffed with spicy meats. Accompany all of this with fresh rum punch — as only the island home of Angostura Bitters can make it — or Carib or Stag beer. The local rum, Old Oak, is made at the House of Angostura, along with a fairly good coffee liqueur called Mokatia.

In the listing below, dinner for two will cost $60 or more, not including drinks and the service charge, at restaurants described as expensive; from about $30 to $60 at moderate places; and $30 or less at inexpensive places. All telephone numbers are in the 809 area code unless otherwise indicated.

TRINIDAD

PORT OF SPAIN AND ENVIRONS

EXPENSIVE

La Boucan Named for the smoking oven used by buccaneers to prepare meat for their voyages, the *Hilton International*'s widely known dining place sports a replica of this cooking apparatus, and many of its dishes are characterized by a subtle, smoky taste. There are also steaks, fish, and mildly flavored island dishes, like *callaloo.* Look for the wall painting by Trinidadian Geoffrey Holder. Open for dinner daily. Reservations advised. Major credit cards accepted. Lady Young Rd., Port of Spain (phone: 624-3211).

China Palace Unlike most North American Chinese restaurants, those on Trinidad don't include vegetables in meat and fish dishes, and rice must be ordered separately. An outstanding starter here is shrimp *souse,* a combination of traditional Trinidadian *souse* and a shrimp cocktail; unfortunately, its tanginess makes most of the other dishes seem bland by comparison. The Wednesday night buffet offers an overview of the kitchen's prowess. Open for lunch and dinner daily except holidays. Reservations unnecessary. Major credit cards accepted. Two locations: 5 Maraval Rd., Port of Spain (phone: 628-6439) and Ellerslie Plaza, St. Clair (phone: 622-5866).

The Orchid The seafood-oriented menu is a tad too cute, but the dishes themselves are more appealing than their descriptions. Seasoning is to local taste, so spicy can be "hot" to the uninitiated. The bar is a popular gathering spot at cocktail hour; there's entertainment on weekends. Open daily for lunch and dinner. Reservations advised. Major credit cards accepted (there is a 10% surcharge on all non-cash transactions). 100 Saddle Rd., Maraval (phone: 628-7007).

Le Poissonnier Located at the *Maraval Shopping Centre,* this eatery serves all sorts of very fresh fish and seafood (there's a retail and take-out shop next door). Though many of the baked and creole preparations of king, dolphin, and swordfish may sound familiar, the freshness of the ingredients makes them special. Two of the more unusual preparations are *carite Portuguese* (fish filet served with tomatoes, onions, chives, and garlic) and fish served with "shadow benny" (a curry sauce of East Indian origin). Open daily; dinner only on Sundays and holidays. Reservations advised. Major credit cards accepted. 3A Saddle Rd., Maraval (phone: 628-8186).

La Ronde The *Holiday Inn*'s revolving rooftop restaurant offers one of the best nighttime views in town. Steaks and other tourist fare are featured menu items. Open for dinner daily. Reservations advised. Major credit cards accepted. Wrightson Rd., Port of Spain (phone 625-3361).

Veni Mange A not-to-be-missed lunch spot renowned for its soups (especially *callaloo,* red bean, pumpkin), lobster, curried crab; some vegetarian dishes, too. Open weekdays for lunch only; also open Friday nights for drinks and snacks. Reservations necessary. No credit cards accepted. 13 Lucknow St., St. James (no phone).

MODERATE

Café Savanna Featuring Caribbean and creole specialties including *callaloo,* grouper baked in banana leaves, and fried flying fish. Open for lunch and dinner; closed Sundays. Reservations advised. Major credit cards accepted. In the *Kapok Hotel,* 16-18 Cotton Hill, St. Clair (phone: 622-6441).

Coconut Village An open-air lounge and dining spot at the Cruise Ship Complex, featuring creole specialties, burgers, and sandwiches at lunch; more elaborate platters for dinner. When there's a live radio broadcast or live jazz in the evening, there's a $2.50 cover charge. Open daily for lunch and dinner. Reservations advised on weekends. Major credit cards accepted. Wrightson Rd., Port of Spain (phone: 627-2648).

La Fantasie This place pioneered *cuisine créole nouvelle,* a reinterpretation and creative updating of Trinidad's diverse, traditional cooking. Try the *poule déshoue viande fin* (pâté of chicken with garlic and bay leaf seasoning) for starters. *Crème de croisse* is a pumpkin and bean soup, and entrées include Manzanilla Morning (fish steak or filet with herbs and sauce) and *petit pap bois* (charbroiled filet mignon with herb bouquet and rum butter). Open daily for dinner. Reservations advised. Major credit cards accepted. In the *Normandie Hotel,* 10 Nook Ave., St. Ann's (phone: 624-1181).

Il Giardino di Luciano Homemade pasta and garlicky Italian-style dishes are served in a garden setting. Don't miss the Caroni mussels alla marinara. Open for lunch and dinner; closed Sundays. Reservations unnecessary. Major credit cards accepted. 6 Nook Ave., St. Ann's (phone: 624-1459).

Monsoon Busy at lunch, but less hectic in the evening this eatery, has a modern, stylish decor with service to match. Trinidadian-Indian dishes are the specialties here, although few are done in the Old World Indian manner. Open for lunch and dinner; closed Sundays. Reservations advised for large parties. Major credit cards accepted. Corner of Tragarete Rd. and Picton St., Port of Spain (phone: 628-7684).

Rafters An eatery that specializes in both seafood and carved meats. Roast beef and lamb top the carvery list, while the seafood menu includes everything from lobster to local mussels and the shellfish called *chip-chip.* The lunch buffet is popular with the locals. Open daily; dinner only on Saturdays and Sundays. Reservations advised, especially for lunch. Major credit cards accepted. 6A Warner St., Port of Spain (phone: 628-9258).

Singho Tucked inside the *Longcircular Mall,* it offers the best Cantonese-style food in the area, excellent service, and entertainment. Try the lemon chicken or lobster in black bean sauce. Buffets on Sundays for lunch; Wednesdays for dinner. Open daily for lunch and dinner. Reservations advised. Major credit cards accepted. St. James (phone: 628-2077).

TOBAGO

EXPENSIVE

Dillon's Owned by local fisherman and charter captain Stanley Dillon, this restaurant has been popular ever since it opened a few years ago; the kitchen can get overwhelmed on busy nights. Seasoning is timid by local standards, but when the place isn't hectic, the lobster thermidor and stuffed kingfish in creole sauce are memorable. Open for dinner only; closed Mondays. Reservations necessary. Major credit cards accepted. Crown Point Rd., Scarborough (phone: 639-8765).

Old Donkey Cart House In an old French colonial house, this first class dining spot serves local fish and meat dishes, along with imported cheeses and excellent German wines. Open for lunch and dinner; closed Wednesdays. Reservations advised for weekends and winter months. Major credit cards accepted. Bacolet St., Scarborough (phone: 639-3551).

Papillon Jakob Straessle's place in the *Old Grange Inn* has long been popular with island visitors and is still going strong. Such dishes as local crayfish, lobster crêpes, and seafood casserole with ginger wine — now island favorites — were introduced here. The largest menu in Tobago also includes *boeuf Chez Jacques* (a French-style cube steak), baby shark marinated in lime and rum, and conch stewed with coconut and rum. Open for lunch and dinner; dinner only on Sundays. Reservations advised. Major credit cards accepted. Buccoo Crossing (phone: 639-0275).

Sugar Mill Dine in a relaxed atmosphere at this 200-year-old converted sugar mill. Guests choose from an à la carte menu or select items from the buffet, both featuring local seafood and creole dishes. Open daily for lunch and dinner. Reservations advised. Major credit cards accepted. At the *Mount Irvine Bay* hotel (phone: 639-8871).

La Tartaruga A small dining room with a cozy, homey atmosphere, this place features seafood and Italian dishes. Open for lunch and dinner; closed

Tuesdays. Reservations advised. Major credit cards accepted. Idlewild Trace, Scarborough (phone: 639-1861).

MODERATE

Blue Crab On a verandah overlooking Rockly, this dining spot features seafood and creole dishes. Specialties include curried goat, crab backs, conch chowder, homemade ice cream, and homemade tropical fruit wines. Open weekdays for lunch; dinner on Wednesdays and Fridays only. Reservations necessary. Major credit cards accepted. At Main and Robinson Sts., Scarborough (phone: 639-2737).

Cocrico Inn A must for trying tempting Tobagonian fare. Spicy seafood dishes are the specialty here, served in a charming dining room. Open daily for lunch and dinner. Reservations advised. Major credit cards accepted. Plymouth (phone: 639-2961).

Gomes Sunrise Nothing fancy, just a great view of the harbor and downtown Scarborough, the cheapest beer on the island (about 60¢), and honest food. Adelia Rodriques serves large portions, in the tradition of her native Portugal, including a dozen different shrimp preparations, steaks, chicken, burgers, and sandwiches. Open daily for lunch and dinner; a DJ plays ballroom dance music on Saturday evenings. Reservations unnecessary. Major credit cards accepted. Lower Scarborough (phone: 639-3477).

Kariwak Village Sample some of the most enticing preparations of local dishes on the island in a rustic bamboo setting. Open daily for lunch and dinner. Reservations necessary. Major credit cards accepted. Crown Point (phone: 639-8545).

Steak Hut If red meat is your thing, dine here; but if you don't like barbecue sauce, say so, because it's slathered on everything. Fish dishes also are served, and there are some good wine choices. It's the island's only seafront restaurant. Open for dinner daily. Reservations advised. Major credit cards accepted. At the *Sandy Point Beach Club,* Crown Point (phone: 639-8533 or 639-8391).

Village Garden The owner specializes in seafood, including barracuda steaks, snapper, and lobster. There's live music on Wednesday and Sunday evenings. Open for dinner; closed Tuesdays. Reservations advised on weekends. No credit cards accepted. Store Bay (phone: 639-0025).

INEXPENSIVE

Miss Esmie One of the food stalls at Store Bay Beach operated by women who until a few years ago cooked right on the beach. For about $5, you can get a plate of three square, flat "dumplings," a good portion of fricasseed conch or crab, plus sweet potato, plantain, *callaloo,* and the vegetable of the day, all swimming in gravy, plus a soft drink. Open daily. No reservations. No credit cards accepted. Store Bay Beach (no phone).

Teaside Originally a teahouse, the menu still includes a good selection of tea, but just as popular now is the pizza, which comes with 10 toppings (you have to specify what you *don't* want). No alcoholic beverages. Open daily; dinner only on Sundays. Reservations unnecessary. No credit cards accepted. Lambeau (phone: 639-4306).

The US Virgin Islands

Among the most beautiful islands in the entire Caribbean are the three siblings that make up the US Virgin Islands — St. Croix, St. John, and St. Thomas. Products of a common history, set in the same sea, they are at once the same and very different — St. Thomas with steep, green mountains and lengths of shining sands; St. John with a cover of jungle and its share of beaches, most within the boundaries of the extraordinary Virgin Islands National Park; and St. Croix, the most underrated of the three, with nostalgic towns, ruins of plantation houses, and rolling, breeze-combed grass hills and valleys.

Despite their insistent greenery and profuse flowers, the USVI are counted among the dry islands of the Caribbean; just why is most evident on St. Croix, where the landscape gradually browns as the dry season wears on. Prickly fingered cacti are the chief botanical feature of its Atlantic tip — the easternmost tip of US territory. This dry weather, however, means lots of sunshine. Breezes temper the humidity so that even late summer days, with midday temperatures in the low 90s, are fairly comfortable.

The blue and green waters around the islands are clean and clear thanks to the national park, which protects 5,650 acres offshore and 9,000 acres of land on St. John. Virgin Islands National Park was established in 1956 after extensive donations of land by Laurance Rockefeller's Rockresort Foundation. It has set the pace for similar preserves on a number of other Caribbean islands.

Since Columbus discovered the islands in 1493, St. Croix, St. John, and St. Thomas have attracted the attention of more outside powers than any other Caribbean isles. The flags of Spain, the Knights of Malta, France, England, Holland, Denmark, and the United States have flown over them. Columbus and his men came ashore near St. Croix's Salt River in search of water but were repulsed by Carib Indians. Columbus hastily named the island for the Holy Cross (Santa Cruz) and shoved off to discover St. Thomas and St. John. He then named the whole group — at that time including the British Virgin Islands — for the legendary 11,000 virgin followers of St. Ursula, and moved on to Puerto Rico.

A century later, in 1593, Sir Francis Drake put in at St. Thomas and St. John on his way to attack the Spanish at San Juan. In 1625 — although the islands were still technically Spanish — British, Dutch, and French colonists established farms on St. Croix. By 1650, the French were gone, and Spain returned to expel the British as well. In 1653, St. Croix was given to the crusaders' Order of St. John, better known as the Knights of Malta. A few years later, France took it over, and for the next half century or so,

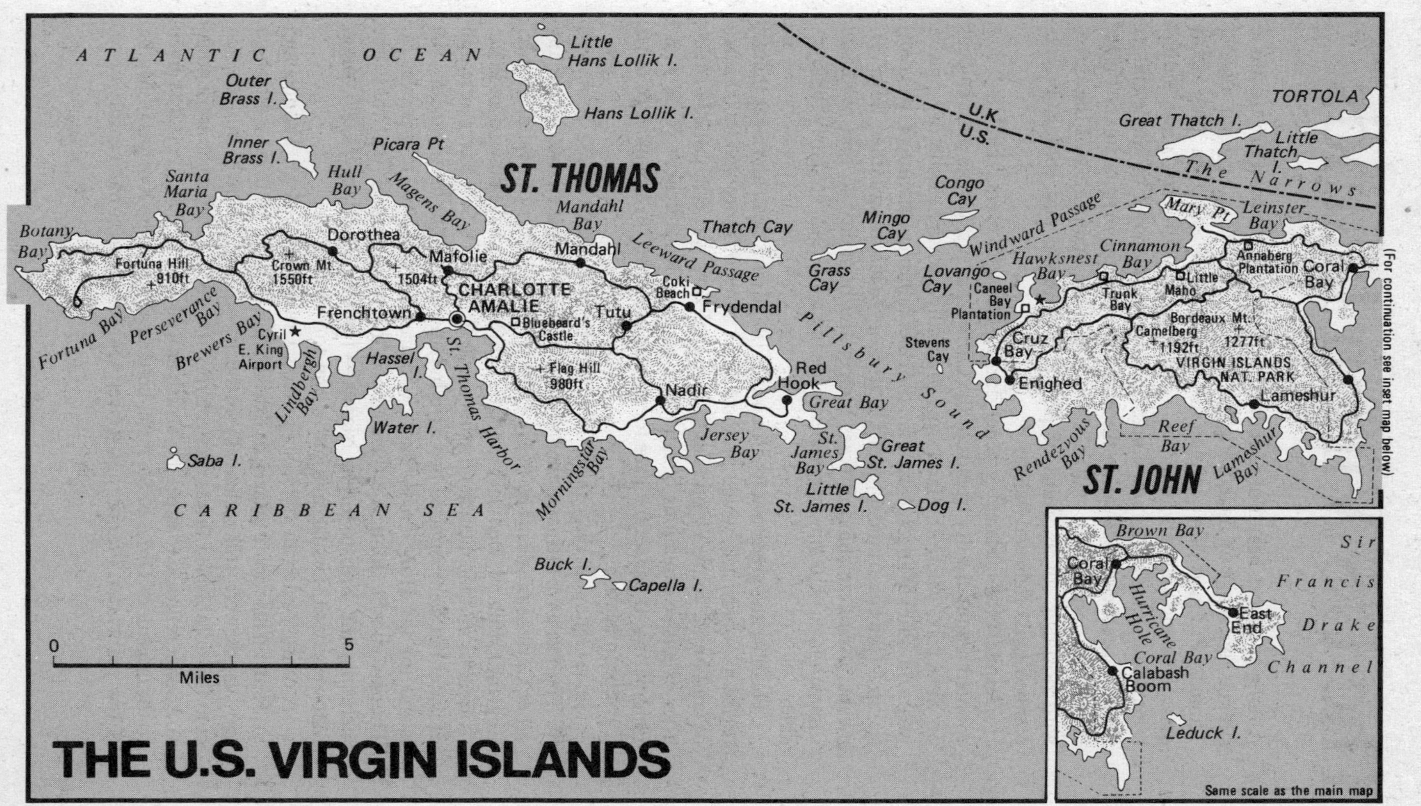
THE U.S. VIRGIN ISLANDS
ATLANTIC OCEAN
CARIBBEAN SEA
ST. THOMAS
ST. JOHN
TORTOLA
U.K.
U.S.
The Narrows
Little Hans Lollik I.
Hans Lollik I.
Outer Brass I.
Inner Brass I.
Picara Pt
Hull Bay
Magens Bay
Santa Maria Bay
Botany Bay
Fortuna Hill 910ft
Crown Mt. 1550ft
Dorothea
Mafolie
1504ft
CHARLOTTE AMALIE
Mandahl Bay
Mandahl
Tutu
Bluebeard's Castle
Frenchtown
Flag Hill 980ft
Nadir
Coki Beach
Frydendal
Red Hook
Great Bay
Jersey Bay
St. James Bay
Great St. James I.
Little St. James I.
Dog I.
Fortuna Bay
Perseverance Bay
Brewers Bay
Cyril E. King Airport
Lindbergh Bay
Hassel I.
Water I.
St. Thomas Harbor
Morningstar Bay
Saba I.
Buck I.
Capella I.
Thatch Cay
Leeward Passage
Grass Cay
Mingo Cay
Congo Cay
Lovango Cay
Stevens Cay
Pillsbury Sound
Windward Passage
Great Thatch I.
Little Thatch I.
Mary Pt
Leinster Bay
Cinnamon Bay
Hawksnest Bay
Caneel Bay Plantation
Trunk Bay
Little Maho
Annaberg Plantation
Coral Bay
Cruz Bay
Enighed
Camelberg 1192ft
Bordeaux Mt. 1277ft
VIRGIN ISLANDS NAT. PARK
Lameshur
Reef Bay
Rendezvous Bay
Lameshur Bay
(For continuation see inset map below)
0
5
Miles
Brown Bay
Coral Bay
Hurricane Hole
Coral Bay
Calabash Boom
East End
Leduck I.
Sir Francis Drake Channel
Same scale as the main map

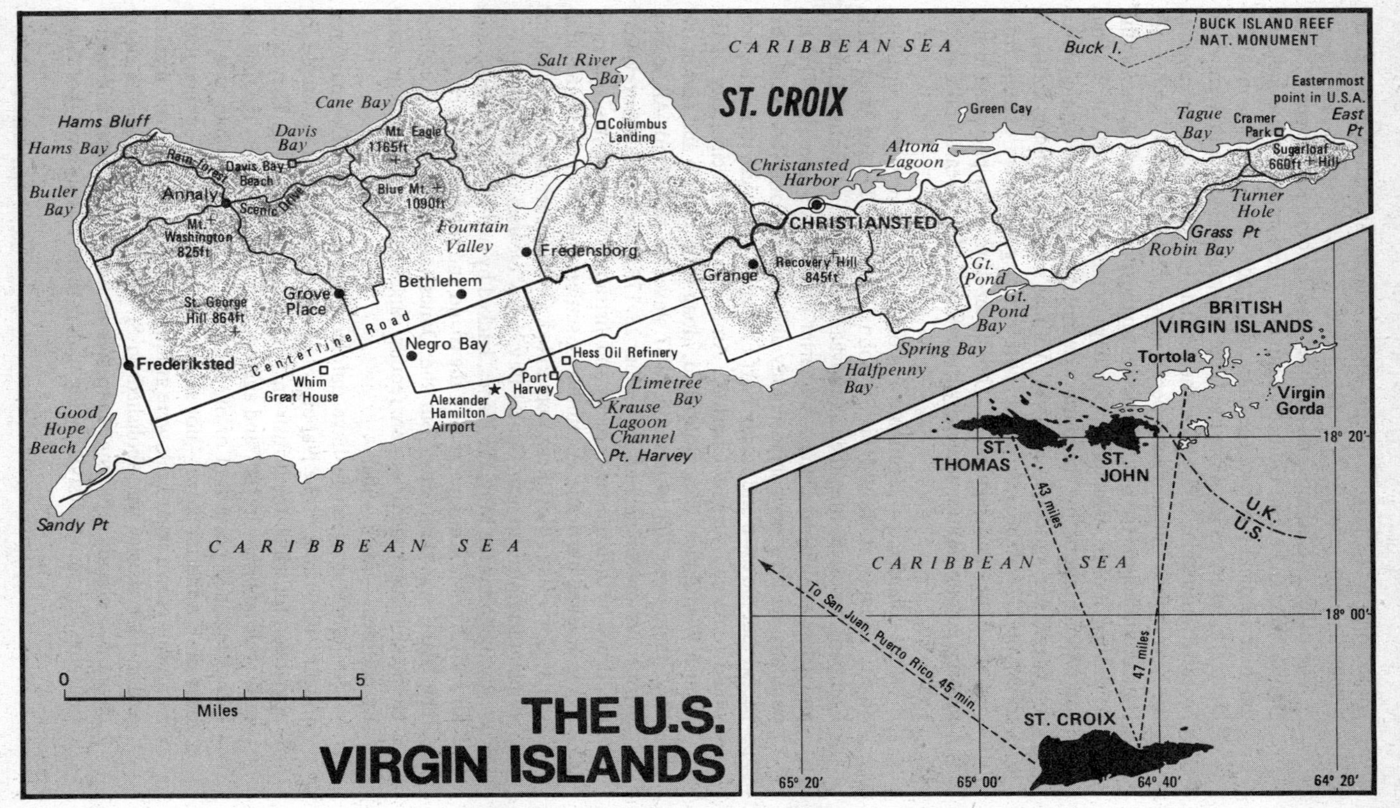
THE U.S.
VIRGIN ISLANDS
ST. CROIX
CARIBBEAN SEA
Buck I.
BUCK ISLAND REEF
NAT. MONUMENT
Salt River
Bay
Cane Bay
Hams Bluff
Hams Bay
Davis
Bay
Davis Bay
Beach
Rain Forest
Butler
Bay
Annaly
Scenic Drive
Mt. Eagle
1165ft
Blue Mt.
1090ft
Mt.
Washington
825ft
Fountain
Valley
Fredensborg
Columbus
Landing
Christiansted
Harbor
Altona
Lagoon
Green Cay
CHRISTIANSTED
Recovery Hill
845ft
Grange
Bethlehem
Grove
Place
St. George
Hill 864ft
Negro Bay
Centerline Road
Frederiksted
Whim
Great House
Alexander
Hamilton
Airport
Port
Harvey
Hess Oil Refinery
Limetree
Bay
Krause
Lagoon
Channel
Pt. Harvey
Good
Hope
Beach
Sandy Pt
Halfpenny
Bay
Spring Bay
Gt.
Pond
Gt.
Pond
Bay
Robin Bay
Grass Pt
Turner
Hole
Tague
Bay
Cramer
Park
Sugarloaf
660ft Hill
Easternmost
point in U.S.A.
East
Pt
CARIBBEAN SEA
0
5
Miles
BRITISH
VIRGIN ISLANDS
Tortola
Virgin
Gorda
ST.
THOMAS
ST.
JOHN
U.K.
U.S.
43 miles
47 miles
CARIBBEAN SEA
To San Juan, Puerto Rico, 45 min.
ST. CROIX
18° 20′
18° 00′
65° 20′
65° 00′
64° 40′
64° 20′

possession of this largest of the Virgin Islands alternated between the French and the Spanish.

The other two islands, meanwhile, had become the property of the Danish West India and Guinea Company. The company name indicates the three cardinal points of the triangular trade in which it was involved: Denmark, where its investors lived; the West Indies, where they grew and processed sugarcane; and Africa (then called Guinea), where they captured the slaves whose labor made operations profitable. On St. Thomas, the Danes founded the town of Charlotte Amalie (pronounced Ah-*mahl*-yah). At the height of its sugar-producing days in the 17th century, St. Thomas had 170 plantations, but the number dwindled quickly. The terrain proved too rugged for agriculture, and St. Thomas's economic focus shifted to trade. In 1724 it became a free port where goods were exempt from customs duties and regulation. The laissez-faire atmosphere made it a favorite among pirates, especially the infamous Blackbeard and Captain Kidd.

While commerce — legitimate and otherwise — outstripped sugarcane on St. Thomas, it thrived on St. John. When the Danish West India Company first took title, the island was shared by some British squatters and a few established Danes. A quarter of a century later, in 1717, the company set up a permanent colony and port at Coral Bay. It was expected that the town and sturdy Fort Frederiksvaern, with its fine harbor, would some day surpass Charlotte Amalie as the principal city of the Danish West Indies. Cane flourished, along with tobacco and cotton. By 1733, there were 208 whites and 1,087 slaves on the island. All seemed prosperous and serene until November 23, 1733, when the slaves revolted, maddened by their masters' cruelty and distraught by drought, plague, and a crop-leveling hurricane. A number of settlers and the entire white garrison at Coral Bay's Fort Berg were killed. On the other side of the island, 40 planters holed up near Caneel Bay; many escaped to St. Thomas.

By the following May, the Danes, backed by two French warships and an army from Martinique, retook the island and subdued the rebel slaves. The island was devastated, but the Danes (and capitalism) prevailed. Homes and sugar factories were rebuilt, cane was replanted, and prosperity returned — for a while.

St. John's story might have unfolded differently had Denmark not fought with France in the Napoleonic Wars. This was just the excuse for aggression for which the British on Tortola had been waiting. They occupied St. John briefly in 1801 and again for 7 years in 1807. By the time the Danes regained possession of St. John, the island's economic base had been dealt a mortal blow — not so much by the British as by time itself. European-grown sugar beets were gradually taking over the sugar market, and in 1848 slavery was abolished on St. John. Even though the steam engine was already replacing manpower in some island sugar mill operations, the plantation lifestyle couldn't adapt to the loss of slave labor. Soon after abolition, the Danish planters who hadn't already left because of failing cane markets sailed for home.

If it had not been for World War I, St. Croix, St. John, and St. Thomas might still be Danish. But when the sugar industry began to crumble, Denmark started looking for buyers. In 1917, the United States, worried about possible unfriendly bases in the Caribbean that might threaten the Panama Canal or the US mainland, bought the three islands for $25 million. Today, although some fine old Danish buildings remain and streets have Danish *gade* (street) signs, the atmosphere of the US Virgin Islands is distinctly American.

St. Croix became better known when the *Carambola Beach Resort and Golf Club* opened in 1986, and the condominium developers moved in. The resort has recently reopened as a Radisson property after being closed for nearly 2 years (the result of damage from 1989's Hurricane Hugo), and future plans include building a conference center elsewhere on the island. In addition, shallow-draft cruise ships are now docking at Christiansted, and a new, state-of-the-art dock that will accommodate most ships is being built in Frederiksted. In spite of the increase in development, however, St. Croix is a surprisingly livable island. Neither as developed as St. Thomas nor as rural and raw as St. John, it boasts a number of historical sites, plenty of water sports facilities, and enough restaurants, hotels, and night-spots to keep most visitors happy.

St. John, which pulled a blanket of jungle over its head when the Danish planters left in 1848, is reawakening. This process first started in 1956, when the national park was established and Laurance Rockefeller built his *Caneel Bay* resort, allowing visitors to enjoy the park in ultra comfort. A second stage of development was launched in 1976 with the camp-in-comfort *Maho Bay* resort. This attracted a new wave of more adventuresome travelers, intrigued with the park and the island's history. The third stage began in the late 1980s with the opening of the *Virgin Grand* — now the *Hyatt Regency* — and the inevitable appearance of condominiums.

St. Thomas, liveliest of the island trio, takes its quickened pace from active visitors who swim, sail, windsurf, dive, and water-ski off its spectacular beaches and explore its up-hill-and-down-dale roads in cars and jeeps. They gather in seafront watering spots and choose from an array of restaurants and nightclubs in the evenings. The press of local hawkers and the onslaught of cruise passengers (often thousands a day) make Charlotte Amalie a good place to avoid on days when there are several ships in port (Wednesdays and Fridays are generally busiest). But St. Thomas's boosters believe that the island's beauty and fun more than make up for the inconvenience of crowds.

Residents of all three islands are somewhat ambivalent about the changes wrought by new development. There is controversy concerning the effects of tourism on the environment, and nowhere is that more evident than on St. John, which fears for the future of the National Park and is fighting to keep the cruise ships away. (The owners of the *Maho* resort have broken ground on the island's east end for a condominium complex that will follow in the resort's environmentally aware footsteps — however, at press time, construction plans were still on hold due to lack of funds.) Many black citizens feel they are underrepresented in management positions within the tourism industry and, as elsewhere in the Caribbean, there is an undercurrent of racially rooted resentment. Lonely nighttime walks down dark streets in Virgin Island towns are not recommended; unfortunately, such warnings, sensibly and sensitively applied, have become a "given" of contemporary travel.

But understanding that few places are exempt from the tensions of modern life and nature's wrath, savvy travelers continue to return to the US Virgins, because they also recognize that few, if any, islands anywhere in the world offer so much in the way of natural beauty and potential pleasure.

US Virgin Islands At-a-Glance

FROM THE AIR

In addition to the three major US Virgin Islands — St. Croix, St. John, and St. Thomas — there are approximately 50 smaller islets and cays, most of them uninhabited. Spread over some 14,000 square miles of Caribbean and Atlantic waters, the US Virgin Islands are part of the Leeward Islands in the Lesser Antilles and have a total population of over 150,000. The center of the island group is about 60 miles east of Puerto Rico and just west of the smaller British Virgin Islands. St. Croix (pronounced *Croy*) is the largest (23 miles long and 6 miles across at its widest point) of the group, 40 miles south of the other two main islands and entirely surrounded by the Caribbean Sea. Long, narrow St. Thomas (12 miles long and 3 miles wide) and little St. John (9 by 3 miles) are next-door neighbors, only 3 miles apart, both with northern coasts washed by the Atlantic and southern sides bathed by the Caribbean Sea.

St. Croix looks like a caveman's club floating northeast (handle end) to southwest (round end) in the Caribbean. Its rolling land is still laid out in fields where cane used to grow. About 150 chunky stone towers — former plantation windmills — still dot the hills of St. Croix. Most island areas are still identified by names of the original plantations.

St. Croix has two towns: Christiansted, tucked into a reef-protected harbor a little east of center on its north coast, and Frederiksted, its deep-water port, in the middle of its western coast. Alexander Hamilton Airport is about a 10-minute drive due east of Frederiksted. Farther east along the south shore is St. Croix's major industrial development: the Hess Oil Refinery. The northern road out of Frederiksted leads toward the island's small rain forest and the Scenic Drive. An unpaved road follows along the crest of these hills, overlooking Fountain Valley to the south and, to the north, Cane Bay and Davis Bay, two of St. Croix's many handsome beaches. St. John, amoeba-shaped and indented with beach-lined bays, rises to inland heights covered with tropical forest. In the early 1800s, it boasted more than a hundred sugar plantations; now ruins of the old greathouses and sugar mills lie hidden in the undergrowth of the Virgin Islands National Park, which covers nearly 60% of the island's 20 square miles. One of the island's most beautiful beaches is Francis Bay, at the end of the road past Little Maho. While Cruz Bay lacks the sophistication of a modern mainland city, its pace is more frenetic now than it has been.

St. Thomas has an elongated hourglass shape, its waist cinched by a deep-water harbor on the south and horseshoe-shaped Magens Bay on the north. A ridge of mountains forms its spinal column. Surrounding the harbor and climbing the green hills beyond are the red-roofed houses of Charlotte Amalie, St. Thomas's only city and the capital of the US Virgin Islands, with a population of about 25,000. Since it has a major cruise port and an excellent shopping center, Charlotte Amalie's population swells by thousands of visitors whenever ships come into port, which is usually every day. Beyond the town, St. Thomas is a scenic collection of hills rising up to 1,500 feet and sloping steeply down to beaches cupped in curved bays on the jagged southern coast, or down to longer sweeps of white sand on the northern shore. Cyril E. King Airport (with its recently built, air conditioned terminal and spiffy shops) is on the south shore, about a 10-minute drive west of town. About 20 minutes to the east, at the end of the island, Red Hook Harbor has marina facilities for pleasure and deep-sea fishing boats and docks for ferries and launches that make the trip across Pillsbury Sound to St. John.

SPECIAL PLACES

ST. CROIX — Christiansted St. Croix's largest town, Christiansted is a cozy and culturally active community. Begin your sightseeing tour in the heart of town, where handsome 18th-century buildings stand near the harbor. Built by the Danish West India and Guinea Company, they're now a US National Historic Site. The Old Scalehouse, where Danish customs officers once weighed imports and exports, faces the waterfront; it now houses the visitors' bureau, where a free *Walking Tour Guide,* a map of the 4-square-block historic area, and a number of brochures on the island are available.

Just east of the Scalehouse, across a small park, stands Fort Christiansvaern, painted yellow and built on the foundations of a 1645 French fortress. Inside there are fine harbor views from battlements lined with cannon (never fired at an invader). A free booklet/guide provides information about the dungeons, powder magazine, barracks, officers' kitchen, and battery. Five rooms have been designed to look as they did in the

1840s. The fort's single non-military exhibit tells all about Buck Island reef. Tours are available on request. Open daily from 8 AM to 5 PM; from 9 AM to 5 PM weekends and federal holidays; there's an admission charge except for those under 16 or over 62 (phone: 773-1460). A block from the fort, on Company Street, stands the Steeple Building. Originally a Lutheran church, it has served as a military bakery, a hospital, and a school; today it's a historical museum with a small collection of Carib and Arawak artifacts, old uniforms, a diorama showing Christiansted as it was around 1800, an exhibit on black urban history during the Danish period, a display of drawings and photos of Christiansted's historic Danish architecture, and a visitors' orientation center. Open daily from 9 AM to 5 PM; admission charge (phone: 773-1460). Diagonally across the street, the post office does business in what was once the Danish West India and Guinea Company warehouse, built in 1749.

From the post office, head back toward the Scalehouse, turn left, and walk 1 block up King Street to Government House, the impressive cream-and-white former residence of the Danish governor-general. A small red Danish guardhouse still stands at the foot of the formal staircase, which leads from the courtyard to a grand ballroom with chandeliers, chimneyed sconces, and a dining table — copies of the originals — presented by the King and Queen of Denmark when the building was restored several decades ago. Official receptions are still held here, and visitors can look in daily from 8 AM to 6 PM.

At the outdoor market at "Shan" Hendricks Square, a short stroll away on Company Street, stalls are full of island-grown vegetables and fruit, including the pulpy green genips that are island favorites. Be sure to try one. Saturday morning is the best time to check out the market. Between Company Street and the harbor, old buildings, arcades, patios, and walkways are full of shops; a number of them are branches of St. Thomas stores. The harbor itself, with its bustling small boat traffic, is a fascinating sight.

FREDERIKSTED Seventeen miles from Christiansted at the west end of the island, this town comes to life when a cruise ship ties up at its deep-water pier. At other times, the town snoozes, especially during the summer when a number of its restaurants and shops hang out "Closed for the season" signs. Still, it's worth some browsing time because it is so different from Christiansted.

First of all, it looks different — more Victorian gingerbread than colonial Danish — though a few of its landmarks do date from the 1700s. Most buildings of that era were destroyed in a devastating fire in 1878, however, and Frederikstedders rebuilt the city with wood framing rather than stone, elaborate curlicued fretwork replacing the straightforward lines and arches of earlier Danish architecture. Try to go on a day when no cruise ship is in port, so that you'll be able to park at the north end of town near the pier.

The visitors' bureau at the end of the Frederiksted pier can provide a free *Walking Tour Guide* and a map. Fort Frederik, on the other side of Lagoon Street, is the logical place to begin a walking tour. Built in 1752 and now restored and repainted (Danish-fort red and white, naturally), it was the site of the 1848 proclamation freeing the slaves. It also claims to have been the first foreign fort to have fired a salute to the American flag — flown by a US merchant ship — on October 25, 1776. The Dutch island of St. Eustatius files a counterclaim by virtue of its salute to the Stars and Stripes aboard the US man-of-war *Andrew Doria* on November 16, 1776. The issue seems to hinge on the ownership (private or federal) of the vessel involved. At the fort, you can inspect the courtyard, the stable, the canteen, and the art exhibit in the old garrison. It's open weekdays from 8:30 AM to 4 PM; closed weekends and holidays. There's no admission charge.

Two blocks south and 1 block east of the fort, at the corner of Prince and Queen Streets, is the Market Place. Islanders have sold locally grown produce and herbs here since the town's founding in 1751. A block farther down Prince Street, at the corner of Market, is an interesting, though unrestored, antique masonry and frame residence, beyond which is St. Patrick's Catholic church, erected in 1843. On Hospital Street (parallel to Prince Street, 1 block east) stands an 18th-century building that was originally a residence, then a school. On Strand Street, which runs along the waterfront, the Old Customs House (late 18th century), now the headquarters of the Energy Commission, and Victoria House, with its elaborate gingerbread trim, are prime examples of Frederiksted's two favorite building styles. Children especially will enjoy the *St. Croix Aquarium* (Strand St.; phone: 772-1345). It's open Fridays, Saturdays, and Sundays from 10 AM to 6 PM; admission charge.

ELSEWHERE ON ST. CROIX

NORTH OF FREDERIKSTED The shore road north passes *Sprat Hall,* an old plantation home that's now a guesthouse with cottages, to the rain forest, the Scenic Drive (see *From the Air,* above), and 150-foot-high Creque Dam (pronounced *Creeky*), surrounded by yellow cedar, mahogany trees, and lilies.

SUGAR COUNTRY The Centerline Road heads northeast from Frederiksted across what was once St. Croix's sugar country. The land is green and rolling, still neatly divided into fields, though it has been a number of years since sugarcane was cultivated here. (Local distilleries now make their rum from imported molasses.) Old stone mill towers (at Bodkin, Jolly Hill, Mount Eagle) seem to watch through window eyes as you drive past. The map of this area is scribbled with antique plantation names like Upper and Lower Love, Jealousy, Sally's Fancy, Anna's Hope, and John's Rest. The last is the site of *Estate Whim Plantation Museum,* off Centerline Road a few minutes from Frederiksted. Distinctive in shape, it is a long graceful oval with rounded ends. Inside there are only 3 rooms in the main part of the house: a large dining room and a large bedroom, divided by a central reception or living room. It's small — only 1 story high — but the 16½-foot ceiling and many tall windows give it an airy feeling. The Landmarks Society has furnished it with 17th- and 18th-century pieces. Outside there's a watchhouse, the ruins of the sugar boiling factory, a mule mill, a steam chimney, and a windmill with grinding machinery. The slave quarters have recently been restored, and fields of sugarcane planted. On an island of now vaneless towers, it is satisfying to see all four of the mill's big sail arms restored. This place provides visitors with a good explanation of how a sugar plantation operated; the demonstrations of johnnycake making are especially interesting. There's also a small museum, including an apothecary from 1832, and a shop (see *Shopping*). Open from 10 AM to 4:30 PM Mondays through Saturdays; admission charge (phone: 772-0598).

CRUZAN RUM FACTORY Not far from Christiansted (West Airport Rd.; phone: 772-0280) the factory offers guided tours Mondays through Fridays from 9 to 11:30 AM and from 1 to 4:15 PM. The admission charge includes rum drink samples.

JUDITH'S FANCY Located off Route 751, northwest of Christiansted, there are impressively proportioned ruins of the onetime home of the Governor of the Knights of Malta. From the hill beyond the structure there's an overview of the mouth of the Salt River, where Columbus was driven off by resident Carib Indians in 1493 (he later called the place the Cape of Arrows).

ST. GEORGE VILLAGE BOTANICAL GARDEN Off Centerline Road, Frederiksted, this is a historically interesting combination of trees, blooms, and village ruins, including slave quarters. The newest addition is a walk-through tropical rain forest. It is open Tuesdays through Fridays from 9 AM to 4 PM and additional times when cruise ships are in port; closed holidays. There's an admission charge (phone: 772-3874). The fine, airy central building is the site of frequent concerts and special events and also houses a gift shop with a fine selection of Cruzan crafts and edibles.

SPECIAL PLACES

ST. JOHN A tour of this island can take no time or forever — it all depends on how interested you are in nature.

CRUZ BAY The island's town is tiny and informal, with a harbor, St. John's Square, a communications center, and a Chase Manhattan Bank. It also has a scattering of boutiques, and the *Mongoose Junction* marketplace, which houses one of the island's best restaurants (see *Eating Out*). First check the bulletin board at the ferry dock for news of local happenings, then have a cup of coffee at the *Back Yard*, the *Lime Inn*, or *Joe's Diner* to pick up some local color.

VIRGIN ISLANDS NATIONAL PARK This is the real place of interest on St. John. Start explorations at the park headquarters on the National Park Service dock (along the waterfront to the left as you leave the ferry dock). Regular briefings and slide talks about the park and its flora, fauna, and history take place here. Rangers know all about the area's native birds (from pelicans to sandpipers), trees (including stands of mahogany and bay — from which the "bay" of bay rum comes), and flowers (tamarind, flamboyant, shower of gold). They'll also tell you about the mongooses, imported to hunt rats. Park guides lead nature walks and set up evening programs on a flexible schedule at *Maho Bay Camps, Cinnamon Bay, Caneel Bay,* and other locations. Call 776-6201 for a complete rundown of park activities.

You can rent a car or take a safari bus tour into the park, but you'll have more fun and come home with a better sense of the island if you make your first tour with one of the native drivers who gather near the ferry dock around mid-morning. The classic route takes in Trunk Bay; Annaberg Plantation, the ruins of a greathouse that have been marked for self-guided tours; and assorted lookout points. An alternate tour follows the old Danish Centerline Road to the almost forgotten settlement of Coral Bay, with its 18th-century Moravian church and Fort Berg Hill ruins. Tour rates are standard — about $30 for two people for 2 hours; the accompanying commentary is not. The park is also crisscrossed with clearly mapped hiking trails, some of which were old Danish roads and all of which — except the steep climb to see the plantation ruins and the petroglyphs above Reef Bay — are reasonably easy going.

If you sail, you can take the sea way to Hurricane Hole, a postcard-perfect harbor surrounded by park wilderness, as well as to Coral Bay, Lameshur Bay, Reef Bay, and Chocolate Hole. Ask at the visitors' bureau in Cruz Bay (phone: 776-6450) for information about local skippered or bareboat rentals. Don't forget that almost a third of the park is under water. There is a spectacular underwater trail at Trunk Bay, which the park service administers and which allows you to snorkel along coral reefs amid schools of tropical fish. In the past, the sheer number of tourists had largely destroyed its appeal; to remedy this situation, the National Park Service has set a maximum number of visitors to Trunk Bay to 500 at one time; the limit for smaller beaches is 75.

SPECIAL PLACES

ST. THOMAS — Charlotte Amalie Charlotte Amalie's harbor has been a haven for ships — merchantmen, naval vessels, and buccaneer galleons — since the 1600s. The town's white and pastel buildings cover the waterfront and three steep hills called, west to east, Denmark Hill, Synagogue Hill, and

Government Hill. Along the harbor, warehouses that in another age held pirates' loot are now chock-full of duty-free shops stocked with imported luxuries that lure shiploads of shoppers docked at the deep-water pier out toward the harbor's east end.

Start your walking tour in the narrow streets near the Charlotte Amalie waterfront at the *Grand* hotel. Built in 1841, it no longer takes guests but still dispenses hospitality in the Project St. Thomas ground-floor visitors' center. Next door is Emancipation Park, a tiny plot that commemorates the 1848 proclamation that freed the slaves. Across the street to the west of the park is the post office, embellished inside with murals by the illustrator Stephen Dohanos. Beyond the post office lies Main Street and the alleys and passages of the principal shopping district.

Southeast of the park stands Fort Christian, a venerable monument painted rust red and topped with a clock tower. Built by the Danes in 1671, it has served as a jail, courthouse, church, rectory, and governor's residence. Now a national landmark, its dungeons house a small museum with a modest collection of Arawak and Carib relics, and displays depicting the life of the early Danish settlement, including a re-creation of a Danish plantation and merchants' furniture made from local mahogany. Though the fort is still being restored, parts of it may be open at various times; contact the tourism office before you go. The Legislative Building is on the harbor side of the fort; visitors can observe when the Senate is in session.

High on Government Hill, overlooking the town and the waterfront, the white brick and wood Government House, built in 1867 as a meeting place for the Danish Colonial Council, is now the official residence of the Governor of the US Virgin Islands. The first 2 floors, where murals portray significant moments in the islands' history, are open to the public. There's also a collection of oil paintings by St. Thomian artists, including French Impressionist Camille Pissarro, who lived in the building that now houses the *Tropicana Perfume Shop* before moving to Paris. His relatives are buried in the Jewish cemetery, Savan, on the low peninsula to the west of town. Its epitaphs date from 1792.

On the same street as Government House (Kongens Gade, Danish for King's Street), overlooking Emancipation Park, stands *Hotel 1829,* a mansion built in that year by a French sea captain named Lavalette. (His initials appear entwined in the hotel's wrought-iron balcony.) Between the hotel and Government House, the staircase known as the Street of 99 Steps (actually, there are 103) climbs to the summit of Government Hill.

Not far from the stairs are remnants of 17th-century fortifications originally known as Fort Skytsborg, now a 17-room hotel called *Blackbeard's Castle.* Historically, the name Blackbeard refers to the pirate Edward Teach, who frequented St. Thomas in the 1700s. Confusingly, there's also a Bluebeard's Tower atop another 300-foot hill at the eastern edge of town. This one — its historic origins are vague — has a honeymoon suite on its top floor and is a part of *Bluebeard's Castle* hotel. At the foot of

Government Hill on Norre Gade stands the yellow-brick Frederik Lutheran church, built in 1826. Its serene interior is decorated with white pews, a mahogany altar, and impressive antique chandeliers; the church still uses 18th-century ecclesiastical silver brought from Denmark.

The synagogue of St. Thomas's Jewish congregation — B'racha V'Shalom U'Gemiliut-hasadim ("Blessing and Peace and Loving Deeds") — overlooks the town from neighboring Synagogue Hill. It is reached by a steep climb from Main Street up to Krystal Gade. Built by Sephardic Jews in 1833, it is one of the Western Hemisphere's oldest synagogues (the oldest is on Curaçao). Benches in the traditional arrangement face inward along three sides. It also has the traditional sand-covered floor.

Farther west, where Main Street intersects Strand Gade, is Market Square. A slave market before emancipation, it is now a roofed-over, open-air block of stalls where island farmers and gardeners sell their produce. It's open every day but Sunday. (Saturday is the biggest market day.) Action is liveliest and the light for picture taking best in the early morning. After your market rounds, follow Strand Gade to the waterfront, where you can buy a fresh coconut; ask the seller to lop off its top so you can drink the sweet milk from the hull.

ELSEWHERE ON ST. THOMAS

Having seen Charlotte Amalie on foot, get wheels (rental or taxi) to tour the rest of St. Thomas. Head west out of town on Main Street, connecting with Harwood Highway. You also may want to follow Veterans Drive along the waterfront and turn off to the left at the Villa Olga sign to visit Frenchtown (also called Cha Cha Town for the peaked straw hats called "cha chas" that are made and worn there). It is an enclave of descendants of refugees from the Swedish invasion of St. Barthélemy in the late 18th century, who still speak a Norman French dialect.

Farther west off Harwood Highway, turn right at Contant Hill, and climb Crown Mountain Road for super views of green hills, white beaches, and blue seas. For a stunning view of Drake's Passage, which separates the British and US Virgin Islands, stop at the perch called Drake's Seat, where Sir Francis himself allegedly watched the galleons go by. From this point, there's a splendid view of the passage Drake first navigated in 1580, plus an entire panorama of almost 100 Virgin Islands — both US and British. Another option is to drive higher, to *MountainTop,* a shopping complex with spectacular views.

Continue east along northern roads with fine views of Magens Bay, Mandahl Bay, and others. At the T-shaped intersection near the *Green Parrot* restaurant in the *Magens Point* hotel, continue east, following the signs to the intriguing manmade attraction called *Coral World* (at Coki Beach), a completely remodeled marine park with an underwater observatory tower planted on the sea floor. You climb down 14 feet for a wide-windowed view of reef life. The best time to visit is at 10 and 11 AM, when the fish are being fed. Geodesic domes housing an aquarium, restaurant, shops, and a museum are also part of the complex. It's open daily from 9 AM to 6 PM; admission charge (phone: 775-1555). There's also a dinner theater program on Thursday through Sunday evenings, with performances by the local *Pistarckle Theatre Co.* (see *Nightlife*).

On your way to or from *Coral World,* stop at *Jim Tillett's Art Gallery and Boutique* (on Rte. 38; phone: 775-1405), built around an old sugar mill. Watch the silk screeners work, browse through the gallery (it sells silk-screen graphics, some paintings, ceramics, and lengths of Tillett fabric), shop the boutiques, and sample tacos and *refritos* in the Mexican patio restaurant, *El Papagayo.* Rhoda Tillet also stages arts festivals several times a year.

In a clockwise direction, the road leads past Pineapple, Pelican, and Sapphire beaches, and Red Hook (where the ferries leave for St. John). Before finishing the circle — back to home base in Charlotte Amalie — stop at the Cultural Center of the Caribbean on Flag Hill across from Havensight (phone: 800-874-6251). Here, a 6-story-high IMAX screen colorfully projects the history of the eastern Caribbean, emphasizing the Virgin Islands; shops sell local crafts; eateries feature Caribbean food; and steel drum players and "moko jumbis" — costumed men on stilts — add to the carnival atmosphere.

At the east end of the island, near Balongo and Bovoni Bays, *Carifest,* a 30-acre cultural theme center, is set to open early this year. It will depict Caribbean history from its geological beginnings to its settling by Indians, Europeans, and Africans. Plans for the development include restaurants, shops, and music performances. For more information, contact the tourism office in New York (phone: 212-582-4520).

Sources and Resources

TOURIST INFORMATION

The US Virgin Islands Division of Tourism maintains a number of Visitors Information Bureaus to provide on-the-spot information: *On St. Croix:* Tourist bureaus are located at the airport, in the Scalehouse at Christiansted's harbor (phone: 773-0495), and at the end of Frederiksted's cruise ship pier (phone: 772-0357).

On St. John: The tourist office is around the corner from Cruz Bay ferry dock by the post office (phone: 776-6450).

On St. Thomas: Offices are at the airport, on the waterfront in Charlotte Amalie, and in *Havensight Mall* near the cruise ship pier. As part of their Project St. Thomas, merchants maintain a Hospitality Lounge in the *Old Customs House* next to *Little Switzerland,* where visitors can pick up information, rest, even check shopping bags for a small fee; closed Sundays (phone: 774-8784).

The Division of Tourism also has branch offices in numerous US cities (see GETTING READY TO GO).

LOCAL COVERAGE There are several sources of up-to-the-minute information: *Here's How,* with editions for each island, is a yearly 16-page guide to sightseeing, hotels, nightlife, and especially shopping. It's free on the islands or is available by mail (send a $4 check to *Here's How,* PO Box 1795, St. Thomas, Virgin Islands 00801; specify edition). *WHERE, St. Thomas This Week* (which includes St. John information), *St. Croix This Week,* and *Today in St. Thomas* cover special events, shopping, restaurants, and nightlife. *Best Buys* is another source of shopping information, while *What to Do in St. Thomas and St. John* (published biannually) highlights activities. All are free in airports, hotels, and shops.

St. Thomas's *Daily News,* St. Croix's *Avis,* and St. John's *Tradewinds* cover local, national, and international news. The *San Juan Star* (Virgin Islands edition), *The New York Times, New York Daily News, Wall Street Journal,* and *Miami Herald* are available on newsstands daily. The annual *Virgin Islands Playground* is a tourist-oriented magazine.

Island Insight, a 30-minute cable TV program featuring information on hotels, shopping, and car rentals for all three islands, runs continuously from 6 AM to 10 PM on channels 4 and 6.

For history buffs, Florence Lewisohn's lively *The Romantic History of St. Croix* is required reading, and a booklet, *The Undiscovered Gifts of the Caribbean,* a historical guide to the entire region, is available free (although there is a shipping fee) from Partners for Livable Places, 1429 21st St. NW, Washington, DC 20036 (phone: 202-887-5990).

RADIO AND TELEVISION

In addition to CBS television programming on WBNB, an ABC Newsfeed on St. Croix's WSVI, and PBS on WTJX, many hotels on St. Thomas and St. Croix have satellite reception, which brings in movies and wider TV programming. On St. Croix there is one FM radio station, WSTY, and two AM stations, WRRA and WSTX. On St. Thomas there are two AM stations, WSTA and WVWI, and two FM stations, WSTX and WIBS.

TELEPHONE

The area code for the USVI is 809.

ENTRY REQUIREMENTS

No passports or visas are required of US citizens. If you're contemplating a side trip to the neighboring British Virgin Islands, however, bring proof of citizenship (passport or birth certificate and photo ID). Canadians must have a current passport.

CLIMATE AND CLOTHES

The average winter temperature is 77F (25C), with lows around 69F (21C) and highs of up to 84F (29C). The average summer temperature, dehumidified by the trade winds from the east, is 82F (28C), sometimes dropping to 75F (24C). Summer can bring some extremely hot days, but there's usually a brief shower to cool off the evenings. Average annual rainfall is 40 inches, but even in the rainiest months (September through January), days with no sunshine are rare.

"Casual chic" is the tourist office's description of the islands' dress code. In practice, attire is more casual than chic — even the toniest hotels and restaurants rarely hold fast to the tie and jacket rule, even in season. However, wearing shorts indoors after dark in public places is *verboten* at *Caneel Bay.* For men and women, sports clothes are the daytime rule. Cutoffs, jeans, and T-shirts are okay if you're camping or sporting, but not for resort hotels or sit-down restaurants. Wearing an uncovered bathing suit away from the beach is against the law. Evenings call for something a little dressier, and women may want a shawl or sweater on winter nights.

MONEY

US dollars are the local currency.

LANGUAGE

English is the official language, but you'll still hear Norman French spoken in French Town, and islanders also speak a local patois — English creole — that's a puzzling but musical mix of English, African, and Spanish. As there is a large Puerto Rican population — particularly on St. Croix — Spanish can be considered the islands' second language.

TIME

The US Virgin Islands are on atlantic standard time, 1 hour ahead of eastern standard time. When it's noon in Charlotte Amalie, it's 11 AM in New York. When the mainland is on daylight saving time, Virgin Island and East Coast times are the same.

CURRENT

Current is 110 AC, the same as on the mainland US, so US-made appliances don't need adapters.

TIPPING

When your hotel adds an automatic 10% to 15% service charge, you need not leave tips for the room maid, dining room waiter or waitress, or other hotel personnel. Tips are customary, however, for service above and beyond the expected: give $1 to the bellboy who runs a special errand; $1 to $2 or so to the maid who presses the skirt or slacks it's too late to send to the valet; $2 to the wine steward who brings and serves your wine. When no service charge is added, give the maid $1 to $2 for each day of your stay, your dining waiter 15% of the check — or $2.50 to $3 per person a day, depending on the class of hotel and number of meals included. Bartenders and bar waiters should be tipped 10% to 15% whenever they serve you. Bellboys and porters get at least 50¢ per bag, and never less than $1 on arrival or departure. Tip taxi drivers 15% of the fare.

GETTING AROUND

ST. CROIX — Car Rental Ideal for exploring on your own, but hardly inexpensive. Rates run about $50 and up per day with no mileage charge. Weekly rates average slightly less per day. *Avis* (phone: 778-9365; 800-331-1084 from the US), *Budget* (phone: 773-2285; 800-472-3325 from the US), *Hertz* (phone: 778-1402; 800-654-3131 from the US), and local agencies have offices in Christiansted; some firms also have branches in Frederiksted. *Olympic* (phone: 773-2208; 800-344-5776 from the US) is a good local agency with somewhat lower rates, as is *Caribbean Jeep & Car Rentals* (phone: 773-9162). The latter's cars are in good shape, but not necessarily the latest models. Most car rental agencies will deliver a car to your hotel within 2 hours of your call. But since demand sometimes exceeds supply, especially in high season, reserve well ahead through your travel agent or the larger rental companies' toll-free reservation services. Driving in the US Virgin Islands is on the left side of the road.

SEA EXCURSIONS *Mile Mark Charters'* sleek trimaran *Viti Viti* runs personable full- and half-day charters at reasonable rates (phone: 773-2285, 773-2628; 800-524-2012 from the US). The three-masted 118-foot schooner *Elinor* offers half-day, full-day, and sunset cruises with refreshments (phone: 772-0919, 778-0037, or 778-0461), while only six passengers enjoy the sunset cruises aboard the *Junie Bomba* (phone: 772-2482). Your hotel travel desk will have up-to-date information on twilight sails, cocktail cruises, and special excursions.

The all-day sail to Buck Island reef — the country's only underwater national monument — is a must. The US Park Service has laid down an underwater trail marked with surface floats and blue sea floor signs that identify coral formations and plants for passing snorkelers. The fish are fantastic — 90 species swim alongside hawksbill sea turtles. The coral reef, with some of the world's largest specimens of elkhorn coral, rises 30 feet from the sea floor. Guides aboard day-trip boats help beginners get used to the gear and lead snorkelers along the reef (it's easy). Non-swimmers can ride in a glass-bottom dinghy or catch a life preserver tow. Your hotel can book you on your choice of a big or small boat. (You also can wander down to the harbor and make your own arrangements on the spot.) Figure about $30 for a half day, $48 for a full day, which sometimes includes a barbecue. Beer and soft drinks are provided (sometimes at additional charge), but bring your own picnic, towel, and an extra T-shirt for sunburn protection while you're swimming along the trails.

Among the charterers offering Buck Island excursions: the *Jolly Roger* (phone: 773-0754), the *Snowflake* (phone: 773-8520), *Teroro II* (phone: 773-3161 or 773-4041), *Big Beard's Adventure Tours* (phone: 773-4482), *Low Key Watersports* (776-7718), *Mile Mark Charters* (phone: 773-2285 or 773-2482), and the glass-bottom *Reef Queen* (phone: 773-0754). All operate out of Christiansted Harbor.

SIGHTSEEING BUS TOURS Mostly timed and organized with cruise ship passengers in mind. *Travellers' Tours* (at the Alexander Hamilton Airport; phone: 778-1636) runs a 3-hour island tour for about $20 per person; *St. Croix Safari Tours* (44 Queen Cross; phone: 773-6700) offers an especially well-guided 4-hour bus tour for about $25 per person, and can arrange minibus tours; and *Smitty's* (King St.; phone: 773-9188) gives 4½-hour tours for $20.

SIGHTSEEING TAXI TOURS A good way to see the island. Drivers are usually good guides. Ask your hotel travel desk to recommend one and negotiate a price for the length of tour you'd like.

TAXI Cabs are easy to find in towns and at the airport. No matter how far out your hotel may be, the desk usually can get a taxi within half an hour. Fares for most trips run about $8 to $12 per passenger, with the fare from the airport to Christiansted or Frederiksted hotels averaging about $10 and $8, respectively for one or two persons, $4.50 to $5 for each additional passenger. As cabs are unmetered, it's best to settle on a price before you get in. At the airport, a list of rates is posted by the baggage counter.

GETTING AROUND

ST. JOHN — Car Rental Agencies include *St. John Car Rental* (phone: 776-6103) in Cruz Bay; *Hertz* (phone: 776-6695; 800-654-3001 from the US) at the dock; *St. John Development Corporation* (phone: 776-6343) at the gas station in Cruz Bay; *Budget* (Cruz Bay; phone: 776-7575; 775-0815 at night; 800-626-4516 from the US); *Delbert Hill Taxi & Jeep Rental* (Cruz Bay; phone: 800-537-6238 from the US); *Spencer's Jeeps & Cars* (Cruz Bay; phone: 776-6628); and *Denzil Clyne Jeeps & Cars* (Cruz Bay; phone: 776-6715). Daily rates for a car or jeep run about $45 to $50 a day plus an insurance fee ($10 and up a day), with unlimited mileage (you pay for gas). Four-wheel-drive is not essential for exploring.

FERRY SERVICES Ferries cross Pillsbury Sound to Red Hook on St. Thomas. The trip takes half an hour; one-way fare is $3 per adult, $1.25 per senior citizen, $1 per child under 12. Check the visitors' bureau or dockside bulletin board for current schedule. Ferry boats also travel to Charlotte Amalie on St. Thomas (near the Coast Guard dock) and to Tortola from Cruz Bay. The trip to Tortola takes about 45 minutes; one-way fare is $7 per adult, $3 per child. There's also launch service from the *Caneel Bay* dock to the National Park Dock at Red Hook. One-way fare is $9 per person, and the trip takes about 20 minutes. For complete ferry schedules, call 776-6282.

SEA EXCURSIONS Several outfits offer *PADI* scuba instruction and certification, equipment rentals, and reef and wreck dives: *Cruz Bay Watersports Co.* in Cruz Bay (phone: 776-6234); *Low Key Watersports* in Wharfside Village, which also arranges sport fishing and day sailing excursions (phone: 776-7048; 800-835-7718 from the US); and *St. John Water Sports/Hinkley Charters* in *Mongoose Junction* (phone: 776-6256).

TAXI Available, but not always where and when you want them. If you find a driver you like, take his card so you can get in touch by phone. Fares run about $2 to $10 from Cruz Bay to outlying points, depending on the number of passengers. The standard 2-hour tour is $30 for one or two people, $12 per person for three or more. Night fares are 40% higher.

GETTING AROUND

ST. THOMAS — Bus Public bus service exists — just barely — and it's not recommended. However, there is a *Manassah Country Bus* that makes one trip about every hour between town and Red Hook (fare: 75¢ per person). A safari bus also shuttles between downtown Charlotte Amalie and Red Hook hourly during the day for about $3 per person each way. Check your hotel or the tourist office for schedules; ask, too, about shuttle service to *Jim Tillett's Art Gallery and Boutique* and *Coral World.*

CAR RENTAL Easily arranged, but relatively expensive. Rates start at about $50 a day for a compact with unlimited mileage up to $75 a day for an air conditioned sedan, plus gas. Honda scooters are rented by the hour, or $25 to $40 a day. Weekly rentals cost somewhat less per day. *Avis* (phone: 774-1468; 800-331-1084 from the US), *Budget* (phone: 776-5774; 800-626-4516 from the US), *Hertz* (phone: 774-0841, 774-1879; 800-654-3001 from the US), *National* (phone: 776-3616), *Dollar* (phone: 776-0850), and *Discount* (phone: 776-4858) have offices at or near the airport. *Avis, Budget, Hertz,* and a number of local operators, such as *Paradise Car Rental* (phone: 775-7282), have downtown offices, too. *Econo-Car*'s base (phone: 775-6763) is by the marina at Red Hook. *ABC* (phone: 776-1222), *Dependable* (phone: 774-2253; 800-522-3076 from the US), *Cowpet Auto Rental* (phone: 775-7376; 800-524-2072 from the US), *Sea Breeze Car Rental* (phone: 774-7200), *V.I. Auto Rental* (phone: 776-3616; 800-843-3571 from the US), *Al's Honda and Jet Ski Rentals* (phone: 774-2010), and *Sun Island Car Rentals* (phone: 774-3333; 800-774-3333 from the US) are good local firms that offer bargain rates. The usual $100 to $150 deposit is not required for major credit card holders. Your driver's license is good for up to 90 days on the islands. Just remember to keep left.

FERRY SERVICES There is service between Red Hook and St. John (see listings for St. John, above), as well as launch service from Red Hook to Charlotte

Amalie (near the Coast Guard dock). The *Reefer* connects Charlotte Amalie and *Frenchman's Reef* for $3 one-way. It leaves on the hour from the waterfront and on the half hour from the hotel (phone: 776-8500, ext. 625 or 445).

SEA EXCURSIONS Highly individualized glass-bottom boats leave from a number of docks. Cost is about $10 for adults, $5 for children under 12. In addition, the *Atlantis* submarine offers a comfortable 2-hour cruise at a depth of 90 feet with good views. The 46-passenger sub with large port-holes reveals a world of coral shapes and brilliantly colored fish. It's the next best thing to scuba diving, and even those in wheelchairs can enjoy day and night dives. Children under 4 are not allowed. Cruises are $58 per adult; $29 or $15 per child; reservations are required (phone: 776-5650; 800-253-0493 from).

The motor ships *Bomba Charger* (phone: 775-7292) and *Native Son* (phone: 774-8685) both make the scenic run to another small world — the British Virgin Island of Tortola. The trip takes 45 minutes each way, and the round-trip fare is about $27. Schedules leave time for a look around, lunch, a pint at the *Sir Francis Drake Pub,* and a chance to meet some nice people. For a day trip to St. John, there are a number of boats that sail from Charlotte Amalie every morning. A park tour and a chance to explore the Trunk Bay underwater trail are built into most itineraries. Prices run from $35 to $65 per person, including lunch and drinks; sunset sails are $25. Smaller yachts handle parties of six. Ask at *Sea Tours Transfers* at *Frenchman's Reef* (phone: 774-2990) or at the visitors' bureau for information on available boats. Or try a trip on one of the picturesque tall ships: the *Schooner Alexander Hamilton* (phone: 775-6500) charges $90 for a full day, including lunch; a 2½-hour dinner cruise on the *Resolution* (phone: 690-7351) costs $85.

SIGHTSEEING BUS TOURS These are not a big deal on St. Thomas. Cruise passengers are their principal customers. *Tropic Tours,* with its main office in the International Plaza at The Waterfront (phone: 774-1855) and branches in major hotels, runs 2½-hour safari bus tours for about $15 per person, including hotel pickup and drop-off. A $30 tour includes *Coral World, Bluebeard's Castle,* and shopping at *Havensight Mall;* they also run a $40 full-day tour of St. John, including ferry and lunch at *Cinnamon Bay. Greyline* (phone: 776-1515) offers a 2-hour tour for $13, a trip to *Coral World* for $20, and an outing to St. John — similar to *Tropic*'s but including snorkeling gear — for $35.

SIGHTSEEING TAXI TOURS A pleasantly effortless way to see island sights. Many St. Thomas drivers are good guides and can suggest half- and full-day itineraries, including likely lunch spots if you have nothing specific in mind. But don't rely on the luck of the taxi-stand draw. As soon as you know when you want to go, ask your hotel tour desk to make arrangements with a driver they know. The charge for a standard 2-hour trip is about $30 per couple, $12 for each additional passenger.

TAXI Plentiful, unmetered, and inexpensive. Rates, based on destination rather than mileage, run $3.50 to $8.50 for most trips. If your hotel is in Charlotte Amalie, the fare from the airport is about $4.50 for one passenger; $3.50 for each additional passenger. (It's considered okay for the driver to pick up additional people en route if they're going your way.) There's also an after-midnight surcharge of $2 for in-town fares and $1.50 for out of town. The ubiquitous *Virgin Islands Taxi Association* may be reached at 774-7457. *Hint:* If you're downtown shopping and want to taxi back to your hotel, head for the waterfront drive. No cab driver in his right mind would voluntarily tangle with Main Street or Back Street traffic — especially on a cruise ship day.

INTER-ISLAND FLIGHTS

American Eagle provides local service, flying approximately every hour to San Juan, Puerto Rico, and frequently each way from St. Thomas to St. Croix and Tortola. *Sunaire Express* flies 22 daily flights from St. Croix to St. Thomas, San Juan, Tortola, and Virgin Gorda. *LIAT* carries passengers from and to the islands to the south. *Virgin Air* (phone: 776-2992) handles small-plane charters. There are several helicopter operators, among them *Air Center Helicopters* (phone: 775-7335), *Air There Helicopters* (phone: 776-9464), and *Antilles Helicopters* (phone: 776-7880).

SPECIAL EVENTS

In addition to all the US national holidays (*New Year's Day, Martin Luther King's Birthday, President's Day, Easter, Memorial Day, Independence Day, Labor Day, Columbus Day, Veterans' Day, Thanksgiving,* and *Christmas*), the Virgin Islands celebrate *Three Kings' Day* (January 6); *Transfer Day* (March 31, the day the US flag first flew in the islands); *Holy Thursday; Good Friday; Organic Act Day* (June 16, the day in 1936 when the US Congress granted home rule and suffrage to the Virgin Islands); *Emancipation Day* (July 3, the anniversary of the 1848 day when slaves were freed in the Danish West Indies); *Supplication Day* (third Monday in July, a day of prayer for protection from hurricanes); *Puerto Rico Friendship Day* (October 12, same as *Columbus Day*); *Hurricane Thanksgiving Day* for the end of hurricane season (third Monday in October); and *Liberty Day* (November 1, honoring Judge David Hamilton Jackson, who secured freedom of the press and assembly from King Christian X of Denmark). Cruzans make a 2-week fiesta of *Christmas* (from December 25 to January 6, *Three Kings' Day*). Also on St. Croix, the *Mumm's Cup Regatta* (phone: 773-9118) and the *St. Croix Jazz Festival* liven things up in October. St. Thomians celebrate *Carnival* (the last 2 weeks of April) with stilt-walking "moko jumbis" and steel bands that reverberate all day and night; on St. John, *Independence Day* is the Big Time, celebrated with music, "moko jumbis," a *Miss St. John* contest, plus the traditional fireworks. A smaller carnival is celebrated on St. John during the last week of June. For more information about events on the three islands, call 800-USVI-INFO.

SHOPPING

A little planning will help you through the maze of shops so that you end up with the goodies you want without spending your entire vacation shopping. Check prices in your hometown stores before you leave so you know whether the Virgin Islands prices are worth the time and effort of long-distance hauling. Currently, for example, savings are minimal on photographic and electronic equipment (at best, a few dollars less than at mainland discount outlets), more substantial on fine china and crystal (savings from 30% to 50%). Perfume, watches, gold jewelry, and imported beauty products (makeup, bath gels) can sometimes be real bargains. Everybody buys liquor at half to two-thirds (for scotch, liqueurs) less than New York prices, and almost everybody buys cigarettes at carton prices 40% or so below New York levels.

Three things have made US Virgin Islands shopping famous: low prices (on a list of 20 or so categories of most-wanted merchandise); wide selections; and the fact that US citizens are allowed to carry home, untaxed, triple the value in goods purchased ($1,200 instead of the usual $400 per person) that is permitted when returning from most foreign countries, and five fifths of liquor (six, if one fifth is locally produced) instead of the usual one liter. In addition, stateside residents may ship home from the US Virgin Islands, each day, up to $100 worth of goods as gifts, over and above the $1,200 individual exemption. Products manufactured in the US Virgin Islands are completely tax exempt and do not count in the duty-free allowance.

The low prices are a legacy from the Danes, who stipulated as part of their 1917 treaty of sale that island retailers be forced to pay no more than 6% *ad valorem* duty (property tax) on incoming goods. This is so much less than the tax paid elsewhere that Virgin Islands merchants can afford to sell their luxury imports for 5% to 60% less than most mainland US stores. Selections are large because volume is enormous, swelled by hundreds of thousands of cruise ship passengers' purchases.

ST. CROIX

Shopping is better than ever on this island. More cruise ships are adding St. Croix to their itineraries; most call at Frederiksted (which still has only a few stores), but some shallow-drafted ships dock at Christiansted's Gallows Bay. Hope for future business is evident in several new, upscale stores, such as the *St. Croix Shoppes*.

Bear in mind that Christiansted's shopping area, although colorful, may pose a problem for those who have difficulty walking: Sidewalks are made of brick or stone, and there are numerous short flights of steps to maneuver. Navigation is easier at some of the newer complexes close to the water, such as the *Pan Am Pavilion* or *Caravelle Arcade.*

Most shops in St. Croix are open Mondays through Saturdays from 9 AM to 5 PM. The following shops are in Christiansted, unless otherwise noted:

AMERICAN WEST INDIA COMPANY All products made or grown in the Caribbean, including spices and coffee, gourmet food, batik clothing, Sea Island cotton fabric, and artworks. Strand St. (phone: 773-7325).

ANYTHING GOES The place to pick up fancy fixings for a sail or beach picnic. Near the docks at Gallows Bay (phone: 773-2777).

AY AY GOLD Gold and jeweled rings, earrings, bracelets, and necklaces. 59 King's Wharf near the Old Scalehouse (phone: 773-8305).

CARIBBEAN CLOTHING CO. Designer duds, featuring men's and women's sportswear (including Bally men's shoes). 41 Queen Cross St. (phone: 773-5012).

COLOMBIAN EMERALDS The gorgeous green gems in varied settings. At two locations: 43 Queen Cross St. (phone: 773-1928 or 773-9189) and 2A Strand St., Frederiksted (phone: 772-1927).

COURTSHIP & SEDUCTION Lingerie, beauty oils, romantic cards, and games, mixed in with wide assortment of handmade, contemporary jewelry. *Caravelle Arcade,* 38 Strand St. (phone: 778-8401).

CRUCIAN GOLD Original fine gold jewelry made on the spot. 57A Company St. (phone: 773-5241).

1870 TOWNHOUSE SHOPPES Attractive, reasonably priced beachwear and sportswear, and Chinese and African giftware. 52 King St. (phone: 773-2967).

GROG & SPIRITS Portable potables — wine, liquor, beer, and mixers to go, plus picnic fixings. At two locations: 59 King's Wharf (phone: 778-8400) and Chandlers Wharf at Gallows Bay (phone: 773-8485).

JAVA WRAPS Dozens of hand-blocked pareos (sarongs), no two alike, in terrific colors; also shirts, sundresses, jumpsuits, and all sorts of resortwear in the same great Indonesian batik prints. October clearance sale yields savings of 50% and more. *Pan Am Pavilion* (phone: 773-3770).

JELTRUP'S BOOKS Specializing in Caribbean lore — histories, cookbooks, and gardening; paperbacks, too. 2132 Company St. (phone: 773-1018).

LAND OF OZ Children's and adult games, including backgammon and wari (an ancient African game that's an island favorite), plus jigsaw puzzles, kites, and lots more. 52A Company St. (phone: 773-4610).

LITTLE SWITZERLAND For fine imported china, perfume, watches, crystal, and porcelain figures. 1108 King St. (phone: 773-1976 or 773-5366).

MANY HANDS Imaginative graphics and crafts at wonderfully non-shock prices; cards, shells, jams and spices, enchanting *Christmas* ornaments, too. 21 *Pan Am Pavilion* (phone: 773-1990).

NANCEE'S LEATHER AWL All sorts of good-looking leather goods, some Nancee-made, some imported. 57 Company St. (phone: 773-7801).

PEGASUS Original jewelry made with gemstones. 58 Company St. (phone: 773-6926).

ROYAL POINCIANA A potpourri of coffees, teas, spices, Caribbean condiments, herbal bath gels and soaps, and tropical perfume. 38 Strand St. (phone: 773-9892).

S & B LIQUOR The place to stock up on alcohol in Frederiksted. 9 A King St., Frederiksted (phone: 772-3934).

ST. C. JEWELRY DESIGNER Ladies' clothing with such labels as Donna Karan, and discounted jewelry. 69A King St., Frederiksted (phone: 772-5888).

ST. CROIX SHOPPES All of Estée Lauder's products, including Clinique, Aramis, and Prescriptives, in two sparkling side-by-side stores. Other fragrances and makeup are available as well. 53B Company St. (phone: 773-2727).

SIMPLY COTTON Colorful cotton knit clothing for women and kids. 36C Strand St. (phone: 773-6860).

SMALL WONDER Fine children's clothing (such as Florence Eiseman and Oshkosh togs) and high-quality toys. 4 Company St. (phone: 773-5551).

VIOLETTE'S BOUTIQUE Downstairs is an enormous perfume and cosmetics selection, featuring popular imports; upstairs are Cartier, Fendi, and Gottex boutiques. *Caravelle Arcade,* 38 Strand St. (phone: 773-2148).

WAYNE JAMES BOUTIQUE Native son Wayne James, who has designed clothing for the likes of the Queen of Denmark (and even the pope), has opened a new shop to sell his fashions. 42 Queen Cross St. (phone: 773-8585).

WHIM MUSEUM SHOP Antique reproductions (door knockers, hurricane globes) and some period pieces (silver, paperweights, Cantonware). All profits go to the St. Croix Landmarks Restoration. At *Estate Whim Plantation Museum,* Rte. 70, east of Frederiksted (phone: 772-0598).

WRITER'S BLOCK Excellent bookstore, with a good travel section. 36 S. Strand St. (phone: 773-5101).

ST. JOHN

Shops on St. John, primarily clustered around Cruz Bay, are generally open Mondays through Saturdays from 9 AM to 5 PM.

BATIK CARIBE Hand-painted clothing for men and women. Cruz Bay (phone: 776-6465).

CANEEL BAY BOUTIQUE Sportswear and a few sundries for the casual — but chic — good life. Selection is small, prices very high. Try the products made exclusively for the property, such as the wonderful Caneel Appeal coconut shampoo. At the *Caneel Bay* resort (phone: 776-6111).

MONGOOSE JUNCTION A complex of smart brick and wood studio shops (many open daily; hours vary) in Cruz Bay sheltering such crafts emporia as *R. and I. Patton* (contemporary gold and silver jewelry; phone: 776-6548), *Donald Schnell Studio* (original pottery and hand-blown glass; phone: 776-6420), *Wicker, Wood & Shells* (gifts, decor items; phone: 776-6909), *Canvas Factory* (seaworthy totes, bags, clothing, as well as sail repair; phone: 776-6196), *Fabric Mill* (batiks, silk screen prints; phone: 776-6194), *The Clothing Studio* (hand-painted garments; phone: 776-6585), *Colombian Emeralds* (a branch of the one on St. Thomas; phone: 776-6007), *Mongoose Trading Co.* (hand-painted dinnerware and state-of-the-art kitchen items; phone: 776-6993), and *Seasons Boutique* (ladies' and men's beachwear; phone: 776-6130).

SPARKY'S One of a chain of gleaming shops featuring perfume, jewelry, liquor, and cigarettes. This branch is smaller than its St. Thomas cousin, but is handy for liquor purchases, which they'll deliver to the airport or your ship. 6B Cruz Bay (phone: 776-6284).

WHARFSIDE VILLAGE A cluster of pastel-painted stores at the water's edge (many open daily; hours vary), includes *Barracuda Bistro* (freshly baked bread and picnic sandwiches; phone: 779-4944), *Blue Caribe Gems* (phone: 693-8244), *Colombian Emeralds* (phone: 776-6999), *Cruz Bay Clothing Company* (women's and children's casual clothing; phone: 776-7611), *Freebird Creations* (jewelry; phone: 776-7512), *Let's Go Bananas* (women's clothing; phone: 776-7055), *Sailor's Delight* (men's sports clothes and beachwear; phone: 776-3033), and *Third World Electronics* (CDs and tapes; phone: 776-6600).

ST. THOMAS

If shopping is your favorite sport, you can spend days searching glassy-eyed through the offerings — though true bargains are relatively scarce — in Charlotte Amalie's restored warehouse shops. Of the three US Virgin Islands, St. Thomas has the biggest stores (most in Charlotte Amalie) and the largest stocks (and crowds). Before heading downtown, check *Here's How, This Week,* or *Best Buys* to find out which store sells the most of the brands or kinds of merchandise you want. In general, prices for similar items are the same throughout the islands, so the more items found in a single store, the fewer stops and the less time spent in cash register lines.

(Included in the listing below are available toll-free numbers so that visitors can check prices before leaving home.)

Avoid shopping on crowded cruise ship days whenever possible, and go early in the day — while you and the salespeople are still fresh — or during mealtimes, when many cruisers head back to their ships to eat. Most stores are open from 9 AM to 5 PM, but numerous shops on St. Thomas remain open until 10 or 11 PM for cruise ship passengers. Many close on Sundays, unless ships are in port. Main Street, also called Dronningens Gade, is the main shopping street. Also check out the shops in *Bakery Square,* Charlotte Amalie's restored shopping complex on Back Street, and the 50 air conditioned stores at *Havensight Mall* near the West Indian Co. dock, just steps from the ships' gangways (thus avoiding the long, traffic-congested ride into town). There's also the *International Plaza* complex at The Waterfront and *The MountainTop* shopping and cultural complex.

The *Vendors Plaza,* an outdoor flea market, is held at Emancipation Park Mondays through Saturdays from 6 AM to 6 PM and Sundays from 7 AM to 3 PM when cruise ships are in port. You'll find plenty of T-shirts and designer knockoffs; try your hand at bargaining here. A number of St. Thomas shops have St. Croix branches where the choices may be somewhat smaller, but so are the crowds. If you're planning to island hop, you may want to plan your shopping accordingly.

A discordant note on the St. Thomas shopping scene: The crowds and frequent discourtesy of Charlotte Amalie shopkeepers have been joined by street hawkers and vendors who seem bent on making a sale — regardless of how many times prospective purchasers decline their entreaties. St. Thomas is fast becoming the Mexico City of the Caribbean for shoppers — and that's no compliment.

Here are some of the best-stocked Charlotte Amalie stores:

A. H. RIISE Stacks of top-quality china (Wedgwood), crystal (Waterford), watches, jewelry, objets d'art, antiques, and decorator accessories, as well as a large stock of liquor. Nice, helpful people. Two locations: an enormous complex at 37 Main St. (phone: 776-2303) and *Havensight Mall* (phone: 776-2303; 800-524-2037 from the US).

AL COHEN'S Huge liquor warehouse at *Havensight,* with prices 30% to 60% below US prices, and a few cents below other town shops. Across from the West India Co. dock, Long Bay Rd. (phone: 774-3690).

AMSTERDAM SAUER Internationally known South American jewelry firm shows wares to buyers by appointment only. 14 Main St. (phone: 774-2222) and *Havensight Mall* (phone: 776-3828; 800-345-3564 from the US).

APERITON For fine furs, leather clothing for men and women, and jewelry of Greek and Italian design. 3A Main St. (phone: 776-0780).

BAKERY SQUARE A complex of stores (hours may vary from shop to shop) housed in an old brick bakery, including *Blue Carib Gems* (a workshop to tour, gemstones and jewelry to buy — they sometimes let you design your own; phone: 774-8525); *Down Island Traders* (homemade Virgin Island goods that are tax-exempt — mango chutney and preserves, sea grape jelly, papaya and lime marmalades, as well as spices and fancy teas, Caribbean cookbooks, and more; phone: 774-4265); *Marni* (ladies' cotton clothing and vintage jewelry; no phone); *Orchid Boutique* (eelskin and leather items; no phone); and *Sand Dollars* (gift items, clocks, and Virgin Islands–made jewelry; phone: 774-5038). On Back Street at Nye Gade.

BALLY OF SWITZERLAND The famous line of men's and women's shoes, handbags, and other leather goods. *Havensight Mall* (phone: 774-4370).

BOLERO Daum and Danish crystal, English bone china, Omega and Tissot watches, French perfume, men's and women's fashions, liquor. 21 Main St. and 34 Main St. (phone: 776-0551).

CARDOW Long established, claims the Caribbean's biggest precious and semiprecious gem collection. Thirteen locations, including 25-26 Main St. (phone: 776-1140) and on the waterfront.

CARTIER Stunning jewelry at 15% below mainland prices. Main St. at Trumpeter Gade (phone: 774-1590).

CHINA EMBROIDERY ARTS Large selection of embroidered linen. Two locations: 17 Main St. (phone: 776-2521); and the large, air conditioned warehouse at 6-C Wimmelskaft Gade (phone: 776-0726).

COLOMBIAN EMERALDS Large selection of both set and unset gemstones and famous-name watches. At four locations: Main St. (phone: 774-0581), The Waterfront (phone: 774-1033), *The MountainTop* (phone: 774-3400), and *Havensight Mall* (phone: 774-3400).

CORAL BAY FOLK ART GALLERY Wonderful handmade items crafted in the Virgin Islands, from fabric dolls and baskets to oil paintings and mahogany furniture. *Frenchman's Reef* hotel (phone: 776-7665).

COSMOPOLITAN Bally shoes, a large selection of Gottex bathing suits, and Ellesse and Fila sportswear at discount prices. At Drake's Passage on the waterfront (phone: 776-2040).

DOCKSIDE BOOK SHOP A reliable source of reading matter, with a good travel section. *Havensight Mall* (phone: 774-4937).

ENGLISH SHOP China, porcelain, and crystal with brands such as Wedgwood, Boehm, and Royal Bierley. On the waterfront above *Cardow* (phone: 776-5399) and *Havensight Mall* (phone: 774-3495; 800-524-2013 from the US).

GUCCI The one and only at substantial savings; the October end-of-season clearance sale is worth a trip in itself. On the waterfront and *Havensight Mall* (phone: 774-7841).

H. STERN The prestigious South American jewelry outfit. (Advantage: branches worldwide in case anything goes wrong.) Six locations: 12 Main St., Main St. at Raadets Gade, *Havensight Mall,* and at the *Frenchman's Reef, Bluebeard's Castle,* and *Stouffer Grand Beach* resorts (phone: 776-1939; 800-524-2024 from the US).

JAVA WRAPS Wonderful hand-screened batik clothing printed in Indonesia. Sale during first 2 weeks in October offers 50% to 75% off regular prices. 5141 Palm Passage (phone: 774-3700).

JONNA WHITE ART GALLERY Unique etchings on handmade paper. Palm Passage, above *Bared Jewelers* (phone: 774-3098).

LEATHER SHOP Fendi, Bottega Veneta, Desmo, and Furla items at 40% below mainland prices. 2 Main St. (phone: 776-3995) and *Havensight Mall* (phone: 776-0040).

LINEN HOUSE Tablecloths and blouses imported from China. Three locations: Main St., *Royal Dane Mall,* and Palm Passage (phone: 774-8117).

LION IN THE SUN Eclectic selection of American and European designer labels, including Donna Karan, Yves Saint Laurent, Sonia Rykiel — some items priced low — for men and women. Riis Alley (phone: 776-4203).

LITTLE SWITZERLAND As might be expected, a high concentration of watches (including Omega and Rolex), music boxes, cuckoo clocks; also elegant china (Rosenthal and Royal Worcester), crystal, jewelry, binoculars. At four locations: 5 Main St., 38 Main St., 48A-B Norre Gade, and the *Havensight Mall* (one phone for all: 776-2010).

LOCAL COLOR Silk-screened knits and artworks in vibrant colors and designs seen all around the island, but the largest selection is here. 2A Garden St. (phone: 774-3727).

LOUIS VUITTON The famous initials — leather products made in Europe, discounted 20% below stateside prices. 24 Dronningens (phone: 774-3644).

MR. TABLECLOTH Discount prices on table and bed linen; aprons and crocheted scarves. 6 Main St. (phone: 774-4343).

MODAMARE Izod/Lacoste clothing at 20% discounts. *Havensight Mall* (phone: 776-5067).

MOUNTAINTOP An air conditioned shopping and cultural center atop a mountain in the center of the island. Its 18 colorful shops include some branches of in-town stores plus independents such as *Parfum de Paris,* featuring Christian Dior and Givenchy scents, *West Indian Museum Shop,* with prints and antique map reproductions, and a local jam and spice shop. Scratch bands and weavers of palm hats demonstrate local arts and crafts. There's also an aquarium, a terrarium, an outdoor observation deck, and a snack bar. And it's all on one level, providing easy access for the disabled.

PARADISE POINT Up Flag Hill above Havensight, the first building of a four-building complex has opened with several shops and the *Bar at Paradise Point,* offering a spectacular view. A tramway to transport guests from the foot of the hill to the complex was being constructed at press time; until it is ready, shuttle buses will be used. The first stores feature locally made items; eventually a broader selection will be available, along with a horticultural center, local shows, and a historical exhibit. Flag Hill.

POLO/RALPH LAUREN FACTORY STORE Men's and women's clothing by the famous designer, some items at one-third off. 2 Garden St., above *Local Color* on Garden St. (phone: 773-4388).

SCANDINAVIAN CENTER Collection of fine wares from top names in Sweden, Finland, Denmark, and Norway, including Royal Copenhagen china, Kosta Boda crystal, and jewelry by Georg Jensen. At two locations: 4 Main St. (phone: 777-4656) and *Havensight Mall* (phone: 776-5030; 800-524-2063 from the US).

SIGNATURES An elegant boutique featuring daily fashion shows at 5141 Palm Passage (phone: 776-5900).

SPARKY'S Several gleaming shops with a variety of best-selling merchandise such as perfume and jewelry, including Gucci and Ebel watches. Best known for liquor and cigarettes. 29-31 Main St. (phone: 776-7510).

TILLETT GARDENS CRAFT STUDIOS Jim Tillett's silk-screened fabrics, wall hangings, and paintings are fresh and fun. His compound at Estate Tutu on the road to *Coral World* — where they do the screen printing — is a sightseeing must even if you don't buy. Arts and crafts festivals are held here three times each year: *Thanksgiving* weekend, March, and August. Rte. 38 (phone: 775-1405 or 775-1929).

TROPICANA PERFUME SHOP The world's largest scents store, it has cosmetics, bath oils, and men's and women's toiletries as well. At two locations: 2 Main St. (phone: 774-0010), and 14 Main St. (phone: 774-1834; 800-233-7948 from the US).

ZORA OF ST. THOMAS Custom-made leather sandals and belts, and canvas bags. 34 Norre Gade (phone: 774-2559).

SPORTS

ST. CROIX — Boating *Caribbean Sea Adventures* (phone: 773-5922) handles small boat rentals and arranges charters for larger boats, bareboat and crewed. At *Green Cay Marina,* try *Bay Boat Rentals* (phone: 773-9933). Sunfish and Hobie Cats can be rented at the water sports activity centers of most beach hotels.

For those captains of their own ships, there are repair, service, and docking facilities at *St. Croix Marina* at Gallows Bay (phone: 773-0289;

fax: 778-8944), *Salt River Marina* at Salt River (phone: 778-9650; fax: 772-3059), and *Green Cay Marina* on the northeast coast (phone: 773-1453; fax: 773-9651).

GOLF While the number of courses on the island is limited, one stands out from the rest.

TOP TEE-OFF SPOT

Carambola For more than 20 years, this course was known as *Fountain Valley,* one of the most challenging golf courses in the Caribbean, and this Robert Trent Jones, Sr. course is in better shape than ever. The course is mostly notable for its route through a deep valley, full of abundant water hazards and an inordinate number of deep ravines. From its championship tees, it plays to a length of more than 6,900 yards, which should be sufficient to exhaust even the most inveterate ball pounder. With the expanded clubhouse, a good challenge has been made into a great one. Players staying at the *Carambola Beach* resort pay $35 daily for greens fee and a cart, or $175 for a week's unlimited play and use of a cart; non-guests pay $50 for the greens fee and $12 per person for a cart (phone: 778-4848). The pro shop (in the rebuilt clubhouse) has rental clubs and lockers, and there's a restaurant where the steak sandwiches and the view make it a recommended lunch stop even if you don't play golf.

In addition, the public also is welcome to play the far shorter course at the *Buccaneer* hotel. For 18 holes, greens fees run about $30; cart rental, $12 for two. There is a 9-hole course at the *Reef* (phone: 773-8844). Greens fees are $12 for 9 holes, $20 for 18; carts, $12 and $18.

HORSEBACK RIDING At *Sprat Hall,* a plantation homestead-turned-hotel, *Paul and Jill's Equestrian Stable* (phone: 772-2880) offers trail riding through the rain forest and over the hills beyond. The 2-hour ride is $40 per person. After you've made a daylight excursion, you may qualify for one of their highly memorable moonlight expeditions; reserve at least a day in advance. *Sprat Hall* has riding packages.

HORSE RACING Thoroughbred horses race about twice a month at *Flamboyant Race Track* on Airport Road; check newspapers for race schedules. There's informal betting, food, drink, live music, and a party atmosphere.

PARASAILING Rides are offered by *Mile Mark Charters* at the *King Christian* hotel in Christiansted and *Paradise Parasailing* (phone: 773-7060). The latter operates from several hotels as well as the Christiansted boardwalk.

SNORKELING AND SCUBA Waters are so clear and warm and there are so many dive sites to see that you could spend a whole vacation under water and still cover only a fraction of what's there. St. Croix has become known as a top diving destination, offering all types of diving — beach dives, wall dives, reef dives, wreck dives, and nighttime dives. In addition to the underwater trails off Buck Island, the island's most intriguing sites include its coral canyons and the drop-offs at Salt River, Cane Bay, and Davis Bay (site of the 12,000-foot-deep Puerto Rico Trench, the fifth-deepest body of water in the world). For scuba instruction, day and night dives, and equipment rental, contact *Mile Mark Charters* (phone: 773-2285 or 773-2628). Outfits offering *PADI* certification include *Dive Experience* (1 Strand St., Christiansted; phone: 773-3307; 800-235-9047 from the US); *Anchor Dive Center* (Salt River, Sunny Isle; phone: 778-1522; 800-532-DIVE from the US); *Cruzan Divers* (12 Strand St., Frederiksted; phone: 772-3701; 800-352-0107 from the US); *V.I. Divers* (*Pan Am Pavilion,* Christiansted; phone: 773-6045; 800-544-5911 from the US); and *Cane Bay Dive Shop* (phone: 773-9913). Plan to spend about $55 for a two-tank dive and $45 for a night dive.

Snorkeling doesn't require any formal arrangements. There are plenty of good snorkeling spots right off the coast, and even the smallest hotels are likely to have equipment on hand, which they will lend gratis or rent for a small fee. However, most visitors to St. Croix — snorkelers and non-snorkelers alike — make at least one trip to see the Buck Island reef. A number of boats make half- or full-day excursions to Buck Island that include snorkeling in the underwater park and provide the equipment and, frequently, a guide (see "Sea Excursions" above).

SPORT FISHING Cruzan fisherman go deep for mahimahi, wahoo, snapper, grouper, and blue dolphin (the fish, not the mammal), using light tackle for sporty jack or bonefish closer to shore. Islanders claim to hold the world billfishing record. Two-chair, two-line boats charge from about $375 for a half day to $600 for a full day, with bait, tackle, and soft drinks included. A 3-hour light-tackle trip runs about $20 per person. *Mile Mark Charters* (phone: 773-2628 or 773-2285) arranges deep-sea trips. Since fleet members are limited, advance reservations are always a good idea; most places require a 50% deposit.

SWIMMING AND SUNNING Beach names to know are Cane, Sugar, Pelican, Davis, and Grapetree bays, as well as La Grange — all pleasant, none spectacular. People staying in Christiansted tend to use the small, pretty beach on Protestant Cay or take a short shuttle out to one of the three beaches at the *Buccaneer* hotel. Cramer Park, near the island's eastern tip, has a beach, picnic tables, and changing rooms — but on weekends, it's crowded with locals.

TENNIS The island has courts galore, making it a great locale for both novices and experienced players.

CHOICE COURTS

Buccaneer Unarguably the best tennis in the Virgin Islands. Good for watching (with several annual tournaments) as well as playing. Facilities: 8 all-weather (2 lighted) Laykold courts; ball machine; newly expanded pro shop. Private lessons with the resident pro are $22 per half hour; The *Virgin Islands Tennis Championships* usually take place in July; several other tournaments are held during the year (phone: 773-2100; for reservations only, 800-223-1108 from the US).

Sugar Bay Plantation boasts the USVI's first stadium tennis court, 6 additional lighted courts, and a pro shop. Here's the private court count: *Bluebeard's Castle* (2), *Bolongo Bay* (4), *Elysian* (1), *Frenchman's Reef* (4), *Grand Palazzo* (4), *Limetree Beach* (2), *Mahogany Run* (2), *Point Pleasant* (1), *Sapphire Beach* (4), and *Stouffer Grand Beach* (6). The courts at *Cowpet Bay, Magens Point, Secret Harbour,* and *Watergate* are for members and hotel guests only. Some condominium complexes limit play to club members, owners, and guests.

In addition, the *Carambola Beach* resort has 9 courts with a *Peter Burwash* instructional operation. Other setups include *St. Croix by the Sea,* 4 courts; Chenay Bay, 2 courts; the *Club St. Croix,* 3 courts; *Hotel on the Cay,* 2 courts; and *The Reef* golf course, 2 courts (phone: 773-8844). There also are 3 public courts at Canegata Ball Park.

WATER SKIING Boats, skis, and lessons are available through most hotels, or *Trade Windsurfing* (phone: 773-7060) at about $90 per hour of boat time for up to three skiers.

WINDSURFING A very popular sport in these parts, it is available at many hotels, with lessons and rentals at the *Chenay Bay Beach* resort, *Mile Mark Charters* at the *King Christian* hotel, and *Paradise Parasailing* (phone: 773-7060). Boards can be rented for $25 for 2 hours.

SPORTS

ST. JOHN — Boating *Low Key Watersports* (phone: 776-7048; 800-835-7718 from the US), *Cinnamon Bay Watersports* (phone: 776-6330), and *Cruz Bay Watersports* (phone: 776-6234) will arrange daily sails, as will the water sports centers at *Caneel Bay* and *Maho Bay. St. John Water Sports/ Hinkley Charters* (phone: 776-6256) handles both day sails and longer crewed charters.

HIKING An extensive network of trails covers the national park. Take a four-wheeled tour first to get oriented, then ask for the free park service trail map and literature and set out on your own. Two or three times a week — on a flexible schedule — a park service guide leads nature walks.

SNORKELING AND SCUBA There is a fine marked underwater trail at Trunk Bay, with guided snorkel tours on Wednesday mornings. Other top spots are Hawksnest Bay, Waterlemon Cay, and Salt Pond. For snorkeling and scuba trips, equipment rental, and instruction, try *St. John Water Sports/ Hinckley Charters* in Cruz Bay (phone: 776-6256), *Low Key Watersports* (phone: 776-7048; 800-835-7718 from the US), or *Cruz Bay Watersports* (phone: 776-6234). *Caneel Bay* has its own facilities.

SPORT FISHING Book through *Caneel Bay* (phone: 776-6111) or check with *Cruz Bay Watersports* (phone: 776-6234) or *Low Key Watersports* (phone: 776-7048; 800-835-7718 from the US). Mary's Creek, near Maho Bay, has excellent bonefishing.

SWIMMING AND SUNNING For such a small island, St. John has more than its share of super, sandy stretches.

DREAM BEACH

Trunk Bay Success hasn't spoiled it one iota, thanks to the diligence of the National Park Service rangers who keep watch. Its most famous asset is the underwater trail, with markers to guide you along the reef just off the beach. It's been named one of the Ten Best time and again. A favorite escape destination for *Caneel Bay* guests, it has picnic tables, changing facilities, restrooms, beverage and snack service. Part of the Virgin Islands National Park, and open during the daytime only.

In addition, *Cinnamon Bay* and *Maho Bay* campgrounds have their own beaches, and seven more stunning beaches scallop the waters around *Caneel Bay*. Elsewhere, swim and sun at Hawks Reef and Lameshur bays.

TENNIS *Caneel Bay* has 11 courts, a pro shop, and a *Peter Burwash International* pro staff. *Cinnamon Bay* and *Maho Bay* campers can arrange to play there. There are also 2 public courts in downtown Cruz Bay.

SPORTS

ST. THOMAS — Boating Virgin Islanders do the biggest charter business in the Caribbean. St. Thomas, with its sizable yacht harbors at the *Ramada Yacht Haven Marina* and Red Hook marina, is the heart of the business. Moving out of the Sunfish/Hobie Cat class (both of which can be rented at bathing beach centers), you can rent just about anything that floats — from a 13-foot power boat to an 80-foot schooner, and houseboats, cabin cruisers, and trimarans in between. Cruising vacations aboard a charter yacht with skipper, crew, meals, and liquor included can cost as little as $85 or as much as $1,000 and up per person a day in winter, 10% to 20% less in summer. Or you can go bareboat and sail yourself for a per-person cost of about $100 a day in winter, roughly 15% less in summer. (*Note:* A proficiency check is a standard pre-takeover requirement.)

For information on day or night sails and boat charters, ask at your hotel's travel desk, or contact *Club Nautico* (Red Hook; phone: 775-6265), *V.I. Charteryacht League* (Flagship, Anchor Way, St. Thomas, USVI 00802; phone: 774-3944; 800-524-2061 from the US), or *American Yacht*

Harbor (Red Hook; phone: 775-6454); all can put you in touch with any one of the abundant charter operators in the area.

Day sails, which generally include snorkeling and a picnic lunch while anchored in an out-of-the-way cove, are very popular. *Sea Tours Transfers* at the *Frenchman's Reef* hotel (phone: 776-8500, ext. 145 or 774-2990) and the activities desk at the *Sapphire Beach* hotel (phone: 775-6100) will charter half- or full-day sails. You also can book directly on a variety of craft, including the schooner *True Love* (the very yacht on which Bing Crosby sang to Grace Kelly in the film *High Society*), which has a champagne buffet that sets the standard for day sail elegance (phone: 775-6547 or 775-6374); *Nightwind,* a 55-foot yawl (phone: 775-6666 or 775-6110); and the sloop *Tijou* (phone: 775-6135). Dozens of other craft are advertised in local publications; also check with your hotel.

GOLF There's only one course on St. Thomas, but it is a beauty.

TOP TEE-OFF SPOT

Mahogany Run One of the Caribbean's newer golf courses, designed by George and Tom Fazio, it runs along some of the most picturesque parts of the island, through scenery that makes it well worth enduring the few dull stretches. Especially picturesque is the "Devil's Triangle" (holes 13 through 15). Relatively tight and hilly, with small greens, this is not a course for the lover of classic hole configuration. But it provides 18 good reasons for making a Virgin Islands visit. The greens fee is $75, including cart (phone: 775-5000; 800-524-2038 from the US).

HORSE RACING At the *Estate Nadir Race Track* (Bovari Rd.; no phone), there are meets roughly once a month — usually on a holiday or a Sunday. Check the papers for the schedule.

PARASAILING The *Skyrider* is available at the *Point Pleasant, Sapphire Beach,* and *Stouffer Grand Beach* resorts, and *Tradewinds Para-sail* can be reached at the *Point Pleasant* resort and near the cruise ship dock. Also ask at *Frenchman's Reef.*

SNORKELING AND SCUBA You can rent masks and fins for a small fee at all major hotels and on tourist beaches. Snorkel gear is standard equipment on sailing and yacht excursions as well. Off St. Thomas there are good beginners' dive spots (Cow and Calf, St. James Island, Stevens Cay, Coki Bay) plus any number of underwaterscapes (Congo Cay's lava archways, Thatch Cay's tunnels, Eagle Shoal's submerged mountain) fascinating for more advanced divers. From St. Thomas (or St. John) you can make the all-day dive trip to the wreck of the Royal Mail packet boat *Rhone* (now a British national park) off the British Virgin Islands. Night dives are available for intermediate and advanced divers only (about $50 per person).

Some firms that offer diving trips, instruction, and equipment on St. Thomas are *Aqua Action* at Secret Harbour (phone: 775-6550), *Caribbean Divers* at Red Hook (phone: 775-6384), the *Coki Beach Dive Club* at Coki Beach (phone: 775-4220), the *Watersports Center* at the *Sapphire Beach* resort (phone: 775-6100), *Virgin Island Diving Schools and Divers' Supplies* (phone: 774-8687), and *Joe Vogel Diving Company* (phone: 775-7610) at the *Galleon House* in Frenchtown. The *St. Thomas Diving Club* (phone: 776-2381) sponsors daily dives from a choice of three island take-off points — its own dock at Bolongo Bay or satellites at Elysian and Limetree. The club offers instruction and certification aboard dive boats *Let's Dive* and *Christmas Wind.*

SPORT FISHING There's year-round fishing for wahoo, Allison tuna, bonito, sailfish, and marlin. Blue marlin angling is best between June and August, white marlin in spring and fall, tarpon and bonefish in spring, wahoo from September to May, and sailfish and blackfin tuna in January and February.

American Yacht Harbor (phone: 775-6454) at Red Hook is prime deep-sea headquarters with boats in fine fighting trim. They can arrange on- or offshore fishing for half days, full days, or longer. Captain Al Petrosky skippers angling trips on the *Fish Hawk,* out of East End Lagoon (phone: 775-9058). The *Sapphire Beach* resort and *Sea Tours Transfers* (phone: 776-8500, ext. 145, or 774-2990) also arrange deep-sea fishing.

SWIMMING AND SUNNING Most resorts, hotels, condominiums, and cottage colonies are on sandy stretches of beach stocked with chaises, towels, and beach toys (snorkel gear, float boards, Sun- or Sailfish and/or Hobie Cats and the like, all for rent at small fees). All US Virgin Islands beaches are public. Magens Bay, a wide, protected stretch of golden sand thickly edged with palms, is probably best known. In fact, it may be a little too popular on weekends and on cruise ship arrival days, but it is gorgeous. There are changing rooms and a good but tacky-looking snack bar (small admission and parking fees). Sapphire, Morningstar, and Lindbergh beaches have the same facilities, and are well known and beautiful. But for leisurely picnicking and putting some space between you and the crowds, head for Cowpet Bay or Nazareth Bay, both on the Caribbean side of St. Thomas; or, on the Atlantic side, Mandahl Bay, Hull Bay, or Stumpy Bay (axle fracturing road, but a good beach).

TENNIS Laykold or all-weather courts are the rule; many are lighted for night play and have pro shops and pro instruction.

CHOICE COURTS

Sugar Bay Plantation This resort may give the *Buccaneer* on St. Croix some competition for the tennis crowd, with the USVI's first stadium tennis court (capacity: 220), plus 6 additional Laykold lighted courts, lessons under the supervision of Vic Braden, and a pro shop (phone: 777-7100; 800-HOLIDAY from the US). In addition, there are 2 free public courts at Sub Base, available on a first-come, first-served basis.

All hotel courts require players to wear standard whites or clothes designed for the game. Hotel guests are charged no fee (or a very small one) for court use. Non-guests pay a nominal hourly fee to play. Lessons run $16 to $30 for a half-hour's instruction.

NIGHTLIFE

On St. Croix, the *Buccaneer* hotel schedules music most nights, limbo shows and reggae at least once a week; on Saturday nights, Jimmy Hamilton — who played lead clarinet and tenor sax with Duke Ellington's orchestra for 30 years — plays here with his own quartet. *Café Madeleine* at *Villa Madeleine* provides music every night, with a piano player Wednesdays through Fridays, a jazz group Saturdays, and a steel band on Sundays. In Christiansted, the *King's Alley* hotel's *Marina Bar* is the place for sunset and people watching. Also downtown, there's West Indian music every night at *Calabash* (Strand St.; phone: 778-0001); nightly entertainment at the *Moonraker Lounge* (43-A Queen Cross St.; phone: 773-1535). Softer sounds of "oldies" and guitar selections can be heard nightly at the *Tivoli Gardens* (upstairs at the corner of Queen Cross and Strand Sts.; phone: 773-6782). The *Caravelle* features jazz Fridays and Saturdays (44A Queen Cross St.; phone: 773-0687), as does the *Captain's Table* (55-56 Company St.; phone: 773-2026). Just west of town on Northside Road is *Two Plus Two,* a disco (Rte. 75; phone: 773-3710) with dancing to taped music Sundays to Thursdays, live calypso band on Fridays and Saturdays, when there's a cover charge. North of Frederiksted, the *Sand Bar* (Rte. 63; phone: 772-9906) features entertainment on Fridays and Sundays. Other Friday night jazz spots are *Villa Morales* (Estate Whim; phone: 772-0556) and *Blue Moon* (17 Strand St.; phone: 772-2222). St. Croix's *Quadrille Dancers* are a special treat. In bright yesteryear costumes, they move to the old plantation-days calls, and before the performance ends, you're invited to try a few steps yourself. The amateur group's schedule is erratic, but watch *This Week* for date, time, place, and go if you get a chance. They also perform for private parties; contact Bradley Christian (phone: 772-2021).

Not a lot is happening on St. John. There are fish fries at *Fred's* on Cruz Bay (phone: 776-6363) on Fridays and occasionally Saturdays, and live music nightly; *Sputnik Bar* at Coral Bay (no phone) offers native food and a live reggae/calypso band. The *Caneel* band plays at the *Beach Terrace* at *Caneel Bay.* For just hanging out, there's *The Backyard,* Cruz Bay (phone: 693-8886).

St. Thomas boasts no star-spangled nightclub shows, no big-deal casinos. One big hotel — *Frenchman's Reef* — offers a nightly Calypso Carnival of island music and dance (with perhaps the Caribbean's most entertaining limbo dancer) at its *Top of the Reef* nightclub. In addition, *Coral World Marine Park and Underwater Observatory* offers dinner theater Thursdays through Sundays, with performances by the local *Pistarckle Theatre Co.* Entrance to the park, the show, and dinner and drinks at the *Tropical Terrace* restaurant is $45 per person; the show alone is $20 per person (phone: 775-1560). Elsewhere, entertainment is simpler. Hotels provide music — songs and a guitar or a small combo — most nights, and many host outdoor barbecues with a steel band and limbo show (usually with a bit of fire-eating or broken-glass walking thrown in) at least one evening a week. If you've never seen a limbo show, check one out; but if you've seen one . . . . Other options: *Frenchman's Reef* has dance music at *La Terraza,* and there's later dancing at the *Top of the Reef, while Bluebeard's* features dancing Sunday night. *Barnacle Bill's* at Sub Base (phone: 774-7444) has bands nightly (except Mondays and Wednesdays) and during happy hour on Fridays, while *Raffles* (Rte. 32 at Compass Point; phone: 775-6004) plays softer music Tuesdays through Saturdays. *Agave Terrace,* also outside town (Rte. 38; phone: 775-4142), features steel bands Tuesday and Thursday evenings, with a jazz concert held out on the pool terrace monthly — on full-moon night. *Blackbeard's* offers jazz Fridays through Sundays. *Harbor View* (Frenchman's Hill; phone: 774-2651) offers piano music Thursdays through Sundays. At the *Green House* restaurant on the waterfront in town (phone: 774-7998) a DJ plays oldies on Monday nights; on Wednesdays, Thursdays, and Fridays, there's live reggae or rock bands. At *Iggy's,* a *karaoke* bar in the *Limetree* hotel, guests can get up on stage and sing along to their favorite songs, as 15 TV screens project videos. Upstairs there is a nightclub with a calypso band and a disco for dancing. *The Old Mill* (Upper Constant; phone: 776-3004) features local music, the *East Coast Bar and Grill* (Red Hook; phone: 775-1919) is a sports bar with local rock 'n' roll bands on Saturday evenings, and *For the Birds* draws a young crowd with its calypso and reggae beats (Scott Beach; phone: 775-6431).

Best on the Islands

CHECKING IN

The US Virgin Islands have just about everything in the way of accommodations except high-rises. Among the nicest properties are condominiums, which, though not inexpensive, can be real money savers for families or a couple of couples sharing an apartment — the usually well-stocked kitchens can really cut down on dining expenses. There are also modest guesthouses and small inns on all three islands. Rates range from as little as about $55 for two with breakfast at a 19th-century guesthouse in summer, to $495 and up for two without meals at the *Grand Palazzo* in winter. (A very inexpensive option is pitching a tent at *Cinnamon Bay*'s campgrounds; visitors pay as little as $10 a night for a bare tent site.) In the lists that follow, very expensive is defined as $300 or more per day for a room for two with no meals during the winter season; expensive is $175 to $300; moderate, $125 to $175; and inexpensive, under $125. Summer rates are 25% to 45% less. Modified American Plan (MAP, which includes breakfast and dinner) is usually available at a $25 to $35 per person per day surcharge. All telephone numbers are in the 809 area code unless otherwise indicated. The central toll-free telephone number for making hotel reservations on St. Croix is 800-524-2026; for St. John and St. Thomas hotel reservations call 774-6835.

For an unforgettable island experience, we begin with our favorites, followed by our recommendations of cost and quality choices of hotels large and small, listed by area and price category.

REGAL RESORTS

Caneel Bay, St. John Perfect serenity is the most enticing amenity offered here. This 170-acre resort estate in one small part of the 7,028 forested acres that Laurance S. Rockefeller gave to the US to become the Virgin Islands National Park is still operated by the Rockresorts folk (though Rockresorts is now owned by a Chicago real estate group). The only thing flamboyant on the property is the tree of the same name, and only the colors of the flowers — scarlet hibiscus, yellow trumpet vine, purple morning glories — are loud. There are 7 superb beaches, and swimming, basking, snorkeling, and small-boat sailing occupy most days; tranquillity is further protected by the national park's ban on water skiing. Just next door is Trunk Bay, with its marked underwater nature trail for snorkeling; more ambitious dive trips are also available, as are ranger-led tours through the park. Amenities also include *Peter Burwash International* tennis. Elegant dinners are served at the *Turtle Bay* restaurant (see *Eating Out*), with cocktails on the terrace overlooking gardens that sweep down to the sea. The noon buffet on the *Garden Terrace* is a tradition, but when you've ingested one you've experienced them all; so you may want to opt for a meal at the *Sugar Mill Dining Room* (specializing in fresh seafood), a picnic at Trunk Bay, or a bite at one of Cruz Bay's native restaurants (the hotel offers an EP option). Room refurbishing has refreshed the accommodations quite nicely. A steel band arrives to play for dinner-dancing several times a week, and there are nightly movies. Otherwise, it is happily, serenely, and early to bed. Caneel Bay (phone: 776-6111; 800-928-8889 from the US; fax: 776-2030).

Grand Palazzo, St. Thomas The stunning new beachfront resort at Great Bay, on the east end of St. Thomas, is laid out in three sections featuring Italian Renaissance–style architecture. Guests relax among marbled and tiled splendor in 154 upscale rooms and suites (2 equipped to accommodate the disabled). All rooms feature cable TV, hair dryers, coffee makers, and in-room safes, among other luxury amenities. In addition, there is a magnificent 125-foot pool that looks as though it merges with the ocean, a smaller children's pool, a fitness center, *Peter Burwash International* tennis on 4 lighted courts, and water sports. Of the 2 restaurants, the most romantic is the *Palm Terrace* (see *Eating Out*), where ceiling fans stir the large palms and guests view the ocean through large windows as they feast on elegantly presented continental specialties. Great Bay (phone: 775-3333; 800-283-8666 from the US; fax: 775-4444).

ST. CROIX

CHRISTIANSTED AND ENVIRONS

VERY EXPENSIVE

Buccaneer Sprawling down a hillside outside Christiansted, it has the most extensive facilities on the island — 3 beaches, an 18-hole golf course, 8 highly rated tennis courts, basketball courts, a 2-mile jogging trail, a spa and fitness center, shops, plus a full roster of activities. There's a lot happening, but the atmosphere is easygoing. The 150 rooms, all with private terraces, are large and nicely furnished. Favorites are the beachside rooms with fieldstone terraces right on the water. The 1653 sugar mill on the property is a popular wedding site. There are also 4 restaurants; the view of Christiansted from the open-air *Terrace* is unequaled. Estate Shoy (phone: 773-2100; 800-223-1108 from the US).

Club St. Croix This stylish beachfront property has 52 air conditioned studio and 1-bedroom units, all with modern decor, rattan furnishings, ceiling fans, and telephones. The suites also have full kitchens and balconies with sea views. There are 3 tennis courts, a lap pool, and water sports facilities. The resort launch brings guests to town; day sails can be arranged. The pleasant poolside restaurant/bar overlooks the sea. One mile west of downtown Christiansted (phone: 773-4800; 800-635-1533 from the US; fax: 773-4805).

EXPENSIVE

Colony Cove Here are 60 large, good-looking apartments, each with a washer and dryer, a microwave oven, and a dishwasher. There's a solar-tiled pool (it keeps the water warm for dips after dark) and a good water sports center. The extra-large terraces, all facing the ocean, are especially nice. About 10 minutes from Christiansted (phone: 773-1965; 800-828-0746 from the US; fax: 773-5377).

Hotel on the Cay On its own island in Christiansted Harbor, with a white sand beach and lush grounds, this place has a good water sports center, Olympic-size pool, 2 tennis courts on the water, and dining with 360-degree views. The 55 smallish rooms are comfortably contemporary, with tile floors, platform beds, and wet bars. Only 2 minutes from town by ferry (phone: 773-2035; 800-524-2035 from the US; fax: 524-2035).

St. Croix by the Sea A pretty, popular spot with 65 rooms, a great view of the ocean, a huge saltwater pool, tennis (4 courts), and 3 very good restaurants. Close to downtown (phone: 778-8600; 800-524-5006 from the US; fax: 778-8002).

MODERATE

Anchor Inn Thirty refurbished harborfront rooms in the heart of Christiansted, each with a balcony and refrigerator. There is also a restaurant. Day trips to Buck Island are available. King St. (phone: 773-4000; 800-524-2030 from the US; fax: 773-4408).

Club Comanche This old-fashioned, 3-story, 15-room hotel in the heart of Christiansted has quirky, unique rooms. The newer wing houses some split-level suites (4 penthouses). There's also a breakfast porch, an attractive pool deck, and a very popular restaurant. No beach, but very convenient for shopping. 1 Strand St. (phone: 773-0210; 800-524-2066 from the US).

Waves at Cane Bay A small seaside hotel, it's in a beautiful natural setting near the *Carambola Beach* resort. The 11 spacious studios and 1 villa feature kitchens, balconies with ocean views, and air conditioning. There's a saltwater grotto pool, a small beach area, and superior snorkeling and scuba diving right in front of the property. Beautiful Cane Bay beach, a golf course, and tennis courts are nearby. There's no restaurant (though guests may use the grill by the pool). The location is a bit remote; a car is a necessity. Cane Bay (phone: 778-1805; 800-545-0603 from the US; fax: 778-1895).

INEXPENSIVE

Caravelle Sitting on the water in Christiansted's historic district, the 43 rooms here have air conditioning and phones. A freshwater pool, a variety of water sports, and the *Banana Bay Club,* a harbor-view open-air restaurant, complete the picture. 44A Queen Cross St. (phone: 773-0687; 800-524-0410 from the US; fax: 778-7004).

Hilty House Near the jungle, this small, charming hotel is housed in a former 18th-century rum factory. Hugh and Jacquie Hoare-Ward, the owners, take great pains to make their guests feel at home. The building has 2-foot-thick outer walls and interior rooms decorated with hand-painted Italian tiles and dark beams. There are 5 guestrooms and 3 cottages, tastefully furnished and featuring ceiling fans and private baths or showers. There's also a large pool and sun deck. A delicious continental breakfast, prepared with garden-fresh ingredients, is included. Hermon Hill (phone/fax: 773-2594).

King Christian Its wharfside location in a former historic warehouse couldn't be more convenient. The 39 rooms (25 with ocean views) are basic, but large; the newer rooms are a bit more refined. The hotel, which draws many repeat visitors, also sports a freshwater pool with a deck. Guests can use *Hotel on the Cay* sports facilities for a nominal fee. The *Chart House* restaurant (see *Eating Out*) is on the property. 59 King's Wharf (phone: 773-2285; 800-524-2012 from the US; fax: 773-9411).

Pink Fancy Encompassing a restored 18th-century Danish townhouse and its attendant buildings, this small gem is a mosaic of white-shingled, pink-shuttered buildings; walled courtyards; gardens; and terraces on different levels. The 13 large, attractive, studios — with living areas, air conditioning, and fully stocked kitchenettes — are meant for solid comfort. There's a pretty tiled swimming pool and 24-hour complimentary bar where guests help themselves to continental breakfast and drinks. A 5-minute walk from the Christiansted wharf (phone: 773-8460; 800-524-2045 from the US; fax: 773-6448).

FREDERIKSTED

EXPENSIVE

King Frederik A stroll from Frederiksted on a nice strand of beach, this 13-room hostelry offers modest accommodations. Request one of the 5 tidily attractive 1-bedroom apartments with a cool, ocean-facing terrace with tropical gardens. There are also 4 courtyard villas under construction; each will have 2 bedrooms and will share a pool and whirlpool. There's a beach bar and restaurant serving breakfast, lunch, and dinner. On the southern end of town (phone: 772-1205; 800-524-2018 from the US; fax: 809-772-1757).

INEXPENSIVE

Paradise Sunset Beach Drive through a rugged strip of woods to find this pink complex perched above the road. The pool looks like it's hanging over Estate Ham's Bay. Grounds include 17th-century sugar mill ruins. One of the few island hotels facing the spectacular sunsets, it has 11 rooms and 2 cottages, all air conditioned. A poolside restaurant serves three meals daily. On Rte. 63 (phone: 772-2499; fax: 772-0001).

ELSEWHERE ON ST. CROIX

VERY EXPENSIVE

Carambola Beach Nestled on 28,000 acres overlooking the Caribbean, this property — dealt a severe blow by Hurricane Hugo in 1989 — reopened last year and is now a fully operational hotel run by the Radisson group. Its 157 rooms and suites are distributed among several villas around the pristine white sand beach. Several 2- and 3-bedroom villas can be rented as well. There are 3 dining rooms whose menus run the gamut from casual, light meals to elegant continental fare. Sports facilities include 9 tennis courts and the marvelous 18-hole Robert Trent Jones, Sr. championship course (see *Top Tee-Off Spot* in *Golf* in this chapter). On the northeastern part of the island (phone: 778-3800; 800-333-3333 from the US).

Villa Madeleine This stunning resort has 43 villas (3 one-bedroom and 40 two-bedroom), each with its own pool, marble baths, and ocean views. The main building, with the restaurant, music room, and gameroom, was built to resemble a sugar plantation greathouse. All villas have kitchens with microwave ovens and are air conditioned. Tennis, golf, horseback riding, and all water sports may be arranged. The beach is within walking distance of units on the lower hill. *Café Madeleine* (see *Eating Out*) serves outstanding continental and Italian food. On the east end of the island (phone: 778-7377).

EXPENSIVE

Cormorant Beach Club On a 1,600-foot palm-fringed beach, it has 34 double rooms and 4 one-bedroom suites, all beautifully furnished and boasting air conditioning, fresh flowers daily, and private patio and/or balcony overlooking the beach. There is a pool, tennis, and snorkeling; also a restaurant (see *Eating Out*) and a bar. Rates include morning coffee or tea and afternoon tea and pastries; an optional plan includes breakfast, lunch, and all drinks until 5 PM. Adjacent *Cormorant Cove* has 6 high-rise luxury condominium units, some with marble baths and Jacuzzis, and its own freshwater pool. 4126 La Grande Princesse, 10 minutes west of Christiansted (phone: 778-8920; 800-548-4460 from the US; fax: 778-9218).

MODERATE

Cane Bay Reef Club Surfers and snorkelers like this place's proximity to the beach, while other guests choose to play golf at *Carambola Beach.* It's small, informal, and friendly, with kitchens in the 9 one-bedroom apartments, and balconies with spectacular views of the sea. The beach is just down the road; there's a pool on the property. There's also a bar and grill. Optional maid service is available. A car is recommended. On the north shore, close to the *Carambola Beach* resort and midway between Christiansted and Frederiksted (phone: 778-2966; 800-253-8534 from the US; fax: 778-1017).

Hibiscus Beach Built on the site of the former *Cathy's Fancy,* its 38 immaculate, well-appointed rooms feature air conditioning, a fine ocean view that includes Buck Island, and in-room safes. Guests can walk right onto the beach, and from there to a coral reef; there's also a swimming pool. Many guestrooms are fully or partially equipped for the disabled, and there is a poolside wheelchair lift. The open-air restaurant/bar and casual indoor dining room serve good continental fare. Snorkeling equipment is complimentary. 4131 La Grande Princesse, 10 minutes west of Christiansted (phone: 773-4042; 800-442-0121 from the US; fax: 773-7668).

ST. JOHN

VERY EXPENSIVE

Hyatt Regency St. John This modern, luxury property has 285 air conditioned rooms, suites, and townhouses perched on 34 acres of tropical, lush hillside. Highlights include a huge pool, excellent white sand beach, tennis on 6 lighted courts, water sports, shops, 3 restaurants (including *Chow Bella* and *Café Grand;* see *Eating Out*), a bar, a health club, and an airport shuttle to and from St. Thomas. Beachfront and poolside rooms are the best choices for disabled guests because of steep steps elsewhere. Just outside Cruz Bay (phone: 693-8000; 800-233-1234 from the US; fax: 775-3858).

EXPENSIVE

Estate Zootenvaal An intimate complex of 2 one-bedroom cottages and 2 two-bedroom cottages on the water's edge close to the isolated town of Coral Bay. This is a quiet bargain spot with simple, tasteful furnishings and fully equipped kitchens, ceiling fans, and private beach, but no air conditioning or in-room phones. Hurricane Hole (phone: 776-6321).

Gallows Point A 60-unit West Indian–influenced condominium complex overlooking Pillsbury Sound and Cruz Bay. The tastefully furnished 2-story cottages house 1-bedroom suites with ceiling fans and sea views. *Ellington's* restaurant is long on atmosphere, short on service. There's also a pool. Convenient location near town (phone: 693-8788; 800-323-7229 from the US).

INEXPENSIVE

Cinnamon Bay Campground Back to the basics, for island lovers on a limited budget: this offers tents and cottages with cooking gear, a commissary, a cafeteria, and bathhouses, as well as bare sites on a beachside campground owned by the National Park Service and managed by Rockresorts. Extremely popular, so book well in advance. Dive packages and National Park snorkeling instruction and hikes available. Near the Virgin Islands National Park (phone: 776-6330; 800-223-7637 from the US).

Cruz Inn A cozy, family-run, West Indies–style guesthouse, it has 15 one- and two-bedroom suites with kitchens (baths are shared); one unit has air conditioning. Complimentary breakfast; the *Bamboo Bar* is a friendly watering hole. Convenient to town (phone: 776-7688 or 776-9762; fax: 776-7449).

Maho Bay Camps A truly laid-back escape from the shoppers and cruise ship passengers. There are 114 tents that serve as small canvas houses — with good beds, kitchen areas, refrigerators, sun decks — dotting the 14-acre hillside, with the beach below, and the national park all around. Ecologically sensitive (non-erosive boardwalks, pick-yourself herb gardens), it now offers expanded water sports. Simple fare is served at an open-air, island-style restaurant. There's live entertainment Friday evenings; a pavilion, with magnificent view and massage facilities, hosts weddings and meetings. A shuttle to Cruz Bay is available. Some units are reserved a year in advance. Near the Virgin Islands National Park (phone: 776-6226 or 776-6240; 212-472-9454 from New York; 800-392-9004 from elsewhere in the US).

ST. THOMAS

Those who can't find available hotel rooms below should check out *Property Management Caribbean,* which handles seven properties that rent condominiums (phone: 800-524-2038 from the US).

CHARLOTTE AMALIE AND THE SOUTHERN COAST

VERY EXPENSIVE

Bolongo Limetree Beach The main house is above a pleasantly untrammeled stretch of sand; 84 good-looking contemporary guestrooms (some split-level) line the hill, all with ocean views. Everything is included — meals, drinks, tips, tennis on 2 lighted courts, 1-day use of a car, water sports, shuttles to *Elysian* and *Bolongo* beaches, and a trip to *Coral World.* At night, the casual restaurant downstairs turns into a *karaoke* bar. A calypso band plays at the nightclub upstairs, alongside the disco. Bolongo Bay Rd. (phone: 775-1800; 800-524-4746 from the US; fax: 776-3208).

Elysian Bolongo Beach On the beach at Cowpet Bay (cowpets are baby whales, which sometimes migrate past the bay), this pretty pink resort offers 169 stunning condos with kitchens, balconies, and mini-bars. There's a large freshwater pool with waterfall and whirlpool, plus a beach, fitness center, tennis, day-cruises, and water sports. The complex has 3 restaurants; continental breakfast is included in the rate. Cowpet Bay (phone: 775-1000; 800-524-4746 from the US; fax: 775-3208).

Frenchman's Reef This huge, very modern Marriott resort complex has 421 rooms; most popular are the 96 additional luxurious rooms at the *Morning Star Beach Club,* each with a private entrance, tropical decor, and many special amenities. The resort also offers several restaurant choices, including the open-air *Caesar's Ristorante* (see *Eating Out*). For sports-minded guests, there are 4 lighted tennis courts and a pro shop, 2 freshwater pools, a health club, Jacuzzis, and a beautiful beach. The panoramic ocean view is stunning; the water sports setup is the island's most extensive. Other services include a water taxi into Charlotte Amalie and tour and car rental desks in the lobby. MAP and all-inclusive plans are offered. Ten minutes from town (phone: 776-8500; 800-524-2000 from the US; fax: 774-6249).

EXPENSIVE

Bluebeard's Castle A historic setting with a terrific view, lush gardens, tennis courts, and 170 rooms. We're sentimentally attached to the old tower (request Room 139 or 140), although a newer building, with 48 rooms and suites and 8 condominium units and meeting rooms, has taken away some of the charm here. Not for beach buffs — it has none — but it does provide 2 night-lighted tennis courts, a freshwater pool, beach transportation, and 2 restaurants (including the outstanding *Entre Nous* — see *Eating Out*). Near town (phone: 774-1600; 800-524-6599 from the US; fax: 774-5734).

Secret Harbour Beach Contemporary and casual, here are 60 suites with expansive sun decks and kitchenettes overlooking Nazareth Bay. A $2-million restoration has spruced up the guestroom and bathroom decor, and a pool and fitness center have been added. Right on the beach with water sports, tennis on 2 courts, and 2 restaurants. Complimentary continental breakfast. Five miles east of Charlotte Amalie, on a secluded beach (phone: 775-6550; 800-524-2250 from the US; fax: 775-1501).

Secret Harbourview Villas This property has 25 studio and 1- and 2-bedroom condominium units available for rental. Each unit is attractively furnished and air conditioned and has a private bath for each bedroom, full kitchen, telephone, and a balcony with a view of the Caribbean. There are all-weather tennis courts, a freshwater pool, Jacuzzi, and a fitness center. On the beach there's a fabulous water sports center, plus a cocktail pavilion and delicious food at the waterfront restaurant/bar. One of the prettiest locations on St. Thomas, just 20 minutes from Charlotte Amalie (phone: 775-2600; 800-874-7897 from the US; fax: 775-5901).

MODERATE

Admiral's Inn Formerly the *West Indies Inn,* it's located in a 19th-century building that served as a Russian consulate. It offers 16 rooms (4 with ocean views), all air conditioned but lacking phones and TV sets. Complimentary continental breakfast is served. The view is across the harbor to town. There's a recently restored beach and pool, an informal restaurant/bar, and the *Chart House* (see *Eating Out*). At Villa Olga in French Town (phone: 774-1376; 800-544-0493 from the US; fax: 774-8010).

Blackbeard's Castle Small and intimate, it has 20 rooms and apartments in a restored 17th-century Danish mansion. The watchtower in the center of the complex was built in 1679 by Blackbeard so he could spot ships to plunder. The room decor is unassuming, but there's air conditioning and phones. Also on the premises are an Olympic-size pool and an excellent restaurant (see *Eating Out*). There also are great views of Charlotte Amalie and the cruise ship area. Rte. 35 at the top of Blackbeard Hill (phone: 776-1234; 800-344-5771 from the US; fax: 776-4321).

Hotel 1829 Long a landmark in historic Charlotte Amalie, this pretty pink building with the green awning and the wrought-iron gate is small and utterly charming, with lots of ancient tile, stone, and wooden louvers. Everything about it bespeaks graciousness — a shady verandah for daytime reading, a sunny courtyard with a small swimming pool, 15 rooms decorated with taste and imagination, and an excellent, popular restaurant (see *Eating Out*). A 15-minute drive to the beach. Government Hill (phone: 776-1829; 800-524-2002 from the US; fax: 776-4313).

Mafolie A quiet place with a lovely view of the harbor. There are 23 air conditioned rooms (no phones), 2 restaurants, and a pool; beach transportation and continental breakfast are included. On Mafolie Hill (phone: 774-2790; 800-225-7035 from the US; fax: 809-774-4091).

Ramada Yacht Haven Excellent for sailing buffs, it offers very attractive charter yacht packages from its own private, 200-slip marina, the largest on St. Thomas. There are 210 rooms and suites, a good-size pool, 3 restaurants, complimentary transportation to the beach, and evening entertainment. At the mouth of the cruise ship port (phone: 774-9700; 800-228-9898 from the US; fax: 776-3410).

INEXPENSIVE

Danish Chalet On a hill overlooking the bay and cruise ship docks, this 15-room bed and breakfast establishment offers a breezy deck and Jacuzzi. Some rooms are air conditioned and have private baths; all have phones. Continental breakfast is included in the rate. Five-minute walk to town. Solberg Rd. (phone: 774-5764; 800-635-1531 from the US; fax: 777-4886).

NORTHERN COAST

VERY EXPENSIVE

Magens Point On a hill above the famous beach; there are 52 trim contemporary rooms (ask for the one in the new section with the cathedral ceiling), a pool, 2 tennis courts, water sports, and the popular *Mona's Place* restaurant. Close to *Mahogany Run* golf. Free transportation to beach; slight charge to Charlotte Amalie (phone: 775-5500; 800-524-2031 from the US; fax: 776-5524).

Sapphire Beach On one of the island's loveliest beaches, this huge complex has a 67-slip marina, a hotel, 2 restaurants, a pool, and 4 tennis courts. The 171 suites and villas face either the beach or the marina and have kitchens, microwave ovens, coffee makers, and patios. All water sports are complimentary; lessons cost extra. On Sapphire Beach (phone: 775-6100; 800-524-2090 from the US; fax: 775-4024).

Stouffer Grand Beach The architecture here is a departure from that of other island hotels, with wood-shingled dormers, awnings, and French doors.

There are 290 rooms and suites, 2 restaurants, shops, a fitness center, 6 lighted tennis courts, 2 swimming pools, a daily activities program for children of all ages, and a dock, marina, and water sports center on 34 acres of landscaped grounds. Rooms in the Bougainvillea area are conveniently grouped behind the beach and the great beachfront pool, while those in the hillside Hibiscus area have the better view (the resort runs a continuous shuttle up and down and a complimentary shuttle to *Coral World*). Whichever area you choose, specify a second-floor or higher room for maximum privacy on your terrace. On an inviting stretch of sand on the island's northeast shore (phone: 775-1510; 800-468-3571 from the US; fax: 775-2185).

EXPENSIVE

Sugar Bay Plantation This Holiday Inn Crowne Plaza resort sweeps down the hill to the sea near Red Hook, with 300 luxury rooms and suites with ocean views. Decorated in elegant plantation style, it boasts the USVI's first stadium tennis court, plus 6 additional lighted courts and pro shop. Other amenities include 3 connected pools with a waterfall and Jacuzzi, access to golf, 3 restaurants, a nightclub, a beach, and a view of a 1.6-acre historic area with archaeological remains. A lavish buffet breakfast is included, as are nightly cocktail parties and a shuttle service. Rte. 38, Smith Bay Rd. (phone: 777-7100; 800-HOLIDAY from the US).

Point Pleasant A small, secluded, 15-acre ecologically minded world of gardens with great charm, quiet style, and 134 spacious villas overlooking the sea — all with balconies, many with kitchens. The beach is tiny, but guests may use the beach facilities at *Stouffer Grand Beach* next door. There's also an excellent restaurant and a swimming pool. Use of a car (mandatory insurance charge is extra), tennis court, boats, and snorkel gear are included in rates. The *Agave Terrace* restaurant has a fabulous view and chic clientele (see *Eating Out*). In the northeastern part of the island, on the Atlantic (phone: 775-7200; 800-524-2300 from the US; fax: 776-5694).

EATING OUT

Menus run from genuine, elegant French and continental to casual deli — with Mexican, Italian, Chinese, American steaks and seafood, and a touch of "soul" sandwiched between. Island fare is limited but good. Staples are delicious fish (red snapper, dolphin, wahoo, yellowtail, grouper) poached or broiled and served with a choice of sauces (we're partial to the hot lime, but creole and spicy West Indian are good, too), and sweet lobster with lemon butter. Mushrooms or *funghi,* dumplings made of cornmeal, are likely side dishes. An alternative main course might be a curry (conch or lamb or goat) or boiled chicken with vegetables. The best soup around is *callaloo,* thick with greens and bits of ham and crab, spiced with okra and pepper. For dessert: guava or pineapple tart, or soothing soursop ice cream. The *vin du pays* (light Cruzan rum) goes nicely with most everything.

One place to get all this together is at a fish fry, a y'all-come superpicnic with music and dancing, and a favorite island social event. They're held at varying intervals on the beaches of all three islands. Admission, drinks, and food come to about $15 per person, and you really are welcome.

Expect to pay $110 or more for a meal for two (including tip) at a restaurant we list as very expensive. Dinner for two at expensive places costs $75 to $110; moderate places run about $40 to $60; less than $40 at spots we describe as inexpensive. All telephone numbers are in the 809 area code unless otherwise indicated. A timely note: Call ahead to be sure the restaurant is open, since some close during the off-season.

ST. CROIX

EXPENSIVE

Café Madeleine Elegant dining on a floral canopied terrace, with arguably the best food on the island. Arrive for cocktails while it's still light enough to appreciate the view down the hill to the sea. Try the wild mushroom ravioli with pepper boursin sauce, or roasted chicken with hazelnut and starfruit stuffing. Open daily for dinner only. Reservations necessary. Major credit cards accepted. At the *Villa Madeleine* resort on the east end of the island (phone: 778-7377).

Captain's Table Formerly the *Mahogany Inn,* this dining spot is set in a partially roofed courtyard surrounded by 18th-century buildings. The menu features fine West Indian and French fare, including quail with raspberry sauce and linguini with lobster. Save room for the outstanding chocolate mousse. Open for dinner only; closed Sundays. Reservations advised. Major credit cards accepted. 55-56 Company St., Christiansted (phone: 773-2026).

Chart House Part of the US restaurant chain that specializes in historic locations and in dishes such as teriyaki chicken, Australian lobster tails, prime ribs, fine steaks, and grilled local fish such as wahoo, tuna, and kingfish, plus an all-you-can-eat soup and salad bar. Open daily for dinner only. No reservations. Major credit cards accepted. 59 King's Wharf in the *King Christian* hotel overlooking the harbor (phone: 773-7718).

Cormorant Beach Club This dining spot encompasses two places side by side: a beachside dinner restaurant and an open-air beachfront restaurant. The menu features such creations as grouper with a coconut crust, lobster medallions with passion-fruit hollandaise, and for dessert, homemade ice cream with island fruit. Open daily for lunch and dinner; Sunday brunch is also served. Reservations advised. Major credit cards accepted. 4126 La Grande Princesse, 10 minutes west of Christiansted (phone: 778-8920).

Kendrick's Set in an authentic old Danish home, this establishment offers excellent service and an attractive, antiques-filled decor. Diners enjoy superb angel hair pasta with sun-dried tomatoes, grilled rack of lamb, and enticing appetizers such as baked brie with wild mushrooms. Open for dinner only; closed Sundays in the off-season. Reservations advised. Major credit cards accepted. 52 King St., Christiansted (phone: 773-9199).

Tivoli Gardens Prettiest at night when lights twinkle and greenery ruffles in the harbor breeze. Zesty soups and *coquilles St. Jacques* are fine starters; noteworthy entrées include steak Diane, fresh local fish, and various lobster dishes; the chocolate velvet dessert is superb. Open daily; dinner only on weekends. Reservations advised. Major credit cards accepted. Strand St. and Queen Cross, Christiansted (phone: 773-6782).

Top Hat One of the best eateries on the island, it's located in a small space above shops in an 18th-century merchant's home. Chef Bent Rasmussen prepares superb Danish specialties such as Danish meatballs with red cabbage, and pâtés, as well as seafood and Cruzan coffee. Open Mondays through Saturdays; dinner only on Mondays and Saturdays. Reservations advised. Major credit cards accepted. 53 Company St., Christiansted (phone: 773-2346).

MODERATE

Club Comanche On a breezy terrace, this eatery is close to Christiansted Harbor near an old sugar mill. Neither all continental nor all native — just some of the best of both, and reliably good. Choose hamburgers and steaks or Cruzan meat loaf and curried chicken salad. Live piano music is played nightly. Open daily; no dinner on Sundays. Reservations advised in season. Major credit cards accepted. 1 Strand St. (phone: 773-2665).

Duggan's Reef Overlooking the beach and Buck Island, this informal dining spot serves soups, salads, burgers, and grilled fish at lunch; escargots, rack of lamb, shrimp tempura, and lobster pasta in the evening. Open daily. Reservations necessary. Major credit cards accepted. Rte. 82 at Reef Beach (phone: 773-9800).

Sprat Hall Great House Island dishes (pork chops in orange sauce, baked breadfruit, coconut beef) are served by candlelight in the island's oldest continuously lived-in plantation house. The menu changes nightly. Friendly atmosphere; jackets and ties for men and dresses for women are preferred but not mandatory. Open for dinner only; closed Sundays. Reservations necessary. No credit cards accepted. On Rte. 63, 1 mile north of Frederiksted (phone: 772-0305).

Tutto Bene Café One of the newest eateries in Christiansted is this charming Italian bistro that is usually packed with enthusiastic patrons. Its atmosphere is informal; the menu (which changes daily) presents classic dishes such as veal parmigiano, lasagna, and seafood fra diavolo, as well as more unusual specialties, such as grilled mahimahi and crabmeat ravioli. Open daily. Reservations advised. Major credit cards accepted. 2 Company St., Christiansted (phone: 773-5229).

INEXPENSIVE

Brady's Well-prepared, authentic island dishes, including salt fish, *callaloo,* and *funghi* are served in a spacious location. Open daily for breakfast, lunch, and dinner. Reservations unnecessary. No credit cards accepted. 15 Queen St., Christiansted (phone: 773-2505).

Pizza Mare Pizza, calzone, lasagna, overstuffed Italian sandwiches are the bill of fare here. Open for lunch and dinner; closed Sundays. No reservations. No credit cards accepted. Located in *Sunny Isle Shopping Center* (phone: 778-5556).

Sundowner Beach Bar A casual, alfresco place on the waterfront, it's great for breakfast or lunch when you're touring the west end of the island. Lunch is basic burgers and sandwiches; the dinner menu usually includes a nightly special (lobster, barbecue, prime ribs, among others). This is *the* local hangout on Sunday evenings. No reservations. No credit cards accepted. Strand St., Frederiksted (phone: 772-9906).

Villa Morales This family-owned eatery serves local dishes such as stewed salt fish, steamed goat, conch, and rice and beans. Try the fried plantains; they taste like candy. Open for lunch and dinner Tuesdays through Saturdays. Reservations unnecessary. No credit cards accepted. Near Frederiksted, south of Queen Mary Hwy. (phone: 772-0556).

ST. JOHN

VERY EXPENSIVE

Chow Bella Formerly *Fronds,* this premier restaurant on the top of the *Hyatt Regency St. John* offers a choice of two menus: Italian selections include fried calamari and sambuca shrimp, while Oriental dishes feature wok-roasted duck and sizzling yellowtail snapper. Live piano music provides a soothing atmosphere every night. Open daily for dinner only. Reservations advised. Major credit cards accepted. Great Cruz Bay (phone: 693-8000).

Turtle Bay The best dining spot at *Caneel Bay* offers elegant decor and an equally special menu. Highly recommended are the Turtle Bay pasta pepperpot and the beef tournedos with shiitake mushrooms. *Note:* open daily for lunch and dinner, but to hotel guests only. Reservations advised. Major credit cards accepted. *Caneel Bay* (phone: 776-6111).

EXPENSIVE

Café Grand The fare served at this open-air eatery covers a wide range of dishes, from burgers to osso buco. Theme nights and Sunday brunch are also featured. Open daily for lunch and dinner. Reservations advised for dinner. Major credit cards accepted. At the *Hyatt Regency St. John* (phone: 693-8000).

Lucy's The ribs and conch are well known, but shrimp curry and lobster also rate highly. Open daily for lunch and dinner. Reservations advised. No credit cards accepted. Coral Bay (phone: 776-6804).

Paradiso An upscale Italian eatery with an extensive wine list. Good menu choices are crab cakes *Paradiso* and seafood *fra diavolo.* Open for dinner and cocktails only; closed Mondays. Reservations advised. Major credit cards accepted. In *Mongoose Junction,* Cruz Bay (phone: 776-8806).

Sugar Mill A round restaurant at *Caneel Bay*'s original sugar mill, it offers a widely varied American and Caribbean-style buffet. Open daily; guests only for breakfast, but non-guests are welcome for the buffet lunch and dinner. Reservations advised. Major credit cards accepted. *Caneel Bay* (phone: 776-6111).

MODERATE

Café Roma Italian specialties are featured at this dining spot with a café atmosphere. The menu includes standard pasta dishes, seafood, and pizza. Open daily for dinner only. No reservations. Major credit cards accepted. Cruz Bay (phone: 776-6524).

Fish Trap Known for its seafood, especially the island fish chowder and conch fritters. The fresh homemade desserts are also a treat. Open for dinner only; closed Mondays. No reservations. Major credit cards accepted. At *Raintree Inn,* Cruz Bay (phone: 693-9994).

Lime Inn A casual spot serving salads and sandwiches. The patio is a great place for people watching. Wednesday nights are all-you-can-eat shrimp feasts. Open for lunch and dinner; closed Sundays. Reservations advised for dinner. Major credit cards accepted. Cruz Bay (phone: 776-6425).

Pusser's of the West Indies Informal food in an open-air setting overlooking Cruz Bay. The *Crow's Nest* (located upstairs) sees lots of action for burgers, steaks, seafood, and drinks. Open daily for lunch and dinner. Reservations advised for parties of six or more. Major credit cards accepted. *Wharfside Village,* Cruz Bay (phone: 774-5489).

INEXPENSIVE

Garden of Luscious Licks This tiny place serves vegetarian foods, including homemade soups and muffins, both for takeout and dining in. Open daily. Reservations unnecessary. No credit cards accepted. Cruz Bay (phone: 776-6070).

Vie's Local to the core, this spot has an ever-changing menu that includes homemade juices, pâté, and tarts. Open for lunch only; closed Sundays,

Mondays, and Fridays. Reservations unnecessary. No credit cards accepted. On the fringes of Coral Bay (phone: 693-5033).

ST. THOMAS

VERY EXPENSIVE

Agave Terrace A delightful terrace room opens on one side to reveal a spectacular view of the Caribbean dotted with a dozen Virgin Islands. Wonderful appetizers include lobster Angelina, pasta Palamero, or gazpacho; fresh seafood is prepared according to the diner's choice. A member of Chaîne des Rôtisseurs. Open daily for dinner only. Reservations advised. Major credit cards accepted. At the *Point Pleasant* resort (phone: 775-7200).

Bay Winds A dining spot that offers fine continental food. Popular dishes include chicken fettucine, grilled lobster, and fried plantain served with lemon grass béarnaise. Don't miss their famous fudgesickle cocktail — a decadent treat made with rum, crème de coconut, crème de banana, and assorted chocolates. Open daily for lunch and dinner. Reservations advised for dinner. Major credit cards accepted. At the *Stouffer Grand Beach* resort (phone: 775-1510).

Café Normandie This small, popular place features French food beautifully presented — beef Wellington, veal, duck, game, local seafood — and a well-chosen wine list. Don't miss the Normandie chocolate fudge pie for dessert. Smoking allowed only at the *Porch Bar.* Open for dinner only; closed Mondays. Reservations necessary. Major credit cards accepted. French Town (phone: 774-1622).

Palm Terrace A luxurious dining room with windows overlooking the ocean; there's no air conditioning, but ceiling fans keep things pretty cool. Besides, you'll be too absorbed in feasting upon grilled breast of duck with foie gras sauce or salmon filet braid with halibut to notice the temperature. Open daily for dinner only. Reservations advised in season. Major credit cards accepted. At *Grand Palazzo,* Great Bay (phone: 775-3333).

EXPENSIVE

Blackbeard's Castle The setting above Government Hill is stunning, with wooden louvers opening to a view of the city and docked cruise ships. Star appetizers include poached jumbo shrimp with fried tortilla strips and *penne* (quill-shaped pasta) with sautéed radicchio and roasted garlic. The poached seafood medallions with saffron-Pernod sauce and grilled New York strip steaks are outstanding entreés, and the richest dessert anywhere must be the flourless chocolate cake with raspberry sauce. Check out the Sunday brunch. Open daily; no lunch on Saturdays. Reservations advised. Major credit cards accepted. Rte. 35, at the top of Blackbeard Hill (phone: 776-1234).

Caesar's Ristorante Just steps from the ocean, this open-air eatery serves wonderful, gigantic portions of tri-colored lobster ravioli and other Italian-style seafood dishes. The cannoli with chocolate mousse filling is a dynamo. Open daily; no dinner on Tuesdays. Reservations advised in season. Major credit cards accepted. At the *Morning Star Beach Club, Frenchman's Reef* (phone: 776-8500).

Entre Nous This elegant place is perfect for a romantic dinner. The bill of fare includes Caesar salad, chateaubriand, and fresh local fish prepared in a variety of ways. Open daily for dinner. Reservations advised. Major credit cards accepted. In *Bluebeard's Castle* (phone: 776-4050).

L'Escargot Offers fine French food and a wine cellar to match. Dover sole, rack of lamb, and chocolate mousse remain favorites. Closed Sundays; no lunch on Saturdays. Reservations necessary for dinner. Major credit cards accepted. The Sub Base, near Crown Bay dock (phone: 774-6565).

Frigate at Mafolie A small hotel terrace with a large reputation for charcoal-grilled steaks, lobster, and local seafood, but known especially for its view. *Frigate East,* a spin-off branch with a similar menu, is across from *Red Hook Marina.* Open daily for dinner only. Reservations advised. Major credit cards accepted. On Mafolie Rd., Mafolie, overlooking Charlotte Amalie (phone: 774-2790) and 18-8 Red Hook (phone: 775-6124).

Hotel 1829 The elegant setting — on a verandah with a view of the harbor or inside this handsome old townhouse — complements the fine food. Try the brie and sun-dried tomatoes in phyllo dough as an appetizer, then veal with lobster medallions and champagne and wild mushroom sauce. The chef also has a delicious way with seafood and Black Angus prime ribs. Save room for the raspberry chocolate soufflé. Open daily for dinner only. Reservations necessary. Major credit cards accepted. Government Hill, Charlotte Amalie (phone: 776-1829).

Tavern on the Beach The current hot spot for regional American fare. Perched above the pounding surf, this romantic place is ideal for sampling such eclectic dishes as roasted Nantucket scallops and grilled salmon served with passion-fruit sauce. Open daily; no dinner on Fridays. Reservations advised in season. Major credit cards accepted. At the *Morning Star Beach Club, Frenchman's Reef* (phone: 776-8500).

Virgilio's An intimate room, it's popular with the business community at lunch. Virgilio himself oversees the preparation of specialties such as fried calamari, veal marsala, fettuccine Alfredo, and osso buco. Open for lunch and dinner; closed Sundays. Reservations advised. Major credit cards accepted. 18 Main St., Charlotte Amalie (phone: 776-4920).

Windjammer The specialties here are fresh seafood and veal dishes. Dolphin, a sautéed seafood platter for two, Wiener schnitzel, and generous-size steaks also are on the menu. Open for dinner only; closed Sundays. Reservations advised. Mastercard and Visa accepted. At Compass Point, off Rte. 32 (phone: 775-6194).

MODERATE

Alexander's Café Delicious Austrian/German fare — Wiener schnitzel, roast pork, strudel, plus pasta and seafood — in a café setting. Open for lunch and dinner; closed Sundays. Reservations advised. Major credit cards accepted. French Town (phone: 776-4211 or 774-4349).

Café Havensight Continental fare served indoors and outdoors, just off the exit from the docked cruise ships. Sandwiches and salads for lunch, stir-fries and steaks for dinner, with smaller portions available for kids. Closed Sundays. Reservations advised for dinner. Major credit cards accepted. At *Havensight Mall* (phone: 774-5818).

Chart House A terrace dining spot featuring an impressive salad bar, beef kebabs, Hawaiian chicken, lobster, prime ribs, fresh fish, shrimp, and sirloin teriyaki. A must-try: the mud pie. Open daily for dinner only. Reservations advised. Major credit cards accepted. Villa Olga, French Town (phone: 774-4262).

Diamond Barrel This eatery is known for its conch and other local fare, plus steaks and seafood. Open daily for breakfast, lunch, and dinner. Reservations unnecessary except for parties of more than six. Major credit cards accepted. 18 Norre Gade, Charlotte Amalie (phone: 774-5071).

East Coast Bar & Grill A sports bar featuring choice beef, fresh fish, chicken, and their famous "Coast Burgers." Open daily for dinner; brunch on Sundays. No reservations. Major credit cards accepted. Red Hook (phone: 775-1919).

Green House This shady terrace right on the waterfront is a great place to cool off when shopping or sightseeing. Burgers, omelettes, salads, and tall frozen drinks are the specialties. A great happy hour spot with live entertainment. Open daily for lunch and dinner. Reservations unnecessary. Major credit cards accepted. On the waterfront, Charlotte Amalie (phone: 774-7998).

El Papagayo Red Hook, the parrot, presides over tacos, enchiladas, and *chiles rellenos.* Open daily; no lunch on Sundays. Reservations usually unnecessary. No credit cards accepted. 126 Annas Retreat, in the garden of Jim Tillett's sugar mill (phone: 775-1550).

Piccola Marina Café This lively open-air spot, which spills right down to the dock of the Red Hook Marina, is a popular stop for boaters. Dinner emphasis is on pasta, served hot with classic sauces (seafood marinara, pesto, Alfredo) or cold in sometimes unlikely combinations. Also good are steaks, fish, and herb-marinated mesquite-grilled chicken. The lunch menu features salads and sandwiches. Brunch is served on Sundays. Open daily. Reservations advised. Major credit cards accepted. 16-3 Smith Bay (phone: 775-6350).

Provence At this harborfront restaurant, country-style French cooking is served in a large but intimate dining room decorated with brightly painted murals on the walls, crisp tablecloths, and candles. The food is simply superb: Begin with one of the tasty appetizers, such as onion soup au gratin, chicken liver pâté, or grilled squid; then move on to the roasted free-range chicken prepared with garlic, the duck cassoulet, or the sauteéd shrimp. A fitting end to the meal is the Chocolate Sin, which lives up to its name. Open daily. Reservations advised. Major credit cards accepted. French Town (phone: 777-5600).

Romano's A popular spot that doesn't advertise, it serves such traditional Italian specialties as veal marsala and osso buco. Open for dinner only; closed Sundays. Reservations advised. Major credit cards accepted. On the road to *Coral World* at 97 Smith Bay Rd. (phone: 775-0045).

Victor's New Hideout Extraordinary seafood dishes are turned out with West Indian flair. Lobster Montserrat is served in a white sauce with chunks of pineapple. For meat eaters, the pork chops marinated in ginger sauce are a must. Open daily; no lunch on Sundays. Reservations advised. Major credit cards accepted. 103 Sub Base, near Crown Bay dock (phone: 776-9379).

Zorba's Chicagoans Jim and Steve Boukas turn out traditional Greek dishes — kebabs, moussaka, lamb specialties — that some consider the best in the islands. The home-baked breads and pastries are also delicious. The setting here recalls the Greek isle of Mykonos. Open for lunch and dinner; closed Sundays. Reservations advised. Major credit cards accepted. 1854 Hus, Government Hill (phone: 776-0444).

INEXPENSIVE

Eunice's Terrace This eatery serves some of the best West Indian food on-island. Menu choices, listed on a blackboard, change daily. Locals love the conch soup and *funghi* (cornmeal dumplings); also broiled fish or roast chicken with tomatoes accompanied by fried plantains and beans and rice. Don't miss the sweet potato pie if it's available. Open daily for lunch and dinner. Reservations unnecessary. Major credit cards accepted. Located next to the *Stouffer Grand Beach* in the Smith Bay area (phone: 775-3975). A second branch, seating 60, is in the Sub Base region at Crown Bay. Called *Eunice's* (phone: 774-4776), it serves similar fare; also inexpensive.

For the Birds Serves ribs and Tex-Mex foods to a mostly young crowd; there's also a children's menu. Open daily for lunch and dinner, and later for dancing. Reservations necessary for parties of six or more. Major credit cards accepted. At Scott Beach (phone: 775-6431).

Sinbad's Garden An informal eatery serving Middle Eastern dishes, plus burgers and sandwiches. Open for breakfast and lunch; closed Sundays. Reservations unnecessary. *Bakery Square,* Charlotte Amalie (phone: 774-2434).

Venezuela's Caribbean Coast

The string of Caribbean islands known as the Lesser Antilles seems to lead inexorably to Venezuela's 1,750-mile Caribbean coast. The Spanish originally followed that trail to Venezuela in the early 1500s, and that's still how many tourists come, looking for a new experience after repeated visits to more familiar Caribbean vacation spots. Yet over the past several years, a growing number of first-time Caribbean vacationers have been lured here by super-affordable travel packages, and if favorable word of mouth continues to spread, even more can be expected.

The Spanish first came to Venezuela for gold and pearls, but the coast itself became even more valuable as a convenient pick-up point for the great wealth that poured from Spain's other New World possessions, and as a base from which to protect its Caribbean holdings. Tourists today come primarily for Caracas, Venezuela's cosmopolitan capital city nestled in a mountain valley less than an hour from the coast; Margarita, the country's best-known island possession; and the increasingly popular beach area of Puerto La Cruz

The first Spanish settlement in the New World was officially founded in 1521 on the site of what is today the town of Cumaná, across from Margarita Island. The coast hardly was enticing: a series of swamps, inlets, jungles, and bays dotted with tiny Indian villages filled with people ravaged by malaria and fever. The Spanish named the country Venezuela — Little Venice — because of the stilt-perched houses of the villages on the shore of Lake Maracaibo. While the coastal Indians were too sick to fight the Spanish invaders, Venezuela's inland mountain tribesmen resisted ferociously, and it took 20 years for the Spanish to establish settlements inland.

From the beginning, the Spanish were obsessed with finding gold. They used conquered Indian tribes as slaves in mines; as the empire grew, they imported African slaves, too. Yet the results were consistently disappointing. Spain also had a voracious appetite for the huge pearls found off Margarita and the mainland coast. So abundant were they that the island of Margarita was named for *margarites,* the Greek word for pearl. Indians were forced to dive several times a day off Margarita, Cubagua, and Cumaná, and if they did not bring back enough pearls, they were punished severely. By the 1530s, the oyster beds had been all but depleted and the Spanish abandoned their efforts.

Venezuela participated in the wars of liberation that swept Latin America from the time of the American and French revolutions until Spain gave

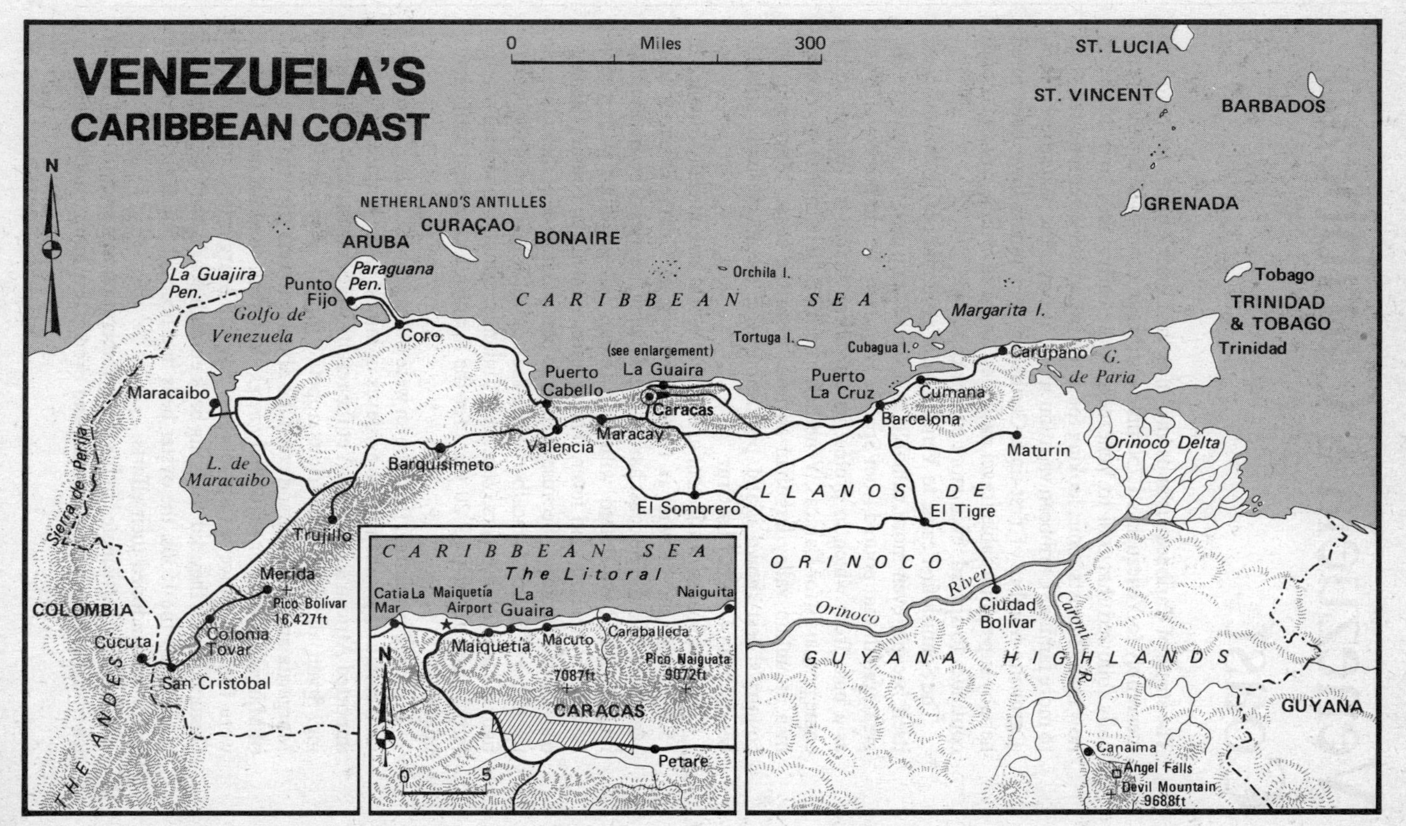

VENEZUELA'S
CARIBBEAN COAST
N
0
Miles
300
ST. LUCIA
ST. VINCENT
BARBADOS
GRENADA
NETHERLAND'S ANTILLES
ARUBA
CURAÇAO
BONAIRE
Orchila I.
Tobago
TRINIDAD & TOBAGO
Trinidad
La Guajira Pen.
Punto Fijo
Paraguana Pen.
Golfo de Venezuela
CARIBBEAN SEA
Margarita I.
Tortuga I.
Cubagua I.
Coro
(see enlargement)
La Guaira
Puerto Cabello
Puerto La Cruz
Carupano
G. de Paria
Maracaibo
Caracas
Cumana
Barcelona
Maracay
Valencia
Maturín
Orinoco Delta
Barquisimeto
L. de Maracaibo
Sierra de Perijá
LLANOS DE
El Sombrero
El Tigre
Trujillo
ORINOCO
Merida
Pico Bolívar 16,427ft
COLOMBIA
Colonia Tovar
Cúcuta
San Cristobal
THE ANDES
Orinoco River
Ciudad Bolívar
Caroni R.
GUYANA HIGHLANDS
GUYANA
Canaima
Angel Falls
Devil Mountain 9688ft
CARIBBEAN SEA
The Litoral
Catia La Mar
Maiquetía Airport
La Guaira
Naiguita
Maiquetía
Macuto
Caraballeda
Pico Naiguata 9072ft
7087ft
CARACAS
Petare
N
0
5

up its New World possessions in 1823. Violent slave rebellions always had been a part of Venezuelan life, but by the beginning of the 19th century, the resentment of the dispossessed classes was fed by the frustration of the Creoles, people of pure Spanish blood born in South America and prevented from participating freely in colonial government. Between 1805 and 1811 a Creole man named Francisco de Miranda led two attempts to take over the Spanish government of Venezuela. When he finally was captured, leadership of the revolt passed to a native Venezuelan who came to be known as the Great Liberator — Simón Bolívar.

Bolívar's wars for the liberation of South America are legendary; he is the Venezuelan equivalent of George Washington. He helped free not only Venezuela, but also Bolivia, Colombia, Ecuador, Peru, and Panama. His dream had been to create a self-governing, democratic republic composed of all those nations — the Republic of Gran Colombia. But his grand alliance never happened; the revolution succeeded, but the newly independent colonies did nothing but squabble among themselves. Bolívar retired to the estate of some friends in Colombia, and there he died, penniless and heartbroken.

The next 100 years were violent and difficult for Venezuela; government changed hands by coup, and the country struggled to become a self-supporting entity. Much of this struggle ended earlier this century. When huge stores of oil were discovered at Lake Maracaibo, the political and economic life of the country stabilized. Since 1959, Caracas has been the seat of a democratic government and has become a sophisticated business-oriented metropolis. Lately, however, concern about government corruption and the lagging economy has spurred social unrest.

Political troubles began brewing in late 1989, when President Carlos Andres Pérez introduced an economic austerity program that caused a series of protest riots. In February 1992, a disgruntled military officer named Hugo Chávez led a handful of men in an unsuccessful coup attempt. Despite his failure and resulting incarceration, Chávez enjoyed a fair amount of public support, and tension continued to build. Later that same year, a second coup was attempted, reportedly engineered by Chávez from his jail cell. This too failed, but several shops in downtown Caracas were looted and government buildings attacked. The most severely damaged structures were Miraflores, the presidential palace, and La Carlota, the small military airport. Despite this continuing unrest, at press time President Pérez planned to complete his term; elections are scheduled for this year.

Today, gold prospectors are still at work, hoping to strike it rich, and oil exportation has made Venezuela the richest South American country. But the true value of Venezuela isn't in gold or even oil; it lies in the country itself, which, as its cities and economy move toward modernization, struggles to protect its forests from the blade of the ax and its beaches from the advance of the bulldozer. The perfect introduction to the complex world that is Venezuela is its Caribbean coast, where everything began.

Venezuela's Caribbean Coast At-a-Glance

FROM THE AIR

The contrasts along Venezuela's 1,750-mile Caribbean coast are startling: sandy beaches, tiny fishing villages, lagoons fed by mountain streams that run down the slopes of the Andes toward the sea, and, just beyond the horizon, uncounted miles of jungles interspersed with open plains. Caracas is in a valley formed by the southern slopes of the coastal range and the northern slopes of the mountains of the central highlands. To the west, in the plains beyond a spur of the Sierra Nevada range, lies oil-rich Lake Maracaibo, the source of Venezuela's prosperity.

Inland, south of the central highlands (which are parallel to the central section of the Caribbean coast), lie the *llanos* of the Orinoco, the grassy plains that make up about a third of Venezuela. From here southward the country becomes increasingly mountainous, and patches of jungle begin to mingle with the forests and plains. This area has proven to be rich in gold, diamonds, oil, and many commercially valuable minerals.

Venezuela occupies a central position on South America's northern coast, bordered by Colombia to the west, Guyana and Brazil on the east and south. Its southern border stretches into the Amazon region, and its 352,150 square miles include Pico Bolívar (Bolívar Peak), which rises more than 16,000 feet above sea level, and the 3,212-foot-high Angel Falls, the tallest waterfall in the world (15 times as high as Niagara Falls).

Caracas shows all the marks of its recent and rapid jump into the 20th century. Large sections of the city have been razed to make way for modern high-rise office buildings, and the installation of the Metro de Caracas (subway) has helped alleviate at least some traffic congestion. However, slums of wooden shacks still line dirt roads in the hills above the city. Of the 20 million residents of Venezuela, roughly 5 million live in Caracas; more than half of the total population is under the age of 19.

SPECIAL PLACES

Until recently, Venezuela's Caribbean coast missed most of the tourist invasion that has overtaken much of the Caribbean; its recent development has been inspired primarily by the influx of oil money and international business. As a result, there wasn't the same emphasis on protecting historical landmarks as in more tourist-conscious countries; nor has there been much development of tourist-oriented amusements. But Venezuelans have realized that their share of the Caribbean tourism boom can help them recover from a sharp currency devaluation and help pay off the country's hefty foreign debt.

CARACAS Simón Bolívar is Venezuela's greatest hero, and almost all of the city's notable landmarks pay homage to the Great Liberator. In the center of the oldest section of town is the Plaza Bolívar, surrounded by government buildings, many of which are renovated colonial homes. In its time, it was the focus of all activity in the colony, the site of revolts against Spanish rule and of executions of revolutionaries by the Spanish governors. Today, under the watchful eyes of the Great Liberator, mounted on horseback in the 1874 statue, *caraqueños* (as residents are called) gather to gossip and discuss the latest news. To the east stands the city's church, a colonial structure granted cathedral status in 1637. The building was nearly demolished by earthquakes early in the 19th century, and large sections were reconstructed in 1876.

A block south and west of Plaza Bolívar is the Capitol, easily distinguished by its gold dome. The building was constructed in 114 days in 1874. The interior is filled with paintings of the country's leaders as well as scenes of the Battle of Carabobo on June 24, 1821 (which solidified the country's independence from Spain). A formal garden at the rear contains a beautiful fountain — itself worth the visit. The Capitol is open to the public from 9 AM to noon and from 2 to 5:30 PM; it's closed on Mondays and on Wednesday and Thursday afternoons when Congress is in session.

Two blocks south of the Plaza Bolívar, at the intersection of San Jacinto and Traposos, is the *Casa Natal del Libertador* (phone: 2-545-7693), the birthplace of Bolívar. The original adobe dwelling was damaged in an earthquake, rebuilt, abandoned, then rescued by a local patriotic organization in the 1900s and restored. The building houses the font in which Bolívar was baptized, his bed, and many paintings by Venezuelan artists depicting the major military campaigns of the War for Independence and other events of the warrior's life. The house is open from 9 AM to noon and from 2:30 to 5:30 PM daily except Mondays. Directly next door is the *Museo Bolívariano* (Bolívar Museum; phone: 2-545-9828), the largest collection of the Great Liberator's war memorabilia ever assembled, including gifts from the Washington family (the two heroes often are associated in South America). The museum is open from 9 AM to noon and from 2:30 to 5:30 PM daily except Mondays.

The *Panteón Nacional,* or National Pantheon, several blocks north of the Plaza Bolívar, at Plaza Panteón, contains the mortal remains of Bolívar as well as those of other national heroes. There is an open tomb in memory of Francisco de Miranda, whose unsuccessful attempts at freedom gave strength to Bolívar's movement. Miranda died in prison; this resting place awaits the body that was never recovered. (*Note:* Venezuelans have an almost religious attitude toward this monument, so dress respectfully when visiting the tomb. In fact, restrained attire is recommended for visits to most of the national monuments and historic buildings in Caracas, particularly those honoring Bolívar.)

Simón Bolívar was given the title of the Great Liberator in 1813 in the Church of San Francisco, which stands at the corner of Avenida Universidad and Avenida San Francisco. Most of the building dates from 1574, and many of the paintings and hand-carved wooden altars are from the 17th century.

The *Museo de Arte Colonial* (Colonial Art Museum; phone: 2-518517 or 2-518650), in the former residence of the Marqués del Toro (also known as the Quinta Anauco), dates from the 17th century and also is highly recommended. It is located on Avenida Panteón, San Bernardino, and is open Tuesdays through Saturdays from 9 AM to noon and from 3 to 5 PM; and on Sundays from 10 AM to 5 PM. Separating Caracas proper from its port town of La Guaira is El Avila, the mountainous national park. La Guaira is the working port familiar to any cruise passenger en route to Caracas. However, the beach resort of Caraballeda, east of La Guaira, is more interesting with its excellent hotels and deluxe resort complexes. The beach facilities of the *Macuto Sheraton* hotel are open to non-guests, and there are also public beaches (for sunning; the water is polluted).

PUERTO LA CRUZ Dynamic Puerto La Cruz has all the ingredients of paradise — a modern city known for its good service and friendly people; an attractive seaside boulevard with outdoor cafés, handicrafts vendors, and benches for people watching; and a number of postcard-perfect beaches blessed with fine sand and crystalline waters. Other excellent beaches, including the fabulous Playa Colorada, are a taxi ride away. You can bargain with one of the local fishermen for a boat outing to otherwise inaccessible pristine beaches, book a yacht tour, or sample the local fish and shellfish dishes at a seaside restaurant. If you simply want to laze around, buy a hammock (*chinchorro*) and string it between two trees; beach vendors will soon appear with ice-cold cans of ever-present Polar beer. Puerto La Cruz is the site of several impressive resorts (see *Checking In*).

MARGARITA ISLAND This getaway spot in the Caribbean Sea, about 30 miles north of the coastal town of Cumaná, is popular with *caraqueños* for its shopping bargains and among foreign visitors for its lovely beaches. Most activity centers around the port area of Porlamar, on the southeast coast, where duty-free shops abound. The beaches near town are not the best, but there are several sandy strands not far away, including Playa El Agua (accessible by bus or taxi), and exploring the rest of Margarita is well worth the time. Or sip a cool rum drink at a local open-air restaurant and stop and chat with the local children; for a small tip, some will recite the history of the area, and even if you don't understand them, the performance is well worth the price. An hour before sunset, hop into your car (or hire a taxi) and head to Juangriego, the fort above the bay, to watch the sun dip into the sea. Then enjoy dinner at one of the bayside restaurants.

Margarita is really two little islands joined Siamese-twin fashion by a long, narrow spit of land that forms the north side of a central lagoon, La Restinga. The curvature of the two islands forms the narrow mouth of the lagoon to the south, whose floor was once lined with pearl-bearing oysters. It's a perfect spot for wetting a line or just drifting. The lagoon is also a refuge for the rare, beautiful scarlet ibis.

La Asunción, the capital of this island-state, contains several colonial buildings, including two 16th-century churches, the Catedral de Santa Ana and the Iglesia de Nuestra Señora de la Asunción.

CUBAGUA On this small island off Margarita's coast are the ruins of Nueva Cádiz, a Spanish settlement that was destroyed by earthquakes and tidal waves in 1541. However, the beaches, the quiet, isolated lagoons and inlets, the fishing, and the water sports are Cubagua's real attractions.

The ghost-town atmosphere here may soon be a thing of the past. A Venezuelan investment group is working on a $4.9-billion development project — the largest ever in the country — that would turn the island into a resort with hotels, nautical clubs, cottages, spas, swimming pools, and recreation areas.

LOS ROQUES The country's most pristine — and remote — beaches are found in this cluster of tiny cays 100 miles offshore from La Guaira. White sand, turquoise waters, and coral reefs await the intrepid sun worshiper who is willing to get to the cays — which have been designated a national park — by plane, chartered helicopter, or yacht. Don't expect any luxuries in this archipelago; be sure that the charter or package you choose includes all meals and drinks. *Aerotuy* has daily service to Gran Roque from Simón Bolívar International Airport at Maiquetía, Barcelona (near Puerto La Cruz), and Porlamar on Margarita. The flight takes 35 minutes. *Aerotuy* offers both day trips and overnight stays in small guesthouses with beach and/or fishing excursions.

Other ways to get to Los Roques include flying via the local air carrier *CAVE* (phone: 2-952-1840); booking a package with a Caracas tour operator such as *Chapi Tours and Fishing* (phone: 2-781-2108) or *Alpi Tours* (phone: 2-283-1433); chartering a helicopter from *Helicópteros del Caribe* at Maiquetía (phone: 31-28217); or calling *Lost World Adventures* in Atlanta, Georgia (phone: 800-999-0558 from the US or 404-971-8586). You can also charter a yacht. Check *The Daily Journal* or inquire at the *Caraballeda Marina* near the *Macuto Sheraton* hotel at El Litoral. It takes 6 to 8 hours of hard sailing against the current, but the return trip is smoother.

ELSEWHERE IN VENEZUELA

COLONIA TOVAR Less than 2 hours from Caracas, the alpine village of Colonia Tovar, built by German immigrants in the 1840s, seems like 19th-century Bavaria. The town is filled with German-style handicrafts and — a surprising sight to those accustomed to seeing darker Latin Venezuelans — a number of blue-eyed, blond residents. Black Forest farmers, carpenters, and masons colonized this area when the Venezuelan government was seeking immigrant workers to labor in the fields. For more than 100 years, the villagers here remained isolated; a road finished in 1963 finally linked them to the rest of the country. Much of the traditional German culture brought by these settlers survives today, although it is rapidly being supplanted by an international, modern way of life. For a taste of the old country, try Freiburg or Selva Negra (Black Forest), the local German-style beers, and perhaps some sauerbraten or wurst.

MORROCOY NATIONAL PARK To the west of El Litoral, 85 miles from Caracas, the cays of this park are idyllic for scuba diving, snorkeling, fishing, and bird watching. The drive takes 2½ hours because of the poor condition of the small back roads; for this reason, most visitors prefer to stay here one or more days rather than visiting the park as a day trip. There are several choices of accommodations in nearby Chichiriviche; the best are the 90-room *Mario,* a full-service hotel with a pool and dining room (on Av. Principal de Chichiriviche between Calles 6 and 7; phone: 42-86114 or 42-86115) and *Náutico,* a rustic 20-room establishment popular with divers (Sector Playa Sur; phone: 42-86024; 2-312953 in Caracas).

EXTRA SPECIAL **Those who really want to escape civilization and are willing to endure a little discomfort should consider a trip to Canaima and Angel Falls. Few things in Venezuela match the sight of these falls. They are 3,212 feet high — 15 times the height of Niagara Falls and two-and-a-half times as tall as the Empire State Building — and they crash down a sheer drop of 2,648 feet past layers of multicolored rock, and then onto the seven lower falls of La Hacha, before creating the calm lagoon that washes the beach. The Gran Sabana, a raised savannah in the jungle with rivers and *tepuís* (flat-topped mountain formations), also is memorable.**

Although the outside world did not learn of the falls until 1935, both the falls and the Auyan Tepuí, the tabletop mountain from which they tumble, have been worshipped by area Indians since prehistoric times. Jimmy Angel, the pilot for whom these falls are named, was hired in 1928 to fly a prospector named Robert McCracken into the jungle and back. On his return, McCracken carried 20 pounds of gold estimated to be worth $27,000. It took Angel until 1935 to locate the area again, and although he never found the source of McCracken's gold, he did discover the falls (which had been so shrouded in mist that Angel hadn't seen them when he was first in the area with the miner).

The area is inaccessible except by plane, and the landing strip is small. Visitors must fly from Caracas to Camp Canaima, run by *Avensa Airlines* (phone: 2-562-3022), and then travel to the falls by canoe and on foot through virgin forest (not an easy trip). The camp's cabins have electricity, running water, and a convenient outdoor restaurant and bar; nearby a pink sand beach, boats, and jungle walks provide diversion. The falls themselves can be viewed by air on the incoming or departing flight, and are an unforgettable sight. *Aerotuy* (phone: 2-717375, 2-716231, or 2-716247) also offers

flights over Angel Falls as part of day tours or in combination with overnight stays at rustic huts owned by area Indians. Bilingual guides accompany tourists on the small propeller planes that fly over the falls, a lunch is included, and arrangements can be made to take an easy hike to the waterfalls and gorge at Kavac Cave. *Aerotuy* flights depart daily from Porlamar (Margarita Island) and other points in Venezuela — Barcelona, Cumaná, Ciudad Bolívar, Puerto Ordaz, and Caracas's Maiquetía Airport.

Sources and Resources

TOURIST INFORMATION

In Caracas, the office of Corpoturismo (Corporación de Turismo de Venezuela), the government tourist bureau, is on the 37th floor of Torre Oeste in Parque Central (phone: 2-574-1513). Hours are 8:30 AM to noon and 2 to 5 PM weekdays. There are branch offices at Simón Bolívar International Airport in Maiquetía (phone: 31-551060, international terminal; 31-551191, national terminal). Tourism officials will answer questions and provide literature as well as make hotel reservations. For information on Venezuelan tourist offices in the US, see GETTING READY TO GO.

LOCAL COVERAGE Of the 11 daily newspapers, only one, *The Daily Journal,* is published in English and is a handy reference for movies, plays, and musical events. Both *The New York Times* and *The Miami Herald* cost about $3 and make their way to newsstands in the larger hotels (usually a day late), as do a number of US news magazines. The biggest local newspapers, *El Diario de Caracas, El Universal,* and *El Nacional,* carry complete coverage of current events.

RADIO AND TELEVISION

Some of the larger hotels receive CNN programming.

TELEPHONE

When calling from the US, dial 011 (international access code) + 58 (country code) + (city code) + (local number). The city code for Caracas is 2; for Caraballeda, 31; for Puerto La Cruz, 81; and for Margarita Island, 95. To call from elsewhere, the access code may vary, so call the local operator. When dialing from one place to another in Venezuela, you must dial the city code (with a zero in front of 1-digit codes) plus the local number. Dial only the local number when calling from within the same city.

ENTRY REQUIREMENTS

A passport, tourist card, and return or ongoing ticket are required for US and Canadian citizens entering the country. Tourist cards are issued by the

Venezuelan consulate, or by airlines serving Venezuela, upon presentation of a current passport. Also, it's helpful if your ticket has a *localizador* number assigned to it; this is a computerized number that speeds processing. There is an airport departure tax of about $16 for international flights.

CLIMATE AND CLOTHES

Although Venezuela is a tropical country, weather is almost entirely dependent upon altitude. At about 3,000 feet, Caracas has one of the finest climates in the world, an eternal spring that requires only light wraps in the evening. In the warm zone — from sea level to about 2,000 feet — temperatures range from the upper 70s (20s C) to the 90s (30s C). The rainy season is from May through November; you'll want to keep an umbrella on hand for sudden showers. If you're thinking of traveling into the mountains, regardless of the season, bring raincoats or ponchos and warm sweaters. Otherwise, summer resortwear is acceptable all year; no-iron polyester-cotton blends are recommended. Caracas tends to be fashionable, and women dress smartly for daytime and evening; a jacket and tie often are mandatory for men in good restaurants and night clubs. At resorts, however, life is more casual, and the jacket/tie rule is relaxed.

MONEY

The monetary unit is the bolívar, written as a B. The fluctuating exchange rate was about 70 Bs to the US dollar at prcss time. Traveler's checks and major credit cards are accepted by most hotels, restaurants, and stores, but converting traveler's checks to bolívars sometimes involves massive amounts of red tape. ATMs are found all over Caracas and credit card advances using the machines (or in banks) are simple. Currency can be changed in banks or *casas de cambio,* change houses. Banking hours are 8:30 to 11:30 AM and 2 to 4:30 PM weekdays; closed Saturdays, Sundays, and holidays. All prices in this chapter are quoted in US dollars.

LANGUAGE

Spanish is the official language of the country, although English generally is understood and spoken in the larger hotels, finer restaurants, and better shops of cities like Caracas, which attracts an international group of travelers. In the rural areas, English is seldom spoken (or understood). Venezuelans are friendly and helpful, and with the aid of a phrase book and some basic gestures, you should get along okay.

TIME

Venezuela is on atlantic standard time. When New York is on eastern standard time, Caracas time is 1 hour ahead. During daylight saving time in New York, the two cities are on the same time.

CURRENT

Electricity is 110 volts, 60 cycles, AC, the same as in North America. No need for converters.

TIPPING

Widespread in Venezuela. A 10% tip usually is included on restaurant bills, but add more if you think your waiter has been especially attentive. Taxi drivers, however, are not tipped unless they help with luggage; bellhops should get about $1 per bag. Attendants who pump gas at service stations should be tipped the equivalent of 25¢.

GETTING AROUND

BUS Caracas buses come in various colors, which indicate the routes they serve, and can take you to almost any part of the city for about 20¢. The buses usually are crowded, however, and bus travel requires a basic knowledge of the city and Spanish. The bus ride from Macuto to Caracas takes 45 minutes and costs about $1.50.

Minibuses called "por puestos" ("by the way" in Spanish) also pick up and discharge passengers along designated routes through Caracas. Most of the city can be reached for about 20¢, but here, also, it is necessary to know Spanish and your way around.

CAR RENTAL The roads in Venezuela are in good condition, and gasoline is incredibly inexpensive. Almost every major rental company is represented here. *Hertz* has offices at Simón Bolívar Airport in Maiquetía (phone: 31-552758, national terminal; 31-551197, international terminal); on the island of Margarita (phone: 95-691274); and in a number of smaller cities. *National Car Rental* has offices at the Simón Bolívar Airport (phone: 31-522777, national terminal; 31-551183, international terminal); at the hotels *Avila, Tamanaco,* and *Eurobuilding* in Caracas; and at the airport on Margarita Island (phone: 95-691171). *Budget Rent-A-Car* has locations in Caracas (phone: 2-283-4333) and on Margarita Island (phone: 95-691047). *Fiesta Car Rentals* in Caracas (phone: 2-781-6965) is a reputable local agency. Rental costs vary according to make of car and agency rates, but figure on about $35 a day with limited mileage, plus gas. Insurance may be included. A credit card will be required. US and Canadian driver's licenses are valid for drivers over 18. Rush hours in and around Caracas should be avoided (7 to 9 AM, noon to 2 PM, and 4 to 7 PM). Also, steer clear of beach traffic on weekends — especially Sunday afternoons. *Note:* Venezuelan driving can be downright hazardous; tourists should be very careful.

FERRY SERVICES The ferry to Margarita Island leaves from Cumaná (3 hours) twice a day and from Puerto La Cruz (4 hours) six times a day, depending on the traffic. Rates are about $7.50 per person and $13 per car. The service is run by *Conferry* (Av. Casanova in Sabana Grande, Caracas; phone: 2-782-8544 for current sailing information). In Porlamar, on Margarita, the firm's office (phone: 95-616397) is opposite the *Bella Vista.* In Puerto la Cruz, call 81-668767; in Cumaná, 93-314262.

METRO It's by far the fastest and easiest way to get to the center of Caracas. Fares vary according to the distance traveled, starting at about 10¢. Operational between Propatria in the west and Palo Verde in the east, the system also runs from El Silencio (where it connects to the principal line) south to the Caricuao Zoo. The subway and metro bus system run daily from 5:30 AM to 11 PM. To avoid long lines at the ticket booth, have coins ready to use in the automatic ticket machines.

SIGHTSEEING BUS TOURS There are many tour operators in Caracas, and most offer similar trips for about the same prices, although each has a favorite or exclusive outing. Let your hotel desk make the arrangements for you, or check tour company ads in *The Daily Journal.* Tours in and around Caracas average about $25. A full-day tour to Colonia Tovar costs about $40.

TAXI More often than not, taxi meters are turned off. If that's the case, negotiate the fare before entering the cab. The minimum charge in the capital is $1, and you should be able to go anyplace in the city for less than $10 (there's a 10% surcharge on Sundays, holidays, and at night). The 45-minute trip to Caracas from the airport costs about $25; you can purchase a ticket for a taxi at the airport at the window marked *Venta de Boletos.* The trip from the airport to El Litoral's Caraballeda resort area costs about $20, and on the island of Margarita the ride into Porlamar from the airport is about $7.

Taxi sightseeing tours with English-speaking drivers are available and are best arranged through your hotel or travel agency. Rates are about $8 an hour.

INTER- AND INTRA-ISLAND FLIGHTS

Venezuela has some 287 airports, including some small landing strips in the far reaches of the jungle and eight international airports. It's a big country, and all of it is served by the domestic carriers *Avensa,* its subsidiary *Servivensa* (phone: 2-562-3022 for both), and *Línea Aeropostal* (phone: 2-573-6511 or 2-575-2511). An especially interesting package is a 2-day excursion to Angel Falls and Canaima for about $200 per person. Due to the easy availability of low-priced fuel, airfares to Margarita and other beach resort areas are inexpensive. The small carrier *Aerotuy* (phone: 2-717375, 2-716231, or 2-716247) also serves Angel Falls and Canaima, plus Los Roques, Kavac, the Amazon, and the cities of Valencia, Ciudad Bolívar, Barcelona, and Porlamar on Margarita Island. *CAVE,* another small carrier, serves Los Roques and other Venezuelan points (phone:

2-952-1842). Charters in Venezuela and the Caribbean can be arranged. *Viasa* and *American* fly from San Juan, Puerto Rico, to Maiquetía's Simón Bolívar International Airport, and *Viasa* connects Santo Domingo, Domincan Republic, and Caracas.

SPECIAL EVENTS

Carnaval takes over parts of Venezuela, with dancing in the streets, costumes, and parades, for the 2 days and nights before *Ash Wednesday*. Caracas virtually closes down during *Semana Santa* (Holy Week). All of the major Roman Catholic holidays are observed, plus *Declaration of Independence Day* (April 19), *Labor Day* (May 1), *Anniversary of the Battle of Carabobo* (June 24), *Independence Day* (July 5), *Bolívar's Birthday* (July 24), *Columbus Day* (October 12), and *New Year's Day*. Remember, too, that practically everything shuts down on *New Year's Eve,* a holiday traditionally celebrated with family parties at home.

SHOPPING

The coast's selection of *típico* handicrafts is wider and less expensive than in Caracas. Margarita Island's duty-free zone has the best buys in liquor, perfume, and gold jewelry. On the coast, there are also fine-quality hammocks (*chinchorros*). Still, Caracas's shopping scene is worth a go-round for the people watching and style sampling in its appealing collection of super-sleek centers and malls. *Centro Comercial Ciudad Tamanaco* (Latin America's largest shopping mall), *Paseo Las Mercedes, Centro Comercial Concresa, Centro Comercial Chacaíto,* and *Centro Plaza* not only showcase all the latest Venezuelan/international luxuries, but shelter dozens of restaurants and nightspots that serve as meeting and greeting grounds. *Centro Comercial Ciudad Tamanaco* (*CCCT*), is the smartest in fashion sense and also is full of eating and entertainment possibilities.

Venezuela produces fine aged rum (*ron añejo*) and coffee; both make excellent gifts. It is also one of the biggest recording centers on the continent and is a great place to pick up salsa and merengue tapes, as well as South American pop music. If you aren't familiar with the artists, ask the record store attendants to play sample tracks — they'll be happy to do it. Throughout the city, costume jewelry, leather bags, and shoes are major bargains. (Keep in mind that some shops will offer a discount if you pay in cash; it's always a good idea to ask.)

The Sabana Grande pedestrian mall offers clothing, music, and jewelry stores galore — plus theaters, clubs, and cafés, including the famous *Gran Café*. (But watch out for pickpockets here.) Caracas shops to explore include the following:

ARTESANÍA VENEZUELA Full of folk art and crafts, including weavings by Guajira Indians and wicker basketry from Orinoco regions. Fine-quality hammocks and the famous painted devil masks worn at the *Feast of*

Corpus Christi in June are sold, along with just about everything else produced by craftspeople across the country. *Plaza Venezuela* (phone: 2-782-6143).

CHARLES JOURDAN/GUCCI Casual and dressy shoes, bags, belts, and wallets from these two famous European sources, at bargain prices. *CCCT* (phone: 2-925405).

LA FRANCIA A 9-story building filled with small jewelry shops — 18-karat gold is a specialty. Most jewelry is sold by weight. There are some real buys here. No credit cards accepted. Off Plaza Bolívar at Esquina Las Monjas.

NARDI High-quality shoes at low prices. *CCCT* (phone: 2-959-2137).

EL TALLER DE LA ESQUINA Venezuelan arts and crafts. A good place to buy gifts. Paseo Las Mercedes, Nivel Galerias (phone: 2-926308)

TREVI Shop here for well-made and well-designed leather purses. Branches in *CCCT* and at *Centro Comercial Chacaíto* (no phone).

SPORTS

BASEBALL The Venezuelan season runs during the US off-season — October through February. Games at the stadium at Universidad Central in Caracas generally are played at night, although afternoon games are held some Sundays and Mondays. Reserved seats are about $2. For information on schedules, either check newspapers or call the tourist office.

BOATING Day coastal cruiser tours are available, starting at around $50, including food and drink. Check *The Daily Journal* ads for packages, stop by the *Macuto Sheraton* marina for rentals, or contact *Alpi Tours* (phone: 2-283-1433 or 2-283-9837) or *Caribbean Nimbus Tours* (phone: 2-310001), both in Caracas.

BULLFIGHTS Traditional Sunday afternoon bullfights are held at the *Plaza de Toros Nuevo Circo* in Caracas (Calles San Martín and San Roques; no phone). Normally tickets cost about $5 for seats in the sun, $10 for shaded areas, but if there's a big-name fighter on the bill, seats can go up to $15.

GOLF In Caracas, your hotel can arrange for you to play at the nearby courses at the *Junko, La Lagunita,* or *Caracas* country clubs. Greens fees start at about $20 (and are whopping for non-members); caddies and club rental (if available) are extra. In Caraballeda, the *Macuto Sheraton* and *Meliá Caribe* have a standing arrangement that enables guests to play on the 9-hole course at the *Caraballeda Golf Club.* The *Tamanaco* hotel can arrange for guests to play at the 18-hole *Valle Arribe* golf course. César Quijada at *Arelys Tours* (phone: 2-828192 or 2-442-6437) can arrange privileges, including greens fees and equipment, at *Junko, Caraballeda,* and, on the eastern outskirts of Caracas in the Federal district, at *Iz-*

caragua. Watch it, César's services rarely come cheap, and arrangements usually start at $100.

HORSE RACING *La Rinconada* in El Valle, Caracas, holds races Saturday and Sunday afternoons, as well as every second Thursday evening. Evening races, beginning at 5 PM, are held on the first Thursday of each month in Valencia. Admission is about $1.50. Check the local papers for details (or call 2-681-3333 in Caracas).

SNORKELING AND SCUBA For independent dives, the cays of Morrocoy National Park or Cubagua Island near Margarita Island, provide the best reefs (see *Special Places*). The *Macuto Sheraton* rents scuba gear and provides guides, as does *Marina Mar* beside the *Sheraton.*

SPORT FISHING Chartering a cruiser for fishing, complete with crew, drinks, lunch, and all the needed gear, for up to six people, will cost between $100 and $175 a day at *Marina Mar* alongside the *Macuto Sheraton* (phone: 31-527097) in Caraballeda. Rates on Margarita are similar, but with the recent growth on the island, some operators are willing to go out for less. Shop around the Porlamar waterfront for the best deal. For sport fishing at Los Roques, try *Chapi Tours and Fishing* (phone: 2-781-2108) or *Lost World Adventures* (phone: 2-717859; 404-971-8586 from Georgia; 800-999-0558 from elsewhere in the US).

SWIMMING AND SUNNING Venezuela's Caribbean coastline provides fine beaches for swimming and lazing in the sun. Just a short drive from Caracas, or a quick hop over the coastal mountains, will put you at El Litoral, as the entire coast is called. The beach at Caraballeda, Caracas's favorite weekending place, is not remarkable, nor is the polluted Catia La Mar. But farther jaunts from Caracas can lead to the lovely, still largely unspoiled Puerto La Cruz to the east and Puerto Cabello and Morrocoy National Park to the west. Margarita Island, just 30 miles from the coast town of Cumaná, literally is surrounded with magnificent beaches. A hundred miles offshore from La Guaira are the pristine, undeveloped cays of Los Roques.

TENNIS Non-guests can arrange to play for a nominal fee at the *Caracas Hilton International* or the *Tamanaco* in Caracas, or at the *Macuto Sheraton* or the *Meliá Caribe* in Caraballeda. Hotel guests are given priority.

WINDSURFING On Margarita, the *Concorde* and the *LagunaMar Beach* hotels provide water sports facilities.

NIGHTLIFE

The best thing about Caracas after dark is its restaurants, which are numerous and excellent (see *Eating Out*). A superb range of plays and concerts is offered at the *Teresa Carreño* complex (across from the *Caracas*

Hilton International; phone: 2-574-9122). English-speaking theater is limited to occasional amateur productions by the *Caracas Playhouse* (Calle Chivaloa in San Román, Caracas; phone: 2-911311). Movies — including week-long foreign film festivals — are cheap and abundant. Check *The Daily Journal* movie guide for listings. *The Daily Journal* also lists local bars, music clubs, and discos, which sometimes admit only couples (no singles of either sex). Some Latins still labor under the impression that women shouldn't go out after dinner, or even for dinner, unescorted, but many restaurants don't agree (check with your concierge). In the city, drinks can be expensive — so keep the running tab in mind to avoid embarrassing finales. Some of the livelier options include *Le Club* in *Centro Comercial Chacaíto* (phone: 2-952-0807); *Magic* in *Las Mercedes* (phone: 2-928704); *New York, New York* in *Centro Comercial Concresa* (phone: 2-979-7745); *1900 My Way* in the *CCCT* (phone: 2-959-0441); and *Madison Puf* (Av. Principal, Bello Campo; phone: 2-331164). Where membership is required, tourists wearing jackets and ties usually can enter by presenting a passport.

Full of French atmosphere, *Montmartre* (phone: 2-93-1060), in the near suburb of Baruta, is an old favorite for more romantic dancing. *La Cota 880* (phone: 2-571-0486), on the *Caracas Hilton*'s top floor, offers two orchestras, continuous dancing, and an incredible view. After dinner, the *Crystal Club* (phone: 2-314973) in La Castellana is worth checking out. At the *Juan Sebastian Bar* (Av. Venezuela in El Rosal, Caracas; phone: 2-951-5575), live jazz starts cooking at about 9:30; from the first note, the place bustles with singles, couples, and jazz lovers in general.

Best on the Coast

CHECKING IN

Hotel and resort prices in Venezuela are not subject to the seasonal fluctuations that are the rule throughout the rest of the Caribbean. However, Caracas is primarily a business center, so prices at the best hotels, though not as high as those of the most luxurious Caribbean resorts, can be steep. Reservations are recommended. The National Reservation System guarantees bookings at more than 300 hotels nationwide (phone: 2-782-8433; fax: 2-782-4407). If you arrive at the airport without lodging, a representative from the Venezuelan Tourism Corporation (Corpoturismo) can assist you. Expect to pay more than $150 for a double room in hotels listed below as very expensive; $80 to $150 in those listed as expensive; $40 to $80 in those listed as moderate; and under $40 in inexpensive places. Telephone numbers listed below include both the city code and the local number. When calling within a city, use only the local number.

CARACAS

VERY EXPENSIVE

Anauco Hilton The more residential of the Hilton chain's two Caracas properties, featuring balconied suites overlooking the city's fine arts neighborhood. There are 317 suites, some 2 stories. Other features include an outdoor pool, 2 restaurants, a bar, and use of facilities at its sister hotel, the *Caracas Hilton International.* Edificio Anauco, Parque Central, El Conde District (phone: 2-573-4111; 800-HILTONS from the US; fax: 2-573-7724).

Caracas Hilton International A very modern 912-room property favored by businesspeople. Features *La Cota 880* nightclub on the top floor and a wide variety of restaurants. Also a pool, tennis courts, a gym, a sauna, and lounges on executive floors. Service, however, is spotty. Av. 25 Sur, near Parque Central, El Conde District (phone: 2-571-2322; 800-HILTONS from the US; fax: 2-575-0024).

Eurobuilding This luxury high-rise features nearly 800 rooms and suites, 3 restaurants, 2 coffee shops, 3 bars, a shopping gallery, a sun deck, a gym, a sauna, and a nightclub. Calle La Guairita in Urbanización Chuao (phone: 2-959-1133; fax: 2-922069).

Tamanaco Inter-Continental One of the best in South America, this 600-room place has both resort and city hotel assets. There's a nightclub, several bars with city views, a pool, tennis, a gym, a sauna, and every hotel service. Av. Principal de Las Mercedes, Las Mercedes District (phone: 2-914555; 800-327-0200 from the US; fax: 2-208-7951).

EXPENSIVE

Lincoln Suites Service is uneven here, but the location can't be beat — the back of the building opens onto the Sabana Grande Boulevard pedestrian walkway, and two subway stops are within walking distance. The 128 units at this all-suite hotel are upscale; ask for a quiet room. There's a restaurant and a bar on the premises. Av. Francisco Solano between Jerónimo and Los Jabillos (phone: 2-728576 through 2-728579; fax: 2-725502).

MODERATE

Avila Small by the standards of either of the *Hilton*s or the *Tamanaco* (only 107 rooms), but pleasantly situated on a hill overlooking the city, this gracious older hotel has a pool, a relaxing piano bar, and plenty of old-fashioned Venezuelan charm. Av. Jorge Washington, San Bernardino (phone: 2-515128; fax: 2-523021).

Continental Altamira Well situated in Altamira, it features 77 rooms, a swimming pool, a restaurant, a bar, and room service. Av. San Juan Bosco, Altamira (phone: 2-261-6019; fax: 2-262-2163).

El Cóndor Next to the Metro in Chacaíto, this up-and-coming 73-room place offers an Italian restaurant and bar. 3ra. Av. Las Delicias de Sabana Grande (phone: 2-729911).

CARABALLEDA

EXPENSIVE

Macuto Sheraton A natural choice for sun worshipers, this 492-room property features 2 pools, all aquatic sports, and a sandy beach. Other bonuses: restaurants, a disco, and nightclub. Service, however, is seldom up to par, and nightly music at the poolside bar can be heard in nearby rooms. On the beach (phone: 31-781-1508 or 31-944300; 800-325-3535 from the US; fax: 31-944318).

Meliá Caribe This link in the famous Spanish chain boasts fascinating indoor architecture; much swankier and sleeker, more tropical and original than the *Sheraton* next door. Set in beautiful gardens, this 290-unit (rooms and suites) property has a pool, water sports, and a sauna; tennis courts and golf privileges in the neighborhood. There are also 3 bars and 3 restaurants (phone: 31-945555; 800-336-3542 from the US).

PUERTO LA CRUZ

EXPENSIVE

Doral Beach Villas A massive resort with 1,312 apartments on the coast at Ponzuelo Bay. Facilities include an 18-hole golf course, tennis, water sports, restaurants, and bars. Av. Américo Vespucio, Complejo Turístico El Morro (phone: 81-812222; 305-759-8071 from the US).

Golden Rainbow Maremares This 500-room resort offers a range of daytime activities, including golf, tennis, and water sports. The hotel's pool is designed like a lagoon banked with foliage. Five restaurants, a dinner theater, 3 lounges, and a nightclub offer a variety of evening choices. Complejo Turístico El Morro (phone: 81-813022; 800-3-GOLDEN from the US).

Meliá Located on the beach, this deluxe 222-unit property has a bar and restaurant, sauna, 2 tennis courts, a pool, a nightclub, and a disco. All rooms have private balconies. Golf facilities are available. Paseo Colón (phone: 81-691311; 800-336-3542 from the US; fax: 81-691241).

Rasil Here are 348 luxurious, air conditioned rooms, a pool, several restaurants, a gym, sauna, tennis courts, and a gallery of shops. Calle Monagas at Paseo Colón (phone: 81-672422; fax: 81-673121).

Vista Real A 112-room hotel, it offers spectacular Caribbean views, a restaurant, and most of the expected luxuries and amenities. Zona Turística El Morro (phone: 81-811721; fax: 81-675058).

MARGARITA ISLAND

EXPENSIVE

Bella Vista Centrally located and relatively modern, this government-owned 321-room property has a disco as well as a bar and restaurant. Insist on a room in the new wing. Av. Santiago Mariño in Porlamar (phone: 95-614831).

Flamingo Beach A luxury hotel with 163 rooms, 2 restaurants, 2 bars, and a disco. The elevated pool gives the impression that it was dropped into the middle of the Caribbean; in fact, a bridge connects the pool area to the sea. There are also facilities for tennis, snorkeling, sailing, and windsurfing. Calle El Cristo, Sector La Caranta in Pampatar (phone: 95-616301; 800-44U-TELL from the US).

LagunaMar Beach The largest hotel on the island, it has 401 rooms, 6 restaurants, 7 pools (including slide and wave), as well as a beach and saltwater lagoon, a spa, and tennis courts. Windsurfers, Sunfish, and water skiing equipment also are available. There is free shuttle service to the airport and to the duty-free shopping areas. Near Porlamar on Via Pompatar, Sector Apostadero (phone: 95-620711; 800-44U-TELL from the US).

Margarita Concorde Towering over a sweep of beach on this simple, sandy island, this 475-room luxury establishment offers a pool, tennis, a marina — and among the best accommodations in town. You may want to dine and dance at its rooftop restaurant/club and savor the view. El Morro Bay in Porlamar (phone: 95-613333).

Margarita Hilton International On the waterfront, there are 280 rooms and 11 suites, all with air conditioning, ocean views, a balcony or terrace, satellite TV, and a mini-bar. There's also a pool, a health club and fitness center, tennis, water sports facilities, 2 restaurants, 2 bars, a nightclub, a cluster of shops, and all the other amenities generally associated with the chain's name. Calle Los Uveros at Playa Moreno, Porlamar (phone: 95-615387 or 95-615822; 800-HILTONS from the US; fax: 95-614801).

MODERATE

Club Cotoperix This intimate, colonial-style inn has 25 rooms. Traditional criollo (Spanish-American) meals, drinks, and local excursions are included in the room rate. Calle El Saco in Urb. La Otra Banda, La Asunción (phone: 95-422674).

EATING OUT

The restaurants in Caracas are excellent, with several superior choices in every culinary category. Expect to pay at least $60 for two at the restaurants listed below as expensive; from $40 to $60 in our moderate range; and under $40 for two at a restaurant listed as inexpensive. Prices don't include drinks, wine, or tips. Eating outside the capital generally costs less. The telephone numbers listed below include both the city code and the local number. When calling within a city, use only the local number.

CARACAS AND ENVIRONS

EXPENSIVE

La Atarraya One of the few truly classy restaurants in the city's center and a great favorite with the governmental elite. Traditional criollo (Spanish-American) menu; *pabellón* (shredded beef, beans, rice, plantains), *cazon* (ground shark meat), *natilla* cheeses with *arepas* (corn cakes), and the house sangria are highlights. Open daily for lunch and dinner. Reservations advised. Major credit cards accepted. Esquina de San Jacinto at Plaza El Venezolano (phone: 2-545-8235).

Aventino Housed in a gracious villa, this spot features a French kitchen and the most extensive wine cellar in the city. The specialty — pressed duck — is considered such an event that every diner who orders it receives a special certificate and his or her meal is recorded in a gold book. Open daily for lunch and dinner. Reservations essential. Major credit cards accepted. Av. San Felipe at José Angel Llamas, La Castellana (phone: 2-322640).

El Barquero The spot for Spanish-style dining with the accent on seafood. It's also known for its *pasapalos* (generous rations of sausage, clams, shrimp, and mushrooms in garlic sauce). Open daily for lunch and dinner. Reservations advised. Major credit cards accepted. Av. Luis Roche at 5th Transversal, Altamira (phone: 2-261-4645).

La Belle Epoque Elegantly French, this dining enclave offers a romantic atmosphere, classic entrées (the trout is especially tasty), and particularly piquant appetizers (*sopa de pesca,* artichoke, asparagus). Music at night. Jackets preferred. Open for lunch and dinner; closed Sundays. Reservations advised. Major credit cards accepted. In Edificio Century on Av. Leonardo da Vinci, Colinas de Bello Monte (phone: 2-752-1342).

El Bogavante A fishing-boat decor and an outstanding marine menu featuring lobster, crab, shrimp, and fresh fish are highlights here. The Italian and Spanish wine list is quite good. Open daily for lunch and dinner. Reservations advised. Major credit cards accepted. Av. Venezuela, El Rosal (phone: 2-718624).

Casa Juancho The menu is Spanish at this large popular establishment in a garden setting. *Especialidad de la casa* is suckling pig. There's live guitar music in the evenings. Open daily for lunch and dinner. Reservations advised. Major credit cards accepted. Av. San Juan Bosco, Altamira (phone: 2-334614).

Da Emore This charming family-run eatery offers a very special variety of Italian dishes on a prix fixe menu. Open for lunch and dinner; closed Mondays. Reservations advised. Major credit cards accepted. In *Centro Comercial Concresa* (phone: 2-979-3242).

Hereford Grill This steakhouse does prime meat to perfection. *Medallón de lomito al oporto* (steak in port) and *pollo deshuasado* Hereford (boned chicken) are special. Open daily for lunch and dinner. Reservations advised. Major credit cards accepted. Calle Madrid, Las Mercedes (phone: 2-925127).

Lasserre Classic French food is served in elegant surroundings. Of special note: the fine cellar of French wines. Open for lunch and dinner; closed Sundays. Reservations advised. Major credit cards accepted. Av. 3, near 3ra. Transversal, Los Palos Grandes (phone: 2-283-4558 or 2-283-3079).

Il Padrino An Italian experience: The place is big, with a fascinating decor — vaulted ceilings, Italian hardwood, Toledo lamps — and an ambience full of music and festive feeling. The vast menu and antipasto selections are worthy of Godfatherly gusto. Open daily for lunch and dinner. Reservations advised. Major credit cards accepted. Plaza Altamira Sur (phone: 2-327684).

MODERATE

L'Arbalette A wide variety of fondues is featured at this new Swiss restaurant in the lovely colonial town of El Hatillo. The decor is charming, and the splendid, panoramic view and luscious desserts combine to make the dining experience pleasant and elegant. Open daily for lunch and dinner. Reservations advised. Major credit cards accepted. Calle Santa Rosalía, Local 34, El Hatillo (phone: 2-963-4718).

Dama Antañona Housed in a beautifully converted colonial home, its original rooms intact, this spot offers a genuine criollo (Spanish-American) menu. Best at midday for business lunches. Open for lunch and dinner; closed Saturdays. Reservations unnecessary. Major credit cards accepted. 14 Jesuitas at Maturín (phone: 2-563-5639 or 2-837287).

Lee Hamilton Steak House A US-style steak and potatoes place, it also serves prime ribs and has an impressive salad bar. Good value, agreeable setting. Open daily for lunch and dinner. Reservations unnecessary. Major credit cards accepted. Av. San Felipe in La Castellana (phone: 2-325227).

El Portón A must on all visitors' restaurant lists: This place is tops for creole atmosphere and cookery. Try the *pabellón* (the national dish of shredded beef with rice and black beans), *lomito con queso* (steak with cheese), or *hallacas* (leaves stuffed with a mix of cornmeal, meats, olives, and onions). The Spanish colonial setting is enhanced by *típico* Venezuelan music. Open daily for lunch and dinner. Reservations advised. Major credit cards accepted. 18 Av. Pichincha, El Rosal (phone: 2-716071).

Seoul Conveniently located, this Korean eatery serves food that is hot, hot, hot. Open daily for lunch and dinner. Reservations unnecessary. Major credit cards accepted. 10 Calle El Cristo, Sabana Grande (phone: 2-762-3222).

ON THE COAST

EXPENSIVE

Timotes Tastefully decorated in colonial style, it is famous for fine criollo seafood; the *sancocho* alone is worth the cab ride from Macuto. The service is pleasant as well. Open daily for lunch and dinner. Reservations unnecessary. Major credit cards accepted. In the *Centro Comercial CADA* in Maiquetía (phone: 31-22618).

MODERATE

Aimara Indoor and outdoor patio dining in a delightfully restored colonial house overlooking the sea; seafood and *típico* dishes are featured. Open daily for lunch and dinner. Reservations unnecessary. Major credit cards accepted. Near both the *Meliá Caribe* and *Macuto Sheraton* hotels. Av. La Playa, Caraballeda (phone: 31-943876).

Cookery An informal spot with an international flavor — scampi, pasta, steaks, and French dishes are specialties. There's an air conditioned dining room, disco and bar upstairs. Open daily for lunch and dinner. Reservations unnecessary. Major credit cards accepted. Near the *Macuto Sheraton,* on Av. Principal del Caribe, Caraballeda (phone: 31-944643).

El Portón de Timotes The younger brother of *Timotes* in Maiquetía, this large, colonial style dining spot has a criollo menu featuring seafood. Open for lunch and dinner; closed Tuesdays. Reservations advised. Major credit cards accepted. Near both the *Sheraton* and *Meliá Caribe,* Blvd. Naiguatá, Caraballeda (phone: 31-22618 or 31-26643).

INEXPENSIVE

Tomaselli Everyone's favorite snack source, here's the place for pizza, burgers, hot dogs, ice cream, the works. Good breakfasts, too. Open daily. Reservations unnecessary. No credit cards accepted. Av. Principal del Caribe, Caraballeda (phone: 31-91832).

MARGARITA ISLAND

MODERATE

Da Gaspar This Italian eatery featuring homemade pasta has a loyal following — no wonder, it's consistently good. It's also the best place in town for seafood. Open daily for lunch and dinner. Reservations unnecessary. Major credit cards accepted. Av. 4 de Mayo (phone: 95-613486).

Martín Pescador Crowded and raucous, this small seafood eatery is nonetheless a great place to sample Margarita's luscious vine-ripe tomatoes; locals say the tomato salad is the best to be had on the island. Open daily for lunch and dinner. Reservations unnecessary. Major credit cards accepted. Av. 4 de Mayo (phone; 95-611120 or 95-616697).

Diversions

Exceptional Experiences for the Mind and Body

Introduction

Few committed sailors, swimmers, or divers can resist the urgent call of the sea, and nowhere in the Western Hemisphere is that voice stronger than in the islands and along the coastal shores of the Caribbean. Traditionally, vacations in the Caribbean are schizophrenic affairs, with periods of the most intense activity — tacking through clusters of tiny land dots in a strong wind; fighting tarpon or, in deeper water, marlin; following the twisting patterns of a coral reef into the depths — redeemed by the unabashed luxury of beachside do-nothingism, sipping cool drinks in the hot sun, enjoying the latest best seller unharried by anything more pressing than a date with some suntan oil.

But the islands of the Caribbean are much more than beaches wrapped around volcanoes and dropped into the sea for the convenience of ocean addicts. Their history is a weltering confusion of languages, cultures, and modes of government. The profusion of influences and peoples strewn throughout the area seems almost profligate. An embarrassment of riches, the Caribbean is as lushly endowed with manmade leisure activities as it is with natural ones. When the pleasures of the water begin to pale and even the most devoted sun worshiper has soaked up enough rays for one day, there are a multitude of other distractions — physical and cerebral — with which to pass the time.

What follows are our choices of the best places in the islands in which to enjoy some unexpected pleasures and treasures — from sampling the islands' most splendid natural wonders to discovering the most fascinating historic sites and the most elegant casinos. In each section, the emphasis is firmly on the quality of experience, doing what you want to do in the best possible environment.

Natural Wonderlands

To most urban dwellers, the island world is one vast natural wonder — a serendipitous embrace of land, sea, and sun that is wide enough to include anyone who ventures into the area. They aren't all that wrong. But even in paradise there are superlatives, and the spots below give a special sense of the islands' splendor.

BARBADOS *The Andromeda Gardens,* overlooking the Atlantic coast, feature an exotic collection of hybrid orchids and other tropical plants in a maze-like, rock garden setting. The 45-acre *Turner's Hall Woods* are all that remains of the primeval forest that once covered the island. It is part of the Barbados National Trust, as is *Welchman Hall Gully,* a botanical ravine about 3 miles from the stalagmites and stalactites of *Harrison's Cave.*

BELIZE *Crooked Tree Wildlife Sanctuary,* just 33 miles northwest of Belize City, is a refuge for thousands of birds and many other varieties of fauna and flora. Visitors may tour the network of lagoons, swamps, and waterways. *Cockscomb Basin Wildlife Sanctuary and Forest Reserve* in southern Belize was set aside by the government of Belize as the first reserve specifically for the protection and management of jaguars. There are many other species here, including the puma, ocelot, margay, and jaguarundi, as well as the Central American tapir and the scarlet macaw. *Guanacaste National Park,* near Belmopan, is home to numerous species of birds, including woodcreepers, woodpeckers, tanagers, toucans, wood thrushes, kingfishers, and orioles. *Half Moon Cay Natural Monument,* a sanctuary for the red-footed booby, is located on the southeastern corner of Lighthouse Reef, Belize's outermost coral atoll. Near Half Moon Cay is the famous *Blue Hole,* formed when the roof of an ancient cave collapsed. *Hol Chan Marine Reserve* covers 5 square miles and is centered around a break in Belize's barrier reef off Ambergris Caye. *Caracol Archaeological Reserve* — a significant Maya excavation site — is located within the *Chiquibul Forest Reserve* of southern Belize. The *Rio Bravo Conservation Area* in northwestern Belize is a part of the proposed three-country "Maya Peace Park." *Las Milpas* is a Maya city within the area that is in the process of being excavated. Information: *Belize Audubon Society,* PO Box 1001, Belize City (phone: 501-2-77369).

DOMINICA Trails have been restored in Edenesque *Morne Trois Pitons National Park,* where giant ferns and bromeliads surround trunks of trees and weave through their limbs, forming latticeworks of foliage that seem to climb to the sky. A water-filled grotto, fed by a waterfall and surrounded by beautiful plants, flowers, and ferns, lies hidden deep within the park. So do three remarkable lakes: Boeri, rimmed with volcanic rock; Fresh Water, with sweeping coastal views; and Boiling Lake, kept bubbling by the volcanic heat of the crater in which it is cupped. The park is at the southeast end of the island; the tourist office or the Forestry Department in Roseau will supply current information on trail conditions, tours, and guides.

Not far from Roseau, in the south-central section of Dominica, is a magnificent area where twin waterfalls, surrounded by tree-covered cliffs, converge in a cluster of rocky ponds studded with ferns and orchids. Near Trafalgar Falls, north and east of Roseau, and in the south of Soufrière, are the *Sulfur Springs,* hot pools of volcanic mud where the earth bubbles and steams like a huge vat of sorcerer's brew.

GUADELOUPE A day's journey to the *Parc Naturel* in the heart of Basse-Terre, now an official national park of France, is not one you are likely to forget. The tropical rain forests, lakes, waterfalls, natural mountain pools, steaming fumaroles, and the well-marked trails make this one of the loveliest hiking spots in the Caribbean. There is an excellent booklet, *Walks & Hikes,* which lists 18 trails in the park with maps and difficulty ratings. You can obtain it from the tourist office or the *Organisation des Guides de Montagne* in Basse-Terre (phone: 590-800579).

JAMAICA Off the main road from Kingston to Ocho Rios, on Route A-3, a 3-mile stretch of road winds down an old riverbed surrounded by giant ferns. This stretch is called *Fern Gully,* a deep forest area that offers a taste of cool air and an opportunity to ride beneath the tall ferns — the first complex plant life to populate the island.

While driving along a 2-mile stretch of road in St. Elizabeth Parish, close to Black River, you suddenly feel surrounded by something that looks like a soft yellow-green feathery umbrella or veil. You are driving through *Bamboo Avenue,* a continuous arch of feathery bamboo that seems to appear out of nowhere. To reach this avenue you pass through Holland Estate, a former sugar factory.

PUERTO RICO *El Yunque* is a 28,000-acre tropical rain forest and national bird sanctuary where you will see more than 250 different species of native trees, many primeval. While wandering beneath a towering pine or sierra palm you might catch a whiff of white ginger or find a wild orchid as you hear the call of the coqúi, the tiny tree frog that is Puerto Rico's official mascot. Be on the alert, for there are many delicate, beautifully colored wildflowers that hide behind, beneath, and around the more conspicuous trees and shrubs. Although more than 100 billion gallons of rain fall in the forest annually, the showers are usually short, and the park provides adequate shelter for visitors caught in a downpour. On Route 191 there's the Sierra Palm Visitors Center, where you can obtain information or guides. The park is about 25 miles east of San Juan via Route 3, then south on Route 191.

TRINIDAD If you arrive at the *Caroni Bird Sanctuary* at sunset or late afternoon, you might see a large cluster of bright red feathers swooping through the sky like a gigantic flame. Within moments, hundreds of scarlet ibis (Trinidad's national bird) descend onto the 450-acre sanctuary, where they live and nest amid vast stretches of mangrove trees. The inner sanctuary of Caroni, where the birds nest, is open to the public from May to October;

the rest of the sanctuary stays open all year. If you arrive during the fall, you might find a sea of red mangroves that match the feathers of the birds they house. The sanctuary is about 7 miles south of Port of Spain.

US VIRGIN ISLANDS About two-thirds of the island of St. John is a natural haven. In fact, there is little to do on the island but enjoy the scenery, particularly the *Virgin Islands National Park.* Don't hesitate to ask the rangers to fill you in on the flora and fauna that abound in the park — pelicans and sandpipers, mahogany and bay, tamarind, flamboyant, and shower of gold are among the native inhabitants you are likely to run across. Park guides also lead nature walks and give nature talks several times a week.

VENEZUELA The highest waterfall (and one of the most beautiful) in the world lies deep in the Venezuelan jungle and is called Angel Falls, after the American pilot Jimmy Angel, who discovered it in 1935. Approximately 3,212 feet high (15 times as tall as Niagara), the falls are most often seen during a breath-catching flight en route to *Avensa Airline*'s Canaima camp/resort or Kavac, the Pemón Indian camp, in the Venezuelan interior. Steeped in swirling mists and rainbows, the falls tumble down layers of multicolored rock to the jungle floor. They also can be reached by a fairly arduous walking-canoeing trip from the comfortably simple cottage resort at the edge of Canaima lagoon — itself fed by a spectacular ring of seven falls. But most guests prefer shorter treks, swimming, or relaxing in the immensely beautiful jungle surroundings. For details on getting there and available accommodations, see *Venezuela's Caribbean Coast* in ISLAND-BY-ISLAND HOPPING.

Testaments in Stone: Historic Sites

With the exception of the ancient Maya and Toltec ruins of Mexico and scattered Indian relics, most historic sites of the Caribbean and Atlantic islands date from the colonial period after the arrival of Columbus. These sites reflect the course of European colonialism in the New World — the presence and influence of the French, English, Dutch, and Spanish on the islands, and the struggles for control.

ANTIGUA *Nelson's Dockyard* was the major British naval yard in the Caribbean from 1707 until 1899, when ships simply became too large to negotiate the entrance to its harbor. It got its name (and its reputation) from the 4-year period (1784–87) when Captain Horatio Nelson was in command. The dockyard area includes the *Admiral's Inn,* a hotel and restaurant made from bricks that came to Antigua as ships' ballast; the *Admiral's House* (now a museum), which never actually housed Admiral Nelson; the Officers' Quarters; and the *Copper and Lumber Store,* now a hotel.

BARBADOS Some of the finest antique greathouses in the Caribbean can be found on Barbados. *Villa Nova, Porters, Mullins Mill, Drax Hall, St. Nicholas Abbey,* and *Francia* are all elegantly preserved and occasionally or regularly open to the public; check with the tourist board or the Barbados National Trust. *Farley Hill* and the *Morgan Lewis Mill* are also relics of the old plantation days.

CURAÇAO *Mikve Israel-Emanuel,* the oldest synagogue extant in the Western Hemisphere, is in Willemstad on the corner of Columbusstraat and Kerkstraat. Built in 1732 in the Dutch colonial architectural tradition, the interior is carpeted with a layer of white sand, symbolizing the journey of the Jews across the desert to the Promised Land. Next door is the *Jewish Historical and Cultural Museum,* which served as a rabbinical house and, later, a Chinese laundry, until the remains of an ancient *mikvah* (ritual bath) were uncovered in its courtyard. The museum contains exhibits of centuries-old religious relics, tools, and artifacts. Open weekdays from 9 to 11:45 AM and 2:30 to 5 PM. Admission charge (phone: 5999-611633).

DOMINICAN REPUBLIC As a center of activity in the gold-hunting days, Santo Domingo became a city of elegant living. All along the Calle Las Damas in old Santo Domingo you will find buildings from these gilded days — the *Bastidas House,* the *Chapel of Our Lady of Remedies,* the *Museum of the Royal Houses,* and others. Also on Calle Las Damas is the *National Pantheon,* formerly a Jesuit monastery, built in 1714.

The oldest cathedral in the Western Hemisphere is the *Cathedral of Santa María la Menor,* also in Santo Domingo. Its 450-year-old nave once housed what are said to be the mortal remains of Christopher Columbus (the reputed remains have since been moved to the Columbus Lighthouse Monument). It is on the south side of Columbus Square.

HAITI Perhaps the most astounding single spectacle in the Caribbean is the *Citadelle,* on a remote mountaintop more than 3,000 feet above the sea. This amazing structure, with its 12-foot-thick walls, required the labor of 200,000 citizens, all former slaves and all conscripted by King Henri Christophe to drag thousands of tons of rocks and hundreds of cannon up the tortuous road to build a fort that would protect him and his court from an anticipated invasion. Although the journey, made partly on muleback, may take its toll in bottom-bruising, the monumental site itself is worth it. Before starting the climb, explore the ruins of King Henri's *Palais de Sans Souci,* intended to be the most regal building ever raised in the New World. The *Citadelle* and *Palais* are near the town of Milot, a short drive from Cap-Haïtien. Both were recently restored.

JAMAICA Across the harbor from Kingston, *Port Royal* was called "the world's wickedest city" while it served as headquarters for the privateer (pirate) Henry Morgan. Although a good part of the town was toppled into the harbor by a treacherous tidal wave and earthquake in 1692, several remnants from those ribald days remain intact, including *St. Peter's Church, Fort Charles,* the old *Naval Hospital* (now a museum of Port Royal relics), and the *National Trust Tower.*

MARTINIQUE *La Pagerie,* in Trois-Ilets, was once a busy plantation and thriving sugar factory. It was also the birthplace of Marie-Josèphe Rose Tascher de la Pagerie, who became the Empress Josephine, wife of Napoleon. Her childhood bed, clothes, and letters are on display in the kitchen, which occupies a separate building beside the crumbled plantation house foundations. Closed Mondays. Admission charge (phone: 596-683455).

Another site worth visiting is the town of *St. Pierre,* "the Pompeii of the West Indies," which was devastated by a volcano in 1902. What remains of this once-flourishing city of stately villas, mansions, and gardens are the ruins of the theater and cathedral and the broken walls of the homes.

MEXICO *Chichén Itzá* was a flourishing Maya and Toltec center that dominated the entire Yucatán Peninsula until 1224. Many of the ruins at this major archaeological site reflect the bellicose nature of the Toltec culture — including the ritual practice of human sacrifice. Among those buildings of particular interest are the *Temple of the Warriors,* the *Group of a Thousand Columns,* the *Tzompantiti,* the *Temple of the Chac-Mool,* and the ball court. Bus tours from Cancún and Cozumel visit the site daily. *Tulum,* a walled seaside city-fort, and *Cobá,* a jungle city that is still being excavated, are two other Maya centers near Cancún and Cozumel; a number of tour operators offer half- or full-day excursions to the sites.

PUERTO RICO The 7-block-square area of Old San Juan, in the westernmost part of the city, contains myriad interesting sites dating back to Spanish colonial days, when this harbor was considered essential to Spanish supremacy in the New World. Today, you can still explore the moats, turrets, and tunnels of *Fuerte San Cristóbal* and *El Morro,* the two forts that were part of the wall built around the city to protect it from unfriendly visitors like Sir Francis Drake. Two blocks from El Morro's exit, at the Plaza de San José, you will find the *Church of San José,* and heading west on Calle San Sebastián, you will reach *Casa Blanca,* the intended home of Juan Ponce de León, which served as the residence of his descendants and several Spanish and American military commanders before it was turned into a museum. Nearby is *La Fortaleza,* the Western Hemisphere's oldest executive mansion, the home of more than 200 Puerto Rican governors. Built in 1540 and given palatial additions in the 19th century, it is open to the public for guided tours. *La Casa del Libro,* an 18th-century house, contains thousands of ancient books. Farther on, *La Princesa,* the restored 1837 prison, mounts changing art exhibits.

ST. KITTS The landmark that gave St. Kitts its reputation as "the Gibraltar of the Caribbean" is *Brimstone Hill.* On top of a 750-foot cliff, this enormously impressive fortress took the British more than 100 years to build. Although the French captured Brimstone Hill in 1782, the fort returned to British hands, as did the island, under the conditions of the Treaty of Versailles in 1783.

US VIRGIN ISLANDS In the heart of Christiansted on St. Croix stands a group of 18th-century buildings that the Danes built after buying St. Croix from the French. The US now maintains this area as a National Historic Site. At the Visitors' Information Bureau in the Old Scalehouse near the harborfront, you can pick up a *Walking Tour Guide. Fort Christiansvaern,* which contains military treasures, battlements, and dungeons, is one of the site's attractions with particular appeal to children.

Sunken and Buried Treasure

It doesn't take too much imagination for a Caribbean vacationer to begin dreaming about discovering sunken or buried treasure. The area is alive with tales and relics of pirates, Spanish gold, sunken ships, and yellowed parchment maps that seem to cry out for some adventurous diver or explorer to dig deeper, look further, dive farther offshore — and discover a wealth of gold and precious stones. Estimates of the number of ships sunk in the Caribbean and western Atlantic are as high as 4,000; in the Anegada Channel of the British Virgin Islands alone, some 134 ships are supposed to have gone down between 1523 and 1833.

The Spanish kept excellent records of the treasure ships transporting the wealth of the New World across the Atlantic and Caribbean. The cargo manifest of a single ship, the *Nôtre Dame de Déliverance,* shows 1,170 pounds of gold bullion (packed into 17 chests), 15,399 gold doubloons, 153 gold snuff boxes weighing 6 ounces each, more than a million pieces of eight, 764 ounces of silver, 31 pounds of silver ore, 6 pairs of diamond earrings, a diamond ring, and several chests of precious stones.

Bear in mind that most of the ships that went down during this period either ran aground or tore out their bottoms on the numerous coral reefs that lie just beneath the surface of the water. Those treasure-laden ships sent to the bottom by pirate cannon fire (or pirate ships sunk by other vessels) were a total loss to all involved. Many of the ships that were sunk by enemy fire were warships or light cargo and messenger packets, not huge treasure galleons. Tides and sifting sands can cover a ship or move the wreck miles from its original site. These same tides can cause lost treasure to rise to the surface, too, as in the case of the woman who happened upon an estimated $100,000 in gold and diamond jewelry, gold, silver, and platinum on Grand Cayman Island some years ago.

What follows is a list of the best treasure-hunting spots in the Caribbean; we ask only a modest percentage of your findings as recompense:

BELIZE Originally a colony of shipwrecked pirates, with the world's second-longest barrier reef just off its well-traveled coastline, there is every reason to believe that more than one wreck lies among these treacherous shoals. Try the area just outside the reef. Prior permission by the Archaeology Commission, Belmopan, Belize (phone: 501-8-22106) is required for any excavations.

BRITISH VIRGIN ISLANDS Robert Louis Stevenson's *Treasure Island* is based on activities rumored to have taken place on Norman Island or Dead Chest, both near Tortola, which was a pirate stronghold for quite some time. Also check both Anegada and Virgin Gorda as well as the Anegada Channel between them; the channel is known to be the site of over 130 wrecks. Waters of any of the surrounding isles could hold sunken cargo.

CAYMAN ISLANDS As local legend has it, during a dark night in November 1788, a convoy of British merchant ships was sailing to the east of Grand Cayman. Due to the inaccuracy of the navigating charts in those days — and the coral reefs that lie just beneath the surface — this was a particularly hazardous route in these treacherous waters. The lead ship, the *Cordelia,* struck a reef and raised flags of warning and distress. The other ships misunderstood the signal in the darkness, and nine more ships struck the reef before anything could be done. Many of the passengers (one rumored to be royal) were rescued by the residents of the island's East End area. The fluke of an anchor, said to be a relic of this Wreck of Ten Sails, can be seen today from land, but the reef is known to be infested with sea urchins (which effectively prevents much treasure hunting there). In addition to the jewelry found on the beach here, a platinum bar (dated 1521) was recovered from a shipwreck just off Grand Cayman.

COLOMBIA Morgan would have been one successful pirate if he really buried treasure on all the islands that claim to be the site of one of his hidden fortunes. But because it is strategically located between the old Spanish treasure ports of Porto Bello and Cartagena, San Andrés Island is a likely possibility. The odds are even better on adjacent Providencia Island or on one of the others around San Andrés.

DOMINICAN REPUBLIC and HAITI In the opening days of Spain's presence in the Americas, the city of Santo Domingo (Dominican Republic) was its Caribbean headquarters. Explorers departed from here on their quests for gold and silver, and ships put in here before journeying to Spain. Ships leaving the port city (on the southern crescent of the island) had to pass through the narrow passages at either end of the island in order to return to Spain. If they passed through the Windward Passage to the west end, they had to skirt the reefs and shallows around the Caicos Islands and pass through the Mouchoir (Silver) Bank (northeast of Hispaniola) before heading for the open sea. Once through the eastern channel (Mona Passage), they were in open waters. Ile de la Tortue, off the northwest side of the island (now

Haiti), made a perfect hiding place for pirates and could easily be the legendary stronghold of Tortuga. From here they watched the western passage, and if a prize should make for the sea through the eastern channel, a pirate ship could be dispatched from the island to intercept a treasure-laden galleon before it made open water. Ile de la Tortue itself is a good place to look for buried treasure, and there have been reports of wrecks near Silver Bank. The wreck of the *Concepción,* discovered here late in 1978, carried about $40 million in silver and antiques. Some of the pieces may be found for sale at Dominican museums and jewelry shops.

JAMAICA On June 7, 1692, an earthquake and tidal wave hit the island of Jamaica, and the city of Port Royal literally sank beneath the waves. Long before the city was flooded, it often had been compared with the biblical Sodom, for there was one tavern, alehouse, or winery for every ten people. During the 1960s, divers brought up hundreds of pieces of silver, pewter, and ceramics, and enough ethnographic evidence to prove Port Royal's rightful claim to being the former center of sin in the West Indies. The remains of this lively city have been picked through by many divers, but something new is always being brought to the surface. There are also reports of several wrecks off Negril, and records show that six ships went down in Montego Bay (1780). The Seranilla Bank, about 250 miles southeast of Jamaica (about halfway between Jamaica and the coast of Honduras), is reputed to be where an entire Spanish treasure fleet went down during a hurricane in 1655.

ST. EUSTATIUS The Dutch pirates were as successful at sea as the Dutch merchants were on land; with financial encouragement from the Dutch West Indies Company (which bought plundered goods for resale), Dutch pirates managed to take a goodly number of Spanish (and other) ships. The entire yield of one successful 1717 expedition, estimated at 1 million pieces of eight, was placed in a cave on Statia for storage; later, the mouth of the cave was sealed by an earthquake and the treasure has never been recovered. The *Zeelander,* a Dutch warship, went down off the northern tip of the island in 1792 carrying 500,000 guilders in gold and silver with it.

ST. MARTIN/ST. MAARTEN The Portuguese galleon *Santissimo Trinidade,* carrying some 2.5 million cruzados in gold, is believed to have been lost off the eastern coast of St. Martin in 1781.

Shopping

There are three distinct kinds of shopping opportunities available in the Caribbean: *duty-free* (or almost), wherein imported goods are offered at relatively low prices because they are not taxed (or taxed at a very low rate) as imports; *in-bond,* where specified goods are sold to tourists as if the merchandise had never entered the vending country and where delivery is usually made to your departing plane or ship; and what can be called *"limited duty-free,"* whereby the island does not tax imports from its mother country, although goods from other countries are charged an import tax. This means that on British islands, English goods will be cheaper than the same brands in the US (which taxes foreign imports); French goods on French islands always represent bargains and in some cases are actually cheaper than the same goods available in France.

In addition, there are fine stores and boutiques as well as native markets for browsing. The markets are marvelous places to meet and mingle with local people, absorb atmosphere, tune your ear to the island's patois, bargain for crafts and homemade treats (mango chutney, hot sauce, preserves), and — not incidentally — have a great time. Remember that market dealing in the islands is done on the spot, and you should feel free to haggle a little for the price's sake and for the fun of it. Local vendors enjoy a friendly negotiation, and while they will take your money for the price asked, everyone will have a better time engaging in the close, good-natured give-and-take of striking a final price. A few islands produce mostly straw and shell work, but on Jamaica, Haiti, Puerto Rico, Barbados, the Dominican Republic, and the Dutch islands, there is a rich choice of fine European and Asian imports and/or colorful native fashions, crafts, and art. For detailed information on the best places to shop in the Caribbean, see the *Shopping* entries in the individual island reports in ISLAND-BY-ISLAND HOPPING.

In general, customs regulations allow US citizens to bring home $400 worth of goods for personal use duty-free (with a limit of a liter of liquor, 1 carton of cigarettes, and 100 cigars). However, the allowance is more generous for travelers returning from certain Caribbean destinations. For example, the duty-free allowance for those returning from the US Virgin Islands is $1,200, including five fifths of liquor per person; there is a $600 limit for travelers returning from the following islands: Antigua, Aruba, Barbados, Belize, Dominica, the Dominican Republic, Grenada, Haiti, Jamaica, Montserrat, the Netherlands Antilles (including St. Maarten), St. Kitts and Nevis, St. Lucia, St. Vincent and the Grenadines, Trinidad and Tobago, and the British Virgin Islands.

If you have already used part of your exemption within the past 30 days, or if your trip is less than 48 hours long, the duty-free allowance is cut to $25 (with a limit of 10 cigars, 50 cigarettes, and 4 ounces of perfume). Families traveling together may make a joint declaration to customs; this permits a family member to exceed his or her duty-free exemption to the extent that another family member falls short. An across-the-board duty fee of 10% (5% from the USVI) is levied on the next $1,000 worth of goods above the duty-free level. Beyond that amount, fees vary; consult the *Tariff Schedules of the United States* in any library or US Customs office.

You also can mail home an unlimited number of gifts individually valued at $50 or less ($100, from the USVI), but no more than one per day to any single recipient. These must be marked "Unsolicited Gift," with value and item listed on the outside of the package. More information on mailing packages home from abroad is contained in the US Customs Service pamphlet *Buyer Beware, International Mail Imports* (see GETTING READY TO GO for details about where to write for this and other useful brochures).

Antiques purchased abroad are duty-free (you must have written proof of that fact from the seller), as are paintings and drawings done entirely by hand. In addition, you are allowed to bring crafts and handmade goods into the US duty-free from a number of Caribbean countries and dependencies under the Generalized System of Preferences (GSP), a program established to encourage local industries in developing countries. Virtually all the islands and countries covered in this book are GSP beneficiaries, with the exception of the French West Indies and Venezuela. The list of eligible goods includes the following categories: baskets and woven bags; cameras and other photographic equipment; candy; china and silverware; cigarette lighters; earthenware; some furniture; games and toys; golf and ski equipment; some jewelry, unset precious or semi-precious stones and pearls; jewelry and music boxes; musical instruments, radios, tape recorders, records, and tapes; paper goods and printed matter; perfume and toilet preparations; electric shavers; items made of cork, jade, or shell (other than tortoiseshell); wigs; and woodcarvings. *Note:* Federal laws prohibit the import of certain articles into the US, including the furs or hides of animals on the endangered species list. For more information, see GETTING READY TO GO.

Horse Races

There are only four places in the whole Caribbean where a bookie stands a chance of making an honest living: Puerto Rico, the Dominican Republic, Venezuela, and Jamaica — all of which schedule flat racing on a regular basis. There's pari-mutuel betting at all four; the time-honored British tote-board system also operates at Jamaica's *Caymanas* track. On other islands where racing exists, though there's all kinds of formal and informal betting, it's a long time between meetings. And when they are off and running — once a month or four times a year — the scene is much more like a county fair and/or a big barbecue than the ritualized proceedings at *Belmont* or *Churchill Downs.* Racing fans don't just watch, they *participate* — snacking, tippling, betting, gossiping, and toe tapping to steel bands and calypso (they probably have more fun than the toffs in the boxes). By all means go to the track if you get a kick out of racing, wherever you find it. But if there's island-style racing, go — even if you never follow the ponies back home. Odds are, it'll be a great party.

CONVENTIONAL RACES

DOMINICAN REPUBLIC The *Hipodromo Perla Antillana* in Santo Domingo has races on Tuesdays, Thursdays, and Sundays, all year. The track is in town near the *Quisqueya* baseball stadium.

JAMAICA There's racing at *Caymanas Race Track,* Kingston. Races are held every Wednesday, Saturday, and some holidays; check newspapers for times.

PUERTO RICO *El Comandante Race Track* is a modern track about 45 minutes from downtown San Juan on Route 3. It has 18,000 seats and an attractive restaurant. Races are held Wednesdays, Fridays, Sundays, and holidays at 2:30 PM.

VENEZUELA *La Rinconada* in Caracas runs day races every Saturday and Sunday afternoon and the second Thursday evening of the month. The first Thursday of each month there's racing at Valencia starting at 5 PM.

THE PARTIES

BARBADOS The *Barbados Turf Club* holds race meetings on alternating Saturdays during the island's two racing seasons — from January to April and from August to November — on the *Garrison Savannah* in Christ Church. Thoroughbred horses are not the only attraction — there are also steel bands, food and drink stands, and a pervasive party atmosphere. Meets usually start at 1 PM and end about 6 PM.

BRITISH VIRGIN ISLANDS There are holiday and *Festival* (last week of July, first week of August) meets at the Tortola track, with informal betting, music, food, and fun. See the *Welcome Guide* and the local paper for dates and times.

US VIRGIN ISLANDS The activities at the *Flamboyant* racetrack in Frederiksted on St. Croix are usually flamboyant. Although the event is organized, few horses bear the certified markings or demeanor of a purebred. But the races are always entertaining and amusing, especially when accompanied by lively reggae, rock, soul music, and abundant refreshments. Races are held twice a month, usually on Sundays — check local papers for exact times. Over on St. Thomas, races at the *Estate Nadir Track* are similar to those on St. Croix — amusing and lively, with down-home horses, good music, and plenty of food and drink. Check the local paper for monthly date, time.

Casino Countdown

Island gambling takes one of two forms: action or distraction. The presence of junkets (trips organized to deliver high rollers to the tables by the planeload) and several casinos (rather than just one or two) usually indicates serious play. Otherwise, it's lowercase stuff — something to do with your evenings in town besides eating, dancing, or watching another island floor show.

Only 13 island countries offer casino gambling. In these, certain generalizations apply: Basic games are roulette, craps, and 21 (or blackjack). The minimum bet is $2 (exceptions: baccarat tables, where the stakes are usually *big,* and Haiti and Colombia, where $1 qualifies), but this can vary slightly (with the designation of certain $5 tables, for example) according to the night, the crowd, and who's in charge. Most islands prohibit their own nationals from gambling, but tourists aren't stopped at the door or charged admission except on the French islands, where they're very serious about rules. (There, you must have identification with a photograph that proves you are 21 — everywhere else, it's 18 — and there is a 50- to 80-franc admission charge.) Once inside, there may or may not be drinks (which may or may not be free to players).

Judged by breadth of equipment, intensity of action, and the proportion of tourists who list casinos among their prime reasons for choosing a particular destination, Puerto Rico and Aruba are the islands' top gaming spots; Curaçao, St. Maarten, and St. Kitts — all of which attract some junkets — come next; then the French islands, where interest seems to be growing even though there is no junket traffic. These are the best bets:

ANTIGUA There are four casinos: one at the *Ramada Renaissance,* one at the *Halcyon Cove Beach Resort* at Dickenson Bay, one at the private *St. James's* on Mamora Bay, and another at *King's Casino* in Heritage Quay. There is considerable junketing. Baccarat and backgammon are played in addition to usual games. Players buy their own drinks. Hours: 9 PM to 4 or 5 AM.

ARUBA The island's big tourist parlay is a combination of beaches and casinos at the major Palm Beach hotels: *La Cabaña All Suite Beach* (with the largest gaming facility in the Caribbean), the *Golden Tulip Aruba Caribbean,* the *Aruba Palm Beach,* the *Americana Aruba,* the *Aruba Concorde,* the *Hyatt Regency Aruba,* the *Sonesta Beach,* and the *Holiday Inn,* several of which have adjacent cabarets in season. There's also the *Harbour Town* casino in downtown Oranjestad, and the *Alhambra* (part of an entertainment complex), where betting limits are low and the atmosphere, pleasantly relaxed. Frequent junkets are available. Drinks are free while you play; people under 18 are not admitted. Hours: 1 PM until 4 AM.

BONAIRE There's a "Barefoot Casino" at the *Divi Flamingo Beach.* More casual fun than real glitter; junkets are not encouraged. Drinks are free for players; people under 18 not admitted. Hours: 4 PM until 3 or 4 AM.

COLOMBIA'S CARIBBEAN COAST The *Casino del Caribe* in Cartagena's *Pierino Gallo Shopping Center* has one room devoted to slot machines and another for roulette and blackjack. Minimum table bets are 700 pesos (about $1). Casino hours are from early evening to 3 AM. Stakes start at $1 on San Andrés at the *Casino Internacional* and *Casino El Dorado–Monte Carlo.* No jackets are required, and the hours are 9 PM to 3 AM.

CURAÇAO The chicest crowds play at the plush-lined *Princess Beach* casino; there are also active gaming rooms at the *Holiday Beach,* the *Curaçao Caribbean,* the *Holland* hotel, the *Sonesta Beach,* the *Otrabanda,* the *San Marco* hotel, and the *Van der Valk Plaza* (formerly the *Curaçao Plaza*). There is also a small casino at the *Las Palmas* hotel. This island is one of the few Caribbean spots where you can lose your blackjack boodle to machines. Junkets are allowed. Players get free drinks. Hours: noon to 4 AM.

DOMINICAN REPUBLIC *Naco, El Embajador,* the *Ramada Renaissance Jaragua,* the *Sheraton,* the *Hispaniola,* the *Lina,* the *San Gerónimo,* and the *Dominican Fiesta* hotels in the capital have casinos, as does *Maunaloa,* a nightclub in the Centro de los Héroes section of Santo Domingo. Casinos at Puerto Plata are in *Jack Tar Village,* the *Puerto Plata Beach* resort, the *Punta Cana Beach* resort, the *Bavaro Beach* resort, and the *Playa Dorada.* Other casinos on the island are at the *Matun* hotel in Santiago and *De Cameron Club* in Juan Dolio. All have all table games, no slot machines. US tourists seem to favor *El Embajador, Jaragua,* and the *Sheraton.* There is little junket action. Hours: 4 PM to 6 AM.

GUADELOUPE The *Casino de la Marina* at St. François (hours: 9 PM to 3 AM) is near both the *Méridien* and the *Hamak;* the *Gosier-les-Bains* (hours: 9 PM to dawn), on the grounds of the *PLM Azur Arawak,* is handy to Gosier and Bas du Fort hotels. Strict French rules apply for admission. Admission charge is about $12. No junkets allowed. There are drinks, but they're not free.

HAITI The most ambitious casino is located in the *El Rancho* hotel, high up in the cool hills of Pétionville, above Port-au-Prince. Once owned by Albert Silvera, one of Haiti's most flamboyant hoteliers, the casino boasted the most liberal craps rule in the Caribbean, "liberal Las Vegas returns on all slot machines," and $50,000 keno payoffs. However, with tourism reversals in Haiti and Silvera's death in 1988, the casino has lost much of its former cachet. There's a second casino in Pétionville in the *Christophe* hotel. The two casinos serve sandwiches, snacks, and occasional free drinks. Both also host junkets. Hours: The *Christophe*'s casino opens at 3 PM, the *El Rancho*'s at 8 PM; both close at 4 AM, but when the action's hot, they'll stay open later.

MARTINIQUE The casino at the *Méridien Trois-Ilets* is more accessible than Guadeloupe's casinos. Standard French admission rules apply. Games are roulette and blackjack. Jackets and ties are not required. Croupiers are European-trained islanders; minimum bet is about $5. Admission charge: $12. Hours: 9 PM to 3 AM nightly.

PUERTO RICO The government carefully supervises the casinos at the *Caribe Hilton, Clarion, Condado Plaza, Ambassador, Dutch Inn,* and *Ramada Inn* in the Condado section; the *El San Juan, Holiday Inn,* and the *Sands* in Isla Verde; the *Palmas del Mar* in Humacao;, the *Hyatt* duo — *Dorado Beach* and *Cerromar Beach* — in Dorado; the *El Conquistador* in Las Croabas; the *Ponce Hilton;* and the *Holiday Inn, Mayagüez* and *Mayagüez Hilton* in Mayagüez. Men must wear jackets after 8 PM, and no drinking is allowed at the tables. If asked, you must be able to produce identification that proves you are at least 18. Hours: variable, but 1 PM to 4 AM is most common.

ST. KITTS All the action is at the casino of the *Jack Tar Village* at Frigate Bay. There's no charge for admission to the casino, and gamblers are given complimentary drinks at the gaming tables. All the usual games are offered, plus slot machines. Hours: 5 PM to 4 AM.

ST. MARTIN/ST. MAARTEN The Dutch side has the gambling monopoly: at *Treasure Island, Mullet Bay, Great Bay Beach, Pelican, Divi Little Bay, Belair Beach,* and *Maho Reef Beach* hotels (hours: 8 PM to 3 AM). At *Seaview* and other in-town casinos, gaming starts in the afternoon. Some French-side hotels provide free casino transport. There are some junkets, but they're minor in the overall tourist picture. Roulette, 21, craps, and slot machines are all there; check the rules before you play for slight differences between casinos. (Minimum age is 21.) Since gambling is only an incidental reason for most people's trips, the atmosphere is pleasantly relaxed.

ST. VINCENT The *Emerald Valley* hotel has a small gaming room with blackjack, craps, roulette, and slots. Minimum age, 18; no photo ID required. Admission charge: $5 EC. Casino hours: 9 PM to 3 AM daily.

Climbing and Hiking

Nowhere in the islands is there the kind of mountain climbing that is likely to draw a serious mountaineer off the more challenging precipices elsewhere in the world. Many of the islands are of volcanic origin, however, and some of these are still rather threatening — dormant, but hot. And that means extremely interesting climbs are available up, into, and through volcanic craters and bubbling sulfur pits, mud pots, and steam vents to summits that, while hardly high in the eyes of the world, at least provide breathtaking views of the islands.

Less arduous but no less spectacular scenery is open to hikers who avail themselves of rain forest preserves and parks in the islands. Many islands have some kind of park system, but the rain forests of St. Lucia, Puerto Rico, and Guadeloupe offer an unparalleled sense of the island environment.

Since most of the islands are either coral formations or are of volcanic origin, there is a great disparity between their heights. Mt. Christoffel, on

Curaçao, is the highest point of the six islands in the Netherlands Antilles group at only 1,250 feet above the sea; on St. Lucia, the smaller of the Pitons stands 2,460 feet tall (the larger is 2,619 feet, and the highest point on that island is Mt. Gimie, at 3,145 feet). Remember, where there are summits, there are guides. Passing through sulfur pits is a fascinating experience with a guide (a favorite trick is to boil eggs in fuming potholes); without a guide it can be dangerous.

Below, our choice of the best hiking and climbing spots in the islands and along the Caribbean coast:

BELIZE The Maya Mountains in the southwest quarter of Belize present a challenging goal to the most avid climbers. *Victoria Peak* tops Belize's Cockscomb range, at 3,680 feet. As in all the inland areas of this country, which tend to be densely jungled, no expedition should be attempted without a guide. The Chief Forest Officer, Ministry of Natural Resources, Belmopan, Belize, will help you get in touch with a qualified expert.

DOMINICA The central rain forests, and especially the Emerald Pool in the *Morne Trois Pitons National Park,* provide beautiful day trips; *Morne Diablotin* (4,747 feet) should not be attempted without a guide — mists the islanders call "liquid sunshine" make it impossible to judge direction near the crest.

GRENADA Hiking along the *Grand Etang National Park*'s improved trails (phone: 809-440-7425) is a favorite sport of islanders and visitors alike. The government has helped by grading trails, mapping, and organizing. The tourist office (phone: 809-440-2279) will brief you on routes, level of skill required, and — with a day's notice — put you in touch with expert guides. Several hiking excursions are offered by several touring groups, including *Henry's Tours, Ltd.* (phone: 809-443-5313).

GUADELOUPE The lush rain forest scenery (lakes, waterfalls, pools, steaming fumaroles) plus a system of well-marked trails make Basse-Terre's giant *Parc Naturel* exotically beautiful hiking terrain. *Walks & Hikes,* a booklet outlining 18 beckoning trails with maps and difficulty ratings, is available through the *Organisation des Guides de Montagne* (phone: 590-800579) or the tourist office (phone: 590-820930).

HAITI The vigorous 30-minute hike (or muleback) trip up to the recently restored *Citadelle* is breathtaking — the old fortifications near Cap-Haïtien are set on the crest of a mountain 3,000 feet up. There are also several peaks worth climbing in the Kenscoff area (*Morne La Selle* and *Chaîne-des-Mattheux* among them), south of Port-au-Prince. Have your hotel desk arrange for a guide in advance.

JAMAICA The 7,402-foot-tall *Blue Mountain Peak* is a rough climb, even for those in good condition. You can make arrangements with John Allgrove (8 Armon Jones Crescent, Kingston 6; phone: 809-927-0986 after 5 PM). Or contact *Jamaica Alternative Tourism, Camping & Hiking Association* (*JACHA*; PO Box 216, Kingston 7; phone: 809-927-2097), about *Blue Mountain* camping trips.

MARTINIQUE For those who wish to stay closer to sea level, there's the peninsula of *Presqu'île de la Caravelle,* part of the island's *Parc Naturel,* with trails covering a wide range of terrain but nothing very difficult. Serious climbers should contact *Parc Régional de la Martinique* (Quartier Bouillé, Rue Redoute du Marouba, Fort-de-France; phone: 596-731930) to arrange for a guide to take them to the top of *Mt. Pelée* (the dormant volcano whose 1902 eruption took 30,000 lives), through the *Gorges de la Falaise,* or to the rain forest between Grand' Rivière and Le Prêcheur.

MONTSERRAT Chance Peak, the island's highest point, makes an excellent viewing tower from which to plan island excursions, since almost the entire island can be seen from its 3,002-foot elevation.

ST. LUCIA Rising half a mile from the shore of the Caribbean, with the waves crashing upon their feet, the peaks of the *Pitons* have been a landmark for mariners since the pirate days. Climbers have been challenging these mountains for just as long. *Gros Piton* stands 2,619 feet above the sea and *Petit Piton* just 2,460 feet; but the high point of the island is *Mt. Gimie* — 3,145 feet tall. None of these peaks should be attempted without a guide, as the mists and rains which frequently and suddenly cover the island's dense rain forest areas can make visibility a problem. (*Petit Piton* is closed until 1996 because of fire damage caused by climbers.) The *St. Lucia National Trust* (phone: 809-452-5005) and the *Forestry Division* (phone: 809-452-3231) both have nature walks.

ST. VINCENT A climb to the top of St. Vincent's *Soufrière,* 4,048 feet high, takes about 3 hours of walking along the steep volcanic ridges and rocky streams, through lush rain forests, and over loose volcanic ash. Since its 1979 eruption, new trails have been blazed. This climb should not be attempted without a guide. Arrangements can be made through hotel desks or the island tourist board, which also books the easier *Buccament Valley Nature Trail.* The tour winds through tropical rain forest, and there are pre-Columbian stone writings at Buccament Cave.

Hunting

There was a time when all the islands were completely open to hunters and the killing of birds and wild animals was not controlled. Today, many island species are protected, and where it is allowed at all, most hunting is restricted to waterfowl and certain other species of birds. Though the days of the big bang are gone, hunting is still available on some islands.

Before planning an expedition, be aware that even in countries that still allow visitors to hunt, the paperwork involved in bringing your own guns onto certain islands can be more arduous than a 5-day trek across the Sahara. After rechecking that the country you're about to visit still allows hunting (regulations often change), contact the consulate to arrange to transport your weapons into the area. The consulate will require information on the make, model, caliber (or bore), and serial number of your guns; your expected arrival and departure dates; and where, what, and with whom you intend to hunt. In addition, you will have to contact either a minister of game or forestry in the island and/or the local police. Some countries will not allow you to bring in any handguns; others limit the number of rounds of ammunition as well as the number of weapons you can bring.

ANTIGUA/BARBUDA There are some wild duck and deer on Barbuda. Contact the Commissioner of Police (American Rd., St. John's, Antigua, WI; phone: 809-462-0125), for information on importing firearms. In addition, check with the Barbuda Council (phone: 809-460-0217).

BELIZE The jungles of Belize teem with wild pig, deer, game birds, and coastal waterfowl. It is necessary to contact the Chief Forest Officer (Ministry of Natural Resources, Belmopan, Belize; phone: 501-8-22166), before attempting to organize an expedition, as well as the Commissioner of Police, Police Headquarters, Belmopan, Belize, if you wish to bring guns into the country.

COLOMBIA For the foreseeable future, species depletion has forced the government to close hunting on all game and fowl except doves. Limited expeditions can be arranged through *Fish and Game Frontiers* (PO Box 161, Pearce Mill Rd., Wexford, PA 15090; phone: 412-935-1577 in Pennsylvania; 800-245-1950 elsewhere), or through *Alberto Lleras* (PO Box 3444, 79-51 Carrera 15, Office 102, Bogotá, Colombia). Firearm rentals can be arranged by the same sources; if you wish to bring your own guns, contact the nearest Colombian consulate, advise them of the number of guns, including full descriptions of each with serial numbers, number of rounds of ammunition, and dates of arrival and departure (you have to submit eight copies of this information).

DOMINICAN REPUBLIC More hunting is allowed here than on any other Caribbean island. With an abundance of birds (doves, duck, pigeons), even the two national birds — cignas and tortolas — are fair game. However, there are specific hunting seasons and restrictions on certain birds and other animals. Contact the Dominican Tourist Information Center, 1 Times Square, New York, NY 10036 (phone: 212-768-2481 or 212-768-2482).

Index